The Routledge Encyclopedia of Second Language Acquisition

The Routledge Encyclopedia of Second Language Acquisition offers a user-friendly, authoritative survey of terms and constructs that are important to understanding research in second language acquisition (SLA) and its applications. The Encyclopedia is designed for use as a reference tool by students, researchers, teachers and professionals with an interest in SLA. The Encyclopedia has the following features:

- 255 alphabetized entries written in an accessible style, including cross references to other related entries in the Encyclopedia and suggestions for further reading.
- Among these, 9 survey entries that cover the foundational areas of SLA in detail: Development in SLA, Discourse and Pragmatics in SLA, Individual Differences in SLA, Instructed SLA, Language and the Lexicon in SLA, Measuring and Researching SLA, Psycholinguistics of SLA, Social and Sociocultural Approaches to SLA, Theoretical Constructs in SLA.
- The rest of the entries cover all the major subdisciplines, methodologies and concepts of SLA, from "Accommodation" to the "ZISA project."

Written by an international team of specialists, *The Routledge Encyclopedia of Second Language Acquisition* is an invaluable resource for students and researchers with an academic interest in SLA.

Peter Robinson is Professor of Linguistics and Second Language Acquisition, Department of English, Aoyama Gakuin University, Tokyo, Japan.

The Routledge Encyclopedia of Second Language Acquisition

Edited by
Peter Robinson

LONDON AND NEW YORK

First published 2013
by Routledge
711 Third Avenue, New York, NY 10017

Simultaneously published in the UK
by Routledge
2 Park Square, Milton Park, Abingdon, Oxon OX14 4RN

Routledge is an imprint of the Taylor & Francis Group, an informa business

Library of Congress Cataloging in Publication Data
Routledge encyclopedia of second language acquisition / edited by Peter Robinson.
p. cm.
Includes index.
1. Second language acquisition. 2. Language and languages. I. Robinson, Peter Jake.
II. Title: Encyclopedia of second language acquisition.
P118.2.R67 2012
401′.9303–dc23
2011043255

ISBN: 978-0-415-87751-0 (hbk)
ISBN: 978-0-203-13594-5 (ebk)

Typeset in Times New Romans and Helvetica
by Taylor & Francis Books

Printed and bound in the United States of America on acid-free paper.

Printed and bound in the United States of America
by Edwards Brothers Malloy

Table of Contents

List of Illustrations

Figures

Tables

Editorial Advisory Board

List of Contributors

Rebekha Abbuhl
California State University at Long Beach

Niclas Abrahamsson
Stockholm University

Michel Achard
Rice University

Phillip L. Ackerman
Georgia Institute of Technology

Agnes Albert
Eötvös Loránd University

Eva Alcón-Soler
Universitat Jaume I

Jeanette Altarriba
University at Albany, State University of New York

Dwight Atkinson
Purdue University

Kathleen Bardovi-Harlig
Indiana University

Robert Bayley
University of California, Davis

Alessandro Benatti
University of Greenwich

Tej K. Bhatia
Syracuse University

Ellen Bialystok
York University

Henrike K. Blumenfeld
San Diego State University

Melissa Bowles
University of Illinois at Urbana-Champaign

Diana Boxer
University of Florida

Charles Browne
Meiji Gakuin University

Christopher D.B. Burt
University of Canterbury

Heidi Byrnes
Georgetown University

Teresa Cadierno
University of Southern Denmark

Marcus Callies
Johannes-Gutenberg-Universität Mainz

Helen Carpenter
Upper-Story Educational Services and Consulting

Mary Carroll
University of Heidelberg

Susanne E. Carroll
University of Calgary

Devin M. Casenhiser
York University

Micheline Chalhoub-Deville
University of North Carolina at Greensboro

Andrew Cohen
University of Minnesota

KimMarie Cole
SUNY Fredonia

Joseph Collentine
Northern Arizona University

Vivian Cook
Newcastle University

Albert Costa
Universitat Pompeu Fabra

Alister Cumming
Ontario Institute for Studies in Education, University of Toronto

Jim Cummins
Ontario Institute for Studies in Education, University of Toronto

Saadiyah Darus
Universiti Kebangsaan Malaysia

Maria C.M. de Guerrero
Inter American University of Puerto Rico

Nel de Jong
Free University Amsterdam

Tamar Degani
University of Pittsburgh

Robert M. DeKeyser
University of Maryland

Tracey M. Derwing
University of Alberta

Jean-Marc Dewaele
Birkbeck College, University of London

Bruno Di Biase
University of Western Sydney

Bryan Donaldson
University of Texas at Austin

Margaret A. DuFon
California State University, Chico

Paola E. Dussias
Pennsylvania State University

Fred R. Eckman
University of Wisconsin-Milwaukee

Nick C. Ellis
University of Michigan

Soren Eskildsen
University of Southern Denmark

Hossein Farhady
American University of Armenia

J. César Félix-Brasdefer
Indiana University

Pauline Foster
St. Mary's University College

Patricia Friedrich
Arizona State University

María del Pilar García-Mayo
Universidad del País Vasco

Robert C. Gardner
University of Western Ontario

Susan Gass
Michigan State University

Ronald Geluykens
University of Oldenburg

Pauline Gibbons
University of Technology Sydney

Roger Gilabert
University of Barcelona

Christina Gitsaki
University of Queensland

Aline Godfroid
Michigan State University

Donald F. Graves
University at Albany, State University of New York

Elena Grigorenko
Yale University

Rosa E. Guzzardo Tamargo
Pennsylvania State University

Stefan Th. Gries
University of California, Santa Barbara

Henk Haarmann
University of Maryland

Gisela Håkansson
Lund University

Joan Kelly Hall
Pennsylvania State University

Björn Hammarberg
Stockholm University

ZhaoHong Han
Columbia University, Teachers College

Linda Harklau
University of Georgia

Ruth Harman
University of Georgia

Eric Hauser
Tokyo University of Electro-communications

Alice F. Healy
University of Colorado

John Hellermann
Portland State University

Henriëtte Hendriks
University of Cambridge, RCEAL

Julia Herschensohn
University of Washington

Thom Heubner
San Jose State University

Gregory Hickok
University of California, Irvine

Richard Hudson
University College London

Paul Ibbotson
University of Manchester

Tomohito Ishikawa
Soka Women's College

Shinichi Izumi
Sophia University

Daniel O. Jackson
University of Hawai'i at Mānoa

Eunice Eunhee Jang
Ontario Institute for Studies in Education, University of Toronto

Scott Jarvis
Ohio University

Geoff Jordan
Leicester University

Satomi Kawaguchi
University of Western Sydney

Chieko Kawauchi
Kurume University

Wolfgang Klein
Max Planck Institute for Psycholinguistics, Nijmegen

Keiko Koda
Carnegie Mellon University

Joel Koeth
University of Maryland

James A. Kole
University of Colorado

Judit Kormos
Lancaster University

Silvia Kouwenberg
University of the West Indies

Claire Kramsch
University of California, Berkeley

Anthony John Kunnan
California State University, Los Angeles

Hye-Young Kwak
University of Hawai'i

Usha Lakshmanan
Southern Illinois University Carbondale

Donna Lardiere
Georgetown University

Diane Larsen-Freeman
University of Michigan

Jenifer Larson-Hall
University of North Texas

David Lasagabaster
University of the Basque Country

Batia Laufer
University of Haifa

Sunyoung Lee-Ellis
University of Maryland

Mietta Lennes
University of Helsinki

Ronald P. Leow
Georgetown University

Ping Li
Pennsylvania State University

Patsy M. Lightbown
Concordia University

Jeannette Littlemore
University of Birmingham

Shawn Loewen
Michigan State University

Wander Lowie
University of Groningen

Zoe Luk
University of Pittsburgh

Roy Lyster
McGill University

Ernesto Macaro
University of Oxford

Peter D. MacIntyre
Cape Breton University

Brian MacWhinney
Carnegie Mellon University

Theodoros Marinis
University of Reading

Numa Markee
University of Illinois at Urbana-Champaign

Clara Martin
Laboratoire de Psychologie Cognitive, CNRS and Université de Provence

Kim McDonough
Concordia University

Jürgen M. Meisel
University of Hamburg and University of Calgary

J. Dean Mellow
Simon Fraser University

Renata Meuter
Queensland University of Technology

Silvina Montrul
University of Illinois at Urbana-Champaign

Kara Morgan-Short
University of Illinois at Chicago

Junko Mori
University of Wisconsin-Madison

Carmen Muñoz
Universitat de Barcelona

Hitoshi Muranoi
Tohoku Gakuin University

Pieter Muysken
Radboud University Nijmegen

Hossein Nassaji
University of Victoria

Paul Nation
Victoria University of Wellington

Helen Neville
University of Oregon

Shuichi Nobe
Aoyama Gakuin University

Kimberly Noels
University of Alberta

Bonny Norton
University of British Columbia

Terence Odlin
Ohio State University

William O'Grady
University of Hawai'i

Luca Onnis
University of Hawai'i

Frederick L. Oswald
Rice University

Rebecca L. Oxford
Air Force Culture and Language Center and University of Maryland

Hiromi Ozeki
Reitaku University

Eric Pakaluk
University of Oregon

Jenefer Philp
University of Auckland

Teresa Pica
University of Pennsylvania

Luke Plonsky
Northern Arizona University

Matthew E. Poehner
Pennsylvania State University

Charlene Polio
Michigan State University

Graeme Porte
Universidad de Granada

Anna Giacalone Ramat
Università di Pavia

Patrick Rebuschat
University of Wales, Bangor

Daniel J. Reed
Michigan State University

Andrea Revesz
Lancaster University

Håkan Ringbom
Abo Akademi University

William C. Ritchie
Syracuse University

Leah Roberts
University of York

Karen Roehr
University of Essex

Ute Römer
Georgia State University

Kenneth R. Rose
City University of Hong Kong

Ralph L. Rose
Waseda University

Rebecca Sachs
Georgetown University

Jasmin Sadat
Institució Catalana de Recerca i Estudis Avançats (ICREA)

Yasuyo Sawaki
Waseda University

Norbert Schmitt
University of Nottingham

Barbara Schulz
Goethe-Universität Frankfurt am Main

John Schumann
University of California, Los Angeles

Norman Segalowitz
Concordia University

Jeff Siegel
University of New England

Larry Selinker
New York University and Research Production Associates

Ali Shehadeh
United Arab Emirates University

Yasuhiro Shirai
University of Pittsburgh

Roumyana Slabakova
University of Iowa

Nina Spada
Ontario Institute for Studies in Education, University of Toronto

Richard Sparks
College of Mount St. Joseph

Charles Stansfield
Second Language Testing, Inc.

Robert Sternberg
University of Oklahoma

David Stringer
Indiana University

Naoko Taguchi
Carnegie Mellon University

Satomi Takahashi
Rikkyo University

Sauli Takala
University of Helsinki

Steven Talmy
University of British Columbia

Elaine Tarone
University of Minnesota

Parvaneh Tavakoli
London Metropolitan University

John Taylor
University of Otago

Steven L. Thorne
Portland State University and University of Groningen

Tomoko Tode
Niigata University of Health and Welfare

Minna Toivola
University of Helsinki

Natasha Tokowicz
University of Pittsburgh

Michael Tomasello
Max Planck Institute for Evolutionary Anthropology

Shigeo Tonoike
Aoyama Gakuin University

Pavel Trofimovich
Concordia University

John Truscott
National Tsing Hua University

Ianthi Maria Tsimpli
Aristotle University of Thessaloniki

Andrea Tyler
Georgetown University

Michael T. Ullman
Georgetown University

Ema Ushioda
University of Warwick

Kris Van den Branden
Katholieke Universiteit Leuven

Leo van Lier
Monterey Institute of International Studies

Larry Vandergrift
University of Ottawa

Bill VanPatten
Michigan State University

Marjolijn Verspoor
University of Groningen

Christiane von Stutterheim
University of Heidelberg

Michiko Watanabe
University of Tokyo

Joanna White
Concordia University

Lydia White
McGill University

Jessica Williams
University of Illinois at Chicago

Alison Wray
Cardiff University

Stefanie Wulff
University of North Texas

Hongzhi Yang
University of New South Wales

Richard F. Young
University of Wisconsin-Madison

List of Entries

Note: Thematic overview entries are in bold.

Acknowledgments

The preparation of this encyclopedia has taken place over two and a half years, beginning in mid 2009 when I contacted colleagues who would become members of the advisory board, asking them if they would be willing to look over my rationale for the content and organization, and give feedback on suggestions for entries and thematic areas, before I submitted the proposal. I am grateful for all of their work at that initial stage and, in many cases, for entries they have themselves written, and for their reviews of entries submitted by others. In addition to the advisory board members, Nick C. Ellis (University of Michigan), Jaemyung Goo (Georgia State University), Lourdes Ortega (University of Hawai'i), and Dick Schmidt (University of Hawai'i), also reviewed and made comments for authors on one or more entries, and I am grateful to them for that. I am very grateful too, to each of the many entry authors for agreeing to contribute, and for taking the time needed to prepare their submissions following the guidelines provided. Chloe Wandler, an exchange student from the University of Oregon helped to prepare the large spreadsheet with contributor information and keep it up to date while she was at Aoyama Gakuin University. That has been a great help. Finally, Ivy Ip and Mike Andrews, and more recently Elysse Preposi and Paola Celli, at Routledge have been very efficient and easy to work with in answering email queries from various contributors, and keeping them updated on the progress of the book, and in dealing with details of the production process.

Introduction to the encyclopedia

The Routledge Encyclopedia of Second Language Acquisition aims to provide readers with a user-friendly, authoritative survey of terms and constructs that are currently thought to be important to understanding research in second language acquisition (SLA) and its applications. As such this encyclopedia can be used as a reference tool by students, researchers, teachers and professionals with an interest in SLA. As described in a number of recent introductions to SLA (e.g., Ellis, 2008; Ortega, 2009), theoretical thinking about, and empirical research into SLA has accumulated over the last forty years, with the result that there are now a number of Handbooks of SLA (e.g., Doughty and Long, 2003; Gass and Mackey, 2012; Ritchie and Bhatia, 2009) providing valuable in-depth chapter length treatment of many of the topics covered in this encyclopedia. However, the number of chapters in these handbooks is limited (24 chapters in Doughty and Long, 2003; 35 in Gass and Mackey, 2012; and 27 in Ritchie and Bhatia, 2009) and each of these chapters often deals simultaneously with many of the terms and topics addressed separately by entries in this encyclopedia. Consequently, the more broadly presented, concise, and focused treatment of terms and topics in this encyclopedia should be useful for readers to consult either in preparation for, or whilst reading the in-depth surveys provided by various introductions to SLA, or by contemporary handbook chapters on SLA.

Organization of entries

The encyclopedia contains over 250 entries, written in an accessible, concise style, followed by references, and recommended further readings. The length of each entry differs, reflecting differences in what is known of each entry term and topic, and the extent of SLA research into it to date, with approximately equal numbers of entries consisting of 500 words, 1,000 words, 1,500 words, and 2,000 words. Each entry is also followed by a "*see also*" list of six related entries, which should help readers navigate among entries dealing with similar issues in SLA research. In addition, there are also nine *survey entries*, of around 4,000 words in length, describing different *thematic areas* in SLA research, which relate the terms and topics addressed in separate entries to broader issues. These thematic survey entries are a good starting point for readers wishing to navigate between entries, and broaden their search for information, and can be read in any order, as suits the individual reader's interests. A brief summary of the scope of each survey entry is given below.

Survey entries

- The thematic survey entry on *Social and sociocultural approaches on SLA*, is written by Dwight Atkinson. An example of an entry in this area is "scaffolding," a term used to describe how a more knowledgeable partner can help a learner construct their knowledge of the second language (L2). This survey also relates issues such as "communicative competence" and "second language socialization" to socially oriented approaches to SLA research such as "conversation analysis."

- The survey entry on *Psycholinguistics of SLA*, written by Ping Li and Natasha Tokowicz, deals with such issues as "Age effects in SLA" and "The critical period" as well as with mechanisms and stages in language processing, such as the phonological loop, which is where sounds of the L2 are stored and rehearsed temporarily in "phonological short-term memory." This entry also describes mental processes such as "inhibitory control," or the ability to not think about one thing (for example, words in the L1) while processing another (words in the L2).
- There are many sources of *Individual differences in SLA*, and inhibitory control is one of them. Bilinguals have very good inhibitory control when it comes to language selection. Another, rather different source of differences between learners is "willingness to communicate," as is measured by responses to questionnaires by L2 learners. In this survey entry Rebecca Oxford describes a number of areas of individual differences between learners that have been researched for their effects on successful SLA.
- The survey entry on *Discourse and pragmatics in SLA* concerns issues such as "politeness," and how perceptions of it are affected by choice of L2 words and phrases for "speech acts" such as apologizing or requesting in the L2. In this entry Eva Alcón-Soler describes the broader notion of "pragmatic competence" and how it may be implicated in learning during interaction in the L2.
- Of course, the area of discourse and pragmatics is closely related to *Language and the lexicon in SLA*, and the differences between languages, for example, in whether they have "inflectional morphology" for marking the past tense, or the object of a sentence. This survey entry, by Marjolijn Verspoor and Norbert Schmitt, also addresses choices that exist within any language, such as the use of "Wh-questions" in English, versus other "constructions" for asking questions, and describes the processes that contribute to "construction learning" and the establishment of "form-meaning connections" in the L2.
- The study of *Development in SLA* is the study of stages in the L2 emergence of e.g., morphemes, WH words, and multi-word constructions. In his survey entry, Jürgen Meisel considers to what extent there are "morpheme acquisition orders" that are shared across L2 learners with a wide variety of L1s, and to what extent there is "transfer" of L1 knowledge to the L2 while learning them. Large-scale projects such as the "European Science Foundation Project" and the "ZISA project" in the 1980s and 1990s studied these issues during "naturalistic" untutored learning of L2s in European countries.
- *Instructed SLA* differs from naturalistic learning in its broadly defined social setting, and aims to speed up learning through various pedagogic interventions. In their survey entry Patsy Lightbown and Nina Spada describe some of these techniques that aim to focus learner attention on aspects of the L2 that are infrequent in the input, or easy to overlook, such as "input enhancement." In this technique forms can be underlined or italicized to increase their perceptual salience in reading materials. Alternatively "flooding" is a technique for providing many examples of the forms, above their usual level of frequency, in spoken or written input.
- *Measuring and researching SLA* involves, for example, assessing the "variance" between learners in any group in their accuracy in using a form, or identifying the "hesitation phenomena" that occur during spoken performance, and contributing to "fluency." In their survey entry Andrew Cohen and Ernesto Macaro describe these and other issues, such as measurement options appropriate to "qualitative research" and "quantitative research" procedures, and the tasks that are often used as instruments to test the extent of L2 knowledge and ability.
- Finally, *Theoretical constructs in SLA* include such terms as "interlanguage," "motivation," "aptitude," and "noticing." As Geoff Jordan describes in his survey entry, these constructs are used in the service of theories which attempt

> to explain phenomena and he describes three criteria which can be used for assessing constructs used in SLA theories, relating these to Krashen's "Monitor Model," Schmidt's "Noticing Hypothesis," "aptitudes" and "variationist approaches to SLA."

In summary, this encyclopedia aims to provide accessible, authoritative entries on terms which are often used in descriptions of research to date on SLA, and also to help organize links between them in a way that allows readers to fashion their own understanding of the issues addressed in this important field of enquiry.

Peter Robinson

References

Doughty, C.J. and Long, M.H. (2003). *The Handbook of Second Language Acquisition.* Oxford: Blackwell.

Ellis, R. (2008). *The Study of Second Language Acquisition*, 2nd edn. Oxford: Oxford University Press.

Gass, S. and Mackey, A. (2012). *The Routledge Handbook of Second Language Acquisition.* New York: Routledge.

Ortega, L. (2009). *Understanding Second Language Acquisition.* London: Hodder.

Ritchie, W.C. and Bhatia, T.K. (2009). *The New Handbook of Second Language Acquisition*, 2nd edn. Bingley: Emerald.

Accommodation

KimMarie Cole
SUNY Fredonia

In the field of sociolinguistics, accommodation is valued for its explanations and predictions of individual variation. As described below, second language acquisition (SLA) researchers have used accommodation to account for differences in learners' language use with native speakers and how it accounts for some linguistic features of input. While empirical studies are relatively few in number, Tarone's (2007) review includes accommodation among sociolinguistic theories of SLA.

Beebe and Giles (1984) first present an overview of Speech Accommodation Theory (SAT) and its applications to second language acquisition. Its key propositions include convergence and divergence, active strategies used by learners based on their assessment of the perceived relationship between their language and that of their interlocutors. When speakers like or identify with their speakers or have an instrumental purpose for speaking, their speech converges. They are likely to model their speech on that of their interlocutor, using similar linguistic features. Conversely, when speakers feel a lack of identification or a perceived threat to their language, they accentuate linguistic differences, or diverge from their interlocutors. In terms of SLA, the model suggests that those learners who perceive the new language as a threat to their first language would not seek opportunities to practice the second and would therefore not develop second language proficiency. Conversely, learners, who see the second language as complementary to their first would achieve higher proficiency. Early SLA accommodation studies predicted learners' convergence or divergence from target language forms usually based on factors such as the perceived ethnolinguistic vitality or relative status of the first language with respect to the target language.

With additional developments, SAT gave way to Communication Accommodation Theory (CAT) to account for an expanded notion of accommodation and a greater number of features included in the model. Giles, Coupland and Coupland (1991) explain that CAT accounts for intergroup variables and language use in naturalistic settings. Zuengler's (1991) review of CAT in SLA in the same volume discussed empirical studies and offered a grounded explanation for foreigner talk (FT), a form of input considered beneficial for SLA. CAT predicts that if a native speaker has a functional reason for interacting with a language learner, there would be greater amounts of converging FT. Someone who wished to highlight social or personal distinctions, would diverge from facilitative FT. In this way, CAT's relevance for SLA expands beyond learners' identifications to include contextual features of input and demonstrates that language acquisition can depend on complex relationships in the learning context as much as within the learner.

SAT and CAT rely heavily on the idea of strategic language use based on perceived notions of interlocutors and language groups. Recent challenges argue that this identification of the "other" can be static or stereotypical given new models of personal and group identity affiliation within cultural studies. Ylanne-McEwen and Coupland (2000) review this critique and counter that CAT is a multi-faceted perspective that recognizes language as both symbol of cultural identification and as the medium through which individuals negotiate their identities (p. 211). In their view CAT accommodates the full complexity of speakers in interaction.

See also: alignment, attitudes to the L2, bilingualism and SLA, context of situation, identity theory, social and sociocultural approaches to SLA

References

Beebe, L. and Giles, H. (1984). Speech Accommodation Theories: a discussion in terms of second-language acquisition. *International Journal of Sociology of Language*, *46*, 5–32.

Giles, H., Coupland, N. and Coupland, J. (1991). Accommodation theory: communication, context and consequence. In H. Giles, J. Coupland and N. Coupland (eds), *Contexts of Accommodation: Developments in Applied Sociolinguistics*, pp. 1–68. Cambridge: Cambridge University Press.

Tarone, E. (2007). Sociolinguistic approaches to second language acquisition research, 1997–2007. *Modern Language Journal*, *91*, 837–48.

Ylanne-McEwen, V. and Coupland, N. (2000). Accommodation theory: a conceptual resource for intercultural sociolinguistics. In H. Spencer-Oatey (ed.), *Culturally speaking: managing rapport through talk across cultures*, pp. 191–216. London: Continuum.

Zuengler, J. (1991). Accommodation in native-nonnative interactions: going beyond the "what" to the "why" in second language research. In H. Giles, J. Coupland, and N. Coupland (eds), *Contexts of accommodation: developments in applied sociolinguistics*, pp. 223–44. Cambridge: Cambridge University Press.

Acculturation Model

John Schumann
University of California, Los Angeles

The acculturation model (AM) (Schumann, 1978) is an exploration of social (i.e., group) and psychological (i.e., individual) influences on second language acquisition (SLA). The model identifies factors affecting an immigrant group's and an individual immigrant's interaction with the target language speakers and the resultant acquisition of the target language by the learners.

Social variables

From this perspective seven factors to consider: dominance, integration patterns, enclosure, cultural congruence, group size, group attitudes, and intended length of residence. The first factor considers dominance relations between the immigrant group and the target language group. If one of the groups is considered politically, economically, culturally, or militarily superior, that group would be unlikely to acquire the other group's language. For example, when Turkish workers immigrated to Germany, it was the Turks who acquired German, not the other way around. The second factor involves integration patterns. The immigrant group might adopt an assimilation strategy in which it is willing to give up its lifestyle and values and adopt those of the target language group. Or the immigrant group might choose an adaptation strategy in which they maintain their native language and culture for intragroup use and adapt to the lifestyle and values of the target language group for intergroup interaction. For example, Armenian immigrants throughout their diaspora have retained their native language and acquired the local TLs. It is very difficult to find a monolingual Armenian. Finally, an immigrant group might choose a preservationist strategy in which they reject the lifestyle and values of the TL group, retain their own, and learn little of the target language. This strategy is perhaps starkly exemplified by military personnel living on American bases in countries such as Germany, Japan, and South Korea. Another example might be French colonists living in urban areas of North Africa and by early German immigrants to the Midwest in the United States. The next factor to consider in the AM is enclosure. If the immigrant group and the TL group participate in different crafts, professions, trades, if they attend different schools, churches, and recreational facilities, and if they do not intermarry, then enclosure is said to be high, contact and interaction between groups is restricted, and therefore, opportunity for acquisition of the target language by the immigrant group is limited. A related factor is cohesion. If the members of the immigrant group associate mostly or even exclusively with each other, then the group is said to be cohesive, and again opportunities for contact and interaction with members of the TL group are diminished. Cultural congruence is another issue. If the two groups have cultural values that are similar (e.g., Western/Christian, Eastern/Muslim), then the potential for interaction is increased. Additionally, if the size of the immigrant group is large (e.g., the Mexican or Korean communities in Los Angeles, California) group contact will likely be much greater than if the immigrant group were small and scattered. If the two groups have positive attitudes towards each other interaction is more likely. And finally if the immigrant group intends to remain in the TL area for a long period (perhaps forever) they are more likely to make an effort to acquire the target language than if they believe they will be there only temporarily.

Psychological variables

Affective factors. The second part of the AM consisted of four affective variables: language shock, culture shock, motivation, and ego permeability.

Stimulus appraisal dimensions. Schumann *et al.* (2004) replaced these affective factors with the more general notion of stimulus appraisal (Scherer, 1984). This construct consists of five domains in which an individual assesses the emotional and motivational relevance of stimuli and stimulus situations in SLA according to their novelty, pleasantness, goals/needs significance, coping potential, and self and social image. The novelty check assesses whether simulation contains new or unexpected patterns. An assessment of intrinsic pleasantness determines whether an event is pleasant and thus fosters approach or whether it is unpleasant and thus promotes avoidance. The goals/needs significance check assesses the relevance of the event to the individual's needs and goals. The coping potential check determines an individual's ability to cope intellectually, psychologically or physically with stimulus event. Finally the self and social compatibility check assesses compatibility of the event with one's self-image and with social norms and the expectations of significant others. Schumann (1997) argued that all items on questionnaires measuring motivation in SLA can be reduced to these five dimensions of stimulus appraisal.

The social and the affective factors in the AM are neither independent nor mutually exclusive. They all highlight slightly different aspects of acculturation and its influence on SLA, but there is also considerable overlap among them. This makes acculturation very difficult to measure. Therefore, the model is best considered a conceptual-theoretical perspective that allows one to think about success or lack of it in SLA. This kind of reflection can usefully be applied to case studies of SLA. One such case (Schmidt, 1983) has been considered counter evidence to the acculturation (indeed by Schumann himself, see Schumann, 1986). Schmidt studied the acquisition of English over a three-year period by Wes, a 33-year-old Japanese artist who ultimately settled in Hawaii. Wes had substantial contact and interaction with English-speaking friends and customers. His English proficiency developed in the areas of sociolinguistic, discourse, and strategic competence; however, he showed little development in grammatical proficiency. Nevertheless, in terms of acculturation variables, Wes had a profile that would predict a higher efficiency in all aspects of English. However, Schumann (1993), in light of neuropsychological research, pointed out that Wes may constitute an exceptional case that needed another explanation. Based on research by (Humes-Bartlo, 1989; Novoa *et al.*, 1988; Schneiderman and Desmaris, 1988), Schumann suggested that the visuo-spatial talent that Wes had as an artist may have existed alongside a deficit in his ability to acquire a grammatical code in an L2. From this perspective, positive acculturation may have facilitated the development of his communicative ability in English, and his deficit in code learning may have diminished his ability to acquire the L2 grammar. From this perspective, Wes is actually evidence for the AM.

See also: amygdala, motivation, theoretical constructs in SLA, social and cultural influences on SLA, attitude, and motivation test battery, individual differences in SLA

References

Humes-Bartlo, M. (1989). Variation in children's ability to learn second languages. In K. Hyltenstam and L.K. Ober (eds), *Bilingualism across the Lifespan*. New York: Cambridge University Press.

Novoa, L., Fein, D. and Obler, L.K. (1988). Talent in foreign languages: A case study. In L.K. Obler and D. Fein (eds), *The Exceptional Brain*. New York: The Guilford Press.

Scherer, K.R. (1984). Emotion is a multi-component process: A model and some cross cultural data. In P. Shaver (ed.), *Review of Personality and Psychology*. Vol. 5: *Emotions, Relationships and Health*. Beverly Hills, CA: Sage.

Schmidt, R. (1983). Interaction, acculturation, and the acquisition of communicative competence: A case study of an adult. In N. Wolfson and E. Judd (eds), *Sociolinguistics and Language Acquisition*, Rowley, MA: Newbury House Publishers.

Schneiderman, E.I. and Desmaris, C. (1998). A neuropsychological substrate for talent in second language acquisition. In L.K. Obler and D. Fein (eds), *The Exceptional Brain*. New York: The Guilford Press.

Schumann, J.H. (1978). The acculturation model for second language acquisition. In R.C. Gingras (ed.), *Second Language Acquisition and Foreign Language Teaching*. Washington, DC: Center for Applied Linguistics.

——(1986). Research on the acculturation model for second language acquisition. *Journal of Multilingual and Multicultural Development*, *7*(5), 379–92.

——(1993). Some problems with falsification: An illustration from SLA research. *Applied Linguistics*, *14*(3), 295–306.

——(1997) *The Neurobiology of Affect in Language*. Malden, MA: Blackwell.

Schumann, J.H., Crowell, S.E., Jones, N.E., Lee, N., Schuchert, S.A. and Wood, L.A. (2004). *The Neurobiology of Learning: Perspectives from Second Language Acquisition*. Mahwah, NJ: Lawrence Erlbaum.

Acquisition of motion expressions

David Stringer
Indiana University

Second language research into the linguistic expression of motion events has drawn largely on Talmy's well-known typology of motion: V(verb)-framed languages, such as those in the Romance, Semitic and Polynesian families, generally encode Path in verbs; while S(satellite)-framed languages, such as those in the Indo-European family (apart from Romance), usually do so in adpositions, affixes or particles. Thus in Spanish one must *cruzar la calle corriendo* 'cross the road running' (Path in the verb, Manner in an adjunct); while in English one can *run across the road* (Path in the preposition, Manner in the verb). Systematic differences in the ways typical V- and S-framed languages encode Path and Manner have been used to argue for the hypothesis that our perception of events as we engage in language use is partly determined by the language we speak (see **Thinking for speaking**).

Such typological differences raise questions for second language research. Cadierno (2010) addressed the issue of transfer of thinking-for-speaking patterns from the first to the second language. She found that low-intermediate learners of Danish (S-framed) whose first language was German or Russian (also S-framed) used more characteristic motion constructions and had a larger vocabulary of motion verbs than those whose first language was Spanish (V-framed). This finding suggests that transfer may be apparent in the earlier stages of acquisition, despite previous evidence that advanced learners are able to converge on target-like expression of motion events. Thinking-for-speaking patterns in motion events have also been observed to transfer in terms of the gestures that synchronically accompany speech. Stam (2006) found that Spanish learners of English had an overall gesture pattern somewhere between the typical alignments for Spanish and English, and produced interesting speech-gesture mismatches.

Taking a generative approach to issues of learnability, Inagaki (2001) argued that English allows both S-framed and V-framed grammar, while Japanese strictly allows only V-framed grammar, thus creating a subset problem in acquisition. His experimental evidence revealed that English learners of Japanese transfer S-framed grammar, leading him to predict that a retreat from such overgeneralization is impossible, as appropriate positive evidence is not available. This interpretation was questioned by Stringer (2007), who found evidence of both patterns in Japanese, and argued that the problem is one of lexical relativity: analogous verbs in each language differ in argument structure, such that learners must fine-tune individual predicates in a general process of relexification.

More recent research in both cognitive linguistic and generative frameworks recognizes that the original binary typology is too strict; many, if not most, languages fall somewhere on a cline between these two characteristic means of expression. Chinese, originally characterized as S-framed, is now considered to be somewhere in-between. Wu (2010) examined how English-speaking learners come to grasp the dual functions of Chinese spatial morphemes as Path satellites and as independent verbs, and proposed a sequence of development in the second language grammar. In line with previous studies, the results were interpreted as revealing initial problems in adjusting to new patterns of thinking for speaking in a second language.

See also: cognitive linguistics and SLA, conceptual transfer, gestures and SLA, linguistic relativity, linguistic transfer, thinking for speaking

References

Cadierno, T. (2010). Motion in Danish as a Second Language: Does the Learner's L1 make a Difference? In Z.-H. Han and T. Cadierno (eds), *Linguistic Relativity in SLA: Thinking for Speaking*. Clevedon: Multilingual Matters.

Inagaki, S. (2001). Motion Verbs with Goal PPs in the L2 Acquisition of English and Japanese. *Studies in Second Language Acquisition, 23*, 153–70.

Stam, G.A. (2006). Thinking for Speaking about Motion: L1 and L2 Speech and Gesture. *International Review of Applied Linguistics, 44* (2), 143–69.

Stringer, D. (2007). Motion events in L2 acquisition: A lexicalist account. In H. Caunt-Nulton, S. Kulatilake and I.H. Woo (eds), *BUCLD 31: Proceedings of the 31st annual Boston University Conference on Language Development, Vol. II*, 585–96. Somerville, MA: Cascadilla.

Wu, S.L. (2010). Learning to Express Motion Events in an L2: The Case of Chinese Directional Complements. *Language Learning*, no. doi: 10.1111/j.1467–9922.2010.00614.x

Further reading

Berman, R.A. and Slobin, D.I. (eds) (1994). *Relating Events in Narrative: A Crosslinguistic Developmental Study*. Hillsdale, NJ: Lawrence Erlbaum Associates. (A classic volume investigating the linguistic expression of motion events by children and adults, using the now-famous "frog story" elicitation technique.)

Han, Z.-H. and Cadierno, T. (eds) (2010). *Linguistic Relativity in SLA: Thinking for Speaking*. Clevedon: Multilingual Matters. (Recent edited volume with several papers on motion events and spatial relations in second language acquisition.)

Slobin, D.I. (1996). Two ways to travel: Verbs of motion in English and Spanish. In M. Shibatani and S.C.A. Thompson (eds), *Grammatical Constructions: Their Form and Meaning*. Oxford: Oxford University Press. (An insightful analysis of V-framed and S-framed means of expression, drawing on developmental data as well as literary texts in translation.)

Strömqvist S. and Verhoeven, L. (eds) (2004). *Relating Events in Narrative: Typological and Contextual Perspectives*. Mahwah, NJ: Lawrence Erlbaum. (An excellent collection of research reports inspired by Berman and Slobin, 1994, which goes beyond the original binary typology.)

Talmy, L. (2000). *Toward a Cognitive Semantics, Vol. 1: Concept Structuring Systems; Vol. 2: Typology and Process in Concept Structuring*. Cambridge, MA: MIT Press. (A collection of Talmy's most influential research, with revised and expanded versions of several classic papers on motion events.)

Acquisition of tense and aspect

Kathleen Bardovi-Harlig
Indiana University

Interest in the second language acquisition of tense and aspect dates back to the earliest studies in the field. Before studies of acquisition as we know them, tense and aspect figured prominently in pedagogical curricula of languages, and this continues today. Studies that include tense and aspect consist of two types: studies of tense and aspect as morphology (in which the semantic characteristics of tense-aspect systems are largely irrelevant), and studies of tense and aspect as temporal semantics (in which the form-meaning associations are paramount).

Tense locates an event or situation on the time line. In English, *John loves Mary* (present) and *John loved Mary* (past) show a difference in tense. *Grammatical aspect* provides a means of expressing one's view of a situation or event. For example, an event may be viewed as completed, as in *John walked down the road* (simple past), or as continuous, as in *John was walking down the road* (past progressive); both are past, but differ in grammatical aspect. The choice of grammatical aspect reflects the function of the sentence in evolving discourse.

Studies of tense and aspect as morphology include studies of morpheme order, phonetic constraints, and universal grammar. They generally employ a supplied in obligatory context (SOC) analysis. The first studies to include tense-aspect morphology were the morpheme order studies in which verbal morphemes (notably, present, progressive, and past) were included among other grammatical morphemes (e.g., noun markers, prepositions, auxiliaries, and the copula). Separating verbal morphology from other morphemes reveals a single order of verbal morphemes for both children and adults: *-ing*, irregular past, and third person singular. (See morpheme acquisition order.)

Interest in the acquisition of regular and irregular past has continued beyond the morpheme order studies; longitudinal studies have supported the irregular-before-regular order in a variety of languages and have argued that this order does not characterize the learning of rules, but individual lexical items (Dietrich *et al.*, 1995).

Studies of phonetic constraints on past-tense use in English have shown that phonetic realization of the past tense is dependent on phonological environments and make two main claims: 1) irregular verbs will show greater tense marking than regular verbs and 2) the phonetic shape of the past tense of the verb and the following phonological environment will determine the likelihood of past-tense realization (Wolfram, 1989). Bayley (1994) posited the following hierarchy, from the most likely to be marked to the least: suppletive (*be*), doubly marked (*sleep/slept*), internal vowel (*sing/sang*), change in final segment (*send/sent*), weak syllabic (*pat/patted*), and modals.

Tense-aspect morphology has also been investigated in the generative framework, with a focus on whether optionality in the L2 use of tense and agreement morphology is due to impaired knowledge of functional categories, or a mapping problem from existing abstract features to their surface representations (Ionin and Wexler, 2002; Lardiere, 2006).

Studies of tense-aspect as a semantic system span a range of target languages dividing into two main strands of inquiry: the form-oriented approach, which investigates the distribution of verbal morphology and its interlanguage function, and the meaning-oriented approach, which investigates the expression of semantic concepts. Both the form-oriented and meaning-oriented approaches take an interlanguage perspective, describing the interlanguage as a system independent of the target language (e.g., Dietrich *et al.*, 1995; Bardovi-Harlig, 2000).

Form-oriented inquiry has taken three perspectives: acquisitional sequences, the influence of lexical aspect, and the influence of discourse structure. Studies of acquisitional sequences describe via longitudinal studies the order of emergence of tense-aspect morphology and the meaning associated with each form and the contrasts between form-meaning associations (e.g., Bardovi-Harlig, 2000; Dietrich *et al.*, 1995).

The aspect hypothesis predicts that the lexical aspect of predicates—their inherent temporal properties—will determine the distribution of tense-aspect morphology in the earlier stages of acquisition (Andersen, 1991). Predicates will attract semantically compatible tense-aspect morphology, reflecting prototype associations. For example, a predicate expressing a state (e.g., *John seemed happy*) will attract the imperfective and a predicate expressing an action with no inherent endpoint, called an activity (e.g., *John swam*) will attract the progressive in languages that have one. In contrast, predicates that have inherent endpoints such as *John changed the tire* (an accomplishment) and *John recognized Mary* (an achievement) will attract the perfective past. Following the initial, exclusive associations with semantically compatible predicates, tense-aspect morphology then spreads across lexical categories (see **Aspect Hypothesis**).

Following Hopper's observation that competent (native) users of a language "mark out a main route through the narrative and divert in some way those parts of the narrative that are not strictly relevant to this route" (1979: 239), the Discourse Hypothesis predicts that learners use emerging verbal morphology to distinguish the main route (the foreground) from the background in narratives. For example, learners of English show greater use of simple past in foreground than in the background. Moreover, they show greater use of progressive in the background than in the foreground. Unlike the past which can occur in both foreground and background, the progressive generally occurs in the background in targetlike use (Bardovi-Harlig, 1998).

Aspectual categories and discourse structure interact (Bardovi-Harlig, 1998): achievements are most likely to be inflected for simple past, regardless of grounding; accomplishments are the next most likely to exhibit the simple past with foreground accomplishments showing higher rates of use than background accomplishments; and, activities are the least likely of all the dynamic predicates to carry simple past, but foreground activities show higher rates of simple past inflection than background activities. Activities also show use of progressive in the background.

The concept-oriented, or meaning-oriented, approach investigates all means of expression for a particular concept such as the past or the future (von Stutterheim and Klein, 1987). Temporality may be expressed (in order of appearance in second language acquisition) by pragmatic devices (e.g., use of chronological order or scaffolding), lexical means (e.g., temporal adverbials), and verbal morphology. Form-oriented inquiry concentrates only on the third stage, whereas the concept-oriented approach situates the development of tense-aspect morphology in the larger context of second language acquisition.

See also: Aspect Hypothesis, concept-oriented approach to SLA, developmental sequences, European Science Foundation (ESF) project, form-meaning connections, morpheme acquisition orders

References

Andersen, R.W. (1991). Developmental sequences: The emergence of aspect marking in second language acquisition. In T. Huebner and C.A. Ferguson (eds), *Crosscurrents in Second Language Acquisition and Linguistic Theories*. Amsterdam: Benjamins.

Bardovi-Harlig, K. (1998). Narrative structure and lexical aspect: Conspiring factors in second language acquisition of tense-aspect morphology. *Studies in Second Language Acquisition*, *20*, 471–508.

——(2000). *Tense and Aspect in Second Language Acquisition: Form, Meaning, and Use*. Oxford: Blackwell.

Bayley, R.J. (1994). Interlanguage variation and the quantitative paradigm: Past tense marking in Chinese-English. In S. Gass, A. Cohen, and E. Tarone (eds), *Research Methodology in Second Language Acquisition*. Hillsdale, NJ: Erlbaum.

Dietrich, R., Klein, W. and Noyau, C. (1995). *The Acquisition of Temporality in a Second Language*. Amsterdam: Benjamins.

Hopper, P.J. (1979). Aspect and foregrounding in discourse. In T. Givón (ed.), *Syntax and Semantics: Discourse and Syntax*. New York: Academic Press.

Ionin, T. and K. Wexler (2002). Why is 'is' easier than '-s'?: acquisition of tense/agreement morphology by child second language learners of English. *Second Language Research*, *18*, 95–136.

Lardiere, D. (2006). *Ultimate Attainment in Second Language Acquisition: A Case Study*. Mahwah, NJ: Erlbaum.

von Stutterheim, C. and Klein, W. (1987). A concept-oriented approach to second language studies. In C.W. Pfaff (ed.), *First and Second Language Acquisition Processes*. Cambridge, MA: Newbury House.

Wolfram, W. (1989). Systematic variability in second-language tense marking. In M.R. Eisenstein (ed.), *The Dynamic Interlanguage: Empirical Studies in Second Language Variation*. New York: Plenum.

Further reading

Kempchinsky, P. and R. Slabakova, R. (eds) (2005). *Aspectual Inquiries*. Dordrecht: Kluwer. (Empirical and theoretical treatments of aspect.)

Labeau, E. (ed.) (in press) *Development of Tense, Aspect and Mood in L1 and L2*. Amsterdam: Rodopi/Cahiers Chronos. (Acquisitional studies on a range of languages including non-Indo-European languages.)

Li, P. and Shirai, Y. (2000). *The Acquisition of Lexical and Grammatical Aspect*. Berlin: De Gruyter. (Acquisition of aspect in Chinese and Japanese.)

Salaberry, R. and Shirai, Y. (eds) (2002). *Tense-aspect Morphology in L2 Acquisition*. Amsterdam: John Benjamins. (Covers many issues in a range of European languages.)

Salaberry, R. and L. Comajoan, L. (eds) (in press). *Research Design and Methodology in Studies on Second Language Tense and Aspect*. Mouton. (Comprehensive coverage of tense-aspect research designs.)

Activity theory and SLA

Hongzhi Yang
University of New South Wales

Activity theory, or cultural historical activity theory (CHAT), is an interdisciplinary approach to human sciences and a commonly accepted name for a line of theorizing and research established by the founders of the cultural-historical school of Russian psychology, L.S. Vygotsky, A.N. Leont'ev, and A R. Luria, during the 1920s–1930s. Vygotsky proposed that consciousness is constructed through a subject's interactions with the world and is an attribute of the relationship between subject and object. Activity theory is used as a framework for analysis of an object-oriented, collective and culturally mediated human activity, emphasizing the mediation of human action by 'cultural artefacts'. It is not only a psychological theory *per se*, but also a broad approach that develops novel conceptual tools for tackling theoretical and methodological questions in the social sciences today. In this way, activity theory has much to contribute to the growing wave of multidisciplinary interest in cultural practices and practice-bound cognition (Engeström and Miettinen, 1999).

The first generation of activity theory centres on Vygotsky's development of the concept of *cultural mediation*. In the second generation theory developed by A.N. Leont'ev, division of labour, rules, and community were incorporated into the activity theory framework, determining how subjects must fit into the community (Engeström, 1987). The third generation of activity theory concerns the development of conceptual tools to address dialogue, a multiplicity of perspectives, and the interrelations between defined activity systems (Engeström, 2001). Language, being determined by the broader socio-historical milieu, is realized in dialogues by interlocutors whose multiple perspectives are constructed according to the structure of the activity they are engaged in (Moro, 2007).

The elements of this activity system include the object, subject, mediating artefacts, rules, community, and division of labour (Engeström, 1987). The internal contradictions within the elements of an activity system are the potential force of development if they are properly resolved. This development happens as a result of continuous transitions and transformations between these components of an activity system (Engeström and Miettinen, 1999). At the same time, there are two basic intertwined processes operating at every level of human activity: internalization, the reproduction of culture; and externalization, the creation of new artefacts and production of new activity structures during the process of transformation. Internalization relates to self-regulation where individuals develop new linguistic resources that can potentially mediate their mental and social activity during this process (Lantolf and Thorne, 2006).

Activity and agency

From the activity theory perspective, one's agency is constantly constrained and empowered by social groupings, material and symbolic resources, as well as other social and personal factors. Agency is not only intentionality but also a cultural informed attribute shaped by participation in specific community of practices. It is a relationship which is co-constructed and negotiated with others in a social setting (Lantolf and Thorne, 2006). Agency can explain why and how learners act. Therefore, teachers should be aware of the difference between the cognitive target of learning and learners' agency in determining activities. In addition, agency is shaped in response to the transformation of activities, and is influenced by learner's personal histories of language learning (Lantolf and Thorne, 2006), and the language ideologies that are part of the implicit and explicit discourse produced at institutional and nation-sate levels (Lantolf and Pavlenko, 2001). Therefore, the outcomes of a language classroom should not only pertain to language development, but also enhance an individual's sense of agency for adaptation and action, as well as facilitate the development of learners' agency in response to educational requirements.

Second language education and activity theory

Language learning is connected with cultural, social, institutional and discursive forces, where language is considered a cultural artefact that mediates thinking and communication between people and within an individual. This cultural historical perspective caused an epistemological shift away from Cartesian-derived theories of cognition that isolate the individual mind from the culture and society, to the perception that historical, institutional and discursive forces mediate a person's activity (Thorne, 2004). Activity theory proposes more holistic approaches to SLA research and praxis (Lantolf and Thorne, 2006). It aims to transform practices in the way that might improve the conditions and outcomes of teaching and learning, by providing additional mediation, offering different rules of engagement, and gathering individuals/communities with different previous histories. In the classroom, even when operationally learners appear to be adopting the same behaviours, cognitively they are always engaging in the activity differently and even direct the activity in specific ways according to their different individual history, goals and motives. It is not necessary that all learners in the classroom have the same goal of learning. What matters to learning is the activity, how learners construct the task, because it shapes the learners' orientation to learn or not (Lantolf and Thorne, 2006). The process of intersubjectivity, or shared understanding in collaboration, and the support intersubjectivity provides to language-mediated communication, are elements of developing communicative abilities which are often missing in the SLA research (Lantolf and Thorne, 2006).

Limitations

Activity theory has given rise to alternative ways of conceiving of situated cognition that is mediated by its social context and culturally shaped meditational tools. However, researchers in sociocultural psychology fall victim to the circumstances that Vygotsky had warned about at the outset of his career; namely, activity cannot be an object of study and simultaneously serve as an explanatory principle of consciousness, unless it has its own unit of analysis as well as its own explanatory principles (Lantolf and Appel, 1994). Activity theory, like many other theories, has a number of unresolved problems (e.g. see Davydov, 2007). Some philosophers and psychologists dismiss it altogether due to its alleged expression of totalitarian ideology, representing human beings as mere executors of plans, orders and standards imposed from the outside. However, the third generation activity theory tries to bridge the outside and inside by including sensuous aspects, such as emotions, identity and moral dimensions of action into the unit of analysis (Engeström, 2009). While the formulation and elaboration of some ideas of this theory were influenced by the ideological and political climate at the time and place of its origin, there is great potential for new directions to be forged, and SLA is a fruitful ground for this to happen.

See also: development in SLA, identity theory, qualitative research, motivation, social and sociocultural approaches to SLA, theoretical constructs in SLA

References

Davydov, V.V. (1999). The content and unsolved problems of activity theory. In Y. Engestrom, R. Miettinen and R.-L. Punamaki (eds), *Perspectives on Activity Theory*, pp. 39–52. Cambridge: Cambridge University Press.

Engeström, Y. (1987). *Learning by Expanding: An Activity-theoretical Approach to Developmental Research*. Helsinki: Orienta-Konsultit.

——(2001). Expansive learning at work: Toward an activity theoretical reconceptualization. *Journal of Education and Work*, *14*, 133–156.

Engeström, Y. (2009). The future of activity theory: A rough draft. In A. Sannino, H. Daniels and D. Gutierrez (eds), *Learning and Expanding with Activity Theory*, pp. 303–28. Cambridge: Cambridge University Press.

Engeström, Y. and Miettinen, R. (1999). Introduction. In Y. Engestrom, R. Miettinen and R.-L. Punamaki (eds), *Perspectives on Activity Theory*, pp. 1–16. Cambridge: Cambridge University Press.

Lantolf, J. and Pavlenko, A. (2001). (S)econd (L)anguage (A)ctivity theory: understanding second language learners as people. In M.P. Breen (ed.), *Learner Contributions to Language Learning: New Directions in Research*, pp. 141–58. London: Longman.

Lantolf, J.P. and Thorne, S.L. (2006). *Sociocultural Theory and the Sociogenesis of Second Language Development*. New York: Oxford University Press.

Lantolf, J.P. and Appel, G. (1994). Theoretical framework: An introduction to Vygotskian perspectives on second language research. In J.P. Lantolf and G. Appel (eds), *Vygotskian Approaches to Second Language Research*, pp. 1–32. Norwood, NJ: Ablex.

Moro, Y. (2007). The expanded dialogic sphere: Writing activity and authoring of self in Japanese classrooms. In Y. Engestrom, R. Miettinen and R.-L. Punamaki (eds), *Perspectives on Activity Theory*, pp. 165–82. Cambridge: Cambridge University Press.

Thorne, S.L. (2004). Cultural historical activity theory and the object of innovation. In O. St. John, K. Esch and E. Schalkwijk (eds), *New Insights into Foreign Language Learning and Teaching*. Frankfurt: Peter Lang Verlag.

Affordance

Leo van Lier

Monterey Institute of International Studies

During the last decade or so, the concept of affordance has gradually made its entry into second language acquisition (SLA), and it has by now become a regularly used term in the field. I began using it in my teaching and in presentations in the early 1990s, and proposed using the ecological notion of *affordance* to replace the information-processing term *input* (van Lier, 1996; 2000). I first encountered the term in a paper by the psychologist Thomas Natsoulas (1993), in which he described the work on the ecology of visual perception by Gibson (1979). The notion seemed immediately useful, since I was working at the time on the ways in which language students worked collaboratively on computer projects (such as designing simple web pages) and learned language at the same time, often using deictic gestures and cursor movements on the screen as integral components of their interactive co-constructions. I initially incorporated the construct in my 1996 book on the importance of interaction in the language curriculum, and published a paper in 2000 arguing that the mechanistic information-processing term input could and should be replaced by the ecological notion of affordance. The term affordance is still relatively new in our field, and its raison d'être, as well as its core meaning, are as yet not widely understood. The purpose of this entry is to trace the origin and meaning of the term affordance, and discuss its relevance for language education.

The word affordance was coined by the psychologist James Jerome Gibson (1979), who defined it as "what the environment *offers* the animal, what it *provides* or *furnishes*, either for good or ill" (p. 127, emphasis in the original). For Gibson, the construct of affordance is a central component of an ecological theory of visual perception. This theory signals a radical break with traditional theories that are characterized by individual cognitive processes enriching "fleeting fragmentary scraps of data signaled by the senses" (Gregory, 1991: 512). J.J. Gibson and E. Gibson referred to their new theory as a *differentiation* theory, as opposed to traditional *enrichment* theories (Gibson and Pick, 2000). Briefly, enrichment theories assume, with Gregory, that the real work of perceiving is done in the brain. Perceptual experience, in this view, is cognitive, not environmental. The Gibsonian differentiation approach, on the other hand, assumes that the environment is richly specified, and the work of perceptual learning consists of increasingly learning to interact with this real world of affordances.

The main characteristics of an affordance-based, differentiation theory of perception are as follows:

1) Perception and action are inseparable, they co-specify one another, and thus form an action-perception system.
2) Perception is reciprocal (or dialogical), that is, other-perception is contingent on self-perception.
3) Affordances are neither objective nor subjective, they are *relational*, that is, affordances refer to relations among entities, not the entities themselves.
4) Affordances are primarily perceived directly or immediately, not indirectly or in mediated form. In other words, they do not have to go through a mental processing cycle, before being perceived, though mediation may enter into their subsequent interpretation.

Language is an inseparable part of a much broader array of meaning making resources, patterns and practices (in other words, semiotics) and occasions of language use are concretely specified in the environment in which language users and learners are active. Linguistic expressions and actions, much like gestures, facial expressions and other semiotic phenomena of the physical, social and symbolic worlds that we inhabit, carry arrays of potential affordances that can be turned into meanings (and possibilities for further action) depending on the access and engagement that a language user enjoys with the phenomena in question.

The relevance of affordances for language education

Gibson (1979) distinguishes several modes of visual perception: snapshot, ambient and ambulatory.

Traditional perceptual psychology is based on phenomena observed when an observer is stationary (snapshot). Gibson added two other modes of perception in actual contexts: ambient, when an observer is looking around, and ambulatory, when an observer is moving around in three-dimensional space.

We can suggest that all three play a role in language learning (see also, Forman, 2005).

At the risk of some oversimplification, snapshot perception is the scrutiny of grammatical rules and sentences for analysis, memorization, and subsequent application on exercises and tests. Ambient perception implies looking around, seeing rules and sentences in context (discourse), and examining the before, after, above, and below of a particular linguistic impression.

Ambulatory perception pertains to a perceiving agent who moves around and picks up information while pursuing a particular goal. One can see this as the most natural environment for picking up affordances for learning, and the most appropriate curriculum from this perspective is a project-based (or action-based – see van Lier 2007) one.

The suggested hierarchy of perceptual experience in the above scenarios is that ambulatory perception is primary and natural, and the others are merely artifacts of instructional traditions (say, of stationary learners at desks who are provided with static exemplars of linguistic practice). However, in practice things are perhaps not quite so simple. Moving around the spatio-temporal landscape of learning while picking up affordances for instructional purposes (the ambulatory scenario) may indeed be richly fruitful, but for learning to be shaped and consolidated in an instructional environment it is also necessary to require the ambient analysis of genres and registers of expression, and these in turn require much detailed (snapshot) scrutiny of grammatical and lexical patterning.

The theory of language learning affordances, in a wider ecology of learning, therefore accords a place for a variety of meaning-making resources, all of which may activate different kinds of affordances that the learning environment can enable, if this environment is set up to provide a rich semiotic budget (van Lier, 2000).

Now that the notion of affordance is gaining traction in the applied linguistics literature, it is perhaps worth concluding with the recommendation that the term affordance should be used only in the context of its twin defining features: its inseparability from *agency*, and its *dialogicity* or *reciprocity*. A third feature, the immediacy or directness of affordances (as opposed to the contribution of mediation or indirectness of various kinds) will no doubt be the subject of much debate for some time to come (Forrester, 1999; van Lier, 2004).

See also: awareness, dialogic inquiry, discourse and pragmatics in SLA, ecology of language learning, social and sociocultural approaches to SLA, symbolic mediation

References

Forman, R. (2005). *Teaching EFL in Thailand: A Bilingual Study*. Unpublished PhD thesis. University of Technology, Sydney, Australia.

Forrester, M. (1999). Conversation and instruction within apprenticeship: Affordances for learning. In Ainley, P. and Rainbird, H. (eds), *Apprenticeship: Towards a New Paradigm of Learning*, pp. 86–97. London: Kogan Page.

Gibson, E.J. and Pick, A.D. (2000). *An Ecological Approach to Perceptual Learning and Development*. Oxford: Oxford University Press.

Gibson, J.J. (1979). *The Ecological Approach to Visual Perception*. Hillsdale, NJ: Erlbaum.

Gregory, R. (1991). Seeing as thinking: An active theory of perception. In E.J. Gibson (ed.), *An Odyssey in Learning and Perception*, pp. 511–19. Cambridge, MA: MIT Press.

Natsoulas, T. (1993). Perceiving, its component stream of perceptual experience, and Gibson, J.J.'s ecological approach. *Psychological Research*, *55*, 248–57.

van Lier, L. (1996). *Interaction in the Language Curriculum: Awareness, Autonomy and Authenticity*. London: Longman.

——(2000). From input to affordance: Social-interactive learning from an ecological perspective. In J.P. Lantolf (ed.), *Sociocultural Theory and Second Language Learning: Recent Advances*, pp. 245–59. Oxford: Oxford University Press.

——(2004). *The Ecology and Semiotics of Language Learning: A Sociocultural Perspective*. Boston, MA: Kluwer Academic.

——(2007). Action-based teaching, autonomy and identity. *International Journal of Innovation in Language Learning and Teaching*, *1*, 46–65.

Age effects in SLA

Carmen Muñoz
Universitat de Barcelona

The influence that learners' age may have on their acquisition of a second or additional language has become a crucial issue in debates in both theoretical and applied areas of SLA research. Its relevance has increased as second language (L2) learning has become a common phenomenon in different political situations and varied exposure conditions, such as mass immigration (naturalistic language learning), compulsory schooling (instructed language learning), or school immersion programs. It was in the context of the latter, the Canadian immersion programs, that the debate about the best or most effective starting age began with Penfield's notion that "for the purposes of learning languages, the human brain becomes progressively stiff and rigid after the age of nine" (Penfield and Roberts, 1959: 236).

Lenneberg (1967) maintained a similar perspective with his formulation of the Critical Period Hypothesis (CPH). According to this hypothesis, there is a period in life – between the age of two and puberty – in which first language (L1) acquisition must necessarily take place, otherwise it will be impossible or incomplete. Although Lenneberg's only evidence at the time was based on his observations concerning different recovery patterns of patients with brain injuries, his biological hypothesis concurred with the Chomskyan conception of language innateness. As for L2 acquisition, it was argued that it may resemble L1 acquisition and approach nativelike attainment only if it begins during this privileged period (Johnson and Newport, 1989).

The first review of the literature on age differences dates back to the 1979 publication by Krashen, Long and Scarcella. Two findings appeared consistently across the studies then available: older starters proceed through early stages of morphological and syntactic development faster than younger starters; and child starters outperform adult starters in the long run. Hence, a distinction may be made between two types of advantage: a rate advantage for older starters, and an ultimate attainment advantage for younger starters. The latter advantage was deemed more important because it was related to the possibility that child starters, but not late starters, could achieve nativelike command of a second language. This suggests differences in learning mechanisms between children and adults that should be accounted for by a theory of language and language learning.

Research in recent decades has accumulated rich and complex evidence of age effects in L2 learning, but it has not ended the dispute about the existence, scope and characteristics of a critical period. One crucial issue in the discussion centers on the shape of the decline of age effects: whereas an elbow shape showing abrupt discontinuity after a certain age would strongly argue for the end of a privileged period for L2 acquisition, a smooth linear decline would instead suggest an age-related decline that is consistent with the contour of general cognitive deterioration (see Birdsong, 2006). Another significant point in question is that of the existence and interpretation of cases of nativelike achievement in late learners, a matter that has been expected to provide final evidence for the existence of maturational constraints.

While the jury is still out on such central issues, a number of specific research questions have sought answers in behavioral evidence, such as: are all aspects of language similarly affected by starting age of learning? Is an early starting age an absolute guarantee for nativelikeness in a second language? What is the effect of language learning aptitude? And what is the effect of learning context? Other questions have their roots in linguistic theory, psycholinguistics, or neurobiological investigation.

The issue of whether all aspects of language are similarly affected by starting age of learning is related to the existence of either one critical period or of several sensitive periods for the acquisition of the different components of a language. In view of research findings that indicate that age-related declines may be variable in onset in relation to the area of language under study, Long (1990) suggested that not all areas of language may be affected at the same time. He claims that the supposed closure for phonology may be as early as age six while it may be around 15 for morphology and syntax. Moreover, while Long holds that all aspects of language are affected by maturational constraints, including lexis as well, a different standpoint is offered by Scovel (1988), who argues that phonology is the only aspect affected by age constraints because of its neuromotor etiology.

In fact, the influence that age has on the various language dimensions seems to affect phonological development in a distinctive way. To illustrate, in the area of L1 perception, evidence sustaining a very early schedule has mounted up. In the first months of life infants are endowed with universal discrimination abilities, which decline or, more specifically, become attuned to the native language as early as one year of age. In second language acquisition, older learners may be less likely to perceive differences between L1 and L2 sounds, once the L1 categories are fully developed. As a consequence, learners may perceive and produce non-native sounds under a greater influence of their native language. Moreover, research has also shown that L2 input (its quantity and quality) and L1 use are predictive factors of L2 speech mastery (e.g., Flege, 1995).

The second question above – whether L2 learning that begins in childhood inevitably results in nativelikeness – has been addressed only recently. Findings from studies with increasingly demanding tests and measures seem to show that this is not the case, and that an early age of onset is a necessary although not sufficient requirement for nativelike ultimate attainment in a second language (Abrahamsson and Hyltenstam, 2009). Whereas such a finding does not deny the existence of a critical period as such, it introduces some complexity to the former, more deterministic prediction. Another factor that has added complexity to the critical period debate is the possible interaction between age effects and language aptitude. Mixed results have been obtained in research so far: while some findings seem to show that having superior language analytical skills is a condition for late learners' nativelike attainment in a second language (DeKeyser *et al.*, 2010), other studies have observed that a superior language learning aptitude may also be a characteristic of successful child L2 acquisition (Abrahamsson and Hyltenstam, 2008).

The role played by language learning context has not traditionally been addressed in the work inspired by maturational constraints issues. However, some authors have argued that the critical period hypothesis might only apply to language acquisition under sustained conditions of naturalistic or informal exposure, thereby excluding its generalization to situations of instructed foreign language. A reason for this may lie in the scarcity of the input learners receive in an instructed foreign language learning setting. According to DeKeyser (e.g., 2000), the lack of massive exposure to the target language does not allow children to use their superior implicit learning mechanisms, the possibility for implicit learning (acquisition from mere exposure to the language) being the critical difference between children and adults.

A number of studies have been recently conducted in instructed language learning settings that have obtained some consistent findings. First, it has been confirmed that, where exposure to the target language is limited, older children and adolescents are more efficient learners than younger children. That is to say, after the same amount of instructional hours older children are observed to attain higher levels of proficiency than younger children, especially in those areas that are more cognitively demanding (Muñoz, 2006). This finding confirms the older starters' short-term rate advantage also found in naturalistic language learning settings (Snow and Hoefnagel-Höhle, 1978). The older learners' advantage in learning rate may be the result of their superior cognitive maturity relative to younger learners, which grants older learners greater efficiency in learning. In contrast, the younger starters' advantage in ultimate attainment found in naturalistic exposure settings may be the result of the younger learners' superior implicit learning skills, but implicit learning is slow and requires massive exposure to the target language (DeKeyser, 2000). In the absence of massive exposure, younger learners in instructional settings seem to be deprived of this long-term advantage (see Muñoz, 2008).

The comparison of early and late school immersion programs has also brought evidence of age effects. In such a context, an early start has been observed to result in superior levels of language comprehension and oral production skills, relative to a late start, but not of reading comprehension and writing skills (Turnbull *et al.*, 1998). In sum, results from different learning contexts seem to show that age effects are mediated by context, so that findings from L2 learning under naturalistic exposure conditions – which provided empirical evidence for the widely extended belief that "younger is better" – are not generalizable to all L2 learning contexts.

Researchers debating age-related issues from a Chomskyan perspective are concerned with the question of whether late learners have total, partial, or no access to Universal Grammar (UG), which, according to Chomsky, informs and guides language acquisition. An active research agenda from a partial access standpoint has tried to isolate precisely which linguistic modules, submodules, features, or interface areas are affected by maturation. On the other hand, other researchers' findings indicate that late learners have full access to the target formal features or to particular UG-derived mental representations. As can be seen, the UG perspective is less concerned with nativelike performance or behavior than with underlying competence and whether the associated mental representations can continue to be induced from L2 data with advancing maturation.

A different view on the study of age effects is taken by a psycholinguistic perspective that claims that differences between younger and older learners may reside in their respective processing mechanisms. For example, work on grammatical processing seems to indicate that adult language learners under-use syntactic information and assign representations to the input that lack grammatical detail (Felser and Clashen, 2009). From a neurobiological perspective, researchers have been looking for confirmatory evidence for the claim that a late-acquired L2 is represented in the brain differently from the L1. At present, findings highlight the role of L2 proficiency and exposure as well (see Abutalebi, 2008), but despite the recent technical advances this type of research is still in its infancy.

A last concern to note from the current debate of issues revolving around age factors in SLA relates to the appropriateness of the native speaker model in the examination of L2 attainment. In brief, the important differences existing between a monolingual and a bilingual, such as the possession of knowledge of another language by the latter, suggest that there is no intrinsic reason why the L2 user's attainment should be the same as that of a monolingual native speaker (Cook, 1995). From this standpoint, some researchers argue that a more appropriate comparison might be one between later L2 beginners and those who begin to acquire an L2 in early childhood (see Muñoz and Singleton, 2011).

To conclude, the vast number of studies on age effects conducted in recent decades has enriched our knowledge of the age factor while revealing a complexity that is greater than previously suspected. In that respect, researchers from different perspectives have argued that initial age of learning may be considered a macrovariable that includes, among other factors, state of neurobiological maturation, stage of cognitive development, levels of L1 proficiency, L1 and L2 use, and language dominance. In addition, a number of factors, such as the socio-cultural context, the quality of the L2 learning experience, and learners' attitudes and orientations have been observed to combine with initial age of learning, resulting in differences in L2 attainment. Hence, research is needed that integrates quantitative and qualitative methods in order to better grasp the individual and social determinants that interplay with age of learning. In the end, the isolation of age effects on L2 acquisition may be neither possible nor the most adequate aim in age-related investigation.

See also: child second language acquisition, cognitive aging, Critical Period Hypothesis (CPH), implicit learning, native speaker, psycholinguistics of SLA

References

Abutalebi, J. (2008). Neural aspects of second language representation and language control. *Acta Psychologica*, *128*, 466–78.

Abrahamsson, N. and Hyltenstam, K. (2008). The robustness of aptitude effects in near-native second language acquisition. *Studies in Second Language Acquisition*, *30* (4), 481–509.

——(2009). Age of onset and nativelikeness in a second language: Listener perception versus linguistic scrutiny. *Language Learning*, *59* (2), 249–306.

Birdsong, D. (2006). Age and second language acquisition and processing. A selective overview. *Language Learning*, *56* (1), 9–49.

Cook, V. (1995). Multicompetence and effects of age. In D. Singleton and Z. Lengyel (eds), *The Age Factor in Second Language Acquisition*, pp. 51–56. Clevedon: Multilingual Matters.

DeKeyser, R. (2000). The robustness of critical period effects in second language acquisition. *Studies in Second Language Acquisition*, *22* (4), 499–533.

DeKeyser, R., Alfi-Shabtay, I. and Ravid, D. (2010). Cross-linguistic evidence for the nature of age effects in second language acquisition. *Applied Psycholinguistics*, *31* (4), 413–38.

Felser, C. and Clashen, H. (2009). Grammatical processing of spoken language in child and adult language learners. *Journal of Psycholinguisti Research*, *38* (3), 305–19.

Flege, J.E. (1995). Second-language speech learning: Theory, findings, and problems. In W. Strage (ed.), *Speech Perception and Linguistic Experience: Issues in Cross-language Research*, pp. 229–73. Timonium, MD: York Press.

Johnson, J.S. and Newport, E.L. (1989). Critical period effects in second language learning: The influence of maturational state on the acquisition of ESL. *Cognitive Psychology*, *21* (1), 60–99.

Krashen, S., Long, M. and Scarcella, R. (1979). Age, rate and eventual attainment in second language acquisition. *TESOL Quarterly*, 9, 573–82. Reprinted in S.D. Krashen, R.C. Scarcella and M.H. Long (eds) (1982). *Child-Adult Differences in Second Language Acquisition*, pp. 161–72. Rowley, MA: Newbury House Publishers.

Lenneberg, E.H. (1967). *Biological Foundations of Language*. New York: Wiley.

Long, M. (1990). Maturational constraints on language development. *Studies in Second Language Acquisition*, *12* (3), 251–85.

Muñoz, C. (ed.) (2006). *Age and the Rate of Foreign Language Learning*. Clevedon: Multilingual Matters.

——(2008). Symmetries and asymmetries of age effects in naturalistic and instructed L2 learning. *Applied Linguistics*, *24* (4), 578–96.

Muñoz, C. and Singleton, D. (2011). A critical review of age-related research on L2 ultimate attainment. *Language Teaching*, *44* (1), 1–35.

Penfield, W. and Roberts, L. (1959). *Speech and Brain Mechanisms*. Princeton, NJ: Princeton University Press.

Scovel, T. (1988). *A Time to Speak. A Psycholinguistic Inquiry into the Critical Period for Human Speech*. Rowley, MA: Newbury House.

Snow, C. and Hoefnagel-Höhle, M. (1978). The critical period for language acquisition: Evidence from second language learning. *Child Development*, *49*, 1114–28.

Turnbull, M., Lapkin, S., Hart, D. and Swain, M. (1998). Time on task and immersion graduates' French proficiency. In S. Lapkin (ed.), *French Second Language Education in Canada: Empirical Studies*, pp. 31–55. Toronto, ON: University of Toronto Press.

Agreement

J. Dean Mellow

Simon Fraser University

Agreement occurs when a word's form depends upon the inherent grammatical categories of another word or phrase (Anderson, 1985: 172). For example, the English verb *write* has the variants *write* and *writes*. The use of these forms agrees with the person (first, second, third) and number (singular, plural) of the subject of the sentence (i.e. *I write*; *she writes*). Other agreement patterns involve grammatical categories such as noun class (e.g., grammatical genders including masculine, feminine, and neuter) and case (e.g., subject, nominative). Compared to other languages, Modern English tends to use relatively fixed word order rather than agreement to indicate which words are members of the same phrase or clause. Bill VanPatten (personal communication) provided the following Spanish sentence in which number and gender agreement involves most major language elements (agreement is indicated in italics): "L*as* típic*as* casas roman*as* era*n* pequeñ*as* y construíd*as* de ladrillo." – "Typical Roman houses were small and built with bricks."

In second language acquisition (SLA), some agreement patterns are difficult to acquire and are learned relatively later or never fully mastered. As a result, agreement phenomena have been widely considered in research, theory development, and application. For example, a review of foundational empirical studies of morpheme order acquisition led Krashen and Terrell (1983: 29) to conclude that the third person singular non-past (3sg)-*s* suffix is usually one of the last morphemes to be acquired by English as a second language (L2) learners, supporting their hypothesis that language is learned in a Natural Order. Chen *et al.* (2007) found that advanced Chinese learners of English could accurately judge the grammaticality of agreement patterns, but exhibited neural responses (electrophysiological data in an ERP study) that were distinct from native speakers. Agreement patterns have also been incorporated into testing materials. The Language Proficiency Index (LPI) is a test for determining university-level language proficiency (University of British Columbia Applied Research and Evaluation Services, 2004). To distinguish between developing proficiency and adequate proficiency in essay writing, the LPI criteria include the number of subject–verb agreement errors.

The relatively late acquisition of patterns such as English subject–verb agreement results from the interaction of many factors. Functionally, the verbal variant is often redundant with marking of the subject and therefore non-target-like uses do not often result in a breakdown of communication. In addition, there are many variations of form and use. A variety of forms indicate agreement, including a suffix that has three phonetic variants (e.g., *write-s* [s]; *jog-s* [z]; *fish-es* [əz]), suppletive forms of some verbs (e.g., *be*: *am*, *are*, *is*; *was*, *were*), and clitics (or contracted copula and auxiliary verbs; e.g., *I'm*, *you're*, *he's*). Across English verb paradigms, agreement contrasts are relatively limited: Only 3sg is expressed as a suffix and only a few suppletive forms have additional contrasts. In some constructions, the category of the subject is not indicated by the noun that is adjacent to the verb, leading to processing and acquisition difficulties (e.g., *The group of drunk, angry, young men is rioting*). Although the verb agrees with a preceding subject in declarative sentences, in many constructions the agreeing verb precedes the nominal (e.g., *What are the answers?*; *There are two answers*).

SLA researchers have investigated agreement in relation to a variety of issues and theories. For example, researchers have examined agreement in relation to redundancy (i.e., grammatical and semantic meanings expressed by more than one element in a construction). Mellow and Cumming (1994) investigated multiple expressions of number in a noun phrase, including agreement of demonstrative pronouns (e.g., *this*, *these*), as well as the use of a variety of free morphemes (e.g., numerals, quantifiers). In essays written by French and Japanese learners of English, Mellow and Cumming found that the use of the inherent plural-*s* suffix on nouns was more accurate when plural number had previously been expressed. Schmidt (1983) reported a case study of a 33-year-old Japanese learner of English, Wes, whose spoken grammatical competence, including 3sg agreement, was very limited. However, Schmidt found that Wes had strengths in discourse and strategic competence and did not need the redundancy of grammar in communication to be successful interacting about relationships and business. VanPatten (2004) proposed a set of principles that explain the use and acquisition of constructions in which semantic and grammatical information is expressed by more than one element, including patterns affected by the attentional requirements of language tasks (e.g., essays vs. spoken interaction). VanPatten's model of Input Processing provides guidelines for language teaching and builds from a range of empirical studies including instructional experiments.

Researchers have also investigated agreement in relation to the complex syntactic constructions in which it appears. For example, Hoshino *et al.* (2010) examined sentences with a mismatch between grammatical number and conceptual number (e.g., in *The drawing on the posters is colorful*, the conceptual interpretation is that there is more than one drawing). In sentence completion tasks, Hoshino *et al.* found that highly proficient bilinguals showed greater sensitivity to both grammatical and conceptual number agreement in their L2 than did bilinguals who were less proficient in their L2. Many theoretical analyses have been proposed to explain agreement patterns within complex syntactic constructions. Hawkins (2008) and O'Grady (2008) explicitly compared the analyses provided by Minimalism, which assumes that innate linguistic knowledge is needed to explain the patterns (e.g., Prévost and White's (2000) Missing Surface Inflection Hypothesis), to the analyses provided by emergentism, which explains agreement patterns in terms of efficient sentence processing, grammaticalization, and frequency of usage.

The interaction of the factors that affect the SLA of agreement was investigated by Goldschneider and DeKeyser (2001). They conducted a meta-analysis of 12 studies of the acquisition of English grammatical morphemes, including 3sg agreement. They found that the combination of perceptual salience, semantic complexity, morphophonological regularity, syntactic category, and frequency in input accounts for a substantial portion of the order in which these elements are acquired. Through findings such as these, agreement provides a window into the complex nature of SLA and into the many ways that it can be studied.

See also: error analysis, functional categories, functional linguistics, inflectional morphemes, morpheme acquisition orders, Processing Instruction (PI)

References

Anderson, S. (1985). Inflectional morphology. In T. Shopen (ed.), *Language Typology and Syntactic Description Volume III: Grammatical categories and the lexicon*, pp. 150–201. Cambridge: Cambridge University Press.

Chen, L., Shu, H., Liu, Y., Zhao, J. and Li, P. (2007). ERP signatures of subject–verb agreement in L2 learning. *Bilingualism: Language and Cognition*, *10*, 2 161–74.

Goldschneider, J. and DeKeyser, R. (2001). Explaining the 'natural order of L2 morpheme acquisition' in English: A meta-analysis of multiple determinants. *Language Learning*, *51*, 1–50.

Hawkins, R. (2008). Commentary: Can innate linguistic knowledge be eliminated from theories of SLA? *Lingua*, *118*, 613–19.

Hoshino, N., Dussias, P. and Kroll, J. (2010). Processing subject–verb agreement in a second language depends on proficiency. *Bilingualism: Language and Cognition*, *13*, 2 87–98.

Krashen, S. and Terrell, T. (1983). *The Natural Approach: Language Acquisition in the Classroom*. Oxford: Pergamon Press.

Mellow, J.D. and Cumming, A. (1994). Concord in interlanguage: Efficiency or priming? *Applied Linguistics*, *15*, 442–73.

O'Grady, W. (2008). Commentary: Innateness, universal grammar, and emergentism. *Lingua*, *118*, 620–31.

Prévost, P. and White, L. (2000). Missing surface inflection or impairment in second language acquisition? Evidence from tense and agreement. *Second Language Research*, *16*, 2 103–33.

Schmidt, R. (1983). Interaction, acculturation, and the acquisition of communicative competence: A case study of an adult. In N. Wolfson and E. Judd (eds), *Sociolinguistics and Language Acquisition*, pp. 137–74. Rowley, MA: Newbury House.

Van Patten, B. (2004). Input processing in second language acquisition. In B. VanPatten (ed.), *Processing instruction: Theory, research, and commentary*, pp. 5–31. Mahwah, NJ: Lawrence Erlbaum.

University of British Columbia Applied Research and Evaluation Services (2004). *Preparing to Write the Language Proficiency Index (LPI)*, 3rd edn. Vancouver: University of British Columbia.

Alignment

Eric Hauser

Tokyo University of Electro-communications

As used by the sociologist Goffman (1981), *alignment* is basically synonymous with several other terms. In discussing *footing*, he states that, "Participants' alignment, or set, or stance, or posture, or projected self is somehow at issue" (p. 128). *Alignment* is taken toward participants, including self, and changes in alignment are implied by changes in footing or *frame* (Goffman, 1981; Tannen and Wallat, 1993). While alignment is not developed as a technical term in Goffman, it is so developed in linguistically oriented spoken discourse analysis. Schiffrin (1993), drawing heavily on Goffman, in particular on footing and *participation structure*, states that, "Participant alignments are related to the way that interactants position themselves relative to one another, e.g., their relationships of power and solidarity, their affective stances, their footing … " (p. 233). She places the concept within "the broader notion of participation structure (or framework), i.e., the way that speaker and hearer are related to their utterances and to one another" (p. 233). A point of continuity with Goffman is that alignment involves how participants position themselves toward one another and what they say.

Work in Conversation Analysis (CA) focuses on alignment as related to action, in particular to the actions of *recipients*. (Much of the use of this concept has been with story-telling (e.g., Stivers, 2008), but it is not only relevant to this activity.) Hutchby and Wooffitt (1998) discuss how Harvey Sacks showed that a story preface is used to align the recipients to the story as, for example, a funny story. Story recipients can then display their alignment with the teller through their response to the preface and to the story itself. They also discuss how *repair* is important for maintaining and re-establishing *interpersonal alignment*, which they treat as synonymous with *intersubjectivity*, or mutual orientations to and understandings of what participants are doing in interaction. Stivers (2008) has gone further in developing alignment as a technical term to describe actions which are responsive "to the activity in progress" (p. 34). What may be treated as an aligning response varies according to the activity that it is responsive to and the current state of the activity. For example, in the midst of a story-telling, a *continuer* would be an *aligning response*, while at the end of the story-telling, it would be a *disaligning response*. Stivers (2008) distinguishes *alignment* from *affiliation*, stating that, "In contrast to alignment, with the term *affiliation* I mean that the hearer displays support of and endorses the teller's conveyed stance" (p. 35, italics in original). Within CA, then, alignment involves how a recipient's actions fit the (ongoing) activity to which they are responsive.

Within SLA, alignment has been developed in the work of Atkinson (2011) and colleagues, who focus on alignment among participants in interaction, alignment between participants and semiotic resources, and learning as a process of alignment. How participants display alignment may also be seen as an aspect of *interactional competence*.

See also: Conversation Analysis (CA), discourse and pragmatics in SLA, pragmatics, self repair, social and socio cultural approaches to SLA, turn taking

References

Atkinson, D. (2011). A sociocognitive approach to second language acquisition. In D. Atkinson (ed.), *Alternative Approaches to Second Language Acquisition*. New York: Routledge.

Goffman, E. (1981). *Forms of Talk*. Philadelphia, PA: University of Pennsylvania Press.

Hutchby, I. and Wooffitt, R. (1998). *Conversation Analysis*. Cambridge: Polity.

Schiffrin, D. (1993). 'Speaking for Another' in sociolinguistic interviews: Alignments, identities, and frames. In D. Tannen (ed.), *Framing in Discourse*. Oxford: Oxford University Press.

Stivers, T. (2008). Stance, alignment, and affiliation during storytelling: When nodding is a token of affiliation. *Research on Language and Social Interaction*, *41*, 31–57.

Tannen, D. and Wallat, C. (1993). Interactive frames and knowledge schemas in interaction: Examples from a medical examination/interview. In D. Tannen (ed.), *Framing in Discourse*. Oxford: Oxford University Press.

Further reading

Atkinson, D. (2010). Extended, embodied cognition and second language acquisition. *Applied Linguistics*, *31*, 599–622. (Develops alignment as a theoretical concept specifically relevant to SLA. Defines learning as "a process of alignment—of continuously and progressively fitting oneself to one's environment, often with the help of guides" (p. 611), e.g., tutors.)

Churchill, E., Nishino, T., Okada, H. and Atkinson, D. (2010). Symbiotic gesture and the sociocognitive visibility of grammar in second language acquisition. *The Modern Language Journal*, *94*, 234–53. (Looks at alignment between two participants and between participants and semiotic resources in a grammar tutoring session.)

Ohta, A.S. (2001). *Second Language Acquisition Processes in the Classroom: Learning Japanese*. Mahwah, NJ: Lawrence Erlbaum. (Discusses the learning of aligning expressions in classroom learning of Japanese as a foreign language.)

Sacks, H. (1995). *Lectures on Conversation, Volumes I and II*. Oxford: Blackwell. (Contains several lectures on the activity of story-telling.)

Schegloff, E.A. (2007). *Sequence Organization in Interaction: A Primer in Conversation Analysis*. Cambridge: Cambridge University Press. (Though not the main focus, contains a concise review of CA work on repair.)

Amygdala

John Schumann
University of California, Los Angeles

The amygdala is a set of nuclei located bilaterally in the temporal lobes of the brain. Most of the research on the amygdala has been with stimuli that generate fear or threat. However, it has also been shown to be important in making appropriate character judgments, in determining the direction of another's gaze, in recognizing blended emotions and the intensity of emotions, and in appraising the reward value of stimuli. Additionally, it is seen as important in mediating cognitive functions involved in perception, attention, and memory (Damasio, 1994; Schumann, 1997; LeDoux, 2008). The standard view, based on the rodent visual system, has been that sensory information enters the brain and is transmitted to the thalamus and then to the neocortex for detailed processing, but there is also a short route that runs directly from the thalamus to the amygdala. This route makes quick and partial analyses of the emotional relevance of the stimuli which are then further processed at the cortical level (LeDoux, 1996).

Schumann (1997, 2004) suggested that the amygdala, along with the orbitofrontal cortex, and the body proper (the autonomic nervous system, the endocrine system, and the musculoskeletal system) (Damasio, 1994), the ventral striatum, the dopamine system, and now possibly the insula and the pulvinar constitute a stimulus appraisal system that learners use to evaluate the emotional and motivational relevance of stimuli in SLA (i.e., the target language culture, its speakers, the language itself and the teacher methods and texts) according to their novelty (a new or unexpected stimulus), pleasantness, goal significance, coping potential and self and social image. Schumann (1997, 2004) argues that these dimensions of stimulus appraisal and the neural mechanism that supports them are what underlies the motivational constructs that have been studied in second language acquisition research (e.g., integrative, instrumental, intrinsic, value-expectancy, etc.). Thus the amygdala focuses attention on stimuli and stimulus situations. It has connections to the nucleus basalis of Meynert which is a source of acetylcholine which is widely distributed in the cortex and facilitates the processing of information and therefore may mediate aspects of cognition and learning.

SLA research frequently dichotomizes affect and cognition. From a neural perspective, this distinction is difficult to maintain. For example, the amygdala certainly mediates affect via its appraisal functions, but it also mediates cognition and learning through its attentional and memory functions. The numerous case studies of SLA (Schumann, 1997) based on learner autobiographies suggest that the enhancing and inhibiting effects of the amygdala and related areas guide the learners' cognitive efforts in acquiring the L2. It must be noted, however, that the relationship of this neural appraisal system and SLA remains hypothetical until appropriate imaging technology is available to test it.

See also: Acculturation Model, attention, emotion, motivation, psycholinguistics of SLA, willingness to communicate (WTC)

References

Damasio, A.R. (1994). *Decartes' Error: Emotion, Reason, and the Human Brain*. New York: Grosset/Putnam.

LeDoux, J. (1996). *The Emotional Brain: The Mysterious Underpinnings of Emotional Life*. New York: Simon and Schuster.

——(2008). Amygdala. *Scholarpedia*, *3*(4): 2698.

Schumann, J.H. (1997). *The Neurobiology of Affect in Language*. Malden, MA: Blackwell Publishers.

——Crowell, S.E., Jones, N.E., Lee, Namhee, Schuchert, S.A. and Wood, L.A. (2004). *The Neurobiology of Learning: Perspectives from Language Acquisition*. Mahwah, NJ: Lawrence Erlbaum.

Further reading

Pessoa, L. and Adolphs, R. (2010). Emotion processing and the amygdala: from a 'low road' to 'many roads' of evaluating biological significance. *Nature Reviews Neuroscience*, *11*, 773–82. (Research on the visual system of primates indicates that cortical inputs to the amygdala via the visual thalamus (pulvinar) are more important than previously thought.)

Analogical mapping in construction learning

Paul Ibbotson and Michael Tomasello
University of Manchester and Max Planck Institute for Evolutionary Anthropology

All theories of language acquisition agree that from an early age children do not just work with concrete words and phrases, but they also use some kinds of linguistic abstractions. Traditionally, this has meant mainly lexical categories like nouns and verbs, or possibly syntactic categories like subjects and direct objects. In these cases, the cognitive processes for acquisition would be straightforward categorization, based on similarities of either form or function. Traditionally, such categories were thought to be "glued together" into sentences with abstract rules.

Construction grammar offers a different approach in which utterances or sentences as wholes are categorized, and this process replaces rules as such (Goldberg, 1995). In cognitive science, finding the common relational structure of complex entities – that is, similarities not of the items involved but of the relations among items – is called analogy (Gentner and Markman, 1997). In construction grammar, young children construct not only lexical and syntactic categories, but also abstract constructions. These include whole utterance level constructions such as the transitive, intransitive, ditransitive and caused motion. When the learner is trying to comprehend the two transitive sentences the "*the goat ate the woman*" and "*a woman tickled a goat,*" they do not begin by aligning elements on the basis of the literal similarity between the two goats, but match the goat and the woman because they are both construed as playing similar roles in the event, such as *actor* or *undergoer*. There is much evidence that people, including young children, focus on these kinds of relations in making analogies across linguistic constructions, the most important being the meaning of the words involved, especially the verbs, and the spatial, temporal, and causal relations they encode (e.g., Gentner and Markman, 1997; Gentner and Medina, 1998; Tomasello, 2003).

Analogy also operates in a more abstract sense, by extending the prototypical meaning of constructions. For example, the meaning of the ditransitive construction is closely associated with "transfer of possession" as in "*John gave Mary a goat.*" Metaphorical extensions of this pattern, such as "*John gave the goat a kiss*" or even "*Cry me a river*" are understood by analogy to the core meaning of the construction from which they were extended, which in the case of the ditransitive is something like "X causes Y to receive Z" (Goldberg, 2006).

Analogy also functions at the level of words and sounds. When a learner says "*I goed to shops*" it is by analogy to a set of verbs which mark past tense in English with-*ed*. Likewise, "*I brung it*" is produced by analogy to "phonological neighbours" which show similar sound alternations, such as "*sing-sung*"→"*bring-brung.*" When a number of exemplars show systematic variation they can be analogized as instances of a more general pattern where the linguistic items play similar communicative roles, in what Tomasello has called functionally based distributional analysis (Tomasello, 2003). So, whether children or second language learners are learning syntactic, morphological, or phonological patterns, analogical mapping plays a central role in learning and in using constructions.

See also: construction learning, form-meaning relations, frequency effects, language and the lexicon in SLA, development in SLA, metaphor.

References

Gentner, D. and Markman, A. (1997). Structure mapping in analogy and similarity. *American Psychologist*, *52*, 45–56.

Gentner, D. and Medina, J. (1998). Similarity and the development of rules. *Cognition*, *65*, 263–97.

Goldberg, A. (1995). *Constructions*: *A Construction Grammar Approach to Argument Structure*. Chicago, IL: University of Chicago Press.

——(2006). *Constructions at Work*: *The Nature of Generalisations in Language*. Oxford: Oxford University Press.

Tomasello, M. (2003). *Constructing a Language*: *A Usage-based Theory of Language Acquisition*. Cambridge, MA: Harvard University Press.

Further reading

Tomasello, M. (2003). *Constructing a Language: A Usage-based Theory of Language Acquisition.* Cambridge, MA: Harvard University Press. (How a uniquely human ability to comprehend intention is interwoven with cognitive abilities, such as pattern-finding and analogical mapping, to learn language.)

Analysis of variance (ANOVA)

Jenifer Larson-Hall
University of North Texas

Analysis of variance (ANOVA) is a statistical technique that tests for group differences. The basic logic is to compare the ratio of differences between groups (how much the groups differ from each other) to the differences within groups (how much variation there is within the group itself). If the groups come from the same population, this ratio will be approximately 1. However, if the differences between groups are much larger than the differences within groups, this ratio will increase to 2 or larger. In such cases the probability of finding this large of a ratio becomes very small and we conclude that differences between groups are statistically significant.

Different types of ANOVA are used depending on how many dependent and independent variables are examined. The dependent variable should be measured on an interval-level scale, and in the SLA field is often obtained through means of a test (such as a cloze test for grammar), a count (how many times each participant uses the correct tense out of all of the verbs produced, for example), a measure of reaction time, or judges' ratings (how pragmatically appropriate responses are, for example). Most often ANOVA are conducted with only one dependent variable (an analysis with more than one dependent variable is a MANOVA).

It is more common that ANOVA will differ in number of independent variables (IV). IVs are categorical (nominal) variables that name some division of interest to the researcher, such as gender, membership in an experimental group, or proficiency level. An ANOVA with only one IV is a one-way ANOVA. An ANOVA with more than one IV can be a factorial ANOVA or a repeated-measures ANOVA, depending on whether the same people are included in more than one level of the categorical variable. If the same people are tested at more than one time or on more than one related category (such as phonological contrasts), a repeated-measures ANOVA should be used. Such ANOVAs can show the interaction of IVs. Generally, no more than three IVs should be used in one ANOVA.

A good online calculator for one-way ANOVA is www.physics.csbsju.edu/stats/anova_NGROUP_NMAX_form.html. No reliable calculators for more complex ANOVA are available online—use statistical software such as SPSS or R.

All ANOVAs return several pieces of information on the main (omnibus) test:

- the F statistic (this is the ratio mentioned above)
- the probability of the F (the p-value)
- the degrees of freedom of the ratio numerator (the between-groups calculation) and denominator (the within-groups calculation, also called the error).

Additionally, include information on effect size using eta-squared statistics. For example:

> A one-way ANOVA found no differences between experimental groups ($F_{3,68} = 0.78$, $p = 0.69$, $\eta^2 = 0.03$). The effect size was negligible.

A finding that an ANOVA is statistically significant simply means that not all of the groups come from the same population. If there are more than two levels of the IV, further testing with post hoc tests or more simplified ANOVAs is necessary to determine exactly whether and how the levels differ from one another.

See also: correlation, effect size, mixed methods research, quantitative research, significance level, variance

Further reading

Hatch, E.M. and Lazaraton, A. (1991). *The Research Manual: Design and Statistics for Applied*

Linguistics. New York: Newbury House. (Uses examples from SLA; Chapters 11–13 cover ANOVA design.)

Howell, D.C. (2009). *Statistical Methods for Psychology*, 7th edn. Pacific Grove, CA: Duxbury/ Thomson Learning. (Thorough statistical coverage; Chapters 11, 13 and 14 cover ANOVA design.)

Larson-Hall, J. (2010). *A Guide to Doing Statistics in Second Language Research Using SPSS*. New York: Routledge. (Uses examples from SLA and shows how to use SPSS and R statistical software; Chapters 10–12 cover ANOVA design.)

Perry, F.L. (2005). *Research in Applied Linguistics: Becoming a Discerning Consumer*. Mahwah, NJ: Lawrence Erlbaum Associates. (Chapter 7 helps readers understand research results from statistics.)

Analysis-control model

Ellen Bialystok
York University

The analysis-control model was conceptualized as a means of understanding variation in the development of metalinguistic ability in children and acquisition of second-language proficiency in adults. In both cases, language proficiency depended on features of the task that interacted with ability levels of the learners, although both the process and progress of language learning were different for children and adults. The main claim of the model was that language learning appeared to progress in a unitary manner, characterized by steady increases in proficiency, but was in fact based on two separable component skills (later called processes). Because advance in each of these skills was largely correlated, it was difficult to see their independent influences on development. However, targeted comparisons, such as between children learning a first language and adults learning a second language, and monolingual and bilingual children learning a first language, provided a means to disentangle these two skills.

The model was first presented by Bialystok and Ryan (1985) and was further developed over the next several years (e.g., Bialystok, 1993). The model distinguished between metalinguistic tasks in terms of their demand for detailed or explicit knowledge of language structure, as in grammaticality judgment and correction tasks, and their demand for attention to ignore misleading information, as in repetition of sentences with errors. The first task demand required *analysis of linguistic knowledge* – the developmental progress in which the representation for knowledge of language became increasingly explicit. The idea was that information is first acquired in a rather implicit manner with the corresponding representations being unarticulated and general. With development, the representations reorganize and become more explicit, with clear relations between connecting information. As the representations become more explicit, specific details can be accessed, evaluated, and manipulated, making linguistic knowledge available for the type of scrutiny required by some metalinguistic tasks. The second task demand required *control of linguistic processing* – the emergence of the ability to control attention to relevant information when irrelevant information is competing for attention. In different contexts of language use, such as speaking, reading, or writing, attention must be focused on form or meaning according to specific protocols. The ability to carry out the appropriate attentional procedures depends primarily on mechanisms of attention rather than on the richness of the linguistic representations (although the two are related).

Research following from the model was used to explain discontinuities in adult second language learning (Bialystok, 1982) and differences between monolingual and bilingual children in metalinguistic development (Bialystok, 1986, 1988). The key discovery was that bilingualism promoted the development of control but had little impact on analysis. This idea was extended to nonverbal tasks, beginning with a study of children (Bialystok and Majumder, 1998) and eventually demonstrated across the lifespan (e.g., Bialystok *et al.*, 2004). As the terms of the model have been continually refined, the applicability has become more general. A current version of the analysis-control model, now called representation and control, is the basis for a description of cognitive change across the lifespan (Craik and Bialystok, 2006).

See also: automaticity, attention, awareness, bilingualism and SLA, explicit learning, implicit learning

References

Bialystok, E. (1982). On the relationship between knowing and using linguistic forms. *Applied Linguistics*, *3*, 181–206.

——(1986). Factors in the growth of linguistic awareness. *Child Development*, *57*, 498–510.

——(1988). Levels of bilingualism and levels of linguistic awareness. *Developmental Psychology*, *24*, 560–67.

——(1993). Metalinguistic awareness: The development of children's representations of language. In C. Pratt and A. Garton (eds), *Systems of representation in children: development and use*, pp. 211–33. London: Wiley and Sons.

Bialystok, E., Craik, F.I.M., Klein, R. and Viswanathan, M. (2004). Bilingualism, aging, and cognitive control: Evidence from the Simon task. *Psychology and Aging*, *19*, 290–303.

Bialystok, E. and Majumder, S. (1998). The relationship between bilingualism and the development of cognitive processes in problem-solving. *Applied Psycholinguistics*, *19*, 69–85.

Bialystok, E. and Ryan, E.B. (1985). Towards a definition of metalinguistic skill. *Merrill-Palmer Quarterly*, *31*, 229–51.

Craik, F.I.M. and Bialystok, E. (2006). Cognition through the lifespan cognition: Mechanisms of change. *Trends in Cognitive Sciences, 10,* 131–38.

Anxiety

Jean-Marc Dewaele
Birkbeck College, University of London

Foreign Language Anxiety (FLA) has attracted a lot of attention in Second Language Acquisition (SLA) research because of its perceived negative effect on learning and using the foreign language. MacIntyre and Gardner (1994: 284) defined FLA as "the feeling of tension and apprehension specifically associated with second language contexts, including speaking, listening, and learning." FLA that occurs within the foreign language classroom has been labeled Foreign Language Classroom Anxiety (FLCA) and defined as "a distinct complex of self-perceptions, beliefs, feelings and behaviors related to classroom learning arising from the uniqueness of the language learning process" (Horwitz *et al.*, 1986: 128). The authors illustrate it with a statement of one of their participants: "When I'm in my Spanish class I just freeze! I can't think of a thing when my teacher calls on me. My mind goes blank" (Horwitz *et al.*, 1986: 125). FLCA is typically highest for speaking the foreign language (FL), but it can also affect comprehension. It affects learners at all levels although it levels off after years of practice in the FL (Dewaele *et al.*, 2008). Foreign language teachers have been warned to recognize explicit anxiety-indicating cues, so as to identify learners who struggle with high levels of FLCA. This is not an easy task, as some learners are silent because they are frozen with FLCA while others might be shy, introvert, tired, sad, sulking, or simply bored with the topic (Horwitz *et al.*, 1986). Tackling FLCA is very important because it can impede learning and performance (Horwitz, 2001). Feelings of displeasure and FLCA are obstacles in FL learning: reciprocal paths seem to exist between language anxiety and motivation. High levels of motivation abate FLCA, and high levels of FLCA inhibit motivation, which in turn affects progress in FL learning. High levels of FLCA in the classroom have been linked with a wish to drop the study of FLs (Dewaele and Thirtle, 2009). However, Marcos-Llinas and Juan Garau (2009) have argued that FLCA can also have a facilitative effect and push learners to higher levels of FL achievement.

Early research on the link between success in SLA and FLCA reported contradictory findings which have been linked to a confusion in levels of abstraction, more specifically the distinction between trait anxiety, situation-specific anxiety, and state anxiety. Traits refer to stable, general patterns of behavior. In other words, an individual with a high level of trait anxiety is likely to feel anxious in a variety of situations, but may feel particularly anxious in FL classroom (FLCA is a situation-specific anxiety).

One consistent finding in research on FLA/FLCA is the huge amount of variation between learners. The precise reasons why learners suffer from FLCA are diffuse, but the most frequently cited reasons are fear of making mistakes, being laughed at, pursuing high expectations, showing low self-esteem, or failing the language class (Marcos-Llinas and Juan Garau, 2009). Investigations into the possible psychological and sociobiographical causes of FLA/FLCA have revealed complex interactions of different clusters of independent variables.

Onwuegbuzie *et al.* (1999) identified seven variables that were significantly linked to FLA among American students enrolled in FL courses (i.e. age, academic achievement, prior history of visiting foreign countries, prior high school experience with foreign languages, expected overall average for current language course, perceived scholastic competence, and perceived self-worth). Freshmen and sophomores reported the lowest levels of FLA, and FLA levels increased linearly as a function of year of study. A further study by Onwuegbuzie, Bailey and Daley (2000) on a similar population identified the same independent variables as being linked to higher levels of FLA, with the addition of perceived intellectual ability and perceived job competence.

Multilinguals who score high on the Trait Emotional Intelligence scale have been found to suffer significantly less from FLA (Dewaele *et al.*, 2008), possibly because they are better at gauging the emotional state of their interlocutor and feel more confident (and hence less anxious) about their ability to communicate effectively. The history of the learning of the FL also plays a role, with later starters and formally instructed learners suffering more from FLA than early starters and learners who had also used their language outside the classroom. The knowledge of more languages, a higher frequency of use of the FL, a stronger socialization in the FL, the use of the FL with a larger network of interlocutors, and a higher level of self-perceived proficiency in the TL are also linked to lower levels of FLA (Dewaele *et al.*, 2008).

The FL teacher is a crucial factor in FLCA for FL language learners whose only contact with the FL is through classroom instruction. FL teachers who are comprehensible, can convince the learners of the value of learning a language in a "safe" and positive learning environment where nobody is afraid to speak up for fear of ridicule are more likely to have less anxious learners (Arnold and Fonseca, 2007). The friendly classroom environment, the use of humor, the choice of pertinent and appealing subject matter linked to the learners' interests can reduce FLCA (Ewald,2007) and establish a good "rapport" between teacher and learners. Teachers can also help combat students' FLCA through particular techniques. Arnold (2000) showed that visualization-relaxation training exercises can lower FLCA and improve listening performance of advanced FL learners.

See also: attitudes to the L2, Attitudes and Motivation Test Battery (AMTB), emotions, individual differences in SLA, instructed SLA, motivation

References

Arnold, J. (2000). Seeing through listening comprehension exam anxiety. *TESOL Quarterly*, *34*, 777–86.

Arnold, J. and Fonseca, C. (2007). Affect in teacher talk. In B. Tomlinson (ed.), *Language Acquisition and Development*. London: Continuum.

Dewaele, J.-M. and Thirtle, H. (2009). Why do some young learners drop foreign languages? A focus on learner-internal variables. *International Journal of Bilingual Education and Bilingualism*, *12*, 635–49.

Dewaele, J.-M., Petrides, K.V. and Furnham, A. (2008). The effects of trait emotional intelligence and sociobiographical variables on communicative anxiety and foreign language anxiety among adult multilinguals: A review and empirical investigation. *Language Learning*, *58*, 911–60.

Ewald, J. (2007). Foreign language learning anxiety in upper-level classes: Involving students as researchers. *Foreign Language Annals*, *40*, 122–43.

Horwitz, E.K. (2001). Language anxiety and achievement. *Annual Review of Applied Linguistics*, *21*, 112–26.

Horwitz, E.K., Horwitz, M.B. and Cope, J. (1986). Foreign language classroom anxiety. *Modern Language Journal*, *70*, 125–32.

MacIntyre, P.D. and Gardner, R.C. (1994). The subtle effects of language anxiety on cognitive processing in the second language. *Language Learning*, *44*, 283–305.

Marcos-Llinas, M. and Juan Garau, M. (2009). Effects of language anxiety on three proficiency-level courses of Spanish as a foreign language. *Foreign Language Annals*, *42* (1), 94–111.

Onwuegbuzie, A., Bailey, P. and Daley, C.E. (1999). Factors associated with foreign language anxiety. *Applied Psycholinguistics*, *20*, 217–39.

——(2000). Cognitive, affective, personality, and demographic predictors of foreign-language achievement. *The Journal of Educational Research*, *94*, 3–15.

Further reading

Dewaele, J.-M. (2009). Perception, attitude and motivation. In V. Cook and Li Wei (eds), *Language Teaching and Learning*, pp. 163–92. London: Continuum.

——(2010). *Emotions in Multiple Languages*. Basingstoke: Palgrave Macmillan.

Dörnyei, Z. and Ushioda, E. (eds) (2009). *Motivation, Language Identity and the L2 Self*. Bristol: Multilingual Matters.

Kramsch, C. (2009). *The Multilingual Subject. What Foreign Language Learners Say about their Experiences and Why it Matters*. Oxford: Oxford University Press.

MacIntyre, P.D. (2002). Motivation, anxiety and emotion. In P. Robinson (ed.), *Individual Differences and Instructed Language Learning*, pp. 45–68. Amsterdam: Benjamins.

Aptitude-trait complexes

Phillip L. Ackerman
Georgia Institute of Technology

From an individual-differences perspective in psychology, a complex represents some combination of traits (i.e., relative stable individual characteristics) that share common variance. That is, a complex would represent two or more characteristics of individuals that are found to "go together" in the sense that they are positively correlated with one another. The term "aptitude complex" was developed by Snow (1963) in the context of a hypothesis that specific combinations of abilities might be "particularly appropriate or inappropriate for efficient learning." Aptitudes, in the framework articulated by Cronbach (1957) and later extrapolated by Cronbach and Snow (1977), refer to a wide variety of individual traits, not just those in the cognitive domain. The more generic term "trait complex" was coined by Ackerman and Heggestad (1997) to make explicit that there is significant common variance among a variety of personal characteristics, including cognitive (aptitudes, intelligence, and achievement), affective (personality and emotions), and conative traits (interests and motivation). One trait complex has been called "intellectual/cultural," and it represents the shared variance among such traits as verbal abilities, artistic and investigative interests, and personality characteristics of openness to experience and typical intellectual engagement. Another trait complex has been called "social" and it consists of social and enterprising interests and extroversion and social dominance personality characteristics, but no cognitive abilities (partly because there are few indicators of "social intelligence").

Some trait complexes, such as the intellectual/cultural trait complex, have been found to be positive predictors of the acquisition of knowledge in academic and everyday domains. Others, such as the social trait complex, have been found to be negative predictors for the acquisition of academic domain knowledge, but not in the acquisition of everyday knowledge (e.g., current events or health and nutrition knowledge).

Traditional approaches to individual differences in learning and skill acquisition have taken a piecemeal approach – they focus only on aptitudes or interests or personality. The aptitude-trait complex approach takes account of the fact that, some learners may have an aptitude for acquisition of a particular skill, but have little motivation or interest in that skill. Other learners may have modest aptitudes, but high levels of motivation and interest. Such learners may compensate for cognitive limitations by devoting more time and effort for out-of-the-classroom activities that lead to better achievement outcomes. The aptitude-trait complex approach takes account of the "whole person" in a way that traditional piecemeal approaches do not.

Knowing an individual's abilities allows one to predict learning, when other variables are equal, such as when interest in the topic area and motivation for success in learning are equally high. This is a situation that mostly occurs in maximal performance situations. Predicting maximal performance is useful, but aptitude variables only explain a part of the variance in learning, when one considers the individual's "typical" behaviors. Understanding the interactions among traits may enhance prediction of success in learning contexts, and may also be used in tailoring instructional treatments, to best match the characteristics of the individual to the structure and context of the instruction.

See also: aptitude, Aptitude treatment interaction (ATI) research, individual differences in SLA, instructed SLA, motivation, variance

References

Ackerman, P.L. and Heggestad, E.D. (1997). Intelligence, personality, and interests: Evidence for overlapping traits. *Psychological Bulletin*, *121*, 219–45.

Cronbach, L.J. (1975). Beyond the two disciplines of scientific psychology. *American Psychologist*, *30*, 116–27.

Cronbach, L.J. and Snow, R.E. (1977). *Aptitudes and Instructional Methods: A Handbook for Research on Interactions*. New York: Irvington Publishers.

Snow, R.E. (1963). *Effects of Learner Characteristics in Learning from Instructional Films*. Unpublished doctoral thesis. Purdue University. University Microfilms #6404928.

Further reading

Ackerman, P.L. (1996). A theory of adult intellectual development: process, personality, interests, and knowledge. *Intelligence*, *22*, 229–59.

Ackerman, P.L. and Lohman, D.F. (2006). Individual differences in cognitive functions. In P.A. Alexander, P.R. Pintrich, and P.H. Winne (eds), *Handbook of Educational Psychology*, 2nd edn, pp. 139–61. Mahwah, NJ: Lawrence Erlbaum Associates.

Goff, M. and Ackerman, P.L. (1992). Personality-intelligence relations: Assessing typical intellectual engagement. *Journal of Educational Psychology*, *84*, 537–52.

Robinson, P. (2001). Individual differences, cognitive abilities, aptitude complexes, and learning conditions in second language acquisition. *Second Language Research*, *17*, 368–92.

Snow, R.E. (1989). Aptitude-treatment interaction as a framework for research on individual differences in learning. In P.L. Ackerman, R.J. Sternberg, and R. Glaser (eds), *Learning and individual differences. Advances in theory and research*, pp. 13–59. New York: W.H. Freeman.

Aptitude

Robert M. DeKeyser
University of Maryland

Any layman knows that some people are better at learning languages than others, and decades of research have confirmed the importance of aptitude for learning a foreign language. Many questions remain, however: about the relative importance of aptitude compared to other factors such as motivation, personality, age, instruction and practice; about the nature of aptitude and its components, about the best ways to measure it, and about its interaction with other variables. For a variety of reasons, little empirical work on aptitude for L2 learning was carried out in the last couple of decades of the twentieth century, but several new lines of research are budding, and a major effort to develop a better test battery is underway. This article will first explain the relationship between aptitude and several related concepts, then provide a short overview of the research in the middle of the twentieth century, go on to describe some of the research efforts currently underway and end with some considerations about why research on aptitude is important for various theoretical and practical reasons.

A terminological roadmap

Aptitude is most commonly thought of as a specialized form of intelligence. Some people have more aptitude for math, others for languages, still others for music or for mechanics. For some individuals the differences between these various aptitudes can be dramatic, but for the population as a whole aptitudes of various kinds tend to correlate fairly strongly, which enables us to think of something like general cognitive aptitude, often called intelligence. For most kinds of learning, however, whether in school or in informal learning contexts, more than merely cognitive aptitude is required. Motivation, personality traits and previous experiences are often equally or more predictive, and some educational psychologists use the term aptitude to refer to this constellation of factors that makes somebody "ready" to learn a particular kind of thing at a particular point in time. From there it is only a small step to adding "under particular conditions", which leads to the concept of aptitude-treatment interaction: aptitudes, even in the wider sense of the word, are not predictive of all learning in some abstract sense, but rather of a particular kind of learning, which can be encouraged and facilitated or discouraged and hampered by teaching methodologies and other learning contexts. For reasons of space, this article is limited to cognitive aptitude; interaction with the learning context will be discussed briefly, however, towards the end.

Aptitude is definitely not to be confused with achievement or proficiency, which are the results of a learning process that was enabled by aptitude. Ability is a more ambiguous term, sometimes used as a synonym of aptitude, other times to refer to the skills that result from the learning process.

Early work on aptitude for L2 learning: pursuing predictive validity

Just as the First World War provided a great impetus to the development of tests for mental abilities in general, the Second World War created an urgent need for a test that would predict chances of success in short-term language learning. Crash courses for military personnel were being developed in a variety of languages, and given the time pressure and the variety of languages involved, it was very important to determine who would benefit from intensive training and in what languages. Tests were developed by starting from educated guesses about what kinds of learning a language learner should be good at and what tasks would give a good indication that a potential student was promising on these points, and then working on the internal consistency of these tasks (by eliminating and replacing test items that did not correlate well with the others) and, most importantly, selecting the tasks that proved to correlate most with rapid progress in classroom language learning. Various iterations of these processes led to three tests that are currently still in use, one restricted to the US government (the Defense Language Aptitude Battery or DLAB), the other two also available to civilian researchers and administrators (the Modern Language Aptitude Test (MLAT, published by Carroll and Sapon in 1959) and the Pimsleur Language Aptitude Battery (PLAB, published by Pimsleur in 1966). The MLAT was later adapted/translated for a variety of native languages, and a children's version was developed (EMLAT). The US government developed the VORD (cf. Parry and Child, 1990), but its predictive validity was lower than that of the MLAT, and a new version of the DLAB is now being developed (DLAB-2) instead. In an effort to avoid limiting a test to speakers of one native language, Meara developed the LLAMA, which offers the additional advantage that it can be taken on the internet, but no reliability or validity data are available yet.

All these tests have essentially the same problem, which they share with the testing of aptitude or intelligence in general: the tests were developed with – understandably – predictive validity as their main concern. This implies that they are not particularly revealing about the nature or the components of aptitude. Just like for measures of intelligence, the test results have been subjected to a number of factor-analytic studies, which show that a) various relatively independent components underlie the results on the test and b) these components of aptitude do not correspond neatly to the various parts of the test (see Carroll, 1990).

Current work on aptitude for L2 learning

In recent years, various researchers have tried to provide a better conceptualization for language aptitude than "what is measured by a language aptitude test." These developments have been driven by developments in both the study of second language acquisition and in cognitive psychology. As a result, more attention is given now to working memory, to implicit learning processes (cf. Kaufman *et al.*, 2010), and to more specialized aspects such as aptitude for learning phonetics or pragmatics, or aptitudes that are particularly relevant at certain stages of the learning process (Skehan, 1998: Ch. 5). Many studies in the last couple of decades have shown the importance of working memory for various aspects of first and second language learning and use (for a summary see DeKeyser and Koeth, 2011). Some evidence suggests that musical ability predicts the acquisition of phonology, even after partialing out various other factors (cf. Slevc and Miyake, 2006). There is also evidence of the genetic basis (i.e. heritability) of second language learning aptitude (Dale *et al.*, 2010) and of the predictive validity of first language skills at various ages for second language learning aptitude and achievement (Sparks *et al.*, in press). Finally, neuroimaging techniques are brought to bear on the aptitude issue, as they are on many others (e.g. Reiterer, 2009).

The only new test that is available so far as a result of these theoretical and empirical developments is the CANAL-FT (cf. Grigorenko *et al.*, 2000). It differs from the previous generation of tests in essentially three ways: it is grounded in cognitive theory (Sternberg's triarchic theory of intelligence); it is dynamic, that is, it involves the ability to learn at the time of the test, rather than some inherent ability; and it is a simulation of the learning of a language, proceeding through a number of stages that are built on the previous ones, so that vocabulary and grammar learned early on play a role in later learning. The language learned during the test is one designed for this specific purpose and called Ursulu. Because the test components are based on theory, scores on the various components can be used for diagnostic purposes and to match students with treatments. In spite of all these improvements, however, the predictive validity does not seem much different so far from that of the MLAT or the PLAB, and the test has the disadvantage of taking much longer to administer, about three hours.

New test development is underway at the University of Maryland's Center for the Advanced Study of Language. The Hi-Lab test battery is designed to be a better predictor than the existing tests for learning of harder languages at higher levels (Doughty *et al.*, 2010). While predictive validity is clearly the main goal, and while the test is not based on any specific theory, it is, of course, more informed by contemporary views of second language acquisition and learning processes more generally than older tests. Various aspects of working memory, as well as individual differences in implicit learning ability are incorporated, along with aspects of language that were underrepresented in previous tests, in particular phonetics. At the time of writing, it is undergoing validity testing. The current version takes about two hours.

Besides new theorizing about aptitude and new test development, an important new tendency is visible in the empirical work. While before almost all researchers limited themselves to reporting correlations between (various components of) aptitude and (various components of) proficiency, recent experimental research often involves interactions between aptitude (components) and other independent variables, whether they be treatment variables or variables inherent to the learner.

The importance of aptitude has been shown to vary dramatically depending on the number of instances presented for inductive learning of a pattern (Brooks *et al.*, 2006), on whether the learning process is largely explicit or largely implicit ("incidental") (Robinson, 1996), or on the amount of metalinguistic information provided. Research on this last point can appear contradictory, because aptitude was more important in the more explicit treatment in Sheen (2007), and less important in the more explicit treatment in Erlam (2005), but this is probably an indication that the explicit information in the latter relieved some of the inductive burden for the less able learners, whereas in Sheen's study, because of the time pressure involved, it was helpful only for the ablest learners. This illustrates two points often made by educational psychologists who study aptitude-treatment interaction (Corno *et al.*, 2002): that aptitude becomes more important as the treatment puts more of a burden of information processing on the learners, and that many second-order interactions occur, in this case aptitude × explicitness × time pressure. Interactions can also occur between constellations of aptitude ("aptitude complexes") and treatment conditions (see esp. Robinson [2007] for discussion of this issue in the second language context).

Aptitude has also been shown repeatedly to interact with age of second language acquisition: DeKeyser (2000) and Abrahamsson and Hyltenstam (2008) both showed that only high-aptitude learners do well past puberty, while high aptitude is not a requirement for success in younger learners; DeKeyser *et al.* (2010) show that for learners below 18 aptitude plays little role, but age is a strong predictor, while after age 18 (at least up to age 40) age plays little role and aptitude is an important predictor.

The importance of research on aptitude for second language learning

In the past research on aptitude has been used mainly for two obvious goals: for theoretical reasons, to determine the role of aptitude in language learning, and for practical goals, mainly to select learners for specific programs, in particular in the US government. Both in the practical and theoretical realms, however, the importance of aptitude research goes far beyond that.

The interaction between aptitudes on the one hand and treatments or other elements of the learning context on the other hand reveals much more about aptitudes and treatments than a study on only one of the two can provide, not only in the obvious practical sense of showing that certain treatments are better for certain types of learners, suggesting differential instruction (at least in part) for different individuals, but also by providing evidence for exactly HOW certain treatments work (as suggested by what aptitudes they interact with and how) and exactly WHAT certain aptitudes contribute to the learning process (as suggested by the conditions under which they do or do not play a role). These kinds of insights into the process of learning a second language are even more fundamental and more generalizable in their applicability than the direct implications in the sense of how to adapt instruction to individuals (or at least to groups of learners).

At the same time, the increasing sophistication and internal differentiation of the aptitude tests being developed should make them more useful for the traditional purpose of selection, allowing for more precise prediction of who would be a good learner of what aspects of what language at what level.

See also: age effects in SLA, Aptitude-treatment interaction (ATI) research, attention, dynamic assessment, individual differences and SLA, Triarchic Theory of intelligence

References

Abrahamsson, N. and Hyltenstam, K. (2008). The robustness of aptitude effects in near-native second language acquisition. *Studies in Second Language Acquisition*, *30*(4), 481–509.

Brooks, P.J., Kempe, V. and Sionov, A. (2006). The role of learner and input variables in learning inflectional morphology. *Applied Psycholinguistics*, *27*(2), 185–209.

Carroll, J.B. (1981). Twenty-five years of research on foreign language aptitude. In K.C. Diller (ed.), *Individual Differences and Universals in Language Learning Aptitude*, pp. 83–118. Rowley, MA: Newbury House.

——(1990). Cognitive abilities in foreign language aptitude: Then and now. T. Parry and C. Stansfield (eds), *Language Aptitude Reconsidered*, pp. 11–27. Englewood Cliffs, NJ: Prentice Hall.

Carroll, J.B. and Sapon, S. (1959). *Modern Language Aptitude Test. Form A*. New York: The Psychological Corporation.

Corno, L. (2002). Aptitude: The once and future concept. In L. Corno *et al.* (eds), *Remaking the Concept of Aptitude. Extending the Legacy of Richard E. Snow*, pp. 1–34. Mahwah, NJ: LEA.

Dale, P.S., Harlaar, N., Haworth, C.M. A. and Plomin, R. (2010). Two by two: A twin study of second-language acquisition. *Psychological Science*, *21*(5), 635–40.

DeKeyser, R.M. (2000). The robustness of critical period effects in second language acquisition. *Studies in Second Language Acquisition*, *22*(4), 499–533.

DeKeyser, R.M., Alfi-Shabtay, I. and Ravid, D. (2010). Cross-linguistic evidence for the nature of age effects in second language acquisition. *Applied Psycholinguistics*, *31*(3), 413–38.

DeKeyser, R.M. and Koeth, J. (2011). Cognitive aptitudes for second language learning. In E. Hinkel (ed.), *Handbook of Research in Second Language Teaching and Learning*, Vol. 2, pp. 395–406. London: Routledge.

Doughty, C., Campbell, S., Mislevy, M., Bunting, M., Bowles, A. and Koeth, J. (2010). Predicting near-native ability: The factor structure and reliability of Hi-LAB. In M.T. Prior, Y. Watanabe and S.-K. Lee (eds), *Proceedings of the 2008 Second Language Research Forum*, pp. 10–31. Somerville, MA: Cascadilla Press.

Erlam, R. (2005). Language aptitude and its relationship to instructional effectiveness in second language acquisition. *Language Teaching Research*, *9*(2), 147–71.

Grigorenko, E., Sternberg, R.J. and Ehrman, M.E. (2000). A theory-based approach to the measurement of second-language learning ability: The CANAL-F theory and test. *The Modern Language Journal*, *84*(3), 390–405.

Kaufman, S.B., DeYoung, C.G., Gray, J.R., Jiménez, L., Brown, J. and Mackintosh, N. (2010). Implicit learning as an ability. *Cognition*, *116*, 321–40.

Meara, P. (2005). *LLAMA Language Aptitude Tests. The Manual*. www.lognostics.co.uk/tools/llama/llama_manual.doc

Parry, T.S. and Child, J.R. (1990). Preliminary investigation of the relationship between VORD, MLAT and language proficiency. In T. S. Parry and C.W. Stansfield (eds), *Language Aptitude Reconsidered*, pp. 30–66. Washington, DC: Center for Applied Linguistics.

Pimsleur, P. (1966). *Pimsleur Language Aptitude Battery (PLAB)*. New York: The Psychological Corporation.

Reiterer, S.M. (2009). Brain and language talent: a synopsis. In G. Dogil and S.M. Reiterer (eds), *Language Talent and Brain Activity*, pp. 155–91. Berlin: Mouton de Gruyter.

Robinson, P. (1996). Learning simple and complex second language rules under implicit, incidental, rule-search, and instructed conditions. *Studies in Second Language Acquisition*, *18*(1), 27–67.

——(2007). Aptitudes, abilities, contexts, and practice. In R.M. DeKeyser (ed.), *Practice in a Second Language. Perspectives from Applied Linguistics and Cognitive Psychology*, pp. 256–86. Cambridge: Cambridge University Press.

Sheen, Y. (2007). The effect of focused written corrective feedback and language aptitude on ESL learners' acquisition of articles. *TESOL Quarterly*, *41*(2), 255–83.

Skehan, P. (1998). *A Cognitive Approach to Language Learning*. Oxford: Oxford University Press.

Slevc, L.R. and Miyake, A. (2006). Individual differences in second-language proficiency: Does musical ability matter? *Psychological Science*, *17*(8), 675–81.

Sparks, R., Patton, J., Ganschow, L. and Humbach, N. (in press). Do L1 Reading Achievement and L1 Print Exposure Contribute to the Prediction of L2 Proficiency? *Language Learning*.

Further reading

Carroll, J.B. (1993). *Human Cognitive Abilities: A Survey of Factor-analytic Studies*. New York: Cambridge University Press.

Corno, L., Cronbach, L.J., Kupermintz, H., Lohman, D.F., Mandinach, E., Porteus, A., *et al.* (eds), (2002). *Remaking the Concept of Aptitude. Extending the Legacy of Richard E. Snow*. Mahwah, NJ: Erlbaum.

Dogil, G. and Reiterer, S.M. (eds) (2009). *Language Talent and Brain Activity*. Berlin: Mouton de Gruyter.

Dörnyei, Z. (2005). *The Psychology of the Language Learner. Individual Differences in Second language acquisition*. Mahwah, NJ: Erlbaum.

Robinson, P. (ed.). (2002). *Individual Differences and Instructed Language Learning*. Amsterdam: Benjamins.

Aptitude-treatment interaction (ATI) research

Karen Roehr
University of Essex

Aptitude-treatment interaction (ATI) research tries to answer the question of whether different methods of second language (L2) learning and teaching or different types of exposure to L2 input are differentially associated with (components of) language learning aptitude (Dörnyei, 2005). Thus, ATI research is aimed at identifying whether there is an interaction between aptitude and treatment in the sense of input (naturalistic, instructed, or both). Another way of phrasing this research issue would be to ask how situation-dependent language learning aptitude is (Dörnyei, 2005).

In the 1970s and 1980s, many researchers tended to be critical of the concept of language learning aptitude and its measurement by means of the Modern Language Aptitude Test (MLAT) (Carroll and Sapon, 1959, 2002) and similar instruments developed in the United States in accordance with the empiricist psychometric approach common in the 1950s. Critics argued that such tests would only predict speed of L2 learning in formal instructional settings, especially audiolingual classrooms (e.g. Krashen, 1981; see also reviews by Sawyer and Ranta, 2001; Skehan, 1998).

Contrary to this theoretical line of argument, empirical evidence suggests that measures of language learning aptitude such as the MLAT can reliably predict L2 learning outcomes in a range of environments and learning conditions, that is, it appears that their predictive validity is not restricted to specific learning situations or teaching methods (Dörnyei, 2005; Nagata *et al.*, 1999; Ranta, 2002; Sawyer and Ranta, 2001; Skehan, 2002). Three studies from three decades by Wesche (1981), Ehrman and Oxford (1995), and Erlam (2005) serve to illustrate this finding.

Studying a large sample of experienced and educated adult L2 learners undergoing intensive training in a range of languages at the Foreign Service Institute in the United States and thus arguably staying fairly close to the teaching and learning conditions in which classic measures of aptitude were originally conceptualized, Ehrman and Oxford (1995) found significant correlations of around 0.5 between MLAT performance and end-of-training L2 proficiency measures in reading and speaking.

In another approach to ATI research involving a comparatively large sample of participants, Wesche (1981) reports on a program of intensive L2 instruction in which an attempt was made to match Canadian civil servants at the start of their language training with specific teaching methods – audio-visual, deductive-analytical, or functional – according to their aptitude profiles as well as their learning style preferences and educational background. For instance, learners with particularly high scores on language-analytic components of aptitude and sophisticated L1 knowledge were allocated to a deductive-analytical classroom, while learners with weaker language-analytic scores but particularly strong auditory, phonetic-coding, and memory abilities as measured by relevant aptitude subtests were allocated to a functional classroom. Learners with relatively even aptitude profiles and without strong stylistic preferences were allocated to an audiovisual classroom, which constituted the default approach and accommodated the majority of students.

When L2 achievement and student attitudes were measured at the end of the program and compared with measures from learners who had been placed in an audiovisual classroom regardless of their specific profiles, it was found that learners who were exposed to an instructional method which matched their aptitude profile both performed better and felt more comfortable with their learning situation than learners who had been mismatched, thus experiencing a conflict between their aptitude profile and the instructional method used in the classroom.

Erlam (2005) addressed the question of whether a learner's ability to benefit from a particular instructional method depends on their aptitude in a study with high school students in New Zealand. Adolescent learners participated in three sessions of instruction targeting French direct object pronouns. Teaching was either deductive, inductive, or based on structured input as used in a processing instruction paradigm. Deductive instruction was explicit and included metalinguistic explanations; learners engaged in form-focused activities and output practice, and the teacher provided corrective feedback. Inductive instruction did not include explicit metalinguistic explanations; instead, practice activities were designed to encourage hypothesis testing on the part of the learners; students participated in consciousness-raising activities and engaged in output practice. Structured input instruction was based on explicit metalinguistic information, aural and written input-based activities, and error identification activity; corrective feedback was provided, but there was no output practice.

Learning outcomes were measured by assessing participants on the four skills of L2 reading, writing, listening and speaking. Results suggest that deductive instruction benefited all learners, but there was little evidence that deductive instruction was more beneficial for students with high overall aptitude scores than for the others. Learners with strong language-analytic ability gained more from inductive and structured-input instruction than other learners.

With regard to the question ATI research seeks to answer, the findings from these three example studies all point in the same direction: language learning aptitude appears to play a role in different teaching and learning environments. The educational implications of these studies are perhaps less clear, though. Wesche's (1981) research indicates that teaching learners in accordance with their strengths is most effective. By contrast, Erlam's (2005) study seems to suggest that a compensatory approach may be advisable; after all, providing deductive instruction which included rule explanations, form-focused activities, output practice and corrective feedback was equally beneficial to all students, including those with weaker language-analytic ability. At the same time, and arguably more importantly, it was not more beneficial to students with stronger language-analytic ability.

Indeed, recent reviews of aptitude research agree that the issue of whether instruction should accommodate learners' aptitude profiles by playing to their strengths or by aiming to compensate for their weaknesses still remains to be resolved empirically (e.g. Sawyer and Ranta, 2001). Some researchers seem to lean towards a compensatory approach (e.g. Ranta, 2005), while others appear to favor a matching approach (e.g. Robinson, 2005; Sheen, 2007). Most recently and perhaps most wisely, Ranta (2008) proposed a mixed approach combining compensatory and matched classroom activities.

Since the 1990s, ATI research has sought to move away from studying teaching methods in the broad sense and towards empirically investigating finer-grained processes of L2 learning. Laboratory-based research examining the role of aptitude whilst exposing learners to language training in carefully manipulated and highly controlled learning conditions is representative of this type of work. A study by Robinson (1997) serves as an illustration.

In Robinson's (1997) investigation, university-level learners of L2 English in the United States participated in two short training sessions conducted under four different conditions labeled implicit, rule-search, incidental and instructed. In each condition, participants were presented with English sentences exemplifying two structural patterns described by associated pedagogical rules. In the implicit condition, learners were asked to perform a memory task; in the rule-search condition, by contrast, they were asked to actively search for rules that might underlie the example sentences. In the incidental condition, learners were asked to respond to comprehension questions which focused on the meaning of the example sentences; conversely, in the instructed condition, they were explicitly taught the pedagogical rules describing the two target structures. Learning outcomes were measured by means of an immediate post-test consisting of grammaticality judgments. Furthermore, in addition to testing the participants' aptitude, Robinson assessed their self-reported level of awareness of rules during the training sessions.

The study resulted in significant correlations between aptitude and learning outcomes in all conditions except the incidental learning condition. At the same time, large numbers of participants in all learning conditions reported looking for rules, including participants in the incidental and implicit conditions. Finally, in the implicit learning condition, participants with high levels of language-analytic ability were more likely both to report having searched for rules and to be able to verbalize rules. Taken together, these findings suggest, first, that some participants may have taken an explicit approach to learning in any of the conditions, regardless of task instructions; and second, that aptitude had a role to play not only in explicit learning conditions (rule-search and instructed), but also in the implicit learning condition.

This research provides further evidence that can speak to the question ATI research is concerned with. In consonance with findings arising from classroom-based studies, findings from laboratory-based experiments suggest that language learning aptitude plays a role in different learning conditions. Crucially, aptitude appears to be implicated in an implicit learning condition, that is, a condition which arguably bears some resemblance to untutored L2 learning in an immersion setting.

It is worth bearing in mind that controlled laboratory research is necessarily selective in terms of L2 aspects that can be targeted as well as necessarily restrictive in terms of time on task. As yet, there is no published research available which has sought to identify the role of language learning aptitude in naturalistic L2 learning while at the same time attempting to maintain ecological validity by studying participants in long-term L2 immersion who are not exposed to any regular instruction.

Over and above the empirically supported claim that aptitude seems to impact on L2 learning in different situations, it has been suggested that the role of aptitude may actually be more central in naturalistic L2 learning than in formal classroom settings (Skehan, 1998, 2002). Classroom activities may focus the learner's attention on form and may thus help them notice and analyze relevant aspects of the linguistic input, as Erlam's (2005) results indicate. Conversely, untutored L2 learning provides no scaffolding; it is up to the learner to focus their attention appropriately and identify relevant patterns in the input. Arguably, a high level of language learning aptitude or strong language-analytic ability at the very least will allow them to do this particularly successfully.

Since the beginning of the twenty-first century, ATI research has also moved forward in terms of theoretical conceptualization. In an attempt to develop theorizing in the field, researchers have aimed to identify direct links between aptitude as an individual difference variable and specific processes of L2 acquisition. Robinson's concept of aptitude complexes (Dörnyei, 2005, 2009; Robinson, 2001, 2005, 2007) exemplifies this trend.

Robinson (2001, 2005, 2007) conceptualizes aptitude as clusters of situation-specific abilities which differentially relate to L2 processing under different learning conditions. These clusters are termed aptitude complexes. The model comprises four such complexes labeled (1) aptitude for focus on form via recasts, (2) aptitude for incidental learning via oral content, (3) aptitude for incidental learning via written content and (4) aptitude for explicit rule learning.

Each aptitude complex is associated with certain ability factors. For instance, (1) aptitude for focus on form via recasts is associated with the ability to notice the gap between one's oral production and an interlocutor's recast. A range of primary cognitive abilities are thought to underlie the various ability factors associated with each of the four aptitude complexes. Thus, it is proposed that the ability to notice the gap is determined by perceptual speed, pattern recognition ability and phonological working memory capacity. Robinson (2007) further proposes specific ability tests which may be employed to measure the various primary cognitive abilities thought to underlie the ability factors associated with different aptitude complexes. To exemplify, it is suggested that an inspection time task could be used to assess an individual's perceptual speed and a listening span test to assess phonological working memory capacity.

The aptitude complexes model has the advantage of being based on a detailed theoretically driven analysis of cognitive factors which are likely to interact with L2 learning processes. The model is of potential interest to both researchers and educators. Researchers may wish to apply the concept of aptitude complexes in order to examine the precise role of various cognitive abilities underlying language learning aptitude in L2 learning under different conditions and by different individuals; educators may eventually be able to benefit from the model by being able to obtain more detailed aptitude profiles of learners than has hitherto been possible.

Whilst these are promising developments, it is worth noting that the model of aptitude complexes is currently still awaiting empirical validation. Therefore, at this point in time, it is probably best described as a model indicating a promising way forward for both theoretical and empirical ATI research.

See also: aptitude, individual differences in SLA, instructed SLA, Modern Language Aptitude Test (MLAT), naturalistic and instructed learning, theoretical constructs in SLA

References

Carroll, J.B. and Sapon, S. (1959). *The Modern Language Aptitude Test*. San Antonio, TX: Psychological Corporation.

——(2002). *Modern Language Aptitude Test: MLAT*. N. Bethesda, MD: Second Language Testing Inc.

Dörnyei, Z. (2005). *The Psychology of the Language Learner: Individual Differences in Second Language Acquisition*. Mahwah, NJ: Erlbaum.

——(2009). Individual differences: Interplay of learner characteristics and learning environment. *Language Learning*, *59*(s1), 230–48.

Ehrman, M.E. and Oxford, R.L. (1995). Cognition Plus: Correlates of language learning success. *Modern Language Journal*, *79*(1), 67–89.

Erlam, R. (2005). Language aptitude and its relationship to instructional effectiveness in second language acquisition. *Language Teaching Research*, *9*(2), 147–71.

Krashen, S.D. (1981). *Second Language Acquisition and Second Language Learning*. Oxford: Pergamon.

Nagata, H., Aline, D. and Ellis, R. (1999). Modified input, language aptitude and the acquisition of word meanings. In R. Ellis (ed.), *Learning a Second Language through Interaction*. Amsterdam: John Benjamins.

Ranta, L. (2002). The role of Learners' language analytic ability in the communicative classroom. In P. Robinson (ed.), *Individual Differences and Instructed Language Learning*. Amsterdam: John Benjamins.

——(2005). Language analytic ability and oral production in a second language: Is there a connection? In A. Housen and M. Pierrard (eds), *Investigations in Instructed Second Language Acquisition*. Berlin: Mouton de Gruyter.

——(2008). Aptitude and good language learners. In C. Griffiths (ed.), *Lessons from Good Language Learners*. Cambridge: Cambridge University Press.

Robinson, P. (1997). Individual differences and the fundamental similarity of implicit and explicit adult second language learning. *Language Learning*, *47*(1) 45–99.

——(2001). Individual differences, cognitive abilities, aptitude complexes and learning conditions in second language acquisition. *Second Language Research*, *17*(4) 368–92.

——(2005). Aptitude and second language acquisition. *Annual Review of Applied Linguistics*, *25*, 46–73.

——(2007). Aptitudes, abilities, contexts, and practice. In R.M. DeKeyser (ed.), *Practice in a Second Language: Perspectives from Applied Linguistics and Cognitive Psychology*. Cambridge: Cambridge University Press.

Sawyer, M. and Ranta, L. (2001). Aptitude, individual differences, and instructional design. In P. Robinson (ed.), *Cognition and Second Language Instruction*. Cambridge: Cambridge University Press.

Sheen, Y. (2007). The effect of focused written corrective feedback and language aptitude on ESL Learners' acquisition of articles. *TESOL Quarterly*, *41*(2) 255–83.

Skehan, P. (1998). *A Cognitive Approach to Language Learning*. Oxford: Oxford University Press.

——(2002). Theorising and updating aptitude. In P. Robinson (ed.), *Individual Differences and Instructed Language Learning*. Amsterdam: John Benjamins.

Wesche, M.B. (1981). Language aptitude measures in streaming, matching students with methods, and diagnosis of learning problems. In K.C. Diller (ed.), *Individual Differences and Universals in Language Aptitude*. Rowley, MA: Newbury House.

Artificial Language Learning (ALL)

Luca Onnis

University of Hawai'i

Artificial Language Learning (ALL) is an experimental paradigm used to investigate the learning capabilities of individuals, both in infancy and adulthood. An artificial language can be any miniature linguistic system constructed by the researcher according to rules and properties (deterministic or probabilistic) that generate language-like sentences using pseudowords. In a typical scenario where ALL is used to mimic language learning, learners are exposed to made-up sentences such as *pel wadim jik*, *rud beefle tood*, etc. In a subsequent test phase, learning is assessed by presenting participants with novel sentences that either respect or violate the underlying rules or properties. These rules typically resemble structural properties and relations found in natural languages. For example, the researcher may have defined a grammar containing non-adjacent grammatical dependencies such as *pel – jik*, and *rud – tood*, similar to the non-adjacent noun-verb number agreement in the English sentence *The boys[PLUR] who work[PLUR] in the building are[PLUR] all under age*. Here a sentence like *pel gubam jik* would be grammatical, while **pel gubam tood* would not. Various measures of sensitivity can be used, from asking participants to rate the grammaticality or familiarity of a sentence, to providing them with a forced-choice preference task, to more implicitly measuring the time it takes to press a button after presentation of each word or sentence.

There are numerous advantages to using ALL to study language processes. First, as with natural languages, rules and probabilistic tendencies in ALL can be designed to mimic structural regularities. In addition, words and sentences can be meaningfully associated to real-world scenarios, like a visual scene. However, in terms of placing learners in similar initial conditions, minimizing outside exposure and learners' prior knowledge, ALL has a much better control of these factors, which might otherwise affect the interpretation of results. Furthermore, the paradigm allows for testing hypotheses about specific language-like properties and structures that would be difficult to study systematically in naturalistic scenarios given the complexity of real natural languages. In addition, despite their small scale, the rules and lexicon of an artificial language can generate a large number of possible sentences, maintaining the generative aspect of natural languages and allowing for testing learners' ability to generalize beyond the input they receive. Finally, ALL is a flexible paradigm: underlying structural properties can be initially defined as abstract relations, and then instantiated in different modalities, such as tones or shapes, to test whether learning processes are modality specific or underlie more general cognitive abilities.

Brief history of ALL

The origins of the paradigm can be traced back to the1950s, when George Miller (1958) found that participants presented with two lists of letter strings – one generated randomly, the other containing strings generated by an artificial grammar – memorized grammatical strings much more quickly than random strings. Arthur Reber (1967) extended the paradigm using what has become the standard approach for artificial grammar learning experiments. His subjects could discriminate grammatical and ungrammatical sequences of symbols even for novel stimuli not experienced during training, suggesting that they had extracted the underlying rules of the system. Importantly, they did so even though they could not verbally express their knowledge about any of the grammatical rules that produced the sequences.

These pioneering studies paved the way for research of implicit versus explicit learning in psychology, but had relatively little impact on linguistic studies. It was not until the 1990s that infants, toddlers and children were shown to be sensitive to statistically relevant cues and used them to learn structural aspects of artificial languages – from phonological categories and word-units, to abstract lexical categories and phrase structure (Gomez and Gerken, 1999; Saffran *et al.*, 1996).

Since then, ALL studies have multiplied in several directions, from addressing processes of creolization, to language evolution and second language acquisition. For example, Hudson-Kam and Newport (2005) exposed children and adults to artificial languages of varying degree of regularity, and found that while adults reproduce the inconsistencies in their output, children regularized the language through generating patterns that are different from the initial input. They suggest that children play a vital role in Creole formation from a more basic Pidgin by regularizing and stabilizing language patterns. ALL is also employed to study the evolution of linguistic properties such as word order in computer simulations (Christiansen, 2000), and in experimental language games. In the latter studies, the question is how a novel communication system may emerge over time to solve a particular task (Galantucci, 2005; Scott-Philipps and Kirby, 2010) or through repeated interaction (Selten and Warglien, 2007).

Key questions in ALL research

The nature of what is being learned in ALL has been the subject of extensive investigation. The *abstractive* view proposes a mechanism that encodes and extracts the abstract rules of the grammar (e.g., Marcus *et al.*, 1999; Peña *et al.*, 2002; Reber, 1993). The *exemplar-based* instead suggests that artificial language stimuli are encoded and stored in memory (e.g., Vokey and Brooks, 1992). Participants implicitly or explicitly compare the test items to their memory of the stored exemplars and make their decision based on similarity. The *fragment-based* view posits that participants learn small fragments or chunks of information, consisting of pairs and triples of elements (e.g., Perruchet and Pacton, 2006). These chunks are explicitly available to participants and guide them in the classification task. The *distributional/statistical* view asserts that learning accrues from sensitivity to distributional regularities among sequenced events. This type of statistical learning has been demonstrated across a variety of language-like learning situations, including segmenting speech, detecting the orthographic and phonotactic regularities of words, constraining speech production errors, acquiring morphological features such as number or tense, locating syntactic phrase boundaries, using function words to delineate phrases, integrating prosodic and morphological cues in the learning of phrase structure, and detecting long-distances relationships between words. Thus, the *abstractive* view relying exclusively on abstract, rule-based knowledge is no longer the only paradigm, and the exact nature of what is learned is yet to be settled (see Perruchet and Pacton, 2006; Pothos, 2007, for reviews).

Another key question is whether the mechanisms underlying artificial language learning are domain-specific or domain-general. On the one hand, neuroimaging responses to ALL stimuli have elicited similar brain signatures as natural language stimuli, strengthening the case that artificial languages constitute valid simulations of natural languages, and suggesting that the same domain-specific mechanisms are at play when processing both natural and artificial languages (e.g. Friederici *et al.*, 2002). On the other hand, recent brain imaging studies have shown that structural incongruencies in non-language sequential stimuli, such as sounds and visual objects, elicit brain responses similar to those observed for syntactic anomalies in natural language, suggesting the existence of more general-domain processes (Christiansen *et al.*, in press). In general, the learning of artificial grammars has been demonstrated in non-language domains, including visual processing, visuomotor learning, tactile sequence learning, and non-linguistic auditory processing, so it is possible that mechanisms involved in processing structural regularities are shared in both language and non-language learning.

Relevance of ALL for second language acquisition

ALL is gaining popularity in the study of second language acquisition and processing. To the extent that artificial languages constitute miniature systems to be learned by adults in addition to and after the first language has been acquired, they can be considered miniature artificial second languages in their own right, and as such they can yield important insights into various issues of interest to SLA. For example, Ellis and Schmidt (1998) found a frequency effect for irregular pseudowords equivalent to that found for morphosyntactic processes in natural language: production latencies were affected by the frequency of plural forms when generating irregular inflections, but not when generating regular ones. Other studies have explored the implicit learning of form-meaning mappings (Williams, 2005), and the differential impact of implicit and explicit training regimes on learning outcomes in artificial second languages (Robinson, 2005).

ALL can be particularly useful to investigate the conditions leading to *enhanced learning* of particularly difficult aspects of language. For example, morpho-syntactic agreement is hard to master by second language learners even at advanced levels of proficiency. Studies of ALL simulating agreement dependencies suggest that the variability of the material intervening between non-adjacent dependent elements (such as *pel – jik*, and *rud – tood*) plays a central role in determining how easy it is to detect a particular dependency (Gómez, 2002, Onnis *et al.*, 2003). Learning of non-adjacencies improves as the variability of elements that occur between two dependent items increases. When the set of items that participate in the dependency is small relative to the set of elements intervening, the non-adjacent dependencies stand out as invariant structures against the changing background of more varied material. A general principle that is emerging in the literature is that learners seek invariant structure in the input (Onnis *et al.*, 2008).

How can these laboratory studies inform L2 instruction practices? It is possible to construct L2 teaching materials that reflect the principles of variability versus invariant structure described above. At least with respect to the instructed components of L2 learning, the input to an L2 learner can be manipulated to a large extent. For instance, applying the concept of large variability to morphosyntactic relations in Spanish might involve input with sentences like:

Tengo **las** bot**as** para el matrimonio.
Tengo **las** películ**as** para el fin de semana.
Tengo **las** pelot**as** para el niño.

In these examples the female gender and plural number agreements (las -as) are repeated while the intervening lexical items are modified (bot-, películ-, pelot-). The prediction is that a large enough number of intervening words should facilitate the extraction of the invariant non-adjacent relations (las -as), either implicitly or by promoting the explicit noticing of the target structure. Thus, ALL can inform the design of exercises and teaching practices to pinpoint specific areas for improvement in L2 learning. In addition, ALL principles can be effectively implemented as supportive solutions to enhancing instruction and curricula.

In conclusion, despite its seemingly 'toy-like' nature, the ALL paradigm can provide principled conceptions of learning and learnability for particular aspects of real language. The paradigm further allows for empirical measurement of the utility of potential sources of information in language. Future L2 research could then apply such mechanisms and principles to more naturalistic situations of real language learning, providing empirical predictions about the time course and process of L2 acquisition, and bridging the gap between the laboratory and the classroom (Onnis, 2011).

See also: connectionism, emergentism, input enhancement, implicit learning, psycholinguistics of SLA, statistical learning

References

Christiansen, M.H., Conway, C.M. and Onnis, L. (in press). Similar neural correlates for language and sequential learning: Evidence from event-related brain potentials. *Language and Cognitive Processes*.

Ellis, N.C. and Schmidt, R. (1998). Rules or associations in the acquisition of morphology? The frequency by regularity interaction in human and PDP learning of morphosyntax. *Language and Cognitive Processes*, *13*, 307–36.

Friederici, A.D., Steinhauer, K. and Pfeifer, E. (2002). Brain signatures of artificial language processing: Evidence challenging the critical period hypothesis. *Proceedings of the National Academy of Sciences of the United States of America*, *99*, 529–34.

Galantucci, B. (2005). An experimental study of the emergence of human communication systems. *Cognitive Science*, *29* (5), 737–67.

Gómez, R.L. (2002). Variability and detection of invariant structure. *Psychological Science*, *13*, 431–36.

Gómez, R.L. and Gerken, L.A. (2000). Infant artificial language learning and language acquisition. *Trends in Cognitive Sciences*, *4*, 178–86.

Hudson-Kam, C. and Newport, E. (2005). Regularizing unpredictable variation: The roles of adult and child learners in language formation and change. *Language Learning and Development*, *1* (2), 151–95.

Marcus, G.F., Vijayan, S., Bandi Rao, S., and Vishton, P.M. (1999). Rule-learning in seven-month-old infants. *Science*, *283*, 77–80.

Miller, G.A. (1958). Free recall of redundant strings of letters. *Journal of Experimental Psychology*, *56*, 485–91.

Onnis, L. (2011). The potential contribution of statistical learning for second language acquisition. In P. Rebuschat, and J.N. Williams (eds), *Statistical Learning and Language Acquisition*. Berlin: Mouton de Gruyter.

Onnis, L., Christiansen, M.H., Chater, N. and Gómez, R. (2003). Reduction of uncertainty in human sequential learning: Evidence from artificial grammar learning. In *Proceedings of the 25th Annual Conference of the Cognitive Science Society*, pp. 886–91. Mahwah, NJ: Lawrence Erlbaum.

Onnis, L., Waterfall, H. and Edelman, S. (2008). Learn locally, act globally: Learning language from variation set cues. *Cognition*, *109*, 423–30.

Peña, M., Bonatti, L.L., Nespor, M. and Mehler, J. (2002). Signal-driven computations in speech processing. *Science*, *298* (5593), 604–7.

Perruchet, P. and Pacton, S. (2006). Implicit learning and statistical learning: One phenomenon, two approaches. *Trends in Cognitive Sciences*, *10*, 233–38.

Pothos, E.M. (2007). Theories of artificial grammar learning. *Psychological Bulletin*, *133*, 227–44.

Reber, A.S. (1967). Implicit learning of artificial grammars. *Journal of Verbal Learning and Verbal Behavior*, *6*, 855–63.

Robinson, P. (2005). Cognitive abilities, chunk-strength, and frequency effects in implicit artificial grammar and incidental L2 learning: Replications of Reber, Walkenfeld, and Hernstadt (1991) and Knowlton and Squire (1996) and their relevance for SLA. *Studies in Second Language Acquisition*, *27*, 2, 235–68.

Selten, R. and Warglien, M. (2007). The emergence of simple languages in an experimental coordination game. *Proceedings of the National Academy of Sciences of the United States of America*, *104*, 18, 7361–66.

Scott-Phillips, T.C. and Kirby, S. (2010). Language evolution in the laboratory. *Trends in Cognitive Sciences*, *14*, 9, 411–17.

Williams, J.N. (2005). Learning without awareness. *Studies in Second Language Acquisition*, *27*, 269–304.

Aspect Hypothesis (AH)

Yasuhiro Shirai
University of Pittsburgh

Since the 1970s, L1 acquisition researchers have observed that children's use of tense-aspect marking is not applied evenly to all obligatory contexts, but appears to be restricted according to its temporal semantics. Brown (1973) for English, Bronckart and Sinclair (1973) for French, and Antinucci and Miller (1976) for Italian were the initial studies to show that when children use past tense marking (English simple past, French *passé composé*, Italian *passato prosimo*) it is not applied to all types of verbs but rather is selectively attached to instantaneous, change of state verbs that denote clear end-results, and that progressive marking is only attached to activity verbs, and it is not incorrectly attached to stative verbs.

Andersen (1991) extended this research to second language acquisition. His work on Spanish, as well as work on other languages such as English and French (Bardovi-Harlig and Bergström, 1996), among many other languages, confirmed this semantic bias. This line of research usually uses Vendler's (1957) classification of verbal semantics: States, Activities, Accomplishments (durative change-of-state verbs) and Achievements (punctual change-of-state verbs).

Shirai (1991: 9–10) proposed the following descriptive generalizations, which are now called the Aspect Hypothesis (Andersen and Shirai, 1994), noting that (4) does not necessarily hold for SLA.

Learners first use past marking (e.g. English) or perfective marking (Chinese, Spanish, etc.) on achievement and accomplishment verbs, eventually extending its use to activities and stative verbs.

In languages that encode the perfective/imperfective distinction, imperfective past appears later than perfective past, and imperfective past marking begins with stative verbs, then extending to accomplishments and activity verbs.

In languages that have progressive aspect, progressive marking begins with activity verbs, then extends to accomplishment or achievement verbs.

Progressive markings are not incorrectly overextended to stative verbs.

This observation of semantic bias is also referred to as the Aspect-Before-Tense Hypothesis, the Defective Tense Hypothesis, the Primacy of Aspect Hypothesis, the Lexical Aspect Hypothesis, and the Aspect First Hypothesis.

Second language acquisition researchers have extensively investigated semantic bias in the use of tense-aspect markers, mostly supporting hypotheses (1) to (3). Researchers generally agree on the descriptive generalizations of the Aspect Hypothesis. However, a hypothesis has been advanced as a counterexample to the Aspect Hypothesis: the Default Past Tense Hypothesis (Salaberry, 1999). It predicts that during the first stages of L2 development, learners will attempt to mark tense distinctions rather than aspectual distinctions, and in so doing will initially rely on a single marker of past tense, most typically the perfective form.

Empirical evidence for this hypothesis comes from Salaberry's work on L2 Spanish, which shows that learners' use of perfective past (preterit) is spread across various lexical aspectual classes at the beginning stage, not just restricted to telic verbs (i.e. accomplishments and achievements), while association with telicity increases as the learner's proficiency increases. This deviation from the prediction of the Aspect Hypothesis appears to be the combination of three factors. First, the learners' L1 (English) has a simple past tense marker, which is less aspectual compared with Spanish preterit (perfective past). Therefore, assuming transfer, learners at the beginning stage will show a lesser degree of association with telicity, since perfective past in the learners' L1 is more strongly associated with telic verbs than is simple past in the target language, English. Second, learners in classroom settings can use their monitor when telling a story in the past tense. Third and related, the task (film retell) allows learners to use their monitor in the sense that it is a past narrative and they know they should tell it in the past tense. Importantly, most of the studies that are consistent with the Default Past Tense Hypothesis come from L1 English learners learning a foreign language in classroom settings.

Although the research on the Aspect Hypothesis has generally focused on the universality of tense-aspect acquisition, the effect of the L1 is gaining increasing attention, and it appears to be stronger than previously thought. Nishi (2008), in investigating the acquisition of the Japanese imperfective aspect marker–*teiru* by L1 English, Chinese, and Korean learners, has shown that L1 influence is much stronger than previously thought, and suggests that the pattern of acquisition that is consistent with the Aspect Hypothesis in Japanese may come from the fact that progressive is represented in all three languages.

Finally, the explanation for the empirical generalizations predicted by the Aspect Hypothesis is still wide open. One important proposal is input frequency: the semantic bias found in the learner data is also present in native speech albeit to a less marked degree, which in turn results in more absolute semantic bias in learner language (the Distributional Bias Hypothesis, Andersen and Shirai, 1994).

It may also be possible that empirical evidence found so far supporting the Aspect Hypothesis can also be partially attributed to L1 influence. Most of the L1s studied to date have corresponding past or perfective marking, for which the prototype is telic and punctual, which may transfer to L2 learning of past or perfective marking. This may facilitate early acquisition of past tense with telic verbs. Likewise, acquisition of progressive marking with activities may be facilitated because in most languages, progressive marking marks action in progress that is obtained when imperfective aspect marking is combined with activity verbs, whereas other meanings (such as habitual, futurate) are not always present.

Future study should systematically investigate the effect of the L1 by comparing different L1 groups acquiring the same language to tease out the effect of natural acquisitional processes from the effect of the L1. For example, what are the differences between L1 German learners (simple past) versus L1 Spanish learners (perfective past) of English in their acquisition of English past tense? How about L1 German learners (no progressive) versus Chinese learners (restrictive progressive, with action in progress meaning only) in the acquisition of the highly grammaticized, polysemous English progressive? These studies would contribute to an explanation of why learners generally follow the prediction of the Aspect Hypothesis and why sometimes they do not.

See also: acquisition of tense and aspect, development in SLA, frequency effects, functional typological linguistics, linguistic transfer, prototypes

References

Andersen, R.W. (1991). Developmental sequences: The emergence of aspect marking in second language acquisition. In T. Huebner and C.A. Ferguson (eds), *Crosscurrents in Second Language Acquisition and Linguistic Theories*. Amsterdam: John Benjamins.

Andersen, R.W. and Shirai, Y. (1994). Discourse motivations for some cognitive acquisition principles. *Studies in Second Language Acquisition*, *16*, 133–56.

Antinucci, F. and Miller, R. (1976). How children talk about what happened. *Journal of Child Language*, *3*, 169–89.

Bardovi-Harlig, K. and Bergström, A. (1996). The acquisition of tense and aspect in SLA and FLL: A study of learner narratives in English (SL) and French (FL). *Canadian Modern Language Review*, *52*, 308–30.

Brown, R. (1973). *A First Language*. Cambridge, MA: Harvard University Press.

Bronckart, J.P. and Sinclair, H. (1973). Time, Tense and Aspect. *Cognition*, *2*, 107–30.

Nishi, Y. (2008). *Verb Learning and the Acquisition of Aspect: Rethinking the Universality of Lexical Aspect and the Significance of L1 Transfer*. Ph.D. dissertation, Linguistics, Cornell University, Ithaca, NY.

Salaberry, M.R. (1999). The development of past tense verbal morphology in classroom L2 Spanish. *Applied Linguistics*, *20*, 151–78.

Shirai, Y. (1991). *Primacy of Aspect in Language Acquisition: Simplified Input and Prototype*. Ph.D. dissertation, Applied Linguistics, University of California, Los Angeles.

Vendler, Z. (1957). Verbs and times. *Philosophical Review*, *66*, 143–60.

Further reading

Bardovi-Harlig, K. (2000). *Tense and Aspect in Second Language Acquisition: Form, Meaning, and Use*. London: Blackwell. (Comprehensive review of tense-aspect acquisition in SLA, in which chapter 4 is devoted to the Aspect Hypothesis.)

Li, P. and Shirai, Y. (2000). *The Acquisition of Lexical and Grammatical Aspect*. Berlin: Mouton de Gruyter. (An extensive treatment of the semantic bias in L1 and L2 acquisition.)

Shirai, Y. (2009). Temporality in First and Second Language Acquisition. In W. Klein and P. Li (eds), *The Expression of Time*. Berlin: Mouton de Gruyter. (A survey of the Aspect Hypothesis.)

Attention in SLA

Ronald P. Leow

Georgetown University

The role of attention in the early stages of the acquisitional process of input to output finds its roots in the earliest studies in the field of second language acquisition (SLA). Many researchers have generally assumed that their experimental conditions (instruction, exposure or interaction) that exposed participants to the L2 input (be it in the written or aural mode, modified or authentic) elicited learners' attention paid to the targeted item(s) in the L2 input. This assumption is clearly seen in the type of research design employed in the studies, which is the classical pretest – experimental condition – posttest design that did not methodologically gather concurrent or online data to establish whether learners did indeed pay attention to the targeted items in the input. However, it was from the 1980s that the SLA field began to witness theoretical underpinnings postulating an important role for attention at the initial stage of L2 development and addressing attention in relation to the role of awareness or lack thereof (e.g., Gass, 1997; McLaughlin, 1987; Robinson, 1995; Schmidt, 1990; Tomlin and Villa, 1994). Mainly based on works in cognitive psychology and cognitive science, these theoretical underpinnings of the role of attention in input processing arguably propelled several researchers to probe deeper, both methodologically and empirically, into the construct of attention (and awareness) and its role in L2 development.

McLaughlin's (1987) cognitive theory, derived from cognitive psychology, is one of the earliest theories in SLA that has posited a role for attention in input processing. This theory is generally based on the concepts of controlled and automatic processes, allocation of attention, the notion of cognitive effort, and the role of consciousness or unconsciousness, among others. Cognitive theory views the early stage adult L2 learner as limited capacity processors of information, that is, they are limited to what they can attend to at a given point in time (selective or focal attention) and what they can process on the basis of previous knowledge and expectations (McLaughlin *et al.*, 1983). During the early stages of SLA, learners' information processing mechanism is regulated by controlled processes. Controlled processes require a large amount of cognitive effort, are generally conscious, and under voluntary control of the learners. These controlled processes are used with any new or inconsistent information learners receive in the input. Automatic processes, on the other hand, require little cognitive effort, occur rapidly and presumably do not require consciousness. Consequently, the amount of attention paid to the L2 data by L2 learners is largely dependent upon the amount of cognitive effort required by their processing of the input. Thus, when conscious attention is viewed as processing capacity, it is found to be flexible and the amount of attention can be deployed dependent upon the difficulty of the task and the amount of controlled or automatic processing involved.

Gass (1988) posits two stages in her Model of Second Language Acquisition to account for the input to intake stages of the acquisitional process, namely, apperceived input and comprehended input. Apperceived input is based on learners' recognition that there is a gap between what they know and do not know. According to Gass, it is that piece of language that is noticed (a la Schmidt, cf. below) by the learner due to some recognizable features that are linked to their prior knowledge. Apperception is "an internal cognitive act in which a linguistic form is related to some bit of existing knowledge (or gap in knowledge)" (p. 4). Once the particular piece of input has been apperceived, the potential for intake to take place depends upon what she calls comprehended input. Comprehended input may be analyzed at different levels, for example, global comprehension versus a more linguistic focus, and these analyses have an impact on what becomes intake, which is controlled by the learner.

Schmidt's (1990) noticing hypothesis was the first theoretical postulation in the SLA field to address the role of attention in direct relation to the construct of awareness in L2 input processing. Drawing from works in cognitive psychology (e.g., Bowers, 1984) and his own personal experience while learning Portuguese (Schmidt and Frota, 1986), Schmidt's noticing hypothesis postulates that attention controls access to awareness and is responsible for noticing. According to Schmidt, to learn any linguistic feature of the L2, for example, sounds, words, grammar, pragmatics etc., this feature in the L2 input must be noticed with minimally a low level of awareness by learners, even though they may lack understanding of the underlying rule associated with this linguistic feature. Given that attention, according to Schmidt, is isomorphic with awareness, he rejects the idea of learning without awareness. However, given the methodological problem of establishing zero awareness at the point of noticing or processing, Schmidt has withdrawn from his original postulation of noticing as "the necessary and sufficient condition for the conversion of input into intake" (Schmidt, 1993: 209) to one of "more noticing leads to more learning" (Schmidt, 1994: 129), underscoring the facilitative nature of noticing in the early stages of the acquisitional process. In addition, Schmidt proposes a level of awareness that is higher than awareness at the level of noticing, namely, awareness at the level of understanding. Whereas awareness at the level of noticing leads to mere intake, this higher level of awareness promotes deeper learning marked by restructuring and system learning and is underscored by learners' ability to analyze, compare and test hypotheses at this level.

While concurring with Schmidt's noticing hypothesis on the important role of attention in learning, Tomlin and Villa's model of input processing in SLA differs sharply from Schmidt's regarding the role of awareness in the input to intake process. Drawing on works in cognitive science (e.g., Posner and Petersen, 1990), Tomlin and Villa (1994) propose a functionally based, fine-grained analysis of attention for input processing in SLA. In their model, attention has three components (all of which have neurological correlates): (1) alertness (an overall readiness to deal with incoming stimuli); (2) orientation (the direction of attentional resources to a certain type of stimuli); and (3) detection (the cognitive registration of stimuli). According to Tomlin and Villa, it is detection alone that is necessary for further processing of input and subsequent learning to take place. The other two components can enhance the chances that detection will occur, but neither is necessary. Crucial to understanding Tomlin and Villa's claims is that, in their model, detection does *not* imply awareness, that is, awareness does not play a crucial role in the preliminary processing of input into intake during exposure.

The fine-grained analysis of attention proposed by Tomlin and Villa (1994) was empirically tested by Leow (1998). Leow concurred with Tomlin and Villa's critique that previous SLA research had not addressed the actual role attention played during exposure to the L2 data by pointing out the typical offline postexposure tasks employed by most SLA studies to operationalize attention (1998: 134). To this end, Leow employed concurrent verbal reports to first operationalize and then measure attention before addressing which attentional functions or mechanisms were crucial for intake and subsequent processing to take place *while* adult learners interact with L2 data on subsequent behavior. Results indicated that participants who detected the targeted forms were able to take in and produce in writing significantly more targeted forms than those who did not demonstrate this cognitive registration. This superior effect for detection was also found on the immediate posttest and two delayed posttests administered five and eight weeks after exposure (that is, after completion of the crossword puzzle). These findings lend empirical support for Tomlin and Villa's fine-grained analysis of attention at a morphological level without addressing the issue of the role of awareness at the level of detection.

A third model of attention in relation to awareness proposed for SLA is that of Robinson (1995). Drawing from Cowan's (1988) unified model of memory and attention, Robinson's model of the relationship between attention and memory brings together Tomlin and Villa's (1994) notion of detection (which does not involve awareness) and Schmidt's (1990 and elsewhere) notion of noticing (which does involve awareness). Robinson constructs a model in which detection is one early stage in the process, sequentially prior to noticing. More specifically, linguistic information may be detected and taken in by the learner but if this information is not accompanied by awareness, then the chance of this information being further processed is relatively minimal. Noticing, in Robinson's model, is "detection plus rehearsal in short-term memory, prior to encoding in long-term memory" (Robinson, 1995: 296). To Robinson, noticing does involve awareness, as in Schmidt's model, and it is crucial for learning to take place.

As can be seen from the different theoretical models of attention, the facilitative role of attention in L2 development is generally accepted, but the role of awareness still remains debatable. More specifically, Schmidt's noticing hypothesis and Robinson's model of the relationship between attention and memory posit a crucial role for awareness, whereas Tomlin and Villa's functional model of input processing does not. What is not controversial, then, is that attentional resources need to be allocated to specific linguistic data in the input, but whether learner awareness is required for the grammatical information to be processed by the learner is open to debate.

There are several strands of SLA research that are explicitly or implicitly premised on the role(s) of attention and/or noticing (attention plus a low level of awareness) in L2 development. These strands of research typically manipulate the L2 input in the hope of drawing learners' attention to targeted items in the input. Strands include processing instruction, interaction or feedback, learning or training conditions, input/textual enhancement, input flooding, focus on form, and so on. Attention/noticing has been measured by a variety of instruments in SLA studies that include off-line questionnaires, online uptake charts, learning diaries, online verbal reports, and offline verbal reports such as stimulated recall protocols. In addition, in some studies participants were prompted to take notes while reading an L2 text, to underline, circle, or check targeted linguistic structures in written text, or to make a check mark every time a targeted item was heard.

Quite a large range of linguistic items has also been empirically investigated and these include Spanish imperatives, imperfect and preterit forms, present perfect forms, relative pronouns, past conditional; Finnish locative suffixes; English possessive determiners, relative clauses; French past participle agreement, and so on. Different levels of language experience have also been explored, ranging from beginner learners of an L2 to intermediate to advanced levels. Amount of exposure has also been differential, ranging from less than an hour to over several days.

Overall, the findings of these studies provide strong support for the role of attention and/or noticing in L2 development, especially research with a focus on classroom-based learning that employed concurrent data elicitation procedures (e.g., online verbal reports or think aloud protocols to establish the process of learner attention e.g., Leow, 2001; Rosa and O'Neill, 1999).

Given its crucial role in any further processing of L2 data to take place, the centrality of learner attention in the acquisitional process is well accepted by the SLA field together with its four main characteristics: its capacity is limited, it is selective, it is voluntary, and it controls access to consciousness. While current research findings are indeed promising, more robust research designs are clearly needed to address the issue of L2 development premised on the roles of attention/noticing given the wide variety of variables that can potentially impact learners' processes while interacting with L2 data. Such findings can only improve our understanding of the attentional and cognitive processes involved in foreign/second language learning.

See also: awareness, automaticity, depth of processing, eye-tracking, intake, Noticing Hypothesis

References

Bowers, K. (1984). On being unconsciously influenced and informed. In K. Bwers and D. Meichenbaum (eds), *The Unconscious Reconsidered*. New York: Wiley.

Cowan, N. (1988). Evolving conceptions of memory storage, selective attention, and their mutual constraints within the human information-processing system. *Psychological Bulletin, 104* (2), 163–91.

Gass, S. (1988). Integrating research areas: A framework for second language studies. *Applied Linguistics*, *9*, 198–217.

Gass, S. (1997). *Input, Interaction, and the Second Language Learner*. Mahwah, NJ: Erlbaum.

Leow, R.P. (2001). Attention, awareness and foreign language behavior. *Language Learning, 51*, 113–55.

——(1998). Toward operationalizing the process of attention in second language acquisition: Evidence for Tomlin and Villa's (1994) fine-grained analysis of attention. *Applied Pyscholinguistics*, *19*, 133–59.

McLaughlin, B. (1987). *Theories of Second Language Learning*. London: Edward Arnold.

McLaughlin, B., Rossman, T. and McLeod, B. (1983). Second language learning and information processing perspective. *Language Learning*, *33*, 135–58.

Posner, M.I. and Petersen, S.E. (1990). The attention system of the human brain. *Annual Review of Neuroscience*, *13*, 25–42.

Robinson, P. (1995). Attention, memory, and the 'noticing' hypothesis. *Language Learning, 45*, 283–331.

Rosa, E. and O'Neill, M. (1999). Explicitness, intake, and the issue of awareness: Another piece to the puzzle. *Studies in Second Language Acquisition*, *21*, 511–56.

Schmidt, R.W. (1994). Deconstructing consciousness in search of useful definitions for applied linguistics. *AILA Review*, *11*, 11–26.

——(1993). Awareness and second language acquisition. *Annual Review of Applied Linguistics*, *13*, 206–26.

——(1990). The role of consciousness in second language learning. *Applied Linguistics*, *11*, 129–58.

Schmidt, R.W. and Frota, S.N. (1986). Developing basic conversational ability in a second language: A case study of an adult learner of Portuguese. In R.R. Day (ed.), *Talking to Learn: Conversation in Second Language Acquisition*. Rowley, MA: Newbury.

Tomlin, R.S. and Villa, V. (1994). Attention in cognitive science and second language acquisition. *Studies in Second Language Acquisition*, *16*, 183–203.

Further reading

Leow, R.P. (2007). Input in the L2 classroom: An attentional perspective on receptive practice. In R. DeKeyser (ed.), *Practice in Second Language Learning: Perspectives from Applied Linguistics and Cognitive Psychology*, pp. 21–50. Cambridge: Cambridge University Press. (This article takes a critical look at three major strands of research in SLA in relation to the role of attention.)

Schmidt, R.W. (2001). Attention. In P. Robinson (ed.), *Cognition and Second Language Instruction*, pp. 3–32. Cambridge: Cambridge University Press. (A must read for an in-depth review of this construct.)

Attitudes and Motivation Test Battery (AMTB)

Robert C. Gardner

University of Western Ontario

The Attitudes and Motivation Test Battery was developed initially in the 1970s to assess affective variables associated with learning a second language. The associated research gave rise to the socio-educational model of second language acquisition (Gardner, 1985a). The original AMTB, concerned with learning French as a second language, is available in Gardner (1985b), while other versions have appeared in some journal articles (see Gardner, 2010). The most recent version is the International AMTB for learning English as a foreign language (see Gardner, 2010). To date, this has been translated (and adapted) into seven languages (Catalan, Croatian, Japanese, Polish, Portuguese, Romanian, and Spanish), available at http://publish.uwo/~gardner/.

The International AMTB is comprised of 12 scales, all but two of which assess four complex variables. The complex variables and the scales assessing them are as follows:

1. Integrativeness:
   a. Integrative Orientation (four items)
   b. Attitudes toward English Speakers (eight items)
   c. Interest in Foreign Languages (10 items)
2. Attitudes toward the Learning situation
   a. English Course Evaluation (10 items)
   b. English Teacher Evaluation (10 items)
3. Motivation
   a. Motivational Intensity (10 items)
   b. Desire to Learn English (10 items)
   c. Attitudes toward Learning English (10 items)
4. Language Anxiety
   a. English Class Anxiety (10 items)
   b. English Use Anxiety (10 items)

The two additional scales assessing unitary constructs are:

a. Instrumental Orientation (four Items)
b. Parental Encouragement (eight items)

The 104 items are presented in a random order and are responded to on a six alternative scale with item scores ranging from 1 to 7. The alternatives and relative values are strongly disagree (1), moderately disagree (2), slightly disagree (3), slightly agree (5), moderately agree (6) and strongly agree (7). The three scales with less than 10 items are each positively keyed such that a high score reflects the attribute. For those scales with 10 items, five are positively keyed while five are negatively keyed so that disagreement indicates a high level. For scoring, the negatively keyed items are recoded (i.e., 1 = 7, 2 = 6, etc.) so that high scores for all scales indicate high levels of the attribute in question.

Research has investigated both test/retest and internal consistency reliability for the scales (see Gardner, 2010). In addition, validity has been assessed in a number of ways varying from correlations with alternative measures (eg., the mini-AMTB), correlations with subsequent achievement, relationships to classroom behavior, persistence in language study, participation in bicultural excursions, language loss after training ends, rate of vocabulary acquisition, etc. (see Gardner, 2010). Most recently, the question of validity has been directed toward the predictive validity of an integrative motive score based on an aggregate defined as integrativeness plus attitudes toward the learning situation plus motivation minus language anxiety. The median correlation with subsequent grades in the language course is 0.44, while that with self-ratings of achievement is 0.57 (Gardner, 2010). These values correspond closely to a large effect size (i.e., 0.50), indicating a high level of association between integrative motivation and achievement in another language, supporting the socio-educational model of second language acquisition.

See also: effect size, individual difference in SLA, measuring and researching SLA, motivation, questionnaire research, theoretical constructs in SLA

References

Gardner, R.C. (1985a). *Social Psychology and Second Language Learning: The Role of Attitudes and Motivation*. London: Edward Arnold. Available at http://publish.uwo.ca/~gardner/

——(1985b). *The Attitude/Motivation Test Battery: Technical Report*. Unpublished manuscript, London, Canada: The University of Western Ontario. Available at http://publish.uwo.ca/~gardner/

——(2010). *Motivation and Second Language Acquisition: The Socio-Educational Model*. New York: Peter Lang Publications.

Attitudes to the L2

David Lasagabaster
University of the Basque Country

In recent times the impact of affective variables on successful L2 learning has engaged teachers' and researchers' attention. Factors such as anxiety, personality, willingness to communicate, self-esteem, inhibition, motivation and attitudes have been the subject of much research, but the last two variables – motivation and attitudes – by virtue of their interrelation, are both more recurrent and conspicuous in L2 learning theories. Attitudes have motivational implications and play a key role in most theoretical models seeking to explain individual differences in second language learning. An attitude is a positive or negative feeling towards a person (teacher or speakers of the L2), object (textbook) or issue (methodology) acquired through social interaction. There are three main reasons why attitude is a central explanatory variable (Baker, 1992): it is a term in common usage beyond the limited scope of specialists; it provides an indicator of learners' thoughts, beliefs and preferences; it has maintained an influential position in L2 learning theories for over 70 years.

Measurement

Because quantitative survey methods to collect and evaluate data on attitudes to the L2 have traditionally reigned supreme, more qualitative approaches are needed to complement this largely quantitative tradition. The questionnaire is by far the most widely used instrument because it is versatile, easy to construct and much information is readily available to process. The Attitudes and Motivation Test Battery (AMTB), whose validity and reliability have been widely reported, is the most popular. However, questionnaires are too often *ad hoc* instruments without sufficient psychometric reliability and validity (Dörnyei, 2003), resulting in a discrepancy between attitudes and learners' actual behavior. Reliable instrument construction is therefore a prerequisite for reliable data assessment.

Attitudes and achievement

Although positive attitudes are generally believed to facilitate second language acquisition, the assumption is far from straightforward. In fact, the relationship between attitude and second language achievement can be represented by two different hypotheses. On the one hand, the resultative hypothesis claims that positive attitudes are caused by good results and progress in second language learning, a line of causation which may come about when the learner has low initial motivation. On the other hand, the motivational hypothesis claims that attitudes will exert their influence on the success or failure of the L2 language learning process. Attitudes may therefore play a double role, as is the case in Gardner's (1985) socio-educational model, in which they have a triggering effect on bilingual proficiency (together with intelligence, aptitude and anxiety), but they also appear as an outcome alongside bilingual proficiency. This is why researchers endeavor to measure both the direction of attitudes and their intensity. Even so, causality is still a slippery fish to catch. Notwithstanding, the importance of attitudes in L2 acquisition cannot be underestimated.

Attitudes and age

The relationship between attitudes and age is well worth considering, especially at a time when the early learning of an L2 is becoming commonplace all over the world. Interestingly enough, research studies focused on the documentation of attitudes over time have consistently shown that positive attitudes to the L2 tend to decline with age. This is especially so at school, as students become increasingly disenchanted with school in general and the L2 in particular. The more years students spend learning an L2, the more unfavorable attitudes they harbor (Heining-Boynton and Haitema, 2007). The challenge is therefore how to better harness the positive desire of young students to learn an L2 and maintain this enthusiasm over an extended period of time.

Language attitudes

People hold language attitudes at many different levels (word, accent, grammar, dialect, etc.) and, consequently, language attitudes are ubiquitous. Although we are not always aware of them, attitudes are particularly noticeable when they are negative and explicitly articulated (Garrett, 2010). The positive/negative distinction is thus the first to arise when speaking about attitudes.

However, traditionally a second distinction between integrative and instrumental attitudes has been made. The former implies attachment and identification with a language group and their culture, whereas the latter involves economic benefits or the desire to gain social recognition through knowing an L2, that is, the individual's self-interest in utilitarian terms. This distinction has lately been challenged, especially with regards to English as a global language. In many L2 learning contexts the world over there has been limited contact with native speakers and their culture and, on top of that, L2 culture may be an issue of little interest to younger learners, which should end up affecting both teaching methods and the design of materials (Lamb, 2003). The integrative viewpoint can be useful in the Canadian context, where this integrative/instrumental distinction originally came to the fore, but may not be feasible in many other contexts where there is limited or no contact with the L2 speaking community.

Since globalization and ever increasing migratory movements have led to varied contexts where the coexistence of different languages has become the norm, language attitudes have recently gained considerable importance in research on multilingualism (Lasagabaster and Huguet, 2007), as most previous studies focused on bilingualism.

Final considerations

Attitudes are not static but rather dynamic, which is why longitudinal studies on attitude change are much needed. The relationship between attitudes and success in L2 learning seems not to be stable or unidirectional, as the social context and attitudes constantly influence each other, which is why societal processes and ideologies have to be considered. Attitudes are part of a dynamic scenario in which individual, group and societal dimensions intertwine (Pavlenko, 2002) and wherein learners sometimes show an ambivalent desire to learn and practice their L2 (Norton, 1997).

Attitudes are political as much as purely educational; cultural and historical as often as sociolinguistic. This is what makes attitudes to the L2 a really challenging field of research.

See also: anxiety, Attitudes and Motivation Test Battery (AMTB), bilingualism and SLA, individual differences in SLA, motivation, questionnaire research

References

Baker, C. (1992). *Attitudes and Language*. Clevedon: Multilingual Matters.

Dörnyei. Z. (2003). *Questionnaires in Second Language Research*. Mahwah, NJ: Lawrence Erlbaum.

Gardner, R.C. (1985). *Social Psychology and Second Language Learning: the Role of Attitudes and Motivation*. London: Edward Arnold.

Garrett, P. (2010). *Attitudes to Language*. Cambridge: Cambridge University Press.

Heining-Boynton, A.L. and Haitema, T. (2007). A ten-year chronicle of student attitudes toward foreign language in the elementary school. *The Modern Language Journal, 91*, 149–68.

Lamb, M. (2003). Integrative motivation in a globalizing world. *System, 32*, 3–19.

Lasagabaster D. and Huguet, A. (eds) (2007). *Multilingualism in European Bilingual Contexts. Language Use and Attitudes*. Clevedon: Multilingual Matters.

Norton, B. (1997). Language, identity, and the ownership of English. *TESOL Quarterly, 31*, 409–429.

Pavlenko, A. (2002). Poststructuralist approaches to the study of social factors in second language learning and use. In V. Cook (ed.), *Portraits of the L2 User*. Clevedon: Multilingual Matters.

Attrition

David Stringer

Indiana University

Language attrition is the term given to loss of language knowledge and skills, the reasons for which may vary considerably in different populations. Languages may attrite in individuals due to prolonged lack of use, or to physical trauma. At the level of communities, shared linguistic knowledge may suffer in situations of language shift, or following displacement of communities in times of social upheaval. In the context of second language research, studies of attrition have focused primarily on individuals who have learned a second language in either "naturalistic" or classroom settings, and who have subsequently been deprived of input as they return to a first language environment (most published studies have been conducted in predominantly monolingual societies). Even with this narrower focus, the variables in such studies are striking, as participants have ranged from schoolchildren to university students, from soldiers to missionaries, and from diplomats to citizens of decolonized countries. Although research on second language attrition has been conducted since the early decades of the twentieth century, it did not fully emerge as a recognized subfield of SLA until the first groundbreaking conference on the topic was held in 1980. In the subsequent proceedings volume, Lambert (1982) made an enduring distinction between criterion variables and predictor variables, which can be respectively thought of as linguistic (e.g. loss of morphological complexity, morphosyntactic transfer from the dominant language, reduction in registers), and extralinguistic (age, motivation, the period of time without input). In order to understand processes of language attrition, it is generally recognized that both linguistic and extralinguistic factors must be taken into account, and that multiple hypotheses are necessary as part of a broadly grounded approach to the phenomenon.

Attempts to explain second language loss have all drawn, at least in part, on hypotheses originally proposed for first language attrition (for an overview of approaches to first language attrition, see Köpke and Schmid, 2004). Here, discussion is restricted to the three hypotheses that have proven most influential in research on second language attrition. First, the regression hypothesis predicts that the path of attrition will be the reverse of the path of acquisition. In an early investigation of this idea, Cohen (1975) examined patterns of attrition in three children acquiring Spanish in an immersion program, administering an oral elicitation task before and after the summer vacation, and examining the results with reference to prior assessments. The grammatical contrasts only acquired in the months leading up to the summer vacation did appear to be more vulnerable to attrition. Another study used to support this claim was conducted by

Hansen and Chen (2001), who studied knowledge of numerical classifiers (grammatical morphemes denoting properties of objects in counting systems). Their participants were 703 Mormon missionaries who were living or who had lived in Japan or Taiwan, and who were categorized in terms of the learners' length of residence and the attriters' period of language disuse. Patterns of acquisition and attrition generally followed the predictions of the proposed Numeral Classifier Accessibility Hierarchy (animate human > animate non-human > shape > function), with two notable exceptions: the classifiers for books (e.g. the bible) and large mechanical objects (e.g. bicycles), both of which were high-frequency terms in this population. This suggests another plausible explanation of the patterns found; in general, classifier accessibility is consistent with a frequency explanation, as the authors note.

Frequency of reinforcement plays an important role in the second proposal considered here: the critical threshold hypothesis (which is distinct from the Threshold Hypothesis discussed elsewhere in this volume). The idea is that what is least vulnerable to language loss is not what is learned first but what is learned best. Neisser (1984) suggested that if a certain threshold of use is achieved, a representation may be less susceptible to or even immune from attrition, citing as evidence Bahrick's (1984) report on language retention in learners of Spanish even after 25 years of disuse. Another variant of this proposal is that once learners have achieved a certain level of proficiency, knowledge of language is more easily maintained. On this assumption, Clark and Jorden (1984) excluded first-year foreign language students from their study, arguing that for beginners "attrition is almost total after a comparatively short period of time away from the classroom" (pp. 16–17). As yet, empirical testing of this hypothesis for second language attrition has not been as rigorous as in first language attrition, where results may have implications for future second language research. Interesting evidence for this general approach is presented in terms of the "activation threshold hypothesis" discussed by Paradis (2007), who found that the facility of reactivation of lexical representations by aphasic patients is at least partly dependent on frequency of use prior to brain damage. However, she cautions that linguistic subsystems sustained by declarative memory appear to be much more vulnerable to frequency effects than those sustained by procedural memory. As the latter include the core linguistic systems of syntax and phonology, it is unlikely that this hypothesis applies across all submodules of the language faculty. Nevertheless, types of second language knowledge that involve domain-general information and a role for declarative memory, such as the lexicon or principles of pragmatics, may be strongly susceptible to frequency effects.

Quite apart from questions of sequences of attrition is the issue of what happens to knowledge of language once it has been "lost". The dormant language hypothesis maintains that knowledge that appears to have been erased from the mind may be reactivated in a situation of relearning. Evidence that this might be so for phonology in first language attrition is found in studies such as Tees and Werker (1984) and Oh *et al.* (2009). This general hypothesis is found in the concept of "savings" in second language studies of relearning (e.g. Hansen *et al.*, 2002). If relearning a language takes less time than learning it for the first time, this appears to implicate access to unconscious linguistic knowledge, rather than a second acquisition process after total loss. Given the need for further empirical research on this issue, which kinds of knowledge are prone to erasure and which might be subject to reactivation remains an open question. Of course, both outcomes are possible simultaneously for different linguistic representations. Anecdotally, many second languages learners who have experienced attrition report the language "coming back" after a few days' re-immersion in the country where the language is spoken. However, pending more rigorous examination of this issue, little is known about what exactly occurs in such situations. That language retrieval may occur in a context of more general retrieval of memories raises the question of how episodic memories might trigger unconscious procedural knowledge, at least parts of which have been argued to be modular and informationally encapsulated. This is an area rich for future exploration. Research to date has been more general in outlook: Clark and Jorden

(1984) and Russell (1999) employed simple attrition assessment interviews, which appear to confirm that highly advanced learners can retrieve items in the unused language with relative ease during relearning sessions.

In a comprehensive review of previous research on second language attrition, Bardovi-Harlig and Stringer (2010) note that many studies have addressed skill maintenance (reading, listening, speaking and writing) rather than examining linguistic knowledge; only about half of reports published to date include analysis of language samples. The general findings that emerge from the literature thus reflect the skills-dominated approach to attrition, and include the following: (i) production (speaking and writing) is more susceptible to attrition than comprehension (listening and reading); (ii) literacy supports retention; (iii) the lexicon appears to be more vulnerable than grammar, although formulas and conventional expressions may prove robust (Berman and Olshtain, 1983); (iv) motivation is implicated in processes of both learning and attrition; and (v) there is a general decrease in fluency. Bardovi-Harlig and Stringer suggest that more fine-grained analysis would be facilitated by defining populations in terms of sets of linguistic and extralinguistic variables, each of which may be subject to change over time; in this way, attrition may be accurately measured by comparing learners as individuals to themselves in longitudinal designs.

While attrition is usually conceived of as an independent process, occurring in the absence of acquisition and experienced by specific types of populations, it might also be thought of as a normal part of the second language experience. Arguably all learners go through periods in which their use of the language declines, whether for a few weeks or a few years, often followed by a resumption of the general acquisition process. Even in periods of continuous use, learners do not regularly exercise all aspects of second language knowledge, so that gain and loss may sometimes proceed in parallel. It is to be hoped that future studies of extreme shifts in input of the type experienced by populations going from continuous input to no input will also shed light on strategies for language maintenance in second language learning more generally.

See also: crosslinguistic influence, declarative memory and knowledge, developmental sequences, frequency effects, heritage language acquisition, procedural memory and knowledge

References

Bahrick, H. (1984). Fifty years of second language attrition: Implications for programming research. *Modern Language Journal*, *68*, 105–11.

Bardovi-Harlig, K. and Stringer, D. (2010). Variables in second language attrition: Advancing the state of the art. *Studies in Second Language Acquisition*, *32* (1), 1–45.

Berman, R.A. and Olshtain, E. (1983). Features of first language transfer in second language attrition. *Applied Linguistics*, *4*, 222–34.

Clark, J.L. D. and Jorden, E.H. (1984). *A Study of Language Attrition in Former U.S. Students of Japanese and Implications for Design of Curriculum and Teaching Materials: Final Project Report* [Online]. Retrieved November 1, 2008, from ERIC Document Reproduction Service, http://www.eric.ed.gov, No. ED243317.

Cohen, A.D. (1975). Forgetting a Second Language. *Language Learning*, *25*, 127–38.

Hansen, L. and Chen, Y.-L. (2001). What Counts in the Acquisition and Attrition of Numeral Classifiers? *JALT Journal*, *23*, 90–110.

Hansen, L., Umeda, Y. and McKinney, M. (2002). Savings in the relearning of second language vocabulary: The effects of time and proficiency. *Language Learning*, *52*, 653–78.

Köpke, B. and Schmid, M.S. (2004). First language attrition: The next phase. In M.S. Schmid, B. Köpke, M. Keijzer, and L. Weilemar (eds), *First Language Attrition: Interdisciplinary Perspectives on Methodological Issues*, Amsterdam: John Benjamins.

Lambert, R.D. (1982). Setting the agenda. In R.D. Lambert and B.F. Freed (eds), *The Loss of Language Skills*. Rowley, MA: Newbury House.

Neisser, U. (1984). Interpreting Harry Bahrick's Discovery: What Confers Immunity against Forgetting? *Journal of Experimental Psychology: General*, *113*, 32–35.

Oh, J., Au, T.K. and Jun, S.-A. (2009). The nature of childhood language memory: Korean adoptees learning Korean as adults. In J. Chandlee, M. Franchini, S. Lord, and G.-M. Rheiner (eds), *Proceedings of the 33rd Annual Boston University Conference on Language Development*. Somerville, MA: Cascadilla Press.

Paradis, M. (2007). L1 attrition features predicted by a neurolinguistic theory of bilingualism. In B. Köpke, M.S. Schmid, M. Keijzer, and S. Dostert (eds), *Language Attrition: Theoretical Perspectives*. Amsterdam: John Benjamins.

Russell, R.A. (1999). Lexical maintenance and attrition in Japanese as a second language. In L. Hansen (ed.), *Second Language Attrition in Japanese Contexts*, Oxford: Oxford University Press.

Tees, R.C. and Werker, J.F. (1984). Perceptual flexibility: Maintenance or recovery of the ability to discriminate nonnative speech sounds. *Canadian Journal of Psychology*, *38*, 579–90.

Autistic savants

Ianthi Maria Tsimpli
Aristotle University of Thessaloniki

Savants are individuals with an atypical and strongly asymmetrical pattern of behavior: their verbal and non-verbal performance is at or below the lower end of the average scale, and their communication is severely deficient; at the same time they excel in some special skill. There is extensive literature on athetoid musicians, calendrical calculators and retarded artists with little or no language ability (Hermelin, 2002). Savants are more frequently found in individuals with autism spectrum conditions than in any other group (Howlin *et al.*, 2009). Moreover, the majority of savants reported in the literature are autistic.

Autism involves a spectrum of communication disorders associated with impairments in three domains: social interaction, social communication and imagination, and a restricted repertoire of activities and interests (Wing, 1997). Deficient social interaction is at the heart of autistic behaviour and it can dissociate from linguistic and cognitive abilities. Thus, within autistic populations various levels of linguistic ability are found although many children in the autistic spectrum are non-verbal. Of the autistic children with some language ability, many exhibit language impairments affecting both vocabulary and morpho-syntax.

There are various, alternative or complementary, cognitive approaches to autism. Baron-Cohen's (1995) idea of *mind-blindness* views autism as a deficit in Theory of Mind (ToM), that is, the ability to interpret other people's intentions, beliefs and attitudes through interpreting discourse, context, facial expressions and body language. Frith's (1989/2003) theory of *weak central coherence* (WCC) characterizes autism as an inability to integrate relevant pieces of information drawn from perceptual evidence and/or from previous knowledge, preventing the autistic individual from seeing the "big picture." Accordingly, the typical autist shows *excellent attention to detail* both in terms of processing and memory. A more recent version of WCC attributes this attention to detail to a local processing bias. Finally, autism has also been characterized as a deficit in executive functions leading to limited or no cognitive flexibility. This executive dysfunction is responsible for the inability to abandon decisions or misguided interpretations of actions (Ozonoff *et al.*, 1991).

All of the above approaches seek to account for the basic properties of autism spectrum conditions concentrating on the deviance from the average individual in terms of abilities and behavior. However, the frequent co-occurrence of savantism and autism presents an interesting challenge to the above theories: why is autism associated with excellence in some aspect of cognition?

Autism and savantism: what is the link?

The shared characteristic of all individuals with autism spectrum conditions, including high-functioning autists, Asperger' syndrome individuals and savants is this excellent attention to detail analyzed as *strong systemising* (Baron-Cohen *et al.*, 2009). Systemizing crucially involves a higher cognitive ability to extract patterns, rules and generalizations from perceptual input. As a result, autists are good at extracting repeating patterns in stimuli while strong systemising is also evident in their actions and overall behavior.

Savantism is thus viewed as a strong ("hyper") version of the common autistic trait of strong systemising (Baron-Cohen *et al.*, 2009): sensory hypersensitivity, hyper-attention to detail and hyper-systemizing. The first property characterises low-level perception, aspects of which (tactile, visual, auditory) seem to be enhanced in savants. Hyper-attention to detail is a necessary prerequisite for hyper-systemizing, that is, for extracting the detailed ingredients of an association which enter into *modus-ponens* ($p \rightarrow q$) patterns from a complicated and highly integrated form of the input. Hyper-systemizing is a basic inferential ability which, if meticulously applied to perceptually accessible systems, can lead to excellent knowledge of the system's ingredients and operations. A memory system dedicated to the domain of hyper-systemizing in the savant enables the build-up, storage and retrieval of a highly sophisticated and detailed system of knowledge in this cognitive domain.

Music, arithmetic, art (drawing, sculpture) are systems in which savants have been found to exhibit "gifted" behavior. They are highly complex, detailed systems which are good candidates for the savant hyper-systemizing mind. Language is also a highly complex cognitive system with properties such as recursion and discrete infinity that appear similar to other aspects of human cognition, such as music and mathematics (Berwick and Chomsky, forthcoming). On the other hand, language enjoys a privileged position in the human mind in that it underlies thought and communication. Since autism typically involves a deficit in social interaction and communication but also a deficit in thought processes, language is not expected to be a domain of hyper-systemizing in savants (cf. Howlin *et al.*, 2009). Christopher is a unique case of a polyglot-savant (Smith and Tsimpli, 1995; Smith *et al.*, 2010 and references therein).

Christopher

Christopher has been institutionalized during almost all of his adult life. He has severe apraxia, visuo-spatial deficits, very poor drawing abilities and motor coordination skills. His behavior shows autistic features in the limited use of facial expression and intonation, in the avoidance of eye contact and in the resistance to social, verbal and non-verbal, interaction. His performance on ToM tasks (cognitive and social affect) is mixed and inconsistent. Turning to language, the picture is different.

Christopher speaks and understands around 20 languages most of which he learned without spoken interaction. His "obsessive" interest in the written form of language allowed him to learn vocabulary, morphology and, to some extent, syntactic variation in these languages while gathering encyclopaedic information on a variety of topics ranging from football and politics to history and meta-language. Teaching Christopher British Sign Language was a challenge: limited eye-contact, insensitivity to facial expression and the lack of a written form of BSL were all predictive of failure. Nevertheless, a strong asymmetry between comprehension and production as well as between BSL classifiers and other domains of morphosyntax (agreement, negation, questions) was found in his BSL learning. Christopher's savantism could be attributed to his hyper-attention to linguistic detail, hyper-sensitivity to written language input and hyper-systemising in the discovery of rules, patterns and generalisations that make languages similar and at the same time different from each other. Crucially, however, Christopher's savantism shows multiple dissociations among Language, Thought and Communication.

See also: aptitude, executive control and frontal cortex, individual differences in SLA, inhibitory control, modularity, procedural memory and knowledge

References

Baron-Cohen, S. (1995). *Mindblindness: An Essay on Autism and Theory of Mind.* Cambridge, MA: MIT Press.

——(2008). Autism, hypersystemizing and truth. *Quarterly Journal of Experimental Psychology, 61*, 64–75.

Baron-Cohen, S., Ashwin, E., Ashwin, D., Tavassoli, T. and Chakrabarti, Bhismadev (2009).

Talent in autism: hyper-systemizing, hyper-attention to detail and sensory hypersensitivity. *Philosophical Transactions of the Royal Society B*, *364*, 1377–83.

Berwick, R. and Chomsky, N. (forthcoming) The biolinguistic program: The current state of its evolution and development. In A.M. Di Sciullo and C. Boeckx (eds), *The Biolinguistic Enterprise: New Perspectives on the Evolution and Nature of the Human Language Faculty*. Oxford: Oxford University Press.

Frith, U. (1989/2003). *Autism: Explaining the Enigma*. Oxford: Blackwell.

Hermelin, B. (2002). *Bright splinters of the mind: a personal story of research with autistic savants*. London: Jessica Kingsley.

Howlin, P., Goode, S., Hutton, J. and Rutter, M. (2009). Savant skills in autism: Psychometric approaches and parental reports. *Philosophical Transactions of the Royal Society of London B*, *364*, 1359–1367.

Ozonoff, S., Pennington, B. and Rogers, S. (1991). Executive function deficits in high-functioning autistic children: relationship to theory of mind. *Journal of Child Psychology and Psychiatry*, *32*, 1081–1106.

Smith, N. and I.M. Tsimpli (1995). *The Mind of a Savant: Language Learning and Modularity*. Oxford: Blackwell.

Smith, N., Tsimpli, I., Morgan, G. and Woll, B. (2010). *The Signs of a Savant: Language Against the Odds*. Cambridge: Cambridge University Press.

Wing, L. (1997). *The Autistic Spectrum*. Oxford: Pergamon.

Automaticity

Norman Segalowitz
Concordia University

Automaticity is a theoretical concept central to cognitive psychology and psycholinguistics, and more recently to social psychology. *Automaticity* has also been imported into theories of second language (L2) acquisition and L2 performance (DeKeyser, 2007a; Mitchell and Myles, 2004; Segalowitz, 2010) where it continues to be used widely. In its most general sense, *automaticity* has been used to refer to those properties of behavior that reflect the individual's ability to perform very rapidly and with little or no (conscious) effort. For example, a literate adult's recognition of letters of the alphabet in the first language (L1) is usually automatic in the sense of being extremely rapid and requiring little or no attention due to massive overlearning, whereas the ability to recognize letters drawn from a different alphabet in an L2 is usually not automatic, especially during the early phases of learning the language. Pashler (1998) suggests that the core propositions generally agreed upon in automaticity theories are the "lack of interference with competing tasks; functioning without voluntary control" (p. 358).

Several milestone contributions provide background for understanding how automaticity has been operationalized for research purposes in general and for L2 acquisition research in particular. Kahneman (1973) elaborated upon the idea that some behaviors can come to require little or no attention for their execution. Schneider and Shiffrin (1977) studied the effect of repetition on response times (RTs) in learning stimulus-response connections, by comparing the results of learning involving *consistent* mapping (when a given stimulus is always the target and never a non-target) with learning involving *varied* mapping (when a given stimulus is a target on some trials and a non-target on others). In tasks with massive practice over hundreds of trials involving consistent mapping, they found that responses became fast, relatively effortless and immune to interference from distracting stimuli – that is, processing had become automatic – in contrast to learning involving varied mapping. Schneider *et al.* (1984: 1) defined this automaticity as "a fast, parallel, fairly effortless process that is not limited by short-term memory (STM) capacity, is not under direct subject control, and is responsible for the performance of well-developed skill behaviors."

In short, the mental activities underlying a learned skill appear to take on new features as a result of massive practice – they are said to become more automatic. The process involved in this change is sometimes called *automatization*. Questions about automatization are relevant to learning in every skill domain, including L2 acquisition where automatization is assumed to be important in fluency development (for implications of automaticity for L2 pedagogy see DeKeyser, 2001, 2007b; Johnson, 1996; Segalowitz, 2010; Skehan, 1998). It is important, therefore, for L2 researchers to find ways to distinguish automatic from non-automatic processing for measuring the automatization that results from learning and practice, and for studying the conditions leading to the development of automatic processing in L2 use.

While there is agreement on some of the general characteristics of automatic behaviors, consensus on how to operationally define automaticity for research purposes has proven elusive. The following ideas about what distinguishes automatic from non-automatic (sometimes called control) processes have motivated different researchers' operational definitions: automatic processing proceeds faster, it consumes little or no attentional resources (it is effortless), it reflects a change from a serial to a parallel mode of processing and it is ballistic (unstoppable once initiated and cannot be interrupted by other ongoing processes). As well, in the process of automatization, RTs improve over time in a pattern following a power law distribution. These properties of performance correspond to what many would normally expect *automatic processing* to refer to. However, the psychological literature also reveals that so-called automatic behaviors do not necessarily always exhibit all of the above features at the same time. Automaticity, therefore, is not a well-defined construct in the sense that there is no criterial feature or set of features that can be used to unambiguously distinguish all automatic from non-automatic behavior. This poses a problem for researchers wishing to investigate the acquisition of high-level skills in which automatic processing – in some sense of the word – plays a role. Pashler (1998: 357–89) provides a very useful discussion of the relevant issues here, one that challenges some widely held assumptions about automaticity. We turn now to discussion of automaticity in relation to L2 processing.

Automaticity and the L2

Some L2 theorists have used automaticity generically without proposing an operational definition or explicitly specifying what the contrasting non-automatic behavior might be. For example, Bybee (2008), in discussing fossilized features of L2 speech commented on how difficult it is to change the structure of a fossilized chunk of language 'once it has become automatized' (p. 221). Presumably this means that the "chunk of language" has become so embedded in the speaker's behavioral repertoire that it is difficult or impossible to modify. Others have provided more concrete operational definitions for automaticity, and these fall into four general categories, depending on whether automaticity is identified in terms of *speed* of processing, *unstoppable* processing, the *power law* or *efficient* processing.

Speed. Early on, cognitive researchers recognized that L1 processing was in some sense more automatic than L2 processing. Lambert, a pioneer in bilingualism research, wrote "automatic behavior is characterized chiefly by its speed" (1955: 197), explicitly focusing on processing speed as what chiefly distinguishes automatic from non-automatic behavior. Magiste (1986), in a study of interference across languages in bilinguals and learners of a third language, also explicitly used processing speed to make inferences about automaticity. Segalowitz (2010) further discusses how people have linked automaticity with processing speed, arguing that making such a link is an error. He argues that while automatic behavior is likely to be faster than non-automatic behavior, this cannot be the whole story because, if it were, then *automatic* would reduce to becoming a mere synonym for *fast*. If speed were the primary criterion for automaticity then we would need to establish some absolute speed-of-processing millisecond threshold that separates automatic from non-automatic performance, and it seems unlikely that this can be done. Segalowitz (2010; Segalowitz and Segalowitz, 1993) argues, instead, that the speed usually associated with automaticity is really a consequence of some other more critical feature of automatic behavior, namely the way the underlying processes are organized. According to this view, one should distinguish *speed-up* from *restructuring* (or re-organisation) explanations for so-called non-automatic and automatic behaviors respectively.

Unstoppable (ballistic) processing. An alternative to speed as a criterion for distinguishing automatic from non-automatic behavior is processing independence – that is, the immunity of automatic mechanisms to interference from other ongoing processing. The idea here is that once a process has been triggered (e.g., retrieving a word's meaning), it cannot be stopped in midstream and will run – *automatically* – to completion. Tzelgov, Henik, Sneg and Barch (1996) reported a study that illustrates just such automatic processing. They showed that Hebrew-English bilinguals could not override the processing of a word in their dominant language, even when that word was technically irrelevant to the primary task at hand. The task was a color-word interference task requiring the participant to name the color of the font of a color name word (e.g., *red* written in a green font). In the Tzelgov *et al.* study, the word itself was written with the orthography of one language (say, non-dominant English) with the phonology of the other (say, dominant Hebrew), as in the case of *adom* ["red"] in a green font where the orthography is English, the phonology is Hebrew (dominant language) and the word-color pair is incongruent (respond "green" for the font colour and ignore the meaning "red" of *adom*). They found a strong interference effect for incongruent Hebrew-phonology/English-orthography stimuli, but not for English-phonology/Hebrew-orthography, presumably because Hebrew was the participants' dominant language. This illustrates how once there had been activation of a dominant-language phonological code linked to a particular meaning, processing could not be stopped. Favreau and Segalowitz (1983) reported similar processing with French–English bilinguals in a study dissociating ballistic processing from speed of processing effects. They used a lexical decision task (judge whether a target item is a real word or not), where the target word was sometimes preceded by a to-be-ignored prime stimulus whose meaning could potentially interfere with judging the target. Participants who were more fluent in the L2 demonstrated ballistic processing in both languages whereas less fluent participants showed this in the L1 only, indicating that L2 automatic processing, but not L2 speed as such, to be associated with fluency. The upshot of these two studies is that one can operationally define automatic processing in a meaningful way as ballistic or unstoppable processing.

Power Law. Newell and Rosenbloom (1981), in a highly influential paper, argued for *a power law* of learning, according to which RT in performing a task is related to the number of practice trials; as the number of practice trials increases, RT becomes faster but with a decreasing rate of gain in speed. The exact mathematical form of the relationship has been a matter of debate (see, among others, Heathcote *et al.*, 2000; Rickard, 1997). Some L2 researchers have used the power law pattern in RT data to interpret results as evidence for automatization (DeKeyser, 1997; Ellis and Schmidt, 1997).

Efficiency. Segalowitz (2010) argued that even if there is little consensus on how best to operationalize automaticity, the construct of automaticity nevertheless does serve a useful purpose. This is because to claim that some behavior (e.g., retrieving L2 word meaning) is automatic beyond simply being very fast, is to claim that the behavior reflects a noteworthy level of cognitive efficiency. This efficiency is achieved, presumably, through some as-yet-unspecified cognitive organization that is different from some appropriate reference point of non-automatic behavior. Segalowitz and Segalowitz (1993; Segalowitz, 2010) discuss how analysis of *intra*-individual RT variability (as opposed to *inter*-individual variability) can be used to operationalize these distinctions. This involves using the coefficient of variation (CV) of the RT – that is, the standard deviation of a person's RT divided by that person's mean RT. The CV is claimed to be a reflection of "noise" in the processing system, that is, processing variability after correcting for response speed. The lower the "noise" level, the more efficient the system can be claimed to be. Segalowitz (2010) reviews L2 processing research using this measure of processing efficiency and discusses conditions under which one can claim that a case of fast processing is more than just a reflection of simple speed-up but rather is a reflection of highly efficient processing. It is claimed that, under this view, automaticity can be operationalized by the CV when used with appropriate control procedures.

The future of automaticity in L2 acquisition research

As definitions of automaticity become more sophisticated and differentiated, the term itself seems to be evolving into more of a general umbrella construct for highly efficient performance. In this sense, automaticity appears to be losing its original sense of referring to a specific feature of cognitive processing such as parallel processing, ballistic processing, effortless processing, etc. Nevertheless, automaticity remains useful when understood in this more general sense of indicating performance reflecting more than just speed-up (where speed-up would be the null hypothesis explanation for the observed fast behavior), as long as there is a way to operationalize speed-up so that it can be rejected as the explanation for the case at hand. Of course, after rejecting a speed-up explanation in a given case, it may still be important to investigate further the exact nature of what is responsible for the significantly efficient performance. However, even without an immediate answer to that question, it is still useful to know whether a particular L2 learning context (e.g., a particular approach to instructed learning; immersion in a community of native speakers) is able to improve performance efficiency in ways that require explanation beyond simple speed-up.

As indicated in the above discussion, the meaning of automaticity in L2 research (and more generally in cognitive psychology) appears to be evolving. On the one hand, the original sense of the term may have lost some usefulness because there were too many different interpretations of what it meant to say that a behavior was automatic. It is nevertheless possible to think of automaticity as generally referring to *processing efficiency* in a way that makes possible asking whether some target behavior can be differentiated meaningfully from some reference point (such as, that the behavior can be explained in terms of simple speed-up). In this way, the study of automaticity can be useful in the study of L2 acquisition and L2 pedagogy.

See also: attention, declarative memory and knowledge, fluency, inhibitory control, procedural memory and knowledge, psycholinguistics of SLA

References

Bybee, J. (2008). Usage-based grammar and second language acquisition. In P. Robinson and N.C. Ellis (eds), *Handbook of Cognitive Linguistics and Second Language Acquisition*, pp. 216–36. New York: Routledge.

DeKeyser, R. (1997). Beyond explicit rule learning: Automatizing second language morphosyntax. *Studies in Second Language Acquisition*, *19*, 195–221.

——(2007a). Skill acquisition theory. In B. VanPatten and J. Williams (eds), *Theories in Second Language Acquisition*, pp. 97–113. Mahwah, NJ: Erlbaum.

DeKeyser, R. (ed.). (2007b). *Practice in a Second Language: Perspectives from Aapplied Linguistics and Cognitive Psychology*. Cambridge: Cambridge University Press.

Ellis, N.C. and Schmidt, R. (1997). Morphology and longer distance dependencies: Laboratory research illuminating the A in SLA. *Studies in Second Language Acquisition*, *19*, 145–71.

Favreau, M. and Segalowitz, N. (1983). Automatic and controlled processes in the first and second language reading of fluent bilinguals. *Memory and Cognition*, *11*, 565–74.

Heathcote, A., Brown, S. and Mewhort, D. (2000). The power law repealed: The case for an exponential law of practice. *Psychonomic Bulletin and Review*, *7*, 185–207.

Johnson, K. (1996). *Language Teaching and Skill Learning*. Oxford: Blackwell.

Kahneman, D. (1973). *Attention and effort*. Englewood Cliffs, NJ: Prentice-Hall.

Lambert, W.E. (1955). Measurement of linguistic dominance in bilinguals. *Journal* of *Abnormal and Social Psychology*, *50*, 197–200.

Magiste, E. (1986). Selected issues in second and third language learning. In J. Vaid (ed.), *Language Processing in Bilinguals: Psycholinguistic and Neuropsychological Perspectives*, pp. 97–122. Hillsdale, NJ: Lawrence Erlbaum Associates.

Mitchell, R. and Myles, F. (2004). *Second Language Learning Theories*, second edn. London: Hodder Arnold.

Newell, A. and Rosenbloom, P.S. (1981). Mechanisms of skill acquisition and the law of practice.

In J.R Anderson (ed.), *Cognitive Skills and their Acquisition*, pp. 1–55. Hillside, NJ: Laurence Erlbaum Associates.

Pashler, H. (1998). *The Psychology of Attention*. Cambridge, MA: MIT Press.

Rickard, T.C. (1997). Bending the power law: A CMPL theory of strategy shifts and the automatization of cognitive skills. *Journal of Experimental Psychology: General, 126*, 288–311.

Robinson, P. (2001). Task complexity, task difficulty, and task production: Exploring interactions in a componential framework. *Applied Linguistics, 22*, 27–57.

Schmidt, R. (1992). Psychological mechanisms underlying second language fluency. *Studies in Second Language Acquisition, 14*, 357–85.

Schneider, W., Dumais, S. and Schiffrin, R. (1984). Automatic and control processing and attention. In R. Parasuraman (ed.), *Varieties of attention*, pp. 1–27. New York: Academic Press.

Schneider, W. and Shiffrin, R.M. (1977). Controlled and automatic human information processing: I. Detection, search, and attention. *Psychological Review, 84*, 1–66.

Segalowitz, N. (2010). *Cognitive Bases of Second Language Fluency*. New York: Routledge.

Segalowitz, N. and Segalowitz, S.J. (1993). Skilled performance, practice, and the differentiation of speed-up from automatization effects: Evidence from second language word recognition. *Applied Psycholinguistics, 14*, 369–85.

Skehan, P. (1998). *A Cognitive Approach to Language learning*. Oxford: Oxford University Press.

Tzelgov, J., Henik, A., Sneg, R. and Baruch, O. (1996). Unintentional word reading via the phonological route: The Stroop effect with cross-script homophones. *Journal of Experimental Psychology: Learning, Memory and Cognition, 22*, 336–49.

Further reading

Bargh, J.A. and Williams, E.L. (2006). The automaticity of social life. *Current Directions in Psychological Science, 15*(1), 1–4. (This paper provides a good entry into the literature on automaticity as it relates to social psychology, thereby extending the discussion to an area that goes beyond general cognitive information processing issues.)

DeKeyser, R. (2001). Automaticity and automatization. In P. Robinson (ed.), *Cognition and Second Language Instruction*, pp. 125–51. Cambridge: Cambridge University Press. (This chapter provides a wide-ranging discussion of automaticity issues as they relate to second language instruction.)

Meyer, A., Wheeldon, L. and Krott, A. (eds). (2007). *Automaticity and Control in Language Processing*. New York: Psychology Press. (The 11 chapters in this volume discuss automaticity from different perspectives, providing the reader with an appreciation of the applicability of the construct to a wide variety of language-based situations.)

Moors, A. and De Houwer, J. (2006). Automaticity: a theoretical and conceptual analysis. *Psychological Bulletin, 132*(2), 297–326. (This article provides a detailed look into the concept of automaticity from a general cognitive psychological perspective.)

Segalowitz, N. and Hulstijn, J. (2005). Automaticity in bilingualism and second language learning. In J.F. Kroll and A.M. B. De Groot (eds), *Handbook of Bilingualism: Psycholinguistic Approaches*, pp. 371–88. Oxford: Oxford University Press. (This chapter provides an extended overview of automaticity issues as they relate specifically to second language acquisition and to bilingualism).

Autonomous Induction Theory

Susanne E. Carroll
University of Calgary

The Autonomous Induction Theory (AIT) is a theory of second language acquisition. It asks: how does new knowledge come to be represented in the learner's mind/brain? What changes in the learner's mental representations? What inputs do learning mechanisms draw on? What are the operations and mechanisms of language acquisition?

One basic premise is that explicit formal descriptions of learning problems are required.

Every learning problem has a logical structure. Some representations must be in place before new ones can come into existence. Stating what they are helps to define necessary inputs to acquisition. A second premise is that learners don't acquire "language" or a "behavior"; they acquire a structural description from which the ability to act and understand speech will ultimately follow. Consider English speakers asked to listen to German sentences while looking at pictures and who are told: "Learn the names of the people depicted." Participants hear speech (approximately rendered as in (1a)). The target name is shown in (1b)

(1) a. [dasɪstbɛno]
Das ist Benno
"That is Benno"

b.

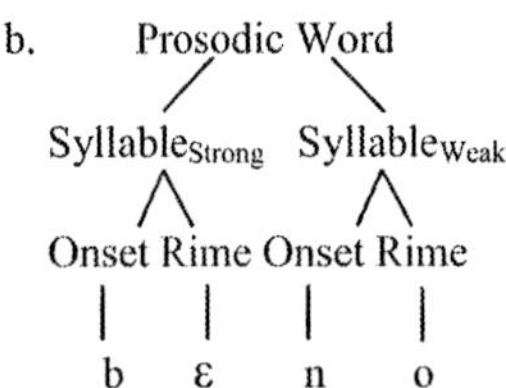

To learn the name, the learner must segment the continuous signal into discrete units: not just sound "forms" but prosodic words. However, the signal does not directly indicate where one prosodic word begins and another ends, how many syllables the word contains, where the syllables begin and end, and so on. This information must be induced. Current research suggests that some of this induction will be based on distributional computations (statistical learning), if the learner is exposed repeatedly to enough speech. However, distributional learning cannot explain how (1b) emerges from minimal exposure to speech. Current work shows that ab initio learners have no difficulty in immediately segmenting sound forms from sentences, forming representations of both syllables, consonants and vowels, and exhibiting sensitivity to novel acoustic features in the signal, even when their own pronunciations are strongly influenced by the organization of the L1 lexicon and the articulation of English syllables (Carroll, 2010). Indeed not only simple words but also complex words and constructions can be acquired on minimal exposure (Widjaja, 2010).

The AIT explains rapid learning by hypothesizing that the learner comes armed with implicit knowledge of the primitives of language (phonetic features, units like onset, syllable, morpho-syntactic features, heads, etc.), and universal processes of structure-building (feature unification, feature copying, indexing, etc.). However, since the composition of units varies across languages, language-specific structures must be acquired from cues in the signal and information deduced "top-down." SLA involves a mix of data-driven and knowledge-based processes.

This mixture of bottom-up and top-down processes is predicted by the tripartite modular functional architecture in which the AIT is rooted (Jackendoff, 1997; see Carroll, 2001). The architecture necessitates an indexing process linking autonomous representations outputted by distinct processing modules. Thus (1b) must be indexed both to (2a), a simplified syntactic representation, and (2b), its conceptual structure.

(2) a.
$$\begin{pmatrix} \text{CAT : NP} \\ \text{VALENCE :<>} \\ \begin{pmatrix} \text{HEAD: N} \\ \text{Count: Sg} \\ \text{Person: 3rd} \end{pmatrix} \end{pmatrix}$$

b. PERSON x, x BEARS NAME [bɛno]
(cf. Katz, 2001)

Linguistic approaches to SLA have emphasized acquired language-specific constraints: the verb-second constraint of German, vowel harmony constraints of Turkish, and so on. These are constraints on structure-building within an autonomous module (morpho-syntactic structure and prosodic structure, respectively). The AIT also emphasizes constraints on the correspondences *across modules*, an issue usually relegated to processing research. Thus, French requires that its functional categories (determiners, pronouns, auxiliaries) be clitics and not prosodic words. When English learners of French pronounce determiners with stress and full vowels, this is clear evidence that they have constructed a structure that violates this constraint.

The AIT grew out of work seeking to understand how structure and processing interact. Why do Anglophones have such trouble producing French gender accurately despite ample input? The AIT's answer is twofold: they parse determiners as distinct prosodic words (as in English), stripping off privileged cues to gender when they build lexical entries of nouns. When they speak, they have no feature to base determiner selection on. They also treat the phonological variation between *un/une* and *le/la* as "noise" irrelevant to the construction of a semantic representation (Carroll, 1989). Since production demands a choice between determiners, learners must find alternative solutions, either a default selection strategy (Hawkins, 1998), or concept-form mappings that are only a partial solution (Carroll, 1999). This solution involves linking conceptual structures directly to prosodic structures, bypassing the morpho-syntactic structure. Learners construct a representation like (2a), not one that includes a gender feature.

Such problems led to the conclusion that learning is triggered only when parsing fails. If learners can parse their way to an interpretation, they need not construct target-like structures. Additional support comes in MacDonald's (2010) study of intermediate and advanced Korean learners who failed to learn English morpho-syntactic cues to number, despite ample evidence. MacDonald showed in a two-picture interpretation task asking: *Who has more?* that Koreans' interpretations were indistinguishable from those of native Anglophones choosing volume with mass nouns and counting with count nouns. Only in the case of ambiguous nouns (*more stones* versus *more stone*) where sensitivity to number marking was required did Koreans fail to get the right interpretation.

Recent AIT work explores claims that certain input properties are more perceptually salient than others: sentence position, word length, and focal accent. Carroll (to appear) showed that sentence position is not a factor in word learning once focal accent is controlled for. Salience is in the mind, not in the signal. Longer words are learned as easily as short words (Carroll, 2010). Yet other work asks if learners themselves perceive words they have learned as perceptually salient.

The AIT has been formulated in the belief that general and descriptive linguistics have a contribution to make to theories of SLA but they play a supporting role, embedded in processing models. The primary goal has to be to define the multiple learning mechanisms at work in specific learning problems, among specific populations.

See also: form-meaning connections, input enhancement, modularity, psycholinguistics of SLA, speech perception, statistical learning, Universal Grammar (UG) and SLA

References

Carroll, S.E. (1989). Second language acquisition and the computational paradigm. *Language Learning*, *39*(4), 535–94.

——(1999). Adults' sensitivity to different sorts of input. *Language Learning*, *49*(1), 37–92. Reprinted in R. DeKeyser (ed.) (2005). *Grammatical Development in Language Learning. Best of Language Learning Series*, pp. 79–138. Malden, MA: Blackwell.

——(2001). *Input and Evidence: The Raw Material of Second Language Acquisition*. Amsterdam: John Benjamins.

——(2010) Interactions of statistical learning and form-meaning mappings in second language learning. Paper to *Multilingual Individuals & Multilingual Societies Conference*. Universitaet Hamburg, October 6–8.

——(to appear). When is input salient? An exploratory study of the Sentence Location Principle and word length. *International Review of Applied Linguistics*.

Hawkins, R. (1998). Explaining the difficulty of gender attribution for speakers of English. Paper to *EUROSLA* 8. Paris, France.

Jackendoff, R. (1997). *The Architecture of the Language Faculty*. Cambridge, MA: MIT Press.

Katz, J.J. (2001). The end of Millianism: multiple bearers, improper names and compositional meaning. *Journal of Philosophy*, *98*(3), 137–66.

MacDonald, D. (2010). *Second Language Acquisition of English Mass-count Nouns by Koreans*. M.A. thesis, Linguistics Department, University of Calgary.

Widjaja, E. (2010). *Second Language Acquisition Order of Indonesian Reduplication and Numeral*

Classifiers. M.A. thesis, Linguistics Department, University of Calgary.

Awareness

Melissa Bowles
University of Illinois at Urbana-Champaign

Awareness has been defined as "a particular state of mind in which an individual has undergone a specific subjective experience of some cognitive content or external stimulus" (Tomlin and Villa, 1994, p. 193). There are three major theoretical positions regarding the relationship between awareness and L2 development in second language acquisition (SLA). Schmidt's (1990 and elsewhere) Noticing Hypothesis states that a low level of awareness is necessary for linguistic input to become intake. This low level, which he refers to as awareness at the level of noticing is defined as "conscious registration of the concurrence of some event" (Schmidt, 1995: 29). There is a higher level, awareness at the level of understanding, which Schmidt defines as "recognition of a general principle, rule or pattern" (Schmidt, 1995: 29), which is not required for initial input processing. A second theoretical position, Tomlin and Villa's (1994) functionally based, fine-grained analysis of attention, involves three components, each with neurological correlates – alertness, orientation, and detection. Tomlin and Villa contend that detection, defined as the "cognitive registration of stimuli" (p. 190) is necessary for input to be processed. Awareness is not required for detection, and therefore is not needed for language development. A third theoretical position, that of Robinson (1995), reconciles the two previous views of the role of awareness. Specifically, Robinson contends that detection is an important precursor to noticing, and that linguistic input is only available for further processing at the noticing phase.

According to Allport (1988), one of three criteria must be met in order for the presence of awareness to be established: 1) a sign of some behavioral or cognitive change due to the experience, 2) a report of being aware of the experience, or 3) a metalinguistic description of an underlying rule for the targeted linguistic form. Nevertheless, the operationalization and measurement of awareness in SLA is methodologically thorny (Hama and Leow, 2010). Since the 1980s, several different instruments have been used to measure awareness, including offline questionnaires (Alanen, 1995), offline uptake recall charts (Slimani, 1989), online uptake charts (Mackey *et al.*, 2001), free recall (VanPatten, 1990), and learning diaries (Schmidt and Frota, 1986). In some studies, learners were instructed to take notes as a measure of awareness while reading an L2 text (Izumi, 2002), or to underline or otherwise mark targeted linguistic structures in L2 text (Fotos, 1993).

Recently, studies have used protocol analysis (PA) to gain insight on learners' cognitive processes online (while they engaged in language tasks). A majority of studies have supported a link between awareness and either subsequent language modifications, such as modified output (Egi, 2010), or between awareness and language development (Sachs and Suh, 2007). Specifically, these studies have demonstrated that higher levels of awareness, such as what Schmidt refers to as awareness at the level of understanding, were related to greater linguistic gains than lower levels of awareness.

It is uncontroversial, therefore, that learning can occur in the presence of, and is facilitated by, awareness. The central question is not whether learning is possible in the *presence* of awareness but rather whether it is possible in the *absence* of awareness. To date, there have been three studies in SLA (Hama and Leow, 2010; Leow, 2000; Williams, 2005) that set out to investigate language development by unaware participants.

Leow (2000), the first SLA study to address the question of unawareness and learning in SLA, found that his unaware college-level L2 learners of Spanish did not learn targeted third-person stem-changing preterit morphology whereas aware learners showed gains in both intake and production of those forms. Specifically, the 32 participants completed a crossword puzzle that required them to fill in the correct endings of 10 irregular verbs but did not make them to attend to the stem-change in the incomplete targeted verb form (e.g., *mur* –). Once they completed the crossword puzzle, the participants completed a four-option multiple-choice recognition task with items identical to the crossword clues, as well as a written production (fill-in-the-blank) task that required them to produce the targeted forms in novel contexts. Think-aloud protocols (TAPs) were collected while participants completed the crossword and post-tests. The protocols were then used to code each participant as either aware or unaware, using the criteria for levels of awareness from Leow (1997, 2001). Specifically, participants were coded as aware if they "provided a report of being aware of the target forms [a simple reference to the target forms which does not require mentioning of rules] or some form of metalinguistic description of the underlying rule" (p. 564). Participants who did not meet this criterion were coded as unaware. A post-exposure questionnaire and interview also provided data triangulating the group assignment. Aware participants scored significantly higher on both post-test measures than they did on the pre-test, whereas unaware participants' post-test scores were not significantly different from their pre-test scores.

In a series of experiments, Williams (2005) provided evidence to the contrary. Williams (2005) conducted two experiments to test whether unaware participants were able to learn miniature noun class systems. The 41 participants in the experiments were from a variety of language backgrounds. The target noun phrases were four nonce determiners, *gi*, *ro*, *ul*, and *ne*. *Gi* and *ro* are the English translation equivalents of "near," and *ul* and *ne* are equivalents of "far." However, the determiners also specify animacy: *Gi* and *ul* are animate and *ro* and *ne* are inanimate. Participants were provided with the translations of the four novel determiners for "near" or "far." However, they were not informed about the animacy feature. Then, during the training phase, the participants listened to individual sentences containing noun phrases consisting of one of the determiners and an English noun (e.g., *gi* dog, "near dog"). As they heard each sentence, participants a) indicated if the determiner meant "near" or "far," b) repeated the sentence aloud, and c) were asked to create a mental image of the situation described by the sentence. The participants were told that the main focus of the study was memory, so that they would be less likely to attend to the animacy feature. After the training phase, participants completed a multiple-choice post-test that required them to select the noun phrase that seemed "more familiar, better, or more appropriate" on the basis of what they had heard during the "training task" from a pair of noun phrases, one of which was animate and the other of which was inanimate (pp. 282–83). Finally, participants were asked what criteria they had used to make their choices on the multiple-choice task. Anyone who did not make "any references to living or non living, moves or does-not-move, and so forth" (p. 283) was classified as unaware. Results showed that many of the participants who were classified as unaware were able to choose the correct noun phrase on the post-test at a level significantly higher than chance (50 percent).

The contrasting findings of Leow's (2000) study and Williams' (2005) experiments are likely due to methodological differences in the research designs. As discussed in Hama and Leow (2010), many factors could have contributed to the differing findings. For instance, the participants are from different language backgrounds and were exposed to different targeted items and experimental learning tasks. Specifically, the learners in Leow's experiment were exposed to morphology in a natural language context, whereas those in Williams' experiments were exposed to a much more restricted number of artificial language morphemes that were embedded in sentences in their L1. Furthermore, the post-test measures in the two studies were quite different: whereas Leow used a four-option multiple-choice recognition task and a written production task to measure any pre-posttest gains, Williams used only one measure, a two-option multiple-choice recognition test. Furthermore, the criteria used to establish awareness were different: in Williams' study participants were coded as aware only if they demonstrated awareness at the level of understanding, whereas in Leow's study they were coded as aware if they demonstrated even the lower level of awareness at the level of noticing. Most importantly, the measures of awareness were different. Williams relied on participants' free recall after task completion to determine (un)awareness, whereas Leow relied on both online TAP data and post-task questionnaires and interviews.

Hama and Leow (2010) is a partial replication and extension of Williams (2005) that set out to address these discrepant findings. It included both online and offline data elicitation procedures to gather data on learners' awareness both during the testing phase, and after the experimental exposure. The study also made the multiple-choice post-test measure more robust, increasing each item from two options to four; added a production test; and used the same modality for both the training and testing phases. Results showed that the 34 learners who were coded as unaware, both based on their TAPs and on the information they provided in the post-task questionnaire, were not capable of selecting or producing the correct determiner-noun combination at an above-chance level when required to do so from options that included both animacy and distance information.

The findings of these studies, taken as a whole, suggest that learning of the sort that happens in natural languages is not possible in the absence of awareness. They also highlight the importance of using multiple measures of awareness, both during the task (at the time of encoding) and after the task (at the time of retrieval), since no one measure was able to correctly classify all of the participants in Hama and Leow's (2010) study as unaware.

Leow, Johnson, and Zárate-Sández (in press) have advocated a more fine-grained investigation of awareness that specifically focuses on a) what is being learned (e.g., artificial grammars, sequences of letters or numbers, lexical items), b) where awareness is measured (i.e., at the stage of construction, when participants are processing information, or at the stage of reconstruction, after information has been processed), and c) how awareness is measured (i.e., what type of experimental task is being used, what type of measurement instrument is used, and whether the measurement is online or offline). They argue that only with more detailed measurement and reporting will our understanding of the role of awareness in SLA develop.

See also: attention, instructed SLA, intake, Noticing Hypothesis, protocol analysis, researching and measuring SLA

References

Alanen, R. (1995). Input enhancement and rule presentation in second language acquisition. In R. Schmidt (ed.), *Attention and awareness in foreign language learning*, pp. 259–302. Honolulu, HI: University of Hawai'i Press.

Allport, A. (1988). What concept of consciousness? In A.J. Marcel and E. Bisiach (eds), *Consciousness in Contemporary Science*, pp. 159–182. London: Clarendon Press.

Egi, T. (2010). Uptake, modified output, and learner perceptions of recasts: Learner responses as language awareness. *The Modern Language Journal*, *94*(1), 1–21.

Fotos, S. (1993). Consciousness-raising and noticing through focus on form: Grammar task performance versus formal instruction. *Applied Linguistics*, *14*, 385–407.

Hama, M. and Leow, R.P. (2010). Learning without awareness revisited. *Studies in Second Language Acquisition*, *32*(3), 465–491.

Izumi, S. (2002). Output, input enhancement, and the noticing hypothesis: An experimental study on ESL relativization. *Studies in Second Language Acquisition*, *24*(4), 541–577.

Leow, R.P. (1997). Attention, awareness, and foreign language behavior. *Language Learning*, *47* (3), 467–505.

——(2000). A study of the role of awareness in foreign language behavior: Aware versus unaware learners. *Studies in Second Language Acquisition*, *22*(4), 557–584.

——(2001). Attention, awareness, and foreign language behavior. *Language Learning*, *51*(supplement 1), 113–155.

Leow, R.P., Johnson, E. and Zárate-Sández, G. (in press). Getting a grip on the slippery construct of awareness: Toward a finer-grained methodological perspective. In C. Sanz and R. P. Leow (eds), *Implicit and Explicit Conditions, Processes, and Knowledge in SLA and Bilingualism*. Washington, DC: Georgetown University Press.

Mackey, A., McDonough, K., Fujii, A. and Tatsumi, T. (2001). Investigating learners' reports about the L2 classroom. *IRAL*, *39*, 285–308.

Robinson, P. (1995). Attention, memory, and the "noticing" hypothesis. *Language Learning, 45* (2), 283–331.

Sachs, R. and Suh, B.R. (2007). Textually enhanced recasts, learner awareness, and L2 outcomes in synchronous computer-mediated interaction. In A. Mackey (ed.), *Conversational Interaction in Second Language Acquisition: A Collection of Empirical Studies*, pp. 197–227. Oxford: Oxford University Press.

Schmidt, R. (1990). The role of consciousness in second language learning. *Applied Linguistics*, *11*(2), 129–158.

——(1995). Consciousness and foreign language learning: A tutorial on the role of attention and awareness in learning. In R.W. Schmidt (ed.), *Attention and Awareness in Foreign Language Learning*. Honolulu, HI: University of Hawai'i.

Schmidt, R. and Frota, S. (1986). Developing basic conversational ability in a second language. In R. Day (ed.), *Talking to learn*, pp. 237–326. Rowley, MA: Newbury House.

Slimani, A. (1989). The role of topicalization in classroom language learning. *System*, *17*, 223–234.

Tomlin, R.S. and Villa, V. (1994). Attention in cognitive science and second language acquisition. *Studies in Second Language Acquisition*, *16*(2), 183–203.

VanPatten, B. (1990). Attending to form and content in the input: An experiment in consciousness. *Studies in Second Language Acquisition*, *12*, 287–301.

Williams, J.N. (2005). Learning without awareness. *Studies in Second Language Acquisition*, *27*(2), 269–304.

B

Basic variety

Wolfgang Klein
Max Planck Institute for Psycholinguistics, Nijmegen

In a large longitudinal and cross-linguistic examination of how adults acquire a second language by everyday communication, the European Science Foundation (ESF) Project (see e.g., Dietrich *et al.*, 1995; Perdue, 1993), it was found that all learners develop a structurally simple, but communicatively efficient linguistic system – the "Basic Variety" (BV). Lexically, it is mainly derived from the L2, but structurally, it is largely independent of L1 and L2 (Hendriks, 2005; Klein and Perdue, 1992, 1997). It has three main features:

A. There is no inflection, hence no morphological marking of case, number, gender, tense, aspect, or agreement.

B. Its lexicon primarily consists of noun-like and verb-like words, a few adjectives, and a few adverbs. The pronoun system is rudimentary, but allows reference to speaker, listener, and a third person. There are some determiners, but at best an incipient determiner system, and a few function words, such as a negation particle. Subordinators and relative pronouns are mostly absent; Hence, there is hardly any subordination. There are no semantically empty elements, such as existential *there*.

C. Complex expressions are formed according to a few phrasal, semantic, and pragmatic constraints. Three phrasal patterns prevail (subscripts relate to varying NP types):

P1a. $NP_1 - V$
P1b. $NP_1 - V - NP_2$
P1c. $NP_1 - V - NP_2 - NP_2$

P2. NP_1 – COPULA – NP_2/ADJ/ PP

P3. V/COPULA - NP_2

All patterns may be preceded or followed by an adverb or words like *and/or*.

A pattern like NP – V – NP does not imply that the first NP is the "subject" and the second NP is the "object" (as speakers of English would normally assume). In the BV, the relation between position and role is primarily defined by the "control asymmetry," that is, the greater or lesser degree of control which an NP referent exerts or intends to exert over the referents of the other argument(s). The most important *semantic constraint* of the BV is:

> SEM1. The NP referent with the highest control comes first ("Controller first")

Pragmatic constraints relate to information status (new vs given) or to the topic-focus structure; most important is:

> PRAG1. The focus expression comes last ("Focus last")

The various constraints interact according to the particular constellation. In P1a or P3, there is only one NP, thus no control asymmetry, and "Controller first" cannot apply. Hence, only PRAG1 and phrasal constraints interact: if NP-referent is topical, then pattern P1 is used; if it is in the focus, then "focus last" applies and pattern P3 is used. The same constraint determines the position of NPs in copula constructions. But constraints may also pull in opposite directions, for example, if the agent (high degree of control) happens to be in focus. Such conflicts are resolved in different ways. Some learners weigh the constraints, for example by a principle like "Semantic constraints outweigh pragmatic constraints." Or they use additional devices that allow them to mark either what is in focus or what is the controller, for example intonation or a special particle. In fact, such conflicts are often a germ for development beyond the BV.

See also: agreement, development in SLA, European Science Foundation (ESF) project, inflectional morphemes, language and the lexicon in SLA, topicalization

References

Dietrich, R., Klein, W. and Noyau, C. (1995). *The Acquisition of Temporality in a Second Language Acquisition*. Amsterdam: Benjamins.

Hendriks, H. (ed.) (2005). *The Structure of Learner Varieties*. Berlin and New York: de Gruyter

Klein, W. and Perdue, C. (1992). *Utterance Structure*. Amsterdam: Benjamins.

——(1997). The Basic Variety (or: Couldnt natural languages be much simpler?). *Second Language Research*, *13*, 301–47.

Perdue, C. (ed.) (1993). *Adult language acquisition: Cross-linguistic perspectives, Vol. 1. Field Methods*. Cambridge: Cambridge University Press.

BICS and CALP

Jim Cummins
Ontario Institute for Studies in Education, University of Toronto

The distinction between *basic interpersonal communicative skills* (BICS) and *cognitive academic language proficiency* (CALP) was introduced by Cummins (1979) to draw educators' attention to the timelines and challenges that second language learners encounter as they attempt to catch up to their peers in academic aspects of the school language. BICS refers to conversational fluency in a language while CALP refers to students' ability to understand and express, in both oral and written modes, concepts and ideas that are relevant to success in school. Conversational language typically relies on high-frequency vocabulary and relatively common grammatical and discourse structures. By contrast, academic language draws on low-frequency vocabulary and less common discourse and grammatical structures (e.g., passive voice) reflecting the increasing conceptual and linguistic complexity of academic content taught at different grade levels.

The initial BICS/CALP distinction was elaborated (Cummins, 1981) into two intersecting continua that highlighted the range of contextual support and cognitive demands involved in particular language tasks or activities. The horizontal continuum ranged from context-embedded to context-reduced, while the vertical continuum ranged from cognitively undemanding to cognitively demanding, resulting in four quadrants that varied in the degree of contextual support and cognitive demand associated with language activities. This quadrants framework extended the BICS/CALP distinction into the realm of pedagogy. Specifically, it was argued that effective instruction for second language learners should focus primarily on context-embedded and cognitively demanding tasks.

In more recent elaborations of the distinction (Cummins, 2000), the terms *conversational fluency* and *academic language proficiency* have been used interchangeably with BICS and CALP. In addition, the construct of *discrete language skills* was identified as a distinct component of language proficiency. Discrete language skills involve the learning of rule-governed aspects of language (including phonology, phonics, grammar, spelling, punctuation, etc.) where acquisition of the general case permits generalization to other instances governed by that particular rule. Discrete language skills can sometimes be learned in virtual isolation from the development of academic language proficiency, as illustrated in the fact that some students who can "read" English fluently may have only a very limited understanding of the words they can decode.

Conversational and academic language proficiencies can be viewed as instances of Gee's (1990) distinction between *primary* and *secondary* discourses. Primary discourses are acquired through face-to-face interactions in the home and represent the language of initial socialization. Secondary discourses are acquired in social institutions beyond the family (e.g., school, business, religious, and cultural contexts) and involve acquisition of specialized vocabulary and functions of language appropriate to those settings.

Although controversial (e.g., Edelsky *et al.*, 1983; Rolstad and MacSwan, 2008), the distinction has been invoked to account for the longer time periods typically required for immigrant students to catch up academically in English (typically at least five years) as compared to acquiring fluent conversational skills in English (typically less than two years). It has also drawn attention to the potential for discriminatory assessment of bilingual students when their L2 conversational fluency is conflated with the development of L2 academic skills.

See also: bilingualism and SLA, content-based language teaching, Interdependence Hypothesis, proficiency, second language socialization

References

Cummins, J. (1979). Cognitive/academic language proficiency, linguistic interdependence, the optimum age question and some other matters. *Working Papers on Bilingualism*, *19*, 121–29.

——(1981). The role of primary language development in promoting educational success for language minority students. In California State Department of Education (ed.), *Schooling and Language Minority Students: A Theoretical Framework*. Los Angeles, CA: Evaluation, Dissemination and Assessment Center California State University.

——(2000). *Language, Power and Pedagogy: Bilingual Children in the Crossfire*. Clevedon: Multilingual Matters.

Edelsky, C., Hudelson, S., Flores, B., Barkin, F., Altweger, B. and Jilbert, K. (1983). Semilingualism and language deficit. *Applied Linguistics*, *4*, 1–22.

Rolstad, K. and MacSwan, J. (2008). BICS/CALP: Theory and critique. In J. Gonzalez (ed.), *Encyclopedia of Bilingual Education*. Thousand Oaks, CA: Sage Publishers.

Bilingualism and SLA

William C. Ritchie and Tej K. Bhatia
Syracuse University

Though there are many characterizations of bilingualism in the research literature, all of them imply some notion of second- or double-language acquisition. This article addresses issues in the empirical study of bilingualism. What is bilingualism and who is bilingual? Defining bilingualism and measuring it are very complicated tasks because of the number and variety of types of input conditions, biological, socio-psychological, and other non-linguistic parameters which can lead to varying degrees and forms of bilingual competence. As a consequence of the complexity of these parameters, there is no widely accepted definition or measure of bilingualism. Instead, a rich range of scales, dichotomies, and categories has appeared in the research literature in attempts to characterize bilinguals. For example, if a bilingual can understand but cannot speak a second language, such an individual is called a "receptive" bilingual, whereas a "productive" bilingual demonstrates a spoken proficiency in his/her two languages. If the second language is acquired naturally before the age of five, that individual is termed an "early" bilingual, in contrast with a "late" bilingual who learns his/her second language after the age of five whether in the home or at school. Labels such as "fluent" versus "non-fluent," and "functional" versus "non-functional," "balanced" versus "unbalanced," "primary" versus "secondary," and "partial" versus "complete" refer, either to a varying command in different types of language proficiency (e.g. speaking, listening, writing, etc.), or an asymmetrical, dominant/subordinate relationship between two languages. The distinction between "compound" and "coordinate" bilingualism refers to the ways in which the two languages of a bilingual are processed in the mind/brain.

The list of distinctions among types of bilingualism given above is by no means exhaustive. Other major distinctions such as that between "simultaneous" and "sequential" bilingualism will be discussed in the next section. Similarly, bilingualism can be viewed from the perspective of the individual, of society at large (including social attitudes towards bilingualism), and of political issues (i.e. government policies toward bilingualism). But in general, a bilingual person exhibits many complex attributes rarely seen in a monolingual person beyond the obvious difference between knowing two languages rather one. For that reason, a bilingual is not equivalent to two monolinguals, but, rather, is something entirely different.

Providing a natural environment for language acquisition in monolingual or dominant-language speech communities is not a challenging task. The same is also true for those societies where social and political systems are conducive to bilingualism. For instance, in India, where bilingualism is viewed as natural, approved by society, and further nurtured by government language policies, linguistic groups and communities do not need to take any special measures to assure that their children receive input from two languages.

In sharp contrast, in societies where bilingualism is not valued or where the language of a minority is distinct from that of the surrounding majority community, it becomes imperative for families to plan meaningful strategies to ensure natural exposure to the family language if they wish use of this language to continue. One such strategy that families employ in this second setting – referred to by Bhatia and Ritchie (1999) as "Discourse Allocation" – restricts the use of one language to one social agent or social setting and the other language to other social situations. The various manifestations of such strategies are these: one-parent/one-language (e.g. the child's mother speaks one language and the child's father speaks the other). This strategy was employed by Leopold in his classic study of bilingual language development of his daughter, Hildegard (published 1939–1949). Another strategy used is the one-place/one-language strategy (e.g. speaking one language in the kitchen and the other elsewhere); another is a language/time approach; and, finally, some parents use a topic-related approach. Although the discourse allocation approach is better than providing no bilingual input at all to the child and thus raising a monolingual child, it leads to somewhat different patterns in bilingual language development from the development of bilingualism in a natural setting. For instance, during the early stages of Hildegrard's bilingualism, she developed a rule that fathers speak German and mothers speak English, which was, of course, modified over time.

Other factors such as age and amount of exposure to the two languages also result in differences in the pattern of childhood bilingualism. The distinction between simultaneous and sequential bilinguals in research on bilingual language acquisition is based on age and the degree of exposure to two languages. When the child is exposed to the languages to more or less the same degree from birth onward, the pattern of language development is referred to as "simultaneous," whereas "sequential" bilingualism describes the attainment of one language first and the second language later, generally before the age of seven. Relatedly, the terms early bilingual and late bilingual are used to distinguish those sequential bilinguals who acquire their second language earlier and later, respectively, but all at a younger age than adults learning a second language. Although there is unanimous agreement among researchers concerning the validity of the simultaneous/sequential distinction, there is no consensus among scholars about the exact line of demarcation between the two (see McLaughlin, 1984, and De Houwer, 1995 on theoretical and methodological grounds for the distinction).

One of the most intriguing aspects of childhood bilingualism is how children learn to separate the two languages, particularly in a natural setting in the initial stages of simultaneous bilingual acquisition. After all, when parents provide input, they do not tag or prime their input with a language identification label. Even if parents were to go to the absurd length of identifying the language of each word or sentence they use, these labels would be semantically empty for the child. Furthermore, bilingual parents unwittingly make the task of separating the two languages even harder for children because of their normal tendency to mix the two languages. In short, a child is provided with three distinct types of linguistic input: two languages, each in an unmixed/"pure" form, and one with a mixture of two languages. Given this state of affairs, how does the child learn to separate the two languages in question? The two hypotheses which attempt to shed light on this question are: the unitary system hypothesis and the dual system hypothesis.

According to the unitary system hypothesis (Volterra and Taeschner, 1978), the child undergoes three stages before s/he is able to separate two input languages. During the first two stages, the child experiences confusion. During the first stage, s/he is unable to distinguish the two lexicons and grammars of the linguistic systems. At this stage, they have a single lexicon made up of items drawn from the lexicons of both languages. Hence, no translational equivalents or synonyms are found in their vocabulary. Volterra and Taeschner claim that their two bilingual subjects at the ages of 1;10 and 1;6 had a hybrid list of 137 words with no translational equivalents. During the second stage, the child slowly learns to separate the two lexicons, but is still unable to separate the grammatical systems. Cross-linguistic synonyms emerge, but the child applies the same set of syntactic rules to both languages. It is only during the third stage that the child becomes capable of separating the two lexicons and grammars. However, under the scrutiny of succeeding research, the evidence motivating the three stages of bilingual language development claimed by the unitary system hypothesis has been found to suffer from shortcomings and contradictions on both methodological and empirical grounds (for a summary of these problems, see Bhatia and Ritchie, 1999).

The dual system hypothesis states that bilingual children, based on their access to Universal Grammar and language-specific parameter settings, have the capacity to separate the two grammars and lexical systems right from the beginning. A wide variety of cross-linguistic studies (e.g. different input conditions – one-parent/one language and mixed input conditions; and different word order types) lends support to this hypothesis. For instance, in a study devoted to the language development of a Hindi-English bilingual child, it is clear that at age 2, the child is capable of developing two distinct lexicons using a syllabification strategy. At the age of 1;7, two different word orders develop – SVO [subject-verb-object] for English and SOV for Hindi. (For a more detailed treatment of both the shortcomings of the unitary system hypothesis and the strengths of the dual system hypothesis, see Bhatia and Ritchie, 1999: 598–614.)

Another prominent feature of bilingual speech is this: not only are bilinguals capable of keeping the two linguistic systems separate as they put them to use, but they often mix them either within a sentence or inter-sententially. This behavior is generally termed "code-mixing" or "code-switching" in the sociolinguistic research literature. Depending upon the theoretical and empirical objectives of their research, researchers do not distinguish between the two terms and use them interchangeably; for those researchers who distinguish between the two, code-mixing refers to intrasentential mixing while code-switching refers to the intersentential mixing in bilinguals. Both bilingual children and bilingual adults show this behavior. What explains this behavior of language mixing? Earlier research attempted to explain it in terms of the language deficiency hypothesis: it was claimed that bilinguals in general and children in particular have language gaps. As claimed by the unitary system hypothesis the lack of synonyms compels bilinguals to mix the two lexical systems – particularly during stage-I of acquisition. Similarly, stage-II yields the mixing of two language systems due to "confusion." In other words, the lack of proficiency in either one language (i.e. the absence of "balanced bilingualism") or both languages (i.e. "semi-bilingualism") leads to mixing.

The language augmentation hypothesis offers deeper insights into bilingual mixing behavior. As was concluded earlier in the discussion of the dual system hypothesis, children do not go through the initial stages of treating the two linguistic systems as if they were one system, but begin to distinguish them immediately. The consideration of optimization leads bilinguals to mix language with an aim to get maximum mileage from the two linguistic systems at their disposal. Research on the linguistic and sociolinguistic motivations for language mixing both in children and in adults shows that such considerations as semantic domains and semantic complexity (an item less complex or salient in one language than in the other), stylistic effects, clarification, elaboration, relief (i.e. a linguistic item being temporarily unavailable in one language), interlocutor's social identity, discourse strategies based on participants/topics, addressee's perceived linguistic capability and speaker's own linguistic ability, and other complex socio-psychological reasons such as attitudes, societal values, and personality prompt bilinguals to mix two languages. This list of motivations is by no means exhaustive (see Bhatia and Ritchie, 2009 for more details).

In conclusion, a number of diverse and complex conditions and factors lead to life-long bilingualism. These factors – biological, social, psychological, and linguistic – account for a varied pattern amongst bilinguals, witnessed around the world. Thus, a bilingual is neither two monolinguals in the brain, nor are two bilinguals clones of each other. These complexities indicate why no current theory of language learning and/or teaching is capable of fully explaining bilingual verbal behavior and the mechanisms leading to bilingual language development.

See also: age effects in SLA, child second language acquisition, code-switching, cognitive aging, development in SLA, Interdependence Hypothesis

References

Bhatia, T. and Ritchie, W. (2009). Bilingual language mixing, Universal Grammar, and second language acquisition. In Ritchie, W.C. and Bhatia, T.K. (eds), *The New Handbook of Second Language Acquisition*, pp. 591–621. Bingley: Emerald Group Publishing Ltd.

——(1999). The bilingual child: Some issues and perspectives. In Ritchie, W.C. and Bhatia, T.K. (eds), *Handbook of Child Language Acquisition*, pp. 569–643. San Diego, CA: Academic Press.

Bloomfield, L. (1933). *Language*. New York: Holt.

De Houwer, A. (1995). Bilingual language acquisition. In Fletcher, P. and MacWhinney, B. (eds), *Handbook of Child Language*, pp. 569–643. Oxford: Basil Blackwell Ltd.

Grosjean, F. (1982). *Life with Two Languages*. Cambridge, MA: Harvard University Press.

Leopold, W. (1939–49). *Speech Development of a Bilingual Child: A Linguist's Record*, 4 volumes. Evanston, IL: Northwestern University Press.

McLaughlin, B. (1984). Early bilingualism: Methodological and theoretical issues. In Paradis, M. and Lebrun, Y. (eds), *Early Bilingualism and Child Development*, pp. 19–45. Lisse: Swets and Zeitlinger.

Volterra, V. and Taeschner, T. (1978). The acquisition and development of language by bilingual children. *Journal of Child Language*, 5, 311–26.

C

Case studies

Thom Heubner
San Jose State University

A case study has been defined as a process of qualitative inquiry commonly used in such diverse fields as psychology, anthropology, sociology, history, political science, economics, education, medicine, law, and other social science-related disciplines as well as in applied linguistics. It has also been defined as the product of such an inquiry (Merriam, 1998: 27). As a method, case study research is characterized by a common set of assumptions and practices across disciplines.

One of these assumptions is that case study design provides an understanding of "the complexity and dynamic nature of the particular entity" and the discovery of "systematic connections among experiences, behaviors, and relevant features of the context" (Johnson, 1992; cited in Duff, 2008: 32). At issue in all case study research is its boundedness, or focus on a single unit, be that an individual language learner, a classroom, a school program, an educational policy, etc., "usually selected for study on the basis of specific psychological, biological, sociocultural, institutional, or linguistic attributes" (Duff, 2008: 32). Case studies can be purely descriptive; they can raise questions and propose hypotheses; or they can test hypotheses and provide causal relationships between the entity studied and the larger context. Regardless, they share the notion of the centrality of context.

To explore a given entity in depth and given the complexity of context, multiple perspectives need to be presented. To do this, case studies draw on multiple sources of data, including recorded interviews and transcriptions, observations and notes, questionnaires and surveys, historical records and accounts, journals, etc., resulting in a process of triangulation. Because case studies are intensive and require extended investigation, they often contain a longitudinal component.

Case studies also vary across a number of parameters. They may be contemporary or historical. They may be single-case studies, as in most of the earlier ones in applied linguistics, or of multiple-case design. The former may be chosen for its uniqueness or its prototypicality, and there may be multiple foci within a given single-case study. Multiple case studies involve two or more objects of investigation, usually for comparative or contrastive purposes (e.g., Huebner, 1987). Both single and multiple case studies can provide evidence supporting or challenging hypotheses, but evidence from the latter type is usually more compelling. While qualitative by definition, case studies often contain quantitative and descriptive statistics, and they may involve a treatment or intervention.

In the field of applied linguistics, the subject of a case study could be an individual or family, a classroom or school, even a government or corporate entity. The earliest case studies in applied linguistics were longitudinal studies of the linguistic development of individual second language learners, focusing on evolving form-function relationships, such as tense and aspect or the system of reference (see the discussion in Duff, 2008: 61–62). Data consisted primarily of interviews and transcripts, with little or no triangulation. An exception is Schmidt and Frota, 1986. More recent case studies have been much more far-ranging in scope and have paid greater attention to the larger socio-cultural context, focusing, for example, on issues of socialization and identity, or on the evolution, practices, and consequences of language policy.

Case studies have often been criticized for their lack of generalizability, sophisticated statistical analyses, and objectivity. Yet despite their labor intensity and the dangers of attrition, the unique advantages of case studies, including their thick descriptions and triangulation, their exploratory, innovative potential and role in theory building, and their exploration of unique, atypical cases, offer insights and understandings not afforded by other approaches to research.

See also: ethnographic research, longitudinal research, mixed method research, qualitative research, questionnaire research, time-series designs

References

Duff, Patricia (2008). *Case Study Research in Applied Linguistics*. New York: Routledge.

Huebner, Thom (1987). A socio-historical approach to literacy acquisition, language shift, and language maintenance: A comparative case study from the Pacific. In J. Langer (ed.), *Language, Literacy and Culture*. Norwood, NJ: Ablex.

Merriam, Sharan B. (1998). *Qualitative Research and Case Study Applications in Education*. San Francisco, CA: Jossey-Bass.

Schmidt, Richard and S. Frota. (1986). Developing basic conversational ability in a second language: A case study of an adult learner of Portuguese. In R. Day (ed.), *Talking to Learn: Conversation in Second Language Acquisition*, pp. 237–326. Rowley, MA: Newbury House.

Stake, Robert E. (1995). *The Art of Case Study Research*. Thosand Oaks, CA: Sage publications.

Yin, Robert K. (2009). *Case Study Research: Design and Methods*. Thousand Oaks, CA: Sage publications.

Child Second Language Acquisition

Usha Lakshmanan
Southern Illinois University Carbondale

The term Child Second Language Acquisition refers to the successive acquisition of a second language (L2) during childhood, where exposure to the L2 occurs after the age of 3 years, when the core aspects of the first language (L1) have been largely established (McLaughlin, 1984; Lakshmanan, 1995: 322). This lower age boundary distinguishes child L2 from simultaneous bilingualism, where two languages are acquired concurrently from birth, and other forms of early sequential bilingualism, where exposure to the L1 occurs at birth, but exposure to the L2 is delayed, but occurs prior to age 3. As certain complex aspects of a child's L1 may emerge only in late childhood, the child L2 learner at a given stage may exemplify successive L2 acquisition with respect to certain properties, and depending on continued exposure to the L1, also exemplify simultaneous acquisition of two languages in relation to other properties.

Age at onset of puberty (10–13 years), which marks the offset of the critical period for language development (Lenneberg, 1967), is generally used to distinguish child L2 from adult L2 acquisition. A lower upper-boundary (7 years) has also been assumed in the recent literature (Schwartz, 2004), based on the findings of studies on critical-period effects in L2 acquisition, which found that only those learners whose age at onset of exposure to the L2 was between 3–7 performed like native-speakers with respect to ultimate attainment (e.g. Johnson and Newport, 1989).

The child L2 learner is cognitively more mature than the L1 child, although less so than the adult; similar to adults, the child L2 learner already has an L1 in place prior to onset of exposure to the L2. In the 1970s, when SLA emerged as a field in its own right, the child L2 learner was at the center of debates concerning the similarities and differences between the processes characterizing SLA and child L1 acquisition (see McLaughlin, 1984 for comprehensive review). In the 1980s, the focus shifted to the adult L2 learner. Since the 1990s, however, there has been renewed interest in child L2 acquisition, as witnessed by the growing number of longitudinal and cross-sectional studies of child L2 acquisition, with emphasis largely on morphosyntax and to a lesser extent phonology (for a review, see Lakshmanan, 1995, 2009). Within generative approaches to SLA, researchers have increasingly adopted a developmental perspective in addressing the issue of whether child L2 is more similar to adult L2 or child L1 (for discussion, see Schwartz, 2004; and also chapters in Haznedar and Gavruseva, 2008). SLA researchers espousing functional and social/interactional approaches to language have also begun paying increasing attention to the development of these aspects in the L2 child (e.g. Rocca, 2007; see also chapters in Philp *et al.*, 2008).

Factors influencing child L2 development

Adult L2 learners, because of greater cognitive maturity, may initially learn at a faster rate. However, child L2 learners (especially younger children) do better in the long run. The advantages associated with exposure to an L2 during childhood have been found for various linguistic aspects. But it is in phonology, even more than morphology and syntax, that age-related effects have been robust; only very young children (below the age of six years) succeed in acquiring an L2 pronunciation and accent that is indistinguishable from their native-speaker peers, although even in this domain, child L2 learners may differ in subtle ways from native speakers. It is generally believed that the observed age-related effects stem from the maturation of the brain. With increasing age, there is a steady decline in the plasticity of the brain, rendering it difficult to attain native-like abilities in an L2, unless exposure to it occurs within the critical period for language acquisition. For an extensive review of the role of maturational factors, see Hyltenstam and Abrahamsson (2003).

Other factors also impact children's success in L2 learning. The child's exposure to L2 input can vary depending on whether the context involves naturalistic exposure (through social interaction with native speakers and/or through school immersion) or formal instruction in a classroom setting. Instruction can differ depending on whether it emphasizes implicit processes, favoring children, or explicit processes, favoring adolescents and adults. Another factor is the *extent* to which the L2 (and L1) are used and supported in the home and the school environment. Other variables that can impact L2 development include L1 and L2 congruence, attitudes toward the target L2 (and the L1), motivation, personality, aptitude, the local and global status of the L2 and the L1, whether the learner is a language minority child learning a majority language of the community or a language majority child learning a minority language, as well as the status of the target L2 dialect (i.e. a prestige or non-prestige variant). For discussion of individual differences in child L2 development, see Jia and Aaronson, 2003; McLaughlin, 1984, 1985; Paradis *et al.*, 2011).

Acquiring an L2 is an effortful activity and not necessarily an easy task for children. Typically, children take 2 to 3 years to achieve fluency in the conversational or social uses of the L2 and about 5 to 7 years to attain proficiency in the academic uses of the L2, at levels comparable to their native-speaker peers (Cummins, 2000; see also Hakuta *et al.*, 2000). While children, overall are more successful at L2 learning compared to adults, their eventual L2 attainment, especially in relation to monolingual native-speaker criterial levels, is not an inevitable outcome (Pladevall-Ballester, 2010). As Grosjean (1989) has stated, a bilingual is not two monolingual speakers in the same person.

Universal Grammar

Learnability theories within child L1 acquisition research have been driven by the logical problem of language acquisition. How do children, through the course of language acquisition, attain complex knowledge states in their L1 that are vastly underdetermined by the input available to them? A solution to the logical problem is that children are equipped with a biological blueprint for language (i.e. Universal Grammar), which constrains their acquisition of their native language/s. SLA researchers have debated the issue of the availability of Universal Grammar (UG) for L2 acquisition. These debates have centered on adult rather than child L2 learners. Primarily because of children's greater success in relation to ultimate L2 attainment, compared to adults, a general assumption has been that child L2 acquisition, like child L1 acquisition, is constrained by UG (Lakshmanan, 1994, 1995).

Language minority children, acquiring a majority language as the L2, typically encounter L2 input outside the home and L1 input within the home. Similar to simultaneous bilingual children (Yip and Mathews, 2007), the total quantity of input available to child L2 learners in their L2 (and L1) is typically greatly reduced, compared to the total input available to monolingual children. Although child L2 learners may not be identical to monolingual native-speakers in terms of the end-states attained, they succeed in attaining complex knowledge states that go well *beyond* the L2 input, which serves to exacerbate the logical problem and strengthen the long-standing assumption that UG continues to be available for the acquisition of an L2 during childhood.

Within child L1 acquisition research, it has been proposed that certain properties of UG that characterize the adult grammar (e.g. functional categories associated with clausal structure), are maturationally triggered and become available only later (e.g. around 24 months). A growing body of morphological and syntactic evidence from child L2 acquisition suggests that once functional categories and their projections have emerged for L1 acquisition, they are operative from the very beginning for subsequent acquisition; therefore, child L2 learners do not regress to a stage, where only lexical projections (e.g. Noun Phrase and Verb Phrase) are present, but not functional or non-thematic systems. In relation to clausal structure, child L2 learners are more like "architects," with a full-blown clausal structure in place from the earliest stages of their L2 development (for extensive review, see Lakshmanan, 1995, 2009). Additionally, the evidence suggests that the relationship between the development of syntax and morphology in child L2, unlike in the case of child L1, is more indirect than direct (Lakshmanan, 1994; Meisel, 2008).

Language transfer

When two languages come in contact in the same individual, each language can potentially influence the development of the other language. Similar to simultaneous bilingualism (Yip and Mathews, 2007), the directionality of language transfer effects in child L2 acquisition may depend on language dominance. During the initial stages of child L2 acquisition, it is the L1, already established for the most part, that is dominant. The directionality of potential transfer effects will likely be from the L1 onto the developing L2. Subsequently, particularly in L2 immersion contexts, the L2 child may become more dominant in the L2, leading to a reversal of the directionality of transfer effects (i.e. from the L2 to the L1); this can result in L1 attrition, particularly in subtractive contexts of bilingualism, where there is no continued support for the L1 (Wong-Fillmore, 1991).

In the child L2 literature, researchers have largely addressed the language transfer issue, from a unidirectional perspective (from the L1 onto the developing L2). The findings provide mixed evidence regarding the role of the L1 (for discussion see Lakshmanan, 2009; McLaughlin, 1984; and chapters in Haznedar and Gavruseva, 2008). Several studies have found that L1 transfer is not operative and that errors produced by child L2 learners are L2-based developmental errors, similar to the L1 child. As in the case of child L1, invariant or natural developmental sequences have been attested for certain aspects (e.g. grammatical morphemes, negation, interrogatives) for children with different L1s, acquiring the same L2 (e.g. Dulay and Burt, 1974). Some studies have indicated that L1 influence in child L2 is a selective one, found only at certain points in L2 development, as well as affecting only certain linguistic aspects. Other researchers have argued for a "full-transfer" position in child L2 acquisition, similar to adult L2 (e.g. Schwartz, 2004), although the typological distance between the L1 and the L2 (actual or perceived) likely plays a role in facilitating L1 transfer effects.

Child L2 learners, unlike adolescent and adult L2 learners, appear to be able to successfully override negative L1 transfer effects (for discussion, see Lakshmanan, 2009). Children (especially younger children), but not adults, typically go through an initial "silent period," when they do not speak in the L2. The length of the silent period varies across children (e.g. 2–6 months) and also based on L1 and L2 congruence (Lakshmanan, 1994). To the child, the silent period may help in preempting any potential L1 transfer effects resulting from their producing utterances in the L2 before they are ready for it, through the use of L1 borrowing as a strategy to meet their communicative demands. The silent period also enables children to attend to the ambient L2 input without being hampered by their own productions. Furthermore, although child L2 learners already have an L1 in place, their knowledge of the L1 may not be as firmly established compared to adults. Certain complex properties of the L1 may not yet have emerged at the onset of exposure to the L2. If exposure to the L1 is not sustained, child L2 learners may eventually become monolingual users (of the L2).

The L1, depending on the level of its development, also plays a facilitative role in child L2 acquisition (Lakshmanan, 2009: 393). Moreover, in relation to literacy development, proponents of strong forms of bilingual education have emphasized the importance of children learning to read in the language in which they are orally proficient in (i.e. the L1). Literacy and other academic language skills based upon the child's L1 can be drawn upon to facilitate academic language development in the L2 (Cummins, 2000).

Conclusion

Many countries have witnessed a steady increase in the number of minority language children who acquire an L2 sequentially. Research on child L2 acquisition is of direct relevance in educational and clinical settings; it can help inform parents and professionals involved in the care and education of children about the stages that typically developing children go through in acquiring the target L2, as well as help identify and treat language learning difficulties in sequential bilingual children (Paradis *et al.*, 2011).

See also: age effects in SLA, bilingualism and SLA, Critical Period Hypothesis (CPH), development in SLA, linguistic transfer, Universal Grammar (UG) and SLA

References

Cummins, J. (2000). *Language, Power and Pedagogy: Bilingual Children in the Crossfire*. Clevedon: Multlingual Matters.

Dulay, H. and Burt, M. (1974). Natural sequences in child second language acquisition. *Language Learning*, *24*, 37–53.

Grosjean, F. (1989). Neurolinguists, beware! The bilingual is not two monolinguals in one person. *Brain and Language*, *36*, 3–15.

Hakuta, K., Goto Butler, Y. and Witt, D. (2000). *How Long Does it Take English Learners to Attain Proficiency?* University of California Linguistic Minority Research Institute Policy Report 2000–2001. Retrieved on October 15, 2010, from www.stanford.edu/~hakuta/.

Haznedar, B. and Gavruseva, E. (eds) (2008). *Current Trends in Child Second Language Acquisition: A Generative Perspective*. Amsterdam: John Benjamins.

Hyltenstam, K. and Abrahamson, N. (2003). Maturational constraints in second language acquisition. In C. Doughty and M.H. Long (eds), *Handbook of Second Language Acquisition*, pp. 539–88. Oxford: Blackwell.

Jia, G. and Aaronson, D. (2003). A longitudinal study of Chinese children and adolescents learning English in the United States. *Applied Psycholinguistics*, *24*, 131–61.

Johnson, J. and Newport, E. (1989). Critical period effects in second language learning: the influence of maturational state on the acquisition of English as a second language. *Cognitive Psychology*, *21*, 60–99.

Lakshmanan, U. (1994). *Universal Grammar in Child Second Language Acquisition*. Amsterdam: John Benjamins.

——(1995). Child second language acquisition of syntax. *Studies in Second Language Acquisition*, *17*, 301–29.

——(2009). Child second language acquisition. In Ritchie, W. and Bhatia, T. (eds). *The*

New Handbook of Second Language Acquisition pp. 377–399. Sheffield: Emerald Publishers.

Lenneberg, E. (1967). *Biological Foundations of Language*. New York: Wiley.

McLaughlin, B. (1984). *Second Language Acquisition in Childhood, Second Edition, Vol. 1: Preschool Children*. Hillsdale, NJ: Lawrence Erlbaum Associates.

McLaughlin, B. (1985). *Second Language Acquisition in Childhood, Second Edition, Vol. 2: School-age Children*. Hillsdale, NJ: Lawrence Erlbaum Associates.

Meisel, J. (2008). Child second language acquisition or successive second language acquisition? In B. Haznedar and E. Gavruseva (eds). *Current Trends in Child Second Language Acquisition*, pp. 55–80. Amsterdam: John Benjamins.

Paradis, J., Genesee, F. and Crago, M. (2011). *Dual Language Development and Disorders: A Handbook on Bilingualism and Second Language Learning, second edition*. Baltimore, MD: Brookes Publishing Company.

Philp, J., Oliver, R. and Mackey, A. (eds) (2008). *Second Language Acquisition and the Younger Learner*. Amsterdam: John Benjamins.

Pladevall-Ballester, E. (2010). Child L2 development of syntactic and discourse properties of Spanish subjects. *Bilingualism: Language and Cognition, 13,* 185–216.

Rocca, S. (2007). *Child Second Language Acquisition: A Bidirectional Study of English and Italian Tense and Aspect Morphology*. Amsterdam: John Benjamins.

Schwartz, B.D. (2004). Why child L2 acquisition? In J. van Kampen and S. Baauw (eds), *Proceedings of Generative Approaches to Language Acquisition 2003*, vol. 1, pp. 47–66. Utrecht: LOT Publications.

Wong-Fillmore, L. (1991). When learning a second language means losing the first. *Early Childhood Research Quarterly*, *6*, 323–46.

Yip, Y. and Mathews, S. (2007). *The Bilingual Child: Early Development and Language Contact*. Cambridge: Cambridge University Press.

Chunking and prefabrication

Tomoko Tode
Niigata University of Health and Welfare

Both chunking and prefabrication refer to processing, storing, and retrieving language sequences as a unit, though the terms themselves derive from different academic disciplines. Historically prefabrication was treated as a peripheral issue in the field of second language acquisition (SLA) study. Recently, however, the importance of this process in second language (L2) performance and acquisition has been recognized. The importance is confirmed when we discuss chunking, the term from psychology. This entry begins with clarification of the terms prefabrication and chunking, and follows with a redefinition of prefabrication within the framework of the usage-based account of chunking.

Prefabrication

Prefabrication has been usually understood in contrast to generation (e.g., Skehan, 1998). Generation refers to producing or decoding language analytically by rules. It enables creative construction of language that has not been heard or said before. Prefabrication, on the other hand, is a holistic process. Meaningful units segmented from speech stream are memorized and retrieved as wholes in performance.

Originally, prefabrication implied a pre-grammatical communication strategy employed by learners lacking sufficient L2 knowledge. In a longitudinal study of a child naturalistically learning L2 English, Hakuta (1974), who coined the term "prefabricated patterns" (i.e., slot-and-frame patterns), showed that prefabrication was pervasive at initial stages. For example, the child initially used the prefabricated pattern "*how to* Verb" as a single unit; later the pattern was replaced with the embedded question with inversion (e.g., *I know how do you write this*), which Hakuta infers would be probably generated by her interlanguage rule. Hakuta considers prefabricated language to be "props which temporarily give support until a firmer foundation is built (p. 288)."

Through different strands of research, it has been acknowledged that prefabrication performs functions beyond the communication strategies mentioned above (for review see Wray, 2001). First, prefabrication promotes fluency. Drawing on memorized sequences eases processing demands and allows for faster processing (Skehan, 1998). Considering that adult native speakers and advanced L2 learners rely considerably on memorized sequences, prefabrication cannot be restricted to pregrammatical strategies at initial stages of acquisition. Skehan (1998) considers prefabricated chunks at advanced stages to be analyzable language, that is, exemplars stored as wholes after occasional generation by rules.

Another important function of prefabrication is to promote learning. It has been discovered in some studies that unanalyzed chunks memorized at initial stages serve as the basis for creative construction (for review see Wray, 2001). Those studies involve studies not only on naturalistic L2 learning but also on classroom L2 learning of linguistic adults (e.g., Myles *et al.*, 1999). Myles *et al.* (1999) demonstrate that classroom learners who developed proficiency had actively experimented with their memorized chunks by breaking down and combining them together to produce novel utterances. It is suggested that prefabrication may contribute to such creative construction.

In sum, it can be said that prefabrication plays more significant roles in language performance and learning than has been thought. These roles are elaborated below in the review of literature on chunking.

Chunking

In psychology, chunking is a means for efficient information processing within working memory. According to Miller (1956), chunks (defined as cognitive units) that human beings can store within working memory (immediate memory in Miller's terms) are limited in number, but the amount of information contained in one chunk can be increased. Thus, in order to organize a large amount of information efficiently in memory, human beings group and weld a set of already formed chunks together into a larger unit recursively (Newell, 1990). This process is called chunking. For example, the string UNNYUSA consisting of seven letters can be chunked into three meaningful units UN-NY-USA.

Language is comprehended and produced through chunking (Ellis, 2001; Fukaya and Tanaka, 1996; MacWhinney, 2001). In comprehension, language users parse "the speech stream into chunks which reliably mark meaning" instead of conducting word-by-word (or morpheme-by-morpheme) analysis (Ellis, 2001: 40). Take, for example, the parsing of the speech stream, *A hurricane is coming to Florida, the reporter said.* After comprehending the first chunk *a hurricane is coming*, the next chunk *to Florida* is added and welded to the previous chunk to form a larger chunk, *A hurricane is coming to Florida*. Then the last chunk *the reporter said* is added, and sentence comprehension is completed (Fukaya and Tanaka, 1996). In production as well, language is dynamically produced through a chain-reaction of chunking. The preceding chunk evokes the next chunk recursively like "avalanches" (MacWhinney, 2001: 459).

MacWhinney (2008) holds that the definition of chunking should be extended to allow for more abstract levels of chunking. It is true that storing and retrieving phrasal chunks contributes to fluency, but this alone is not sufficient. In addition to retrieving chunks, learners have to learn to integrate the combination of one chunk with another in real time to achieve full fluency. What is necessary is to chunk the creation process as well as the actual phrase. For this reason, MacWhinney (2008: 358) argues that learners need to learn "more schematic chunks" involving the constructional schema.

How do learners form schematic chunks? According to Ellis (2001), chunking is the language acquisition process in itself. Elements co-occurring frequently become associated and chunked together (e.g., *gimme*), and label-meaning pairings are formed. Repeating this associative process with a number of exemplars (e.g., *give her*; *send me*), frequency-sensitive implicit analysis of sequences takes place. Learners gradually discover sequential patterns immanent in exemplar chunks.

Ellis's argument (2001) can be delineated in terms of token and type frequency in the usage-based framework. The phrasal chunks entrenched in memory due to high token frequency perform an anchoring function as prototypes (Ellis, 2009; Goldberg, 1999). As children or learners encounter other exemplars of the same type (i.e., as type frequency increases), the exemplars center around the prototype. The prototypical meaning comes to be associated with the form that is common among the exemplars. In this bottom-up fashion, the constructional schema, the abstract chunk as a form-meaning pairing, is formed. Even after the schema is formed, however, its instances entrenched in memory continue to exist. Thus it can be said that the linguistic system is a massive and redundant inventory consisting of constructional schemas with varying degrees of abstraction (e.g., V NP NP; *give* NP NP) and their instances (e.g., *gimme milk*) (Langacker, 2000).

In this theoretical framework, fluency development can also be explained in terms of chunking frequency. To comprehend or produce language, an appropriate unit, whether schema or exemplar, needs to be activated and selected among competing units stored in the mind (Langacker, 2000). The more strongly particular exemplars are entrenched due to high token frequency, the more easily the exemplars tend to be activated and selected, resulting in fluency. In addition, high type frequency in chunking particular constructions facilitates strengthening the schemas instead of actual instances, also resulting in automatic activation of the schemas (Bybee, 1995).

Prefabrication revisited

Here prefabrication needs to be redefined in terms of chunking in the usage-based framework. Under the original definition, prefabrication was defined in contrast to generation. However, the usage-based account of chunking suggests that this dichotomy is invalid. First, prefabrication itself results in developing schematic knowledge, which enables generation of novel utterances. As Ortega (2009: 114) states, frequency-sensitive implicit analysis of prefabricated exemplars is "not only a springboard to communication and grammatical analysis at the beginning stages, but the stuff of acquisition." Second, the process of generating new utterances cannot be distinguished clearly from prefabrication. The usage-based model (Langacker, 2000) posits that the constructional schema is interconnected with its subschemas and exemplars in a single system. Language users comprehend and produce language by activating and retrieving appropriate levels of units, whether schematic chunks or exemplar chunks. Thus, underlying processes in generation and holistic use of specific expressions might be the same, in the sense that both of them involve activating chunks in memory. In this contemporary framework, therefore, distinction between generation and prefabrication is blurred. It follows from the discussion above that chunking or prefabrication is the central process of language performance and learning.

Although chunking guides an essential part of the acquisitional task, it needs to be noted that multiple factors make L2 learning processes complex. In particular, it should be recalled that the abstraction process in chunking takes place implicitly. Since adult L2 learners tend to be oriented toward explicit learning (Wray, 2001), the interaction of the two types of learning should be examined. For a more comprehensive understanding of SLA, complexity of L2 learning needs to be explored from multiple perspectives.

See also: construction learning, formulaic language, frequency effects, phonological short term memory (PSTM), statistical learning, type and token frequency in SLA

References

Bybee, J. (1995). Regular morphology and the lexicon. *Language and Cognitive Processes, 10*, 425–55.

Ellis, N.C. (2001). Memory for language. In P. Robinson (ed.), *Cognition and Second Language Instruction*. Cambridge: Cambridge University Press.

——(2009). Optimizing the input: Frequency and sampling in usage-based and form-focused learning. In M.H. Long and C.J. Doughty (eds), *The Handbook of Language Teaching*. Oxford: Willey-Blackwell.

Fukaya, M. and Tanaka, S. (1996). *Kotoba no Imizukeron: Nichijogengo no nama no itonami*

(Meaning-Making Theory: Dynamism in Daily Language), Tokyo: Kinokuniya.

Goldberg, A.E. (1999). The emergence of the semantics and argument structure constructions. In B. MacWhinney (ed.), *The Emergence of Language*. Mahwah, NJ: Lawrence Erlbaum.

Hakuta, K. (1974). Prefabricated patterns and the emergence of structure in second language acquisition. *Language Learning*, *24*, 287–97.

Langacker, R.W. (2000). A dynamic usage-based model. In M. Barlow and S. Kemmer (eds), *Usage-Based Models of Language*. Stanford, CA: CSLI Publications.

MacWhinney, B. (2001). Emergentist approaches to language. In J. Bybee and P. Hopper (eds), *Frequency and the Emergence of Linguistic Structure*. Amsterdam: John Benjamins.

——(2008). A unified model. In P. Robinson and N.C. Ellis (eds), *Handbook of Cognitive Linguistics and Second Language Acquisition*, New York: Routledge.

Miller, G.A. (1956). The magical number seven, plus or minus two: Some limits on our capacity for processing information. *The Psychological Review*, *63*, 81–97.

Myles, F., Mitchell, R. and Hooper, J. (1999). Interrogative chunks in French L2: A basis for creative construction. *Studies in Second Language Acquisition*, *21*, 49–80.

Newell, A. (1990). *Unified Theories of Cognition*. Cambridge, MA: Harvard University Press.

Ortega, L. (2009). *Understanding Second Language Acquisition*. London: Hodder Education.

Skehan, P. (1998). *A Cognitive Approach to Language Learning*. Oxford: Oxford University Press.

Wray, A. (2001). *Formulaic Language and the Lexicon*. Cambridge: Cambridge University Press.

Further reading

Bush, N. (2001). Frequency effects and word-boundary palatalization in English. In J. Bybee and P. Hopper (eds), *Frequency and the Emergence of Linguistic Structure*. Amsterdam: John Benjamins. (A study of phonological reduction from the perspective of frequency-dependent chunking.)

Ellis, N.C. (1996). Sequencing in SLA: Phonological memory, chunking, and points of order. *Studies in Second Language Acquisition*, *18*, 91–126. (An account of chunking in terms of phonological long-term and short-term memories.)

——(2003). Constructions, chunking, and connectionism: The emergence of second language structure. In C.J. Doughty and M.H. Long (eds), *The Handbook of Second Language Acquisition*. Malden, MA: Blackwell. (A proposal for chunking as the process for developing constructions.)

Classroom interaction research

Hitoshi Muranoi
Tohoku Gakuin University

Interaction refers to the verbal exchange of messages between two or more speakers. In a second language classroom, a teacher interacts with a group of students or an individual student and students interact with one another. Interaction is important for teachers and learners not only to establish rapport and a sense of community in a classroom but also to develop learners' interlanguage systems. As such, second language researchers have examined how interaction contributes to second language development using a variety of approaches, both descriptive and experimental.

Interaction in the second language classroom was first examined descriptively starting in the 1970s. As a result of these early efforts, researchers devised various instruments for classroom observation and interaction analysis to identify the manner in which teachers interacted with their students (Chaudron, 1988; Malamah-Thomas, 1987). For instance, Moskowitz's (1971) Foreign Language interaction (FLINT) system, one of the most well-known interaction analysis instruments, was designed to meticulously code teacher–student interactions in three-second intervals. Within this system, teacher talk is divided into two types: indirect influence (e.g., the expression of feelings, praise, encouragement, and jokes; use of students' ideas, repetition; and the asking of questions) and direct influence (e.g., the giving of information, corrections, directions, and criticisms; and the use of pattern drills). Also within this system, student talk is categorized into different types of verbal and non-verbal responses (e.g., specific response, choral response, open-ended or student-initiated response, silence, confusion, laughter, etc.).

Fanselow's (1987) Foci for Observing Communication Used in Settings (FOCUS) is another example of a multidimensional system that aims at analyzing teacher–student interaction within a classroom setting. FOCUS identifies the source/target (e.g., teacher, individual students, group of students, entire class, other, text, test), move type (e.g., structuring, soliciting, responding, reacting), medium (e.g., linguistic, aural, visual, paralinguistic, silence), use (e.g., attend – listen, read, smell, taste, touch, view; characterize – differentiate, evaluate, examine, illustrate, label; present – elicit, query, question, sate; relate – explain, infer; reproduce – change medium, same medium), and content (e.g., life, procedure, study – language and other areas). According to Chaudron (1988), Fanselow's FOCUS system is useful for classroom interaction analysis, because it considers "pedagogical events as … a sequence of moves of some sort, the most typical in the classroom being the well-known 'teaching cycle' – solicit (elicit)/respond/react (evaluate)" (p. 37).

A classroom analysis instrument designed to evaluate second language teaching programs was developed by Allen *et al.* (1984). It is called the Communicative Orientation of Language Teaching (COLT). The COLT instrument has two parts. Part A is designed for real-time coding of classroom activities analyzed in terms of activity types (e.g., drill, translation, game, discussion, and dialogue), participant organization (whole class, group work, or individual work), content (management, language, and other topics), student modality (skills), and materials. Part B, designed for post-lesson analysis, uses tape recordings to assess the relative frequency of communicative behaviors and activities depending on several communicative features. COLT is useful for examining the kinds of interaction which occur in different types of classrooms.

Chaudron (1988), however, points out that such descriptive systems have certain methodological weaknesses. For example, the unit of analysis in the segmentation of classroom events is underspecified. In addition, the definition of the meaning/category of specific segments depends on observer interpretation. Chaudron argues that empirical validation should be required in order to assess whether or not a consistent relationship exists between coded events in second language classrooms and actual teaching and learning behaviors and outcomes.

Other descriptive approaches to second language interaction include the analysis of second language teachers' talk to their students. The role of teacher talk has been underscored by L2 researchers who subscribe to the assumption, termed the Interaction Hypothesis, that interactional modifications in response to communication difficulty help make input more comprehensible and thereby promote acquisition (Long, 1983). Chaudron (1988), for example, reviewed nine studies on second language teacher modifications of their talk and listed the following characteristic phenomena found in teacher speech: slower rate of speech, more frequent and longer pauses, exaggerated and simplified pronunciation, more basic vocabulary use, less subordination, more declaratives and statements than questions, more frequent self-repetition. In short, Chaudron's research suggests that by using such modifications, teachers adjust their speech in order to aid learners' comprehension.

Such attempts to make input more comprehensible have been termed "negotiation for meaning," a process in which interlocutors engage when misunderstanding occurs in interaction. For instance, L2 learners signal the incomprehensibility of an interlocutor's utterance with clarification requests such as "Sorry?" and "Could you say that again?," to which their interlocutor likely responds by repeating, segmenting and or rewording so that the communication problem can be resolved. In other words, negotiation for meaning helps learners understand what they have had difficulty comprehending.

In the 1990s, classroom interaction researchers began investigating additional functions of negotiation beyond the enhancement of comprehensibility. In an updated version of the Interaction Hypothesis, Long (1996) summarizes his expanded view of the role of interaction by claiming:

"negotiation for meaning, and especially negotiation work that triggers interactional modifications by the NS or more competent interlocutor, facilitates acquisition because it connects input, internal learner capacities, particularly by selective attention, and output in productive ways" (pp. 451–52). That is, interaction promotes not only comprehension but also L2 learners' awareness of target forms as well as their awareness of the output they produce.

In a similar vein, Pica (1992) argues that the negotiation process provides learners with: "(1) L2 input adjusted or modified for their comprehension needs; (2) feedback on semantic and structural features of interlanguage; (3) opportunities to adjust, manipulate, or modify semantic and structural features of their interlanguage; and (4) a source of L2 data that highlights L2 semantic and structural relationships" (p. 205). In other words, during interaction, L2 learners are given comprehensible input, negative evidence in the form of feedback, opportunities to produce modified output, and information on form-meaning-use connections.

Among these functions of negotiation, what has arguably received the most attention from second language researchers is feedback. Based on the updated Interaction Hypothesis, a number of second language researchers have empirically investigated the effects of various types of feedback, ranging from explicit to implicit and direct to indirect. Evidence of the beneficial effect of a type of implicit negative feedback, called corrective recast, has been reported in multiple classroom interaction studies. Corrective recast has been defined as "a reformulation of all or part of a learner's immediately preceding utterance in which one or more nontarget-like (lexical, grammatical, etc.) items is/are replaced by the corresponding target language form(s), and where, throughout the exchange, the focus of the interlocutors is on meaning, not language as objects" (Long, 2007: 77). Corrective recasts are considered to be beneficial for the acquisition of certain grammatical forms, especially when the target of recasting is specified, because they lead L2 learners to compare their interlanguage forms with immediately contingent correct utterances in a conversation where the form-meaning-use connection is clearly understood (Gass, 1997; Long, 2007).

As a result of these research findings, numerous instructional treatments aimed at promoting L2 learners' active involvement in the interaction process have been proposed. For example, L2 researchers and teachers have recognized the utility of focus-on-form treatments that create natural opportunities to negotiate meaning with other speakers of the target language by using communication tasks (e.g., problem-solving tasks, information-gap tasks, decision-making tasks) (Doughty and Williams, 1998). For example, Muranoi (2000) reports on the beneficial effects of focus-on-form treatments designed to enhance interaction by providing interactional modifications such as request for repetition and recasts in a second language classroom.

In interpreting the results of instruction studies, however, we must keep in mind that the impact of interaction on the development of L2 grammar is dependent upon the characteristics of the target grammar as well as a vast number of learner factors. Long (2007), for example, points out that the complexity of the target grammatical forms and their perceptual saliency determine the effectiveness of recasts. Also, Mackey (2007) claims that "there is more than one route to L2 development through interaction, with learners perceiving feedback differently depending on the type, relevant area of language (e.g., morpho-syntax, lexis, phonology), and possibly the specific target of the feedback" (p. 87). Recent SLA studies have even revealed that the impact of feedback (e.g., recasts) is influenced by cognitive and psychological factors such as working-memory capacity, analytical ability, and communication anxiety (Mackey, 2007; Robinson, 2002, 2007; Sheen, 2008).

It should also be noted that classroom interaction is affected by task variables such as required versus optional information exchange tasks, one-way versus two-way information exchange tasks, and open versus closed tasks. Though the results are not clear-cut, findings of the studies on these task variables suggest that required information, two-way, and closed tasks are likely to promote more negotiation than optional information exchange, one-way, and open tasks (see Ellis, 2008; Gass, 1997; for a review of studies on the relation between interaction and task types).

Current classroom research into the role of interaction in second language acquisition provides insight into the complex nature of the relationship between interactional and linguistic features of the target forms, characteristics of tasks, and individual differences. The ability to extend as well as come up with effective applications of these findings for second language learners remains as both a challenge and potential reward of continued efforts in this field.

See also: corrective feedback, Focus on Form (FonF), individual differences in SLA, interaction and the interaction hypothesis, measuring and researching SLA, negotiation of meaning

References

Allen, F., Fröhlich, M. and Spada, N. (1984). The communicative orientation of language teaching: An observation scheme. In J. Handscombe, R. Orem, and B. Taylor (eds), *On TESOL '83: The Question of Control*. Washington, DC: TESOL.

Chaudron, G. (1988). *Second Language Classrooms: Research on Teaching and Learning*. Cambridge: Cambridge University Press.

Doughty, C. and Williams, J. (eds) (1998). *Focus on Form in Classroom Second Language Acquisition*. Cambridge: Cambridge University Press.

Ellis, R. (2008). *The Study of Second Language Acquisition*, 2nd edn. Oxford: Oxford University Press.

Fanselow, J. (1987). *Breaking Rules: Generating and Exploring Alternatives in Language Teaching*. New York and London: Longman.

Gass, S. (1997). *Input, Interaction, and the Second Language Learner*. Mahwah, NJ: Lawrence Erlbaum.

Leeman, J. (2007). Feedback in L2 learning: Responding to errors during practice. In R. DeKeyser (ed.), *Practice in a Second Language: Perspectives from Applied Lnguistics and Cognitive Psychology*. Cambridge: Cambridge University Press.

Long, M. (1983). Native speaker/non-native speaker conversation and the negotiation of comprehensible input. *Applied Linguistics*, *4*, 126–41.

——(1996). The role of the linguistic environment in second language acquisition. In W. Ritchie and T. Bhatia (eds), *Handbook of Research on Second Language Acquisition*. New York: Academic Press.

——(2007). *Problems in SLA*. Mahwah, NJ: Lawrence Erlbaum Associates.

Mackey, A. (2007). Interaction as practice. In R. DeKeyser (ed.), *Practice in a Second Language: Perspectives from Applied Linguistics and Cognitive Psychology*. Cambridge: Cambridge University Press.

—— (ed.) (2007). *Conversational Interaction in Second Language Acquisition*. Oxford: Oxford University Press.

Mackey, A. and Goo, J. (2007). Interaction research in SLA: A meta-analysis and research synthesis. In Mackey, A. (ed.), *Conversational Interaction in Second Language Acquisition*. Oxford: Oxford University Press.

Malamah-Thomas, A. (1987). *Classroom Interaction*. Oxford: Oxford University Press.

Moskowitz, G. (1971). Interaction analysis: A new modern language for supervisors. *Foreign Language Annals*, *5*, 211–21.

Muranoi, H. (2000). Focus on form through interaction enhancement: Integrating formal instruction into a communicative task in EFL classrooms. *Language Learning*, *50*, 4, 617–73.

Pica, T. (1992). The textual outcomes of native speaker-non-native speaker negotiation: What do they reveal about second language learning?. In C. Kramsch and S. McConnell-Ginet (eds), *Text and Context*. Cambridge, MA: Heath.

Robinson, P. (ed.) (2002). *Individual Differences and Instructed Language Learning*. Amsterdam and Philadelphia, PA: John Benjamins.

Robinson, P. (2007). Aptitudes, abilities, contexts, and practice. In R. DeKeyser (ed.), *Practice in a Second Language: Perspectives from Applied Linguistics and Cognitive Psychology*. Cambridge: Cambridge University Press.

Sheen, Y. (2008). Recasts, language anxiety, modified output, and L2 learning. *Language Learning*. *58*, 4, 835–74.

Further reading

Chaudron, G. (1988). *Second Language Classrooms: Research on Teaching and Learning*.

Cambridge: Cambridge University Press. (A comprehensive introduction to classroom interaction research.)

Ellis, R. (2008). *The Study of Second Language Acquisition*, 2nd edn. Oxford: Oxford University Press. (Chapter 15 is a comprehensive review of descriptive and confirmatory classroom interaction studies.)

Mackey, A. (ed.) (2007). *Conversational Interaction in Second Language Acquisition*. Oxford: Oxford University Press. (A collection of empirical studies on classroom interaction.)

Malamah-Thomas, A. (1987). *Classroom Interaction*. Oxford: Oxford University Press. (A survey of instruments that have been used when conducting classroom interaction analysis research.)

Code-switching

Jean-Marc Dewaele

Birkbeck College, University of London

Code-switching (CS) – changes from one language to another in the course of conversation (Li Wei, 2007: 14) – is a typical feature of bilinguals' speech and a generally accepted practice in many multilingual societies. It has become clear from the research that CS is not necessarily the sign of a problem, but rather the illustration of "skilled manipulation of overlapping sections of two (or more) grammars, and that there is virtually no instance of ungrammatical combination of two languages in code-switching, regardless of the bilingual ability of the speaker" (Li Wei, 2007: 15).

CS has attracted the attention of both psycholinguists and sociolinguists. The former focus on how multilinguals process words from different languages and the neurocognitive cost associated with CS, the latter analyze CS behavior between speakers in various situations within various speech communities.

There is a large body of research on the reasons underlying CS (Gardner-Chloros, 2009; Isurin *et al.*, 2009). One area of research has focused on the phenomenon of triggering in CS. It seems that overlap between languages at any level (i.e. conceptual, syntactical, discourse, gesture, syllable and phoneme) can trigger CS at almost any point in the sentence.

CS can happen spontaneously and unintentionally, but it can also be planned. Indeed, a speaker can have pragmatic reasons for CS. It can signal that the speaker is reporting someone else's speech. It can also serve to highlight particular information, indicate a change in the speaker's role, qualify a topic or single out one person to direct speech at.

The reasons for CS may also be linked to specific contexts. For example, classroom CS is closely linked with teaching and learning activities where CS to the learners' L1 may signal a metalinguistic explanation or the translation of a word in the target language. Family interactions are also conducive to CS, with parents and children displaying different patterns of CS linked to different socializations and displays of identity (Lanza, 1997). CS has also been described as a mixed language that became conventionalized within certain speech communities as the result of a complex interaction of sociolinguistic factors. Foreign words used in CS (such as English swearwords) can become part of the repertoire of speakers of the borrowing language at which point it could be argued that their use no longer constitutes an instance of CS. CS patterns within certain immigrant communities have been analyzed from a synchronic and diachronic perspective.

CS has also been linked to the specialized knowledge individuals have of specific topics in different languages. Multilinguals may CS to a preferred language for a particular topic.

CS can also have affective functions. CS to the L1 is posited to signal intimacy, group membership, and is favored to express strong emotions, while CS to the L2 has been found to mark distance, an out-group attitude, or to describe emotions in a detached way. Dewaele (2010) found that self-reported frequency of CS is much higher when talking about more emotional topics with familiar interlocutors compared to neutral topics being discussed with unknown interlocutors.

See also: attitudes to the L2, bilingualism and SLA, emotions, identity theory, second dialect acquisition, World Englishes

References

Dewaele, J.-M. (2010). *Emotions in Multiple Languages*. Basingstoke: Palgrave-Macmillan.

Gardner-Chloros, P. (2009). *Code-switching*. Cambridge: Cambridge University Press.

Bullock, B.E. and Toribio, A.J. (2009). *The Cambridge Handbook of Linguistic Code-switching*. Cambridge: Cambridge University Press.

Isurin, L., Winford, D. and de Bot, K. (2009). *Multidisciplinary Approaches to Code Switching*. Amsterdam and Philadelphia, PA: Benjamins.

Lanza, E. (1997). *Language Mixing in Infant Bilingualism. A Sociolinguistic Perspective*. Oxford: Clarendon Press.

Li Wei (2007). *Dimensions of Bilingualism. The Bilingualism Reader*, 2nd edn. London: Routledge.

Cognition Hypothesis (CH)

Tomohito Ishikawa

Soka Women's College

The Cognition Hypothesis (CH) is that in task-based syllabi, pedagogic tasks should be sequenced solely on the basis of increases in their cognitive complexity and that such sequences provide optimal support for learners in their attempts to use accurate and complex language at the level needed to meet real-world target task demands (Robinson, 2001, 2005). To guide research into these claims, and also pedagogy, Robinson proposes an operational taxonomy of task characteristics (Robinson, 2007). This taxonomic, Triadic Componential Framework (TCF) distinguishes three categories of task demand implicated in real-world task performance. Task *condition* refers to interactive demands of tasks, including participation variables (e.g., open vs. closed tasks) and participant variables (e.g., same vs. different gender). Task *difficulty* concerns individual differences in learner factors (such as working memory capacity). Task *complexity* refers to the intrinsic cognitive complexity of tasks (such as their reasoning demands).

In the TCF, task features affecting the cognitive complexity of tasks are distinguished along two dimensions. Resource-*directing* dimensions of complexity affect allocation of cognitive resources to specific aspects of L2 code. For instance, tasks which increase in their intentional-reasoning demands require linguistic reference to the mental states of others. These demands should therefore direct learners' attention to forms needed to meet them during communication, such as psychological state terms in English ("believe", "wonder", etc.). These forms may be currently known, but not well controlled, or if they are unknown, then attempts to complete the task may make them salient, and "noticeable." In contrast, resource-*dispersing* dimensions do not do this: making a task complex by removing planning time does not direct the learner's attention to specific aspects of L2 code, but rather disperses attention over many linguistic and other features.

The *pedagogic* claim of the CH – that tasks should be sequenced on the basis of increases in cognitive complexity – is supported by some *theoretical* claims about second language acquisition (SLA). Increasing the cognitive demands of pedagogic tasks along resource-directing dimensions will: (i) push learners to greater accuracy and complexity of L2 production in order to meet the greater conceptual and communicative demands they make. Along resource-directing and resource-dispersing dimensions, increasing task complexity will also (ii) promote greater amounts of interaction, heightened attention to and memory for input, and incorporation of forms made salient in the input; and (iii) promote longer-term retention of input. The CH also predicts that (iv) performing simple to complex sequences will lead to automaticity and efficient scheduling of the cognitive components of complex task performance; and that (v) individual differences between learners in cognitive abilities and affective states will progressively differentiate their performance and learning as pedagogic tasks increase in complexity.

Based on this resource-directing/dispersing distinction, and the TCF, Robinson (2010) proposes two *operational principles* for sequencing tasks in a task-based syllabus: (i) sequencing should be based only on increases in cognitive complexity, (ii) increase resource-dispersing dimensions of task complexity first (to promote access to current interlanguage), then increase resource-directing dimensions of complexity (to promote development of new form-function mappings, and destabilize the current interlanguage system).

See also: attention, classroom interaction research, instructed SLA, planning time, task-based learning, units of analysis for measuring L2 speech

References

Robinson, P. (2001). Task complexity, cognitive resources, and syllabus design: A triadic framework for examining task influences on SLA. In P. Robinson (ed.), *Cognition and Second Language Instruction*, pp. 287–318. Cambridge: Cambridge University Press.

——(2005). Cognitive complexity and task sequencing: A review of studies in a Componential Framework for second language task design. *International Review of Applied Linguistics*, *43*, 1–33.

——(2007). Criteria for grading and sequencing pedagogic tasks. In M. del Pilar Garcia-Mayo (ed.), *Investigating Tasks in Formal Language Learning*, pp. 7–27. Clevedon: Multilingual Matters.

——(2010). Situating and distributing cognition across task demands: The SSARC model of pedagogic task sequencing. In M. Putz and L. Sicola (eds), *Cognitive Processing in Second Language Acquisition: Inside the Learner's Mind*, pp. 239–64. Amsterdam and Philadelphia, PA: John Benjamins.

Further reading

Garcia-Mayo, M.P. (ed.) (2007). *Investigating Tasks in Formal Language Learning*. Clevedon: Multilingual Matters. (A collection of empirical studies, many of them addressing the theoretical claims of the Cognition Hypothesis.)

Robinson, P. and Gilabert, R. (eds) (2007). Task complexity, the cognition hypothesis and second language instruction. (Special issue) *International Review of Applied Linguistics*, *45* (3). Berlin: Mouton de Gruyter. (A collection of theoretical papers and empirical studies of the claims of the Cognition Hypothesis.)

Robinson, P. (ed.) (2011). *Second Language Task Complexity: Researching the Cognition Hypothesis of Language Learning and Performance*. Amsterdam: John Benjamins. (Contains theoretical papers and empirical studies of predictions of the Cognition Hypothesis concerning spoken and written production, interaction, uptake of negative feedback, and the effects of individual differences on simple and complex task-based learning and performance.)

Cognitive aging

Henrike K. Blumenfeld

San Diego State University

Given current population trends, the ability of older adults to attain and maintain a second language is likely to be of increasing interest among language teachers and providers of social and healthcare services. The general population is aging, with 12 percent of the US population above age 65 in 2004 and a projected 20 percent above 65 in 2030. In 2000, 10 percent of the US population 65 and older was foreign-born, and 13 percent of the population 65 and over spoke a language other than English at home. Therefore, the acquisition and maintenance of a second language is likely to play a pivotal role in the lives of a growing number of older adults.

The ability to learn and maintain new skills, including language, is a central cognitive ability that is affected by age-related declines. For example, among 2,492 Israeli participants aged 50 and above, individuals above age 70 showed significantly higher odds of impairment on a verbal learning task than individuals between ages 50–70 (Ayalon *et al.*, 2010), with new immigrants showing higher impairment rates in Hebrew verbal learning than individuals who had been in the country longer. This finding suggests that learning of a new language (as opposed to material within previously learned languages) may be especially challenging for older adults.

Age-related changes in the ability to learn, process, and maintain a second language are likely influenced by a variety of factors, including age-related changes in perception (hearing and vision, see Baltes and Lindenberger, 1997), cognitive changes, as well as social and motivational factors. Age-related cognitive changes that are particularly relevant to language learning include changes in the memory and cognitive control systems.

Cognitive factors

The memory systems that support language learning include procedural and declarative components (Paradis, 2009; Ullman, 2005), with procedural components underlying incidental and effortless learning that is typical of childhood acquisition and declarative components underlying effortful and content-based acquisition that is thought to dominate learning in adults. Crucially, declarative memory undergoes more decline than procedural memory with cognitive aging, with decreased performance evident in both encoding and retrieval processes (Connor, 2001). Extreme cases of declines in declarative memory are evident in frequently reported greater losses in the second language (L2) versus the native language (L1) in late L2 learners with dementia (Paradis, 2009).

When information is learned explicitly, the ability to automatize newly acquired language skills plays an important role in language attainment. Young adult learners are able to automatize rule-based information with practice (Ullman, 2005). Yet, even after extensive training, older adults may continue to perform slower on newly learned tasks, and may show less evidence of automatization (Maquestiaux *et al.*, 2010). Age-related declines in automatization are more marked for perceptual learning than for learning that involves rote memorization (Rogers, 2000), suggesting that perceptual aspects of language learning may be especially affected. A reduced ability to automatize newly acquired linguistic skills, such as grammatical rules, may limit foreign language learning in older adults.

In addition to changes in memory, age-related changes in cognitive control (the ability to support effortful processing) are also likely to influence the ability to learn and maintain a second language. Age-related changes in cognitive control result in a decreased ability to ignore irrelevant information while focusing on relevant information. Changes in executive function may be related to general cognitive slowing, rendering the processing system overall less efficient (Hasher and Zacks, 1988). Together, these cognitive changes may reduce a learner's ability to parse novel input, and to identify and encode relevant information. Moreover, the native/dominant language may become increasingly more likely to interfere with the learning and processing of a new language, rendering learning and maintenance of an L2 more difficult (e.g., Hernandez and Kohnert, 1999).

To summarize, age-related declines in the ability to attain and maintain a second language can be related to at least four cognitive factors: declines in the ability to acquire an L2 implicitly, declines in the declarative memory system, declines in the ability to automatize processes, and declines in cognitive control. Therefore, the cognitive architecture underlying second language learning in older adults typically becomes less efficient with age, constraining the cognitive resources that are available for second language learning and maintenance.

Levels of second language attainment with increased age

While extensive research exists on second language acquisition in early versus later childhood (e.g., Birdsong, 2006), little systematic research is available on ultimate attainment levels when older adults learn a second language. Large-scale analyses that compare age of immigration with attained self-reported proficiency have yielded linear declines, with increased age of immigration associated with decreased proficiency (Chiswick and Miller, 2008, Hakuta *et al.*, 2003). DeKeyser (2000) found negative correlations between attainment (grammaticality judgments) and both age of acquisition and age of testing, with partial correlations suggesting that age of testing accounts for patterns of age-related decline more in older adults (18–40 and 40+) than younger participants. In sum, across currently available studies, an age-related linear decline in attainment seems to exist, with some studies showing a linear pattern and others showing increased variability with age (for a review, see Birdsong, 2006).

Regardless of specific patterns of decline, the existing age of acquisition literature suggests that the language domains particularly affected by later age of acquisition include syntax and morphosyntax (grammaticality judgments), and phonology (accentedness). It is likely that these language domains remain particularly difficult to acquire to a native-like level as cognitive aging progresses, given that they rely most heavily on automatization for optimal processing. Nevertheless, while declines in the ability to *learn* rule-based aspects of language may be present, age-related declines in *previously attained* L2 abilities may not be significant in all linguistic domains. For example, in individuals who had immigrated to Canada from Italy at similar ages, chronological age at the time of testing did *not* correlate with L2 accent (Mackay *et al.*, 2006). This finding suggests that, once acquired, accent may remain a stable feature of a second language.

In contrast to other linguistic domains, successful vocabulary learning may not be constrained by age until clear memory-related declines appear in the 70s and 80s. Older adults may outperform younger adults on vocabulary tests, with only subtle declines in vocabulary in old age (Kavé *et al.*, 2010). In fact, it is conceivable that extensive vocabulary, acquired across a lifetime, may scaffold learning of new second-language vocabulary. Nevertheless, word retrieval difficulties during language production are typically more persistent in older adults. Decline in both encoding and retrieval are likely to have marked influences on the new learning of vocabulary and the maintenance of L2 vocabulary with advanced age. In particular, retrieval of lexical items with lower frequencies, or in areas of low expertise seems particularly vulnerable to advanced age. Since vocabulary in a later-acquired language may have subjectively lower frequencies than native-language words, it can be expected that L2 vocabulary is more vulnerable to age-related decline.

In general, declines in language abilities with age have been found to be more marked for language production than comprehension (Schrauf, 2008), likely because production requires more cognitive resources and because less context-based scaffolding is provided (Craik, 1986), yielding greater demands on word retrieval. Accordingly, older adults may find particular difficulties in second language production.

Social and motivational factors

Older adults may not have the same opportunities for second language immersion as younger adults. In addition, where opportunities are available, the nature of the input may be qualitatively and quantitatively different from that received by younger adults. Social theories, such as the Communication Predicament of Aging Model, posit that the activation of age-related stereotypes in intergenerational communication may result in simplified and significantly limited language input for older adults as opposed to younger adults (Harwood, 2007). Reduction in the quality of language input, including grammatically less complex and shorter sentences and limited conversation topics due to younger adults' goals to accommodate the older conversation partner, may potentially lead to fewer opportunities in learning and maintaining a second language. Such changes in the social context may in turn influence motivational and self-esteem factors in the older language learner.

Methodological concerns and future directions

In examining language learning and attainment in older adults, it is important to separate age of acquisition effects from age of testing effects in order to distinguish the *ability to learn* language from the *ability to maintain and process* it. The influence of chronological age on second language attainment is notably difficult to study within the framework of research approaches that dominate the field, where second language learners are examined who have immigrated to the country of their second language as adults. In such contexts, chronological age is frequently strongly related to other factors such as length of residence in the country where L2 is spoken and the age of L2 acquisition (Stevens, 2006). To differentiate these factors and reach a fuller understanding of the role of chronological age in second language attainment, studies are needed where the chronological age of learning is manipulated as an independent variable in more controlled environments, and with clear language learning and cognitive profiles in participants.

See also: age effects in SLA, attrition, Declarative Procedural Model, explicit learning, individual differences in SLA, inhibitory control

References

Ayalon, L., Heinik, J. and Litwin, H. (2010). Cognitive functioning in a national sample of Israelis 50 years and older. *Research on Aging*, *32* (3), 304–22.

Baltes, P.B. and Lindenberger, U. (1997). Emergence of powerful connection between sensory and cognitive functions across the adult life span: A new window to the study of cognitive aging? *Psychology and Aging*, *12*, 12–21.

Birdsong, D. (2006). Age and second language acquisition and processing: A selective overview. *Language Learning*, *56*, 9–49.

Chiswick, B.R. and Miller, P.W. (2008). A test of the critical period hypothesis for language learning. *Journal of Multilingual and Multicultural Development*, *29* (1), 16–29.

Craik, F.I.M. (1986). A functional account of age differences in memory. In F. Klix and H. Hagendorf (eds), *Human Memory and Cognitive Capabilities*, pp. 409–42. New York: Elsevier Science.

DeKeyser, R.M. (2000). The robustness of critical period effects in second language acquisition. *Studies in Second Language Acquisition*, *22*, 499–533.

Hasher, L. and Zacks, R.T. (1988). Working memory, comprehension and aging: A review and a new view. In G.H. Bower (ed.), *The Psychology of Learning and Motivation*. Vol. 22, pp. 193–225. San Diego, CA: Academic Press.

Hakuta, K., Bialystok, E. and Wiley, E. (2003). Critical evidence: A test of the critical-period hypothesis for second-language acquisition. *Psychological Science*, *14*, 31–38.

Hernandez, A.E. and Kohnert, K.J. (1999). Aging and language switching in Bilinguals. *Aging, Neuropsychology, and Cognition*, *6* (2), 69–83.

Kavé, G., Knafo, A. and Gilboa, A. (2010). The rise and fall of word retrieval across the lifespan. *Psychology and Aging*, *25* (3), 719–24.

Maquestiaux, F., Laguë-Beauvais, M., Ruthruff, E., Hartley, A. and Bherer, L. (2010). Learning to bypass the central bottleneck: Declining automaticity with advancing age. *Psychology and Aging*, *25* (1), 177–92.

Paradis (2009). *Declarative and Procedural Determinants of Second Languages*. Amsterdam: John Benjamins.

Rogers, W.A. (2000). Attention and aging. In Park, D. and Schwartz, N. (eds), *Cognitive Aging: A Primer*, Ch. 4, pp. 57–73. New York: Psychology Press.

U.S. Census (2004). *We the People: Aging in the United States, Census 2000 Special Reports*. Retrieved from www.census.gov/prod/2004pubs/censr-19.pdf 1–15–2011.

Ullman, M.T. (2005). A cognitive neuroscience perspective on second language acquisition: the declarative/procedural model. In C. Sanz (ed.), *Mind and Context in Adult Second Language Acquisition: Methods, Theory, and Practice*. Ch. 5, pp. 141–78. Washington, DC: Georgetown University Press.

Further reading

Connor, L.T. (2001). Memory in old age: Patterns of decline and preservation. *Seminars in Speech and Language*, *22* (2), 117–25. (An overview of patterns of decline in memory with cognitive aging.)

Harwood, J. (2007). *Understanding Communication and Aging*. Thousand Oaks, CA: Sage Publications. (An extensive treatment of communication and aging, including social and cultural aspects that are relevant to understanding second language acquisition and maintenance in older adults.)

Mackay, I.R.A., Flege, J.E. and Imai, S. (2006). Evaluating the effects of chronological age and sentence duration on degree of perceived foreign accent. *Applied Psycholinguistics*, *27*, 157–83. (Examination of the influence of chronological age, as opposed to other factors such as age of acquisition or duration of immersion, on perceived foreign accent.)

Schrauf, R.W. (2008). Bilingualism and aging. In Altarriba, J, and Heredia, R. (eds), *An Introduction to Bilingualism: Principles and Processes*. Ch. 5, pp. 105–23. New York: LEA.

(An overview of changes in the linguistic systems of bilinguals vs. monolinguals with cognitive aging.)

Stevens, G. (2006). The age-length-onset problem in research on second language acquisition among immigrants. *Language Learning*, *56* (4), 671–92. (A description of confounding variables in studying the influence of chronological age on second language attainment, and potential methodological solutions to isolate confounding variables from each other.)

Cognitive Linguistics and SLA

Andrea Tyler
Georgetown University

Cognitive Linguistics (CL) is a usage-based approach to language with well-articulated, integrated analyses of language structure, use and change that offers many potential insights into L2 development. Two core principles involve the Cognitive commitment (i.e., linguistic theory should conform to general human cognitive processes, including perceptual processes) and the Generalization commitment (i.e., recurrent reflexes of cognitive processes exist at all levels of language, thus obviating distinct subsystems of semantics, lexicon, pragmatics, syntax, etc.) (Lakoff, 1990). Together these two principles redefine language as a reflection of general human cognition, with its tendency to create dynamic, interconnected, patterned memory and respond in finely tuned fashion to frequency of the input, rather than as a set of language-specific rules.

Within CL, language is understood as being constructed by the learner from individual instances of contextualized language input (e.g., Tomasello, 2003). As the learner encounters more instances of contextualized language, she begins to construct more abstract generalizations, which often evidence prototype effects and hierarchically organized schemas. The formation of such conceptual linguistic structure is understood as drawing on the same cognitive processes used in category formation for non-linguistic phenomena. For instance, syntactic patterns are taken to be abstract schema formed over multiple exposures of contextualized instances of language. All linguistic units are held to be symbolic units with a phonological pole and a semantic pole. Crucially, syntax itself is meaningful (Goldberg, 1995). Syntactic patterns which are seemingly semantic equivalents, such as the active versus the passive, are understood as distinct constructions, which allow the speaker to offer different interpretations (or construals) on the scene/event under discussion. Thus, constructions, that is, conventionalized linguistic patterns, "structure concepts and window attention to aspects of experience through the options specific languages make available to speakers" (Talmy, 2000a).

CL places contextualized meaning-making at the center of language use and structure. Language is likened to a set of tools from which speakers draw in order to appropriately shape the message in order to make mental contact with the listener(s) (e.g. Langacker, 1987). Thus, the approach offers specific support to contextualized, communicatively oriented L2 learning, along with explanations of how particular language forms (e.g., articles, modals, competing syntactic constructions) serve as choices that speakers exploit in crafting their message.

CL is unique in its emphasis on embodied meaning, that is, the notion that the particularities of human neuro-physical architecture and the way humans interact with the physical world, crucially shape human cognition and language. One of the most intensively studied connections between the human perceptual system, cognition and language involves the visual system. (e.g., Talmy, 2000a, 2000b). Reflexes of focus and background perception prevalent in the visual system are found in a variety of subsystems of language, such as the prepositional system and clause structure. Cognitive linguists (e.g., Lakoff and Johnson, 1989; Grady, 1999) also argue that one of the most pervasive cognitive processes reflected in language is humans' tendency to think asymmetrically about experiences and events in one domain in terms of spatial-physical domains. This is thinking metaphorically. Linguistic reflexes of conceptual metaphor include use of spatial language, such as "up," to refer to abstract concepts, such as "more," as well as conceptual metaphors such as "words are objects" to explain otherwise unexpected uses of various syntactic patterns (Goldberg, 1995). Metaphorical analysis provides principled, meaning-based explanations for the fit between particular verbs and argument structures, as well as providing systematic accounts for semantic extensions of all lexical items (Sweetser, 1990). The precision of these predictions allows for examination of many specific aspects of L2 learning, ranging from general vocabulary, the article system, and syntactic constructions.

An additional aspect of embodied meaning is that humans appear to conceptualize the world and their experiences in it in terms of spatial scenes. CL recognizes that any spatial scene can be construed in multiple ways; thus, each speech community has the potential to construe a spatial scene in numerous ways, accounting for the variations we find within and across languages. Extensive, cross-linguistic work on how languages typically articulate motion events by researchers such as Berman and Slobin's (1994) shows that different languages lead speakers to prioritize different aspects of events in narrative discourse. "Because languages achieve these attention-directing outcomes in different ways, learning another language involves learning how to construe the world like natives of the L2" (Robinson and Ellis, 2008: 124–29).

Learning an L1 and an L2 are understood to involve the same general processes. A crucial difference is that learning the L1 involves learning the categories and their linguistic labels favored by the community of speakers who surround the young child. The L2 learner begins with myriad categories and schema from their L1 in place; these are often at variance with the categories and schema of the L2. CL provides the analytical tools for fine-grained analyses of cross-linguistic differences in some of the most challenging areas of language. This usefully revives a much refined notion of contrastive analysis.

Frequency of the input, with the learner actively interpreting and creating form-meaning mappings, is another key factor in language learning. Ellis and his colleagues (e.g., Ellis and Fernando Ferreira-Junior, 2009), as well as Gries and Stefanowitch (2006), have established the importance of frequency effects in L2 learning. For instance, Ellis (e.g., 2008) has written persuasively about the consistency between the tenets of CL and associative learning. He argues that CL helps predict the effects of "frequency, contingency, competition between multiple cues, and salience" in both L1 and L2. Moreover, aspects of the L2 that are typically not learned are "those, however available in the input, fall short of intake because of one of the factors of contingency, cue competition, salience, interference, overshadowing, blocking or perceptual learning, all shaped by L1 entrenchment" (Ellis and Cadierno, 2009: 373).

The focus on frequency bears on the importance of learning collocations, including learning which verbs more frequently occur in particular syntactic patterns. For instance, Goldberg found a strong correlation between the frequency of the word *give* and the ditransitive construction, both in general corpora of English and in adult language directed at young children. The fact that the meaning of the verb *give* closely parallels the meaning of the ditransitive construction (X causes Y to receive Z) serves as an anchor for learning the meaning of the syntactic pattern. Ellis and Fernando Ferreira-Junior (2009) found similar skewed frequency of anchor verbs occurring in all the syntactic patterns they investigated.

The issue of sufficient, appropriate, salient contextualized input, in conjunction with the recognition that L2 learners already have entrenched L1 categories and routines in place, raises important questions for L2 learners so-called "end state." Associative processes such as competition and blocking "explain why form focused instruction is a necessary component of L2 learning and why successful L2 learning necessitates a greater level of explicit awareness of the L2 constructions" (Ellis and Cadierno, 2009: 373). Evidence is beginning to emerge that even very advanced learners whose L2 appears to have stabilized can move towards more nativelike competence when given CL-based instruction on recalcitrant forms, such as prepositions and complex grammatical constructions (Tyler, 2010).

See also: construal and perspective taking, construction learning, corpus analysis, entrenchment, metaphor, schemata

References

Berman, R. and Slobin, D. (1994). *Relating Events in Narrative: A Cross-linguistic Developmental Study*. Hillsdale, NJ: Lawrence Erlbaum Associates.

Ellis, N. (2008). Usage-based and form-focused language acquisition: The associative learning of constructions, learned attention and the limited L2 endstate. In P. Robinson and N. Ellis (eds), *Handbook of Cognitive Linguistics and Second Language Acquisition*, pp. 372–405. New York: Routledge.

Ellis, N. and Cadierno, T. (2009). Constructing a second language: Introduction to the Special Section. *Annual Review of Cognitive Lingusitics. 7*, 111–39.

Ellis, N. and Ferreira-Junior, F. (2009). Constructions and their acquisition: Islands and the distinctiveness of their occupancy. *Annual Review of Cognitive Linguistics*, *7*, 187–220.

Goldberg, A. (1995). *Constructions: A Construction Grammar Approach to Argument Structure*. Chicago, IL: Chicago University Press.

——(2006). *Constructions at Work: The Nature of Generalization in Language*. Oxford: Oxford University Press.

Grady, J. (1999). A typology of motivation for conceptual metaphor: Correlation vs. resemblance. In R.W. Gibbs and G. Steen (eds), *Metaphor in Cognitive Linguistics*, pp. 79–100. Amsterdam: John Benjamins.

Gries, S. and Stefanowitch, A. (2006). (eds), *Corpora in Cognitive Linguistics*. Berlin: Mouton de Gruyter.

Lakoff, G. (1990). The invariance hypothesis: Is abstract reason based on image schemas? *Cognitive Linguistics*, *1*, 39–74.

Lakoff, G. and Johnson, M. (1999). *Philosophy in the Flesh*. New York: Basic Books.

Langacker, R. (1987). *Foundations of cognitive grammar, Vol. I: Theoretical prerequisites*. Stanford, CA: Stanford University Press.

——(1991). *Foundations of Cognitive Grammar: Vol. II. Descriptive application*. Stanford, CA: Stanford University Press.

Robinson, P. and Ellis, N. (eds) (2008). *Handbook of Cognitive Linguistics and Second Language Acquisition*. New York: Routledge.

Sweetser, E. (1990). *From Etymology to Pragmatics: Metaphorical and Cultural Aspects of Semantic Structure*. Cambridge: Cambridge University Press.

Talmy, L. (2000a, b). *Toward a Cognitive Semantics: Volume I and II Concept Structuring Systems*. Cambridge, MA: MIT Press.

Tomasello, M. (2003). *Constructing a Language: A Usage-Based Theory of Language Acquisition*. Cambridge, MA: Harvard University Press.

Tyler, A. (2010). Usage-based approaches to language and their applications to second language learning. *Annual Review of Applied Linguistics. 30*, 270–93.

Cohesion and coherence

Ronald Geluykens

University of Oldenburg

The notions of cohesion and coherence are indispensable for defining the concept of "discourse". Whether a chunk of speech or writing is merely a jumble of unconnected clause, or a piece of connected discourse, will depend on the degree to which it is judged to be coherent, which in turn may depend on the use of cohesive devices. This formulation already shows that, despite the fact that the two terms are often used in the same breath (as indeed they are here), they are conceptually quite distinct. Cohesion refers to the ways in which parts of a piece of discourse are linked by the use of formal (i.e. lexical, grammatical, and, in the case of spoken discourse, prosodic) devices. Cohesion, in other words, refers to *observable properties of texts.*

Coherence, on the other hand, is a far less tangible phenomenon. Crystal defines it as "the underlying functional or logical connectedness of a use of language; contrasts with incoherence" (Crystal, 2004: 459); this means that the extent to which discourse is coherent is a matter of *interpretation.* As Sanders and Spooren point out (2007: 918), coherence is a "mental phenomenon" rather than a property of texts: language users attempt to build up a coherent mental representation of a piece of discourse by linking pieces of information and drawing inferences.

Cohesion, then, appears to be the more straightforward notion in terms of linguistic analysis, and it is not surprising that there have been various attempts at classifying cohesive devices within the discourse-analytic literature. One of the most comprehensive of these attempts, the one by Halliday and Hasan (1976), distinguishes between two main types of cohesion. The first of these, *grammatical cohesion*, in turn consists of four subtypes of devices: Reference (e.g. use of anaphoric pronouns, such as "he" in (1a)), Substitution (e.g. "did" substituting for "came in" in (1b)), Ellipsis (e.g. part of the proposition being implicit, as in (1c)) and Conjunction (e.g. use of clausal connectives such as "after" in (1d)):

(1) (a) John came in. He closed the door.
(b) John came in and then Bill did.
(c) John came in but I don't know how.
(d) After John had come in, he closed the door.

Lexical cohesion, the second major type, is "the cohesive effect achieved by the selection of vocabulary" (Halliday and Hasan, 1976: 274), and refers to the way writers may use devices such as repetition of nouns, use of synonyms and exploit certain semantic relationships (such as antonymy or hyperonymy) to create cohesion. Other classifications have been proposed over the years, but it is fair to say that these are all comparable to some degree to Halliday and Hasan's model.

A question which might be raised at this point is whether cohesion and coherence are intrinsically linked. First of all, is the use of cohesive devices a necessary condition for obtaining coherence? Clearly not: in (1a), for example, there is no explicit marking of any temporal link between the two clauses by means of a Conjunction (unlike (1d)). Nevertheless, most language users would interpret this as a temporal sequence of events (i.e. John closed the door after coming in), possibly due to a Gricean implicature based on the Maxim of Manner (Grice, 1975). Conversely, it is entirely possible that a text which is loaded with cohesive devices is still interpreted as incoherent by language users, so cohesion cannot be a sufficient condition for coherence either.

As was already pointed out, *coherence* is not an an intrinsic property of texts, but rather a "comprehension-based, interpretive notion" (Bublitz, 1999: 2). Whether a text is coherent or not ultimately depends on its interpretation by the hearer (or reader, or analyst). This interpretation may (but need not) correspond to the speaker's or writer's intention while producing the text. In other words, coherence is a cognitive process rather than a textual feature. Nevertheless, there have been various attempts at constructing a classification of coherence relations in discourse (e.g. Sanders, 1997).

One such attempt towards a comprehensive descriptive framework is Rhetorical Structure Theory (henceforth RST; see Mann and Thompson, 1988, among others). RST is an attempt to describe the coherence of a text in functional terms, by explicating its underlying relational propositions. These relations can be described in terms of a finite number of nucleus-satellite relationships between textual units (usually clauses). So, for instance, in example (2) (slightly simplified from Mann and Thompson, 1988: 255), units (b) and (c) stand in a Concessive relationship, with (c) at its nucleus. In its turn, the larger chunk formed by (b) and (c) together is Justification for the proposition expressed in (a).

(2) (a) The next music day is scheduled for July 21st.
(b) I'll post more details later,
(c) but this is a good time to reserve the place on your calendar.

This example also nicely demonstrates that an RST analysis tries to go beyond a description of semantic links between adjacent clauses (often in a hypotactic relationship), by working out the potential hierarchy involved in larger text stretches.

A few promising further research domains suggest themselves. First of all, coherence is clearly a key concept not just for discourse interpretation, but also plays an important role in models of (automated) text *generation*. Secondly, much work on cohesion and coherence is based on the analysis of, often written, monologic discourse (RST being a case in point). This raises the question as to how coherence is achieved in *spoken interaction,* and to what degree this differs significantly from written discourse (see also Gernsbacher and Givón:, 1995). Geluykens (1999), for instance, argues that coherence, and in particular the way this is achieved via the flow of topics in a conversation, depends on speaker–hearer collaboration, and needs to be negotiated. A final important issue which needs to be addressed is the *acquisition* of both cohesion and coherence (in L1 as well as in interlanguage). A representative, and continually updated, bibliography of research on coherence, compiled by Wolfram Bublitz (2008), is available online.

See also: discourse processing, discourse and pragmatics in SLA, implicature, pragmalinguistics, systemic-functional linguistics

References

Bublitz, W. (1999). Introduction: Views of coherence. In W. Bublitz, U. Lenk and E. Ventola (eds), *Coherence in Spoken and Written Discourse*. Amsterdam: Benjamins.

——(2008). *A Bibliography of Coherence and Cohesion*. [latest update March 2008] At www.philhist.uni-augsburg.de/lehrstuehle/anglistik/sprachwissenschaft/bibliography

Crystal, D. (2004). *The Cambridge Encyclopedia of Language*. Cambridge: Cambridge University Press.

Geluykens, R. (1999). It take two to cohere: The collaborative dimension of topical coherence in conversation. In W. Bublitz, V. Lenk and E. Ventola (eds), *Coherence in Spoken and Written Discourse*, pp. 35–53. Amsterdam: Banjamins

Gernsbacher, M.A. and T. Givón (eds) (1995). *Coherence in Spontaneous Text*. Amsterdam: Benjamins.

Grice, H.P. (1975). Logic and conversation. In P. Cole and J. Morgan (eds), *Speech Acts* (Syntax and Semantics 3), pp. 41–58. New York: Academic Press.

Halliday, M.A.K. and R. Hasan (1976). *Cohesion in English*. London: Longman.

Mann, W.C. and S.A. Thompson (1988). Rhetorical structure theory: Toward a functional theory of text organisation. *Text*, *8*, 243–81.

Sanders, T. (1997). Semantic and pragmatics sources of coherence: On the categorization of coherence relations in context. *Discourse Processes*, *24*, 119–47.

Sanders, T. and W. Spooren (2007). Discourse and text structure. In D. Geeraerts and H. Cuyckens (eds) *Handbook of Cognitive Linguistics*, pp. 916–41. Oxford: Oxford University Press.

Collostructions

Stefan Th. Gries
University of California, Santa Barbara

Corpus-linguistic methods are now one of the standard tools in many areas of linguistics. Linguists routinely use distributional data to describe and explain linguistic phenomena. However, the discipline is still evolving and (new) tools are constantly developed and refined. One new development involves studying what is sometimes called *colligation*, that is, the co-occurrence of lexical and grammatical elements, or words and patterns/constructions, using methods that were before only applied to *collocation*, that is, the co-occurrence of words. This approach is called *collostructional analysis*, a blend of *collocation* (for co-occurrence) and *construction* (for Construction Grammar, the framework this method has come to be associated with most). Collostructional analysis is a family of methods based on measures of association strength applied to co-occurrence data from corpora, and the following two sections will (i) explain the logic underlying this method and (ii) point to applications relevant to SLA.

The method and its results

Like most measures of association strength in corpus linguistics, collostructional analysis is based on 2×2 tables of observed of (co-)occurrence frequencies such as Table 1.

For the first method, *collexeme analysis* (cf. Stefanowitsch and Gries, 2003), *A* corresponds to a

Table 1 Schematic frequency table of two elements *A* and *B* and their co-occurrence

	B	$\neg B$	*Totals*
A	$nA \& B$	$nA \& \neg B$	nA
$\neg A$	$n\neg A \& B$	$n\neg A \& \neg B$	$n\neg A$
Totals	nB	$n\neg B$	$nA \& B \& \neg A \& \neg B$

construction (e.g., the ditransitive NP V NP1 NP2), $\neg A$ corresponds to all other constructions in the corpus (on the same level of specificity), *B* corresponds to a word (e.g., *give*) occurring in a syntactically defined slot of such constructions, and $\neg B$ corresponds to all other words in that slot. A collexeme analysis requires that such a table be created for all *x* different types of *B* occurring in the relevant slot of Construction *A*. For an example such as a table, the frequency table of *give* and the ditransitive, consider Table 2 (based on data from the British Component of the International Corpus of English).

Each of these *x* tables is then analyzed with one of many possible association measures that have been used in the context of collocational strength. The most widely used measure is the negative log10 of a *p*-value of a Fisher-Yates exact test (other statistics have been used, too). For this table, this test returns a very small *p*-value (< 4.94e-324), indicating that the mutual attraction between *give* and the ditransitive is in fact very strong. When that association measure is computed for each verb type in the ditransitive and the verbs are ranked according to their attraction to the ditransitive, the rank-ordering in (1) emerges:

(1) *give, tell, send, offer, show, cost, teach, award, allow, lend, deny, owe, promise, earn, grant, allocate, wish, accord, pay, hand*

The results not only show that verbs are not distributed randomly across constructions, but also help identifying semantic characteristics of the construction. In this case, the verbs in (1) reflect the ditransitive's meaning of transfer very clearly (since most strongly attracted verbs involve transfer), but they also reflect the other (related) senses this construction has been associated with: (non-) enablement of transfer, communication as transfer, perceiving as receiving, etc.

For the second main method, *distinctive collexeme analysis* (cf. Gries and Stefanowitsch 2004a), the 2×2 table is set up differently: *A* corresponds to a construction (e.g., the ditransitive), $\neg A$ corresponds to another functionally similar construction (e.g., the prepositional dative NP V NP PP*for/to*), *B* corresponds to a word (e.g., *give*) occurring in a syntactically defined slot of that construction and $\neg B$ corresponds to all other words in that slot. While the computation of association measures is as before, the rank-ordering of the words now reflects which word "prefers" to occur with which construction how strongly, that is, subcategorization preferences.

There is now some experimental evidence supporting this approach. For example, Gries *et al.* (2005, 2010) showed that the verbs that, according to a collexeme analysis, are strongly attracted to the *as*-predicative (e.g., *Politicians regard themselves as being closer to actors*) are better predictors of

Table 2 Observed of *give* and the ditransitive in the ICE-GB (with expected frequencies in parentheses)

	Verb: give	*Other verbs*	*Totals*
Construction: ditransitive	461 (9)	574 (1,026)	1,035
Other clause-level constructions	699 (1,151)	136,930 (136,478)	137,629
Totals	1,160	137,504	138,664

subjects' sentence-completion preferences and self-paced reading times than frequencies alone. The above methods of analysis as well as extensions (*multiple distinctive collexeme analysis* to test more than two alternative constructions), additional methods (*covarying collexeme analysis* to test for co-occurrence preferences within one construction) (cf. Gries and Stefanowitsch 2004b), and different association measures can now be computed easily with an interactive R script by the author (cf. http://tinyurl.com/collostructions).

Some applications in SLA

Collostructional studies of these kinds have been applied in numerous contexts: structural/syntactic priming, the study of morphosyntactic alternations, first language acquisition, diachronic constructional change, and more. However, there are now also studies in SLA using these methods. For example, Gries and Wulff (2005) showed that advanced German learners exhibit verb-specific priming effects that are highly correlated with distinctive collexeme strengths of verbs participating in the English "dative alternation." In a similar vein, Gries and Wulff (2009) illustrated that the *to-* versus *ing-* complementation alternation exhibits similar effects: advanced German learners sentence-completion priming was more influenced by the preference of the verb in the sentence fragment than any other variable included in the experimental design. Ellis and Ferreira-Junior (2009) showed how the verbs learners learn first in several argument structure constructions are highly associated with these constructions (using collexeme analysis and a directional measure called ΔP) and are, thus, pathbreaking verbs for the acquisition of constructions. Wulff *et al.* (2009) compared learners' tense-aspect marking patterns in the British National Corpus and the Michigan Corpus of Academic Spoken English; Gilquin (to appear) studies causatives in English; and Wulff and Gries (submitted) show how verb-specific constructional preferences of German and Dutch learners of English correspond to native speakers' preferences and how this approach allows to identify learners' behavioral outliers for subsequent analysis. These applications show that this method has a lot to offer to SLA research, especially to SLA research that involves, or is based on, exemplar-based approaches to language learning, representation, and processing.

See also: cognitive linguistics and SLA, construction learning, corpus analysis, formulaic language, frequency effects, priming

References

Ellis, N.C. and F. Ferreira-Junior. (2009). Constructions and their acquisition: islands and the distinctiveness of their occupancy. *Annual Review of Cognitive Linguistics*, *7*, 187–220.

Gilquin, G. (to appear). The non-finite verb slot in English causative constructions: comparing native and learner collostructions. In J. Leino and R. von Waldenfels (eds), *Analytical Causatives*. München: Lincom Europa.

Gries, S.Th., B. Hampe, and D. Schönefeld. (2005). Converging evidence: bringing together experimental and corpus data on the association of verbs and constructions. *Cognitive Linguistics*, *16*(4), 635–76.

——(2010). Converging evidence II: more on the association of verbs and constructions. In John Newman and Sally Rice (eds), *Empirical and Experimental Methods in Cognitive/Functional Research*, pp. 59–72. Stanford, CA: CSLI.

Gries, S.Th. and A. Stefanowitsch. (2004a). Extending collostructional analysis: a corpus-based perspective on "alternations". *International Journal of Corpus Linguistics*, 9(1). 97–129.

——(2004b). Co-varying collexemes in the *into*-causative. In M. Achard and S. Kemmer (eds), *Language, Culture, and Mind*, pp. 225–36. Stanford, CA: CSLI.

Gries, S.Th. and S. Wulff. (2005). Do foreign language learners also have constructions? Evidence from priming, sorting, and corpora. *Annual Review of Cognitive Linguistics*, *3*, 182–200.

——(2009). Psycholinguistic and corpus linguistic evidence for L2 constructions. *Annual Review of Cognitive Linguistics*, *7*, 163–86.

Stefanowitsch, A. and S.Th. Gries. (2003). Collostructions: investigating the interaction between words and constructions. *International Journal of Corpus Linguistics*, *8*(2), 209–43.

Wulff, S., N.C. Ellis, U. Römer, K. Bardovi-Harlig, and C. LeBlanc. (2009). The acquisition of tense-aspect: converging evidence from corpora, cognition, and learner constructions. *Modern Language Journal*, *93*(3), 354–69.

Wulff, S. and S.Th. Gries (2011). Corpus-driven methods for assessing accuracy in learner production. In P. Robinson (ed.), *Second Language Task Complexity: Researching the Cognition Hypothesis of Language Learning and Performance*, pp. 61–87. Amsterdam: Benjamins.

Communicative competence

Patricia Friedrich
Arizona State University

To investigate the origins and the contributions of the concept of communicative competence to language studies, it is necessary to travel a bit further into the past of linguistic theory, before the concept's inception, and revisit Noam Chomsky's influential notions of competence and performance. According to Chomsky:

> Linguistic Theory is concerned primarily with an ideal speaker-listener, in a completely homogeneous speech community, who knows its language perfectly and is unaffected by such grammatically irrelevant conditions as memory limitations, distractions, shifts of attention and interest, and errors (random or characteristic) in applying his knowledge of the language in actual performance.
>
> (Chomsky, 1965: 3)

As Miller (1975), points out, the historical precedent for Chomsky's theorizing is Saussure's distinction between *langue* and *parole*, or the collective, more abstract norm and the individual, situational realization of language.

For Hymes (1972) social forces are at the center of language studies, and who quotes Chomsky in a 1972 seminal work, finds the latter's characterization of linguistic theory, or the space where that theorizing occurs, restrictive. Hymes also appreciates that the idea of performance is irrevocably connected to imperfection in the context of Chomsky since actual performance can never match abstract knowledge. While Chomsky makes references to "a completely homogeneous speech community," perfect knowledge, and does not focus on context-specific differences of performance by the same listener-speaker, Hymes:

> concludes that a linguistic theory must be able to deal with a heterogeneous speech community, differential competence and the role of sociocultural features. He believes that we should be concerned with performance, which he defines as the actual use of language in a concrete situation, not an idealized speaker-listener situation in a completely homogeneous speech community.
>
> (Ohno, 2006: 26)

That necessity to include forces within and among speech communities as pertinent to the investigation of linguistic theory results in a disambiguation of competence. It can be seen as referring on the one hand to linguistic competence, more and the coding and decoding of strings of language as grammatical or not, and also to communicative competence, or the ability to gauge situational acceptabiliıy and appropriateness of discourse. In that sense, Hymes is interested in the "social meaning of language" and not in the abstract conceptualization of language as it *could be* if forces outside of language were not at play at all times. According to Spolsky (1989), Hymes's framework is a direct result of his application of Jakobson's ideas which he was exposed to in a conference about style (Spolsky, 1989: 138–39), a possibility only afforded by Jakobson's assertion that language could be studied as it changes (i.e. diachronically). Hymes then goes on to write the 1972 article bringing the problem of the social construction of language into light. In Hymes's own words:

> The heart of the argument was that "language" and "culture" could not be successfully related by comparing the end-products of the work of linguists and anthropologists. Each abstracted into a partial hypostatized frame of reference, grammar on the one hand, cultural analyses on the other, from the actual relation between language and culture in living speech.
>
> (Hymes, 1985: 13)

To Hymes, it was necessary to merge the two – grammar and culture – as in living speech they cannot be separated without significant loss in insight. Spolsky also acknowledges that "Communicative competence, as Hymes proposed it, seemed a particularly relevant idea to those interested in second language learning," (p. 139) and, accordingly, Savignon (1972) applies Hymes's idea in that context.

Of her own earlier work, Savignon (1991: 264) writes that she employed the term communicative competence "to characterize the ability of language learners to interact with other speakers, to make meaning, as distinct from their ability to perform on discrete-point tests of grammatical knowledge." She further explains that his "communicative competence may be seen as the equivalent of Halliday's meaning potential. Similarly, his focus was not language learning but language as social behavior." Halliday (1993: 113) actually frames learning vis-à-vis the ability to communicate in context. To him, "learning **is learning to mean,** and to expand one's meaning potential" (emphasis in the original). Therefore, despite both scholars having a view of language as unequivocally connected to social life, as Berns (1990: 31) points out, "for Halliday, it is unnecessary to speak of *communicative competence*; knowing how to use language is the same as knowing what one can do with language" (italics in the original).

It is several years after Hymes's observations that Canale and Swain (1980) establish that "Communicative competence is to be distinguished from communicative performance, which is the realization of these competencies and their interaction in the actual production and comprehension of utterances" (p. 6). They go on to propose that communicative competence be seen as made out of constitutive parts, namely grammatical, sociolinguistic, discourse and strategic competencies or rules governing lexical items, syntax, phonology and the like; rules of use and discourse (coherence and cohesion); and verbal and non-verbal strategies to be used to compensate for insufficient or imperfect knowledge of the other elements. Their framework, like the work of Savignon before them, is particularly concerned with second language acquisition and English Language Teaching (ELT). As Leung points out:

> Communicative competence, in this formulation, represented a considerable broadening of the conceptual base of second language curriculum and pedagogy. The attempt to embrace social, discoursal and interactional dimensions in language teaching was both challenging and stimulating.
>
> (Leung, 2005: 124)

In the case of ELT, the advent of communicative competence as a workable, pedagogically noteworthy model signified a movement away from a purely grammatical emphasis in the language classroom and toward a more situation-focused teaching as indicative of an understanding that knowledge of the structure of the target language alone does not result in effective communication in context. At the same time, such realization complicates and invites new complexity into the realm of second language acquisition. Suddenly, preoccupations with context-specific appropriateness, usefulness of instructional varieties, and the relative unpredictability of individual responses in real situations of communication must be dealt with.

But communicative competence is not important only for language teaching. Overall, sociolinguistic discussions progressed because of it, even in corners where it might have been met with suspicion. Romaine (1994: 30) explains that "The notion of communicative competence in sociolinguistics is intended to replace the dichotomy between competence and performance central to mainstream linguistics," and, in many respects, the way it has been intertwined with notions of appropriateness, speech communities and contextual choices has helped define sociolinguistics as a field on inquiry.

However, over the years, the idea of communicative competence, regardless of its widespread use and perceived usefulness, has also been questioned. One of the most common pieces of criticism relates to the possibility that communicative competence, despite its attempt at capturing facets of language in its social milieu, still upholds native speaker norms as a sort of standard. To some, the idea of communicative competence has replaced Chomsky's ideal (native) speaker-listener with a "real" (native) speaker-listener, and not all are content with that possibility either; after all, as Alptekin (2002: 60) asks, "Who then is the 'real' native speaker-listener typifying accurate and proper language use, if not another abstraction, or an idealization?"

Others are concerned for the possibility that communicative competence becomes an uncritically examined concept in language teaching and an unchanging pillar in communicative teaching methodologies. Kramsch, for example, points out that:

> Not only has communicative competence become reduced to its spoken modality, but it has often been taken as an excuse largely to do away with grammar and to remove much of the instructional responsibility from the teacher who becomes a mere facilitator of group and pair work in conversational activities.
>
> (Kramsch, 2006: 250)

As a result, she calls for an expansion of the concept to include symbolic competence. She argues that a language user (especially in situations of power inequality), "Might need much more subtle semiotic practices that draw on a multiplicity of perceptual clues to make and convey meaning" and claims that "What is at stake is not only the communicative competence of nonnative speakers, but how they are to position themselves in the world, that is, find a place for themselves on the global market of symbolic exchanges."

While one could claim that the strategic level of communicative competence is able to accommodate not only "imperfect knowledge" as a lack of (traditionally viewed) linguistic competence but any compensatory strategies given any number of possible non-commonalities among speakers, it is clear that current questionings of the role of society in linguistic models increasingly focus on issues of power, negotiation of meaning in context, and the questioning of the native speaker of English (or any language) as a model of language production. With the political nature of linguistic exchanges more and more in the forefront of language study concerns, the years ahead will certainly bring fascinating discussions and reformulations of the paradigm-shifting concept of communicative competence.

See also: cross-linguistic influence, functional-typological linguistics, generative linguistics, second language socialization, grammatical encoding, social and sociocultural influences on SLA

References

Alptekin, C. (2002). Toward intercultural communicative competence in ELT. *ELT Journal, 56* (1), 57–64.

Berns, M. (1990). *Contexts of Competence: Social and Cultural Considerations in Communicative Language Teaching*. New York: Plenum.

Canale, M. and Swain, M. (1980). Theoretical bases of communicative approaches to second language teaching and testing. *Applied Linguistics, 1*(1), 1–47.

Chomsky (1965). *Aspects of the Theory of Syntax*. Cambridge, MA: MIT Press.

Halliday, M.A.K. (1993). Towards a language-based theory of learning. *Linguistics and Education, 5*, 93–116.

Hymes, D. (1972). On communicative competence. In J.B. Pride and J. Holmes (eds), *Sociolinguistics*. Harmondsworth: Penguin Books.

——(1985). Toward linguistic competence. *Revue de l'AILA: AILA Review, 2*, 9–23.

Kramsch, C. (2006). From communicative competence to symbolic competence. *Modern Language Journal, 90*(2), 249–52.

Leung, C. (2005). Convivial communication: recontextualizing communicative competence. *International Journal of Applied Linguistics, 15* (2), 119–44.

Miller, G.A. (1975). Some comments on competence and performance. In D. Aaronson and R. W. Rieber (eds), *Developmental Psycholinguistics and Communication Disorders*. New York: New York Academy of Sciences.

Ohno, A. (2006). Communicative competence and communicative language teaching. Internal publication of the Bunkyo Gakuin University. Tokyo, Japan.

Romaine (1994). *Language in Society: An Introduction to Sociolinguistics*. Oxford: Oxford University Press.

Savignon, S. (1972). *Communicative Competence: An Experiment in Foreign-language Teaching*. Philadelphia, PA: Center for Curriculum Development.

——(1991). Communicative Language Teaching: state of the art. *TESOL Quarterly*, *25*(2), 261–77.

Spolsky (1989). Communicative Competence, Language Proficiency and Beyond. *Applied Linguistics*, *10* (2), 138–56.

Community of Practice

John Hellermann
Portland State University

Community of Practice is a learning theory developed by social and cognitive anthropologists who were interested in the complex interactions of context of situation, activity, and expertise during informal learning settings. The term Community of Practice (hereafter, CoP) was coined by Lave and Wenger (1991) in their outline of learning in apprenticeship situations of (among others) tailors, recovering alcoholics, and midwives. CoP theory highlights the importance of heterogeneous knowledge levels and negotiation for learning through practice. Rather than focusing on an individual learner or even a teacher-learner dyad, CoP investigates the setting, participants, and their activity as an organization.

Learning and participation are considered mutually constitutive and occur because of the nature of a group and the activities of the group. The community facilitates learning in practice while the learning of members of the community constructs and shapes the community.

In CoP theory, learning is practice-oriented and socially-situated. The theory views cognition as inseparable from practice. The CoP is not simply a physical location but rather a group of individuals, heterogeneous with respect to expertise, who come together to accomplish goal-oriented tasks such as language learning. The social practice aspect of the CoP is inseparable from the cognitive learning aspect. Although the theory was developed to explain learning in informal settings, outside of school contexts, it suggests that even learning abstract, decontextualized conceptual knowledge in formal settings is often mediated by social practice in a CoP. Key constructs in the theory are *mutual engagement, joint enterprise, shared repertoire, reification and participation* (Wenger, 1998)*, and legitimate peripheral participation* (Lave and Wenger, 1991).

Mutual engagement

The CoP is characterized as an inherently cooperative enterprise in which members share a commitment to one another and the community of which they are members. This cooperative orientation allows for the development of local understanding of the roles of the members and their levels of participation in the CoP. This local understanding and co-constructed shared history is important for the maintenance of the CoP when the levels of participation of different members in the CoP change. Examples of mutual engagement in a CoP are students who must cooperate in tasks in a language-learning classroom (Hellermann, 2008) or the novice writer and journal editor working toward publication of a peer-reviewed journal article (Flowerdew, 2000).

Joint enterprise

The CoP is made up of a collection of individuals who share some of the same goals and motivations for participating in the CoP. Those motivations may be to learn, to produce a product, or to earn money. However, because the community is a collection of individuals, the goals of the CoP as a whole are continually negotiated. In classrooms, we see the differing goals when participants with different language proficiencies and language-learning needs (due to heterogeneous language proficiency levels) negotiate interactions explicitly designed for learning (tasks). These may be the interaction of teachers and students or students in small-group projects.

Shared repertoire

This third construct is particularly relevant for investigations of language learning. Wenger's conceptualization of a shared repertoire is broad and includes "routines, words, tools, ways of doing things, stories, gestures, symbols, genres, actions, or concepts" (1998: 83). Given the nature of the history and relationships of the members in a CoP, a repertoire of practices both sustains and grows out of the mutual engagement and joint enterprise of the CoP. Language practices that develop for particular situations are examples: the use of a *lingua franca* (Brower and Wagner, 2004), responding to teacher requests (Toohey, 2000).

Reification and participation

This dialectic highlights the need for CoP members to use static, established forms while simultaneously co-creating new ways of using language for the contingencies that arise when using language for social practices. Members in a newly developed CoP that lacks a shared history may find that they lack established forms for meaning making while the interactions of members in a CoP with a long shared history may be ritualistic and lack an impetus for participation and change.

Interactions between language learning students are an example of how this dialectic plays out. A school's curriculum, an academic journal's genre and style requirements illustrate the reified aspect of a CoP. In a classroom, students must use established language and interactional forms provided by texts and instructors so that they can participate in the use of the language in language learning tasks. Language learners in a CoP, whether speakers or writers, must negotiate their participation in a CoP through the dialectic of reified language structure used for participating in interactions using language.

Change in participation: "peripheral" but "legitimate" members

The key construct in CoP is *legitimate peripheral participation* and the conceptualization of learning as the movement from legitimate peripheral participation toward full participation in a CoP. The theory considers that all collections of individuals (communities) are, by nature, heterogeneous with respect to competencies. In such groups, members with less competencies (novices) are not passive recipients of knowledge but active, legitimate participants (though peripheral) in the work of the CoP. In language learning research, this has been illustrated by tracing learners' level of participation in particular language practices in classroom tasks (Hellermann, 2008).

Studies of language learning using CoP

Previous language learning research using CoP theory has focused on both in classroom (Toohey, 2000; Leki, 2001; Morita, 2004; Hellermann, 2008) and out of classroom contexts (Flowerdew, 2000; Brouwer and Wagner, 2004). Some are ethnographic in design capturing the social practices of the community as they are embedded in cultural and historical trajectories. Others are focused on the micro-level language practices that are constitutive of the CoP. Critical perspectives on the use of CoP for research on language learning can be found in Canagarajah (2003) and Haneda (2006).

See also: activity theory and SLA, communicative competence, discourse and pragmatics in SLA, ethnographic research, qualitative research, social and sociocultural approaches to SLA

References

Brower, C. and Wagner, J. (2004). Developmental issues in second language conversations. *Journal of Applied Linguistics, 1*, 1, 29–47.

Canagarajah, A.S. (2003). A somewhat legitimate and very peripheral participation. In C. Casanave and S. Vandrick (eds), *Writing for scholarly Publication*. Mahwah, NJ: Lawrence Erlbaum.

Flowerdew, J. (2000). Legitimate peripheral participation, and the nonnative-English-speaking scholar. *TESOL Quarterly, 34*, 1, 127–50.

Haneda, M. (2006). Classrooms as communities of practice: a reevaluation. *TESOL Quarterly*, *40*, 4, 807–17.

Hellermann, J. (2008), *Social Actions for Classroom Language Learning*. Clevedon: Multilingual Matters.

Lave, J. and Wenger, E. (1991). *Situated Learning: Legitimate Peripheral Participation*. Cambridge: Cambridge University Press.

Leki, I. (2001). "A narrow thinking system": nonnative English-speaking students in group projects across the curriculum. *TESOL Quarterly, 35*, 1, 39–67.

Morita, N. (2004). Negotiating participation and identity in second language academic communities. *TESOL Quarterly*, *38*, 4, 573–603.

Toohey, K. (2000). *Learning English at School: Identity, Social Relations, and Classroom Practices*. Clevedon: Multilingual Matters.

Wenger, E. (1998). *Communities of Practice: Learning, Meaning, and Identity*. Cambridge: Cambridge University Press.

Competition Model (CM)

Brain MacWhinney
Carnegie Mellon University

The Competition Model provides an account of language learning and processing that is compatible with recent developments in usage-based linguistics (Bybee, 2010), emergentist development psychology (MacWhinney, 1999), and constraint satisfaction psycholinguistics (MacDonald *et al.*, 1994). The first statement of the model was provided in (Bates and MacWhinney, 1982). The most recent version, called the Unified Competition Model, is found in MacWhinney (2012). The newer model adds the term "unified" to express the idea that L1 and L2 learning relies on a single underlying set of language learning mechanisms. In this sense, the Unified Competition Model can be contrasted with accounts such as the Fundamental Difference Hypothesis (Bley-Vroman, 1989) that emphasize the differences between L1 and L2 learning.

Before discussing the Unified Model, it is good to review the basic concepts of cues, cue strength, cue validity, and competition from the original Competition Model.

Cues

The Competition Model views sentence comprehension as the decoding of linguistic cues. It views sentence production as the compilation of messages that contain these cues. Cues are associations between forms and meanings in which the form is the cue to the selection of the meaning or interpretation. For example, the suffix -t at the end of a Hungarian noun is a strong and reliable cue to the fact that the preceding noun is the direct object and that it plays the thematic role of the patient. Most of the experimental work in the Competition Model has focused on the use of cues for marking thematic roles such as agent, patient, or recipient. However, the model also deals with cues for choosing lexical items to name actions, cues for interpreting coreference, cues for syntactic attachment, and cues for marking pragmatic contrasts. Work on the interpretation of cues for thematic roles has typically relied on sentences with transitive verbs. For example, in the sentence *the boys chase the ball,* the two nouns (*boys* and *ball*) are possible candidates for the role of the agent or subject of the verb. However, the candidacy of boys for this role is favored by three strong cues – preverbal positioning, subject-verb agreement, and animacy. None of these cues favors the candidacy of *ball*. Therefore, we assume that *the boys* are the agents. However, in ungrammatical sentences such as *the ball are chasing the boys*, the competition between the noun phrases becomes tighter. In this sentence, the strong cue of preverbal positioning favors *the ball* as agent. However, the cues of subject–verb agreement and animacy favor *the boys* as the agents. Given this sentence, listeners are often quite unsure which of the two noun phrases to choose as agent, since neither choice is perfect. As a result, listeners, as a group, are slower to make this choice and their choices are nearly evenly split between the two possibilities.

Competition Model experiments use sentences in which cues have been randomly combined to measure the strength of the underlying cues. The same method has been used for experiments in 45 empirical studies involving 18 different languages. Across these various experiments and languages, the cues involved come from a very small set of linguistic devices. There are basically five possible cue types: word order, case marking, agreement, intonation, and verb-based expectations. For simple transitive sentences, the possible word orders are NNV, NVN, and VNN. Case marking can be achieved by affixes on the noun (as in Hungarian or Turkish), postpositions (as in Japanese), prepositions (as in Spanish), or articles (as in German). Agreement marking displays correspondences between the subject and the verb (as in English) or the object and the verb (as in Hungarian and Arabic). Agreement features include number (as in English), definiteness (as in Hungarian), gender (as in Arabic), honorific status (as in Japanese) and other grammatical features in other languages. Intonation is seldom a powerful cue in thematic role identification, although we have seen that it plays a role in some non-canonical word order patterns in Italian and in the topic marking construction in Hungarian. Verb-based expectations vary markedly across verb types. High activity transitive verbs like *push* and *hit* tend to serve as cues for animate agents and inanimate patients. Stimulus-experiencer verbs like *amaze* and *surprise* cue animate patients and either animate or inanimate agents.

Cue strength

The Competition Model holds that, during comprehension, interpretations compete with each other, as in the example sentences given above. During production, cues compete with each other as ways of marking functions. Although cues are used in both processes, it is easier to control the shape of comprehension experiments. As a result, most Competition Model work looks at comprehension, although there are also several studies of production. In comprehension experiments, the various cues are placed into systematic conflict with one another using orthogonalized analysis of variance designs. The major goal of these studies is to determine the relative strength of each of the competing cues, when they are placed into competition. This strength can be expressed in terms of statistics such as significance levels, percentage variance accounted for, or numerical strength as measured through maximum likelihood estimation (MLE).

Cue validity: Availability and reliability

The core theoretical claim of the Competition Model is that cue strength is determined by cue validity. Cue strength is defined through experimental results; cue validity is defined through corpus counts. Using conversational input data such as those available from the CHILDES (http://childes.psy.cmu.edu) or TalkBank (http://talkbank.org) corpora, we can define *cue reliability* as the proportion of times the cue is correct over the total number of occurrences of the cue. Cue *availability* is the proportion of times the cue is available over the times it is needed. The product of cue reliability and cue availability is overall *cue validity*. Early in both L1 and L2 learning, cue strength is heavily determined by availability, because beginning learners are only familiar with cues that are moderately frequent in the language input (Matessa and Anderson, 2000; Taraban and Palacios, 1993). As learning progresses, cue reliability becomes more important than cue availability. In adult native speakers, cue strength depends entirely on cue reliability. In some cases, we can further distinguish the effects of *conflict reliability*. When two highly reliable cues conflict, we say that the one that wins is higher in conflict reliability. For example, in the case of Dutch pronouns, only after age 8 do L1 learners begin to realize that the more reliable cue of pronoun case should dominate over the more frequent, but usually reliable, cue of word order (McDonald, 1986).

Cue cost

When adult native speakers are given sufficient time to make a careful decision, cue strength is nearly perfectly predicted by cue reliability. However, when cue strength is measured online during the actual process of comprehension, before the sentence is complete, other factors come into play.

During online processing, listeners tend to rely initially on a single cue with good reliability and high availability without integrating the effects of that core cue with other possible cues. This happens, for example, during online processing of sentences in Russian (Kempe and MacWhinney, 1999). Cue strength is also heavily influenced during the early phases of learning by the factors of *cue cost* and *cue detectability*. Cue cost factors arise primarily during the processing of agreement markers, because these markers cannot be used to assign thematic roles directly. For example, in an Italian sentence such as *il gatto spingono i cani* (the cat push the dogs), the listener may begin by thinking that *il gatto* is the agent because it occurs in preverbal position. However, because the verb *spingono* requires a plural subject, it triggers a search for a plural noun. The first noun cannot satisfy this requirement and the processor must then hope that a plural noun will eventually follow. In this example, the plural noun comes right away, but in many cases it may come much later in the sentence. This additional waiting and matching requires far more processing than that involved with simple word order or case marking cues. As a result of this additional cost for the agreement cue, Italian children are slow to pick it up, despite its high reliability in the language (Bates *et al.*, 1982).

Cue detectability

Cue detectability issues arise primarily during the very earliest stages of learning of declensional and conjugational patterns. For example, although the marking of the accusative case by a suffix on the noun is a fully reliable cue in both Hungarian and Turkish, 3-year-old Hungarian children show a delay of about 10 months in acquiring this cue, when compared to young Turkish children. The source of this delay seems to be the greater complexity of the Hungarian declensional pattern and the more difficult detectability of the Hungarian suffix. However, once Hungarian children have "cracked the code" of accusative marking, they rely nearly exclusively on this cue. Because of its greater reliability, the strength of the Hungarian case-marking cue eventually comes to surpass the strength of the Turkish cue.

The Unified Model

The Unified Competition Model preserves the concepts and methods of the original model, but supplements the model with additional features that impact the core competition. The additional components of the model include specific auxiliary theories for these dimensions: maps, chunking, transfer, resonance, connectivity, codes, and mental models. The articulation of each of these additional components relies on additional traditions of research. The account of lexical and grammatical maps is based on work on the DevLex model of self-organizing lexical learning (Li *et al.*, 2007), as well as evidence from this work regarding the processes of *entrenchment* in neural networks. The account for chunking derives from the theory of item-based learning (MacWhinney, 1975, 1982). The model of connectivity derives from recent work in neuroimaging (Friederici, 2009). The role assigned to codes and social participation comes from studies of the social bases of learning (Firth and Wagner, 1998); and the role of mental models comes from recent work in cognitive linguistics (MacWhinney, 2008).

The Unified Model addresses the issue of the similarities between L1 and L2 learning by emphasizing the extent to which second language learners must deal with the risk factors of entrenchment, negative transfer, mismatched connectivity, and social isolation. It also shows how learners can make use of preventive factors to overcome these risks. The preventive factors include reorganization through resonance, positive transfer, social participation, and active thinking in the second language. The interaction between these risk factors and preventive factors is reviewed in recent accounts of the model (MacWhinney, in press).

See also: automaticity, chunking and prefabrication, conceptual transfer, frequency effects, linguistic transfer, emergentism

References

Bates, E. and MacWhinney, B. (1982). Functionalist approaches to grammar. In E. Wanner and

L. Gleitman (eds), *Language Acquisition: The State of the Art*, pp. 173–218. New York: Cambridge University Press.

Bates, E., McNew, S., MacWhinney, B., Devescovi, A. and Smith, S. (1982). Functional constraints on sentence processing: A cross-linguistic study. *Cognition, 11*, 245–299.

Bley-Vroman, R. (1989). What is the logical problem of foreign language learning? In S. Gass and J. Schachter (eds), *Linguistic Perspectives on Second Language Acquisition*. Cambridge: Cambridge University Press.

Bybee, J. (2010). *Language, Usage, and Cognition*. New York: Cambridge University Press.

Firth, A. and Wagner, J. (1998). SLA territory: No trespassing! *Modern Language Journal, 72*, 8–22.

Friederici, A. (2009). *Brain Circuits of Syntax: From Neurotheoretical Considerations to Empirical Tests. Biological Foundations and Origin of Syntax*. Cambridge, MA: MIT Press.

Kempe, V. and MacWhinney, B. (1999). Processing of morphological and semantic cues in Russian and German. *Language and Cognitive Processes, 14*, 129–171.

Li, P., Zhao, X. and MacWhinney, B. (2007). Dynamic self-organization and early lexical development in children. *Cognitive Science, 31*, 581–612.

MacDonald, M.C., Pearlmutter, N.J. and Seidenberg, M.S. (1994). Lexical nature of syntactic ambiguity resolution. *Psychological Review, 101*(4), 676–703.

MacWhinney, B. (1975). Pragmatic patterns in child syntax. *Stanford Papers And Reports on Child Language Development, 10*, 153–165.

——(1982). Basic syntactic processes. In S. Kuczaj (ed.), Language acquisition: Vol. 1. *Syntax and semantics*, pp. 73–136. Hillsdale, NJ: Lawrence Erlbaum.

——(2008). How mental models encode embodied linguistic perspectives. In R. Klatzky, B. MacWhinney and M. Behrmann (eds), *Embodiment, Ego-space, and Action*, pp. 369–410. Mahwah, NJ: Lawrence Erlbaum.

——(in press). The logic of the Unified Model. In S. Gass and A. Mackey (eds), *Handbook of Second Language Acquisition*. New York: Routledge.

MacWhinney, B. (ed.). (1999). *The Emergence of Language*. Mahwah, NJ: Lawrence Erlbaum Associates.

Matessa, M. and Anderson, J. (2000). Modeling focused learning in role assignment. *Language and Cognitive Processes, 15*, 263–292.

McDonald, J.L. (1986). The development of sentence comprehension strategies in English and Dutch. *Journal of Experimental Child Psychology, 41*, 317–335.

Taraban, R. and Palacios, J.M. (1993). Exemplar models and weighted cue models in category learning. In G. Nakamura, R. Taraban and D. Medin (eds). *Categorization by Humans and Machines*. San Diego, CA: Academic Press.

Complexity Theory/Dynamic Systems Theory

Diane Larsen-Freeman
University of Michigan

Complexity Theory (CT) and Dynamic Systems Theory (DST) originated in the disciplines of the natural sciences and mathematics, respectively. Despite their different origins, underlying both theories are common theoretical understandings to account for the behavior of complex, nonlinear, dynamic systems. As general approaches, rather than single theories (van Geert, 2003), they have been widely applied to model change in the evolution of animal species, in the rise and fall of the stock market, in the spread of diseases, and so forth. Its explanation for the development of language is the focus of this entry.

One of CT/DST's basic premises is that real-time language processing, language development, and language change can be characterized by the same dynamic process. The process operates across different nested levels of complexity and at different timescales: from the milliseconds of neural activity in one individual's brain to the diffusion of linguistic features over months and years across a speech community, to the evolution of the same language by generations of speakers over millennia. It is in using the language that it evolves, is transformed, and is developed. The act of playing the game has a way of changing the rules, as Gleick (1987) put it. Thus, "language development is no longer seen as a process of acquiring abstract rules, but as the *emergence* of language abilities in *real time*" (Evans, 2007: 128) through the use of the language.

CT/DST holds that it when speakers "soft assemble" (Thelen and Smith, 1994) their language resources that the resources change. Speakers construct "successive make-do solutions" to make meaning under the pressures of communication in real time, given their abilities, goals, and history at the time. In their make-do solutions, speakers iteratively adapt their language resources to a changing environment so that the solutions that emerge are tailored to the idiosyncracies of the context. When they adapt their resources through interaction with others, it is said to be co-adaptation (Larsen-Freeman and Cameron 2008), the language resources of each participant adapting to the other. As new forms emerge through adaptation and co-adaptation, they self-organize into coherent patterns without the need for an external executive or an innate faculty to direct the patterning. Language is a complex adaptive system (Ellis and Larsen-Freeman, 2009; Kretzschmar, 2009).

Preferred patterns become stable with frequent use. It is important to note, however, that even stable patterns are subject to change. In fact, stable patterns must become unstable for development to continue because it is the instability that allows for the components of the system to reorganize in new ways. "Development can be envisioned, then, as a series of evolving and dissolving patterns of varying dynamic stability, rather than an inevitable march towards maturity" (Smith and Thelen, 2003: 344). As Larsen-Freeman has put it "there is no end, and there is no state" in language development (2006a: 189).

While language development may look like a discrete stage-like progression toward more complex language forms, it is often characterized by progress and regress from a target-language perspective. This is best seen at the level of the individual because when developmental data are averaged across learners, variability among them is obscured, and the averages may represent none of them. What often results from averaging is a picture of linear development, when, in fact, individuals' paths are nonlinear, each unique (Larsen-Freeman 2006b).

Thus, development does not always lead to more target-like language. Growth and decline are normal phenomena in developing systems (Herdina and Jessner, 2002); both are developmental, but the direction of change depends on the availability of internal resources, such as memory, attention, motivation, and of external resources, such as the opportunity for interaction and the degree of co-adaptation that takes place between interlocutors which facilitates the learner's participation in interactions. Development is a sociocognitive process.

Variability is intrinsic in complex, dynamic systems. Variability gives a system degeneracy, increasing its complexity and robustness against perturbations (Mason, 2010). In addition, variability in a language system gives speakers choices among forms to use to create meaning and to express themselves pragmatically as they intend. It also enhances speakers' ability to adapt to new situations. Further, performance "variability in the developmental process is not simply 'noise' in the system but instead provides valuable insights into the nature of language development and may in fact be the actual mechanism of change in development … " (Evans, 2007: 132).

Because the development of complex, dynamic systems is highly dependent on their initial conditions, even small differences in developmental histories can amplify and lead to large individual differences. The present level of development depends critically on the previous level of development. Thus, "the same learning operation may lead to very different outcomes in the long run, depending on the starting point and the learning rate. So a similar 'learning' procedure, rather than having a homogenizing effect, could actually lead to highly diverging patterns of development" (de Bot *et al.*, 2007: 13–14).

When it comes to second language research on individual differences, the normal practice has been to look for simple linear correlations between a non-linguistic variable and language proficiency at one point in time. From a CT/DST perspective, this practice can lead to misleading inferences. Such correlations may be significant but spurious, for two reasons. One is that statistical significance can result from averaging the behavior of individual learners. Second, the correlations may be misleading because as the system progresses, the contributions of the variables shifts. So, for example, while language aptitude might be important initially, its importance may diminish later. Furthermore, since a complex system interacts with the environment, language aptitude may only be important in the context of formal instruction – but less so in immersion outside the classroom.

From a CT/DST perspective, then, it is important to understand the processes by which the everyday activities of learners create developmental change – both the common attainments and the individual pathways. CT/DST emphasizes the importance of interaction in real time, where the intrinsic dynamics of the system and its interaction with the environment lead to new order, amidst the inherent variability of a dynamic system.

See also: connectionism, construction learning, development in SLA, emergentism, psycholinguistics of SLA, sociocognitive approaches to SLA, theoretical constructs in SLA

References

de Bot, K., Lowie W. and Verspoor, M. (2007). A Dynamic systems approach to second language acquisition. *Bilingualism: Language and Cognition*, *10*, 7–21.

Ellis, N.C. and Larsen-Freeman, D. (eds) (2009). *Language as a Complex Adaptive System*. Malden, MA: Wiley-Blackwell.

Evans, J. (2007). The emergence of language: A dynamical systems account. In E. Hoff and M. Shatz (eds), *Handbook of Language Development*. Malden, MA: Blackwell.

Gleick, J. (1987). *Chaos: Making a New Science*. New York: Penguin Books.

Herdina, P. and Jessner, U. (2002) *A Dynamic Model of Multilingualism*. Clevedon: Multilingual Matters.

Kretzschmar, W. (2009). *The Linguistics of Speech*. Cambridge: Cambridge University Press.

Larsen-Freeman, D. (2006a). Second language acquisition and fossilization: There is no end, and there is no state. In Z.-H. Han and T. Odlin (eds), *Studies of Fossilization in Second Language Acquisition*. Clevedon: Multilingual Matters.

——(2006b). The emergence of complexity, fluency, and accuracy in the oral and written production of five Chinese learners of English. *Applied Linguistics*, *27*, 590–619.

—— and Cameron, L. (2008). *Complex Systems and Applied Linguistics*. Oxford: Oxford University Press.

Mason, P. (2010). Degeneracy at multiple levels of complexity. *Biological Theory*, *5*, 277–88.

Smith, L. and Thelen, E. (2003). Development as a dynamic system. *TRENDS in Cognitive Sciences*, *7*, 343–48.

Thelen, E. and Smith, L. (1994). *A Dynamic Systems Approach to the Development of Cognition and Action*. Cambridge, MA: The MIT Press.

van Geert, P. (2003). Dynamic systems approaches and modeling of developmental processes. In J. Valsiner and K. Connolly (eds), *Handbook of Developmental Psychology*. London: Sage.

Further reading

de Bot, K. (2008). Introduction: Second language development. *Modern Language Journal*, *92*, 166–78. (A special issue of the *Modern Language Journal* devoted to DST.)

Dörnyei, Z. (2009). *The Psychology of Second Language Acquisition*. Oxford: Oxford University Press. (Discusses individual differences from a dynamic perspective.)

Ellis, N.C. and Larsen-Freeman, D. (2006). Language emergence: Implications for applied linguistics—Introduction to the Special Issue. *Applied Linguistics*, *27*, 558–89. (Applies insights from CT/DST to a variety of phenomena of concern to applied linguists.)

van Geert, P. (1994). *Dynamic Systems of Development: Change between Complexity and Chaos*. London: Harvester Wheatsheaf. (One of the first works to apply DST to development.)

Verspoor, M., de Bot, K. and Lowie, W. (2011). *A Dynamic Approach to Second Language Development*. Amsterdam and Philadelphia,

PA: John Benjamins. (Offers research methods and techniques from a CT/DST perspective.)

Computer Assisted Language Learning (CALL)

Christina Gitsaki
University of Queensland

Computer Assisted Language Learning (CALL) is a specialized field in applied linguistics concerned with the use of technology in language teaching and learning. CALL covers a diverse area of study not only in terms of the range of technologies and software available for language learning, but also in terms of the principles and theories underlying CALL design, research and practice.

In its early days, about half a century ago, CALL was synonymous with drill-and-practice-oriented software framed around behaviorism and the audiolingual approach to language teaching. With the widespread availability and accessibility of computers and multimedia and the advent of the Internet at the end of the last century, CALL diversified, expanded and evolved. Today, CALL encompasses not only the use of specialized and sophisticated English Language Teaching (ELT) multimedia software, but also a vast array of web resources (ELT and authentic websites), Web 2.0 tools and social networking software (blogs, wikis, chat, podcasts, twitter, virtual learning environments (VLE), audio/video conferencing, etc.), learning management systems (LMS) and instructional tools (BlackBoard, Moodle, Interactive Whiteboards), and mobile technologies (laptops, iPads, smart phones), that are utilized in various degrees both inside and outside of the classroom for language teaching and learning purposes. This diverse application of CALL has given rise to a number of terms used to refer to the utilization of technological tools in the language classroom, such as:

NBLT – Network-Based Language Teaching
CMC – Computer Mediated Communication
WELL – Web-Enhanced Language Learning
MALL – Mobile Assisted Language Learning
ICALL – Intelligent Computer Assisted Language Learning
CALT – Computer Assisted Language Testing
eLearning – Learning with Technology

Despite the wide range of CALL applications and the equally wide list of acronyms in the field, 'CALL' remains the umbrella term for the use of technology in language teaching and research.

CALL and Language Learning

Early on, CALL was seen as a distinct and largely subordinate area of ELT, with books on second language acquisition and pedagogy devoting little, if any, space on the use of technology for language teaching and learning (see Chapelle, 2003: 128). Today with several publications devoted exclusively to CALL (including four major international CALL journals: *CALICO, Computer-Assisted Language Learning*, *ReCALL* and *Language Learning and Technology*), CALL is a well-established field with an extensive research agenda and diverse practice applications across all areas of second language acquisition (SLA).

Practice is at the heart of CALL and computers have been utilized in all areas of language teaching largely due to their technological affordances and their ability to motivate and engage learners. Computers are considered particularly useful for the teaching of grammar, vocabulary, reading and writing, listening and pronunciation, and they have been widely utilized in language assessment. In reading, CALL provides access to authentic materials through the Internet rich with multimedia annotations (such as visual and audio input, hyperlinked glosses) that can enhance both language development and cultural understanding. For writing practice, learners can access advanced writing tools (such as a word processor) that make text editing easy, while through CMC and social networking software (e.g. blogs and wikis) they can practice asynchronous text production that can enhance the development of their writing skills. Practicing speaking through computers is largely taking place through synchronous audio/video-conferencing with other learners or native speakers. Computer-learner open interaction is an area that is still developing as Natural Language Processing (NLP), Automatic Speech Recognition (ASR) and Intelligent Language Tutoring Systems (ILTS) are becoming more sophisticated and closer to being able to parse learner spoken input for errors and provide individualized feedback (see Heift and Schulze, 2007). Still, certain aspects of speaking, such as pronunciation, accent and intonation, can be practiced through software applications that provide instruction and graphic annotations to help learners compare their output to the target output and identify specific areas of difficulty (see Neri *et al.*, 2008). Listening is also a skill that has benefited by the latest developments in technology. The ability to digitize audio files has resulted in a vast array of audio resources (such as podcasts) that offer learners endless opportunities to practice listening and become aware of different varieties of English spoken around the world. In grammar, the most popular usage of computers is through drill-based grammar tutorial exercises (much like the early applications of CALL) that provide instant feedback allowing the learner to repeat drills, select grammar topics and keep practicing according to their needs. Similarly, vocabulary can be practiced through software specifically designed to teach vocabulary, through reading text with glosses, or even looking up vocabulary items in online corpora. Hyperlinks allow instant access to word definitions, pronunciations, translations and audiovisual input that can enhance vocabulary acquisition (see Xu, 2010). Concordancing and the use of corpora have also been applied in CALL as they allow learners to view target expressions and vocabulary used in naturalistic contexts that can lead to a better understanding of these expressions and how they are used in different linguistic contexts (see Chambers, 2005; Chang and Sun, 2009). Finally, computers are increasingly used for language assessment due to their practicality, speed and efficiency (see Chapelle and Douglas, 2006; Dooey, 2008). As newer technologies emerge, practitioners constantly reassess the capabilities of the new technological tools and consider how to best apply them in the classroom.

At times CALL enthusiasts have been criticized for being too techno-centric, eager to use the latest technological tools and all the bells and whistles that come with them, overlooking vital aspects of pedagogy and task design principles that are necessary for language acquisition to occur. While CALL undoubtedly has the potential to immerse learners to authentic and up-to-date target language input, exposure by itself is not enough for the development of language skills (for a discussion see Skehan, 2003). The effectiveness of CALL tasks for language development is largely dependent upon the pedagogical and language acquisition principles guiding their design (see Chapelle, 2003). This is especially crucial when web-based authentic language resources are used with second language learners. The web can be overwhelming for learners, it has no structure and no underlying pedagogical framework or syllabus. Therefore, the onus is on the teacher to adequately prepare and support the learners for language tasks that involve authentic web resources.

Throughout its 50-year history, CALL practitioners and researchers have utilized a number of different learning theories to guide the design and use of computer-based tasks. For example, the interactionist theory has been largely used as a theoretical basis for CMC tasks (see Peterson, 2009), and sociocultural theory has been applied on collaborative CALL tasks to draw focus on learning in social groups (see Gnem-Gutirrez, 2009). Constructivism has also been used to support the use of collaborative learning tools and the design of activities that emphasize the centrality of the learner in the learning process and involve learners in investigation, discovery and discussion. While activity theory has been used to examine the integration of technology in curricula and schools and the systemic changes that result from technology use and integration, Focus-on-Form principles have been used to provide a principled basis for the design and teaching of individual CALL tasks (see Yilmaz and Granena, 2010). Such theories provide a methodological framework that, in terms of practice, guides the selection of technologies to be used in the classroom, the task design and the role of the teacher and the learners, while in terms of research, it dictates the use of specific research tools and methods, and justifies second language learning outcomes.

CALL research

Much of the early research in the field of CALL lacks an underlying conceptual framework making CALL research results difficult to generalize and compare across studies. More recently CALL research studies have been firmly grounded on one or multiple theoretical perspectives, making research results easier to interpret, justify and integrate with mainstream SLA research.

The design of CALL materials has been a central issue in CALL research especially since the widespread availability of user-friendly authoring software and the use of the web by teachers and learners as a publishing tool. Levy and Stockwell (2006) classified CALL research into two major categories: survey studies and comparative studies. Survey studies are primarily concerned with learner attitudes and perceptions towards the use of technology for learning. Studies in this category are pre-occupied with showcasing how a new software or technological tool was used for teaching language and measuring its effect on student motivation and engagement through survey-type instruments (see for example, Taylor and Gitsaki, 2003). The overwhelming majority of these studies show a positive influence of technology on students' attitudes and engagement, but they do not address adequately the issue of "novelty effects", that is, learners who are surveyed immediately after using a new application tend to react favourably to it because it is new and different to their regular classroom routine (see Levy and Stockwell, 2006: 159), or the psychometric validation of the survey instrument (see Vandewaetere and Desmet, 2009). Comparative studies can be broad-based, comparing CALL to non-CALL contexts (see Alabbad *et al.*, 2010), or narrowly focused, comparing the effectiveness of specific software design features for language learning (see Al-Shehri and Gitsaki, 2010). Broad-based comparative studies have been criticized for making "broad-brush" comparisons between technology-based and face-to-face teaching that are not particularly helpful (see Levy and Stockwell, 2006: 162; Chapelle, 2003: 180), and they are largely irrelevant these days since the question today is no longer "*if* technology should be used for language teaching" but rather "*how* it can be best utilized for teaching." Comparative studies that describe the conditions under which different technology-based task design features are more effective for language learning are extremely helpful and can provide important information to task designers (for a review see Felix, 2008). A number of experimental SLA-focused studies have also used technology for investigating the effectiveness of specific conditions for instructed SLA, such as implicit versus explicit instruction (see Robinson, 1996). The use of technology in such research studies allows precise control and accurate measurement of a specific SLA variable under strict experimental conditions, which strengthens the validity of the research findings.

Further issues in CALL

Longitudinal studies of learners' attitudes towards CALL (see Lenders, 2008) and comparative CALL research studies with a focus on how to best utilize the affordances of technology for language learning are needed and greatly encouraged as long as they have a well-defined scope and are informed by theory and practice. The following are some representative issues that warrant further research.

- With technology evolving continuously and new tools and software becoming widely accessible by second language learners, more research is needed to enhance our understanding of how the different affordances of modern technology can be used to enhance language acquisition. Which attributes of technology are the most effective for language development?
- How does the use of technology in language tasks affect the development of complexity, accuracy and fluency of learner output?
- What CALL-based task designs are most effective for drawing learners' attention to language form (FonF)?
- What strategies do second language learners use when they engage in CALL-based language tasks?
- How can technology improve language assessment?
- How does computer-generated feedback affect student language development?

- What effect does the use of Web 2.0 tools and social networking software have on second language acquisition and student motivation?
- How does the expanding use of mobile technologies (e.g. iPads, smart phones, laptops) affect task design and student learning?
- How does learning through VLEs affect language development?

Research in CALL is as diverse as the applications of CALL. What is urgently needed is a focus on studies that connect more closely the application of CALL with the field of SLA. As SLA evolves and expands with new theories and new findings adding vital pieces to the puzzle of the second language acquisition process, CALL research needs to enhance our understanding of how technology affects this process. Unlocking the potential of technology for language learning is imperative in a technology-rich world where learning with technology is part of everyday life.

See also: corpus analysis, corrective feedback, focus on form, instructed SLA, interaction and the interaction hypothesis, task-based learning

References

Alabbad, A., Gitsaki, C. and White, P. (2010). CALL course design for second language learning: A case study of Arab EFL learners. In D.L. Pullen, C. Gitsaki, and M. Baguley (eds), *Technoliteracy, Discourse and Social Practice: Frameworks and Applications in the Digital Age*. Hershey, PA: IGI Global.

Al-Shehri, S. and Gitsaki, C. (2010). Online reading: The impact of integrated and split-attention formats on L2 students' cognitive load. *ReCALL*, *22*(3), 356–75.

Chambers, A. (2005). Integrating corpus consultation in language studies. *Language Learning and Technology*, *9*(2), 111–25.

Chang, W.-L. and Sun, Y.-C. (2009). Scaffolding and web concordancers as support for language learning. *Computer Assisted Language Learning*, *22*(4), 283–302.

Chapelle, C. (2003). *English Language Learning and Technology: Lectures on Teaching and Research in the Age of Information and Communication*. Amsterdam: John Benjamins.

Chapelle, C. and Douglas, D. (2006). *Assessing Language Through Computer Technology*. Cambrisge: Cambridge University Press.

Dooey, P. (2008). Language testing and technology: Problems of transition to a new era. *ReCALL*, *20*(1), 21–34.

Felix, U. (2008). The unreasonable effectivness of CALL: What have we learned in two decades of research? *ReCALL*, *20*(2), 141–61.

Gnem-Gutirrez, G.A. (2009). Repetition, use of L1 and reading aloud as mediational mechanism during collaborative activity at the computer. *Computer Assisted Language Learning*, *22*(4), 323–48.

Heift, T. and Schulze, M. (2007). *Errors and Intelligence in Computer-Assisted Language Learning: Parsers and Pedagogues*. New York: Routledge.

Lenders, O. (2008). Electronic glossing – is it worth the effort? *Computer Assisted Language Learning*, *21*(5), 457–81.

Levy, M. and Stockwell, G. (2006). *CALL Dimensions: Options and Issues in Computer-Assisted Language Learning*. Mahwah, NJ: Lawrence Erlbaum Associates, Publishers.

Neri, A., Cucchiarini, C. and Strik, H. (2008). The effectiveness of computer-based speech corrective feedback for improving segmental quality in L2 Dutch. *ReCALL*, *20*(2), 225–43.

Peterson, M. (2009). Learner interaction in synchronous CMC: A sociocultural perspective. *Computer Assisted Language Learning*, *22*(4), 303–21.

Robinson, P. (1996). Learning simple and complex second language rules under implicit, incidental, rule-search, and instructed conditions. *Studies in Second Language Acqusition*, 18, 27–67.

Skehan, P. (2003). Focus on form, tasks, and technology. *Computer Assisted Language Learning*, *16*(5), 391–411.

Taylor, R. and Gitsaki, C. (2003). Teaching WELL in a Computerless Classroom. *Computer Assisted Language Learning*, *16*(4), 275–94.

Vandewaetere, M. and Desmet, P. (2009). Introducing psychometrical validation of questionnaires in

CALL research: The case of measuring attitude towards CALL. *Computer Assisted Language Learning, 22*(4), 349–80.

Yilmaz, Y. and Granena, G. (2010). The effects of task type in Synchronous Computer-Mediated Communication. *ReCALL, 22*(1), 20–38.

Xu, J. (2010). Using multimedia vocabulary annotations in L2 reading and listening activities. *CALICO, 27*(2), 311–27.

Further reading

Chapelle, C. (2001). *Computer Applications in Second Language Acquisition: Foundations for Teaching, Testing and Research.* Cambridge: Cambridge University Press. (A comprehensive analysis of past work in the field of computer-assisted instruction, SLA, language teaching and language testing.)

Hubbard, P. (2009). *Computer Assisted Language Learning: Critical Concepts in Linguistics.* London: Routledge. (A four-volume collection consisting of 74 of the most influential published papers throughout the history of the field of CALL.)

Kárpáti, A. (2009). Web 2 technologies for Net Native language learners: A "social CALL". *ReCALL, 21*(2), 139–56. (The paper outlines differences in competence structures of Net Natives (who came of age in the twenty-first century) and the Net Generation of the 1980s and 1990s who evolve in response to changes between Web 1 and Web 2 technologies.)

Kukulska-Hulme, A. (2009). Will mobile learning change language learning? *ReCALL, 21*(2), 157–65. (The paper offers reflections on what mobile learning has to offer and considers whether it is likely to change how languages are taught and learnt.)

Oxford, R. and Oxford, J. (2009). *Second Language Teaching and Learning in the Net Generation.* Manoa, HI: National Foreign Language Resource Center University of Hawai'i at Manoa. (The book describes empirical studies involving different innovative technologies and state-of-the-art tools, offering pedagogical ideas, effective strategies, and useful suggestions on how these technologies could be applied to enhance language teaching and learning.)

Concept-oriented Approach to Second Language Acquisition (CoA)

Christiane von Stutterheim and Mary Carroll
University of Heidelberg

Second language acquisition is determined by a multitude of factors. The general goal of SLA research is to disentangle the interplay of these factors and their respective force in order to understand the *what, when* and *why* and *why not* of L2 acquisition and use. A number of different theoretical approaches have been developed and applied, rooted in general views on language. The concept-oriented approach views language as a system for the expression of meaning in the service of communication. It thus shares basic assumptions with cognitive and functional approaches to language in which the linguistic system in all its components is taken as a symbolic representation of meaning (cf. Gass and Selinker 2008: Ch. 7; Berman and Slobin 1994; Robinson and Ellis, 2008). "(Cognitive linguistics) is an approach to language description which sees linguistic expression and conceptualization to be mutually dependent, and interfaced with other cognitive and social systems in adult language use and language development" (see Robinson and Ellis, 2008:497).

In contrast to first language acquisition, the learner in SLA comes to the starting point with a more or less fully fledged conceptual system and knows how to communicate in the L1. What is needed are new expressive devices which can serve to get the message across. The learners have, for example, temporal concepts such as past, present, or future. What they have to learn is that these concepts are expressed in different ways, by lexical means, by particles, by auxiliaries rather than suffixes, or by a certain combination of these means. The key idea of the Concept-oriented Approach (CoA) is therefore not to focus on how, for example, tense morphology evolves but on how "pastness" is expressed by a particular combination of linguistic devices: "We may gain some insight into the 'logic' of the acquisition process as well as into the organization of learner languages by looking at the way in which specific concepts, such as temporality, are expressed at various stages of the acquisition process" (von Stutterheim and Klein, 1987: 194). The CoA thus looks at the learning process through the lenses of the learner who, in a given communicative situation when expressing a message with its conceptual structure, will to this purpose draw on means available from different components of the L2 linguistic system in an integrated fashion (cf. Bardovi-Harlig, 2008). The CoA is in many ways linked to approaches in first language acquisition (Tomasello, 2003) which also implement typological contrasts, as in the large-scale study by Berman and Slobin (1994).

Research goals and major topics

Overarching research goals can be formulated at different levels. At a first level, linguistic facts in SLA have to be systematized across time, across individuals, and across languages. At a second level, these facts have to be explained in relation to the underlying conceptual system which itself is subject to constraining and modifying variable factors. At a third level, results and assumptions on specific learning processes and conditions (e.g. language combinations, learning conditions, learner population) have to be integrated into what might be a partial theory of SLA. At the final level, insights gained in SLA will serve to enrich our knowledge of language and language processing in general.

Major topics in this field of SLA cover the conceptual domains of temporality, spatial categories, modality, causation, possession, object categorization, and discourse functional concepts such as foreground/background, as well as categories of information structure (Robinson and Ellis, 2008: 494 et.). The CoA assumes that the structure of a conceptual domain, which is probably universal at the most abstract level, but language (and culture) specific in its conceptual ramifications, provide criteria for the intake of linguistic form. Conceptual categories drive attention and thus the learning process in a selective way (cf. Bardovi-Harlig, 2008).

Previous work and key findings

Research in this framework has its roots in early work on SLA among immigrant populations in Europe. This period was followed by a large-scale longitudinal study across languages which marked the beginnings of a cognitive shift in SLA. Selected typological contrasts profiling relevant conceptual and structural differences between the L1s and targeted L2s of the learners were thereby varied on a systematic basis. Analyses of how learners proceed focused not only on formal development (e.g. acquisition of word order, negation, pronouns) but also on the acquisition of means to express *temporal* and *spatial* relations, as required when locating events and entities in space and time, as well as formal means which serve to encode the *informational status* of different parts of the message (word order, topic, focus, downgrading) (Perdue, 1984). Using both controlled data as well as relatively "free" speech, findings on the acquisition process reveal how adult learners build up a linguistic system starting with fundamental notional categories in the relevant domains, while acquisition beyond this *basic language variety* is increasingly modulated by core typological differences between the L1 and the targeted L2 of the learner, as well as the internal logic of the learner system (see Klein, this volume).

Subsequent studies within the CoA framework address language acquisition at more advanced stages of SLA. Focus has been placed on the role of typological differences between the L1 and targeted L2 with regard to patterns of grammaticalization versus lexicalization in the domains of temporality and spatial cognition. In the domain of temporality, which will serve to illustrate work carried out within CoA, the frame of reference relates to abstract levels of distinction such as "completion" or "progression." Relevant analyses of the role of semantic and grammatical differences are used in order to pinpoint core differences between the language pairs at issue, and with this to identify the conceptual underpinnings of the learner language at different stages of development.

On this basis, a CoA allows for tracking the path of grammatical markers into the learner system. Grammatical rules are not acquired in one step. Rather, as studies have shown (cf. Dietrich *et al.*, 1995; Bardovi-Harlig, 2000), the door is first opened on the basis of semantic triggers. Tense, aspect and modal morphology enter the L2 system showing sensitivity to the specific semantics of verbs and their use in a given communicative context, while extending over time to other verbs and finally to a grammatical rule without semantic constraints based on a cognitive logic. This logic cannot be understood in taking a form-based approach.

Factors governing the acquisition of temporal aspectual concepts and their function in context at advanced stages of SLA were first investigated on the basis of how learners proceed in tasks which require the implementation of temporal relations to present sets of events as occurring in sequence; the findings show that for a language pair with next to no aspect in the L1 (German) and a highly grammaticalized form in the other member of the pair (progressive in English), and relatively flexible (German) versus relatively rigid word order constraints (English), advanced learners of English do not acquire the implications of an aspectual system with a marked progressive for the way events are sequenced at text level, whereas the advanced English learners of German studied do not acquire the implications of specific word order distinctions for information structure and reference management (use of ellipsis, pronouns, passives, downgrading) (see, on the role of aspect Carroll and von Stutterheim, 2003; von Stutterheim and Lambert, 2005; Carroll and Lambert, 2006); on the role of word order constraints for information structure ("deciding what to say," subject mapping, downgrading) for German as well as French learners of English.

From classical empirical methods to brain imaging

Based on initial findings in narrative (temporal) and descriptive tasks (spatial), further studies were developed using controlled elicitation procedures to test hypotheses on factors relevant for acquisition. They include reaction time measures, eye tracking, picture-word matching, all with statistical evaluations. For example, eye tracking studies on the way speakers segment motion events (motion of an entity along a trajectory to a goal) investigate the extent to which event segmentation is driven by aspectual distinctions such as the progressive. Relevant cross-linguistic differences in the domain of temporal aspect between languages such as German and English are used to investigate different phases of language planning from the conceptualization phase (information intake and "deciding what to say" when thinking for speaking) to the relation between vision and speech during the formulation phase. Similarities and contrasts between L1 and L2 speakers are investigated in order to gain insight into questions relating to language processing in SLA, compared with monolingual speakers (von Stutterheim and Nüse, 2003; von Stutterheim and Carroll, 2006 on advanced learners of German-English; Flecken, 2010 on early Dutch-German bilinguals). Studies in this field of inquiry are conducted with brain imaging, using EEG for priming and mismatch, fMRT for questions relating to the interrelation between conceptual and linguistic knowledge.

See also: acquisition of tense and aspect, conceptual transfer, cross-linguistic influence, functional typological linguistics, psycholinguistics of SLA, thinking for speaking

References

Bardovi-Harlig, K. (2000). *Tense and Aspect in Second Language Acquisition: Form, Meaning, and Use*. London: Blackwell.

——(2008). One functional approach to second language acquisition: The concept-oriented approach. In B. VanPatten and J. Williams (eds), *Theories in Second Language Acquisition*, New York and London: Routledge.

Berman, R. and Slobin D.I. (eds) (1994). *Relating Events in Narratives: A Crosslinguistic Developmental Study*. Mahwah, NJ: Erlbaum.

Carroll, M. and Lambert, M. (2006). Reorganizing Principles of Information Structure in Advanced L2s: A Study of French and German Learners of English. In H. Byrnes, H. Weger-Guntharp and K. Sprang (eds), *Educating for Advanced Foreign Language Capacities*. Georgetown, DC: Georgetown University Press.

Carroll, M. and von Stutterheim, C.v. (2003) Typology and information organisation: Perspective taking and language-specific effects in the construal of events. In A. Giacalone Ramat (ed.), *Typology and Second Language Acquisition*. Berlin: Mouton de Gruyter.

Dietrich, R., Klein, W. and C. Noyau (ed.) (1995). *The Acquisition of Temporality in a Second Language*. Amsterdam: Benjamins.

Flecken, M. (2010). *Event Conceptualization in Language Production of Early Bilinguals*. Utrecht: LOT dissertation publications 256.

Gass, S.M. and Selinker. L. (2008). *Second Language Acquisition*. New York and London: Routledge.

Perdue. C. (ed.) (1984). *Second Language Acquisition by Adult Immigrants: A Field Manual*. Rowley, MA: Newbury House.

Robinson, P. and Ellis, N. (2008). Conclusion: Cognitive linguistics, second language acquisition and L2-Instruction – Issues for research. In P. Robinson and N. Ellis (eds), *Handbook of Cognitive Linguistics and Second Language Acquisition*. New York and London: Routledge.

Stutterheim, C. von and Klein, W. (1987). A Concept-oriented approach to second language studies. In C. Pfaff (ed.), *First and Second Language Acquisition Processes*. Rowley, MA: Newbury House.

Stutterheim, C. von and Nüse, R. (2003). Processes of conceptualisation in language production, *Linguistics* (Special Issue: Perspectives in language production), 851–81.

Stutterheim, C. von and Lambert, M. (2005). Crosslinguistic analysis of temporal perspectives in text production. In H. Hendriks (ed.), *The Structure of Learner Varieties*, pp. 203–30. Berlin: de Gruyter.

Stutterheim, C. von and Carroll, M. (2006). The Impact of grammatical temporal categories on ultimate attainment in L2 learning. In H. Byrnes, H. Weger-Guntharp and K. Sprang (eds), *Educating for Advanced Foreign Language Capacities*. Georgetown, DC: Georgetown University Press.

Tomasello, M. (2003). *Constructing a Language: A Usage-based Theory of Language Acquisition*. Cambridge, MA: Harvard University Press.

Conceptual span

Henk Haarmann

University of Maryland

Conceptual span is an index of semantic short-term memory (STM) (Haarmann *et al.*, 2003), the semantic storage component within working memory. Semantic STM is a system that maintains the meanings of words in a highly activated state above their resting level in long-term memory (Haarmann and Usher, 2001). It is separate from phonological STM, which stores words in their phonological form (Haarmann *et al.*, 2003). Research with the conceptual span test has shown that semantic STM is subject to age-related declines and that it supports several cognitive and language functions (Haarmann *et al.*, 2003, 2005): on-line integration of the meaning of words, maintenance of task context, and protection from pro-active interference (i.e., confusion with previously presented similar words). The role of semantic STM in second language processing has yet to be addressed (but see Signorelli *et al.*, in press). The conceptual span test is a promising candidate for such research, as are similar category-cued recall tests (Haarmann and Usher, 2001).

The conceptual span involves the presentation of a series of words followed by a category name. The task of the subject is to try to recall all the words in the named category (i.e., category-cued recall) in any order (i.e., free recall). For example, when presented with the words *lamp, pear, tiger, apple, grape, elephant, horse, fax, phone*, and the category cue *FRUIT?* a correct answer would be *pear grape apple*. The conceptual span score is the average number of words that have been correctly recalled. There are two versions of the conceptual span test, a clustered version in which words are presented grouped by category and a non-clustered version without such grouping, as in the above example.

Like word span, the conceptual span test is a simple-span or storage-only (i.e., STM) measure of working memory, contrasting with complex-span or storage-plus-processing measures of working memory. Complex (but not simple) span measures include an explicit task instruction to manipulate information (i.e., processing) beyond the storage component of the task. For example, in reading span, subjects are presented with a set of sentences and have to read aloud each sentence (processing) and retain each sentence-final word for recall (storage). The use of the clustered over the non-clustered version is recommended if minimizing internal processing demands is desirable.

Several properties of the conceptual test help ensure that it is sensitive to storage in semantic STM, including the use of semantic category cue and aspects of material and task design that make it difficult to recall items from LTM due to pro-active interference and thereby encourage retrieval from STM (Davelaar *et al.*, 2005). The conceptual span test should not be regarded as a pure test of only semantic STM, since it may also receive contributions from phonological STM. Instead, it should be regarded as a test in which the contribution of semantic STM is greater than in other storage-only span tasks such as digit span and word span (Haarmann *et al.*, 2003).

See also: individual differences in SLA, phonological short term memory (PSTM), prototypes, psycholinguistics of SLA, semantic processing, working memory

References

Davelaar, E.J., Goshen-Gottstein, Y., Ashkenazi, A., Haarmann, H.J. and Usher, M. (2005). The demise of short-term memory revisited: empirical and computational investigations on recency effects. *Psychological Review*, *112* (1), 3–42.

Haarmann, H.J. and Usher, M. (2001). Maintenance of semantic information in capacity-limited item short-term memory. *Psychonomic Bulletin and Review*, *8*(3), 568–78.

Haarmann, H.J., Davelaar, E.J. and Usher, M. (2003). Individual differences in semantic short-term memory capacity and reading comprehension. *Journal of Memory and Language*, *48*, 320–45.

Haarmann, H.J., Ashling, G.E., Davelaar, E.J. and Usher, M. (2005). Age-related declines in context maintenance and semantic short-term memory. *The Quarterly Journal of Experimental Psychology* (special issue on aging), *55A* (1), 34–53.

Signorelli, T., Haarmann, H.J. and Obler, L.K. (in press). Working memory in professional interpreters. *International Journal of Bilingualism*.

Suggested reading

Bunting, M.F. and Cowan, N. (2005). Working memory and flexibility in awareness and attention. *Psychological Research*, *69*(5–6), 412–19. (Presents data that suggests that internal processing, in addition to storage, contributes to performance on clustered conceptual span, when there are attention demands from a conflicting retrieval cue.)

Kane, M.J. and Miyake, T.M. (2007). The validity of conceptual span as a measure of working memory capacity. *Memory and Cognition*, *35*, 1136–50 (Reports a failure to replicate the finding that conceptual span is a stronger test of some individual differences than other span measures, but does not mimic the original conceptual span task by Haarmann *et al.*, 1993, in critical aspects.)

Koutstaal, W. and Aizpurua, A. (2010). Aging and flexible remembering: contributions of conceptual span, fluid intelligence, and frontal functioning. *Psychological Aging*, *25*(1), 193–207 (Replicates age-related declines in conceptual span and its relation with fluid intelligence.)

Martin, R.C., Shelton, J.R. and Yaffee, L.S. (1994). Language processing and working memory: Evidence for separate phonological and semantic capacities. *Journal of Memory and Language*, *33*, 83–111 (Presents neuropsychological evidence for a separation between phonological and semantic short-term memory.)

Vernon, D., Engner, T., Cooper, N., Compton, T., Neilands, C., Sheri, A. and Gruzelier, J. (2003). The effect of training distinct neurofeedback protocols on aspects of cognitive performance. *International Journal of Psychophysiology*, *47*, 75–85. (Presents findings that show that electroencephalographic (EEG) neurobiofeedback improves semantic short-term memory performance as indexed by conceptual span.)

Conceptual transfer

Scott Jarvis
Ohio University

Conceptual transfer refers to cases where language learners', bilinguals', and multilinguals' language behavior exhibits crosslinguistic effects (or transfer) that are interpreted as having taken place in the speakers' conceptual systems prior to the conversion of their preverbal messages into language (Jarvis, 2007). Conceptual transfer deals largely with the elements of meaning that people choose to express in given contexts, and is therefore a type of meaning transfer, but is not limited to semantic transfer. Whereas semantic transfer arises largely out of the different ways in which meaning is lexicalized and grammaticized in different languages, conceptual transfer is assumed to originate from language-specific characteristics of a person's conceptual system rather than from his or her linguistic (including semantic) knowledge per se. A distinction is consequently drawn between conceptual transfer and *linguistic transfer* (q.v.) (see also Jarvis, 2007; Jarvis and Pavlenko, 2008). Meaning transfer also encompasses pragmatic transfer, which has both conceptual and linguistic dimensions (see the articles on pragmatics and pragmalinguistics).

Transfer in the language use of language learners, bilinguals, and multilinguals can be identified and confirmed on the basis of rigorous criteria (e.g., Jarvis, 2000, 2010), but whether those cases represent conceptual transfer instead of or in addition to various types of linguistic transfer is a matter of theoretical interpretation. For this reason, any investigation of conceptual transfer will necessarily be grounded in a theoretical or empirical framework that explicates the nature of the human conceptual system, how it relates to language use, and how it might differ for speakers of different languages. Studies on conceptual transfer can generally be viewed as attempts to investigate crosslinguistic influence within the theoretical framework of cognitive linguistics, which allows researchers to formulate and test specific hypotheses concerning the nature of language-specific conceptual structures and processes and their likelihood of affecting a person's use of another language. This line of inquiry shares much in common with Slobin's (1996) *thinking for speaking* framework, as well as with Levelt's (1989) speech production model and the work by von Stutterheim and colleagues on information structure and conceptualization (e.g., von Stutterheim and Nüse, 2003). However, whereas these other frameworks were originally developed to account for other phenomena, such as monolingual speech production and differences across languages in the organization and expression of information, the conceptual transfer framework has been formulated to focus exclusively on crosslinguistic influence.

Within that focus, conceptual transfer actually has a broader scope than these other frameworks in the sense that, as the examples below will show, conceptual transfer deals not just with conceptualization, which is the process of forming temporary mental representations of complex situations and events, but it also deals with mental concepts themselves, or in other words, the structure and content of mental categories. Both phenomena fall within the purview of conceptual transfer, but the terms *conceptualization transfer* and *concept transfer* are sometimes used, when necessary, to differentiate the two (Jarvis, 2007).

Although it is difficult at present to establish with certainty whether particular instances of transfer originate from a person's conceptual system, the empirical evidence for conceptual transfer has accumulated substantially over the past few years. The evidence for concept transfer includes the finding that there exist crosslinguistic differences and corresponding crosslinguistic effects in bilinguals' and multilinguals' patterns of naming, categorizing, and judging the similarity and typicality of various colors, shapes, substances, and objects (Athanasopoulos, 2009; Cook *et al.*, 2006; Pavlenko and Malt, in press). It also includes the finding that there exist transfer-related differences in how learners from different language backgrounds interpret the meanings of tense and aspect markers in both the L1 and L2, how well they can distinguish between completed and non-completed actions (Boroditsky and Trusova, 2003), and how well they can remember certain types of information, such as object-name pairs in languages that have grammatical gender (Boroditsky *et al.*, 2003; see Jarvis and Pavlenko, 2008 for a review of these findings).

The continually accumulating evidence for conceptualization transfer shows that language learners with different language backgrounds display differential effects in how they segment strings of continual action into discrete events (von Stutterheim and Nüse, 2003), how they construe motion events in terms of manner and path of movement (Hohenstein *et al.*, 2006), and which components of these events they select for verbalization (von Stutterheim, 2003). Crucially, these findings are bolstered by additional evidence from language learners' gestures (Brown and Gullberg, 2008), as well as eye fixations and ability to recall certain characteristics of events they have witnessed (von Stutterheim *et al.*, in press). These additional forms of evidence seem to confirm that the transfer effects in question do indeed occur at the conceptual level, perhaps often in combination with simultaneous transfer effects at the linguistic level.

Most research associated with conceptual transfer has focused on the construal of motion events in narrative tasks. There is a great deal that we do not yet know about what types of transfer might occur in language learners' conceptualization of scenes, situations, arguments, and forms of reasoning and problem-solving in tasks other than narratives. There is also a great deal still to be discovered about the relationship between conceptualization transfer and concept transfer, particularly with respect to the mental templates (or schemas) that people rely on when conceptualizing or forming temporary representations of events and situations in their working memory (Langacker, 2008). These schemas are presumably stored in long-term memory and therefore constitute concepts, so crosslinguistic differences in event construal may very well reflect not just conceptualization (or processing) differences, but also concept (that is, knowledge) differences. It is important to discover whether speakers of different languages actually have differently structured event schemas, or whether they differ simply in terms of which schemas they tend to access in particular contexts.

See also: cognitive linguistics and SLA, crosslinguistic influence, lexical concepts, linguistic relativity, linguistic transfer, thinking for speaking

References

Athanasopoulos, P. (2009). Cognitive representation of colour in bilinguals: The case of Greek blues. *Bilingualism: Language and Cognition*, *12*, 83–95.

Boroditsky, L., Schmidt, L. and Phillips, W. (2003). Sex, syntax, and semantics. In D. Gentner and S. Goldin-Meadow (eds), *Language in Mind: Advances in the Study of Language and Thought*, pp. 61–79. Cambridge, MA: MIT Press.

Boroditsky, L. and Trusova, E. (2003). *Cross-linguistic Differences in the Representation of Events: Verb Aspect and Completion in English and Russian.* Paper presented at the 25th Annual Conference of the Cognitive Science Society, July, Boston, MA.

Brown, A. and Gullberg, M. (2008). Bidirectional crosslinguistic influence in L1-L2 encoding of manner in speech and gesture: A study of Japanese speakers of English. *Studies in Second Language Acquisition*, *30*, 225–51.

Cook, V., Bassetti, B., Kasai, C., Sasaki, M. and Takahashi, J. (2006). Do bilinguals have different concepts? The case of shape and material in Japanese L2 users of English. *International Journal of Bilingualism*, *10*, 137–52.

Hohenstein, J., Eisenberg, A. and Naigles, L. (2006). Is he floating across or crossing afloat? *Bilingualism: Language and Cognition*, *9*, 249–61.

Jarvis, S. (2000). Methodological rigor in the study of transfer: Identifying L1 influence in the interlanguage lexicon. *Language Learning, 50*, 245–309.

——(2007). Theoretical and methodological issues in the investigation of conceptual transfer. *Vigo International Journal of Applied Linguistics (VIAL), 4*, 43–71.

——(2010). Comparison-based and detection-based approaches to transfer research. In L. Roberts, M. Howard, M. Ó Laoire, and D. Singleton (eds), *EUROSLA Yearbook, 10*,169–92. Amsterdam: Benjamins.

Jarvis, S. and Pavlenko, A. (2008). *Crosslinguistic Influence in Language and Cognition*. New York and London: Routledge.

Langacker, R. (2008). *Cognitive Grammar: A Basic Introduction*. New York: Oxford University Press.

Levelt, W. (1989). *Speaking: From Intention to Articulation*. Cambridge, MA: MIT Press.

Pavlenko, A. and Malt, B.C. (in press). Kitchen Russian: Cross-linguistic differences and first-language object naming by Russian–English bilinguals. *Bilingualism: Language and Cognition, 14* (1).

Slobin, D. (1996). From "thought and language" to "thinking for speaking. In J. Gumperz, and S. Levinson (eds), *Rethinking Linguistic Relativity*, pp. 70–96. Cambridge: Cambridge University Press.

von Stutterheim, C. (2003). Linguistic structure and information organisation: The case of very advanced learners. In S. Foster-Cohen and S. Pekarek Doehler (eds), *EuroSLA Yearbook*, pp. 183–206. Amsterdam: John Benjamins.

von Stutterheim, C., Bastin, D., Carroll, M., Flecken, M. and Schmiedtova?, B. (in press). How grammaticized concepts shape event conceptualization in the early phases of language production: Insights from linguistic analysis, eye tracking data and memory performance. *Linguistics*.

von Stutterheim, C., and Nüse, R. (2003). Processes of conceptualization in language production: Language specific perspectives and event construal. *Linguistics, 41*, 851–81.

Further reading

Han, Z.-H. and Cadierno, T. (eds) (2010). *Linguistic Relativity in SLA: Thinking for speaking*. Bristol: Multilingual Matters. (This is an edited collection of recent empirical studies on conceptual transfer, thinking for speaking, and the relationship between linguistic relativity and second language acquisition.)

Jarvis, S. (in press). Conceptual transfer: Crosslinguistic effects in categorization and construal. *Bilingualism: Language and Cognition, 14* (1). (This is the introduction to a special issue of the journal that features recent empirical investigations of conceptual transfer and related phenomena in the language use and language-related behavior of language learners and bilinguals.)

Odlin, T. (2010). Conclusion: On the interdependence of conceptual transfer and relativity studies. In Z.-H. Han and T. Cadierno (eds), *Linguistic relativity in SLA: Thinking for speaking*, pp. 183–94. Bristol: Multilingual Matters. (This paper insightfully elucidates the relationship between transfer and relativity, as well as the relationship between meanings and concepts, and discusses the existing and still needed types of evidence for conceptual transfer.)

Pavlenko, A. (ed.) (2011). *Thinking and Speaking in Two Languages*. Bristol: Multilingual Matters. (This is an edited collection of papers that summarize and synthesize the sustained work by several researchers on issues related to conceptual transfer, thinking for speaking, and the more general relationship between language and thought in bilinguals.)

Connectionism and SLA

Luca Onnis
University of Hawai'i

Connectionism proposes an explanation of the mind by exploring how higher-level cognitive faculties like language may emerge from simpler processes. It provides explanations implemented in computer simulations inspired by neural principles of brain functioning and architecture. These artificial neural networks are formed by several simple processing units – often called nodes – that mimic the activity of groups of neurons. Each node can be excited or inhibited by activation coming from other nodes to which it is connected, mimicking synaptic connectivity in the brain. A set of nodes can collectively represent linguistic information, for example phonetic, phonemic, or semantic cues. Connectionist models have been applied to model-specific language tasks such as perceiving speech and identifying spoken words (e.g., McClelland and Elman, 1986), inferring the syntactic category of words and phrasal structure (e.g., Elman, 1990; Redington and Chater, 1998), learning regular and irregular forms of verbs (e.g., Plunkett and Marchman, 1993), learning to read words (e.g., Seidenberg, 2005), developing semantic knowledge (Rogers and McClelland, 2008), etc. Importantly, connectionist models are not static representations of knowledge, but rather are capable of learning to form input–output mappings that eventually develop into systematic knowledge. In addition, such knowledge is not stored in any specific node, but is distributed over the set of nodes and connections of the entire network. As such, connectionist models lend themselves naturally to investigate the dynamics of cognitive processes at different time scales, from the perception of a word within a few hundred milliseconds, to the development of language skills in childhood, and even to the evolution of language over generations of learners. Learning proceeds by progressively modifying the initially random synaptic-like connection strengths between nodes in a fashion that reduces the error between the actual and the desired output, or in ways that strengthen the connection among nodes when both are active at the same time.

Implementing ideas and theories in connectionist simulations is advancing knowledge of cognitive functions beyond abstract verbal theorizing. Akin to preparing a food recipe that requires the exact type and amount of ingredients and step-by-step procedures to turn raw ingredients into the final product, a connectionist model necessarily requires specifying every step and every assumption for its implementation, including the type of linguistic data to be input, the type of learning conditions, as well as the architectural properties of their networks, and the type of learning output to be expected. The implementation of such procedures yields a product of learning (an output) that can be matched against actual human psycholinguistic data (such as specific developmental knowledge, sensitivity to grammatical structure, ability to perform a reading task, types of errors produced by second language learners, etc.). When the simulated output data do not meet the empirical data, the model's results can be questioned, and the specific implementation falsified or modified. When the simulated data do match closely the psycholinguistic facts, it is possible to inspect the actual processes that lead to successful learning. Failures to learn successfully are also illuminating in understanding the processes underlying linguistic disorders. In this sense, connectionist models can be seen as a form of reverse engineering, when the cognitive recipe that leads to the end product is unknown.

Connectionist models of language

Various aspects of neural networks are particularly valuable for understanding language acquisition and processing. Networks learn to perform some specific task from being exposed to relatively unanalyzed raw input, or from input that is typically less structured than the knowledge to be attained. For example, in learning to read printed words, the raw input could be a series of horizontal and vertical lines corresponding to the printed letters in a word (e.g., M I N T), with the network having to learn the correct phonetic output (e.g., /mint/ as opposed to /maint/). Structural properties of language can emerge out of simpler tasks. Networks that are simply required to predict the next word in a sentence can develop implicit knowledge of syntactic categories, phrase structure configurations, and grammatical relations. As a by-product of learning to map input and output, the models *reorganize* the input they receive (e.g., simple word tokens) into more abstract categories, corresponding to semantic and syntactic groupings like nouns and verbs. Such knowledge is not represented explicitly, but rather emerges as a pattern of neuronal activity between the interconnected nodes in a parallel distributed fashion (meaning the knowledge acquired is not stored in any single node – just like no single brain cell in the brain stores a unique symbol such as the word MINT or its lexical category of NOUN). This behavior contrasts with more traditional views that see language processing as transforming static symbolic representations according to pre-wired grammatical rules.

Insights into bilingualism and second language acquisition

While most connectionist efforts have focused on monolingual acquisition and processing of language in normal and impaired populations, recent models have started to investigate mechanisms of early and late bilingualism, often re-examining "common wisdom" assumptions (e.g., Seidenberg and Zevin, 2006; Thomas and Johnson, 2008). One such assumption holds that a biologically determined critical period must be responsible for differences in language acquisition between children and adults. Connectionist models have provided a concept proof that a critical period need not be invoked. Rather, there may be sensitive periods influenced by the processes of learning itself. By keeping the network architecture unchanged in a given simulation (equivalent to the absence of biological changes), age-related differences can emerge as a by-product of learning itself. Three types of processes are responsible for a reduction in plasticity driven by learning. First, "younger" networks are more plastic – they are more sensitive to experience and change driven by the input they receive. Later learning (as in the case of a second language) may be harder or suboptimal not because of any structural change in the network properties dictated by an external biological program, but because of *competition* for resources that have already been claimed in earlier learning (Hernandez et al., 2009). Second, by modifying their synaptic connections, networks find an optimal solution to a given learning problem, and their internal representations stabilize becoming *entrenched*. Later learning may be sub-optimal, especially when it requires a reorganization of already committed (entrenched) neural states. If the introduction of an L2 is delayed significantly, the consolidated representations for the L1 may prevent the network from establishing new distinct representations for the L2 (e.g., McCandliss *et al.*, 2002). Third, initial learning may reduce the networks' ability to detect changes in the environment. This leads to processes of *assimilation*, as when two phonemes in a second language are indistinguishable perceptually, or the system is unable to develop new fine-tuned motor representations to produce a novel sound.

Because connectionist models are sensitive to properties of the input and order of presentation, they lend themselves naturally to simulate differences between early and late bilingualism. Outcomes of bilingual language learning in neural networks are different when networks are trained on two sets of linguistic stimuli simultaneously, corresponding to conditions of early bilingualism (e.g, Li, 2009; Zhao and Li, 2010). Here the early mixing of two input languages can produce distinct patterns, such that representations for the two languages become separated and can naturally coexist. The bilingual input itself may suffice for the development of distinct mental representations for each language of the bilingual mind.

While much work remains to be done to illuminate the mechanisms involved in early and late bilingualism, connectionist models are providing fresh insights into how different patterns of experience can have a dramatic effect on learning outcomes without invoking separate mechanisms for different languages or different ages of acquisition.

See also: age effects in SLA, competition model, Critical Period Hypothesis (CPH), emergentism, implicit learning, statistical learning

References

Elman, J. (1990). Finding structure in time. *Cognitive Science, 14*, 179–212.

Hernandez, A., Li, P. and MacWhinney, B. (2005). The emergence of competing modules in bilingualism. *Trends in Cognitive Sciences, 9*, 220–25.

Li, P. (2009). Lexical organization and competition in first and second languages: Computational and neural mechanisms. *Cognitive Science, 33*, 629–64.

McCandliss, B.D., Fiez, J.A., Protopapas, A., Conway, M. and McClelland, J.L. (2002). Success and failure in teaching the [r]–[l] contrast to Japanese adults: Tests of a Hebbian model of plasticity and stabilization in spoken language perception. *Cognitive, Affective, and Behavioral Neuroscience*, *2*, 89–108.

McClelland, J.L. and Elman, J.L. (1986). The TRACE model of speech perception. *Cognitive Psychology*, *18*(1), 1–86.

Plunkett, K. and Marchman, V. (1993). From rote learning to system building: acquiring verb morphology in children and connectionist nets. *Cognition, 48,* 21–69.

Redington, M. and Chater, N. (1998). Connectionist and statistical approaches to language acquisition: a distributional perspective. *Language and Cognitive Processes, 13*, 129–92.

Rogers, T.T. and McClelland, J.L. (2008). Precis of semantic cognition, a parallel distributed processing approach. *Behavioral and Brain Sciences*, 31, 689–749.

Seidenberg, M.S. (2005). Connectionist models of word reading. *Current Directions in Psychological Science*, *14*, 238–42.

Seidenberg, M.S. and Zevin, J.D. (2006). Connectionist models in developmental cognitive neuroscience: Critical periods and the paradox of success. In Y. Munakata and M. Johnson (eds), *Attention and Performance XXI: Processes of Change in Brain and Cognitive Development*, pp. 585–612. Oxford: Oxford University Press.

Thomas, M. and Johnson, M.H. (2008). New advances in understanding sensitive periods in brain development. *Current Directions in Psychological Science*, *17*, 1, 1–5.

Zhao, X. and Li, P. (2010). Bilingual lexical interactions in an unsupervised neural network model. *International Journal of Bilingual Education and Bilingualism*, *13*, 505–24.

Further reading

McMurray, B. (2000). Connectionist Modeling for … er … linguists. In K.M. Crosswhite and J. McDonough (eds), *University of Rochester Working Papers in the Language Sciences*, Vol. Spring 2000, no. 1. Available at: http://homepage.psy.utexas.edu/homepage/class/psy338k/gough/chapter4/mcmurray.pdf (An introduction to the major terms and concepts of connectionism geared to an audience of linguists.)

Strauss, T.J., Harris, H.D. and Magnuson, J.S. (2007). jTRACE: A reimplementation and extension of the TRACE model of speech perception and spoken word recognition. *Behavior Research Methods*, *39*, 19–30. (Introduces principles of computational modeling of human speech processing with freely downloadable modeling tools.)

Construal and perspective taking

Michel Achard

Rice University

In Cognitive Grammar (CG Langacker, 1987, 1991, 2008), the meaning of an expression includes at the same time and in equally important parts the conceptual content that entity evokes and the specific way in which this content is construed, or in other words, the way in which the conceptualizer chooses to think about it and represent it: "Linguistic expressions and grammatical constructions embody conventional imagery, which constitutes an essential aspect of their semantic value. In choosing a particular expression or construction, a speaker construes the conceived situation in a certain way, i.e. he selects a particular image (from a range of alternatives) to structure its conceptual content for expressive purposes" (Langacker, 1988: 7). The notion of construal can be divided into four broad classes of phenomena, namely specificity, focusing, prominence, and perspective (Langacker 2008: 55).

Specificity refers to "the level of precision and detail at which a situation is characterized" (Langacker 2008: 55). A CG grammar consists of a large number of expressions which describe a situation at different levels of granularity. Highly specific expressions describe a situation in fine-grained details and resolution (*cute little kitten*), while more schematic ones reveal only coarse-grained and general features which can be instantiated by several more specific expressions (*feline*). In the lexicon, this organization produces a large number of taxonomies of conventionally recognized types [*thing* → *object* → *tool* → *hammer* → *claw hammer* (from Langacker 2008: 56)]. In the grammar, specific expressions (*Mary made her sister smile*) cohabitate with the schematic templates or rules which sanction their existence (the causative construction [X MAKE Y INF]).

Focusing "includes the **selection** of conceptual content for linguistic presentation, as well as its arrangement into what can broadly be described (metaphorically) as **foreground** vs. **background**" (Langacker, 2008: 57, emphasis in the original). The foreground/background distinction is manifested at various levels of linguistic organization, including information structure (given versus new) and topic versus focus. Focusing also restricts the conceptual content for linguistic presentation. The meaning of linguistic expressions is characterized with respect to a matrix of cognitive domains, and it has a particular scope (i.e. covers a particular portion) in these domains. It is often necessary to distinguish between an expression's different scopes, often organized in a hierarchy. For example, the expression *finger* maximally evokes the human body (its maximal scope), but more immediately the conception of a hand (its immediate scope).

Prominence mainly refers to profiling and trajector/landmark alignment. The meaning of linguistic expressions is characterized by the imposition of a profile on a base. The base consists of the immediate scope of each active domain in its matrix; the profile refers to the substructure within that base which is singled out for specific attention. For example, the conception of a wheel constitutes the base with respect to which *hub*, *spoke*, and *rim* profile different substructures. Profiling is critical to the definition of grammatical categories because "what determines an expression's grammatical category is not its overall conceptual content, but the nature of its profile in particular" (Langacker, 2008: 98, emphasis in the original), and consequently, grammatical categories are characterized with respect to what they profile. Schematically, a noun profile a "thing," or more precisely a set of interconnected entities manipulated as a conceptual whole or reified. The members of other grammatical classes profile simple or complex relationships, namely the connections that exist between participants. For example, the preposition *in* profiles the simple relation which obtains between the container and the entity it contains. It is frequent for a specific participant in a relationship to receive focal prominence as the entity being located or evaluated. That participant is called the "trajector" (tr). When a second focal participant is present, it is called the "landmark" (lm). For example, in *John ate the sandwich*, the nominals *John* and *sandwich*, respectively, elaborate the trajector and landmark of the relationship the verb profiles.

Finally, perspective describes the viewing arrangement, or in other words the relationship which exists between the conceptualizers who apprehend the meaning of a linguistic expression and the object of their conceptualization (Langacker, 1985, 1990). In the default arrangement, the vantage point from which the object of conceptualization is entertained is the location of the speaker and hearer, but the same objective situation can be construed from a variety of vantage points. Deictic entities make necessary reference to a specific vantage point as a part of their meaning. For example, "*in front of* and *behind* rely on vantage point to specify the trajector's location vis-à-vis the landmark" (Langacker, 2008: 75–76). Closely related to vantage point, the objectivity or subjectivity imposed on a conceptualized scene pertains to the specific relation that exists between the conceptualizing subject and the object of her conceptualization. The Optimal Viewing Arrangement (Langacker, 1985, 1990) maximizes the asymmetry between the subject and object roles. Because it is strictly confined to its subject role, the conceptualizing subject is subjectively construed. By contrast, the object of conceptualization is construed with maximal objectivity. The Egocentric Viewing arrangement (Langacker, 1985, 1990) blurs the asymmetry of the subject and object roles. The subject itself functions as an object of conceptualization at varying degrees, and is thus construed more objectively. The most extreme objective construal of a conceptualizing subject is observed in the case of personal pronouns (*I, you, we*) where the speaker and hearer are put onstage and objectively construed. The perspective from which a given entity is conceptualized has been shown to account for a wide range of grammatical phenomena including the grammaticalization of motion verbs into future auxiliaries (Langacker, 1990) and the distribution of French infinitival and finite complements (Achard, 1998).

The centrality of construal to the description of linguistic phenomena clearly points to the central role of the speaker in the distribution of linguistic expressions in discourse. "It is not the linguistic system per se that constructs and understand novel expressions, but rather the language user, who marshals for this purpose the full panoply of available resources" (Langacker, 2000: 9). Consequently, successful grammatical instruction amounts to providing students with clear guidelines that allow them to express their linguistic choice. This involves making available to them the whole range of conventionalized options, as well as the precise parameters which determine the native usage of each particular construction (Achard, 2008).

See also: cognitive linguistics and SLA, Competition Model, concept-oriented apprioach to SLA, construction learning, language and the lexicion in SLA, semantic processing

References

Achard, M. (1998). *Representation of Cognitive Structures: Syntax and Semantics of French Sentential Complements*. Berlin: Mouton de Gruyter.

——(2008). Teaching construal: Cognitive pedagogical grammar. In P. Robinson, and N. Ellis (eds), *Handbook of Cognitive Linguistics and Second Language Acquisition*, pp. 432–56. Mahwah, NJ: Lawrence Erlbaum Associates.

Langacker, R.W. (1985). Observations and speculations on subjectivity. In J. Haiman (ed.). *Iconicity in Syntax*, pp. 109–50. Amsterdam and Philadelphia, PA: John Benjamins.

——(1987). *Foundations of Cognitive Grammar*. Vol. 1: *Theoretical Prerequisites*. Stanford, CA: Stanford University Press.

——(1988). A usage-based model. In B. Rudzka-Ostyn (ed.), *Topics in Cognitive Linguistics*, pp. 127–61. Amsterdam and Philadelphia, PA: John Benjamins.

——(1990). Subjectification. *Cognitive Linguistics*, *1*, 5–38.

——(1991). *Foundations of Cognitive Grammar*. Vol. 2: *Descriptive Application*. Stanford, CA: Stanford University Press.

——(2000). A dynamic usage-based model. In M. Barlow and S. Kemmer (eds), *Usage Based Models of Language*, pp. 1–63. Stanford, CA: CSLI.

——(2008). *Cognitive Grammar: A Basic Introduction*. Oxford: Oxford University Press.

Construction learning

Devin M. Casenhiser
York University

A fundamental issue facing language acquisition researchers is the question of how language learners are able to translate the ideas that are formulated in their minds into strings of sounds in order to convey those ideas to other people. The question gets even more interesting when we consider that the strings of sounds must represent both simple concrete things like objects, or actions, but abstract things ranging from concepts (e.g., like) to propositions (Ted likes chocolate). It is clear that speakers and listeners must conform to a common set of conventions in expressing these ideas. Generativist theory, for example, proposes that there are two quite different components to answering this question. The first is a set of culturally determined strings (lexical items). The second is a set of universal and innate "linking rules" that specify how the surface items are to be arranged. Linking rules connect the surface ordering of words to an underlying representation of the utterance. The meaning of the utterance is determined by the conjunction of the meaning of the underlying representation and the meaning of the culturally determined lexical items. In generativist theory, then, the learning issue is simplified since the language learner only has to learn the meaning of lexical items, and then select the proper underlying form and linking rules that correspond to the spoken language.

In the last 20 years, however, a new approach to understanding abstract patterns of language has developed. This approach, called construction grammar, holds that the patterns of argument structure (constructions) are learned on the basis of surface patterns in much the same way that other patterns perceived in the environment are learned – that is, through the use of general cognitive abilities.

Constructions are learned pairings of form and function and may take the form of partially or fully filled words (dog, V-ed), idioms (up to my <body part> in <noun>), or general linguistic patterns (Subj V Obj1 Obj2 *Jan gave Steve a book.*) (Goldberg, 1995, 2006). The formal patterns may be specified using semantic categories, grammatical relations, grammatical categories, or lexical items alone or in combination.

Constructions may themselves be made up of constructions – as they are in multi-word phrases – and both the component constructions as well as the larger, containing construction contribute to the meaning. In the phrase *John tossed the paper into the box* each component construction, such as the lexical items (*tossed*, *paper*), and phrases (e.g., NP, PP), contributes to the meaning of the sentence. But the overall pattern of the sentence, which may be specified as <agent> <verb> <obj/theme> <$PP_{loc/path}$>, also contributes to the meaning of the utterance: an <agent> causes an <object/theme> to move to the location specified in the <$PP_{loc/path}$> in the manner specified by the <verb>. Thus, even in the face of much missing lexical information, we are still able to glean a general "caused-motion" meaning from an utterance such as: *The birt mooped the fleek onto the plurp,* a feat that would not be possible if the utterance's meaning were entirely dependent on the meaning of its constituent parts (say, the lexical items, for example).

Early research designed to show that constructions are learned on the basis of input rather than being innate required learners to assign a familiar meaning to a new linguistic form (e.g., Abbot-Smith *et al.*, 2001; Akhtar, 1999; Childers and Tomasello, 2001; Hudson *et al.*, 1999). Research such as this is helpful in establishing the item-specific nature of how constructions are learned. However, while they require children to learn novel words and/or morphemes, they do not require the children to learn both a novel form and a novel meaning, and to map one onto the other. This is a substantially more complex task, and one that critically could not be influenced (for better or worse) by patterns of language that the child already knows.

Together with colleagues, Adele Goldberg and I have conducted a number of studies in an attempt to address this gap in the research. We have produced evidence that children are in fact able to assign a novel meaning to a novel construction, have looked at what is learned from these patterns, and have investigated parameters that affect this learning. Recently, these results have begun to be picked up by second language acquisition researchers, and we review the data below.

The general paradigm used in each of the studies to date is reminiscent of the preferential looking paradigm used to test children's understanding of linguistic constructions (e.g., Fisher, 1996; Gleitman, 1994; Naigles, 1990). In it, we created a novel construction whose meaning indicated that an NP theme appeared in an NP location in the manner specified by a nonsense verb. The form was as follows:

Noun $phrase_{theme}$ noun $phrase_{location}$ nonsense verb

The utterances generated by this construction were then paired with video-taped scenes depicting their meaning. For example, *the spot the king moopoed* indicated that the spot (NP_{theme}) appeared on the king ($NP_{location}$) in the manner indicated by the verb (in this case, "fading into existence"). The paradigm is rounded out by using a training phase in which participants are exposed to the utterances paired with the video-taped examples of the utterance's meaning. The intent is to simulate in a controlled manner the sorts of pairings between scenes and utterances that a learner would experience in being exposed to a novel construction (cf. Hauser *et al.*, 2002). In the testing phase of the experiment, two minimally different scenes are placed side-by-side while an utterance is played. The child is instructed to touch the scene that corresponds to the utterance. In this paradigm, only the meaning of the noun phrases is known. Thus participants had to determine from context, the meaning of the verb, the meaning of the construction, and the form of the construction. In fact, they also had to determine that the word order did in fact have a meaning rather than being haphazard.

In one early experiment, Casenhiser and Goldberg (2005) trained six-year-olds on the novel construction above for a total of 3 minutes during which time they say 16 scenes, each lasting approximately 10 seconds. These children were then tested by asking them to distinguish between a simple transitive scene and a scene of appearance. The children were able to do so reliably above chance. Moreover, when compared to the performance of a control group of children who received no training on the novel construction, their performance on the novel construction was significantly better. These results suggest that children did in fact correctly match the novel construction to the novel meaning. Moreover, since both the scenes and verbs in the testing phase were new, children had to generalize beyond the input they had received. That is, the evidence suggests that participants had learned a generalized construction rather than a set of idioms. Moreover, Boyd and colleagues (2009) have found evidence that participants are able to use such newly acquired constructions productively – even when mappings run counter to specifications which are claimed to be universal (Pinker, 1989).

In other work, we and other researchers have investigated construction learning as an instance of category learning that is subject to the same sorts of facilitative and inhibitory effects as other types of category learning (Goldberg *et al.*, 2007). For example, we have found a facilitative effect on construction learning when the token frequency of a prototypical verb is disproportionately higher than the token frequency of other verbs occurring in the construction – a so-called Zipfian distribution (Casenhiser, 2005; Goldberg *et al.*, 2004). That natural language input tends to mirror this effect has been suggested by a number of studies (e.g., Gries, 2005; Goldberg, 2004; Cameron-Faulkner *et al.*, 2003; Hunston and Francis, 1999; Goldberg, 1999; Goldberg, 1995, 1996), and Elio and Anderson (Elio and Anderson, 1984; Elio, Anderson, and Carnegie-Mellon, 1980) have shown a similarly facilitative pattern for category learning in general. The effect is not to be overstated however, since the importance of type frequency in generalization may overshadow the effects of Zipfian distributions. In ESL studies, McDonough and Kim (2009) found a facilitative effect of greater type frequency in priming *wh*-questions, and Collins and colleagues (2009) also found type frequency (along with perceptual salience) to reliably distinguish early-learned L2 constructions from those that are learned later. Indeed, the facilitative effect of skewed input may well be an early one that becomes washed out by extended training. In teaching the English ditransitive construction to Korean speakers, for example, Year and Gordon (2009) trained participants for a total of 200 minutes. Though participants did learn the construction, the authors failed to find a facilitative effect for skewed input.

To date the findings support the notion that both children and adults are able to learn constructions on the basis of relatively little input, and recent research is consistent with the notion that construction learning is a specific instance of category learning. Although proponents of Universal Grammar may rightly contend that the evidence presented here is not conclusively supportive of a constructionist approach to language learning over a generativist approach, the findings indicating that constructions can be learned from the input alone suggest that Universal Grammar may be an unnecessary construct.

See also: analogical mapping in construction learning, child second language acquisition, cognitive linguistics and SLA, frequency effects, type and token frequency, Universal Grammar (UG) and SLA

References

Abbot-Smith, K., Lieven, E. and Tomasello, M. (2001). What children do and do not do with ungrammatical word orders. *Cognitive Development*, *16*, 1–14.

Akhtar, N. (1999). Acquiring word order: Evidence for data-driven learning of syntactic structure. *Journal of Child Language*, *26*(2), 339–56.

Boyd, J.K. and Goldberg, A.E. (2009). Input effects within a constructionist framework. *The Modern Language Journal, 93*(3), 418–29.

Cameron-Faulkner, T., Lieven, E. and Tomasello, M. (2003). A construction-based analysis of child-directed speech. *Cognitive Science, 27*, 843–73.

Casenhiser, D. (2005). Children's resistance to homonymy: An experimental study of pseudo-homonyms. *Journal of Child Language, 32*(2), 319–43.

Casenhiser, D. and Goldberg, A. (2005). Fast mapping of a phrasal form and meaning. *Developmental Science, 8*(6), 500–8.

Childers, J.B. and Tomasello, M. (2001). The role of pronouns in young children's acquisition of the english transitive construction. *Developmental Psychology, 37*, 739–48.

Collins, L., Trofimovich, P., White, J., Cardoso, W. and Horst, M. (2009). Some input on the easy/difficult grammar question: An empirical study. *The Modern Language Journal, 93*(3), 336–53.

Elio, R. and Anderson, J.R. (1984). The effects of information order and learning mode on schema abstraction. *Memory and Cognition, 12*(1), 20–30.

Elio, R., Anderson, J.R. and Carnegie-Mellon, U. U.P.P.D.O. (1980). *The Effects of Category Generalizations and Instance Similarity on Schema Abstraction*. Defense Technical Information Center.

Fisher, C. (1996). Structural limits on verb mapping: the role of analogy in children's interpretation of sentences. *Cognitive Psychology, 31*, 41–81.

Gleitman, L. (1994). The structural sources of verb meanings. In P. Bloom (ed.), *Language acquisition: Core readings*, pp. 174–220. Cambridge, MA: MIT Press.

Goldberg, A.E. (1995). *Constructions: A Construction Grammar Approach to Argument Structure*. Chicago, IL: Chicago University Press.

——(1999). The emergence of the semantics of argument structure constructions. In B. MacWhinney (ed.), *The Emergence of Language*, pp. 197–212. Hillsdale, NJ: Erlbaum.

——(2004). But do we need Universal Grammar? *Cognition, 97*, 77–84.

——(2006). *Constructions at work: The nature of generalization in language*. Oxford: Oxford University Press.

Goldberg, A.E., Casenhiser, D. and White, T.R. (2007). Constructions as categories of language. *New Ideas in Psychology, 25*(2), 70–86. doi:10.1016/j.newideapsych.2007.02.004

Goldberg, A.E., Casenhiser, D.M. and Sethuraman, N. (2004). Learning argument structure generalizations. *Cognitive Linguistics, 15*(3), 289–316.

Gries, S. Th. (2005). Syntactic priming: A corpus-based approach. *Journal of Psycholinguistic Research, 34*(4), 365–99.

Hauser, M.D., Chomsky, N. and Fitch, W.T. (2002). The faculty of language: What is it, who has it, and how did it evolve? *Science, 298*, 1569–79.

Hudson, C., Newport, E.L., Greenhill, A., Littlefield, A. and Tano, C. (1999). Creolization: Could adults really have done it all? In *Proceedings of the Boston University Conference on Language Development*, pp. 265–76. Somerville, MA: Cascadilla Press.

Hunston, S. and Francis, G. (1999). *Pattern grammar: A Corpus-driven Approach to the Lexical Grammar of English*. Amsterdam: Benjamins.

McDonough, K. and Kim, Y. (2009). Syntactic priming, type frequency, and EFL learners' production of wh-questions. *The Modern Language Journal, 93*(3), 386–98.

Naigles, L. (1990). Children use syntax to learn verb meanings. *Journal of Child language, 7*, 357–74.

Pinker, S. (1989). *Learnability and Cognition: The Acquisition of Argument Structure*. Cambridge, MA: MIT Press and Bradford Books.

Year, J. and Gordon, P. (2009). Korean speakers. *Modern Language Journal, 93*(3), 19.

Content-based language teaching

Roy Lyster
McGill University

Content-based language teaching (CBLT) refers to an instructional approach in which non-linguistic curricular content such as geography or mathematics is taught to students through the medium of a language that they are learning at the same time as an additional language. The additional languages promoted by CBLT run the gamut from second and foreign languages to regional, heritage, and indigenous languages.

Contexts of CBLT

Met (1998) described a range of CBLT settings along a continuum varying from content-driven programs, such as immersion, to language-driven programs, which include language classes either based on thematic units or with frequent use of content for language practice. Towards the middle of the continuum are program models in which students study one or two subjects in the target language along with a more traditional language class.

School-based language immersion programs aim for additive bilingualism by providing a significant portion of students' subject-matter instruction through the medium of an additional language (e.g., at least 50 percent during elementary school years). The term "immersion" was first used in this way by Lambert and Tucker (1972) to describe a parent-driven initiative that launched the first French immersion classes in 1965 in Montreal, Quebec, and then a proliferation of immersion programs across Canada. Immersion programs have since been adapted to teach various languages around the world (Johnson and Swain, 1997), although the term "immersion" is not used consistently to describe such programs, which can be identified more generically, for example, as Gaelic-medium or Welsh-medium education in Scotland and Wales, respectively, or as *classes bilingues* in the case of Breton and Occitan in France. Many programs have been implemented for the purpose of language revitalization and in these cases include some learners who already speak the target language at home and others who do not.

Two-way immersion programs normally integrate a similar number of children from two different mother-tongue backgrounds (e.g., Spanish and English in the US) and provide curricular instruction in both languages (Lindholm-Leary, 2001). CLIL programs (Content and Language Integrated Learning; see Mehisto *et al.*, 2008) are similar to immersion insofar as CLIL also aims to integrate content and language instruction. Immersion programs, however, target languages other than only English and are usually implemented throughout a learner's elementary school education and often in secondary schooling as well.

CBLT has been used as well to refer to school settings in which newcomers to a country are learning the new language while also studying curricular content through that language, yet without necessarily any first language support, as in the case of content-based ESL and "sheltered instruction" in the US. In content-based ESL, "teachers seek to develop the students' English language proficiency by incorporating information from the subject areas that students are likely to study," and sheltered instruction entails content courses for ESL learners taught normally by content (rather than ESL) specialists (Echevarría *et al.*, 2008: 13). CBLT thus crosses a wide range of international contexts and instructional settings, including elementary, secondary, and post-secondary institutions. In spite of the tremendous differences across these contexts (some including majority-language and others minority-language students), there are some common pedagogical issues that arise at the interface of language and content teaching.

Pedagogical Issues

Swain (1988) proposed that content teaching on its own is not necessarily good language teaching and needs to be complemented and manipulated to maximize language learning. Students can otherwise understand content by drawing on world knowledge and extra-linguistic information while bypassing redundant grammatical information in order to process input for comprehension. Accordingly, research on outcomes of CBLT has generally revealed relatively high levels of comprehension abilities and content knowledge but comparatively lower levels of production abilities especially with respect to linguistic accuracy.

Researchers concur that, for CBLT to be effective, it must be language-rich and discourse-rich, but also that such an integrated approach requires a great deal of systematic planning and does not necessarily come naturally to content-based teachers. For example, observation studies of immersion classrooms revealed that a typical way to approach CBLT is to focus exclusively on content and to refer to language only incidentally as the need arises by chance. Then, if more attention to language is called for, a traditional approach is adopted in language arts classes to engage in structural analyses of the target language out of context. These decontextualized grammar lessons appeared to have minimal effect on students whose exposure to the target language was primarily message-oriented and content-based. Observations in other CBLT contexts revealed that content-trained teachers tend to focus mainly on content at the expense of language while language-trained teachers tend to focus more on language but often at the expense of greater in-depth exploration of content (Kong, 2009).

Proposals for improving the quality of CBLT designed to teach additional languages can be found in the research literature. One is for a more systematic integration of form-focused and content-based instruction through "counterbalanced instruction" (Lyster, 2007), which promotes continued language growth by inciting learners to shift their attentional focus in a way that balances their awareness of learning both language and content together. Drawing on systemic-functional linguistics, Schleppegrell *et al.* (2004) advocated CBLT that emphasizes how linguistic features of disciplinary texts construe particular kinds of meanings. From a similar perspective, Kong's (2009) comparative study of teachers in Hong Kong late immersion classrooms and in content-based foreign language classrooms in China revealed that effective teachers explored content with students from multiple perspectives rather than covering a list of facts; they also conveyed complex subject matter through knowledge relationships (i.e., cause-effect, hypothesis, and comparison) that were actualized in target language forms made salient by the teacher through consistent and explicit use.

The seemingly paradoxical endeavor of learning and teaching language through non-linguistic curricular content continues to be of interest to researchers and of concern to educators. Much remains to be done in contexts where key pedagogical issues might be taken for granted and left up to the devices of individual teachers or overshadowed by larger socio-political concerns for securing and defending rights to implement educational innovations to revitalize and maintain local languages.

See also: bilingualism and SLA, Focus-on-Form (FonF), instructed SLA, naturalistic and instructed learning, systemic functional linguistics, teacher talk

References

Echevarría, J., Vogt, M. and Short, D. (2008). *Making Content Comprehensible for English Learners: The SIOP Model*. Boston, MA: Pearson Education.

Johnson, K. and Swain, M. (1997). *Immersion Education: International Perspectives*. Cambridge: Cambridge University Press.

Kong, S. (2009). Content-based instruction: What can we learn from content-trained teachers' and language-trained teachers' pedagogies? *The Canadian Modern Language Review*, *66*, 233–69.

Lambert, W. and Tucker, R. (1972). *Bilingual Education of Children: The St. Lambert Experiment*. Rowley, MA: Newbury House.

Lindholm-Leary, K. (2001). *Dual Language Education*. Clevedon: Multilingual Matters.

Lyster, R. (2007). *Learning and Teaching Languages through Content: A Counterbalanced Approach*. Amsterdam: John Benjamins.

Mehisto, P., Frigols, M. and Marsh, D. (2008). *Uncovering CLIL: Content and Language Integrated Learning in Bilingual and Multilingual Education*. Oxford: Macmillan.

Met, M. (1998). Curriculum decision-making in content-based language teaching. In J. Cenoz and F. Genesee (eds), *Beyond Bilingualism: Multilingualism and Multilingual Education*, pp. 35–63. Clevedon: Multilingual Matters.

Schleppegrell, M., Achugar, M. and Orteíza, T. (2004). The grammar of history: Enhancing content-based instruction through a functional focus on language. *TESOL Quarterly*, *38*, 67–93.

Swain, M. (1988). Manipulating and complementing content teaching to maximize second language learning. *TESL Canada Journal*, *6*, 68–83.

Context of situation

Joseph Collentine
Northern Arizona University

Context-sensitive accounts of language acquisition complement cognitive models, which explain second language (L2) development via the interaction between psycholinguistic processes and input-oriented, output-oriented, interactional, and task-based instructional techniques. Greater explanatory adequacy results when researchers also consider the variables defining the learning context. The importance of complementing psycholinguistic with context-sensitive perspectives reflects the Firthian perspective that understanding linguistic behavior – and thus language development – requires a consideration of language's function in a larger social and cultural context (Berns, 1989).

An important distinction for understanding contextual effects on acquisition is between communicative context and learning context (Batstone, 2002). Communicative contexts require that learners use the L2 to exchange information as well as to affect social and interpersonal functions. Learning contexts manage input and output for learners. The domestic foreign-language classroom heavily favors learning contexts. Intensive domestic immersion settings provide a heavy dose of learning contexts with some communicative contexts. Study abroad presumably provides a balance between communicative and learning contexts, and so a great deal of the literature on learning contexts focuses on the effects and efficacy of study abroad.

It seems that to benefit from a study abroad experience learners must first attain certain pre-programmatic thresholds in their overall grammatical abilities, metalinguistic awareness, word-recognition abilities, lexical-access abilities, phonological-memory capacity with the L2, and in their repertoire of communicative strategies (cf. Collentine, 2009). Study abroad yields better outcomes in terms of L2 fluency (e.g., how much learners can say within a given timeframe) whereas domestic foreign-language instruction may facilitate more grammatical and metalinguistic development, although some contend that formal classroom study is a necessary precursor for overall success in a study abroad context (cf. Dekeyser 2007). The implications are: (i) learning and communicative contexts have differential effects on acquisition; (ii) the learning context supports linguistic development in the communicative context.

Sociocultural research indicates that an underrepresented theme in the research on learning context is learner identity (cf. Kinginger, 2008). When learners' sense of identity with the target culture (e.g., defined with the home-stay family or the institution abroad) is distant or when the learner senses that s/he has too many obstacles to attaining higher levels of proficiency (either through negative interactions or from a sense of linguistic inadequacy), the learner may abandon his/her role as a "language learner," thus impeding the development process.

Two related strands of L2 acquisition research focus on learning context. On the one hand, researchers interested in the effects of positive and negative evidence often consider the influence of naturalist versus instructed learning contexts, examining the effects of explicit and implicit instruction on acquisition. Additionally, sociocultural research often considers the effects of situated learning, such as the extent to which learners attain legitimate peripheral participation in the target culture when they become "members" of the L2 community.

See also: discourse and pragmatics in SLA, fluency, naturalistic and instructed learning, person in situation approaches to SLA, social and sociocultural influences on SLA, study abroad and SLA

References

Batstone, R. (2002). Contexts of engagement: A discourse perspective on intake and pushed output. *System*, *30*, 1–14.

Berns, M. (1989). Learning and using English in West Germany: A Firthian perspective. *International Review of Applied Linguistics*, *85*, 51–65.

Collentine, J. (2009). Study abroad research: Findings, implications and future directions. In M. Long and C. Catherine (eds), *The Handbook of Language Teaching*, New York: Wiley.

Dekeyser, R. (2007). Study abroad as foreign language practice. In R. Dekeyser (ed.), *Practice in a Second Language. Perspectives from Applied Linguistics and Cognitive Psychology*, Cambridge: Cambridge University Press.

Kinginger, C. (2008). Language learning in study abroad: Case studies of Americans in France. *The Modern Language Journal, 92* (supplement), iii–131.

Further reading

Collentine, J. (2009). Study abroad research: Findings, implications and future directions. In M. Long and C. Doughty (eds), *The Handbook of Language Teaching*. New York: Wiley. (Provides a state-of-the-art presentation of study-abroad research, updating the seminal 1995 work of Freed).

Freed, B. (1995). *Second Language Acquisition in a Study Abroad Context*. Philadelphia, PA: John Benjamins. (An extensive, historical overview of the research on learning contexts up to 1995.)

Contrastive Analysis Hypothesis (CAH)

Terence Odlin
Ohio State University

"The Contrastive Analysis Hypothesis" (CAH) is the title of a 1970 article by Ronald Wardhaugh in *TESOL Quarterly*, and ever since then the term has been widely used. Wardhaugh defined the CAH as "the claim that the best language teaching materials are based on a contrast of the two competing linguistic systems" (p. 123). Wardhaugh also distinguished what he said are two versions of the CAH, a "strong" and a "weak" form. Although he did not define these explicitly, his discussion implies that they differ mainly in two ways: 1) in the strong version, predictions of difficulty in learning a second language are essential, while in the weak version they are possible but not essential (p. 127); 2) in the strong version, nothing beyond a thorough comparison of two languages is needed to make predictions, whereas the weak version "starts with the evidence provided of linguistic interference and uses such evidence to explain the similarities and differences between systems" (p. 126).

Wardhaugh deemed the strong version "unrealistic and impracticable" (p. 124), but he considered the weak version possibly useful (even while noting reasons for concern). The alleged untenability of the strong version is largely due to the difficulties of deciding how best to describe the two languages and to compare them when, for example, the phoneme /p/ in French is not phonetically the same as English /p/. Whether one were to adopt a structuralist or a generative analysis, Wardhaugh believed, the theoretical question of what the best comparisons might be remains unanswered and indeed unanswerable (at least for the near future). Although the weak version of the CAH was more viable for Wardhaugh, he thought that the uncertainties about what linguistic theories to use could affect the assessment of difficulties. He also noted that even while many teachers take seriously the possible influence of, for example, Spanish phonology on a learner's attempts to pronounce English sounds, many teachers also have a sense that some parts of a language are more easily learned than others. However, the sequencing of what to present earlier or later in instruction remains, Wardhaugh judged, problematic because of the theoretical uncertainties. While he considered most contrastive studies as closer to the weak than to the strong version of the CAH, he believed that such work would have less influence in the 1970s (than it did in the 1950s and 1960s) on second language teaching.

Wardhaugh's definition of the general CAH paraphrases a statement from Charles Fries (1945) that does indeed claim that "the most efficient materials are those that are based upon a scientific description of the language to be learned, carefully compared with a parallel description of the native language of the learner" (p. 9). A statement by Robert Lado in the preface to his *Linguistics Across Cultures* likewise shows something close to the "strong" version of the CAH inferred by

Wardhaugh: "The plan of the book rests on the assumption that we can predict and describe the patterns that will cause difficulty in learning, and those that will not cause difficulty, by comparing systematically the language to be learned with the native language and culture of the student" (p. vii). In one sense, however, Wardhaugh's discussion is anachronistic because Fries and Lado did not use the term *Contrastive Analysis Hypothesis*. It is also noteworthy that the term *contrastive* predates the claims of Fries and Lado, having been used at least as early as 1941 by Benjamin Lee Whorf, who wrote of "contrastive linguistics" ([1941] 1956: 240).

Subsequent discussions invoking the CAH have often cited Fries and Lado, but their definitions of the CAH often differ considerably from Wardhaugh's, as in one textbook: "Where two languages were similar, positive transfer would occur; where they were different, negative transfer, or interference would result" (Larsen-Freeman and Long (1991: 53). Dulay *et al.* (1982) offer yet another definition: "The CA hypothesis held that where structures in the L1 differed from those in the L2, errors that reflected the structure of the L1 would be produced" (p. 97). Neither of these post-1970 definitions mentions instructional materials and neither discusses in detail the strong/weak distinction made by Wardhaugh, while the one of Larsen-Freeman and Long comes closer to the strong version and that of Dulay, Burt, and Krashen to the weak.

Along with taking on different definitions, the CAH has been associated with terms and theoretical concerns not found in Wardhaugh's article. For Schachter (1974), the strong and weak versions were equivalent to *a priori* and *a posteriori* contrastive analysis. Schachter viewed her own study of transfer as support for the *a priori* approach (for her, the strong version of the CAH), although one could possibly see her investigation as consistent with the weak version. In any case, the terms *a priori* and *a posteriori* have become at least rough equivalents for Wardhuagh's distinction. In historical discussions, two theoretical issues not addressed by Wardhaugh have been the perceived association of CA with behaviorist psychology and the relation between first and second language acquisition. Dulay *et al.*, for instance, cite the claim of Fries in his foreword to Lado's book that adult SLA is quite different from child language acquisition because of the "special 'set' created by the first language habits" (1957: v). The word "habits" does seem consistent with the interpretation of Dulay *et al.* that Fries was a behaviorist, and Larsen-Freeman and Long likewise associate the CAH with behaviorism. However, Selinker (2006), who studied with both Fries and Lado, states that only the latter was a behaviorist. Selinker nevertheless uses *contrastive analysis* to refer to the structuralist era even while other researchers (e.g., Schachter) have used it without any structuralist or behaviorist connotations. The term *contrastive analysis*, one might add, is also found in other fields such as anthropological linguistics and translation studies. The variable uses of *CA* and *CAH* thus illustrate how the presumably scientific terminology of linguistics is susceptible, as Lehrer (1983) observed, to the ambiguities of everyday semantics.

See also: cross-linguistic influence, interlanguage, linguistic transfer, development in SLA, language and the lexicon in SLA, theoretical constructs in SLA

References

Dulay, H., Burt, M. and Krashen, S. (1982). *Language Two*. New York: Oxford University Press.

Fries, C. (1945). *Teaching and Learning of English as a Foreign Language*. Ann Arbor: University of Michigan Press

Lado, R. (1957). *Linguistics across Cultures*. Ann Arbor: University of Michigan Press.

Larsen-Freeman, D. and Long, M. (1991). *An Introduction to Second Language Acquisition research*. London: Longman

Lehrer, A. (1983). *Wine and Conversation*. Bloomington: Indiana University Press.

Schachter, J. (1974). An error in error analysis. *Language Learning*, *24*, 205–14.

Selinker, L. (2006). Afterword: Fossilization or 'Does your mind mind'? In Z.-H. Han and T. Odlin (eds), *Studies of Fossilization in Second Language Acquisition*, pp. 201–10. Clevedon: Multilingual Matters.

Wardhaugh, R. (1970). The contrastive analysis hypothesis. *TESOL Quarterly*, *4*, 123–30.

Whorf, B.L. (1956). *Language, Thought, and Reality*. In J. Carroll (ed.), Cambridge, MA: MIT Press.

Further reading

Luk, Z. and Shirai, Y. (2009). Is the acquisition order of grammatical morphemes impervious to L1 knowledge? Evidence from the acquisition of plural *-s*, articles, and possessive *'s*. *Language Learning*, *59*, 721–54. (This article reevaluates the evidence that was often cited as a rebuttal of the CAH.)

Odlin, T. (2006). Could a contrastive analysis ever be complete? In J. Arabski (ed.), *Cross-linguistic Influence in the Second Language Lexicon*, pp. 22–35. Clevedon: Multilingual Matters. (The paper considers the problem of prediction as well as the problem of comprehensiveness in CA.)

Ringbom, H. (1987). *The Role of the First Language in Foreign Language Learning*. Clevedon: Multilingual Matters. (This book cites numerous studies that validate the importance of language distance, that is, the degree of relatedness among languages as a major factor in ease or difficulty.)

Selinker, L. (1992). *Rediscovering Interlanguage*. London: Longman. (Fries and Lado are among the linguists considered in depth in this reflection on the history of SLA.)

Weinreich, U. (1953). *Languages in Contact*. The Hague: Mouton. (Despite some claims to the contrary, many of the studies cited in this volume show that cross-linguistic influence was an area of study long before Fries and Lado, moreover, Weinreich's own analysis had little to do with behaviorism.)

Conversation analysis (CA)

Junko Mori

University of Wisconsin-Madison

Conversation analysis (CA) has burgeoned as a unique form of sociological inquiry under the leadership of Harvey Sacks and his colleagues, Emanuel Schegloff and Gail Jefferson. A variety of scholarly traditions, most notably ethnomethodology and Goffmanian sociology, influenced the inception of CA, but CA distinguishes itself from other forms of inquiry because of its vigorous attention to the details of participants' conduct observed in audio- or video-recorded conversations and other kinds of talk-in-interaction. The aim of CA is to describe "the competences which ordinary speakers use and rely on when they engage in intelligible, conversational interaction" (Heritage, 1984: 241) or "the procedural infrastructure of interaction" (Schegloff, 1992: 1338). Earlier CA studies reported how turn-taking is organized among participants (Sacks, Shegloff, and Jefferson, 1974); how problems in speaking, hearing, and understanding are managed (Schegloff, Jefferson, and Sacks, 1977); how a particular sequence of talk is initiated, extended, and closed (Schegloff and Sacks, 1973); or how turns performing socially affiliative or disaffilitive actions are structured differently (Sacks, 1987 [1973]). These findings were generated based on careful examinations of recurrent patterns observed in a large database consisting of interactions occurring in varying contexts.

During the last four decades, CA has been adopted by an increasing number of researchers in various fields, where the nature of human language occupies the central position in their academic pursuit; they include anthropology, communication studies, education, and linguistics. Within SLA, CA has gained recognition since the mid 1990s, along with the rapid growth of studies informed by various sociolinguistic or sociocultural frameworks, offsetting the field that had been skewed towards psycholinguistic or cognitive orientations. Firth and Wagner's (1997) call for the reconceptualization of fundamental concepts widely adopted in SLA research, such as *nonnative speaker, language,* and *interlanguage*, for instance, was by and large informed by their background in CA. Namely, CA resists the analyst's imposition of preconceived categories when approaching interactional data and strives to explicate how the participants of interaction themselves engage in a moment-by-moment analysis of the co-participants' conduct and design their own subsequent conduct accordingly. Thus, the analyst's task is to uncover how a particular speaker's competence is evaluated and treated in situ by the co-participants, rather than assuming that nonnative speakers' underdeveloped linguistic facility is inherently problematic. CA researchers consider that second language is one of many resources for accomplishing social actions, and that participants often perform indigenous deployments of linguistic and non-linguistic resources, which may appear unconventional to a third party, but nevertheless are treated as inconsequential by the parties involved.

While no one seems to disagree that CA is one of the best tools available for analyzing how language is used in talk-in-interaction, disagreement remains over whether or not, or to what extent, CA can contribute, either alone or combined with other theories, to the study of how a second language is acquired or learned (e.g. Gass, 1998; Larsen-Freeman, 2004). The appreciation of CA's potentials in SLA research largely depends on one's ontological perspective on language and learning. CA is not likely a useful tool for those who conceptualize language learning as the development of knowledge concerning second language structures as an autonomous system because CA is not concerned with each individual's inner mental states gauged in isolation from social contexts. Instead, CA excels in its investigation of how interactants display cognitive processes, such as noticing, forgetting, remembering, or understanding through their observable verbal or nonverbal conduct in situated social interaction (Mori and Markee, 2009). Thus, those who are interested in the process of how language is acquired through interaction, or those who conceptualize language learning as an increased level of participation in a wider variety of social activities, would likely find CA to be a powerful tool for microanalysis of any type of interaction, including mundane conversations, classroom interactions, or interviews.

One of the critiques of SLA research discussed by Firth and Wagner's aforementioned article concerns the limited scope of its traditional database, primarily consisting of classroom, experimental, or quasi-experimental interactions involving second language learners receiving formal instruction. When collecting and analyzing such data, researchers tend to start with preconceived research questions and hypotheses and approach the data from specific angles. CA, on the other hand, underscores the importance of "unmotivated looking;" that is, analysts are recommended not to dismiss any detail of the participants' conduct as trivial, but to describe and discover phenomena, which might have been unimaginable prior to the meticulous observation of the data. This process helps researchers expand the understanding of the nature of language as a vehicle of interaction. The exploration of data collected outside of educational or experimental contexts reveals different types of social actions that second language speakers need to perform, as well as different types of competences required for their accomplishment.

Some studies included in a volume edited by Gardner and Wagner (2004), for instance, demonstrate that errors and mistakes concerning grammar, vocabulary, or pronunciation are rarely treated as consequential outside of educational or experimental settings. Others in the volume also document how second language speakers, despite their limited linguistic proficiency, can be versatile and persistent interactants by utilizing a wide range of interactional resources. Further, as mentioned earlier, the management of problems in speaking, hearing, and understanding in talk-in-interaction, or more technically *repair organization*, has long been investigated by CA researchers, who examined interactions among first language speakers. Insights from CA literature on repair organization propose how *communication strategies* or *comprehension checks,* which had often been described as peculiar to second language interaction, are indeed commonly seen in first language interaction, as well. CA techniques enable researchers to delve further into the details of how exactly a particular action taken in a particular manner at a particular moment of an interaction indicates the participants' treatment of a given speaker's non-native status. In fact, second language speakers assume a variety of professional, social, or situated identities, and being second language speakers is just one of many possible attributes, which may or may not be made relevant in any given moment of interaction. CA takes the view that the participants' identities, including their native or non-native statuses, are co-constructed and reflexively indexed through their conduct in interaction.

Not only has the CA approach been applied to a new set of data collected outside of educational or research settings, but it has also enriched the study of institutional talk, such as classroom interaction (Markee, 2004; Seedhouse, 2004), oral proficiency interview tests (Lazaraton, 2002), and qualitative interviews conducted for the purpose of research (Talmy and Richards, 2011). Similar to its approach regarding the speaker's native or non-native statuses, CA does not assume that the fact that the participants are teachers, students, interviewers, or interviewees is always relevant to the ways in which they conduct themselves; rather, it attempts to describe how particular ways in which they take turns, design their talk, or respond to their co-participants demonstrate their orientation to the institutional nature of a particular interaction and to their situated identities associated with the setting. Namely, how participants are *doing being* X, or treating the others as X, is what CA researchers explore, while also acknowledging that there are moments when their other identities may become more salient.

With this mindset, CA-based classroom interaction research has examined how teachers and students participate in, or co-construct, different phases of classroom activities, including teacher fronted plenary talk, peer-to-peer interaction promoted by task instructions, or off-task talk; how transitions from one type of activity to another is negotiated by the participants; or how the participants' conduct demonstrates their orientation towards particular instructional designs determined in advance while simultaneously attending to the contingent nature of unfolding interaction. Corrective feedback observed in classrooms has also been reexamined with reference to CA literature on repair. Similarly, CA-based studies of oral proficiency interviews or qualitative interviews underscore the co-constructed nature of interaction. Namely, while the tendency has been to focus primarily on the interviewees' performance or narrative, CA-based studies of interviews investigate how the interviewees' performances are shaped by the interviewers' conduct. Namely, how questions are designed, delivered, and sequenced in situ and what kinds of uptakes are provided or withheld largely influence the ways in which the interviewees construct their responses.

Finally, the wealth of CA findings has also informed language pedagogy and teacher training in a number of ways (Wong and Warning, 2010). Attention to how naturally occurring interactions are organized and co-constructed by the participants aided by CA helps language teachers and material developers critically examine model dialogs in textbooks, design of classroom activities, and methods of error corrections, as well as forms, actions, and sequences to be introduced in classrooms.

In summary, an increasing number of CA-based studies have paid greater attention to multimodal resources, including talk, gaze, and gesture, as well as texts and other artifacts, which can be brought in to accomplish tasks at hand and achieve mutual understanding during institutional and non-institutional talk-in-interaction. These studies should continue to advance our understanding of such key concepts in SLA research as language, competence, cognition, and participation.

See also: classroom interaction research, institutional talk, qualitative research, second language socialization, self-repair, turn taking

References

Firth, A. and Wagner, J. (1997). On discourse, communication, and (some) fundamental concepts in SLA research. *Modern Language Journal*, *81*, 285–300.

Gass, S.M. (1998). Apples and oranges: Or, why apples are not oranges and don't need to be. *Modern Language Journal*, *82*, 83–90.

Gardner, R. and Wagner, J. (2004). *Second Language Conversations*. London: Continuum.

Heritage, J. (1984). *Garfinkel and Ethnomethodology*. Cambridge: Polity Press.

Larsen-Freeman, D. (2004). CA for SLA? It all depends .... *Modern Language Journal*, *88*, 603–7.

Markee, N (ed.) (2004). Special Issue: Classroom talks. *Modern Language Journal*, *88* (4).

Mori, J. and Markee, N. (eds) (2009). Special Issue: Language learning, cognition, and interactional practices. *International Review of Applied Linguistics in Language Teaching*, *47* (1).

Sacks, H. (1987 [1973]) On the preferences for agreement and contiguity in sequences in conversation. In G. Button and J.R. E. Lee (eds), *Talk and Social Organization*. Clevedon: Multilingual Matters.

Sacks, H., Shegloff, E.A. and Jefferson, G. (1974). A simplest systematics for the organization of turn-taking for conversation. *Language, 50*, 696–735.

Seedhouse, P. (2004). *The International Architecture of the Language Classroom: A Conversation Analysis Perspective*. Malden, MA: Blackwell.

Schegloff, E.A. (1992). Repair after next turn: The last structurally provided defense of intersubjectivity in conversation. *American Journal of Sociology, 97*, 1295–1345.

Schegloff, E.A., Jefferson, G. and Sacks, H. (1977). The preference for self-correction in the organization of repair in conversation. *Language, 53*, 361–82.

Schegloff, E.A. and Sacks, H. (1973). Opening up closings. *Semiotica*, 8, 289–327.

Talmy, S. and Richards, K. (eds) (2011). Special issue: Qualitative interviews in applied linguistics: Discursive perspectives. *Applied Linguistics, 32*(1).

Wong, J. and Warning, H.Z. (2010). *Conversation Analysis and Second Language Pedagogy: A Guide for ESL/EFL Teachers*. New York: Routledge.

Further reading

Hellermann, J. (2008). *Social Actions for Classroom Language Learning*. Clevedon: Multilingual Matters. (An extensive classroom research that combines CA and sociocultural approaches.)

Hutchby, I. and Wooffitt, R. (2008). *Conversation Analysis*. Cambridge: Polity Press. (A comprehensive introduction to CA.)

Richards, K. and Seedhouse, P. (2005). *Applying Conversation Analysis*. Basingstoke: Palgrave Macmillan. (A collection of studies that illustrate how CA analysis of institutional talk can inform professional practices.)

Schegloff, E.A., Koshik, I., Jacoby, S. and Olsher, D. (2002). Conversation analysis and applied linguistics. *Annual Review of Applied Linguistics, 23*, 3–31. (An extensive discussion of how CA can contribute to applied linguistics research.)

Sidnell, J. (2010). *Conversation Analysis: An Introduction,* Malden, MA: Wiley-Blackwell. (A comprehensive introduction to CA.)

Corpus analysis

Ute Römer
Georgia State University

A corpus (plural corpora) can be defined as a systematic collection of texts from spoken and/or written sources (nowadays usually in electronic format) that is used in language-related scholarship. Corpus applications range from linguistic research over dictionary making to language acquisition and language teaching. In language teaching, corpora of native speaker and learner language are used as interactive inductive learning tools in the classroom and to improve pedagogical materials (Römer, 2011). Corpus analysis refers to the ways in which corpora are accessed as sources of data in research and teaching.

Web-based tools and offline software packages or computer scripts can be used to analyze a corpus in several ways, thus providing different views on the data captured in the corpus. Without such tools, corpora would be of no use to the analyst other than being electronic repositories of texts that could be read on screen (or on paper printouts) in the normal linear fashion. Corpus analysis can be regarded as *corpus transformation* (Barlow, 2004) in that words in the corpus texts are sorted, rearranged, and highlighted in different ways, depending on the analytic step that is applied. The resulting text transformations enable insights into the type of language under analysis that the mere input files could not provide.

Central steps in corpus analysis

The most important steps in corpus analysis (or corpus transformation) are: creating a frequency word list, creating a keyword list, compiling and sorting a concordance, creating a distribution plot for a word or phrase, extracting collocates, and extracting fixed and variable phraseological items.

A useful first step in approaching a corpus is to generate a list of all the words (types) that occur in it together with their token frequencies. *Frequency word lists* are useful because they highlight which words are most common in a corpus and may be worth investigating. Such lists either give all distinct words separately or they are lemmatized which means that inflected forms are grouped under their headword (e.g. the count for *think* covers the occurrences of *think*, *thinks*, *thinking*, and *thought*).

While a word list highlights what is frequent in a corpus, it does not necessarily show what is important or unusually frequent. To identify the most unexpectedly frequent words, corpus users can compare a frequency wordlist based on a target corpus with another frequency wordlist based on a reference corpus (usually larger and of a more general type) and thus create a *keyword list* (see Scott and Tribble, 2006). In such a list, words or phrases are usually listed in order of their keyness values. Items get a high keyness value if they occur considerably more (positive keyness) or less frequently (negative keyness) in a selected corpus than they would be expected to occur on the basis of figures derived from a reference corpus. A keyword list based on a corpus of Biology journal articles, for example, might include words such as *genes*, *cells*, and *species*.

Another central analytic step results in the core tool in corpus linguistics: the *concordance* (see Figure 1). A concordance provides a contextualized view of a word or phrase by listing all its instances in the selected corpus in the middle of the computer screen with a few words of context on the left and on the right. This format of displaying language examples is referred to as *KWIC*, or keyword in context. Depending on the type of analysis, it may be necessary to look at more context than fits in one line on the computer screen. In such cases, most corpus tools enable the user either to expand the context (from a line to a paragraph of text) or toggle between concordance line and text. Unlike a text that we usually read horizontally, line by line, a concordance is read vertically, focusing on the search word (or "node") in the middle of the screen (Tognini-Bonelli, 2001: 3). By looking at the context words on the left and right of the node, we get access to phraseological patterns and to the meanings expressed by the search word or phrase (Sinclair, 2003). What we search for in the concordance are repeated events – repetitions of words in combination with other words. *Sorting the context* in a concordance facilitates the identification of repeated events and makes patterns visible. When we sort a concordance, the order of the concordance lines is rearranged according to predefined sorting criteria and lines that contain the same words to the left or right of the search term are grouped together (e.g. *important consideration* in Figure 1).

```
268 terial in these languages is another important consideration. As well, it is the reality th
269 ion potential (Texas GLO).  It is an important consideration because grading and excavating
270 aken from Hansell, 2000)     Another important consideration for the success of a nest is t
271 d the support system and peers is an important consideration for the midwife (Low et al.).
272 higher temperatures. [12]    Another important consideration in aqueous cleaning is the amo
273 e outsource our materials is also an important consideration.  We propose to use a mechanis
274 t thought that the case presented an important constitutional question about the State's du
275 iculate and defend certain basic and important constraints on, or enablers for, a big-pictu
276 theories     In my opinion, the most important contribution of behavioral theories is the e
277 model for the future.      The other important contribution to the 'Prisoner of the Caucasu
278 evidence; while Jacobson provided an important contribution to whiteness theory in another
279 ts is possible.    We summarized the important contributions in each simulation in the tabl
280  movement is another one of the most important contributions of postmodern feminist theory:
281 What issues and areas have been most important contributions of these theories? What issues
282 ere, it is important to discuss some important contributions on prior hypotheses of vicaria
283  fuel, and Russian peacekeepers make important contributions to the local economies.  There
284 ble yields, and is believed to be an important contributor to forest degradation. Fuel wood
285  often cited in gender studies as an important contributor to heterosexism, homophobia, and
286 developed by the Psych. Corp.  Other important contributors to I/O psychology have been Haw
287  to analyze the interactions between important controllable factors in the creation of high
```

Figure 1 Part of a right-sorted concordance of *importance* in the Michigan Corpus of Upper-level Student Papers (MICUSP)

If we want to trace repeated instances of a word or phrase across texts and find out where in a corpus file a word or phrase occurs, we can create and examine its *distribution plot*. It may, for example, be interesting to know whether a selected word has a preference to occur at the beginning or end of a text, if it clusters in a certain section of a text or is evenly distributed across a text. Several software packages for corpus analysis offer tools that visualize repeated instances of an item in a text, usually in the form of a barcode (one for each text in the corpus). Each line in the barcode represents an occurrence of the search term in a text. Alternatives to using the distribution plot function in a software program are to divide corpus files in customized ways and carry out separate searches in sections of texts (e.g. Römer, 2010) or to extract items from corpus files together with information on their location in the sentence, paragraph and text (e.g. O'Donnell and Römer submitted).

As mentioned above, concordances (especially when they are sorted) can help to highlight patterns in language. Another means to uncover word associations in texts is the *extraction of collocates* of a search word or phrase. Collocate lists (or collocation lists) consist of words which frequently co-occur with the search term, often within a fixed span of four or five words to the left and right of the node. In a collocation list collocates can be sorted by raw frequency of occurrence or by a statistical measure, for example Mutual Information or t-score. These measures capture the relationship between expected and attested frequencies of the collocate near the search term. Depending on the selected statistical measure, the collocate list for a word or phrase can look very different (Hoffmann *et al.*, 2008: Ch. 8).

Further insights into language patterns and common co-occurrence phenomena are enabled by analytic techniques that center around *extracting fixed and variable phraseological items* from corpora. Several current corpus tools retrieve lists of fixed word sequences of different lengths, often referred to as *n-grams* or clusters (e.g. *you know*, *in terms of*, *on the one hand*), from corpora. To create a list of all n-grams in a corpus, the user simply specifies a length or span, for example n = 3 to extract repeatedly used sequences of three words. The specification of a search word around which n-grams are formed is optional (e.g. a span = 3 search for n-grams with *interesting* in a corpus of academic writing would retrieve items including *it is interesting* and *would be interesting*). A final corpus-analytic step involves the extraction of phraseological items that are not entirely fixed (like n-grams) but allow for internal variation. The third position in the 4-gram *on the one hand*, for example, is variable in that it can be occupied by the word *one* or by the word *other*. The software tool kfNgram (see below) derives lists of so-called *phrase-frames* (short p-frames), that is sets of n-grams which are identical except for one word in the same position (e.g. *on the * hand*, *at the * of*). P-frames provide insights into pattern variability and highlight to what degree language items are fixed. A related concept is *concgram* – a word association pattern that captures constituency variation and positional variation (Cheng *et al.*, 2006). A concgram of the words *seems* and *that*, for example, would not only list the 2-gram *seems that* but also cover the patterns *that seems*, *seems likely that* and *seems to suggest that*, among many others. Variable phraseological items are also the focus of attention in *Collostructional Analysis*, a corpus linguistic approach that investigates how lexical items interact with grammatical structures, involving measures of association strength between words and the constructions they tend to occur in Stefanowitsch and Gries (2003).

Useful corpus-analytic tools

A growing number of available software tools, usually referred to as "concordance programs" or "concordancers," provide easy electronic access to the texts stored in a corpus. They offer a range of functions to highlight interesting aspects about the language captured in the corpus, and enable the user to carry out the steps described above. These tools can be divided into two groups: offline tools which the user installs and runs on her/his local computer, and online tools which are accessible through the internet.

Tools for offline corpora use

Offline corpus tools can generally process any corpus that is stored locally on the user's computer, provided the files are in a format that is supported by the selected tool (usually txt, xml, or html). Table 3 presents a list of tools that are widely used in corpus analysis, their functions and weblinks to more information. Corpus researchers who wish to go beyond the functionality of available tools may also write their own scripts to perform corpus-analytic steps tailored to their specific needs. Scripting languages that lend themselves well to this task include Perl and Python.

Conclusion

Corpora have become invaluable in linguistic description, language teaching, and SLA research. With the help of the right tools and analytic techniques, a corpus can highlight aspects of the distribution, function, and use of important language features and provide exciting insights into the patterned nature of different types of texts.

See also: collostructions, Computer Assisted Language Learning (CALL), formulaic language, frequency effects, quantitative research, type/token frequency

References

Anderson, W. and J. Corbett (2009). *Exploring English with Online Corpora. An Introduction.* London: Palgrave Macmillan.

Barlow, M. (2004). Software for Corpus access and analysis. In J.M. Sinclair (ed.) *How to Use Corpora in Language Teaching*, pp. 205–21. Amsterdam: John Benjamins.

Cheng, W., C. Greaves and M. Warren (2006). From N-gram to skipgram to concgram. *International Journal of Corpus Linguistics*, *11*(4), 411–33.

Table 3 Selected software tools for corpus analysis (offline use)

Tool name	*Tool generates*	*Requires license*	*Download/purchase information*
AntConc	Word frequency lists, keyword lists, concordances, distribution plots, collocate lists, n-gram lists	No	http://www.antlab.sci.waseda.ac.jp/antconc_index.html
Collocate	N-gram lists	Yes	http://www.athel.com/colloc.html
ConcGram	Concgram displays, concordances	Yes	http://www.edict.com.hk/pub/concgram/
Concordance	Word frequency lists, concordances, collocate lists	Yes	http://www.concordancesoftware. co.uk/
kfNgram	N-gram lists, phrase-frame lists	No	http://www.kwicfinder.com/kfNgram/kfNgramHelp.html
MonoConc Pro	Word frequency lists, keyword lists, concordances, distribution plots, collocate lists	Yes	http://www.athel.com/mono.html
TextSTAT	Word frequency lists, concordances	No	http://neon.niederlandistik.fu-berlin.de/en/textstat/
WordSmith Tools	Word frequency lists, keyword lists, concordances, distribution plots, collocate lists, cluster lists, concgrams	Yes	http://www.lexically.net/wordsmith/

Table 4 Selected online corpus tools

Tool name	*Brief description*	*URL*
BNC Simple Search	Provides simple access to the British National Corpus and creates sample concordances in sentence (not KWIC) format	http://www.natcorp.ox.ac.uk/using/index.xml.ID=simple
BNCweb	A sophisticated interface to the British National Corpus, allowing for complex searches and user annotation	http://bncweb.info
Brigham Young University (BYU) corpus interface	Provides access to the following corpora: British National Corpus (BYU BNC), Oxford English Dictionary (BYU OED), Corpus of Contemporary American English (COCA), Corpus of Historical American English (COHA), Corpus del Español, Corpus do Português, TIME Magazine Corpus	http://corpus.byu.edu
COBUILD Concordance and Collocations Sampler	Creates concordance samples and collocate lists based on subsets of the Bank of English	http://www.collins.co.uk/Corpus/CorpusSearch.aspx
Compleat Lexical Tutor	Tool collection focused on teaching/learning vocabulary; includes a concordancer to several English, French and German corpora	www.lextutor.ca
Just the Word	A simple interface which extracts word combinations from the British National Corpus; also checks how appropriate a user-specified word combination is and suggests alternatives	http://www.sle.sharp.co.uk/JustTheWord
MICASE	A search and browse interface providing access to the transcripts in the Michigan Corpus of Academic Spoken English	http://quod.lib.umich.edu/m/micase
MICUSP Simple	Allows users to browse and search in all texts included in the Michigan Corpus of Upper-level Student Papers	http://search-micusp.elicorpora.info
Phrases in English (PIE)	Extracts n-grams consisting of words or part-of-speech tags from the British National Corpus	http://phrasesinenglish.org
Research Centre for Professional Communication in English (RCPCE) online corpora	Provides tools to search a set of profession-specific corpora or a corpus uploaded by the user	http://rcpce.engl.polyu.edu.hk
Sketch Engine	Allows to search (and create word sketches based on) a large set of corpora of a range of different languages	http://www.sketchengine.co.uk

Table 4 (continued)

Tool name	*Brief description*	*URL*
Web as Corpus	Creates concordances of web pages in different languages	http://webascorpus.org
WebCorp	Allows access to the web as a corpus; generates concordances, using different search engines	http://www.webcorp.org.uk
Wmatrix	A tool for corpus analysis, comparison, and complex structural/semantic annotation	http://ucrel.lancs.ac.uk/wmatrix

O'Donnell, M.B. and Römer, U. (Submitted). Investigating the interaction between phraseological items and textual position.

Römer, U. (2010). Establishing the phraseological profile of a text type: The construction of meaning in academic book reviews. *English Text Construction*, *3*(1), 95–119.

——(2011) Corpus research applications in second language teaching. *Annual Review of Applied Linguistics*, *31*, 205–25.

Römer, U. and Wulff, S. (2010). Applying Corpus methods to written academic texts: Explorations of MICUSP. *Journal of Writing Research*, 2(2), 99–127. Available at www.jowr.org/articles/vol2_2/JoWR_2010_vol2_nr2_Roemer_Wulff.pdf [Accessed 9 September 2010].

Sinclair, J.M. (2003). *Reading Concordances*. London: Longman.

Stefanowitsch, A. and Gries, S.Th. (2003). Collostructions. Investigating the interaction between words and constructions. *International Journal of Corpus Linguistics*, *8*(2), 209–43.

Tognini-Bonelli, E. (2001). *Corpus Linguistics at Work*. Amsterdam: John Benjamins.

Further reading

Hoffmann, S., Evert, S., Smith, N., Lee, D. and Berglund Prytz, Y. (2008). *Corpus Linguistics with BNCweb – a Practical Guide*. Frankfurt: Peter Lang. (Provides a detailed introduction to central topics in corpus methodology using the BNC and the BNCweb interface.)

Lindquist, H. (2009). *Corpus Linguistics and the Description of English*. Ediburgh: Edinburgh University Press. (A concise introduction to corpora use in language analysis with numerous hands-on examples.)

McEnery, T., Xiao, R. and Tono, Y. (2006). *Corpus-based Language Studies. An Advanced Resource Book*. London: Routledge. (A comprehensive introduction to corpus linguistics, including key readings and interesting case studies.)

Scott, M. and Tribble, C. (2006). *Textual Patterns. Key Words and Corpus Analysis in Language Education*. Amsterdam: John Benjamins. (Focuses on corpus resources and analytic techniques, and shows how they can be profitably used in different educational contexts.)

Sinclair, J.M. (1991). *Corpus Concordance Collocation*. Oxford: Oxford University Press. (A seminal text in corpus linguistics which discusses the rationale behind and key notions in analyzing corpora.)

Corrective feedback (oral)

Nina Spada

Ontario Institute for Studies in Education, University of Toronto

Corrective feedback (CF) is a fundamental feature of second/foreign language instruction. While different types of CF have been associated with particular teaching methods, CF is an instructional strategy that has been a constant throughout the history of second language (L2) teaching. Within the grammar translation approach, the use of explicit metalinguistic CF predominated with its focus on grammar rules. In audio-lingual teaching with its roots in behaviorist learning theory, CF remained explicit but with less metalinguistic information and more emphasis on modeling correct forms for learners to repeat. With the introduction of communicative approaches to L2 instruction, less explicit CF was advocated so as not to interfere with communication. In fact, some versions of communicative language teaching actively discouraged any type of CF. Below is a summary of descriptive and experimental research investigating the effects of *oral* CF on L2 learning between 1970 and 2010.

Descriptive CF research

The late 1970s witnessed several observational studies of CF in L2 classrooms resulting in different descriptive models (e.g. Chaudron, 1977; Fanselow, 1977). This research investigated questions about how much CF teachers provided, in what contexts, and whether some errors received more attention than others. The overall results revealed that teachers tended to correct learners' errors more during formal language-based activities than in communicative practice, the greatest amount of CF was devoted to errors that interfered with communication and somewhat paradoxically, the more a particular type of error was produced, the less likely the teacher was to correct it. Other findings pointed to inconsistency and ambiguity in the CF teachers provided and a tendency for L2 teachers to provide more CF earlier rather than later in the learners' development. In an early large-scale descriptive study of CF in Canadian French immersion classes, Chaudron (1977) investigated relationships between different types of teacher repetition and the rate of correct learner response. The results indicated that repetitions served different functions (e.g. correcting and agreeing) and that learners were more likely to repair their errors when the repetition included emphasis either through rising intonation or stress. This observation was an early indicator of the need for precise definitions and operationalizations of different CF types when investigating their effects on L2 learning.

In the 1980s few studies focused on CF in the L2 classroom. This was related to the arrival of communicative language teaching (CLT) and the widespread acceptance that exposure to comprehensible input was sufficient for successful L2 learning (Krashen, 1982). By the 1990s, however, there was concern that the pendulum may have swung too far pointing to a need for more attention to language form in communicative and content-based approaches to L2 instruction. In another large-scale study to examine CF in French immersion classes, Lyster and Ranta (1997) described six types provided by teachers and learners' immediate responses to them. The findings indicated that the most frequently occurring type of CF was a recast – a reformulation of a learner's incorrectly formed utterance while maintaining a focus on meaning, illustrated below:

STUDENT: Julie like science.
TEACHER: Yes, Julie likes science. (Recast)
STUDENT: Me too.

The findings also revealed that recasts led to few immediate learner responses and repairs. This suggested that learners may not have perceived the recasts as corrective in nature but as confirmations of what they had said leading Lyster and Ranta to characterize recasts as ambiguous particularly when provided in classrooms where the focus is on meaning and content-based instruction. In other classroom studies of CF in which the instruction has been more language focused, learners' immediate responses to recasts have been more frequent and resulted in higher levels of repair (e.g. Sheen, 2004). However, this research was descriptive and thus, no conclusions could be drawn about the long-term effects of recasts or any other type of CF on L2 learning. Furthermore, subsequent studies revealed that immediate responses to CF are not reliable predictors of L2 learning (McDonough and Mackey, 2006). The need for experimental research on the effectiveness of CF was evident and this led to a burst of research activity in the 1990s that has continued to the present.

Experimental CF research

Experimental studies in laboratories and classrooms have been conducted to examine the contributions of different CF types on L2 learning. Most of them have targeted grammatical structures and focus on how implicit CF (e.g. recasts) compares with explicit CF (e.g. prompts). Prompts indicate that an utterance is ill-formed and offer learners the opportunity to self-correct as illustrated below.

STUDENT: Julie like science.
TEACHER: Can you say it again? Julie. (Prompt)
STUDENT: ...likes? ... science.

The majority of laboratory studies have reported benefits for recasts when compared with other types of CF (e.g. Long *et al.*, 1998; Leeman, 2003). Explanations for these findings are that recasts enable learners to notice the gap between what they say and hear in the input and to incorporate this information into their developing grammars without interrupting the flow of communication. There have been fewer experimental/quasi-experimental classroom studies of the effects of CF on L2 learning but all of them have provided evidence for the benefits of explicit over implicit CF. Explicit CF in the form of prompts and metalinguistic cues (e.g. What's the past tense of "go"?) was found to be more effective than recasts in a study by Ellis *et al.* (2006) and prompts were reported to be more effective than recasts by Yang and Lyster (2010).

The conflicting results of classroom and laboratory studies appear to be related to differences between the two contexts. The laboratory setting is controlled and the delivery of CF is intense and consistent likely making implicit types of CF (i.e. recasts) more salient to the learner. On the other hand, the classroom is not a controlled environment and the provision of CF is often diffuse and inconsistent. Furthermore, if the instructional approach focuses on content and meaning this can make implicit CF less noticeable to the learner.

Current interests and future research

Several themes have emerged in CF research and five are identified below. The first concerns the definition and operationalization of CF types. It has been demonstrated that the explicit/implicit dichotomy is not useful in distinguishing CF types because many of them can be delivered in explicit and implicit ways. For example, a recast with emphasis can be explicit whereas a recast without emphasis can be implicit. An alternative dichotomy proposed by Lyster and Saito (2010) is that CF types be differentiated in terms of whether they place demands on the learner to push themselves to self-correct (i.e. output generating) or provide learners with models to reproduce (i.e. input providing). More research is needed to further identify the specific components of CF that contribute to their effectiveness. A second theme is the increased attention given to the synthesis of CF research. In the first meta-analysis to examine the effectiveness of CF on L2 learning, Russell and Spada (2006) investigated classroom and laboratory studies of both oral and written CF and obtained large effect sizes indicating positive effects of CF. However, they did not investigate the effectiveness of different types of CF. Lyster and Saito (2010) limited their meta-analysis to different types of oral CF in classroom settings and also report large effect sizes for CF with advantages for output-generating CF (i.e. prompts) over input-generating CF (i.e. recasts). In a meta-analysis with different inclusion/exclusion criteria than previous studies, Li (2010) reports medium effect sizes for CF showing better maintenance of the effects of implicit CF (i.e. recasts) as well as stronger effects for laboratory compared with classroom studies. Two other meta-analyses, one by Keck *et al.* (2006) and another by Mackey and Goo (2007) examined the effects of different types of interaction on L2 learning and both report large effect sizes for interaction compared with no interaction. The latter study obtained large effect sizes for recasts but could not determine whether they were more beneficial than other types of CF due to an insufficient number of studies. These research syntheses have been critical in moving the research agenda forward. A third theme concerns the interaction between type of target feature and CF raising the question as to whether certain features of language (e.g. vocabulary, grammar) might benefit from different types of CF. A fourth theme relates to the type of L2 knowledge that results from CF. The findings from the Lyster and Saito (2010) and Mackey and Goo (2007) meta-analyses present evidence that CF contributes positively to different types of L2 knowledge including learners' performance on more and less constrained measures (e.g. grammar tests and oral communicative tasks). Nonetheless, there remains a need for studies to include more L2 measures that can tap into learners' unanalyzed/spontaneous ability. The fourth and final theme relates to individual differences. Learner characteristics are well known to effect L2 development yet few studies (e.g. Sheen, 2007) have investigated interactions between CF, learner characteristics, and their combined effects on L2 development. It will be important in future research to investigate the impact of CF in relation to factors such as learner age, proficiency level and L1 background.

See also: classroom interaction research, Focus on Form (FonF), instructed SLA, interaction and the interaction hypothesis, Noticing Hypothesis, recasts

References

Chaudron, C. (1977). A descriptive model of discourse in the corrective treatment of learners' errors. *Language Learning*, *27*, 29–46.

Ellis, R., Loewen, S. and Erlam, R. (2006). Implicit and explicit corrective feedback and the acquisition of L2 grammar. *Studies in Second Language Acquisition*, *28*, 339–68.

Fanselow, J. (1977). Beyond *Rashomon* – conceptualizing and describing the teaching act. *TESOL Quarterly*, *11*, 17–39.

Keck, C.M., Iberri-Shea, G., Tracy-Ventura, N. and Wa-Mbaleka, S. (2006). Investigating the empirical link between task-based interaction and acquisition: A meta-analysis. In J. Norris, and L. Ortega (eds), *Synthesizing Research on Language Learning and Teaching*, pp. 91–131. Amsterdam: Benjamins.

Krashen, S. (1982). *Principles and Practice in Second Language Acquisition*. Oxford: Pergamon.

Leeman, J. (2003). Recasts and second language development: Beyond negative evidence. *Studies in Second Language Acquisition*, *25*, 37–63.

Li, S. (2010). The effectiveness of corrective feedback in SLA: A meta-analysis. *Language Learning*, *60*, 309–65.

Long, M.H., Inagaki, S. and Ortega, L. (1998). The role of implicit negative feedback in SLA: Models and recasts in Japanese and Spanish. *The Modern Language Journal*, *83*, 357–71.

Lyster, R. and Saito, K. (2010). Oral feedback in classroom SLA: A meta-analysis. *Studies in Second Language Acquisition*, *32*, 265–302

Lyster, R. and Ranta, L. (1997). Corrective feedback and learner uptake: Negotiation of form in communicative classrooms. *Studies in Second Language Acquisition*, *19*, 37–66.

Mackey, A. and Goo, J. (2007). Interaction research in SLA: A meta-analysis and research synthesis. In A. Mackey (ed.), *Conversational Interaction in Second Language Acquisition: A Series of Empirical Studies*, pp. 407–52. Oxford: Oxford University Press.

McDonough, K. and Mackey, A. (2006). Responses to recasts: Repetitions, primed production and linguistic development. *Language Learning*, *56*, 693–720.

Russell, J. and Spada, N. (2006). Corrective feedback makes a difference: A meta-analysis of the research. In J. Norris and L. Ortega (eds), *Synthesizing Research on Language Learning and Teaching*. Amsterdam: John Benjamins.

Sheen, Y. (2004). Corrective feedback and learner uptake in communicative classrooms across instructional settings. *Language Teaching Research*, *8*, 263–300.

——(2007). The effect of corrective feedback, language aptitude, and learner attitudes on the acquisition of English articles. In A. Mackey (ed.), *Conversational Interaction in Second Language Acquisition: A Series of Empirical Studies*, pp. 301–22. Oxford: Oxford University Press.

Yang, Y. and Lyster, R. (2010). Effects of form-focused practice and feedback on Chinese EFL learners' acquisition of regular and irregular past tense forms. *Studies in Second Language Acquisition*, *32*, 235–63.

Correlation

Hossein Farhady
American University of Armenia

Correlational analyzes are used to find out the extent to which two sets of scores go together or co-vary. Consider the following sample data from 10 pairs of scores on tests of language proficiency (LP), and vocabulary knowledge (VK).

Applicant	LP	VK
1.	50.0	40.0
2.	44.0	38.0
3.	40.0	36.0
4.	36.0	35.0
5.	32.0	30.0
6.	30.0	32.0
7.	28.0	30.0
8.	25.0	20.0
9.	23.0	18.0
10.	20.0	16.0

These data show that as the scores on LP increase, so do the scores on VK. It is easy to visualize the relationship by plotting the scores on a scatterplot, as illustrated in Figure 2. The scatterplot provides significant pieces of information about the relationship between the two variables. First, pairs are presented as a cluster of points whose density shows the strength of correlation. Second, there is a slope which moves from bottom left to top right indicating a positive correlation. If the direction of the slope is from top left to bottom right, it indicates a negative correlation. Third, the scatterplot shows that as the scores on one variable increase, the scores on the other variable either decrease or increase consistently and in a linear manner. Not all

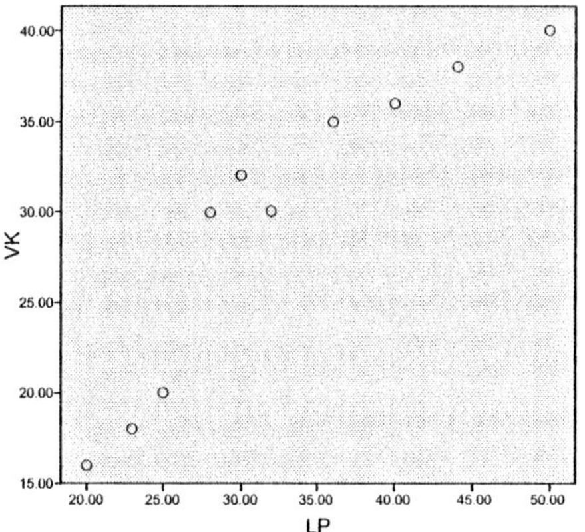

Figure 2 A correlation of language profeciency and vocabulary knowledge

correlations are linear and sometimes the relationship between two variables is nonlinear or curvilinear. For example, there is a curvilinear relationship between anxiety and performance on LP tests. That is, as anxiety level increases to a certain level, called facilitative anxiety, scores on LP increase as well, but when the anxiety level increases beyond the facilitative level and moves into the debilitative level, the scores on LP start to decrease.

Although scatterplots are useful means of understanding the direction and strength of relationship, they do not provide quantitative value for the magnitude of the correlation. There are many types of correlations and many ways of quantifying them. A major factor in determining the way to calculate correlation is the scale of variables in the research project. The variables may be measured on interval, ordinal, or nominal scales. For each case, a specific computation formula should be used.

Two most frequently used correlation types are Pearson's Product Moment correlation and Spearman Brown's rank order correlation. The former is used to calculate the correlation between two variables measured on an interval scale and the latter for two variables measured on an ordinal scale. If the variables are on nominal scales or a combination of an ordinal, an interval, or a nominal scale, other types of correlations, referred to as nonparametric correlations are used. Nowadays, user friendly computers programs such as SPSS have made the calculation process quite manageable.

To interpret the coefficient of correlation, it is squared to be converted into variance term. Square of correlation is interpreted as the amount of common variance between the two variables. For example, if the correlation between two variables is 0.80, they share 0.64 percent of the variance and this much variance in one variable can be accounted for by the other variable. In other words, performance on one measure can be predicted from another measure by the extent of the square of correlation between the two measures. Therefore, the higher the correlation between the two variables, the more common variance between them, and thus more prediction can be made on one variable from the other. This raises the question of how high a correlation coefficient should be to which there is no clearcut answer. Although statistical significance of a coefficient of correlation can be taken as a criterion, it is not always meaningful because statistical significance is a function of the number of pairs in the calculation and sometimes a small correlation may turn out to be significant. Therefore, it is recommended that in interpreting correlation, the extent of common variance along with some logic regarding the nature of the variables should be employed.

See also: Factor Analysis (FA), hypothesis testing, inter-rater reliability, quantitative research, significance level, variance

Further reading

Clark-Carter, D. (2004). *Quantitative Psychological Research: A Student's Handbook*. Hove: Psychology Press.

Cohen, L., Manion, L. and Morrison, K. (2000). *Research Methods in Education*, 5th edn. London and New York: Routledge Flamer.

Hatch, E. and Farhady, H. (1982). *Research Design and Statistics for Applied Linguistics*. Newbery House Publishers.

Larson-Hall, J. (2010). *A Guide to Doing Statistics in Second Language Research Using SPSS*. New York: Routledge.

Creativity

Agnes Albert
Eötvös Loránd University

Creativity is a term that is often used by laypeople in everyday speech; everyone seems to know what it means, but scientific definitions of the term are numerous and diverse. According to recent summaries, it is becoming generally accepted that creativity refers to the production of ideas that are both novel and useful (Mumford, 2003; Sternberg and Lubart, 1999). The task of providing a generally accepted comprehensive definition is not made any easier by the fact that the term creativity is generally used to refer to four distinct but interrelated phenomena: the *processes* involved in creativity, the *person* and the personality traits that are in the background, the properties of the creative *product*, and the *pressures* or characteristics of the environment.

Historical overview

Although philosophers of the Antiquity already dealt with the concept of "inspiration," they considered creativity as a highly individualistic and unpredictable process that is qualitatively different from normal mental processes and is brought about by the intervention of gods. The age of Enlightenment brought the dominance of scientific explanations, which has led to the formulation of numerous theories of creativity. Galton's book "*Hereditary Genius*" published towards the end of the last century was the first attempt to account for the individual differences in people's abilities. Nevertheless, during the first half of the twentieth century, probably due to its great potentials for practical application in institutionalized education and the army, it was the research of intelligence that flourished not creativity.

This does not mean, however, that there were no theories of creativity at all. Almost all the different schools and approaches of personality psychology interpreted this phenomenon in their own way. Psychoanalysis used the term "sublimation" (Freud, 1908/1959) and authors of the psychodynamic approach talked about "regression in service of the ego" (Kris, 1952). These approaches regard creativity as a way of reducing psychic tension: a special means to escape mental illness, neurosis. Other schools of personality psychology have more optimistic views of creativity; in their view it is the greatest fulfillment of human potentials. Authors within the humanistic approach used different terms to describe it: Rogers (1954) calls it "fully-functioning person" and Maslow (1968) refers to it as "self-actualization" and "peak experience." What they all refer to is that creativity can only be achieved through the realization of one's own potentials, instead of living up to the expectations and constraints imposed upon us by others.

Creativity became a topic of psychometric research after 1950 when Guilford in his famous

APA address opened the research agenda. Guilford (1950) argued for the importance of identifying talented individuals and pointed out that tests of intelligence are not suitable for this purpose. Indeed, while it seems that intelligence and creativity are positively correlated up to a certain level, the relationship between them ceases in the case of high creativity and high intelligence scores. According to the threshold theory (Torrance, 1962) very creative people can have average IQs and vice versa; therefore, very intelligent people will not necessarily be very creative. Guilford believed that creativity can be described as a stable set of traits normally distributed in the population, and hypothesized that divergent thinking, the ability to produce many different ideas in response to a problem, is its cognitive background. He contrasted divergent thinking with convergent thinking, the ability to find the correct solution to a problem; this is the cognitive process that he believed is tapped by the majority of intelligence tests. His divergent thinking tests, still in use today, attempt to measure the following four aspects of creativity: fluency, the ability to produce a large number of ideas; flexibility, the ability to produce a wide variety of ideas; originality, the ability to produce unusual ideas; and elaboration, the ability to develop or embellish ideas, to produce many details.

Current models of creativity tend to be more complex; the area is dominated by multi-componential approaches. Besides cognitive components, these models heavily rely on personality and motivational variables as well. These multi-componential theories hypothesize that multiple components must converge for creativity to occur; one such theory is Sternberg and Lubart's (1996) investment theory. These authors propose that creative people pursue ideas that are unknown or unpopular but have growth potential, and having developed these ideas further they are eventually able to make profit by persuading others of the value of their ideas. According to this theory creativity requires six distinct but interrelated resources: intellectual abilities, knowledge, styles of thinking, personality, motivation, and environment. Three intellectual abilities are judged essential with respect to creativity: synthetic ability, which makes it possible for the individual to see problems in new ways and escape the bounds of conventional thinking; analytic ability, which is useful for recognizing those ideas that are worth pursuing; and the practical–contextual ability, which helps in persuading others of the usefulness of the individuals' ideas.

Another new feature of current theories of creativity is that contrary to earlier models, where the assumed position was content generality, some recent theories of creativity argue for domain specificity. They state that creative activity within one content area is independent of creativity in others. This line of argumentation seems to be supported by findings that people capable of producing truly creative products usually perform this in one certain area only, and that in many cases a large base of knowledge is needed on which creativity can operate. Amabile's componential approach (Amabile, 1996) can serve as an example of the domain-specific approach, since besides the groups of creativity-relevant skills and task motivation, she introduces a third group of variables called domain-relevant skills. These include: knowledge about the domain, technical skills required, and special, domain-relevant talent.

Creativity and SLA

It seems that changes in language instruction initiated by communicative and task-based approaches resulted in greater reliance on learners' creativity, positing creativity as a potentially important ID variable within SLA research. Albert and Kormos (2004) found that greater creativity positively affected aspects of L2 narrative performance, such as the amount of talk produced. Dornyei (1995) argues that it is a variable "to be aware of in future studies" (p. 207). However, the fact that creativity has been almost entirely neglected in the SLA field so far can probably be ascribed to the definitional and measurement difficulties associated with the construct.

See also: European Science Foundation (ESF) project, individual differences in SLA intelligence, measuring and researching SLA, motivation, Triarchic Theory of intelligence

References

Albert, A. and Kormos, J. (2004). Creativity and narrative task performance: An exploratory study. *Language Learning, 54*, 277–310.

Amabile, T.M. (1996). *Creativity in Context.* Boulder, CO: Westview Press.

Freud, S. (1959). Creative writers and daydreaming. In J. Strachey (ed. and trans.), *The Standard Edition of the Complete Psychological Works of Sigmund Freud*, Vol. 9, pp. 143–53. London: Hogarth Press. (Original work published 1908.)

Guilford, J.P. (1950). Creativity. *American Psychologist, 5*, 444–54.

Kris, E. (1952). *Psychoanalytic Exploration in Art.* New York: International Universities Press.

Maslow, A. (1968). *Toward a Psychology of Being*. New York: Van Nostrand.

Mumford, M.D. (2003). Where have we been, where are we going? Taking stock in creativity research. *Creativity Research Journal, 15*, 107–20.

Rogers, C.R. (1954). Toward a theory of creativity. *ETC: A Review of General Semantics 11*, 249–60.

Sternberg, R.J. and Lubart, T.I. (1996). Investing in creativity. *American Psychologist*, 51, 677–88.

——(1999). The concept of creativity: Prospects and paradigms. In R.J. Sternberg (ed.), *Handbook of Creativity*, pp. 3–15. New York: Cambridge University Press.

Torrance, E.P. (1962). *Guiding Creative Talent.* Englewood Cliffs, NJ: Prentice Hall.

Further reading

Albert, Á. (2011). When individual differences come into play: The effect of learner creativity. In P. Robinson (ed.), *Second Language Task Complexity: Researching the Cognition Hypothesis of Language Learning and Performance.* Amsterdam: John Benjamins. (An empirical study investigating the relationship between creativity and oral narrative task performance within the framework of task-based instruction.)

Dörnyei, Z. (2005). *The Psychology of the Language Learner: Individual Differences in Second Language Acquisition.* Mahwah, NJ: Lawrence Erlbaum. (This book offers a brief discussion of creativity as a potentially important ID variable.)

Kaufman, J.C. and Sternberg, R.J. (eds) (2010). *The Cambridge Handbook of Creativity.* New York: Cambridge University Press. (A comprehensive overview of current issues in creativity research.)

Ottó, I. (1998). The relationship between individual differences in learner creativity and language learning success. *TESOL Quarterly, 32*, 763–73. (An empirical study investigating the relationship between learner creativity and language learning success.)

Runco, M.A. (1991). *Divergent thinking.* Norwood, NJ: Ablex Publishing Corporation. (A collection of empirical studies about divergent thinking tests.)

Critical Period Hypothesis (CPH)

Niclas Abrahamsson
Stockholm University

The Critical Period Hypothesis (CPH) refers to a now half-century old discussion in linguistics and SLA on whether the human ability to acquire language is maturationally constrained and limited to a critical period in childhood. According to this hypothesis, first exposure to a language that takes place within the critical period results in normal levels of attainment in the case of first language (L1) acquisition and (in most cases) nativelike levels of attainment in the case of second language (L2) acquisition. However, if first exposure to a language takes place after the critical period, the end result will be non-normal/non-nativelike in the case of L1 and L2 learning, respectively.

The term *critical period* originated in the biological sciences and refers to a limited time span in the early life of an organism during which exposure to or stimulation of a certain behavior must take place for that precise behavior to develop in the organism. If exposure or stimulation only takes place after the critical period is closed, abnormal (if any) behavior will result. For example, for certain sparrows and finches, there is a short critical period after birth (ca. 10–50 days) during which young birds must be exposed to the parents' song if characteristic, species-specific singing is to be reproduced. If exposed only after the end of the critical period, the young bird will eventually sing, but not in the proper way (e.g., Marler, 1970). However, for other songbirds, such as canaries, a critical period cannot be observed – in fact, canaries are so-called open-ended learners who learn new songs throughout their lives (Nottebohm, 1984). The question is, then, whether the human ability to acquire language is constrained by a relatively short critical period in childhood, as with the singing of sparrows and finches, or whether this capacity remains unaffected by brain maturation, making it similar to the ability of the canary bird to learn new songs at any age.

Language is by far the most complex and abstract system of knowledge we will ever learn during our lives – yet, it is fully acquired in only a few years time, and at an age at which our general cognitive abilities are not developed enough to handle even the simplest cognitive puzzles. No other animal species exhibit communication systems that come even close to the human language in terms of abstraction, depth, and complexity. Furthermore, children around the world acquire their mother tongues in the same order and during the same timeframe, irrespective of language and social, cultural, and educational circumstances. For many (e.g., generativist or otherwise Chomsky-influenced) linguists, these facts are convincing enough to assume that language is modular and autonomous (i.e., separate and independent from other cognitive systems) and that the human ability to acquire language is possible only through the guidance of an innate and specialized *language acquisition device* (LAD) or *universal grammar* (UG). From such a nativist assumption it follows that the human language is in some way genetically endowed and neurologically hardwired. The commonplace observation that children are far more successful second-language learners than adults are, therefore, makes it natural to assume that the specific, innate ability for language acquisition is also maturationally constrained and is effective only during a limited, critical period in childhood. After such a period has ended, language learning must instead be handled by the general cognitive system, with the result being less efficiency and poorer ultimate attainment. For nativist linguistic theories, the CPH is a natural, or even necessary, component.

The first researchers to scientifically acknowledge children's specialized capacity for acquiring language as biologically determined were the Canadian neurosurgeons Leslie Penfield and Lamar Roberts, who stated that linguistically "there is a biological clock of the brain" (Penfield and Roberts, 1959: 237). They suggested a time span ending at approximately age 9, during which cerebral flexibility allowed direct learning from input. Penfield and Roberts further argued that "for the purposes of learning languages, the human brain becomes progressively stiff and rigid" (p. 236) between ages 9 and 12, after which children become more analytical (Piaget's *formal operations stage*) and begin to learn indirectly via their L1 rather than directly from language exposure, inevitably making learning less efficient and less successful.

A few years later, Eric Lenneberg, an American neurolinguist and specialist in aphasia, postulated what has become known as the (original) Critical Period Hypothesis (CPH). Lenneberg wrote that:

> automatic acquisition from mere exposure to a given language seems to disappear [after puberty], and foreign languages have to be taught and learned through a conscious and labored effort. Foreign accents cannot be overcome easily after puberty. However, a person *can* learn to communicate at the age of forty. This does not trouble our basic hypothesis on age limitations because we may assume that the cerebral organization for language learning as such has taken place during childhood, and since natural languages tend to resemble one another in many fundamental aspects [...], the matrix for language skills is present.
>
> (Lenneberg, 1967: 176)

A careful reading of this quote from Lenneberg potentially renders a great deal of information about what the CPH is all about – and, just as importantly, what it is *not* about.

The first and perhaps most important aspect of the hypothesis can be found in the first sentence, namely what kind of language learning the hypothesis covers. Lenneberg specifically mentions "automatic acquisition" resulting from "mere exposure," which is comparable to Penfield and Roberts' "direct learning from input." This aspect is much too often ignored, not least of all in studies that have claimed to test the CPH in formal, foreign language classrooms, where children generally experience *less* success than older children and teenagers (Ekstrand, 1979). However, if the CPH concerns only the kind of natural acquisition from input that pre-school-aged children engage in, then these results from school settings should be of no relevance for it. Note that Lenneberg uses the acquisition-learning distinction in much the same way as proposed by Krashen a decade later (e.g., 1977).

The literature on the potentially different systems/mechanisms used by child and adult language learners include Selinker (1972), who distinguished between the *latent language structure*, comparable to Chomsky's LAD/UG and used by child L1 and child L2 acquirers, and the *latent psychological structure*, that is, the general cognitive system/ general learning strategies used by adult L2 learners; Felix (1985), who, with his *competing systems hypothesis*, suggested that LAD/UG does not disappear, atrophy or become immature *per se*, but rather becomes "blocked" at a certain age by general cognitive strategies; Bley-Vroman (1989; see also DeKeyser, 2000), who, with his *fundamental difference hypothesis*, suggested that LAD/UG becomes inaccessible/disappears with the termination of the critical period, leaving post-critical period learners with only general learning strategies; and Paradis (2004, 2009), who, by adopting the acquisition-learning distinction, maintain that children up to age 5 automatically and incidentally acquire *implicit knowledge* through *procedural memory* only, while adults consciously and intentionally learn *explicit (meta-linguistic) knowledge* through the *declarative memory* system. For all these authors and theoretical positions, children benefit from some kind of innate and specialized language acquisition mechanism (although not necessarily in the Chomskyan sense, including preprogramed universal grammatical structures or principles), while adults are left with general learning strategies that are seen as less efficient means for developing language.

A second, crucial part of the Lenneberg passage above informs us that it is the *ultimate attainment* of a given language that is of relevance to the hypothesis, or, more specifically, the possibility to reach a *nativelike* ultimate attainment. Lenneberg's statement that "a foreign accent cannot be overcome easily" clearly points to the nativelikeness criterion, especially when contrasted with the statement that older learners can "learn to communicate" at any age. Empirical studies reveal that, while there seem to be short-term initial advantages for adult and adolescent L2 learners (e.g., Snow and Hoefnagel-Höhle, 1978), the typical long-term effect of naturalistic L2 acquisition is, first, a strong correlation between the age of onset of L2 acquisition and ultimate attainment (e.g., Abrahamsson, 2012; Asher and García, 1969; DeKeyser, 2000; Flege, 1999; Johnson and Newport, 1989; Munroe and Mann, 2005; Oyama, 1976, 1978; Patkowski, 1980), and, second, nativelike levels of L2 proficiency in child learners only. From the early 1990s to the present, there has been a certain focus on the potential counter-evidence to the CPH, namely post-critical period L2 learners who, despite a late start, seem to have attained a nativelike command of the L2. However, the typical result from such studies is that, despite more-or-less nativelike language behavior in everyday, oral communication, no adult or adolescent learners have ever been shown to pass for native speakers if a variety of tests – covering both pronunciation and grammar and both production and perception – has been employed to assess their L2 proficiency (e.g., Abrahamsson, 2012; Abrahamsson and Hyltenstam, 2009; Hyltenstam and Abrahamsson, 2003). In addition, members of this category of adult near-native L2 learners always seem to possess an above-average, sometimes extraordinary, innate talent/aptitude for linguistic structure and language learning, through which they have compensated for the disadvantage of having learned the L2 beyond childhood (Abrahamsson and Hyltenstam, 2008; DeKeyser, 2000).

The Lenneberg quote also contains the most criticized part of the CPH, namely the assertion of *puberty*, or age 12–13, as the closure of the critical period. According to Lenneberg's observations of the recovery from aphasia, full recovery seemed possible for pre-pubescent but not for post-pubescent patients, which Lenneberg related to the closure of the hemispheric lateralization process. After lateralization, the brain seemed less *plastic* (or *flexible*, in Penfield and Roberts' terminology) than before, and hence less prone to acquire language. However, subsequent research would soon show that the lateralization process is completed much earlier than at puberty (Krashen, 1973; Lamendella, 1977), perhaps as early as the fetal stage (e.g., Paradis, 2004). This should not automatically invalidate the CPH, since other neurological correlates to "brain maturation" and "maturational constraints" have been suggested over the years. One of the more solid and promising ones is the differentially timed process of *myelination* of different cortical areas. Myelin is a nutritious white matter that is wrapped around the neuronal axons and serves to speed up the execution of electrochemical signals between neurons of different cortical areas. However, a negative but interesting by-product is that new, short-distance connections between neurons within the same local cortical area become more difficult to establish when neuronal axons are covered in myelin (while new long-distance connections between different cortical areas can still be made with the same efficiency as before). According to this account, the primary sensory, motor, and auditory areas around the central fissure in the left hemisphere are fully developed and fully myelinated at age 1, while the grammatical/systematic linguistic (i.e. Broca's and Wernicke's) areas around the Perisylvian fissure are fully myelinated at around age 5–6. Still other, so-called higher-order association areas (responsible for vocabulary, meaning/semantics, facts/knowledge of the world), which are spread out over the entire cortex, become myelinated much later – if at all (see Pulvermüller and Schumann, 1994).

The above neurolinguistic theory, where the successive myelination of different cortical areas more or less equals the successive maturation of the brain, fits well with the discussion within SLA of whether the CPH concerns everything included in the concept of "language" (i.e. everything from phonetics and grammar to pragmatics and literacy), or only certain aspects of language, for example, pronunciation, as suggested by Scovel (1988), or core elements of UG, as suggested by White (1989). Even though Lenneberg himself did not take a clear stand on these matters, his mention of "foreign accent" and his statement above that "natural languages tend to resemble one another in many fundamental aspects," together with the use of the term "the matrix for language skills," makes his position similar to the present-day consensus among CPH proponents that only abstract and core systemic-linguistic parts of language (often boiled down to *phonology* and *grammar*) could be subject to age constraints and the CPH, while vocabulary and other language-specific, peripheral aspects are not affected by maturation but continue to develop throughout life. Even within such a view, it is possible to assume *multiple critical* periods, as proposed by Seliger (1978), for example, one for phonology and one for grammar (Long, 1990), or even different periods for different subcomponents, such as prosody, phonemics, inflectional morphology, word order, etc.

See also: age effects in SLA, cognitive aging, declarative memory and knowledge, Fundamental Difference Hypothesis (FDH), implicit learning, procedural memory and knowledge

References

Abrahamsson, N. (2012). Age of onset and native-like L2 ultimate attainment of morpho-syntactic and phonetic intuition. To appear in N. Abrahamsson and K. Hyltenstam (eds), *High-Level L2 Acquisition, Learning and Use*. (Thematic issue of *Studies in Second Language Acquisition*, *34*, 2, June, 2012.) Cambridge: Cambridge University Press.

Abrahamsson, N. and Hyltenstam, K. (2008). The robustness of aptitude effects in near-native second language acquisition. *Studies in Second Language Acquisition*, *30*, 481–509.

——(2009). Age of onset and nativelikeness in a second language: listener perception versus linguistic scrutiny. *Language Learning*, *59*, 249–306.

Asher, J. and García, G. (1969). The optimal age to learn a foreign language. *Modern Language Journal*, *38*, 334–41.

Bley-Vroman, R. (1989). What is the logical problem of foreign language learning? In S. Gass and J. Schachter (ed.), *Linguistic Perspectives on Second Language Acquisition*, pp. 41–68. Cambridge: Cambridge University Press.

DeKeyser, R.M. (2000). The robustness of critical period effects in second language acquisition. *Studies in Second Language Acquisition*, *22*, 499–533.

Ekstrand, L.H. (1979). Replacing the Critical Period and Optimum Age Theories of Second Language Acquisition with a Theory of Ontogenetic Development Beyond Puberty. *Educational and Psychological Interactions*, *69* (School of Education, Malmö).

Felix, S. (1985). More evidence on competing cognitive systems. *Second Language Research*, *1*, 47–72.

Flege, J.E. (1999). Age of learning and second language speech. In D. Birdsong (red.), *Second Language Acquisition and the Critical Period Hypothesis*, pp. 101–31. Mahwah, NJ: Lawrence Erlbaum.

Hyltenstam, K. and Abrahamsson, N. (2003). Age of onset and ultimate attainment in near-native speakers of Swedish. In K. Fraurud and K. Hyltenstam (ed.), *Multilingualism in Global and Local Perspectives. Selected papers from the 8th Nordic Conference on Bilingualism*, pp. 319–40, November 1–3, 2001, Stockholm Rinkeby. Stockholm: Centre for Research on Bilingualism, Stockholm Universitey, and Rinkeby Institute of Multilingual Research.

Johnson, J.S. and Newport, E.L. (1989). Critical period effects in second language learning: The influence of maturational state on the acquisition of English as a second language. *Cognitive Psychology*, *21*, 60–99.

Krashen, S.D. (1973). Lateralization, language learning, and the critical period: some new evidence. *Language Learning*, *23*, 63–74.

——(1977). Some issues relating to the Monitor Model. In H.D. Brown, C. Yorio and R. Crymes (red.), *On TESOL '77: Teaching and Learning English as a Second Language: Trends in Research and Practice*, pp. 144–58. Washington DC: TESOL.

Lamendella, J. (1977). General principles of neurofunctional organization and their manifestations in primary and non-primary language acquisition. *Language Learning*, *27*, 155–96.

Lenneberg, E. (1967). *Biological Foundations of Language*. New York: Wiley and Sons.

Long, M. (1990). Maturational constraints on language development. *Studies in Second Language Acquisition*, *12*, 251–86.

Marler P. (1970). A comparative approach to vocal learning: song development in white-crowned sparrow. *Journal of Comparative Physiology and Psychology Monographs*, *71*, 1–25.

Munroe, M. and Mann, V. (2005). Age of immersion as a predictor of foreign accent. *Applied Psycholinguistics*, *26*, 311–41.

Nottebohm, F. (1984). Birdsong as a model in which to study brain processes related to learning. *Condor*, *86*, 227–36.

Oyama, S. (1976). A sensitive period for the acquisition of a nonnative phonological system. *Psycholinguistic Research*, *5*, 261–85.

——(1978). The sensitive period and comprehension of speech. *Working Papers on Bilingualism*, *16*, 1–17.

Paradis, M. (2004). *A Neurolinguistic Theory of Bilingualism*. Amsterdam: John Benjamins.

——(2009). *Declarative and Procedural Determinants of Second Languages*. Amsterdam: John Benjamins.

Patkowski, M.S. (1980). The sensitive period for the acquisition of syntax in a second language. *Language Learning*, *30*, 449–72.

Penfield, W. and Roberts, L. (1959). *Speech and Brain Mechanisms*. New York: Atheneum.

Pulvermüller, F. and Schumann, J.H. (1994). Neurobiological mechanisms of language acquisition. *Language Learning*, *44*, 681–734.

Scovel, T. (1988). *A Time to Speak: A Psycholinguistic Inquiry into the Critical Period for Human Speech*. Cambridge: Newbury House.

Seliger, H. (1978). Implications of a multiple critical period hypothesis for second language learning. In W. Ritchie (ed.), *Second Language Research: Issues and Implications*. New York: Academic Press.

Selinker, L. (1972). Interlanguage. *International Review of Applied Linguistics, 10*, 209–31.
Snow and Hoefnagel-Höhle, 1978.
White, L. (1989). *Universal Grammar and Second Language Acquisition*. Amsterdam: John Benjamins.

Cross-linguistic influence (CLI)

Terence Odlin
Ohio State University

The phrase *cross-linguistic influence* (CLI) means roughly the same thing as certain other terms, including *language transfer* and *interference*: each signifies the metaphoric notion of one language influencing another. All three function as cover terms, and the phenomenon is multi-faceted. For example, *transfer* is often subcategorized into *positive* and *negative transfer*. The former occurs when the influence of one language in acquiring another proves helpful, as when students literate in English can easily recognize certain vocabulary items in a language with a similar writing system, for instance, the English word *doubt* and the French word *doute*. Negative transfer, can arise when there is some kind of mismatch between the two languages, as will be considered below. Yet another synonym for *CLI*, one that often appears in language contact studies, is *substrate influence*, such as in analyzes of features of Celtic languages evident in the English of various parts of the British Isles (Filppula *et al.*, 2008).

As stated above, *CLI*, *transfer*, and *interference* are only rough equivalents. *Interference*, for example, usually suggests some kind of negative transfer, especially production errors, as when a native speaker of Vietnamese says, *She has managed to rise the kite fly over the tallest building* instead of *She has managed to fly a kite over the tallest building*, where the learner's use of *rise ... fly* indicates influence from Vietnamese syntax (Helms-Park, 2003). The Vietnamese speakers studied by Helms-Park were recent immigrants to Canada, but similar cases of CLI have also been evident in historical studies of language contact (especially creolist studies), as Helms-Park observes. The mutual relevance of SLA and historical contact studies is sometimes ignored, but what researchers in the former field call negative transfer and what researchers in the latter call substrate influence may often be indistinguishable. On the other hand, SLA researchers have paid more attention to the importance of positive transfer even though it is occasionally considered in historical studies (often going by the name *convergence*).

The *cross-* in *cross-linguistic influence* suggests a metaphor of motion, as does the Latin etymology of *transfer*, the *-fer* meaning "carry" and the *trans-* "across"). Similarly, the German philosopher Wilhelm von Humboldt (1767–1835) used *hinübertragen* (carry over), which may be a deliberate calque of the Latin word. Critics have sometimes expressed concern over the transfer metaphor of something moving somewhere despite the psychological, not physical, nature of the phenomena in question. Even so, the metaphor will not mislead anyone who remembers that *transfer* (or any synonym) serves merely as a cover term. *Transfer* thus resembles the term *metaphor*, which in fact shows a similar etymology, and also the term *translate*, which is from the same Latin verb as *transfer*, even though *metaphor* and *translate* certainly indicate rather different phenomena (Odlin, 2008).

The notion of "influence" is not confined to the positive/negative distinction. Thus, the transfer metaphor is often employed to characterize both influence of a first language on a second (e.g., L1 Russian on L2 English) and the influence of a second language on the first (L2 English on L1 Russian). Whenever a second language is acquired (however incompletely), either kind of CLI is possible, and both are common. Such mutual influence is occasionally investigated and often called *bidirectional transfer* (e.g., Jarvis and Pavlenko, 2008). Nevertheless, many researchers concentrate on either L1→L2 influence (e.g., Han, 2010) or L2→L1 influence (e.g., Porte, 2003). Along with second language research, a growing number of studies focus on CLI involving the acquisition of a third language (e.g., DeAngelis 2007). The influences can include L1→L2 or L2→L3, as well as combined L1 and L2 effects. Reverse influences (e.g., L3→L1) are likewise possible. Influences beyond L2 in the contexts of a third, a fourth, or some additional language (e.g., L7) often go by the name of *multilingual transfer*. While bidirectional and multilingual transfer easily fit under the rubric of cross-linguistic influence, a related phenomenon known as code-switching is somewhat more problematic, especially as to where one should draw the line between L2→L1 influence and bona fide switching (Jarvis and Pavlenko, 2008). Even so, some differences are clear, especially the significance of positive transfer for CLI but not for switching.

Comprehension and production

Both the comprehension and production of a second language can be affected by cross-linguistic influence. Although there seem to be fewer studies of CLI in comprehension than in production, evidence of such influence does exist (e.g., Grabe, 2002). In speech production and writing, vestiges of L1 pronunciation, vocabulary, and grammar are well attested (Weinreich, 1953; Odlin, 2003, 2008; Kormos, 2006; Jarvis and Pavlenko, 2008). Less considered has been how CLI affects the relation between comprehension and production. However, a recent analysis (Ringbom, 2007) suggests that when two languages such as English and Swedish share many features, the similarity will prove especially helpful in comprehension; native speakers of Finnish, though comparable to the Swedish speakers in certain other ways, showed no such advantage, which is consistent with the much greater language distance between Finnish and English. Ringbom's main conclusion is that the special advantages of positive transfer in comprehension will free up processing resources to cope with the challenges of trying to speak or write in a new language.

Hypercorrection, avoidance, and simplification

Errors such as use of the *to rise the kite fly* seen in the English of Vietnamese are especially salient, but negative transfer takes other forms as well. There are, for instance, hypercorrections, which can occur when the L1 has just one phoneme, for example, the Finnish voiceless velar /k/, while the target language has more than one, as with the two English velar stop phonemes, /k/ and /g/. A misspelling such as *crass* for *grass* could be analyzed as the substituting of Finnish /k/ for English /g/, but another error, the spelling of English *comes* as *gomes*, requires a different analysis. Because there is no /g/ in Finnish, *gomes* (but not *crass*) is a hypercorrection. Still another possible manifestation of negative transfer is avoidance, when something in the target language seems incompatible with something in the native language. For example, speakers of Nootka and Thai prove averse to speaking particular English words due to coincidental similarities: the words sound like taboo words in the native languages (Haas, 1951).

Somewhat different from hypercorrection or avoidance is simplification, when the absence of something in the target language is consistent with a similar absence in the L1. In a sentence written by a Finnish learner of English, for instance, there are no articles before the nouns, nor does a preposition mark the direction of motion after the verb: *And man go cafeteria* (this example as well as ones above comes from a database discussed by Jarvis and Pavlenko). One might argue that such reductions are part of natural learning processes also found in child language acquisition. However, the argument does not account for the much greater success of native speakers of Swedish given the same task (narrating events of a film). Since Swedish has a robust system of articles and prepositions and since Finnish has no articles and only a marginal prepositional system, the outcome is largely positive transfer among the Swedish speakers and simplification among the Finnish speakers (Jarvis and Pavlenko, 2008). Such comparisons of two different L1 groups have often shown significant differences (e.g., Helms-Park, 2003; Luk and Shirai, 2009), and the methodology pioneered by Jarvis extends the comparisons to differences seen in the L1s when individuals perform similar tasks. In article use, for example, Swedish speakers writing in their native language tended to use articles much the same way that Swedish speakers writing in English did, which argues for positive transfer, especially in light of the contrast with Finnish speakers who perforce did not use articles when writing in their native language, and with

Finns who frequently omitted obligatory articles when writing in English (Jarvis and Pavlenko, 2008: 192).

Individual variation and constraints

Uriel Weinreich observed that "the bilingual speaker is the ultimate locus of language contact" (1953: 71). While the metaphor of one language influencing another can prove useful, individual learners inevitably mediate any CLI. Weinreich's commonsense observation puts in perspective all appeals to theoretical constructs such as systems, parameters, and constraints, which after all must be able to reconcile group tendencies with individual experiences and behaviors. There have been various claimed constraints on transfer, but exceptions to such claims abound (Odlin, 2003: 454–67). One example of the importance of individual judgment appears in a study of the transferability of Dutch idioms in the judgment of EFL students. Kellerman (1977) emphasized the skepticism of many learners that collocations such as *to have victory in the bag* (which has a close analog in Dutch) were bona-fide idioms. Although several learners deemed such expressions too similar to Dutch to seem genuine English, Kellerman's statistics (pp. 118–19) indicate that several other learners were actually inclined to consider such expressions as real. The kind of skepticism found among some of Kellerman's students indeed suggests the importance of learner perceptions, yet the variation in such perceptions seems no less important.

CLI and the notion of habits

Textbooks of SLA have usually examined controversies over CLI including the perceived connection between transfer and behaviorist theories of language learning (e.g., Larsen-Freeman and Long, 1991). However, the link between structuralists in linguistics interested in CLI (e.g., Charles Fries and Robert Lado) and behaviorists in psychology seems less firm than is sometimes claimed. While Lado was a behaviorist, Fries was not, according to Selinker (2006), who himself studied with both. Another structuralist, Benjamin Lee Whorf, also rejected behaviorism yet saw as very significant what he called the "binding power" of CLI (1956). Although many structuralists (including Fries and Whorf) subscribed to some vague notion of "habits" as relevant to language, only some such as Lado would specify habits in terms of a behaviorist stimulus/response model.

The term *habit* seems less frequent nowadays, but concerns suggested by the word remain prominent in SLA, and terms related to those concerns include *activation*, *automaticity*, and *entrenchment*. Activation can occur in varied contexts such as the use of a word in the second language that evokes more than one meaning in the native language. For example, Elston-Güttler and Williams (2008) found that among Germans the L2 English word *bag* seems to evoke the joint L1 notions of a pouch and a container (German *Tasche* can indicate either a pocket or a bag). The needs for speed and economy underlie automaticity, which may also contribute to a foreign accent. Hammarberg (2001) found that the Swedish of an English/German bilingual initially showed greater phonetic influence from her L2 German but later there was more from her L1 English as she grew fluent in Swedish, with the change apparently due to the automaticity of motor patterns early acquired in English. CLI can result in entrenchment where the influence makes difficult or perhaps impossible the full acquisition of structures such as English articles, which are formally simple yet semantically and pragmatically complex (e.g., Han, 2010). The precise nature of the relationships between activation, automaticity, and entrenchment remains an empirical issue.

Entrenchment and related phenomena went by other names in the structuralist era, as in Whorf's use of "binding power" to characterize L1 English influence in acquiring L2 French. Regardless of terms, how powerful CLI actually is remains unclear, and one reason is the challenge of specifying the relation between language and thought (a.k.a. the "Whorfian" problem). Recent research reviewed by Jarvis and Pavlenko (2008) and Odlin (2008) suggests that there indeed are language-specific effects on cognition. Accordingly, there may also be subtle cognitive influences varying from one language to another that form part of CLI in second language acquisition. Even though Whorf has often been considered a "linguistic determinist," he was quite confident about the potential of linguistics to promote second language learning, his optimism contrasting with some recent thinking in cognitive linguistics. It remains an empirical question as to how well or poorly founded Whorf's optimism was.

See also: conceptual transfer, Contrastive Analysis Hypothesis (CAH), interlanguage, linguistic transfer, language typology and language distance

References

DeAngelis, G. (2007). *Third or Additional Language acquisition*. Clevedon: Multilingual Matters.

Elston-Güttler, K. and Williams, J. (2008). L1 polysemy affects L2 meaning interpretation: Evidence for L1 concepts active during L2 reading. *Second Language Research*, *24*, 167–87.

Filppula, M., Klemola, J. and Paulasto, H. (2008). *English and Celtic in Contact*. New York: Routledge.

Grabe, W. (2002). Reading in a second language. In R. Kaplan (ed.), *Oxford Handbook of Applied Linguistics*, pp. 49–59. New York: Oxford University Press.

Haas, M. (1951). Interlingual word taboos. *American Anthropologist*, *53*, 338–44.

Hammarberg, B. (2001). Roles of L1 and L2 in L3 production and acquisition. In J. Cenoz, B. Hufeisen, and U. Jessner (eds), *Cross-linguistic Influence in Third Language Acquisition: Psycholinguistic Perspectives*, pp. 21–41. Clevedon: Multilingual Matters.

Han, Z. (2010). Grammatical inadequacy as a function of linguistic relativity: A longitudinal case study. In: Z. Han and T. Cadierno (eds), *Linguistic Relativity in Second Language Acquisition: Evidence of First Language Thinking for Speaking*, pp. 154–82. Clevedon: Multilingual Matters.

Helms-Park, R. (2003). Transfer in SLA and creoles: The implications of causative serial verbs in the interlanguage of Vietnamese ESL learners. *Studies in Second Language Acquisition*, *25*, 211–44.

Jarvis, S. and Pavlenko, A. (2008). *Cross-linguistic Influence in Language and Cognition*. New York: Routledge.

Kellerman, E. (1977). Towards a characterisation of the strategy of transfer in second language learning. *Interlanguage Studies Bulletin*, 2, 58–145.

Kormos, J. (2006). *Speech Production and Second Language Acquisition*. Mahwah, NJ: Erlbaum.

Larsen-Freeman, D. and Long, M. (1991). *An Introduction to Second Language Acquisition*. New York: Longman.

Luk, Z. and Shirai, Y. (2009). Is the acquisition order of grammatical morphemes impervious to L1 knowledge? Evidence from the acquisition of plural-*s*, articles, and possessive *'s*. *Language Learning*, *59*, 721–54.

Odlin, T. (2003). Cross-linguistic influence. In C. Doughty and M. Long (eds), *Handbook of Second Language Acquisition*, pp. 436–86. Oxford: Blackwell.

——(2008). Conceptual transfer and meaning extensions. In P. Robinson and N. Ellis (eds), *Handbook of Cognitive Linguistics and Second Language Acquisition*, pp. 306–40. New York: Routledge.

Porte, G. (2003). English from a distance: Code-mixing and blending in the L1 output of long-term resident overseas EFL teachers. In V. Cook (ed.), *Effects of the Second Language on the First*, pp. 103–19. Clevedon: Multilingual Matters.

Ringbom, H. (2007). *Cross-linguistic Similarity in Foreign Language Learning*. Clevedon: Multilingual Matters.

Selinker, L. (2006). Afterword: Fossilization or 'Does your mind mind?' In Z.-H. Han and T. Odlin (eds), *Studies of Fossilization in Second Language Acquisition*, pp. 201–10. Clevedon: Multilingual Matters.

Weinreich, U. (1953). *Languages in Contact*. The Hague: Mouton.

Whorf, B.L. (1956). *Language, Thought, and Reality*. J. Carroll (ed.). Cambridge, MA: MIT Press.

Further reading

Andersen, R. (1983). Transfer to somewhere. In S. Gass and L. Selinker (eds), *Language Transfer in Language Learning*, pp. 177–201. Rowley, MA: Newbury House. (This classic paper considers the problem of constraints on CLI.)

Ellis, N. (2008). Usage-based and form-based language acquisition. In P. Robinson and N. Ellis (eds), *Handbook of Cognitive Linguistics and Second Language Acquisition*, pp. 372–405. New York: Routledge. (The discussion of CLI in part of this chapter offers a view of influence in terms of constructs widely used in psychology such as inhibition and blocking.)

Jarvis, S. (2000). Methodological rigor in the study of transfer: Identifying L1 influence in the interlanguage lexicon. *Language Learning, 50*, 245–309. (As the title suggests, this article considers the means of verifying CLI.)

Migge, B. (2003). *Creole Formation as Language Contact*. Amsterdam: Benjamins. (The book-length study of substrate influence in certain South American creoles illustrates the relevance of creolist studies for second language research on CLI.)

Odlin, T. (2010). Nothing will come of nothing. In B. Kortmann and B. Szmrecsanyi (eds), *Linguistic Complexity in Interlanguage Varieties, L2 Varieties, and Contact Languages*. Frankfurt: Walter de Gruyter. (The problem of the relation between CLI and simplification is considered in detail.)

Cross-sectional research

Daniel O. Jackson
University of Hawai'i at Mānoa

The term cross-sectional is a label for research in which measures are taken at a single point in time. The assumption is that simultaneously collecting data on potential explanatory variables and outcomes may provide a snapshot of a population (Kutner *et al.*, 2005). Such observational designs are widely used in other fields, so, naturally, they have been employed in SLA. Cross-sectional research is distinct from longitudinal research, which employs measurement of key variables over time.

One does not need to look far for examples of L2 research employing the short-term measurement procedures typical of cross-sectional designs. The tendency to investigate L2 outcomes this way is so strong that commentators have noted an over-reliance on cross-sectional studies. For instance, in their handbook of second language acquisition, Doughty and Long (2003) argued that the prevalence of cross-sectional research represents a weakness in SLA. To understand why this approach is problematic, it helps to consider a classic example that focused on measuring L2 performance in a broad sample, rather than observing changes across time.

In the 1970s, Dulay and Burt (1974, *inter alia*) conducted a series of cross-sectional studies to investigate whether schoolchildren learning English as an L2 exhibit a regular sequence of acquisition for a variety of morphosyntactic structures. These researchers analyzed speech samples elicited from learners who differed in age, location, and L1 background, among other factors. Their findings resulted in a hypothesized morpheme acquisition order, whereupon researchers used similar techniques to examine this order in adult L2 learner populations. However, it was not long before criticisms arose; in particular, some investigators cautioned that the cross-sectional rankings did not correlate with longitudinal data on the same L2 phenomena (e.g., Rosansky, 1976). Thus, many researchers now hold that cross-sectional designs obscure the dynamic nature of L2 development.

It should also be noted that cross-sectional studies may employ stratified samples to uncover associations between learner subpopulations and specific dimensions of L2 performance. For example, a researcher might design a study to randomly sample from groups of learners whose age of onset ranged from childhood to adulthood. The analysis would examine how well the age factor corresponds to scores on a grammaticality judgment test. Obviously, there are numerous potential confounds that could hinder interpretations of this study (e.g., L1 transfer). Thus, the researcher would attempt to control for these confounding factors. These additional controls would negatively affect the study's generalizability.

To summarize, cross-sectional research entails (a) one-time measurement of variables and (b) sampling to recruit a cross-section of learners. Although the former characteristic severely limits the usefulness of cross-sectional studies for explicating acquisition processes, the latter has relevance in terms of making fundamental observations about SLA. Furthermore, evaluating basic findings from multiple reports though narrative or meta-analytic reviews may extend and refine the knowledge gained through cross-sectional examinations, as demonstrated by Goldschneider and DeKeyser's (2001) meta-analysis of the morpheme order studies. In this regard, maintaining study quality and reporting usable statistics are strategies which can ultimately enhance the value of cross-sectional research.

See also: longitudinal research, measuring and researching SLA, meta-analysis, quantitative research, questionnaire research, replication research

References

Doughty, C.J. and Long, M.H. (2003). The scope of inquiry and goals of SLA. In C.J. Doughty and M.H. Long (eds), *The Handbook of Second Language Acquisition*, pp. 3–16. Malden, MA: Blackwell.

Dulay, H.C. and Burt, M.K. (1974). Natural sequences in child second language acquisition. *Language Learning*, *24*, 37–53.

Goldschneider, J.M. and DeKeyser, R.M. (2001). Explaning the "natural order of L2 morpheme acquisition" in English: A meta-analysis of multiple determinants. *Language Learning*, *51*, 1–50.

Kutner, M.H., Nachtsheim, C.J., Neter, J. and Li, W. (2005). *Applied Linear Statistical Models*, 5th edn. Boston, MA: McGraw-Hill.

Rosansky, E.J. (1976). Methods and morphemes in second language acquisition research. *Language Learning*, *26*, 409–425.

D

Declarative memory and knowledge

Kara Morgan-Short
University of Illinois at Chicago

Two types of long-term memory are understood to underlie general human cognition: declarative and nondeclarative memory (Squire and Knowlton, 2000; Eichenbaum and Cohen, 2001). Here we focus on declarative memory and aim to define and describe aspects of this particular type of memory as well as to provide an overview of the role that it is posited to play in second language (L2) acquisition. (See the *procedural memory and knowledge* entry in the current volume for information on nondeclarative memory.) Declarative memory comprises the knowledge that we have about facts and events related to our world. It is typically characterized as "knowledge that" and encompasses representations of both semantic and episodic memory. Semantic memory includes our knowledge of facts about our world. For example, it includes our knowledge that Washington, DC is the capital of the United States, that the character "a" is on the left side of a computer keyboard, and that the word "cat" refers to a particular four-legged animal. Episodic memory includes our knowledge of events that we have experienced and allows us to re-experience these events. For example, it includes the knowledge that we visited Washington, DC, that we learned how to type in a high school class, and that we were at a particular location when a historical event occurred. Because declarative memory consists of all our semantic and episodic knowledge about the world, the total amount of a person's declarative knowledge is quite large (Chi and Ohlsson, 2005), containing approximately one million pieces of knowledge, according to one estimation.

Researchers interested in declarative memory have proposed at least three ways in which declarative memory representations may be organized (Chi and Ohlsson, 2005). First, declarative memory may be represented as semantic networks, in which all knowledge (represented as nodes) is interconnected through links. Second, declarative memory may be organized as theories, in which core, abstract knowledge represents the fundamental elements of a "theory" and peripheral knowledge represents specific instantiations that are representative of the core. Finally, declarative memory may also be represented as schemas, in which patterns represent a set of relations between variables. Exactly how these apparent types of organization of declarative memory relate to each other is not yet well understood, but each seems to capture sets of relationships among certain types of declarative memory.

There are several characteristics of declarative memory that together distinguish it from other types of memory. First, declarative memory is often characterized as being available to conscious recall such that the knowledge can be expressed or "declared" by the person who knows a particular piece of information (Eichenbaum and Cohen,

2001). In this regard, declarative memory is thought to be explicit because the knowledge is available to conscious awareness. Note, however, that not all types of information encoded by declarative memory are available for conscious recall (Chun, 2000). Second, the learning of declarative knowledge in most domains appears to depend on attention. Evidence suggests that when information is learned under a condition that diverts or splits attention, the learning of declarative knowledge is impaired (Foerde *et al.*, 2006). In effect, learning declarative knowledge is subject to interference in dual-task situations. Third, information that has been learned and that has become part of one's declarative memory is not informationally encapsulated: It is accessible to other non-declarative memory systems, and it may be applied to contexts different than the one under which it was learned (Eichenbaum and Cohen, 2001). Fourth, learning in declarative memory can occur quickly and on the basis of only one exposure to new information, although the memory may continue to be consolidated over time (Eichenbaum and Cohen, 2001). Finally, one's ability to learn declarative knowledge changes over the lifespan. Declarative memory ability is known to increase during childhood, remain fairly stable during middle adulthood and decrease in later stages of life (DiGiulio *et al.*, 1994; Ronnlund *et al.*, 2005).

Apart from this distinct set of characteristics, declarative memory has been distinguished from other types of memory, such as procedural memory, working memory, and emotional memory, through evidence of double dissociations. In particular, double dissociations between declarative and procedural memory have been repeatedly evidenced in patient populations (Poldrack and Foerde, 2008). For example, amnesic patients with damage to the medial temporal lobe are not able to show improvement on declarative learning tasks, but are capable of demonstrating learning on nondeclarative tasks. In contrast, patients with Parkinson's disease, which is caused by basal ganglia malfunction, show the opposite pattern: they do not evidence learning on a nondeclarative task but perform well on tasks of declarative memory. This double dissociation clearly shows that one type of memory can remain intact even as another type of memory is affected by a particular condition. Such evidence leads one to logically conclude that these types of memory are separate.

The dissociations evidenced by patient populations have also elucidated the regions of the brain associated with declarative memory. The first indication about the neural substrates that underlie declarative memory came from the famous patient H.M. (Eichenbaum and Cohen, 2001). H.M. suffered from severe epileptic seizures. In 1953, his doctor performed a surgery which removed a large portion of his medial temporal lobe in both hemispheres. After the surgery, H.M. could no longer form new memories about facts, events, or people. In other words, he had lost his ability to form new declarative memories. This incident led to the discovery that the brain structures found in the medial temporal lobe are crucial for the formation of new declarative representations. Since this discovery, memory research with patients who have suffered some type of trauma- or disease-induced brain damage and with healthy research participants using neuroimaging techniques has revealed the architecture of the neurocognitive system that underlies declarative memory. This memory system consists primarily of three major components: the hippocampus, the parahippocampal gyrus, and association cortex (Eichenbaum, 2002; Squire and Knowlton, 2000). These structures have been shown to support the formation of memory and its reorganization and consolidation. New declarative representations are formed as highly processed sensory information comes into the parahippocampal region from association cortex. The parahippocampal region allows isolated representations of information to persist in memory for several minutes and serves as a pathway to the hippocampus. The hippocampus appears to compare and relate incoming representations to other memory representations in such a way that it creates organization among memory representations. Finally, the hippocampus outputs this representation to the parahippocampal region, which relays it back to association cortex where the new declarative memory is stored and consolidated. Although other brain areas interact with the hippocampal system in the formation and retrieval of declarative memory, the hippocampus and its related structures are the primary structures involved in forming and storing new declarative representations.

Declarative memory and knowledge has been invoked in several domain-general perspectives of adult L2 acquisition (e.g., Ullman, 2001; Ullman, 2005; DeKeyser, 2007). One of these perspectives is DeKeyser's skill acquisition theory (2007), which maintains that L2 acquisition is similar to the acquisition of other types of skills, such as learning new dance moves. This perspective maintains that skill acquisition passes through three stages, with the first stage necessarily being a declarative stage in which learners acquire declarative knowledge about a skill through observation or instruction. This position has been supported by research that finds that successful acquisition of a linguistic form depends on having initially learned it declaratively (Ferman *et al.*, 2009). Another perspective of L2 acquisition that posits a role for declarative memory is Ullman's declarative/procedural model (Ullman, 2001, 2005). This model ties language acquisition and processing to specific neurocognitive memory systems and posits that L2 acquisition of the mental grammar is particularly dependent on the declarative memory system at low levels of proficiency and experience, but may come to rely on procedural memory at higher levels of L2 proficiency and experience. Declarative memory is expected to underlie the mental lexicon in L2 at all levels of proficiency. (See the **Declarative/Procedural Model** entry in the current volume for more information.) Specific neurocognitive predictions have been made by this model and have found support from research that examines L2 processing at different levels of proficiency using methods such as frequency effects (Bowden *et al.*, 2010) and event-related potentials (Morgan-Short *et al.*, 2010). Although the precise role of declarative memory in L2 acquisition remains an open question, it is likely to contribute to adult acquisition at least for some forms.

In conclusion, declarative memory is a type of memory that is well defined and well studied in cognitive science. Exploring the role that declarative memory may play in L2 acquisition may elucidate the processes involved in late-learned L2 acquisition because what is known about declarative memory can then be applied to particular aspects of L2 acquisition. In the same vein, given a particular link between aspects of L2 acquisition and declarative memory and knowledge, research in L2 acquisition may also prove informative to cognitive science.

See also: Declarative/Procedural Model, episodic memory, explicit learning, frequency effects, procedural memory and knowledge, psycholinguistics of SLA

References

Bowden, H.W., Gelfand, M.P., Sanz, C. and Ullman, M.T. (2010). Verbal inflectional morphology in L1 and L2 Spanish: A frequency effects study examining storage Vs. composition. *Language Learning*, *60*, 44–87.

Chi, M.T. H. and Ohlsson, S. (2005). Complex Declarative Learning. In Holyoak, K.J. and Morrison, R.G. (eds), *The Cambridge Handbook of Thinking and Reasoning*. Cambridge: Cambridge University Press.

Chun, M.M. (2000). Contextual Cueing of Visual Attention. *Trends in Cognitive Sciences*, *4*, 170–8.

Dekeyser, R. (2007). Skill Acquisition Theory. In Vanpatten, B. and Williams, J. (eds), *Theories in Second Language Acquisition: An Introduction*. Mahwah, NJ: Erlbaum.

Digiulio, D.V., Seidenberg, M., O'Leary, D.S. and Raz, N. (1994). Procedural and Declarative Memory: A Developmental Study. *Brain and Cognition*, *25*, 79–91.

Eichenbaum, H. (2002). *The Cognitive Neuroscience of Memory: An Introduction*. New York: Oxford University Press.

Eichenbaum, H. and Cohen, N.J. (2001). *From Conditioning to Conscious Recollection: Memory Systems of the Brain*. New York: Oxford University Press.

Ferman, S., Olshtain, E., Schechtman, E. and Karni, A. (2009). The Acquisition of a Linguistic Skill by Adults: Procedural and Declarative Memory Interact in the Learning of Articifical Morphological Rule. *Journal of Neurolinguistics*, *22*, 384–412.

Foerde, K., Knowlton, B.J. and Poldrack, R.A. (2006). Modulation of competing memory systems by distraction. *Proceedings of the National Academy of Science*, *103*, 11778–83.

Morgan-Short, K., Sanz, C., Steinhauer, K. and Ullman, M.T. (2010). Second Language Acquisition of Gender Agreement in Explicit and Implicit Training Conditions: An Event-Related Potential Study, *Language Learning*, *60*, 154–93.

Poldrack, R.A. and Foerde, K. (2008). Category Learning and the Memory Systems Debate, *Neuroscience and Biobehavioral Reviews*, *32*, 197–205.

Ronnlund, M., Nyberg, L., Nilsson, L.-G. and Backman, L. (2005). Stability, Growth, and Decline in Adult Life Span Development of Declarative Memory: Cross-Sectional and Longitudinal Data from a Population-Based Study. *Psychology and Aging*, *20*, 3–18.

Squire, L.R. and Knowlton, B.J. (2000). The medial temporal lobe, the hippocampus, and the memory systems of the brain. In Gazzaniga, M.S. (ed.), *The New Cognitive Neurosciences*. Cambridge, MA: MIT Press.

Ullman, M.T. (2001). The neural basis of lexicon and grammar in first and second language: The Declarative/Procedural Model. *Bilingualism: Language and Cognition*, *4*, 105–22.

——(2005). A cognitive neuroscience perspective on second language acquisition: The declarative/Procedural Model. In C. Sanz, (ed.), *Mind and Context in Adult Second Language Acquisition: Methods, Theory and Practice*. Washington, DC: Georgetown University Press.

Declarative/Procedural Model (DP)

Michael T. Ullman
Georgetown University

The Declarative/Procedural (DP) model posits that both first and second language (L1 and L2) depend on two long-term memory systems in the brain: declarative and procedural memory (Ullman, 2001b, 2004, 2005). Because the computational, anatomical, physiological, molecular and genetic substrates of these systems are well studied in both animals and humans, this theoretical approach generates a wide range of well-motivated, specific and testable predictions about the neurocognition of both L1 and L2 that one might have no reason to make based on the study of language alone.

This entry summarizes the two memory systems and their interactions, presents the basic predictions of the model for first and second language, provides an overview of the evidence, and discusses future directions.

The two memory systems

The *declarative memory system* underlies the learning, representation, and use of knowledge about facts and events, such as the fact that Kilimanjaro is the highest mountain in Africa, or that you had onion soup for lunch yesterday (Eichenbaum and Cohen, 2001; Squire *et al.*, 2004, Ullman, 2004). The system may be specialized for learning arbitrary bits of information and associating them. Knowledge in this system is learned rapidly, and is at least partly, though *not* completely, explicit – that is, available to conscious awareness.

The hippocampus and other medial temporal-lobe structures learn and consolidate new knowledge, which ultimately depends largely on neocortical regions, particularly in the temporal lobes. Other brain structures play a role in declarative memory as well, including a region in the frontal neocortex corresponding to Brodmann's Areas (BAs) 45 and 47 (within and near classical Broca's area), which underlies the selection or retrieval of declarative memories. (Note that for both the declarative and procedural memory systems, the DP model refers to the *entire* neurocognitive system involved in the learning, representation, and processing of the relevant knowledge, not just to those parts underlying learning and consolidating new knowledge.)

Declarative memory is modulated by various factors (Eichenbaum and Cohen, 2001; Ullman, 2004, 2005; Ullman *et al.*, 2008). Molecular factors include estrogen (higher levels improve declarative memory in women, men, and rodents) and variability in the genes for at least two proteins, BDNF (brain derived neurotrophic factor) and APOE (apolipoprotein E). Other factors also affect it, including sex (females seem to have an advantage at declarative memory over males), sleep (memory consolidation is improved by sleep), and – of particular interest for the study of second language acquisition – age (declarative memory improves during childhood, plateaus in adolescence and early adulthood, and then declines).

The *procedural memory system* underlies the implicit (non-conscious) learning of new, as well as the control of already-learned, perceptual-motor and cognitive skills, such as typing, riding a bicycle, or video game playing (Eichenbaum and Cohen, 2001; Henke, 2010; Ullman, 2004; Ullman and Pierpont, 2005). It may be specialized, at least in part, for sequences and rules. Learning in the system requires extended practice, though it seems to result in more rapid and automatic processing of skills and knowledge than does learning in declarative memory. Note that the term "procedural memory" is used by the DP model to refer only to *one* implicit non-declarative memory system, *not* to all such systems.

The procedural memory system is composed of a network of interconnected brain structures rooted in frontal/basal-ganglia circuits, including premotor cortex and BA 44 (within Broca's area) in the frontal cortex. Although procedural memory is generally less well understood than declarative memory, evidence suggests that the neurotransmitter dopamine plays an important role in this system, as do certain genes, including *FOXP2*. Other factors may also affect procedural memory, including age – unlike declarative memory, procedural memory seems to be well established early in life, after which learning and consolidation in this system may attenuate (Ullman, 2005).

These two memory systems *interact* both cooperatively and competitively in learning and processing (Poldrack and Packard, 2003, Ullman, 2004). First, the two systems can complement each other in acquiring the same or analogous knowledge, including knowledge of sequences and rules. Declarative memory may acquire knowledge initially, thanks to its rapid acquisition abilities, while the procedural system gradually learns analogous knowledge, which is eventually processed rapidly and automatically. Second, animal and human studies suggest that the two systems also interact competitively, resulting in a "see-saw effect." Thus, the dysfunction of one system may result in enhanced functioning of the other. Along the same lines, estrogen seems not only to improve declarative memory, but also to suppress procedural memory.

Predictions of the model

According to the DP model, each of the two memory systems plays roles in language analogous to those they play in other domains in animals and humans (Ullman, 2001a, 2001b, 2004, 2005).

In L1, declarative memory underlies all idiosyncratic knowledge in language – that is, the mental lexicon – across linguistic sub-domains (e.g., simple words and their meanings, irregular morphology, syntactic complements). Procedural memory can underlie the rule-governed sequencing of complex forms, again across sub-domains, including phonology, morphology, and syntax (e.g., *walk* + *-ed*, *the* + *cat*). Crucially, however, complex forms can *also* be learned and processed in declarative memory, for example as chunks (e.g., "walked," "the cat"). Thus, complex forms can rely on either memory system. Which one they rely on should depend on various subject-, task- and item-level factors. For example, individuals or groups with superior declarative memory abilities (e.g., women as compared to men), or worse procedural memory abilities (e.g., those with developmental disorders that affect this system, such as Specific Language Impairment, or those with FOXP2 mutations; Ullman and Pierpont, 2005) should rely more on declarative and less on procedural memory.

The pattern expected for L2 is similar in some respects to that expected for L1 but different in others (Ullman, 2001a, 2005). First, as in L1, lexical knowledge in L2 should be learned in declarative memory. However, the strength of this knowledge should be weaker in later-learned L2 than in earlier-learned L2 or L1: When matched for age, L1 and early L2 learners have had more years of exposure to lexical input than late L2 learners. Moreover, unlike in L1, lexical learning in L2 may be impeded by difficulties with L2 phonology or proactive interference from the L1.

Second, the improvement of declarative memory and possible attenuation of procedural memory during childhood leads to the expectation that complex forms should rely more on declarative and less on procedural memory in later-learned L2 than in L1 or earlier-learned L2. In L1 and even early-learned L2, adult speakers should rely heavily on procedural memory because this system was readily available during childhood learning of the language, and many years of exposure should have allowed for substantial proceduralization. By contrast, adult speakers of later-learned L2 should rely heavily on declarative memory for complex forms because procedural memory may be attenuated in adults, while declarative memory is in its prime; moreover, as compared to age-matched L1 subjects, L2 learners have had fewer years or exposure to the language and thus less opportunity for proceduralization.

Crucially however, proceduralization of the grammar should nonetheless occur in L2, even in adult learners. Although procedural memory is attenuated in adults, it is certainly not afunctional, and indeed procedural learning is well studied in adults. Thus, although L2 grammar should rely heavily on declarative memory (particularly at lower L2 exposure, and especially in later learners), with increasing exposure it should be increasingly proceduralized, and thus increasingly L1-like (contrary to strict versions of the critical period hypothesis). However, the speed and degree of the proceduralization of grammatical abilities should vary substantially as a function of many intrinsic and extrinsic factors, including not only the amount of L2 exposure (i.e., practice with the L2), but also the type of input and the kinds of grammatical rules and relations (some should be easier to proceduralize), as well as intrinsic factors such as sex and genotype.

Note that it is *not* the case that such changes in the relative reliance on the two memory systems are due to any "transformation" of knowledge from one to the other system. The two systems *independently* acquire knowledge, even though knowledge acquired in one system may enhance or inhibit the learning of analogous knowledge in the other. Thus, proceduralization of grammar does *not* constitute the "transformation" of declarative into procedural representations, but rather the gradual acquisition of grammatical knowledge in procedural memory: this system is increasingly relied on, with an accompanying decrease in reliance on declarative memory.

Finally, although the DP model is similar in some respects to other SLA approaches that refer to "declarative memory" and "procedural memory" or to explicit and implicit knowledge (e.g., DeKeyser, 2003, Paradis, 2004), it also differs from them. In particular, the DP model defines the two memory systems according to their neurocognitive bases, whereas most SLA conceptions of declarative and procedural memory treat them – contrary to the neurocognitive evidence – as isomorphic to explicit and implicit memory, respectively (for further discussion see Morgan-Short and Ullman, 2012; Ullman, 2005).

Evidence

Here we discuss evidence related to the DP model's predictions about L2 and its relation to L1. We focus primarily on evidence from Event-Related Potentials (ERPs), whose L2-related findings are more consistent and comprehensive than those from other methodological approaches, such as hemodynamic neuroimaging with PET or fMRI, or neurological studies of adult-onset brain damaged patients. (For more in-depth reviews of all these lines of evidence, see e.g., Abutalebi, 2008; Indefrey, 2006; Kotz, 2009; Morgan-Short and Ullman, 2012; Steinhauer *et al.*, 2009; Ullman, 2001a, 2005.)

In L1, different types of processing difficulties elicit different ERP components. Lexical/semantic processing elicits central/posterior bilaterally distributed negativities (N400s) that often peak about 400 ms after the onset of the word. N400s reflect aspects of lexical/semantic processing, depend at least partly on declarative memory brain structures, and appear to reflect the processing of knowledge learned in declarative memory. In contrast, difficulties in (morpho)syntactic processing often produce two components: first, early (150–500 ms) left-to-bilateral anterior negativities (LANs), which appear to reflect aspects of rule-governed automatic structure-building, and may depend on the procedural memory brain system; and second, late (600 ms) centro-parietal positivities (P600s), which are linked to controlled (conscious) processing and structural reanalysis (and are not posited to depend on procedural memory).

In L2, lexical/semantic processing also elicits N400s, even after minimal L2 exposure – though N400s in L2 learners can be delayed and have reduced amplitudes. This is consistent with the DP model's predictions that L2 is like L1 in depending on declarative memory for lexical acquisition and processing, even though the lexical knowledge may be weaker than in L1. In contrast, L2 differs from L1 in (morpho)syntactic processing, in particular at lower levels of exposure and proficiency. (Proficiency and exposure are generally correlated and difficult to tease apart in L2 studies; following many L2 neurocognitive studies, below we refer only to proficiency levels rather than to both proficiency and exposure.) At lower levels, LANs are typically absent, with subjects instead showing no negativity at all or N400s or N400-like posterior negativities. This is consistent with a lack of reliance on procedural memory for grammar, and a possible dependence on declarative memory instead. However, recent studies have reported LANs in higher proficiency L2, consistent with eventual proceduralization of the grammar. Finally, P600s are generally found in L2, particularly at higher proficiency.

Studies of artificial languages can further elucidate the neurocognition of L2, especially because these languages can be rapidly learned (in the order of hours to days, likely due to their reduced vocabulary and rule inventory) and thus the neurocognition of L2 can be easily compared longitudinally between lower and higher proficiency levels. ERP studies of artificial languages have shown that whereas at lower proficiency adult L2 learners under certain training conditions can show N400s in response to syntactic violations, at higher levels they show a LAN/P600 response, consistent with the expected shift from declarative to procedural memory (Morgan-Short *et al.*, 2012). In an fMRI study of an artificial language (Opitz and Friederici, 2003), adult learners initially depended on the hippocampus and temporal neocortical regions for syntactic processing. Subsequently, activation in these brain structures *decreased* with increasing proficiency, while activation in BA 44 *increased*. Again, this suggests a switch from declarative memory to procedural memory during L2 learning.

Summary and future directions

In sum, the DP model is a useful theoretical approach for generating novel specific predictions, and has a fair degree of empirical validity thus far. Yet much remains to be examined. For example, there has been little work on the model's endocrine or genetic predictions in either L1 or L2. Additionally, the model's pharmacological and pedagogical ramifications may prove important for second language learning. Future studies will provide a better understanding of the model and its implications.

See also: declarative memory and knowledge, explicit learning, implicit learning, procedural memory and knowledge, psycholinguistics of SLA, semantic processing

References

Abutalebi J. (2008). Neural aspects of second language representation and language control. *Acta Psychologica, 128*, 466–478.

DeKeyser, R.M. (2003). Implicit and explicit learning. In C.J. Doughty and M.H. Long (eds) *The Handbook of Second Language Acquisition*, pp. 313–348. Malden, MA: Blackwell.

Eichenbaum, H. and Cohen, N.J. (2001). *From Conditioning to Conscious Recollection: Memory Systems of the Brain*. New York: Oxford University Press.

Hatch, E. and Farhady, H. (1982). *Research Design and Statistics for Applied Linguistics*. Rowley, MA: Newbery House.

Henke., K. (2010). A model for memory systems based on processing modes rather than consciousness. *Nature Reviews Neuroscience, 11*, 523–532.

Indefrey, P. (2006). A meta-analysis of hemodynamic studies on first and second language processing: which suggested differences can we trust and what do they mean? *Language Learning, 56*, 279–304.

Kotz, S.A. (2009). A critical review of ERP and fMRI evidence on L2 syntactic processing. *Brain and Language*, *109*, 68–74.

Larson-Hall, J. (2010). *A Guide to Doing Statistics in Second Language Research Using SPSS.* New York: Routledge.

Morgan-Short, K., Steinhauer, K., Sanz, C. and Ullman, M.T. (2012). Implicit but not explicit second language training leads to native-language brain patterns. *PNAS*.

Morgan-Short K. and Ullman, M.T. (Under Review). The neurocognition of second language. In A. Mackey and S. Gass (eds), *The Routledge Handbook of Second Language Acquisition*. New York: Routledge.

Opitz, B. and Friederici, A.D. (2003). Interactions of the hippocampal system and the prefrontal cortex in learning language-like rules. *NeuroImage*, *19*, 1730–1737.

Paradis, M. (2004). *A Neurolinguistic Theory of Bilingualism*. Amsterdam: John Benjamins.

Poldrack, R.A. and Packard, M.G. (2003). Competition among multiple memory systems: Converging evidence from animal and human brain studies. *Neuropsychologia*, *41*, 245–51.

Squire, L.R., Stark, C.E. and Clark, R.E. (2004). The medial temporal lobe. *Annual Review of Neuroscience*, *27*, 279–306.

Steinhauer, K., White, E.J. and Drury, J.E. (2009). Temporal dynamics of late second language acquisition: Evidence from event-related brain potentials. *Second Language Research*, *25*, 13–41.

Ullman, M.T. (2001a). The neural basis of lexicon and grammar in first and second language: The declarative/procedural model. *Bilingualism: Language and Cognition*, *4*, 105–122.

——(2001b). A neurocognitive perspective on language: The declarative/procedural model. *Nature Reviews Neuroscience*, *2*, 717–726.

——(2004). Contributions of memory circuits to language: The declarative/procedural model. *Cognition*, *92*, 231–270.

——(2005). A cognitive neuroscience perspective on second language acquisition: The declarative/procedural model. In C. Sanz (ed.) *Mind and Context in Adult Second Language Acquisition: Methods, Theory and Practice*, pp. 141–178. Washington, DC: Georgetown University Press.

Ullman, M.T., Miranda, R.A. and Travers, M.L. (2008). Sex differences in the neurocognition of language. In J.B. Becker, K.J. Berkley, N. Geary, E. Hampson, J. Herman and E. Young (eds), *Sex on the Brain: From Genes to Behavior*, pp. 291–309. New York: Oxford University Press.

Ullman, M.T. and Pierpont, E.I. (2005). Specific language impairment is not specific to language: the procedural deficit hypothesis. *Cortex*, *41*, 399–433.

Depth of processing

Alice F. Healy and James A. Kole
University of Colorado

Students can take different approaches when acquiring second language vocabulary. Specifically, they can focus on the sound (phonology), spelling (orthography), or meaning (semantics) of the words. These can be viewed as different levels, or depths, of processing, and the depth of processing has been shown to influence learning and retention (Craik and Lockhart, 1972). One way that researchers have used to vary processing depth is to give the student an orienting task when exposed to the vocabulary items, with no explicit mention of any future memory test. For example, to elicit orthographic processing, students could judge whether a given word contains a specific target letter, and to elicit semantic processing, students could judge instead the pleasantness of the word. It has been shown that semantic processing leads to better memory than does orthographic processing. More generally, material is learned better with deeper levels of processing.

Although the type of processing that occurs at the time of encoding information influences memory, that is not the only factor of importance. Also critical is the type of processing that occurs at the time of retrieving the information. In fact, it has been shown that a more shallow level of processing at encoding leads to better retention than a deeper level of processing at encoding if the retention test also demands a shallow processing level. To illustrate the importance of such *transfer appropriate processing*, Morris *et al.* (1977) compared two types of word orienting tasks, one involving semantic and the other phonological processing. They also examined two different types of recognition tests, one standard and the other requiring recognition of words that rhymed with the to-be-remembered words. As expected on the basis of depth of processing, the semantic orienting task led to better performance than the phonological orienting task for the standard test. However, contrary to predictions based on depth of processing, phonological processing led to better performance than semantic processing for the word-rhyming recognition test.

Another way to vary processing depth is to promote multiple types of processing rather than a single type. For example, using imagery as well as semantic processing would be more effective than using either processing type alone, according to a *dual-coding* account (Paivio, 2007). By dual coding, information is stored in memory using two different representations, one verbal and the other visual. When trying to retrieve information, students who have used dual coding can search their memory using two different routes, thereby increasing their success at finding the information.

Another method for promoting deep processing is based on the *testing effect*, which employs tests rather than pure study episodes. For example, instead of simply viewing the foreign word and its translation at the same time, students could see just the foreign word and be required to translate it themselves. The test requirement leads to better learning and retention than does study alone (Karpicke and Roediger, 2008). This method for enhancing learning also benefits from transfer appropriate processing when the testing during learning matches the final testing.

See also: declarative memory and knowledge, Involvement Load Hypothesis (ILH), rehearsal, semantic processing, transfer appropriate processing, vocabulary learning

References

Craik, F.I. and Lockart, R.S. (1972). Levels of processing: A framework for memory research. *Journal of Verbal Learning and Verbal Behavior*, *11*, 671–84.

Karpicke, J.D. and Roediger, H.L. III (2008). The critical importance of retrieval for learning. *Science*, *319*, 966–68.

Morris, C.D., Bransford, J.D. and Franks, J.J. (1977). Levels of processing versus transfer appropriate processing. *Journal of Verbal Learning and Verbal Behavior*, *16*, 519–33.

Paivio, A. (2007). *Mind and Its Evolution: A Dual-Coding Theoretical Approach*. Mahwah, NJ: Erlbaum.

Further reading

Healy, A.F. and Bourne, L.E. Jr. (eds) (1998). *Foreign Language Learning: Psycholinguistic Studies on Training and Retention*. Mahwah, NJ: Erlbaum. (A summary of specific psychology experiments on foreign language learning.)

Kroll, J.F. and de Groot, A.M.B. (eds) (2005). *Handbook of Bilingualism: Psycholinguistic Approaches*. New York: Oxford University Press. (A comprehensive summary of psychology research on bilingualism, including relevant neuroscience.)

Menn, L. (2011). *Psycholinguistics: Introduction and Applications*. San Diego, CA: Plural Publishing. (Introduction to research accomplishments in the psychology of language.)

Roediger, H.L. III (ed.) (2008). *Cognitive Psychology of Memory*, Vol. 2 of *Learning and Memory: A Comprehensive Reference*, 4 vols. (J. Byrne, Editor). Oxford: Elsevier. (A broad summary of cognitive psychology research on memory.)

Development in Second Language Acquisition

Jürgen M. Meisel
University of Hamburg and University of Calgary

Ordered Sequences in Language Acquisition

The very notion of (second) language acquisition as implying that learners' knowledge of the target language changes over time, from the *initial* towards the *final state*, draws attention to the idea of linguistic *development*. It might also justify acquisition research restricting its attention to these two states, disregarding the question of how learners proceed from start to endpoint. Second language (L2) research, up to the late sixties of the twentieth century, indeed focused primarily on the end result and the ability to use the L2, rather than on the process of acquisition or the cognitive capacity underlying it. Moreover, this ability was claimed to be shaped by forms, meanings and habits of the native language. In the early 1960s, L1 (first language) research started to entertain the idea of an innate Language Acquisition Device (LAD) (McNeill, 1966; Chomsky, 1981) which not only defines the initial state of L1 development, that is, the implicit knowledge which children bring to the task of acquisition prior to experience, but also determines the course of development since it requires that children's grammars conform to principles of Universal Grammar (UG), the core unit of the LAD, at each point of acquisition (see **Initial state**, and **Universal Grammar (UG)**, this volume).

The question of whether the LAD or the human Language-Making Capacity (LMC), more generally, also guides L2 acquisition, was not addressed in a systematic fashion until the late 1960s. Corder (1967) was among the first to suggest that L1 and L2 acquisition are shaped by the same underlying mechanism, and he demanded that the focus of L2 research should therefore be on these mechanisms and on the changing knowledge of the learner, that is, on the "interlanguage." From early on, a crucial issue pursued by this research paradigm as whether the "transitional competence" of L2 learners differs in fundamental ways from the linguistic knowledge developed by L1 children.

Soon after Corder's (1967) programmatic paper, a series of L2 interlanguage studies, the *Morpheme Order Studies*, set out to test empirically the hypothesis predicting substantial similarities between first and second language acquisition, inspired by the research of Roger Brown and his students. Brown (1973) found in a longitudinal study of three children, known as Adam, Eve, and Sarah, that English grammatical morphemes which are initially lacking in L1 child utterances emerge in a specific order in the children's speech. Brown's list contained 14 items, including bound morphemes like present progressive–*ing*, plural–*s*, third person singular–*s*, possessive–*'s* and past tense–*ed*, as well as free morphemes like prepositions (*in*, *on*), articles (*a*, *the*), and specific forms of verbal elements (*went*, *be*, *has*). Rank-order correlations among the orderings observed in the data from these three children exhibited a high degree of invariance. This discovery of cross-individually similar *ordered sequences* represents one of the most significant insights into language development. Importantly, it confirms the suspicion that grammatical development is determined by an underlying logic common to all children, in spite of considerable differences between them with respect to the primary linguistic data to which they are exposed, the socio-cultural environment in which they are raised, or individual properties (personality, intelligence, etc.) which they bring to the task of language acquisition (see **Developmental sequences** and **Morpheme acquisition orders**, this volume).

Morpheme Order Studies investigating child and adult L2 learners revealed that in second language acquisition too, the emergence of grammatical morphemes follows a specific order, exhibiting very little variation across individuals. This finding is particularly important because it is based on studies of learners with different first languages. Dulay and Burt (1974), for example, analyzing the acquisition of English by Spanish- and Chinese-speaking children aged five to eight years, found a common acquisition order for 11 grammatical morphemes, including nine of those studied by Brown (1973). Research results of this kind speak strongly against transfer from the L1 as a predominant mechanism determining L2 acquisition. Dulay and Burt suggested instead that the course of L2 acquisition is shaped by "creative construction." Although this term is not defined precisely, it clearly refers to innate capacities with which the human mind is endowed, enabling L2 learners to actively organize their knowledge about the L2; cf. Dulay *et al.* (1982). The lack of cross-individual variation in the emergence of grammatical morphemes indeed supports the idea of a common underlying logic for L2 acquisition. Interestingly, however, the invariant sequences in L2 are not identical to the ones in L1 development. Thus, although these findings demonstrate that grammatical development in both types of acquisition is guided by general, possibly universal principles, doubts remain as to whether the underlying logic emanates in both cases from the same acquisition device.

In fact, the sequences established by Morpheme Order Studies for L2 acquisition have been subject to criticism, primarily concerning methodological issues which will not be dealt with. What matters here is whether the proposed acquisition orders are merely artefacts of the methods of collecting, analyzing, and interpreting the data. Larsen-Freeman and Long (1991) showed that this is not the case, and they concluded that the morpheme studies provide strong evidence in support of common accuracy/acquisition orders. A more serious concern, alluded to by this way of phrasing it, is whether "accuracy order" can indeed be interpreted as "order of acquisition." The problem is that the major criterion in deciding on the point of emergence of a morpheme was whether or not it appeared in the required context (see **Emergence criterion**, this volume). In cases where L2 learners use target-deviant "interlanguage" forms, their acquisition achievement will be underrated by a criterion which requires correct use in adequate contexts. Conversely, overrating happens if correct forms are used although the relevant grammatical knowledge has not been acquired, for example, in cases of rote learning. However, these problems are not specific to the Morpheme Order Studies. Moreover, it has been shown that orders of emergence postulated in the morpheme studies do capture acquisition sequences rather than merely reflecting accuracy of use; see Andersen (1978), among others.

Another potentially serious problem is that orderings are not equally well motivated for each possible pair of elements within a sequence. Studies investigating different groups of learners yielded statistically significantly related orders, but some orderings are more robust than others. In addition, the individual items are not equidistant on the assumed chronological hierarchy, that is, some cluster around almost identical values whereas others exhibit more varied rankings. In order to capture this fact, morphemes exhibiting similar rank orderings have been ranked together; see Dulay and Burt (1975). The idea is that items in an earlier group are acquired before those in a later one and, conversely, the acquisition of an element in a later group implies the acquisition of all those displayed in all earlier ones (see **Implicational scaling**, this volume). However, no claim is made with respect to the order of acquisition of morphemes within one group.

Note that this changes our perspective on linguistic development in a second language in a substantive way since it replaces the idea of an order of emergence of linguistic items by the concept of an ordered sequence of acquisition phases. The underlying developmental logic thus applies exclusively to the ordering of the phases of a sequence, not to the set of elements emerging during a given phase. This observation draws attention to the fact that nothing has been said, so far, about the nature of the developmental logic. In other words, morpheme orders are justified based on empirical facts. Informally speaking, certain items happen to be acquired in a specific order, and since the developmental regularities go beyond what can reasonably be expected to occur coincidentally, one may plausibly assume that an acquisition mechanism is at work. The nature of the mechanism remains opaque, however; see section 3. At this point, one can conjecture that the developmental logic will relate either to *what* is acquired, that is, properties of grammatical items, or to *how* something is acquired, that is, possibly referring to increasing learning difficulties.

When dealing with the acquisition of grammatical elements, describing and explaining developmental sequences in grammatical terms should probably be the first option. Yet the grammatical heterogeneity of the set of morphemes studied by Brown (1973) has proven to be an insurmountable obstacle, cf. Meisel (2011: Ch. 3.2), and even the less heterogeneous set of items studied by Dulay and Burt (1974, 1975) cannot be accounted for systematically in grammatical terms alone. It is, for example, not obvious which properties are shared by plural–*s*, present progressive–*ing*, articles, auxiliaries, and the copula, causing them to emerge more or less simultaneously during the same phase, as suggested by Krashen (1977). Andersen (1978) took a first step towards solving this problem, demonstrating that variation across learner groups and across individuals can be reduced to a minimum if the single order of emergence is split into distinct sequences, defined in terms of the categorial status (nominal-verbal) and the combinatorial type (bound-free) of the morphemes.

In sum, a significant finding concerning development in L2 acquisition is that learners proceed in some domains of grammar through invariant sequences. However, their descriptive characterization still needs to be refined, and their explanation remains a *desideratum*.

Developmental sequences in second language acquisition

The notion of "developmental sequence" can thus be defined as a sequence of grammatically related and chronologically strictly ordered phases; see Wode (1976) or Felix (1982), among others. Each phase, in turn, is defined in terms of grammatical properties acquired during the period in question. "Strict ordering" of phases implies that learners are predicted not to violate the ordering established by the sequence, that is, no learner will acquire features characteristic of phase x+1 before those characterizing phase x; however, not all these phenomena must appear in the speech of all learners.

Although developmental sequences and the phases characterizing them are defined by newly emerging grammatical properties, it is not possible to rely solely on empirical findings when attempting to identify sequences in a given target language. The first reason leading to this conclusion is the one already mentioned, namely that the defining criteria need to be motivated theoretically. They should, for example, constitute a grammatically coherent set, as suggested by Andersen (1978). This amounts to disentangling the sequences proposed by morphological studies, splitting them into separate ones.

As an illustration, assume that the acquisition device indeed operates separately on the grammatically defined (e.g. verbal, nominal, etc.) sets of elements: {a, b, c, ... z}, {1, 2, 3, ... n}, {A, B, C, ... Z}, etc., causing them to appear in a fixed order within each set. Since the first elements of the sets need not emerge simultaneously and the elements within a set have been shown not to be chronologically equidistant, the causally connected orders can emerge as is illustrated in (1) rather than in a synchronized fashion.

(1) Disentangling empirically motivated sequences

	1	
a	2	
b		A
	3	B
c		C

The vertical ordering in (1) depicts the chronology of emergence. Since at every point of development, that is, within the five phases in (1), the elements are not ordered, this allows for different acquisition orders, for example [1 a 2 b A 3 B c C], [1 2 a A b B 3 C c]. Analyses of different data sets will thus not necessarily come up with completely identical orders, and a search for a single developmental logic must fail. If these orders are reinterpreted as sequences of phases, the result reflects the facts more accurately, but it is still not satisfactory, as becomes apparent when the phases in (1) are represented as unordered sets: {1}, {a 2}, {b A}, {3 B}, {c C}. It shows correctly the ordering within the grammatical domains – 1 < 2 < 3, a < b < c and A < B < C – but it also suggests an underlying logic causing 1 < a, 2 < b, b < B, and so forth, although these elements are not logically related in this hypothetical example. The problem in real life is that one does not know from the start whether an empirically detected sequence reflects a single underlying logic or several, and if several, how many. Rather, this has to be determined by theoretically guided analyses which must also reveal the nature of the underlying forces causing particular elements to emerge in specific orders.

Another reason why L2 developmental sequences cannot be identified on the basis of empirical findings alone is that not every feature attested in the speech of learners necessarily characterizes a developmental phase, not even if it is used regularly and at a specific point of acquisition. L2 acquisition exhibits more variability than L1 development, across learners as well as intra-individually, and learner-type specific variation can complicate considerably the task of identifying properties which characterize grammatical developmental. Considerations of this type led to the *multidimensional model* of L2 acquisition, proposed by Meisel *et al.* (1981); see also Clahsen *et al.* (1983). It distinguishes between a *developmental dimension* defining the invariant sequence through which all learners of a given L2 proceed and a *dimension of variability* characterizing the variation space explored by different types of learners.

As an illustration, one can mention the fact that it has repeatedly been suggested in L2 research that learners, during an early period of acquisition, proceed through a phase in which they use a "pidginized" version of the target language (cf. Schumann, 1978; Andersen, 1983) or a "Basic Variety" (Klein and Perdue, 1997) (see **Basic Variety, Simplification**, and **Pidginization and creolization**, this volume). This is commonly characterized as structurally reduced or "simplified" (Meisel, 1977), typically lacking elements which are obligatory in the target languages, for example, copulas, auxiliaries, verbs, prepositions, or articles. Yet although the use of simplified structures during initial phases of L2 acquisition is well documented, a number of studies have demonstrated that learners vary considerably in the extent to which they resort to this kind of use and that certain elements are never omitted by some learners; cf. Meisel *et al.* (1981), Pienemann (1981). Thus, rather than characterizing an early phase through which all L2 learners proceed, structural simplification seems to reflect a specific approach to L2 acquisition and use, that is, a learner-specific strategy rather than a developmental mechanism. A similar argument can be made for other types of L2 uses, for example, preverbal placement of negators (Meisel, 1997) or syntactic transfer from the L1 (Meisel, 2000). These strategies are applied to varying degrees by different learner types, and although they tend to be used at specific points of acquisition (e.g. simplification during early phases), they are not restricted to certain developmental phases.

Based on research findings with Italian and Spanish learners of German, see Clahsen *et al.* (1983), (2) is an illustration of how L2 learners at different developmental phases differ with respect to how strongly they rely on strategies of the type just mentioned. Those plotted towards the left on a vertical axis use them heavily, those towards the right rarely or not at all. Since simplification and similar strategies arguably facilitate using the available grammatical knowledge, one may expect learners to cluster at the lower left and the upper right corner of the diagram: Pepita who has acquired only basic grammatical knowledge, omits elements frequently, places the negator invariably in preverbal position, etc.; an advanced learner like Janni, on the other hand, does not resort to these options at all. But learners may rely on them although they have acquired the target system successfully, for example, Lolita, Franco, and Benito, whereas others refrain from doing so, in spite of limited knowledge, for example, Rosemarie. Thus, changes over time in the speech of learners do not necessarily indicate increasing knowledge; they may instead reflect decreasing reliance on facilitating strategies.

In sum, properties defining phases of developmental sequence should be identified by means of theoretical, empirical, and methodological criteria. The phases in (2), for example, refer to verb placement in German. I: invariant SVO/Adv order; II: non-finite verbal items appear in clause-final

Table 5

(2) *Development and learner-specific variation in L2 acquisition*

Phase IV	Benito I	Janni I		
Phase III	Franco I		Carlo	
Phase II		Lolita S		Angelina S
Phase I	Pepita S		Rosemarie S	

position; III: finite verbs precede subjects when a constituent other than the subject appears in initial position; IV: finite verbs are placed clause-finally in subordinate constructions. These properties thus constitute a coherent set, defined by grammatical theory. Their order of acquisition has been detected in longitudinal and in cross-sectional studies of child as well as adult L2 learners and it represents one of the most robust empirical findings in L2 research. Methodologically, the sequence is corroborated by the fact that its phases can be plotted on an implicational scale of the form A ⊃ B ⊃ C ⊃ D ⊃ E ⊃ F ⊃ … Z, cf. Hyltenstam (1977), Andersen (1978), Meisel *et al.* (1981), meaning that learners who have acquired C have also acquired D, E, F, and so forth but not A or B. Put differently, strict order is the psycholinguistic correlate of implicational scales.

Explaining developmental sequences

Developmental sequences can thus be considered as a crucial characteristic of development in both first and second language acquisition. This conclusion is supported by robust empirical evidence, but up to this point sequences are merely descriptive tools, for the observation that certain grammatical phenomena emerge in a fixed order does not yet reveal what causes them to appear in just this order. Attempts at explaining development are scarce.

As for the morpheme order, Brown (1973) considered grammatical complexity as a likely explanatory factor for their order of acquisition in L1, and Dulay and Burt repeatedly referred to “universal language processing strategies” as an explanation of the L2 orders. Although these authors did not actually provide solid evidence supporting their suggestions, there can be no doubt that system-internal properties and processing mechanisms are factors which can plausibly be suspected to determine the course of acquisition. In fact, grammatical and processing complexity may conspire, as was suggested indirectly by Andersen (1978) who argued that categorial status (nominal-verbal) and combinatorial type (bound-free) of morphemes together explain their order of acquisition; the assumption here is that free morphemes are processed more easily.

In L1 acquisition, the relevance on system-internal properties for an explanation of the course of linguistic development is widely acknowledged, even if this does not necessarily imply increasing grammatical complexity. Given that sentence structures consist of layers of lexical and functional categories (FC, e.g. D(ET), T(ENSE) and C(OMP)) and considering that FC have been identified in UG theory as the locus of intra- and inter-linguistic variation, it has been argued that FC may be lacking in early grammars (see **Functional categories**, this volume). Developmental phases could then be defined in terms of successively implemented FC, their order of emergence resulting from the functional layering of sentence structures; cf. the Structure Building Hypothesis (Guilfoyle and Noonan, 1992). Postulating an initial lack of FC may however be a too radical claim. A more parsimonious explanation suggests that functional categories are initially underspecified for uninterpretable features and that specific developmental sequences reflect incremental feature specification of functional heads, determining the strength or the distribution of these features across FC; see Meisel (2011: Ch. 2.3). Although the Structure Building Hypothesis is controversial, the idea of a grammatically guided logic of L1 development is widely accepted, and it is in line with the assumption that principles of UG, the core component of the LAD, constrain developing grammars at every point of acquisition.

In L2 acquisition, on the other hand, the hypothesis of incremental structure building fares less well. Zobl and Liceras (1994), for example, argue that the SBH can account for L1 acquisition orders, and they succeed reasonably well in demonstrating that these orders are determined by the functional layering of sentence structure. Importantly, they show that the developmental logic is category-specific and that elements related to DP appear before those related to IP. In their analysis of L2 orders, on the other hand, they find cross-categorical development; morphemes dependent on different functional categories appear simultaneously whereas others are scattered over the acquisition sequence although they are related to the same functional domain. Zobl and Liceras (1994) contend that this is due to the fact that, in L2, functional projections are available from the beginning, possibly due to grammatical transfer from the L1 (see **Linguistic transfer**, this volume).

That L1 and L2 sequences are not identical has indeed been observed repeatedly (see section 1) not only for morpheme order but also for syntactic phenomena like those displayed in (2) (see Pienemann, 1981), among others. Whether these differences are caused by transfer from the L1 grammar during early phases of L2 acquisition is a more controversial issue. That the initial states are markedly different in the two acquisition types and that L2 learners can rely to some extent on previously acquired knowledge are widely accepted facts. Attributing the observed differences in development to the fact that the starting points are different, is, however, not a convincing solution – even less so if one wants to claim that L2 learners have full access to the LAD, much like children acquiring an L1; see Schwartz and Sprouse (1996). If principles of UG indeed guided L2 acquisition in more or less the same way as in the L1, they should enable learners to make corrections compensating for the false start. A detailed discussion of the availability of the LAD in L2 acquisition is beyond the scope of this article. More importantly, this issue is not directly relevant for the current discussion because UG by itself does not explain the course of development and what triggers it, anyway; it merely constrains the properties of grammars at each point of acquisition; cf. Gregg (1996).

Structure building might offer a solution to this *developmental problem*, but in the case of L2 acquisition it is less convincing than in L1. This comment also applies to the Minimal Trees Hypothesis, proposed by Vainikka and Young-Scholten (1996). Inspired by the SBH, it claims that L2 structures initially only contain lexical categories transferred from the L1, together with their head directionality. An underspecified head-initial functional projection is said to emerge subsequently and to develop into a target-conforming functional projection, once the appropriate grammatical features are acquired. Yet these claims stand in conflict with the observation by Zobl and Liceras (1994), Parodi (1998) and others who provided strong empirical evidence showing that L2 grammars do contain functional elements from early on. These findings speak against the plausibility of a developmental logic based on grammatical properties alone. If, moreover, Clahsen and Muysken (1986) are correct in claiming that not all L2 transitional grammars are fully constrained by UG, a purely grammatical explanation must be abandoned; see Meisel (2011: Ch. 4.4) for a discussion of this issue.

A more promising solution seems to be to rely on processing mechanisms as well as on grammatical properties of sentences. In L2, acquisition order of elements related to FC does not follow a logic determined solely by properties of functional heads. Meisel *et al.* (1981) and Clahsen *et al.* (1983) argued therefore that developmental sequences reflect increasing processing costs of syntactic constructions defining the respective developmental phases, a proposal confirmed and explained in more detail by the Processability Theory; cf. Pienemann (1998) (see **Processability Theory**, this volume). It builds on the insight that language acquisition implies the acquisition of procedural skills necessary for the processing of the target language. An alternative would involve examining the prosodic properties of morphemes, an idea implicit in Andersen's (1978) distinction between bound and free morphemes.

Summary and conclusion

Invariant properties of development, across individuals and across languages, demonstrate that grammatical development in naturalistic as well as in tutored L2 acquisition follows an underlying logic. This supports the assumption that the human Language Making Capacity is also operative in L2 acquisition. However, differences between the two types of acquisition, especially with respect to the course of development, suggest that there also exist differences in how the LAD guides acquisition. Linguistic research can explain many linguistic properties of developmental sequences, but more (psycho-)linguistic research is needed in order to solve the developmental problem.

See also: child second language acquisition, linguistic transfer, morpheme acquisition orders, Processability Theory (PT), simplification, Universal Grammar (UG) and SLA

References

Andersen, R.W. (1978). An implicational model for second language research. *Language Learning*, *28*, 221–82.

—— (ed.) (1983). *Pidginization and Creolization as Language Acquisition*. Rowley, MA: Newbury House.

Brown, R. (1973). *A First Language*. Cambridge, MA: Harvard University Press.

Chomsky, N. (1981). Principles and parameters in syntactic theory. In N. Hornstein and D. Lightfoot (eds), *Explanation in Linguistics: The Logical Problem of Language Acquisition*, pp. 32–75. London: Longman.

Clahsen, H., Meisel, J.M. and Pienemann, M. (1983). *Deutsch als Zweitsprache: Der Spracherwerb ausländischer Arbeiter*. Tübingen: Narr.

Clahsen, H. and Muysken, P. (1986). The availability of Universal Grammar to adult and child learners: A study of the acquisition of German word order. *Second Language Research*, *2*, 93–119.

Corder, S.P. (1967). The significance of Learner's errors. *International Review of Applied Linguistics*, *5*, 161–70.

Dulay, H.C. and Burt, M.K. (1974). Natural sequences in child second language acquisition. *Language Learning*, *24*, 37–54.

——(1975). A new approach to discovering universals of child language acquisition. In D. Dato (ed.), *Developmental Psycholinguistics*, pp. 209–33. Washington, DC: Georgetown University Press.

Dulay, H.C., Burt, M.K. and Krashen, S. (1982). *Language Two*. Oxford: Oxford University Press.

Felix, S.W. (1982). *Psycholinguistische Aspekte des Zweitsprachenerwerbs*. Tübingen: Narr.

Gregg, K. (1996). The logical and developmental problems of second language acquisition. In W.C. Ritchie and T.K. Bhatia (eds), *Handbook of Second Language Acquisition*, pp. 49–81. San Diego, CA: Academic Press.

Guilfoyle, E. and Noonan, M. (1992). Functional categories and language acquisition. *The Canadian Journal of Linguistics*, *37*, 241–72.

Hyltenstam, K. (1977). Implicational patterns in interlanguage syntax variation. *Language Learning*, *27*, 383–411.

Klein, W. and Perdue, C. (1997). The basic variety (or: Couldn't natural languages be much simpler?), *Second Language Research*, *13*, 301–47.

Krashen, S.D. (1977). Some issues relating to the monitor model. In H. Brown, C. Yorio and R. Crymes (eds), *On TESOL '77*, pp. 144–58. Washington, DC: TESOL.

Larsen-Freeman, D. and Long, M.H. (1991). *An Introduction to Second Language Acquisition Research*. London: Longman.

McNeill, D. (1966). Developmental psycholinguistics. In F. Smith and G. Miller (eds), *The Genesis of Language*, pp. 15–84. Cambridge, MA: MIT Press.

Meisel, J.M. (1977). Linguistic simplification: A study of immigrant workers' speech and foreigner talk. In S.P. Corder and E. Roulet (eds), *The Notions of Simplification, Interlanguages and Pidgins and their Relation to Second Language Pedagogy*, pp. 88–113. Geneva: Droz.

——(1997). The acquisition of the syntax of negation in French and German: Contrasting first and second language development. *Second Language Research*, 13, 227–63.

——(2000). On transfer at the initial state of L2 Acquisition. In C. Riemer (ed.), *Kognitive Aspekte des Lehrens und Lernens von Fremdsprachen – Cognitive Aspects of Foreign Language Learning and Teaching, Festschrift für Willis J. Edmondson*, pp. 186–206. Tübingen: Narr.

——(2011). *First and Second Language Acquisition: Parallels and Differences*. Cambridge: Cambridge University Press.

Meisel, J.M., Clahsen, H. and Pienemann, M. (1981). On determining developmental stages in natural second language acquisition. *Studies in Second Language Acquisition*, *3*, 109–35.

Parodi, T. (1998). *Der Erwerb funktionaler Kategorien im Deutschen. Eine Untersuchung zum bilingualen Erstspracherwerb und zum Zweitspracherwerb*. Tübingen: Narr.

Pienemann, M. (1981). *Der Zweitspracherwerb ausländischer Arbeiterkinder*. Bonn: Bouvier.

——(1998). *Language Processing and Second Language Development: Processability Theory.* Amsterdam: John Benjamins.

Schumann, J. (1978). *The Pidginization Process: A Model for Second Language Acquisition.* Rowley, MA: Newbury House.

Schwartz, B.D. and Sprouse, R.A. (1996). L2 Cognitive States and the Full Transfer/Full Access Model. *Second Language Research, 12*, 40–77.

Vainikka, A. and Young-Scholten, M. (1996). Gradual development of L2 phrase structure. *Second Language Research, 12*, 7–39.

Wode, H. (1976). Developmental sequences in naturalistic L2 acquisition. *Working Papers in Bilingualism, 11*, 1–31.

Zobl, H. and Liceras, J. (1994). Functional Categories and Acquisition Orders. *Language Learning, 44*, 159–80.

Developmental sequences

Niclas Abrahamsson
Stockholm University

One of the most significant breakthroughs in second language acquisition (SLA) research was the discovery in the early-to-mid 1970s that second language (L2) learners develop their L2 in very similar ways, irrespective of socio-economic status, education, personality, and even first language (L1). This is not to suggest that everyone learns an L2 at the same speed or with the same ease, nor that they ultimately enjoy the same success, but that people of various ages, origins, and L1 backgrounds seem to follow the same developmental route when learning a new language. A crucial aspect of this discovery was the recognition that the path L2 learners take toward the target grammar closely resembles the natural development that had previously been documented for children acquiring their L1, hence the postulation of the *L2 = L1 hypothesis* (or *identity hypothesis*), which boldly states that (adults') L2 acquisition might actually be the same process as (children's) L1 acquisition.

In several studies, Dulay and Burt (e.g., 1973, 1974) found that L2 children (aged 5–8) of different L1 and social backgrounds acquired English morphemes in the same order and that this order, while not identical, was quite similar to that of children acquiring English as their L1 (e.g., Brown, 1973). These results were later corroborated for adult L2 learners by Bailey, Madden and Krashen (1975) and others. The findings of these studies contrasted sharply with assumptions that had gone unquestioned during the heyday of *Behaviorism* and *Contrastive Analysis*, namely (1) that L2 learning was constrained primarily (or only) by the learner's previous language habits (causing interference), hence (2) that the character of a person's language development was uniquely colored by the L1 (via transfer), and therefore (3) that L2 learning and L1 development must be fundamentally different and incomparable. Conversely, these findings aligned perfectly with the new mentalist research paradigms, whether in the realm of Chomskyan generative/nativist linguistics or more general cognitive/process-oriented approaches to language acquisition.

An important branch of developmental research in SLA has been the investigation, description, and (to some extent) explanation of *developmental sequences*. In contrast to acquisition order, which denotes the order that *different* features, structures, and elements appear/are acquired, developmental sequences constitute the typical stages in which *individual* features, structures and elements develop/are acquired. In other words, the acquisition order is the order in which different linguistic forms are acquired in relation to each other, while developmental sequences are the sequences of interlanguage variants through which each of these different linguistic forms approximate targetlike manifestations.

Often mentioned in this regard is negation development in L2 English, as shown in (1). At first, learners use an external negator (*no* or *not*) placed either before or after a phrase or sentence. Second, negation is integrated with the internal sentence structure and is manifested preverbally; also at this stage, *don't* is used as a negator with no analysis of its constituents (i.e. *do* + *not*). Third, negation is acquired for modal auxiliary contexts, and at the fourth and final stage, it is acquired for all auxiliary contexts; also during this last stage, *don't* is analyzed by its constituents, as evidenced by the use of inflected forms such as *doesn't* and *didn't*.

(1) Developmental sequence: English negation (based on Schumann, 1979)

	Stage	*Example*
1.	External NEG	* *No* this one. * *No* you playing here.
2.	Internal preverbal NEG, unanalyzed *don't*	*Mariana *not coming* today. *Juana *don't have* job
3.	NEG w/modal AUX	I *can't* play that one. I *won't* go.
4.	NEG w/AUX, analyzed *don't* believe me.	He *doesn't* know anything. She *didn't*

The developmental sequence for Swedish negation is similarly well documented. As illustrated in (2), learners of L2 Swedish first pass through a general preverbal stage, comparable to stage 2 in the English sequence in (1) above. Second, the negator (*inte*) appears post-verbally in auxiliary contexts, expanding to main verb contexts during the third stage. At stages 4 and 5, negator placement is acquired in subordinate clauses, but in reverse order between auxiliaries and main verbs in comparison to main clauses.

(2) Developmental sequence: Swedish negation (after Hyltenstam, 1977, 1978; Bolander 1987, 1988a, 1988b)

	Stage	*Example*
1.	Preverbal NEG	*Lisa *inte* går / *inte* kan gå.
	Lisa NEG goes / NEG can go.	
2.	AUX + NEG Lisa can NEG go.	Lisa kan inte gå.
3.	Main verb + NEG Lisa goes NEG.	Lisa går inte.
4.	NEG + main verb in subordinate clause	... att Lisa inte går. ... that Lisa NEG goes.
5.	NEG + AUX in subordinate clause	... att Lisa inte kan gå. ... that Lisa NEG can go.

Another well-documented sequence is the development of English question formation, as shown in (3). The first stage is characterized by Yes/No-questions in declarative form with rising intonation. Next, Wh-questions appear with a sentence-initial Wh-element but without subject-verb inversion. Third, the inversion rule is acquired for main clauses but is overgeneralized to subordinate clauses. At stage 4, the learner differentiates between clause types and can therefore cancel inversion in subordinate clauses, as the target grammar does. Except for a few language-specific features, the developmental sequence for L2 Swedish question formation is very similar to that of L2 English, containing features like uninverted word order in main clauses, as well as over-inversion followed by cancel inversion in subordinate clauses (see, e.g., Hyltenstam, 1978; Philipsson, 2007).

(3) Developmental sequence: English question formation (based on, e.g., Cazden *et al.*, 1975; Cancino *et al.*, 1978)

	Stage	*Example*
1.	Canonical word order + rising intonation	*He work today? ↑
2.	Uninverted WhX question	*What he (is) saying?
3.	Overinversion in subordinate clause	*Do you know where is it?
4.	Sentence differentiation, cancel inversion	Does she like where she lives?

A fairly well-established *phonological* developmental sequence is the acquisition of final consonants/consonant clusters in languages such as English or Swedish, both of which permit relatively complex syllable codas. In the interlanguage development of learners with highly restrictive L1 syllable structure conditions (such as Mandarin Chinese, which allows only /n/ and /ŋ/ in final position), the sequence shown in (4) is typically salient. A simplification process used in principle by all learners, at least to some extent, is final consonant deletion, which is typical for stage 1. At stage 2, the learner simplifies syllable structure by inserting epenthetic vowels rather than by deleting consonants. At the third stage, the learner manages to launch the final consonant without adding a supportive vowel, but usually at the cost of some internal feature of the consonant being changed instead (through, e.g., devoicing). At the final stage, final consonants and clusters are pronounced without modification.

(4) Developmental sequence: word-final consonants/clusters (alt. closed syllables) (after, e.g., Abrahamsson, 2003; Hammarberg, 1988; Hansen, 2001)

	Stage	*Example*
1.	Consonant deletion	*dog* →→ [dɒː]
2.	Vowel epenthesis	*dog* →→ [dɒːgə], [dɒːgᵊ]
3.	Feature change (e.g., devoicing)	*dog* →→ [dɒːkʰ], [dɒːg̊]
4.	Target value	*dog* →→ [dɒːg]

These developmental sequences have all been observed for L1 acquisition also – that is, L1 acquisition of English and Swedish negation, question formation and final consonants exhibit the same forms, stages and general sequences as in L2 acquisition. However, some research has reported specific sequences differing for L1 and L2 acquisition. For example, Håkansson (2001; see also Håkansson and Nettelbladt, 1993, 1996) claimed that the developmental sequence for Swedish subject-verb inversion, as shown in (5), relates only to L2 learners, since Swedish L1 children rarely show evidence of the second stage (i.e. lack of inversion in topicalized clauses), while child and adult L2 learners frequently do. However, this difference could be explained in that (child) L1 development is generally more rapid than (adult) L2 development. The functionality of topicalization and the formal rule of inversion apparently develop more or less simultaneously in L1 children, or with a brief intermittent delay, hence the rare overt manifestations of non-inversion. In adult L2 learners, conversely, development is slow, and the functionality of topicalization is already fully developed, while the linguistic rule of inversion is not, hence the prolonged duration at this stage and the numerous manifestations of non-inversion that follow. Evidence supporting this interpretation is that non-inversion *does indeed occur* in normally developed children, although *rarely*, and, furthermore, that non-inversion is quite common in children with Specific Language Impairment (SLI), which, like L2 acquisition, is characterized by slower structural/linguistic development but normal cognitive/functional development. In other words, if we could study normal L1 development in slow motion, or if each stage of the developmental sequence could be expanded temporally, the manifestations of non-inversion would suddenly be observable. For a similar discussion concerning the sparse use of vowel epenthesis by normally developed L1 children compared to adult L2 learners and linguistically delayed L1 children, see Weinberger (1994) and Abrahamsson (2003).

(5) Developmental sequence: Swedish subject-verb inversion (after, e.g., Hyltenstam, 1978; Håkansson, 2001)

	Stage	*Example*
1.	No topicalization	Jag gick till skolan (igår).
	I walked to school (yesterday).	
2.	Topicalization without inversion	*Igår jag gick till skolan.
	Yesterday I walked to school.	
3.	Topicalization with inversion (= target structure)	Igår gick jag till skolan. Yesterday walked I to school.

Another question concerns whether certain stages exist only for learners with particular L1s. This issue is especially relevant for phonological sequences, where the phonological process at a certain stage, for example, the epenthesis stage in example (4) above, is shared by all learners, but the exact manifestation of it can vary in terms of the quality of the added vowel. For example, rather than using [ə] (i.e. schwa), L2 learners with Portuguese as their L1 frequently add an [i]-like vowel in accordance with the Portuguese lexical pattern, while for Turkish learners, the added vowel is frequently colored by a preceding vowel, thus following Turkish rules of vowel harmony. However, it is important to remember that developmental sequences are invariant in terms of length, complexity, and stage order as a function of the learner's L1; as Larsen-Freeman and Long (1991) report: "Modifications due to L1 influence (…) may delay initiation of a sequence, delay or speed up passage through it, or even add sub-stages to it, but never seem to involve either omission of stages or changes in the sequence of stages" (p. 96). The same can be said concerning the role of formal instruction: learners with or without formal instruction in the L2 apparently go through identical developmental sequences (see, e.g., Fathman, 1978; Norrby and Håkansson, 2007; Pica, 1983). In addition, experimental studies by Pienemann (e.g., 1984) showed that school children benefited significantly from L2 instruction of grammatical features matching their current developmental stage, while instruction of features from more advanced stages was not effective.

This last issue concerning the (non-)teachability of alternative sequences raises the question of what the underlying explanations are for the shape and existence of developmental sequences. Why are stages sequenced the way they are, and why can they not be altered? Developmental sequences are reported to be universal in nature; therefore, typological markedness relations might shed some light on them. As shown above, the first stages in the acquisition of English and Swedish negation include preverbal negation, while postverbal negation appears later. This is in accordance with the typological finding that most languages have unmarked preverbal negation, while postverbal negation is considered unusual and is therefore relatively marked. Similarly, early stages in the phonological sequence in (4) above produce open, unmarked CV syllables as output, while later stages yield closed and relatively marked CVC syllables. In other words, developmental sequences apparently conform to universal principles, ushering learners from the relatively unmarked to the relatively marked.

Another kind of explanation is based in cognition and processing. For example, in L2 Swedish, attributive agreement between noun and adjective develops before predicative agreement (see Glahn *et al.*, 2001), and an explanation is offered by *Processability Theory* (Pienemann, 1998). According to this theory, language production involving local grammatical processing (e.g. grammatical agreement *within* the noun phrase) is automatized much earlier than processes involving distant processing (e.g. grammatical agreement *across* phrase boundaries). This also explains why negation is mastered in main clauses before subordinate clauses, since sentence differentiation (involving grammatical exchange across clause boundaries) appears relatively late in development. In other words, both typological markedness and processing seem to be strong factors determining the shape of sequences.

See also: agreement, development in SLA, markedness, morpheme acquisition orders, Processability Theory (PT), Wh-questions

References

Abrahamsson, N. (2003). Development and recoverability of L2 codas: A longitudinal study of Chinese/Swedish interphonology. *Studies in Second Language Acquisition*, *25*, 313–49.

Bailey, N., Madden, C. and Krashen, S. (1974). Is there a "natural sequence" in adult second language learning? *Language Learning*, *24*, 235–43.

Bolander, M. (1988). Is there any order? On word order rules in Swedish as a second language. *Journal of Multilingual and Multicultural Development*, *9*, 97–113.

Brown, R. (1973). *A First Language: the Early Stages*. Cambridge, MA: Harvard University Press.

Cancino, H., Rosansky, E. and Schumann, J. (1978). The acquisition of English negatives and interrogatives by native Spanish speakers. In E. Hatch (ed.), *Second Language Acquisition*, pp. 207–30. Rowley, MA: Newbury House.

Cazden, C., Cancino, E. Rosansky, E. and Schumann, J. (1975). *Second Language Acquisition in Children, Adolescents and Adults. Final Report.* Washington DC: National Institute of Education.

Dulay, H. and Burt, M. (1973). Should we teach children syntax? *Language Learning, 23*, 245–58.

——(1974). Natural sequences in child second language acquisition. *Language Learning, 24*, 37–53.

Fathman, A. (1978). ESL and EFL learning: similar or dissimilar? In C.H. Blatchford and J. Schachter (ed.), *On TESOL '78*, pp. 207–30. Washington DC: TESOL.

Glahn, E., Håkansson, G., Hammarberg, B., Holmen, A., Hvenekilde, A. and Lund, K. (2001). Processability in Scandinavian second language acquisition. *Studies in Second Language Acquisition, 23*, 389–416.

Håkansson, G. (2001). Tense morphology and verb-second in Swedish L1 children, L2 children and children with SLI. *Bilingualism: Language and Cognition, 4*, 85–99.

Håkansson, G. and Nettelbladt, U. (1993). Developmental sequences in L1 (normal and impaired) and L2 acquisition of Swedish syntax. *International Journal of Applied Linguistics, 3*, 131–57.

——(1996). Similarities between SLI and L2 children: Evidence from the acquisition of Swedish word order. In J. Gilbert and C. Johnson (ed.), *Children's Language. Vol. 9*, pp. 135–51. Mahwah, NJ: Lawrence Erlbaum.

Hammarberg, B. (1988). *Studien zur Phonologie der Zweitsprachenerwerbs*. Stockholm: Almqvist and Wiksell International.

Hansen, J. (2001). Linguistic constraints on the acquisition of English syllable codas by native speakers of Mandarin Chinese. *Applied Linguistics*, 22, 338–65.

Hyltenstam, K. (1977). Implicational patterns in interlanguage syntax variation. *Language Learning, 27*, 383–411.

——(1978). *Progress in Immigrant Swedish Syntax. A Variability Analysis*. Doktorsavhandling, Lunds universitet.

Larsen-Freeman, D. and Long, M. (1991). *An Introduction to Second Language Acquisition Research*. London: Longman.

Norrby, C. and Håkansson, G. (2007). *Språkinlärning och språkanvändning. Svenska som andraspråk i och utanför Sverige*. Lund: Studentlitteratur.

Philipsson, A. (2007). *Interrogative Clauses and Verb Morphology in L2 Swedish. Theoretical Interpretations of Grammatical Development and Effects of Different Elicitation Techniques.* Ph.D. dissertation, Centre for Research on Bilingualism, Stockholm University.

Pica, T. (1983). Adult acquisition of English as a second language under different conditions of exposure. *Language Learning, 33*, 465–97.

Pienemann, M. (1998). *Language Processing and Second-Language Development: Processability Theory*. Amsterdam: John Benjamins.

Schumann, J. (1979). The acquisition of English negation by speakers of Spanish: a review of the literature. In R. Andersen (ed.). *The Acquisition and Use of Spanish and English as First and Second Languages*, pp. 3–32. Washington, DC: TESOL.

Weinberger, S.H. (1994). Functional and phonetic constraints on second language phonology. In M. Yavaş (ed.), *First and Second Language Phonology*. San Diego, CA: Singular Publishing Group.

Dialogic inquiry

Joan Kelly Hall
Pennsylvania State University

Dialogic inquiry is an approach to pedagogy that considers teaching and learning to be an integrated, collaborative, and purposeful process in which teachers and learners together engage in the construction of knowledge. The curriculum is typically organized around topics or questions for investigation and the central role of teachers is to facilitate and guide students' participation in collaboratively designed activities, which serve to foster exploration of the topic. The goal is not to find the right answer but instead to seek appropriate resolutions to the questions. The activities typically involve whole group teacher–student interaction and small group student–student interaction in which students are afforded frequent opportunities to share opinions, and reflect on and refine their understandings. In the process of interacting, teachers actively guide learners by evoking ideas and views, reformulating questions and interpretations, and building connections among the various contributions to form coherent strands of thinking (cf. Wells, 1999). A related term for this approach is *dialogic teaching* (cf. Alexander, 2006).

Dialogic inquiry draws heavily on Vygotsky's (1978) sociocultural theory of development and, in particular, on two key premises. The first locates the source of learning in joint activity between individuals with varying levels of expertise, with knowledge arising as an emergent product of interaction among the participants. A second premise considers language to be the quintessential sociocognitive tool for intellectual development. In their interactions, more expert members assist less competent participants in developing particular understandings of and ways of talking about that which is to be learned. The more one is required to "explain, elaborate or defend one's position to others" in these interactions (Vygotsky, 1978: 158), the more likely there will be cognitive growth.

A fairly large body of work has examined classroom interaction from this perspective. Findings from studies by Wells (1999) and Nystrand and his colleagues (2003), for example, reveal a strong link between the dialogic quality of classroom interaction and learning. Interaction rating high on dialogic quality fosters more open discussion of ideas among students and contains a higher proportion of authentic questions and follow-up questions by the teacher. Mercer and his colleagues (e.g. Mercer and Littleton, 2007) have also examined links between dialogic interaction and learning, with a particular focus on "exploratory talk," that is, high-quality dialogic interaction in which participants jointly consider ideas and opinions in forming understandings. A key finding of this research reveals that learners' extended involvement in such talk enhances their problem-solving and reasoning skills. Taken together, findings linking dialogic inquiry to enhanced learning help us to understand more fully how we can create effectual communities of learners in our classrooms. Since English language arts classrooms, and to a lesser extent, math and science classrooms, have received the bulk of research attention, it is hoped that future research will be extended to other subject matters such as second and foreign language classrooms, where the role of language as a tool for learning and a curricular outcome takes on heightened importance.

See also: classroom interaction research, interaction and the interaction hypothesis, scaffolding, second language socialization, social and socio-cultural approaches to SLA, teacher talk

References

Alexander, R. (2006). *Towards Dialogic Teaching: Rethinking Classroom Talk*. Cambridge: Dialogos.

Mercer, N. and Littleton, K, (2007). *Dialogue and the Development of Children's Thinking: A Sociocultural Approach*. London: Routledge.

Nystrand, M., Wu, L., Gamoran, A., Zieser, S. and Long, D. (2003). Questions in time: Investigating the structure and dynamics of unfolding classroom discourse. *Discourse Processes*, *35*, 135–198.

Vygotsky, L.S. (1978). *Mind in Society: The Development of Higher Psychological Process*. Cambridge, MA: Harvard University Press.

Wells, G. (1999). *Dialogic Inquiry: Towards a Sociocultural Practice and Theory of Education*. Cambridge: Cambridge University Press.

Discourse and pragmatics in SLA

Eva Alcón-Soler
Universitat Jaume I

The study of discourse and pragmatics has grown into a heterogeneous field of research drawing on different disciplines to examine the potential meaning of utterances in different contexts. Halliday's (1978) notion of language as choice, Grice's (1975) cooperative principle and maxims, and Austin's (1962) and Searle's (1969) theory of language as social action contributed to generate the idea of language as a cooperative effort in which interlocutors choose linguistic devices both to understand and to be understood. Following this idea, discourse-based studies focus on the analysis of language beyond the level of the sentence, and pragmatics deals with language in use in particular social contexts (see **Pragmatics**, and **Speech acts**, this volume). Work on discourse analysis focuses primarily on textual aspects of messages while pragmatics deals with the situational factors that influence how people communicate with each other. On the one hand, discourse analysis has provided information, for example, on the use of cohesive ties, the coherence of discourse and the management of information and turn-taking in a coherent way. On the other hand, pragmatics takes into account the point of view of the users of a language, that is to say, both the speaker's intention and the hearer's interpretation of the utterances. From this perspective, language users' perception and performance of speech acts, the management of conversation or the cooperative and politeness principles have been the focus of attention of pragmatics-based studies (see **Politeness**, this volume). It can be safely said that within the field of applied linguistics, both discourse- and pragmatics-based studies have influenced our growing understanding of language use in context.

Drawing on these studies, the idea of communication as both an end and a means toward language learning was emphasized in the field of language education in the 1980s, and since then it has influenced both language teaching and research on second language acquisition (SLA). From this perspective, and taking speech act theory into account, the language learning content was designed following a functional-notional syllabus, and Hymes's (1975) original definition of communicative competence was taken into account in several pedagogically motivated models of communicative competence. In these models pragmatics, discourse, and strategic competence have been target learning aims. Moreover, our increasing interest in examining language in contexts has undoubtedly influenced our understanding of oral and written skills, which has also been applied to the field of language teaching. As far as the teaching of oral skills is concerned, observations of how people behave in spoken discourse have helped to further our understanding of native/non-native and non-native/non-native communication, although questions remain about how to apply this knowledge in language teaching (see **Discourse processing**, this volume). With regard to the written skills, the analysis of language has contributed to a better understanding of the texture and structure of texts, and how both texture and structure illustrate the interactive nature of reading and writing. Such analysis of written discourse has also illustrated the different mechanisms we have at our disposal for teaching reading and writing.

Moreover, in the educational context, the study of discourse and language learning can be approached from a descriptive point of view or from an SLA perspective. In the first case, discourse is viewed as "talk-in-interaction" or as ways of understanding the social world (see Martin-Jones *et al.*, 2008, for research on discourse and education). Following a SLA perspective, two main concerns have been: (a) how discourse can provide opportunities for language learning, and (b) how learners acquire pragmatic competence. Both issues have been widely examined following either an information-processing perspective or a socially oriented approach to language learning. In this chapter we will refer to these two questions by addressing research that has been conducted and major contributions. Finally, further issues to be considered in future research will be suggested.

Discourse and second language acquisition

Early research on discourse in SL (second language) contexts was conducted in classroom settings with the aim of evaluating the effectiveness of the teaching method or providing a description of classroom discourse rather than due to a concern for describing the discourse in which learners participate and its potential for language learning. In the 1960s and 1970s, following research on child language development, and the baby-talk register in particular, studies on NS-learner interaction provided descriptions of how NS tended to use a simplified variety of the language when addressing foreigners, the so-called foreigner talk register. In the late 1970s descriptive studies of SL discourse provided a view of discourse as interaction, and

Hatch (1978) argued that the learning of the L2 evolved out of communication. Drawing on Hatch's (1978) claim that second language learning occurs through the process of interacting, and understanding discourse as the interaction constructed by participants, SLA studies began to examine how interaction facilitates language learning from different theoretical perspectives (see **Interaction and the Interaction Hypothesis**, this volume).

Research carried out during the 1980s and 1990s aimed to test Hatch's (1978) claims about language learning through interaction, together with Krashen's (1985) Input Hypothesis, pointing out that comprehensible input is both a necessary and sufficient condition for L2 learning. The empirical studies followed an information-processing approach and examined learners' opportunities for input, output, and feedback, as the three theoretical conditions for language learning. Within the framework of Long's Interaction Hypothesis (1981, 1996), Long used the term "negotiation of meaning" in his early research to describe the conversational exchanges that arise when interlocutors try to avoid communication breakdowns and facilitate comprehension (see **Negotiation of meaning**, this volume). The use of clarification requests, comprehension checks, and confirmation checks were described in NS-NNS and NNS-NNS conversation, thereby suggesting that they might play a role in comprehension and deducing that those linguistic adjustments could promote SLA. However, the claim that comprehension of input promotes acquisition was questioned on the grounds that (a) learners may fake comprehension in meaning-negotiation sequences; (b) some aspects of languages such as inflectional morphology are not subject to negotiation; and (c) there are other ways in which interaction can provide conditions for language learning.

One piece of evidence questioning the claim that comprehension of input correlates with SLA is the findings from research conducted in a wide range of immersion acquisition studies. These studies show that when second language learning is solely based on communicative success, some linguistic features like accuracy do not develop until the target is reached, and this was reported to occur in spite of years of being exposed to meaningful input and having opportunities for interaction. These research outcomes triggered the perspective adopted by Swain (1995) in her proposed Output Hypothesis (see **Output Hypothesis**, this volume). The author claims that output is not only the result of learning, but an important factor to promote L2 learning. In the same vein, in his revised Interaction Hypothesis, Long (1996) acknowledged that learners' output and feedback play a role in the way negotiation of meaning can assist language learning. The three functions that, according to Swain (1995), output plays in the process of L2 learning (noticing, hypothesis testing, and metalinguistic function) have been examined in a number of empirical studies. Findings from these studies reveal that learners' output is influenced by the type of feedback and that learners are able to respond to feedback in conversational interaction with learners. In addition, research has shown that on the basis of interlocutors' feedback (explicit versus implicit) learners may notice mismatches between their production and target-like forms, and modify their output accordingly.

An interesting line of research within the interaction approach is that of examining how some degree of focus on form in classes that are primarily focused on meaning and communication can have some advantages over purely meaning-focused instruction. The framework for these studies can be found in Long's (1996: 40) definition of focus on form as " … interactional moves directed at raising learner awareness of forms by briefly drawing students' attention to linguistic elements (words, collocations, grammatical structures, pragmatic patterns, and so on), in context, as they arise incidentally in lessons whose overriding focus is on meaning, or communication" (see **Focus on Form**, this volume). Descriptive research on focus on form instruction has been undertaken to conceptualize and describe the procedures for teaching form in the context of a communicative activity, with a distinction being made between planned versus incidental focus on form. The former involves the use of communicative tasks designed to elicit forms which have been pre-selected by the teacher, while in the latter tasks are designed to elicit and use language without any specific attention to form, although the role of participants in performing the task will determine whether a reactive or pre-emptive focus on form is accomplished. Furthermore, the effectiveness of both planned and incidental focus on form has stimulated recent research in the field of SLA. Planned focus on form instruction has been tested empirically by measuring gains in learners' ability to use the targeted structures. For instance, Mackey and Oliver (2002) reported that, in immediate and delayed post-tests, learners who received recasts after non-target-like question forms outperformed learners who did not. Similar results were reported by Mackey and Silver (2005) in a study conducted in the multilingual context of Singapore. The effectiveness of incidental focus on form has been tested in second and foreign language learning settings. Loewen (2005) used incidental focus on form episodes in a second language context as a basis for individualized test items. Results of this study showed that learners were able to recall the targeted linguistic information correctly or partially correctly nearly 60 percent of the time one day after the focus on form episode, and 50 percent of the time two weeks later. In addition, the results suggest that incidental focus on form might be particularly beneficial if learners incorporate the linguistic items into their production. In a foreign language context, Alcón and García Mayo (2008) measured the effectiveness of learners' incidental focus on vocabulary items on subsequent written production. The authors used individualized, tailor-made sentences for translation based on the vocabulary items that arose in incidental focus on form episodes, and reported that focus on form was effective in raising learners' awareness of lexical items and to facilitate immediate language use.

A cognitive approach has also been adopted in analyzing whether factors such as task type, task implementation or individual differences influence learners' discourse and SLA. As far as task type is concerned, both task design variables (required versus optional information exchange; one-way versus two-way or open versus closed tasks) and task complexity have been reported to influence SLA according to the Interaction Hypothesis. Following Robinson's (2001) Cognition Hypothesis, inconclusive results have been found on how the complexity of the task is likely to promote interactional modification, thus suggesting that further research is needed on task-related features and interaction (see **Cognition Hypothesis**, and **Task-based learning and teaching**, this volume). Similarly, task implementation variables such as the extent to which learners lead the interaction, interlocutor familiarity, or type of feedback have stimulated research on task-based interaction, recasts being one type of implicit feedback that has recently aroused special interest. Another factor that is opening a line of research within the study of interaction is the role of individual differences. Different studies explore the extent to which individual differences affect learners' performance and language learning gains. Although factors such as personality traits, motivation, gender or individual cognitive factors (especially working memory capacity) seem to point out that these factors play a significant role in interaction, further studies need to address how methods of data collection and research design may capture a more direct influence of these factors on interaction and language learning (see **Individual differences in SLA**, this volume). For instance, the use of self-reported data on how learners' individual variables affect their discourse behavior is an issue in need of further examination.

As can be seen from the research reported above, the primary aim of the study of discourse and SLA from an information-processing perspective has been to provide explanations for linguistic development and how different factors may contribute to facilitate language learning through interaction. However, it has to be acknowledged that, in the 1990s, sociocultural and language socialization approaches began to explain the role of discourse in SLA in much broader terms (see **Social and socio-cultural approaches to SLA**, this volume). On the one hand, drawing on work by Vygotsky (1978), sociocultural studies view language learning as a mediated process that prepares learners to do independently what they have first accomplished in a particular social setting. As reported by Lantolf (2000), three general categories are considered: mediation by others in social interaction, mediation by self through private speech, and mediation by artifacts. In the case of studies with a focus on discourse and language learning, the behavior of experts (the teacher) and novices (the learner) has provided insights on the nature of interaction in different educational contexts. Research has also examined the role of interaction during collaborative tasks, and how the collaborative dialogue in which participants engage provides opportunities for metalinguistic reflection on language use. Findings from studies that have adopted a sociocultural perspective report that learners' collaborative dialogue is as effective for learning as interaction between teacher and learners. On the other hand, current research on interaction and language learning following a language socialization perspective addresses issues such as the co-construction of cultural identity, power, or agency (see Duff, 2010, for a review of research issues in language socialization and SLA, and see **Identity Theory** and **Second language socialization**, this volume). Language socialization approaches dealing with discourse in educational contexts is also one of the approaches used to examine our second question: How is L2 pragmatic ability acquired?

Pragmatics and second language acquisition

Pragmatics has been reported to be difficult to acquire on the grounds that learners often focus on the sentence-level message, they are unaware of pragmatic errors, or they are not familiar with cultural conventions. The field of inquiry of Interlanguage Pragmatics (ILP) has provided explanations on learners' use, perception and acquisition of L2 pragmatic ability. Regarding learners' use and perception, most of the studies have been comparative given its closeness to cross-cultural pragmatics and they have focused mainly on speech acts. In accounting for an acquisitional perspective, ILP research has been concerned with the study of language users' acquisition of linguistic actions, pragmatic norms and conventions. One particularly interesting line of investigation has been the factors that influence the development of learners' pragmatic competence. Those factors, which include availability of input, L2 proficiency, length of stay, transfer and instruction, have been addressed in different studies dealing with the acquisition of pragmatics. Regarding availability of input, the use of audiovisual materials, rather than classroom discourse and textbook conversations, has been reported as a useful resource for addressing the knowledge of a pragmatic system, and the knowledge of its appropriate use in settings with limited exposure to the target language, such as foreign language contexts. In relation to the other factors, research shows that the level of proficiency and length of stay influence pragmatic learning, although there is no consensus on whether other variables, such as learners' individual characteristics, play a role when dealing with the effect of these factors on learners' pragmatic ability. In contrast, there seems to be general agreement on the positive effects of instruction on learners' acquisition of pragmatic competence. Most research dealing with the teachability of pragmatics focuses on speech acts, pointing out that pragmatics is teachable and that pedagogical intervention plays a facilitative role in learning pragmatics. In the same vein, the overall outcome of studies on the effect of different teaching approaches reports the advantage of explicit over implicit instruction, although evidence for the benefits of both types of instruction seems to occur when the implicit treatment is properly operationalized.

The analysis of factors that potentially influence learners' acquisition of pragmatic ability has been carried out within the framework of understanding pragmatic learning as a cognitive activity. For instance, taking into account Schmidt's (2001) noticing hypothesis, different studies have provided evidence that high levels of attention-drawing activities are more helpful for pragmatic learning than exposure to positive evidence (see **Awareness, Positive and negative evidence,** and **Noticing Hypothesis**, this volume). However, sociocultural and language socialization work on the development of pragmatic learning has been gaining ground in the last decade. Both theories place great importance on the social and cultural context of learning and they focus on learners' development of pragmatics by examining language use between experts and novices over time. From a sociocultural perspective, and among the three domains of mediation, ILP research has mostly focused on mediated learning in interaction, with special attention being paid to Vygotsky's (1978) concept of zone of proximal development (ZPD), which in turn points to individual learning potential. Examples of research motivated by sociocultural theory are, for instance, those conducted by Shea (1994) and Ohta (1999). Shea (1994) analyzed Japanese ESL speakers' and native English speakers' interactions within the dimensions of perspective and production, and four interactional patterns were obtained: incongruous perspective and asymmetric production; incongruous perspective and symmetric production; congruent perspective and asymmetric production; and congruent perspective and symmetric production. According to Shea, the four participation structures provide different opportunities for learners' development of conversational ability and the author also points out the relevant role of native speakers' responses in the construction of non-native speakers' discourse. Ohta's (1999) study focused on the acquisition of extended assessments and the initiation-response-follow-up moves in a foreign language classroom, more specifically in a Japanese language classroom at an American university. Results from her study show that in teacher–students interaction learners had few opportunities to produce assessments, but when they did occur teachers used them to produce an affective response, thus producing alignment sequences that resemble those found outside the classroom, and as a result provided opportunities to develop learners' ZPD. Likewise, and following a longitudinal microanalysis of classroom discourse, Hall (1998) and Ohta (2001) showed, respectively, that opportunities for participation affect the devel opment of interactional competence and that pragmatic knowledge may emerge from assisted performance, in both teacher and peer interaction.

In a similar vein to the sociocultural approach, language socialization theory views social interaction as being crucial to the acquisition of language (see Schieffelin and Ochs, 1986, for the twofold relationship between language and socialization). However, in contrast to the interest of sociocultural theory in exploring the mediating role of language in the process of language learning, language socialization focuses on the integration of culture and language. Studies conducted within the setting of language socialization theory have demonstrated that the theory provides an appropriate framework for researching pragmatics. For instance, Kanagy (1999) illustrated how American children learning Japanese in an immersion program were learning the routines of greetings, taking attendance and personal introductions at the same time as they were learning about Japanese values and behaviors. The integration of the acquisition of language and culture is also evident in Duff's and her colleagues' investigations on the acquisition of pragmatics at the secondary school level. Of special interest is the research that the author conducted in Hungary after the dissolution of the Soviet Union, in which one can observe how different models of discourse socialization evolve and may be either in conflict or in harmony with existing cultural practices.

More recently, conversation analysis (CA), which represents another perspective on language learning as a social practice, has provided information about how learners constitute their roles and identities through classroom talk (see **Conversation Analysis (CA)**, this volume). Following a CA approach, research has provided information about how learners' interactional competencies are both resources and objects of learning. For instance, Kasper (2004) examined a dyadic conversation for learning conducted between a learner of German as a foreign language at beginner level and a native speaker of German, pointing out that the metalingual exchanges stood out for their acquisitional potential. In a similar vein, Young and Miller's (2004) study focused on tracking a student's changing participation in revision talk, and revealed how the student eventually starts to take over tasks which were initially performed by the teacher. Although the benefits of CA to explain pragmatic learning are less apparent, CA focuses both on how learners use language in interaction and on how they learn language when interacting. This can be observed in the attempt to link CA as a methodological tool with some of the above-mentioned socially oriented theories. For example, He (2004) argued for CA and language socialization as complementary approaches. According to this author, CA may help us to understand how classroom activities are accomplished interactionally and what opportunities are provided through these interactions. Similarly, Mondada and Pekarek Doethler (2004) drew from both sociocultural theory and CA to suggest what they called a "socio-interactionist approach." From this perspective, pragmatic learning is viewed in this study as situated practice explained by learners' participation and adaptation to the activities that constitute talk in interaction.

Contributions and future directions for research on discourse and pragmatics in SLA

Focusing on the role of discourse in SLA it can be claimed that theoretically derived hypotheses on the role of interaction have been tested in laboratory and in classroom settings, providing information on how interaction works in particular language learning environments, and showing evidence on how learners' engagement in discourse provides the theoretical conditions for language learning, that is to say, opportunities for input, output, and feedback. In addition, interaction research has shown that negotiation of meaning during interaction offers learners the opportunity to connect input, noticing, and output in educational contexts. In spite of empirical research supporting these claims, the cause and effect of interaction and SLA has not been proven, and instead what we know is that interaction can be a facilitator of the learning process. In the case of pragmatics and SLA, learners' development of pragmatic ability has been framed within two views of understanding pragmatic learning, that is, as either a cognitive or a socially oriented activity. Following a cognitive theoretical approach, the development of pragmatic competence has been considered as an individual mental process, and different factors influencing pragmatic learning have been reported and generalized as potential factors influencing learners' development of pragmatic ability. Following the socially oriented approaches, more holistic explanations on how pragmatic ability develops within a specific context have been put forward. In doing so, CA has the advantage of allowing us to examine the microanalysis of discourse and present findings related to particular settings, but research outcomes are difficult to generalize.

In spite of these contributions much work remains to be done in dealing with discourse and pragmatics in SLA. One area to be explored further is that of language-learning opportunities in different contexts. The emergence of new language-learning environments, where language is used and thus learned, offers new settings for researching discourse and language learning. Among these, content and language integrated learning (CLIL) classrooms, computer-mediated communication, and multilingual settings are potential environments where learners may find opportunities to negotiate discourse and develop their pragmatic ability (see **Content based instruction**, this volume). Further research is needed to explore whether interaction provides opportunities for connecting input, output, and noticing in content and integrated language learning environments. Similarly, how learners express pragmatic meanings as the interaction unfolds in CLIL contexts, and whether the nature of these settings offers opportunities for pragmatic learning are some of the research challenges. In the same vein, computer-mediated communication (see **Computer Assisted Language Learning (CALL)**, this volume) and the multilingual environment of most classrooms may offer different perspectives on how learners negotiate meaning, use speech acts or develop their interactional competence in different languages, English as a lingua franca being one of them.

Additionally, the theoretical and methodological approaches followed in the analysis of learners' discourse will continue to prompt a lot of discussion. On the one hand, the main argument of the cognitive view is that, although the social context may exert an influence, the process of learning is essentially cognitive. Following this theoretical framework, cognitive-oriented research on discourse and pragmatics in SLA has tested theoretical claims on the role of interaction in language learning and conditions for pragmatic learning. This has been done in experimental or quasi-experimental research with the aim of generalizing research findings. In contrast, the socially oriented approaches share a concern for examining the microanalysis of discourse, thus providing more holistic insights on how linguistic and other forms of knowledge, such as cultural and social norms, develop in particular settings. We acknowledge that cognitive- and socially oriented approaches represent two different ontological positions with regard to SLA, but research needs to explore whether and, if so, how the cognitive and socially oriented theories can be complementary for understanding pragmatic learning in particular educational contexts. And one of these contexts is the classroom setting, where both cognitive and social-oriented approaches may merge so as to understand patterns of participation and link them to learning outcomes.

See also: classroom interaction research, instructed SLA, pragmatics, pragmalinguistics, sociopragmatics, speech acts

References

Alcón Soler, E. and García Mayo, M.P. (2008). Focus on form and learning outcomes in the foreign language classroom. In J. Philp, R. Oliver and A. Mackey (eds), *Child's play? Second Language Acquisition and the Younger Learner*, pp. 173–92. Amsterdam: John Benjamins.

Austin, J.L. (1962). *How to do Things with Words.* London: Clarendon Press.

Duff, P. (2008). Language socialization theory and the acquisition of pragmatics in the foreign language classroom. In E. Alcón and A. Martínez-Flor (eds), *Investigating Pragmatics in Foreign Language Learning, Teaching and Testing*, pp. 25–44. Clevedon: Multilingual Matters.

Grice, H. (1975). Logic and conversation. In P. Cole and J. Morgan (eds), *Syntax and Semantics, vol. 3: Speech acts*, pp. 41–58. New York: Academic Press.

Hall, J.K. (1998). Differential teacher attention to student utterances: The construction of different opportunities for learning in the IRF, *Linguistics and Education*, *9*(3), 287–311.

Halliday, M.A. K. (1978). *Language as Social Semiotic.* London: Edward Arnold.

Hassall, T.J. (1997). *Requests by Australian Learners of Indonesian*, unpublished doctoral dissertation, Canberra: Australian National University.

Hatch, E. (1978). Discourse analysis and second language acquisition. In E. Hatch (ed.), *Second Language Acquisition. A book of readings,* pp. 401–35, Rowley, MA: Newbury House.

He, A.W. (2004). CA for SLA: Arguments from the Chinese language classroom. *The Modern Language Journal*, *88*(iv), 568–82.

Hymes, D. (1975). On communicative competence. In J.B. Pride and J. Holmes (eds), *Sociolinguistics: Selected Readings*, pp. 269–93. Harmondsworth: Penguin.

Kanagy, R. (1999). Interactional routines as a mechanism for L2 acquisition and socialization in an immersion context. *Journal of Pragmatics*, *31*(11), 1467–92.

Kasper, G. (2004). Participant orientation in German conversation-for-learning. *The Modern Language Journal*, *88*(iv), 551–67.

Krashen, S. (1985). *The Input Hypothesis: Issues and implications*. London: Longman.

Lantolf, J. (2000). Second language learning as a mediated process. *Language Teaching Journal*, *33*, 79–96.

Loewen, S. (2005). Incidental focus on form and second language learning. *Studies in Second Language Acquisition*, *27*(3), 361–86.

Long, M.H. (1981). Input, interaction and second language acquisition. In H. Winitz (ed.), *Native language and foreign language acquisition*, pp. 259–78. New York: Annals of the New York Academy of Sciences.

——(1996). The role of the linguistic environment in second language acquisition. In W. Ritchie and T. Bhatia (eds), *Handbook of Research on Second Language Acquisition*, pp. 413–68, New York: Academic Press.

Mackey, A. and Oliver, R. (2002). Interactional feedback and children's L2 development. *System*, *30*, 459–77.

Mackey, A. and Silver, R.E. (2005). Interactional tasks and English L2 learning by immigrant children in Singapore. *System*, *33*, 239–60.

Martin Jones, M., De Mejía, A. and Hornberger, N. (eds) (2008). *Encyclopedia of Language and Education*. New York: Springer.

Mondada, L. and Pekarek Doehler, S. (2004). Second language acquisition as situated practice: Task accomplishment in the French second language classroom. *The Modern language Journal*, *88*(iv), 501–18.

Ohta, A.S. (2001). *Second Language Processes in the Classroom: Learning Japanese*. Mahwah, NJ: Lawrence Erlbaum Associates.

——(1999). Interactional routines and the socialization of interactional style in adult learners of

Japanese. *Journal of Pragmatics*, *31*(11), 1493–1512.

Robinson, P. (2001). Task complexity, cognitive resources, and syllabus design: A triadic framework for examining task influences on SLA. In P. Robinson (ed.), *Cognition and Second Language Instruction*, pp. 287–318. Cambridge: Cambridge University Press.

Schieffelin, B. and Ochs, E. (1986). Language socialization. *Annual Review of Anthropology*, *15*, 163–91.

Schmidt, R. (2001). Attention. In P. Robinson (ed.), *Cognition and Second Language Instruction*, pp. 3–33, New York: Cambridge University Press.

Searle, J.R. (1969). *Speech Acts: An Essay in the Philosophy of Language*. Cambridge: Cambridge University Press.

Shea, D.P. (1994). Perspective and production: structuring conversational participation across cultural borders. *Pragmatics*, *4*(3), 357–89.

Swain, M. (1995). Three functions of output in second language learning. In G. Gook and B. Seidlhofer (eds), *Principle and Practice in Applied Linguistics*, pp. 125–44. Oxford: Oxford University Press.

Vygotsky, L.S. (1978). *Mind in Society*. Cambridge, MA: Harvard University Press.

Young, R.F. and Miller, E.R. (2004). Learning as changing participation: Discourse roles in ESL writing conferences. *The Modern language Journal*, *88*(iv), 519–35.

Further reading

Alcón-Soler, E. and Martínez-Flor, A. (eds) (2008). *Investigating Pragmatics in Foreign Language Learning, Teaching and Testing*. Clevedon: Multilingual Matters.

Duff, P. (2012). Identity, agency and second language acquisition. In S.M. Gass and A. Mackey (eds), *The Routledge Handbook of Second Language Acquisition*. London: Routledge.

Ellis, R. (2003). *Task-based Language Learning and Teaching*. Oxford: Oxford University Press.

García Mayo, M. P. and Alcón Soler, E. (in press). *Negotiated Input and Output. Encyclopedia of Second Language Acquisition*. Cambridge: Cambridge University Press.

Mackey, A. and Polio, C. (eds) (2009). *Multiple Perspectives on Interaction*. New York: Routledge.

Discourse Completion Task (DCT)

Kathleen Bardovi-Harlig
Indiana University

DCTs, or discourse completion tasks, are one type of production questionnaire used to study pragmatic knowledge and performance. DCTs typically present a description of a situation (called a scenario) and ask the participant to respond. Most DCTs are written and are best described as "an indirect means for assessing spoken language in the form of a written production measure" (Cohen and Shively, 2007: 196). There are at least two types of DCTs, "open questionnaires" in which no conversational turns are provided (Example 1), and "dialogue completion tasks" in which an initiating turn or a rejoinder is provided (Bardovi-Harlig and Hartford, 1993: Examples 2 and 3).

(1) Open Questionnaire (Pearson, 2006: 494)
Your roommate has left the kitchen a mess after cooking. You want him/her to clean it up.
What do you say to your roommate?

____

(2) Dialogue Completion with initial turn (Shardakova, 2005: 450–51)
It is winter and you are in Moscow. You have a meeting with your advisor at the university at noon and you are a half-hour late because of the traffic delays caused by the snowstorm. Your bus that was taking you to the metro station was cancelled. Since you couldn't get a taxi, you had to walk and it took you thirty minutes longer to get to the metro station. When you arrived to the office your professor greeted you with the phrase: "Вы опаздали на 30 минут." ["You are 30 minutes late.]
You: ________________________

(3) Dialogue Completion with rejoinder (Blum-Kulka, House, and Kasper, 1989: 14)
At the university
Ann missed a lecture yesterday and would like to borrow Judith's notes.
Ann: ____________________
Judith: Sure, but let me have them back before the lecture next week.

The DCT introduced a means by which the performance of speech acts could be compared cross-linguistically and cross-culturally, thus offering an avenue for empirical investigation that was understandably absent from a tradition derived from philosophy. The introduction of the DCT (Blum-Kulka, 1982) and the subsequent publication of the results of the Cross Cultural Speech Act Realization Project (Blum-Kulka, House, and Kasper, 1989) left an indelible mark on pragmatics research: as an elicitation task, the DCT dominated interlanguage pragmatics research for at least 20 years and is still a popular means of data collection, favored for its potential to collect data from relatively large numbers of respondents in a short amount of time, by-passing transcription. In addition to ease of administration, the DCT allows maximal researcher control over the variables presented in the scenarios resulting in high comparability of items including degrees of differences among addresses and speakers, topic, setting, tone, and speech acts. DCTs have been used to investigate such speech acts as requests, apologies, refusals, complaints, compliments, disagreements, and expressions of gratitude.

Well-constructed DCTs used culturally plausible scenarios, and over time, evolved to having respondents take only roles with which they were familiar (for example, students playing a student or a visitor to a health center, rather than a police officer or a CEO of a company; they may have a host brother who speaks the L2, but not a brother). Scenarios generally do not mention the speech act that is being investigated, but instead use the general cue "you say:" rather than "you refuse" or "you agree," thus allowing the respondent some flexibility in response without raising awareness. The use of rejoinders in Example (3) shows one way in which the expectation of compliance is conveyed to the participant, avoiding a statement such as "you agree." In contrast, a rejoinder such as "I need them to study" would indicate that a refusal should be offered in the second turn. The use of "you say" to prompt simulation of speech encourages "live" responses rather than conjectures "I would probably say," so that the turns supplied reflect speech (e.g., "Can you take the trash out?") rather than reported speech (e.g., "I would ask him to take the trash out.").

In spite of the wide popularity of DCTs – and the measures taken to assure optimal responses – researchers also noted many ways in which DCTs differed from the natural conversations which they hoped to invoke. Acknowledgment of these differences led to modifications to the DCT, allowing researchers to retain advantages of the DCT while addressing some of the weaker points of the instrument. The differences include the ability of a speaker to a) not say anything in a given situation (called *opting out*), b) take turns, c) speak, d) take in multiple facts about the situation.

Opting out. DCTs show how speakers perform a given speech act when asked to do so, but the instrument does not give respondents an opportunity to decline to perform the speech act (in other words, they show how, but not if, a speaker would perform a particular speech act given a particular scenario). One of the issues faced in task construction is that "opting out" may take less effort than providing a verbal answer, especially for second language learners. Bonikowska (1988) avoided that problem by asking for the reasons behind opting out. She presented potential complaint scenarios differing in likelihood of a direct complaint followed by a set of questions (Example 4).

(4) "Landlady" Complaint Scenario (Bonikowska, 1988)
You're renting a room, but because the landlady's son is coming back home, you'll have to move out next term. Your landlady promised to help you find new accommodation. She was to have a word with some of her friends and let you know last week. She didn't. You haven't started looking for a

room on your own as you hoped to find a new place to stay through her.

Would you react/say anything in this situation?

If not, why not?

If so, what would you say?

Garton (2000) used an integrated prompt, in which saying and doing were presented as equivalent options, both requiring a verbal response: "What would you say or do?" Yu (2004) combined a production task and multiple choice (Example 5) reminiscent of Rose and Ono's (1995) multiple choice questionnaire where opting out and verbal responses are given equal weight.

(5) After you present your final project in class, a female classmate says to you, "I think you really did a good job."

A. You would say:_________________

or

B. You would not say anything about it.

Taking turns. Lack of turn taking in DCTs has been a serious issue not only for face validity, but because respondents are likely to produce more on the written DCT than they say in a single conversational turn. Turns allow speakers to distribution information depending on the responses of their interlocutors. The Interactive DCT offered a technology-based solution to this problem. Kuha (1997) devised a computer program to investigate complaints which read typed responses and gave and took up to three turns. Another means of creating turns was used a computer-delivered oral DCT (Bardovi-Harlig, *et al.*, 2010). A recorded voice took the first turn, then the participant replied, resulting in one turn exchange.

A second approach to collecting turns using DCTs was what Barron (2007) called the Free DCT: like all DCTs, these variants provide a scenario, but respondents write both parts of a conversation, providing either one exchange (Rose and Ng, 2001) or a whole conversation (Barron, 2007; Example 6, translated from the German by Barron, p. 160).

(6) You are in the airport. You see a girl your own age with two huge bags. As you haven't much luggage yourself, you offer to help. She REFUSES.

You:_________________

Girl:_________________

Speaking. For SLA researchers, mode is perhaps the most sensitive difference between written DCTs and conversation because general SLA data collection has handled them distinctly, whereas for at least two decades interlanguage pragmatics research as allowed writing to represent oral production. Early examples of oral DCTs were used by Murphy and Neu (1996) and Yuan (2001). Advances in technology, including the ability to record sound files directly to computers, facilitate the collection of oral data while retaining the highly valued advantages of ease of administration of the written DCT. The availability of computer labs and computerized language labs in major universities allows researchers to collect oral data from many respondents at the same time (Bardovi-Harlig *et al.*, 2010).

Knowing the situation. Context clearly plays an important role in pragmatics; in DCTs context has generally been represented by scenarios. Whereas native speakers may be generally aware of context and may need only a short scenario which evokes a setting, learners and nonnative speakers may need more specific scenarios, including speech turns (Bardovi-Harlig and Hartford, 1993). Billmyer and Varghese (2000) investigated the efficacy of short versus elaborated scenarios in DCTs. Lengthy descriptions could cause fatigue and favor advanced learners. In contrast, visual enhancement delivers certain details quickly and more naturally. Visual enhancements of DCTs which have been used to overcome the limits of verbal description include the use of drawings in the cartoon oral production task (COPT) designed for younger L2 learners (Rose, 2000), photographs (Nickels, 2006), and digitized, computer-delivered film excerpts (Leary, 1994).

See also: discourse and pragmatics in SLA, interlanguage, pragmatics, pragmalinguistics, speech acts, sociopragmatics

References

Bardovi-Harlig, K., Bastos, M.-T., Burghardt, B., Chappetto, E., Nickels, E. and Rose, M. (2010). The use of conventional expressions and utterance length in L2 pragmatics. In G. Kasper, H. t. Nguyen, D.R. Yoshimi, and J. K. Yoshioka (eds), *Pragmatics and Language Learning* (Vol. 12), Honolulu: University of Hawai'i, National Foreign Language Resource Center.

Bardovi-Harlig, K. and Hartford, B.S. (1993). Refining the DCT: Comparing open questionnaires and dialogue completion tasks. In L. F. Bouton and Y. Kachru (eds), *Pragmatics and Language Learning*, Vol. 4, pp. 143–65. Urbana-Champaign, IL: University of Illinois, Division of English as an International Language.

Barron, A. (2007). 'Ah no honestly we're okay:' Learning to upgrade in a study abroad context. *Intercultural Pragmatics*, *4*, 129–66.

Billmyer, K. and Varghese, M. (2000). Investigating instrument-based pragmatic variability: Effects of enhancing discourse completion tasks. *Applied Linguistics*, *21*, 517–52.

Blum-Kulka, S. (1982). Learning to say what you mean in a second language: A study of the speech act performance of learners of Hebrew as a second language. *Applied Linguistics*, *3*, 29–59.

Blum-Kulka, House, J., and Kasper, G. (eds). (1989). *Cross-cultural pragmatics: Requests and apologies*. Norwood, NJ: Ablex.

Bonikowska, M.G. (1988). The choice of opting out. *Applied Linguistics*, *9*, 169–81.

Cohen, A.D. and Shively, R. (2007). Acquisition of requests and apologies in Spanish and French: Impact of study abroad and strategy-building intervention. *The Modern Language Journal*, *91*, 189–212.

Garton, M. (2000). *The interlanguage pragmatics of learners of Hungarian as a second language*. Unpublished Indiana University PhD Dissertation, Bloomington, IN.

Kuha, M. (1997). The computer-assisted Interactive DCT: A study in pragmatics research methodology. In L. Bouton (ed.), *Pragmatics and Language Learning, Monograph* 8, Urbana-Champaign, IL: University of Illinois, Division of English as an International Language.

Leary, A. (1994). *Conversational replicas on computer for intermediate-level Russian: A Theoretical Model of a Design Paradigm*. Unpublished masters thesis, University of Iowa, Iowa City.

Murphy, B. and Neu, J. (1996). My grade's too low: The speech act set of complaining. In S.M. Gass, and J. Neu (eds), *Speech acts across cultures: Challenge to communication in a second language*. Berlin: Mouton de Gruyter.

Nickels, E.L. (2006). Interlanguage pragmatics and the effects of setting. In K. Bardovi-Harlig, C. Félix-Brasdefer, and A. Omar (eds), *Pragmatics and Language Learning*, vol. 11. Honolulu: University of Hawai'i, National Foreign Language Resource Center.

Pearson, L. (2006). Patterns of development in Spanish L2 pragmatic acquisition: An analysis of novice learners' production of directives. *The Modern Language Journal*, *90*, 473–95.

Rose, K. (2000). An exploratory cross-sectional study of interlanguage pragmatic development. *Studies in Second Language Acquisition*, *22*, 27–67.

Rose, K.R. and Ng, C.K. (2001). Inductive and deductive teaching of compliments and compliment responses. In K. Rose, and G. Kasper (eds), *Pragmatics in Language Teaching*. Cambridge: Cambridge University Press.

Rose, K. and Ono, R. (1995). Eliciting speech act data in Japanese: The effect of questionnaire type. *Language Learning*, *45*, 191–223.

Shardakova, M. (2005). Intercultural pragmatics in the speech of American L2 learners of Russian: Apologies offered by Americans in Russian. *Intercultural Pragmatics*, *2*, 423–51.

Yu, M.-C. (2004). Interlinguistic variation and similarity in second language speech act behavior. *The Modern Language Journal*, *88*, 102–19.

Yuan, Y. (2001). An inquiry into empirical pragmatics data-gathering methods: Written DCTs, oral DCTs, field notes, and natural conversations. *Journal of Pragmatics*, *33*, 271–92.

Discourse processing

Leah Roberts
University of York

In order to understand spoken and written discourse in real time, one must perform lexical-semantic and grammatical analyses of each word as it is encountered in the input, and integrate this "bottom-up" knowledge with the mental representation of the situation that has been built up so far on the basis of "top-down" discourse-pragmatic and world knowledge (Singer, 2007). The question of how this complex skill is affected during second language (L2) comprehension has only recently become a topic of interest. Most researchers investigate learners' interpretations of referring expressions such as pronouns, used to link phrases and clauses together in coherent discourse and on the extent to which learners' are sensitive to discourse-related constraints on grammatical processing. As well as informing current debates on the underlying causes of L1-L2 processing differences (Clahsen and Felser, 2006), these topics are set within the context of questions that are familiar from traditional applied linguistics research: whether L2 learners process the input like native speakers, and what the effects are of a learner's first language (L1) and of factors such as amount of experience/ level of proficiency.

L2 learners' resolution of pronouns in discourse

L2 discourse processing studies have investigated how learners resolve dependencies between pronouns and an antecedent in the preceding discourse, specifically addressing the question of potential L1 influences. Using eye-tracking during reading, Roberts, Gullberg, and Indefrey (2008) compared advanced Turkish and German L2 learners of Dutch in their processing of texts containing subject pronouns like in (1), where native speakers prefer to co-refer the pronoun *hij* with the most recently mentioned referent *Peter*, singled out from a conjoined noun phrase (NP) in the earlier discourse (*Peter en Hans*). This is because the most reduced referring expressions tend to refer to highly cognitively accessible referents (Ariel, 2001).

(1) Peter$_i$ en Hans zitten in het kantoor. Terwijl Peter$_i$ aan het werk is, eet hij$_i$ een boterham.
"Peter and Hans are in the office. While Peter is working, he is eating a sandwich."

Dutch and German are similar in that subject pronouns are obligatory, whereas in Turkish (a *null-subject* language) they are optional. Thus, a direct translation of (1) into Turkish (2) shows that the overt subject pronoun (*o*, "he") cannot refer to the local referent (*Peter*), but must refer to somebody else, most readily with *Hans* in the previous discourse. Co-reference with the most recently mentioned (and cognitively salient) referent would be achieved with a zero pronoun.

(2)

Peter ve Hans$_j$	Peter$_i$	o$_{*i/j}$ sandeviç
ofiste oturuyorlar.	çalışırken,	yiyor.
Peter and Hans	Peter	[he] sandwich
office sit-PL.	work,	eats.

"Peter and Hans are in the office. While Peter is working, he is eating a sandwich"

The results of a questionnaire task showed that this L1 difference affected the learners' final interpretations: the Germans patterned like the Dutch, linking the subject pronoun to the most recent referent, whereas the Turkish learners had an optional interpretation, with the majority linking the pronoun with the sentence-external referent *Hans* at least once. Interestingly, however, the eye-tracking data revealed a different pattern: both groups spent longer reading the region with the subject pronoun in (1), in comparison to a condition where the conjoined NP was replaced by a plural noun (*De Werknemers,* "the workers"), and thus where only one potential referent (*Peter*) was grammatically available for co-reference. Thus, irrespective of their final interpretation of the pronoun, both learner groups' linking of the pronoun to a discourse referent was disrupted by the potential competitor antecedent (*Hans*) in the earlier discourse (see also, Felser, Sato and Bertenshaw, 2009, for similar results with English reflexive pronouns).

Using the visual-world paradigm, where pictures are presented on a screen and participants' eye movements are recorded while they hear spoken input, Ellert, Järvikivi, and Roberts (in press) examined Finnish L2 learners' real-time interpretations of the German subject pronoun *er* and the demonstrative *der* ("he"), both of which being able to resolve towards a masculine, singular antecedent (3).

(3) Der Zauberer wollte den Arzt umarmen, weil die Sonne schien. Aber er (der)
war viel zu klein.
The doctor-ACC wanted the magician-NOM to-hug, because the sun-NOM
was-shining. But he-NOM/he-DEM-NOM
was much too small.
"The doctor wanted to hug the magician because the sun was shining. But he was much too small."

On hearing *er*, the German natives looked more often at the picture of the syntactic subject (also the topic, *Der Zauberer*), and for *der*, towards the accusative-marked second referent *den Arzt*. In the information-structurally marked condition, created by reversing the word order of the antecedents (*Den Arzt. ... der Zauberer*), the native speakers still preferred the fronted accusative antecedent as a referent for *der*, but in this marked context, *er* was less consistently interpreted as co-referential with the nominative-marked antecedent (*der Zauberer*): there was more optionality in the interpretation of *er* versus *der* for non-canonical word-order antecedent sentences. Testing Finnish L2 learners allowed for a direct investigation of potential L1 influences, since Finnish has a demonstrative (*tämä*) similar to *der*, as well as a masculine, singular subject pronoun (*hän*). However, despite the similarity between Finnish and German, the learners patterned with the native Germans only with *der*, resolving it towards the accusative-marked referent irrespective of word order, whereas for *er*, they had no resolution preference at all. These data suggest that the distribution of the subject pronoun *er* in German is only reliable in neutral (canonical) contexts and thus poses more of a learning problem than *der*, which appears to be consistent, even though it is the "marked" form (for similar results with English learners of German, see Wilson, 2009).

L2 learners' sensitivity to information structure constraints

In the above study, the marked object-subject word order might have caused difficulty overall, because it was not licensed by the discourse context. Also with German as the target language, Hopp (2009) specifically investigated whether lower- and higher-proficient L2 learners would be sensitive to information-structure factors licensing either canonical or non-canonical object-subject (*scrambling*) constructions. In German, a fronted object functions as *given* information, and occurs in discourse contexts where the subject is new information. In a self-paced reading study, participants were presented with a short text plus a *wh*-question: one that was felicitous for an object-first sentence, the "subject-focus" condition "In the factory, the worker was distracted by someone last Monday. Who distracted the worker?" (4b), and one in which the subject was old information and the object was new ("In the factory, the apprentice distracted someone last Monday. Who did the apprentice distract?"), and thus which the canonical subject-object word order sentence would be most appropriate (4a).

(4) a. Ich glaube, dass der Lehrling am Montag den Arbeiter abgelenkt hat. (SO).
I believe that the.NOM apprentice on Monday the.ACC worker distracted has.
b. Ich glaube, dass der Lehrling am Montag den Arbeiter abgelenkt hat. (OS).
I believe that the.ACC worker on Monday the.NOM worker distracted has.

The L1 background of the learners had an interesting effect. Like the German natives, the Russian learners' reading times were higher for the critical sentences (4) when they were in conflict with the information structure of the preceding discourse, arguably because scrambling is similar in the two languages. Interestingly, the more advanced English group, with no such phenomenon in the L1, showed similar sensitivity to the grammar-IS relation, suggesting that scrambling is acquirable, at least at higher levels of proficiency. However, the Dutch learners showed no sensitivity to the experimental manipulations, despite object-scrambling being permitted in Dutch. The author argues that L1 interference was the cause, the fronted object functions as a contrastive topic in Dutch, and so differs from the function of object-scrambling in German and Russian. Therefore, in comparison to the English group who had to acquire new IS-grammatical knowledge, a restructuring of knowledge was necessary for the Dutch learners of German, which may cause difficulty even at advanced levels of proficiency.

L2 learners' use of referential context in resolving structural ambiguities

Hopp's (2009) study shows that learners can make use of discourse information to constrain their real-time analyses of the unfolding input. Other studies have looked at whether such information can influence L2 learners' resolution of fully ambiguous sentences like (5), where a prepositional phrase (PP) can modify either the verb phrase (VP) (*the policeman had the binoculars* [5a]) or the noun phrase (NP) (*the man had the binoculars* [5b]). Native English speakers prefer VP-attachment, following a parsing principle that pushes for the structurally simplest analysis (*cf. Minimal Attachment,* Frazier and Rayner, 1982).

(5) a. The policeman [VP saw [NP the man] [PP with the binolulars.]]
(VP-modification)
b. The policeman [VP saw [NP the man [PP with the binolulars.]]]
(NP-modification)

This preference for VP-attachment can be reduced, however, with a preceding referential discourse context in which more than one referent for the postverbal definite NP is provided and thus renders the restrictive modifier meaning of the PP more felicitous (e.g., *There was one man with binoculars and one man without. The policeman saw the man with the binoculars*), as one specific referent is selected from a set (Altmann and Steedman, 1998). Pan and Felser (2011) investigated whether Chinese L2 learners of English would be sensitive to referential context in their processing of such ambiguities, and using self-paced reading, asked when such information would come into play during interpretation, given that there is controversy in the monolingual literature as to whether discourse-pragmatic information guides sentence processing, or whether such information is accessed in a stage following syntactic analysis (see Vasishth and Lewis, 2006). The materials comprised VP-supporting (6a) and NP-supporting (6b) contexts, and the critical sentences were semantically consistent with either VP (*Bill glanced at the customer with strong suspicion.*) or NP-modification interpretation (*Bill glanced at the customer with ripped jeans.*).

(6) a. *VP-supporting context*
Bill walked into a shop that he knew the police were keeping an eye on. There was only one other customer in the shop. The customer was wearing old and filthy clothes, whereas the sales assistant was very smartly dressed.
b. *NP-supporting context*
Bill walked into a shop that he knew the police were keeping an eye on. There were two other customers in the shop. One customer was wearing old and filthy clothes, whereas the other one was dressed very smartly.

The learners patterned like natives in the questionnaire task, with the overall preference for VP-modification reduced following an NP-modification context (see also Ying, 2006). Interestingly, though, this effect of discourse context was observed in the reading of the critical PP segment only for the L2 learners; the native speakers' reading times showed only a facilitation for VP attachment, even though their final interpretations were affected by the referential context. Therefore, the learners' real-time use of discourse information came into play earlier than that of the native speakers.

Conclusion

In sum, L2 learners' discourse processing may be disrupted in comparison to native speakers when encountering ambiguity that needs to be resolved by accessing and integrating grammatical with discourse-pragmatic information, and this is often the case irrespective of how typologically close the source and target language are, although L1 effects may come into play at later stages of interpretation (c.f., Roberts *et al.*, 2008), or cause problems where there are subtly different effects of information structure on grammatical function (c.f., Hopp, 2009). However, overall, L2 discourse processing is rather similar to that of native speakers: learners are sensitive to referential context, and discourse information rapidly affects on-line processing of the input. In fact, some argue that L2 learners are more sensitive to discourse-pragmatic information than native speakers, which compensates for their compromised grammatical processing as stated in the *Shallow Structure Hypothesis*, a fundamental-difference account of L1-L2 processing (Clahsen and Felser, 2006). Furthermore, such sensitivity to discourse constraints is argued to go against a processing capacity limitation account for differences between L1 and L2 processing (e.g., Hopp, 2009). Whether or not L2 processing is qualitatively or quantitatively different, it does appear that differences observed in L1-L2 processing, for instance in the processing of ambiguities (e.g., Felser, Roberts, Gross and Marinis, 2003) can be eradicated when learners are provided with a supporting discourse context (Dekydtspotter, Edmonds, Fultz, Liljestrand, and Petrusch, 2008), as found in most naturally occurring language situations.

See also: psycholinguistics and neurolinguistics, parsing and processing, discourse and pragmatics in SLA, cohesion and coherence, eye-tracking, reading

References

Altmann, G. and Steedman, M. (1988). Interaction with context during human sentence processing. *Cognition*, *30*, 191–238.

Ariel, M. (2001). Accessibility theory: An overview. In T. Sanders, J. Schilperoord and W. Spooren (eds), *Text Representation: Linguistic and Psycholinguistic Aspects*. Amsterdam: Benjamins.

Clahsen, H. and Felser, C. (2006). Grammatical processing in language learners. *Applied Psycholinguistic*, *27*, 3–42.

Dekydtspotter, L., Edmonds, A.C., Fultz, A.L., Liljestrand, A. and Petrusch, R.A. (2008). Syntactic and prosodic computations in the resolution of relative clause attachment ambiguity by English-French learners. *Studies in Second Language Acquisition*, *30*, 453–80.

Ellert, M., Järvikivi, J. and Roberts, L. (in press) Information structure affects the resolution of the subject pronouns *er* and *der* in spoken German discourse. In L. Sarda, S.C. Thomas and B. Fagard (eds), *Linguistic and Psycholinguistic Approaches to Text Structuring*. Amsterdam: John Benjamins.

Felser, C., Roberts, L, Gross, R. and Marinis, T. (2003). The processing of ambiguous sentences by first and second language learners of English. *Applied Psycholinguistics*, *24*, 453–89.

Felser, C., Sato, M. and Bertenshaw, N. (2009). The on-line application of binding Principle A in English as a second language. *Bilingualism: Language and Cognition*, *12*, 485–502.

Frazier, L. and Rayner, K. (1982). Making and correcting errors during sentence comprehension: Eye movements in the analysis of structurally ambiguous sentences. *Cognitive Psychology*, *14*, 178–210.

Hopp, H. (2009). The syntax-discourse interface in near-native L2 acquisition: Off-line and on-line performance. *Bilingualism: Language and Cognition*, *12*, 463–83.

Pan, H-Y. and Felser, C. (2011). Referential context effects in L2 ambiguity resolution: Evidence from self-paced reading. *Lingua*, *121*, 221–36.

Roberts, L., Gullberg, M. and Indefrey, P. (2008). Online pronoun resolution in L2 discourse: L1 influence and general learner effects. *Studies in Second Language Acquisition*, *30*, 333–57.

Singer, M. (2007). Inference processing in discourse comprehension. In G. Gaskell (ed.), *Oxford Handbook of Psycholinguistics*. Oxford: Oxford University Press.

Vasishth, S. and Lewis, R.L. (2006). Symbolic models of human sentence processing. In *Encyclopedia of Language and Linguistics*, 2nd edn. Oxford: Elsevier.

Wilson, F. (2009). *Processing at the syntax-discourse interface in second language acquisition*. Unpublished PhD thesis, University of Edinburgh, Edinburgh.

Ying, I. (1996). Multiple constraints on processing ambiguous sentences: Evidence from L2 learners. *Language Learning*, *46*, 681–711.

Further reading

Cook, A.E. and Guéraud, S. (2005). What have we been missing? The role of general world knowledge in discourse processing. *Discourse Processes*, *39*, 265–78. (An overview and discussion of current theories/debates in the monolingual discourse comprehension literature.)

Roberts, L. (2012) Sentence Processing in Bilinguals. In R. van Gompel (ed.), *Sentence Processing*. Hove: Psychology Press. (For overview and discussion of debates on underlying differences between L1 and L2 processing.)

Ward, G. and Birner, B.J. (2001). Discourse and Information Structure. In D. Schriffrin, D. Tannen and H. Hamilton (eds), *Handbook of Discourse Analysis*. Oxford: Basil Blackwell. (An overview of the topic of Information Structure.)

Distributed cognition

Steven L. Thorne
Portland State University and University of Groningen

Distributed cognition (also called extended and social distributed cognition) refers to a framework for understanding human action, such as thinking and communicating, as processes that are fundamentally supra-individual and which include, but importantly are seen to extend beyond, neuronal activity of the brain. The term "distribution" is meant to highlight the idea that thinking and doing involve the body (see Embodiment) and coordination between human as well as non-human artifacts and environments. In this sense, neither the brain nor the individual are the exclusive loci of cognition; rather, the focus is on understanding the organization of systems, or "cognition in the wild" (Hutchins, 1995), which presumes an ecological view of cognitive activity as organized by the interplay between persons and resources that are distributed across social and material environments.

Approaches to extended and distributed cognition posit that humans are open systems that function and develop within complex, historically formed, and dynamically changing social, symbolic, and material ecologies. When viewed this way, human activity and development are seen to form an "ensemble" process that plays out along a brain-body-world continuum (e.g., Spivey, 2007). This understanding of human cognition as distributed includes a number of entailments, one of which is a focus on mediation – that objects and other people in the environment co-produce action and thinking in unison with individual human agents. Another is that cognition, action, and communication are processes that are inherently shared across individuals, artifacts, environments, and through individual and collective memory, across time periods as well (e.g., Wertsch, 2002).

An important constraint is that the principle of distribution is not meant to suggest symmetry or equal division between individual humans and other people, artifacts, or environments; rather, the suggestion is that the density of cognitive activity can shift from brains to bodies and to a range of physical and representational media in the flow of activity. The notion of distribution suggests an additional entailment, namely that of units of analysis such as 'organism-environment systems' (e.g., Järvilehto, 2009), which describe how change within an organism is accompanied by change to the environment and a reorganization of organism–environment relations. In these ways, distributed cognition suggests that human action and development are fundamentally emergent of, and enmeshed with, specific temporal, social, and material conditions.

Examples of distributed cognition in the literature include the use of alarm clocks and timers as external regulators of human action, shopping lists and online translators as forms of distributed memory, collaboratively produced utterances that are common to multiparty verbal interaction, and coordination among humans that involves mediation via sophisticated navigation equipment on large ships and aircraft. Within applied linguistics, Atkinson (2010) has proposed distributed or "extended," cognition principles to SLA that call for a focus on the inseparability of mind-body-world ecologies, processes of adaptation to complex environments, and dynamics of alignment through which humans effect interaction.

See also: context of situation, dynamic assessment, ecology of language learning, embodiment, social and sociocultural approaches to SLA, variationist approaches to SLA

References

Atkinson, D. (2010). Extended, embodied cognition and second language acquisition. *Applied Linguistics*, *31*(5), 599–622.

Hutchins, Edwin (1995). *Cognition in the wild.* Bradford, MA: MIT Press.

Järvilehto, T. (2009). The theory of the organism-environment system as a basis of experimental work in psychology. *Ecological Psychology*, *21*, 112–20.

Spivey, M. (2007). *The Continuity of Mind.* New York: Oxford University Press.

Further reading

Cowley, S. (ed.) (2009). Distributed language. Special issue of *Pragmatics & Cognition*, *17*, 3. (A collection of articles that outline a view of distributed language in a variety of communication and developmental contexts.)

Norman, D. (1993). *Things that make us smart.* New York: Addison-Wesley. (A seminal text that focuses on mental tools, or "cognitive artifacts," and their capacity to enhance as well as constrain thinking and action.)

Salomon, G. (ed.) (1993). *Distributed cognitions: Psychological and educational considerations.* Cambridge: Cambridge University Press. (An edited volume with chapters that describe distributed cognition from psychological, cultural-historical, and situated perspectives.)

Dynamic assessment

Matthew E. Poehner
Pennsylvania State University

Regardless of the context in which they occur, all assessments, at least implicitly, are concerned with a future beyond the immediacy of the current activity. Classroom assessments frequently aim to provide insights into learners' current understanding so as to inform subsequent instruction. In more formal assessments, the notion of generalizability addresses the confidence one can have in claims about individuals' likely performance in other contexts on the basis of their assessment performance. Even when the stated purpose is to measure the products of prior learning, as with achievement tests, this measurement is in fact undertaken to inform judgments of what may reasonably be expected of individuals in the future. Dynamic Assessment (henceforth, DA) aims to glimpse this future in the process of its formation, constructing a model of an individual's future independent functioning on the basis of performance undertaken cooperatively with an assessor, or mediator.

DA unfolds at precisely the point that many assessments are concluded, that is, the point at which individuals reach the threshold of their independent functioning and begin to experience problems (Poehner, 2008). In DA, the mediator functions jointly with learners, offering hints and prompts, leading questions, suggestions, models, and feedback to support learner efforts to overcome problems. In this way, the present interaction creates a dialogic site bringing together the results of the learners' past development, manifested in independent performance, as well as their immediate future development, interpreted according to their success in resolving difficulties with mediator support. DA is thus predicated upon a dialectic tension between what learners can do independently and what they are capable of doing only in cooperation with a mediator. The synthesis in this dialectic, or resolution of this tension, is brought about as development moves forward and what was once possible only in cooperation now comes to characterize learner independent functioning.

This dialectical understanding of human abilities and their development originated with the Russian psychologist, L.S. Vygotsky. Vygotsky (1978) famously distinguished between the range of abilities that characterize what we can do independently, which he termed the *zone of actual development* (ZAD), and those abilities that have not yet developed to a point where individuals are capable of full, independent control. These latter abilities, which are still in the process of forming, constitute the *zone of proximal development* (ZPD). In practice, the ZPD may be understood according to what learners are capable of during cooperative interaction with a mediator. As a consequence, these abilities are missed by conventional approaches to assessment, which reveal only the ZAD. For Vygotsky (1987), who rejected the view that development proceeds along a linear, pre-determined path, the ZAD is an inadequate basis for explaining an individual's future. Proceeding from the perspective that development is a social process driven by participation in activities, he argued that a cooperative rather than observational orientation is required on the part of the assessor. In this way, an individual's proximal, or near future, independent functioning is reflected in mediator-learner dialoguing, and at the same time this cooperation begins to create the path toward realizing those abilities.

Vygotsky and his colleagues conducted the first applications of DA more than eighty years ago in their work to diagnose causes underlying children's poor school performance and design appropriate educational plans (Poehner, 2008). The subsequent introduction of Vygotsky's theory outside Russia has led to a variety of DA practices around the world (see Haywood and Lidz, 2007). DA has only recently been taken up by L2 researchers, who have broken with the widespread view that DA is primarily relevant to psychologists operating in clinical settings. L2 DA has been placed directly in the hands of classroom teachers as a framework for conceptualizing instruction and assessment in relation to learner development. As a framework rather than a set of techniques, DA applications with L2 learners have emerged through cooperation between researchers and teachers and have been responsive to particular classroom contexts. Poehner (2008) reports a highly dialogic approach to DA with advanced undergraduate university learners of French struggling to control verbal tense and aspect in oral production. Ableeva (2010) employed DA principles to diagnose phonological, lexical, and cultural difficulties experienced by intermediate level undergraduate learners of French engaged in listening activities. Lantolf and Poehner (to appear) describe how a primary school teacher of Spanish structured her daily interactions with learners around DA and supported their ability to correctly mark noun-adjective concord. Among the important findings in these studies is that the value of implicit and explicit feedback to learners, an ongoing topic of debate in the field of SLA, is relative to the point at which it occurs in mediator-learner interaction. That is, the degree of implicitness or explicitness in DA is determined by learner responsiveness, with mediation becoming more explicit only as needed to stimulate a correct response from the learner. This is important not only because the quality of mediation and learner responsiveness form part of the diagnosis in DA but also because it is through learners' struggle to stretch beyond their current capabilities that development occurs (Poehner and Lantolf, to appear).

Current L2 DA research addresses the need to move beyond dyadic interactions to engage with larger numbers of learners while remaining attuned to their emerging needs and abilities. Poehner (2009) argues for a group ZPD, with teachers designing activities that no individual can complete independently but that each may carry out with mediation. It is recognized that individuals will vary with regard to the amount of mediation they require, but the argument is that through participation in activities in which the group is mediated, individuals as well as the group itself will develop.

Poehner and Lantolf (in preparation) are developing a set of computerized L2 proficiency tests that include scripted mediation in the form of prompts proceeding from implicit to explicit and that are made available to learners as they respond to multiple-choice items. Through such projects, DA's contributions to L2 teaching, learning, and assessment may be better understood.

See also: development in SLA, language testing and SLA, measuring and researching SLA, scaffolding, social and socio-cultural approaches to SLA

References

Ableeva, R. (2010). *Dynamic Assessment of Listening Comprehension in Second Language Learning*. Unpublished doctoral dissertation. The Pennsylvania State University.

Haywood, H.C. and Lidz, C.S. (2007). *Dynamic Assessment in Practice. Clinical and Educational Applications*. New York: Cambridge University Press.

Lantolf, J.P. and M.E. Poehner. (2011). Dynamic Assessment in the Classroom: Vygotskian Praxis for L2 Development. *Language Teaching Research*, *15*(1), 11–33.

Poehner, M.E. (2008). *Dynamic Assessment: A Vygotskian Approach to Understanding and Promoting Second Language Development*. Berlin: Springer Publishing.

——(2009). Group dynamic assessment: Mediation for the L2 classroom. *TESOL Quarterly*, *43* (3), 471–91.

Poehner, M.E. and J.P. Lantolf. (in preparation). Bringing development into the equation: Dynamic assessment as a principled approach to assessing learners of L2 French.

Vygotsky, L.S. (1978). *Mind in Society. The Development of Higher Psychological Processes*. Cambridge, MA: Harvard University Press.

——(1987). *The collected works of L.S. Vygotsky. Volume 1. Problems of General Psychology. Including the Volume Thinking and Speech*. New York: Plenum.

Further reading

Kozulin, A. (1998). *Psychological Tools: A Sociocultural Approach to Education*. Cambridge, MA: Harvard University Press. (An elaboration of Vygotsky's theory and how it serves as a foundation for education aimed at promoting learner development through engagement in the ZPD.)

Lantolf, J.P. and Poehner, M.E. (2006). *Dynamic Assessment in the Foreign Language Classroom: A Teacher's Guide*. University Park, PA: CALPER. [149pp. and Video DVD: version 1.0]. (A practical introduction to DA and guide for L2 teachers interested in implementing DA principles in their classrooms.)

Lidz, C.S. and J.G. Elliott (eds) (2000). *Dynamic assessment: Prevailing Models and Applications*. Amsterdam: Elsevier. (A representation of a range of DA studies from around the world and with diverse populations and learning contexts.)

Poehner, M.E. and P. Rea-Dickins (eds) (to appear). Addressing issues of access and fairness in education through Dynamic Assessment. Special Issue of *Assessment in Education: Principles, Policy and Practice*. (A collection of studies addressing a variety of DA approaches in L2 classrooms, cognitive education programs, and early childhood education.)

Ecology of language learning

Leo van Lier
Monterey Institute for International Studies

The transdisciplinary field of ecology was first established in biology, in the nineteenth century, by the German biologist Ernst Haeckel. The term ecology is based on the Greek word "oekos," which means household. Haeckel's innovative proposal was to study the environment in terms of the *relations* among all organisms, rather than simply as collections of objects that may act upon one another in linear cause-effect ways (1866). Some time later the Estonian biologist Jakob Johann von Uexküll established his influential notion of "Umwelt," as distinct from "Umgebung" or simply environment (context). The Umwelt is the subjective spatio-temporal world that organisms live in, rather than an objective reality. The notions of ecology and Umwelt also share a close resemblance to Lewin's (1943) "life space," Wittgenstein's (1958) "forms of life" and also, arguably, to the work of Vygotsky, Bakhtin, Peirce, and Gibson, among others (see van Lier, 2004).

The term *transdisciplinary* mentioned above means that ecology does not merely claim relevance to several different established fields such as psychology, sociology, or linguistics, but that it operates at both a higher (metatheoretical) and a lower (metapractical) level than the various disciplines addressed. *Higher*, in the sense that it seeks deeper theoretical understandings that transcend disciplinary boundaries, and *lower*, in the sense that it proposes guidelines for clinical and interventionist work that apply to a range of practitioners' real-world tasks.

There are two primary aspects of an ecology of language learning that we have to consider: first, the more *macro* notion of language diversity, issues of language contact, Lingual Franca languages, language policies and politics (often called eco-linguistics, see e.g. Fill and Mühlhäusler, 2001); and second, the more *micro* issue of an ecological perspective on language learning and language using, that is, the behavior of learners as they perceive, act on and in, and interpret the world. Although the terms macro and micro may invite unwarranted dichotomizing, it is useful to look at these as two different spatiotemporal scales. The first scale is one of languages at work in the world (much like biological ecosytems and climates) in the form of speech communities and their interconnections, including processes leading to stabilization and change. The other, at the more micro end of the scalar spectrum, looks at individuals and the ways in which they negotiate their being and becoming in the world. These two scales are not independent or separate but are intertwined in a multitude of ways. In actual fact, just as in biology, scales in ecological linguistics are not either macro or micro, rather there are a multitude of scales that range across degrees of distances in spatiotemporal terms. Any particular focal point in time and space is an intersection of diachrony and synchrony, of temporal and spatial influences.

Modern general linguistics, influenced by Saussure's (1986 – original publication 1916) structuralism, is based on a-temporal and non-spatial slice of language at a given time, and is thus blind to the essential "structure/process" tensions that inhere in all natural phenomena. As a more recent subfield, sociolinguistics is also essentially synchronic, but focuses primarily on spatial (e.g. regional variation, contact) and stratal (social and institutional genres and registers) phenomena. An ecological perspective looks at the intersection of temporal and spatial planes, just as a field ecologist must look both at climatic and geophysical shifts over time, and at current dynamics of intra- and inter-systemic developments.

Ecology, language, language use and learning

So what does an ecological perspective on language, language use, and language learning look like in the practical world? I will answer in four parts, addressing the ecological view of language, of language use, of learning, and finally of research.

First, then, what is language in an ecological perspective? It is not an autonomous or even quasi-autonomous system that can be studied in isolation from its connections to context and all the multifarious ways of making meaning that people and communities invent and employ. In other words, language is an integral part of semiotics, that is, the science of making and using signs. Second, language use defines language. As such it is essentially dialogical in nature, born from communicative intentions and realized in communicative settings. Third, and following from the above, language learning is accomplished by participating in language-rich events. It is not primarily a matter of learning words and stringing together sequences. It is fundamentally a matter of making stories, talking about places and times, shaping identities, projecting futures, reliving pasts, negotiating work and leisure, and a million other things. It is not about making grammatical sentences, although they do occur from time to time, of course. Finally, ecological research is characterized by the following criteria:

1 It is oriented towards intervention (improvement of a particular ecosystem)
2 It is ecologically valid
3 It is longitudinal in nature
4 It studies relations among elements in the setting
5 It addresses an intact ecosystem at a particular focal scale
6 It also addresses at least one scale above and one scale below the focal scale.

These principles are in need of elaboration and further definition, and in this brief overview they are merely presented as part of a blueprint for future specification. However, there are some research frameworks that exemplify some or all of the criteria listed. The most well-known example is Bronfenbrenner's bioecological research (2005), and particularly the model of nested ecosystems that he developed.

The ecology of langage learning and SLA

In SLA and applied linguistics, van Lier (2004), Leather and van Dam (2003), and Kramsch (2002) have been prominent in pointing towards ecological approaches in language learning and teaching. What such studies have in common is a concern with dynamic processes in context, detailed descriptions of events, a dialogical view of language embedded in a larger semiotics, and a rejection of linear causal information-processing assumptions, as manifested in much of the traditional research in SLA. A clear statement of this rejection is the recent collection of studies published under the heading of "language as a complex adaptive system," spearheaded by the "Five Graces" group (Beckner *et al.*, 2009).

Of particular importance in an ecological view of language, language learning, and language teaching are the notions of perception, agency, and interpretive processes. The centrality of perception in language learning and teaching is argued in van Lier (2004), and emphasizes a departure from the narrowly defined experimental constructs of attention and noticing in SLA based on information processing theory. In particular, van Lier (1996) proposes that the notion of "input" should be replaced by Gibson's ecological construct "affordance," which is a relation between observer and observed that originates in interaction and that constitutes a potential for further action (Gibson, 1979). Similarly, the monological term "output" is increasingly replaced by "languaging" and "translanguaging" (e.g. Creese and Blackledge, 2010).

Conclusion

In summary and conclusion, the influence of an ecological perspective on language and language education is still relatively young in applied linguistics and SLA. Time will tell if the ecological perspective will have a lasting impact on our field. If it does, I predict that it will be in the areas of the redefining of language as part of a broader semiotics; the insight that language learning is defined in large measure by perception and agency; and that teaching is a matter of creating favorable conditions for learning to happen.

See also: affordance, Complexity Theory/ Dynamic Systems Theory, dialogic inquiry, ethnographic research, social and sociocultural approaches to SLA, sociocognitive approaches to SLA

References

Beckner, C., Blythe, R., Bybee, J., Christiansen, M., Croft, W., Ellis, N., Holland, J., Ke, J., Larsen-Freeman, D. and Schoenemann, T. (2009). The "Five Graces group." In N. Ellis and D. Larsen-Freeman (eds), *Language as a Complex Adaptive System*. Malden, MA: Wiley-Blackwell.

Bronfenbrenner, U. (2005). *Making Human Beings Human: Bioecological Perspectives on Human Development*. Thousand Oaks, CA: Sage Publications.

Creese, A. and Blackledge, A. (2010). Translanguaging in the bilingual classroom: A pedagogy for learning and teaching? *The Modern Language Journal*, *94*, 1, 103–115.

Fill, A. and Mühlhäusler, P. (eds) (2001). *The Ecolinguistics Reader: Language, Ecology and Environment*. London: Continuum.

Gibson, J.J. (1979). *The Ecological Approach to Visual Perception*. Hillsdale, NJ: Erlbaum.

Haeckel, E. (1866). *Allgemeine Anatomie der Organismen*. Berlin: Reimer.

Leather, J. and van Dam, J. (2003). Towards an ecology of language acquisition. In J. Leather and J. van Dam (eds), *The Ecology of Language Acquisition*, pp. 1–29. Dordrecht: Kluwer Academic Publishers.

Kramsch, C. (ed.) (2002). *Language Acquisition and Language Socialization: Ecological Perspectives*. London: Continuum.

Lewin, K. (1943). Defining the 'field at a given time.' *Psychological Review*, *50*, 292–310.

Saussure, F. de (1986/1916). *Course in General Linguistics*. La Salle, IL: Open Court Classics.

van Lier, L. (1996). *Interaction in the Language Curriculum: Awareness, Autonomy and Authenticity*. London: Longman.

——(2004). *The Ecology and Semiotics of Language Learning*. Dordrecht: Kluwer Academic.

von Uexküll, J. (1902). Psychologie und Biologie in ihrer Stellung zur Tierseele. *Ergebnisse der Physiologie*, *1* (2), 212–233.

Wittenstein, L. (1958). *Philosophical Investigations*. Oxford: Blackwell.

Effect size

Luke Plonsky
Northern Arizona University

An effect size is a descriptive statistic that indicates the strength of a relationship as measured and is therefore critical to interpreting quantitative results. There are two main types of effect sizes in SLA research: correlation coefficients (r) and standardized mean differences between or within groups (Cohen's d), defined as

$$d = M_1 - M_2 \ / \ \text{SD pooled}$$

where M_1 and M_2 refer to the means of the treatment and comparison groups, respectively, and SD refers to the pooled standard deviation (Grissom and Kim, 2005). Like a z-score, a d value expresses the difference between two means in standard deviation units.

Discussions of effect sizes are often contextualized within the decades-long controversy in the social sciences over null hypothesis significance testing (Cohen, 1994). In contrast to *p* values, which reduce continuous data to a dichotomy of statistical significance or non-significance based on an arbitrary cut-off for the acceptable level of Type I error (usually 0.05), effect sizes provide greater precision by quantifying the magnitude of the relationship in question.

Because SLA researchers often employ instruments unique to a particular study with their own scales, effect sizes are particularly useful in that they provide a common metric for comparing findings across studies. This feature of effect sizes enables the results of multiple studies to be averaged, that is, meta-analyzed. To be included in a meta-analysis, however, each study must report an effect size or sufficient data to calculate an effect size, a condition frequently unmet in SLA research (Plonsky, 2011). Nevertheless, reporting of basic descriptive statistics and effect sizes has increased recently and in parallel to the use of meta-analysis thanks in part to recent editions of the APA publication manual (2010; see pp. 33–34) as well as several prominent applied linguistics journals that now encourage or require authors to report effect sizes.

Effect sizes can also be used for power analysis, a procedure designed to determine a priori the sample size necessary to reliably detect whether or not an effect will be found using inferential statistics. When previous research and/or theory predict a relatively small effect, for example, a large sample of participants is needed to have sufficient power to reject a false null hypothesis. Unfortunately, power is very rarely considered in SLA research (see Plonsky, 2011; Plonsky and Gass, 2011).

Finally, although more informative than *p* values and other descriptive statistics alone, effect sizes place the burden of interpretation upon researchers who must translate the numerical value into a meaningful, qualified description. In addition to researchers' expertise and understanding of the designs and variables in question, interpretations of effect sizes might consider the following: (a) effect sizes from previous/related studies, (b) magnitude of relationships as predicted by theory, (c) the SD units they represent (for *d* values), (d) benchmarks proposed for interpreting effect sizes, both those specific to SLA (d = .4, .7, and 1.00 for small, medium, and large, respectively; Oswald and Plonsky, 2010) and those applied across the social sciences (d = 0.2, 0.5, 0.8; Cohen, 1988), and (e) practical significance.

See also: hypothesis testing, measuring and researching SLA, meta-analysis, quantitative research, significance level, variance

References

American Psychological Association (2010). *Publication Manual of the American Psychological Association* (6th edn). Washington, DC.

Cohen, J. (1994). The Earth Is Round (p < .05), *American Psychologist, 49*, 997–1003.

Grissom, R J. and Kim, J.J. (2005). *Effect Sizes for Research: A Broad Practical Approach.* Mawhah, NJ: Lawrence Erlbaum Associates.

Oswald, F.L. and Plonsky, L. (2010). Meta-analysis in Second Language Research: Choices and Challenges. *Annual Review of Applied Linguistics, 30*, 85–110.

Plonsky, L. (2011). Study Quality in SLA: A Cumulative and Developmental Assessment of Designs, Analyses, Reporting Practices, and Outcomes in Quantitative L2 Research. Unpublished doctoral dissertation, Michigan State University.

Plonsky, L. and Gass, S. (2011). 30 years of interaction: Research methods, study quality, and outcomes. *Language Learning, 61*, 325–66.

Further reading

Cohen, J. (1988). *Statistical Power Analysis for the Behavioral Sciences.* Hillside, NJ: Lawrence Erlbaum Associates.

Journal Article Reporting Standards Working Group (2008). Reporting standards for research in psychology: Why do we need them? What might they be? *American Psychologist, 63*, 839–51.

Lazaraton, A. (1991). Power, effect size, and second language research: A researcher comments. *TESOL Quarterly, 25,* 759–62.

Vacha-Haase, T. and Thompson, B. (2004). How to estimate and interpret various effect sizes. *Journal of Counseling Psychology*, *51*, 473–81.

Wilkinson, L. and Task Force on Statistical Inference (1999). Statistical methods in psychology journals: Guidelines and explanations. *American Psychologist*, *54*, 594–604.

Embodiment

Steven L. Thorne
Portland State University and University of Groningen

Embodiment (also called embodied and/or embedded cognition) has many meanings across disciplines such as cognitive science, linguistics, neuroscience, philosophy, psychology, and sociology. In broad relief, the term embodiment underscores the importance of understanding intelligent behavior as a function of enmeshment between the brain, body, and the social-material world. Embodied views of cognition and emotion are often contrasted with modular and more hermetically bounded and computational conceptions of cognition as a brain-local phenomenon.

Within cognitive science and linguistics, conceptual metaphor theory proposes the view that human conceptual systems are a consequence of bodily-kinesthetic experience in physical and social environments. Lakoff (1987) has argued that cognitive models, which include metaphorical mapping of bodily and perceptual experience to abstract conceptual domains, structure thought and are fundamentally embodied with respect to their content. Examples are the metaphors "Affection is warmth," which emerges when infants are held by caregivers and hence link body heat to affection, and "More is up," based on the visual perception of greater volume equating with verticality (i.e., water level in a container rises and piles of objects increase in height with greater volume).

In psychology, Barsalou (2008) has proposed an approach called "grounded cognition," which contends that bodily states and cognitive states have mutually influencing effects on one another. Using the experience of sitting in a chair as an example, Barsalou explains that the brain integrates immediate experience with multimodal representations stored in memory, such as prior instances of sitting on chairs, how they feel, and associations with comfort and relaxation. In future instances of sitting, these multimodal representations are reactivated and construct the category of "chair" based on accrued bodily experiences situated in specific sociocultural settings.

Recent cognitive neuroscience research has argued that the body is foundational to consciousness. Taking an evolutionary position, Damasio (2010) contends that "brain and body bond" (p. 21), especially in the domain of emotions, and that cognitive activity is phylogenetic emergent of bodies engaged in perception, action, and real-time adaptation to cultural and physical environments. Neuroscience research related to language and communication supports arguments for embodied cognition through the discovery that somatic and linguistic processes often recruit overlapping neural systems. Examples include language about bodily action co-activating with somatotopic representations in the motor system, neural representations of action-related language affecting the bodily performance of these actions, and that perception and production of language and gesture are all subserved by the same neural networks and brain regions, the conclusion being that "[bodily] action and language processing share a high-level neural integration system" (Willems *et al.*, 2007).

In the realm of sociology, Bourdieu's notions of *habitus* and *body hexis* outline the idea that cognition, communication, perception, and appraisal are culturally organized and result in "a durable way of standing, speaking, walking and thereby of feeling and thinking" (1990: 70), a view which unites embodiment with subjective experience in the context of differentiated subject positions in society.

See also: Cognitive Linguistics and SLA, distributed cognition, dynamic assessment, ecology of language learning, social and sociocultural approaches to SLA, variationist approaches to SLA

References

Barsalou, L. (2008). Grounded cognition. *Annual Review of Psychology*, *59*, 617–645.

Bourdieu, P. (1990). *The Logic of Practice*. Cambridge: Polity.

Damasio, A. (2010). *Self Come to Mind: Constructing the Conscious Brain*. London: William Heinemann.

Lakoff, G. (1987). *Women, Fire, and Dangerous things: What Categories Reveal about the Mind*. Chicago, IL: University of Chicago Press.

Willems, R., Özyürek, A. and Hagoort, P. (2007). When language meets action: The neural integration of gesture and speech. *Cerebral Cortex*, *17*, 2322–2333.

Further reading

Bates, E. and Dick, F. (2002). Language, gesture, and the developing brain. *Developmental Psychology*, *40*, 293–310. (This article examines the relationship between language and gesture in early childhood language acquisition.)

Clark, A. (2008). *Supersizing the Mind: Embodiment, Action, and Cognitive Extension*. Oxford: Oxford University Press. (This book outlines an embodied-embedded framework for understanding mind and action.)

McNeill, D. (2005). *Gesture and Thought*. Chicago, IL: University of Chicago Press. (McNeill explores the relationship between gesture and speech, showing that they form an imagery (gesture)-language dialectic in which gesture is co-expressive with speech.)

Wilson, M. (2002). Six views of embodied cognition. *Psychonomic Bulletin and Review*, *9*, 625–636. (This review article critically examines six claims emerging from embodied cognition research.)

Emergence criterion

Gisela Håkansson
Lund University

The emergence criterion is one of the measures used to gauge grammatical development in language acquisition. It is based on a cognitive theory of language acquisition that assumes language to be acquired by learners systematically building up the target language grammar in a series of interlanguage stages. In order to distinguish stages it is important to be able to tell that one structure is acquired before another.

The emergence criterion is known as an important tool within Processability Theory (Pienemann, 1998). According to Processability Theory learners develop their internal version of the target grammar by a gradual automatization of the skills needed to process the target language. Each stage in the developmental hierarchy serves as a prerequisite for the next, higher stage. When the processing prerequisites for a given stage are in place, the linguistic structures emerge in the learners' production. Thus, the emergence of the structure is the point when the processing operations can be carried out, and it marks an important phase of acquisition:

> From a descriptive viewpoint one can say that this is the beginning of an acquisition process, and focusing on the start of this process will allow the researcher to reveal more about the rest of the process
>
> (Pienemann, 1998: 138)

The use of an emergence criterion instead of a mastery criterion with percentage of correctness marks a shift of perspective in language acquisition research. Instead of a target language perspective, where the distance to the goal is measured, the focus is on how the individual learner proceeds from one stage to another. One of the first to apply an emergence criterion was the ZISA study (Meisel *et al.*, 1981). The correctness criterion was criticized for not capturing the dynamics of language development, since it only takes standard-like usage into consideration. The results of the ZISA projects were analyzed by counting "the number of actual occurrences relative to the total number of possible occurrences" (Meisel *et al.*, 1981: 112), and then plotted on an implicational scale (see Implicational scaling). This method demonstrated that certain given word order structures emerged before other word order structures in L2 German.

When applying the emergence criterion to spontaneous data it is important to find evidence for systematic and productive use and avoid memorized formulas. Pienemann (1998) suggests that in order for inflectional morphology to be regarded as productive the affix must be used with different lexical items. For example, the same noun must occur in both singular and plural (dog – dogs) and the plural suffix is added to different nouns (dogs, cars, friends). The exact amount of lexical items necessary for deciding productiveness depends on the variation found in the data and it differs between different researchers (Pallotti, 2007). The strictest emergence criterion of just one occurrence is more common for syntax than for morphology, since the probability of formulaic use is greater for morphology than for syntax.

See also: development in SLA, developmental sequences, implicational scaling, Processability Theory (PT), Target-Like-Use (TLU) Analysis, ZISA project

References

Meisel, J., Clahsen, H. and Pienemann, M. (1981). On determining developmental stages in natural second language acquisition. *Studies in Second Language Acquisition*, *3*, 109–35.

Pallotti, G. (2007). An operational definition of the emergence criterion. *Applied Linguistics*, *28*, 361–82.

Pienemann, M. (1998). *Language processing and second language development: Processability theory*. Amsterdam: Benjamins.

Emergentism

J. Dean Mellow
Simon Fraser University

Emergentism is a scientific approach to explanation in which a complex phenomenon is hypothesized to result from the aggregation, organization, and interaction of its basic component parts and processes within a particular context (e.g., Sawyer, 2002; Stephan, 1999). For example, an emergentist explanation of consciousness proposes that it arises from a very complex (and not yet fully understood) interaction of neurophysiological elements and processes within perceptual contexts, rather than from the Cartesian dualist proposal that the mind is a distinct nonphysical substance that is independent of a physical body (e.g., Churchland, 1988: 7–8, 180; Ellis, 2011: 671). Within second language acquisition (SLA), O'Grady *et al.* (2009: 70) provided the following definition of the central emergentist thesis: "The complexity of language must be understood in terms of the interaction of simpler and more basic nonlinguistic factors." Ellis (1998: 657) provided a parallel definition: "Emergentists believe that simple learning mechanisms, operating in and across the human systems for perception, motor-action and cognition as they are exposed to language data as part of a communicatively-rich human social environment by an organism eager to exploit the functionality of language, suffice to drive the emergence of complex language representations."

Within the study of language, emergentism is often contrasted with the Universal Grammar (UG) theory. The UG theory hypothesizes that language abilities result from a large number of abstract, innate principles and concepts that are used only for language and not for any other cognitive functions. Emergentists argue that these hypothetical, genetically encoded language capacities are implausible and unnecessary. Instead, human language systems are hypothesized to result from historical developments that were affected by cognitive processes such as generalization and efficient processing and by evolving cultural expressions of concepts and functions. Individuals gradually acquire these language systems through a variety of cognitive and social processes.

Different varieties of emergentism are possible, depending upon the linguistic elements and factors that are included. Two complementary strands of emergentist SLA research have developed, each focusing on different aspects of the complexity of language. One approach, substantially developed by Nick Ellis (e.g., Ellis, 1998, 2003, 2011; Ellis and Larsen-Freeman, 2006, 2009), focuses on the breadth of linguistic complexity, including a wide range of linguistic elements and factors. The second approach, primarily developed by William O'Grady (e.g., O'Grady, 2005, 2008; O'Grady *et al.*, 2008, 2009), focuses on what can be described as the depth of linguistic complexity: the linguistic phenomena that have been characterized as challenges for learnability due to "poverty of the stimulus," and which are the focus of UG research. Although this distinction highlights different tendencies within these strands, both approaches contribute understanding to both types of complexity.

Breadth of complexity

As an approach that incorporates a large number of linguistic elements and factors, emergentism is, in many ways, a continuation of the development of earlier multi-factorial SLA theories (e.g., Anderson, 1990; MacWhinney, 1997). Given the range of elements and factors that are considered, emergentist analyses of SLA do not fit into only one of the theoretical categories that are often discussed in overviews of SLA research (i.e., functional, cognitive, interactional/social, or linguistic theories; e.g., Mitchell and Myles, 2004). As a general theoretical approach, linguistic emergentism has much in common with a number of other approaches to the study of language and language acquisition, including chaos/complexity theory, cognitive linguistics, the Competition Model, complex adaptive systems, connectionism, construction grammar, corpus linguistics, dynamic systems theory, functional linguistics, and usage-based theories (e.g., Ellis, 1998, 2011).

The investigation of the breadth of linguistic elements occurs within and across individual empirical studies. Within one study, the researchers may investigate multiple language elements, revealing differing acquisition trajectories across elements and interactions between elements. Ellis and Larsen-Freeman (2009) summarized studies that examined the relationship between the ESL acquisition of specific types of words, such as the verbs *go*, *put*, and *give*, and the acquisition of three types of syntactic verb-argument constructions: verb locative, verb object locative, and ditransitive. Mellow (2008) described the longitudinal acquisition of all of the dependent, verb-headed constructions that an ESL learner used, including relative clauses, elliptical constructions, and a variety of non-finite complements and modifiers. Larsen-Freeman (2006) analyzed the longitudinal acquisition of four variables: fluency (average number of words per t-unit), grammatical complexity (average number of clauses per t-unit), accuracy (the proportion of error-free t-units to t-units), and vocabulary complexity (a type–token measure). Larsen-Freeman argued that valid measurement of language variables requires a breadth of measurement types, including both central tendencies (e.g., averages for groups of learners and sets of data points) and variation (e.g., individual variation, variation of use over time).

Across studies such as these three, a wide range of lexical and grammatical elements have been studied from an emergentist perspective. Other emergentist studies have investigated semantic and pragmatic elements, including idiomatic expressions. For example, Cameron and Deignon (2006) examined metaphorical expressions, including the example of *look like a lollipop* developing into *lollipop trees* in elementary school classroom discourse. By including such a wide breadth of linguistic elements, emergentism provides a comprehensive framework for research and application.

In addition to the breadth of language elements, emergentist SLA research also investigates a wide range of factors that contribute to acquisition, including (but not limited to) input frequency, usage in interactional contexts, schematization, and compositional development. (An additional cognitive factor, efficient linear processing, is discussed in relation to depth of complexity.) Humans learn the language that they hear and therefore input frequency is an important factor affecting SLA. Ellis and Larsen-Freeman (2009: 95) summarized the claims that "frequency promotes learning" and that "language learners are exquisitely sensitive to input frequencies of patterns at all levels (Ellis, 2002)." Ellis and Larsen-Freeman further explained that associative learning involves more than frequency: learning is affected by the properties of the language items (e.g., prototypicality, redundancy, reliability of the form-function mapping [contingency]) and of the social and discourse context (e.g., coadaptation between conversation partners) (see also O'Grady *et al.*, 2009: 71–72). Because these properties affect attention and comprehension, they also affect acquisition. Ellis and Larsen-Freeman summarized analyses of a corpus of conversations between ESL learners and native speakers, finding support for and specification of these aspects of associative learning.

Because emergentism investigates the effects of attention to and comprehension of input, the interactional use of language is a second general factor that is part of an emergentist approach to acquisition. In relation to first language acquisition, Mellow (2010) provided an example of mother–daughter conversation (in the Algonquian language Anihshininiimowin) in which meaning was clarified and expanded across turns and in which turn-taking created a communicative context that encouraged and facilitated the use of more complex utterances. In this way, the emergentist approach is consistent with the large body of SLA research that investigates interactions and conversations by learners both within and outside of classrooms (e.g., Mitchell and Myles, 2004).

Emergentism also investigates cognitive factors that contribute to acquisition. One of these processes is schematization, the gradual transition from concrete items to abstract linguistic schemata (Ellis, 2011: 668). Ellis (2003) argued for an acquisition sequence that begins with formulae (unanalyzed chunks of frequent collocations) that gradually lead to low scope patterns (limited, lexically specific combinatorial patterns) that may ultimately become constructions (syntactic generalizations). This acquisition results from a top-down process of decomposition in which the shared features of many exemplars of formulaic constructions emerge in a cognitive representation.

In addition to top-down decomposition of chunks, emergentist development is also hypothesized to be compositional or cumulative. The acquisition of complex constructions is hypothesized to be facilitated by the acquisition and use of the component parts of these constructions. Mellow (2006) reported that relative clause (RC) constructions were used by an ESL learner after component elements were acquired (i.e. simpler dependent, modifying constructions such as non-finite post-nominal modifiers) and that more complex RC constructions (direct object RCs) were used only after simpler RCs (subject RCs) were used.

In order to understand the acquisition of complex phenomena that have a large number of component elements and that are affected by a large number of factors, emergentists can use connectionist simulations to understand the interaction and development of these elements and factors over time. Ellis and Larsen-Freeman (2009) created connectionist simulations that used the same learning cues available to learners. These simulations learned abstract verb argument constructions in the same order of emergence as ESL learners. Future simulations can manipulate the frequency and properties of the language elements, providing insight into the contributions of the different properties of language elements to acquisition processes.

Depth of complexity

With respect to breadth of complexity, emergentism is generally compatible with the other SLA theories and approaches listed above. With respect to depth of complexity (learnability issues), emergentism is not compatible with the UG theory. The UG theory is very controversial and has been criticized as psycholinguistically uninterpretable, evolutionarily implausible, circularly unlearnable, Eurocentric, and colonialist (a review of these criticisms was provided in Mellow, 2010; see also O'Grady *et al.*, 2009: 69). In spite of these criticisms, the abstract formalisms within the UG theory have been extensively developed to include many complex morphosyntactic elements (e.g., the nature, use, and interpretation of: pronouns, relative clauses, content [or *wh-*] questions, and "subjects" of complement clauses). The UG theory has also been used to interpret a large body of empirical SLA research. The morphosyntactic phenomena that have been studied by UG researchers have not often been studied within other theoretical approaches to acquisition. As a result, it is especially important that the strand of emergentist research developed by O'Grady has considered and provided explanations for these morphosyntactic phenomena.

The key emergentist factor that O'Grady has used to explain these morphosyntactic phenomena is that sentences are produced and comprehended by a linear, efficiency-driven processor that interacts with working memory that has a limited capacity. The processing of language requires certain computational operations, such as the resolution of lexical requirements or dependencies (e.g., the verb *help* implies the existence of an entity that is the helper). The processor carries out these operations at the first opportunity, shaping the nature of the constructions that are used and acquired in human languages.

An example of this analysis is the explanation of the difference between subject relative clauses (e.g., *the girl who helped the boy*) and direct object RCs (e.g., *the girl who the boy helped*) (O'Grady, 2005: 199–203). In the subject RC, the filler-gap dependency triggered by the relative pronoun is resolved at the adjacent verb, when *who* is identified as the agent (ag) argument of *help*. In the direct object RC, the filler-gap dependency extends across the subject NP *the boy* and is resolved only after *who* is identified as the verb's second (patient [pat]) argument.

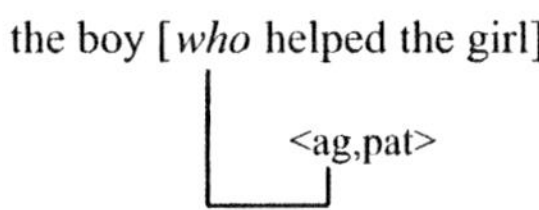

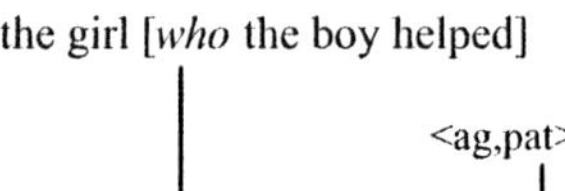

More working memory resources thus are required to process the direct object RC. The necessity of these additional resources is manifested in acquisition data in which direct object RCs are more difficult to comprehend and are acquired later (see also Mellow, 2006).

O'Grady's emergentist analysis accounts for the nature and acquisition of relative clauses without using abstract, unlearnable UG constructs such as universal phrase structures and right-to-left movement of elements. O'Grady and his colleagues have also provided emergentist analyses of the acquisition of a wide range of phenomena including pronominal coreference, *want-to* contraction, plural agreement, regular and irregular morphology, and aspects of negation and quantification.

Future directions

With respect to breadth of complexity, emergentism reveals the compatibility of a variety of approaches to SLA research, encourgaging theoretical collaborations that address the multi-factorial nature of acquisition. With respect to depth of complexity, emergentism offers an innovative approach that can minimize or eliminate the language-specific biological capacities that have been hypothesized in UG research. In these ways, emergentism provides a theoretical approach that is useful for the broad scope of issues within SLA, while simultaneously providing an approach for refining and narrowing the number of theoretical models within the field.

See also: Complex Systems Theory/Dynamic Systems Theory, Competition Model (CM), construction learning, frequency effects, theoretical constructs in SLA, Universal Grammar (UG) and SLA

References

Anderson, R. (1990). Models, processes, principles and strategies: Second language acquisition inside and outside the classroom. In B. VanPatten and J. Lee (eds), *Second Language Acquisition/ Foreign Language Learning*, pp. 45–68. Philadelphia, PA: Multilingual Matters.

Cameron, L. and Deignan, A. (2006). The emergence of metaphor in discourse. *Applied Linguistics*, *27*, 4 671–90.

Churchland, P.M. (1988). *Matter and Consciousness*, rev. edn. Cambridge, MA: The MIT Press.

Ellis, N. (1998). Emergentism: Connectionism and language learning. *Language Learning*, *48*, 631–64.

——(2003). Constructions, chunking, and connectionism: The emergence of second language structure. In C. Doughty and M. Long (eds), *Handbook of Second Language Acquisition*, pp. 33–68. Oxford: Blackwell.

——(2011). The emergence of language as a complex adaptive system. In J. Simpson (ed.), *Handbook of Applied Linguistics*, pp. 666–79. London: Routledge/Taylor & Francis.

Ellis, N. and Larsen-Freeman, D. (2006). Language emergence: Implications for applied linguistics. Introduction to the Special Issue. *Applied Linguistics*, *27*, 558–89.

——(2009). Constructing a second language: Analyses and computational simulations of the emergence of linguistic constructions from usage. *Language Learning*, *59*, Suppl. 1, 90–125.

Larsen-Freeman, D. (2006). The Emergence of Complexity, Fluency, and Accuracy in the Oral and Written Production of Five Chinese Learners of English. *Applied Linguistics*, *27*. 590–619.

MacWhinney, B. (1997). Second language acquisition and the competition model. In A. de Groot and J. Kroll (eds), *Bilingualism: Psycholinguistic Perspectives*, pp. 113–42. Mahwah, NJ: Erlbaum.

Mellow, J.D. (2006). The emergence of second language syntax: A case study of the acquisition of relative clauses. *Applied Linguistics*, *27*, 645–70.

——(2008). The emergence of complex syntax: A longitudinal case study of the ESL development of dependency resolution. *Lingua*, *118*, 4, 499–521.

——(2010). Fostering diversity and minimizing universals: Toward a non-colonialist approach to the acquisition of algonquian languages. *Native Studies Review*, *19*, 1 67–100.

Mitchell, R. and Myles, F. (2004). *Second Language Learning Theories*, 2nd edn. London: Arnold.

O'Grady, W. (2005). *Syntactic Carpentry: An Emergentist Approach to Syntax*. Mahwah, NJ: Lawrence Erlbaum.

——(2008). Commentary: Innateness, Universal Grammar, and emergentism. *Lingua*, *118*, 620–31.

O'Grady, W., Lee, M. and Kwak, H. (2009). Emergentism and second language acquisition. In W.C. Ritchie and T.K. Bhatia (eds), *The New Handbook of Second Language Acquisition*, pp. 69–88. Bingley: Emerald.

O'Grady, W., Nakamura, M. and Ito, Y. (2008). *Want-to* contraction in second language acquisition: An emergentist approach. *Lingua*, *118*, 478–98.

Sawyer, R.K. (2002). Emergence in psychology: Lessons from the history of non-reductionist science. *Human Development*, *45*, 2–28

Stephan, A. (1999). Varieties of emergentism. *Evolution and Cognition*, *5*, 49–59.

Further reading

MacWhinney, B. (1998). Models of the emergence of language. *Annual Review of Psychology*, *49*, 199–227. (An overview of how emergentist concepts can apply to various levels of language learning.)

——(ed.) (1999). *The Emergence of Language*. Mahwah, NJ: Lawrence Erlbaum. (An edited collection of sixteen foundational articles about emergentism and language.)

Ortega, L. (2009). *Understanding Second Language Acquisition*. London: Hodder. (An analysis of emergentism is provided within this overview of SLA research.)

Emotions

Jean-Marc Dewaele

Birkbeck College, University of London

Emotions play a crucial part in our lives. The sharing of emotions, whether in face-to-face interactions or through written communications is an important social activity, and the ability to do so helps us maintain physical and mental health (Fussell, 2002). Fussell points out: "The interpersonal communication of emotional states is fundamental to both everyday and clinical interaction. One's own and others' affective experiences are frequent topics of everyday conversations, and how well these emotions are expressed and understood is important to interpersonal relationships and individual well-being" (Fussell, 2002: 1).

Expressing one's emotions accurately in one native (or dominant) language requires a good understanding of the situation and of the local norms concerning emotional speech. Jelling abuse at the players of an opposing team during a football match may be considered socially acceptable by fervent football supporters, but insulting someone in the same way in a face-to-face situation would be considered inappropriate by the same supporters. The communication of emotion in a socially acceptable way does require a good mastery of linguistic, sociolinguistic, sociopragmatic and sociocultural information. Native speakers can get it wrong, embarrassing themselves and their interlocutor(s). The challenge is even greater for Foreign Language (FL) learners and users who rely on incomplete linguistic and pragmatic resources to express the full range of their emotions (Dewaele 2008a). It typically takes years of practice in authentic interactions before FL users can be quite sure that their communicative intentions in expressing emotions will be decoded as they intended, and they are capable to infer the emotions expressed by their interlocutors unerringly. I have compared the communication of emotion in an FL to trying to get hold of a bar of soap in a bathtub (Dewaele, 2010). A relentless and continuous effort is needed to bridge the emotional communication gap and to achieve smooth emotional interactions. The initial inability to express emotions appropriately is doubly frustrating because FL users are usually able to express their own emotions, and interpret other people's emotions, without much difficulty in their first or dominant language, yet they may struggle in another language. Part of the difficulty lies in the fact that a more limited number of conventional implicatures in our FL means it is both harder to signal the emotional state, and it takes longer to interpret those of interlocutors. Rintell (1984) showed that FL learners scored significantly lower than a native speaker control group in identifying the emotion verbalized by actors in tape-recorded conversations, with Asian learners scoring lower than Arab learners which in turn scored lower than Spanish learners. This also showed that cultural distance between the L1 and the FL is an important obstacle in the communication of emotion. If the emotion is not expressed as would be expected by a native speaker interlocutor, the FL user might be misinterpreted. Native speakers themselves can consciously deviate from the norm when expressing emotions but this may have very different illocutionary consequences compared to FL users deviating in a similar way (Dewaele, 2008b, 2010). An emotional expression, a swearword, or a risqué joke uttered by a native speaker may be judged appropriate by his/her peers, but the same words in the mouth of a foreigner risk to be judged negatively or even considered gross by native speaker interlocutors. In other words, when in Rome, do as the Romans do (except the swearing and the bitching about the government).

Much of the early work in the field of emotion and multilingualism has pointed to the more limited emotional resonance of the L2 compared to the L1 (Bond and Lai, 1986).

Pavlenko (2005) argues that different languages can have different affective meanings depending on the interlocutors and the situation. In other words, the L1 is not always the language of intimacy and the L2 the language of detachment: "Speakers may use these languages to index a variety of affective stances, and they may also mix two or more languages to convey emotional meanings" (p. 131).

Harris *et al.* (2003) found that different types of words elicit different galvanic skin responses in both monolingual and Turkish–English bilingual speakers who were students at Boston University, with taboo words and reprimands eliciting the strongest responses. A comparison of the adult offspring of Latin American immigrants in the US, for whom English was considered L2 but was the dominant language, and more recently arrived immigrants from Latin America to the US showed that only the latter group reacted more strongly to reprimands in Spanish. The early learners of English had similar patterns of electrodermal responding in their two languages (Harris, 2004).

Dewaele (2008) looked specifically at the perceived emotional weight of the phrase "I love you" in the multilinguals' different languages. A majority of speakers who filled out a web questionnaire reported that "I love you" was strongest in their L1, a third reported that the phrase was equally strong in their L1 and an LX, and the remaining quarter of participants said that the phrase was stronger in an LX which showed that the language of the heart can shift.

Dewaele (2010) presented a systematic analysis of the effect of three clusters of independent variables (participants' linguistic history, present language use, sociobiographical and psychological variables) on language perception and language choice for the communication of feelings in general, for anger and swearing, as well as self-perceived proficiency and Foreign Language Anxiety. It showed that linguistic history and particularly present language use (i.e. the degree of socialization in a FL) are linked to the choice of the FL to express emotions, and to positive attitudes and low anxiety in using the FLs.

An analysis of participants' comments showed that emotionality of speech acts is often culture-specific (Dewaele, 2010). Verbalizing certain emotions is appropriate in Western countries but not in Asia. Bicultural multilinguals reported strategic use of code-switching with other multilinguals, especially when talking about more emotional topics with familiar interlocutors. However, multilinguals also reported uncontrolled code-switching in cases of strong emotional arousal. A striking finding was also the dynamic aspect of language choice to express emotion (Dewaele, 2010).

See also: anxiety, implicature, individual differences in SLA, multicompetence, pragmatics, second language socialization

References

Bond, M.H. and Lai, T.M. (1986). Embarrassment and code-switching into a second language. *Journal of Social Psychology*, *126*, 179–86.

Caldwell-Harris, C.L. and Ayçiçeği-Dinn, A. (2009). Emotion and lying in a non-native language. *International Journal of Psychophysiology*, *71*, 193–204.

Dewaele, J.-M. (2008a). Appropriateness in foreign language acquisition and use: Some theoretical, methodological and ethical considerations. *International Review of Applied Linguistics*, *46*, 235–55.

——(2008b). The emotional weight of 'I love you' in multilinguals' languages. *Journal of Pragmatics*, *40*, 1753–80.

——(2010). *Emotions in Multiple Languages*. Basingstoke: Palgrave Macmillan.

Fussell, S.R. (2002). The verbal communication of emotion: Introduction and overview. In S.R. Fussell (ed.), *The Verbal Communication of Emotions: Interdisciplinary perspectives*. Mahwah, NJ: Lawrence Erlbaum.

Harris, C.L. (2004). Bilingual speakers in the lab: Psychophysiological measures of emotional reactivity. *Journal of Multilingual and Multicultural Development*, *25*, 223–47.

Harris, C.L., Ayçiçegi, A. and Gleason, J. (2003). Taboo words and reprimands elicit greater autonomic reactivity in a first than in a second language. *Applied Psycholinguistics*, *24*, 561–79.

Pavlenko, A. (2005). *Emotions and Multilingualism*. Cambridge, MA: Cambridge University Press.

Rintell, E. (1984). But how did you feel about that? The learner's perception of emotion in speech. *Applied Linguistics*, *5*, 255–64.

Entrenchment

John Taylor
University of Otago

Entrenchment is an important concept in usage-based theories of language. Repeated use of a linguistic form, whether in production or reception, increases the strength of its representation in memory. It is not only words as such which can become entrenched through frequent use; this also goes for combinations of words. The implication, for theories of language and language learning, is that speakers of a language not only know the basic words and morphemes of their language, they also have varying degrees of familiarity with a vast number of multi-word expressions. Compare *a large amount* and *a large quantity*. These share the same syntactic structure and have roughly the same meaning. As a result of its frequent use in the language, however, the first expression is probably highly entrenched in the minds of English speakers. *A large amount* has the status of a unit, and speakers do not need to consciously assemble it from its components. *A large quantity* is less entrenched, and speakers may need to make a conscious choice about both adjective and noun. The number of highly entrenched expressions probably runs into the tens, if not the hundreds of thousands. Since they are readily available as units to speakers and hearers, their use makes an important contribution to the speed and fluency of linguistic interactions.

Entrenchment has some further effects. Repeated use of a linguistic form tends to obscure its internal structure; it is accessed as a whole and the contribution of the parts may be overlooked. As a consequence, the form is liable to take on a life of its own, independent of the meanings of its parts. Words such as *dirty* and *filthy* are so entrenched that we may not be immediately aware of their relation with *dirt* and *filth*. If we describe a room as "dirty," we may simply mean that it is untidy – it is not necessarily covered with dirt. The phonological structure of entrenched units also tends to be obscured, resulting in a higher incidence of reductions and assimilations. The highly entrenched *I don't know* is likely to be pronounced "I dunno," where the contribution of the word *don't* is obscured, whereas the syntactically identical *they don't know* is less likely to be pronounced "they dunno."

The entrenchment of irregular forms contributes to their persistence in the language. It is inconceivable that the past tense form of *drive* (i.e. *drove*) would ever be regularized to *drived*; the past tense form, being very frequent, is highly entrenched. For many speakers, however, the past tense form of *strive* (i.e. *strove*) is so infrequent that it is scarcely entrenched at all. Consequently, the form *strived* is often heard. Syntactically odd phrases, such as *I think not, Far be it from me (to V), If I were you*, and the like, are preserved because of their entrenchment.

Entrenchment may also play a role in the persistence of learners' fossilizations. Repeated use by the learner of an "incorrect" form serves to further entrench the form in the speaker's mental grammar, thereby increasing the probability that the incorrect form will be used on future occasions.

See also: construction learning, formulaic language, fossilization, frequency effects, language and the lexicon in SLA, type and token frequency in SLA

References

Bybee, J. (2007). *Frequency of Use and the Organization of Language*. Oxford: Oxford University Press.

Langacker, R. W. (1987). *Foundations of Cognitive Grammar, vol. 1: Theoretical Prerequisites*. Stanford, CA: Stanford University Press.

Taylor, J. R. (2002). *Cognitive Grammar*. Oxford: Oxford University Press.

Episodic memory

Christopher D.B. Burt
University of Canterbury

The term episodic memory was proposed by Tulving (1972) when he described the distinction between episodic and semantic memory. Episodic memory is one of the five major memory systems, the other four being semantic memory, procedural memory, perceptual representation, and short term memory (Tulving, 1993). Episodic memory can be generally defined by its contents, in that it stores representations of unique, personal past experiences, and by the phenomenological aspects of re-experiencing and imagery associated with recall. Most cognitive psychologists and neuroscientists assume that episodic memory is unique to humans, but attempts have been made to study episodic-like memory in a wide range of species (Salwiczek *et al.*, 2010).

Early studies of episodic memory provided the foundation for the development of the study of autobiographical memory (Rubin, 1998), and the terms are often used interchangeably. The autobiographical aspect of episodic memory is reflected in the nine properties which collectively define an episodic memory, and distinguish it from other types of memory representation. An episodic memory generally contains a summary record of sensory-perceptual-conceptual-affective processing, retains activation/inhibition over long periods, is represented in the form of visual images, is recalled from a field or observer perspective, represents a time slice of experience, can be represented on temporal dimensions, can be subject to rapid decay (forgetting), makes autobiographical remembering experience specific, and is recollectively experienced when accessed (Conway, 2009).

While episodic memories clearly represent an individual's past experiences, they are typically not retrieved as literal records of experience. Access to specific details is often lost within a few days of formation. Thus many aspects of episodic retrieval appear to involve complex reconstructive processes based on schematic knowledge of the way events typically happen. Schematic knowledge develops through repeated experiencing of events and represents the typical features which are likely to occur, as in the classic restaurant script which defines the key features of eating at a restaurant. Reconstructive processes do allow for coherent episodic narratives to be developed when the veridical details of the actual experience have decayed from memory. Retrieval of episodic memories also appears to be language specific, with research on bilingualism suggesting that a memory is retrieved in, and/or its retrieval is influenced by, the language spoken at the time of the event experience (see Schrauf *et al.*, 2003).

In contrast to other forms of memory, such as semantic memory, episodic memory of past experiences does not develop until at least late in the second year of life (Howe *et al.*, 2003). Howe and colleagues have argued that the prerequisite for episodic memory development is the establishment of the cognitive self, while others have suggested it requires the ability to establish a personal life story via linguistic and narra'ive competence, or the emergence of a *theory of mind.* The later theory argues that awareness or *knowing* an experience happened, rather than *remembering* an experience happened is central to episodic memory (Tulving, 1984), and this transition occurs around the age of 4. The delayed development of episodic memory equates to the phenomenon known as *infantile amnesia*, where most people when queried about the events of childhood fail to recall their very early experiences.

The retrieval of an episodic memory typically is a phenomenological complex experience with the individual being conscious of a prior conscious experience, what Tulving terms auotnoetic consciousness or what might simply be described as reliving a past experience. This distinguishes episodic recall from other seemingly event-related cognitive activities, such as imagining, dreaming, or the retrieval of an autobiographical fact. Visual imagery is generally a central component of an episodic memory, with the vividness of the imagery typically dependent on the age of the memory. Exceptions are so called *flashbulb memories*, which are generally of significant life events and are characterized by vivid recall over very long time periods. Episodic memory imagery tends to take either a *field* or *observer* perspective. An episodic memory with a field perspective seems to preserve the person's original perspective, whereas in the observer perspective the rememberer looks into the memory and sees themselves in the memory. Field episodic memories have been found to be more strongly associated with recollective or re-living experiences.

The re-experiencing of a past experience or mental-time-travel back to when the experience occurred, which occurs when an episodic memory is retrieved, places temporal organization at a central point in our understanding of episodic memory. As such, episodic memories are unique in the complexity of the temporal information which can be either associated directly with them, as in *landmark events*, or reconstructed as an episodic memory is retrieved. Temporal aspects such as specific position in time (date), sequential relationship with other experiences, order of the activities within an experience, and experiential duration have all received considerable research attention (Burt, 2008). These temporal features often play an important part in the way episodic memories are described to others, and play an important role in helping others understand episodic narrative.

The majority of episodic memory access stems from deliberate and controlled retrieval processes: the individual wants to remember an experience. However, there is evidence of seemingly spontaneous or *involuntary* recall of episodic memories (Berntsen, 2009), and this can be a specific symptom of *post traumatic stress disorder* (*PTSD*). There is also clear evidence supporting the so called *reminiscence bump* phenomenon. This term is used to describe the disproportionate number of episodic memories recalled from the adolescence and early adulthood years when individuals are asked to recall important, vivid or first to come to mind events.

A large body of evidence from functional magnetic resonance imaging (fMRI) studies has investigated the neural basis of episodic memory recall. This work has shown that a consistent, and distributed, network of associated brain regions are involved. Furthermore, these brain networks are also active during other activities, such as *thinking about the future*, *navigation*, and *theory of mind*, suggesting that all these cognitive functions may share common underlying processes.

Episodic memory is central to humans' ability to remember their past and relive life events. As such episodic memory has many unique features which distinguish it from other forms of memory. Reminiscence, story-telling, and simple conversations about the day's events, all require access to episodic memory, making it a central feature of human cognitive functioning.

See also: bilingualism and SLA, declarative memory and knowledge, developmental sequences, procedural memory and knowledge, psycholinguistics of SLA, semantic processing

References

Berntsen, D. (2009). *Involuntary Autobiographical Memories: An Introduction to the Unbidden Past*. Cambridge: Cambridge University Press.

Burt, C.D. B. (2008). Time, language and autobiographical memory. In Idenfrey, P. and Gullberg, M. (eds), *Time to Speak: Cognitive and Neural Prerequisites for Time in Language*. Oxford: Blackwells.

Conway, M.A. (2009). Episodic memories. *Neuropsychologia*, *47*, 2305–13.

Howe, M.L., Courage, M.L. and Edison, S.C. (2003). When autobiographical memory begins. *Developmental Review*, *23*, 471–94.

Rubin, D.C. (1998). Beginnings of a theory of autobiographical remembering. In C.P. Thompson, D.J. Hermann, D. Bruce, J.D. Read, D.G. Payne, and M.P. Toglla (eds), *Autobiographical memory: Theoretical and Applied Perspectives*. Mahwah, NJ: Lawrence Erlbaum.

Salwiczek, L.H., Watanabe, A. and Clayton, N.S. (2010). Ten years of research into avian models of episodic-like memory and its implications for development and comparative cognition. *Behavioural Brian Research*, *215*, 221–34.

Schrauf, R.W., Pavlenko, A. and Dewaele, J. (2003). Bilingual episodic memory: An introduction. *The International Journal of Bilingualism*, *3*, 221–33.

Tulving, E. (1993). What is episodic memory? *Current Directions in Psychological Science*, *2*, 67–70.

——(1984). Precis of elements of episodic memory. *Behavioral and Brian Sciences*, *7*, 223–38.

——(1972). Episodic and semantic memory. In E. Tulving and W. Donaldson (eds), *Organization of memory*. New York: Academic Press.

Error analysis

Saadiyah Darus
Universiti Kebangsaan Malaysia

The field of error analysis in second language acquisition was given impetus by a seminal paper by Corder (1967) entitled "The significance of learner's errors," and was subsequently an area of extensive research throughout the 1970s. Error analysis was "promoted as an alternative (and superior) approach to *contrastive analysis* for understanding language learning" (Ellis and Barkhuizen, 2005: 52) since it attempted to identify and explain errors which could not simply be attributed to negative transfer from the first language (L1). An important finding of these early error analysis studies is that there are similarities across all learners in the specific *type* of errors they make at certain stages of development. Dulay *et al.* (1982) provided an extensive summary of the results of this research, showing errors in, for example, the use, or non-suppliance, of morphology, and in negation and question forms, occurring at different stages of development of L2 English by speakers of many different L1s.

Selinker (1972) introduced the term *interlanguage* to refer to the systematic knowledge of a second language which is independent of the learner's first language and the second language. Nemser (1971) refers to this knowledge as an *Approximate System*, and Corder (1967) referred to it as the learner's *Idiosyncratic Dialect* or *Transitional Competence*. Corder (1974) viewed error analysis as having implications for both theory and pedagogy. The investigation of learner errors can serve two pedagogic purposes; diagnostic (to pinpoint a problem in learner production) and prognostic (to guide pedagogic decision-making about how to solve a specific problem once identified). However, with respect to diagnosis, one limitation of error analysis identified by Schachter (1974) is that since error analysis only investigates what learners do, it cannot reveal what learners are avoiding when producing language (for whatever reason) and therefore that error analysis underdetermines the extent of problems that learners actually have in producing the L2.

Following Corder (1967), error analysts distinguish between *errors* and *mistakes*. Errors are systematic while mistakes are not. Mistakes are temporary lapses in control of the L2 (such as slips of the tongue), are not consistently made, and are often the focus of immediate self-repair. An error refers to a systematic and consistent deviance from the norms of the second language, revealing a gap in underlying knowledge or L2 competence. Errors can be classified into various levels; discourse (the communicative use that sentences are put to), lexicon (vocabulary), morphology (the internal structure of words), phonetics/phonology (pronunciation), and syntax (the construction of sentences).

Errors can be categorized into two groups; inter-lingual and intra-lingual errors. Inter-lingual errors are caused by the interference of the learners' first language. Brown (1994) states that especially in the early stages of learning a second language, before the L2 system is familiar, the first language is the only linguistic system upon which the learner can draw. Brown (1994) explains that when features of the L1 and L2 correspond exactly, there may be positive transfer from the first language to the second language. When they do not correspond exactly, there may be negative transfer, that is, interference.

Intra-lingual errors are defined by Richards (1971:198) as those "which reflect the general characteristics of rule learning, such as faulty generalization, incomplete application of rules and failure to learn conditions for rule application, the learner attempting to build up hypothesis about English from his limited experience of it in the classroom or textbook." Richards (1971) further states that intra-lingual errors are those that originate within the structure of the second language itself, as a result of misinterpretation of grammatical rules of the L2. Early stages of language learning are characterized by a predominance of inter-lingual error, but once learners have begun to acquire parts of the new L2 system, more and more intra-lingual error is manifested (Brown, 1994).

Errors are usually analyzed following the three steps described by Ellis (1999: 15–20): *sampling* of learner production data, *identification* of errors, and *description and classification* of errors. An example of an error analysis project is Maros *et al.* (2007) who analyzed interference effects of Malay as the first language on the acquisition of English as a foreign language by students from rural schools in Malaysia. The results of that study showed that the use of articles, subject–verb agreement, and copula "be" were the most frequent errors in students' writing. Darus and Khor (2009) analyzed essays written in English by Chinese L1 speaking learners. In contrast to the Malay L1 speaking population studied by Maros *et al.*, the most common errors in this sample were mechanics, tenses, preposition, and subject–verb agreement. As in all of the early error analysis studies in the 1960s and 1970s, errors were analyzed manually in Maros et al.'s (2007) study. On the other hand, errors were analyzed semi-automatedly using Markin 3.1 software in Darus and Khor's (2009) study. In automated error analysis (see e.g., De Felice and Pullman, 2008; Omar *et al.*, 2009) an error annotation scheme needs to support unambiguous and consistent identification of errors. In other words, a unique representation of the identified error is necessary. Lee *et al.* (2011) developed an automated scoring system that grades writing tests in English as a second language for Korean L1 speaking junior high school students. The automated scoring system consists of a morphological analyzer and a syntactic analyzer that detects errors within a single sentence. Another component of the system is the inter-sentential error detection module that compares the sentences and identifies the sections that do not match. The system can detect word errors (e.g., noun plural form error, idiom usage error, verb inflectional form error), syntax errors (e.g., preposition type error, relative clause subject error, relative pronoun type error) and mapping errors (e.g., incomplete sentence error).

It is possible that with the further development of automated scoring systems for detecting errors, second language learners will increasingly benefit from the feedback given by such systems, thus helping them to improve their writing skills in the L2. An automated system is not only able to give feedback to learners in a short time, it also ensures that feedback is given in a consistent and *reliable* manner—more so than when errors are identified and described by human raters, where estimates of interrater reliability are sometimes low, and inevitably fluctuate across populations of raters.

See also: Contrastive Analysis Hypothesis (CAH), cross-linguistic influence, developmental sequences, interlanguage, linguistic transfer, Target-Like-Use (TLU) Analysis

References

Brown, H.D. (1994). *Principles of Language Learning and Teaching*. Eaglewood Cliffs, NJ: Prentice Hall.

Corder, S.P. (1967). The significance of learner's errors. *International Review of Applied Linguistics*, *5*, 162–70.

——(1974). Idiosyncratic Dialects and Error Analysis. *International Review of Applied Linguistics*, *9*, 147–59.

Darus, S. and Khor, H.C. (2009). Common errors in written English essays of form one Chinese students: A case study. *European Journal of Social Sciences*, *10*(2), 242–53.

De Felice, R. and Pullman, S.G. (2008). A classifier-based approach to preposition and determiner error correction in L2 English. In *Proceedings of the 22nd International Conference on Computational Linguistics (COLING 2008)*, pp. 169–76.

Dulay, H., Burt, M. and Krashen, S. (1982). *Language Two*. Oxford: Oxford University Press.

Ellis, R. (1999). *Second Language Acquisition*. Oxford: Oxford University Press.

Ellis, R. and Barkhuizen, G. (2005). *Analysing Learner Language*. Oxford: Oxford University Press.

Lee, K.J., Choi, Y. and Kim, J.E. (2011). Building an automated English sentence evaluation system for students learning English as a second language. *Computer Speech and Language*, *25*, 246–60.

Maros, M., Tan, K.H. and Salehuddin, K. (2007). Interference in learning English: Grammatical errors in English essay writing among rural Malay secondary school students in Malaysia. *Jurnal e-Bangi*, *2*(2), 1–15.

Nemser, W. (1971). Approximate systems of foreign language learners. *International Review of Applied Linguistics*, *9*, 115–23.

Omar, N., Mohd Razali, N. A., and Darus, S. (2009). Automated grammar checking of tenses for ESL writing. In P. Wen *et al.* (eds). *Rough Sets and Knowledge Technology. Lecture Notes in Computer Science*, 5589, pp. 475–82. Berlin and Heidelberg: Springer-Verlag.

Richards, J.C. (1971). Error analysis and second language strategies. *Language Science*, *17*, 12–22.

Schachter, J. (1974). An error in error analysis. *Language Learning*, *24*, 205–14.

Selinker, L. (1972). Interlanguage. *International Review of Applied Linguistics*, *10*, 209–31.

Ethnographic research

Ruth Harman and Linda Harklau
University of Georgia

Developed in the field of anthropology, the primary focus of ethnography is the description and interpretation of culture. How cultural practices are conceptualized and analyzed in this type of qualitative research, however, varies according to the disciplinary tradition and theoretical lens of the researcher (Salzman, 2001). Notwithstanding differences in interpretive paradigms, ethnography can be defined as a sustained first-person naturalistic study and written account of the cultural patterns and practices of a group of people who are bound by language or culture. Primary methods include participant observation and interviews (Denzin and Lincoln, 2000).

Over the past thirty years, ethnography has become an increasingly popular approach among second language researchers. SLA ethnographers have explored and continue to explore a wide range of issues, including intercultural relations, language socialization and learning, and social constructions of race, class, and gender. This entry provides a brief history of ethnography, a description of its methodologies and epistemological stances, and discussion of research in second language acquisition.

Overview

Ethnography developed as a primary research approach in anthropology in the early twentieth century. Malinowski's extensive fieldwork on the Trobiand Islands in the 1920s was highly influential in establishing sustained participant observation as a methodology in social anthropology (Heath and Street, 2008). In North America, influenced by Malinowski's student Boas, early ethnographies were conducted on the rituals, life styles, and languages of Native American communities. Through systematic description and interpretation of the complex organization of kinship, institutions, and language in colonial and neocolonial societies, these early studies counteracted social Darwinist claims about biological and racial determinism (Goldschmidt, 2000).

Over time, ethnographers narrowed their focus and purpose in conducting research. Drawing on G. H. Mead's work and symbolic interactionism, researchers in the Chicago school of sociology during the 1920s and 1930s conducted ethnographies on urban life and poverty with an emphasis on naturalistic life story and slice-of-life approaches. In the 1940s, applied anthropologists used the approach to highlight the disruptive influence of governmental bodies (e.g., Bureau of Indian Affairs) on the lives and schooling of Native American communities (Heath and Street, 2008). In the 1960s to the 1980s, informed by cognitive and interpretive anthropology, ethnographers explored the symbolic beliefs and knowledge systems that underlie cultural practices. Language study was also incorporated into ethnographic studies at this time, with the influence of Levi Straus and structural linguistics in sociology and with the emergence of approaches such as sociology of language and ethnography of communication in anthropology. The linguistic turn in ethnography led to a "crisis in representation" in the mid 1980s, when ethnographic representation was critiqued for its historic collusion with discourses of colonial and imperialist expansionism and its lack of reflexivity (see, e.g., Clifford, 1986).

Methodologies

Despite paradigm shifts over recent years in how ethnography has been conceptualized, participant observation has remained a primary feature of its methodology. Over a sustained period of time in the field, the participant observer collects a corpus of field notes that serves as a primary record of the events. Researchers also conduct interviews that provide a lens on informants' perceptions of events. Other methods may include taking photographs, audio and video recordings, the collection of life histories or written documents, and narrative analysis.

A key feature of ethnography is to understand cultural practices from an emic, or insider perspective, making manifest the implicit knowledge of beliefs and practices of participants. Data analysis involves an inductive process that begins with data collection. Ethnographers informed by an interpretive or critical perspective of meaning making tend to use a cross-comparison approach in analyzing multiple data sources, a process commonly known as triangulation (Denzin and Lincoln, 2000).

Language-oriented ethnographers often integrate discourse analysis with ethnographic methods. In the interdisciplinary fields of linguistic ethnography and anthropology, for example, researchers draw from divergent language approaches including interactional sociolinguistics and ethnography of communication to explore language use in specific cultural and intercultural contexts (Wortham and

Rymes, 2003). Ethnographic work in SLA also has incorporated conversation analysis and related traditions of ethnomethodology. Combined ethnographic and discourse analytic approaches always include audio and video recordings of interactions, detailed transcriptions, and microanalysis of data supported by ethnographic contextualization.

Stance

The ontological and epistemological orientation of the researcher shapes the ethnographic approach. Early twentieth-century anthropologists established a realist tradition, portraying culture as a unified and static system of kinship and institutions that could be analyzed and represented in a cohesive manner. Contemporary ethnographies in this vein often supplement participant observation with quantifiable data and statistical analyses (Salzman, 2001: 8). On the other hand, theorists who assume an interpretivist or phenomenological stance view culture as a set of tacit understandings woven into symbolic significance over time by members of a discourse community. To understand the laminated web of social significance of which they are also part, ethnographers co-construct understanding of cultural phenomena with participants and write their research through a complex process of reflexivity and description. Dyson's ethnographic studies (see e.g., 2003) investigated the complex symbolic repertoire of young children in diverse elementary classrooms. Through her multilayered study of their creative processes and products, she found that they participated in a wide range of intertextual practices that involved interweaving of voices from media, community, and art.

Critical ethnographers are interested in exploring the underlying systemic reasons why and how certain cultural groups are selected and favored over others in a particular society. In other words, they are interested in exploring the nexus among local cultural events, social practices, and societal structures. In a longitudinal study, Talmy (2010) investigated the marginalization of incoming Micronesian students by more veteran Asian students in an ESL program in Hawaii. He found that the negative social constructions of the new "off the boat" Micronesian group were informed by larger institutional and societal practices of racial hierarchies in Hawaii.

The linguistic turn in postmodernism has led to further epistemological divides in ethnographic theory. Some ethnographers, concerned about the historic lack of examination of the ethnographer's own cultural values and assumptions in analysis and written accounts, attempt to integrate postmodern critiques and notions of representation with more traditional ethnographic modes of inquiry. Others use alternative forms such as performance and auto-ethnography to research and represent the fluidity and multifaceted nature of identity and the problematic dynamics between researcher and the researched. Epistemological divisions are further overlaid with a number of "schools" (Salzman, 2001). For example, neo-Marxist studies focus their investigation on the material conditions that underlie social and cultural change whereas feminist poststructuralist studies problematize issues of identity and power by incorporating a polyphony of voices in the research process and writing. Lather and Smithies (1997), for example, highlighted the multiple, fragmented and contradictory nature of ethnographic narrative when they interwove the voices of women affected by AIDS with their own voices.

SLA research

In the height of the post Civil Rights era, applied linguists saw ethnography as an optimal way to research the lack of support for culturally and linguistically diverse students in public schools (Heath and Street, 2008). Ethnography of communication (EOC) provided researchers with tools to explore how language learners were socialized not only into a system of language use but also into the socio-cultural assumptions and values of a specific community (e.g., Cazden *et al.*, 1972), as well as mismatches between home and school sociolinguistic norms and interactional practices for bilingual children. Recent ethnographies in this vein, informed by a hybrid view of social identities, have focused on the proficiencies and "funds of knowledge" of multilingual learners. For example, Moll *et al.* (2001) highlighted how bilingual kindergartners, when given the opportunity, produced bilingual texts even before learning the alphabet.

Other recent ethnographic research on second language learning has focused on a wide variety of issues such as gender and language learning, post-colonial student resistance and the experiences of multilingual students in immersion programs. For example, in his critical ethnography of a Sri Lankan EFL classroom, Canagarajah (1993) analyzed the oppositional strategies of rural EFL students. He found that the language learners used resistance tactics to challenge underlying cultural assumptions and ideologies of the class textbooks imported from the United States. Research has also focused on out-of-school or other informal, self-selected activities. Lam's ethnographic work (2009) showed how immigrant youth who were marginalized in school expanded their communities and status through online communication and creative web design.

In the 1990s and 2000s, SLA ethnographers also began to investigate the complex interplay between language learning and social context. Studies, for example, explored how classroom literacy events were socially constructed within a specific range of institutional and societal discourses. In her institutional ethnography, Gebhard (2004) examined how language learners and their teachers responded to post-Fordist school reform policies in the Silicon Valley in the 1990s and how these responses shaped their academic and teaching trajectories. Informed by feminist poststructuralist theories of identity, investment, and language, Norton (2000) showed how the language learning experiences of a group of immigrant women varied according to their subject positioning in different social contexts.

Challenges and future directions

Contemporary ethnographic research may suffer from a clash between increasingly complex views of culture and dated methodologies for conducting, analyzing, and reporting research (Eisenhart, 2001). In addition, although it is widely accepted that researcher ethnolinguistic background impacts ethnographic data collection and analysis, research in applied linguistics and other fields often fails to adopt a reflexive stance on the role and identities of the researcher.

Other frequent weaknesses in ethnographic work include a lack of explicit articulation of an epistemological orientation or the use of research methods that clash with an espoused epistemological or theoretical frame (see Harklau, 2011). In addition, SLA researchers may identify research as ethnography when in fact it only borrows certain ethnographic tools – particularly interviewing and observations – for a more broadly defined qualitative study. The lack of clear definition leads to concerns in the field about the misapplication of the term "ethnography" to inadequately conceptualized or designed research (Watson-Gegeo, 1988).

Another important challenge for ethnography in SLA research is to overcome the overwhelming dominance of White Anglophone researchers. There likewise remains a paucity of ethnographic research on language learning outside of North America and Britain (but see, e.g., Lin, 1999). In addition, a continuing challenge for current and future ethnography is the favoring of quantitative over qualitative research by the SLA field as well as by policy makers. Harklau (2011) notes a clear bias towards quantitative studies in top peer-reviewed journals in applied linguistics. Calls for "rigor" and "accountability" in recent government initiatives are also typically met with quantitative research and overlook qualitative approaches. This challenge may very well continue to undercut the status and influence – if not the quantity – of qualitative research on second language acquisition.

Despite these challenges, new directions for ethnography proliferate in the field. Recent SLA ethnographic research increasingly has adopted a critical perspective on social equity issues that may enhance the academic trajectory and lives of second language learners and their communities. In addition, new studies on immigrant and post-colonial identities from poststructuralist and critical feminist perspectives push the boundaries on how to conceptualize and research issues of language, power, and culture.

See also: discourse and pragmatics in SLA, institutional talk, longitudinal research, qualitative research, second language socialization, social and sociocultural approaches to SLA

References

Canagarajah, A.S. (1993). Critical ethnography of a Sri Lankan classroom: Ambiguities in student opposition to reproduction through ESOL. *TESOL Quarterly*, *27*, 601–26.

Cazden, C., John, V. and Hymes, D. (eds) (1972). *Functions of Language in the Classroom*. New York: Teachers College Press.

Clifford, J. (1986). Introduction. In J. Clifford and G.E. Marcus (eds), *Writing Culture: The Poetics and Politics of Ethnography*, pp. 1–26. Berkeley: University of California Press.

Denzin, N.K. and Lincoln, Y.S. (2000). *Handbook of Qualitative Research*, 2nd edn. Thousand Oaks, CA: Sage Publications.

Dyson, A. (1997). *Social Worlds of Children Learning to Write in an Urban Primary School*. New York: Teachers College Press.

Eisenhart, M. (2001). Educational ethnography past, present, and future: Ideas to think with. *Educational Researcher*, *30*, 8, 16–27.

Gebhard, M. (2004). Fast Capitalism, School Reform, and Second Language Literacy Practices. *Modern Language Journal*, *88*, 245–265. doi:10.1111/j.0026-7902.2004.t01-4-.x

Goldschmidt, W. (2000). A perspective on anthropology. *American Anthropologist*, *102*, 789–807.

Harklau, L. (2011). Approaches and methods in recent qualitative research. In E. Hinkel (ed.), *Handbook of Research in Second Language Teaching and Learning*, volume II. New York: Routledge.

Heath, S.B. and Street, B.V. (2008). *On Ethnography: Approaches to Language and Literacy Research*. New York: Teachers College Press; NCRLL/National Conference on Research in Language and Literacy.

Lam, W.S. E. (2009). Multiliteracies on instant messaging in negotiating local, translocal, and transnational affiliations: A case of an adolescent immigrant. *Reading Research Quarterly*, *44*, 4, 377–397.

Lather, P. and Smithies, C. (1997). *Troubling the Angels: Women Living With HIV/AIDS*. Boulder, CO: Westview/HarperCollins.

Lin, A. (1999). Doing-English-lessons in the reproduction or transformation of social worlds? *TESOL Quarterly*, *33*, 393–412.

Moll, L.C., Saez, R. and Dworin, J. (2001). Exploring biliteracy: Two student case examples of writing as a social practice. *Elementary School Journal*, *101*, 4, 435–449.

Norton, B. (2000). *Identity and Language Learning: Gender, Ethnicity, and Educational Change*. Harlow: Pearson Education.

Salzman, P.C. (2001). *Understanding Culture: An Introduction to Anthropological Theory*. Prospect Heights, IL: Waveland Press.

Talmy, S. (2010). Becoming 'local' in ESL: Racism as resource in a Hawai'i public high school. *Journal of Language, Identity, and Education*, *9*, 1, 36–57.

Watson-Gegeo, K.A. (1988). Ethnography in ESL: defining the essentials. *TESOL Quarterly*, *22*, 575–592.

Wortham, S. and Rymes, B. (eds) (2003). *Linguistic Anthropology of Education*. Westport, CT: Praeger.

Further reading

Heller, M. (2006). *Linguistic Minorities and Modernity: A Sociolinguistic Ethnography*, 2nd edn. New York: Continuum. (A sociolinguistic ethnography that traces the linguistic and identity struggles for diverse French-speaking communities in Ontario, Canada.)

Kamberelis, G. and Dimitriadis, G. (2005). *Qualitative Inquiry: Approaches to Language and Literacy Research*. New York and London: Teacher's College, Columbia University. (An exploration of different interpretive paradigms that developed through a nexus of material, discursive, and social practices.)

Menard-Warwick, J. (2005). Intergenerational Trajectories and Sociopolitical Context: Latina Immigrants in Adult ESL. *TESOL Quarterly*, *39*, 2, 165–185. (A critical ethnography that uses life-history narratives and participant observation to explore the academic trajectory of two Central American immigrant women in an ESL family literacy program.)

Pacheco, M. (2010). Performativity in the bilingual classroom: The plight of English learners in the current reform context. *Anthropology and Education Quarterly*, *41*, 1, 75–93. (A feminist poststructuralist ethnography that use theories of performativity to investigate the discursive constitution of bilingual learners.)

Samy, A., Ibrahim, A. and Pennycook, A. (eds) (2009). *Global Linguistic Flows: Hip Hop Cultures, Youth Identities, and the Politics of Language*. London and New York: Routledge. (A network of ethnographic studies that explore the cultural and linguistic practices of Hip Hop across a diverse range of geographical and societal contexts.)

European Science Foundation (ESF) project

Wolfgang Klein
Max Planck Insitute for Psycholinguistics, Nijmegen

By nature, languages are acquired in the daily interaction of learners with their social environment, rather than by classroom instruction. In these contexts, the learners use the input to build linguistic systems ("learner varieties"), which are initially very simple, then become richer in lexicon and grammar, and end at a stage where they are more or less similar and in the ideal case identical to the language used in the learning environment. This fact was first noted in the early Seventies (Nemser, 1991), but its echo in acquisition research has been limited, due to two reasons. First, acquisition research is traditionally done from the perspective of a language teacher, who is primarily interested in how learners still deviate from the target, rather in the systems they build themselves and how they do it. Second, it is much easier to study language acquisition in a classroom setting than to follow the developmental route of a learner in those environments for which the human language capacity was made. Only a few projects ventured such an investigation (such as Heidelberger Forschungsprojekt Pidgin-Deutsch, 1975; Schumann, 1987; Klein und Dittmar, 1979; Clahsen *et al.*, 1983). They inspired the most comprehensive endeavour to date in the area of natural second language acquisition, the European Science Fondation project "Second language acquistion of adult immigrants". It was run from 1981 to 1987 by seven research centres in five European countries (England, France, Germany, the Netherlands and Sweden), under the coordination of the Max-Planck-Institut for Psycholinguistics (Nijmegen). The project was cross-linguistic and longitudinal. For each of the following ten L1-L2 pairs, four adult foreign immigrants, mostly workers, with minimal or no L2-knowledge at the beginning, were observed and recorded over a period of about 30 months:

Various types of data collection were used, ranging from free conversation and personal narratives to more controlled methods, such as film retellings, instructions ('stage-directions'), role-plays, picture descriptions and self-confrontation. Rigidly controlled experiments were avoided, such as to ensure ecological validity (Perdue, 1993, vol 1). All techniques were ordered into three data-collection cycles of about 10 months each, such that each task was performed at least three times. Data were audio- or video-recorded, transcribed and to a large extent computerized (see ESF under http://corpus1.mpi.nl/ds/imdi_browser/).

These data show all the richnesses and deficiencies of extensive field work: they are comprehensive, ecologically valid and a unique source of observations, but also heterogenous and not always comparable with each other. Thus, their analysis can best be characterised as a number of parallel case studies. This analysis initially focused on six major themes: the structure of utterances (Perdue and Klein, 1992), the expression of temporal relations (Dietrich *et al.*, 1994), the expression of spatial relations (Becker and Carroll, 1995), developments in the lexicon, feedback behavior in interaction and the ways in which speakers try to achieve understanding in intercultural discourse

(Bremer *et al.*, 1997). Subsequent studies, often completed by additional data, extended this to topics such as the expression of modality, the role of finiteness, negation, adverbial scope, or the use of focus particles (see, e.g. Giacalone Ramat and Crocco Galeas, 1995, Hendriks, 2005).

The ESF project still stands out in its radical attempt to investigate language acquisition under natural conditions, to ascertain a high degree of ecological validity, and to look at acquisition from the learner's, rather than the teacher's or the linguist's, point of view. Second language acquisition is not seen as a more or less perfect replication of a set norm – a "real language," as decribed in grammar books and dictionaries, but as a continuous attempt to construct linguist systems which allow the learner to communicate efficiently and thereby to advance their linguistic competence. Both the internal organization of these "learner varieties" at a given time as well as the way in which they move towards the target, that is, the language of the learner's social environment, as the learners actually hear it, follow certain regularities. These vary according to a number of factors, such as type and amount of the input, properties of L1 or L2, type of social interaction, or the particular motivation of the learner. Under this perspective, learner varieties are no less "real languages" than, for example, the L1 or the L2; in fact, the latter are only a special case of a learner variety, rather than the yardstick against which imperfections and deviations are measured.

See also: basic variety, concept-oriented approach to SLA, development in SLA, functional-typological linguistics, thinking for speaking, longitudinal research

References

Becker, A., and Carroll, M. (2005). *The Acquisition of Spatial Relations in a Second Language*. Amsterdam: Benjamins.

Bremer, K., Roberts, C., Broeder, P., Vasseur, M.-T., and Simonnot, M. (1996). *Achieving Understanding Discourse in Intercultural Encounters*. London: Longman.

Clahsen, H., Meisel, J., and Pienemann, M. (1983). *Deutsch als Zweitsprache. Der Spracherwerb ausländischer Arbeiter*, Tübingen: Gunter Narr.

Dietrich, R., Klein, W., and Noyau, C. (1995). *The Acquisition of Temporality in a Second Language Acquisition*. Amsterdam: Benjamins.

Giacalone Ramat, A. and Crocco Galeas, G. (eds) (1995). *From Pragmatics to Syntax: Modality in Second Language Acquisition*. Tübingen: Narr.

Hendriks, H. (ed.) (2005). *The Structure of Learner Varieties*. Berlin and New York: de Gruyter.

Heidelberger Forschungsprojekt "Pidgin-Deutsch". (1975). *Sprache und Kommunikation ausländischer Arbeiter*. Kronberg: Scriptor.

Klein, W. and Dittmar, N. (1979). *Developing Grammars: the Acquisition of German Syntax by Foreign Workers*. Berlin: Springer.

Klein, W., and Perdue, C. (1992). *Utterance structure*. Amsterdam: Benjamins.

Nemser, W. (1971). Approximate systems of foreign language learners. *International Review of Applied Linguistics*, *9*, 115–23.

Perdue, C. (ed.) (1993). *Adult Language Acquisition: Crosslinguistic Perspectives*, Two volumes. Cambridge: Cambridge University Press.

Schumann, J. (1978). *The Pidginization Process*. Rowley, MA: Newbury House.

Event-related potentials (ERP)

Eric Pakaluk and Helen Neville

University of Oregon

Recent advances in neuroimaging allow for the investigation of the neurobiological bases of language and the effects of environmental factors, such delays in second language acquisition (SLA), on neural organization for specific subsystems of language. The present, selective overview will focus on two subsytems extensively examined using the event-related potential methodology in the study of second language acquisition: semantics and syntax.

Event-related potentials

Event-related potentials (ERPs) are measurements of continuous brain electrical activity (electroencephalogram) time-locked to the presentation of a stimulus. ERPs provide an online, non-invasive index of cognitive processes with a temporal resolution of milliseconds. The ERP response typically consists of a series of positive and negative deflections, known as components. As these components vary on a number of dimensions, such as amplitude, polarity, and latency, ERPs provide a multidimensional index of cognitive processes. This degree of temporal resolution is crucial in the study of language given the rapid pace of information processing in natural language processing, and thus ERPs are arguably the most powerful methodologies in examining online language processing. While this methodology has been used more extensively in studies of language processing in monolinguals, a growing number of studies have used ERPs to examine SLA.

Most ERP studies of SLA are framed in the context of an ongoing debate concerning the critical period hypothesis. Based on evidence from the development of sensory and motor systems, Lenneberg (1967) proposed that similar maturational processes might constrain language development such that there may be sensitive periods during which the effects of language experience are maximal on ultimate linguistic proficiency and neural organization for language. This hypothesis is supported by behavioral data from both first and second language acquisition which suggest that proficiency decreases with delays in language immersion (e.g., Johnson and Newport, 1989). Other evidence suggests that a small number of non-native speakers who acquire a second language after a hypothesized sensitive period, around the onset of puberty, can attain a level of proficiency in syntactic processing which is similar to that of native speakers (e.g., White and Genesee, 1996), though the question of whether such individuals recruit the same neural mechanisms as native speakers to achieve such a level of proficiency is an open one. The ERP methodology permits the examination of these questions with a greater degree of specificity.

Semantic processing

Consistent with other methodologies, ERP studies in monolinguals have demonstrated that semantic and syntactic subsystems are mediated by non-identical neural mechanisms: numerous studies in both the visual and auditory modalities have found that semantic anomalies elicit a neural response distinct from that elicited by syntactic violations (discussed in more detail below). Kutas and Hillyard (1980) first discovered that a semantically unexpected word in a sentence elicited a negative-going potential peaking around 400 ms (the N400) after the onset of the word compared to contextually appropriate words (e.g., *He spread the warm bread with* *__butter__* compared to **He spread the warm bread with* *__socks__*). The N400 has since been replicated in numerous studies of monolinguals across languages and modalities (e.g., Friederici *et al.*, 1993, Holcomb and Neville, 1991), leading to the hypothesis that the N400 component indexes semantic integration processes.

Evidence from several ERP studies suggests that neural systems important for semantic processing are less sensitive to delays in language acquisition than other subsystems. An early study of bilinguals showed that semantic anomalies elicited a similar N400 response in both native and non-native speakers, even with delays in SLA of more than 12 years, though this response was delayed in bilinguals (Ardal *et al.*, 1990). Weber-Fox and Neville (1996) found similar results in a study of native speakers of Chinese who began learning English at different ages in development. Even with delays in acquisition of more than 16 years, bilinguals showed a native-like N400, though this response was delayed slightly in participants with delays in acquisition greater than 11 years. A similar pattern of results was found in two studies of non-native speakers of German: groups of native speakers of Japanese (Hahne and Friederici, 2001) and native speakers of Russian (Hahne, 2001), both of whom learned German after puberty, showed an N400 response to semantic anomalies in German. In a study of two groups of native speakers of Japanese who started learning English around age 12, Ojima and colleagues (2005) reported that semantic violations elicited an N400 in both higher and lower proficiency non-native speakers. This pattern also holds for manual languages, as non-native signers who acquired American Sign Language (ASL) after the age of 17 showed an N400 to semantic anomalies in ASL similar to that in native signers (Neville *et al.*, 1997).

Syntactic processing

Studies of monolinguals have identified at least two components hypothesized to index syntactic processing, typically elicited by syntactic violations in a biphasic response. The first is a negative-going wave between 100 and 500 ms, often larger over left anterior scalp regions (left anterior negativity; LAN). The LAN has been elicited by a variety of syntactic violation types, such as phrase structure (e.g., Neville *et al.*, 1991, Friederici *et al.*, 1993, Hahne and Friederici, 1999) and morphosyntactic violations (e.g., Friederici *et al.*, 1993, Coulson *et al.*, 1998). The second component that has been observed in ERP studies of syntactic processing is a large positive-going wave usually maximal between 500 and 1000 ms over bilateral posterior regions referred to as the P600 (e.g., Osterhout and Holcomb, 1993). The P600 is consistently elicited by syntactic violations (e.g., Hagoort *et al.*, 1993, Hahne and Friederici, 1999) as well as by violations of preferred syntactic structure (Osterhout and Holcomb, 1993) or in well-formed sentences of higher syntactic complexity (e.g., Kaan *et al.*, 2000).

Several ERP studies of bilinguals have provided evidence that neural systems important for syntactic processing are more sensitive to delays in language acquisition than other subsystems. In the first ERP study of online syntactic processing in bilinguals, Weber-Fox and Neville (1996) examined the processing of phrase structure violations (e.g., *The scientist criticized Max's proof __of__ the theorem* compared to **The scientist criticized Max's __of__ proof the theorem*) in Chinese-English bilinguals who differed in their ages of first exposure to English. Systems involved in syntactic processing were found to be sensitive to delays of even four years: while syntactic violations elicited a biphasic anterior negativity-P600 response in all groups, the anterior negativity was left-lateralized only in groups with earlier ages of acquisition (i.e., 1–3 years), bilateral in groups with later ages of acquisition, and right-lateralized in participants who acquired English after age 16. Two subsequent studies examined the ERP response to phrase structure violations in late learners of German who were native speakers of Japanese (Hahne and Friederici, 2001) or Russian (Hahne, 2001). In both studies, phrase structure violations failed to elicit an anterior negativity, and only in the group of Russian native speakers, who had higher second language proficiency, did violations elicit a P600.

While these results provide neurophysiological evidence that neural systems underlying semantic and syntactic processing may be differentially affected by delays in second language, there was a confound in these studies between age of exposure and proficiency. Several recent studies have attempted to address the role of second language proficiency in online syntactic processing using both less traditional ERP paradigms featuring artificial and miniature languages and more traditional natural language ERP paradigms.

Artificial and miniature language paradigms employed constrained sets of words and sentence structures to train participants to a high level of proficiency, after which ERPs are examined to syntactic violations created using the same stimulus sets. These paradigms have both advantages (e.g., they permit participants to reach a high level of proficiency in a short time frame, they permit more control over potentially confounding variables than natural languages) and disadvantages (e.g., the degree to which they are comparable and relevant to natural languages) compared to natural language paradigms (for a more detailed discussion, see Steinhauer *et al.*, 2009). Using a 14-word artificial language, Friederici and colleagues (2002) found that word category violations elicited ERP effects only in a high proficiency group: a small early anterior negativity followed by a posterior negativity and a P600-like posterior positivity. While these results were interpreted as evidence that native-like neural organization for syntactic processing can be achieved with an extremely high level of proficiency, the constrained nature of the artificial language limits the degree to which these results can be generalized to natural language. Mueller and colleagues (2005) used a miniature version of Japanese to train a group of native German speakers to a high level of proficiency then examined ERPs elicited by several Japanese violation types. After training, violations elicited a P600 in the non-native learner group which was similar to that in native Japanese speakers, suggesting that more controlled syntactic processes can be acquired after a short training period with a constrained set of natural language stimuli.

Several recent studies have used more traditional natural language ERP paradigms to explore the relationship between second language proficiency and online syntactic processing. Ojima and colleagues (2005) examined native speakers of Japanese who started learning English around age 12 and found that verb agreement violations elicited a left-lateralized negativity between 350 and 550 ms in both native speakers and high proficiency late learners. However, as the stimuli were short, simple, active sentences presented visually at a slower rate than is typical in ERP studies, violations were very predictable and the interpretability of the results is limited. Rossi and colleagues (2006) examined low and high proficiency late learners of both German and Italian. Agreement errors elicited a biphasic LAN-P600 response in high proficiency late learners, and word category violations elicited an extended bilateral anterior negativity followed by a P600 in both proficiency groups. The authors attribute this finding to the use of simple, active sentences with only two violation types with no variability in the position of violation point, which likely increased predictability and allowed participants to concentrate on the processing of a limited number of syntactic rules.

Pakulak and Neville (2011) examined the effects of delayed second language acquisition while controlling for proficiency differences by examining late learners of English who had achieved a high enough level of proficiency to match a group of native speakers from a previous study of proficiency in monolinguals (Pakulak and Neville, 2010). Crucially, the paradigm in this study was designed to limit predictability and increase difficulty by using naturally spoken speech and varying sentence length, violation type and position, and participant task to limit the degree to which participants could focus on one violation point. While in native speakers phrase structure violations elicited a bilateral and prolonged early anterior negativity followed by a P600, in proficiency-matched non-native speakers violations did not elicit the early anterior negativity, but did elicit a large and widespread P600. This study provided evidence that neural organization for syntactic processing is sensitive to delays in language acquisition independently of proficiency level.

Conclusion

While ERP studies of SLA provide some degree of consistency, there also remains a level of inconsistency. Overall, the results provide general support for the critical period hypothesis, while also suggesting that proficiency may be an important factor in neural organization for a second language. However, it is also clear that methodological differences between laboratories are a confounding factor. With increasing use of this powerful methodology in the study of SLA, and increased collaboration between laboratories, future studies will provide more clarity on these important questions.

See also: artificial language learning, Critical Period Hypothesis (CPH), measuring and researching SLA, psycholingustics of SLA, proficiency, semantic processing

References

Ardal, S., Donald, M., Meuter, R., Muldrew, S. and Luce, M. (1990). Brain responses to semantic incongruity in bilinguals. *Brain and Language*, *39*, 187–205.

Coulson, S., King, J.W. and Kutas, M. (1998). Expect the unexpected: Event-related brain response to morphosyntactic violations. *Language and Cognitive Processes*, *13*, 21–58.

Friederici, A.D., Pfeifer, E. and Hahne, A. (1993). Event-related brain potentials during natural speech processing: Effects of semantic, morphological and syntactic violations. *Cognitive Brain Research*, *1*, 183–92.

Friederici, A.D., Steinhauer, K. and Pfeifer, E. (2002). Brain signatures of artificial language processing: evidence challenging the critical period hypothesis. *Proc. Natl. Acad. Sci. U.S. A.*, *99*, 529–34.

Hagoort, P., Brown, C. and Groothusen, J. (1993). The Syntactic Positive Shift (SPS) as an ERP measure of syntactic processing. *Language and Cognitive Processes*, *8*, 439–83.

Hahne, A. (2001). What's different in second-language processing? Evidence from event-related brain potentials. *Journal of Psycholinguistic Research*, *30*, 251–66.

Hahne, A. and Friederici, A. (2001). Processing a second language: Late learners' comprehension mechanisms as revealed by event-related brain potential. *Bilingualism: Language and Cognition*, *4*, 123–41.

Hahne, A. and Friederici, A.D. (1999). Electrophysiological evidence for two steps in syntactic analysis: Early automatic and late controlled processes. *Journal of Cognitive Neuroscience*, *11*, 194–205.

Holcomb, P.J. and Neville, H.J. (1991). Natural speech processing: An analysis using event-related brain potentials. *Psychobiology*, *19*, 286–300.

Johnson, J. and Newport, E. (1989). Critical period effects in second language learning: The influence of maturational state on the acquisition of English as a second language. *Cognitive Psychology*, *21*, 60–99.

Kaan, E., Harris, A., Gibson, E. and Holcomb, P. (2000). The P600 as an index of syntactic integration difficulty. *Language and Cognitive Processes*, *15*, 159–201.

Kutas, M. and Hillyard, S.A. (1980). Reading senseless sentences: Brain potentials reflect semantic incongruity. *Science*, *207*, 203–5.

Lenneberg, E.H. (1967). *Biological Foundations of Language*. New York: Wiley.

Mueller, J.L., Hahne, A., Fujii, Y. and Friederici, A.D. (2005). Native and nonnative speakers' processing of a miniature version of Japanese as revealed by ERPs. *Journal of Cognitive Neuroscience*, *17*, 1229–44.

Neville, H.J., Coffey, S.A., Lawson, D.S., Fischer, A., Emmorey, K. and Bellugi, U. (1997). Neural systems mediating American sign language: Effects of sensory experience and age of acquisition. *Brain and Language*, *57*, 285–308.

Neville, H.J., Nicol, J., Barss, A., Forster, K. and Garrett, M. (1991). Syntactically based sentence processing classes: Evidence from event-related brain potentials. *Journal of Cognitive Neuroscience*, *3*, 155–70.

Ojima, S., Nakata, H. and Kakigi, R. (2005). An ERP study of second language learning after childhood: Effects of proficiency. *Journal of Cognitive Neuroscience*, *17*(8), 12–1228.

Osterhout, L. and Holcomb, P.J. (1993). Event-related potentials and syntactic anomaly: Evidence of anomaly detection during the perception of continuous speech. *Language and Cognitive Processes*, *8*, 413–37.

Pakulak, E. and Neville, H. (2010). Proficiency differences in syntactic processing of monolingual native speakers indexed by event-related potentials. *Journal of Cognitive Neuroscience*, *22*, 2728–2729.

——(in press) Maturational constraints on the recruitment of early processes for syntactic processing. *Journal of Cognitive Neuroscience*, *23*(10), 2752–2765.

Rossi, S., Gugler, M.F., Friederici, A.D. and Hahne, A. (2006). The impact of proficiency on syntactic second-language processing of German and Italian: Evidence from event-related potentials. *Journal of Cognitive Neuroscience*, *18*, 2030–48.

Steinhauer, K., White, E.J. and Drury, J.E. (2009). Temporal dynamics of late second language acquisition: Evidence from event-related brain potentials. *Second Language Research*, *25*, 13–41.

Weber-Fox, C. and Neville, H.J. (1996). Maturational constraints on functional specializations for language processing: ERP and behavioral evidence in bilingual speakers. *Journal of Cognitive Neuroscience*, *8*, 231–56.

White, L. and Genesee, F. (1996). How native is near-native? The issue of ultimate attainment in adult second language acquisition. *Second Language Research*, *12*, 238–65.

Executive control and frontal cortex

Henk Haarmann
University of Maryland

Executive control refers to the attention- and goal-directed guidance of multiple domains of human information processing. It relies crucially upon a well-functioning frontal lobe, particularly, the pre-frontal cortex (PFC) and its subsections, such as the ventro-lateral, medial-lateral, and orbitofrontal PFC, and the anterior cingulate cortex (ACC) (Miller and Cohen, 2001; Roelofs and Hagoort, 2002). Other brain regions that are connected to but outside the frontal lobe, particularly the attention networks in the parietal lobe, are also involved in executive control (Alvarez and Emory, 2006).

The brain's system for executive control is also known as the central executive. Human information processing can be subdivided into different content domains, for example, perception and attention, learning and memory, speech and language, visual-spatial and tactile processing, problem-solving and reasoning, judgment and decision-making, and planning and action. But regardless of the specific content of the domain, certain aspects of the information processing in each domain need to be modulated (i.e., controlled) so that the person's needs are met.

Executive control functions and examples

Executive control includes aspects of several multiple functions. These functions include initiating, interrupting, and stopping an information process (e.g., stopping an utterance midway), prioritizing cognitive activities in accordance with one's goals (e.g., correcting a grammatical error in one's speech in order to meet the requirements of a formal setting before proceeding), sequencing (e.g., greeting and then asking a sales person for a ticket to a particular movie before entering a movie theater), organizing behavior hierarchically (e.g., continuing a movie ticket sales transaction after interruption by and responding to a text message), controlling the allocation of attention to storage and manipulation of information in working memory (e.g., encoding the greeting of a sales person and deciding how to respond in a pragmatically appropriate manner, considering his or her gender, age, status, and culture), controlling the allocation of attention to retrieval from long-term memory (e.g., continuing attempts to retrieve an infrequently used word after failing to find it initially), deploying selective attention (e.g., focusing on the form over the meaning of an utterance or vice versa) and its counterpart inhibition (e.g., suppressing the processing of distracting speech in the background), alternating attention (e.g., listening to different successive speakers in a conversation), and dividing attention (e.g., simultaneous analyzing a person's spoken language and non-verbal visual-spatial gestures), task switching (e.g., changing from a speaking to a listening mode, while negotiating meaning with an interlocutor in a foreign language), multi-tasking (e.g., translating while keeping track of topic changes), error monitoring (e.g., realizing a violation of pragmatics from an interlocutor's facial expression), and conflict monitoring and resolution (e.g., observing a conflict between two interpretations of the same utterance and resolving it in favor of the interpretation that best fits the context) (e.g., Miller and Cohen, 2001; Roelofs and Hagoort, 2002; Novick *et al.*, 2010). This list of functions in which executive control plays a role illustrates the critical role of executive control in human cognition. Moreover, the various examples clearly illustrate how important executive control of language is for first and second language processing and acquisition.

Brain basis of executive control

Executive control relies for the most part on the pre-frontal cortex and other regions of the frontal lobe (e.g., the anterior cingulate cortex on the medial surface of the frontal lobe and Broca's area) plus on networks for controlling attention in the parietal cortex (Novick *et al.*, 2010). The pre-frontal lobe makes up the anterior portion of the frontal lobe. It takes up about more than one-third of total brain volume and half of the volume of the frontal lobe, which in turn is the largest lobe of the human brain and much larger than the frontal lobe of other mammals, including higher order primates. As such, the frontal lobe and especially its pre-frontal portion are believed to be responsible for the largely superior cognitive abilities of humans compared to other animals. The other lobes of the brain include the parietal lobe, temporal lobe, and occipital lobe and each of these lobes has a left and right brain counterpart.

Much is currently known about the particular brain regions that support many of the executive control functions outlined above, as well as what variables (e.g., memory load, absence/presence of error) they respond to, and how they are connected to and work together with other brain regions in a network to accomplish a task. This knowledge stems in large part from the availability of non-invasive cognitive neuroscience methods. Neuroimaging methods employed during the performance of a task or while at rest enable observing the anatomical structure and activation of the contributing regions (e.g., Magnetic Resonance Imaging or MRI). Still other neuroscience methods are used to change the activity of the brain (e.g., Transcranial Magnetic Stimulation or TMS) as an independent variable by interfering with it very briefly (TMS) or by elevating or decreasing it through repeated stimulation (e.g., repetitive TMS or rTMS or repetitive Direct Current Stimulation or tDCS).

Various well-controlled and well-understood experimental task paradigms employed during neuroimaging allow brain regions supporting particular sub-functions of the executive control system to be indentified. One such task paradigm is the n-back task. In each trial on this task, a person is given a sequence of stimuli (typically, letters or numbers), presented one at a time, and has to detect any stimulus that repeats a stimulus that was presented n positions back in the same sequence (e.g., in the 2-back version of this task with letter stimuli a person would respond with *yes* upon detecting the second letter *m* in the sequence of letters: *l k b **m** r **m** s*). This task is made more difficult when the working memory load is increased by placing more intervening stimuli between a pair of repeating stimuli (e.g., l k b **m** r h **m** s in a 3-back task) or by presenting distracting pairs of identical stimuli that are not separated by the required distance (e.g., l k b **m** r **m** h s in a 3-back task) and therefore should not be responded to. Since the dorso-lateral PFC (DL-PFC) is one of the regions that responds selectively to this manipulation of working memory load, it is believed to support maintenance of information in working memory (Miller and Cohen, 2001). Another example of a task used to study executive control and its neurobiological basis is the color-word version of the Stroop task in which a subject must name the ink color of a color word in a congruent condition (i.e., name of color word and name of ink color are the same, e.g., the word "red" written in red) or incongruent condition (i.e., name of ink color is different from the name of the color word, e.g., the word "red" written in blue). Reaction times are typically slower in the incongruent than congruent condition, an effect known as the Stroop effect. The Stroop effect has been found to impact the activation of the DL-PFC and also of the anterior cingulate gyrus inside the pre-frontal lobe, resulting in the proposal that both areas are involved in the attention control of conflict between representations and/or responses (Roelofs and Hagoort, 2002).

For the executive control system to function well its individual contributing brain regions must function well. In addition, good connections of pre-frontal brain regions with one another and with regions elsewhere in the brain are crucial for exerting executive control. The neuropsychological case of Phineas Gage is often cited to illustrate the importance of good pre-frontal connections for proper executive control. Phineas Gage was a railroad foreman in 1848 when a tamping iron penetrated his brain after a pre-mature explosion of a charge, severing connections inside the pre-frontal lobe. One prominent account of his impairment is that Gage had lost the ability to bring emotional evaluation of the consequences of actions to bear on action selection, destroying his social life due to poor decision-making. Although we will never know for sure the details of this historical case (MacMillan, 2008), the guidance of thought and action by emotion is considered a crucial function of the executive control system (Bechara *et al.*, 1994). This function is believed to be supported by the ventro-medial PFC within the orbitofrontal PFC.

Neuropsychological impairment of the pre-frontal lobe is diagnosed with behavioral tests such as the IOWA gambling test, the Wisconsin Card Sort

Testing, and fluency tests (Bechara *et al.*, 1994; Alvarez and Emory, 2006). In the IOWA gambling test, subjects must learn to avoid monetary losses by shifting their selection of playing cards from high-reward, high-risk to lower-reward, lower-risk cards since the long-term profit of the latter can be anticipated to be higher. Individuals with deep lesions of the pre-frontal lobe, while experiencing being upset over large losses just like unimpaired individuals, have difficulties shifting to the less risky optimal strategy on this task. On the Wisconsin Card Sort Test, individuals must sort cards by one of several possible criteria, which they must uncover through trial and error, and they must quickly learn to adopt a new criterion when the experimenter shifts it unannounced. Unlike unimpaired individuals, persons whose pre-frontal lobe is neurologically damaged have a hard time letting go of a sorting criterion when it is no longer appropriate. Such a tendency to perseverate or continue to provide previous responses when they are no longer appropriate is a symptom that is indicative of impairment of the pre-frontal lobe and poor executive control. Performance decrements on fluency tests, in which a subject must produce as many responses as possible within a certain category (e.g., starting with a specific letter or belonging to a certain semantic category), can also be indicative of an impaired executive system (e.g., decreased monitoring and retrieval of new items), provided that other explanations (e.g., decreased vocabulary size) are excluded. By contrast a well-functioning central executive enables overcoming of habitual responses and cognitive flexibility.

Cognitive neuroscience studies of the frontal lobe in neurologically unimpaired adults have furthermore revealed decrements in the neurological functioning of the pre-frontal lobe and its corresponding executive control functions during the process of healthy aging. Compared to young adults, older adults have more problems with storing and manipulating information in working memory, inhibiting task irrelevant and distracting information, memory retrieval, and selective and divided attention (Haarmann *et al.*, 2005). There is evidence that physical fitness exercise can provide some protection against these age-related cognitive decrements in healthy aging and their negative impact on executive control.

Attempts have been made to formulate integrative accounts of executive control that explain many of its various functions with a single underlying set of neurocognitive principles. One prominent account, which has been supported by empirical evidence and neurocomputational modeling, proposes that an integral function of the PFC is to selectively enhance and suppress the activation of mental representations and thereby bias and modulate the flow of high-level information processing elsewhere in the brain in all relevant domains (e.g., perception, action, memory, decision-making, emotion, language) (Miller and Cohen, 2001). Alternatively, executive control may be accomplished by different cognitive functions and corresponding brain regions that contribute relatively independently to task performance (e.g., task switching versus inhibition).

Executive control and language

Executive control plays an important role in first and second language processing, as many of the above listed examples of the various executive functions illustrate. Laboratory-controlled psycholinguistic and cognitive neuroscience studies on the role of executive control in language processing have focused on the importance of working memory and conflict monitoring, detection, and resolution in both production and comprehension. There is strong evidence that the anterior cingulate cortex in the frontal lobe is involved in conflict monitoring and detection when during lexical access a target word is competing for production with a non-target word (Roelofs and Hagoort, 2002). There is furthermore evidence that Broca's area, at the back of the lower portion of the frontal lobe, helps to resolve conflict between competing syntactic readings of the same sentence (Novick *et al.*, 2010). Experience with language is known to confer advantages upon the executive control function. In several studies, Bialystok and her colleagues have shown that individuals who grow up bilingual are better at inhibition, particularly the kind of inhibition that enables a person to cope with interference from distracting information (Bialystok and Viswanathan, 2009; Luk *et al.*, 2010). Cognitive neuroscientists have recently begun to examine the nature and role of individual differences in the patterns of structural and functional connectivity among brain regions that are networked together, using magnetic resonance imaging (MRI). Such studies could be applied to second language acquisition. They hold much promise because they will be able to elucidate (a) the contribution of connectivity patterns involved in the executive control of domain-specific language functions to individual differences in aptitude and proficiency and (b) also how malleable such differences are to training.

See also: attention, bilingualism and SLA, Event-related potentials (ERP), explicit learning, inhibitory control, psycholinguistics of SLA

References

Alvarez, J.A. and Emory, E. (2006). Executive function and the frontal lobes: a meta-analytic review. *Neuropsychological Review*, *16*(1), 17–42.

Bechara, A., Damasio, A.R., Damasio, H. and Anderson, S.W. (1994). Insensitivity to future consequences following damage to human prefrontal cortex. *Cognition*, *50*, 7–12.

Bialystok, E. and Viswanathan, M. (2009). Components of executive control with advantages for bilingual children in two cultures. *Cognition*, *112*(3), 494–500.

Haarmann, H.J., Ashling, G.E., Davelaar, E.J. and Usher, M. (2005). Age-related declines in context maintenance and semantic short-term memory. *The Quarterly Journal of Experimental Psychology* (special issue on aging), *55A* (1), 34–53.

Luk, G., Anderson, J.A., Craik, F.I., Grady, C., and Bialystok, E. (2010). Distinct neural correlates for two types of inhibition in bilinguals: Response inhibition versus interference suppression. *Brain and Cognition*, *74*(3), 347–57.

Macmillan, M. (2008). Phineas Gage: Unravelling the myth. *The Psychologist*, *21*(9), 828–31.

Miller, E.K. and Cohen, J.D. (2001). An integrative theory of prefrontal cortex function. *Annual Review of Neuroscience*, *24*(1), 167–202.

Novick, J.M., Trueswell, J.C. and Thompson-Schill, S.L. (2010). Broca's area and language processing: Evidence for the cognitive control connection. *Language and Linguistics Compass*, *4*(10), 906–24.

Roelofs, A. and Hagoort, P. (2002). Control of language use cognitive modeling of the hemodynamics of Stroop task performance. *Cognitive Brain Research*, *15*, 85–97.

Further reading

Cohen, M.X. (2010). Error related medial frontal theta activity predicts cingulate-related structural connectivity. *Neuroimage*, *55*(3), 1373–83. (Illustrates an advanced brain-region connectivity approach to individual differences in executive control in the domain of error detection.)

Jackson, G.M., Swainson, R., Cunnington, R. and Jackson, S.R. (2001). ERP correlates of executive control during repeated language switching. *Bilingualism: Language and Cognition*, *4*, 169–78. (Illustrates the collaboration between prefrontal and parietal lobe areas during language switching in bilinguals.)

Risberg, J. and Grafman, J. (2006). *The Frontal lobes: Development, Function, and Pathology*. Cambridge: Cambridge University Press. (Provides a systematic scholarly introduction to the frontal lobes including its various executive control functions and their normal and impaired functioning.)

Thompson-Schill, S.L., Bedny, M. and Goldberg, R. (2005). The frontal lobes and the regulation of mental activity. *Current Opinion in Neurobiology*, *15*, 219–24. (Argues for domain-general principles of pre-frontal executive control, which govern different domain-specific processes in the frontal lobe and elsewhere in the brain.)

Explicit learning

Karen Roehr
University of Essex

In second language acquisition (SLA), explicit learning refers to situations in which "the learner has online awareness, formulating and testing conscious hypotheses in the course of learning" (N. Ellis, 1994: 38). Put differently, explicit learning occurs when a learner consciously and deliberately attempts to master language material or solve a language-related problem (Dörnyei, 2009). By contrast, implicit learning takes place without conscious awareness.

Both explicit and implicit learning are often defined with reference to the nature of the knowledge acquired, so implicit learning refers to the acquisition of implicit knowledge, whilst explicit learning refers to the acquisition of explicit knowledge (Hulstijn, 2005). Implicit knowledge can perhaps most easily be understood as intuitive knowledge in the non-technical sense of the term. Conversely, explicit knowledge is conscious knowledge that can be expressed in a verbal statement. In the human mind, explicit knowledge is represented declaratively and accessed during controlled processing (Dörnyei, 2009; R. Ellis, 2004).

Examples of explicit knowledge in SLA are a learner's knowledge of pedagogical grammar rules (metalinguistic knowledge) and a learner's knowledge of vocabulary in the sense of form-meaning pairings underlying lexical units (semantic knowledge). Thus, specific instances of explicit knowledge are my knowledge that English verbs in the third person present tense typically end in *–s* as well as my knowledge that the English noun *night* has the French translation equivalent *nuit*, the German translation equivalent *Nacht*, and the Polish translation equivalent *noc*.

In second language (L2) instruction, teachers and learners often draw on explicit knowledge and explicit learning. However, it is worth bearing in mind that in SLA, whether instructed or untutored, whether adult or child, both implicit and explicit learning contribute to the development of language proficiency; accordingly, both implicit and explicit knowledge have a role to play.

SLA research concerned with explicit learning has focused on three topic areas, that is, (1) the learning difficulty of specific linguistic constructions as either implicit or explicit knowledge, (2) the effects of different levels of learner awareness on L2 learning, and (3) the interaction of explicit and implicit processes in L2 learning.

Learning difficulty

Research addressing the issue of learning difficulty has sought to characterize the nature of linguistic constructions and pedagogical grammar rules describing these constructions. Constructions vary in terms of complexity, perceptual salience, and communicative redundancy, for instance. Pedagogical grammar rules likewise vary along a range of parameters, including complexity, scope, and reliability. Based on such considerations, researchers have attempted to predict which L2 constructions and which pedagogical grammar rules might be more or less difficult for learners to acquire and, depending on their difficulty, more or less amenable to explicit learning and teaching (DeKeyser, 2003; Hulstijn and de Graaff, 1994).

Recently, DeKeyser (2005) proposed a revised list of characteristics believed to impact on the relative learning difficulty of aspects of L2 morphosyntax, arguing that a lack of transparency in form-meaning mappings constitutes a primary source of difficulty. Lack of transparency can be attributed to three factors: communicative redundancy of form, optionality of form, and opacity, which refers to the reliability of a form-meaning mapping. Opacity (and learning difficulty) is high when different forms denote the same meaning, or when the same form stands for different meanings. Additional factors responsible for the learning difficulty of L2 form-meaning mappings are frequency in the input, phonological salience of the form, and regularity of the form-meaning relationship in the sense of scope, or the number of cases covered (DeKeyser, 2005).

The latter three characteristics, that is, frequency, salience, and regularity, are also listed by R. Ellis (2006), but, together with processability, they are presented as specifically contributing to implicit learning difficulty. R. Ellis (2006) posits a further set of characteristics accounting for explicit learning difficulty, that is, systematicity, which refers to the rule-based versus item-based nature of the form-meaning mapping described by a pedagogical grammar rule, the relative technicality of the metalanguage used in a pedagogical grammar rule, and conceptual complexity of the form-meaning mapping described by a pedagogical grammar rule.

Conceptual complexity is understood as a composite notion which includes formal and functional complexity.

Most recently, Roehr and Gánem-Gutiérrez (2009) proposed a taxonomy of learning difficulty which combines parameters from DeKeyser (2005) and R. Ellis (2006). According to their taxonomy, the variables frequency in the input, perceptual salience, communicative redundancy, opacity of form-meaning mapping (one form, x meanings), and opacity of meaning-form mapping (one meaning, x forms) refer to the characteristics of linguistic constructions and are thought to impact on implicit learning difficulty. The variable schematicity refers to the characteristics of both linguistic constructions and pedagogical grammar rules and affects both implicit and explicit learning difficulty. Schematicity describes the extent to which a linguistic construction is schematic in the sense of "general" or specific in the sense of "concrete." It likewise refers to whether a pedagogical grammar rule covers a schematic or specific linguistic construction. The variables conceptual complexity, technicality of metalanguage, and truth value refer to the characteristics of pedagogical grammar rules and are thought to impact on explicit learning difficulty. It should be noted that this taxonomy arose out of a small-scale study and requires further empirical validation.

Learner awareness

Research investigating the effects of different levels of learner awareness on L2 learning has been inspired by the Noticing Hypothesis (e.g. Schmidt, 1990) as well as by investigations into implicit versus explicit learning in the field of cognitive psychology. The Noticing Hypothesis states that noticing has to take place for L2 input to become intake. Noticing is defined as a momentary subjective experience which can be reported by the learner; it requires focused attention at the level of stimulus detection with awareness and thus goes beyond the pre-conscious registration of stimuli, or detection without awareness (Schmidt, 2001). Noticing is distinguished from understanding, which involves metalinguistic reflection, comprehension, and insight and thus represents a higher level of awareness (Schmidt, 1990).

Empirical studies investigating different levels of learner awareness typically draw on verbal reports such as think-aloud protocols and stimulated recall to operationalize concepts such as understanding, noticing, or lack of awareness. Overall, findings suggest not only that reported noticing is often associated with more successful L2 learning than apparent lack of awareness (e.g. Camps, 2003), but also that high levels of reported awareness typically result in significantly improved performance on L2 outcome measures (e.g. Leow, 1997; Rosa and O'Neill, 1999).

Work in the field of cognitive psychology has sought to establish whether structural regularities underlying a set of stimuli can be acquired without conscious awareness on the part of the learner and subsequently be applied to a novel set of stimuli. In SLA, researchers have followed up the claim that such learning seems to be possible by studying the short-term acquisition of selected aspects of L2 morphosyntax and morphophonology in different training conditions. It was found that learners trained in explicit conditions involving input enhancement, explicit instruction in the rules underlying the targeted L2 aspects, or explicit instruction plus output practice outperformed learners trained in implicit conditions involving exposure to exemplars of the targeted L2 aspects. Learners in implicit conditions were either tasked with memorizing instances or answering meaning-focused comprehension questions. Outcome measures required learners to judge the grammaticality of both known and novel instances of the targeted L2 aspects. Even though there was evidence of learning in all conditions, participants trained in explicit conditions showed better generalizable knowledge than participants trained in implicit conditions (e.g. N. Ellis, 1993; Robinson, 1997).

It is evident that studies investigating the effects of different levels of learner awareness as well as studies carefully manipulating learning conditions in order to encourage either implicit or explicit learning are of interest to instructed SLA. L2 instruction in the classroom often draws on explicit knowledge, thus facilitating or perhaps even actively encouraging explicit learning. A recent meta-analysis of the findings arising from 49 empirical studies conducted between 1980 and 1998 focused on this close relationship between explicit learning and instruction. Norris and Ortega (2001) analyzed the cumulative results of experimental and quasi-experimental research investigating the effects of various kinds of L2 instruction. They concluded that L2 instruction is more effective than mere exposure to L2 input. Thus, instructed learners consistently, significantly, and substantially outperformed learners who had received no instruction of any kind.

When different types of instruction were compared with one another, it was found that treatments involving an explicit focus on the rule-like nature of L2 structures were most effective. However, Norris and Ortega (2001) also report that the nature of the outcome measures used appear to have favored learners in explicit instructional conditions. Typical outcome measures consisted of grammaticality judgments or other similarly constrained response formats; by contrast, extensive communicative use of the L2 was not required. Norris and Ortega's (2001) analysis suggested that effect sizes were directly related to the type of outcome measure employed. Despite this caveat, though, the analysis also indicated that the nature of the outcome measures could not account for the magnitude of the cumulative differences between instructional treatments. In other words, while effect sizes were influenced by the type of outcome measure used, the observed effects themselves were robust.

Potentially biased outcome measures aside, (quasi-)experimental studies comparing explicit and implicit instruction or explicit and implicit learning conditions are subject to a further caveat: the typically short duration of the treatment, which often lasts only one or two hours in total. Implicit learning is gradual and slow; for implicit learning to be effective, extensive, long-term exposure to input is needed. By contrast, explicit learning is fast and efficient, although it requires effort and is constrained by the limits of focused attention and working memory. The short but intensive treatment administered in experiments can therefore be expected to work in favor of explicit learning and against implicit learning (DeKeyser, 2003).

The interaction of explicit and implicit processes

As both explicit and implicit learning contribute to the development of L2 proficiency, the question arises whether explicit and implicit processes can interact. Is there an interface between explicit and implicit knowledge? Recent reviews of the topic (Dörnyei, 2009; R. Ellis, 2005) distinguish three so-called interface positions: a strong-interface, a weak-interface, and a no-interface position.

According to the no-interface position, explicit and implicit knowledge and learning are entirely independent from each other; acquisition of one type of knowledge has no influence on the acquisition of the other type of knowledge. Conversely, the strong-interface position argues that explicit knowledge can gradually be converted into implicit knowledge through long-term practice.

Currently, most scholars appear to subscribe to a weak-interface position. This position assumes that explicit and implicit knowledge are separate and distinct, but that explicit learning can nonetheless impact on implicit learning and vice versa. It is argued that the explicit registration of linguistic material facilitates its subsequent implicit fine-tuning. Explicit output practice creates further input for the learner and thus provides additional opportunities for implicit learning. Explicit knowledge in the form of pedagogical grammar rules or in the form of corrective feedback can increase the accuracy of, or fill gaps in, a learner's implicit knowledge (Dörnyei, 2009). When listening to or reading the L2, the learner may deliberately and consciously analyze the input. When speaking or writing the L2, the learner may deliberately and consciously construct an utterance or monitor and self-correct the output of their implicit system (N. Ellis, 2005).

In the weak-interface position, explicit and implicit processes "meet" in working memory, at the point when we are consciously aware of an experience: "Consciousness *is* the interface, and like consciousness, the interface is dynamic: it happens transiently during conscious processing, but the influence upon implicit cognition endures thereafter" (N. Ellis and Larsen-Freeman, 2006: 569, emphasis in original). The weak-interface position is in keeping with the statement that the key to effective L2 learning appears to be the successful cooperation of explicit and implicit systems (Dörnyei, 2009).

See also: attention, awareness, declarative memory and knowledge, implicit learning, instructed SLA, noticing hypothesis

References

Camps, J. (2003). Concurrent and retrospective verbal reports as tools to better understand the role of attention in second language tasks. *International Journal of Applied Linguistics, 13* (2) 201–21.

DeKeyser, R.M. (2003). Implicit and explicit learning. In C.J. Doughty and M.H. Long (eds), *The Handbook of Second Language Acquisition*. Malden, MA: Blackwell.

——(2005). What makes learning second-language grammar difficult? A review of issues. *Language Learning*, *55*(s1), 1–25.

Dörnyei, Z. (2009). *The Psychology of Second Language Acquisition*. Oxford: Oxford University Press.

Ellis, N.C. (1993). Rules and instances in foreign language learning: Interactions of explicit and implicit knowledge. *European Journal of Cognitive Psychology*, *5*(3), 289–318.

——(1994). Consciousness in second language learning: Psychological perspectives on the role of conscious processes in vocabulary acquisition. *AILA Review*, *11*, 37–56.

——(2005). At the interface: Dynamic interactions of explicit and implicit language knowledge. *Studies in Second Language Acquisition*, *27*(2), 305–52.

Ellis, N.C. and Larsen-Freeman, D. (2006). Language emergence: Implications for applied Linguistics. *Applied Linguistics*, *27*(4), 558–89.

Ellis, R. (2004). The Definition and Measurement of L2 Explicit Knowledge. *Language Learning*, *54*(2), 227–75.

——(2005). Measuring implicit and explicit knowledge of a second language: A psychometric study. *Studies in Second Language Acquisition*, 27(2), 141–72.

——(2006). Modelling learning difficulty and second language proficiency: The differential contributions of implicit and Explicit Knowledge. *Applied Linguistics*, *27*(3), 431–63.

Hulstijn, J.H. (2005). Theoretical and empirical Issues in the study of implicit and explicit second-language learning: Introduction. *Studies in Second Language Acquisition*, *27*(2), 129–40.

Hulstijn, J.H. and de Graaff, R. (1994). Under what conditions does explicit knowledge of a second language facilitate the scquisition of implicit knowledge? A research proposal. *AILA Review*, *11*, 97–112.

Leow, R.P. (1997). Attention, awareness, and foreign language behavior. *Language Learning*, *47*, 467–505.

Norris, J.M. and Ortega, L. (2001). Does type of instruction make a difference? Substantive findings from a meta-analytic review. *Language Learning*, *51*(1) 157–213.

Robinson, P. (1997). Generalizability and automaticity of second language learning under implicit, incidental, enhanced, and instructed conditions. *Studies in Second Language Acquisition*, *19*, 223–47.

Roehr, K. and Gánem-Gutiérrez, G.A. (2009). Metalinguistic knowledge: A stepping stone towards L2 proficiency? In A. Benati (ed.), *Issues in Second Language Proficiency*. London: Continuum.

Rosa, E. and O'Neill, M.D. (1999). Explicitness, Intake, and the Issue of Awareness. *Studies in Second Language Acquisition*, *21*, 511–56.

Schmidt, R.W. (1990). The Role of Consciousness in SLA Learning. *Applied Linguistics*, *11*, 129–58.

——(2001) Attention. In P. Robinson (ed.), *Cognition and Second Language Instruction*. Cambridge: Cambridge University Press.

Further reading

DeKeyser, R. M. (2003). Implicit and explicit learning. In C.J. Doughty and M.H. Long (eds), *The Handbook of Second Language Acquisition*. Malden, MA: Blackwell. (An informative review summarizing research on implicit and explicit learning.)

Ellis, N.C. (2005). At the interface: Dynamic interactions of explicit and implicit language knowledge. *Studies in Second Language Acquisition*, *27*(2), 305–52. (An in-depth discussion of how explicit and implicit knowledge interact in language learning.)

Ellis, R. (2004). The definition and measurement of L2 explicit knowledge. *Language Learning*, *54* (2), 227–75. (A comprehensive review of the state of research on explicit knowledge in language learning.)

Ellis, R., Loewen, S., Elder, C., Erlam, R., Philp, J. and Reinders, H. (2009). *Implicit and Explicit Knowledge in Second Language Learning*. Bristol: Multilingual Matters. (A collection of recent empirical studies on implicit and explicit language learning.)

Schmidt, R.W. and Hulstijn, J.H. (eds) (1994). *AILA Review 11: Consciousness in Second Language Learning*. (A volume of insightful contributions from some of the leading researchers in implicit and explicit language learning.)

Eye tracking

Aline Godfroid

Michigan State University

Eye tracking, the online registration of language users' eye movements, is a research methodology that is used to examine visual attention and other cognitive processes in a variety of areas, including scene perception, visual search, and language processing. Eye-tracking data inform researchers with regard to two basic components of eye movement behavior: (i) eye *fixations* (i.e. where and for how long a subject is looking) and (ii) *saccades* or eye movements (i.e. where the eyes move next).

The use of eye-tracking data in psychologically oriented research rests on the assumption that overt attention (as manifested by the exact eye location) and covert attention are tightly linked, in other words, that there is a close relationship between the eyes and the mind (Rayner, 2007). This principle has been termed the "eye-mind link" (Reichle *et al.*, 2006: 4). It embodies the idea that cognitive processing is a major determinant of when and where the eyes move during complex task performance.

The emphasis of this article will be on the use of eye tracking to study second-language (L2) written input processing. By way of background, we will first review some general findings about eye movements from first-language (L1) reading research.

Basic characteristics of eye movements

During reading, saccades move the eyes across the text in order to optimize the ocular resolution of the word that is in the focus of attention and, thus, process it more efficiently. Starting from the point of fixation, the visual field can be functionally divided into three regions: (i) the *fovea* spans the central 2° of vision where visual acuity is best. It is flanked by (ii) the *parafovea*, which extends out 3° to either side of the foveal region and then turns into (iii) the *periphery*. As we move away from the center of the visual field, visual acuity steadily declines. Although most processing is done while foveating word *n*, preliminary processing of the non-fixated word *n + 1* also occurs when word *n* is easy (i.e. high-frequency, short and/or predictable; e.g. Henderson and Ferreira, 1990). This phenomenon is known as *parafoveal processing* or *parafoveal preview*.

In some cases, identification of word *n + 1* is completed during parafoveal preview, which eliminates the need to fixate it next. Approximately 15 percent of content words and about 65 percent of function words are skipped during normal L1 reading (Rayner, 2007). In contrast, words may also be fixated more than once (i.e. refixated), for example because they are low frequency or syntactically ambiguous. The number of fixations on a given target is expressed in the measure *fixation count*. Higher fixation counts typically give rise to higher values for the different eye fixation time measures, which we present in the next section.

Fixation time measures

Fixation times are collected for predefined *interest areas*, which correspond to words, phrases or any other elements in the visual display. *First fixation duration* is the duration of the first fixation made in an interest area when that area is encountered during "forward" (in English: left-to-right) reading for the first time (i.e. during first pass). While the eventual fixation count for a given interest area is irrelevant to first fixation duration, the related variable *single fixation duration* is only reported for those interest areas that receive exactly one fixation.

Also with respect to first-pass reading, *gaze duration* represents the sum of all fixations made in an interest area before the eyes leave that area. First fixation duration and gaze duration are the two most frequently reported dependent variables in psycholinguistic eye-movement research (Rayner, 1998).

In some cases, the eyes exit an interest area or skip it initially but *regress* to it later on. The sum of the fixations made during this second pass equals *second pass time*. *Total time*, then, is defined as the sum of all fixations over first, second, and possibly further passes.

Eye movements and L2 written language processing

A handful of L2 eye-tracking studies have looked into syntactic ambiguity resolution by bilinguals. In a prototypical study of this kind, participants are presented with an ambiguous target structure in the L2 (e.g. an ambiguous subject pronoun; Roberts *et al.*, 2008) for which the preferred resolution differs between the participants' L1 and their L2. By comparing fixation times between trials that enforce an L2 interpretation and trials which impose an L1 reading, researchers can investigate the influence of the L1 on L2 processing (or *vice versa*; cf. Dussias and Sagarra, 2007), with higher fixation times taken to be indicative of less preferred processing strategies.

In the area of L2 vocabulary acquisition, Siyanova-Chanturia *et al.* (2011) have compared native and nonnative speakers' fixation times for figuratively used idioms (e.g. "*ring a bell*" = *sound familiar*), literally used idioms (e.g. "*ring a bell*" = *sound a small metal object*) and matched novel phrases. Their analyses revealed that the well-known processing advantage for idioms in the L1 did not hold in the L2, with non-native speakers actually taking longer to read figuratively used idioms than literally used ones.

Finally, eye tracking has also been proposed as one of the means for measuring learners' "noticing" (Schmidt, 1995) of new forms in written L2 input. In a study of incidental vocabulary learning while reading, Godfroid *et al.* (forthcoming) found learners' noticing of novel lexical items to be enhanced when these items were followed by a known synonym (e.g. *paniplines or boundaries*). Also, the total reading time for a novel word was shown to be a predictor of subsequent vocabulary recognition, which is consistent with the idea that attention is beneficial for learning.

In sum, eye tracking is still a novel methodological procedure in second language acquisition research, which may explain why it has been employed for such different ends and purposes. However, the millisecond precision and high spatial accuracy of the technique make it a very valuable research tool (cf. Frenck-Mestre, 2005). Current lines of research are likely to be further developed and new alleys explored, as SLA researchers' familiarity with eye tracking increases.

See also: attention, awareness, measuring and researching SLA, psycholinguistics of SLA, reading, Noticing Hypothesis

References

Dussias, P.E. and Sagarra, N. (2007). The effect of exposure on syntactic parsing in Spanish-English bilinguals. *Bilingualism: Language and Cognition*, *10*, 101–16.

Frenck-Mestre, C. (2005). Eye-movement recording as a tool for studying syntactic processing in a second language: A review of methodologies and experimental findings. *Second Language Research*, *21*, 175–98.

Godfroid, A., Boers, F. and Housen, A. (in press) An eye for words: Gauging the role of attention in L2 vocabulary acquisition by means of eye tracking. *Studies in Second Language Acquisition, 35*.

Henderson, J.M. and Ferreira, F. (1990). Effects of foveal processing difficulty on the perceptual span in reading: Implications for attention and eye movement control. *Journal of Experimental Psychology: Learning, Memory, and Cognition*, *16*, 417–29.

Rayner, K. (1998). Eye movements in reading and information processing: 20 years of research. *Psychological Bulletin*, *124*, 372–422.

——(2007) Attention and eye movements in reading, scene perception, and visual search. *Bartlett Lecture to the Experimental Psychology Society*, Edinburgh, July.

Reichle, E.D., Pollatsek, A. and Rayner, K. (2006). *E-Z* Reader: A cognitive-control, serial-attention model of eye-movement behavior during reading. *Cognitive Systems Research*, *7*, 4–22.

Roberts, L., Gullberg, M. and Indefrey, P. (2008). Online pronoun resolution in L2 discourse: L1 influence and general learner effects. *Studies in Second Language Acquisition*, *30*, 333–57.

Schmidt, R.W. (1995). Consciousness and foreign language learning: A tutorial on the role of attention and awareness in learning. In R.W. Schmidt (ed.), *Attention and Awareness in Foreign Language Learning*. Honolulu: University of Hawai'i.

Siyanova-Chanturia, A., Conklin, K. and Schmitt, N. (2011). Adding more fuel to the fire: An eye-tracking study of idiom processing by native and nonnative speakers. *Second Language Research, 27,* 251–72.

F

Factor analysis (FA)

Jenifer Larson-Hall
University of North Texas

Factor analysis (FA) is a data reduction technique used to shrink a large number of variables into coherent categories. Suppose that a researcher gives 17 tests of proficiency to a group of learners of Chinese, including grammar, listening, and speaking tests. Using factor analysis the researcher might be able to reduce the 17 tests to two or three categories of language proficiency. The researcher would then need to examine which tests fell into which categories and assign an appropriate label for the abilities underlying the performance on the tests (such as grammar vs vocabulary abilities). The factors that emerge from the analysis are relatively independent of each other, but the variables within each factor are closely related.

FA is different from other types of statistical tests in that it does not seek to test a hypothesis (such as whether groups are different), but rather explore the existing data and generate hypotheses about patterns. Data snooping is encouraged here! FA is often used in creating tests, where a large number of questions can be reduced and grouped into different clusters of factors. Within SLA, many studies of literacy, reading, and writing employ FA to find factors which form the basis of these abilities.

FA encompasses a number of related reduction techniques, of which the best known are Principal Components Analysis and FA. Both of these approaches also have exploratory and confirmatory techniques. Exploratory FA is useful in theory development and confirmatory FA is used for theory testing—exploratory techniques simply allow factors to emerge while confirmatory techniques test different models to see which provide better fits (Thompson and Daniel, 1996).

Sample sizes used in FA must be large for the analysis to have validity. Tabachnik and Fidell (2001: 588) say 300 cases is "comforting" although 150 may be sufficient if solutions with factor loadings on several variables are high (over 0.80). Note that one would not know whether factor loadings were high until they had already done the analysis, in which case an insufficient number of cases might be too late to remedy!

The requirements for an FA are too complicated to spell out, but here are a few basics that should be followed in any analysis:

- intercorrelations between all variables should have several correlations over $r = 0.3$ (otherwise an FA approach is not advised)
- factors should have an Eigenvalue above 1
- factor loadings should be reported
- rotation may be used after factor loadings are extracted to maximize correlations
- the proportion of variance accounted for by the factors should be listed
- each factor should have a label

Reports should also explain what type of FA and rotation, if any, was used. There are an overwhelming number of choices for doing FA using statistical software but Tabachnik and Fidell (2001) note that most researchers start by using PCA and varimax rotation, then may experiment with different extraction techniques and rotation types. This can result in different solutions even with the same data.

See also: Analysis of Variance (ANOVA), correlation, effect size, mixed methods research, quantitative research, variance

References

Tabachnick, B.G. and Fidell, L.S. (2001). *Using Multivariate Statistics*, 4th edn. Boston, MA: Allyn and Bacon.

Thompson, B. and Daniel, L.G. (1996). Factor analytic evidence for the construct validity of scores: A historical overview and some guidelines. *Educational and Psychological Measurement*, *56*(2), 197–208.

Further reading

Isemonger, I.M. (2007). Operational definitions of explicit and implicit knowledge. *Studies in Second Language Acquisition*, *29*, 101–18. (Explores issues of FA in relation to a specific language acquisition study.)

Pallant, J. (2001). *SPSS Survival Manual*. Philadelphia, PA: Open University Press (Chapter 15 is a quick introduction to how to do PCA using SPSS.)

Thompson, B. (2004). *Exploratory and Confirmatory Factor Analysis*. Washington, DC: APA. (A thorough book covering FA.)

Flooding

Joanna White
Concordia University

Input flooding is a type of Focus-on-Form (FonF) that provides learners with positive evidence about what is possible in the second language (L2). There is no metalinguistic teaching or corrective feedback. The flooding can be provided by the teacher or the pedagogical materials, or both, and can be spoken or written. The objective of this implicit input enhancement technique is to increase the salience of a target linguistic form by increasing its frequency in the input. The assumption is that the increased frequency will attract the learners' attention and promote incidental learning of a form known to pose difficulties without seeming unnatural or disrupting meaning-based activities. While an input flood includes more instances of the target form than would normally be available in the instructional input, the optimal ratio of targets to total number of words in the text is unspecified in the research literature.

The pedagogical activities in input flood studies vary, depending on the form in focus and the instructional context. Since input flooding is typically combined with other FonF techniques like textual enhancement, rule presentation, corrective feedback, and output practice, the impact of the flood itself is difficult to determine. Three studies that have investigated input flooding as an independent variable are discussed here. The first two were conducted in intact intensive ESL classes with francophone learners in upper elementary school grades. The third was carried out in university ESL composition classes with learners from a variety of L1 backgrounds.

Spada and Lightbown (1999) explored how an input flood might help learners move along a developmental continuum of interlanguage stages in their acquisition of English questions. Children in five classes were exposed to hundreds of correct stage 4 and stage 5 English questions (Pienemann *et al.*, 1988) during a variety of classroom activities such as games, surveys, projects, and questionnaires. The intervention lasted for two weeks, for a total of eight hours out of a total of about 40 hours of English instructional time. Post-tests showed that on oral tasks, learners progressed through the acquisition sequence slowly and without skipping stages. Those at stage 2 on the pre-test advanced one stage, while most learners at stage 3 did not. Learners made more progress on written preference tasks, showing evidence of knowledge of stage 4 and 5 forms. However, they were more likely to accept subject-verb inversion with pronouns than with nouns, the former allowed, the latter disallowed, in

French. Spada and Lightbown compared these findings with earlier research (1993) that included corrective feedback on question formation. They speculated that the input flood was too implicit to help learners identify the gaps in their knowledge and that they would have benefited more from contrastive metalinguistic information.

Trahey and White (1993) saturated the input with adverbs of manner (e.g. quietly, carefully) and frequency (e.g. always, usually), which they knew to be uncommon in communicative classrooms. The learning problem for French L1 learners was that French allows SVAO word order, but not SAVO, whereas English allows SAVO but not SVAO. The activities included listening to stories, reading poems, answering comprehension questions, matching sentences to pictures, and playing a variety of games. They were designed to provide positive evidence showing learners all the possible word orders that English allows, but they did not draw learners' attention to the absence of SVAO in English. Two input flood groups had one hour of adverb activities each day for two weeks, for a total of ten hours. Learners' performance on written correction and preference tasks, as well as sentence manipulation and oral production measures, revealed that the input flood led to a significant increase in use and acceptance of SAVO order, but it did not cause the SVAO order to disappear. Trahey (1996) found that one year later, learners' knowledge of adverb placement had not changed. It appears that both positive and negative evidence were necessary to promote interlanguage development.

Williams and Evans (1998) investigated two linguistic features in their input flood study: participial adjective pairs, such as boring and bored, which learners produced incorrectly, and passive verbs, which were rare in the instructional materials and in learners' written output. The input flood activities were integrated into two regular instructional units. In a unit on education, the written input was modified to contain three times the number of participial adjectives as had occurred in the original texts. The passive flood was part of a unit on cultural values in which the active verbs in an interview questionnaire were changed to passives. Pre-test to post-test gains of the flood group were compared to those of a control group working with unflooded versions of the same materials and to a third group receiving explicit instruction and corrective feedback on the target forms. The findings for the two target features differed. For passives, the input flood was as effective as explicit instruction, and both had a greater impact on learning than the control condition. For participial adjectives, explicit instruction was more effective than input flooding or unflooded texts. The researchers attributed the differential development of the two forms to the fact that the rule for participial adjectives is relatively easy to explain, and learners were able to apply it on the post-test tasks. Passives, on the other hand, are more complicated, and if learners were not ready to make use of explicit instruction on this feature, the input flood was equally effective.

One advantage of input flooding is that it is an unobtrusive type of input enhancement which does not disrupt communicative activities. However, as Sharwood Smith (1991) noted, input enhancement is "engineered" by the teacher, and attempting to increase the saliency of a form in the instructional input does not guarantee that learners will notice it, especially if the pedagogical activity requires them to focus on meaning. The characteristics of the L2 feature, cross-linguistic influence, and the developmental readiness of individual learners are other factors that can have an impact on the effectiveness of input flooding.

See also: attention, developmental sequences, Focus on Form (FonF), implicit learning, input enhancement, positive and negative evidence

References

Pienemann, M., Johnston, M. and Brindley, G. (1988). Constructing an acquisition-based procedure for second language acquisition. *Studies in Second Language Acquisition*, *9*, 92–122.

Sharwood Smith, M. (1991). Speaking to many minds: On the relevance of different types of language information for the L2 learner. *Second Language Research*, *7*, 118–32.

Spada, N. and Lightbown, P. (1993). Instruction and the development of questions in the L2

classroom. *Studies in Second Language Acquisition*, *15*, 205–21.
——(1999). Instruction, L1 influence and developmental readiness in second langauge acquisition. *Modern Language Journal*, *83*, 1–22.
Trahey, M. (1996). Positive evidence in second language acquisition: Some long-term effects. *Second Language Research*, *12*, 111–39.
Trahey, M. and White, L. (1993). Positive evidence and preemption in the second language classroom. *Studies in Second Language Acquisition*, *15*, 181–204.
Williams, J. and Evans, J. (1998). What kind of focus and on which forms? In C. Doughty and J. Williams (eds), *Focus on Form in Classroom Second Language Acquisition*, pp. 139–55. New York: Cambridge University Press.

Further reading

Book flood studies

Book floods are input floods that aim to increase comprehensible input in the second language classroom. They do not target specific linguistic features, but rather aim to promote general proficiency. In the studies reviewed by Elley, the primary goal is to increase literacy; for Lightbown, and to some extent for Elley, the book flood is an alternative to a more traditional/audiolingual pedagogical approach.

Elley, W. (1991). Acquiring literacy in a second language. *Language Learning*, *41*, 374–411.
——(2000). The potential of book floods for raising literacy levels. *International Review of Education*, *46*, 233–55.
Lightbown, P. (1992). Can they do it themselves? A comprehension-based ESL course for young children. In J.S. J.R. Courchene, C. Therien, and J. Glidden (ed.), *Comprehension-based language teaching: Current trends*, pp. 353–70. Ottawa: University of Ottawa Press.

Typographical (textual) input enhancement studies

Typographical enhancement is a type of input flood in which specific linguistic features are made more salient through increased frequency combined with techniques such as enlargement, bolding, italicizing, and/or underlining. The article by Han reviews a number of textual enhancement studies. The chapter by J. White reports a study combining textual enhancement with a book flood.

Han, Z. (2008). Textual enhancement of input: Issues and possibilities. *Applied Linguistics*, *29*, 597–618.
White, J. (1998). Getting the learners' attention: A typographical input enhancement study. In C. Doughty and J. Williams (eds), *Focus on form in classroom second language acquisition*, pp. 85–113. Cambridge: Cambridge University Press.

Fluency

Norman Segalowitz
Concordia University

Fluency is a key component of second language (L2) ability. Yet, there is considerable debate on how best to operationally define *fluency*. Different authors define it differently; moreover, in some languages (e.g., French, Russian) the exact equivalent to the term *fluency* does not even exist. All this creates a challenge for researchers interested in L2 fluency: what exactly is one studying and how does one communicate this to colleagues from other linguistic communities? For most, the qualities that make speech fluent include fast speech rate, and the relative absence of undue hesitations, pausing, repetitions, and repairs. For some, fluent speech is also speech that is accurate, appropriate, and natural in terms of the conventions of language use. Each of these features, of course, may or may not prove to be linked to the others in a meaningful way, and so the utility of the construct *fluency* may itself be open to question. Important discussions regarding what may be meant by fluency can be found in De Bot (1992), Fillmore (1979), Kormos (2006), Levelt (1989), Kaponen and Riggenbach (2000), Schmidt (1992), and Segalowitz (2010).

Nevertheless, as with many scientific constructs, as work progresses in the field, the original natural language term has come to take on a more precise meaning within the scientific community. While it might be overly optimistic to claim there is consensus, for purposes of this overview a useful formulation may be the following. Goldman-Eisler (1968), in addressing fluency issues in first language (L1) production, wrote, "the complete speech act is a dynamic process, demanding the mobilization in proper sequence of a series of complex procedures and is the temporal integration of serial phenomena" (p. 6). And further, she wrote, "Hesitation is thus shown to be an indicator of the internal act of generating information ... " (p. 57). In other words, behind the oral manifestations of fluency (the temporal characteristics of fluency) lie cognitive processes responsible for creating an utterance with its specific features of fluency. Taking a cue from Goldman-Eisler (1968) and others, a working definition of L2 fluency can be synthesized as follows:

> L2 fluency refers to the "features of L2 oral performance that serve as reliable indicators of how efficiently the speaker is able to mobilize and temporally integrate, in a nearly simultaneous way, the underlying processes of planning and assembling an utterance in order to perform a communicatively acceptable speech act".
>
> (Segalowitz, 2010: 47)

An important feature of the above definition is that it distinguishes between two sets of temporal phenomena, those of the observable features of oral performance—the *utterance fluency*—and those of the underlying processes responsible for the utterance—the *cognitive fluency*. Thus, the emerging definition of L2 fluency is one that identifies separate, operationally definable phenomena linking a speaker's utterance fluency to an underlying cognitive fluency.

Utterance fluency

Most research on L2 utterance fluency has focused on the features of oral production that differentiate more from less fluent speakers. In such research it is necessary, of course, to first independently distinguish the more fluent from the less fluent speakers in the first place. Many studies have attempted to do this by comparing L2 speakers with more versus less experience in the target language (e.g., by age of acquisition; length of study; number of years exposed to the language). Others have examined judgments by native-speaking listeners of the fluency levels the L2 users have attained (Derwing *et al.*, 2004). Other studies have compared L2 speech against the presumably more fluent L1 speech. The methods just enumerated may have intuitive appeal, but it is easy to see that they differ from one another in important ways and therefore may yield different results. Moreover, in order to avoid circularity, a method of distinguishing speakers of different fluency levels is needed that is independent of the speech features being examined. We will return to this problem below.

As for how to operationally define utterance fluency, the list of potentially interesting speech features to look at is relatively long (see, for example, summaries in Ellis and Barkhuizen, 2005; Kormos, 2006; Luoma, 2004). These features include speech rate (syllables per second), its inverse (milliseconds per syllable), silent pauses per minute (where silent pause has been defined variously as 200 msec, 250 msec or 400 msec of silence), filled pauses per minute (pauses containing ums, ers, etc.), mean length of runs (mean number of syllables between silent pauses), dysfluencies per minute (repetitions, restarts, repairs), measures of speech rhythm, etc. Studies by Lennon (1990), Towell *et al.* (1996), and by Iwashita *et al.* (2008) (among others) illustrate the range of measures used. A feature of the fluency literature is that no one measure has emerged as *the* best way to characterize fluency.

One important point to emerge from studies of utterance fluency is that it is necessary to take into account how the speech samples have been elicited. It turns out that it matters whether speech samples are taken from spontaneous speech, from reading samples, from story retelling, from tasks allowing or preventing pre-planning of what to say, from tasks that are simple versus complex, etc. This is because speakers can use many different strategies to cope with the demands of communicating in a non-fluent language (Dörnyei and Kormos,1998). The issue of how speech fluency characteristics reflect the way the speech sample was obtained and the speakers' strategies is itself an important topic of study (see, for example, Robinson, 2001; Tavakoli and Skehan, 2005). The findings from such studies further complicate the study of fluency because they show that manifestations of fluency reflect, to a great degree, the conditions under which the speech samples have been obtained.

As a result of the multiplicity of operational definitions of utterance fluency, and the performance variability resulting from different speech elicitation techniques, and also the small sample sizes used in many studies, research on fluency has not always yielded consistent results. Part of the problem no doubt has been the large effort required to obtain measures from large speech samples, including the need to transcribe spoken samples and to make spectrographic measurements of various temporal phenomena by hand. Because of the costs, the study of large samples of participants can be impractical in many situations. However, in recent years new techniques have emerged that allow for some automated measurements of utterance features (Cucchiarini *et al.*, 2002; De Jong and Wempe, 2009) and this may help to make the study of large samples more feasible.

One recent study using automated speech analysis software (e.g., De Jong *et al.*, 2009) revealed that speakers' measures of speech rate and of silences were strongly correlated between the L1 and L2. This result underscores the need to keep in mind that, when searching for reliable and valid measures of L2 utterance fluency, there are individual differences between L2 speakers that do not reflect differences in proficiency as such but general individual differences in speaking. These differences will be reflected in the corresponding features of the speakers' L1. Thus, a good way to take this source of individual differences into account, and hence to remove a source of unwanted noise in the L2 fluency data, is to use L1 speech data as a control measure. To date, very few studies have attempted to do this, and this might be one of the reasons for the poor record of consistency between studies of L2 fluency (an issue that merits addressing in future research).

As mentioned earlier, most research on L2 utterance fluency is premised on the assumption that there exist underlying cognitive processes that are responsible for speech production. These processes themselves unfold over time; therefore they too can be characterized in terms of fluency considerations. This cognitive fluency is discussed in the next section.

Cognitive fluency

To date little empirical research has aimed at identifying the features of cognitive fluency that might underlie utterance fluency. Some theoretical accounts of speech production, however, do provide a basis for thinking about this. For example, the model of speech production proposed by Levelt (1989; De Bot, 1992) identifies a number of cognitive processes that underlie speech production. These include conceptualizing what is to be said, formulating the ideas to be expressed in a manner compatible with the specific requirements of the language, accessing word meanings from a mental lexicon, and encoding the information into appropriate phonological and articulatory codes. If any of these cognitive processing activities is highly inefficient, this could result in reduced oral fluency. A challenge for researchers, then, is to operationalize these various aspects of the underlying cognitive system in such a way that allows measuring cognitive fluency and relating this to utterance fluency.

One approach to doing this is to assess how *automatic* a given cognitive process is, under the assumption that automatic processing contributes to fluent utterance production. Here there are different ways of operationalizing what is meant by *automatic*, including speed of processing, stability of processing, the ballistic (unstoppable) nature of the processing, the effortlessness of it, etc. Another feature of cognitive fluency that is relevant to oral fluency is the flexibility of the underlying cognitive processing—that is, the ability to refocus attention as needed in order to keep the flow of speech smooth and fluid. Flexibility of attention control complements the automaticity of processing; the cognitive system underlying speech production should be both highly efficient (able to execute processing in a fast, effortless, automatic manner) but not so rigidly as to be unable to correct itself or change direction without compromising the fluidity of speech.

One aspect of cognitive processing where automaticity may be important for utterance fluency is lexical access—linking words with meanings. Clearly, word-finding problems can compromise oral fluency. Other relevant considerations are the ability to process grammatical structure efficiently and to process fixed or formulaic expressions. Each of these can be characterized in terms of fluency—that is, in terms of their temporal characteristics—and this can be done in different ways (processing speed and stability; priming effects; etc.). This leads to a situation similar to the one described earlier for utterance fluency. Although any given measure of cognitive fluency may be of intrinsic interest to the researcher (e.g., the efficiency of word finding), a way needs to be found to help researchers decide which of the many possible measures of cognitive fluency will truly contribute to a larger theory of L2 fluency.

Bringing cognitive and utterance fluency together

Which of the many potentially useful measures of utterance and cognitive fluency should be the focus of research? Segalowitz (2010: 167) proposes two criteria for retaining measures for a theory of L2 fluency:

(1) Retain those measures of L2 utterance fluency (e.g., speech rate, hesitation rate) and of L2 cognitive fluency (e.g., processing speed, processing stability) that are L2 specific—that is, that take into account corresponding L1 baseline values.
(2) Retain those measures of L2-specific utterance fluency that are linked to L2-specific measures of cognitive fluency.

This proposal reflects the idea that utterance fluency reflects a speaker's underlying cognitive fluency in the planning and assembling of communicative acts. The idea is that in this way a set of operationally well-defined measures will emerge that can be said to usefully define what is meant by L2 fluency.

The bigger picture

Recent research results suggest that fluency and its attainment is more than just a matter of the efficient operation of cognitive and speech processes. One can ask questions about the neurophysiological mechanisms involved in L2 production fluency. Social, attitudinal, and motivational factors also enter into the picture (Dörnyei and Ushioda, 2009). In fact, it may be more appropriate to approach L2 fluency in a way that goes beyond piecemeal studies of cognitive and articulatory issues and to adopt a broader cognitive science framework (Segalowitz, 2010). This has the potential of raising new and exciting questions related to L2 skill acquisition in different contexts, in different populations, with implications for L2 fluency instruction.

See also: automaticity, intelligibility in SLA, pausology and hesitation phenomena, speech rate, units for analyzing L2 speaking, units for analyzing L2 writing

References

Cucchiarini, C., Strik, H. and Boves, L. (2002). Quantitative assessment of second language learners' fluency: Comparisons between read and spontaneous speech. *Journal of the Acoustical Society of America, 111*, 2862–73.

De Bot, K. (1992). A bilingual production model: Levelt's 'Speaking' model adapted. *Applied Linguistics, 13,* 1–24.

De Jong, N.H., Schoonen, R. and Hulstijn, J. (2009). *Fluency in L2 is Related to Fluency in L1.* Paper presented at the Seventh International Symposium on Bilingualism (ISB7), Utrecht, The Netherlands.

Derwing, T., Rossiter, M., Munro, M. and Thompson, R. (2004). Second language fluency: Judgments on different tasks. *Language Learning, 54,* 655–79.

Dörnyei, Z. and Kormos, J. (1998). Problem-solving mechanisms in L2 communication: A psycholinguistic perspective. *Studies in Second Language Acquisition*, *20*, 349–85.

Dörnyei, Z. and Ushioda, E. (eds) (2009). *Motivation, Language Identity and the L2 Self.* Bristol: Multilingual Matters.

Ellis, R. and Barkhuizen, G. (2005). *Analysing Learner Language.* Oxford: Oxford University Press.

Fillmore, C. (1979). On fluency. In Fillmore, C., Kempler, D. and Wang, W.S.-Y. (eds), *Individual Differences in Language Ability and Language Behavior*, pp. 85–101. New York: Academic Press.

Goldman-Eisler, F. (1968). *Psycholinguistics Experiments in Spontaneous Speech.* London: Academic Press.

Iwashita, N., Brown, A., McNamara, T. and O'Hagan, S. (2008). Assessed levels of second language speaking proficiency: How distinct? *Applied Linguistics*, *29*, 24–49.

Kaponen, M. and Riggenbach, H. (2000). Overview: Varying perspectives on fluency. In H. Riggenbach (ed.), *Perspectives on Fluency*, pp. 5–24. Ann Arbor, MI: University of Michigan Press.

Kormos, J. (2006). *Speech Production and Second Language Acquisition.* Mahwah, NJ: Lawrence Erlbaum Associates.

Lennon, P. (1990). Investigating fluency in EFL: A quantitative approach. *Language Learning*, *40*, 387–417.

Levelt, W. (1989). *Speaking: From Intention to Articulation.* Cambridge, MA: MIT Press.

Luoma, S. (2004). *Assessing Speaking.* Cambridge, MA: Cambridge University Press.

Robinson, P. (2001). Task complexity, task difficulty, and task production: Exploring interactions in a componential framework. *Applied Linguistics*, *22*, 27–57.

Schmidt, R. (1992). Psychological mechanisms underlying second language fluency. *Studies in Second Language Acquisition*, *14*, 357–85.

Segalowitz, N. (2010). *Cognitive bases of second language fluency.* New York: Routledge.

Tavakoli, P. and Skehan, P. (2005). Strategic planning, task structure, and performance testing. In R. Ellis (ed.), *Planning and Task Performance in a Second Language*, pp. 239–73. Amsterdam: John Benjamins.

Towell, R., Hawkins, R. and Bazergui, N. (1996). The development of fluency in advanced learners of French. *Applied Linguistics*, *17*, 84–119.

Focus on Form (FonF)

Shinichi Izumi
Sophia University

"Focus on form" (Long, 1991, 2009; henceforth referred to as FonF) is a pedagogical approach that aims to integrate attention to meaning and attention to form in second/foreign language (L2) learning. The notion of FonF arose out of a historical context in which two dominant approaches to language teaching—traditional language teaching characterized with predominant focus on language forms on the one hand (termed "focus on form*s*" by Long, 1991), and the communicative language teaching characterized with the main focus on transaction of meaning on the other hand (termed "focus on meaning")—have been tried and failed in many places in the world to produce balanced L2 users who are simultaneously fluent, accurate, and versatile.

To rectify the problems in these earlier approaches, Long (1991) introduced the notion of FonF, which attempts to capture the strengths of the communicative approach while dealing with its limitations. The FonF approach tries to ensure the provision of plenty of comprehensible input and interaction in L2 learning, while at the same time incorporating grammar teaching in supplementary and often incidental ways. Instead of having an extended separate grammar explanation and exercises, FonF tries to integrate attention to form and meaning by drawing the learner's attention to form in the course of communicative language use. FonF does not assume that language acquisition occurs instantaneously after the teaching, nor does it assume that learners can pick up language forms without any external help. The expectation is that if the teaching intervention is introduced in such a way as to respect the learner's social, psycholinguistic, and emotional/affective needs, it is likely to promote L2 learning even if the immediate outcome may not be realized as the learner's target-like use of the form.

Cognitive rationale for FonF

An important cognitive rationale of FonF is succinctly summarized by Doughty (2001: 211) as follows:

> The factor that consistently distinguishes FonF from the other pedagogical approaches is the requirement that FonF involves learners' briefly and perhaps simultaneously attending to form, meaning, and use during one cognitive event. This kind of joint processing is claimed to facilitate the cognitive mapping among form, meaning, and use that is fundamental to language learning.

In other words, by drawing the learner's attention to form as it is used to convey meaning in context, FonF encourages learners to make the necessary connections among the three essential elements of language—form, meaning, and functions—without which the development of learners' communicative competence cannot be expected. In terms of the allocation of the learner's focal attention, such join processing is often referred to as "noticing" and "noticing the gap" (Schmidt, 2001). Based on her review of literature on memory and language processing, Doughty (2001) argues that L2 learners, though maturationally constrained, are nevertheless psycholinguistically equipped with abilities to enable such processing, which makes FonF a cognitively viable intervention procedure for post-puberty L2 learners.

The ideas of joint processing and noticing are in sharp contrast to the foregoing two dominant approaches to language teaching. In FonFs, forms are highlighted first for analysis, and meaning and functions are added, though not always, in later activities. Such isolation of forms, while arguably making focused analysis easier, renders the establishment of form-meaning-function connections difficult. Focus on meaning, on the other hand, gives the foremost priority to meaning and communicability, and form is considered learnable without any assistance from the teacher—an assumption that is not well supported by existing SLA research on adult IL development. In both of these approaches, the notion of learner-initiated noticing is either completely ignored or belittled, or otherwise wrongly equated with teacher's teaching.

FonF taxonomy

In its original formulation (Long, 1991; Long and Robinson, 1998), FonF is conceptualized as mainly a reactive attempt on the part of the teacher (or other learners) to draw learners' attention to forms which cause problems in comprehension or production. In this sense, FonF is considered to occur only incidentally, not intentionally, as language problems should arise in the course of natural communication, rather than by means of the teacher's imposition of a predetermined linguistic agenda in teaching. While the basic stance remains that any attempt to teach form must be situated within communicative contexts of some kind, recent research on FonF has resulted in the broadening of the FonF procedures.

Doughty and Williams (1998), for instance, included proactive approaches to FonF to allow for the prior teacher/researcher preparation of FonF activities to introduce in class. Focusing on overall lesson planning, they also distinguished integrated FonF and sequential FonF. While the former is closely aligned to Long's original formulation of FonF as described above, the latter allows for the option of prior isolated teaching of form so that any subsequent attempt to FonF during communication can occur without excessive interruption or disruption of processing of meaning. The sequential FonF is claimed to be particularly suited for forms that are semantically lightweight and highly redundant in communication. However, since such FonF can easily cross over to FonF*s*, it may be necessary to contextualize advance teaching of the form, make it brief, and employ subsequent tasks that allow for natural use of the form. Ultimately, the effectiveness of different FonF procedures, it is argued, is contingent on whether joint attention to form, meaning, and function can be effectively achieved during language processing.

To cope with the proliferation of FonF definitions, Williams (2005) argued that three features are particularly important for any pedagogical attempts to qualify as FonF: (1) an overall emphasis on the communicative meaning, (2) a brief diversion from that emphasis on communication to focus on language form, and (3) a problem-based trigger for the diversion, be it a real-time problem-trigger or based on the teachers' prior analysis and assessment of learners' IL profiles. With these core features in mind, Williams classified FonF in four stages in terms of advance planning, the timing at which FonF takes place, the specification of the instructional target, and the initiator of FonF, as shown in Figure 3.

While useful such classification may be in capturing diversity of FonF, it should be kept in mind that not all FonF types can be classified so neatly and in a mutually exclusive manner. For example, planned reactive FonF with general focus (b) and spontaneous reactive teacher-initiated FonF (e) may not be so clearly distinguishable, as the definition can differ depending on what one considers to be advance planning. In addition, learner-initiated FonF (f) is classified here as spontaneous FonF, but in actuality planned proactive FonF with general focus (d) can often be learner-initiated as well. There is also another issue regarding whether it is appropriate to label preemptive FonF as FonF because teacher's anticipation of learner problems may not in fact be problems for the learners at all.

FonF types introduced above can further be distinguished at the level of the actual technique to be used, in terms of how explicitly to draw the learner's attention to form. FonF techniques often categorized as implicit include recasts (the provision of correct reformulation of the learner's error), input flood (artificial increase of the targeted form in the input given to learners), and input enhancement

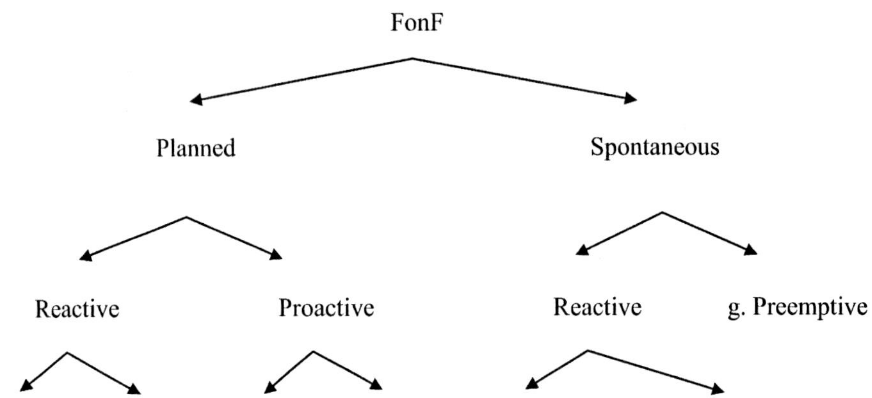

Examples of activities/instructional sequences:

a. Narrow recasting of preselected form(s)
b. General recasting of learner error
c. Enhanced input, focused communicative tasks
d. Increased planning time for task; negotiation tasks
e. Scattershot response to learner error, e.g., "mini-lessons" in response to learner problems
f. Learner requests for assistance
g. Mini-lessons in anticipation of learner problems

Figure 3 FonF taxonomy (adapted from Williams, 2005: 677)

(typographical or intonational highlighting of the targeted form in the input). Explicit FonF includes such techniques as brief grammar explanation, processing instruction (the use of receptive activity that requires attention to the target form for its completion), and consciousness-raising tasks (the use of inductive grammar tasks). Some techniques are situated somewhere in the middle, such as prompts (requests to learners to correct their own errors), and interaction enhancement (a combination of prompt and recast in an interactive sequence). As can be imagined, explicit-implicit distinction here is a matter of degree and relative explicitness/implicitness can be manipulated according to the learners' needs.

Empirical research on FonF

Since Long first introduced the notion of FonF, a number of empirical studies have been conducted to investigate the effectiveness of FonF. Following Williams' taxonomy outlined in Figure 3, research on planned reactive FonF includes those that investigated recasts and prompts (e.g., Doughty and Varela, 1998; Lyster, 2007). Research on planned proactive FonF includes investigation on input flood, input enhancement, and processing instruction (e.g., Lee and Huang, 2008; VanPatten, 2004; Williams and Evans, 1998). Also included in this category are studies on pretask planning, task repetition, insertion of brief grammar explanation in otherwise content- or task-based lessons, and output enhancement (e.g., Ellis, 2005; Izumi, 2002; Samuda and Bygate, 2008). Although the number is still limited compared to planned FonF, research on spontaneous FonF is increasing (e.g., Ellis *et al.*, 2001). With regard to integrated and sequential FonF, although conceptual research has been reported (e.g., Spada and Lightbown, 2008), empirical investigation into their relative effectiveness is still scarce. There are also studies that investigated the interaction of FonF techniques and timing of FonF (e.g., Williams and Evans, 1998).

While many of these primary studies found effectiveness of FonF procedures, particularly noteworthy is the study by Norris and Ortega (2000), which synthesized previous effect-of-instruction studies by means of statistical meta-analysis. It was found that FonF treatments in which form and meaning are somehow integrated in teaching are superior to FonF*s* treatments in which form and meaning are separated. Furthermore, for both FonF and FonF*s*, explicit teaching produced higher learning outcomes than implicit teaching. These results were corroborated by a recent meta-analyitic study by Spada and Tomita (2010). This study, though not specifically concerned with FonF per se, found that explicit instruction was more effective than implicit instruction for both simple and complex features, not only in explicit-knowledge tests, but also in tests that arguably tapped learners' implicit knowledge. Another recent meta-analytic study by Li (2010), however, showed that the effect of implicit corrective feedback was more durable than that of explicit feedback, the former showing greater improvement over time, and the latter showing signs of attenuation.

Further issues in FonF

For further investigation of FonF, future research needs to pursue rigorous research methodology as suggested by Norris and Ortega (2000), particularly with regard to the use of longitudinal study designs that employ assessment instruments that tap learners' implicit L2 knowledge. In addition, given that L2 learning involves complex processes that elude capture as an either-or issue, future research needs to examine complex interactions that likely exit between many relevant variables. The following are some representative issues:

- What kind of forms should be chosen as targets for FonF? How should FonF procedures or techniques differ for different forms? What might be principled criteria that can be used in such decision making?
- What is the best timing for FonF in the overall curriculum? Which forms should be targeted for FonF and at what point in the curriculum? How should the timing decision be made in an informed manner?
- Which FonF procedure is more effective, integrated FonF or sequential FonF? How do

their effectiveness differ depending on the choice of form?

- What is the relationship between FonF procedures/techniques and differences among learners (e.g., ages, aptitude, proficiency)? How can FonF take learner differences into account in systematic ways?
- What is the relationship between FonF procedures/techniques and types of learning-outcome measures used (e.g., explicit and implicit tests)?

FonF research has started only relatively recently. Research is needed not only for those conducted in second-language or immersion situations, but also in foreign-language contexts where language learning opportunities are more restricted, yet the need for proficiency in an L2 is increasingly becoming important in the globalized world.

See also: corrective feedback, form-meaning relations, input enhancement, instructed SLA, Noticing Hypothesis, recasts

References

Doughty, C. (2001). Cognitive underpinnings of focus on form. In P. Robinson (ed.), *Cognition and Second Language Instruction*, pp. 206–57. Cambridge: Cambridge University Press.

Doughty, C. and Varela, E. (1998). Communicative focus on form. In C. Doughty and J. Williams (eds), *Focus on Form in Classroom Second Language Acquisition*, pp. 114–38. New York: Cambridge University Press.

Doughty, C. and Williams, J. (1998). Pedagogical choices in focus on form. In C. Doughty and J. Williams (eds), *Focus on Form in Classroom Second Language Acquisition*, pp.197–261. New York: Cambridge University Press.

Ellis, R. (ed.) (2005). *Planning and Task Performance in a Second Language*. Amsterdam: Benjamins.

Ellis, R., Basturkmen, H. and Loewen, S. (2001). Learner uptake in communicative ESL lessons. *Language Learning, 51*, 281–318.

Izumi, S. (2002). Output, input enhancement, and the Noticing Hypothesis: An experimental study on ESL relativization. *Studies in Second Language Acquisition, 24,* 541–77.

Lee, S.-K. and Huang, H.-T. (2008). Visual input enhancement and grammar learning: A meta-analytic review. *Studies in Second Language Acquisition, 30*, 307–31.

Li, S. (2010). The effectiveness of corrective feedback in SLA: A meta-analysis. *Language Learning, 60,* 309–65.

Long, M. (1991). Focus on form: A design feature in language teaching methodology. In K. de Bot, C. Kramsch, and R. Ginsberb (eds), *Foreign Language Research in Crosscultural Perspective*, pp. 39–52. Amsterdam: John Benjamins.

Long, M. (2009). Methodological principles for language teaching. In M.H. Long and C.J. Doughty (eds), *The Handbook of Language Teaching*, pp. 373–94. Malden, MA: Wiley-Blackwell.

Long, M. and Robinson, P. (1998). Focus on form: Theory, research, and practice. In C. Doughty and J. Williams (eds), *Focus on Form in Classroom Second Language Acquisition*, pp. 15–41. New York: Cambridge University Press.

Lyster, R. (2007). *Learning and Teaching Language through Content: A Counterbalanced Approach.* Amsterdam: John Benjamins.

Norris, J. and Ortega, L. (2000). Effectiveness of L2 instruction: A research synthesis and quantitative meta-analysis. *Language Learning, 13*, 417–528.

Samuda, V. and Bygate, M. (2008). *Tasks in second language learning.* London: Palgrave.

Schmidt, R. (2001). Attention. In P. Robinson (ed.), *Cognition and Second Language Instruction*, pp. 3–32. Cambridge: Cambridge University Press.

Spada, N. and Lightbown, P. (2008). Form-focused instruction: Isolated or integrated. *TESOL Quarterly, 42,* 181–207.

Spada, N. and Tomita, Y. (2010). Interactions between type of instruction and type of language feature: A meta-analysis. *Language Learning, 60,* 263–308.

VanPatten, B. (ed.) (2004). *Processing Instruction: Theory, Research, and Commentary*. Mahwah, NJ: Lawrence Erlbaum.

Williams, J. (2005). Form-focused instruction. In E. Hinkel (ed.). *Handbook of Research in Second Language Teaching and Learning*, pp. 671–91. Mahwah, NJ: Laurence Erlbaum.

Williams, J. and Evans, J. (1998). What kind of focus and on which forms? In C. Doughty and J. Williams (eds), *Focus on Form in Classroom Second Language Acquisition*, pp. 139–55. New York: Cambridge University Press.

Further reading

DeKeyser, R. (2007). *Practice in a Second Language: Perspectives from Applied Linguistics and Cognitive Psychology*. Cambridge: Cambridge University Press. (A good overview of the notion of practice in instructed SLA from different perspectives.)

Doughty, C. (2003). Instructed SLA: Constraints, compensation, and enhancement. In Doughty, C. and Long, M. (eds), *The Handbook of Second Language Acquisition*, pp. 256–310. Malden, MA: Blackwell. (The author discusses the role of instruction in SLA and suggests a research agenda for future empirical studies.)

Doughty, C. and Williams, J. (eds) (1998). *Focus on Form in Classroom Second Language Acquisition*. New York: Cambridge University Press. (The first collection of important empirical, as well as conceptual, studies on FonF.)

Long, M. (2007). *Problems in SLA*. Mahwah, NJ: Laurence Erlbaum. (A critical overview and analysis of important issues in SLA, with particularly relevant chapters on negative feedback and tasks in language teaching.)

Van den Branden, K., Bygate, M. and Norris, J. (2009). *Task-based Language Teaching: A Reader*. Amsterdam and Philadelphia, PA: John Benjamins. (An excellent collection of must reads on TBLT and FonF.)

Form-meaning connection (FMC)

Jessica Williams
University of Illinois at Chicago

Form-meaning connection (FMC) is both a process and the result of that process. The process takes place at the syntax–semantics interface, where learners need to determine the meanings that should be mapped onto forms in the input. Learners are exposed to a wide range of forms in second language (L2) input, yet they only notice a portion of them and take still fewer of them in for further processing to eventually connect them with specific meanings.

In general, a form is considered to be a surface feature of a language or a surface manifestation of an underlying representation. These include lexemes, inflections, functors, or larger chunks of language to which meaning can be assigned, for example, *chair,-ing, that, dja* (as in *dja eat yet*?). Meaning includes referential, grammatical, or social meaning. For example, *chair* refers to a piece of furniture, *a* marks accusative case for animates in Spanish, and the choice of particular pronouns or honorifics in some languages signals respect or deference. As learners read or listen to L2 input, they generally focus on meaning first (VanPatten, 2011), trying to extract meaning from the stream of input and to assign meaning to the forms they have noticed.

These form-meaning mappings, or constructions, as they are sometimes called, may be simple or multiplex. In the simplest case, one surface form maps consistently onto one meaning. Frequently, however, the relationships are more complex, with one form encoding multiple and separate meanings For example, third person singular marking on verbs, plural marking on nouns, and genitive case marking on full nouns all map onto *–s* in English. Or, a form may encode multiple and overlapping meanings. For instance, habitual activity, ongoing action, and past time all map onto imperfect aspects in Romance languages, yet these meanings cannot be separated easily. There may also be multiple forms that encode similar or overlapping meanings; for example, *yesterday* and *–ed* both encode past time in English. These are examples of what Slabokova calls Simple Syntax-Complex Semantics, and they present significant acquisition "bottlenecks" (2008) for L2 learners. Finally, there is no guarantee that form-meaning mappings are the same in the first language (L1) and the L2. For example, case may map onto specific forms in the L1 but not in the L2. Such mismatches can pose further learning challenges.

In general, FMCs are not established completely in a single encounter with the relevant input. Rather, the process is incremental and recursive. It is useful, however, to think of the process in stages: the initial noticing of a construction in the input, and then subsequent processing, which itself takes place over time and multiple encounters. Once a form is noticed in the input, the next step is to establish the FMC, that is, learners attempt to attach the form to a meaning. As VanPatten (2011) points out, although noticing is an important first step, it may come to nothing if the noticed form is not connected to meaning. Learners may notice, while reading a text, for example, that *the* occurs frequently, but have no idea of its function. Further, because it is not crucial for establishing meaning, any memory trace left as a result of this encounter would likely be weak.

It is unlikely that the construction can be considered to be "acquired" even after this initial processing. It may be weak, or incomplete and/or nontargetlike. A weak FMC may facilitate comprehension at a subsequent encounter, thus strengthening the connection. However, it may not yet be available for production or subject to introspection. An incomplete FMC might encode less than the full meaning of a form. For example, a perfect verb form might be connected to a temporal meaning but not yet to the aspectual meaning(s) that are integral to the target FMC. Finally, learners may make incorrect FMCs, perhaps as a result of L1 influence, misinterpretation of the L2, or general language learning processes. An example of the last possibility is that learners might assign tense to a more salient lexical item, such as an adverb (e.g., *already*), instead of a less salient inflectional morpheme (*-ed*). This stage of strengthening and elaborating the connection is crucial to establishing more permanent FMCs.

Several factors may facilitate noticing and the subsequent processing, resulting in stronger and more complete FMCs. These factors fall into the following categories: (1) nature of the input, (2) learner characteristics, and (3) learning context and instruction. Second language acquisition theories vary in the importance that they place on these factors. Most acknowledge input as a key driver of acquisition. Frequency in the input is a significant factor in the noticing and processing of FMCs. Repeated exposure increases the chances of noticing and is also likely to strengthen FMCs. Rich and varied contexts of exposure are likely to lead to more complete FMCs (N. Ellis, 2006). Yet even a high level of frequency may not be enough to result in complete and target-like FMCs. DeKeyser (2005) maintains that some FMCs pose increased difficulty due to complexity of form or meaning, or of the connection between form and meaning. Some forms may lack perceptual salience or may not be noticed because mapping their meaning is not crucial to message comprehension, or because they are blocked by redundant and more salient forms (N. Ellis, 2006). In such cases, instruction may be useful, or in some cases, perhaps even necessary to direct learners to the target FMC.

Probably the most important learner factor that affects FMCs is the L1. Adult learners' linguistic systems are already optimally tuned—to the L1. L2 learners' prior L1 knowledge will affect their perception of salience and may at times prevent them from noticing and processing L2 forms in the input. N. Ellis (2006) calls this *learned attention*. For example, if L2 learners know from their L1 that adverbs are reliable markers of tense, they may ignore the intricacies of verbal inflections yet still communicate reasonably well. This may delay the noticing and acquisition of inflectional morphology. L2 proficiency has also been claimed as an important factor in a learner's ability to notice forms in the input and to connect them to target meanings. Low proficiency learners may be too focused on meaning to notice less salient forms. In addition, it has been suggested that learners must be developmentally ready to notice and process more advanced L2 forms (Ortega, 2007).

There are also likely to be individual learner differences, such as aptitude, motivation, and memory capacity, which affect FMCs. Working memory has been a focus of recent research on these individual differences. Working memory constrains noticing generally (Robinson, 2003). Learners with higher working memory capacity are more likely to notice novel forms in the input, in particular, those that are redundant, than learners with lower memory capacity (Sagarra, 2008). They are also more likely to notice and process interactional feedback relevant to FMCs (Mackey *et al.*, 2002).

Learners will eventually make many, if not most, FMCs in naturalistic learning contexts, but there is increasing evidence, from a variety of theoretical perspectives, that instruction can facilitate this process in a number of ways. The interaction approach suggests that encouraging interaction and negotiation in the classroom can lead learners to focus on form even in meaning-oriented classrooms. During form-focused episodes, learners may receive crucial information about FMCs (Mackey and Goo, 2007). During these episodes they may also receive feedback from peers, but more important, from teachers. Corrective feedback, in particular, can help them understand that they have made non-target-like connections and assist them in making more target-like FMCs (Loewen, 2011).

There are other ways in which instruction can be designed to facilitate FMCs. Input may be structured and input-processing activities can be designed to make forms and their meanings more salient and to prompt learners to attend to the connection between them (VanPatten, 2011). There is also increasing support for (1) more explicit approaches to instruction, even including the provision of L1 lexical equivalents and grammatical explanations, in which learners are specifically instructed about FMCs (DeKeyser, 2005; R. Ellis, 2006; Hulstijn, 2001; Slabakova, 2008) and (2) structured output activities, which push learner to retrieve and reflect on FMCs they have made (Swain, 2005; Toth, 2006). Retrieval, especially for production, is thought to further strengthen these connections.

See also: corrective feedback, explicit learning, Focus on Form (FonF), individual differences and SLA, input enhancement, learned inattention and blocking

References

DeKeyser, R. (2005). What makes second language learning difficult? A review of the issues. *Language Learning*, *55*, Supplement 1, 1–25.

Ellis, N. (2006). Cognitive perspectives on SLA: The associative-cognitive CREED. *AILA Review*, *19*, 100–121.

Ellis, R. (2006). Researching the effects of form-focussed instruction on L2 acquisition. *AILA Review*, *19*, 18–41.

Hulstijn, J. (2001). Intentional and incidental second language vocabulary learning: A reappraisal of elaboration, rehearsal and automaticity. In P. Robinson (ed.), *Cognition and second language instruction*, pp. 258–86. Cambridge: Cambridge University Press.

Loewen, S. (2011). The role of feedback. In S. Gass and A. Mackey (eds), *Handbook of Second Language Acquisition*. New York: Routledge.

Mackey, A. and Goo, J. (2007). Interaction research in SLA. In A. Mackey (ed.), *Conversational Interaction in Second Language Acquisition*, pp. 407–52. Oxford: Oxford University Press.

Mackey, A., Philp, J., Egi, T., Fujii, A. and Tatsumi, T. (2002). Individual differences in working memory, noticing of interactional feedback and L2 development. In P. Robinson (ed.), *Individual Differences and Instructed Language Learning*, pp. 181–209. Amsterdam: Benjamins.

Ortega, L. (2007). Sequences and processes in language acquisition. In M. Long and C. Doughty (eds), *Handbook of Language Teaching*, pp. 81–105. Oxford: Blackwell.

Robinson, P. (2003). Attention and memory during SLA. In C. Doughty and M. Long (eds), *Handbook of Second Language Acquisition*, pp. 631–78. Oxford: Blackwell.

Sagarra, N. (2008). Working memory and L2 processing of redundant forms. In S. Han (ed.), *Understanding Second Language Processes*, pp. 133–47. Clevedon: Multilingual Matters.

Slabakova, R. (2008). *Meaning in the Second Language*. Berlin: Mouton de Gruyter.

Swain, M. (2005). The output hypotheses: Theory and research. In E. Hinkel (ed.), *Handbook of*

Research in Second Language Teaching and Learning, pp. 471–83. Mahwah, NJ: Erlbaum.
Toth, P. (2006). Processing instruction and a role for output in second language acquisition. *Language Learning*, *56*, 319–85.
VanPatten, B. (2011). Input processing. In S. Gass and A. Mackey (eds), *Handbook of Second Language Acquisition*. New York: Routledge.

Formulaic language

Alison Wray
Cardiff University

Definitions of 'formulaic language' differ, but everyone agrees that it refers to strings of more than one word that are fluently retrieved and have a special status as a whole. There are several potential bases for this status, some more generally accepted than others. Least contentious is where there is no alternative within the linguistic system for understanding or producing the string than having learned it whole, because there is no grammatical rule to generate it (e.g. *all of a sudden*). Also generally recognised as formulaic are strings that have a semantic identity as a whole that is different from the combination of the individual words (e.g. *hold water*, meaning 'be plausible or convincing'). In such cases, it is assumed that the wordstring is learned, remembered and used as a combined lexical unit. Some such units are completely fixed, but many allow limited variation, such as the morphology of the verb.

Beyond these two types, the line is drawn in different places, depending on one's theoretical position on what language fundamentally is as a system. Three key positions will be briefly outlined here, because they have considerable impact on how one explains patterns of L2 learning, and on how one anticipates learners would respond to different kinds of learning experience.

One position, developed most strongly in Chomskian generative theory, is that language is an atomistic system. To account for the fact that language is highly flexible, permitting the expression of any idea one might think up, it is hypothezised that words are stored separately and combined as required, using grammatical rules. It follows that wordstrings will not be in the lexicon if it is possible to generate them by rule from their components. An objection to this view is that it requires the rules to do a great deal of work in accommodating often quite subtle oddities of meaning or grammar that belong to the wordstring. For instance, *all being well* would probably not be viewed as formulaic because its words are grammatically assembled without a major change of meaning—yet it is also idiomatic and has a rather specific function and nuance of meaning. Another objection is that the nativelike way of expressing an idea is not privileged over other possible ways of expressing it, for example, *Can I have your attention* over *Can I request/get your attention*; *Thanks for your help* over *Thank you for helping me*. There is nothing wrong with the latter examples, other than that native speakers would probably choose the former ones. Where other approaches would suggest that the former ones are either stored holistically, or are more deeply engrained as a habit because of their frequency, the atomistic approach may have to suggest very fine-grained differences in meaning between words, to account for how they combine into preferred combinations. As discussed below, there are grounds to think that adult L2 learners do apply this kind of atomistic system, thus explaining some of the problems they can have with expressing themselves idiomatically.

A second theoretical position is that there are indeed units and rules, but that they are not necessarily atomistic. By applying the simple criterion that humans prefer to work with larger units than smaller ones if possible, yet want the flexibility to express themselves according to their need, it becomes possible to suggest that, by adulthood, native speakers have stored a range of different types of lexical unit—morphemes, words and phrases—according to how they have needed to break down the language to make it flexible to just the extent needed and no more. Versions of this suggestion have been made by several linguists, including Sinclair (1991) and Wray (2002). An advantage of this view is that it more easily accounts for native speakers' preferred idiomatic ways of expressing ideas. However, it entails that each person develops their own representation of lexicon and rules that is driven by what they encounter and what they need to say—making it more difficult for linguists to talk with clarity about properties of 'the language'.

The third position considered here naturally accommodates formulaic language by conceiving a language system very different to the atomistic model, while holding that language knowledge is a consequence of what we encounter and what we need. Under the umbrella-term of 'usage-based' (e.g. Tomasello, 2003), several models can be recognized, including Emergent Grammar (Hopper, 1998), Pattern Grammar (Hunston and Francis, 2000) and Construction Grammar (Goldberg, 2006). The basic tenet is that wordstrings (including partly lexicalized frames with slots for variation) fall into patterns which carry their own meaning, even if novel words can be put into the slots. For instance, the pattern *VERB SOMEONE SOMETHING* is typically realized by verbs like *give*, but the meaning of the pattern is evidently stronger than the verb's core meaning, for example, *I picked him some carrots; She ran him a marathon*. We learn these patterns by observing them in the language of others. That is, we strengthen our internal representation of a pattern by encountering it repeatedly.

The role of frequency creates a significant interface between usage-based models and corpus linguistics. Those primarily working on corpora take particular interest in the relative frequency of different words and their combinations. Researchers such as Biber (e.g. Biber *et al.*, 1999) have made important observations about 'lexical bundles', wordstrings that are defined in terms of their size and frequency in a corpus. While there is a clear link between lexical bundles and the accounts of formulaicity offered by usage-based models, there is a less clear relationship between lexical bundles and the first two positions described above. The atomistic model does not recognize frequency as a primary determiner of how the language works. Meanwhile, the second position, being driven by the psychological and social needs of speakers and hearers, recognises frequency as only one of several potential determiners of formulaicity—others being the expression of identity, the effect on the hearer, and the burden of production or comprehension (Wray, 2002).

Formulaic language in 2LA

L2 teachers and learners are interested to know whether formulaic language should be targeted, avoided or left to look after itself. The account so far can help explain the different assumptions and views on the role of formulaic language in L2 learning. Individual differences between learners, plus the capacity of any one learner to display a range of behaviors, beliefs and attitudes over time (Dörnyei, 2010), mean that probably no single approach can be the complete answer to learning an L2 perfectly (even if 'perfectly' could be pinned down itself). Nevertheless, certain observations, outlined below, have been made about formulaic language in L2 learning. For a much more detailed evaluation of the evidence, see Wray (2002).

Children learning an L2 seem able to pick up wordstrings and their associated meanings and uses relatively easily (e.g. Wong Fillmore, 1976). This may be because children's focus is on social integration and controlling their environment—both can be achieved by talking the same way as other people (Wray, 2002). Adults, in contrast, seem more driven by learning the linguistic system and by expressing their existing identity, rather than developing a new, L2-based, one. They tend to focus on the language for its own sake, be conscious of their own shortcomings, and monitor what they say. Although this attention to the linguistic detail can mean they progress in an L2 faster than a child would (Murphy, 2010), it also encourages them to break down their input into small units for maximum flexibility, where children might keep them as wordstrings. As a result, it is children that are more likely to develop sensitivity towards the subset of idiomatic ways of expressing ideas.

Older children and teenagers seem to be caught halfway. Even by the age of nine or so, they may be too mature to learn an L2 without adopting a measure of the adult-like self-consciousness and attention to form that creates atomistic storage and processing (Wray, 2008). Yet they may be too immature to cope with form-focused instruction in a classroom. Myles *et al.* (1999) found that 12 year-olds learning French in a British school took a formulaic approach to their learning, and progressed only slowly in developing the flexibility of forms that would allow them to express a wider range of ideas. That is, they had the young child's slower, holistic approach, but, with only limited exposure to the L2, and with their more fully developed sense of identity, they were unable to benefit from the young child's capacity to enter into the world of L2 users. Meanwhile, they could not cope with examining the language more intellectually, as a grammatical and lexical system.

Adult language learners' tendency to produce wordstrings that are grammatical and meaningful but not idiomatic raises the question of they don't produce the idiomatic expressions used by native speakers. Possible reasons include that they have simply not encountered them (a frequency-based explanation), that they have encountered them but not recognized their significance, they find it psychologically difficult to 'sound nativelike' (consistent with the social and psychological approach to explaining formulaicity), or they have broken them down into their smallest constituents for storage, and thereby lost awareness of the privileged status of those particular formulations relative to other possible ones (an atomistic explanation).

The solution for teachers could be to help learners pay attention to the form of multiword strings, so as to maximize the benefit of each encounter, and help specific patterns become associated with their meaning and usage. However, a more general debate continues, about whether teachers should accept and support the atomistic learning style that seems most natural for adults, or attempt to prevent and supplement it with experiences more like those of the young child. See Wray (2008) and Cook (2010) for discussions of this question. One approach to narrowing the gap between a child's and an adult's approach is to encourage the accurate memorization and repetition of wordstrings, enabling learners to become their own source of nativelike input. In cultures with a tradition of text memorization within education, such as China and parts of Africa, schoolchildren, at least, do seem able to progress significantly in an L2 by means of extensive imitation and repetition of wordstrings (Ding, 2007), mastering excellent pronunciation, fluency and intonation, lexical and grammatical knowledge, and idiomaticity. However, this approach only works if learning is accompanied by clear understanding (e.g. Dahlin and Watkins, 2000). It is also time-consuming and can be boring and demotivating unless carefully managed. Memorisation is not popular in Western L2 school classrooms, other than in the context of drama, and its use with adult learners is minimal. However, repetition and drilling have been successfully used in some contexts, including the Hebrew Ulpan and its Welsh Wlpan equivalent. Although drilling, repetition and memorization are viewed by many as contrary to lessons learned in the 1970s and 1980s regarding the shortcomings of behaviorist and structuralist approaches compared with communicative ones, the recent increased recognition of focus-on-form(s) (Macaro, 2003) potentially offers scope for reconsidering their role (Ortega, 2009: 116).

At the intermediate and advanced levels, L2 learners can benefit from being introduced to the specific wordstrings that achieve key discourse functions, such as changing topic and hedging. Corpus research has established which wordstrings most commonly play these roles. One project (Simpson-Vlach and Ellis, 2010) has identified a body of useful expressions for the academic context which teachers can target for learning. More generic approaches to promoting multiword strings in language teaching include those of Nattinger and DeCarrico (1992), Lewis (1993) and Willis (1990).

Interest has also been taken in the formulaic language that non-native speakers produce in their own right—some of it nativelike, some deviating from a nativelike model, some derived from an L1 equivalent, and some indicating fossilisation of erroneous forms—see, for instance, the International Corpus of Learner English (ICLE) www.uclouvain.be/en-cecl-icle.html, which is an excellent resource for comparing and contrasting the formulaic language observed in different L2 learner groups.

See also: automaticity, chunking and prefabrication, construction learning, fossilization, frequency effects, rehearsal

under investigation. In a series of ten 'highly complex, cognitively demanding' tasks spanning a range of linguistic phenomena from phonetic perception to knowledge of proverbs administered to 41 adult near-native speakers of L2 Swedish, Abrahamsson and Hyltenstam (2009) found that none of the late learners (AoA less than 12 years old) performed within the native-speaker range on all tasks. This finding led them to conclude that nativelike ultimate attainment is never attained in principle (and in fact is also less common than assumed even among early learners), thus supporting some form of the critical period hypothesis.

Interestingly, however, there was no linguistic domain or task that was not mastered by at least one late learner in Abrahamsson and Hyltenstam's (2009) study. Other studies that have examined late second language learners' abilities across a variety of language domains have similarly found that at least some of the participants perform within the same range as that of native-speaker controls for at least some or even all of the particular areas tested (e.g., Birdsong, 2006; Birdsong and Molis, 2001; Marinova-Todd, 2003), prompting Birdsong (2006: 182) to propose the theoretically interesting hypothesis that no feature of an L2 is ultimately unlearnable. If that is the case, the burden of proof then rests on critical period proponents to explain why the biological inevitability of maturational constraints nonetheless appears to selectively spare different linguistic phenomena among some late learners even within the same L1 group; that is, why such constraints lead to fossilization for some features in some cases, but not for the same features in all cases. Moreover, one would presumably not like to claim that the aetiological source of the loss of capacity for phonemic discrimination, for instance, is the same as that for lack of knowledge of proverbs in the second language. Birdsong (2005: 321–22) further addresses this point, asking where we should draw the line ('Should every nit be picked?') in determining the scope of possibly defective L2 learning mechanisms.

Establishing fossilization

Because fossilization is defined as a permanent characteristic of (parts of) an endstate grammar (cf. *stabilization*—a related term that connotes the possibility of further development), it is worth examining how the researcher can establish whether an endstate has been reached and whether a particular L2 feature has indeed fossilized. Several researchers (e.g. Birdsong, 2004; Lardiere, 2007; Long, 2003) address this point in some detail. Ideally, a long-term longitudinal study design should be used. Birdsong (2004) observes that 'with a longitudinal approach one could safely conclude that similar performances over Times X, Y, Z, etc. reflect an asymptotic level of attainment' (p. 86).

Long (2003) points out the need to consider 'a constellation of methodological factors' such as longitudinal duration of the study, number and comparability of data samples, the learner's minimum years in the target language environment and extent of motivation and opportunity to learn the L2 and, all other things being equal, a researcher-preference for studying advanced-proficiency learners whose IL errors are more likely to be 'potentially permanent' than those of less proficient learners (p. 498). Long reports on his 16-year case study of Ayako, a native Japanese speaker who emigrated to the USA at the age of 22 and had lived in an L2 English-speaking environment for 37 years at the start of this study. Long notes that Ayako was happily acculturated to life in Hawai'i and used (Hawaiian Creole) English (HCE) 'more frequently' than Japanese (p. 508). Although her Japanese–American husband also spoke Japanese (having served as an interpreter during the US occupation of Japan), she used English with him about 75 per cent of the time, and also used English with her children, friends and neighbors and, before retiring, over the course of 20 years in the workplace. A battery of oral production tasks including free narrative, picture description, and elicited repetition were administered and then repeated 10 years later, and (minus the repetitions tasks) at one-to-two-year intervals after that. Data were supplemented with audiorecordings from family gatherings, verbatim notes on spontaneous utterances, and a written version of the bicycle story. Long observes that although Ayako speaks and understands HCE fluently in familiar and routinized situations, her speech exhibits 'lexical gaps, little complex syntax, and many persistent morphological errors' (p. 509).

Lardiere (2007) discusses a similar range of factors underlying the rationale for her choice of informant in a longitudinal case study on L2 ultimate attainment. That informant, Patty, was a native Chinese (Mandarin and Hokkien) speaker who emigrated to the USA at the age of 22, and had lived, studied and worked in the target-language (English) environment for about 10 years prior to the start of data collection. Patty was married to a native speaker of American English and spoke only English at home with her husband (and later, also her daughter), had completed undergraduate and masters degrees in American universities and was thus highly literate in English, was working in an exclusively English-speaking office environment in a managerial capacity, and participated in various cultural and professional activities nearly exclusively in English. Thus, the quantity and quality of both spoken and written environmental L2 input was not in question (cf. Sorace, 2003 who writes that persistent L2 optionality is a consequence of insufficient exposure to L2 data); nor was her integrative motivation (cf. Schumann, 1997). Naturalistic spoken and written data samples, in addition to elicited written and acceptability judgment task data, were collected over a period of about 15 years. The data revealed that rates of productive affixation for certain morphosyntactic features (such as regular past tense and non-past 3sg agreement marking on verbs) were low and virtually unchanged (fossilized) over that time. Patty did exhibit task-related variability, however; her rate of past tense marking, for example, was much higher in her written than spoken English.

Variability

Persistent variability or optionality is a widely attested phenomenon among the fossilized endstate grammars of late L2 learners. Grammatical morphemes in particular, such as inflectional affixes, determiners, auxiliaries, pronouns, etc. appear highly vulnerable to omission or occasional overgeneralization. This is a characteristic of developing L1 grammars as well, but native speakers eventually attain a stable endstate that generally precludes such variability except in appropriate conditioning environments. In contrast, variability in the L2 endstate often appears to be much more extensive and random, raising the issue of whether such a grammar can be considered truly "fossilized." Long (2003: 510) discusses this question in some detail, concluding that the diachronic and synchronic morphological variability observed in Ayako's production of HCE suggests that her L2 grammar had not even stabilized, much less fossilized. Lardiere (2007: 3–4) agrees that evidence of diachronic change over a certain developmental period may argue against fossilization, but that synchronic variability is often a persistent hallmark of the L2 endstate and is surely compatible with the notion of fossilization as divergence from nativelikeness.

A related and enduring question about endstate variability is whether it reflects L2 knowledge or performance. A full discussion of this issue is beyond the scope of this entry; however, some studies have argued that knowledge of a particular morphosyntactic feature may be reliably represented by an endstate learner whose morphophonological instantiation of it (in production and/or perception) is unreliable (e.g. Hopp, 2010; Lardiere, 1998, 2006; White, 2003).

What fossilizes?

It is not L2 *learners* that are fossilized, but rather particular aspects of their L2 grammars. Fossilization is not a global phenomenon but instead describes an L2 endstate that is non-convergent with that of native speakers in one or more particular domains. The domain may be specified broadly (such as knowledge of L2 phonology, morphology, syntax, etc.) or preferably more narrowly (such as knowledge of final obstruent devoicing, past-tense marking, or restrictions on *wh*-movement), but it must be specified. The choice of which particular domain to investigate is ideally informed by a learning theory or a linguistic theory (or both).

Hawkins (2000: 76), for example, coins the term *persistent selective fossilization* to refer to particular morphosyntactic properties of a target language that are not "used" by L2 speakers in a nativelike way, as opposed to others that are. The source of such selectivity, he proposes, may reside either in a computational or representational deficit among some components of the language faculty. He argues for a representational deficit account within a parameter-setting linguistic theory, in which particular parameterized feature values that are instantiated in the target language but not in the learner's native language(s) are permanently unavailable, resulting in selective fossilization.

Sorace (2011) proposes that language structures involving an interface between syntax and other cognitive domains are less likely to be acquired completely by even the most advanced endstate learners, resulting in non-convergence and 'residual optionality.' She points in particular to the interface between syntax and pragmatics, and the performance difficulty L2 speakers might have in integrating multiple sources of information in real time—that is, language processing inefficiency. An experimental study that tested this proposal is that of Hopp (2010), who examined highly proficient endstate learners of L2 German (all of whom had been extensively exposed to German for more than 10 years) who were L1 speakers of Dutch, English or Russian. He investigated their knowledge and processing of German scrambling, case and subject–verb agreement inflection. Among the near-native-proficiency learners, all three L1 groups showed nativelike convergence on an offline grammaticality judgment task and self-paced reading task, suggesting that they had acquired nativelike representations of inflectional marking as a means to correctly assign syntactic functions to scrambled sentences in German. On a speeded grammaticality judgment task, however, only the L1 Russian near-native group demonstrated nativelike performance on reliably detecting case-marking violations; the L1 Dutch and English near-native L2 groups did not. Hopp attributed this result to persistent L1 influence affecting L2 processing efficiency; that is, the processes used to access and compute grammatical features are less automatized than those of native speakers.

To summarize, these examples from the literature illustrate that fossilization cannot be applied as a global or monolithic descriptor for a non-convergent L2 grammar; rather, such divergence should be more finely articulated and rooted in some theory about the L2 endstate that makes the testing of specific hypotheses possible.

Concluding comments: is the term *fossilization* still necessary or even useful in SLA?

In the decades since its introduction in 1972, the construct of fossilization has largely been subsumed within the study of L2 ultimate attainment, which focuses on acquirability—what can be attained and what cannot be, ideally for a specific domain within a particular theoretical context under carefully circumscribed conditions. In this respect, the construct of fossilization is redundant and not necessary; Long (2003: 520), for instance, questions its reality as a distinct phenomenon, writing that unless it is clearly distinguished from 'mere non-nativelike proficiency' it can be expected to disappear from SLA theory. It may continue to be informally useful, however, to the extent that researchers must account for the obvious differences in outcome between native and non-native language acquisition.

See also: age effects in SLA, critical period hypothesis, Fundamental Difference Hypothesis, interlanguage, proficiency, theoretical constructs in SLA

References

Abrahamsson, N. and Hyltenstam, K. (2008). The robustness of aptitude effects in near-native second language acquisition. *Studies in Second Language Acquisition*, *30*, 481–509.

——(2009). Age of onset and nativelikeness in a second language: Listener perception versus linguistic scrutiny. *Language Learning*, *59*, 249–306.

Birdsong, D. (2004). Second language acquisition and ultimate attainment. In A. Davies and C. Elder (eds), *The Handbook of Applied Linguistics*, pp. 82–105. Malden, MA: Blackwell.

——(2005). Nativelikeness and non-nativelikeness in L2A research. *International Review of Applied Linguistics*, *43*, 319–28.

——(2006). Why not fossilization. In Z.-H. Han and T. Odlin (eds), *Studies of Fossilization in Second Language Acquisition*, pp. 173–88. Clevedon: Multilingual Matters.

Birdsong, D. and Molis, M. (2001). On the evidence for maturational constraints in second language acquisition. *Journal of Memory and Language*, *44*, 235–49.

Bley-Vroman, R. (1990). The logical problem of foreign language learning. *Linguistic Analysis*, *20*, 3–49.

DeKeyser, R.M. (2000). The robustness of critical period effects in second language acquisition. *Studies in Second Language Acquisition*, *22*, 499–533.

Ellis, R. (1985). *Understanding Second Language Acquisition*. Oxford: Oxford University Press.

Hawkins, R. (2000). Persistent selective fossilization in second language acquisition and the optimal design of the language faculty. *Essex Research Reports in Linguistics*, *34*, 75–90.

——(2001). The theoretical significance of Universal Grammar in second language acquisition. *Second Language Research*, *17*, 345–67.

Hopp, H. (2010). Ultimate attainment in L2 inflection: Performance similarities between non-native and native speakers. *Lingua*, *120*, 901–31.

Johnson, J. and Newport, E.L. (1989). Critical period effects in second language learning: the influence of maturational state on the acquisition of English as a second language. *Cognitive Psychology*, *21*, 60–99.

Lardiere, D. (1998). Case and tense in the 'fossilized' steady state. *Second Language Research*, *14*, 1–26.

——(2006). Establishing ultimate attainment in a particular second language grammar. In Z.-H. Han and T. Odlin (eds), *Studies of Fossilization in Second Language Acquisition*, pp. 35–55. Clevedon: Multilingual Matters.

——(2007). *Ultimate Attainment in Second Language Acquisition: A Case Study*. Mahwah, NJ: Lawrence Erlbaum.

Long, M.H. (1990). Maturational constraints on language development. *Studies in Second Language Acquisition*, *12*, 251–85.

——(2003). Stabilization and fossilization in interlanguage development. In C.J. Doughty and M.H. Long (eds), *Handbook of Second Language Acquisition*, pp. 487–535. Malden, MA: Blackwell.

Marinova-Todd, S.H. (2003). Comprehensive analysis of ultimate attainment in adult second language acquisition. Unpublished doctoral dissertation, Harvard University.

Schumann, J.H. (1997). *The Neurobiology of Affect in Language*. Malden, MA: Blackwell.

Selinker, L. (1972). Interlanguage. *International Review of Applied Linguistics*, *10*, 209–31.

Selinker, L. and Lamendella, J.T. (1978). Two perspectives on fossilization in interlanguage learning. *Interlanguage Studies Bulletin*, *3*, 143–91.

Sorace, A. (2003). Near-nativeness. In C.J. Doughty and M.H. Long (eds), *Handbook of Second Language Acquisition*, pp. 130–61. Malden, MA: Blackwell.

——(2011) Pinning down the concept of "interface" in bilingualism. *Linguistic Approaches to Bilingualism*, *1*(1), 1–33.

White, L. (2003). Fossilization in steady state L2 grammars: Persistent problems with inflectional morphology. *Bilingualism: Language and Cognition*, *6*, 129–41.

Frequency effects

Nick C. Ellis
University of Michigan

Usage-based approaches to SLA hold that we learn linguistic constructions while engaging in communication (Collins and Ellis, 2009; Ellis and Cadierno, 2009; Robinson and Ellis, 2008). The last 50 years of psycholinguistic research provides evidence of usage-based acquisition in its demonstrations that language processing is exquisitely sensitive to usage frequency at all levels of language representation from phonology, through lexis and syntax, to sentence processing (Ellis, 2002). Language knowledge involves statistical knowledge, so humans learn more easily and process more fluently high frequency forms and "regular" patterns which are exemplified by many types and which have few competitors. Psycholinguistic perspectives thus hold that language learning is the associative learning of representations that reflect the probabilities of occurrence of form-function mappings. Frequency is a key determinant of acquisition because "rules" of language, at all levels of analysis from phonology, through syntax, to discourse, are structural regularities which emerge from learners' lifetime unconscious analysis of the distributional characteristics of the language input.

Frequency determinants of construction learning

If constructions as form-function mappings are the units of language, then language acquisition involves inducing these associations from experience of language usage. Constructionist accounts of language acquisition thus involve the distributional analysis of the language stream and the parallel analysis of contingent perceptuo-motor activity, with abstract constructions being learned as categories from the conspiracy of concrete exemplars of usage following statistical learning mechanisms (Williams and Rebuschat, forthcoming) relating input and learner cognition.

Psychological analyses of the learning of constructions as form-meaning pairs is informed by the literature on the associative learning of cue-outcome contingencies where the usual determinants include such factors as: construction frequency, type-token frequency, Zipfian distribution, salience of form, prototypicality of meaning, and contingency of form-function mapping (Ellis and Cadierno, 2009). Consider each in turn:

Construction frequency

Frequency of exposure promotes learning and entrenchment. Learning, memory and perception are all affected by frequency of usage: the more times we experience something, the stronger our memory for it, and the more fluently it is accessed. The more recently we have experienced something, the stronger our memory for it, and the more fluently it is accessed (hence your reading this sentence more fluently than the preceding one). The more times we experience conjunctions of features, the more they become associated in our minds and the more these subsequently affect perception and categorization; so a stimulus becomes associated to a context and we become more likely to perceive it in that context. The power law of learning (Anderson, 2000) describes the relationships between practice and performance in the acquisition of a wide range of cognitive skills – the greater the practice, the greater the performance, although effects of practice are largest at early stages of learning, thereafter diminishing and eventually reaching asymptote.

Frequency of exposure also underpins statistical learning of categories. Human categorization ability provides the most persuasive testament to our incessant unconscious figuring or "tallying." We know that natural categories are fuzzy rather than monothetic. Wittgenstein's (1953) consideration of the concept *game* showed that no set of features that we can list covers all the things that we call games, ranging as the exemplars variously do from soccer, through chess, bridge, and poker, to solitaire. Instead, what organizes these exemplars into the *game* category is a set of family resemblances among these members – son may be like mother, and mother like sister, but in a very different way. And we learn about these families, like our own, from experience. Exemplars are similar if they have many features in common and few distinctive attributes (features belonging to one but not the other); the more similar are two objects on these quantitative grounds, the faster are people at judging them to be similar (Tversky, 1977). The greater the token frequency of an exemplar, the more it contributes to defining the category, and the greater the likelihood it will be considered the prototype. The operationalization of this criterion predicts the speed of human categorization performance – people more quickly classify as *birds* sparrows (or other average-sized, average-colored, average-beaked, average-featured specimens) than they do birds with less common features or feature combinations like geese or albatrosses (Rosch and Mervis, 1975; Rosch *et al.* 1976). Prototypes are judged faster and more accurately, even if they themselves have never been seen before – someone who has never seen a sparrow, yet who has experienced the rest of the run of the avian mill, will still be fast and accurate in judging it to be a bird. Such effects make it very clear that although people don't go around consciously counting features, they nevertheless have very accurate knowledge of the underlying frequency distributions and their central tendencies. Cognitive theories of categorization and generalization show how schematic constructions are abstracted over less schematic ones that are inferred inductively by the learner in acquisition.

Ellis' (2002) review illustrates how frequency effects the processing of phonology and phonotactics, reading, spelling, lexis, morphosyntax, formulaic language, language comprehension, grammaticality, sentence production, and syntax. That language users are sensitive to the input frequencies of these patterns entails that they must have registered their occurrence in processing. These frequency effects are thus compelling evidence for usage-based models of language acquisition which emphasize the role of input.

Type and token frequency

Token frequency counts how often a particular form appears in the input. Type frequency, on the other hand, refers to the number of distinct lexical items that can be substituted in a given slot in a construction, whether it is a word-level construction for inflection or a syntactic construction specifying the relation among words. For example, the 'regular' English past tense *-ed* has a very high type frequency because it applies to thousands of different types of verbs, whereas the vowel change exemplified in *swam* and *rang* has much lower type frequency. The productivity of phonological, morphological, and syntactic patterns is a function of type rather than token frequency (Bybee and Hopper, 2001). This is because: (a) the more lexical items that are heard in a certain position in a construction, the less likely it is that the construction is associated with a particular lexical item and the more likely it is that a general category is formed over the items that occur in that position; (b) the more items the category must cover, the more general are its criterial features and the more likely it is to extend to new items; and (c) high type frequency ensures that a construction is used frequently, thus strengthening its representational schema and making it more accessible for further use with new items. In contrast, high token frequency promotes the entrenchment or conservation of irregular forms and idioms; the irregular forms only survive because they are high frequency. These findings support language's place at the center of cognitive research into human categorization, which also emphasizes the importance of type frequency in classification.

Zipfian distribution

In natural language, Zipf's law (Zipf, 1935) describes how the highest frequency words account for the most linguistic tokens. Zipf's law states that the frequency of words decreases as a power function of their rank in the frequency table (the most frequent word occurring approximately twice as often as the second most frequent word, which occurs twice as often as the fourth most frequent word, etc.). If p_f is the proportion of words whose frequency in a given language sample is f, then $p_f \sim f^{-\gamma}$, with $\gamma \approx 1$. Zipf showed this scaling law holds across a wide variety of language samples. Subsequent research provides support for this law as a linguistic universal. Many language events across scales of analysis follow this power law: phoneme and letter strings, words, grammatical constructs, formulaic phrases, etc. Scale-free laws also pervade language structures, such as scale-free networks in collocation, in morphosyntactic productivity, in grammatical dependencies, and in networks of speakers, and language dynamics such as in speech perception and production, in language processing, in language acquisition, and in language change (Solé *et al.*, 2005). Scale-free laws pervade both language structure and usage. And not just language structure and use. Power law behavior like this has since been shown to apply to a wide variety of structures, networks, and dynamic processes in physical, biological, technological, social, cognitive, and psychological systems of various kinds (e.g. magnitudes of earthquakes, sizes of meteor craters, populations of cities, citations of scientific papers, number of hits received by websites, perceptual psychophysics, memory, categorization, etc.) (Kello *et al.*, 2010). It has become a hallmark of Complex Systems theory. Zipfian scale-free laws are universal. Complexity theorists suspect them to be fundamental, and are beginning to investigate how they might underlie language processing, learnability, acquisition, usage and change (Ellis and Larsen-Freeman, 2009). Usage-based theories argue that it is the coming together of these distributions across linguistic form and linguistic function that makes language robustly learnable despite learners' idiosyncratic experience and the "poverty of the stimulus" (Ellis and O'Donnell, in press).

Form (salience)

The general perceived strength of stimuli is commonly referred to as their salience. Low salience cues tend to be less readily learned. Research in associative learning demonstrates that selective attention, salience, expectation, and surprise are key elements in the analysis of all learning, animal and human alike. The amount of learning induced from an experience of a cue-outcome association depends crucially upon the salience of the cue and the importance of the outcome. Many grammatical meaning-form relationships, particularly those that are notoriously difficult for second language learners like grammatical particles and inflections such as the third person singular *–s* of English, are of low salience in the language stream. This can lead to blocking effects. For example, '*today*' is a stronger psychophysical form in the input than is the morpheme '*-s*' marking third person singular present tense, thus while both provide cues to present time, *today* is much more likely to be perceived, and *-s* can thus become overshadowed and blocked, making it difficult for second language learners of English to acquire (Ellis, 2006b).

Prototypicality of meaning

Categories have graded structure, with some members being better exemplars than others. In the prototype theory of concepts (Rosch and Mervis, 1975), the prototype as an idealized central description is the best example of the category, appropriately summarizing the most representative attributes of a category. As the typical instance of a category, it serves as the benchmark against which surrounding, less representative instances are classified. Ellis and Ferreira-Junior (2009) show that the verbs that naturalistic second language learners first use in particular verb-argument constructions are prototypical and generic in function (*go* for Verb Locative, *put* for Verb Object Locative, and *give* for Verb Object Object ditransitive).

Contingency of form-function mapping

Psychological research into associative learning has long recognized that while frequency of form is important, so too is contingency of mapping. Consider how, in the learning of the category of birds, while eyes and wings are equally frequently experienced features in the exemplars, it is wings which are distinctive in differentiating birds from other animals. Wings are important features to learning the category of birds because they are reliably associated with class membership; eyes are neither. Raw frequency of occurrence is less important than the contingency between cue and interpretation. Contingency, and its associated aspects of predictive value, information gain, and statistical association, is a strong determinant of construction learning too (Ellis, 2006a; MacWhinney, 1987).

Conclusions

The primary motivation of usage-based approaches is that we must bring together linguistic form, learner cognition, and usage. Saussure (1916) said, "To speak of a 'linguistic law' in general is like trying to lay hands on a ghost … Synchronic laws are general, but not imperative … [they] are imposed upon speakers by the constraints of common usage … In short, when one speaks of a synchronic law, one is speaking of an arrangement, or a principle of regularity" (pp. 90–91). The frequencies of common usage count in the emergence of regularity in SLA. Usage is rich in latent linguistic structure.

See also: cognitive linguistics and SLA, construction learning, learned inattention and blocking, prototypes, statistical learning, type and token frequency

References

Anderson, J.R. (2000). *Cognitive Psychology and its Implications*, 5th edn. New York: W.H. Freeman.

Bybee, J. and Hopper, P. (eds) (2001). *Frequency and the Emergence of Linguistic Structure*. Amsterdam: Benjamins.

Collins, L. and Ellis, N.C. (2009). Input and second language construction learning: frequency, form, and function. *Modern Language Journal*, *93*, Whole issue.

Ellis, N.C. (2002). Frequency effects in language processing: A review with implications for theories of implicit and explicit language acquisition. *Studies in Second Language Acquisition*, *24*, 143–88.

——(2006a). Language acquisition as rational contingency learning. *Applied Linguistics*, *27*, 1–24.

——(2006b). Selective attention and transfer phenomena in SLA: Contingency, cue competition, salience, interference, overshadowing, blocking, and perceptual learning. *Applied Linguistics*, *27*, 1–31.

Ellis, N.C. and Cadierno, T. (2009). Constructing a second language. *Annual Review of Cognitive Linguistics*, *7*, 111–290.

Ellis, N.C. and Ferreira-Junior, F. (2009). Construction Learning as a function of frequency, frequency distribution, and function. *Modern Language Journal*, *93*, 370–386.

Ellis, N.C. and Larsen-Freeman, D. (2009). Language as a complex adaptive system (Special Issue). *Language Learning*, *59*, Supplement 1.

Ellis, N.C. and O'Donnell, M. (in press). Statistical construction learning: Does a Zipfian problem space ensure robust language learning? In Williams, J. and Rebuschat, J. (eds), *Statistical Learning and Language Acquisition*. Berlin: Mouton de Gruyter.

Kello, C.T., Brown, G.D. A., Ferrer-I-Cancho, R., Holden, J.G., Linkenkaer-Hansen, K., Rhodes, T. and Van Orden, G.C. (2010). Scaling laws in cognitive sciences. *Trends in Cognitive Science*, *14*, 223–232.

Macwhinney, B. (1987). The Competition Model. In Macwhinney, B. (ed.), *Mechanisms of Language Acquisition*. Hillsdale, NJ: Erlbaum.

Robinson, P. and Ellis, N.C. (eds) (2008). *A Handbook of Cognitive Linguistics and Second Language Acquisition*. London: Routledge.

Rosch, E. and Mervis, C.B. (1975). Cognitive representations of semantic categories. *Journal of Experimental Psychology: General*, *104*, 192–233.

Saussure, F.D. (1916). *Cours de linguistique générale*. London: Duckworth.

Solé, R.V., Murtra, B., Valverde, S. and Steels, L. (2005). Language networks: their structure, function and evolution. *Trends in Cognitive Sciences*, *12*.

Williams, J. and Rebuschat, J. (eds) (forthcoming). *Statistical Learning and Language Acquisition*. Berlin: Mouton de Gruyter.

Wittgenstein, L. (1953). *Philosophical Investigations*. Oxford: Blackwell.

Zipf, G.K. (1935). *The Psycho-biology of Language: An Introduction to Dynamic Philology*. Cambridge, MA: The MIT Press.

Further reading

Ellis, N.C. (2002). Frequency effects in language acquisition. Special issue. *Studies in Second Language Acquisition*, *24* (2). (A special issue of SSLA featuring a target article on frequency effects in SLA, commentaries by leading researchers in the field, and a response.)

Collins, L. and Ellis, N.C. (eds) (2009). Input and second language construction learning: frequency, form, and function. Special issue. *Modern Language Journal*, *93* (3). (SLA research has always emphasised input. This special issue presents new ways of analyzing its latent properties.)

Ellis, N.C. and Cadierno, T. (eds) (2009). Constructing a second language. Special section. *Annual Review of Cognitive Linguistics*, *7*, 111–29. (Cognitive Linguistics is a branch of linguistics which analyzes language in terms of the concepts which underlie its forms. It denies any autonomous linguistic faculty or language acquisition device. Instead it holds that language is learned by general cognitive processes, that grammar can be understood in terms of conceptualization, and that language is learned from usage. The papers in this special section consider SLA from this perspective.)

Ellis, N.C. and Larsen-Freeman, D. (eds) (2009). *Language as a complex adaptive system*. Oxford: Wiley-Blackwell. (A special issue of *Language Learning* gathering experts from various language domains who share a CAS / Emergentist perspective.)

Robinson, P. and Ellis, N.C. (eds) (2008). *Handbook of cognitive linguistics and second language acquisition*. London: Routledge. (An edited collection bringing together leading researchers in Cognitive Linguistics and SLA to consider usage-based SLA.)

Functional categories

Pieter Muysken
Radboud University Nijmegen

Traditionally, grammarians have distinguished between function words and content words in the lexicon. Take a New York Times headline, "*Clandestine operatives have been sent into Libya to gather intelligence for military airstrikes and make contacts with rebels battling Col. Muammar el-Qaddafi's forces*." This sentence contains a number of content words, including proper names, nouns, adjectives, and verbs. There are also function words, such as auxiliaries, conjunctions, and prepositions. So far, so good. However, there are also some words, such as the "light verb" *make* and the locative preposition *into*, which have an inbetween status. These elements have a fairly abstract meaning, but not really a grammatical function. Finally, there are elements which do not occur as independent words but which clearly have a grammatical function, and in this sense resemble function words.

To avoid the need to distinguish between function words and grammatical endings linguists use the term "Functional Categories." These are used both for morpho-syntactic categories:

tense past / future / …
number singular / dual / …
person first / second / third / …

and for the words or word endings instantiating these categories:

pronouns *I* [first] / *you* [second], …
conjunctions *that* [finite] / *for-to* [non-finite], …
prepositions *of* [genitive] / *to* [dative], …
past participle *-ed,-en,-t*

Table 6 Content and function words

Content words	*In between content words and function words*	*Function words*	*Grammatical endings*
Muammar el-Qaddafi-'s	make	have	genitive *'s*
Libya	into	be-en	plural *–s*
col.(onel)		to	past participle *–en, -t*
intelligence		and	gerund *-ing*
airstrike-s		for	
contact-s		with	
operative-s			
rebel-s			
force-s			
military			
clandestine			
battl-ing			
sen-t			
gather			

The distinction between content words and functional categories is not exclusive to English. In fact, it is hard to conceive of a language without it. Take the following sentence in Bahasa Indonesia, for instance:

Kemarin Ali men-beli se-ekor kambing
Yesterday Ali AGF-buy one-CLAS goat
'Yesterday Ali bought a goat.'

Without too much doubt we can rank the elements in this sentence in terms of their "content" or "function" status:

Two more things should be noticed, however:

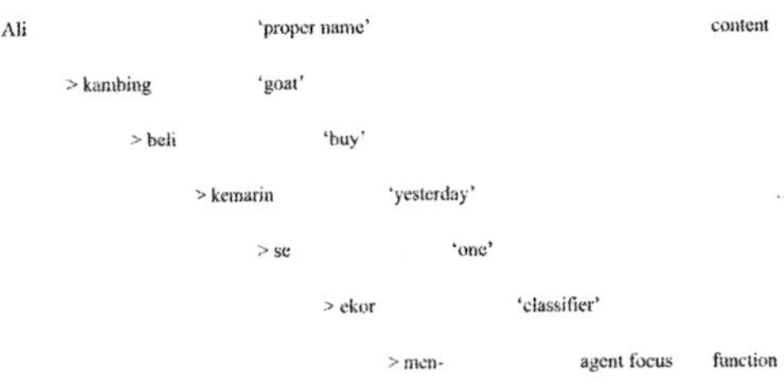

(a) Some elements are again in between "content" and "function": time adverbs such as *kemarin* "yesterday," and numerals such as *se* "one." (b) There are several functional categories in Bahasa that do not have a counterpart in English, such as the classifier *ekor* and the agent focus marker *men-*.

We can conclude that(a) an overall gross distinction between content words and function words is useful in all languages; (b) the exact dividing line is hard to draw; (c) the categories that count as functional may differ from language to language.

Another property of many functional categories is that they can be classified in terms of combinations of binary features. Thus in Bahasa Indonesia, the features [1] "first person," [2] "second person," [plural], and [polite] help define the set of pronouns and address forms (see Table).

Even here, however, the set of address forms is open ended, since various polite forms can be added. The features involved may be general, such as [1] or [2], but sometimes are particular to an individual language.

The criteria used to establish whether a given element is a functional category or not are diverse. Phonologically, they tend to be short elements, often with little stress, and consisting of vowels and consonants that are common in the language in question. Lexically, they are often part of a closed class, which may be paradigmatically structured (cf. the Indonesian pronouns above and English *this / that / these / those*). Morphologically, they tend to have little morphology. Semantically, they have an abstract meaning. Syntactically, they play a role in structuring the sentence. However, none of these criteria is water-tight, and sometimes there is no match in the classification along the different dimensions.

Above, I have stated that languages differ quite a bit in their functional categories. Some theorists,

Table 7 Features distinguishing Bahasa Indonesian pronouns

1	*2*	*plural*	*polite*	
+	-	-	+	saya
+	-	-	-	aku
-	+	-		kamu
-	+	-		engkau
-	+	-	+	saudara, saudari, tuan, …
-	-	-	+	beliau
-	-	-	-	dia, ia
+	-	+		kami
+	+	+		kita
-	+	+		kamu sekalian
-	+	+		engkau sekalian
-	+	+	+	saudara-saudara, …
-	-	+		mereka

particularly some working in the generative tradition, assume, in contrast, that the inventory of categories is universal (a good example is Cinque, 2002 and later work in the so-called cartographic tradition). In this tradition, it is also often assumed that functional categories need not be morphologically realized and can remain abstract. Thus if one assumes that every language has Case, in those languages without overt case marking, such as Bahasa Indonesia and most of English, Case will be an abstract category.

Do functional categories have a special status as a theoretical concept in linguistic theory? Several answers can be given. ***No***, since there is no plausible way in which a separate class of elements can be isolated, on all relevant dimensions, that we can sharply set apart as "functional." ***Yes***, in virtually all domains of linguistics (grammar, historical linguistics, psycholinguistics and acquisition, language contact) the content/function word distinction plays an important role (cf. Muysken, 2008).

In some sense, the functional categories form the sentential skeleton for each language. In second language learning, the challenge is to acquire the categories of another language and internalize their syntactic properties. Several researchers, including Schwarz and Sprouse (1996) and Van de Craats *et al.* (2000, 2002), have assumed that initially the functional skeleton of the first language plays a central role.

See also: agreement, developmental sequences, generative linguistics, inflectional morphemes, morpheme acquisition orders, Universal Grammar (UG) and SLA

References

Cinque, G. (ed.) (2002). *Functional Structure in DP and IP. The Cartography of Syntactic Structures*, vol.1. New York: Oxford University Press.

Craats, I. van de, Norbert C., and R. van Hout (2000). Conservation of grammatical knowledge: On the acquisition of POSSessive noun phrases by Turkish and Moroccan Arabic learners of Dutch. *Linguistics*, *38*, 221–314.

Craats, I. van de, R. van Hout, and N. Corver (2002). The acquisition of possessive HAVE-clauses by Turkish and Moroccan learners of Dutch. *Bilingualism: Language and Cognition*, *5*, 147–174.

Muysken, P. (2008), *Functional Categories*. Cambridge: Cambridge University Press.

Schwartz, B.D. and R.A. Sprouse (1996). L2 cognitive states and the full transfer, full access model. *Second Language Research*, *12*, 40–72.

Functional magnetic resonance imaging (fMRI)

Helen Carpenter
Upper-Story Educational Services and Consulting

Functional magnetic resonance imaging, or fMRI, is a neuroimaging technique used to observe *hemodynamic* (blood flow) activity in the brain. Current fMRI research is considered non-invasive because the technique does not require surgery, ionizing radiation (e.g., x-rays), or administration of pharmaceutical contrast media.

Technique

In fMRI, participants typically lie within the MRI *bore*, a tube lined with different kinds of coils that either create or detect magnetic fields and radio frequency (RF) signals. Magnetic field strength typically ranges from 1.5 tesla (T) to 7T, with stronger magnetic fields (*e.g.*, 9T) undergoing research and development. Stronger magnetic fields yield more detailed images.

fMRI data reflect the activity of *protons*, which in the case of fMRI usually means positively charged hydrogen atoms. Protons are found in hemoglobin, a blood-based protein that carries oxygen to tissues, and are released during the exchange of oxygen between blood and tissue. The most popular use of fMRI involves observing patterns of proton activity. During cognitive or other activities, the exchange of oxygen between blood and tissue increases, resulting in increased proton activity. This is detected and measured, and suggests where, when, and how much hemodynamic activity has occurred. Detection of activity is based on a technique called the *blood-oxygen level dependent* (BOLD) contrast method (Ogawa, 1990). Research on the neuronal circuitry and processes underlying the BOLD response is ongoing (Logothetis, 2008).

Because fMRI can provide data on the locus of neural activation on the order of millimeters, its *spatial resolution* is considered a strength. However, its *temporal resolution* is considered to be relatively weak, as fMRI is unable to index activation on the order of milliseconds.

SLA and fMRI

In SLA, fMRI research is typically used to identify brain regions that become active in response to linguistic tasks. Patterns of activation indicate whether a linguistic activity may rely on brain regions that underlie sensory, emotional, motor, memory, and/or other processes. These data provide insights into how the brain/mind acquires, stores, represents, and retrieves linguistic information. For example, fMRI data may shed light on whether grammar and lexicon are subserved by the same neural resources in different groups of learners. It may also elucidate aspects of affective and/or motivational states experienced during engagement in linguistic activities. Furthermore, fMRI may also provide data on aspects of the networks of brain regions underlying semantic representations of L2 versus L1 lexical items. There are numerous ways to use fMRI to investigate SLA.

As with any research method, the use of fMRI depends on the needs of different paradigms. One group of researchers may examine the neural representation of L2 prosody. Another group may examine how individual differences in working memory affect the representation of L2. Yet another group may observe how aspects of L2 are subserved by the brain at different stages of development for learners at different ages. Finally, others may investigate the neural representation of pragmatic abilities in L1 versus L2. Potential applications for fMRI research span the enormous interface between brain phenomena and SLA research topics.

Regardless of focus, fMRI findings reflect brain-based activity. Such findings cannot be adequately interpreted and evaluated without knowledge of neurocognition and fMRI techniques, which can be obtained through coursework, workshops, and written materials. Rigorous SLA-fMRI research considers cross-disciplinary theories and controls for a range of potential confounding variables (see Neuroimaging). FMRI data are typically interpreted in relation to findings from neurological patients, animals, other neuroimaging methods, and/or other sources.

FMRI may not be appropriate for all SLA research questions. Many considerations exist, but some of the most common are that (a) scanner noise may interfere with participants' abilities to hear; (b) participants must remain still during data acquisition—head movements caused by speech, or hand movements caused by writing, compromise the neural signal; and (c) participants cannot easily interact with other interlocutors in real time interaction during data acquisition. Thus, for SLA, fMRI research currently is best-suited for certain kinds of comprehension and production activities, particularly those considered more 'lab-based,' and less 'authentic.'

See also: Event-related potential (ERP), lateralization, measuring and researching SLA, mirror neurons, neuroimaging, psycholinguistics of SLA

References

Deichmann, R. (2009). Chapter 1. Principles of MRI and Functional MRI. In Filippi, M. (ed.), *fMRI techniques and protocols*, pp. 3–29. New York: Humana Press.

Logothetis, N. (2008). What we can do and cannot do with fMRI. *Nature*, *453*, 869–78.

Ogawa, S., Lee, T.M., Kay, A.R. and Tank, D.W. (1990). Brain magnetic resonance imaging with contrast dependent on blood oxygenation. *Proc. Natl. Acad. Sci. U.S. A.*, *87*(24), 9868–72.

Further reading

Coyne, K. (2010). *MRI: A guided tour*. Retrieved from www.magnet.fsu.edu/education/tutorials/magnetacademy/mri/fullarticle.html

Folia, V., Udden, J., de Vries, M., Forkstram, C., and Petersson, K.M. (2010). Artificial language learning in adults and children. In M. Gullberg and P. Indefrey (eds), *The Earliest Stages of Language Learning*, pp. 188–220. Oxford: Wiley-Blackwell. (An interesting illustration of the use of fMRI to identify areas of the brain activated during implicit artificial grammar learning.)

Hernandez-Garcia, L., Peltier, S. and Grisson, W. (2009). *Introduction to Functional MRI Hardware.* In Filippi, M. (ed.), *fMRI techniques and protocols*, pp. 31–67. New York: Humana Press.

Functional typological linguistics

Anna Giacalone Ramat
Università di Pavia

Functional typological linguistics (henceforth FTL) is both a set of theories and a methodology of linguistic analysis based on the assumption that linguistic structure should be explained primarily in terms of linguistic function (Croft, 2003). The term functional here contrasts with the formal approach of the Chomskyan generative grammar, which follows a quite different conception of language universals. After Joseph Greenberg's (1966) seminal discoveries of universals of word order and morphology, the functional typological approach was taken up by highly influential scholars of linguistics such as J. Haiman, T. Givón, B. Comrie, P. Hopper, E. Traugott, J. Bybee among others and has presently emerged as an alternative to generative grammar.

Goal and methods

The ultimate goal for the typological approach is to offer a framework to describe and explain all types of linguistic variation: synchronic, diachronic, as well as language internal variation. Linguistic diversity is constrained by universals of human language: in order to discover constraints on possible human languages, FTL uses an inductive method of analysis based on an adequate sample of the world's languages. Thus the central role of cross-linguistic comparison is a distinctive characteristic of the FTL approach and a necessary procedure for the search for language universals. Most language universals based on empirical generalizations have exceptions which may show different frequency patterns, some language types being very rare.

Language universals and FTL

Language universals are generalizations observed across languages concerning the distribution of specific phonetic and morphosyntactic features. There are unrestricted universals valid for all languages (of the type: "all languages have oral vowels") and implicational universals that state a correlation between two logically independent grammatical parameters (Croft, 2003). The concept of implicational universals has revealed of primary importance for word order patterns. Developing on Greenberg's proposals typologists have established a number of preferential correlations for VO (Verb Object) and OV (Object Verb) languages, for example the universal correlation between OV order and postpositions and VO order and prepositions. A large body of evidence has been found for combination of implicational universals in implicational hierarchies, such as the Accessibility Hierarchy for relativization (Keenan and Comrie, 1977, Comrie, 1989) or the Prepositional Noun Modifier Hierarchy (Hawkins, 1983).These chains of implicational universals are endowed with high predictive power because they constrain possible language types. At its first stage, research on language universals was synchronic and descriptive leading to the individuation of language types. It was followed by a dynamic perspective according to which language states were reinterpreted as stages of language change processes. Additional concepts in the dynamic perspective are stability and frequency: language are ranked by degree of likelihood that a language will exit a language state, and by frequency for a language to enter a state involving that type (Croft, 2003: 235) (unstable types are exemplified by nasal vowels, which tend to change to oral vowels quite rapidly in comparison to other phonological changes).

Diachronic typology has allowed the extension of typological analysis to the domain of historical linguistics and language change. An increasing attention has been devoted to the typology of diachronic linguistic processes in order to define constraints on language change. The area of grammaticalization studies represents a new domain for functional typology. Grammaticalization is a set of unidirectional grammatical processes through which grammatical morphemes originate from lexical items in specific constructional contexts. An overall classification of processes involved in grammaticalization has been attempted at the phonological and morphosyntactic level, which has shown the strict correlation of changes and allowed to measure the degree of grammaticality of every type of grammatical morpheme (Lehmann, 1995). At the semantic/pragmatic level functional processes usually involve desemanticization (or loss of meaning), but also shifting toward the speaker's subjective beliefs or attitudes toward the proposition, called subjectification (Traugott, 1989).

The issue of explanations

In functional typology the principles motivating the encoding of function into form are functional in origin and are present for all speakers of all languages; they are ultimately motivated by considerations of language processing and by communicative motivations. According to the typological view, iconicity and economy are the major forces determining grammatical structures. The former assumes that the structure of language reflects in some ways the structure of experience: closeness between particular concepts is reflected in formal closeness between grammatical forms (Givón, 1990); the latter is based on the principle that the expression should be minimized where possible. The competition between functional motivations accounts for variation in language types and also for frequency of types across the world. A particular language at some point of its development may present one of the possible ways of resolving the competition at a particular language level. However, a language can change over time reflecting a reassertion of one motivation at the expense of the other (Croft, 2003).

The semantic map model has been recently developed to represent a set of related functions within a conceptual semantic space (Haspelmath, 2003). The structure of the semantic map is empirically constructed via the comparison of different languages. Haspelmath's claim is that similarity in form reflects similarity in function: for example, the conceptual space for indefinite pronouns is shaped by a restricted number of semantic features based on definiteness, specificity, scalarity, and scope of negation. Thus semantic maps are a convenient way of representing similarities in meaning and multifunctionality in grammar; moreover they can make predictions on diachronic developments showing that some changes presuppose others, thus providing evidence for directionality in linguistic change. Some typologists assume a cognitive basis for conceptual spaces which would describe the geography of the human mind.

FTL in a wider context

The functional typological approach may offer theoretical and methodological support to language acquisition research. The typological notions of implicational universals, markedness, and prototypicality may lead to a number of predictions concerning language acquisition: typological patterns such as the Accessibility Hierarchy for relativization have been tested against first and second language acquisition data and have proved to be a universally available option to the language learner, acting in connection with a number of typological and developmental factors (Giacalone Ramat 2003). Cognitive functional linguistics or usage-based models, and construction grammar are among the newly developed linguistic theories the most compatible with typological linguistics.

See also: cognitive linguistics and SLA, implicational universals, language typology and language distance, markedness, relative clauses, Universal Grammar (UG) and SLA

References

Comrie, B. (1989). *Language Universals and Linguistic Typology*, 2nd edn. Oxford: Basil Blackwell.

Croft, W. (2003). *Typology and Universals*, 2nd edn. Cambridge: Cambridge University Press.

Giacalone Ramat, A. (ed.) (2003). *Typology and Second Language Acquisition*. Berlin: Mouton de Gruyter.

Givón, T. (1990). *Syntax. A Functional-Typological Introduction*. Amsterdam: Benjamins.

Greenberg, J.H. (1966). Some Universals of Grammar with Particular Reference to the Order of Meaningful Elements. Iin J.H. Greenberg (ed.), *Universals of Language*, pp. 73–113. Cambridge (MA): The MIT Press.

Haspelmath, M. (2003). The Geometry of Grammatical Meaning. In M. Tomasello (ed.), *The New Psychology of Language*, vol. 2, pp. 211–42. Mahwah, NJ: Erlbaum.

Hawkins, J.A. (1983). *Word Order Universals*. New York: Academic Press.

Keenan, E.L. and Comrie, (1977). Noun Phrase Accessibility and Universal Grammar. *Linguistic Inquiry*, *VIII*, 1, 63–99.

Lehmann, C. (1995). *Thoughts on Grammaticalization*. München: LINCOM EUROPA. Original edition, 1982.

Traugott, E.C. (1989). On the Rise of Epistemic Meanings in English: An Example of Subjectification in Semantic Change. *Language*, *65*, 31–55.

Further reading

Dryer, M.S. (1992). The Greenbergian Word Order Correlations. *Language*, *68*, 81–88.

Greenberg, J.H., Ferguson, C.A. and Moravczik, E. A. (eds) (1978). *Universals of Human Languages*, 4 vols. Stanford, CA: Stanford University Press.

Haiman, J. (1985). *Natural Syntax*. Cambridge: Cambridge University Press.

Hopper, P.J. and Traugott, E.C. (2003). *Grammaticalization*, 2nd edn. Cambridge: Cambridge University Press.

Fundamental Difference Hypothesis (FDH)

Roumyana Slabakova
University of Iowa

Robert Bley-Vroman's (1989, 1990) Fundamental Difference Hypothesis (FDH) is a theoretical proposal purporting to explain the process of second language acquisition (L2A). In a nutshell, it argues that there is a fundamental difference in the way children acquire their mother tongue and the way adult learners acquire a second (or third, etc.) language. The FDH has brought many central issues of L2A theory and practice to the forefront of the field. Most of these issues are still debated today: the critical period hypothesis, domain-specific versus domain-general acquisition processes, implicit versus explicit learning, the use of general problem-solving skills in L2A, and the importance of the native language. This article presents the main ideas of the FDH and its update (Bley-Vroman, 2009), and takes stock of what has been established in the past 20 years with regard to fundamental first language (L1)-L2A differences. The short answer to the fundamental question appears to be: L1 and L2 acquisition are fundamentally different in some respects and fundamentally similar in others.

Bley-Vroman's (1990) *Linguistic Analysis* article starts with a list of 10 differences between L1 and L2 acquisition. Foreign language learning, according to Bley-Vroman, is distinguished from L1 acquisition by these 10 characteristics listed in (1).

(1) a. lack of success
b. general failure
c. variation in success, course, and strategy
d. variation in goals
e. correlation of age and proficiency
f. fossilization
g. indeterminate intuitions
h. importance of instruction
i. negative evidence
j. role of affective factors

The first three characteristics amount to more or less the same claim: the success of L2A is not guaranteed, and individual L2 learners who pass for native speakers may be outliers.

The third difference, in particular, argues that child language is different not only in degree of attainment but in the course and strategy of acquisition as well. The fourth difference captures the fact that an adult learner may decide to learn as much of the L2 as is needed for a job or a specific purpose, which never happens with children. The fifth and sixth differences invoke age effects. The negative correlation of age and proficiency has been attested in study after study (Birdsong, 2005; DeKeyser, 2000; DeKeyser and Larson-Hall, 2005), no matter whether results indicated a true critical period or more prolonged age effects. Fossilization is another phenomenon that just does not happen in normal child language acquisition. The seventh difference alleges that L2 learners have indeterminate intuitions about grammaticality due to the variety of strategies they employ to judge sentences. The eighth and ninth differences are related: the importance of instruction and practice for L2A may be due to the necessity of correction and negative evidence for learning. Finally, affective factors such as personality traits, socialization, motivation, aptitude, and attitude play a role in the L2A process but are not relevant to child language development.

Even the most cursory overview of these contrasts makes one thing obvious: there are indisputable distinctions between the ways children acquire their native languages and the ways adults acquire a L2. However, we could just as easily come up with 10 similarities between the two kinds of acquisition, starting with the most obvious one: SLA is a human language acquisition process, and the grammatical system that L2 learners build in their mind/brain is a natural language system.

Bley-Vroman's FDH has had such a significant impact because it made a coherent, internally consistent proposal that agreed with the existing research data at the time. The central argument is that the domain-specific language acquisition device (i.e., Universal Grammar [UG]) ceases to operate in adults (which leads to critical period effects), and that adult learners use their domain-general problem-solving skills as well as conscious observation of the data and practice to acquire a L2. The latter claim explains several of the observed differences between L1 and L2 acquisition—namely, variation in outcome, the importance of instruction and practice, and the role of affective factors. The major underlying difference between L1 children and L2 adults is that adults already have a native language, so in a sense, their language acquisition device has been activated. This fact gives adult learners access to linguistic principles, properties that are the same in all natural languages. Parameters, or points of linguistic variation, cannot be truly reset to create a native-like linguistic representation. This view has been refined over the years (see the Failed Functional Features Hypothesis; Hawkins and Chan, 1997) and has recently been articulated as the Interpretability Hypothesis (Tsimpli and Dimitrakopoulou, 2007).

The FDH's claim that adults use domain-general problem-solving skills argues specifically against the Fodorian type of informational encapsulation of language acquisition (Fodor, 1983, 2000). Direct observation and pattern noticing also follow from the FDH: whatever properties are observable from the input are learnable without recourse to UG and do not involve grammar restructuring. Another implication has to do with explicit learning: because adults use general problem-solving skills, their cognitive abilities (aptitude, working memory span, etc.) directly impact their language learning skills. The native language is argued by Bley-Vroman (1990) to be the primary source of knowledge about the L2.

An updated version of the FDH (Bley-Vroman, 2009) maintains that L2 and native grammars are different in three crucial ways: L2 grammars make central use of viruses and patches, or idiosyncratic, non-grammar-based mappings of form and meaning, domain-general processes, and shallow parsing (see below). These three practices are also employed by native grammars, but are seen as peripheral phenomena in native language processing. Bley-Vroman (2009) finds that the concept of UG, specifically in the Minimalist Program (Chomsky, 1995, 2005) has evolved in such a way that all grammatical principles are instantiated in all languages and the distinction between the L1 and the L2 is becoming untenable (see also Hale, 1996).

What other linguistic properties, apart from universal principles such as the empty category principle (i.e., a universal syntactic constraint that requires that gaps must be properly licensed and their feature content identifiable), can be gleaned from the native language and from observation? Quite a lot, indeed! The adult L2 learner does not need to acquire anew the fact that the L2 allows recursion; that it has a finite set of phonemes, syllables, feet, and phonological phrases; that syntactic phrases are built according to the X-bar schema and attributed grammatical functions, because there is no natural language without these properties. However, observation of L2 input can also give the learner parameterized properties such as head and complement directionality (the basic word order in the language), the necessity for subjects in embedded clauses, the presence or absence of agreement morphology, tense and aspect marking on the verb, and a whole range of similar important linguistic facts. On the assumption that human beings are excellent pattern-noticing machines, the acquisition of these facts would not represent an insurmountable difficulty to the learner.

What is the burden of proof incumbent on opponents of the FDH? Challengers of the FDH have to show that when adult learners display knowledge of properties standardly attributed to UG, this knowledge is attained by the same means as in L1A. If such success is attested, then a weaker version of the FDH will be supported. It has been argued that Poverty of the Stimulus phenomena can provide the best testing ground for the FDH (Dekydtspotter and Sprouse, 2003; Dekydtspotter, 2009; Schwartz and Sprouse, 2000). In those learning situations, learners have to acquire morphosyntactic and/or interpretive contrasts that are not reliably learnable from available input, are not directly evidenced in their native languages, and are not present in classroom instruction. The pioneering work of Dekydtspotter and Sprouse documents the successful acquisition of a number of such interpretive properties in the absence of positive evidence for them. Particularly convincing are cases where learners manage to acquire the lack of a particular construction (Slabakova, 2002), or a particular interpretation (Slabakova, 2006) in the L2. This line of research argues that the strong version of the FDH is ultimately untenable.

The fundamental difference in processing mechanisms that Bley-Vroman (2009) points to has been discussed widely. Townsend and Bever (2001) proposed that native processing often uses relatively superficial patterns that rely on a SVO template, pragmatic bootstrapping and statistical patterns. Clahsen and Felser (2006) take this proposal further by articulating the Shallow Structure Hypothesis, arguing that this type of processing is the only type that L2 learners engage in. Note that the "shallow processing mechanism" may be widely employed by lower-proficiency native speakers (Pakulak and Neville, 2010), which makes it dependent on exposure to complex language and thus not a fundamentally different mechanism. Dekydtspotter *et al.* (2006) and Juffs (2006) argue that L2 processing mechanisms, although slower, are structure-based and thus fundamentally similar to native ones.

In summary, new findings in the last 20 years directly challenge the FDH and support the "less radical view of the FDH" (Bley-Vroman, 1990: 17). Research points to some parts of linguistic knowledge being innate and other parts being sensitive to regularities and frequency in the input—that is, having commonalities with general types of learning.

See also: Critical Period Hypothesis, generative linguistics, modularity, positive and negative evidence, theoretical constructs in SLA, Universal Grammar (UG) and SLA

References

Birdsong, D. (2005). Interpreting age effects in second language acquisition. In J.F. Kroll and A. de Groot (eds), *Handbook of Bilingualism: Psycholinguistic Approaches*, pp. 109–28. Oxford: Oxford University Press.

Bley-Vroman, R. (1989). What is the logical problem of foreign language learning? In S.M. Gass and J. Schachter (eds), *Linguistic Perspectives on Second Language Acquisition*, pp. 41–68. New York: Cambridge University Press.

——(1990). The logical problem of foreign language learning. *Linguistic Analysis*, 20, 3–49.

——(2009). The evolving context of the Fundamental Difference Hypothesis. *Studies in Second Language Acquisition*, *31*, 2, 175–98.

Chomsky, N. (1995). *The Minimalist Program*. Cambridge, MA: MIT Press.

——(2005). Three factors in language design. *Linguistic Inquiry*, *36*, 1–22.

Clahsen, H. and Felser, C. (2006). Grammatical processing in language learners. *Applied Psycholinguistics*, *27*, 3–42.

DeKeyser, R. (2000). The robustness of critical period effects in second language acquisition. *Studies in Second Language Acquisition*, *22*, 495–533.

DeKeyser, R. and Larson-Hall, J. (2005). What does the critical period really mean? In J.F. Kroll and A. de Groot (eds), *Handbook of Bilingualism: Psycholinguistic Approaches*, pp. 88–108. Oxford: Oxford University Press.

Dekydtspotter, L. (2009). Second language epistemology. *Studies in Second Language Acquisition*, *31*, 2, 291–321.

Dekydtspotter, L., Schwartz, B.D. and Sprouse, R. A. (2006). The Comparative Fallacy in L2 processing research. In M. Grantham O'Brien, C. Shea, and J. Archibald (eds), *Proceedings of the 8th Generative Approaches to Second Language Acquisition Conference (GASLA)*, pp. 33–40. Somerville, MA: Cascadilla Proceedings Project.

Fodor, J. (1983). *Modularity of Mind*. New York: Cambridge University Press.

Fodor, J. (2000). *The Mind Does not Work that Way*. New York: Cambridge University Press.

Hale, K. (1996). Can UG and L1 be distinguished in L2 acquisition? *Behavioral and Brain Sciences*, *19*, 728–730.

Hawkins, R. and Chan, C.Y.-H. (1997). The partial availability of Universal Grammar in second language acquisition. *Second Language Research*, *13*, 187–226.

Juffs, A. (2006). Grammar and parsing and transition theory. *Applied Psycholinguistics*, *27*, 69–71.

Dekydtspotter, L. and Sprouse, R.A. (2003). L2 performance: Interlanguage representations, computations, and intuitions. In J.M. Liceras *et al.* (eds), *Proceedings of the 6th Generative Approaches to Second Language Acquisition Conference (GASLA 2002)*, pp. 45–54. Somerville, MA: Cascadilla Proceedings Project.

Pakulak, E. and H. Neville. (2010). Proficiency differences in syntactic processing of monolingual native speakers indexed by Event-related Potentials. *Journal of Cognitive Neuroscience*, *22*, 2728–44.

Schwartz, B.D. and Sprouse, R.A. (2000). When syntactic theories evolve: Consequences for L2 acquisition research. In J. Archibald (ed.), *Second Language Acquisition and Linguistic Theory*, pp. 156–86. Malden, MA: Blackwell.

Slabakova, R. (2002). The compounding parameter in second language acquisition. *Studies in Second Language Acquisition*, *24*, 507–40.

Slabakova, R. (2006). Learnability in the L2 acquisition of semantics: A bidirectional study of a semantic parameter. *Second Language Research*, *22*, 1–26.

Townsend, D.J. and Bever, T.G. (2001). *Sentence Comprehension: The Integration of Habits and Rules*. Cambridge, MA: MIT Press.

Tsimpli, I. and Dimitrakopoulou, M. (2007). The interpretability hypothesis: Evidence from wh-interrogatives in second language acquisition. *Second Language Research*, *23*, 215–42.

Further reading

Bley-Vroman, R. (1990). The logical problem of foreign language learning. *Linguistic Analysis*, *20*, 3–49.

Bley-Vroman, R. (2009). The evolving context of the Fundamental Difference Hypothesis. *Studies in Second Language Acquisition*, *31*, 2, 175–98.

DeKeyser, R. (2000). The robustness of critical period effects in second language acquisition. *Studies in Second Language Acquisition*, *22*, 495–533.

Dekydtspotter, L. (2009). Second language epistemology. *Studies in Second Language Acquisition*, *31*, 2, 291–321.

Slabakova, R. (2008). *Meaning in the Second Language*. Berlin: Mouton de Gruyter

G

Generalizability

Micheline Chalhoub-Deville
University of North Carolina at Greensboro

Generalizability, acknowledged as a positivist, quantitative concept, is commonly discussed in terms of two inter-related characteristics: external and internal validity. External validity comprises population and setting/ecological validity. Population validity is the degree to which findings obtained with a given sample can be said to apply to the population of interest. The extent to which a study includes participants with pertinent features (e.g., first language, age, motivation, etc.) and a sampling design (e.g., random, cluster, stratified, etc.) that aligns with the purpose of the study impacts the external generalization attained.

In terms of ecological validity, generalizability concerns itself with questions such as the comparability of tasks, raters, and texts in a given research study to those which were not included in the study, but to which we would like to make claims. Ultimately, the basic notion with such comparability is that we are interested in the extent to which research findings/test scores/performances apply to situations other than those where they were initially observed or documented, for example, the lab versus a natural setting. To illustrate, tasks used to elicit samples of language performance affect the type of data obtained but typically researchers would like to speak to learners' language ability or proficiency beyond the specific elicitation tasks.

Meta-analysis is a systematic review of research findings to document the generalizability of a particular intervention across studies (Wolfe, 1986). Meta-analysis helps document the magnitude, practical contribution, or effect size as opposed to the statistical significance of research studies. Effect size measures, the Mantel–Haenszel test, and regression procedures are employed to estimate the *true* contribution of a given intervention beyond that of an individual study with its set of particulars (e.g., sample size, individual characteristics, etc.).

With regard to internal validity, generalizability concerns itself with whether performances are consistent, dependable, replicable, or reliable. In measurement, these terms can be said to refer to the internal consistency of outcomes or scores across various facets, for example, as persons, items/tasks, raters, forms, occasions, etc. (Facets are akin to factors in analysis of variance.)

Generalizability, or G theory, is a statistical approach to estimate the reliability of intended objects of measurement (typically, participants' performances) given specific facets. The purpose of a G study is to quantify the amount of variation that can be attributed to each facet and the interaction of facets. G study results can feed into a decision, or D, study where researchers can document the consistency of facets if altered, for example, if two tasks are used instead of five. G theory is preferred to classical test theory primarily because it also allows for the simultaneous estimation of the reliability of individual facets. G theory also allows for the computation of different generalizability coefficients depending on whether criterion-versus norm-referenced interpretations are warranted. For more information on G theory, see Brennan (2001) and Shavelson and Webb (1991).

In qualitative research (e.g., conversation analysis, case study, and introspection), which tends to favor small and purposeful samples, generalizations is not necessarily sought after. However, the in-depth explorations undertaken in qualitative research afford rich information about a phenomenon, can help denote the generalizability (alternatively, the idiosyncrasies) of the given study. See Chalhoub-Deville *et al.* (2006) for a wide-ranging treatment of generalizability from both a quantitative and qualitative perspective.

See also: effect size, inter-rater reliability, measuring and researching SLA, meta-analysis, qualitative research, quantitive research

References

Brennan, R.L. (2001). *Generalizability Theory*. New York: Springer-Verlag.

Chalhoub-Deville, M., Chapelle, C.A. and Duff, P. A. (eds) (2006). *Inference and Generalizability in Applied Linguistics: Multiple Perspectives*. Amsterdam: John Benjamins Publishing.

Shavelson, R.J. and Webb, N.M. (1991). *Generalizability Theory: A Primer*. Newbury Park, CA: Sage.

Wolf, F.M. (1986). *Meta-analysis: Quantitative Methods for Research Synthesis*. Newbury Park, CA: Sage.

Generative linguistics

Shigeo Tonoike
Aoyama Gakuin University

The term "generative linguistics," also known as "generative grammar" refers to a particular approach to the study of language initiated by Noam Chomsky and its later developments. It also refers to a set of assumptions shared within that approach. Since its inception in 1957 by the publication of Chomsky's seminal work it has gone through a number of major revisions, but it has retained one fundamental hypothesis (often referred to as the innateness hypothesis) that humans are born with a species-specific language faculty, also known as Universal Grammar (UG), which allows each of us to acquire any human language that we are exposed to. Thus the ultimate goal of generative grammar is to clarify what the species-specific language faculty is, and how it is encoded in the human genome.

This approach takes a mentalist view of language, and holds that two notions of language should be strictly distinguished, namely i-language and e-language. I-language (short for internal/individual/intensional language) is the knowledge that a speaker has about his/her language that enables him/her to use it. E-language (e short for external/extensional) is a set of (all) grammatical expressions of that language. E-language is a theoretical construct and is not part of humans or of the world. I-language is the state of each person's mind/brain and hence is part of the world and is the proper object of study in generative grammar. Any explicit system (of rules and other descriptive devices) that defines (or enumerates) all and only the grammatical expressions of a language is a generative grammar of that language and is said to generate expressions of that language.

The earliest model of generative grammar is called the Standard Theory laid out in Chomsky (1957) and (1965). It consisted of a set of phrase structure rules that construct the skeletal clausal structures and the lexicon (collection of lexical items), together forming the base component and a set of transformational rules. The base component generates a deep structure, which is fed to the transformational component and is mapped onto its surface structure. It was assumed that grammar of English, for instance, had such transformation rules as passive transformation, raising transformation, question formation transformation, etc.

Since then generative grammar has gone through a series of stages from a system of rules to a system of general conditions (or constraints), punctuated by major works of Chomsky: Chomsky (1973) marked the model known as the Extended Standard

Theory, characterized by the recognition of the contribution of surface structure word order etc. to the semantic interpretation of the expression as well as the development of a number of general conditions (or constraints) on transformations and a theory of phrase structure known as X-bar Theory (which eliminated phrase structure rules); Chomsky (1977) marks the Revised Extended Standard Theory characterized by trace theory which says that movement leaves the traces of the moved elements, thus allowing surface structure to be the only input to semantic and phonetic interpretation: Chomsky (1980) marks the Government and Binding Theory also known as the Principles-and-Parameters approach, which regards Universal Grammar as consisting of principles invariable across languages and associated parameters allowing crosslinguistic variations. At this stage deep and surface structures were replaced by D- and S-Structure, and various transformational rules were now reduced to one operation called Move a, which maps D-structure onto S-structure, and to the level of semantic representation called Logical Form (LF).

The most recent development of generative grammar is known as the Minimalist Program theory, named after Chomsky (1995). The most important feature of this theory is the insistence on restriction of the use of concepts and descriptive tools to only those with conceptual necessity, eliminating many familiar concepts such as deep and surface structure, transformations, etc. Now the only operations allowed by UG are Merge, which concatenates two syntactic objects including lexical items as well as phrases in accordance with their lexical properties, and Agree, which checks that agreement relations hold properly between relevant elements. Movement is now reinterpreted as an instance of Merge, merging a with an element b that is internal to a (hence it is sometimes referred to Internal Merge: IM) in contrast to the regular Merge referred to as External Merge (EM).

A sample derivation (based on Chomsky 2008) might be in order to help understand how the current theory generates expressions (see Figure 4). An arbitrary set of lexical items is taken out of the lexicon. This is called a lexical array and is the starting point of a derivation. Suppose we have selected {what, say, v*, I, can, C}, where v* is an abstract light verb, C stands for Complementizer, and D for Determiner. The derivation proceeds bottom up as illustrated below, by applying the binary operation of EM and IM, the latter marked by an arrow. IM of *what* to the edge of VP (aka SpecVP) is called A-Movement and results in assigning Accusative Case to *what*. Case assignment is now treated as valuation of Case feature with [Nominative], [Accusative] etc. Notice that the lower v*P contains both the object and the subject; this is referred to as the VP-internal Subject Hypothesis. IM of *say* to v* is called Head Movement. IM of *what* to Specv*P is referred to as A'-Movement (aka Wh-Movement). IM of *I* to SpecTP is another instance of A-Movement, and results in the assignment of Nominative Case to *I*. IM of *can* to C is another instance of Head Movement, resulting in Subject-Aux Inversion. Finally IM of *what* from Specv*P to SpecCP is another instance of A'-Movement. IM results in making a copy of the merged element, but only the last copy is pronounced, which is marked by bold face. These operations are driven by the requirements of each lexical item involved. The derivation is said to converge if one syntactic object is obtained with no lexical item left in the lexical array: otherwise it is said to crash. The sample derivation converges.

See also: functional categories, initial state, language and the lexicon in SLA, minimalist program, scope, Universal Grammar (UG) and SLA

References

Chomsky, N. (1957). *Syntactic Structure*. Mouton: The Hague.

——(1965). *Aspects of the Theory of Syntax*. Cambridge, MA: MIT Press.

——(1973). Conditions on transformations. In S.R. Anderson and P. Kiparsky (eds), *A Festschrift for Morris Halle*, pp. 232–86. New York: Holt, Rinehart and Winston.

——(1977). On Wh-Movement. In P. Culicover, T. Wasow, and A. Akmajian, (eds), *Formal Syntax*, pp. 71–132. New York: Academic Press.

——(1981). *Lectures on Government and Binding*. Dordrecht: Foris Publications.

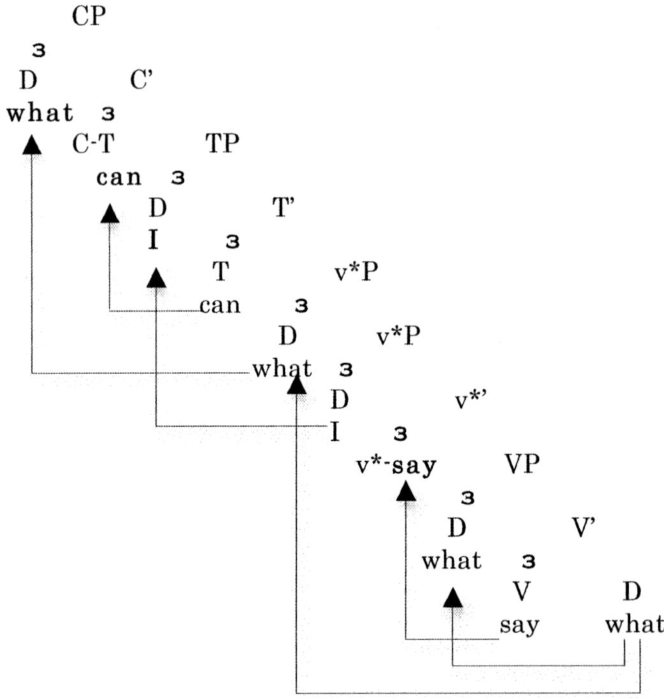

Figure 4 A sample derivation

——(1995). *The Minimalist Program*. Cambridge, MA: MIT Press.

——(2008). On phases. In R. Freidin, C. P. Otero and M. L. Zubizarreta (eds), *Foundational Issues in Linguistic Theory: Essays in Honor of Jean Roger Vergnaud*, pp. 133–66. Cambridge, MA: MIT Press.

Gestures and SLA

Shuichi Nobe
Aoyama Gakuin University

People produce gestures when they speak and they usually do so without being aware of them. Researchers have found that gestures and speech are closely related in meaning, function, and time (Kendon, 1986; McNeill, 1992). Gestures are "active participants in speaking and thinking" (McNeill, 2005: 3). Speakers use gesture as "an integral part of the activity of utterance production, and in everyday co-present interaction it can often have an important role to play in the communicative process, even if only a momentary one" (Kendon, 2004: 361). Many questions have been asked concerning the gestures used by teachers during interaction with learners, and concerning the developmental of gestural abilities in an L2 (see Gullburg, 2006, 2008; Stam and McCafferty, 2008). For example, are gestures by native-speaker teachers always understood by L2 learners, and if not, which gestures cause problems? Are problems in understanding native-speaker teacher gestures attributable to crosslinguistic differences between the L1 and the L2 being learned? Do teachers produce "foreigner gesture" in the same way they sometimes produce "foreigner talk" to help make themselves understood? Do learners produce different gestures when using an L2 than they do when using their L1? Can they produce native-like gestures when becoming proficient in the target language, or do they always retain traces of what

Kellerman and van Hoof (2003) have called "manual accents"?

Understanding of gestures

There are categories of gestures. One of these is emblems, "a direct verbal translation, or dictionary definition, usually consisting of a word or two, or perhaps a phrase" (Ekman and Friesen, 1969: 63). A thumbs up gesture and an OK gesture are emblems. The form-meaning pairs with their well-formed standards are conventionalized within a culture. Emblems can be used with speech, but even when used without speech, members of a given culture understand their meanings. Teachers can use and teach lists of them to learners. Learners learn more of these when taught explicitly than implicitly (Jungheim, 1991).

Another category of gestures is illustrators, "movements which are directly tied to speech, serving to illustrate what is being said verbally" (Ekman and Friesen, 1969: 68). Non-mutually exclusive dimensions are suggested: iconicity, metaphoricity, deixis and temporal rhythms (McNeill, 2005). These dimensions are typically manifested in the following gesture categories: iconics, metaphorics, (abstract) deictics, and beats, and the first three kinds of gestures are especially called representational gestures. "With these kinds of gesture people unwittingly display their inner thoughts and ways of understanding events of the world. These gestures are the person's memories and thoughts rendered visible. Gestures are like thoughts themselves" (McNeill, 1992: 12). Other gesture categories include regulators and adaptors (see McNeill, 2005).

Gestures by teachers are used to help learners understand lexical items and take part in classroom interaction. Learners notice teachers' gestures during instructional episodes, and their gestures helped them to learn more (Sime, 2008). Teachers with higher evaluations from students produced more non-verbal behaviors than those with lower evaluations (Moskowitz, 1976). But sometimes teachers overuse gestures. Whether they are emblems or illustrators, gestures should be fixated at, paid attention to, and processed by learners to facilitate optimal L2 communication (Gullburg and Kita, 2009).

Production of gestures

What is the gestural behavior of L2 learners? Research has shown that they produce more gestures in L2 than in L1 and that their gestures can be regarded as interlanguage while they acquire L2. Lower proficient learners tend to gesture and locate referents in space when mentioning them using a lexical NP for the first time, and anaphorically referred back to the same space with the original gesture when mentioning (without use of the NP) the next time. These anaphoric gestures decrease significantly and are abbreviated once the pronouns were properly used to maintain reference (Gullberg, 2008). Advanced Japanese learners of French tend to use larger, more French-like gesture spaces, and produced more discourse-oriented gestures rather than depictive (i.e., representational) gestures (Kida, 2005).

Beats are simple short and quick flicks of the hand or fingers up and down, or back and forth. These beats are produced with speech rather than without speech. Beats decrease significantly throughout the development of the L2 (Nobe, 1993; 2004). The semiotic value of beats "lies in the fact that it indexes the word and phrase it accompanies as being significant, not for its own semantic content, but for its discourse-pragmatic content. Examples are introducing new characters, summarizing the action, introducing new themes, etc." (McNeill, 1992: 15). Note that beats with speech by these frequent beat users were very prevalent, and they seem to be clearly used for purposes other than introducing new characters, or adding further detail, as in the L1. Although they can be interpreted as manifestations of discourse-pragmatic content, in the sense that difficulties of expression in L2 are an example of discourse-pragmatic content par excellence, most speakers do not appear to seek any help from, or try to negotiate with, their listeners when searching for target words (this is rather common when two interactants who do not know each other well are assigned to a narrative task). One explanation might be that the heavier load (i.e., involved in speaking in the L2) makes it more difficult for these speakers' linguistic processes to operate normally, and thereby makes them overproduce beats and/or use them differently when using the L2. Beats are not just an overflow caused by difficulties in the linguistic processes. Rather, continuously highlighting words by beats might make the speakers speak the target language more effectively. A type of self-feedback may exist. A beat with speech has "a function in the process of verbalization" (Marcos, 1979).

Cross-linguistic influence

When a gesture is produced, how is the division of labor with accompanying speech accomplished? Several researchers argue that cross-linguistic typological differences (e.g., satellite-frame languages vs verb-frame languages) determine not only how motion events are expressed by their gesture and speech (i.e., the degree of coexpressiveness and complementarity), but also how the temporal coordination of gesture and speech are achieved both in L1 and L2. In coexpressiveness, gesture, and speech "are parallel expressions of meaning." In complementarity, gesture and speech "refer to the same event and are partially overlapping, … but each presents a somewhat different aspect of it" (McNeill, 1992: 13).

Speakers' gestural behaviors in English (as a satellite-framed language) and Spanish (as a verb-framed language) have been discussed extensively (Kellerman and van Hoof, 2003; Stam, 2006). Regarding path information, for example, coexpressiveness tends to be achieved both for L1 English speakers (expressing path on the satellite and producing path gestures), and for L1 Spanish speakers (uttering verbs conflating path information and producing path gestures). Spanish learners of English produce path gestures and utter appropriate satellites, and coexpressiveness tends to be achieved in L2. However, Spanish learners of English, unlike L1 English speakers, do not accumulate path gestures with satellite components within a single clause in the L2 (Stam, 2006). These findings show that L1 gestures transfer to the L2.

See also: crosslinguistic influence, Conversation Analysis (CA), discourse and pragmatics in SLA, speaking, thinking for speaking, turn taking

References

Ekman, P. and Friesen, W.V. (1969). The repertoire of nonverbal behavior categories, origins, usage, and coding. *Semiotica*, *1*, 49–98.

Gullberg, M. (2006). Handling discourse: Gestures, reference tracking, and communication strategies in early L2. *Language Learning*, *56* (1), 155–196.

——(2008). Gestures and second language acquisition. Robinson, P. and Ellis, N.C. (eds), *Handbook of Cognitive Linguistics and Second Language Acquisition*, pp. 276–305. New York: Routledge.

Gullburg, M. and Kita, S. (2009). Attention to speech-accompanying gestures: Eye movements and information uptake. *Journal of Nonverbal Behavior*, *33*, 251–77.

Jungheim, N. O. (1991). A study on the classroom acquisition of gesture in Japan. *Journal of Ryutsu Keizai University*, *27*, 61–68.

Kida, T. (2005). *Appropriation du Geste par les Étrangers: Le cas d'étudiants Japonais Apprenant le Français.* Unpublished Dissertation. Aix-en-Provence: Université de Provence.

Kellerman, E. and van Hoof, A. (2003). Manual accents. *International Review of Applied Linguistics*, *41*, 251–69.

Kendon, A. (1986). Some reasons for studying gesture. *Semiotica*, *62*, 3–28.

——(2004). *Gesture: Visible Action as Utterance.* Cambridge: Cambridge University Press.

Marcos, L.R. (1979). Nonverbal behavior and thought processing. *Archive of General Psychiatry*, *36*, 940–43.

McNeill, D. (1992). *Hand and Mind: What Gestures Reveal about Thought.* Chicago, IL: University of Chicago Press.

——(2005). *Gesture and Thought.* Chicago, IL: University of Chicago Press.

Moskowitz, G. (1976). The classroom interaction of outstanding foreign language teachers. *Foreign Language Annals*, *9*, 135–43.

Nobe, Shuichi. (1993). *Cognitive processes of speaking and gesturing: A comparison between first language speakers and foreign language speakers.* Unpublished master's thesis, University of Chicago, IL.

——(2001). On gestures of foreign language speakers. In Cavé, C. Guaïtella, I. and Santi, S. (eds), *Oralité et Gestualité: Interactions et Comportements Multimodaux dans la Communication*, pp. 572–75. Paris: L'Harmattan.

——(2004). Toward a model of gestures of foreign language speakers. In Smith, D., S. Nobe, P. Robinson, G. Strong, M. Tani and H. Yoshiba. *Language and Comprehension: Perspectives from Linguistics and Language Education*, pp. 109–20. Tokyo: Kuroshio Publishers.

Sime, D. (2008). What do learners make of teachers' gestures in the language classroom? *International Review of Applied Linguistics*, *44*, 211–30.

Stam, G. (2006). Thinking for speaking about motion: L1 and L2 speech and gesture. *International Review of Applied Linguistics*, *44*, 145–71.

Stam, G. and McCafferty, S.G. (2008). Gesture studies and second language acquisition: A review. In S.G. McCafferty and G. Stam (eds), *Gesture: Second language acquisition and classroom research*, pp. 3–24. New York: Routledge

Grammatical encoding

Judit Kormos
Lancaster University

The general processes of grammatical encoding can be assumed to be fundamentally similar in first language (L1) and second language (L2). One of the most influential theories of syntactic processing mechanisms which has been adapted in models of speech production (Levelt, 1999) is that of Kempen and Hoenkamp's (1987) theory of Incremental Procedural Grammar. This theory represents the mainstream position in psycholinguistics that syntactic encoding is lexically driven, in other words, lexical items trigger syntactic building procedures. The major difference between L1 and L2 grammatical encoding lies in the extent to which these processes operate automatically. In L1 production, rules are assumed to be automatized and to be part of the encoding systems (Levelt, 1999). In contrast, for L2 speakers many of the phrase- and clause-building rules might not function automatically and might be stored in the form of factual (declarative) knowledge (Ullman, 2001).

Syntactic encoding in speech production consists of two important processes: the retrieval of grammatical information and the initiation of syntactic building procedures. In the first stage, grammatical information related to lexical items such as gender in languages like Spanish and French is activated in the mental lexicon. Optional and obligatory complements of verbs are also accessed at this stage. For highly competent L2 users, L2 lexical items might be stored together with the syntactic information that is specific for the given L2 entry, whereas for less level proficient learners L2 words might be associated with the syntactic information of the corresponding L1 item. This is supported by the frequent occurrence of transfer errors, when syntactic information concerning particular words is transferred from L1. This processing stage draws on declarative knowledge stored in the mental lexicon. The next major phase involves phrase and clause structure building and arranging phrases in the appropriate order. At this stage L1 speakers and balanced bilinguals use knowledge of syntactic and morphological rules of the language automatically. Conversely, L2 learners at lower level of proficiency might proceed in several ways. First of all, some of the rules might be acquired already in the form of procedural knowledge, whereas other rules might be stored in declarative memory and used consciously. It is also possible that some rules are not acquired at all. In this case a communication strategy might be used, with the help of which the L1 rule is transferred to into the L2. Alternatively, lower level L2 speakers might simply juxtapose the lexically encoded concepts after each other to express their intended message.

L1 and L2 syntactic encoding procedures might interact in a number of ways. As already mentioned, L1 syntactic information and encoding procedures might be transferred to the L2. In addition, L1 syntactic encoding procedures can influence the likelihood with which L2 procedures that are similar to the ones in the learners' L1 are used (Meijer and Fox Tee, 2003). Finally, due to the fact that languages might categorize events and concepts in different ways (Slobin, 1996), the grammatical encoding of motion, spatial relations and time can also be affected by the learners' L1.

See also: automaticity, declarative procedural model, Levelt's model of speech production and comprehension, lexical access and selection, linguistic transfer, thinking for speaking

References

Kempen, G. and Hoenkamp, E. (1987). An incremental procedural grammar for sentence formulation. *Cognitive Science*, *11*, 201–58.

Levelt, W.J. M., Roelofs, A. and Meyer, A.S. (1999). A theory of lexical access in speech production. *Behavioural and Brain Science*, *22*, 1–38.

Meijer, P.J. A. and Fox Tee, J.E. (2003). Building syntactic structures in speaking: A bilingual exploration. *Experimental Psychology*, *50*, 184–95.

Slobin, D.I. (1996). From 'thought and language' to 'thinking to speaking.' In J.J. Gumperz and S.C. Levinson (eds), *Rethinking Linguistic Relativity*. Cambridge: Cambridge University Press.

Ullman, T. (2001). The neural basis of lexicon and grammar in first and second language: the Declarative/Procedural Model. *Bilingualism: Language and Cognition*, *4*, 105–12.

Further reading

de Bot, K. (1992). A bilingual production model: Levelt's 'speaking' model adapted. *Applied Linguistics*, *13*, 1–24. (An excellent discussion of how Levelt's speaking model can be adapted to L2 production.)

Kormos, J. (2006). *Speech Production and Second Language Acquisition*. Mahwah, NJ: Lawrence Erlbaum. (Provides a detailed and up-to-date overview of second language speech production processes and proposes a new model for encoding speech in second language.)

Levelt, W.J. M. (1989). *Speaking: From Intention to Articulation*. Cambridge, MA: MIT Press. (A classic overview of speech production processes.)

Pienemann, M. (1998). Developmental dynamics in L1 and L2 acquisition: Processability theory and generative entrenchment. *Bilingualism: Language and Cognition*, *1*, 1–20. (A detailed analysis of grammatical encoding processes and constraints on transfer.)

Heritage Language Acquisition

Silvina Montrul
University of Illinois at Urbana-Champaign

Heritage languages are ethnic minority languages spoken around the world. In North America, Europe and Australia, there are at least two types of minority languages (Cummins, 1995; de Bot and Gorter 1995; Fishman, 1991). One type includes indigenous languages spoken by a group of speakers who have always inhabited the region where the majority language is now spoken: for example, Welsh in Wales, Catalan in Cataluña, Quechua in Peru. The second type includes languages spoken by groups of immigrants who move to a host country where another majority language is spoken: Arabs and Turks in Germany and the Netherlands, Punjabi speakers in the United Kingdom; Spanish, Korean, Japanese, Chinese, Arabic, Hindi, Russian and many other immigrant groups in the United States and Canada.

Definitions of heritage language speakers vary from very broad to very narrow (Hornberger and Wang, 2008). Broad definitions may consider anybody with a distant cultural and affective connection to a language minority group a heritage speaker, even if the person has no proficiency in the language; by contrast, narrower definitions may be as restrictive as to include only highly proficient users of the minority language. In the context of the United States, heritage speakers are individuals who immigrated in early childhood with their parents and other family members, or children of immigrants born in the United States. While the parents are either monolingual or dominant in the family language, the children grow up speaking English and the family language.

Those interested in understanding the nature of heritage speakers' proficiency and competence in the heritage language tend to adopt Guadalupe Valdés's definition of a heritage speaker: "a student who is raised in a home where a non-English language is spoken, who speaks or merely understands the heritage language, and who is to some degree bilingual in English and the heritage language Valdés's (2000: 1)." From a more global perspective, the words "English" and "non-English" could be replaced for any other majority language such as Chinese, German, Dutch, French or Spanish: there are Korean speakers in China, Polish heritage speakers in Germany, Turkish heritage speakers in the Netherlands, Arabic heritage speakers in Spain and France, Italian heritage speakers in Argentina, to name a few.

In the sociolinguistics literature (Silva-Corvalán, 1994), the parents are the first generation immigrants, the children the second generation immigrants, and the grandchildren the third generation. First generation immigrants tend to preserve their native language as they learn the majority language (although there may be borrowings and other lexical changes). At the other extreme is the third generation, who grew up speaking English as a first language and may have very little, if any, knowledge of the heritage language. Those who exhibit most variability in bilingual ability are the second generation, the group most often discussed in studies of incomplete acquisition in heritage language speakers. This group is heterogeneous and may include children of first generation immigrants born in the host country to at least one first generation parent. It also includes immigrant children who come to the host country before the age of 5. In terms of types of bilingual profile, this group may include 1) simultaneous bilinguals, those exposed to the heritage and the majority language before the age of 3–4; 2) sequential bilinguals or child L2 learners, those exposed to the heritage language at home until age 4–5, and to the majority language once they start pre-school; and 3) late child L2 learners, children monolingual in the heritage language, who received some elementary schooling in their home country and immigrated around ages 7–8 or later.

These children are schooled in the majority language and have a strong desire to fit in with the new society. Even when the parents may speak the family language at home with each other and with the children, a very common pattern in these immigrant households is that the children speak the majority language to the parents and their siblings: they do not often use the heritage language with other heritage language speaking children (Anderson, 1999; Bolonyai, 2007; Moag, 1995). As the majority language begins to be used more than the home language, the heritage language lags behind in development. If many of these children are minority language dominant in early childhood, they eventually become dominant in the majority language when they reach adolescence. By college age, the majority language is both stronger and dominant in proficiency and domains of use.

Heritage language speakers are relevant to the study of language acquisition for both theoretical and practical reasons. Normally developing monolingual children eventually attain full command of their native language and, from a purely linguistics perspective (leaving aside dialectal differences), there is little variation in the nature of linguistic knowledge among adult native speakers. However, despite having been exposed to the heritage language early in childhood, the range of linguistic ability and proficiencies reached by heritage language speakers in adulthood varies considerably, from minimal aural comprehension ability to full fluency in written and spoken registers, and everything else in between. For this reason, it has been claimed that many heritage language speakers do not completely acquire their family language in childhood (incomplete acquisition) or may have acquired and later lost parts of their language in childhood (attrition) (Montrul, 2008; Polinsky, 2007). As adults, these children of immigrant families wish to learn, relearn, or improve their current level of linguistic proficiency in their family language and they turn to the classroom.

Recent research has uncovered that adult heritage language speakers display significant gaps in their linguistic knowledge when compared with age-matched peers who possess full command of the language. For example, heritage language grammars exhibit simplification and erosion of morphosyntactic features typically controlled by monolingual children at an early age (Polinsky, 2000). The fact that these speakers have incomplete or partial knowledge of their first language raises several fundamental theoretical questions, such as: 1) the time it takes for a native language to be acquired and solidified so that it does not go away with fluctuations in input, 2) the stability of linguistic knowledge in early childhood, 3) the significant role of input required to develop and maintain language skills, 4) the role of universal linguistic mechanisms that drive linguistic knowledge and restructuring under reduced input conditions, and 5) the role of age and cognitive development in language acquisition and loss, among others. Many of these questions are intrinsically difficult to tease apart in monolingual acquisition when all factors work in tandem, but the study of heritage speaker populations may offer a unique perspective on the relative influence of these factors in the language learning process and outcome.

Heritage language speakers are also relevant for second language acquisition, for both theoretical and pedagogical reasons (Montrul, 2009). An increasing trend in many foreign language classes, originally conceived and developed for second language learners, is the presence of heritage language learners. Among language teachers and program directors, there is growing recognition that heritage language learners are a different breed whose partial knowledge of the language presents a unique set of challenges to language teaching practices. Thus, it is fundamental to understand how and how fast heritage language learners can learn their heritage language in a classroom setting, and whether it is realistic to expect them to become full native speakers.

If the same or different teaching methods and materials utilized in second language classes are to be used with heritage speakers, any pedagogical practice must be informed by a deep understanding of what L2 learners and heritage speakers have or do not have in common. On the one hand, heritage language learners and L2 learners differ in the age of acquisition of the target language, the type of exposure (input), and the context of acquisition (naturalistic vs instructed). For some theoretical accounts, the learning mechanisms deployed in childhood and adulthood are very different, and therefore the outcome of L1 and L2 acquisition is also different. In general, adult heritage speakers have good or better aural comprehension skills than oral production and written skills. By contrast, L2 learners have better written skills than oral skills, by virtue of having learned the language primarily in a formal setting with limited opportunity for interaction with native speakers. Thus, their language learning experience may play a role in how they process and learn the language in the classroom.

But heritage speakers also share some characteristics with L2 learners, including non-native like attainment, fossilization, and transfer errors from the dominant language (Montrul, 2008). In fact, recent research has revealed that many of the problem areas typical of second language learners, like inflectional morphology, for example, seem to be problem areas for heritage speakers as well (Au *et al.*, 2002; Montrul, 2011). Given these findings, it is crucial to carry out systematic comparisons of L2 learners and heritage speakers in order to understand the linguistic ability of the two types of learners, as well as areas of differences and similarities. Therefore, pinpointing specific areas of linguistic knowledge in which the heritage language speakers and L2 learners may differ or not is an important first step in informing any type of classroom-based instructional intervention, materials development, or language program direction. But most importantly for the field of second language acquisition, the study of heritage language learners can also inform classic theoretical debates on the nature of linguistic knowledge as a function of age and experience in L2 learners.

See also: age effects in SLA, attrition, bilingualism and SLA, fossilization, native speaker, ultimate attainment

References

Au, T., Knightly, L., Jun, S. and Oh, J. (2002). Overhearing a language during childhood. *Psychological Science*, *13*, 238–43.

Bolonyai, A. (2007). (In)vulnerable agreement in incomplete bilingual L1 learners. *The International Journal of Bilingualism*, *11*, 3–21.

de Bot, K. and Gorter, D. (1995). A European perspective on heritage languages. *The Modern Language Journal*, *89*, 4, 612–16.

Cummins, J. (1995). A proposal for action: Strategies for recognizing heritage language competence as a learning resource within the mainstream classroom. *The Modern Language Journal*, *89*, 4, 585–91.

Fishman, J. (1991). Three hundred plus years of heritage language education in the United States. In J.K. Peyton, D.A. Ranard and S. McGinnis (eds), *Heritage Languages in America: Preserving a National Resource*, pp. 81–97. McHenry, IL: Center for Applied Linguistics.

Hornberger, N. and Wang, S. (2008). Who are our heritage language learners? In Brinton, D., Kagan, O. and Bauckus, S. (eds), *Heritage Language Education: A New Field Emerging*, pp. 3–35. New York: Routledge.

Moag, R. (1995). Semi-native speakers: How to hold and mold them. In V. Gambhir (ed.), *The Teaching and Acquisition of South Asian Languages*, pp. 168–81. Philadelphia, PA: University of Pennsylvania Press.

Montrul, S. (2008). *Incomplete Acquisition in Bilingualism. Re-examining the Age Factor.* Amsterdam: John Benjamins.

——(2009). Heritage language programs. In C. Doughty and M. Long (eds), *The Handbook of Second and Foreign Language Teaching*, pp. 182–200. Malden, MA: Blackwell.

——(2011). Morphological variability in L2 learners and heritage speakers. *Studies in Second Language Acquisition*, *33* (2), 163–192.

Polinsky, M. (2000). A composite linguistic profile of a speaker of Russian in the U.S. In Kagan, O. and Rifkin, B., S. Bauckus (eds), *The Learning and Teaching of Slavic Languages and Cultures*. Bloomington, IN: Slavica Publishers.

——(2007). Incomplete acquisition: American Russian. *Journal of Slavic Linguistics*, *14*, 191–262.

Silva-Corvalán, C. (1994). *Language Contact and Change: Spanish in Los Angeles*. Oxford: Oxford University Press.

Valdés, G. (2000). Introduction. *Spanish for Native Speakers, Volume I.* AATSP Professional Development Series Handbook for teachers K-16. New York: Harcourt College.

Further reading

Anderson, R. (1999). Noun phrase gender agreement in language attrition. Preliminary results. *Bilingual Research Journal*, *23*, 318–37. (Excellent longitudinal study of language loss in children once they start using the native language less and less with peers.)

Brinton, D., Kagan, O. and Bauckus, S. (2008). *Heritage Language Education. A New Field Emerging*. New York: Routledge. (Comprehensive and multidisciplinary perspectives on heritage languages beyond the United States.)

Kondo-Brown, K. (ed.) (2006). *Heritage Language Development. Focus on East Asian Immigrants*. Amsterdam: John Benjamins. (Sociolinguistic accounts of the state of East Asian heritage languages in Canada and the United States.)

Polinsky, M. and Kagan, O. (2007). Heritage languages in the "wild" and in the classroom. *Language and Linguistics Compass*, *1*, 5, 368–95. (Excellent overview of the linguistic profile of heritage speakers who attend and do not attend language classes.)

Valdés, G., Fishman, J., Chávez, R., and Pérez, W. (2006). *Developing Minority Language Resources: The Case of Spanish in California*. Clevedon: Multilingual Matters. (Comprehensive study of historical, political and educational situation of Spanish heritage speakers in California.)

Hypothesis testing

Ali Shehadeh
United Arab Emirates University

In language learning, hypothesis testing is defined as "the testing of ideas ('hypotheses') about language to see whether they are right or wrong" (Richards *et al.*, 1992: 171). The issue of hypothesis testing has been of interest to second language acquisition (SLA) researchers in light of observations by interlanguage (IL) studies that (a) learners form hypotheses about the structural properties of the target language (TL) based on the second language (L2) input, their first language (L1) knowledge, and Universal Grammar (e.g., Corder, 1981; McLaughlin, 1990), and (b) output is a means of testing these hypotheses. Specifically, SLA researchers argue that learners formulate hypotheses about how the L2 works with respect to pronunciation, word selection, and morphosyntax, for instance. When they produce the L2, they test these hypotheses out to see whether they are correct/accurate or not, or whether they work or not.

For example, Swain (1995: 126), citing evidence from IL research, states: "A considerable body of research and theorizing over the last two decades has suggested that output, particularly erroneous output, can often be an indication that a learner has formulated a hypothesis about how the [target] language works, and is testing it out." Swain (1985, 1995) also argues that learner output contains a series of hypotheses representing the learner's best guess as to how to say or write something in the TL. She further states that "producing output is one way of testing a hypothesis about comprehensibility or linguistic well-formedness" (Swain, 1995: 126).

In a series of articles and studies, Swain (e.g., 1995, 1998, 2000) examined the role of hypothesis testing in L2 learning in conjunction with the other two functions of output within the framework of her comprehensible output hypothesis for SLA (i. e., the noticing function and the metalinguistic function) through collaborative dialogue. Specifically, she investigated how dialogue as a joint activity enables learners to verbalize and test out their hypotheses about the TL. Based on her findings, Swain argues that production enables learners to notice a gap (a problem) in their IL system. To overcome this gap, they verbalize the problem, and jointly start to work on solving it by explicitly engaging in a hypothesis-testing activity and negotiating about TL forms until a satisfactory resolution was reached. For instance, in commenting on the findings of her 1998 study, Swain writes: "students formed hypotheses and tested them against available resources. Vocabulary, morphology, and complex syntactic structures each became the focus of their attention, and in turn, their attention became focused by talking about the problem. Verbalization of the problem allowed them the opportunity to reflect on it and, apparently, served as one source of their linguistic knowledge" (Swain, 1998: 79).

A continuing concern about this hypothesis formation and testing activity for SLA, however, is whether learners might internalize incorrect forms and structures. Seeking to address this question, and to determine if the solutions reached during the dialogue were retained in the students' IL, a dyad-specific posttest one week later administered in Swain's (1998) study referenced above revealed that there was a strong tendency for students to "stick with" the knowledge they had constructed collaboratively the previous week. Students' responses on the posttest showed a 70 to 80 percent correspondence with the solutions – right or wrong – that they arrived at in their dialogues.

In a study specifically designed to investigate learners' hypothesis testing in L2, Shehadeh (2003) found that the eight adult intermediate proficiency level ESL nonnative speakers (NNSs) who participated in his study tested out 39 hypotheses (termed hypothesis-testing episodes, or HTEs) about how the TL works within 72 minutes of interaction, with an average of one hypothesis every 1.8 minutes. Shehadeh also found that of these 39 HTEs, 24 (or 62 per cent) resulted in well-formed output and 15 (or 38 per cent) in ill-formed output. He further found that those 15 HTEs that resulted in ill-formed utterances (phonological, vocabulary, and morphosyntax) went completely unchallenged by interlocutors. That is, Shehadeh's study revealed that unless NNSs sought native speakers' (NSs') help (which was rare), NS interlocutors provided no corrective feedback or negative evidence to NNSs' output, even though the hypothesis testing attempts by NNSs resulted in ill-formed utterances.

Of potentially important consequence for SLA (see below), Shehadeh (2003) observed that some of these hypotheses which resulted in ill-formed language and which were not challenged by the NS interlocutors have resurfaced subsequently in the NNSs' language in the same turn or later in the interaction as confirmed hypotheses about the L2 as in the following example from Shehadeh's study in which an NNS had to describe a picture to an NS partner who had to reproduce the picture as precisely as possible solely on the basis of the NNS's description:

> NNS:
> you have two chairs (0.8) one near of the bed (0.8) near of the bed (0.9) near to the bed (1.0) and the other near to the bottom left corner (2.0) and behind the chair (1.0) you have a door (3.0) now near to the door and go to the left corner
>
> NS:
> yes (0.9) can you see the door full view?
>
> Note: (…) indicates pauses in seconds/fractions of a second.
>
> (Shehadeh, 2003: 163)

All together, research findings suggest that, on the one hand, hypothesis testing does serve the L2 learning process as in the framework of Swain's comprehensible output hypothesis. That is, it may actually result in the internalization or consolidation of linguistic knowledge. On the other hand, it might have other consequences for SLA, namely, it can in part predict fossilization in L2. For instance, Ellis (1994: 354), citing evidence from previous research (e.g., Vigil and Oller, 1976), argues that "positive cognitive feedback (signaling 'I understand you') results in fossilization." According to this explanation, failure to challenge the NNS's output (as in the example above), a fellow learner's output, or solutions in a joint activity that exhibit ill-formed utterances or rules might also lead to the confirmation and internalization of these utterances or rules, resulting in fossilization.

Obviously, more detailed analysis of learner hypothesis testing activity is needed in order to confirm whether and to what extent linguistic knowledge is actually internalized in this way. Also, it remains to be seen if confirmed hypotheses exhibiting ill-formed utterances or rules would lead to permanent internalization of these utterances or rules by L2 learners; or whether these are still open, and to what degree, to further revisions in the light of new or negative evidence.

See also: fossilization, Fundamental Difference Hypothesis (FDH), interlanguage, noticing hypothesis, output hypothesis, positive and negative evidence

References

Corder, P. (1981). *Error Analysis and Interlanguage.* Oxford: Oxford University Press.

Ellis, R. (1994). *The Study of Second Language Acquisition.* Oxford: Oxford University Press.

McLaughlin, B. (1990). Restructuring. *Applied Linguistics*, *11*/2, 113–28.

Richards, J., Platt, J. and Platt, H. (1992). *Longman Dictionary of Language Teaching and Applied Linguistics*. London: Longman.

Shehadeh, A. (2003). Learner output, hypothesis testing, and internalizing linguistic knowledge. *System*, *31*/2, 155–71.

Swain, M. (1985). Communicative competence: some roles of comprehensible input and comprehensible output in its development. In S. Gass and C. Madden (eds), *Input in Second Language Acquisition*, pp. 235–53. Rowley, MA: Newbury House.

——(1995). Three functions of output in second language learning. In G. Cook and B. Seidlhofer (eds), *Principle and Practice in Applied Linguistics: Studies in Honor of H.G. Widdowson*, pp. 125–44. Oxford: Oxford University Press.

——(1998). Focus on Form through Conscious Reflection. In C. Doughty and J. Williams (eds), *Focus on Form in Classroom Second Language Acquisition*, pp. 64–81. Cambridge: Cambridge University Press.

——(2000). The Output Hypothesis and Beyond: Mediating Acquisition through Collaborative Dialogue. In C. Lantolf (ed.), *Sociocultural Theory and Second Language Learning*, pp. 97–114. Oxford: Oxford University Press.

Vigil, F. and Oller, J. (1976). Rule fossilization: A Tentative model. *Language Learning*, *26*, 281–95.

I

Identity theory

Kimberly Noels
University of Alberta

Discussions of identity in second language acquisition research have been informed by a variety of disciplinary and theoretical traditions. Common to most contemporary definitions of identity, however, is the notion that identity is a subjective experience of holding and/or act of claiming a set of characteristics and/or a social position that distinguishes one from other persons, and is important to one's sense of self (Leets *et al.*, 1996).

Identity theories in SLA can be broadly differentiated according to the relative emphasis they place on the socio-structural and socio-constructive aspects of identity. The socio-structural (or "intergroup") perspective partly came about in response to World War II and various civil rights movements and as a reaction to predominant social psychological theories that generally explained these large-scale intergroup dynamics in terms of individual traits or interpersonal interactions. Scholars from this perspective emphasize how the structural relations of groups within a society relate to identity patterns and intergroup behavior, including discrimination, collective action, and social change. For instance, Giles and his colleagues (see Noels and Giles, 2009, for an overview) maintain that we tend to categorize people, including ourselves, into different social groups (e.g., ethnolinguistic, gender, age), and compare these groups on socially important dimensions. Because we know to which groups we belong (termed "social identity"), we also know how our group (and implicitly, ourselves) compares with other groups. We are assumed to have a tendency to see our own group in a relatively positive light and strive to maintain that positive distinctiveness. When a speech style (e.g., language variety, accent, etc.) is a valued component of identification, it can be gainfully used to differentiate one's own group from other groups. If the intergroup comparison results in an unfavorable evaluation of our ethnolinguistic group, then we may try to learn the other language in order to move into the more socially valued group, engage in strategies to overcome the inequities between groups, or reframe the comparison in order to see our group in a more favorable light. Other frameworks, including Lambert's (1978) discussions of "additive and subtractive bilingualism," Gardner's (2010) discussion of the "integrative orientation," and Clément's (1980) discussion of "fear of assimilation" and patterns of identity "integration" and assimilation" also draw on the idea that the relative socio-structural status of groups and intergroup relations have important implications for identity, motivation, and language learning and use.

Socio-constructionist (or "sociocultural") perspectives on identity in SLA refer to a range of conceptualizations that are informed by post-structuralist and critical theory (see Pavlenko and Blackledge, 2004; Ricento, 2005, for overviews). This perspective became prominent partly in response to colonization and increasing globalization and transnational immigration, as well as concerns that some structural theories portray persons as being determined by the social conditions in which they live, and as having relatively immutable characteristics associated with the social groups to which they belong (Block, 2007). At least three themes characterize this perspective, including the interpersonal construction of identities, the indeterminacy of the relation between language and identity, and power and positioning within real and/ or imagined communities.

A first theme is that identities are negotiated through face-to-face or mediated interactions between individuals. Identity is assumed to be a relational and dialogical phenomenon, such that we construct identities through our discursive practices, positioning ourselves and others in order to claim or deny particular identities. Moreover, we generally negotiate multiple, intersecting identities (e.g., language, gender, age) simultaneously. Thus, identity work involves continual positioning and repositioning of the self and others during any given social interaction and/or across different interactions with the same or other people.

A second theme underscores that interactants can use language in diverse, creative ways to make identity claims; eschewed are assumptions of homogeneous language groups with distinct boundaries and of a one-to-one correspondence between language and identity. For instance, some learners live in multilingual contexts, where they might regularly use the target language, but not at all identify with that ethnolinguistic group (e.g., in some ESL contexts). Some learners might use the language to denote identities other than an ethnolinguistic identity (e.g., a professional identity). In addition, learners might create hybrid identities, in which aspects of different ethnolinguistic identities are combined in new ways, perhaps as a way to cope with feelings of ambivalence and conflict that might arise from the instability and contestability of identity positionings. Thus, a multiplicity of language and identities relations are possible.

A third theme is that the positioning of identities occurs within particular contexts, or "communities of practice" (e.g., a language classroom, a language community). Depending on their position within that community, each person is assumed to have more or less "capital," or resources, to make desired identity claims. Identities, then, are shaped by social interactions within a particular social structure, but reciprocally identity negotiations shape those social conditions. Moreover, our understanding of our relationship to others in our social world includes not only our positioning and experience of interactions in the here-and-now, but also how we imagine ourselves to be in the future. Norton (2000) maintains that this vision of a future self in an "imagined community" has considerable motivational significance, as it indicates how much we should "invest" in learning other languages – to the extent that we can envision ourselves as being participants in that community and acquiring the kinds of capital associated with that community, we may be more willing to invest time and energy into learning that group's language. Norton's work highlights learners' agency to make language and identity choices and their capacity to resist identity ascriptions, within the constraints and affordances of the social context and the learner's available resources.

See also: acculturation model, communities of practice, individual differences in SLA, investment, motivation, social and sociocultural influences on SLA

References

Block, D. (2007). *Second Language Identities*. London: Continuum.

Clément, R. (1986). Second language proficiency and acculturation: An investigation of the effects of language status and individual characteristics. *Journal of Language and Social Psychology*, *5*, 271–90.

Gardner, R.C. (2010). *Motivation and Second Language Acquisition: The Socio-Educational Model*. New York: Peter Lang.

Lambert, W.E. (1978). Cognitive and socio-cultural consequences of bilingualism. *Canadian Modern Language Review*, *34*, 537–47.

Leets, L., Giles, H. and Clément, R. (1996). Explicating ethnicity in theory and communication research. *Multilingua*, *15*, 115–47.

Noels, K.A. and Giles, H. (2009). Social identity and language learning. In W. Ritchie and T. Bhatia (eds), *The New Handbook of Second Language Acquisition*, pp. 647–70. Bingley: Emerald.

Norton, B. (2000). *Identity and Language Learning: Gender, Ethnicity and Educational Change*. London: Longman/Pearson Education.

Pavlenko, A. and Blackledge, A. (2004). Introduction: New theoretical approaches to the study of negotiation of identities in multilingual contexts. In A. Pavlenko and A. Blackledge (eds), *Negotiation of Identities in Multilingual Contexts*, pp. 1–33. Clevedon: Multilingual Matters.

Ricento, T. (2005). Considerations of identity in L2 learning. In E. Hinkel (ed.), *Handbook of Research in Second Language Learning*, pp. 895–910. Mahwah, NJ: Lawrence Erlbaum.

Idiomaticity

Stefanie Wulff
University of North Texas

The terms *idiom(aticity)* has two distinct meanings. In linguistic theory, *idiom* is reserved for phrases that behave like single words in some respects and like assembled phrases in others. One the one hand, idioms are not just phrasal lexemes because they can be modified both lexically and syntactically. The idiom *walk a tightrope* ("to act very carefully so that you avoid either of two opposite bad situations") is an example in question: an adjective like *legal* can be inserted before the noun (*to walk a legal tightrope*). On the other hand, idioms do not license the full range of syntactic operations as regular phrases do. (2) and (3) provide examples of idioms that do not allow tense shifting and rephrasing in passive voice, respectively.

(2) a. It takes one to know one.
    b. *It took one to know one.
(3) a. He shot the breeze.
    b. *The breeze was shot (by him).

Given the highly idiosyncratic nature of idioms, they are best defined as a class of phrases that exhibit a range of features to different degrees. Nunberg *et al.* (1994: 492–93) list the following features, with conventionality as the only necessary condition for idiom status:

conventionality: the meaning or use of an idiom cannot be predicted (in full) on the basis of "knowledge of the independent conventions that determine the use of their constituents when they appear in isolation from one another" (Nunberg *et al.*, 1994: 492)
formal inflexibility: idioms are syntactically restricted
figuration: idioms have a non-literal, or figurative, meaning
proverbiality: idioms often describe a more abstract activity in terms of a more concrete activity (consider *climb the wall*, *spill the beans*, or *break the ice*)
informality: idioms tend to be associated with colloquial speech or register
affect: idioms typically entail an evaluative or affective stance

Idioms pose a significant problem for theories of language in which syntax and lexis are strictly separate components. Accordingly, in early generative approaches, idioms were mostly discarded as anomalies (Fraser, 1970). More recent frameworks, on the contrary, attribute idioms a more central role by discarding of a binary distinction between syntax and the lexicon, thereby eliminating the need to draw a sharp distinction between idioms and regular phrases, and instead viewing both as symbolic units which differ with regard to their overall idiomaticity.

In Construction Grammar, for instance, idioms are stored alongside morphemes, words, and abstract grammatical frames in an extended mental lexicon (Goldberg, 2006). Table 8 provides a schematic representation.

Phraseological definitions of idioms and idiomaticity

Idioms have also received considerable attention in the field of phraseology (that is, the study of multiword units). In phraseological models, idioms are

Table 8 A schematic representation of the constructicon (adapted from Goldberg, 2006: 5).

morpheme	*pre-, -ing*
word	*avocado, anaconda, and*
complex word	*dare-devil, shoo-in*
complex word (partially filled)	[N-s] (for regular plurals)
idiom (filled)	*going great guns, give the devil his due*
idiom (partially filled)	*jog* <someone's> *memory, send* <someone> *to the cleaners*
covariational conditional	*the Xer the Yer*(e.g. *the more you think about it, the less you understand*)
ditransitive (double object)	Subj Obj1 Obj2 (e.g. *he gave her a fish taco*; *he baked her a muffin*)
passive	Subj Aux VPpp (PP_{by}) (e.g. *the armadillo was hit by a car*)

defined as a subset of phrases that are maximally conventionalized, and which exhibit the above idiomaticity features different extents (thus resonating with recent grammatical theories like Construction Grammar; see Wulff (2008) for an empirical study of these features in V NP-idioms, adopting a constructionist perspective). Howarth (1998), for example, proposes a model in which phrases can be located on a phraseological spectrum ranging from free combinations to restricted collocations, figurative idioms, and pure idioms (in increasing order of conventionalization, figuration, and formal inflexibility).

This positioning of idioms as one instantiation of phraseological language establishes the link to the second meaning of *idiomaticity* that is of central relevance in a second language acquisition context: the ability to express oneself fluently and accurately *at the same time*. Error-free production alone does not guarantee fluency; conversely, fluent production does not entail accurate production. Advanced level proficiency requires combining the two in a target-like, or idiomatic fashion (Pawley and Syder, 1983). As Howarth (1998) notes,

> [M]any learners fail to understand the existence of the central area of the phraseological spectrum between free combinations and idioms. It is in handling restricted collocations that errors of both a lexical and grammatical structure constantly occur.
>
> (p. 186)

In this sense, idiomaticity can be seen as a major indicator of (advanced) language proficiency (Yorio, 1989).

Psycholinguistic explorations of idiomaticity from an SLA perspective

The wealth of theoretical literature, as well as psycho-linguistic studies of idiom processing by native speakers (see Cacciari and Tabossi, 1995 for an overview) stands at odds with the scarcity of full-fledged theoretical models of L2 idiom processing and acquisition. In line with Howarth's (1998) observation quoted above, there is general agreement that the mastery of idiomatic language characterizes only advanced L2 learners, and that this acquisition process is a gradual one.

Matlock and Heredia (2002) outline an account in which the way idioms are processed shifts with increasing language proficiency: beginner level learners start out translating the idiom back to their native language before the figurative meaning of the expression is accessed; advanced language learners process the figurative meanings increasingly directly. According to Liontas (2002), both the literal and the figurative meaning of an idiom are processed separately, and interpretation defaults to literal interpretations; alternative interpretations are gradually eliminated through cues afforded by the context. Similarly, Cieślicka's *Literal Salience Resonant* (LSR) model of L2 idiom comprehension is based on the assumption that literal meanings are inherently more salient to the learner (Cieślicka,

2010). The learning of figurative meanings is a process of automatization in which the connections between the lexical nodes of the idiom's constituent words in the learner's mental lexicon are gradually strengthened through repeated co-activation until the figurative meaning can be accessed holistically in the lexical network.

See also: automaticity, chunking and prefabrication, formulaic language, fluency, language and the lexicon in SLA, metaphor

References

Cacciari, C. and Tabossi, P. (eds) (1995). *Idioms: Processing, Structure, and Interpretation*. Hillsdale, NJ: Lawrence Erlbaum.

Cieślicka, A. (2010). Formulaic language in L2 storage, retrieval and production of idioms by second language learners. In M. Pütz and L. Sicola (eds), *Cognitive Processing in Second Language Acquisition*, pp. 149–68. Amsterdam and Philadelphia, PA: John Benjamins.

Fraser, B. (1970). Idioms within a transformational grammar. *Foundations of Language*, *6*, 22–42.

Goldberg, A.E. (2006). *Constructions at Work: The Nature of Generalization in Language*. Oxford: Oxford University Press.

Howarth, P. (1998). The phraseology of learners' academic writing. In A.P. Cowie (ed.), *Phraseology*, pp. 161–86. Oxford: Clarendon.

Liontas, J. (2002). *Context and Idiom Understanding in Second Languages*. Amsterdam and Philadelphia, PA: John Benjamins.

Matlock, T. and Heredia, R.R. (2002). Understanding phrasal verbs in monolinguals and bilinguals. In R.R. Heredia and J. Altarriba (eds), *Bilingual Sentence Processing*, pp. 251–174. Amsterdam and Philadelphia, PA: John Benjamins.

Nunberg, G., Sag, I.A. and Wasow, T. (1994). Idioms. *Language*, *70*, 491–538.

Pawley, A. and Syder, F.H. (1983). Two puzzles for linguistic theory: Native-like selection and native-like fluency. In J.C. Richards and R.W. Schmidt (eds), *Language and Communication*, pp. 191–226. New York: Longman.

Wulff, S. (2008). *Rethinking Idiomaticity: A Usage-based Approach*. London and New York: Continuum.

Yorio, C. (1989). Idiomaticity as an indicator of second language proficiency. In K. Hyltenstam K. and L.K. Olber (eds), *Bilingualism Across the Lifespan*, pp. 55–72. Cambridge: Cambridge University Press.

Further reading

Chafe, W. (1968). Idiomaticity as an anomaly in the Chomskyan paradigm. *Foundations of Language*, *4*, 109–27. (A classic paper critiquing early generative approaches to idioms.)

Croft, W. and Cruse, D.A. (2004). *Cognitive Linguistics*. Cambridge: Cambridge University Press. (Detailed discussion of the role of idioms in cognitive-linguistic frameworks.)

Everaert, M, van der Linden, E.-J., Schenk, A., and Schreuder, R. (eds) (1995). *Idioms: Structural and Psychological Perspectives*. Hillsdale, NJ: Lawrence Erlbaum. (Features some of the most influential authors in the field of idiomaticity research.)

Moon, R. (1998). *Fixed Expressions and Idioms in English: A Corpus-based Approach*. Oxford: Clarendon. (A comprehensive, corpus-based study of different idiomaticity features.)

Wray, A. (2002). *Formulaic Language and the Lexicon*. Cambridge: Cambridge University Press. (In-depth overview of phraseological research and its implications for theories of the mental lexicon.)

Implicational scaling

Gisela Håkansson
Lund University

Implicational scaling is a method for the handling of language variation by looking at the distribution of linguistic features. The aim is to describe the implicational relations between certain items, such that the presence of X implies the presence of Y, but not vice versa. Implicational scaling was first introduced by Guttman (1944) to measure social attitudes, but after that the method has come to be used extensively to describe linguistic variation, for example in creole studies (e.g. DeCamp, 1971) and in research on second language acquisition (e.g. Hyltenstam, 1977; Pienemann, 1998).

Most implicational analyses are based on binary judgments – either a presence or a non-presence of a feature, marked by plus or minus. One column is used for each category, and then the rows and columns are shifted in order to find out whether there is a scale pattern. Table 9 below illustrates a hypothesized distribution of variables 1, 2, 3, 4, 5, by the speakers A, B, C, D, E, and F.

Table 9 Distribution of data

	variables				
Speakers	1	2	3	4	5
A	+	-	+	+	+
B	+	+	+	+	+
C	-	-	+	-	-
D	+	-	+	+	-
E	+	-	+	-	-

An implicational scale of the same data is illustrated below:

Table 10 Implicational scale of data

	variables				
Speakers	3	1	4	5	2
B	+	+	+	+	+
A	+	+	+	+	-
D	+	+	+	-	-
E	+	+	-	-	-
C	+	-	-	-	-

The scale above shows a pattern where the presence of a variable to the right implies the presence of a variable to the left. No speaker uses a variable to the right without also using a variable to the left. Speaker B only uses all five variables, Speaker A four variables, Speaker D three variables, Speaker E two variables and Speaker D only one variable. (Such a perfect scale is rarely found in real data, but deviations from the perfect scale can be measured by coefficient of reproducibility, see Guttman, 1944.)

An implicational pattern can be used to show creole continua. For example, DeCamp (1971) demonstrates that certain Jamaican Creole features implies the presence of other features, so that a speaker A using feature 2 also uses feature 1, whereas another speaker only uses feature 1. These linguistic variables occur in a systematic fashion and are related to social class of the speaker.

In the field of second language acquisition, the use of implicational scaling makes it possible to capture the dynamics of interlanguage, or learner language. Hyltenstam (1977) was one of the first researchers to show how learners develop along a series of developmental stages in placement of negation. In Processability Theory (Pienemann, 1998), implicational scales are important tools to illustrate the gradual and systematic development of processing resources for the second language. The learner proceeds through different stages by accumulating rules of the second language.

See also: development in SLA, implicational universals, measuring and researching SLA, Pidginization and creolization, Processability Theory (PI), variationist approaches to SLA

References

DeCamp, D. (1971). Implicational scales and sociolinguistic linearity. *Linguistics*, *9*/73, 30–43.

Guttman, L. (1944). A basis for scaling qualitative data. *American Sociological Review*, *9*, 139–150.

Hyltenstam, K. (1977). Implicational patterns in interlanguage syntax variation. *Language Learning*, *27*, 383–411.

Pienemann, M. (1998). *Language Processing and Second Language Development: Processability Theory*. Amsterdam: Benjamins.

Implicational universals

Anna Giacalone Ramat
Università di Pavia

Two major approaches to language universals have been adopted in recent linguistic research: the

Chomskyan approach, which assumes the existence of a Universal Grammar constrained by a set of principles and parameters meant to be an innate endowment of all human beings and the functional-typological approach, which emerged from J. Greenberg's (1966) seminal work on universals of word order and morphology. The latter approach is based on a typological classification of linguistic phenomena collected from an adequate language sample: thus, cross-linguistic comparison and statistical generalizations are its basic methodological tools.

Language universals based on patterns of generalizations represent constraints on logically possible human language types. Universals can be distinguished into unrestricted and implicational. Unrestricted universals are cross-linguistic generalizations characterizing the distribution of languages along a single parameter: for example, all languages have vowels, but some of them have a larger vowel set than others. Implicational universals define constraints in the occurrence of logically independent grammatical parameters. Consider: "if a language has noun before demonstrative, then it has noun before relative clause" (Hawkins, 1983: 84). This universal can be symbolized: if *p* then *q*, or $P \supset Q$: this means that three types of languages are allowed, and correspond to the attested ones: NDem and NRel, not-NDem and NRel, not-NDem and not-NRel, while the fourth logically possible type NDem and not-NRel is excluded, or extremely rare.

In recent years, typological research has focused on deeper patterns than those described by simple implicational universals, establishing systematic correlations of word order for OV and VO languages:

> "VO type": VO, Prep, NG, NA, NNum, NDem, NRel
>
> "OV type": OV, Postp, GN, AN, NumN, DemN, RelN
>
> (Croft, 2003)

Divergent patterns are however attested: the combination DemN and NRel is present in European languages; the combination OV and NRel is especially frequent in Africa and America (Dryer, 1992). For this last combination a motivation has been proposed in terms of processing ease.

Typological hierarchies derived from a chain of implicational universals have been detected in different aspects of the grammar of human languages, such as accessibility to relativization, animacy, case, and number relations (Croft, 2003). Furthermore, prototypes have been identified based on correlations among values a grammatical category can assume: for example, the prototypical transitive clause results from a cluster of linguistic features, such as number of participants, degree of volitionality, agentivity, etc. (Hopper and Thompson, 1980).

Among the explanatory models used in typology, the notion of competing motivations is of primary relevance: it accounts for the conflict between the functionally based principles of iconicity and economy (see "functional typological linguistics") in the development of languages. For word order patterns Hawkins (1983) has proposed processing principles in the form of competing motivations for noun-modifier order: the heaviness of the modifier is one of such principles: heavier modifiers prefer to follow the head noun.

Explanations of many grammatical phenomena are fundamentally diachronic: for example, in some cases word order correlations are harmonic because a relationship has historically evolved from another, as shown by the correlation between prepositions and noun-genitive order, and postpositions and genitive-noun order, which can be accounted for in diachronic terms since adpositional constructions frequently develop out of genitive phrases (Bybee, 1988: 354).

Not only implicational universals and hierarchies have highly predictive power in synchronic cross-linguistic patterns, but they also govern linguistic change and change in language types.

See also: functional typological linguistics, implicational scaling, language typology and language distance, markedness, prototypes, Universal Grammar (UG) and SLA

References

Bybee, J. (1988). The diachronic dimension in explanations. In J.A. Hawkins (ed.), *Explaining Language Universals*, pp. 350–79. Oxford: Basil Blackwell.

Croft, W. (2003). *Typology and Universals*, 2nd edn. Cambridge: Cambridge University Press.

Dryer, M.S. (1992). The Greenbergian word order correlations. *Language*, *68*, 81–138.

Greenberg, J.H. (1966), Some universals of grammar with particular reference to the order of meaningful elements. In J.H. Greenberg (ed.), *Universals of Language*, pp. 73–113. Cambridge, MA: The MIT Press.

Hawkins, J.A. (1983), *Word Order Universals*. New York: Academic Press.

Hopper, P.J. and Thompson, S.A. (1980), Transitivity in grammar and discourse. *Language*, *56*, 251–99.

Further reading

Comrie, B. (1989), *Language Universals and Linguistic Typology*, 2nd edn. Oxford: Basil Blackwell.

Du Bois, J.A. (1985), Competing motivations. In J. Haiman (ed.). *Iconicity in Syntax*, pp. 343–66 Amsterdam: John Benjamins.

Hawkins, J.A. (ed.) (1988), *Explaining Language Universals*. Oxford: Basil Blackwell.

Haspelmath M., M. Dryer, D. Gil and B. Comrie (eds) (2005). *The World Atlas of Language Structures*. Oxford: Oxford University Press.

Implicature

Naoko Taguchi
Carnegie Mellon University

Paul Grice (1975) first coined the term *implicature* to refer to the implicit meaning we draw based on context of an utterance and our knowledge of how conversation works. Meaning is conveyed on two levels: utterance meaning, or the literal sense of words uttered; and force, or the speaker's intention behind the words (Thomas, 1995). Comprehension of implicature requires decoding linguistic and contextual cues and using them to make inferences of speakers' implied intentions behind the cues. This is a difficult task for L2 learners because they have to recognize the mismatch between the literal utterance and the intended meaning before reprocessing the literal information to infer the implied message. The greater the mismatch is, the greater the comprehension effort becomes.

Early SLA research on implicature goes back to the 1970s, when Carrell (1979) examined comprehension of indirect responses among ESL learners of different proficiency. She used a multiple choice questionnaire in which items had a situational frame followed by alternative statements. Learners were asked to choose the statement that best represents meaning of the indirect reply:

> Bob says: "Did you go to the movies last night?" Ann says: "I had to study last night."

a. Ann went to the movies last night.
b. Ann did not go to the movies last night. (CORRECT)
c. I have no idea at all whether (a) or (b).

Carrell found that the ESL learners' comprehension was significantly weaker than that of native speakers regardless of their proficiency.

The next line of SLA research on implicature is found in a series of studies conducted by Bouton in the mid–late 1990s (1992, 1994). Bouton significantly advanced Carrell's work by designing a test involving different types of implicature based on Grice's maxims. ESL learners took a multiple-choice test consisting of short written dialogues that included different types of implicature: relevance implicature, Pope implicature (saying 'Is Pope catholic?' to mean something obvious), irony, indirect criticisms, and sequence implicature. See the simplified sample items:

Relevance implicature

DAVID: Mandy just broke our date for the play. Now I've got two tickets for Saturday and no one to go with.

MARK: Have you met my sister? She's coming to see me this weekend.

(a) Mark can't remember if David has met his sister.

(b) There is nothing Mark can do to help David.
(c) Mark suggests that David take Mark's sister to the play. (CORRECT)

Indirect criticism

A: What did you think of Mark's term paper?
B: It was well-typed.
(a) He liked the paper; he thought it was good.
(b) He thought it was certainly well typed.
(c) He thought it was a good paper; he did like the form, though not the content.
(d) He didn't like it. (CORRECT)

Four types of implicature that remained difficult after 17 months were indirect criticism, Pope questions, sequence implicature, and irony. ESL learners' comprehension became native-like in relevance-based implicature after four-and-a-half years, but sequence and Pope implicature remained difficult.

Different level of comprehension difficulty found among implicature types lends support to the Relevance Theory (Sperber and Wilson, 1995). According to the theory, the degree of indirectness in an utterance is related to the amount of processing effort required for comprehension. Comprehension is easier when the preceding proposition is immediately accessible. But when the proposition is not salient, listeners need to construct some sort of bridging structure; as a result, comprehension becomes more difficult. Sperber and Wilson introduced the concept of contextual effects to explain processing effort. Although people can interpret a message in many different ways, they select an interpretation that has the greatest contextual effect (i.e., the most relevance in context) for the smallest processing effort. Conventionality is one type of contextual effect that assists comprehension: because they trigger routinized associations in long-term memory, conventional utterances do not require extensive analytical procedures.

These theoretical claims have recently been explored in a series of studies by Taguchi (2008a, 2011) in which a reaction time task with aural input was used to examine L2 English learners' online processing of implicature. Comprehension was tested for two types of implicature: indirect refusals and indirect opinions. Indirect refusals were conventional because they followed a common, predictable discourse pattern (i.e., giving an excuse for refusal). In contrast, indirect opinions were non-conventional because meaning was not embedded in predictable discourse patterns, and linguistic options for expressing the opinion were wide open. See samples:

Indirect refusal

BEN: Hey, what are we doing for dinner tonight?
BARBARA: I don't know.
BEN: How about if we go out to eat tonight. How about Chinese food?
BARBARA: Don't you think we should finish the left over?
QUESTION: Does Barbara want Chinese food?

Indirect opinion

BEN: I can't believe I fell asleep in the middle of the movie last night. Did you watch it till the end?
BARBARA: Yeah, I did.
BEN: Did you like it?
BARBARA: I was glad when it was over.
QUESTION: Did Barbara like the movie?

Supporting the Relevance Theory, results showed that, regardless of participants' learning contexts, indirect refusals were easier and faster to comprehend than indirect opinions. Higher proficiency led to higher accuracy but not speed, and there was no significant relationship between the two dimensions. Learners' comprehension of both implicatures improved over time, but the gains were greater in accuracy than speed for EFL learners, while the pattern was reversed for ESL learners.

In summary, the last three decades have seen a great advancement in studies of L2 comprehension of implicature. Drawing on pragmatic and cognitive processing theories, these research efforts have elevated the status of implicature from linguistic objects to learning objects through which some of the central topics of SLA – developmental patterns, and contextual and individual factors affecting the patterns – are explored. Because previous findings were confined to L2 English (excluding Koike, 1996; Taguchi, 2008b), future research may be prolific if target languages are expanded. In addition, the scope of implicature could go beyond nonliteral utterances to more nuanced implicit meanings, including jokes and sarcasms. Correspondingly, test items could be improved if artificially created dialogues are eliminated and replaced with naturalistic sources such as corpora of conversations, films, and advertisements.

See also: communicative competence, context of situation, discourse processing, pragmatics, pragmalinguistics, speech acts

References

Bouton, L. (1992). The interpretation of implicature in English by NNS: Does it come automatically without being explicitly taught? In L. Bouton (ed.), *Pragmatics and Language Learning Monograph Series*, vol. 3. Urbana-Champaign, IL: Division of English as an International Language, University of Illinois.

——(1994). Can NNS skill in interpreting implicature in American English be improved through explicit instruction?: A pilot study. In L. Bouton and Y. Kachuru (eds), *Pragmatics and Language Learning Monograph Series*, vol. 5. Urbana-Champaign, IL: Division of English as an International Language, University of Illinois.

Carrell, P. (1979). Indirect speech acts in ESL: Indirect answers. In C. Yorio, K. Perkins, and J. Schachter (eds), *On TESOL '79: The Learner I Focus* (pp. 297–307). Washington, DC: TESOL.

Grice, P. (1975). Logic and conversation. In P. Cole and J. Morgan (eds), *Syntax and Semantics*, vol. 3. New York: Academic Press.

Koike, D. (1996). Transfer of pragmatic competence and suggestions in Spanish foreign language learning. In S.M. Gass and J. Neu (eds), *Speech Acts across Cultures*, pp. 257–81. Berlin: Mouton de Gruyter.

Sperber, D. and Wilson, D. (1995). *Relevance: Communication and Cognition*, 2nd edn. Cambridge: Cambridge University Press.

Taguchi, N. (2008a) The role of learning environment in the development of pragmatic comprehension: A comparison of gains between EFL and ESL learners. *Studies in Second Language Acquisition*, *30*, 423–52.

——(2008b) Pragmatic comprehension in Japanese as a foreign language. *Modern Language Journal*, *92*, 558–76.

——(2011). The effect of L2 proficiency and study-abroad experience in pragmatic comprehension. *Language Learning*.

Thomas, J. (1995). *Meaning in Interaction: An Introduction to Pragmatics*. London: Longman.

Implicit learning

Patrick Rebuschat
University of Wales, Bangor

Implicit learning refers to the ability to acquire unconscious knowledge without intending to. The process of implicit learning is assumed to underlie the human capacity to extract knowledge from complex, rule-governed stimulus domains and, as such, appears to be an fundamental process of human cognition (see Cleeremans *et al.*, 1998; Perruchet, 2008; Shanks, 2005, for overviews). Many essential skills, including language comprehension and production, social interaction and intuitive decision-making, are largely dependent on implicit knowledge (Berry and Dienes, 1993; Reber, 1993). The following entry consists of two parts. The first part defines the term *implicit learning* and briefly discusses (lack of) awareness as a criterion of implicitness. The second part then reviews studies that focused on the implicit learning of a second language (L2). The entry concludes with suggestions for future research.

What is implicit learning?

The term *implicit learning* was first employed by Arthur Reber (1967) to describe a process during which subjects acquire knowledge about a complex, rule-governed stimulus domain without intending to and without becoming aware of the knowledge they have acquired. In Reber's (1967, exp. 2) seminal study, subjects were given letter strings such as TPTS, VXXVPS and TPTXXVS and simply asked to memorize them. Unbeknownst to the subjects, the arrangement of letters was determined by a finite-state grammar. After the memorization task, subjects were informed that the previous letter sequences had been generated by a complex system. They were then given new letter sequences, only half of which followed the same grammar, and instructed to judge whether the test sequences were grammatical or not. Reber (1967) found that subjects judged 79 per cent of all letter sequences correctly, which indicated that simple memorization of grammatical strings was sufficient for subjects to derive information about the underlying grammar. Interestingly, when asked to verbalize the rules that generated the letter strings, subjects were unable to do so. In other words, subjects were able to acquire knowledge without intending to (after all, they did not know they were going to be tested, nor were they informed in advance about the existence of the grammar) and without becoming aware of the acquired knowledge (they were unable to verbally describe the grammar). Reber (1967) used the term *implicit learning* to differentiate the process of incidental, unaware learning from that of *explicit learning*, a learning process in which subjects are instructed to actively look for patterns and develop conscious knowledge as a result.

In psychology, the most commonly used criterion for disentangling implicit and explicit knowledge is awareness (see Williams, 2009, for discussion). Implicit knowledge is unconscious knowledge which subjects are generally not aware of possessing. Explicit knowledge is conscious knowledge which subjects will be aware of possessing, though they might still not be able to verbalize it. There are several ways of measuring whether or not the acquired knowledge is conscious or unconscious (see Rebuschat, submitted, for a comprehensive overview). One of the most common procedures is to simply prompt subjects to verbalize any rules they might have noticed while performing on the experimental tasks. In this case, knowledge is considered to be unconscious when subjects show a learning effect (e.g. above-chance performance on a grammaticality judgment task), despite being unable to describe the knowledge that underlies their performance (e.g., Reber, 1967).

The use of verbal reports as a measure of awareness has been criticized for a variety of reasons (see Shanks and St. John, 1994, for an overview). The main point of criticism is that verbal reports constitute a relatively insensitive indicator of awareness, since subjects may be aware of the knowledge they have acquired but simply be unable to verbalize it. Dienes (2004) has advocated the use of subjective measures of awareness instead. In order to determine whether subjects acquired conscious or unconscious knowledge the experimenter collects confidence ratings and source attributions (Dienes and Scott, 2005). This can be done, for example, by asking subjects to perform on a grammaticality judgment task and to indicate, for each judgment, how confident they were in each decision (e.g., guess, somewhat confident, very confident) and what their decision was based on (e.g., guess, intuition, memory, rule knowledge). Subjects' knowledge can be considered unconscious when (i) the grammaticality judgments for which subjects reported to be guessing are actually significantly above chance and (ii) when there is no correlation between the reported confidence level and the observed level of accuracy. In both of these cases, subjects are not aware of having acquired knowledge.

What can be learned implicitly in L2 acquisition?

The field of second language acquisition (SLA) has a long-standing interest in implicit and explicit learning processes. Despite this interest, only very few studies have explored systematically what aspects of language can and cannot be acquired implicitly (Williams, 2009). A significant body of work has investigated incidental language learning (see Hulstijn, 2003 for a review), but these studies tend to concentrate on vocabulary acquisition and do not include measures of awareness, so it is unclear whether the acquired is actually implicit. Many SLA studies have compared implicit and explicit treatment conditions (see Norris and Ortega, 2000, and Spada and Tomita, 2010, for overviews), but it is unclear whether "implicit" methods actually resulted in truly implicit knowledge. There is also a large body of work in developmental psychology, especially in the statistical learning tradition (see Saffran, 2003, for a review), but here the learning conditions are sometimes far from incidental (e.g., subjects might be instructed to actively discover words in a continuous speech stream), nor do these studies include any measures of awareness. The review below will focus on studies that exposed subjects to the target structures under incidental learning conditions and established that the acquired knowledge was implicit according to the awareness criterion.

Williams (2005) focused on the implicit learning of form-meaning connections (see also Leung, 2007; Leung and Williams, 2011). Williams (2005) exposed subjects to a semi-artificial language consisting of English words and four artificial determiners (*gi*, *ro*, *ul* and *ne*) which encoded both distance (near vs far) and animacy (animate vs inanimate). At the beginning, subjects were told that the determiners functioned like English determiners, except that they also encoded distance: *gi* and *ro* were used for near objects, while *ul* and *ne* were used for far objects. Importantly, subjects were not informed that the artificial determiners also encoded animacy: *gi* and *ul* were used with animate objects, whereas *ro* and *ne* were used with inanimate objects. The role of animacy in determiner usage thus served as a hidden regularity. Subjects were exposed to the semi-artificial language under incidental learning conditions, that is they did not know they were going to be tested. Verbal reports served as a measure of awareness. In the testing phase, Williams (2005) observed a significant learning effect: In a sentence completion task, subjects were significantly more likely to select determiners according to the non-instructed meaning dimension (here, animacy) even when they were completely unaware of its relevance to determiner usage.

Support for Williams' (2005) finding that subjects can acquire form-meaning connections implicitly comes from a study conducted by Leung and Williams (2011). Subjects were exposed to an artificial determiner system by means of a novel reaction time task. The study used the same system as Williams (2005), except that here *gi*, *ro*, *ul* and *ne* encoded age (children vs adults) and agency (agent vs patient) instead of distance and animacy. Before the experiment, subjects were told that *gi* and *ro* were used with personal names referring to adults, whereas *ul* and *ne* were used with personal names referring to children. Subjects were not told that the choice of determiner also depended on the thematic role of the noun phrase: *gi* and *ul* were used with agents, while *ro* and *ne* were used with patients. In the experiments, subjects saw a picture on the computer screen that was accompanied by an auditory description. For example, the trial might consist of a picture of a girl kissing a boy on the cheek and an auditory description such as "Kiss ul Mary a boy on the face." The subjects' task was to indicate the location of the named individual in the image (left or right) by pressing the appropriate response key. In the first 114 trials of the experiment, the artificial determiner system followed the rules outlined above, but in the final 16 trials (the violation block) the rules were reversed, that is, *gi* and *ul* were used with patients instead of agents. Learning was assessed by measuring the time it took subjects to identify the location of the named individual. Awareness was assessed by means of verbal reports. The verbal reports showed that, at the end of the experiment, 80 per cent of subjects remained unaware of the simple rules that determined the choice of determiners. Despite remaining unaware of the system these subjects' response times to locate the named individual slowed significantly when the rule system was changed, suggesting that they had learned the relationship between the determiners and the thematic roles implicitly.

Recent research has shown that implicit L2 learning is not restricted to form-meaning mappings. Rebuschat (2008, exp. 3; Rebuschat and Williams, 2009), for example, investigated whether adult learners can acquire novel word order patterns implicitly, that is, without intention and without becoming aware of the knowledge they have acquired. Rebuschat exposed subjects to a semi-artificial language consisting of English words and German word order under incidental learning conditions. The exposure task required subjects to judge the semantic plausibility of 120 sentences, for example, "In the evening explained Rose that the profit below the estimate remained" (plausible) and "Today beheld Chris that the earth around the tomato rotated" (implausible). The exposure task thus required subjects to process the sentences for meaning. In the testing phase, subjects were informed that the word order in the previous sentences was not arbitrary but that it followed a "complex system" instead. They were then instructed to listen to 60 completely new sequences, only half of which followed the same rule system as the one they had just been exposed to. Those sequences that did obey the rules should be endorsed as *grammatical* and those that did not rejected as *ungrammatical*. Importantly, subjects were not only required to judge the grammaticality of each item. They were also asked to report how confident they were in each grammaticality judgment (guess, somewhat confident, very confident) and to indicate what the basis of their judgment was (guess, intuition, memory, rule). The analysis of the grammaticality judgments showed a clear learning effect, that is, subjects were able to acquire the new grammatical system incidentally and to use this knowledge in a transfer task. The analysis of the confidence ratings and source attributions further showed that, while subjects were aware of having acquired some knowledge, this knowledge remained largely unconscious. In other words, subjects displayed intuitive knowledge of the L2.

Future directions

A review of the literature on implicit language learning shows that adult learners are able to acquire form-meaning mappings and L2 syntax implicitly. At the same time, we need to know more about what aspects of the L2 can and cannot be acquired implicitly (see Williams, 2009, for discussion). Several key questions remain unaddressed. For example, the role of individual differences in implicit and explicit L2 learning has received too little attention, despite its relevance for classroom instruction. We also know little about the role of attention in implicit L2 learning, and it is unclear what demands, if any, implicit learning processes place on attentional resources. Finally, we need to know more about the influence of prior knowledge. In other words, how does prior linguistic knowledge (L1, L2, ...) influence the implicit learning of a new language (L2, L3, ...)? Considerably more empirical research is necessary before the precise role of implicit learning in L2 acquisition can be fully specified.

See also: artificial language learning, awareness, explicit learning, procedural memory and knowledge, psycholinguistics of SLA, statistical learning

References

Berry, D.C. and Dienes, Z. (1993). *Implicit Learning: Theoretical and Empirical Issues*. Hove: Lawrence Erlbaum.

Cleeremans, A., Destrebecqz, A. and Boyer, M. (1998). Implicit learning: News from the front. *Trends in Cognitive Sciences*, *2*(10), 406–16.

Dienes, Z. (2004). Assumptions of subjective measures of unconscious mental states: Higher order thoughts and bias. *Journal of Consciousness Studies*, *11*(9), 25–45.

Dienes, Z. and Scott, R. (2005). Measuring unconscious knowledge: Distinguishing structural knowledge and judgment knowledge. *Psychological Research*, *69*(5–6), 338–51.

Hulstijn, J.H. (2003). Incidental and intentional learning, In C. Doughty and M. Long (eds), *Handbook of Second Language Acquisition*, pp. 349–81. Oxford: Blackwell

Leung, J. (2007). *Implicit Learning of Form-Meaning Connections*. Unpublished PhD dissertation. University of Cambridge.

Leung, J. and Williams, J.N. (2011). The implicit learning of mappings between forms and contextually derived meanings. *Studies in Second Language Acquisition*.

Norris, J.M. and Ortega, L. (2000). Effectiveness of L2 instruction: A research synthesis and quantitative meta-analysis. *Language Learning*, *50*, 417–528.

Perruchet, P. (2008). Implicit learning, In J. Byrne and H.L. Roediger, III (eds), *Learning and memory: A comprehensive reference*, Vol. 2:

Cognitive psychology of memory, pp. 597–621. Oxford: Elsevier.

Reber, A.S. (1967). Implicit learning of artificial grammars. *Journal of Verbal Learning and Verbal Behavior*, *6*, 317–27.

——(1993). *Implicit Learning and Tacit Knowledge: An Essay on the Cognitive Unconscious.* Oxford: Oxford University Press.

Rebuschat, P. and Williams, J.N. (2009). Implicit learning of word order, In N.A. Taatgen and H. van Rijn (eds), *Proceedings of the 31th Annual Conference of the Cognitive Science Society*, pp. 425–30. Austin, TX: Cognitive Science Society.

Rebuschat, P. (2008). Implicit learning of natural language syntax, Unpublished PhD dissertation, University of Cambridge.

——(submitted) Measuring awareness in implicit learning research: A review.

Saffran, J.R. (2003). Statistical language learning: Mechanisms and constraints. *Current Directions in Psychological Science*, *12*, 110–14.

Shanks, D.R. (2005). Implicit learning, In K. Lambert and R. Goldstone (eds), *Handbook of Cognition*, pp. 202–20. London: Sage.

Shanks, D.R. and St. John, M.F. (1994). Characteristics of dissociable human learning system. *Behavioral and Brain Sciences*, *17*, 367–447.

Spada, N. and Tomita, Y. (2010). Interactions between type of instruction and type of language feature: A meta-analysis. *Language Learning*, *60*, 263–308.

Williams, J.N. (2005). Learning without awareness. *Studies in Second Language Acquisition*, *27*(2), 269–304.

——(2009). Implicit learning in second language acquisition, In W.C. Ritchie and T.K. Bhatia (eds), *The New Handbook of Second Language Acquisition*, pp. 319–53. Bingley: Emerald Press.

Further reading

Ellis, N.C. (ed.) (1994). *Implicit and Explicit Learning of Languages.* London: Academic Press. (A seminal collection of papers on implicit and explicit L2 learning.)

Ellis, R., Loewen, S., Elder, C., Erlam, R., Philp, J. and Reinders, H. (2009). *Implicit and Explicit Knowledge in Second Language Learning, Testing and Teaching.* Bristol: Multilingual Matters. (A comprehensive description of a major research project on implicit and explicit L2 learning.)

Hulstijn, J.H. and Ellis, R. (eds) (2005). Implicit and explicit second-language learning. Thematic issue of *Studies in Second Language Acquisition*, *27*(2) (An excellent volume with more recent research papers.)

Individual differences in SLA

Rebecca L. Oxford
Air Force Culture and Language Center and University of Maryland

This review of individual differences in language learners focuses on aptitude, gender and age, personality and identity, cognitive development, and affective aspects. All individual differences occur in sociocultural contexts.

Aptitude

Most researchers, such as Carroll and Sapon, creators of the Modern Language Aptitude Battery (MLAT), described aptitude as a stable trait (Ranta, 2008). The MLAT operationally views language aptitude as related to speed and as composed of phonemic coding ability, rote memory, grammatical sensitivity, and inductive ability (see **Modern Language Aptitude Test (MLAT)**, this volume). Skehan (1998) linked MLAT components to different stages in the language learning process, for example, phonemic coding is useful early, and grammatical sensitivity is necessary later. Working memory is crucial in language aptitude. Robinson (2002) portrayed aptitude as a hierarchical system of *aptitude complexes* that influence language learning for specific tasks or situations (see **Aptitude-trait complexes**, and **Working Memory**, this volume). Some learners, compared with others, have greater aptitude to focus on form via recasts, which demand noticing differences between the wrong version and the corrected version. Such noticing requires perceptual speed, pattern recognition, and contingent-speech memory ability. Grigorenko *et al.* (2000) created the CANAL-F (Cognitive Ability for Novelty in Acquisition of Language-Foreign), which emphasizes coping with novelty and ambiguity in "learning" an artificial language. Tare *et al.* (2011) considered aptitude to involve cognitive constructs, such as focusing attention, distinguishing and learning foreign sounds, pattern-learning, meaning association, processing speed, and tolerance of ambiguity, which predict proficiency in particular learning conditions (see **Aptitude-treatment interaction research**, this volume). This idea enables instruction to be matched to aptitude profiles.

Unlike other theorists, Feuerstein argued that aptitude or intelligence is not a stable trait (Kozulin, 2000). He demonstrated that learners can be taught cognitive techniques for thinking and metacognitive techniques for planning, organizing, and evaluating their thinking, with the result of greater ability to learn languages and other subjects.

Gender and age

According to many studies, females invest more time in language learning, report using a wider range of learning strategies, including social strategies and emotionally supportive affective strategies, and use these strategies more flexibly, while males favor rote memorization and translation (Nyikos, 2008). However, gender differences in language learning are not universal. To attain nativelike pronunciation and accent, it is best to learn a second language as a child, but certain other aspects of language learning, such as grammatical understanding, rely on greater cognitive maturity (Griffiths, 2008; Scarcella and Oxford, 1992) (see **Age effects in SLA**, **Child second language acquisition**, and **Critical Period Hypothesis (CPH)**, this volume).

Personality and identity

Personality is especially important in individualist (idiocentric, or individual-focused) cultures, such as mainstream cultures in the USA or the UK, which define personality as the individual's characteristic, unique, special combination of thought, emotion, and behavior, viewed without reference to kinship systems or social groups that hold sway in collectivist (allocentric, other-focused) cultures. Idiocentric cultures urge each person to focus on individuating, self-actualizing, and becoming an authentic self. Idiocentric cultures produce many personality theories, such as Cattell's 16 personality-factor (PF) theory and McCrae and Costa's Big Five theory (factors: extroversion/surgency, agreeableness, conscientiousness, neuroticism, and openness). Using the Myers Briggs Type Indicator, based on the work of Carl Jung, Ehrman (2008) found that introverted, intuitive, thinking, and judging individuals were over-represented among very advanced learners in a large intensive language program in the U.S., causing Ehrman to suggest that personality type and language difficulty interact to predict the highest levels of proficiency. In addition, Ehrman (1996) showed how learners differentially use transference, resistance, and other psychoanalytic mechanisms while learning languages.

In contrast to the detailed theories of personality in individualist/idiocentric cultures, collectivist/allocentric cultures traditionally describe personality in terms of how the person adapts to the group or society, not how he or she stands out (Cross and Markus, 1999). Features such as interdependence, social embeddedness, cooperation, loyalty, and interpersonal sensitivity pervade collectivist views of personality. A language learner who shows these tendencies would fit well into allocentric cultures. However, perhaps as a function of globalization, idiocentric personality theories are now entering China, an allocentric culture. For instance, Ma Xiaomei's team in China is now working with Cattell's 16 PF theory for an online diagnosis and advice system for language learners (Oxford, 2011).

Issues of personality relate to fundamental issues of identity and self, which answer the question, "Who am I?" Language learners differ in their *culturally based self-construals*. In individualist/idiocentric cultures, people largely construe themselves as unique, independent selves, but in collectivist/allocentric cultures, people construe themselves *inter*dependently in relation to family, clan, or group, with boundaries that are permeable, overlapping, and adaptive (Kitayama and Markus,

1994, not to be confused with Hartmann's boundary theory of personality, described in Ehrman, 1996). Some language learners have self-construals that differ from the modal personality tendencies in their cultures. For instance, it is possible to find highly interdependent, relationship-oriented learners in individualist cultures and highly independent individualists in collectivist cultures. These learners might feel somewhat different from those around them (see **Acculturation Model**, this volume).

Language learners have additional beliefs and feelings about themselves that can be placed in a very broad category of *self-perceptions*: self-efficacy, self-concept, and self-esteem (see Oxford, 2011). *Self-efficacy* is a belief about the degree of confidence that one can complete a specific task or meet a chosen goal. Self-efficacy is related to *agency*, that is, belief in one's control over particular outcomes. Some influences on or correlates of self-efficacy include, generally speaking, past experience, vicarious experience (observing others), and social persuasion and, in the language field, learning strategy use. Instruction in learning strategies is related to increases in self-efficacy. *Self-concept,* a cognitive belief about general competence and worth, is shaped by factors similar to the influences on self-efficacy, but another important factor is perceptions by others in the cultural, academic, and sociocultural setting. *Self-esteem,* a largely emotional rather than cognitive self-perception of competence or self-worth, is not necessarily connected to actual language learning performance; one language learner might have high self-esteem while performing poorly, while another language learner might have low self-esteem even though performing very well.

Other people's *recognition or misrecognition* of the learner contributes to but does not determine the learner's self-perceptions. In situations of unequal power, some individuals receive positive recognition while others are ignored or are "misrecognized," that is, demeaningly viewed by others (Oxford, 2011). Some language learners, when encountering a negative image or story about themselves from those in the target culture, successfully create a counter-story and hence achieve greater acceptance in that culture (Norton and Toohey, 2001). When facing negativity related to their language performance, many language learners become socially anxious and avoid taking risks in using the language for communication (see **emotions**).

External images of oneself are connected to the concept of *face,* which is a complex, dynamic variable that involves being judged through the eyes of others and thus being socially influenced by the positive or negative views of others toward oneself. One can gain or lose face, and one can cause someone else to gain or lose it. Face encompasses a sense of honor, respect, and deference from others, and loss of face embodies a sense of humiliation, disrespect, and contempt from others. Face maintenance involves projecting an image of strength or competence or avoiding projecting an image of weakness or incompetence. In general, people from collectivist, high-context cultures are particularly sensitive to potential loss of face, and so they often engage in more "face-honoring" exchanges, that is, building relationships and ignoring conflicts, while people from individualist, low-context cultures are generally less face-conscious and therefore engage in more "face-threatening," confrontive, and competitive behaviors (Ting-Toomey, 2005).

Critical-poststructuralist theorists argued that individuals have many different identities related to their multiple social contexts and that identity is a potential site of struggle, particularly for second language learners and other minorities in settings of unequal power (Norton and Toohey, 2001). Language learners show different degrees of *investment,* defined as the historically and socially constructed, often ambivalent relationship of learners to the target language. Some learners invest more than others in learning the target language, and they generally learn more and perform better in that language than those with less investment (see Identity Theory, and Investment, this volume). Sometimes features of the target culture cause learners not to want to invest or participate (Norton, 2001) and to oppose those features, while other learners engage in more obvious resistance (Canagarajah, 1993).

Cognitive development

Language learners differ in their cognitive development, which involves, among many other factors (see aptitude earlier), schema development, cognitive load, cognitive learning style, and future time perspective.

Schema development. Through cognitive information-processing learners develop, organize, and elaborate their mental frameworks, or schemata (see **Schemata**, this volume). Schemata are initiated in the first stage (declarative) of the process; deepened, elaborated, and strengthened in the second stage (associative); and automatized in the third stage (procedural) (O'Malley and Chamot, 1990). To facilitate this process, successful learners employ *deep processing strategies*, such as metacognitive strategies (e.g., planning, organizing, monitoring, and evaluating) and cognitive "linking" strategies (e.g., reasoning, comparing, contrasting, relating, and synthesizing), but less successful learners employ *surface strategies*, such as repeating without understanding, and they often fail to reach the third or even the second stage of cognitive information-processing (Oxford, 2011). Sociocultural-interactive strategies, often involving gaining help and social interaction, are also important to schema development (see **learning strategies**, this volume; also learner autonomy, Cotterall, 2008) (see **Learning strategies**, and **Social and socio-cultural approaches to SLA**, this volume).

Cognitive load. Cognitive load consists of cognitive demands placed on learners' working memory. If too much cognitive load exists and is not handled well by the learner, schema development suffers and anxiety emerges (Oxford, 2011). Three types of *cognitive load* exist: intrinsic, extraneous, and germane (Clark *et al.*, 2005). *Intrinsic cognitive load* refers to the unchangeable complexity of information elements. Expert language learners use "chunking" (putting related pieces of information together to reduce the number of items to be learned and thus reduce intrinsic cognitive load) and sometimes organize information in memorable sequences or strings (see **Chunking and prefabrication**, this volume). *Extraneous cognitive load* ("split attention" or distraction) is the result of poor design of language materials or programs, resulting in lack of focus. To overcome extraneous cognitive load, skilled language learners intentionally distinguish between relevant and irrelevant information. *Germane cognitive load* creates helpful demands on working memory, for example, calling for the use of multiple senses. Effective language learners embrace the need for multisensory learning.

Cognitive learning style. Several dimensions of cognitive learning style are analytic versus synthesis-oriented, concrete-sequential versus abstract-intuitive, closure-oriented versus open, and field-independent (separating material from its context or field) versus field dependent. Field independence is related to some, but not all, aspects of language learning success (Nel, 2008). Style tendencies that might be ideal for some settings and certain purposes would not be best for others. Though learning styles are rather stable, successful learners flex or adapt their learning styles to immediate task demands (Nel, 2008).

Future time perspective. Learners differ motivationally and metacognitively in terms of *future time perspective* (Simons *et al.*, 2004). Those who have a strong future time perspective are more likely to use strategies such as planning, setting long-term goals, and self-evaluating. Possibly their planning encourages them to use more cognitive and sociocultural-interactive strategies as well (Oxford, 2011).

Affective aspects

Individual differences in the affective domain relate to emotions, attitudes, and motivation.

Emotions. Emotions pervade language learning (MacIntyre, 2002). Emotion combines physiological arousal, subjective experience, and expression. Anxiety, which can harm cognition, performance, and self-efficacy, is the major emotion studied by language researchers. Effective language learners reduce their anxiety through deep breathing, humor, positive self-talk, or making light of a difficult situation, while less effective language learners often experience ongoing anxiety (Horwitz and Young, 1991). Many other emotions, such as happiness, shame, anger, and confusion, emerge in language learners based on situational and personal factors (Dewaele, 2005). These emotions deserve greater study by researchers in our field (Oxford, 2011) (see **Anxiety**, and **Emotions**, this volume).

Attitudes. Learners hold attitudes about language learning, language teachers, peers, the target culture, native speakers of the language, and the language itself (its prestige, aesthetics, richness of sound and writing systems, grammatical complexity or simplicity, metaphors, and communicative value). Positive attitudes help generate motivation, while negative attitudes dampen it (Oxford, 2011) (see **Attitudes to the L2**, this volume).

Motivation. Language learning motivation includes an initial behavior-igniting spark and persistence over time. The learner's motivation is shaped by a host of changeable contextual factors, such as the nature of interactions with teachers, peers, and others, as well as cultural values and social power dynamics, both generally and in specific situations, as well as by personal factors such as emotion and attitude (see **Motivation**, this volume). Motivation can be intrinsic or extrinsic to the learning process itself. *Intrinsic motivation* involves learning the language as an end itself due to a combination of enjoyment, challenge, and interest in the process of developing new skill and knowledge. Intrinsic motivation is often related to higher levels of learning involvement, more creative thinking, a wider range of strategies, and greater retention of information (Ushioda, 2008). The ultimate state of intrinsic motivation is *flow* (Csíkszentmihályi, 1990), or complete engagement with optimal performance. Oxford (2011) conceptualizes "hot cognition," that is, heightened cognition which is related to intrinsic motivation and positive emotion and which results in transformative learning. *Extrinsic motivation* is motivation that is external to the learning process, or the desire to do something for a separable outcome. Both integrative orientation and instrumental orientation (Gardner, 1985) are considered forms of extrinsic motivation (Ushioda, 2008). *Integrative orientation* is the desire to learn the language so as to come closer psychologically or socially to the target language community, while *instrumental orientation* is the desire to learn the language for practical reasons, such as a job. Some wrongly confuse integrative orientation with intrinsic motivation (Ushioda, 2008). Comparing integrative orientation with instrumental orientation, researchers have found that the former often leads to greater proficiency except in situations in which there is no chance of interacting with the target culture, in which case instrumental orientation is often more strongly linked to proficiency (Oxford, 1996).

Motivation is inherent in *willingness to communicate* (WTC), that is, the probability that an individual will choose to initiate communication when free to do so. Factors influencing WTC include the role and vitality of the target language; intergroup motivation, attitudes, and climate; interpersonal motivation; personality, communicative competence, target-language confidence, situational self-confidence, low anxiety, and prior experiences (Clément *et al.*, 2003).

Conclusion

The discussion of individual differences often focuses on cognitive and affective contrasts among individuals or groups of individuals, but I have shown that sociocultural factors are also crucial to consider. Learners develop language competencies within social environments that have certain characteristics, benefits, and limitations.

See also: anxiety, aptitude, identity theory, learning strategies, Willingness to Communicate (WTC)

References

Canagarajah, A.S. (1993). Critical ethnography of a Sri Lankan classroom: Ambiguities in opposition to reproduction through ESOL. *TESOL Quarterly*, *27*(4), 601–26.

Clark, R.C., Nguyen, F. and Sweller, J. (2005). *Efficiency in Learning: Evidence-based Guidelines to Manage Cognitive Load*. New York: Wiley.

Clément, R.C., Baker, S.C. and MacIntyre, P.D. (2003). Willingness to communicate in a second language: The effects of context, norms, and vitality. *Journal of Language and Social Psychology*, *22*(2), 190–209.

Cotterall, S. (2008). Autonomy and good language learners. In C. Griffiths (ed.), *Lessons from Good Language Learners*, pp. 110–20. Cambridge: Cambridge University Press.

Cross, S.E. and Markus, H.R. (1999). The cultural constitution of personality. In L.A. Pervin and O.P. John (eds), *Handbook of Personality*, 2nd edn, pp. 378–96. New York: Guilford.

Csíkszentmihályi, M. (1990). *Flow: The Psychology of Optimal Experience*. New York: Harper and Row.

Dewaele, J.-M. (2005). Investigating the psychological and the emotional dimensions in instructed language learning: Obstacles and possibilities. *Modern Language Journal*, *89*, 367–80.

Ehrman, M.E. (1996). *Understanding Second Language Learning Difficulties*. Thousand Oaks, CA: Sage.

——(2008). Personality and good language learners. In C. Griffiths (ed.), *Lessons from good Language Llearners*, pp. 61–72. Cambridge: Cambridge University Press.

Gardner, R.C. (1985). *Social Psychology and Second Language Learning: The Role of Attitudes and Motivation*. London, ON: Edward Arnold.

Griffiths, C. (2008). Age and good language learners. In C. Griffiths (ed.), *Lessons from good Language Learners*, pp. 35–48. Cambridge: Cambridge University Press.

Grigorenko, E., Sternberg, R. and Ehrman, M. (2000). A theory-based approach to the measurement of foreign language learning ability: The CANAL-F theory and test. *Modern Language Journal*, *83*, 35–50.

Horwitz, E. and Young, D.J. (eds). (1991). *Language Anxiety: From Theory and Research to Classroom Implications*. Englewood Cliffs, NJ: Prentice Hall.

Kitayama, S. and Markus, H.R. (1994). Culture and self: How cultures influence the way we view ourselves. In D. Matsumoto (ed.), *People: Psychology from a Cultural Perspective*, pp. 17–37. Prospect Heights, IL: Waveland Press.

Kozulin, A. (2000). *Experience of Mediated Learning: Impact of Feuerstein's Theory in Education and Psychology*. Bingley: Emerald Group Publishing.

MacIntyre, P.D. (2002). Motivation, anxiety, and emotion in second language acquisition. In P. Robinson (ed.), *Individual Differences and Instructed Language Learning*, pp. 45–68. Amsterdam: John Benjamins.

Nel, C. (2008). Learning style and good language learners. In C. Griffiths (ed.), *Lessons from Good Language Learners*, pp. 49–60. Cambridge: Cambridge University Press.

Norton, B. (2001). Non-participation, imagined communities, and the language classroom. In Breen, M. (ed.), *Learner Contributions to Language Learning: New Directions in Research*, pp. 159–71. London: Longman.

Norton, B. and Toohey, K. (2001). Changing perspectives on good language learners. *TESOL Quarterly*, *35*(2), 307–22.

Norton, B. andToohey, K (eds). (2004). *Critical Pedagogies and Language Learning*. Cambridge: Cambridge University Press.

Nyikos, M. (2008). Gender and good language learners. In C. Griffiths (ed.), *Lessons from Good Language Learners*, pp. 73–82. Cambridge: Cambridge University Press.

O'Malley, J.M. and Chamot, A.U. (1990). *Learning Strategies in Second Language Acquisition*. Cambridge: Cambridge University Press.

Oxford, R.L. (1996). *Language Learning Motivation: Pathways to the New Century*. Manoa: University of Hawaii Press.

——(2011). *Teaching and Researching Language Learning Strategies*. Harlow: Pearson Longman.

Ranta, L. (2008). Aptitude and good language learners. In C. Griffiths (ed.), *Lessons from Good Language Learners*, pp. 142–55. Cambridge: Cambridge University Press.

Robinson, P. (2002). Learning conditions, aptitude complexes, and SLA: A framework for research and pedagogy. In P. Robinson (ed.), *Individual Differences and Instructed Second Language Learning*, pp. 113–33. Amsterdam: John Benjamins.

Scarcella, R. and Oxford, R. (1992). *The Tapestry of Language Learning: The Individual in the Communicative Classroom*. Boston, MA: Heinle and Heinle.

Simons, J., Vansteenkiste, M., Lens, W. and Lacante, M. (2004). Placing motivation and future time perspective theory ina temporal perspective. *Educational Psychology Review*, *16*, 121–39.

Skehan, P. (1998). *A Cognitive Approach to Language Learning*. Oxford: Oxford University Press.

Tare, M., Vatz, K., Freynik, S., Cook, J.G., Jackson, S.R. and Doughty, C.J. (2011). *Tailoring Instruction to Individual Differences: A State of the Science Review of Aptitude-treatment Interaction Studies in Second Language Acquisition*. TTO 82106. College Park, MD: Center for the Advanced Study of Language, University of Maryland.

Ting-Toomey, S. (2005). The matrix of face: An updated face-negotiation theory. In W.B. Gudykunst (ed.), *Theorizing about Intercultural Communication*, pp. 71–92. Thousand Oaks, CA: Sage.

Ushioda, E. (2008). Motivation and good language learners. In C. Griffiths (ed.), *Lessons from Good Language Learners*, pp. 19–34. Cambridge: Cambridge University Press.

Further reading

Ehrman, M.E., Leaver, B.L. and Oxford, R.L. (2003). A brief overview of individual differences in language learning. *System*, *31*(3), 313–30. (This article examines learning styles, strategies, and affect.)

Dörnyei, Z. (2005). *The Psychology of the Language Learner: Individual Differences in Second Language Acquisition*. Mahwah, NJ: Erlbaum. (Dörnyei focuses on psychological elements, such as learning style and motivation.)

Griffiths, C. (2008). *Lessons from Good Language Learners*. Cambridge: Cambridge University Press. (This book provides rich information about individual differences related to culture, age, and gender.)

Robinson, P. (2002). *Individual Differences and Instructed Language Learning*. Amsterdam: John Benjamins. (This is an in-depth look at individual differences in formally instructed learning.)

Inflectional morphemes

Zoe Luk

University of Pittsburgh

Inflectional morphemes are bound morphemes that are used to serve grammatical purposes. As opposed to derivational morphemes, the attachment of an inflectional morpheme does not create a "new" word. Therefore, an inflected word always stays in the same lexical category as the original word (i.e., the stem). Inflectional morphemes are thus more related to properties at a morphosyntactic level, whereas derivational morphemes are more at a lexical level. Examples of inflectional morphemes in English are past tense marker *-ed* and plural marker *-s*. Other examples are aspect markers, case markers, and gender markers. However, it should be noted that there are disagreements among linguists whether these morphemes in isolating languages such as Chinese (see Sun, 2006: 46) are bound and thus inflectional because of the difficulty of defining what a word is in these languages.

The two basic grammatical functions that inflection fulfills are agreement and government (Booij, 2005). Agreement refers to the relation between two members of a phrase or a sentence. For example, in Spanish, an attributive adjective has to agree with the gender of the noun. While "red book" is *libro rojo*, "red pen" is *pluma roja*. In the case of government, the governed member has to inflect to satisfy restrictions imposed by the governing member. For example, in a prepositional phrase in German, the governing member (i.e., the head of the phrase) *auf* "on" forces the following noun phrase *der Tisch* "the table" to inflect for accusative case to become *auf den Tisch*.

Distinguishing inflection from derivation, however, is not always easy. Stump (2001) discusses five criteria:

(1) While derivation may change the lexical category of the stem, inflection does not.

(2) While for inflection the syntactic context determines which particular word in a word's paradigm is to be used, this is not so in the case of derivation.
(3) Inflectional morphemes are generally more productive than derivational morphemes.
(4) Inflection is semantically more regular than derivation.
(5) Inflection prevents additional morphemes, both inflectional and derivational, to be added to the stem, whereas derivation does not.

However, these criteria cannot truly differentiate between inflection and derivation. For example, regarding (1), derivation sometimes may not result in category change. *Screw* and *unscrew* are both verbs. In other words, category change is only a sufficient condition, but not a necessary condition (Stump, 2001). Moreover, agglutinating languages often allow additional morphemes to be added after an inflectional morpheme.

Focusing on the issue crosslinguistically, Bybee (1985) proposes that inflectional and derivational are not two discrete expression types, but a continuous scale, and the likelihood for a semantic notion to be encoded as an inflectional category is determined by two factors, namely 'relevance' and 'generality'. She hypothesizes that the more relevant a semantic notion is to the meaning of the stem, and the more generally application it is, the more likely it will be to be inflectional. It has been suggested in a number of studies (see Goldschneider and DeKeyser, 2001 for review) that there is a relatively fixed second language acquisition order of English inflectional morphemes.

See also: morpheme acquisition orders, developmental sequences, agreement, development in SLA, language and the lexicon in SLA, linguistic transfer

References

Booij, G. (2005). *The Grammar of Words*. New York: Oxford University Press.

Bybee, J. (1985). *Morphology: A Study of the Relation Between Meaning and Form*. Amsterdam and Philadelphia, PA: John Benjamins.

Goldschneider and DeKeyser, R. M. (2001). Explaining the "natural order of L2 morpheme acquisition" in English: A meta-analysis of multiple determinants. *Language Learning, 51* (1), 1–50.

Stump, G. (2001). Inflection. In A. Spencer and A. M. Zwicky (eds), *The Handbook of Morphology*, pp. 13–43. Oxford: Blackwell.

Sun, C. (2006). *Chinese: A Linguistic Introduction*. Cambridge: Cambridge University Press.

Inhibitory control

Joel Koeth
University of Maryland

The existence of more than one language system in bilingual individuals necessitates a mechanism for controlling against the unintended selection of non-target language items. While there is still considerable debate on the specific processes underlying language selection, it is clear that some form of cognitive control is required. Cognitive control refers to a collection of processes within the human cognitive system that allow for the performance of specific tasks through adjustments in perceptual selection, response biasing, and the on-line maintenance of contextual information (Botvinick *et al.*, 2001). One specific type of cognitive control, inhibitory control, has been posited to be critical for language selection and is the focus of several research lines in the fields of Psycholinguistics and Second Language Acquisition.

Inhibitory control can be described as the ability to inhibit responses to irrelevant stimuli during processing of a cognitively represented goal. Applying this concept to bilingual language processing, Green's (1998) Inhibitory Control Model states that non-target lexical items are inhibited to allow for the comprehension and production of the selected, targeted language. According to the Inhibitory Control Model, lexical representations are each associated with a language tag, and non-target lexical nodes can be suppressed in a particular communicative context. It is important to note that Green's (1998) model relies on reactive inhibition of non-target language items. According to the model, lexical items in both languages receive activation, but non-target language items are then reactively suppressed. A key aspect of this reactive suppression is that the amount of inhibition is proportional to the amount of activation. Therefore, non-target items that receive the highest amount of activation are also subjected to the highest levels of inhibition.

Behavioral evidence from psycholinguistic studies supports the claims of the Inhibitory Control Model. In a seminal study, Meuter and Allport (1999) demonstrated that bilinguals performing a number naming language switch task took longer to switch from their second language to their dominant language. Although this may initially seem counterintuitive, it is exactly what Green's (1998) Inhibitory Control Model predicts. Because the first language was the dominant language for the participants in Meuter and Allport's (1999) study, the first language would require a higher degree of inhibition during number naming in the second language. In order to switch back to their first language in the switch condition, participants had to overcome the higher degree of inhibition to access the first language lexicon, resulting in a larger switch cost from the second language to the first. Costa and Santesteban (2004) also found asymmetrical switch costs for low proficiency second language learners. However, when testing balanced bilinguals in a follow-up experiment, the switch costs disappeared. This is also in line with Green's (1998) IC model. As asymmetrical switch costs result from differences in proficiency, cost differences associated with switching between two languages of equal proficiency should be negligible. Interestingly, symmetrical switch costs for balanced bilinguals in Costa and Santesteban (2004) also extended to a much weaker third language. Attributed to unique mechanisms available only to highly proficient bilinguals, this finding highlights the critical importance of learner-related variables, such as proficiency level and age of acquisition, in the study of lexical access and inhibitory control.

In addition to a wide range of psycholinguistic studies focused on lexical selection and inhibitory control, there is also a growing body of neurolinguistic and imaging-based literature targeting this issue. Abutalebi and Green (2007) reviewed a wide range of functional neuroimaging studies, and concluded that the neural representation of a second language converges with that of the first language (they note that the opposite is also possible, under some conditions). Other key findings include identification of both cortical and sub-cortical structures involved in inhibitory control, and further evidence of the critical role of proficiency when examining language control.

Individual differences in cognitive control and inhibition have been demonstrated in the literature. Developmental differences between children and adults result in children being more susceptible to interference and less able to inhibit non-appropriate responses than adults (e.g., Bunge *et al.*, 2002) and the experience of early bilinguals in controlling attention to two languages has been shown to boost the development of inhibitory control processes (e.g., Martin-Rhee and Bialystok, 2008). Recent developments in the literature on bilingual language processing have implicated inhibition as a key cognitive mechanism supporting bilingual language use (e.g., Kroll *et al.*, 2008), and a series of correlational studies have found that highly proficient bilinguals outperform their monolingual counterparts on the Antisaccade task, Simon task, as well as other tasks requiring inhibitory control. This raises the possibility that individuals who demonstrate better inhibitory control skills may be cognitively better equipped to learn a second language, which makes this an issue of potentially great importance to both psycholinguistics and second language acquisition research. More specifically, effects of variation in inhibitory control skills (and executive capacity and control, more generally) might play a significant role in second language learning, and therefore would likely be of interest to SLA researchers investigating aptitude for adult second language acquisition.

It should be noted that not all theories of bilingual lexical selection are tied to the concept of competition between lexemes and inhibition. Several theories pointedly deny any role of competition between lexical items in either monolingual or bilingual processing and attribute asymmetrical switch costs to confounds in methodology and target stimuli valence (e.g, Finkbeiner *et al.*, 2006).

The debate is ongoing, however, with a growing number of studies supporting the existence of competition between lexical items, as well as an integral role for inhibitory control in bilingual language processing. Research on the role of inhibitory control in second language acquisition continues, with recent studies attempting to further specify the role of inhibition, as well as better understand the mechanisms responsible for the bilingual advantage in cognitive control (see, for example, Prior and MacWhinney, 2009).

See also: Analysis-control model, aptitude, attention, language (task) switching, executive control and frontal cortex, psycholinguistics of SLA

References

Abutalebi, J. and Green, D. (2007). Bilingual language production: The neurocognition of language representation and control. *Journal of Neurolinguistics*, *20*, 242–75.

Bialystok, E., Craik, F.I.M, Chau, W., Ishii, R., Gunji, A. and Pantev, C. (2005). Effect of bilingualism on cognitive control in the Simon task: Evidence from MEG. *Neuroimage*, *24*, 40–49.

Botvinick, M.M., Braver, T.S., Barch, D.M., Carter, C.S. and Cohen, J.D. (2001). Conflict monitoring and cognitive control. *Psychological Review*, *108*, 624–52.

Costa, A. and Santesteban, M. (2004). Lexical access in bilingual speech production: Evidence from language switching in highly proficient bilinguals and L2 learners. *Journal of Memory and Language*, *50*, 491–511.

Finkbeiner, M., Almeida, J., Janssen, N. and Caramazza, A. (2006). Lexical selection in bilingual speech production does not involve language suppression. *Journal of Experimental Psychology: Learning, Memory, and Cognition*, *32*, 1075–89.

Green, D.W. (1998). Mental control of the bilingual lexico-semantic system. *Bilingualism: Language and Cognition*, *1*, 67–81.

Kroll, J.F., Bobb, S.C., Misra, M. and Guo, T. (2008). Language selection in bilingual speech: Evidence for inhibitory processes. *Acta Psychologica*, *128*, 416–30.

Martin-Rhee, M.M. and Bialystok, E. (2008). The development of two types of inhibitory control in monolingual and bilingual children. *Bilingualism: Language and Cognition*, *11*(1), 81–93.

Meuter, R.F.I. and Allport, A. (1999). Bilingual language switching in naming: Asymmetrical costs of language selection. *Journal of Memory and Language*, *40*, 25–40.

Prior, A. and MacWhinney, B. (2009). A bilingual advantage in task switching. *Bilingualism: Language and Cognition*, *13*(2), 253–62.

Initial state

Julia Herschensohn
University of Washington

The term initial state of second language acquisition (SLA) can, in principle, refer to the characteristics of the second language learner who is just beginning the acquisition process within any theoretical framework, although it has gained a more specific definition in terms of Universal Grammar (UG) or UG-theoretic explanations.

UG approaches assume that humans are born with a genetic predisposition to learn primary language, a predilection characterized as Universal Grammar, the cross-linguistic properties (e.g. phonetic or syntactic features) and limits (e.g. impossible sounds or syntactic combinations) that human languages do or do not permit. These "guidelines" help the child—whose linguistic competence is initially a tabula rasa—to select the key elements of the native language to which s/he is exposed. The child's grammar matures within the first few years of life, developing a set of morphosyntactic features of lexical categories (e.g. semantic features such as [past] or [plural] necessary for interpretation) and of functional categories (e.g. grammatical features that determine agreement).

Given this view of child native language (NL) acquisition, the availability of UG—that is, the accessibility of second language grammatical properties distinct from the NL for adult learners—is viewed by some as dependent on a critical period threshold (Bley-Vroman, 1990) or not (White, 1989). The initial state of the adult second language learner is then an unknown—is it another tabula rasa, a version of the native grammar, or something in between?

A pivotal publication in the line of UG-theoretic research into the initial state was a 1996 issue of *Second Language Research* (Volume 12, Number 1, edited by Schwartz and Eubank) that sought to explore "the starting point of non-native grammatical knowledge," departing from a comparison to NL development. UG-based approaches to SL—whose goal is to describe and explain the interlanguage competence of the SL learner—had heretofore focused on intermediate and endstate learners, particularly with respect to their abilities to gain SL properties (e.g. parameter settings) that were different from the NL. The 1996 collection posed a foundational question for the interlanguage grammar (or competence) of the SL learner, by asking not only what would be the initial state, but also what trajectory the learner might follow. The three articles in this issue (Vainikka and Young-Scholten, V&YS; Schwartz and Sprouse, S&S; Eubank) and Epstein, Flynn and Martohardjono (EFM 1996) propose four distinct views of the Initial State that they support with empirical evidence from a range of languages and grammatical phenomena.

V&YS adapt a Radfordian Weak Continuity view of NL development to SL acquisition, whereby the initial grammar contains only lexical projections such as VP, but gradually adds the higher functional projections of I[nflection]P and C[omplementizer]P. Their notion of tree building has evolved over the past 15 years, through nomenclatures of Minimal Trees, Structure Building and most recently Organic Grammar. An attractive account of the initial state, transitional mechanisms, and the interdependence of morphology and syntax, it has been adapted by other scholars such as Hawkins (2001) and Myles (Hawkins, 2009). This approach does not explain why functional but not lexical categories should be initially absent, why morphology should trigger syntax, or why production data alone is the basis for determining transitions (White, 2003: 76–78).

S&S argue for Full Transfer/Full Access (FT/FA), a view that assumes the Initial State of the interlanguage is the mature NL grammar containing both lexical and functional projections. The initial grammar can be adjusted to gain SL features and values through "failure to assign a representation to input data" (ibid.: 40). With full access to UG, the learner is capable of, albeit not destined to, gain a complete SL grammar. An intuitively obvious account of the initial state (given the learner's evident mastery of the NL), FT/FA has been broadly accepted by other scholars (e.g. Slabakova, 2000) who use NL functional features as a basis for hypothesis testing regarding SL differing features. FT/FA is not, however, supported by the evidence found in several studies since 1996 that learners whose NLs differ in morphosyntactic feature values go through similar initial states and transitions (White, 2003: 67).

Eubank goes beyond the NL in the Initial State by proposing that Valueless Features are "inert" in having neither NL nor SL values, thus contributing to optionality (variability) of accurate morphosyntax, especially in early SL grammars. The learner's acquisition of inflectional morphology contributes to the activation of SL feature values and functional projections. Although the idea of inert features has not persisted in UG-theoretic studies, the notion of defective SL functional features has done so in views such as Tsimpli's Interpretability or Hawkins' Representation Deficit Hypotheses (Hawkins, 2009). Finally, EFM put forth a kind of SL tabula rasa in that the SL learner initially has full access to UG, a complete starting over in building the SL grammar. Generally, the numerous responses to their keynote article disagree with their stance, which attributes no role for the NL in the initial state. White (2003: 86, 93) points out that Eubank's "inertness" is neither defined nor motivated, and that EFM's model fails to provide any account of NL influence.

Proposals of initial state interlanguage grammars have provided a foundation for theoretical discussions of NL transfer and a launching position from which to project transitions to intermediate and advanced grammatical competence. They have also opened dialogue on the relationship of syntax to morphology and the role of UG in both initial and later stages of SL development.

See also: development in SLA, functional categories, Fundamental Difference Hypothesis (FDH), inflectional morphemes, linguistic transfer, Universal Grammar (UG) and SLA

References

Bley-Vroman, R. (1990). The logical problem of foreign language learning. *Linguistic Analysis*, *20*, 3–49.

Epstein, S.D., Flynn, S. and Martohardjono, G. (1996). Second language acquisition: theoretical and experimental issues in contemporary research. *Behavioral and Brain Sciences*, *19*, 677–758.

Eubank, L. (1996). Negation in early German-English interlanguage: more Valueless Features in the L2 initial state. *Second Language Research*, *12*, 73–106.

Hawkins, R. (2001). *Second Language Syntax*. Oxford: Blackwell.

——(2009). Second language acquisition of morphosyntax. In W.C. Ritchie and T.K. Bhatia (eds), *The New Handbook of Second Language Acquisition*, pp. 211–36. Bingley: Emerald Group.

Schwartz, B.D. and Sprouse, R. (1996). L2 cognitive states and the Full Transfer/Full Access model. *Second Language Research*, *12*, 40–72.

Slabakova, R. (2000). L1 transfer revisited: the L2 acquisition of telicity marking in English by Spanish and Bulgarian native speakers. *Linguistics*, *38*, 739–70.

Vainikka, A. and Young-Scholten, M. (1996). Gradual development of L2 phrase structure. *Second Language Research*, *12*, 7–39.

White, L. (1989). *Universal Grammar and Second Language Acquisition*. Amsterdam and Philadelphia, PA: J. Benjamins.

——(2003). *Second Language Acquisition and Universal Grammar*. Cambridge: Cambridge UP.

Further references

Bohnacker, U. (2006). When Swedes begin to learn German: from V2 to V2, *Second Language Research*, *22*, 443–86. (An initial state study showing evidence of early functional categories, favoring FT/FA.)

Myles, F. (2005). The emergence of morphosyntactic structure in French L2. In J.-M. Dewaele (ed.), *Focus on French as a Foreign Language: Multidisciplinary approaches*, pp. 88–113. Clevedon: Multilingual Matters. (A structure building analysis of L2 French.)

Tsimpli, I.-M. and Dimitrakopoulou, M. (2007). The interpretability hypothesis: evidence from wh-interrogatives in second language acquisition. *Second Language Research*, *23*, 215–42. (A discussion of the interpretability hypothesis.)

Vainikka, A. and Young-Scholten, M. (2007). Minimalism vs. organic syntax. In S. Karimi, V. Samiian and W. Wilkins (eds), *Phrasal and Clausal Architecture: Syntactic Derivation and Interpretation. In Honor of Joseph Emonds*, pp. 319–38. Amersterdam: J. Benjamins. (An updating of Minimal Trees as Organic Grammar.)

Yuan, B. (1998). Interpretation of binding and orientation of the Chinese reflexive *ziji* by English and Japanese speakers. *Second Language Research*, *17*, 248–72. (A study that shows first language differences between English and Japanese in initial state Chinese.)

Input enhancement

ZhaoHong Han

Columbia University, Teachers College

The term "input enhancement" was proposed by Sharwood Smith (1991, 1993) to refer to a pedagogic strategy whereby the input to the second language (L2) learner is highlighted for its certain features so that they become perceptually salient and hence more noticeable. The proposal of input enhancement was, theoretically, a complement – rather than an antithesis – to Krashen's (1982) input hypothesis, which posits that exposure to abundant comprehensible input is all that is needed for L2 acquisition to take place. According to Krashen, second language acquisition (SLA) should follow the suit of first language acquisition. That is, it should largely happen implicitly; explicit manipulation of the learner's consciousness – through rule-based teaching or error correction – is neither all that necessary nor much useful. Krashen's view had rapid ascension to popularity, particularly among second language teachers, only to descend into controversy in second language research circles. While researchers had no objection to the elevated status of comprehensible input, they repudiated it as being a necessary and a sufficient condition for L2 learning, pointing out its lack of validity and falsifiability (e.g., Gregg, 1984). The outcome of this debate was a revived interest in the role of consciousness in L2 learning, overall, and the ensuing conception that consciousness can help where implicit learning fails (e.g., Hulstijn and Schmidt, 1994).

The inception of input enhancement had, in fact, been preceded by another construct, "consciousness-raising" (e.g., Sharwood Smith, 1981), the notion that external manipulation of learner awareness will result in the learner restructuring his/her mental representations, and, in turn, in acquisition. However, this idea was quickly abandoned, for a sensible reason. Externally drawing attention, as Sharwood Smith (1993) later explains, is no guarantee for internal awareness: External manipulation may at best constitute a condition for noticing to occur, but whether or not noticing will subsequently occur resides exclusively with the learner.

Thus, disengaged from prescribing a cognitive correlate, the input enhancement proposal emphasizes what is done externally. Engineered by a third party, say, a researcher or a teacher, via typographic (for written input) or phonologic (for oral input) means, input enhancement seeks only to heighten the chances of detection or noticing (Robinson, 1995). The input enhanced can not only be oral and written, but it may also involve positive evidence (i.e., natural exemplars of target language usage) as well as negative evidence (i.e., information prohibiting certain usage in the target language). Negative input enhancement typically takes the form of error correction, itself assuming multiple ways of conveyance. Strategies of positive and negative input enhancement can be employed singularly or in combination to forge greater or lesser saliency. For example, underlining the relative clause construction as it naturally appears in a reading passage plus explaining the rule governing its formation accords greater salience to the construction than underlining alone.

Sharwood Smith (1991) posits two variables, elaboration (i.e., duration) and explicitness (i.e., metalinguistic depth), to allow permutations of an array of input enhancement strategies. Thus, one-time use of underlining would count as a non-elaborate, non-explicit strategy; one-time use of rule presentation to enhance the target language input would be a non-elaborate yet explicit strategy; and so forth. It follows that strategies embodying varying degrees of elaboration and/or explicitness may exert differential effects on learner noticing, and, potentially, on acquisition, as well.

Throughout his theorizing, Sharwood Smith stresses two potentially competing sources of input enhancement or salience: the external, for instance, a teacher, and the internal, that is, the learner himself, cautioning that mismatch may arise "between the intentions lying behind teacher or textbook generated enhancement of the input and the actual effect it comes to have on the learner system" (1991: 130). The implication of all of this is that the efficacy of external input enhancement rests on its harmony with the salience created by the learner himself.

Much of the empirical research to date has sought to ascertain the effects of external enhancement on learners (see, e.g., Alanen, 1995; Jourdenais *et al.*, 1995; Lee, 2007; Leow, 2001; Overstreet, 1998; Shook, 1994; Simard, 2009; White, 1998), with as yet little attention being given to how the external can be aligned with the internal. The results have been an amalgam of positive and negative findings, due largely to substantial variation by study (Han *et al.*, 2008). Two sets of variables vis-à-vis enhancement (e.g., what was enhanced) and measurement (e.g., what was measured) are at the core of the disparity.

That notwithstanding, a meta-analysis of the empirical research on visual input enhancement over the past decade and a half indicates that "second language readers provided with enhancement-embedded texts barely outperformed those who were exposed to unenhanced texts with the same target forms flooded in them ($d = 0.22$)" (Lee and Huang, 2008, p. 307). However, a parallel, qualitative analysis of the research suggests that, albeit non-categorical, the following findings are systemic:

- Simple enhancement is capable of inducing learner noticing of externally enhanced forms in meaning-bearing input.
- Whether or not it also leads to acquisition depends largely on whether the learner has prior knowledge of the target form.
- Learners may automatically notice forms that are meaningful.
- Simple enhancement is more likely to induce learner noticing of the target form when sequential to comprehension than when it is concurrent with comprehension.
- Simple enhancement of a meaningful form contributes to comprehension.
- Simple enhancement of a non-meaningful form does not hurt comprehension.
- Simple enhancement is more effective if it draws focal rather than peripheral attention.
- Compound enhancement is more likely to induce deeper cognitive processing than simple enhancement, possibly to the extent of engendering "overlearning."

(Han *et al.*, 2008: 16)

Simple enhancement, in this context, involves use of one enhancement strategy, and compound enhancement a combination of strategies, such as underlining and corrective feedback.

More importantly, the qualitative review (Han *et al.*, 2008) reveals a host of issues still beleaguering the input enhancement research. Among these are: first, should acquisition or noticing be measured in the wake of input enhancement? It appears that short-term studies, which have by far been the mainstay in the input enhancement research, should concentrate on measuring noticing and refrain from measuring acquisition. Second, does input enhancement create a trade-off between attention to form and meaning (i.e., comprehension)? It appears that there can be a compromise on comprehension, as a result of input enhancement. Third, should input enhancement occur concurrently or sequentially to comprehension? It appears that a sequential arrangement that allows comprehension to occur before input enhancement should be more conductive to learner noticing. Fourth, is input enhancement appropriate for all linguistic forms? It appears that not all forms are equally amenable to input enhancement. Fifth, does learners' prior knowledge play a role? It appears that input enhancement presupposes some prior knowledge. Sixth, should input enhancement be conflated with input flood? It appears that when the two are conflated, it cancels out the effects of input enhancement (cf. Lee and Huang's conclusion above). Finally, what kind of input enhancement may induce overuse in learners? It appears that compound enhancement is more likely to incur overuse than simple enhancement.

These issues, along with the tentative conclusions, provide pointers for a focused agenda for future research. However, the goal of future research should not be limited to just achieving a deeper and more categorical understanding of input enhancement per se; the impact of input enhancement needs also to be examined more broadly – in relation to issues of general concern, such as learner processing of natural input, role of instruction, role of consciousness, and individual differences, to name a few. To that end, two emerging lines of research are worth noting: recently, a group of researchers have begun to investigate learners' spontaneous processing of input, that is, processing performed by the learner without any instructional guidance (see, e.g., Carroll, 2005; Han and Peverly, 2007; Park and Han, 2008; Rast, 2008). Collective findings from this nascent research have shed light on a series of concerns, including but not limited to what processing strategies the beginning learner resorts to when exposed to a completely new language, what they are capable of processing on their own, and when their first language influence starts kicking in. As this line of research continues, it is likely to lead to a systematic discovery pertinent to what elements in the input are naturally susceptible to noticing (or not), what serve as cues to processing, and how much of that process is aided and/or hindered by their L1. This type of knowledge may, in turn, provide a better basis for default assessment of the usefulness and capacity of (external) input enhancement, as well as, practically, for improving its efficacy.

Another noteworthy line of research relates to applying visual input enhancement to second language instruction of deaf learners, which has consistently yielded positive results. Deaf learners are reported to demonstrate long-term retention of improved grammatical knowledge (see, e.g., Berent *et al.*, 2008). The importance of such finding cannot be underestimated: For hearing learners, because input comes through multiple channels (oral, aural, and visual), input enhancement is arguably not that critical for them, but for deaf learners whose access to input is severely restricted (i.e., visual only), input enhancement may turn out to be an indispensible instructional strategy for easing their difficulty in wrestling with the grammar of a spoken language.

See also: attention, awareness, Focus-on-Form (FonF), instructed SLA, Noticing Hypothesis, recasts

References

Alanen, R. (1995). Input enhancement and rule presentation in second language acquisition. In R. Schmidt (ed.), *Attention and Awareness in Second Language Acquisition*, pp. 259–99. Honolulu: University of Hawai'i Press.

Berent, G.P., Kelly, R.R., Porter, J.E. and Fonzi, J. (2008). Deaf learners' knowledge of English universal quantifiers. *Language Learning, 58* (2), 401–37.

Berent, G., Kelly, R., Schmitz, K. and Kenney, P. (2009). Visual input enhancement via essay coding results in deaf learners' long-term retention of improved English grammatical knowledge. *Journal of Deaf Studies and Deaf Education*, *14*(2), 190–204.

Carroll, S. (2005). Input and SLA: Adults' sensitivity to different sorts of cues to French gender. *Language Learning*, *55*(0), 79–138.

Gregg, K. (1984). Krashen's monitor and Occam's razor. *Applied Linguistics*, *5*, 79–100.

Han, Z.-H., Park, E. and Combs, C. (2008). Textual input enhancement: Issues and possibilities. *Applied Linguistics*, *29*(4), 597–618.

Han, Z.-H. and Peverly, S. (2007). Input processing: A study of *ab initio* learners with multilingual backgrounds *The International Journal of Multilingualism*, *4*(1), 17–37.

Hulstijn, J. and Schmidt, R. (eds) (1994). Consciousness in Second Language Learning. *AILA Review*, *11*.

Jourdenais, R., Ota, M., Stauffer, S., Boyson, B. and Doughty, C. (1995). Does TE promote noticing? A think-aloud protocol analysis. In R. Schmidt (ed.), *Attention and Awareness in Foreign Language Learning*, pp. 182–209. Honolulu: Hawai'i.

Krashen, S. (1982). *Principles and Practice in Second Language Acquisition*. Oxford: Pergamon.

Lee, S. (2007). Effects of textual enhancement and topic familiarity on Korean EFL students' reading comprehension and learning of passive form. *Language Learning*, *57*(1), 87–118.

Lee, S.-K. and Huang, H.-T. (2008). Visual input enhancement and grammar learning: A meta-Analytic review. *Studies in Second Language Acquisition*, *30*(3), 307–31.

Leow, R. (2001). Do learners notice enhanced forms while interacting with the L2? An online and offline study of the role of written input enhancement in L2 reading. *Hispania*, *84*, 496–509.

Overstreet, M. (1998). Text enhancement and content familiarity: The focus of learner attention. *Spanish Applied Linguistics*, *2*, 229–58.

Park, E.S. and Han, Z.-H. (2008). Learner spontaneous attention in L2 input processing: An exploratory study In Z.-H. Han (ed.), *Understanding Second Language Process*, pp. 106–32. Clevedon: Multilingual Matters.

Rast, R. (2008). *Foreign Language Input: Initial Processing*. Clevedon: Multilingual Matters.

Robinson, P. (1995). Review article: Attention, memory and the 'noticing' hypothesis. *Language Learning, 45*, 283–331.

Sharwood Smith, M. (1981). Consciousness-raising and second language acquisition theory. *Applied Linguistics*, *7*(3), 239–56.

——(1991). Speaking to many minds: On the relevance of different types of language information for the L2 learner. *Second Language Research*, *7*(2), 118–32.
——(1993). Input enhancement in instructed SLA. *Studies in Second Language Acquisition*, *15*, 165–79.
Shook, D. (1994). FL/L2 reading, grammatical information, and the input-to-intake phenomenon. *Applied Language Learning*, *5*(2), 57–93.
Simard, D. (2009). Differential effects of textual enhancement formats on intake. *System*, *37*(1), 124–35.
White, J. (1998). Getting the learners' attention. In C. Doughty and J. Williams (eds), *Focus on Form in Classroom Second Language Acquisition*, pp. 85–113. Cambridge: Cambridge University Press.

Institutional talk

Kathleen Bardovi-Harlig
Indiana University

Institutional talk (sometimes referred to as *institutional discourse* or *institutional interaction*) may be understood as talk between an institutional representative and a client (e.g., a faculty advisor and a graduate student, or an interviewer at a job agency and the applicant) or between members of the same institution (also called *workplace talk*, such as talk between a nursing supervisor and a nurse, or among hotel or factory employees). In these cases, the "interaction is institutional insofar as participants' institutional or professional identities are somehow made relevant to the work activities in which they are engaged" (Drew and Heritage, 1992: 3–4).

The interactions between clients and institutional representatives (referred to as *frontstage* by Sarangi and Roberts, 1999: 20) have been studied in a variety of contexts such as business, including employment interviews; law, especially court testimonies; education, including counseling sessions and teacher–student discourse; and medicine, including interviews between doctors and patients. Drew and Heritage (1992) covers a wide range of these settings, as does Sarangi and Roberts (1999). Workplace talk (referred to as *backstage* by Sarangi and Roberts: 20) has been studied in contexts such as disputes between labor and management, pilot and air traffic controller discourse, physician and apprentice discourse, and professional collaborations.

Agar (1985) and Erickson and Schulz (1982) have noted that many institutional encounters share similar structures which are quite different from informal, spontaneous conversations. Institutional discourse differs from ordinary conversations in three primary ways: goal orientation, constraints, and frameworks (Levinson, 1992), which Drew and Heritage (1992: 22) summarize as follows:

1. Institutional interaction involves an orientation by at least one of the participants to some core goal, task or identity (or set of them) conventionally associated with the institution in question. In short, institutional talk is normally informed by *goal orientations* of a relatively restricted conventional form.
2. Institutional interaction may often involve *special and particular* constraints on what one or both of the participants will treat as allowable contributions to the business at hand.
3. Institutional talk may be associated with *inferential frameworks* and procedures that are particular to specific institutional contexts.

In addition to purely goal-oriented contributions, institutional discourse may exhibit comembership talk which reflects participants' shared attributes such as race, ethnicity, or gender (Erickson and Schultz, 1982) or common interests or activities (such as parenting, travel, or sports; Bardovi-Harlig and Hartford, 1993). Similarly, workplace talk may exhibit relational sequences such as evaluations and personal accounts (Koester, 2004).

The characteristic features of institutional talk (goal-orientation, constraints, and inferential frameworks) make institutional talk a valuable context for second language research. The resultant talk is comparable, interactive, authentic, and consequential (Bardovi-Harlig and Hartford, 2005). This means the language samples can be reasonably compared; speakers have the opportunity to take turns; the exchanges take place naturally without intervention of the researcher; and, there is a real-world outcome, or *consequence*, to naturally occurring talk, which often extends beyond the verbal exchange in order to accomplish goals (Drew and Heritage, 1992; Sarangi and Roberts, 1999).

Institutional talk provides a natural laboratory in which learner talk may be observed and potentially generalized to other settings. The study of the acquisition of rules of content, form, turn taking, and timing in institutional talk provides a microcosm for learning the rules of talk of a new culture; and, although institutions are complex themselves, they are more easily describable than an entire culture. While observing one or more institutional interactions with an individual learner at one time provides insight into second language use, observing multiple interactions by the same learner longitudinally can provide insight into acquisition.

One challenge of researching the development of pragmatic, discourse, and interactional competence among second language learners has been satisfying the conflicting desires for both comparable language samples across learners and natural conversations. In traditional interlanguage pragmatics research, conversation has been seen as idiosyncratic and not replicable. In contrast, institutional talk takes place between multiple institutional representatives and multiple clients every day. For example, drivers come to a department of motor vehicles to renew their driver's licenses or license plates, to register new vehicles, and to apply for learner's permits. Each of the resulting conversations is comparable within its category, and the data are enhanced by the number of people who undertake the interactions. The talk in which the speakers are engaged leads to a specific outcome that can be verified in light of the goals of the interaction, and which is often confirmed by written documentation which is so common that Agar (1985) identified report writing as one stage of the institutional interview.

Other features of institutional talk also contribute to its value as a setting for second-language research over general conversation for data collection and comparison. Learners at all levels of proficiency participate in institutional interactions, and this eliminates the bias toward advanced learners found in the other means of elicitation, especially those that provide situational descriptions (see DCTs). Institutional clients and representatives are known to the institution, so participant demographics can be described; institutional talk takes place in specific places at specific times and can be planned for. Recordings of institutional talk often include video as well as audio recording (e.g., Erickson and Schulz, 1982; Tyler, 1995). Analysis of talk, actions, and gestures may be complemented by retrospective interviews in which researchers ask for participant interpretation of potential trouble sources, hesitations, background knowledge, outcomes, or other information (e.g., Erickson and Schulz, 1982; Tyler, 1995).

The goal-oriented nature of institutional talk offers an innovation in evaluating the success of an interaction without a comparison to native-speaker discourse, providing independent assessment. One of the goals of pragmatics research has been to distinguish important differences from trivial ones in the speech of learners, non-native speakers, and native speakers. As Kasper (1998, p.198) notes, "pragmatic divergence itself is not problematic if the social values indexed are acceptable or perhaps even valued by the recipient." Institutional outcomes illustrate that the features contributing to successful interactions can be shared by native-speakers and learners.

See also: communicative competence, discourse and pragmatics in SLA, native speaker, sociopragmatics, pragmalinguistics, pragmatics

References

Agar, M. (1985). Institutional discourse. *Text*, *5*, 147–68.

Bardovi-Harlig, K. and Hartford, B.S. (1993). The language of comembership. *Research on Language and Social Interaction*, *26*, 227–57.

——(2005). Institutional discourse and interlanguage pragmatics. In K. Bardovi-Harlig and B.S. Hartford (eds), *Interlanguage Pragmatics: Exploring Institutional Talk*. Mahwah, NJ: Erlbaum.

Drew, P. and J. Heritage (eds) (1992). *Talk at Work*. Cambridge: Cambridge University Press.

Erickson, F. and J. Shultz (1982). *The Counselor as Gatekeeper*. New York: Academic Press.

Kasper, G. (1998). Interlanguage pragmatics. In H. Byrnes (ed.), *Learning Foreign and Second Language: Perspectives in Research and Scholarship*. New York: The Modern Language Association.

Koester, A.J. (2004). Relational sequences in workplace genres. *Journal of Pragmatics, 36*, 1405–28.

Levinson, S. (1992). Activity types and language. In P. Drew and J. Heritage (eds), *Talk at Work*. Cambridge: Cambridge University Press.

Sarangi, S. and C. Roberts (eds) (1999). *Talk, Work and Institutional Order: Discourse in Medical, Mediation and Management Settings*. Berlin: de Gruyter.

Tyler, A. (1995). The co-construction of cross-cultural miscommunication: Conflicts in perception, negotiation and enactment of participant role and status. *Studies in Second Language Acquisition, 17*, 129–52.

Further reading

Bardovi-Harlig, K. and Hartford, B. (eds) (2005). *Interlanguage Pragmatics: Exploring Institutional Talk*. Mahwah, NJ: Erlbaum. (Empirical studies of learners engaged in institutional talk.)

Kress, G. and Fowler, R. (1979). Interviews. In R. Fowler, B. Hodge, G. Kress, and T. Trew (eds), *Language and Control*. London: Routledge and Kegan Paul. (Analysis of academic interviews with specific reference to multiple challenges faced by students; native speakers.)

Limberg, H. (2008). *The Interactional Organization of Academic Talk: Office Hour Consultation*. Amsterdam: John Benjamins. (Analysis of English-language office hour consultations of English majors at two German public universities.)

Schiffrin, D., Tannen, D. and Hamilton, H.E. (eds) (2001). *The Handbook of Discourse Analysis*. Malden, MA: Blackwell. (Chapters 22–25 address legal, medical, and educational discourse.)

Instructed Second Language Acquisition

Nina Spada and Patsy M. Lightbown
Ontario Institute for Studies in Education, University of Toronto and Concordia University

Instructed second language acquisition (SLA) contrasts with naturalistic SLA. Instructed SLA refers to language acquisition in classrooms, language laboratories, or other settings where language is intentionally taught and/or intentionally learned. Naturalistic language acquisition occurs in informal settings such as the workplace or the playground where learners are expected to "pick up" the second language through observation and interaction with others – in much the same way that children acquire their first language (L1) (see **Naturalistic and instructed SLA**, this volume). A central question motivating research in both domains is how L2 learners process, construct, and develop their knowledge of a second language (L2). It has sometimes been assumed that two different kinds of language learning processes would characterize the two different settings. While it is clear that the context for instructed SLA is different from that of naturalistic SLA, there has been less agreement about whether the cognitive processes that learners engage in to acquire language in the two contexts are also different. Since the 1970s, research on second language acquisition has revealed some important similarities as well as some differences in how learners' language knowledge and language use evolve with and without instruction.

Early research

To understand the nature and goals of instructed SLA, it is useful to consider them within the broader context of SLA theory and research. In the early 1970s SLA studies were influenced by research in L1 acquisition and mentalist (as opposed to behaviorist) theories of language acquisition. These studies, carried out with children and adults, focused on three areas of inquiry: 1) the identification and explanation of the types of errors L2 learners make; 2) the accuracy with which L2 learners produce grammatical morphemes; and 3) the acquisition of some grammatical features such as questions and negative sentences. These early studies showed that contrary to behaviorist assumptions that the primary source of L2 errors was L1 interference, many of the errors that L2 learners made were similar regardless of their L1 background and also similar to those made in L1 acquisition by children (see **Error analysis**, and Interlanguage, this volume). The studies also reported sequences in the development of morpheme accuracy and other grammatical features that were similar across L2 learners from different age groups and L1 backgrounds (see **Development in SLA**, **Developmental sequences**, and **Morpheme acquisition orders**, this volume).

These early research findings suggested that the underlying processes of L2 learning are similar to those of L1 learning, adding strength to mentalist theories of language acquisition and contributing to changes in the way second languages were taught. Findings of these early studies were seen as compatible with the movement away from structure-based approaches (e.g., grammar translation and audio-lingual methods) to communicative language teaching (CLT). There were different versions and implementations of CLT, but they shared a set of common assumptions – that L2 learning could be fostered through exposure to meaningful input, that learners' errors were a natural result of the learning process, and that an emphasis on the exchange of messages and meaning rather than a prescribed sequence of language forms was needed in L2 instruction. Some researchers drew inferences from the early SLA studies that led them to conclude that it was not necessary or desirable for teachers to focus learners' attention on particular language forms or to intervene during communicative activities to provide corrective feedback. The notion was that, with adequate quantities of comprehensible input and motivation to engage in interaction, language acquisition would develop naturally. Indeed, this view came to be so prevalent that some researchers, teachers, and curriculum planners came to question the benefits of instruction that focused on the language itself.

Even though some researchers saw the early SLA findings as relevant to L2 pedagogy, others were skeptical, pointing out that most of the research had been carried out with children and adults learning a second language in a "natural" setting, not in the classroom. Hatch (1978) urged that researchers and educators should "apply with caution" any ideas drawn from research outside instructional contexts until the learning processes had also been investigated inside the classroom. Long (1983) compared the research findings on the relative effects of instruction and exposure on L2 learning. His conclusion, based on the evidence at the time, was that the benefits of instruction "are considerable (although not overwhelming)." He went on to suggest that more research was needed to provide a more certain answer to the question and related questions about how different *types of instruction* might affect SLA as well as how types of instruction might interact with *individual differences* in learners. Such questions have guided much research in instructed SLA since that time.

In the 1980s, a greater number of investigations into L2 development in instructional settings began to be reported. Much of this early research was descriptive, seeking to provide an accurate characterization of how instructed learners acquired language features including grammatical morphemes and questions. These studies provided more empirical data relevant to the question of whether the developmental patterns were similar to or different from those observed in naturalistic L2 acquisition. This marked the beginning of instructed SLA research even though the term "instructed SLA" did not appear in the literature until later. By the end of the 1990s, there was mounting evidence that instruction does "make a difference" and that the difference is a positive one.

Measuring the effects of instruction

Research on instructed SLA has examined three aspects of L2 development: the *route* of L2 acquisition; the *rate* of L2 acquisition, and *levels of ultimate attainment*. As noted above, early studies that investigated the *route* of development found that instructed and naturalistic learners follow similar developmental sequences in their acquisition of grammatical morphemes, questions, and negation. Some studies showed that the learners'

L1 influenced certain details of the developmental sequences, for example, French speakers were slower to acquire some English patterns of question formation that differed from their L1 rules. In addition, L2 instruction was found to lead to some differences in error patterns, for example the overuse of language features that had been extensively drilled and practiced. The general observation was that the overall route of development was more similar than different and that the natural route of SLA was robust and minimally affected by instruction. However, studies of the *route* of L2 development were limited to a few features in a few languages. Subsequent studies have continued to confirm the existence of developmental sequences that do not simply reflect the order in which language features are taught (Lightbown and Spada, 2006). Nevertheless, recent research indicates that even for grammatical morphemes in the so-called "natural" order, the sequence can be influenced by external factors (e.g., frequency and salience in the input) as well as by general processing constraints (Goldschneider and DeKeyser, 2001). Such findings suggest ways in which instruction can influence SLA.

Studies to examine the *rate* of development have indicated that instruction increases the speed with which learners acquire the second language. One series of studies has shown that instruction targeting language patterns that are just beyond learners' current developmental stage can be particularly effective in helping them acquire features and patterns more quickly (Pienemann, 1989). Another aspect of the *rate* of learning is related to L2 learners' age (see **Age Effects in SLA**, this volume). Researchers have found that, in instructional contexts, older children and adolescents appear to progress more rapidly in L2 acquisition than younger children (Muñoz, 2006). This advantage appears to be due to the older learners' ability to use L1 knowledge, metalinguistic awareness, and cognitive maturity to accelerate their progress.

Regarding *ultimate attainment*, the level of L2 proficiency that learners eventually attain varies widely. Nevertheless, some studies have found that instructed learners eventually reach higher levels of proficiency than those who have not had instruction (Pavesi, 1986) (see **Proficiency**, this volume). In some research, instructed learners were observed to reach higher levels of grammatical accuracy in their L2 production but not higher levels of L2 communicative ability when compared with non-instructed learners (Klein, 1986).

Thus, the overall findings from instructed SLA research suggest that while the *route* of L2 development is at least partly determined by learner-internal factors, instruction can have a substantial impact on *rate* and *ultimate attainment.*

Processes in Instructed SLA

Housen and Pierrard (2005) identify three aspects of SLA processes that are known to benefit from L2 instruction: knowledge internalization, knowledge modification, and knowledge consolidation. Research to investigate knowledge internalization includes studies of whether and how instructed learners "notice" features in the input, how they process this information in short-term memory and eventually integrate it into their internal grammars. According to Schmidt (1995) noticing features in the input is essential for SLA and many studies of instructed SLA have investigated this hypothesis (see **Attention, Awareness,** and **Noticing Hypothesis**, this volume). For example, studies examining the effects of corrective feedback on L2 learning are based on the assumption that learners need to notice the difference between what they say and what they hear in the input in order for that input to affect their interlanguage (see **Corrective feedback**, this volume). A number of studies have confirmed that when learners notice this difference they are able to modify their existing knowledge.

L2 learners' ability to fully consolidate L2 knowledge that is acquired through intentional language study and to quickly and efficiently access it in fluent and spontaneous speech is a question that requires further exploration (see **Explicit learning and Fluency**, this volume). However, some studies show that instruction can increase learners' control over their developing knowledge as well as the speed with which they can access that knowledge in L2 production and comprehension. Current thinking is that attaining a level of automaticity required for spontaneous, fluent L2 performance requires numerous opportunities to practise using the L2 in communicative interaction over time (Gatbonton and Segalowitz, 2005) (see **Automaticity**, this volume).

How instruction affects SLA

A conceptual framework that has influenced discussions of how instruction affects SLA is the interface/non-interface contrast (Ellis, 2001). It concerns two different types of L2 knowledge (see **Declarative memory and knowledge** and **Procedural memory and knowledge**, this volume). Explicit knowledge is characterized as conscious, analyzed knowledge; implicit knowledge is seen as intuitive and unanalyzed. Explicit knowledge is reflected in performance on discrete-point grammar tasks or careful performance of tasks without time pressure, for example, in writing as opposed to speaking. Implicit L2 knowledge manifests itself in fluent spontaneous language use.

The *non-interface* position is based on the claim that implicit and explicit knowledge result from two types of learning processes: acquisition and learning. According to this view, *acquisition* occurs through exposure to comprehensible input and opportunities for meaningful interaction, and *learning* is based on intentional learning of language rules or patterns (Krashen, 1982) (see **Implicit learning**, **Negotiation of meaning**, and **Monitor Model**, this volume). It has been hypothesized that these two kinds of knowledge persist as separate systems in the learner's brain and that only explicit linguistic knowledge results from instruction because it is learned in a conscious, analyzed manner. Implicit L2 knowledge cannot be taught but only inferred from naturally occurring input in much the same way that children acquire a first language. Therefore, any development of implicit L2 knowledge in instructional settings is due to the presence of comprehensible and meaningful language rather than to a transfer or evolution of explicit to implicit knowledge.

According to the *weak interface* position, explicit knowledge may not become implicit knowledge. However, with practice learners achieve the ability to retrieve and to use this knowledge so quickly and easily that, in performance, they appear to be operating from implicit knowledge. Furthermore, proponents of the weak interface position argue that explicit knowledge can create opportunities for the development of implicit knowledge. For example, learners' explicit knowledge may help them to notice differences between their output and the instructional input, leading to changes in their implicit knowledge.

The *strong interface* position holds that explicit and implicit knowledge are not distinct entities but that conversion of explicit (declarative) knowledge to implicit (procedural and then automatized) knowledge takes place through practice. Instructed L2 learners start out with explicit declarative knowledge of a particular language feature (i.e., taught via rule presentation) and through subsequent practice in meaningful communication, this knowledge becomes proceduralized and eventually automatized in the learners' L2 (DeKeyser, 2007). Once the automatization has occurred, the knowledge may be indistinguishable from implicit knowledge – both in terms of performance and in terms of a speaker's ability to report on the declarative knowledge that was present at the beginning of the process.

At the core of instructed SLA research are numerous studies that have investigated questions directly relevant to the interface/non-interface positions. This includes research that has explored the contributions of different types of instruction to L2 learning, the effects of instruction on different types of L2 knowledge, and the extent to which individual learner factors interact with instruction to contribute to different learning outcomes. Many studies of the effects of instruction on SLA are associated with cognitive-interactionist theory. In this framework SLA is viewed as an interaction between learner internal and learner external influences with the locus of learning in cognition. Most of the studies are experimental or quasi-experimental and they no longer ask *whether* instruction affects SLA but rather *how* different types of instruction affect learners' progress. In this research, different types of instruction are delivered to different groups of learners, and the effects on L2 development are compared. The majority of instructed SLA studies focus on a specific grammatical feature in which learners are pre-tested on their knowledge of the target feature before the instructional intervention, post-tested immediately following the instruction, and tested again several weeks later to determine the long-term effects of the instructional intervention.

The impetus for many of the instructional intervention studies was the observation that learners who engaged in exclusively meaning-based activities with little or no attention to language form were not developing high levels of proficiency in the L2. This called into question the notion that exposure to comprehensible input and communicative interaction was sufficient for the development of L2 grammar. This led to a series of quasi-experimental classroom studies in the late 1980s and early 1990s to investigate whether more attention to language form within communicative and content-based L2 classrooms would lead to greater accuracy in the L2.

The positive results from these early studies motivated a great deal of instructed SLA research in which "attention to language form" was defined and operationalized in different ways (see **Focus on Form** and **Input enhancement**, this volume). At one end of the explicit/implicit continuum, some studies provided highly explicit metalinguistic instruction (and corrective feedback). At the implicit end of the continuum, other studies provided high frequency exposure (and implicit corrective feedback). Indeed, after 1990, there was a surge in the number of experimental and quasi-experimental studies to investigate the effects of instruction on L2 learning.

While many of these studies were carried out in L2 classrooms, many more were carried out in laboratory settings. Unlike classroom studies which typically involve 20 or more learners and one teacher, the laboratory studies typically consist of dyadic (i.e., one-on-one) interactions that take place between a researcher and an L2 learner. In these interactions learners are encouraged to engage in communicative tasks that are designed to focus attention on or elicit the production of specific L2 forms over a relatively short period of time usually measured in minutes. Although the amount of instruction provided in classroom studies varies considerably, it is usually measured in hours. The majority of instructed SLA laboratory studies have been motivated by the interaction hypothesis (Long, 1996) and questions about how L2 development occurs as a result of the negotiation for meaning in dyadic interactions (see **Interaction and the Interaction Hypothesis**, this volume). Negotiation is traditionally understood as resulting from communication breakdowns when interlocutors are required to restructure their utterances in order to be understood. Most of the early interaction-based research focused on the benefits of negotiation for increasing the comprehensibility of input. However, recent research has investigated how negotiation can focus learners' attention on language form by making the target language input more noticeable and by providing corrective feedback on learner output. This in turn is thought to contribute positively to SLA and a growing number of interaction-based studies have provided evidence to support this claim (e.g., Mackey and Goo, 2007).

The role of corrective feedback has been the subject of numerous studies, particularly with regard to the benefits of particular types. Some researchers argue that recasts (models of the correct form provided as reformulations of a learner's erroneous utterance) work best (e.g., Long, 2007) (see **Recasts**, and **Uptake**, this volume); others argue that prompts (feedback that pushes the learner to retrieve and produce the correct form) are more effective (e.g., Lyster, 2004).

Meta-analyses of instructional effects

By the year 2000 hundreds of instructed SLA studies had been carried out in classrooms and laboratories and a period of research synthesis began. The first meta-analysis of the effectiveness of L2 instruction was published in 2000. In their investigation of 49 studies representing 89 unique instructional treatments, Norris and Ortega (2000) reported that those including explicit instruction were significantly more effective than those in which the instruction was implicit (see **Meta-analysis**, this volume). However, they also pointed out that the majority of the primary studies examined in their meta-analysis consisted of explicit instruction and that there were considerably fewer studies of implicit instruction. In addition, in virtually all the primary studies, L2 progress was measured using discrete-point or declarative knowledge-based tests (i.e., measures of explicit knowledge) rather than tests of fluency or spontaneous speech (i.e., measures of implicit knowledge). This bias led several SLA researchers to argue that until studies include more measures of implicit knowledge, we cannot be confident that instruction leads to L2 competence that is unconscious, unanalyzed, and available for use in rapid, spontaneous communication.

Fortunately, since the Norris and Ortega (2000) meta-analysis, more studies have incorporated measures of spontaneous L2 use in their research design, making it possible to revisit the question of the effectiveness of L2 instruction. In two recent meta-analyses – one reporting the benefits of instruction on simple and complex language features (Spada and Tomita, 2010) and another on the benefits of interaction in SLA (Mackey and Goo, 2007) – over half the language measures used in the primary studies were free production tasks. An increase in the number of studies investigating the effects of implicit instruction on SLA was also reported. While the findings suggest that explicit instruction contributes to the development of both explicit and implicit L2 knowledge, much more research is needed, particularly validation studies of measures of implicit/explicit L2 knowledge.

Instructed SLA and learner factors

It is not uncommon to read in the instructed SLA literature that a particular type of instruction or corrective feedback is beneficial for L2 learning without any acknowledgment of the fact that individual learners respond differently to instruction and that while a particular type of instruction might work well with one learner, it may not with another. The interaction between individual learner differences and type of instruction and their combined effects on SLA is one area of instructed SLA that requires more research (see **Aptitude-treatment interaction research**, and **Individual differences in SLA**, this volume). We know from the broader field of SLA research that many individual learner variables have been observed to contribute to differences in L2 learning including age, aptitude, motivation, attitude and cognitive maturity to name just a few. Yet, few studies have examined these variables in interaction with different types of L2 instruction.

Some early studies found benefits in matching learners with instructional approaches that are compatible with their learning styles (e.g., Wesche, 1981). However, later studies found that young learners (11–12 years old) with good language analytic abilities were more successful in meaning-focused CLT classes than learners with lower analytic abilities (Ranta, 2002). This suggests that strong language analytic ability helps learners compensate for a lack of structured attention to language in CLT. Some researchers have hypothesized that different dimensions of aptitude are more important for learners at different ages. For example, younger learners rely more on memory and implicit learning processes whereas older learners rely more on explicit analytic ability. While there is evidence to support this hypothesis, it is difficult to determine whether the differences are due to the learners' inherent cognitive abilities or to the type of instruction they receive. That is, the curriculum for younger learners often focuses on more implicit activities while the pedagogical activities for older learners includes more explicit focus (Harley and Hart, 1997).

Classroom investigations of the interactions between type of instruction and cognitive orientations of learners are rare but a few "aptitude-treatment-interaction" studies have begun to appear. For example, in a study investigating the relationship between learner aptitude and two types of L2 instruction (deductive/inductive) with high-school learners of French, Erlam (2005) found that differences in aptitude were predictive of outcomes when the instruction was inductive but not when the instruction was deductive. She suggests that this might be related to a leveling off of aptitude-treatment interactions when explicit instruction is provided. In contrast, in another aptitude-treatment-interaction study with young adult learners of English, Sheen (2007) observed a stronger relationship between aptitude measures and L2 progress with learners who received metalinguistic corrective feedback than with learners who received explicit correction without metalinguistic feedback. Before the interaction between L2 aptitude and learning conditions can be understood, more research needs to compare the effects of different types (and durations) of explicit and implicit treatments and perhaps more importantly, better measures of aptitude for implicit learning/teaching conditions need to be developed.

Instructed SLA–beyond grammar

A great deal of instructed SLA research has focused on the acquisition of grammatical aspects of language but it is not limited to this. Research has also investigated the effects of instructional input on the learning of L2 vocabulary, pragmatics, and pronunciation.

In the area of vocabulary learning, it has been hypothesized that the best way to learn new words is to read for pleasure (e.g., Krashen, 1989). While it is true that reading is an important source for vocabulary growth, research has demonstrated that it is difficult to fully understand a text unless the learner is familiar with 95 per cent of the words in it and more difficult to infer the meaning of new words without an even higher percentage of known vocabulary (Nation, 2001). Furthermore, learners need to encounter a word multiple times in order to recognize it in other contexts and begin to produce it themselves. In instructional studies of vocabulary learning through reading, it has been observed that learners are more likely to learn more vocabulary when their attention is focused on the new words and when they are fully engaged in activities to help their comprehension and production of them (e.g., Hulstijn and Laufer, 2001) (see **Vocabulary learning and teaching**, this volume).

In the area of L2 pragmatics, a meta-analysis of 13 studies investigating the effects of instruction on different types of speech acts (e.g., compliments, requests) revealed that learners who received instruction made more progress than learners who did not (Jeon and Kaya, 2006) (see **Discourse and pragmatics in SLA**, this volume).

While there has been less research to investigate the effects of instruction on pronunciation, studies have illustrated a direct and positive effect of instruction on intelligibility and comprehensibility. There is also evidence that pronunciation instruction can be particularly effective when it targets suprasegmental rather than segmental aspects of pronunciation (Derwing and Munro, 2009) (see **Intelligibility in SLA**, **L2 phonology**, and **Speaking**, this volume).

Conclusion

Instructed SLA is the branch of SLA research that has the most direct ties to pedagogical practice. This places particular responsibility on instructed SLA researchers to consider, discuss, and communicate the implications of their research for L2 instruction. To be sure, these connections are more or less direct, more or less applicable, and more or less relevant depending on the nature of the research and the context in which it was carried out. Nonetheless, making these connections in careful and considered ways is a necessary challenge for the instructed SLA researcher in the midst of pressing educational needs related to the teaching and learning of second and foreign languages worldwide.

See also: classroom interaction research, explicit learning, Focus-on-Form (FonF), implicit learning, noticing hypothesis, processing instruction

References

DeKeyser, R.M. (2007). The future of practice. In R.M. DeKeyser (ed.), *Practice in a Second Language: Perspectives from Applied Linguistics and Cognitive Psychology*. Cambridge: Cambridge University Press.

Derwing, T.M. and Munro, M. (2009). Putting accent in its place: Rethinking obstacles to communication. *Language Teaching, 42*, 476–90.

Ellis, R. (2001). Investigating form-focused instruction. *Language Learning, 51*, 1–46.

Erlam, R. (2005). Language aptitude and its relationship to instructional effectiveness in second language acquisition. *Language Teaching Research, 9*, 147–71.

Gatbonton, E. and Segalowitz, N. (2005). Rethinking communicative language teaching: A focus on access to fluency. *Canadian Modern Language Review, 61*, 325–53.

Goldschneider, J.M. and DeKeyser, R.M. (2005). Explaining the natural order of L2 morpheme acquisition in English: A meta-analysis of multiple determinants. *Language Learning, 55*, 27–77.

Harley, B. and Hart, D. (1997). Language aptitude and second language proficiency in classroom learners of different starting ages. *Studies in Second Language Acquisition, 19*, 379–400.

Hatch, E. (1978). Apply with caution. *Studies in Second Language Acquisition, 2*, 123–43.

Housen, A. and Pierrard, M. (2005). Investigating instructed second language acquisition. In A. Housen and M. Pierrard (eds), *Investigations In Instructed Second Language Acquisition*. Amsterdam: Mouton de Gruyter.

Hulstijn, J. and Laufer, B. (2001). Some empirical evidence for the involvement load hypothesis in vocabulary acquisition. *Language Learning, 51*, 539–58.

Jeon, E.H. and Kaya, T. (2006). Effects of L2 instruction on interlanguage pragmatic development: A meta-analysis. In J. Norris and L. Ortega (eds), *Synthesizing Research on Language Learning and Teaching*. Amsterdam: John Benjamins.

Klein, W. (1986). *Second Language Acquisition*. Cambridge: Cambridge University Press.

Krashen, S. (1989). We acquire vocabulary and spelling by reading: Additional evidence for the input hypothesis. *Modern Language Journal, 73*, 440–64.

——(1982). *Principles and Practice in Second Language Acquisition*. Oxford: Pergamon.

Lightbown, P.M. and Spada, N. (2006). *How Languages Are Learned*. Oxford: Oxford University Press.

Long, M. (1996). The role of the linguistic environment in second language acquisition. In W. Ritchie and T. Bhatia (eds), *Handbook of Second Language Acquisition*. New York: Academic Press.

——(1983). Does second language instruction make a difference? A review of research. *TESOL Quarterly, 17*, 359–82.

——(2007). *Problems in SLA*. Mahwah, NJ: Lawrence Erlbaum Associates.

Lyster, R. (2004). Differential effects of prompts and recasts in form-focused instruction. *Studies in Second Language Acquisition, 26*, 399–432.

Mackey, A. and Goo, J. (2007). Interaction research in SLA: A meta-analysis and research synthesis. In A. Mackey (ed.), *Conversational Interaction in Second Language Acquisition: A Series of Empirical Studies*, pp. 407–52. Oxford: Oxford University Press.

Muñoz, C. (ed.). (2006). *Age and the Rate of Foreign Language Learning*. Clevedon: Multilingual Matters.

Nation, I.S.P. (2001). *Learning Vocabulary in Another Language*. Cambridge: Cambridge University Press.

Norris, J.M. and Ortega, L. (2000). Effectiveness of L2 instruction: A research synthesis and quantitative meta-analysis. *Language Learning, 50*, 417–528.

Pavesi, M. (1986). Markedness, discoursal modes, and relative clause formation in a cormal and an informal context. *Studies in Second Language Acquisition, 8*, 38–55.

Pienemann, M. (1989). Is language teachable? Psycholinguistic experiments and hypotheses. *Applied Linguistics, 10*, 52–79.

Ranta, L. (2002). The role of Learners' language analytic ability in the communicative classroom. In P. Robinson (ed.), *Individual Differences and Instructed Language Learning*, Amsterdam: John Benjamins.

Schmidt, R. (1995). Consciousness and foreign language learning: A tutorial on the role of attention and awareness in learning. In R. Schmidt (ed.), *Attention and Awareness in Foreign Language Learning*. Honolulu: University of Hawai'i.

Sheen, Y. (2007). The effect of corrective feedback, language aptitude, and learner attitudes on the acquisition of English articles. In A. Mackey (ed.), *Conversational Interaction in Second Language Acquisition: A Series of Empirical Studies*. Oxford: Oxford University Press.

Spada, N. and Tomita, Y. (2010). Interactions between type of instruction and type of language feature: A meta-analysis. *Language Learning, 60*, 1–46.

Wesche, M. (1981). Language aptitude measures in streaming, matching students with methods, and diagnosis of learning problems. In K.C. Diller (ed.), *Individual Differences and Universals Language Learning Aptitude*. Rowley, MA: Newbury House.

Further reading

Doughty, C. and Williams, J. (eds) (1998). *Focus on Form in Classroom Second Language Acquisition*. Cambridge: Cambridge University Press. (A collection of empirical studies of instructed SLA using different types of instruction in a variety of classroom settings.)

Ellis, R. (2008). *The Study of Second Language Acquisition*, second edn. Oxford: Oxford University Press. (Part 7: an overview of the research literature on instructed SLA.)

Housen, A. and Pierrard, M. (eds) (2005). *Investigations in Instructed Second Language Acquisition*. Amsterdam: Mouton de Gruyter. (A collection of empirical studies of instructed SLA using different types of instruction in a variety of classroom settings.)

Lyster, R. (2007). *Learning and Teaching Language through Content: A Counterbalanced Approach*. Amsterdam: John Benjamins. (A review of research in content-based language teaching (especially immersion) classrooms and a proposal for increasing the effectiveness of instruction by "counterbalancing" the predominant pedagogical model present in different classrooms.)

VanPatten, B. (ed.) (2004). *Processing Instruction: Theory, Research and Commentary*. Mahwah, NJ: Lawrence Erlbaum. (A series of perspectives and empirical studies on Processing Instruction, VanPatten's instructional approach that guides learners to focus on the language itself rather than giving all their attention to the meaning the language conveys.)

Intake

Ronald P. Leow
Georgetown University

The concept of intake was first coined by Corder (1967) to emphasize L2 learners' active role in language acquisition. According to Corder, there is a fundamental difference between input and intake and not all input may be attended to by the learners. The distinction between input and intake has theoretical value given that it postulates that there is at least one intermediate stage of input processing through which the input L2 learners receive must pass before any or all of it can be acquired.

What constitutes intake led to several speculations. Faerch and Kasper (1980) proposed that there might be actually two types of intake: (1) Intake for communication, which is only for the purpose of immediate meaning during a conversational exchange and (2) intake for learning, which refers specifically to an eventual change in the learners' interlanguage or current state of linguistic knowledge. Gass (1988) defined intake as a process that assimilates linguistic material and involves mental psycholinguistic activity prior to being incorporated into the L2 learner's interlanguage.

Chaudron (1985) viewed intake as part of a series of cognitive stages through which input passes until it is fully incorporated in the L2 learners' grammar. According to Chaudron, intake should not refer to a single event or product but to a complex phenomenon that involves several stages. These stages are (1) the initial stages of perception of input, (2) the subsequent stages of recoding and encoding of the semantic (communicated) information into long-term memory, and (3) the series of stages by which L2 learners fully integrate and incorporate the linguistic information in the input into their developing grammars. This process-oriented description of intake was labeled a continuum from *preliminary* intake to *final* intake.

The distinction between the processes involved between preliminary intake and final intake is closely related to a distinction made by Slobin (1985) who proposed two types of processes: (1) those involved in converting input into stored data that may be used for constructing language and (2) those used to organize stored data into linguistic systems. The first type of process is what has been empirically addressed in most studies that investigated the effects of some variable on learners' intake. This definition is encapsulated in Leow's (1993) definition of intake as "that part of the input that has been attended to by the second language learners while processing the input. Intake represents stored linguistic data which may be used for immediate recognition and does not imply language acquisition" (p. 334). Indeed, the postulation that there may be several stages along the acquisitional process is well exemplified in the many studies that have included in the research designs both intake and production assessment tasks.

There is considerable speculation as to the amount of conscious attention or awareness needed to be allocated to linguistic information in the input in order for such information to become intake. There are three major theoretical attentional underpinnings (Robinson, 1995; Schmidt, 1993; Tomlin and Villa, 1994) in the SLA literature that posit a role for awareness, or lack thereof, in the conversion of input into intake. In Tomlin and Villa's (1994) model of input processing in SLA, the conversion of input into intake is dependent upon the linguistic data being "detected" by the learners, that is, while learners pay attention to the linguistic data they undergo some cognitive registration of the detected stimuli in the input. Crucial to their model is the unimportant role played by awareness at the level of detection. Schmidt's (1993) noticing hypothesis contrasts sharply with Tomlin and Villa's (1994) view of the role of awareness at the input to intake stage. According to Schmidt, attention controls access to awareness and is responsible for noticing (attention plus a low level of awareness) that is crucial for intake to take place. Robinson's (1995) model of the relationship between attention and memory reconciled the notions of detection and noticing in relation to the input to intake process. In his model, Robinson posited detection sequentially prior to noticing along the acquisitional process, indicating that awareness may play a more important role in input processing at the stage of intake.

Many assessment tasks designed to measure intake have followed Chaudron's (1985) suggestion to exclude variables that may influence the interaction between the input and learners' capacity for processing it. Most important is the time factor given that the more time available, the more opportunities learners have to engage higher-level, less automatized knowledge sources that would confound the analysis of the early stage of intake processing (p. 9). The two major features of current assessment tasks of intake are (1) a limited time period to respond to test items, including the instruction not to return to any previously completed item and (2) immediate administration of the assessment task after exposure. The most popular task to measure intake is the multiple-choice recognition assessment task that may be form- or sentential-based. For the multiple-choice form recognition task, participants are presented with an incomplete sentence or a sentence with a deleted targeted form that requires the linguistic item under study for its contextual completion, followed by several options. For the multiple-choice sentence recognition tasks, participants are presented with several sentences among which one comes directly from the exposed L2 input. Learners demonstrate their intake of the targeted item in the input by selecting (recognizing) the correct completion or sentence out of a typical number of four choices. Multiple-choice recognition tasks may differ in relation to the content of the items based on whether the content is true or not to the input provided.

To conclude, while the concept of intake is well accepted by SLA researchers, there is a paucity of studies that have qualitatively investigated what constitutes this concept. Future studies may want to probe deeper into concurrent data gathered via the use of verbal reports in an effort to code exemplars of intake addressing issues such as partial versus complete intake, the type of intake available for subsequent processing, the role of type of linguistic data, and so forth.

See also: attention, awareness, depth of processing, development in SLA, noticing hypothesis, psycholinguistics of SLA

References

Chaudron, C. (1985). Intake: On models and methods for discovering learners' processing of input. *Studies in Second Language Acquisition*, *7*, 1–14.

Corder, S. (1967). The significance of Learners' errors. *International Review of Applied Linguistics*, *5*, 161–69.

Faerch, C. and Kasper, G. (1980). Process and strategies in foreign language learning and communication. *The Interlanguage Studies Bulletin – Utrech*, *5*, 47–118.

Gass, S. (1988). Integrating research areas: A framework for second language studies. *Applied Linguistics*, *19*, 198–217.

Leow, R.P. (1993). To simplify or not to simplify: A look at intake. *Studies in Second Language Acquisition*, *15*, 333–55.

Robinson, P. (1995). Review article: Attention, memory, and the Noticing Hypothesis. *Language Learning*, *45*, 283–331.

Schmidt, R.W. (1993). Awareness and second language acquisition. *Annual Review of Applied Linguistics*, *13*, 206–26.

Slobin, D. (1985). Crosslinguistic evidence for the language-making capacity. In D. Slobin (ed.), *The Crosslinguistic Study of Language Acquisition: Theoretical Issues*, Vol. 2. Mahwah, NJ: Lawrence Earlbaum.

Tomlin, R.S. and Villa, V. (1994). Attention in cognitive science and second language acquisition. *Studies in Second Language Acquisition*, *16*, 183–203.

Intelligibility in SLA

Tracey M. Derwing
University of Alberta

Intelligibility, a central feature of successful communication, can be influenced by many factors, including speech disorders, alcohol or other drugs, ambient signal distortion, etc.; however, the discussion here will be limited to normal issues of intelligibility as a result of a second language (L2) accent. Much of the research focusing on intelligibility has been carried out in English, and thus many of the results reported here are language-specific. Whether an utterance is intelligible, that is, whether a message intended by the speaker is understood accurately and fully by the listener, is the responsibility of both interlocutors. L2 researchers have distinguished intelligibility (actual understanding) from comprehensibility (ease of understanding) and accentedness (degree of phonological difference from a local norm), and have shown that these are related but partially independent dimensions (Derwing and Munro, 2009). It is possible to have a heavy accent and yet be relatively intelligible, but unintelligible L2 speech will typically be perceived as being heavily accented. Thus accent reduction per se may have no effect on intelligibility, if the aspects of pronunciation that interfere with it are not addressed. The intelligibility of L2 speakers is most closely associated with pronunciation, but it can also be affected by grammar and lexical choice.

Although L2 pedagogy has been concerned with pronunciation since at least the seventeenth century, it wasn't until much later that intelligibility was seen as an appropriate goal. Abercrombie (1949) argued that L2 speakers should be required to have only "a comfortably intelligible pronunciation ... which can be understood with little or no conscious effort on the part of the listener" (p. 120) rather than "perfect pronunciation" (p. 120). Despite the wisdom of this claim, it has only been in the last two decades that there has been a shift to the view that intelligibility should be the primary aim of L2 speakers (Derwing and Munro, 2009), perhaps in part because there was so little empirical evidence that intelligibility could be improved in adult L2 speakers.

Factors affecting intelligibility

Several factors influence L2 intelligibility, including the L2 speaker's age of learning (Flege, 1988). In several studies, Flege and his colleagues have shown conclusively that most individuals who learned a second language later than early childhood are likely to have a detectable accent, which, in some cases, depending on the nature of the accent, will interfere with intelligibility. Bongaerts *et al.* (1997) demonstrated that a speaker's aptitude and degree of exposure to L2 input also affect accent, and by extension, intelligibility.

One of the earliest comprehensive studies of intelligibility is Gass and Varonis' (1984) examination of listeners' familiarity with four variables: topic, foreign-accented speech, a particular L2 accent, and familiarity with a particular L2 speaker. The authors found that listener familiarity had a facilitating effect on intelligibility for each variable, but that knowledge of the topic had the strongest impact. Bent and Bradlow (2003) found evidence for a "matched interlanguage speech intelligibility benefit" (p. 1600) such that L2 speakers who share a first language (L1) with other L2 speakers have a familiarity advantage. This is an area of intelligibility research that requires further investigation, as there have been other reports of limited or no intelligibility benefit, depending on the L2 accent in question. Listeners' stereotyped perceptions of L2 speakers can have a negative effect on intelligibility. If listeners expect to have difficulties understanding a given speaker on the basis of a photograph of an individual belonging to a visible minority, they will indeed understand less, and perceive an L2 accent, even when presented with utterances in their own L1 dialect (Rubin, 1992). An interesting feature of ambient noise (e.g., cafeteria noise) is its differential effect on L1 and L2 speaker intelligibility. Although all speech is negatively affected by noise, it appears to have a more detrimental impact on L2 accented productions, but it is not clear which features of an accent are most susceptible to distortion in noise (Munro, 1998).

An issue that has recently received increased attention from researchers is the identification of those aspects of L2 accents that have the greatest consequences for intelligibility. Accents can differ from the local variety of a language at suprasegmental (e.g., stress, pitch, intonation, rhythm) and segmental levels (consonants and vowels). Segmental differences include substitutions, deletions, and insertions. Several studies have shown that suprasegmental features generally appear to have more impact on intelligibility than do segmentals (Derwing and Munro, 2009), at least for speakers of English in inner circle countries. Jenkins (2002) has suggested a core of features appropriate for enhancing intelligibility amongst speakers of English as an international language. The proposed core, however, has yet to be tested broadly with large numbers of speakers from a wide range of L1s. Speech rate, nuclear stress, and word stress have been shown to influence intelligibility. Rate can interfere with message clarity if it is either too fast or too slow, and inappropriate placement of stress, both at the sentence and word level, can cause major intelligibility problems. Catford (1987) devised a hierarchy of importance for individual consonants and vowels in English based on functional load, such that the segments which distinguish the greatest number of minimal pairs are most essential for intelligibility. A preliminary study testing this hypothesis suggests that functional load is a significant factor in the determination of intelligibility (Derwing and Munro, 2009).

Can L2 pedagogy enhance intelligibility?

For those L2 speakers who have difficulties with intelligibility, even after years of living and working in an L2 environment, it is possible, through appropriate pronunciation instruction, to make changes that improve listeners' understanding. Furthermore, it is also possible to enhance listeners' willingness to listen to (and therefore understand) accented speech (Derwing and Munro, 2009).

See also: age effects in SLA, L2 phonology, second dialect acquisition, speaking, speech rate, speech perception

References

Abercrombie, D. (1949). Teaching pronunciation. *English Language Teaching, 3* (5), 113–22.

Bent, T. and Bradlow, A.R. (2003). The interlanguage speech intelligibility benefit. *Journal of the Acoustical Society of America, 114* (3), 1600–610.

Bongaerts, T., van Summeren, C., Planken, B., and Schils, E. (1997). Age and ultimate attainment in the pronunciation of a foreign language.

Studies in Second Language Acquisition, *19* (4), 447–65.

Catford, J.C. (1987). Phonetics and the teaching of pronunciation. In J. Morley (ed.), *Current Perspectives on Pronunciation: Practices Anchored in Theory*, pp. 878–100. Washington, DC: TESOL.

Derwing, T.M. and Munro, M.J. (2009). Putting accent in its place: Rethinking obstacles to communication. *Language Teaching*, *42*(4), 476–90.

Flege, J.E. (1988). The production and perception of foreign language speech sounds. In Winitz, H. (ed.), *Human Communication and its Disorders – A Review*, pp. 224–401. Norwood, NJ: Ablex.

Gass, S. and Varonis, E. (1984). The effect of familiarity on the comprehensibility of nonnative speech. *Language Learning*, *34*(1), pp. 65–89.

Jenkins, J. (2002). A sociolinguistically based, empirically researched pronunciation syllabus for English as an international language. *Applied Linguistics*, *23*(1), 83–103.

Munro, M.J. (1998). The effects of noise on the intelligibility of foreign-accented speech. *Studies in Second Language Acquisition*, 20(2), 139–54.

Rubin, D. (1992). Nonlanguage factors affecting undergraduates' judgments of nonnative English-speaking teaching assistants. *Research in Higher Education*, *33*(4), 511–31.

Further reading

Derwing, T.M. and Munro, M.J. (2005). Second language accent and pronunciation teaching: A research-based approach. *TESOL Quarterly*, *39* (3), 379–97. (A review of relevant research indicating that intelligibility and comprehensibility should be the focus of L2 pronunciation instruction.)

Hahn, L. (2004). Primary stress and intelligibility: Research to motivate the teaching of suprasegmentals. *TESOL Quarterly*, *38*(2), pp. 201–23. (This study isolated the effects of primary stress on intelligibility in a format that could and should be replicated for other aspects of L2 pronunciation.)

Levis, J.M. (2005). Changing contexts and shifting paradigms in pronunciation teaching. *TESOL Quarterly*, *39*(3), 369–78. (This article presents a clear explication of the nativist versus the intelligibility principles for language instruction.)

Munro, M.J. (2008). Foreign accent and speech intelligibility. In Hansen Edwards, J.G. and Zampini, M.L. (eds), *Phonology and Second Language Acquisition*, pp. 193–218. Amsterdam: John Benjamins. (A comprehensive overview of second language accent and intelligibility.)

Munro, M.J., Derwing, T.M. and Morton, S.L. (2006). The mutual intelligibility of L2 speech. *Studies in Second Language Acquisition*, *28* (1), 111–31. (This study deals with issues of familiarity and shared responses to elements in the speech stream.)

Interaction and the interaction hypothesis

María del Pilar García-Mayo
Universidad del Pais Vasco

When holding a conversation, whether in a natural environment or in a classroom setting, sometimes there are breaks in the communication flow between the interlocutors. Frequently, one of them wants to solve the breakdown and makes modifications in the language being used. Consider the example in (1):

NATIVE SPEAKER: I am over the deadline for this project
LEARNER: You mean you should have done the job by now?
NATIVE SPEAKER: Exactly

In this short excerpt, the advanced learner of English wants to confirm the meaning of "deadline" before the native speaker goes on with the rest of the conversation. Learners normally interact with other learners or with native speakers (NSs) and use the language they are learning with a communicative purpose in mind.

Early work by Hatch (1978) observed that the study of properties of discourse addressed to learners could provide information about linguistic features relevant to the understanding of the second language (L2) acquisition process. In fact, Hatch's contribution was seminal for all the work to be carried out in later years as she claimed that participation in conversational interaction provided the learners with opportunities to process and produce the L2.

At the beginning of the 80s, Krashen's Input Hypothesis (1985) had a great impact on the L2 field. Krashen (1985) argued that learners acquire a language by understanding input containing structures that are one stage beyond their current level of competence. Comprehensible input was seen as both a necessary and sufficient condition for L2 learning to take place. In Krashen's view, input was made comprehensible by means of simplification and with contextual and extralinguistic cues.

Pioneering work by Long (1983) pointed out that although there were few linguistic differences between the talk produced in NS-NS and NS-learner conversations – as attested by several measures of grammatical complexity – there were crucial changes in the structure of conversational interaction between NSs and learners regarding the use of conversational and linguistic adjustments. Long's main claim was that the changes NSs made to the structure of the conversation were more frequently used in interactional episodes with learners and that those changes might play a role in the provision of comprehensible input. In fact, Long was critical of Krashen's Input Hypothesis and wanted to go beyond descriptive research by proposing a systematic approach to linking those conversational changes to the learners' L2 development. Thus, Long (1985: 378) proposed that research should first show that linguistic and conversational adjustments promote the comprehension of input. Secondly, it should be shown that comprehensible input promotes acquisition and, thirdly, it should be deduced that those linguistic and conversational adjustments promote acquisition.

Long (1983) operationalized conversational adjustments as confirmation checks, clarification requests, and comprehension checks. Confirmation checks are expressions designed to elicit confirmation that an utterance has been correctly understood (*Do you mean that ... ?*); clarification requests are intended to obtain more precise information from the interlocutor's utterance (by asking about specific lexical items, for example); and comprehension checks are attempts to prevent a breakdown in communication (*Do you need me to repeat?*). The goal of most studies carried out in the 90s was to establish a link between the linguistic and conversational adjustments made in conversational interaction and the acquisition of different target forms (Pica, 1994 for a detailed account of that research). In a nutshell then, the main claim of the Interaction Hypothesis (IH) is that interaction, modified through different types of conversational adjustments, enhances the learners' needs to access L2 comprehensible input.

Long (1996) put forward an updated version of the IH and he proposes that:

> [...]environmental contributions to acquisition are mediated by selective attention and the learners' developing L2 processing capacity, and that these resources are brought together most usefully, although not exclusively, during *negotiation for meaning*. Negative feedback obtained during negotiation work or elsewhere may be facilitative of L2 development, at least for vocabulary, morphology, and language specific syntax, and essential for learning certain specifiable L1-L2 contrasts.

In this updated version of the IH, Long pays special attention to cognitive processes such as attention, also to negative feedback the learner might obtain and specifically to the construct of negotiation of meaning, which he also claims might facilitate acquisition because of its potential to connect attention and output (1996: 451–52).

Nowadays, the interaction approach is a well-established framework in the second language acquisition (SLA) field. Numerous studies carried out in laboratory and classroom settings have been published since the 80s, all of them supporting the facilitative role of interaction in the L2 process (see Mackey, 2007, for a list of those studies and Mackey and Goo, 2007 for meta-analysis providing evidence for the positive role of interaction).

However, as noticed by Mackey (2007: 10), research on interaction and negotiation is currently not focused on establishing a connection between conversational interaction and L2 learning but, rather, on the relation between interaction, learner-internal cognitive processes, and L2 learner outcomes.

As expected, the interaction approach has evolved in the past 20 years and it has incorporated new theoretical developments and methodological advances. Gass and Mackey (2007: 175) mention that in its current form the IH subsumes some aspects of Krashen's Input Hypothesis (1985) and of Swain's Ouput Hypothesis (1985). According to Gass and Mackey (2007), the major components of the interaction approach are input (the linguistic forms, both oral, written and the visual signal in sign language, that the learner is exposed to), output (learner production), and feedback (information provided to the learner in response to his/her production). Several studies have provided empirical support for the theoretical claim that interactionally modified input aids comprehension. Specially relevant was the study by Mackey (1999) where she showed that interactionally modified input facilitated the development of question formation in EFL. Other empirical studies have also identified how modified output can impact L2 learning during conversational interaction and that feedback received during interaction facilitates the L2 learning process and is linked to L2 development. Together with research carried out on interactionally modified input, output and feedback, recent developments in the interaction approach stress the importance of combining insights from both cognitive and social perspectives. Thus, current lines of research aim at establishing the impact of cognitive and individual (working memory, aptitude, anxiety, motivation) factors as well as social (setting, interlocutor) ones on the L2 learning process. Mackey *et al.* (2002) showed that learners with larger working and phonological memory spans were more likely to notice errors targeted by recasts than those with smaller spans. Trofimovich *et al.* (2007) examined various individual cognitive factors (phonological memory, working memory, analytical ability and attention control) and concluded that the effect of those factors on the learners' use of information provided in recast was clear.

Motivation is one of the individual differences that has received most attention in SLA. Learners are more willing to communicate if they have a positive motivation toward the activity in need of completion. Dörnyei and Tseng (2009) consider that specific mechanisms making up the learner's motivational system when processing a task might be related to cognitive factors such as attention and noticing, both claimed to be factors that partially account for learning outcomes. Another individual difference that still needs to be researched within the interaction approach is that of gender. Although the topic had been dealt with in previous studies, Ross-Feldman (2007) is designed in such a way that each participant interacted in mixed and matched gender dyads. The researcher showed that the type of dyad did influence interactional patterns.

On the social front, different language learning settings need to be investigated. Research framed within the interaction approach has been mainly focused on English as a Second Language (ESL) settings. Over the past decade, some research has been carried out in English as a Foreign Language (EFL) settings (Alcón Soler and García Mayo, 2009; García Mayo and Alcón Soler, 2002) but more effort is needed to identify other languages taught in foreign language settings. Also, considering the impact the Content and Language Integrated Language (CLIL) approach is having in Europe, it would be worth studying interactional patterns in children who have been exposed to more input hours per week in the foreign language context and compare them with their mainstream partners. A setting that one cannot forget about is the online environment, where languages are increasingly being learned. A way forward in interaction research will be to test whether online interaction will also facilitate language learning.

Regarding interlocutors, an interesting issue to be explored in interaction research carried out in classroom contexts would be to test whether there is a difference in interactional patterns when the learners choose their own partner or the teacher is the one deciding which pairs should be formed.

Another fruitful line of research for the IH is that of interaction and tasks. Over the past years researchers have been interested in tasks as research instruments and task-based language teaching has been primarily informed by the IH. It is by means of tasks that interaction might be modified and thus, characteristics of tasks (task types, task complexity … etc) have been of great interest to researchers (García Mayo, 2007; Robinson, 2007). Future developments in this research line will hopefully shed light on the facilitative effects of interaction.

In conclusion, research over the past three decades has shown that interactional work facilitates L2 learning and has provided empirical support for arguments about its developmental efficacy (see Mackey and Goo, 2007). It seems that it is time now to move on and consider the impact of cognitive and individual variables as well as social ones on the L2 learning process. All the exciting work that is currently underway will provide answers to the questions raised in those two broad realms in the near future.

See also: classroom interaction research, input enhancement, form-meaning relations, negotiation of meaning, output hypothesis, task-based learning

References

Alcón Soler, E. and García Mayo, M.P. (2009). Interaction and language learning in foreign language contexts. *International Review of Applied Linguistics*, *47* (3–4).

Dörnyei, Z. and Tseng, W.-T. (2009). Motivational processing in interactional tasks. In A. Mackey and C. Polio (eds), *Multiple Perspectives on Interaction: Second Language Research in Honor of Susan M. Gass*, pp. 117–34. Mahwah, NJ: Lawrence Erlbaum.

García Mayo, M.P. (ed.) (2007). *Investigating Tasks in Formal Language Learning*. Clevedon: Multilingual Matters.

García Mayo, M.P. and Alcón Soler, E. (2002). The role of interaction in instructed language learning. *International Journal of Educational Research*, 37 (special issue).

Gass, S.M. and Mackey, A. (2007). Input, interaction and output in second language acquisition. In B. VanPatten and J. Williams (eds), *Theories in Second Language Acquisition. An Introduction*, pp. 175–200. Mahwah, NJ: Lawrence Erlbaum.

Hatch, E. (1978). Acquisition of syntax in a second language. In J. Richards (ed.), *Understanding Second and Foreign Language Learning*, pp. 34–70. Rowley, MA: Newbury House.

Krashen, S. (1985). *The Input Hypothesis: Issues and Implications*. London: Longman.

Long, M.H. (1983). Native speaker/non-native speaker conversation and the negotiation of comprehensible input. *Applied Linguistics*, *4*(2), 126–41.

——(1985). A role for instruction in second language acquisition: Task-based language teaching. In K. Hyltenstam and M. Pienemann (eds), *Modelling and Assessing Second Language Acquisition*. Clevedon: Multilingual Matters.

——(1996). The role of the linguistic environment in second language acquisition. In W. Ritchie and T. Bhatia (eds), *Handbook of Research on Second Language Acquisition*, pp. 413–68. New York: Academic Press.

Mackey, A. (1999). Input, interaction and second language development: An empirical study of question formation in ESL. *Studies in Second Language Acquisition*, *21*, 557–87.

Mackey, A. (ed.) (2007). *Conversational Interaction in Second Language Acquisition*. Oxford: Oxford University Press.

Mackey, A. and Goo, J. (2007). Interaction research in SLA: A meta-analysis and research synthesis. In A. Mackey (ed.), pp. 407–72.

Mackey, A., Philp, J., Egi, T., Fujii, A. and Tatasumi, T. (2002). Individual differences in working memory, noticing of interactional feedback, and L2 development. In P. Robinson (ed.), *Individual Differences and Instructed Language Learning*, pp. 181–209. Amsterdam: John Benjamins.

Pica, T. (1994). Review article: Research on negotiation: What does it reveal about second-language learning conditions, processes and outcomes? *Language Learning*, *44*, 493–527.

Robinson, P. (2007). Task complexity, theory of mind, and intentional reasoning: Effects on L2 speech production, interaction, uptake, and perceptions of task difficulty. *International Review of Applied Linguistics*, *45*(3), 193–213.

Ross-Feldman, L. (2007). Interaction in the L2 classroom: Does gender influence learning opportunities? In A. Mackey (ed.), *Conversational Interaction in Second Language Acquisition*. Oxford: Oxford University Press.

Swain, M. (1985). Communicative competence: some roles of comprehensive input and comprehensible output in its development. In S.M. Gass and C. G Madden (eds), *Input in Second Language Acquisition*, pp. 235–53. Rowley, MA: Newbury House.

Trofimovich, P., Ammar, A. and Gatbonton, E. (2007). How effective are recasts? The role of attention, memory and analytical ability. In A. Mackey (ed.), *Conversational Interaction in Second Language Acquisition*. Oxford: Oxford University Press.

Interactional instinct

John Schumann
University of California, Los Angeles

The interactional instinct (Lee *et al.*, 2009) views the structure of language and the ubiquity of its acquisition by children as a consequence of interaction. Complex adaptive systems theory (Larsen-Freeman and Cameron, 2008) maintains that structure can emerge when large numbers of agents interact with a large number of objects. The grammatical structures of language are seen as the product of human agents having developed a lexicon and by their attempts to combine these words to make larger meanings. Those combinations that are efficiently producible, comprehensible, and learnable (Kirby, 1998) become a grammar of the language. On this view, grammatical structure is not determined by a priori linguistic knowledge in the brain but by the vetting of forms in conversational interaction such that the forms are molded to fit the brain (Chater and Christiansen, 2009).

Universality of language acquisition by children is accounted for by positing that human infants have an innate instinct to interact with, attach to, and to become like caregiver conspecifics. This instinct entrains the infant's attention to the faces, voices and body movements of caregivers. It drives them to respond exuberantly to proffers of interaction and to seek it out on their own initiative.

This interaction, whether between child and caregiver, or as overheard by the child from interaction among third parties, contains the language which the child will acquire. Additionally, the child's brain is equipped to perceive and remember patterns in the environment and thus the regularities (grammar) that the child hears are extracted and encoded in the brain (Ellis, 2002). Within this system, the interactional instinct provides attentional and motivational mechanisms that guarantee acquisition of language to which the child is exposed.

This perspective was developed as an alternative to the standard Universal Grammar (UG) view of language. The traditional UG approach maintains that grammar is genetically based and neurobiological instantiated. However, neuroscience has been unable to identify any mechanism in the brain that would subserve a UG. Additionally, it has not been possible to develop an evolutionary scenario that would provide an account for the genetic assimilation of UG. Therefore, Lee *et al.* offer the interactional instinct as a conservative alternative that explores language evolution and first and second acquisition without positing innate abstract information that specifies grammatical structure.

See also: Complexity Theory/Dynamic Systems Theory, emergentism, interaction and the interaction hypothesis, motivation, social and sociocultural approaches to SLA, Universal Grammar (UG) and SLA

References

Chater, N. and Christiansen, M.H. (2009). Language acquisition meets language evolution. *Cognitive Science*, 1–27.

Ellis, N.C. (2002). Frequency effects in language processing. *Studies in Second-language Acquisition*, *24*, 143–188.

Kirby, S. (1998). Fitness and the selective adaptation of language. In J.R. Hurford, M. Studdert-Kennedy, and C. Knight (eds), *Approaches to the Evolution of Language*, pp. 359–383. Cambridge: Cambridge University Press.

Larsen-Freeman, D. and Cameron, L. (2008). *Complex Systems and Applied Linguistics*. New York: Oxford University Press.

Lee, N., Mikesell, L., Joaquin, A.D.L., Mates, A. W. and Schumann, J.H. (2009). *The Interactional Instinct: The Evolution and Acquisition of Language*. New York: Oxford University Press.

Further reading

Christiansen, M.H. and Chater, N. (2008). Language as shaped by the brain. *Brain and Behavioral Sciences*, *31*, 489–558.

Enfield, N.J. and Christiansen, M.H. (2006). Humans sociology as a new interdisciplinary field. In N.J. Enfield and S.C. Levinson (eds), *Roots of Human Sociality: Culture, Cognition and Interaction*. Oxford: Berg.

Tomasello, M. (2008). *Origins of Human Communication*. Cambridge, MA: MIT Press.

Interdependence Hypothesis

Jim Cummins

Ontario Institute for Studies in Education, University of Toronto

The interdependence hypothesis (Cummins, 1978, 1981, 2000) proposed that literacy-related concepts and skills in first and second languages (L1/L2) are interdependent, or manifestations of a common underlying proficiency, such that academic knowledge and skills transfer across languages under appropriate conditions of development (e.g., educational support for both languages). It was argued that this transfer of concepts and literacy-related skills explains the well-documented outcomes of bilingual education programs, specifically the fact that instruction through a minority language exerts no adverse consequences on students' academic development in the majority language despite less instructional exposure to the majority language. This holds true for students from both minority and majority language backgrounds in various kinds of bilingual programs and across a wide range of sociolinguistic contexts (August and Shanahan, 2006).

The interdependence hypothesis (also termed the *developmental interdependence, linguistic interdependence,* and *common underlying proficiency* hypothesis) was formally stated as follows:

> To the extent that instruction in Lx is effective in promoting proficiency in Lx, transfer of this proficiency to Ly will occur provided there is adequate exposure to Ly (either in school or environment) and adequate motivation to learn Ly.
>
> (Cummins, 1981: 29)

In concrete terms, what this hypothesis means is that in, for example, a Basque-Spanish bilingual program in the Basque Country in Spain, Basque instruction that develops Basque reading and writing skills is not just developing Basque skills, it is also developing a deeper conceptual and linguistic proficiency that is strongly related to the development of literacy in the majority language (Spanish). In other words, although the surface aspects (e.g., pronunciation, fluency, etc.) of different languages are clearly separate, there is an underlying conceptual proficiency, or knowledge base, that is common across languages. This common underlying proficiency (or what Genesee, Lindholm-Leary, Saunders, and Christian [2006] call a cross-linguistic *reservoir of abilities*) makes possible the transfer of concepts, literacy skills, and learning strategies from one language to another. This is true even for languages that are dissimilar (e.g., American Sign Language and English, Spanish and Basque; Dutch and Turkish). The transfer of skills, strategies, and knowledge explains why spending instructional time through a minority language entails no adverse consequences for the development of the majority language.

There is extensive empirical research that supports the interdependence hypothesis (see reviews by Dressler and Kamil, 2006; Baker, 2001; Cummins, 2000; Genesee *et al.*, 2006). The most comprehensive review was conducted by Dressler and Kamil as part of the Report of the National Literacy Panel on Language-Minority Children and Youth (August and Shanahan, 2006). They conclude:

> In summary, all these studies provide evidence for the cross-language transfer of reading comprehension ability in bilinguals. This relationship holds (a) across typologically different languages ... ; (b) for children in elementary, middle, and
> high school; (c) for learners of English as a foreign language and English as a second language; (d) over time; (e) from both first to second language and second to first language;
> (ibid.: 222)

The empirical evidence suggests that five types of cross-linguistic transfer are possible:

- Transfer of conceptual elements (e.g., understanding the concept of *photosynthesis*);
- Transfer of metacognitive and metalinguistic strategies (e.g., vocabulary acquisition strategies, mnemonic devices, etc.);
- Transfer of pragmatic aspects of language use (willingness to take risks in communication through L2, ability to use paralinguistic features such as gestures to aid communication, etc.);
- Transfer of specific linguistic elements (knowledge of the meaning of *photo* in *photosynthesis*);
- Transfer of phonological awareness—the knowledge that words are composed of distinct sounds.

The documentation of cross-linguistic transfer of concepts and skills has established a psycholinguistic foundation for the implementation of various kinds of bilingual education programs. It has served to counter the superficially commonsense argument of those ideologically opposed to bilingual programs for minority group students that dilution of the instructional time between students' L1 and the dominant language (L2) would inevitably result in deficient L2 academic development. However, it is important to note certain issues that the interdependence hypothesis does not address. For example, the hypothesis says nothing about the initial language of reading instruction in bilingual programs—the research suggests that, in principle, reading instruction can be delivered initially in L1 or L2 or in both languages simultaneously (Cummins, 2000). Similarly, the hypothesis does not argue that minority students who lack a strong foundation in their L1 will be unable to develop strong L2 skills. It also does not predict that minority students in bilingual programs will necessarily perform better than similar students in monolingual programs. Rather the prediction is that transfer of underlying conceptual and linguistic knowledge and skills across languages will offset any impact of less instructional time through the medium of the majority language.

The pedagogical implications of the interdependence hypothesis are at variance with common assumptions in L2 teaching. Many policy-makers and educators have argued that "best practice" in second language teaching involves instructional use of the target language to the exclusion of students' L1, with the goal of reducing L1 interference. Howatt (1984), in his history of English language teaching, has termed this the "monolingual principle." Similarly, in many bilingual programs the languages remain intentionally isolated from each other in order to minimize interference. The interdependence hypothesis, by contrast, implies that educators should teach for transfer across languages. Numerous researchers (e.g., Jessner, 2006) have pointed out that students are making cross-linguistic connections throughout the course of their second language acquisition, so why not nurture this learning strategy and help students to apply it more efficiently? Language awareness and learning can be enhanced when teachers explicitly draw students' attention to similarities and differences between their languages (e.g., cognate relationships) and reinforce effective learning strategies in a coordinated way across languages.

In summary, the interdependence hypothesis is strongly supported by an extensive body of research. It provides a conceptual foundation for the implementation of bilingual education programs and also suggests that teaching for cross-linguistic transfer should be incorporated into all second language teaching.

See also: awareness, bilingualism and SLA, child second language acquisition, Cross Linguistic Influence (CLI), linguistic transfer, reading

References

August, D. and Shanahan, T. (eds) (2006). *Developing Literacy in Second-language Learners.* Mahwah, NJ: Erlbaum.

Baker, C. (2001). *Foundations of Bilingual Education and Bilingualism*, 3rd edn. Clevedon: Multilingual Matters.

Cummins, J. (1978). Educational implications of mother tongue maintenance for minority language groups. *Canadian Modern Language Review, 34*, 395–416.

——(1981). The role of primary language development in promoting educational success for language minority students. In California State Department of Education (ed.), *Schooling and Language Minority Students: A Theoretical Framework.* Los Angeles, CA: Evaluation, Dissemination and Assessment Center California State University.

——(2000). *Language, Power and Pedagogy: Bilingual Children in the Crossfire.* Clevedon: Multilingual Matters.

Dressler, C. and Kamil, M. (2006). First- and second-language literacy, In D. August and T. Shanahan (eds), *Developing Literacy in Second-language Learners. Report of the National Literacy Panel on Language-Minority Children and Youth.* Mahwah, NJ: Lawrence Erlbaum Associates Publishers.

Genesee, F., Lindholm-Leary, K., Saunders, W. M. and Christian, D. (eds) (2006). *Educating English Language Learners: A Synthesis of Research Evidence.* New York: Cambridge University Press.

Howatt, A. (1984). *A History of English Language Teaching.* Oxford: Oxford University Press.

Jessner, U. (2006). *Linguistic Awareness in Multilinguals: English as a Third Language.* Edinburgh: Edinburgh University Press.

Interlanguage

Larry Selinker
New York University and Research Production Associates

Interlanguages are non-native languages which are created and spoken wherever there is language contact. They are highly structured, contain "new forms"——forms that are neither in the native nor target language—and result from attempted production of a target language. Experience and research show that such interlanguages are *never* perfect in terms of the target language, that they deviate in structured ways from expected target language norms *no matter how much practice or input* is involved. Every research project has shown it to be a fact that there are regular and systematic deviations from interlanguage relevant to target language norms.

Historically, "interlanguage" derives from attempts to understand two primary processes: 1) Transfer from the native language ("language transfer") and 2) learners "getting stuck" in interlanguage patterns, often far from target language norms ("fossilization").

Though transfer was known in Biblical times (the "Shibboleth" story, Judges 12:4–6), the earliest modern reference in English is Whitney (1881), with discussions by many linguists until Harris in 1954 produced a full treatment, "transfer grammar." Weinreich (1953) interpreted transfer in a unique and important way, in terms of "interlingual identifications": speakers in attempting to learn to speak a second language "make the same what cannot be the same." This is cognitively profound. A Weinreich example: if a Russian regularly says [t^yaip] for English [t^haip], "type", he has made FOR HIM a palatalized /t/ *the same as* an aspirated /t/, even though to any observer, they are NOT the same. This fact puzzled Weinreich since it violates classical Saussurean principles of "valeur" and "system." There are many examples in the literature of such identifications as Weinreich's, some very bizarre. It is important to note that such processes occur on all levels of language. Lado (1957) produced a compatible insight spurring much research:

> ... individuals tend to transfer the forms and meanings and the distribution of forms and meanings of their native language and culture to the foreign language and culture."

That view, basically correct, has now been corrected to where transfer occurs NOT directly to any foreign language/culture but to the individuals' developing and more permanent interlanguage (by extension, to interdialect/interculture as described below). Following on from Harris, Weinreich and Lado one of the first detailed attempts to empirically present thousands of exemplars of word order language transfer appears in Selinker (1966) revised as Selinker (1969). Corder (1967), amongst many other seminal concepts, flushed out the fledging language transfer concept.

By contrast, the attempt to understand permanently "getting stuck" is more recent with scholars struggling for several decades to grasp it since it was named "fossilization" in the "Interlanguage" paper that codifies this and other interlanguage processes, developing a research agenda (Selinker, 1972; reframed as Selinker, 1992). Examples occur in Weinreich (1953) and Nemser (1971) but these scholars do not focus on the phenomenon of the cessation of interlanguage development, which occurs in spite of extensive exposure to target language input and massive opportunities for interactive production with such speakers. Without the concept of fossilization, I have long maintained (cf. Long, 2003) that there would be no second language acquisition, that there would only be "language acquisition" with only one underlying cognitive architecture, not potentially two latent psychological mechanisms, as discussed in Selinker (1972). It is Han and Odlin (2006) and Han and Cadierno (2010) who bring fossilization up to date, showing that fossilization is differential or selective by context.

Much of interlanguage research over the decades adds empirical validity to such issues, especially that of transfer (cf. many papers by Kellerman, Odlin, the entry on "cross-linguistic influence"), and attempts to understand the cognition underlying the creation of interlanguage in terms of these two processes as they may or may not intersect with universal grammar principles. There is a long debate in second language acquisition about the place of universal grammar, as to whether interlanguages are formed in terms of these principles, fully or partially, or not at all. Related to this universal issue, there is an interesting number much discussed in the literature, sometimes called "the magical 5 per cent" (passim). Is it indeed *never* the case that interlanguage equals the language of NSs? This was much discussed early on and is still not settled. One methodological suggestion presented in Selinker (1972) involves the estimate of the number of people whose interlanguage *might* equal that of native speakers (NSs) of the target language. Where this number comes from is a story, but one thing is clear and presented there: "the vast majority" of second-language learners do NOT have an interlanguage that equals that of NSs of the target language. The theoretical point is that, if such a subset as the 5% exists, they are on a different track than interlanguage learners and they may be safely ignored when establishing the constructs underlying the "psychologically-relevant" data which control the formation and structure of interlanguage. The setting up of counterfactual conditions has a long history in linguistics, the most notorious one being "the ideal native speaker" of Chomsky, this concept and its thinking being another strand in the initial proposing of the detail of interlanguage theory. There has been at least one attempt to tie language transfer and fossilization together as causative variables in terms of the "multiple effects" principle (cf. Selinker and Lakshmanan, 1992), but there is little empirical validation to date.

A most important characteristic of interlanguages—maybe their prime characteristic—is that they become independent of both native and target language. The empirical fact supporting this view is that speakers attempting to produce a second language produce NEW FORMS that are neither in native nor target language. The [tʸaip] example above is a phonetic example of such a new form. A syntactic example might be the situation of the Spaniard in London overheard at a kiosk asking:

"How much cóst banana?"
NS: *"Pardon?"*

When he is not understood the interlanguage Spanish-English speaker, appearing frustrated, rephrases and says: *"How much dóes cost banana?"*

This is a particularly interesting example as the Spanish speaker has taken two English grammatical rules—do-support and do-emphasis—that NSs use all the time but he uses them in different idiosyncratic ways than NSs would and has thus created a new construction in his interlanguage English, *"How much dóes cost banana?"* Such examples have appeared a thousandfold in the literature. Everyone finds in their production data new forms, not in the native nor in the target language.

Interlanguage is not a monolith. There are various types of interlanguage, though a complete typology is lacking. For example "learner languages" which usually occur in classrooms, often with rapid development, are the type most language teachers are concerned with. There are so-called "fossilized interlanguages" where the linguistic forms in the interlanguage continue for years with little or no change. All sorts of individual sets of variations exist in interlanguage and a needed research project is to produce an empirical typology. Note that various overlapping terms cover different members of the set. The best known are "transitional competence" (Corder, 1967) where development is emphasized versus "approximative system" (Nemser, 1971) where fossilization (unnamed) appears to be more dominant.

Importantly, unlike the productive output of native languages in a particular dialect area, one sees huge variation in the outputs of individual interlanguages. One hypothesis is that the variation is controlled by the learner first creating internally created contexts or "discourse domains" (Selinker and Douglas, 1985). One certainty is that interlanguages are observed as variable across many contexts and that accuracy may be stronger in one domain and weaker in another, and that this will vary by learner. One should not then be surprised that there is belief in the empirical concept of selective fossilization.

Another set of processes which clearly help to shape interlanguage are strategies used by learners to organize input and conduct interaction. Selinker (1972) points out the importance of *learning strategies* versus *communication strategies* as two of the five "central processes" of interlanguage creation, but cautioned that it would be difficult to tease out the distinction and their relative values, and so it has proved. Cohen and Macaro (2007) sum up research in the collapsed field of "learner strategies," but there is scope to tie these variables with interlanguage formation. This area of carefully tying together strategies and interlanguage is crying out for a serious research treatment.

In general, the reality of interlanguage presents a problem in terms of human cognition. Interlanguages are surprising since the capacity to learn where "practice makes perfect" is the expected norm but, for the vast majority of interlanguage learners, this is not the case. Paradoxes of second language learning are nothing new and are discussed in Lawler and Selinker (1971). Here, we note that *practice* is a) necessary to activate interlanguage, but b) no amount of practice ever, or very rarely (that 5 per cent?), makes the interlanguage perfect in terms of desired target language norms.

For a general theory of learning, it may be the case that human learning is different from generally believed, with people NOT "learning" target knowledge but creating/constructing *intersystemS* that are more or less congruent with or different from a desired target. Interlanguages thus become a type or subset of intersystems (Selinker, 2007) with *interdialects* becoming another type of intersystem, since, by extension, there are attested NEW FORMS in interdialect as in interlanguage. (cf. Trudgill, 1988 detail). Other members of the set of intersystems would be *intercultures* and presumably *interliteracies*, though I know of no research on this topic. Studying interlanguage may thus lead to a deeper understanding of human learning since one can argue that one rarely learns the target but, instead, creates or constructs the intersystem we know as interlanguage.

Other issues abound. Early on there were some attempts at studying age effects in the creation of interlanguage (Hakuta, 1975; Selinker *et al.*, 1977). In terms of new media, text analysis on interlanguage has a long history with publishers such as Longman producing large databases. We have explored two other new media areas: distance online interlanguage analysis (Browne *et al.*, 2002) and speech recognition by computer (Selinker and Mascia, 2002). But these efforts are exploratory.

Finally, in order to understand the mechanisms that create linguistic knowledge of interlanguage and drive its restructuring (when it occurs) are many attempts to understand interlanguage grammars/phonologies. But we see no serious attempt to deal with the semantic component of interlanguage. Bley-Vroman (1989) pointed out a series of "Fundamental Differences" between the acquisition and structure of interlanguage versus native language. One semantic example will have to suffice: in discussing some friends, an Italian speaker who "knows" English very well, says:

– "but now they are broken."

The NSs do not understand and it took a while before one said:

– "oh, you mean they are broke."

In terms of this interlanguage-particular idiosyncratic semantics, there is a divergent association where "broken" must be coded as semantically associated with "a person being broke," that is, having no money, in this meaning. This semantic coding involves interlanguage idiosyncratic association, the semantic linking of various forms of particular forms of the word "broke" (but not "break") differently in the native language and interlanguage. Huddleston and Pullum (2002) clearly describe the native English semantics of "break." Take the sentence, "Frank broke the vase"; it entails both "The vase broke" *and* "The vase is broken." But it does not entail other potentially reasonable things; for example, it does not entail "Frank knocked it over."

By extension to interlanguage, in NS English "they are broken" does not entail "Frank has no money" although for the Italian speaker of English referred to above it does have this idiosyncratic entailment. An autonomous "interlanguage-particular semantics" would cover *interlanguage intention* and would include what any serious semantics contains: entailment, truth conditions, ambiguity, and the like, but with items for interlanguage having a *systematic divergent repesentation* from that of the target linguistic system. I am sure readers can think of examples where the semantic knowledge of interlanguage speakers intersects with divergent syntactic knowledge and divergent pragmatic considerations where the speakers have created an interlanguage semantic representation of a word that just is not what NSs know.

See also: age effects in SLA, conceptual transfer, cross-linguistic influence, development in SLA, fossilization, Universal Grammar (UG) and SLA

References

Bley-Vroman, R. (1983). The comparative fallacy in interlanguage studies: the case of Systematicity. *Language Learning*, *33*, 1–17.

Browne, C., Kinahan, C. and Selinker, L. (2002). Distance online interlanguage analysis (DOILA): an aid to language learning. *Thought Currents in English Literature*, *77*.

Corder, S.P. (1967). The significance of learners' errors. *International Review of Applied Linguistics*, *5*, 161–70.

Hakuta, K. (1975). Prefabricated patterns and the emergence of structure in second language acquisition. *Language Learning*, *24*, 287–97.

Han, Z.-H. and Cadierno, T. (eds) (2010). *Linguistic Relativity in Second Language Acquisition: Thinking for Speaking*. Clevedon: Multilingual Matters.

Han, Z.-H. and Odlin, T. (eds) (2006). *Studies of Fossilization in Second Language Acquisition*. Clevedon: Multilingual Matters.

Harris, Z. (1954). Transfer grammar. *International Journal of American Linguistics*, *20*, 259–70.

Lawler, J. and Selinker, L. (1971). On paradoxes, rules, and research in second language learning. *Language Learning*, *21*, 27 43.

Nemser, W. (1971). *An Experimental Study of Phonological Interference in the English of Hungarians*. The Hague: Mouton.

Lado, R. (1957). *Linguistics across Cultures*. Ann Arbor: University of Michigan Press.

Selinker, L. (1966). *A Psycholinguistic Study of Language Transfer*. Unpublished Phd dissertation, Georgetown University.

——(1969). Language transfer. *General Linguistics*, *9*, 67–92.

——(1972). Interlanguage. *International Review of Applied Linguistics*, *10*, 209–31.

——(1992). *Rediscovering Interlanguage*. London: Longman.

Selinker, L. and Douglas, D. (1985). Wrestling with 'context' in interlanguage theory. *Applied Linguistics*, *6*, 190–204.

Selinker, L. and Mascia, R. (2002). Interlanguage speech recognition by computer: implications for SLA and computational machines. *Applied Language Studies*, *1*, 19–55.

Selinker, L., Swain, M. and Dumas, G. (1975). The interlanguage hypothesis extended to children. *Language Learning*, *25*, 139–52.

Weinreich, U. (1953). *Languages in Contact*. The Hague: Mouton.

Whitney, D. (1881). On mixing in language. *Transactions of the American Philological Association*, *12*, 1–16.

Further reading

Cohen, A.D. and Macaro, E. (eds), (2007). *Language Learner Strategies: Thirty Years of Research and Practice*. Oxford: Oxford University Press. (In great detail, the papers in this volume summarize where our knowledge stands in terms of the various types of strategies and their interactions with interlanguage.)

Long, M. (2003). Stabilization and fossilization in interlanguage development. In Doughty, C. and Long, M. (eds) *Handbook of Second Language Acquisition*. Oxford: Blackwell. (An extremely well-researched case for the effect of fossilization (or not) on interlanguages.)

Selinker, L. and Lakshmanan, U. (1992). Language transfer and fossilization: The 'Multiple Effects Principle'. In Gass, S. and Selinker, L. (eds). *Language Transfer in Language Learning*. (Revised edition). Amsterdam: Benjamins. (This paper attempts to tie these two concepts together theoretically and empirically, setting up language transfer as a priviledged effect out of many potential in creating interlanguage.)

Trudgill, P. (1988). *Dialects in Contact*. Cambridge: Blackwell. (This detailed study shows in great detail why interlanguage applies to interdialect in the case with Norwegian dialects.)

Inter-rater reliability

Anthony John Kunnan
California State University, Los Angeles

Reliability or consistency of human ratings is a fundamental concern when test performance in speaking and writing are scored. A human rater may be inconsistent with his/her ratings for the following reasons: type of test tasks, scoring criteria, number and order of performances to rate, amount of training, and fatigue. In addition, when more than one human rater judges test performances, ratings may not be consistent for many additional reasons: they may interpret the scoring criteria differently, pay attention to different features of the performances, have different expectations, and have different reading styles. Ratings in both the above contexts need to be analyzed for their reliability or consistency; in the former case, the concern is with *intra-rater reliability* (how consistent each rater is) and in the latter case, the concern is with *inter-rater reliability* (how similar the ratings of different raters are).

The Classical Test Theory (CTT) approach to estimating the consistency of ratings is to correlate sets of ratings by the same rater or by different raters. This correlation is often reported by itself; however, to be used as a reliability estimate, it should be adjusted using the Spearman–Brown prophecy formula. When there are more than two ratings, the Fisher *Z*-transformation should be applied to each correlation, the correlations then averaged together, and the result then re-transformed to a correlation coefficient. For categorical ratings, the Cohen's Kappa, a measure of inter-rater reliability, can estimate a percentage-of-agreement measure corrected for chance. The main limitation of this overall approach is that only one source of measurement error in ratings can be analyzed at a time.

The Generalizability theory (G-theory) approach overcomes the CTT limitation by providing a means for estimating simultaneously the magnitude of different sources of error. It can estimate person variation (test taker variation due to differences in test takers' ability), rater variation, and task variation and the interactions among these sources of error. A study of the variance components of the sources of error will identify whether a particular source of error exists or not. Similar to the G-theory approach, the Many-Facet Rasch measurement (MFRM) enables researchers to include many facets of measurement such as the difficulty of tasks, the severity of raters, and the interactions between these two facets. Estimates for these two facets are provided through the FACETS software program (Linacre and Wright, 1993).

While test developers and researchers may examine ratings with a view to increasing the reliability of their raters, other procedures that can also contribute to higher reliability include rater training, clear and easy-to-use scoring criteria and multiple tasks instead of a single task with two raters. A soon-to-be pressing concern for many test developers is rater agreements between human and automated ratings where automated language processing and automated speech scoring systems are being implemented.

See also: correlation, quantitative research, language testing and SLA, speaking, writing, measuring and researching SLA

References

Linacre, J. and B. Wright (1993). *FACETS: Many-facet Rasch analysis*. Chicago, IL: MESA Press.

Further reading

Bachman, L.F. (2005). *Statistical Analyses for Language Assessment*. Cambridge: Cambridge University Press.

Investment

Bonny Norton
University of British Columbia

The construct of "investment," first developed by Bonny Norton (Norton Peirce, 1995; Norton, 2000), is a construct that signals the complex relationship between language learner identity and language learning commitment. Inspired by the work of Pierre Bourdieu, Norton argues that if learners "invest" in the target language, they do so with the understanding that they will acquire a wider range of symbolic and material resources, which will in turn increase the value of their cultural capital and social power. The construct helps to explain why a motivated language learner may nevertheless engage in practices of resistance. For example, if target language speakers are racist, sexist, or homophobic, a motivated language learner may have little investment in the language practices of the classroom or community. Unlike more traditional notions of motivation, which often conceive of the language learner as having a unitary, fixed, and ahistorical "personality," the construct of investment conceives of the language learner as having a complex identity, changing across time and space, and reproduced in social interaction. Further, while motivation is a primarily psychological construct (Dornyei, 2001), investment is a sociological construct, and explores how relations of power impact human relationships.

The construct of investment provides for a different set of questions associated with a learner's commitment to learning the target language. In addition to asking, for example, "To what extent is the learner motivated to learn this language?" the teacher or researcher asks, "What is the learner's investment in the language practices of this classroom or community?" Despite being highly motivated, a learner could be excluded from the language practices of a classroom, and in time positioned as a "poor" or unmotivated language learner. Alternatively, the language practices of the classroom may not be consistent with the learner's expectations of good language teaching, and the language learner may not be invested in the language practices promoted by the teacher.

To illustrate, it is instructive to consider a classroom-based study conducted in a multilingual secondary school in Canada, where Duff (2002) found that the teacher's attempts to foster respect for cultural diversity in the classroom had mixed results. In essence, the English language learners in the class were afraid of being criticized or laughed at because of their limited command of

English. As Duff (p. 312) notes, "Silence protected them from humiliation." This silence, however, was perceived by the native English speakers as representing a lack of initiative or agency. It could be argued that while the language learners were highly motivated, they were not invested in the language practices of their classroom, with its unequal relations of power between language learners and native speakers. The investments of the language learners were co-constructed in their interactions with their native speaker peers, and their identities a site of struggle.

The construct of investment has sparked considerable interest in the field of applied linguistics and language education, and Cummins (2006) has argued that the construct has emerged as a "significant explanatory construct" (p. 59) in the second language learning literature.

See also: attitudes to the L2, emotion, identity theory, motivation, social and sociocultural approaches to SLA, theoretical constructs in SLA

References

Cummins, J. (2006). Identity texts: The imaginative construction of self through multiliteracies pedagogy. In O. Garcia, T. Skutnabb-Kangas, and M. Torres-Guzman (eds), *Imagining multilingual schools: Language in education and glocalization*, pp. 51–68. Clevedon: Multilingual Matters.

Dornyei, Z. (2001). *Motivational Strategies in the Language Classroom*. Cambridge: Cambridge University Press.

Duff, P. (2002). The discursive co-construction of knowledge, identity, and difference: An ethnography of communication in the high school mainstream. *Applied Linguistics*, *23*, 289–322.

Norton, B. (2000). *Identity and Language Learning: Gender, Ethnicity and Educational Change*. Harlow: Longman/Pearson Education

Norton Peirce, B. (1995). Social identity, investment, and language learning. *TESOL Quarterly*, *29*(1), 9–31.

Involvement Load Hypothesis (ILH)

Batia Laufer
University of Haifa

It is generally agreed that retention of new vocabulary information depends on the amount and the quality of attention that individuals pay to various aspects of words. However, it is difficult to provide unambiguous, operationable definitions of attention and related notions, be it encoding specificity, distinctiveness of encoding, degree of elaboration, cognitive effort, depth of processing. Involvement is a motivational-cognitive construct proposed by Laufer and Hulstijn (2001) as a first attempt to operationalize the concepts of "attention" and its related notions into concrete and measurable L2 vocabulary learning tasks. Laufer and Hulstijn (L and H) postulate that retention of words is conditional upon three factors in word practice: need, search and evaluation. Taken together, these three factors combine into what L and H call *involvement*.

The *need* component is the motivational, non-cognitive dimension of involvement based on a drive to comply with the task requirements, whereby the task requirements can be either externally imposed or self-imposed. Two degrees of prominence were suggested for need: *moderate* and *strong*. Need is moderate when it is imposed by an external agent. An example is the need to use a word in a sentence that the teacher asked for. Need is strong when it is intrinsically motivated, for instance, by the decision to look up a word in an L1-L2 dictionary when writing a composition. *Search and evaluation* are the two cognitive dimensions of involvement, contingent upon allocating attention to form-meaning relationships (Schmidt, 2001). *Search* is the attempt to find the meaning of an unknown L2 word or trying to find the L2 word form expressing a concept (e.g., trying to find the L2 translation of an L1 word) by consulting a dictionary or another authority (e.g., a teacher). Originally, no distinction was made between moderate or strong search. However, in later discussions of the construct, such a distinction was suggested, whereby a *moderate* search would be a search for meaning of a given word and a *strong* search – a search for word form to express familiar meaning.

Evaluation entails a comparison of a given word with other words, a specific meaning of a word with its other meanings, or comparing the word with other words in order to assess whether a word does or does not fit its context. For example, when a word looked up in a dictionary is a homonym (e.g., bank of a river, or bank as a financial institution), a decision has to be made about its meaning by comparing all its meanings against the specific context and choosing the one that fits best. The kind of evaluation that entails recognizing differences between words (as in a fill-in task with words provided), or differences between several senses of a word in a given context, is referred to as *moderate*. Evaluation that requires a decision as to how additional words will combine with the new word in an original (as opposed to given) sentence or text is referred to as *strong* evaluation.

A real-life communicative situation, or a teacher designed learning task can induce any one, two, or all three of the components of involvement for each word: need, search and evaluation. The combination of components with their degrees of prominence constitutes *involvement load*. Consider two tasks that vary in involvement load. In task one, the learner is asked to write original sentences with some new words and these words are translated or explained by the teacher. The task induces a moderate need (imposed by the teacher), no search (the words are glossed) and strong evaluation because the new words are evaluated against suitable collocations in learner-generated context. If we want to describe the task in terms of an *involvement index*, where absence of a factor is marked as 0, a moderate presence of a factor as 1, and a strong presence as 2, then the involvement index of the task is 3 (1+0+2). In task two, the student has to read a text and to answer comprehension questions. New words, which are relevant to the questions, are glossed. The task will induce a moderate need to look at the glosses (moderate because it is imposed by the task), but it will induce neither search nor evaluation. Its involvement index is 1. Hence, task one induces a greater involvement load than task two.

The Involvement Load Hypothesis (ILH) postulates that words which are processed with higher involvement load will be retained better than words which are processed with lower involvement load (when other word factors, such as phonological, morphological and semantic complexity of the word, learners' L2 proficiency and conceptual development are equal). Hence, teacher/researcher-designed tasks with a higher involvement load will be more effective for vocabulary learning than tasks with a lower involvement load.

All three factors can be manipulated separately and in different combinations by researchers or teachers to create tasks with varying involvement loads. Therefore, as a research paradigm, ILH offers multiple possibilities to explore the relationship between retention and various aspects of deep processing.

The construct of Involvement Load was developed in the context of incidental second language vocabulary learning. Laufer and Hulstijn perceive 'incidental' learning as learning from language input and from word-focused tasks, but without the learner's deliberate intention to commit words to memory. In other words, incidental learning is not necessarily devoid of attention though it is devoid of intention. The authors claim that when learning is intentional, it is impossible to know what strategies learners use when they commit words to memory. Therefore, it is impossible to determine the involvement load of intentional learning. There have now been several pieces of research investigating the hypothesis directly or indirectly and largely confirming its predictive value (Hulstijn and Laufer, 2001; Keating, 2008; Kim, 2008; Webb, 2005).

See also: attention, depth of processing, language and the lexicon in SLA, motivation, theoretical constructs in SLA, vocabulary learning and teaching

References

Hulstijn, J. and Laufer, B. (2001). Some empirical evidence for the involvement load hypothesis in vocabulary acquisition. *Language Learning*, *51*, 539–58.

Keating, G. (2008). Task effectiveness and word learning in a second language: The involvement load hypothesis on trial. *Language Teaching Research*, *12*, 365–86.

Kim, Y.J. (2008). The role of task-induced involvement and learner proficiency in L2 vocabulary acquisition. *Language Learning*, *58*, 285–325.

Laufer, B. and Hulstijn, J. (2001). Incidental vocabulary acquisition in a second language: the construct of task-induced involvement. *Applied Linguistics*, *22*, 1–26.

Schmidt, R. (2001). Attention, In P. Robinson (dd.) *Cognition and Second Language Instruction*, pp. 3–32. Cambridge; Cambridge University Press.

Webb, S. (2005). Receptive and productive vocabulary learning: The effects of reading and writing on word knowledge. *Studies in Second Language Acquisition*, *27*, 33–52.

L

L2 phonology

Wander Lowie
University of Groningen

The study of second language (L2) sound systems has developed as an independent research area with its own specialists and its own types of research focus within the study of second language development. L2 phonology research has especially been discussed in relation to the critical period hypothesis and the claim that it is virtually impossible for older starters of second language acquisition to attain a native-like accent, whereas younger starters generally do manage. The reason for this, it is often argued, is that older starters are more susceptible to influence of the sound system of their mother tongue (L1). The influence of the learner's mother tongue may play a role at all levels within the acquisition of the L2 sound system, ranging from the individual speech sound to the prosodic characteristics of language. L1 influence on L2 phonology has been found to be much more complex than can be predicted by a straightforward comparison of the languages involved, can often be indirect, and occurs in complex interaction with other factors shaping the L2 phonological system. The explanation of L2 phonological development must therefore be found in a complex interplay between a wide range of factors, including the quantity and quality of the input, universal developmental factors, and a number of interacting individual factors.

The acquisition of L2 speech sounds

The similarity of individual speech sounds between L1 and L2 has been an important focus of both theories and empirical investigations. Early approaches to L2 phonology mainly focused on the contrastive analysis of speech sounds in the learner's L1 and L2 (for instance Lado, 1957), which started from the assumption that the difficulty of speech sounds can be predicted by the differences between the target language and the learner's native language. Since then, it has been repeatedly demonstrated that the difficulties of L2 phonology cannot simply be predicted by the differences between the L1 and the L2 (for instance Flege, 1995). Current theories acknowledge that the production of individual L2 speech sounds is influenced by both universal factors and crosslinguistic factors.

Universal factors relate to general phonological principles which are often based in the phonetic specification of speech sounds. For instance, the production of dental fricatives like /ð/ and /θ/ is articulatorily complex, as it requires a very specific position of the tip of the tongue, in combination with the creation of air turbulence. This articulatory difficulty explains why these sounds only occur in a limited number of languages (as compared to sounds like /t/ and /d/) (for an overview, see Maddieson, 1984), why they are acquired relatively late in L1 acquisition (Ohala, 2008), and why their production is unstable by native speakers of languages that have this sound (Schneider, 2004). In the linguistic literature, this general difficulty is often referred to as "markedness"; sounds that are difficult to produce and that do not occur in all languages are referred to as "marked," while very common sounds are referred to as "unmarked." Universal principles have been referred to in accounting for the order in which speech sounds are acquired in L1 (Jakobson, 1941) and have been mentioned as one of the factors that determine the difficulty of the acquisition of speech sounds in L2. An early example of the combination between universal and crosslinguistic influences on L2 sound systems is Eckman's Markedness Differential Hypothesis (Eckman, 2008). In this hypothesis, Eckman argues that the influence of L1 sounds is strongest for marked sounds that do not occur in the native language. For instance, the hypothesis predicted that the acquisition final voiced sounds (which are marked) would be problematic for learners whose L1 does not have these sounds. A more recent combination of markedness and crosslinguistic influence ("transfer") has been proposed by Major (2001) in his Ontogony-Philogeny model. Major emphasizes the interaction between universal principles and transfer. He claims that at early stages of development transfer plays a predominant role, to be replaced by universal principles in later stages, but only for the marked phenomena of the L2 phonology which are not similar to L1.

The observation that differences between languages do not automatically denote areas of difficulty for L2 learners, was made in a number of studies carried out by James Flege and his colleagues (Flege, 1995). Flege's main point was that it is not necessarily the L2 sounds that are most different from the L1 that cause the biggest problems for L2 learners, but the sounds that are phonetically similar, though not identical. The same conclusion had been drawn by Best *et al.* (1988), based on their observation that naïve English adults were very well able to discriminate isiZulu click consonants, in spite of the fact that these sounds are not like any sound in their L1. The cause of, they argued, is in the perception of L2 speech sounds. The main premise of three of the most influential models of L2 speech learning, Best's Perceptual Assimilation Model (PAM) (Best, 1994; Best and Tyler, 2007), Flege's Speech Learning Model (SLM) (Flege, 1995) and Kuhl's Native Language Magnet model (Kuhl, 1992) is that L2 sounds that are phonetically or phonologically similar in L1 and L2 are likely to be perceived as "functionally equivalent" to existing to L1 sounds (Best and Tyler, 2007: 27). Consequently, the similar sounds tend to be problematic for learners in both perception and production.

Suprasegmentals

The development of L2 sound systems has been mostly studied at the level of individual sounds, but is also apparent at other levels of sound systems, like syllable structure and prosody.

While there is a universal preference for the production of open syllables with a syllable onset (CV), languages vary widely in the type of syllable structures allowed as well as in the internal structure of syllables (phonotactics). In some languages, like English, complex onsets clusters occur (as in "strip") as well as complex coda clusters (as in "lengths"). Other languages may show limitations to the type of consonant clusters that can occur (like Spanish), or may show a strong general preference for open (CV-) syllables without complex clusters (like Japanese). The consequences of these crosslinguistic differences can for instance be seen in English loan words in Japanese: "glass" translates to "garasu" (mind the irrelevance of /l/-/r/ in Japanese) and girl translates to "garu." In Spanish, clusters of /sp/ are irregular and are consequently split up into two syllables ("spy" will be pronounced as [əspaɪ]). Compared to segments, research focusing on L2 syllable structure is less strongly represented in recent research. Broselow and Park (1995) have looked into the type and nature of epenthesis (adding a vowel) by Korean learners of English, and found that vowel length plays an important role in this. Eckman (1991) has linked syllable structure to the prevailing theme of perception in L2 phonology. In his Structural Conformity Hypothesis, he claimed that the L1 consonant structure and the related phonotactic characteristics play a role in the perception of phonetic contrasts.

Similar cross-linguistic issues in L2 phonology can also be found at the level of rhythm and intonation. Speakers of languages that have a relatively regular pattern of word stress, like French, are often reported to have great difficulty in acquiring the rhythmic pattern of languages with more complicated and sometimes idiosyncratic word stress, like English. Since word stress strongly affects the speaker's intelligibility, these problems may at least be equally relevant to pay attention to in pronunciation pedagogy (Jenkins, 2000). In the 1990s John Archibald has given prosodic issues some of the attention it deserves (Archibald, 1993, 1997). In recent research, especially the acquisition of tones in Asian languages for learners that do not have tones in their L1 has been given some attention. For instance, Guion and Pederson (2007) have related the acquisition of Mandarin tone to the age issue and to the perception of L2 phonology. They conclude that late learners of Mandarin Chinese are still able to perceive tonal cues when attending to new perceptual dimensions, which corroborates the findings found for segments.

Age-related issues and L2 phonology

Many of the studies discussed above have explicitly or implicitly related crosslinguistic influence on the acquisition of L2 speech to the age issue. Age-related crosslinguistic influence has been accounted for by linking it to perception and the creation of L2 phonetic categories. While neonates are still able to perceive speech sounds in a continuous mode, this becomes increasingly difficult when (L1) phoneme boundaries become established (Flege, 1991; Wode, 1994). The precise moment at which perception become less flexible due to categorization is difficult to determine, as this may be highly individual and dependent on the learning context. Some researchers have shown that vowel categories have become established at around 6 months (Kuhl, 1986), while others have argued that establishment of phonemic categories is not complete until young adulthood (Flege, 1995). In a series of empirical studies, Flege and his colleagues have shown that crosslinguistic influence correlates with the amount of experience in L1 (see, for instance, Flege and Liu, 2001). With increased L1 experience, the L1 phonetic categories become increasingly entrenched, which inhibits the formation of new L2 categories. Consequently, the lower the age of onset of L2 acquisition, the less strong crosslinguistic influence is expected to be. Flege's work did not produce empirical evidence for a critical period, after which no native-like accent can be attained, but implies a continuum. This continuum can account for the observation that most (but not all) young starters develop native-like phonological control but can also account for research findings that show that many older learners can also still become very proficient in pronunciation (cf. Bongaerts, 1999).

Pronunciation pedagogy

Although the study of L2 sound systems has mainly focused on research trying to understand L2 sound development and the factors that affect it, there are pedagogical implications that follow from these studies. First, as research has emphasized the importance of perception, it would be advisable to include perception training, not only for segments, but also for rhythm and intonation (see, for instance, Chun *et al.*, 2008). Second, many authors have stressed that the goals of pronunciation training should primarily be to improve intelligibility (Jenkins, 2000; Munro and Derwing, 1999) rather than attempting to sound "native-like." To achieve intelligibility, Jenkins (2002) has proposed a common core of international English. In spite of the criticism this proposal has met, its focus on intelligibility and the inclusion of suprasegmentals has now been widely accepted. Third, it seems advisable for learners to be exposed to many different speakers and for pronunciation learning to take place in meaningful context (Derwing, 2008). And fourth, in the light of all the evidence for the advantage of early learners discussed above, it would be advisable to start young.

There is one pronunciation issue that deserves additional attention. Several authors have claimed that each language has its own set of characteristics settings of the articulators, called the "articulatory setting" (for instance Collins and Mees, 1995). Many attempts were made to find evidence for the settings, but until recently, references were mainly found in the pedagogical domain, in which learners are instructed about the setting of a particular language (for instance Van Buuren, 1990). The idea behind this being that once the setting is optimal, the quality of pronunciation of the individual sounds will improve dramatically. New techniques of ultrasound imaging (Gick *et al.*, 2008) have now made it possible to visualize the settings and to demonstrate their existence. Besides rhythm and intonation, this seems to be another important global characteristic of pronunciation from which learners may benefit.

See also: age effects in SLA, Critical Period Hypothesis (CPH), intelligibility in SLA, markedness, marked differential hypothesis, speech perception

References

Archibald, J. (1993). The learnability of English metrical parameters by adult Spanish speakers. *Iral-International Review of Applied Linguistics in Language Teaching*, *31*(2), 129–42.

——(1997). The acquisition of English stress by speakers of nonaccentual languages: Lexical storage versus computation of stress. *Linguistics*, *35*(1), 167–81.

Best, C.T. (1994). The emergence of native-language phonological influences in infants: A perceptual assimilation model. In C. Goodman, and H.C. Nusbaum (eds), *The Development of Speech Perception: The Transition from Speech Sounds to Spoken Qords*, pp. 171–204. Cambridge, MA: MIT Press.

Best, C.T., McRoberts, G.W. and Sithole, N.M. (1988). Examination of perceptual reorganization for nonnative speech contrasts: Zulu click discrimination by English-speaking adults and infants. *Journal of Experimental Psychology. Human Perception and Performance*, *14*(3), 345–60.

Best, C.T. and Tyler, M.D. (2007). Nonnative and second language speech perception. In O.S. Bohn, and M.J. Munro (eds), *Language Experience in Second Language Speech Learning*, pp. 13–34. Amsterdam and Philadelphia, PA: Benjamins.

Bohn, O., Munro, M.J. and Flege, J.E. (2007). *Language Experience in Second Language Speech Learning: In Honor of James Emil Flege*. Amsterdam and Philadelphia, PA: Benjamins.

Bongaerts, T. (1999). Ultimate attainment in L2 pronunciation: The case of very advanced late L2 learners. In D. Birdsong (ed.), *Second Language Acquisition and the Critical Period Hypothesis*, pp. 133–59. Mahwah, NJ and London: Erlbaum.

Broselow, E. and Park, H. (1995). Mora conservation in second language prosody. In J. Archibald (ed.), *Phonological Acquisition and Phonological Theory*, pp. 81–109. Hillsdale, NJ: Erlbaum.

Chun, D.M., Hardison, D.M. and Pennington, M.C. (2008). Technologies for prosody in context. In J.G. Hansen Edwards, and M.L. Zampini (eds), *Phonology and Second Language Acquisition*, pp. 323–46. Amsterdam and Philadelphia, PA: Benjamins.

Collins, B. and Mees, I. (1995). Approaches to articulatory setting in foreign-language teaching. In J.W. Lewis (ed.), *Studies in General and English Phonetics: Essays in Honour of Professor J.D. O'Connor*, pp. 415–24. London: Routledge.

Derwing, T.M. (2008). Curriculum issues in teaching pronunciation to second language learning. In J.G. Hansen Edwards, and M.L. Zampini (eds), *Phonology and second language acquisition*, pp. 347–69. Amsterdam and Philadelphia, PA: Benjamins.

Eckman, F.R. (1991). The structural conformity hypothesis and the acquisition of consonant clusters in the interlanguage of ESL learners. *Studies in Second Language Acquisition*, *13*, 23–41.

——(2008). Typological markedness and second language phonology. In J.G. Hansen Edwards, and M.L. Zampini (eds), *Phonology and Second Language Acquisition*, pp. 95–116. Amsterdam and Philadelphia, PA: Benjamins.

Flege, J. and Liu, S. (2001). The effect of experience on adults' acquisition of a second language. *Studies in Second Language Acquisition*, *23*(4), 527–52.

Flege, J.E. (1991). Age of learning affects the authenticity of voice-onset time (VOT) in stop consonants produced in a 2nd language. *Journal of the Acoustical Society of America*, *89*(1), 395–411.

——(1995). Second language speech learning. theory, findings and problems. In W. Strange (ed.), *Speech Perception and Linguistic Experience*, pp. 233–77. Timonium, MD: York Press.

Gick, B., Bernhardt, B.M., Bacsfalvi, P. and Wilson, I. (2008). Ultrasound imaging applications in second language acquisition. In J.G. Hansen Edwards, and M.L. Zampini (eds), *Phonology and Second Language Acquisition*, pp. 309–22. Amsterdam and Philadelphia, PA: Benjamins.

Guion, S.G. and Pederson, E. (2007). Investigating the role of attention in phonetic learning. In O. S. Bohn, and M.J. Munro (eds), *Language Experience in Second Language Speech Learning*, pp. 58–77. Amsterdam and Philadelphia, PA: Benjamins.

Hansen Edwards, J. G., and Zampini, M.L. (2008). *Phonology and Second Language Acquisition*. Amsterdam and Philadelphia, PA: Benjamins.

Ioup, G. and Weinberger, S.H. (1987). *Interlanguage Phonology: The Acquisition of a Second Language Sound System*. Cambridge, MA and London: Newbury House.

Jakobson, R. (1941). *Kindersprache, aphasie und allgemeine lautgesetze*. Uppsala: Almqvist and Wiksell.

Jenkins, J. (2000). *The Phonology of English as an International Language*. Oxford: Oxford University Press.

——(2002). A sociolinguistically based, empirically researched pronunciation syllabus for English as an international language. *Applied Linguistics*, *23*(1), 83–103.

Kuhl, P.K. (1986). Reflections on infants' perception and representation of speech. In J.S. Perkell, and D.H. Klatt (eds), *Invariance and Variability of Speech Processes*, pp. 19–30. Hillsdale, NJ: Erlbaum.

——(1992). Psychoacoustics and speech perception: Internal standards, perceptual anchors, and prototypes. In L. Werner, and E. Rubel (eds), *Developmental psychoacoustics*, pp. 293–332. Washington, DC: American Psychological Association.

Lado, R. (1957). *Linguistics across Cultures: Applied Linguistics for Language Teachers*. Ann Arbor: University of Michigan.

Maddieson, I. (1984). In Disner S.F. (ed.), *Patterns of Sounds*. Cambridge: Cambridge University Press.

Major, R.C. (2001). *Foreign Accent: The Ontogeny and Phylogeny of Second Language Phonology*. Mahwah, NJ: Erlbaum.

Munro, M.J. and Derwing, T.M. (1999). Foreign accent, comprehensibility, and intelligibility in the speech of second language learners. *Language Learning*, *49*, 285–310.

Ohala, D.K. (2008). Phonological acquisition in a first language. In J.G. Hansen Edwards, and M. L. Zampini (eds), *Phonology and Second Language Acquisition*, pp. 19–39. Amsterdam and Philadelphia, PA: Benjamins.

Schneider, E.W. (2004). In Schneider E.W., Kortmann B. (eds), *A Handbook of Varieties of English: A Multimedia Reference Tool*. Volume 1 – Phonology. Berlin and New York: Mouton de Gruyter.

Van Buuren, L. (1990). *The Indispensible Foundation of Linguistic Study*. Amsterdam: University of Amsterdam.

Weinberger, S. (1987). The influence of linguistic context on syllable simplification. In S. Weinberger, and G. Ioup (eds), *Interlanguage Phonology: The Acquisition of a Second Language Sound System*, pp. 401–17. Rowley, MA: Newbury House.

Wode, H. (1994). Nature, nurture, and age in second language acquisition: The case of speech perception. *SSLA*, *16*, 325–45.

Language (task) switching

Renata Meuter
Queensland University of Technology

The ease with which bilinguals (and multilinguals) switch languages belies the cost (i.e., the time taken) associated with making a language switch. The increased response times (RTs) seen when processing and producing bilingually mixed information were first attributed to the greater difficulty in speaking a weaker second language (L_2) (Macnamara, 1967). This intuitively appealing account was based on overall RT comparisons, without regard for switch direction (from the weaker L_2 to the stronger first language (L_1) and vice versa). However, closer examination of language switch costs indicated that the language switch direction is critically important. Detailed analysis of language switch performance by Meuter and Allport (1999) revealed that, while responses in the dominant L_1 are faster for consecutive (repeat) L_1 responses than repeat L_2 responses, the time required to switch back to L_1 is, paradoxically, greater. The asymmetry is reduced for fluent (balanced) bilinguals for who switches in either direction carry similar costs, and decreases also with increased practice (reducing relative proficiency differences). The language switch cost is obtained by subtracting the mean RT for repeat responses (e.g., $L_A \rightarrow L_A$) from the mean RT for switches to that same language (e.g., $L_B \rightarrow L_A$). The repeat and switch RTs used in the calculation are from the same experimental condition (i. e., the bilingual condition). Comparisons across monolingual and bilingual conditions reveal increased RTs on repeat trials in bilingual settings, reflecting the increased task demand associated with switching languages.

The commonly accepted account of language switch costs holds that to speak a given language, L_A, a language set is formed that incorporates the inhibition of responses in the other language, L_B (and activation of L_A). To speak L_B immediately following an L_A response, the inhibition of L_B must be lifted. Doing so requires time. The greater the proficiency in a language (relative to other known language(s)), the greater the inhibition required to prevent its selection and the greater the cost associated with a subsequent switch to that language in response. Other explanations for directional differences in language switch costs include relative activation of selected versus deselected languages (e.g., Poulisse and Bongaerts, 1994) and task nodes controlling language selection (e.g., Green, 1998; see also De Bot, 1992).

Language switching can be viewed as a form of task switching and, experimentally, both paradigms and theoretical accounts are strongly linked to that domain. Consistent with the control processes evident in the behavioral data, hemodynamic studies reveal frontal lobe involvement in language switching (e.g., Hernandez *et al.*, 2000), and the inability of some bilingual aphasic patients to switch languages at will similarly implicate the frontal lobes in the control of language selection. (For reviews, see Meuter, 2009; Van Hell and Witteman, 2009.) The patient data provides compelling evidence that switching between languages also requires speakers to maintain a selected language as the response language and to monitor their performance. Language switch costs reflect a dynamic system in which linguistic context, and relative experience with and proficiency in the languages used, determine the ease with which bilinguals switch between languages.

See also: attention, bilingualism and SLA, executive control and frontal cortex, inhibitory control, psycholinguistics of SLA, reaction time

References

Green, D.W. (1998). Mental control of the bilingual lexico-semantic system. *Bilingualism: Language and Cognition*, *1*, 67–81.

Hernandez, A., Dapretto, M. and Bookheimer, S. (2000). Language switching and language representation in Spanish-English bilinguals: An fMRI study. *NeuroImage*, *11* (5, Supplement 1), S340–S340.

Macnamara, J. (1967). The linguistic independence of bilinguals. *Journal of Verbal Learning and Verbal Behavior*, *6*, 729–36.

Meuter, R.F. I. and Allport, A. (1999). Bilingual language switching in naming: Asymmetrical costs in language selection. *Journal of Memory and Language*, *40*, 25–40.

Poulisse, N. and Bongaerts, T. (1994). First language use in second language production. *Applied Linguistics*, *15*, 36–57.

Further reading

De Bot, K. (1992). A bilingual production model: Levelt's speaking model adapted. *Applied*

Linguistics, *13*, 1–24. (A model of bilingual language selection.)

La Heij, W. (2005). Selection processes in monolingual and bilingual lexical access. In J. Kroll and A.M. B. De Groot (eds), *Handbook of Bilingualism: Psycholinguistic Approaches*. Oxford: Oxford University Press. (A discussion of language selection processes.)

Meuter, R.F. I. (2005). Language selection in bilinguals: Mechanisms and processes. In J.F. Kroll and A.M. B. de Groot (eds), *Handbook of Bilingualism: Psycholinguistics Approaches*. Oxford: Oxford University Press. (A review of the cognitive processes underlying language switching.)

——(2009). Neurolinguistic contributions to understanding the bilingual mental lexicon. In A. Pavlenko (ed.), *The Bilingual Mental Lexicon: Interdisciplinary Approaches*. Bristol: Multilingual Matters. (Includes discussion of the neurolinguistic aspects of language switching.)

Van Hell, J. G. and Witteman, M.J. (2009). The neurocognition of switching between languages: A review of electrophysiological studies. In L. Isurin, D. Winford, and K. de Bot (eds), *Multidisciplinary Approaches to Code-Switching*. Amsterdam: John Benjamins. (A review of the electrophysiological studies of language switching.)

Language and the lexicon in SLA

Marjolijn Verspoor and Norbert Schmitt
University of Groningen and University of Nottingham

When investigating language and the lexicon in second language acquisition (SLA), it is important to know how they are viewed from a theoretical perspective because it establishes what to look at, how to investigate phenomena, how to interpret the results, and what conclusions to draw. There is no single theory that deals with all aspects of what language is, how it is used, organized, processed, or acquired, how it changes, and how it is learned as a second language. However, recently a group of compatible theories has emerged that together could fall under the umbrella of "usage-based" theories, which agree either implicitly or explicitly that language should be seen as a complex dynamic system and that language learning is a dynamic process, in that language emerges through use and changes continually because of interactions at all levels. What follows is a brief description of dynamic, usage-based theory and the implications of such an approach for SLA, with an emphasis on the lexicon.

Language and the lexicon as a complex, dynamic usage-based system

Robinson and Ellis (2008) give an excellent overview of the different approaches involved in usage-based theories. In this chapter, we will draw on Langacker's work (2000), because it describes in detail how language may emerge through use. Langacker assumes that the process involved in language development at the group level is similar to language development at the individual level and we will focus on the latter.

Langacker argues that common cognitive abilities are involved in language learning: the ability to associate things with each other, to compare them, to categorize them, and to abstract away from them. *Association* is the well-known phenomenon in which one kind of experience is able to evoke another. In language use, the ability to associate enables symbolization: the ability to associate sounds, gestures or written marks with observable entities and later on the mental representations of these entities. A symbolic unit is thus a simple association a language user makes between a form (the sound, gesture or written mark) and a meaning (that which it is associated with). For example, the symbolic unit "dog" stands for an animal, first perhaps for only one very specific animal or picture, and there is a direct association between the symbol and the entity. Later, after many exposures to different instances of dog, the learner surmises that the word "dog" can stand for a group of rather similar-looking or -sounding animals. To be able to do so, the learner has shown that she is able to categorize and abstract away from individual instances.

Categorization and *abstraction* are involved at many different linguistic levels. For example, even though each language user may pronounce things somewhat differently, most users will recognize the string of sounds /d 0g/ as being similar enough to categorize it as a particular English word referring to an animal. Later, a string of letters such as [d-o-g-s] will be recognized as referring to more than one dog and after exposure to other words that have an –*s* ending, learners will recognize that an –*s* must refer to "more than one" in general. Such abstraction leads to schematization of a *construction,* which can be defined as a form-meaning pair (see **Construction learning**, and **Form-meaning connections**, this volume).

When humans abstract, attention is not on minute points of difference in multiple experiences, but on their general points of commonality. For example, structures like a plural *-s* may be pronounced numerous different ways when examined in fine-grained detail, but they may sound quite alike in a coarse-grained view in that they are all sibilants. A plural *-s* is thus a *schematization*, or "schema" for short, of a group of similar constructions. A schema is the perceived commonality that has emerged from exposure to distinct constructions.

Symbolic units can be combined into more complex ones by means of a process called *composition*. Composition involves the conceptual integration of two or more component units or constructions (e.g. *dog* and *house*) to produce novel constructions (e.g. *doghouse*). As this example clearly shows, a composition is not simply the sum of the two original units (*dog* + *house*) because both are modified somewhat in the process of combining them. The word *house* does not refer to a typical house and the word *dog* does not refer to an animal but to a possible inhabitant of the non-typical house. The process of composition can occur in various combinations and can be recursive in that one construction becomes integrated into another construction, yielding constituency hierarchies in indefinitely many levels of organization (see **Analogical mapping in construction learning**, this volume).

In this approach, the lexicon of a language is defined as the set of expressions with the status of conventional units (Langacker, 2000). A conventional unit is one that is heard and used frequently and therefore entrenched, which is the result of habit formation, routinization, or automatization. Basically it means that each language event such as hearing or producing a word like *dog* leaves some kind of trace in memory that helps in reactivating it. Eventually it has been heard or used so often that it not likely to change anymore. For example, for fluent language users, most words in a language have conventionalized forms (the way they are pronounced or written), have conventionalized meanings, and are used in conventionalized constructions. Moreover, this works not only with simple words and simple constructions; highly complex events can also become entrenched through enough repetition and practice. For example, long sequences (such as formulaic sequences, idiomatic expressions, or even whole poems) can become automated and become a "pre-packaged" groups of words that no longer require conscious attention to their parts or their order (see **Formulaic language**, and **Idiomaticity**, this volume).

The suggestion that learning the lexicon is all about frequency of input and automaticity is in line with *Activation Theory* (Rumelhart and McClelland, 1987). The more frequently one hears something, the more easily it is activated, the more frequently it is used and the faster it is learned (see **Automaticity**, and **Frequency effects**, this volume). Within activation theory, most work has been done at the lexical level, but MacWhinney also developed a computational model with self-organizing maps (SOMs) at different linguistic levels (morphology, syllable structure, lexicon, syntax and so on). In line with usage-based theories, MacWhinney's unified model (UM) (2008) takes input as the source for learning. It learns by comparing the input, searching for similarities and differences. However, MacWhinney's model emphasizes that in addition to pure frequency, the role of cue availability, validity and reliability play a role in pattern recognition (see **Competition Model**, this volume). Moreover, he argues that salience, which is the degree to which something is noticed, helps determine the course of acquisition.

Language can be regarded as a complex system (cf. de Bot *et al.* (2007), because it involves various components or subsystems that interact with each other over time, and language is a dynamic system because the starting point of each new step is not the first step ever taken but the previous step (see **Complexity Theory/Dynamic Systems Theory**, this volume). This dynamicity can be illustrated as follows: the first step in language acquisition is to make a form-meaning link for a symbolic unit such as DOG as illustrated in Figure 5. Note that the circle is very light, as it represents the initial stage of development of the form-meaning link.

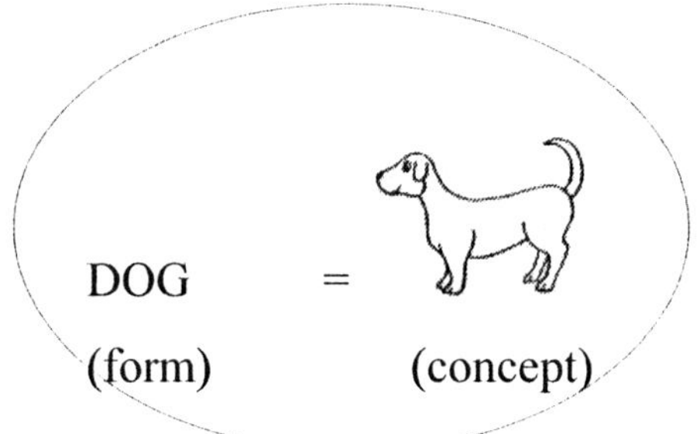

Figure 5 A symbolic unit: a form-meaning link

After multiple exposures of the unit, the form-meaning link will be strengthened, as illustrated in Figure 6. Note that the lines become thicker after each exposure, suggesting that each previous exposure contributes to strengthening the form-meaning link.

Figure 6 Strengthening of form-meaning link over time after multiple exposures

Even at the early stages of learning the word, the learner will probably be aware of some uses of the word, both linguistically and non-linguistically, but because uses of words vary, these connections are probably rather weak, as illustrated in Figure 7. However, just as the form-meaning link, these may strengthen over time. The different uses of the unit can apply to all kinds of interrelated areas such as the types of constructions it may occur in and the types of social situations in which it may be used;

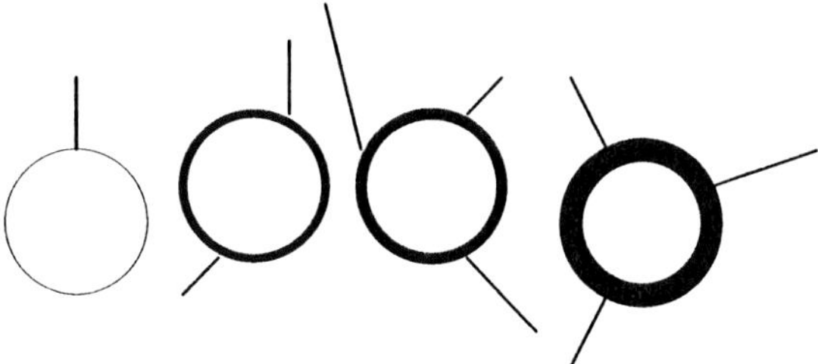

Figure 7 Strengthening of form-meaning link over time after multiple exposures, with weak associations concerning contextualized usage beginning to form

for example, the English unit DOG is a rather basic name (rather than CANINE) for a countable thing and in English such names have to be marked for one or more (*dog* versus *dogs*) and for being definite or non-definite (*the* versus *a dog*). There are certain words such as *barks* or *growls* it occurs with and certain conventionalized expressions such as *it is raining cats and dogs* it may occur in.

We may assume that the different uses of words, which may be called "contextualized aspects of word knowledge," must take massive amounts of exposure to become fully established and are probably never completely mastered by most L2 learners (see **Word knowledge**, this volume). It is not surprising then that they decay more readily than the relatively simple form-meaning link.

We have talked about multiple exposures as if they are all the same, but with each exposure our knowledge of the unit has changed and therefore will affect the new knowledge we absorb at the next exposure. Moreover, as McWhinney (2008) points outs, it is not just pure frequency of exposure but also reliability and salience that helps acquisition. Reliability has to do with the regularity of use and the ease with which the learner can discern a pattern. For example, a dog does not make that many sounds and it may not be difficult for an L2 learner to discover that the most common sound is *bark.* On the other hand, salience is related to how much something is noticed, which brings us to implicit and explicit learning (see **Explicit learning**, **Implicit learning**, and **Noticing Hypothesis**, this volume). It would make perfectly good sense that through skilful instruction, we can focus our learners' attention on certain aspects of word knowledge, thereby strengthening the connections for the form-meaning link, for different meanings, or for different uses of the same word.

To summarize, a dynamic, usage-based view of language defines language as an assembly of meaningful, symbolic units, which can be words, formulaic sequences, idioms, or longer syntactic constructions. They are learned through exposure in a bottom-up process – with the help of some basic cognitive abilities such as association, categorization, and schematization. The more frequently a unit is heard or used and the more meaningful clues the learner has, the more chance initial form-meaning links are made and the more chance the form will be used in conventionalized contexts.

In the next section we show how the dynamic, usage-based view presented above relates to what we know about L2 vocabulary acquisition.

The lexicon and second language acquisition

A usage-based view of language acquisition can pertain to both a first and second language, but it does not tell us how the L1 and the L2 are related. Are they two completely separate systems where words and constructions in the L1 have only associative links with each other, or is it one big system in which all symbolic units in both the L1 and L2 interact and are associated with each other? The best evidence for a single, interconnected network with L1 influence on L2 and vice versa comes from psycholinguistic studies, which demonstrate that the L1 is active during L2 lexical processing in both beginning and more-advanced learners (e.g. Sunderman and Kroll, 2006) (see **Lexical access and selection in bilingual production**, and **Revised Hierarchical Model (RHM)**, this volume). Seeing the L1 and L2 as one overall interconnected conceptual system has implications for L2 acquisition at all levels: associations of different strength can be at the level of form, meaning, and use.

At the form level, there is clearly an L1 influence on the L2. For example, it is difficult to learn L2 sounds that are different from the L1 because the L1 processing of sounds may be entrenched. Through infancy and childhood, the mind becomes attuned to the features and regularities in the L1 input (Ellis, 2006). This *developmental sharpening* applies not only to individual sounds but also their possible combinations (composite structures) such as words, spoken or written, and longer utterances such as phrases or sentences. This L1 specialization makes L1 processing efficient, but can cause problems when there is an attempt to process an L2 in the same way. For example, English speakers use mainly stress to parse words in the speech stream, while French speakers rely more on syllable cues. Cutler and her colleagues have found that both French and English speakers used their L1 cue processing strategies when learning the other language as an L2, causing problems for both groups (e.g. Cutler and Norris, 1988). The same type of mismatch has been found in the processing of written language, for example, between Chinese and English (e.g. Koda, 1997). What this means is that learners not only have to learn new oral and written forms in the L2, but they may also have to develop a completely new way of processing those forms, one which is different from the automatic, entrenched processes in their L1 (see **Entrenchment**, and **Writing**, this volume). The reverse is also true. For example, de Groot (2006) found that L2 words that match L1 orthographical and phonological patterns are easier to learn and are less susceptible to forgetting than L2 words that are atypical.

In addition, because they may be difficult to distinguish, lexical items with similar forms may be difficult to acquire in the L2. For example, Laufer (1988) studied words with similar forms and found that some similarities were particularly confusing for students, especially words that were similar except for suffixes (*comprehensive/comprehensible*) and for vowels (*adopt/adapt*). Another source of difficulty lies in words that have a similar form to a number of others in the L2 (i.e. large *orthographic neighborhoods* (Grainger and Dijkstra, 1992)). For example, the word *poll* may not be difficult in itself, but the fact that there are many other similar forms in English can lead to confusion (*pool, polo, pollen, pole, pall, pill*). Similarly, Bensoussan and Laufer (1984) found that a misanalysis of word forms, which looked transparent but were not, sometimes led to misinterpretation. Their learners interpreted *outline* (which looks like a transparent compound) as "out of line," and *discourse* (which looks as if it has a prefix) as "without direction."

Obviously, depending on different factors such as the learner's L1, age of acquisition and proficiency level, some L2 forms may be difficult to learn and the question is whether only frequent exposure to them is enough to acquire them correctly, as Ellis (1997) argues. There is evidence that attention to form is useful, especially because it can help other aspects of vocabulary learning. For example, Bogaards (2001) found that knowing the form of lexical items aided subsequent vocabulary learning for those items, such as learning additional polysemous meaning senses. So it may well be useful to address form in vocabulary exercises, but if we do, we need to remember that the mind has a finite processing capacity, and any attention given to form will diminish the resources available for attention to meaning, and vice-versa (Barcroft, 2002) (see **Vocabulary learning and teaching**, this volume). Therefore it seems reasonable to focus attention on one or the other of these aspects at any one time.

A form needs to be linked to meaning, which is a very complex, dynamic entity in itself. As early as 1979, Rumelhart suggested that words have no meaning of their own but provide but cues to meaning. In line with this view, Langacker states that symbolic units are labels for concepts, which in turn is nothing but a network of associations, which may be activated depending on context. The associations Langacker refers to can be perceptual, personal, pragmatic, cultural, or linguistics. For example, the word *dog* may be associated with how it looks, smells, and behaves; whether it is appropriate to call a person "a dog" or not, whether a dog is seen as a house pet or a wild animal, and which words usually precede or follow the word *dog*. In other words, all knowledge—experiential and linguistic—is part of the network and may change over time.

When a learner tries to establish a new form-meaning link in the L2, it is likely that initially—just as with sounds—entrenched L1 associations of all kinds are mapped straight onto the L2 words. However, even though there may be a great deal of overlap between L1 and L2 concepts, there may also be differences. For example, a "dog" in one culture may be associated with friendship and loyalty, in another culture with aggression and fiendishness, and yet another culture with work and usefulness (see **Lexical concepts**, this volume). Therefore, in learning the meaning of an L2 word, the learner needs to discover what the similarities and differences are between the L1 and L2.

The question is what the most effective way is to discover the meaning of L2 words. Many experts fear that using the L1 to explain L2 words will cause unnecessary L1 interference and suggest that the L1 should be avoided as much as possible. However, there are also some good arguments to use the L1 at the earliest stages to establish an initial form-meaning link. Because the L1 concept is already established and provides a natural, efficient vehicle to make the form-meaning link, it will allow more cognitive resources to be focused on the form (Barcroft, 2002). Cognitive resources are limited; therefore, it is unlikely that learners will absorb much of the contextualized knowledge at the beginning stages anyway. Once the initial form-meaning link is established, resources can be allotted to discovering the similarities and differences between the L1 and L2 meanings.

Evidence for the benefits of initially establishing form-meaning through the L1 was found in several studies. Prince (1996) found that more newly learned words could be recalled using L1 translations than L2 context, particularly for less-proficient learners. With secondary school Malaysian learners, using L1 translations was much more effective than providing L2-based meanings (Ramachandran and Rahim, 2004). Laufer and Shmueli (1997) found the same trend with Hebrew students. Lotto and de Groot (1998) found that L2–L1 word pairs lead to better learning than L2-picture pairs, at least for relatively experienced foreign language learners. Also learners themselves like to use their L1 in learning an L2, most noticeably in the consistently high usage of bilingual dictionaries (Schmitt, 1997). They also strongly believe that translating helps them to acquire English language skills, such as reading, writing, and particularly vocabulary words, idioms, and phrases (Liao, 2006).

However, after initial form-meaning links have been made, words need to be met many times in order to be learned (Nation, 2001), not just to consolidate the original form-meaning link, but also to developing the other types of word knowledge. Words will have to be met in many different contexts in order to discover their meanings and uses, and this entails a long-term recursive approach to vocabulary learning. Indeed, some research suggests that single episodes of instruction may not only be ineffective, but may actually be counterproductive under certain circumstances. Chang and Read (2006) found that vocabulary instruction before a listening comprehension task helped less than hearing the input twice or reading and discussing the topic beforehand. Crucially, the students reported that they did not learn the target vocabulary well enough to utilize it in the on-line listening task, and for higher proficiency students, a focus on this inadequately learned vocabulary seemed to distract their attention away from a more general understanding of the listening passages.

The discussion so far has implicitly focused on the form-meaning links of single words, but words do not occur in isolation: words are known by the company they keep (Mackin, 1978). If we take a usage-based approach seriously then symbolic units also consist of conventionalized constructions at all kinds of levels, that is, *formulaic language*. Learners need to know various categories of formulaic language to be proficient in the L2, such as collocations, idioms, and lexical bundles. Such combinations are very widespread in language (Wray, 2002) and used for a number of purposes, such as expressing a message or idea (*The early bird gets the worm* = do not procrastinate), realizing functions ([*I'm*] *just looking* [*thanks*] = declining an offer of assistance from a shopkeeper), establishing social solidarity (*I know what you mean* = agreeing with an interlocutor), and transacting specific information in a precise and understandable way (*Blood pressure is 150 over*, 70) (Schmitt and Carter, 2004). Michael Lewis and colleagues (2000) have argued for a language teaching methodology highlighting formulaic language, but the effectiveness of such an approach has not yet been empirically demonstrated to any degree. However, the small amount of research available suggests that highlighting phrasal language to learners can have an impact. Jones and Haywood (2004) focused on formulaic language in a 10-week EAP class, and found that the students became much more aware of formulaic sequences by the end of the course, showed a slight improvement in the production of these sequences in C-tests, but demonstrated no noticeable improvement in their output of these sequences in composition writing. Boers *et al.* (2006) found that learners who were exposed to considerable listening and reading and made aware of the formulaic language in that input were later judged to be more orally proficient than learners who received the same input but were taught with a traditional grammar–lexis dichotomy.

As MacWhinney would predict, learning form-meaning mappings is not only about frequency but also salience. It is a commonsense notion that the more a learner engages with a new lexical item, the more likely they are to learn it. There have been a number of attempts to define this notion more precisely. Craik and Lockhart's (1972) *Depth/Levels of Processing Hypothesis* laid the basic groundwork by stating that the more attention given to an item, and the more manipulation involved with the item, the greater the chances it will be remembered (see **Depth of processing**, and **Rehearsal,** this volume). Hulstijn and Laufer (2001) reviewed a number of studies and found that vocabulary learning tasks with relatively more need, search, and evaluation elements were more effective in remembering vocabulary items (see **Involvement Load Hypothesis**, this volume). Research, however, shows that many other factors make a difference as well. For example, students can scan, engage, and interpret in many different ways, regardless of material design, and there is little way to know in advance exactly how (Joe, 2006). Students' motivation, attitudes, and strategic behavior matter, so even the best teaching materials may be useless if students do not engage with them. It appears that vocabulary learning is part of a cyclical process where one's self-regulation of learning leads to more involvement with and use of vocabulary learning strategies, which in turn leads to better mastery of their use.

Overall, it seems that virtually anything that leads to more exposure, attention, manipulation, or time spent on lexical items adds to their learning. In fact, even the process of being tested on lexical items appears to facilitate better retention, as research designs that include multiple post-tests usually lead to better results on the final delayed post-test than similar designs with fewer or no intermediate post-tests (e.g. Mason and Krashen, 2004). Schmitt (2008) suggests the term *engagement* to encompasses all of these involvement possibilities, and concludes that essentially anything that leads to more and better engagement should improve vocabulary learning. Therefore promoting engagement is the most fundamental task for teachers and materials writers, and indeed, learners themselves.

Summarizing the dynamic process of second language acquisition

Taking a usage-based perspective, we have shown that a second language is learned mainly through making form-meaning links in the L2 and then discovering how these are used by proficient speakers in conventionalized patterns. For the L2 learner, who already has entrenched form-meaning links in the L1, this means that the L1 can be both a help and a hindrance. Similarities at different levels—form, meaning, or use—in the L1 can be used to help uncover the intricacies of the L2, but differences have to be discovered through frequent exposure and/or some form of attention to these differences. There is no single route to master the new L2 conventions but exposure and engagement are essential.

See also: cognitive linguistics and SLA, competition model, Complexity Theory/Dynamic Systems Theory, lexical concepts, vocabulary learning and teaching, word knowledge

References

Barcroft, J. (2002). Semantic and structural elaboration in L2 lexical acquisition. *Language Learning*, *52*, 2, 323–63.

Bensoussan, M. and Laufer, B. (1984). Lexical guessing in context in EFL reading comprehension. *Journal of Research in Reading*, *7*, 1, 15–32.

Boers, F., Eyckmans, J., Kappel, J., Stengers, H. and Demecheleer, M. (2006). Formulaic sequences and perceived oral proficiency: Putting a Lexical Approach to the test. *Language Teaching Research*, *10*, 3, 245–61.

Bogaards, P. (2001). Lexical units and the learning of foreign language vocabulary. *Studies in Second Language Acquisition*, *23*, 321–43.

Chang, A.C.-S. and Read, J. (2006). The effects of listening support on the listening performance of EFL learners. *TESOL Quarterly*, *40*, 2, 375–97.

Craik, F.I.M. and Lockhart, R.S. (1972). Levels of processing: A framework for memory research. *Journal of Verbal Learning and Verbal Behavior*, *11*, 671–684.

Cutler, A. and Norris, D.G. (1988). The role of strong syllables in segmentation for lexical access. *Journal of Experimental Psychology: Human Perception and Performance*, *14*, 113–21.

De Bot, K., Verspoor, M., and Lowie, W. (2007). A dynamic systems theory approach to second language acquisition. *Bilingualism, Language and Cognition*, *10*, 7–21.

de Groot, A.M.B. (2006). Effects of stimulus characteristics and background music on foreign language vocabulary learning and forgetting. *Language Learning*, *56*, 3, 463–506.

Ellis, N.C. (1997). Vocabulary acquisition: Word structure, collocation, word-class, and meaning. In Schmitt, N. (ed.), *Vocabulary: Description, Acquisition, and Pedagogy*. Cambridge: Cambridge University Press.

——(2006). Selective attention and transfer phenomena in L2 acquisition: Contingency, cue competition, salience, interference, overshadowing, blocking, and perceptual learning. *Applied Linguistics*, *27*, 2, 164–94.

Grainger, J. and Dijkstra, T. (1992). On the representation and use of language information in bilinguals. In Harris, R.J. (ed.), *Cognitive Processing in Bilinguals*, pp. 207–20. Amsterdam: North Holland..

Hulstijn, J. and Laufer, B. (2001). Some empirical evidence for the involvement load hypothesis in vocabulary acquisition. *Language Learning*, *51*, 3, 539–58.

Joe, A.G. (2006). *The Nature of Encounters with Vocabulary and Long-term Vocabulary*

Acquisition. Unpublished PhD thesis: Victoria University of Wellington.

Jones, M. and Haywood, S. (2004). Facilitating the acquisition of formulaic sequences: An exploratory study in an EAP context. In N., Schmitt (ed.), *Formulaic Sequences*, pp. 269–300. Amsterdam: John Benjamins.

Koda, K. (1997). Orthographic knowledge in L2 lexical processing. In Coady, J. and Huckin, T. (eds), *Second Language Vocabulary Acquisition*. Cambridge: Cambridge University Press.

Langacker, R.W. (2000). A dynamic usage-based model. In M. Barlow and S. Kemmer (eds), *Usage-Based Models of Language*. Stanford, CA: CSLI, 1–63.

Laufer, B. (1988). The concept of 'synforms' (similar lexical forms) in vocabulary acquisition. *Language and Education*, *2*, 2, 113–132.

Laufer, B. and Shmueli, K. (1997). Memorizing new words: Does teaching have anything to do with it? *RELC Journal*, *28*, 89–108.

Lewis, M. (ed.) (2000). *Teaching Collocation*. Hove: Language Teaching Publications.

Liao, P. (2006). EFL learners' beliefs about and strategy use of translation in English learning. *RELC Journal*, *37*, 2, 191–215.

Lotto, L. and de Groot, A.M.B. (1998). Effects of learning method and word type on acquiring vocabulary in an unfamiliar language. *Language Learning*, *48*, 1, 31–69.

Mackin, R. (1978). On collocations: Words shall be known by the company they keep. In P. Strevens (ed.), *In Honour of A.S. Hornby*, pp. 149–65. Oxford: Oxford University Press.

MacWhinney, B. (2008). A unified model. In P. Robinson and N. Ellis (eds), *Handbook of Cognitive Linguistics and Second Language Acquisition*, pp. 341–71. New York: Routledge.

Mason, B. and Krashen, S. (2004). Is form-focused vocabulary instruction worthwhile? *RELC Journal*, *35*, 2, 179–85.

Nation, I.S.P. (2001). *Learning Vocabulary in Another Language*. Cambridge: Cambridge University Press.

Prince, P. (1996). Second language vocabulary learning: The role of context versus translations as a function of proficiency. *Modern Language Journal*, *80*, 478–93.

Ramachandran, S.D. and Rahim, H.A. (2004). Meaning recall and retention: The impact of the translation method on elementary level learners' vocabulary learning. *RELC Journal*, *35*, 2, 161–78.

Robinson, P. and Ellis, N.C. (eds) (2008). *Handbook of Cognitive Linguistics and Second Language Acquisition*. New York and London: Routledge.

Rumelhart, D.E. and McClelland, J.L. (1987). Learning the past tenses of English verbs: Implicit rules or parallel distributed processing. In B. MacWhinney (ed.), *Mechanisms of Language Acquisition*, pp. 194–248. Mahwah, NJ: Erlbaum.

Rumelhart, D.E. (1979). Some problems with the notion that words have literal meanings. In A. Ortony (ed.), *Metaphor and Thought*, pp. 71–82. Cambridge University Press.

Schmitt, N. (1997). Vocabulary learning strategies. In Schmitt, N. and McCarthy, M. (eds), *Vocabulary: Description, Acquisition, and Pedagogy*. Cambridge: Cambridge University Press.

——(2008). Review article: Instructed second language vocabulary learning. *Language Teaching Research*, *12* (3), 329–63.

Schmitt, N. and Carter, R. (2004). Formulaic sequences in action: An introduction. In Schmitt, N. (ed.), *Formulaic Sequences*. Amsterdam: John Benjamins.

Sunderman, G. and Kroll, J.F. (2006). First language activation during second language lexical processing. *Studies in Second Language Acquisition*, *28*, 387–422.

Wray, A. (2002). *Formulaic Language and the Lexicon*. Cambridge: Cambridge University Press.

Language testing and SLA

Sauli Takala
University of Helsinki

Testing and assessment, which have several functions in the life of individuals and in a variety of institutional domains, have a long history (reference is often made to early examples in China and in the Bible). Language tests also have a long history and some current language examination bodies can trace their origin back to more than a hundred years.

However, more systematic and "modern" approaches to language testing are younger. One of the earliest contributions in the field was John B. Carroll's comprehensive review of achievement testing of foreign languages in the U.S. from the late 1920s through to 1954, the year in which it was produced, but never published, and is therefore unfortunately little known.

Educational measurement had acquired a prominent role relatively early. The first edition of "Educational Measurement" was published in 1951, but it was not until the fourth edition that the first chapter on foreign language testing by Chalhoub-Deville and Deville (2006) was published.

It is common to distinguish three periods or approaches in the history of language testing: *pre-scientific*, *psychometric-structuralist* and *psycholinguistic-sociolinguistic*. This threepartite division was first suggested by Bernard Spolsky in 1975. Later he chose to refer to traditional, modern, and postmodern trends emphasizing the overlap of the trends. The tripartite division continues to be a useful heuristic.

The terms *testing, assessment, evaluation*, and *measurement* are sometimes used as synonyms but they are frequently used to signify partly different activities. What the first three share is the basic idea of collecting information about language ability and interpreting it for various purposes (decisions and actions), whereas the fourth, measurement deals with the general aspects of quantification: the assignment of numbers to an attribute according to a rule of correspondence.

McNamara (2004) provides a perceptive description of language testing and Figure 8 captures much of current thinking of the basic logic of language testing.

Most language testing and assessment is conducted by language teachers in their classrooms, which is not usually noted in the language testing literature. Teachers do this in a variety of ways, not least by observing learners' performance in various tasks and giving feedback using the systems they are familiar with and using the information for making decisions concerning further actions. This can be done without measurement. However, basic principles of good practice in testing and assessment are needed, many of them basically the same that apply to stricter and more large-scale contexts and aims.

Test development

Over the years, test development has become more sophisticated with research and practical experience. The standard reference in our time is the comprehensive and up-to-date *Handbook of Test Development* (edited by Downing and Haladyna, 2006). Downing lists 12 steps for effective test development.

Test development can vary depending on the purposes and uses of testing: selection, placement, feedback, progress/grading, level of proficiency; formative assessment versus summative assessment; norm-referenced versus criterion-referenced testing.

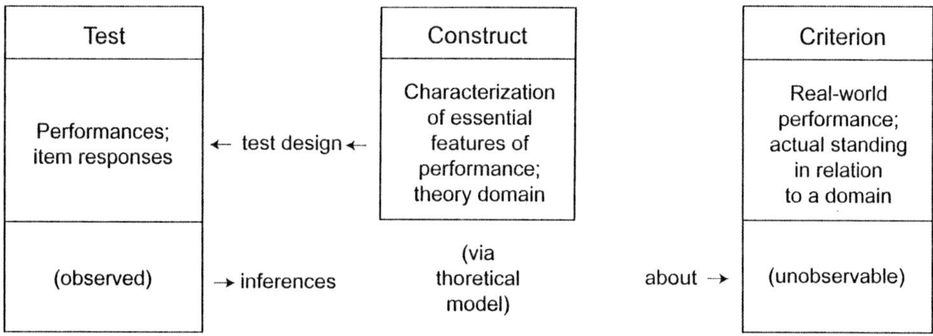

Figure 8 Test, construct, and criterion
McNamara, 2004: 765. Reprinted by permission of Wiley-Blackwell.

One of the key elements in test development is *test specifications*. They may vary from a quite implicit plan by a language teacher to an explicit document which guides the work of examination bodies and testing agencies. Sometimes the specifications are confidential internal documents but usually some information is provided about "less sensitive" principles. Explicit specifications usually contain a definition of the construct to be assessed, the characteristics of the target group, (a) sample item(s), definition of the stimulus characteristics, and a definition of response characteristics. It is in the development of specifications that test developers need to display their *assessment literacy*, their familiarity with what is currently considered a cutting-edge conceptual foundation, and what is good practice in language testing and assessment.

A *test item* is an instruction or question that requires a response, and a rule for scoring that response. The basic difference between items depends on whether the test taker selects the answer or constructs it.

Scoring responses is an easy task in the case of selected answer items. Scoring constructed answer items/tasks is demanding. *Holistic* or *analytic* scoring may be adopted or a combination of the two approaches. In both low-stakes and high-stakes assessment of language ability it is important to define the *scoring rules* at the same time when the items/tasks are constructed. It is bad practice, which may not actually be very uncommon, to delay this work to a stage when scoring is to start. Scoring rules are well defined if they are explicit, easy to understand/interpret, and non-overlapping.

Item/task review plays an important part in test development. It is crucial during both the stimulus construction and after the *piloting* phase. This involves a critical review of content relevance, fairness (lack of bias), the appropriacy of the level of difficulty and technical quality. The review usually leads to some revisions.

Judging tests and assessments

The most important criteria used in judging tests and assessments are validity and reliability. *Validity* concerns the extent to which a claim about a test taker, based on assessment data from that person, is justified (Kane, 2006). *Reliability* concerns how adequately the data can support the claim and how satisfactorily alternative interpretations can be discounted.

Drawing on Toulmin (1958) and Kane (2006), Bachman and Palmer (2010: 103–33) discuss claims and warrants in what they call Assessment Use Argument. The four claims, if warranted, justify the assessment:

- Beneficial consequences.
- Values sensitive and equitable decisions.
- Meaningful, impartial, generalizable, relevant, and sufficient interpretations.
- Consistent assessment records.
- Fairness (equitable treatment and absence of bias) is also discussed as an important requirement in the assessment process.

Issues and future challenges

The nature of the *criterion* is a perennial issue in language assessment. Davies (1990, 2003) has addressed the elusive but ubiquitous concept of the *native speaker* as a criterion in applied linguistics, SLA research and also in language assessment (cf. Abrahamson and Hyltenstam, 2009). Davies concludes that the native speaker is a myth but a useful one. This criterion has, however, been increasingly questioned and the interest in English as a lingua franca (ELF) and "World Englishes" has further problematized this criterion.

A number of other criteria (standards) have been produced in language testing. Important contributions include the Foreign Service Institute's scales developed about 50 years ago for testing proficiency and subsequent scales of proficiency. The Common European Framework for Languages (CEFR, 2001) developed in Europe has acquired a strong position, not only in Europe but also in some other parts of the world. Such standards-based approach to assessment defines *content* as well as *performance standards*.

The role of *self-assessment* has been widely accepted. The ability to assess one's language proficiency is seen as a powerful factor in language learning. The European Language Portolio (ELP), closely linked with the CEFR, is an example of a tool-making use of self-assessment.

Another issue attracting considerable attention is the concern with the *ethics* of language testing. The consequences of assessment were singled out by Messick (1994) as an important aspect of the uniform concept of construct validity. Shohamy (2001) has provided a critical discussion of the power that tests exert in controlling people and institutions. International language testing and assessment associations have developed codes of ethics/guidelines of good practice.

Standard-setting (setting cut scores) is a challenge when assessments, tests, and examinations increasingly are required to report the outcomes in terms of proficiency levels. Cizek and Bunch (2007) is a useful general reference. A Manual for Relating Language Examinations at the CEFR is accessible at www.coe.int/T/DG4/Linguistic/Default_en.asp, and a monograph by Felianka Kaftandjieva (2010) is available at www.ealta.eu.org/resources.

There is a common wish to aim at *simple solutions* and usually it makes sense to start with simplified models. However, *language ability is a complex phenomenon*. In a monumental analysis of human cognitive abilities, Carroll (1993) identified 16 different abilities in the domain of language. We are justified to seek simplicity (practicality) in language assessment but we should be aware of our simplifications. Reckase (2010) notes that the traditional true-score theory and the more recent unidimensional item response theory give good approximations for some test situations. However, in other cases, more complex models are needed to accurately represent the relationships in the test data.

Reckase considers that also *items* are complicated and he points out that they deserve careful attention as the quality of assessment is crucially dependent on the quality of items. Thus training in item writing is needed for teachers as well as for item writers who are commissioned to write items for examinations.

Bachman and Palmer (2010) note that there are frequent *misconceptions and unrealistic expectations* about what language assessments can do and what they should be like. They list (a) a misguided belief in one "best" way to test language ability for any given situation; (b) a belief that language test development depends on highly technical procedures and should be left to experts; and (c) a belief that a test is either "good" or "bad," depending on whether it satisfies *one particular* quality instead of a number of requisite qualities. Davies (2003) has also cautioned about "heresies" of languages testing research, resulting from too enthusiastic embracing of new approaches and leading to loss of proper balance. Therefore, developing *assessment literacy* in a wide sense is a permanent challenge in language testing and assessment.

See also: communicative competence, Modern Language Aptitude Test (MLAT), native speaker, proficiency, qualitative research, quantitative research

References

Abrahamson, N. and Hyltenstam, K. (2009). Age of Acquisition and Nativelikeness in a Second Language: Listener Perception Versus Linguistic Scrutiny. *Language Learning*, *59*, 2249–306.

Bachman, L. and Palmer, A. (2010). *Language Assessment in Practice*. Oxford: Oxford University Press.

Brennan, R.L. (ed.) (2006). *Educational Measurement*, 4th edn. Westport, CT: Praeger.

Carroll, J.B. (1993). *Human Cognitive Abilities. A Survey of Factor-analytic Studies*. Cambridge: Cambridge University Press.

Chalhoub-Deville, M. and Deville, G. (2006). *Old, Borrowed, and New Thoughts in Second Language Testing*. In R.L. Brennan (ed.), *Educational Measurement*, 4th edn. Westport CT: American Council on Education.

Cizek, G.J. and Bunch, M.B. (2007). *Standard Setting. A Guide to Establishing and Evaluating Performance Standards on Tests*. Thousand Oaks, CA: Sage.

Council of Europe (2001). *Common European Framework of Reference for Languages: Learning, Teaching, Assessment*. Cambridge: Cambridge University Press.

Davies, A. (1990). *Principles of Language Testing*. Oxford: Blackwell.

——(2003a) *The Native Speaker: Myth and Reality*. Clevedon: Multilingual Matters.

——(2003b) Three heresies of language testing research. *Language Testing, 20*, 4355–68.

Downing, S.M. and Haladyna, T.M. (2006). *Handbook of Test Development*. Mahwah NJ: Erlbaum.

Kane, M.T. (2006). Validation. In R.L. Brennan (ed.), *Educational Measurement*, 4th edn. Westport, CT: American Council on Education.

Kaftandjieva, F. (2010). *Methods for Setting Cut Scores in Criterion-referenced Achievement Tests: A Comparative Analysis of Six Recent Methods with an Application to Tests of Reading in EFL*. Cito, Arnhem: European Association for Language Testing and Assessment.

Lindquist, E.F. (ed.) (1951). *Educational Measurement*, 1st edn. Washington, DC: American Council on Education.

McNamara, T. (2004). Language testing. In A. Davies and C. Elder (eds), *The Handbook of Applied Linguistics*. Oxford: Blackwell.

Messick, S. (1994) The interplay of evidence and consequences in the validation of performance assessments. *Educational Researcher, 23*(2), 13–23.

Reckase, M.D. (2010). NCME 2009 Presidential Address: What I think I know. *Educational Measurement: Issues and Practice*, 293–97.

Shohamy, E. (2001). *The Power of Tests. A Critical Perspective on the Uses of Language Tests*. Harlow: Pearson Education.

Toulmin, S. (1958). *The Uses of Argument*. Cambridge: Cambridge University Press.

Further reading

Alderson, J.C., Clapham, C. and Wall, D. (1995). *Language Test Construction and Evaluation*. Cambrige: Cambridge University Press. (A user-friendly comprehensive guide to test development based on a solid theoretical foundation.)

Bachman, L.F. (1990). *Fundamental Considerations in Language Testing*. Oxford: Oxford University Press. (Presents a very influential and widely used model for testing communicative language ability.)

Long, M.H. and Doughty, C.J. (eds) (2009). *The Handbook of Language Teaching*. Oxford: Wiley-Blackwell. (In addition to up-to-date discussion of SLA and other relevant topics, includes 13 chapters which address the teaching and testing of different aspects of language proficiency.)

McNamara, T. (1996). *Measuring Second Language Performance*. London: Longman. (An informative discussion of the problems and possible solutions in measuring performance.)

Spolsky, B. (1995). *Measured Words*. Oxford: Oxford University Press. (Provides a thorough and thought-provoking analysis of the emergence of institutionalized language testing, using the U.S. and Britain as two distinct contexts.)

Language typology and language distance

Sunyoung Lee-Ellis
University of Maryland

Language typology is a subfield of linguistics that deals with the classification, generalization, and theorizing of languages or components of languages around the world. There are approximately 7,000 languages in the world, and the language typologists seek to discover the commonalities and points of variation across these diverse languages. Typological research generally involves three aspects: 1) classification of languages based on their structural properties, 2) formulation of generalizations based on this classification, and 3) theoretical explanations of these generalizations.

Recent typological research employs a wide range of linguistic properties such that features of languages are classified rather than the language as a whole. Specific grammatical domains (e.g., word order) are first identified, and individual languages are examined along this property (e.g., SOV, SVO, VSO, VOS, OVS, OSV). Generalizations are then made on the distribution and clustering of typological classifications. A quantitative generalization, for example, can be made about basic word order, in that the majority of the world's languages (more than 75 per cent) have either SOV or SVO word order. Generalizations on co-occurrence are also made: verb-initial languages (VO), for example, tend to have prepositions in the language system, whereas verb-final languages (OV) have postpositions (Song, 2001: 43). Ultimately, typologists seek to explain why such systematic patterns of variation exist.

Examples of cross-linguistic variation

Typological variation can be found in all linguistic domains, including sound systems, word categories, morphological patterns, and semantic, grammatical, and referential components of languages. Within the morphological domain, early work by Sapir (1921) illustrated how languages like Mandarin should be classified as an isolating type (i.e., each word is a morpheme and meanings are clear), whereas languages like Swahili and West Greenlandic are agglutinative, where words may have more than one morpheme with clear boundaries. Fusional languages like Russian and English, finally, may have more than one morpheme, but boundaries are not clear.

Syntactically, languages vary in word order, case marking, relative-clause construction, causative, and passive constructions, and so on. For example, languages are classified into four classes based on case marking. In languages with a nominative-accusative system like English, the agent of the transitive verb and the subject of the intransitive verb take the same case marking (nominative case), whereas the patient of the transitive verb is marked separately (accusative case). On the other hand, so-called ergative-absolutive languages (e.g., Basque, Yalarnnga) mark the agent of the transitive verb separately (ergative) from the patient of the transitive verb and the subject of the intransitive verb (absolutive). Statistically, the nominative-accusative system is the most frequent, with ergative-absolutive second most common (Song, 2001: 156). Extremely rare types include a system that distinguishes all three arguments (i.e., the tripartite system) (e.g., Australian Aboriginal language Wangkumara) and a system where the agent and patient of transitive verbs pattern together againt the subject of intransitive verbs (e.g., Iranian language Rushan) (Comrie, 1989).

These examples of course are not an exhaustive list of typological variations. However, a more comprehensive list can be found via the *World Atlas of Language Structure*, a massive online database containing 2,650 languages, introducing 142 points of linguistic variation.

Typology, language universals, and second language acquisition

Typology and language universals share a close relationship. Linguistic typology examines the range of variation across different languages. Language universals are the generalized principles that hold true for all the languages. In this sense, linguistic typology provides the tools for establishing language universals.

A classic example of a typological universal is implicational universals. Implicational universals are an empirical generalization derived from typological work that states that if a language has a particular feature, it necessarily has another feature.

Once such generalizations are made, they are often extended into something more powerful, a predictive principle that imposes constraints on the limits of possible variation within human language. For example, the noun phrase accessibility hierarchy (NPAH) (Keenan and Comrie, 1977), is a typological generalization about relativization. The hierarchy is "Subject > Direct Object > Indirect Object > Oblique > Genitive > Object of Comparative." Not every language allows relativization of all grammatical relations listed in the hiearchy. For example, many Western Malayo-Polynesian languages (including Javanese, Minang-kabau, Malagasy, and Toba Batak) can relativize only subjects. Welsh, on the other hand, allows subject and direct object relativization; Baque, Tamil, and Roviana allow the three highest grammatical relations to be relativized; Catalan and North Frisian relativize down to oblique; French, German, and Spanish allow down to genitive; English allows all. The generalization made here is that there is an implicational hierarchy in the distribution of relative clause types among the languages of the world, that is, if a language can relativize a noun phrase

(NP) (e.g., indirect object), it necessarily relativizes an NP that is higher in the accessibility hierarchy (e.g., subject and direct object), but not vice versa.

Although the original NPAH had been a descriptive generalization of the implicational distribution of different relative clause types as described, it was later extended to claims for acquisitional sequence and processing difficulty in second language acquisition (SLA) (e.g., Gass, 1979; Eckman, Bell, and Nelson, 1988). The assumption is that what underlies the hierarchy reflects something fundamental in human language faculty: subjects are inherently easier to relativize than, for example, objects, so subject relative clause are easier to process and acquire.

This notion of a natural order of difficulty has also been related to the notion of "markedness." Typological markedness means there is an order of differential naturalness observed in the distribution of features across languages (Eckman, 1977). Over the past couple of decades, a lot of second language research on relativization have been devoted to whether the same implicational generalization found in typology holds for a second language learner's developing grammar (i.e., interlanguage grammar).

The relationship between typology and SLA research and theory

Studying typology is useful for any field of language science. For linguistic analysis, typology can help to determine accidental variation and the deeper property that causes systematic variations across languages. For SLA, typology is often a prerequisite of research design. At a minimum, first language and second language systems should be compared given the widely accepted assumption that first language influences the second language (transfer). Furthermore, typological generalizations help elucidate why certain features are difficult to acquire (e.g., markedness) as well as explain the systematicity of interlanguage development. For some, what exists typologically could also reflect what is learnable: typology determines what the possible range of variation is, while acquisition deals with how learners find their way to the space that their language occupies. In second language processing research, typology specifies the nature of variation in language. One can examine how this plays out in real time, how the language recognition device, the parser, is impacted by surface variation. In SLA theory, any good models of processing, acquisition and representation will have to deal with the kinds of variation that are examined typologically, but it should not be able to deal with the kind of variation never observed in typology.

Although it is undeniable that typology has provided useful theoretical tools to study the nature of SLA process, the relationship between typology and SLA is not unidirectional: SLA research on interlanguage grammar also contributes to typological research for a better understanding of the possible range of language variation (Greenberg, 1991).

Language distance

Related to language typology is the concept of language distance. Language distance means the extent to which languages differ from each other. Language distance has often been thought to be an important factor in the outcome of foreign language learning: English is linguistically closer to West European languages than it is to East Asian languages and it would be easier for English speakers to learn, for example, German than Japanese.

Despite the appeal of this concept to the field of SLA, measuring language distance is often not straightforward because languages are so complex that construction of the measure is not easy. In the applied linguistic context, measurement of language distance has been attempted based on several criteria, including language typology, language trees, and learning difficulty. Rutherford (1983), for example, measured distance from English based on three typological classifications: basic word order, topic-prominence, and pragmatic/grammatical word order, and concluded that Spanish is distance 1, Arabic and Mandarin are 2, and Japanese and Korean are 3. A more applied example of social science research, Chiswick and Miller (1998), used the speaking ability score English native speakers obtained after a certain amount of time spent on foreign language training. The lower the standardized proficiency test score, the greater the distance between the language and English. Some of the resulting scores were 1.00 for Japanese (hardest to learn, thus most distant from English), 1.5 for Mandarin Chinese, 2.0 for Hungarian, 2.5 for Italian and French, and 3.00 for Norwegian and Swedish. The application of language distance has been made in immigration research and international trade research, and in the foreign language education context, the U.S. government bases the length of its training in critical languages on the respective language's distance from English, which is measured by learning difficulty.

See also: functional typological linguistics, implicational universals, interlanguage, linguistic transfer, markedness, relative clauses

References

Chiswick, B.R. and Miller, P.W. (1998). English language fluency among immigrants in the United States. *Research in Labor Economics, 17*, 151–200.

Comrie, B. (1989). *Language Universals and Linguistic Typology*. Oxford: Blackwell.

Eckman, F.R. (1977). Markedness and the contrastive analysis hypothesis. *Language Learning, 27*, 315–30.

Eckman, F.R., Bell, L. and Nelson, D. (1988). On the generalization of relative clause instruction in the acquisition of English as a second language. *Applied Linguistics, 9*, 1–20.

Gass, S.M. (1979). Language transfer and universal grammatical relations. *Language Learning, 29*, 327–44.

Greenberg, J.H. (1991). Typology/universals and second language acquisition. In T. Huebner and C.A. Ferguson (eds), *Crosscurrents in Second Language Acquisition and Linguistic Theories*, Amsterdam: John Benjamins.

Keenan, E. and Comrie, B. (1977). Noun phrase accessibility and Universal Grammar. *Linguistic Inquiry, 8*, 63–100.

Rutherford, W. (1983). Language typology and language transfer. In S. Gass and L. Selinker (eds), *Language Transfer in Language Learning*, Rowley, MA: Newbury House Publishers.

Sapir, E. (1921). *Language: An Introduction to the Study of Speech*. New York: Harcourt, Brace and World.

Song, J.J. (2001). *Linguistic Typology: Morphology and Syntax*. London: Pearson Education.

Further reading

Comrie, B. (1989). *Language Universals and Linguistic Typology*. Oxford: Blackwell. (An introductory account of typology and syntactic-semantic universals.)

Greenberg, J.H. (1991). Typology/universals and second language acquisition. In T. Huebner and C.A. Ferguson (eds), *Crosscurrents in Second Language Acquisition and Linguistic Theories*, Amsterdam: John Benjamin's. (A discussion of the relationship between typology/universals and SLA.)

——(ed.) (1963). *Universals of Language*. Cambridge, MA: MIT Press. (Pioneering research on language typology and universals.)

Keenan, E. and Comrie, B. (1977). Noun phrase accessibility and Universal Grammar. *Linguistic Inquiry, 8*, 63–100. (A seminal piece on the typological generalization on relativization.)

Song, J.J. (2001). *Linguistic Typology: Morphology and Syntax*. London: Pearson Education. (An overview of typological variations in morphology and syntax.)

Lateralization

Helen Carpenter
Upper-Story Educational Services and Consulting

In neuroscience, the term *lateralization* describes localization of a function that depends on one side of the brain more than the other. The brain is divided by the longitudinal fissure into the left and right hemispheres. Terms related to lateralization include *hemispheric dominance* or *specialization* and *cerebral dominance* or *specialization*. An additional term, *neural asymmetry*, refers to anatomic and physiological differences between homolog structures in the two hemispheres.

The Hemispheres and Connectivity. For the cerebral cortex and most subcortical tissue (minus the cerebellum), each hemisphere is predominantly connected to the opposite (contralateral) side of the body (although connections to the same, or ipsilateral, side of the body also exist). Thus the right hemisphere receives input from and sends projections to the left side of the body and vice versa.

Within the brain, the hemispheres communicate across the longitudinal fissure. Structural homologs are connected through white matter tracts (bundles of myelinated axons) called commissures, while structurally unrelated areas are connected through axon bundles called decussations. It is unknown whether interhemispheric connections facilitate bilateral processes or inhibit competing processes (Jäncke and Steinmetz, 2003). Within a single hemisphere, communication is mediated by axon bundles, sometimes called association pathways or fasciculi.

The largest commissure is the corpus callossum. Many, but not all, of the average 200 million callossal axons are very thin, leading to particularly slow interhemispheric signal conduction. One-way messages may take approximately 25ms, while messages that travel longer distances and recruit many axons may take 100ms or more. Additional time is needed for bidirectional, multistage messaging. It may be more expedient for such interactions to take place locally within a hemisphere. Thus, for time-critical functions, hemispheric specialization is potentially advantageous. A factor that may mediate the size of the corpus callosum is brain size (Doty, 2003).

Research Methodology. Research on lateralization derives from several populations and methods. Investigators observe patients with unilateral (one-sided) brain damage, severed corpus callosa ("split-brain" patients), and hemispherectomies; surgical patients; individuals with developmental disorders; individuals who display atypical laterality such as left-handers; and individuals with typical laterality. Temporary loss of unilateral function may be induced for research through transcranial magnetic stimulation or pharmacological means (e.g., amobarbitol). In addition, neuroimaging techniques with good spatial resolution such as fMRI can be used to assess lateralization. Data may comprise anatomical and physiological differences between the hemispheres and/or behavioral responses to stimuli (Kosslyn *et al.*, 1999).

Language Lateralization in the First Language. Typically, the two hemispheres subserve different aspects of language. The left hemisphere alone is sufficient to handle most language functions, while the right hemisphere is much more limited.

Rule-based Grammar. For native language(s), left hemisphere Broca's area and possibly other anterior regions (see **Declarative Procedural Model**) play an important role in rule-based grammar, including decomposition of morphologically complex words and using word order to facilitate comprehension.

Lexicon. The lexicon is subserved by bilateral posterior regions, but lexical organization differs in each hemisphere. The left hemisphere recognizes superordinate relationships. In addition, left hemisphere lexical retrieval is sensitive to priming (Kosslyn *et al.*, 1999).

Auditory input. The left and right hemispheres may process auditory aspects of language on different timescales. The left superior temporal gyrus appears to be sensitive to shorter busts of sound between 25ms and 50ms while the right superior temporal gyrus appears to concurrently analyze somewhat longer sounds between 200ms and 300ms. These temporal differences may underlie the observation that the left hemisphere is specialized for processing speech while the right hemisphere is specialized for processing prosody (Boemio *et al.*, 2005).

Functional specialization may be tied to anatomical asymmetries. For example, there is a tendency for aspects of Broca's area to be enlarged in more than half of all adults, a trend that may begin prenatally (Kosslyn *et al.*, 1999). In addition, during adolescence, the arcuate fasciculus, a white matter tract connecting Broca's and Wernicke's areas, appears to thicken significantly in the left hemisphere and not the right hemisphere (Schmithorst *et al.*, 2002). It is worth mentioning that in a minority of individuals, language-related anatomical asymmetries seem to be reversed or absent, a phenomenon that may truly exist or that may arise from methodological artifacts.

Between 90 and 95 percent of right-handers also display left-lateralization for aspects of language (Rasmussin and Milner, 1977), although the underlying nature of this co-occurrence has not been specified. Language lateralization in left-handers is less predictable. They may exhibit left hemisphere dominance for language (40 percent) or bilateral dominance (40 percent), and to a lesser degree, right-hemisphere language dominance (20 percent; Joanette, 1989). Controlling for hand preference in research studies may increase the probability that all study participants rely on comparable neural processes for language function, a potential consideration when investigating neural or cognitive aspects of language.

Like hand preference, individuals differ in the degree to which they display strong language lateralization. Individual differences may be genetically determined (Anneken *et al.*, 2004), although language lateralization can be determined by non-genetic causes, such as neural damage or surgery. Some research indicates that men tend to display stronger left lateralization than women, although this may be limited to comprehension of story-length discourse (Kitazawa and Kansaku, 2005). Individuals with larger brains may show increased unilateral specialization of functions (Jäncke and Steinmetz, 2003), and this may extend to language.

Language Lateralization in the Second Language. The neural underpinnings of second languages are yet to be determined. Cognitive representation of a second language depends on a number of factors including, but not limited to, age when the second language was learned, the similarity of the second and first languages, the manner and extent to which the second language is used, proficiency level, form of language assessed, and type of language tasks administered. Different models of second language acquisition point to important differences in how second language is represented in the brain. Research on this topic suggests that individuals display a variety of unilateral and bilateral patterns; however, left lateralization for grammar tends to be delayed, if it occurs at all, in adult learners (Ullman, 2005).

See also: child second language acquisition, Critical Period Hypothesis (CPH), Declarative Procedural (DP) model, functional magnetic resonance imaging (fMRI), myelination, neuroimaging

References

Anneken, K., Konrad, C., Dräger, B., Breitenstein, C., Kennerknecht, I., Ringelstein, E.B. and Knecht, S. (2004). Familial aggregation of strong hemispheric language lateralization. *Neurology*, *63*, 2433–35.

Boemio, A., Fromm, S., Braun, A. and Poeppel, D. (2005). Hierarchical and asymmetric temporal sensitivity in human auditory cortices. *Nature Neuroscience*, *8*, 389–95.

Doty, R.W. (2003). Forebrain commissures: Glimpses of neurons producing mind. In E. Zaidel and M. Iscoboni (eds), *The Parallel Brain: The Cognitive Neuroscience of the Corpus Callosum*. Cambridge, MA: MIT Press.

Jäncke, L. and Steinmetz, H. (2003). Brain size: A possible source of interindividual variability in corpus callosum morphology. In E. Zaidel and M. Iscoboni (eds), *The Parallel Brain: The Cognitive Neuroscience of the Corpus Callosum*. Cambridge, MA: MIT Press.

Joanette, Y. (1989). Aphasia in left-handers and crossed-aphasia. In F. Boller and J. Grafman (eds), *Handbook of Neuropsychology*, vol. 2. Amsterdam: Elsevier.

Kitizawa, S. and Kansaku, K. (2005). Letter to the editor: Sex difference in language lateralization may be task-dependent. *Brain*, *128*, E30.

Kosslyn, S.M., Gazzaniga, M.S., Galaburda, A.M. and Rabin, C. (1999). Hemispheric specialization. In M.J. Zigmond, F.E. Bloom, S.C. Landis, J.L. Roberts, and L.R. Squire (eds), *Fundamental Neuroscience*. San Diego, CA: Academic Press.

Rasmussin, T. and Milner, B. (1977). The role of early left-brain injury in determining lateralization of cerebral speech functions. *Annals of the New York Academy of Sciences*, *299*, 355–69.

Schmithorst, V.J., Wilke, M., Dardzinski, B.J. and Holland, S.K. (2002). Correlation of white matter diffusivity and anisotropy with age during childhood and adolescence: A cross-sectional diffusion tensor MR imaging study. *Radiology*, *222*, 212–18.

Ullman, M.T. (2005). A cognitive neuroscience perspective on second language acquisition: The declarative/procedural model. In C. Sanz (ed.), *Mind and Context in Adult Second Language Acquisition*. Washington, DC: Georgetown University Press.

Further reading

Corballis, M.C. (2009). The evolution and genetics of cerebral asymmetry. *Philosophical Transactions of the Royal Society of London B: Biological Sciences*, *364*, 867–79.

Learned attention and blocking

Nick C. Ellis
University of Michigan

Naturalistic SLA tends to stabilize at levels short of nativelike ability. At its most extreme this can present itself as a "Basic Variety" of interlanguage which, although sufficient for everyday communicative purposes, predominantly comprises just nouns, verbs, and adverbs, with closed-class items, in particular grammatical morphemes and prepositions, failing to be put to full nativelike use. Various explanations have been proposed for this limited attainment of adults compared with children, including critical periods for language acquisition, sociocultural differences, motivational differences, and restricted input. Alternative accounts emphasize the associative learning phenomena of learned attention, blocking, and transfer. A number of theories of SLA incorporate notions of learned attention (Schmidt, 2001), for example the competition model (Macwhinney, 1987) and the associative-cognitive CREED (Ellis, 2006c).

Associative learning theory documents a range of effects of transfer and inhibition that shift learners' attention to input as a result of prior experience. Kruschke (2005, 2006) describes the phenomenon of blocking. Associating a particular stimulus A with a particular outcome X makes it more difficult to learn that cue B (subsequently paired with the same outcome) is also a good predictor. Thus, for example, if a pigeon learns that a conditioned stimulus (e.g., a light) is a reliable predictor of an unconditioned stimulus (e.g., the onset of some painful stimulus such as a shock), then it will not become conditioned to or learn that any other conditioned stimulus predicts the unconditioned stimulus (e.g., that a bell predicts the onset of the shock in the same way the light did). Once the animal learns one reliable association with the conditioned stimulus, this essentially blocks further associations. Blocking is an effect of learned attention (Mackintosh, 1975). It is a highly robust and widespread phenomenon that occurs across animal and human learning.

Ellis (2006b) reviews blocking in second language acquisition. There are many situations in natural language in which cues are redundant and thus—as a consequence of blocking—might be less readily learned. If L1 experience has led a learner to look elsewhere for cues to interpretation, he or she might use these cues where available in the L2; the principles of associative learning predict that this reliance on L1 cues will be to the detriment of learning other cues that might also be relevant. For example, L1-derived knowledge that there are reliable lexical cues to temporal reference (words like *yesterday, gestern, hier, ayer*) might block the acquisition of verb tense morphology from analysis of utterances such as *yesterday I walked* or *hier nous sommes allés au cinéma* "yesterday we went to the movies." Given that it is not uncommon in natural language for grammatical cues to be foreshadowed by more salient lexical and discourse cues like this, SLA thus seems to be a problem space that might be particularly susceptible to learned attention effects such as blocking and overshadowing.

Ellis and Sagarra (2010b) explored learned attention in two experiments. The first demonstrated short-term instructional sequence effects in adults learning temporal reference in Latin using the standard blocking experimental paradigm (Kruschke, 2006) but with linguistic content relating to temporal reference in a small set of Latin phrases. In Experiment 1, previous experience with adverbial cues blocked the acquisition of verbal tense morphology, and, in contrast, early experience with tense blocked later learning of adverbs. Experiment 2 demonstrated long-term transfer effects: native speakers of Chinese languages, which do not exhibit verb tense morphology, failed to acquire inflectional cues when adverbial and verbal cues are equally available. These latter findings suggest a long-term attention to language, a processing bias affecting subsequent cue learning that comes from a lifetime of prior L1 usage.

Ellis and Sagarra (2011) replicated and extended these investigations where the participants had to learn a more complicated morphological paradigm. In Experiment 1, salient adverbs were better learned than less salient verb inflections, early experience of adverbial cues blocked the acquisition of verbal morphology, and contrariwise, but to a lesser degree than in Ellis and Sagarra (2010b), early experience of tense reduced later learning of adverbs. Experiment 2 demonstrated long-term transfer: native speakers of Chinese (no tense morphology) were less able than native speakers of Spanish or Russian (rich morphology) to acquire inflectional cues from the same language experience where adverbial and verbal cues were equally available. Learned attention to tense morphology in Latin was continuous rather than discrete, ordered with regard first language: Chinese < English < Russian < Spanish. A meta-analysis of the combined results of Ellis and Sagarra (2010b, 2011) separated out positive and negative learned attention effects: the average effect size for entrenchment was large (+1.23), that for blocking was moderate (–0.52).

Ellis and Sagarra (2010a) demonstrate that such effects extend to the sentence processing strategies of third- and eighth-semester English-Spanish FL learners reading sentences in Spanish containing lexical (adverb) and morphological (verbal inflection) cues to temporal reference. They also show how instructional practices that manipulate learner attention to morphological cues, either in time by means of pre-exposure, or in space by means of typographical enhancement, increase attention to inflections thus to overcome reliance upon adverbial cues.

The findings of such experiments reinforce the possibility that the limited attainment of adult second and foreign language learning follows general principles of associative learning. Adult FL acquirers are limited in working memory and time on task, and they have attentional biases to language. They know that temporal adverbs are more reliable than non-salient and ambiguous verbal inflections and that they can usually satisfice (a cognitive strategy that attempts to meet criteria for adequacy, rather than to identify an optimal solution) and get their message across by lexical means alone—however ungrammatical, the Basic Variety is communicatively effective. An understanding of associative learning theory illuminates both the rationality of L1 fluency and the apparent irrationalities of fragile L2 acquisition and fossilization (Ellis, 2006a, 2006b).

See also: attention, automaticity, frequency effects, inhibitory control, priming, statistical learning

References

Ellis, N.C. (2006a). Language acquisition as rational contingency learning. *Applied Linguistics*, *27*, 1–24.

——(2006b). Selective attention and transfer phenomena in SLA: Contingency, cue competition, salience, interference, overshadowing, blocking, and perceptual learning. *Applied Linguistics*, *27*, 1–31.

——(2006c). The associative-cognitive creed. In Vanpatten, B. and Williams, J. (eds), *Theories in Second Language Acquisition: An Introduction.* Mahwah, NJ: Lawrence Erlbaum Associates.

Ellis, N.C. and Sagarra, N. (2010a). Learned attention effects in L2 temporal reference: The first hour and the next eight semesters. *Language Learning*, *60*, Supplement 1.

——(2010b). The bounds of adult language acquisition: Blocking and learned attention *Studies in Second Language Acquisition*, *32*, 1–28.

——(2011). Learned attention in adult language acquisition: A replication and generalization study and meta-analysis. *Studies in Second Language Acquisition*, *33*, 589–624.

Kruschke, J.K. (2006). *Learned Attention.* Fifth International Conference on Development and Learning. Indiana University.

Kruschke, J.K., Kappenman, E.S. and Hetrick, W. P. (2005). Eye gaze and individual differences consistent with learned attention in associative blocking and highlighting. *Journal of Experimental Psychology: Learning, Memory and Cognition, 31*, 830–845.

Mackintosh, N.J. (1975). A theory of attention: Variations in the associability of stimuli with reinforcement. *Psychological Review, 82*, 276–298.

Macwhinney, B. (1987). Applying the competition model to bilingualism. *Applied Psycholinguistics, 8*, 315–327.

Further reading

Kruschke, J.K. (2010). Models of attentional learning. In Pothos, E.M. and Wills, A. (eds), *Models of Learning and Categorization.* Cambridge: Cambridge University Press. (Blocking from a Bayesian learning perspective.)

Schmidt, R. (2001). Attention. In Robinson, P. (ed.), *Cognition and Second Language Instruction.* Cambridge: Cambridge University Press. (An excellent overview chapter on attention in SLA.)

Shanks, D.R. (1995). *The Psychology of Associative Learning.* New York: Cambridge University Press. (The standard text on associative learning.)

Wills, A.J. (2005). *New Directions in Human Associative Learning.* Mahwah, NJ: Erlbaum.

Learning disabilities and second (foreign) language learning

Richard Sparks
College of Mount St. Joseph

Since the 1960s, foreign language educators have described students who struggle with second language (L2) learning (Dinklage, 1971; Pimsleur, Sundland, and McIntyre, 1964). Likewise, since the 1980s special educators in the learning disabilities (LD) field have noted that some students classified as LD who have difficulties with their native language (L1), especially in the areas of reading and writing, may have difficulties with L2 learning (see Gajar, 1987). Though both fields had addressed the issue separately, it was not until Sparks and Ganschow examined relationships between L1 and L2 learning and presented their Linguistic Coding Differences Hypothesis (LCDH) (Sparks, Ganschow, and Pohlman, 1989) that discussions started across the disciplines. Their research has shown that students, LD or otherwise, who have L1 learning problems have difficulty with L2 learning.

First, a brief review of the LD concept is provided. Then, research is reviewed that summarizes findings on: a) LD and L2 learning problems; b) college students with LD and L2 learning; c) problems with the diagnosis of a "disability" for L2 learning; and d) teaching L2s to students with language learning problems.

Review of the LD concept

Students classified as learning disabled (LD) are those who exhibit severe academic difficulties in reading, mathematics, and/or written language (including spelling). However, since the term was introduced in 1963, LD has been the most contentious and contradictory of the disabilities, primarily because of the failure to develop a valid definition for LD and empirically based diagnostic criteria that are used consistently by professionals in the field (Kavale, 1998). Since the late 1970s, LD has been based on the idea that a student's achievement in reading, mathematics, and/or written language measured by scores on standardized tests should be consistent with his/her "potential," or score on a standardized intelligence (IQ) test. This practice is called the discrepancy concept, the idea that a discrepancy between the IQ score and academic achievement scores is evidence of LD. However, research has falsified the use of IQ-achievement discrepancy for identifying LD on theoretical, empirical, and psychometric grounds (see Dombrowski, Kamphaus and Reynolds, 2004). Because of the problems with definition and evidence which shows that discrepancy fails to identify students with learning problems that are different from the learning problems of students without discrepancies, diagnosticians use different methods to classify students as LD. As a result, numerous studies have found that large numbers of students classified as LD fail to meet even minimum criteria for this diagnosis (e.g., see Kavale, 1998; Sparks and Lovett, 2009). The failure to agree on a standard definition and valid diagnostic criteria for LD has threatened the validity and scientific merit of the LD concept (Stanovich, 2005) and confused L2 educators who teach students with L2 learning problems (Sparks, 2009).

Research on LD and L2 learning problems

In the midst of the debates about the definition and diagnostic criteria for LD, increasing numbers of students classified as LD enrolled in high school L2 courses and entered U.S. colleges and universities, where they often were required to enroll in L2 courses. Most special education and L2 teachers assumed that students classified as LD would have difficulty with the demands of a second language. However, their assumptions had not been tested empirically.

In the late 1980s, Sparks and Ganschow speculated that high- and low-achieving L2 learners have strengths and weaknesses that are language-based and that students' levels of L1 skill were related to their level of L2 proficiency and achievement, that is, the LCDH. The LCDH posits that L1 skills are the foundation for L2 learning and that both L1 and L2 skills run along a continuum of very strong to very weak language learners, that is, above average to average to below average (see Sparks, 1995). In the 1990s, they conducted a series of studies with secondary and postsecondary L2 learners which found that high-achieving L2 learners exhibited significantly stronger L1 skills, most often in the phonological and grammatical components of language, and higher L2 aptitude on the Modern Language Aptitude Test (MLAT) than students classified as LD and low-achieving L2 learners. For example, they found that high-achieving L2 learners exhibited scores in the high average to above average range on measures of L1 skill and L2 aptitude, but low-achieving L2 learners and students with LD exhibited low average to below average scores on these measures. In other studies, they found that high-achieving L2 learners who exhibited significantly higher levels of L1 skills and stronger L2 aptitude achieved higher levels of L2 proficiency than students classified as LD and low-achieving L2 learners. But, they also found that students classified as LD and low-achieving L2 learners exhibited similar performance on all L1 skill and L2 aptitude measures (see review by Ganschow and Sparks, 2001). These results supported their speculation that differences in L2 learning are related to differences in students' L1 skills, but also revealed an important new finding: low-achieving (non-LD) L2 learners exhibited cognitive (IQ, L2 aptitude) and achievement (L1 skills) profiles similar to L2 learners classified as LD. Replication studies with larger numbers of high- and low-achieving L2 learners and students classified as LD in L2 courses have supported the aforementioned findings (e.g., see Sparks, Javorsky, and Humbach, 2008). Furthermore, longitudinal studies have revealed long-term relationships between students' L1 skills in elementary school and their L2 aptitude and L2 proficiency many years later in high school (e.g., see Sparks, Patton, Ganschow, and Humbach, 2009).

Research on college students with LD and L2 learning

In the early 1990s, postsecondary institutions in the U.S. began to offer course substitutions for and waivers from the college L2 requirement for students classified as LD. Initially, educators assumed that students classified as LD would exhibit inordinate problems with L2 learning. To determine whether students classified as LD would exhibit difficulties with L2, Sparks and Ganschow conducted a series of studies with postsecondary students classified as LD who had been granted course substitutions for the college L2 requirement. In these studies, they found that most students with LD had previously passed high school L2 courses with average or better grades and that many had passed college L2 courses before being granted a course substitution (e.g. see Sparks, Philips, and Javorsky, 2002). They also found that students classified as LD with and without IQ-achievement discrepancies did not exhibit significant differences in ACT/SAT scores, college L2 GPA, and/or L2 aptitude on the MLAT. In other studies, they found that students classified as LD who received course substitutions did not exhibit significant differences in IQ, L1 skills, ACT/SAT scores, and college GPA when compared to students classified as LD who had fulfilled the college L2 requirement by passing L2 courses, usually with average to above average grades (e.g. see Sparks, Philips, and Javorsky, 2003). Overall, the findings of these studies showed that students classified as LD, including those with IQ-achievement discrepancies: a) do not always exhibit problems with L2 learning; b) do not exhibit more severe L2 learning problems than low-achieving (non-LD) learners; and c) do not exhibit unique or different L1 skill or L2 aptitude profiles than students without IQ-achievement discrepancies. The lack of empirical evidence linking LD to L2 learning problems with secondary and postsecondary students led them to propose that if an institution allows for course substitutions or waivers, all students (not just LD) should be eligible for these accommodations on the basis of predetermined criteria *or* no students should be permitted substitutions or waivers. However, U.S. colleges and universities continue to grant waivers from and course substitutions for the L2 requirement only to students classified as LD.

Problems with the diagnosis of L2 "disability"

When students classified as LD entered postsecondary institutions and enrolled in L2 courses, a new term, "foreign language learning disability," entered the lexicon of special educators. Although growing evidence had undermined the idea of a link between LD and L2 learning, some educators in both the LD and L2 fields suggested that students with LD may have a specific "disability" for L2s. However, Sparks *et al.* had proposed many years earlier that a specific disability for L2 learning could be operationally defined only by arbitrarily choosing a cutoff score along a continuous distribution of very strong to very weak L2 learners (Sparks, Ganschow, and Javorsky, 1993: 506). More recently, Sparks (2006) proposed that there is not a unique disability for L2 learning and critiqued four methods – IQ-achievement discrepancy, withdrawal from or poor achievement in L2 courses, discrepancy between IQ and L2 aptitude scores, low score on an L2 aptitude test – that were being used by educators to classify students with this hypothetical disability and then reviewed evidence that undermined each method. First, evidence had shown that IQ-achievement discrepancy does not identify a unique group of learners with more severe L2 learning problems nor does one's IQ score accurately predict achievement or proficiency in a L2. Second, poor achievement in L2 courses does not identify a group of students with unique L2 learning problems because students classified as LD (and those without LD) generally achieve average or better grades in L2 courses, withdraw from L2 courses with passing grades, or receive substitutions or waivers after passing L2 courses with average or better grades. Third, comparing a student's IQ to his/her L2 aptitude score requires using an aptitude-aptitude, not aptitude-achievement, comparison because L2 aptitude tests do not measure L2 achievement. Moreover, empirical research does not show that students with IQ-L2 aptitude discrepancies cannot pass L2 courses or achieve a passing level of L2 proficiency. Fourth, use of a low L2 aptitude score alone to diagnose a L2 disability is incongruent with standards teaching diagnosticians not to use a single test score for diagnostic purposes. Also, using an L2 aptitude test to diagnose a disability is inappropriate because these tests were not designed for this purpose and the norms for L2 aptitude tests, for example, MLAT, Pimsleur Language Aptitude Battery, are very outdated.

Teaching L2s to students with language learning problems

Despite evidence that failed to show a link between LD and L2 learning problems, there are students who have overt or subtle difficulties with L2 learning. Unfortunately, there is limited empirical research available on effective methodologies for teaching L2s to students who have problems with L1 learning and corresponding L2 learning difficulties. Researchers who have recommended specific approaches, for example, teaching to learning styles, use of language learning strategies, use of affective strategies to reduce anxiety or increase motivation, have not generated empirical evidence showing that these approaches lead to improvements in L2 achievement with low-achieving students. Because research has demonstrated strong relationships between L1 and L2 learning, Sparks (2009) has recommended that L2 teachers focus on teaching the language skills necessary for learning the L2, not a diagnosis of LD. He and his colleagues have suggested that instruction for low-achieving L2 learners and students classified as LD can best be provided by directly and systematically teaching domain-specific, that is, language, skills in the L2 (e.g., see Sparks, Ganshcow, Kenneweg, and Miller, 1991). Some studies have shown that direct instruction in the phonology and grammar of the new language is effective in teaching L2s to low-achieving and LD learners in L2 classes (e.g., see Demuth and Smith, 1987; Downey and Snyder, 2001). Empirical studies using this approach have shown that low-achieving L2 learners and students with LD in high school L2 courses have: a) significantly increased their L1 skills and L2 aptitude scores over 1–2 years of L2 instruction; b) improved their achievement in L2 classes; and c) achieved levels of oral and written L2 proficiency similar to average- and high-achieving L2 learners after two years of L2 instruction (see Sparks, Artzer, Patton, *et al.*, 1998).

In sum, research has not revealed a direct link between LD and problems with L2 learning or that there is a unique disability for L2 learning. Instead, students with language learning difficulties in L1, LD or otherwise, have been found to have difficulties with L2 learning. Some studies have shown that direct instruction in language skills is beneficial for increasing the proficiency of students with L2 learning problems.

See also: cross-linguistic influence (CLI), individual differences in SLA, language testing and SLA, Linguistic Coding Differences Hypothesis (LCDH), linguistic transfer

References

DeMuth, K. and Smith, N. (1987). The foreign language requirement: An alternative program. *Foreign Language Annals*, *20*, 67–77.

Dinklage, K. (1971). Inability to learn a foreign language. In Blaine, G. and McArthur, C. (eds), *Emotional problems of the student*, pp. 185–206. New York: Appleton-Century.

Dombrowski, S.C., Kamphaus, R.W. and Reynolds, C.R. (2004). After the demise of the discrepancy: Proposed learning disabilities diagnostic criteria. *Professional Psychology: Research and Practice, 35*, 364–372.

Downey, D. and Snyder, L. (2001). Curricular accommodations for college students with language learning disabilities. *Topics in Language Disorders*, *21*, 55–67.

Gajar, A. 1987 Foreign language learning disabilities: The identification of predictive and diagnostic variables. *Journal of Learning Disabilities*, *20*, 327–330.

Ganschow, L. and Sparks, R., (2001). Learning difficulties and foreign language learning: a review of research and instruction. *Language Teaching*, *34* (2), pp. 79–98.

Kavale, K. (1998). The politics of learning disabilities. *Learning Disability Quarterly*, *21*, 245–273.

Pimsleur, P. Sundland, D., and McIntyre, R. (1964). Underachievement in foreign language learning. *International Review of Applied Linguistics*, *2*, 113–150.

Sparks, R. (1995). Examining the linguistic coding differences hypothesis to explain individual differences in foreign language learning. *Annals of Dyslexia*, *45*, 187–214.

——(2006). Is there a 'disability' for learning a foreign language? *Journal of Learning Disabilities*, *39* (6), 544–557.

——(2009). If you don't know where you're going, you'll wind up somewhere else: The case of "foreign language learning disability." *Foreign Language Annals*, *42*, 7–26.

Sparks, R., Artzer, M., Patton, J., Ganschow, L., Miller, K., Hordubay, D. and Walsh, G. (1998). Benefits of multisensory language instruction for at-risk learners: A comparison study of high school Spanish students. *Annals of Dyslexia, 48*, 239–270.

Sparks, R., Ganschow, L. and Javorsky, J. (1993). Perceptions of high and low-risk students and students with learning disabilities about high school foreign language courses. *Foreign Language Annals, 26*, 491–510.

Sparks, R., Ganschow, L., Kenneweg, S. and Miller, R. (1991). Use of an Orton-Gillingham approach to teach a foreign language to dyslexic/learning disabled students: Explicit teaching of phonology in a second language. *Annals of Dyslexia, 41*, 96–118.

Sparks, R., Ganschow, L. and Pohlman, J. (1989). Linguistic coding deficits in foreign language learners. *Annals of Dyslexia, 39*, 79–97.

Sparks, R., Javorsky, J. and Humbach, N. (2008). Individual and longitudinal differences among high and low-achieving LD and ADHD L2 learners. *Learning and Individual Differences, 18*, 29–43.

Sparks, R. and Lovett, B. (2009). Objective criteria for classification of postsecondary students with LD: Effects on prevalence rates and group characteristics. *Journal of Learning Disabilities, 42*, 230–239.

Sparks, R., Patton, J., Ganschow, L. and Humbach, N. (2009). Long-term cross-linguistic transfer from L1 to L2. *Language Learning, 59*, 203–243.

Sparks, R., Philips, L. and Javorsky, J. (2002). Students classified as LD who received course substitutions for the foreign language requirement: A replication study. *Journal of Learning Disabilities, 35*, 482–499, 538.

Sparks, R., Philips, L. and Javorsky J. (2003). Students classified as LD who petitioned for or fulfilled the college foreign language requirement – Are they different?: A replication study. *Journal of Learning Disabilities, 36*, 348–362.

Stanovich, K.E. (2005). The future of a mistake: Will discrepancy measurement continue to make the learning disabilities field a pseudoscience? *Learning Disability Quarterly, 28*, 103–106.

Further reading

Fletcher, J., Lyon, R., Fuchs, L. and Barnes, M. (2007). *Learning disabilities: From identification to intervention*. New York: Guilford. (Book reviews the history of the LD field and presents up-to-date research on identification and treatment of learning disabilities in reading, written language, and mathematics.)

Nijakowska, J. (2010). *Dyslexia in the foreign language classroom*. Bristol: Multilingual Matters. (Book reviews the concept of severe reading disability, i.e., dyslexia. Chapter 3 reviews evidence that students with L1 learning problems also have L2 learning difficulties. Chapter 5 reviews treatment and teaching strategies for students with language learning problems in L2.)

Sparks, R. (2001). Foreign language learning problems of students classified as learning disabled and non-learning disabled: Is there a difference? *Topics in Language Disorders, 21*, 38–54. (Paper reviews evidence and explains that students classified as LD and low-achieving students without LD have similar cognitive and achievement profiles and do not differ in L2 outcomes.)

Sparks, R., Ganschow, L. and Javorsky, J. (1995). I know one when I see one (or I know one because I am one): A response to Mabbott. *Foreign Language Annals, 28*, 479–487, *and*

Sparks, R., Javorsky, J. and Ganschow, L. (1995). Satiating the appetite of the sociologic sponge: A rejoinder to Mabbott. *Foreign Language Annals, 28*, 495–498. (Papers appeared in the same issue of the journal. The first paper explains the importance of using objective diagnostic criteria in classifying students as LD to reduce the heterogeneity in research samples because such samples provide limited generalizability about the difficulties students with L1 learning problems have in learning a L2. The second paper contends that researchers who claim that their research participants have LD must substantiate the diagnoses with objective evidence that the participants meet the definition and diagnostic criteria for LD.)

Sparks, R., Patton, J., Ganschow, L. and Humbach, N. (2009). Long-term relationships among early L1 skills, L2 aptitude, L2 affect, and later L2 proficiency. *Applied Psycholinguistics, 30*, 725–755. (Paper presents the results of a longitudinal study that followed students over 10 years from first–tenth grades when they were completing the second year of L2 study in high school. The findings revealed strong relationships between early L1 skills in elementary school and later L2 aptitude and L2 proficiency in high school, and raised the possibility of long-term, cross-linguistic transfer of L1 skills to L2 learning.)

Learning strategies

Rebecca L. Oxford
Air Force Culture and Language Center and University of Maryland

Second or foreign language (L2) learning strategies are steps the learner consciously takes to reach a learning goal. These strategies (a) involve consciousness (aspects such as awareness, attention, intention, and effort); (b) make learning more efficient and more effective; (c) are frequently manifested through specific tactics for particular tasks and contexts; (d) reflect cognitive, affective, and sociocultural-interactive dimensions of learning; (e) are guided by metastrategies, such as planning, organizing, evaluating, and monitoring; and (f) can be transferred to other tasks as needed (Oxford, 2011). Below I discuss learning strategies in relation to (a) autonomy, (b) self-regulation, (c) the good language learner, (d) typologies, and (e) instruction and assessment.

Strategies and autonomy

Learner autonomy combines (a) belief in the need to take responsibility for learning; (b) ability and willingness to do so; and (c) responsible action in the form of strategies. Holec (1981) stated that L2 learners in self-access centers can make all learning-related decisions, but it is questionable whether ordinary educational settings encourage total autonomy. Though cultural values strongly affect strategy choice and autonomy-related beliefs, Littlewood (1999) incorrectly and prejudicially assumed that Asians are only "reactively autonomous" while Westerners are "proactively autonomous." Holliday (2003) promoted a balanced "social autonomy" approach, which (a) assumes some form of autonomy in students' diverse sociocultural contexts and (b) encourages teachers to learn from students' existing autonomous learning strategies while sharing new learning strategies with students.

Strategies and self-regulation

Self-regulation as a concept arose from Vygotsky's (1978) work on higher psychological processes (similar to strategies), for example, analyzing, synthesizing, planning, monitoring, and evaluating. Learners internalize and automatize these processes through social mediation. Self-regulation strategies can include setting goals; paying attention; organizing, coding, and rehearsing information; establishing a productive setting; using resources effectively; managing time; monitoring performance; seeking help; and managing emotions and attitude (Schunk and Ertmer, 2000). Using different terminology, Rubin (2001) similarly emphasized metacognition in learner self-management (LTM).

The good language learner

Rubin (1975) and others sought to identify the features and strategies of "the good language learner" (GLL). While honoring the pioneering effort to describe "the GLL," Griffiths (2008) and others concluded that many different types of L2 learners are effective, so no singular GLL prototype exists. Even so, some very general features can be identified. Successful L2 learners are highly motivated and use learning strategies relevant to their goals (Oxford, 1990). Key factors in very advanced L2 learning are motivation, use of metacognitive and cognitive strategies, and precise error correction (Leaver, 2003). Oxford (2011) summarized numerous studies in which the relationship between assessed proficiency and reported strategy use was statistically significant, though not all studies show this pattern.

Definitions and typologies of L2 learning strategies

O'Neil (1978) emphasized *cognitive strategies* (for information-processing and schema development), *metacognitive strategies* (for executive management of learning), and *affective strategies* (for managing emotions and motivation). O'Malley and Chamot's 1990 typology of L2 learning strategies consisted of (a) cognitive, (b) metacognitive, and (c) socioaffective strategies. Oxford's 1990 typology was broader, including six categories and a stronger emphasis on affective and social strategies.

Problems have existed about conflicting or vague strategy definitions, different strategy "sizes" and numbers, and lack of identification of tactics. Oxford's (2011) new strategy system addressed many of these problems and included both strategies and metastrategies for cognitive, affective, and sociocultural-interactive dimensions.

Strategy instruction and assessment

Strategy instruction should be based on learners' goals and needs. It is often most effective when integrated into regular language instruction, though non-integration sometimes works. O'Malley and Chamot (1990), Oxford (1990), Wenden (1991), Grenfell and Harris (1999), Macaro (2001), and Cohen and Weaver (2006) offered systematic strategy instruction guidance. Chamot and O'Malley (1994) created the CALLA model, which successfully increased strategy use, proficiency, content knowledge, and self-efficacy in various studies. Oxford (2011) described "strategy assistance," consisting of teacher-led strategy instruction, learner counseling (Rubin, 2007), learner guidebooks, strategy guidance in L2 textbooks, and many other strategy aids. Optimal strategy instruction requires reliable and valid strategy assessment. Oxford (2011), Cohen (2011), and Macaro (2001) have discussed and critiqued numerous strategy assessment techniques.

See also: attitudes to the L2, awareness, individual differences and SLA, instructed SLA, monitoring, motivation

References

Chamot, A.U. and J.M. O'Malley. (1994). *The CALLA Handbook: Implementing the Cognitive Academic Language Learning Approach.* Reading, MA: Addison-Wesley.

Cohen, A.D. (2011). *Strategies in Learning and Using a Second Language*, 2nd edn. Harlow: Longman.

Cohen, A.D. and S.J. Weaver. (2006). *Styles and Strategies-based Instruction: A Teachers' Guide.* Minneapolis, MN: National Language Resource Center, University of Minnesota.

Grenfell, M. and V. Harris. (1999). *Modern Languages and Learning Strategies in Theory and Practice.* London: Routledge.

Griffiths, C. (ed.) (2008). *Lessons from Good Language Learners.* Cambridge: Cambridge University Press.

Holec, H. (1981). *Autonomy and Foreign Language Learning.* Oxford: Pergamon.

Holliday, A. (2003). Social autonomy: Addressing the dangers of culturism in TESOL. In D. Palfreyman and R.C. Smith (eds), *Learner Autonomy across Cultures: Language Education Perspectives*, pp. 110–28. London: Palgrave Macmillan.

Leaver, B.L. (2003). *Achieving Native-like Second Language Proficiency: A Catalogue of Critical Factors. Vol. 1: Speaking.* Salinas, CA: MSI Press.

Littlewood, W. (1999). Defining and developing autonomy in East Asian contexts. *Applied Linguistics, 20*(1), 71–94.

Macaro, E. (2001). *Strategies in Foreign and Second Language Classrooms: Learning to Learn.* London: Continuum.

O'Malley, J.M. and A.U. Chamot. (1990). *Learning Strategies in Second Language Acquisition.* Cambridge: Cambridge University Press.

O'Neil, H.F. (ed.) (1978). *Learning Strategies.* New York: Academic Press.

Oxford, R.L. (1990). *Language Learning Strategies: What Every Teacher Should Know.* Boston, MA: Heinle and Heinle.

——(2011). *Teaching and Researching Language Learning Strategies.* Harlow: Pearson Longman.

Rubin, J. (1975). What the "good language learner" can teach us. *TESOL Quarterly, 9,* 41–51.

——(2001). Language learner self-management. *Journal of Asian Pacific Communications, 11*, 25–37.

——(ed.) (2007). Learner counseling. Special issue. *System: An International Journal of Educational Technology and Applied Linguistics*, 35(1), Mar.

Schunk, D.H. and Ertmer, P.A. (2000). Self-regulation and academic learning: Self-efficacy enhancing interventions. In M. Boeakerts, P.R. Pintrich, and M. Zeidner (eds), *Handbook of Self-regulation*, pp. 631–50. San Diego, CA: Academic Press.

Vygotsky, L. (1978). *Mind in Society: Development of Higher Psychological Processes*. Cambridge, MA: Harvard University Press.

Wenden, A.L. (1991). *Learner Strategies for Learner Autonomy: Planning and Implementing Learner Training for Language Learners*. Englewood Cliffs, NJ: Prentice Hall.

Further reading

Chamot, A.U. (2007). Accelerating academic achievement of English language learners: A synthesis of five evaluations of the CALLA Model. In J. Cummins and C. Davison (eds), *The International Handbook of English Language Learning*, Part I, pp. 317–31. Norwell, MA: Springer. (This article reveals the successes of the CALLA model in school-based studies.)

Cohen, A.D. and Macaro, E. (2007). *Language Learner Strategies: Thirty Years of Research and Practice*. Oxford: Oxford University Press. This landmark book synthesizes research and theory on learning strategies.

Griffiths, C. (ed.) (2008). *Lessons from Good Language Learners*. Cambridge: Cambridge University Press. (Strategies are one of the key themes of this important volume.)

Macaro, E. (2001). *Strategies in Foreign and Second Language Classrooms: Learning to Learn*. London: Continuum. (This highly practical book is very useful regarding strategy instruction.)

Oxford, R.L. (2011). *Teaching and Researching Language Learning Strategies*. Harlow: Pearson Longman. (This book rethinks and expands strategy theory and presents new tools for strategy assistance and assessment.)

Levelt's model of speech production and comprehension

Nel de Jong
Free University Amsterdam

Levelt's model of speech production was described in detail in his 1989 book *Speaking: From intention to articulation*, and updated in a 1999 book chapter. Drawing on a wide range of studies and theories of language knowledge and processing, the model is a blueprint of the speaker that consists of several components from message generation to articulation. For each component it is described what input it takes, what algorithms it involves, and what output it generates. The model is a description of the processes involved in speaking a first language. It is assumed that the process of comprehension is the reverse. The original model does not address second languages, but two adaptations of the model do (see below).

The original model consisted of three main processing components—the Conceptualizer, the Formulator, and the Articulator—and two knowledge stores—Long-Term Memory (the speaker's knowledge of the world and himself) and the Lexicon (lemmas and forms). First, the Conceptualizer engages in macroplanning and microplanning, and produces as output a preverbal message that expresses the communicative intention of the speaker. Macroplanning selects information for expression, and microplanning provides the message with an information structure. Next, the Formulator uses the preverbal message to generate a surface structure. The Formulator consists of a grammatical encoder and a phonological encoder. The grammatical encoder projects the concepts and relations from the preverbal message onto a phrase-structural organization of lemmas and grammatical relations. To do so, it uses the lemmas from the mental lexicon, which contain the meaning, syntactic, morphological, and phonological properties of the words. Grammatical encoding therefore is lexically driven. The next stage within the Formulator is phonological encoding, which takes surface structure as input and generates a phonetic plan, which in turn contains phonetic and prosodic information at different levels, such as phonetic features, syllable structure, syllable stress, and intonation. Finally, the Articulator uses the phonetic plan for motor execution. The phonetic plan is temporarily stored in the Articulatory Buffer until it is articulated. Syllables are assumed to be the basic units of articulatory execution and it is likely that the phonetic plans of syllables are stored. Syllables are organized in such a way that co-articulation is facilitated, even at high speeds, for instance by requiring adjacent segments to be compatible ([sp] is compatible, whereas [pb] is not).

At every point where output is generated, there can be monitoring of what is said or how it is said. Although it is possible to monitor almost any aspect of speech, this cannot happen simultaneously because attention is selective and fluctuating. Speakers may self-interrupt in different ways for different errors, varying what and how much is edited, and if and how editing is signaled. Theories differ in whether they claim monitoring takes place within or outside of the language-production system.

The model has a number of important characteristics. First, its modularity, in that each component only works on its characteristic input and generates a specific type of output that serves as input for the next component. The only possible feedback is from phonological encoding to grammatical encoding, both within the Formulator. Second, processing in the model takes place incrementally: processing in different components can occur in parallel, with minimal fragments of output from one component being sufficient to trigger processing in the next component. Finally, for processing to occur in parallel, it needs to be automatic. In native speakers, algorithms in the Formulator are automatic. Other processes, like conceptualization and monitoring, require attention and therefore require serial processing.

The original model was updated by Levelt (1999). The basic framework is maintained but the model is now partitioned into two systems: the rhetorical/semantic/syntactic system consisting of conceptual preparation and grammatical encoding, and the phonological/phonetic system consisting of morpho-phonological encoding, phonetic encoding, and articulation. There are three knowledge sources: knowledge of the external and internal world, the mental lexicon, and the syllabary. These differences reflect a shift in emphasis from a linguistic to a developmental and processing perspective, and are based on new theoretical insights. Additional publications have further elaborated the model. Levelt, Roelofs, and Meyer (1999), for example, incorporated progress in research on lemma access in a theory and computational model, WEAVER++.

Applications of the model in second language acquisition theories

Even though Levelt's model was of native speakers only, it has been frequently applied in second language hypotheses and research findings. The Output Hypothesis, for instance, was related to the model by De Bot (1996). He explains how monitoring of internal and external speech plays a role in hypothesis testing. It can help the speaker to notice a mismatch between the preverbal message and the phonetic plan (the outcome of the Formulator), as when a second language speaker initially selects a related but inappropriate word. Either a different form needs to be retrieved or the preverbal message needs to be revised. In addition, learning takes place with proceduralization and automatization, as when connections between lemmas and procedures are repeatedly made and strengthened.

A line of SLA research in which the Levelt model features prominently is the study of task demands. Skehan (2009) reviewed findings on task demands (such as type of planning, complexity of information and cognitive operations, and the monologic/dialogic nature of the task) and explained differences in complexity, accuracy, and fluency in relation to the Levelt model. He identified a number of task characteristics that may complexify or pressure task performance on the one hand, or ease and focus on the other hand. Each of these characteristics was discussed in relation to the model's stages. For example, more complex cognitive operations have a complexifying influence on the Conceptualizer and are therefore likely to elicit more complex language.

Time pressure puts pressure on syntactic encoding in the Formulator and will thus be linked to lower fluency and accuracy. On the other hand, pre-task planning may help to organize ideas and thus have an easing influence on lemma retrieval in the Formulator: by priming lexical items this way, their retrieval is smoothed.

Skehan (2009) points out a limitation of the model in its applicability to second language speakers. The model was developed to explain first language speakers' performance, whose processing is mostly modular and parallel (e.g., the Formulator might be processing one part of an utterance, while the Conceptualizer is already processing a subsequent part). However, differences in the mental lexicon of second language speakers—in size, elaborateness, and organization—can necessitate a shift down from parallel processing to serial processing, which has consequences for the complexity, accuracy, and fluency of the speech produced. For example, a preverbal message that requires lexical items that are difficult to access or even absent may disrupt subsequent processing in the Formulator leading to break-down, repair, or replacements. As proficiency increases, second language speakers' performance will gradually approximate that of native speakers. One attempt to explain second language speakers' development of fluency with the Levelt model was by Towell, Hawkins, and Bazergui (1996), who argued that proceduralization of linguistic knowledge affected syntactic processing in the Formulator.

Adaptations of the model to bilingualism and second language acquisition

Levelt does not specifically address second language speakers, but he does indicate at several points how processing may be affected by differences between languages. For example, he points out that conceptualizing is not language independent, because it generates only those concepts for which there are words in the language, and it takes into account the information that is obligatorily expressed in one language but not another, such as tense.

The model was first explicitly adapted for bilingual speakers by de Bot (1992). He only made changes to the original model where necessary, for example to explain code switching or lexical retrieval. While macroplanning in the Conceptualizer can be the same for different languages, microplanning needs to be language-specific because different languages encode information differently like tense and aspect. The Formulator needs separate processing components for each language, while lexical items are all stored and connected in one common mental lexicon. This requires that each part of the preverbal message contains information of what language is to be used. There is probably only one Articulator that works with an extensive set of sounds and pitch patterns for the different languages.

Later, Kormos (2006) adapted the 1999 model for second language learners. Generally, the basic processes are the same for first and advanced second language speakers, and the knowledge stores contain information (concepts, lemmas, lexemes, and syllable programs) from both the first and second language. The major difference lies in the addition of a knowledge store that contains declarative information of syntactic and phonological rules in the L2. In addition, transfer, code-switching, and communication strategies are explained in the L2 model, as well as language acquisition and the encoding of formulaic sequences.

Differences between L1 and L2 speech production include influence of the L1, the speed with which utterances are produced, and incomplete knowledge. When knowledge of the L2 is incomplete, learners need to resort to communication strategies like substitution, modification of the preverbal message, or stalling. In addition, monitoring is different in a L2 because it requires attention, of which less is available because L2 speech processing in general requires more attention than L1 processing. Therefore, L2 speakers will need to prioritize, for example opting for content over form, and lexis over grammar.

Kormos identifies three important aspects that help close the gap between L1 and L2 speakers: the acquisition of declarative knowledge, the development of automaticity, and the memorization of larger production units. First, the acquisition of declarative knowledge concerns vocabulary as well as grammatical, morphological, and phonological rules. The acquisition of a larger number of vocabulary items avoids the need for modifications and substitution strategies. It takes places when memory traces are formed for word forms and their associated characteristics (e.g., semantic, syntactic, phonological, pragmatic). Declarative rule knowledge helps to compensate for procedural knowledge that is lacking or cannot be automatically applied, and involves the creation of new memory traces in the declarative knowledge store. Next, declarative knowledge can be proceduralized and automatized, thus facilitating parallel processing. Finally, the creation of larger production units facilitates processing because strongly connected lemmas can be retrieved as a unit. These units are formed when there is chunking and strengthening of links between items in the Conceptualizer and the lexicon. For example, a learner may establish a concept of requesting, and subsequently associate it with lemmas that are strongly connected: when making a request, the speaker can retrieve the formulaic sequence "Would you mind ... ?" as one unit.

In summary, Levelt's model of speech production is a blueprint of the monolingual speaker that consists of several components, including conceptualization, grammatical and phonological encoding, and articulation. It is assumed that the process of comprehension is the reverse of production. The components make use of knowledge sources such as knowledge of the external and internal world, the mental lexicon, and the syllabary. The model has a modular structure and it involves incremental as well as parallel processing. It has been applied in second language acquisition research to topics like task demands and monitoring. Adaptations have been proposed to account for the situation of the second language speaker, such as separate processing components for different languages, and an additional knowledge source containing declarative information of syntactic and phonological rules.

See also: fluency, grammatical encoding, lexical access and selection, monitoring, psycholinguistics of SLA, speaking

References

De Bot, K. (1992). A bilingual production model: Levelt's 'speaking' model adapted. *Applied Linguistics*, *13*, 1–24.

——(1996). The psycholinguistics of the Output Hypothesis. *Language Learning*, *46*, 529–55.

Kormos, J. (2006). *Speech Production and Second Language Acquisition*. Mahwah, NJ: Lawrence Erlbaum.

Levelt, W.J.M. (1989). *Speaking: From Intention to Articulation*. Cambridge, MA: MIT Press.

——(1999). Producing spoken language: A blueprint of the speaker. In C. Brown and P. Hagoort (eds), *The Neurocognition of Language*, pp. 83–122. New York: Oxford Press.

Levelt, W.J.M., Roelofs, A. and Meyer, A.S. (1999). A theory of lexical access in speech production. *Behavioral and Brain Sciences*, *22*, 1–38.

Skehan, P. (2009). Modelling second language performance: Integrating complexity, accuracy, fluency, and lexis. *Applied Linguistics*, *30*, 510–32.

Towell, R., Hawkins, R. and Bazergui, N. (1996). The development of fluency in advanced learners of French. *Applied Linguistics*, *17*, 84–119.

Lexical access and selection in bilingual language production

Albert Costa, Jasmin Sadat and Clara Martin

Universitat Pompeu Fabra, Institució Catalana de Recerca i Estudis Avançats (ICREA) and Laboratoire de Psychologie Cognitive, CNRS and Université de Provence

Bilingual speakers have the remarkable ability to speak alternatively two different languages with rare involuntary intrusions from the disregarded language to the language in use (see Poulisse and Bongaerts, 1994). During language production, bilinguals do not only have to select the appropriate words to convey information as monolinguals do, but they also have to guarantee that those words belong to the intended language. The extra cognitive process that bilinguals need to put at play during language production is referred to as language control. This language control ability is even more remarkable considering the speed and reliability with which speakers produce language (about 4 words per second, with less than 1 error per 1000 words produced). In the following, we will describe why and how bilingual speakers need language control for lexical access and selection during language production. Then, we will turn to the consequences of mastering two languages, in the linguistic but also in the non-linguistic domain. Finally, we will briefly describe some current limitations of our knowledge on the consequences of being a bilingual in more complex speech production contexts.

How are lexical access and selection controlled in the bilingual brain?

Each time a speaker produces a word, at least three different levels of representations are involved (e.g., Caramazza, 1997; Dell, 1986; Levelt, 1989): production of a word implies the retrieval of semantic, lexical, and phonological information associated to the word. One key assumption concerning the dynamics in the language production system is spreading activation (Collins and Loftus, 1975): when a speaker intends to produce a word (e.g., "apple"), the semantic information related to the intended concept is activated (e.g., concept of apple), but semantic related information is also activated (e.g., concept of pear, orange, etc.). According to most speech production models, the semantic related information which is activated spreads proportional activation to the corresponding lexical and phonological representations.

In the current section, we will focus on two core components of language production: lexical access and selection. Lexical access refers to the retrieval of the appropriate lexical and phonological representations of a given concept. As several lexical representations are activated during lexical access, selection mechanisms are needed to select the appropriate one. This process is called lexical selection: the lexical representation with the highest activation level will be selected among all activated representations. The selection process is more difficult when lexical competitors are highly activated, which results in longer naming latencies and/or spontaneous speech errors.

This system of lexical access and selection becomes especially intriguing in the bilingual brain as bilingual speakers have two different lexical representations (translation words) corresponding to each concept. The main question is then to know how lexical access and selection operate when two lexical and phonological representations are associated to the concept a bilingual speaker wants to express. The most straightforward hypothesis would be to assume that the disregarded language is completely shut down while speaking in the "active" language. This would put bilingual speakers in the same conditions as monolinguals each time they intend to speak in one of their two languages. This hypothesis is unlikely as several experiments showed that lexical and phonological representations of the disregarded language are activated while speaking in the active language (for a review see Costa, 2005). Evidence for this assumption comes for example from studies using cognate words. Cognates are translation words with high phonological overlap across the two languages of a bilingual (e.g., tomato – tomate [in Spanish]). Several studies have shown that cognate words are produced faster in comparison to noncognate words (i.e., apple – manzana [in Spanish]; e.g., Costa, Caramazza, and Sebastián-Gallés, 2000). These findings suggest that during bilingual word production, lexical and phonological representations of the intended and unintended languages become activated. Lexical items of the two languages spread activation to their phonological representations, thereby boosting the processing of phonologically overlapping translations. Assuming this permanent co-activation of both languages, the language production system of a bilingual speaker has to benefit from some sort of control to select the lexical representation of the intended language.

Two different accounts can explain how bilingual speakers avoid interference from the disregarded language while speaking in the other language: according to the Inhibitory Control Model (Green, 1998), lexical selection is language non-specific, meaning that activated representations in the disregarded language would compete with representations from the target language. In order to achieve successful language production, an overall suppression of representations from the disregarded language would be applied, ensuring selection of the lexical representation in the target language. The alternative account assumes a language-specific selection mechanism (e.g., Costa and Caramazza, 1999). According to this account, lexical selection would be a priori restricted to lexical representations from the target language. Lexical representations in the disregarded language would be ignored and not enter into competition.

Language proficiency seems to be the key factor influencing bilingual language control mechanisms. Language control mechanisms put at play during speech production are functionally different between high- and low-proficient bilinguals (Costa and Santesteban, 2004): low proficient bilinguals seem to largely rely on the active suppression of their native language when speaking in their second language (language non-specific selection mechanism). On the contrary, high proficient bilinguals would automatically select their language output without experiencing much interference from the unintended language (language-specific selection mechanism).

We know that being a bilingual involves having specific language control mechanisms to avoid interferences between the two languages during speech production. In the next section, we will give an insight on the consequences of this specific control mechanism implemented in the bilingual brain, at the linguistic and non-linguistic levels.

Consequences of mastering two languages

Although being able to speak two languages has obvious advantages, bilinguals incur some linguistic disadvantages in their two languages, meaning in the non-dominant (L2) but also the dominant language (L1). First of all, speaking in a L2 is overall slower and less accurate than in a L1 as observed in picture naming experiments (for a review see Hanulová, Davidson, and Indefrey, 2011). This L2 naming disadvantage has been observed in many different languages and across different age groups (e.g., Gollan, Montoya, Cera, and Sandoval, 2008). Note that this disadvantage is observed even in bilinguals who are highly proficient in L2 and acquired their L2 early in life (Ivanova and Costa, 2008).

Strikingly, the bilingual disadvantage in picture naming is not only observed when bilinguals have to produce speech in their L2, but also when they speak in their first and dominant language (Ivanova and Costa, 2008). This means that mastering two languages leads to a disadvantage in word production, whatever the proficiency and the language in use.

Apart from picture naming, the bilingual disadvantage has been observed in various language production tasks: bilinguals experience more Tip-of-the-Tongue states than monolinguals (i.e., feeling of knowing an infrequent object's name, but being unable to retrieve it immediately; e.g., Gollan and Silverberg, 2001). When participants have to generate as many exemplars of a given semantic category (e.g., animals), bilinguals have slower first response times and retrieve less category members than monolinguals (e.g., Rosselli and Ardila, 2002). Importantly, when having to classify picture names into categories, monolingual and bilingual speakers perform equally (Gollan, Montoya, Fennema-Notestine, and Morris, 2005). This suggests that the bilingual disadvantage does not originate at the semantic level, but rather at a post-semantic stage, during lexicalisation. Up to now, it is unclear at which post-semantic stage the naming disadvantage occurs. Based on neurophysiological data, some authors propose that the bilingual naming disadvantage originates at a very late post-lexical level during speech production (Indefrey, 2006) while others suggest that it originates at the lexical level (Strijkers, Costa, and Thierry, 2010).

The bilingual disadvantage in language production might be theoretically explained in two ways: it might stem from the fact that bilinguals have to constantly control two languages, and thus be explained in terms of executive control. Given that bilinguals can produce speech in two different languages, their disadvantage can also be explained on a linguistic basis.

According to the executive control account, the bilingual disadvantage is the consequence of applying language control mechanisms during speech production (Green, 1998). Since lexical representations of the two languages are co-activated during lexical access, bilinguals are constantly exposed to potential competition between translations. To avoid interference between languages, bilinguals have to apply some sort of language control. This additional processing would slow down lexical access and selection in bilinguals compared to monolinguals.

The alternative but not mutually exclusive explanation assumes that the bilingual disadvantage is a frequency effect in disguise (linguistic account; Gollan *et al.*, 2008). That is, bilinguals use each of their two languages less frequently than monolinguals use their unique language. Therefore, frequency of use of the bilingual's lexical representations should be lower than those of the monolingual's. Given that word frequency negatively correlates with the speed of lexical retrieval (Oldfield and Wingfield, 1965), bilinguals would show a disadvantage in lexical access relative to monolinguals.

It is important to note that although bilinguals suffer certain linguistic disadvantages, it has been known for a few years that using two languages has positive collateral effects for the development of various cognitive abilities besides language. The general argument is that recruiting executive control processes every time bilinguals produce language (language control mechanisms) results in more efficient development of these processes relative to monolinguals. As a consequence, bilinguals might benefit from better general executive control, even in the non-linguistic domain. This prediction has been confirmed by several studies comparing the performance of bilinguals and monolinguals at different stages of development in non-linguistic tasks requiring executive control. It has been demonstrated that bilingualism enhances executive control abilities such as conflict resolution, monitoring or task switching (see publications on collateral effects of bilingualism; e.g., Costa, Hernandez, and Sebastián-Gallés, 2008).

Bilingualism effects beyond single word production

Up to now, most of the studies comparing linguistic performance of mono- and bilingual speakers have explored simplified experimental contexts, in which single word retrieval is required (e.g., picture naming and verbal fluency tasks). We do not know whether the bilingual disadvantage is also present in contexts where multiword utterances or sentences have to be produced. For example, in order to produce a simple noun phrase in English (i.e., "the red car"), the speaker not only needs to retrieve the two lexical items corresponding to the object (car) and the property (red), but also the grammatical and syntactic rules of the language in use (correct determiner, order of the words, etc.). At present we still do not know whether and how these additional processes (e.g., grammatical and syntactic encoding) modulate the bilingual disadvantage in speech production. If it turns out that the bilingual disadvantage is minimized in more complex utterances, the consequences of this disadvantage for the regular use of language might be negligible. By contrast, if such disadvantages are maximized in multiword utterances, then consequences of bilingualism for speech performance could be even more important than previously thought. Future studies will have to describe in full detail the mechanisms that are sensitive to bilingualism in complex linguistic contexts.

See also: bilingualism and SLA, executive control and frontal cortex, frequency effects, inhibitory control, lexical concepts, Levelt's model of speech production and comprehension

References

Caramazza, A. (1997). How many levels of processing are there in lexical access? *Cognitive Neuropsychology*, *14*(1), 177–208.

Collins, A.M. and Loftus, E.F. (1975). A spreading-activation theory of semantic processing. *Psychological Review*, *82*(6), 407–28.

Costa, A. (2005). Lexical access in bilingual production. In Kroll, J.F. and De Groot, A.M.B. (eds), *Handbook of Bilingualism: Psycholinguistic Approaches*. New York: Oxford University Press.

Costa, A. and Caramazza, A. (1999). Is lexical selection in bilingual speech production language-specific? Further evidence from Spanish–English and English–Spanish bilinguals. *Bilingualism: Language and Cognition*, *2*, 231–44.

Costa, A., Caramazza, A. and Sebastián-Gallés, N. (2000). The cognate facilitation effect: Implications for models of lexical access. *Journal of Experimental Psychology. Learning, Memory, and Cognition*, *26*(5), 1283–96.

Costa, A., Hernandez, M. and Sebastián-Gallés, N. (2008). Bilingualism aids conflict resolution: Evidence from the ANT task. *Cognition*, *106*, 59–86.

Costa, A. and Santesteban, M. (2004). Lexical access in bilingual speech production: Evidence from language switching in highly proficient bilinguals and L2 learners. *Journal of Memory and Language*, *50*(4), 491–511.

Dell, G.S. (1986). A spreading-activation theory of retrieval in sentence production. *Psychological Review*, *93*(3), 283–321.

Gollan, T.H., Montoya, R.I., Cera, C. and Sandoval, T.C. (2008). More use almost always a means a smaller frequency effect: Aging, bilingualism, and the weaker links hypothesis. *Journal of Memory and Language*, *58*(3), 787–814.

Gollan, T.H., Montoya, R.I., Fennema-Notestine, C. and Morris, S.K. (2005). Bilingualism affects picture naming but not picture classification. *Memory and Cognition*, *33*(7), 1220–34.

Gollan, T.H. and Silverberg, N.B. (2001). Tip-of-the-tongue states in Hebrew–English bilinguals. *Bilingualism: Language and Cognition*, *4*(01), 63–83.

Green, D.W. (1998). Mental control of the bilingual lexico-semantic system. *Bilingualism: Language and Cognition*, 1(2), 67–81.

Hanulová, J., Davidson, D.J. and Indefrey, P. (2011). Where does the delay in L2 picture naming come from? psycholinguistic and neurocognitive evidence on second language word production. *Language and Cognitive Processes*, *29*, 902–34.

Indefrey, P. (2006). A meta-analysis of hemodynamic studies on first and second language processing: Which suggested differences can we trust and what do they mean? *Language Learning*, *56*, 279–304.

Ivanova, I. and Costa, A. (2008). Does bilingualism hamper lexical access in speech production? *Acta Psychologica*, *127*(2), 277–88.

Levelt, W.J.M. (1989). *Speaking: From Intention to Articulation*. Cambridge, MA: MIT Press.

Oldfield, R.C. and Wingfield, A. (1965). Response latencies in naming objects. *The Quarterly Journal of Experimental Psychology*, *17*(4), 273–81.

Poulisse, N. and Bongaerts, T. (1994). First language use in second language production. *Applied Linguistics*, *15*, 36–57.

Rosselli, M. and Ardila, A. (2002). A cross-linguistic comparison of verbal fluency tests. *International Journal of Neuroscience*, *112*(6), 759–76.

Strijkers, K., Costa, A. and Thierry, G. (2010). Tracking lexical access in speech production: Electrophysiological correlates of word frequency and cognate effects. *Cerebral Cortex*, *20*(4), 912–28.

Lexical concepts

Natasha Tokowicz and Tamar Degani
University of Pittsburgh

In Levelt's Two-Stage Model of Speech Production (e.g., Levelt, Roelofs, and Meyer, 1999), lexical concepts are concepts for which there exists a lexical item (or label) in an individual's lexicon. According to this model, speech production begins with a conceptual preparation stage in which a relevant lexical concept is activated. This lexical concept then spreads activation to its corresponding lexical entry, which is referred to as a "lemma." The selection of a lemma leads to morphological and phonological encoding, such that a word is prepared for production. According to this model, lexical concepts are undivided wholes and are not decomposable into semantic features, although lexical concepts are connected to other related concepts via labeled links (e.g., "is a" links; see Green, 1998, for further discussion of decomposition). With regard to cross-language variation, Levelt *et al.* point out that lexical concepts vary across languages and that speakers learn through experience which lexical concepts exist in their language. For example, "sibling" is a lexical concept in English that does not exist in Dutch. Instead, Dutch speakers must express this concept as "brother or sister" or "sister or brother" (Green, 1998).

Specifically, languages may differ in how they map mental representations to word forms such that the content of lexical concepts is not necessarily equivalent across languages. According to Pavlenko (2009) such partial or full conceptual non-equivalence has consequences for bilingual conceptual representation and use. These consequences include phenomena such as lexical borrowing and code switching, as well as conceptual restructuring or other changes to the structure or boundaries of conceptual categories. For example, the boundaries and structure of categories of common household objects have been examined by Ameel, Malt, and colleagues (e.g., Ameel, Malt, Storms, and Van Assche, 2009). In particular, they have compared naming patterns across languages, and between monolinguals and bilinguals. The results demonstrate that there is significant cross-linguistic variation in the way that words are mapped to concepts, even for common household objects. Furthermore, bilinguals' naming patterns differ from those of monolinguals of each of their languages and instead tend to converge (Ameel *et al.*, 2009).

Although not all translation equivalents overlap completely in meaning, many models of bilingual memory representation describe the meanings to which words are connected as being fundamentally the same in the two languages, and to be part of the same abstract representational store (e.g., The Revised Hierarchical Model, Kroll and Stewart, 1994; The Word Association Model and The Concept Mediation Model, Potter, So, Von Eckardt, and Feldman, 1984). Two important exceptions are The Distributed Feature Model (De Groot, 1992) and the Distributed Representation Model (Van Hell and De Groot, 1998). These models describe the semantic overlap between translations as varying based on word-specific characteristics. In particular, the models distinguish concrete words (those that refer to perceptible entities) from abstract words (those that refer to imperceptible entities), such that the lexical concepts to which concrete words refer are more similar across languages than the lexical concepts to which abstract words refer. Similarly, cognate translations (translations that share both lexical form and meaning) are thought to refer to more similar concepts across languages than non-cognates. In a series of experiments, faster processing times were found for concrete than abstract words and for cognates than non-cognates, which was taken as evidence for greater semantic similarity for these items (De Groot, 1992; De Groot, Dannenburg, and Van Hell, 1994).

To examine the relative similarity of translations more directly, Tokowicz, Kroll, De Groot, and Van Hell (2002) collected semantic similarity ratings for a set of Dutch–English translation equivalents from a group of proficient Dutch–English bilinguals. Tokowicz *et al.* examined the degree of semantic similarity of translations as a function of their word concreteness and their lexical form overlap. Although concrete words were rated as more semantically similar to their translation equivalents than abstract words, no difference was found as a function of form overlap. It was further observed that translation equivalents were considered more semantically similar the fewer translations they had across languages. If a given lexical concept translates into two lexical concepts in another language, it tends to be less similar in meaning to each of them. For example, the single Dutch lexical concept "duif" corresponds to the two English lexical concepts "dove" and "pigeon," whereas the Dutch lexical concept "aardbei" corresponds uniquely to the English lexical concept "strawberry." Indeed, strawberry and aardbei are rated as more similar in meaning than is duif with each of its English translations (Tokowicz *et al.*, 2002).

The mapping of a lexical concept in one language to more than one in another language also has consequences for the similarity among the representations within a language. For example, the concepts of "home" and "house" are not lexically distinguished in languages like Hebrew ("ba-it") and Spanish ("casa"). Thus, the two lexical concepts (and their corresponding lexical entries) "home" and "house" share a single lexical concept in other languages. An individual who knows a language in which these concepts are denoted by a single lexical concept (e.g., Hebrew or Spanish) will tend to perceive these two words as more similar in meaning, and as more interchangeable, than monolingual speakers of the language that distinguishes the concepts lexically (e.g., English; e.g., Degani, Prior, and Tokowicz, 2011; Elston-Güttler and Williams, 2008). Such cross-linguistic influences are prominent from the native language to a later learned second language, but have also been documented in the reverse direction. Lexical concepts in one language may thus influence the organization of lexical concepts in another language.

A more general influence of lexical concepts on the structure of conceptual representation has been investigated under the "linguistic relativity" hypothesis (or the Sapir-Whorf hypothesis) which posits that language affects thought. In particular, speakers of different languages are hypothesized to perceive or understand the world differently because languages differ in how they semantically partition the world (i.e., the content of their lexical concepts), and because presumably these different semantic structures influence the way we perceive and understand the world. According to Slobin's related Thinking for Speaking Hypothesis (e.g., Slobin, 1996), language forms part of our subjective reality and leads us to interact with the world in particular ways and to think in a manner consistent with how we speak. In that sense, the lexical concepts available in our language shape our thoughts.

See also: conceptual transfer, language and the lexicon in SLA, Levelt's model of speech production and comprehension, linguistic relativity, semantic processing, thinking for speaking

References

Ameel, E., Malt, B.C., Storms, G. and Van Assche, F. (2009). Semantic Convergence in the Bilingual Lexicon. *Journal of Memory and Language*, *60*, 270–90.

De Groot, A.M. B. (1992). Determinants of Word Translation. *Journal of Experimental Psychology: Learning, Memory, and Cognition*, *18*, 1001–18.

De Groot, A.M. B., Dannenburg, L. and Van Hell, J.G. (1994). Forward and Backward Word Translation by Bilinguals. *Journal of Memory and Language*, *33*, 600–29.

Degani, T., A. Prior, and N. Tokowicz. (2011). Bidirectional Transfer: The Effect of Sharing a Translation. *Journal of Cognitive Psychology*, *23*, 18–28.

Elston-Güttler, K.E. and Williams, J.N. (2008). First Language Polysemy Affects Second Language Meaning Interpretation: Evidence for Activation of First Language Concepts During Second Language Reading. *Second Language Research*, *24*, 167–87.

Green, D.W. (1998). Bilingualism and Thought. *Psychologia Belgica*, *38*, 251–76.

Kroll, J.F. and Stewart, E. (1994). Category Interference in Translation and Picture Naming: Evidence for Asymmetric Connections between Bilingual Memory Representations. *Journal of Memory and Language*, 33, 149–74.

Levelt, W.J. M., Roelofs, A. and Meyer, A.S. (1999). A Theory of Lexical Access in Speech Production. *Behavioral and Brain Sciences*, *22*, 1–75.

Malt, B.C. and Wolf, P. (2010). *Words and the Mind: How Words Encode Human Experience*. New York: Oxford University Press.

Pavlenko, A. (2009). Conceptual Representation in the Bilingual Lexicon and Second Language Vocabulary Learning. In Pavlenko, A. (ed.), *The Bilingual Mental Lexicon: Interdisciplinary Approaches*. Tonawanda, NY: Multilngual Matters.

Potter, M.C., So, K.-F., Von Eckardt, B. and Feldman, L.B. (1984). Lexical and Conceptual Representation in Beginning and Proficient Bilinguals. *Journal of Verbal Learning and Verbal Behavior*, *23*, 23–38.

Slobin, D.I. (1996). From 'Thought and Language' to 'Thinking for Speaking'. In Gumperz, J.J. and Levinson, S.C. (eds), *Rethinking Linguistic Relativity*. Cambridge: Cambridge University Press.

Tokowicz, N., Kroll, J.F., De Groot, A.M. B. and Van Hell, J.G. (2002). Number-of-Translation Norms for Dutch-English Translation Pairs: A New Tool for Examining Language Production. *Behavior Research Methods, Instruments, and Computers*, *34*, 435–51.

Van Hell, J. G. and De Groot, A.M. B. (1998). Conceptual Representation in Bilingual Memory: Effects of Concreteness and Cognate Status in Word Association. *Bilingualism: Language and Cognition*, *1*, 193–211.

Further reading

Gentner, D. and Goldin-Meadow, S. (eds) (2003). *Language in Mind: Advances in the Study of Language and Thought*. Cambridge, MA: MIT Press. (Describes current studies on linguistic relativity.)

Gumperz, J.J. and Levinson, S.C. (eds) (1996). *Rethinking Linguistic Relativity*. New York: Cambridge University Press. (Describes recent changes in our understanding of linguistic relativity.)

Hunt, E. and Agnoli, F. (1991). The Whorfian Hypothesis: A Cognitive Psychology Perspective. *Psychological Review*, *98*, 377–89. (Cognitive psychology research on how language shapes thought.)

Whorf, B. (1956). *Language, Thought, and Reality: Selected Writings of Benjamin Lee Whorf*. Cambridge, MA: MIT Press. (Classic writings on linguistic relativity and linguistic determinism.)

Limited Capacity Hypothesis

Chieko Kawauchi
Kurume University

The Limited Capacity Hypothesis refers to an assumption developed in the field of cognitive psychology which suggests that humans have only limited amounts of attention available during intentional learning. The information-processing approach follows this perspective, with McLaughlin, Rossman and McLeod (1983) calling humans "limited-capacity processors" both in terms of what they can attend to and what they can handle on the basis of knowledge. Due to this assumed capacity limitation, if a particularly demanding task surpasses our momentary capacity, we are likely to make an error or may be required to focus our attention on one thing, while forgoing others. Both approaches consider that the amount of information a learner can process is determined by the cognitive demand of the task and the learner's information processing ability, which is controlled and automatic. A task that initially taxes processing capacity may become automatic through practice, reducing the burden on processing capacity accordingly.

The rationale of limited attention capacity on SLA was extensively discussed by a series of studies by Skehan and Foster (Foster and Skehan, 1996; Skehan and Foster, 1997). These authors assumed that tensions exist between different aspects of language use, which require not only fluency but also formal aspects of accuracy and complexity. Based on this assumption, they attempted to establish how learners' limited attention capacity could be extended to allow more opportunities to focus on form by controlling the kind of tasks and by manipulating task conditions. Foster and Skehan (1996), for example, investigated how different tasks as well as different implementation of conditions affected the fluency, accuracy, and complexity of the language produced when a different task is carried out. The tasks they used were personal information exchange (cognitively least difficult), narrative, and decision-making (cognitively most difficult). These tasks were manipulated with and without planning conditions. Any planning was further divided into either a detailed (with guidance) and an undetailed (without guidance) condition. Results showed that planning had a great impact on fluency and complexity, and partial effect on accuracy, particularly in undetailed planning, suggesting that planning enhanced attentional capacity. Overall effects of planning were greater with the narrative and decision-making tasks, implying a greater benefit from planning on cognitively more demanding tasks. More importantly, a trade-off between complexity and accuracy was evident in narrative tasks. When planning time was provided, the narrative task which requires more on-line processing (i.e., constructing a storyline) yielded the highest level of complexity at the expense of accuracy.

It has been argued that fluency, accuracy, and complexity compete with one another due to the limited attention capacity, and that L2 learners seem to allocate attention to particular goals at the expense of other goals. Similar findings have been shown in ESL writing (Li, 2000) in which persuasive tasks indicated more complexity but less accuracy. Thus, the task type and conditions are believed to control the total amount of learner capacity, as well as momentary allocations of effort toward various partial activities.

See also: attention, automaticity, Cognition Hypothesis (CH), fluency, planning time, task-based learning

References

Foster, P. and Skehan, P. (1996). The Influence of Planning and Task Type on Second Language Performance. *Studies in Second Language Acquisition*, *19*, 299–33.

Li, Y. (2000). Linguistic Characteristics of ESL Writing in Task-Based E-Mail Activities. *System*, *28*, 229–45.

McLaughlin, B., Rossman, T. and McLeod, B. (1983). Second Language Learning: An Information-Processing Perspective. *Language Learning*, *33*, 135–57.

Skehan, P. and Foster, P. (1997). Task Type and Task Processing Conditions as Influences on Foreign Language Performance. *Language Teaching Research*, *1*, 185–211.

Further reading

Murdock, B. (1965). A Test of the 'Limited Capacity' Hypothesis. *Journal of Experimental Psychology*, *69*, 237–40.

Schmidt, R. (1992). Psychological Mechanisms Underlying Second Language Fluency. *Studies in Second Language Acquisition*, *14*, 357–85.

Skehan, P. (1998). *A Cognitive Approach to Language Learning*. Oxford: Oxford University Press.

Linguistic Coding Differences Hypothesis (LCDH)

Richard Sparks

College of Mount St. Joseph

The Linguistic Coding Differences Hypothesis (LCDH) developed by Sparks and Ganschow derives its name from native language (L1) research in reading. The major premise underlying the LCDH is that the primary causal factors in successful or unsuccessful L2 learning are linguistic (Sparks and Ganschow, 1991, 1995). Sparks and Ganschow based their hypothesis on the Assumption of Specificity (AOS), a concept in the L1 reading literature, which proposes that students with reading disabilities who have average to superior intelligence have a cognitive deficit reasonably specific to the reading task, and is thus language-related. By connecting the AOS to L2 learning, Sparks and Ganschow propose that students who exhibit strong or weak L2 learning have strengths and weaknesses that are language-related and account for their level of L2 learning (Sparks, 1995; Sparks and Ganschow, 1993). The LCDH posits that L1 skills serve as the foundation for L2 learning and that skill levels in the L1 components of language – phonological, syntactic, semantic, morphological – impact ability (aptitude) for L2 learning. Conceptually, the LCDH is similar to Cummins' Linguistic Interdependence and Threshold Hypotheses. The premises of the LCDH provide an explanation for individual differences in L2 learning. Further, the LCDH posits that problems with one component of language in L1, for example, phonological processing, will have a negative impact on the L1 and L2 in both its oral and written forms.

Initially, Sparks and Ganschow called their hypothesis the Linguistic Coding *Deficit* Hypothesis, developed primarily to explain the L2 learning problems of students classified as learning disabled (LD), who exhibit deficits in L1 skills despite average or better intelligence. As they conducted research on the hypothesis, however, they changed the name from *deficits* to *differences* because their studies revealed no differences in L1 skills and L2 aptitude between low-achieving L2 learners and students enrolled in L2 classes classified as LD (see reviews by Ganschow and Sparks, 2001). In both populations, scores on L1 measures of reading, spelling, writing, and vocabulary were in the average to low average range. As a result, the authors posited that L2 learning skill occurs along a continuum of very strong to very weak learners and that there is not a unique "disability" for learning a L2.

Starting in the 1990s, the authors conducted numerous studies to determine the viability of the LCDH. Their comparison studies demonstrated consistently that L2 learners with significantly stronger L1 skills exhibit higher aptitude on the MLAT and stronger L2 classroom achievement than students with weaker L1 skills. Their prediction studies showed that the best predictors of L2 achievement and proficiency in high school are language-related skills. Their studies that measured oral and written L2 proficiency indicated that students with stronger L1 skills measured prior to L2 study exhibit stronger oral and written L2 proficiency (see reviews by Ganschow and Sparks, 2001). In recent years, their findings have been replicated and supported by researchers who have examined the hypothesis using different age groups and a variety of languages (e.g., see Chung and Suk-Han-Ho, 2010; Dufva and Voeten, 1999).

Recently, Sparks *et al.* described a longitudinal study in which first grade students were administered measures of L1 aptitude, L1 literacy, and L1 oral language and followed over 10 years into high school. Prior to L2 study, they were administered the MLAT; then, measures of L2 proficiency were administered after two years of L2 courses. Overall, the results showed that L1 skills in elementary school, especially L1 literacy, can explain much of the variance in both L2 aptitude and L2 proficiency many years later. In one study L1 word decoding skills, L1 spelling, and L1 phonological awareness in primary school explained over half the variance in first-year L2 word decoding and spelling skills in high school. In another study students classified as high versus low proficiency L2 learners in high school exhibited significant differences on L1 achievement measures as early as second grade. In yet another longitudinal study, high versus low-achieving L2 learners exhibited differences in L1 skills by fourth grade. From these studies, Sparks and colleagues raise the question of whether there may be long-term cross-linguistic transfer of L1 skills to L2. (For reviews of these studies, see Sparks *et al.*, 2009a, 2009b).

Given their findings, Sparks and Ganschow urge L2 researchers to consider that language skill differences in good and poor L2 learners may be a confounding variable. For example, they have questioned explanations based on learning strategies and learning styles because these theories propose explanations for L2 learning that are unrelated to language learning skills (Sparks, 1995). They propose that affective theories, for example, motivation, anxiety about L2 learning are unlikely to provide causal insights into L2 learning differences because low motivation and high anxiety could be used to explain many other learning problems, for example, math, science, not just L2 problems. They have used Horwitz's Foreign Language Classroom Anxiety Scale (FLCAS), the MLAT, measures of L1 skills, and L2 proficiency tests to compare L2 learners with differing levels of anxiety. In several studies, they showed that high anxious students exhibited significantly lower levels of L1 skills, L2 aptitude, and L2 proficiency than students with lower levels of anxiety. In a longitudinal study, they administered the FLCAS after one year of L2 study and found that the FLCAS was negatively correlated with L1 skill measures in first grade several years before the participants began L2 study, and that the negative correlations increased from first through fifth grades. These findings suggest that the FLCAS, and perhaps other affective measures, are measuring L2 learners' perceptions of their language learning skills, and that language skills are likely to play a confounding role in measuring the role of affective in L2 learning. (For review of affective studies, see Sparks and Ganschow, 2007.)

In sum, the LCDH is a research-based hypothesis that focuses on language-based variables for L2 learning and accounts for why students exhibit different levels of L2 learning skill that run along a continuum from very strong to very weak L2 skills. The hypothesis also explains why students who have acquired adequate L1 language and literacy skills exhibit problems with L2 learning.

See also: aptitude, individual differences in SLA, Interdependence Hypothesis, linguistic transfer, phonological short-term memory (PSTM), proficiency

References

Chung, K. and Suk-Han-Ho, C., (2010). Second language learning difficulties: what are the reading-related cognitive skills that contribute to English and Chinese word reading? *Journal of Learning Disabilities*, *43* (3), 195–211.

Dufva, M. and Voeten, M., (1999). Native language literacy and phonological memory as prerequisites for learning English as a foreign language. *Applied Psycholinguistics*, *20* (3), 329–48.

Ganschow, L. and Sparks, R., (2001). Learning difficulties and foreign language learning: a review of research and instruction. *Language Teaching*, *34* (2), 79–98.

Sparks, R., (1995). Examining the linguistic coding differences hypothesis to explain individual differences in foreign language learning. *Annals of Dyslexia*, *45*, 187–214.

Sparks, R. and Ganschow, L., (1991). Foreign language learning differences: affective or native language aptitude differences. *Modern Language Journal*, *75* (1), 3–16.

——(1993) Searching for the cognitive locus of foreign language learning problems: linking first and second language learning. *Modern Language Journal*, 77 (3), 289–302.

——(1995) A strong inference approach to causal factors in foreign language learning: a response to MacIntyre. *Modern Language Journal*, *79* (2), 235–44.

——(2007). Is the Foreign Language Classroom Anxiety Scale measuring anxiety or language skills? *Foreign Language Annals*, *40* (2), 260–87.

Sparks, R., Patton, J., Ganschow, L. and Humbach, N., (2009a). Long-term cross-linguistic transfer from L1 to L2. *Language Learning*, *59* (1), 203–43.

——(2009b). Long-term relationships among early first language skills, second language aptitude, second language affect, and later second language proficiency. *Applied Psycholinguistics*, *30* (4), 725–55.

Further reading

Cummins, J., (1979) Linguistic interdependence and the educational development of bilingual children. *Review of Educational Research*, *49* (2), 222–51. (This paper explains the linguistic interdependence and the linguistic threshold hypotheses.)

Skehan, P., (1998): *A cognitive approach to language learning*. Oxford: Oxford University Press. (This book explains L2 learning and individual differences from a cognitive processing perspective; in particular, Chapters 8 and 9 on language aptitude influenced research on the LCDH.)

Sparks, R. (2001). Foreign language learning problems of students classified as learning disabled and non-learning disabled: is there a difference? *Topics in Language Disorders*, *21* (2), 38–54. (This paper explains the continuum of language learning, describes the primary role of language variables in L2 learning, and summarizes research on LD vs. non-LD L2 learners with L2 learning problems.)

——(2006). Is there a 'disability' for learning a foreign language? *Journal of Learning Disabilities*, *39* (6), 544–57. (This paper explains that there is no evidence to support the notion of a "disability" for L2 learning and reviews the evidence supporting that position.)

Sparks, R., Javorsky, J. and Humbach, N. (2008). Individual and longitudinal differences among high and low-achieving LD and ADHD L2 learners. *Learning and Individual Differences*, *18* (1), 29–43. (This paper reports a longitudinal study that incorporates several premises of the LCDH: individual differences, relationships between L1 and L2 skills, long-term cross-linguistic transfer, and similarities between low-achieving L2 learners and students classified as learning disabled.)

Linguistic relativity in SLA

ZhaoHong Han and Teresa Cadierno
Columbia University, Teachers College and University of Southern Denmark

The term "linguistic relativity" speaks broadly to the influence of language on the thought processes of its speakers, an idea that has been subject to Western intellectual and philosophical debate for centuries dating back to the writings of German Philosopher Wilhelm von Humboldt (1836), and was popularized in modern day by Benjamin Whorf (1956). Whorf's hypothesis, known also as the Sapir-Whorf Hypothesis, stipulates that language determines cognition. Under this view, speakers of Nootka, a language of Vancouver Island, for example, have a "monistic view" on the universe, because of lack of distinction between objects and actions in their language. Such a deterministic view, however, was eventually met with much disbelief leading either to an outright rejection of it, or a much weaker perception that "any such influence is at best negligible, even trivial" (Deutscher, 2010: 445).

Recent years have seen a revival of interest in linguistic relativity. Findings from research employing scientific methods suggest that language can indeed affect the mind such that it can instill habits of the mind on basic cognitive processes such as categorization, memory, attention, perception, and associations, which, taken as a whole, support a weaker version of linguistic relativity, namely that language affects rather than determines cognition.

Contemporary pursuits of the weaker version of linguistic relativity notably includes Slobin's (1996) thinking-for-speaking hypothesis which alleges that language filters and frames our thoughts when we speak or write, directing our attention to certain aspects of our experience of the world. Rather than focusing on the potential influence of language on speakers' habitual thought, that is, on speakers' patterns of attending to, categorizing, and remembering objects and events, the thinking for speaking hypothesis is concerned with the mental processes that occur during the act of interpreting and verbalizing experience. Thinking for speaking (or writing, for that matter) therefore entails "picking those characteristics of objects and events that (a) fit some conceptualization of the event, and (b) are readily encodable in the language" (Slobin, 1996: 76).

This hypothesis has inspired, and gained unambiguous support, from first language research, particularly an array of first language studies examining how speakers of typologically different languages talk about motion events – drawing on Talmy's (1985) typology separating V-languages and S-languages. In this research, cross-linguistic variability is not only amply documented, but, importantly, is found to correlate with the characteristics of spatial reference and motion events that speakers of the languages *habitually* attend to or ignore. Speakers of S-languages versus V-languages reportedly treat "path" and "manner" differently. In terms of encoding of path, speakers of S-languages display a general tendency to provide more elaborated yet tightly packaged descriptions of paths within a single clause than speakers of V-languages, who tend to provide descriptions featuring the static scene in which the movement takes place. In terms of encoding of motion, speakers of S-languages tend to provide more elaborated manner descriptions than speakers of V-languages, as evident both in the frequency with which manner information is supplied and in the variety of manner distinctions made. Speakers of V-languages, on the other hand, typically use neutral motion verbs to describe movement, providing manner information only when the communicative context compels it.

The thinking-for-speaking effects may appear more linguistic than cognitive, if the supporting evidence comes exclusively from studies using linguistic tasks. However, some empirical studies utilizing both linguistic tasks and non-linguistic tasks such as picture categorization and similarity judgments or cognitive tasks alone have suggested that the effects are, in fact, cognitive (Slobin, 2006).

For second language acquisition, the thinking-for-speaking hypothesis predicts that learning a second language entails learning another way of thinking for speaking and that the thinking-for-speaking patterns acquired during first language acquisition, due to their *habitual* nature and cognitive entrenchment, may be particularly resistant to restructuring in adult second language acquisition (Slobin, 1996).

Empirical research by far has largely supported this prognosis. Studies on L2 narratives of motion events (for review, see Cadierno, 2008), for example, have converged on the general finding that intermediate and advanced L2 learners with an L1 S-language background, such as English, and L2 learners of an L1 V-language background, such as Spanish, seem able to learn a new way of thinking for speaking, even when the L1 and the L2 are typologically different, yet with some traces still visible of the learners' L1 thinking-for-speaking patterns. This is true equally of L2 learners from typologically similar backgrounds (see, e.g., Hasko, 2010). Indeed, some researchers have questioned "whether the cognitive as well as the linguistic systems of second language learners can ever be identical" (Han and Odlin, 2006: 11).

The thinking-for-speaking predictions for L2 learners are further borne out in L2 research on motion gestures. Studies investigating the simultaneous use of speech and gesture when talking about motion events in an L2 have reported that "speakers of typologically different languages have different patterns of thinking for speaking about motion not only linguistically, but also gesturally" (Stam, 2010, p. 63). In a longitudinal investigation of an advanced Spanish learner of English, Stam (2010) showed that from 1997 to 2006 the learner's expression of manner in L2 English continued to reflect the Spanish L1 thinking for speaking patterns both linguistically and gesturally. In contrast, her linguistic and gestural expression of path did change towards the target-like English thinking-for-speaking pattern. These results suggest that the development of appropriate L2 thinking-for-speaking patterns may not affect all aspects of a motion event equally. That is, within individual learners, some aspects can become target-like, whereas others may continue to reflect the influence of the learners' L1 thinking-for-speaking patterns, both in linguistic and gestural expression.

While motion talk and gesture have by far been the main test ground for the thinking-for-speaking hypothesis, L2 research has also examined other semantic domains such as temporality and aspect, as well as number and definiteness. Slobin (2003) suggests that it is worthwhile to examine "ways in which one's native language shapes one's mastery of grammatical categories of a foreign language" (Slobin, 2003: 436), positing that grammaticized categories that are independent of "our perceptual, sensorimotor, and practical dealings with the world" such as aspect, definiteness, and voice are the most resistant to restructuring (Slobin, 1996: 91). This prediction is again consistent with the reported results for L2 learning.

Research examining the effect of grammaticized aspect on L2 ultimate attainment has shown that even highly proficient language learners draw on L1 principles of event construal and information organization when narrating in a second language. For example, English-speaking learners of L2 German " … have not uncovered the holistic pattern of construal in German by which events are viewed as bounded" (von Stutterheim and Carroll, 2006: 49). In other words, the learners in question have not acquired the characteristic temporal perspective employed by German native speakers when narrating events, which consists of presenting a series of bounded events related to endpoints or resultant states.

Likewise, a longitudinal case study by Han (2010) examining the acquisition of English articles and plurals in an endstate learner whose L1 was Chinese documented long-term cessation of learning in the subject of these grammatical functors that encode the abstract concepts of number and definiteness. Using a combination of naturalistic data and data clinically elicited via bi-directional translation tasks, the study established the effects of L1 thinking for speaking on the subject's L2 production. Similar findings are reported in Ekiert (2010) focusing on *en route* learners whose L1 was Polish.

Alongside the research on the thinking-for-speaking hypothesis, there is notably another strand of research which pursues a stronger version of linguistic relativity by investigating the non-linguistic cognitive consequences of learning to speak another language. Enlightened by Lucy's (1992) case study of Yucatec, here researchers have sought to address such questions as whether or not there is a correlate between acquiring grammatical categories of another language and general cognitive changes, and whether increased experience with another language can alter one's cognitive processes and behavior (see, e.g., Athanasopoulos, 2006). It appears that at least in certain areas of grammar, L2 learners not only undergo a conceptual restructuring as their proficiency advances, but sometimes do so to the extent of complete reversal of at least parts of the L1-based conception in favor of the L2-based conception, thereby resulting in L1 attrition.

L2 research on linguistic relativity is still in its infancy, and as such, there is ample and fertile ground for future research. One potentially fruitful avenue is to examine relativistic effects on L2 comprehension – to complement the existing research on production. Another avenue is for thinking-for-speaking studies to examine both linguistic and non-linguistic cognitive effects, employing both linguistic and non-linguistic cognitive tasks. This would help ascertain the extent to which L1-based cognition affects the mind of the L2 learner. Additionally, it would be interesting to investigate the extent to which instruction can assist the restructuring of L1-based thinking-for-speaking. Last but not least, broadening the scope of inquiry by subjecting other linguistic and conceptual domains to investigation would directly help to validate the relativistic research as an important source of understanding of human cognition.

See also: acquisition of motion expressions, cognitive linguistics and SLA, concept-oriented approach to SLA, conceptual transfer, cross-linguistic influence, thinking-for-speaking

References

Athanasopoulos, P. (2006). Effects of the grammatical representation of number on cognition in bilinguals. *Bilingualism: Language and Cognition*, *9*(1), 89–96.

Cadierno, T. (2008). Learning to talk about motion in a foreign language. In P. Robinson and N. Ellis (eds), *Handbook of Cognitive Linguistics and Second Language Acquisition*, pp. 239–75. New York: Routledge.

Deutscher, G. (2010). *Through the Language Glass: Why the World Looks Different in Other Languages*. New York: Metropolitan Books.

Ekiert, M. (2010). Linguistic effects on thinking for writing: The case of articles in L2 English. In Z.-H. Han and T. Cadierno (eds), *Linguistic Relativity in Second Language Acquisition: Thinking for Speaking*, pp. 125–53. Clevedon: Multilingual Matters.

Han, Z.H. (2010). Grammatical morpheme inadequacy as a function of linguistic relativity: A longitudinal study. In Z.H. Han and T. Cadierno (eds), *Linguistic Relativity in SLA: Thinking for Speaking*, pp. 154–82. Clevedon: Multilingual Matters.

Han, Z.-H. and Odlin, T. (2006). Introduction. In Z.-H. Han and T. Odlin (eds), *Studies of Fossilization in Second Language Acquisition*, pp. 1–20. Clevedon: Multilingual Matters.

Hasko, V. (2010). The role of thinking for speaking in adult L2 speech: The case of (non)unidirectionality encoding by American learners of Russian. In Z.-H. Han and T. Cadierno (eds), *Linguistic Relativity in Second Language Acquisition: Thinking for Speaking*, pp. 34–58. Clevedon: Multilingual Matters.

Lucy, J. (1992). *Grammatical Categories and Cognition*. Cambridge: Cambridge University Press.

Slobin, D.I. (1996). From 'thought and language' to 'thinking for speaking'. In J. Gumperz. and S. Levinson (eds), *Rethinking Linguistic Relativity*, pp. 70–96. Cambridge: Cambridge University Press.

Slobin, D. (2003). Language and thought online: Cognitive consequences of linguistic relativity. In D. Gentner and S. Goldin-Meadow (eds), *Language in Mind: Advances in the Study of Language and Thought*, pp. 157–92. Cambridge, MA: MIT Press.

——(2006). What makes manner of motion salient? Explorations in linguistic typology, discourse, and cognition. In M. Hickmann and S. Robert (eds), *Space in Languages: Linguistic Systems and Cognitive Categories*, pp. 59–81. Amsterdam: John Benjamins.

Stam, G. (2010). Can an L2 speaker's patterns of thinking for speaking change? In Z.-H. Han and

T. Cadierno (eds), *Linguistic Relativity in Second Language Acquisition: Thinking for Speaking*, pp. 59–83. Clevedon: Multilingual Matters.

Talmy, L. (1985). Lexicalization patterns: Semantic structure in lexical forms. In T. Shopen (ed.), *Language typology and syntactic description*, Vol. 3: Grammatical categories and the lexicon, pp. 57–149. Cambridge: Cambridge University Press.

Von Humboldt, W. (1836/1960). *Über die Verschiedenheit des menschlichen sprachbaues und ihren Einfluss auf die geistige Entwickelung des Menschengeschlechts*. [On the diversity of human language construction and its influence on human development.] Bonn: Dümmler.

Von Stutterheim, C., and Carroll, M. (2006). The impact of grammatical temporal categories on ultimate attainment in L2 learning. In H. Byrmes, H. Weger-Guntharp, and K.A. Sprang (eds), *Educating for Advanced Foreign Language Capacities: Constructs, Curriculum, Instruction, Assessment*, pp. 40–53. Washington, DC: Georgetown University Press.

Whorf, B.L. (1956). Language, thought, and reality. In J. Carroll (ed.), *Selected Writings of Benjamin Lee Whorf*. Cambridge, MA: MIT.

Linguistic transfer

Håkan Ringbom
Abo Akademi University

Transfer, which affects all areas of language, is a narrower term than **cross-linguistic influence**, although the two are often used interchangeably. Similarity is what underlies transfer. Similarities are either perceived or assumed, depending especially on the relationship between source language and target language (TL) (psychotypology) and on whether comprehension or production is involved. Kellerman already emphasized (1977) the importance of what the learner *perceives* to be similar between TL and L1. Cross-linguistic similarity is most obviously perceived in formally similar individual items or words. There are also functional and semantic similarities, without formal similarity, in grammatical categories and semantic units. In comprehension, especially of related languages, learners become aware of TL features they recognize as resembling L1. In production, learners are not engaged in perceiving similarities but in encoding their ideas into language structures either previously learned or created in the absence of learned knowledge. They then rely on similarities they only *assume* exist between the languages. See Ringbom (2007), Ringbom and Jarvis (2009), and cf. Jarvis and Pavlenko (2008).

Linguistic transfer occurs at item level, system level, and overall level. The distinction between items and systems illuminates a basic question in transfer research, what is actually transferred. Before systems are learned, items must be known. Initially, learning takes place on an item-by-item basis in all areas of language: phonological, morphological, syntactic, lexical, and phraseological. An item is an individual form (sound, letter, morpheme, word, phrase, syntactic unit), while system involves organizing forms and mapping meaning onto those forms. Learners initially apply an oversimplified equivalence hypothesis, L2 = L1, applying functions or meanings of L2 items to existing L1 items in comprehension and those of L1 items to L2 items in production. Simplified cross-linguistic one-to-one relationships are thus established. Beginning learners tend to focus on form rather than on abstract concepts of meaning or function, which are less accessible to direct observation and analysis. Perceived formal similarities facilitate the establishment of cross-linguistic relations. Where cross-linguistic similarities of form are perceived, they are combined with an assumed similarity of meaning/function. Across closely related languages, item level transfer generally works well: learners need not expend much effort to attain at least approximate comprehension.

In system transfer, better termed procedural transfer, abstract principles of organizing information are transferred in L2 production. Learners incorporate a productive mechanism, applying L1-based principles to L2. In procedural transfer no formal cross-linguistic similarities are necessarily perceived, learners simply rely on assumptions that L1 and L2 work in more or less the same way. Transfer is thus also found across distant languages, where it frequently results in errors, which provide the most concrete, though not the only, manifestations of transfer.

Overall transfer is an umbrella term referring to learners' reliance on formal similarities across individual items and functional equivalences between the underlying systems. The amount of overall transfer depends on how much cross-linguistic similarity is perceived in items and systems. Overall transfer illustrates a well-known principle in applied linguistics: the whole is more than the sum of individual parts. Many similarities put together produce an even more extensive, generally facilitating effect on learning.

Phonology

Linguistic transfer is clearly manifested in phonology and intonation. Learners initially perceive L2 sounds in terms of the phonological system of their L1. Even learners fluent in speaking generally retain a foreign accent (see Leather and James, 1991; Odlin, 2003).The **Contrastive Analysis Hypothesis** (CAH) originally predicted that linguistic differences between languages make for learning difficulty. At the outset of learning to pronounce a new language great phonological differences certainly pose problems at early stages. Beginning learners show L1 transfer in rhythm, stress and intonation and in individual speech sounds. Yet the CAH remains an oversimplification also in phonology. And transfer clearly relies on similarity, not on difference.

Whether cross-linguistic similarity or cross-linguistic difference causes more difficulties for the learner has been discussed in phonological research (Eckman, 2004; Odlin, 1989: 30f.). Linguists' attempts at defining similarity and difference are, however, not necessarily based on the criteria learners use to perceive similarities and differences. The vagueness of perceived similarity with its individual variability in learners and the generally blurred relation between similarity and difference complicate research. Also, it has not been sufficiently recognized that there must be an underlying similarity for meaningful differences to occur.

As Corder originally suggested (1973: 133), the motor-perceptual skills of phonological reception and production probably behave differently from the organizational language skills. Recognition processes and articulatory processes seem difficult to modify or extend. Learning motor-perceptual skills might be better described as modifying or reshaping existing behavior rather than acquiring a new set of rules. Cross-linguistic similarity facilitates automatization of procedures, and is therefore particularly useful for listening and speaking, where quick and efficient retrieval is required.

Discourse: pragmatic transfer

Discourse and phonology are apparently similar in that L1 patterns in both of these are more resistant to modification and development than grammatical and especially lexical patterns. Transfer in discourse has not been much investigated, partly because no explicitly stated norms exist for discourse. The concept of error is less applicable on units larger than the sentence. Also, investigating transfer in discourse requires studying relatively advanced learners able to produce longish texts. Some types of transfer are not manifested until learners are sufficiently proficient in L2 to notice and rely on certain types of relationships between L1 and L2. Apparently a basic threshold proficiency is needed for pragmatic transfer to appear in production. Once this stage has been reached, assumed similarities to L1 usage at the pragmatic level may be manifested. However, as in other language areas, pragmatic transfer decreases as proficiency develops: advanced learners show less direct L1 influence than intermediate learners (see Kasper and Rose, 2002: 153–57; Takahashi and Beebe, 1987; cf. Ringbom, 2007: 66f.). Pragmatic competence generally tends to lag behind linguistic competence.

Morphology and syntax

In morphology transfer has been said to have little importance. A basic question in transfer-based research on grammar is what type of grammar learners start out from. Their starting point is not L1 grammar but something less complicated. They apparently employ a strategy to reduce the TL to as simple a system as possible. As Ellis suggested (1985: 70), the starting point appears to be the early vocabulary the learner has acquired and which is used in non-grammatical utterances. Initially, learners seek to get their message across without the help of grammar. When TL competence develops, a basic simple grammar is achieved, which is being elaborated in response to exposure to TL data, previous knowledge (L1 and other languages) and communicative needs. Transfer is important in this elaborative process, but its interaction with other processes is not clear. Several studies have found that speakers of Finnish, whose L1 does not have articles, tend to omit these words when they begin their studies of English (Ringbom, 2007; Jarvis and Pavlenko, 2008; cf. **cross-linguistic influence**). Similarly Swedish learners of Finnish at early stages of learning tend to omit many of the 15 case endings of Finnish nouns, since these cases are perceived to be redundant, that is, not found in their L1.

Lexical transfer

Lexical transfer overlaps with **conceptual transfer**. L1 influence is consistently present in comprehension and production of L2 words. Formal cross-linguistic similarities, especially in cognates, facilitate learning a TL related to L1. There are, however, also deceptive cognates, with purely formal but little or no semantic similarity. These often produce ludicrous or memorable effects and easily assume an importance in learners' and teachers' minds unproportional to their significance. But dangers of deceptive cognates should not be exaggerated, since good cognates easily outnumber deceptive ones, for instance between English and French. Cognates classed as deceptive need not have totally different meanings: the meanings often overlap in that some senses of the TL word correspond to the cognate L1 word, while others do not. Cognates in comprehension behave differently compared with production. For L2 comprehension, the context provides cues for inferencing the meaning of an unknown word, while L2 production provides no facilitative context eliminating erroneous interpretations of formally similar but semantically different L2 words. Errors in deceptive cognates therefore occur more frequently in production than in comprehension.

To establish the relative usefulness or hindrance of cognates to learning, at least the following variables should be considered: degree of formal and semantic similarity; whether they occur in similar contexts; frequency and whether they are core, non-core or subject-core items; stage of learning; whether the targeted L2 vocabulary is general or specialized; and whether they are encountered in comprehension or used in production (Granger, 1993: 51).When comprehending a new language, learners at early stages tend to employ lexical item transfer where possible, trying to associate words with natural L1 counterparts.

Lateral (non-native) transfer

Prior linguistic knowledge is not always L1, it can also be another non-native language. Whether knowing one foreign language helps or obstructs learning another foreign language has been frequently discussed (e.g. De Angelis, 2007). Many studies have found that learning a new language is easier if you already know one non-native language, particularly if the two foreign languages are related. Studies of African and Asian learners agree on concluding that previous knowledge of French (or English) influences the learning of English (or French) more than the learner's L1 does. Formally similar items in related non-native languages thus lead to much transfer. Generally this facilitates learning, notably learning for comprehension, while subsequent assumed similarities cause errors especially in production. Good L2 proficiency is, however, probably needed for genuine facilitation of L3 production to occur.

Intrusive, inhibitive and facilitative transfer

While linking errors to L1 is comparatively easy, problems occur in ascertaining the L1 influence in correct expressions of learner language. Transfer studies consistently emphasize negative transfer, whereas positive effects of transfer are mostly commented on only in passing, if at all. The use of the evaluatives positive and negative has also been criticized for being relevant at the product level only, not the process level. Facilitative procedural transfer is often difficult to recognize in language production, because it coincides with successful TL acquisition. Nevertheless, it is clear that learners of a related language regularly outperform learners of an unrelated language (Ringbom, 1987, 2007).

A language the learner knows only superficially generally provides the source of only item transfer but not procedural transfer. Procedural transfer, on the other hand, is predominantly transfer from L1, or possibly from another language the learner knows very well. The negative procedural transfer in learners' TL production is either *intrusive* or *inhibitive*. Intrusive transfer refers to learners' use of inappropriate L1-induced items, while inhibitive transfer prevents or inhibits learning to use new words and structures appropriately. TL words and structures without L1 parallels provide the learner with no concrete item transfer and are therefore often avoided as they are perceived as redundant.

At one stage children learning L1 frequently produce forms like *runned, goed* for *ran, went,* thus avoiding what they apparently perceive as unnecessary redundancy for expressing past tense. Similarly, L2 learners initially also avoid what is perceived as redundant in the TL. They differ, however, in already having a standard against which they can measure redundancy: their L1. Avoidance of perceived redundancy can be considered inhibitive transfer, as in Finnish learners leaving out articles and prepositions in English and Germanic learners dropping case endings when they learn Finnish. Prior knowledge provides a standard for the assessment of redundancy, and learners' assumptions may or may not be correct. More generally, avoidance of redundancy is a subconscious attempt by learners to reduce workload in order to facilitate learning.

Comprehension versus production

Similarities between incoming data and existing knowledge structures in comprehension are more concrete and tangible than similarities between communicative intentions and assumed existing knowledge structures in production. Thus formal cross-linguistic similarities leading to more transfer play a more important role in L2 comprehension than in L2 production. (See **cross-linguistic influence**.)

Conclusion

Transfer-related differences between learning related and unrelated languages apply mainly to early stages of learning. As learning progresses, all learners apply strategies and processes more TL native-like, and the difference between the two types of learners gradually diminishes. The different magnitudes of the learning task are most clearly seen in comprehension, where formal cross-linguistic similarities, especially in lexis, are obvious. Linguistic transfer influences both comprehension and production, albeit in slightly different ways.

See also: cross-linguistic influence, conceptual transfer, Contrastive Analysis Hypothesis (CAH), error analysis, one-to-one principle, vocabulary learning and teaching

References

Corder, S.P. (1973). *Introducing Applied Linguistics*. Harmondsworth: Penguin.

De Angelis, G. (2007). *Third or Additional Language Acquisition*. Clevedon, Buffalo and Toronto: Multilingual Matters.

Eckman, F. (2004). From phonemic differences to constraint rankings: Research on second language phonology. *Studies in Second Language Acquisition*, *26*, 513–49.

Ellis, R. (1985). *Understanding Second Language Acquisition*. Oxford: Oxford University Press.

Granger, S. (1993). Cognates: An aid or a barrier to successful L2 vocabulary development. *ITL Review of Applied Linguistics*, *99–100*, 43–56.

Jarvis, S. and Odlin, T. (2000). Morphological type, spatial reference, and language transfer. *Studies in Second Language Acquisition*, *22*, 535–56.

Jarvis, S. and Pavlenko, A. (2008). *Crosslinguistic Influence in Language and Cognition*. New York and London: Routledge.

Kasper, G. and Rose, K.R. (2002). *Pragmatic Development in a Second Language*. Oxford: Wiley-Blackwell.

Kellerman, E. (1977). Towards a characterisation of the strategy of transfer in second language learning. *Interlanguage Studies Bulletin, Utrecht*, *2*, 58–145.

Leather, J. and James, A.R. (1991). The acquisition of second-language speech. *Studies in Second Language Acquisition*, *13* (1991), 305–41.

Odlin, T. (1989). *Language Transfer: Cross-linguistic Influence in Language Learning*. Cambridge: Cambridge University Press.

——(2003). Cross-linguistic influence. In C.J. Doughty and M.H. Long (eds), *The Handbook of Second Language Acquisition*, pp. 436–86. Oxford: Blackwell.

Ringbom, H. (1987). *The Role of the First Language in Foreign Language Learning*. Clevedon: Multilingual Matters.

——(2007). *Cross-linguistic Similarity in Foreign Language Learning*. Clevedon, Buffalo and Toronto: Multilingual Matters.

Ringbom, H. and Jarvis, S. (2009). The importance of cross-linguistic similarity in foreign language learning. In M.H. Long and C.J. Doughty (eds), *The Handbook of Language Teaching*, pp. 106–18. Chichester: Wiley-Blackwell.

Takahashi, T. and Beebe, L.M. (1987). The development of pragmatic competence by Japanese learners of English. *JALT Journal*, *8*, 131–55.

Further reading

Cenoz, J., Hufeisen, B. and Jessner, U. (eds) (2001). *Cross-linguistic Influence in Third Language Acquisition: Psycholinguistic Perspectives*. Clevedon: Multilingual Matters.

Ellis, R. (2008). *The Study of Second Language Acquisition*, second edn. Oxford: Oxford University Press.

Hammarberg, B. (2009). *Processes in Third language Acquisition*. Edinburgh: Edinburgh University Press.

Kellerman, E. and Sharwood Smith, M. (eds) (1986). *Crosslinguistic Influence in Second Language Acquisition. Language Teaching Methodology Series*. Oxford: Pergamon Press.

Meriläinen, L. (2010). *Language Transfer in the Written English of Finnish Students*. Publications of the University of Eastern Finland. Dissertations in Education, Humanities and Theology 9.

Listening

Larry Vandergrift
University of Ottawa

Listening is an active process of meaning construction in which listeners attend to and process aural input automatically in real time, in order to understand what is unequivocally stated and to make all necessary inferences implied in the input (Buck, 2001). This process is directed by the purpose for listening and may also be influenced by visual input. This brief overview of listening will discuss the 1) cognitive processes involved in listening comprehension; 2) important knowledge sources listeners use to interpret what they hear; and 3) unique features of interactive listening.

Cognitive processes in listening

The cognitive processes that come into play during the process of L2 listening comprehension include: 1) top-down and bottom-up processing; 2) controlled and automatic processing; 3) perception, parsing and utilization; and 4) metacognition.

Fundamental to an understanding of comprehension processes is the distinction between bottom-up and top-down processing. Bottom-up processing involves segmentation of the sound stream into meaningful units to understand the message. This approach to listening, seen as a decoding process, assumes that comprehension begins with information in the sound stream, with minimal contribution from the listener's prior knowledge. An absolute form of this view of the comprehension process is not tenable since listeners could never keep up with the sound stream using this approach only.

Top-down processing, on the other hand, focuses on the use of contextual and prior knowledge to provide a conceptual framework for interpretation of texts. A top-down approach to listening, seen as an interpretation process, assumes that comprehension begins with listener expectations about information in the text. An absolute form of this approach to comprehension is not tenable either, since listeners may not have all the prior knowledge required or share the speaker's perspective on the topic. Top-down and bottom-up processes rarely operate independently, however. Linguistic information gleaned from decoding and prior knowledge applied during interpretation interact in parallel fashion as listeners create a mental representation of what they hear. The degree to which listeners may use one process more than another will depend on their purpose for listening.

Cognitive processing involved in fluent listening comprehension occurs extremely rapidly, moving between top-down and bottom-up processes as required to achieve comprehension. Successful L2 listening depends, obviously, on the degree to which listeners can efficiently coordinate these processes. Depending on their level of L2 proficiency and their familiarity with the topic of the text, listeners may need to consciously focus more on some aspects of the input or learn to selectively attend to basic elements of meaning, such as salient content words. Whatever listeners cannot process automatically is subject to controlled processing, time permitting. Controlled (as opposed to automatic) processing involves conscious attention to and processing of elements in the speech stream. Listening, like other skills, becomes automatic with practice. When conscious attention to specific elements of the sound stream is required, comprehension suffers, given the limitations of working memory and the speed of the incoming input. Controlled processing is not efficient because it cannot keep up with the incoming input and, consequently, comprehension either breaks down or listeners resort to compensatory strategies, contextual factors, and any other relevant information to guess what they did not understand.

Memory plays a crucial role in listening comprehension. Traditionally, the concept of memory has been divided into two components: long-term memory (LTM) and working memory (WM). LTM, as noted in the discussion of top-down processing, is the bank of information that listeners access to interpret what they are trying to understand. It contains the accumulated prior knowledge and life experiences of the listener, organized as schemata. Appropriate schemata are activated when listening to a related topic. While LTM shapes the interpretation of what listeners hear, WM influences the efficiency of the cognitive processing. In contrast to LTM, WM has a limited capacity; listeners can only attend to a restricted number of units before these units are replaced by new information to be processed. Listeners hold these units of information for a few seconds until the sounds are segmented into words or larger chunks of meaningful speech through links with LTM (Baddeley, 2003). The more listeners process information automatically, the more they can allocate the limited resources of WM to processing new information and to thinking about the content.

Another insightful description of how listeners construct meaning while bottom-up and top-down processing occurs is Anderson's (1995) differentiation of listening comprehension into three interconnected phases: perception, parsing, and utilization.

During the perception phase, listeners use bottom-up processing to identify sound categories (phonemes) of the language, pauses, and acoustic emphases, and they hold these in WM. A phonetic representation of what is retained is then passed on for parsing.

During the parsing phase (also bottom-up processing), listeners parse the phonetic representation of what was retained in memory and activate potential word candidates. Meaning is often the principal clue in segmentation and, as language proficiency develops, listeners can more quickly activate successful word candidates related to the context or topic, and hold meaning in increasingly larger chunks of information.

Development of word segmentation skills is a major challenge faced by L2 listeners. Unlike readers, listeners do not have the luxury of spaces to help them determine word boundaries and they may not recognize words they know in connected speech. Furthermore, word segmentation skills are language-specific and involuntarily applied when listening to a non-native language. Finally, in the utilization phase, listeners use top-down processing to relate what is understood to information sources in LTM in order to interpret implied meanings. Listeners monitor their interpretation for congruency with their prior knowledge and the evolving text, as often as necessary within the time available.

The different cognitive processes work neither independently nor in a linear fashion. Cognitive processing at each level can influence and be influenced by the results of processing that precedes or follows. Proficient listeners are better able to regulate these processes through their metacognition, that is, through their awareness of and ability to oversee and direct these processes (Goh, 2008). Judicious application of metacognitive knowledge is a mental characteristic shared by successful learners; in fact, Vandergrift, Goh, Mareschal and Tafaghodtari (2006) found that approximately 13 per cent of variance in listening achievement could be explained by metacognition. Listeners who apply their metacognitive knowledge to the comprehension process are better able to regulate their listening efforts and efficiently draw on relevant knowledge sources to build text comprehension.

Knowledge sources in listening

In order to arrive at a meaningful interpretation of what they hear, listeners must draw on different knowledge sources: linguistic, pragmatic, prior and discourse knowledge.

Linguistic knowledge is fundamental to listening comprehension; in fact, vocabulary knowledge is a strong predictor of L2 listening success (Staehr, 2009). In addition to vocabulary, linguistic knowledge includes phonological knowledge (phonemes, stress, intonation, and speech modifications) and syntactic knowledge (grammar) of the target language. Application of all three elements of linguistic knowledge helps listeners assign meaning to word-level units and to the relationship between words at the discourse level.

Listening involves more than just understanding words. Listeners use pragmatic knowledge to go beyond the literal meaning of a word to interpret the speaker's intended meaning. This involves, for example, interpretation of tone (e.g. sarcasm) or intonation (e.g. rising intonation for a question). Pragmatic knowledge is culturally bound and often needs to be taught.

The critical role of prior knowledge in listening comprehension has long been established (e.g. Macaro, Vanderplank and Graham, 2005). This knowledge base is stored LTM in the form of schemata (complex mental structures that group all knowledge concerning a concept). Providing context for listeners beforehand will help them activate appropriate schemata. They will then have the necessary information to activate their knowledge on the topic and to develop a conceptual framework for purposes of prediction and monitoring. Activation of prior knowledge helps listeners process linguistic input more efficiently, freeing up WM resources to process larger chunks of information. Although prior knowledge is important for facilitating comprehension, it can also be misleading when used inflexibly. Successful listeners continually use a combination of questioning and elaboration (activating prior knowledge) to monitor the emerging interpretation of a text for congruency with their expectations and prior knowledge (Vandergrift, 2003). Listeners use discourse knowledge when they consider and apply knowledge of text types to the comprehension process. It can be used proactively to anticipate the kinds of information that might be found in a text. Discourse knowledge is often used in combination with prior knowledge when, for example, the listener uses knowledge about how an interview with a soccer player might begin, what questions are asked and how the interview will likely end.

Interactive listening

Most accounts of listening focus on one-way listening, that is, contexts where there is no opportunity to intervene for purposes of clarification. Interaction with speakers of the target language, however, is an important goal for language learners. The ability to handle the cognitive and social demands of interactive listening is, therefore, an important component of listening competence. Although one-way and interactive listening share many characteristics (access to the same cognitive processes and knowledge sources) they are also different in important ways. Interactive listening is more contextual. Whether the context is formal or informal, listeners in interactive situations often have a common communicative goal that facilitates interpretation; for example, the job description, the applicant's curriculum vitae and the protocol for a job interview that implicitly specifies the role of applicant and interviewer. The context provides the backdrop to predict information heard, question-types used, and routines followed. Interpretation can be monitored as the interaction unfolds. The highly contextualized nature of interactive situations facilitates perception and parsing, since potential word candidates will be more quickly activated, and connections between words made more quickly. This allows listeners to process the interlocutor's utterances more efficiently. Listeners use metacognition to guide their predictions and to monitor their comprehension for congruence with their expectations. When they are confronted with something unexpected, are unable to resolve a comprehension problem internally, or simply do not understand, listeners can intervene and ask their interlocutor to clarify, repeat or speak slower. The possibility to clarify and/or negotiate meaning is probably the greatest benefit of interactive listening for language learners and has salutary effects on language learning (Eckerth, 2009).

An important variable in the success of interactive listening is the social dynamic. Good listeners do their part to move the interaction forward through culturally acceptable receipt tokens (uptakes or backchannels) or other acknowledgements of comprehension. When listeners face a comprehension problem, however, their response will depend on a number of affective variables such as willingness to take risks, fear of losing face, assertiveness and motivation. The degree to which these variables influence the interaction will depend on the relationship between the interlocutors, since status relationships can affect comprehension and the freedom to negotiate meaning. Differences, for example, in age, gender, language proficiency, and power relationships (employer–employee) often make interactive listening a context where the disadvantaged listener feels powerless. This sense of inferiority affects how much is understood (due to increased anxiety) and the degree to which listeners will dare to clarify comprehension or fake comprehension in order to save face. Furthermore, the face-to-face nature of these events also requires listeners to attend to non-verbal signals (e.g. furrowed eyebrows), body language, and culturally bound cues (e.g. certain gestures) which can add to, or change, the literal meaning of an utterance. Although these cues can be helpful to comprehension (e.g. a gesture that is can be transferred from L1 to L2), they can increase the cognitive demands of interactive listening if they are unique to the target language. Competent L2 listeners are able to coordinate cognitive processing, accessing appropriate knowledge sources and applying metacognitive knowledge as required, for comprehension in all listening contexts. As their language proficiency develops, listeners are able to this more efficiently.

See also: negotiation of meaning, parallel and distributed processing (PDP) models, pragmatics, schemata, speech perception and SLA, working memory

References

Anderson, J.R. (1995). *Cognitive Psychology and its Implications*, 4th edn. New York: Freeman.

Baddeley, A. (2003). Working memory and language: An overview. *Journal of Communication Disorders*, *36*, 189–208.

Buck, G. (2001). *Assessing Listening*. Cambridge: Cambridge University Press.

Eckerth, J. (2009). Negotiated interaction in the L2 classroom. *Language Teaching*, *42*, 109–30.

Goh, C. (2008). Metacognitive instruction for second language listening development: Theory, practice and research implications. *RELC Journal*, *39*, 188–213.

Macaro, E., Vanderplank, R. and Graham, S. (2005). A systematic review of the role of prior knowledge in unidirectional listening comprehension. in *Research Evidence in Education Library*. London: EPPI-Centre, Social Science Research Unit, Institute of Education, University of London.

Staehr, L.S. (2009). Vocabulary knowledge and advanced listening comprehension in English as a foreign language. *Studies in Second Language Acquisition*, *42*, 109–30.

Vandergrift, L. (2003). Orchestrating strategy use: Toward a model of the skilled second language listener. *Language Learning*, *53*, 463–96.

Vandergrift, L., Goh, C., Mareschal, C. and Tafaghodatari, M.H. (2006). The Metacognitive Awareness Listening Questionnaire (MALQ): Development and validation. *Language Learning*, *56*, 431–62.

Further reading

Field, J. (2008). *Listening in the Language Classroom*. Cambridge: Cambridge University Press. (A thorough discussion of the bottom-up dimension of comprehension, with many pedagogical applications.)

Goh, C. (2000). A cognitive perspective on language learners' listening comprehension problems. *System*, *28*, 55–75. (An examination and discussion of comprehension problems faced by ESL learners.)

Lynch, T. (2008). *Teaching Second Language Listening*. Oxford: Oxford University Press. (A readable overview of listening comprehension.)

Vandergrift, L. (1997). The Cinderella of communication strategies: Reception strategies in interactive listening. *Modern Language Journal*, *81*, 494–505. (A good overview of reception strategies and their role in language learning.)

Vandergrift, L. and Goh, C. (in press). *Teaching and Learning Second Language Listening*. New York: Routledge. (A readable and comprehensive overview of listening theory and concrete pedagogical applications with a particular emphasis on metacognition.)

Longitudinal research

Daniel O. Jackson
University of Hawai'i at Mānoa

Longitudinal studies on SLA acknowledge one of its most rudimentary facts: learning a second language takes time. Longitudinal research can be broadly defined in terms of extended study length and data collection at multiple intervals, as well as a focus on describing change by design and an emphasis on contextualized understandings of antecedent–consequent relations (Ortega and Iberri-Shea, 2005). Because they differ in time orientation from cross-sectional studies, longitudinal studies are particularly helpful for understanding developmental change or the long-term effects of individual factors.

Three widely cited examples illustrate how issues addressed by previous longitudinal work remain in focus today. Hakuta's (1976) study of the spontaneous speech of a 5-year old Japanese learner of English over 15 months described the acquisition of prefabricated constructions and morphological markers, in addition to the role of L1 transfer. Schmidt and Frota's (1986) five-month diary study of Schmidt's immersion in Brazilian Portuguese as an adult yielded the observation that noticing facilitates acquisition. Perdue and colleagues (1993; see the companion volume for results) employed a sophisticated design to uncover factors contributing to the acquisition of five target languages by 40 adult immigrants from several L1 backgrounds over a 30-month period. These seminal studies, along with many others, explored issues and constructs which characterize the field of SLA today.

In recent years, more attention has been paid to the diverse perspectives afforded by longitudinal studies. Ortega and Iberri-Shea (2005) reviewed current trends in longitudinal research in SLA, based on 38 studies published between 2002 and 2004. The authors provide definitions and examples of four types of longitudinal study (i.e., descriptive-quantitative studies of development, research on program outcomes, investigations of instructional effectiveness, and qualitative longitudinal research). Shortly afterwards, Ortega and Byrnes (2008) articulated the close relationship between longitudinal research and the study of advanced L2 capacities by compiling theoretical and empirical work on this theme.

Long-term, multi-wave research designs are complex, however, and the dynamics of L2 learning raise concerns which must be addressed in longitudinal studies. First, is the length of the study appropriate to address the emergent L2 phenomena at hand? Standard definitions of "longitudinal" and practical limitations on research notwithstanding, the timescale adopted in a study can drastically influence its conclusions, as described by Ortega and Iberri-Shea (2005, p. 32). Second, does data collection sample L2 phenomena at a rate that allows valid inferences about development? Here, careful task design to ensure comparability across measurement points is important, as is an understanding of the frequency of target behaviors in speech or writing. Participant attrition is yet another concern in this type of research. Lastly, longitudinal data can be analyzed using various approaches along the qualitative–quantitative continuum, thus researchers must consider the assumptions underlying their particular analytical choices.

In conclusion, longitudinal studies have, in a sense, defined the concerns of SLA, while contemporary scholars seek to further refine our notions of longitudinalness. The methodological and empirical insights stemming from recent contributions suggest that innovative, rigorous longitudinal research will continue to enrich our understanding of SLA.

See also: case studies, ethnographic research, measuring and researching SLA, mixed methods research, qualitative research, quantitative research

References

Hakuta, K. (1976). A case study of a Japanese child learning English as a second language. *Language Learning*, *26*, 321–51.

Ortega, L. and Byrnes, H. (eds) (2008). *The longitudinal study of advanced L2 capacities*. New York: Routledge.

Ortega, L. and Iberri-Shea, G. (2005). Longitudinal research in second language acquisition: Recent trends and future directions. *Annual Review of Applied Lingustics*, *25*, 26–45.

Perdue, C. (ed.) (1993). *Adult Language Acquisition: Cross-linguistic Perspectives*. Volume I: Field methods. Cambridge: Cambridge University Press.

Schmidt, R.W. and Frota, S.N. (1986). Developing basic conversational ability in a second language: A case study of an adult learner of Portuguese. In R.R. Day (ed.), *Talking to Learn: Conversation in Second Language Acquisition*, pp. 237–326. Rowley, MA: Newbury House.

Markedness

Marcus Callies
Johannes-Gutenberg-Universität Mainz

Markedness has been a central idea in crosslinguistic research and a popular and widely used construct in linguistics in general. Ascribed to Trubetzkoy and Jakobson of the Prague School of structural linguistics, the term has "developed a multiplicity of sometimes widely diverging senses that linguists who use it are often not aware of," and eventually lost "its association with a particular theoretical approach and became established as an almost theory-neutral everyday term in linguistics" (Haspelmath, 2006: 27). Markedness has been discussed rather controversially (Waugh and Lafford 1994), some criticism as wide-ranging as calling for its complete abandonment since it was "superfluous, because some of the concepts that it denotes are not helpful, and others are better expressed by more straightforward, less ambiguous terms" (Haspelmath, 2006: 25).

Various criteria for a comprehensive definition of markedness have been proposed in the literature. Most definitions assess the relative (un-)markedness of linguistic features in terms of structural, distributional, and frequential parameters in that "the unmarked value has a smaller number of morphemes used to express the value and a greater inflectional range, grammatical and crosslinguistic distribution and textual and crosslinguistic frequency, than the marked value" (Croft, 1990: 92). Additionally, markedness is frequently related to the behavior of linguistic entities in language acquisition and language change. Givón (1991) proposed a definition of markedness that includes three correlates – structural complexity, frequency distribution, and cognitive complexity – considering marked elements structurally more complex, less frequent, and therefore cognitively more salient. The integration of cognitive complexity, postulating a correlation between markedness and the cognitive-physiological complexity of linguistic units, captures the fact that marked structures tend to require more attention, mental effort, and time to be processed.

In SLA research, markedness has been mostly discussed as a predictor of the (non-) occurrence of transfer of linguistic structures from L1 to L2. While Eckman estimates that "linguists have been able to apply this construct to virtually all kinds of linguistic expressions, including […] lexical, morphological, and syntactic structures, in a number of sub-domains of linguistics" (Eckman, 2008: 97), markedness has been most widely applied in research on L2 phonology and the L2 lexicon, but less so in other subsystems like morphosyntax or pragmatics, where only relatively few studies have shown that typological markedness can be a reliable predictor of difficulty in the acquisition and use of linguistic phenomena (Callies, 2006, 2008, 2009).

The application of markedness in SLA theory has been much criticized, partially because of the fact that a straightforward incorporation of the concept into any linguistic theory has been impeded by both its multitude of senses and definitions, and the considerable degree of vagueness and indeterminacy of the term – depending on whether it is used and interpreted in a structural, discourse-motivated, psycholinguistic or typological sense, and depending on the linguistic subsystem it is related to. Eckman aptly summarizes that markedness principles "seemed to be lurking on the fringes as something that had to be recognized and reckoned with but not directly incorporated into a theory" (Eckman, 2004: 534). The usefulness of markedness as an explanatory concept in SLA has been questioned because it has been claimed to be external to the learner (White, 2004), and was not linked to learning mechanisms within the individual (Gregg, 1994). However, markedness has played a significant role in the explanation of various facts about L2 phonology in particular, and provided a precise definition and anchoring in a theoretical framework, it is a valuable research tool with considerable explanatory power.

Markedness has featured most prominently in two linguistic approaches to SLA, Universal Grammar and the Functional-Typological Approach, which will be discussed below. One other approach to SLA phonology in which markedness plays a central role is Optimality Theory (OT), which conceives of a grammar as a ranking of universal and violable constraints. Markedness is a basic tenet of OT, included in the form of markedness constraints that reflect generalizations on linguistic structures which occur frequently (unmarked) or rarely (marked) in natural languages. Highly marked phenomena are characterized by rankings that are very rare in the world's languages, while unmarked phenomena have rankings that are common. Put simply, acquisition is conceptualized as constraint re-ranking. Learners begin L2 learning with their L1 constraint rankings and have to acquire the re-rankings of those constraints according to the L2. It is posited that in the process of re-ranking the constraints from L1 to L2, the least marked structures' re-rankings will emerge before those that are more marked, a principle known as the emergence of the unmarked.

Most SLA research has conceived of markedness as a constraint on L1-transfer and a predictor of the relative ease or difficulty in the acquisition of L2 phenomena. In fact, the explanations and predictions offered through the perspective of language universals and markedness have provided researchers with a fresh look at the role of transfer in SLA. It is generally assumed that marked features, due to their greater structural and cognitive complexity, and comparative infrequency, are less readily transferable, and also more difficult to learn than unmarked features. With regard to making predictions about the acquisition of linguistic structures and their (non-)transferability from the L1, Kellerman (1978, 1983) initiated a re-evaluation of the notion of transfer. In his view, the learner is an active decision-maker on what linguistic structures may be transferable. Transfer is seen as a cognitive process subject to three constraints: (1) the learner's perception of the distance between L1 and L2 ("psychotypology"), (2) the learner's perception of the degree of markedness of a potentially transferable item in the L1 ("perceived transferability"), and (3) the nature of the learner's knowledge of the target language. Kellerman argued that if a linguistic feature was "perceived as infrequent, irregular, semantically or structurally opaque, or in any other way exceptional, what we could in other words call 'psycholinguistically marked', then its transferability will be inversely proportional to its degree of markedness" (Kellerman, 1983: 117). In this view, markedness may be said to resemble prototypicality. Thus, it is important to note that Kellerman's approach to transfer is based on a psycholinguistic understanding of markedness in terms of psychological and perceptual complexity, not structural complexity. Psychotypological aspects of the cognitive organization of interlanguages, such as perceived transferability, are essentially based on subjective learner perception, thus hard to objectify and with limited predictive power for the researcher.

Markedness has been conceptualized quite differently in approaches that employ linguistic universals to explain SLA phenomena: Universal Grammar and the Functional-Typological Approach (FTA). Since markedness has had a wider impact in the latter, I will concentrate on this approach here. The FTA (Eckman, 1977, 1996) is based on the assumption that the findings and generalizations made by language typologists can also be applied to language acquisition, recognizing the significance of universal (implicational) hierarchies for the prediction and explanation of (non-)transfer. It essentially draws on a Greenbergian approach to universals in that markedness is defined and operationalized as typological markedness (TM), an empirically motivated construct determined on the basis of crosslinguistic comparisons (Eckman, 1996). If typological universals are universal to all natural human languages, they should also hold for ILs. Since many universals can be expressed in terms of (implicational) hierarchical relations with respect to TM, it is reasonable to assume that such hierarchical relations between linguistic phenomena should also be present in ILs. Consequently, it should be possible to predict the occurrence of selected linguistic features in ILs, depending on their position in the hierarchy and the relative degree of markedness.

Compared to psycholinguistic markedness (or prototypicality), TM appears a more objective measurement, enabling researchers to assess language distance along typological properties. Eckman (1977) argued that on the basis of a contrastive analysis of L1 and L2, and the inclusion of the concepts of TM and crosslinguistic influence, it should be possible to predict areas of difficulty for L2 learners. He introduced the Markedness Differential Hypothesis (MDH), claiming that L1 structures that are different from L2 structures and typologically more marked will not be transferred, whereas L1 structures that are different from L2 structures and typologically less marked will more likely be transferred. Additionally, predictions can be made to both the order and difficulty of linguistic features in the acquisition process: less marked structures will be acquired first or without difficulty, more marked structures are expected to be acquired later or with greater difficulty. In sum, the MDH identifies potential difficulties in the learning process not merely on the basis of similarities and differences derived from a (traditional) contrastive analysis, but through a combination of the concepts of TM and crosslinguistic influence.

In view of the opportunities that markedness within the FTA offers for SLA research, it has not been utilized to date as much as it could. Despite the fact that a wide range of features has been examined in linguistic typology, only few typological universals have been addressed in SLA research, notably the Noun Phrase Accessibility Hierarchy. Only recently, due the growing interest in advanced stages of acquisition and questions of near-native competence, have studies come to the fore using experimental and learner-corpus data to examine typological universals in advanced ILs, for example, the thematic role hierarchy, a universal hierarchy of raising processes, and focus constructions (Callies, 2006, 2008, 2009).

See also: Contrastive Analysis Hypothesis (CAH), crosslinguistic influence, functional-typological linguistics, implicational universals, language typology and language distance, Markedness Differential Hypothesis (MDH)

References

Callies, M. (2006). Why money can't buy you anything in German: A functional-typological approach to the mapping of semantic roles to syntactic functions in SLA. In J. Arabski (ed), *Crosslinguistic Influences in the Second Language Lexicon*. Clevedon: Multilingual Matters, 111–29.

——(2008). Easy to understand but difficult to use? raising constructions and information packaging in the advanced learner variety. In G. Gilquin, M.B. Diez Bedmar and S. Papp (eds), *Linking Contrastive and Learner Corpus Research*, pp. 201–26. Amsterdam: Rodopi.

——(2009). *Information Highlighting in Advanced Learner English. The Syntax–Pragmatics Interface in Second Language Acquisition*. Amsterdam: Benjamins.

Croft, W. (1990). *Typology and Universals*. Cambridge: Cambridge University Press.

Eckman, F. (1977). Markedness and the contrastive analysis hypothesis. *Language Learning*, *27*, 315–30.

——(1996). A functional-typological approach to second language acquisition theory. In W.C. Ritchie and T.K. Bhatia (eds), *Handbook of Second Language Acquisition*, pp. 195–211. San Diego, CA: Academic Press.

——(2004). From phonemic differences to constraint Rankings. Research on Second Language Phonology. *Studies in Second Language Acquisition*, *26*, 513–49.

——(2008). Typological markedness and second language phonology. In J.G. Hansen Edwards and M.L. Zampini (eds), *Phonology and Second Language Acquisition*, pp. 95–115. Amsterdam: Benjamins.

Givón, T. (1991). Markedness in grammar: Distributional, communicative and cognitive correlates of syntactic structure. *Studies in Language*, *15*, 335–70.

Gregg, K.R. (1994). Second language acquisition: History and theory. In R.E. Asher and J.M.Y. Simpson (eds), *The Encyclopedia of Language and Linguistics*, Volme 5, pp. 3720–26. Oxford: Pergamon Press.

Haspelmath, M. (2006). Against markedness (and what to replace it with), *Journal of Linguistics*, *42*, 25–70.

Kellerman, E. (1978). Giving learners a break: Native language intuitions as a source of predictions about transferability. *Working Papers on Bilingualism*, *15*, 59–92.

——(1983). Now you See it, now you don't. In S. M. Gass and L. Selinker (eds), *Language Transfer in Language Learning*, pp. 112–34. Rowley, MA: Newbury House.

Waugh, L.R. and B.A. Lafford (2006). Markedness. In K. Brown (ed.), *The Encyclopedia of Language and Linguistics*, 2nd edn, pp. 491–98. Amsterdam: Elsevier.

White, L. (2004). 'Internal' vs. 'External' Universals. Commentary on Eckman. *Studies in Language*, *28*(3), 704–6.

Further reading

Eckman, F. (2008). Typological markedness and second language phonology. In J.G. Hansen Edwards and M.L. Zampini (eds), *Phonology and Second Language Acquisition*, pp. 95–115. Amsterdam: Benjamins. (Provides a brief history of typological markedness and an overview of its role in the explanation of facts about L2 phonology, discussing some major issues and counterclaims surrounding the use of markedness as an explanatory principle in SLA in general, and L2 phonology in particular.)

Ellis, R. (2008). *The Study of Second Language Acquisition*, 2nd edn. Oxford: Oxford University Press. (Chapter 12 offers an overview of linguistic approaches that employ universals and markedness to explain SLA phenomena.)

Hancin-Bhatt, B. (2008). Second language phonology in optimality theory. In J.G. Hansen Edwards and M.L. Zampini (eds), *Phonology and Second Language Acquisition*, pp. 117–46. Amsterdam: Benjamins. (Explores the relationship between L2 phonology research and Optimality Theory.)

Haspelmath, M. (2006). Against markedness (and what to replace it with), *Journal of Linguistics*, *42*, 25–70. (Overview of the various senses of markedness used in twentieth-century linguistics and a critical assessment of the usefulness of the concept.)

Markedness Differential Hypothesis (MDH)

Fred R. Eckman
University of Wisconsin-Milwaukee

The purpose of this entry is to describe and exemplify the Markedness Differential Hypothesis (henceforth MDH), as formulated in Eckman (1977). The MDH was proposed to address certain empirical problems with the Contrastive Analysis Hypothesis (henceforth CAH). (Whereas the CAH was formulated by Lado [1957], the hypothesis was given its name by Wardhaugh [1970].) The CAH claimed that structural differences between the learner's native language (NL) and the target language (TL) were both necessary and sufficient to account for difficulty in second-language (L2) acquisition, however, the MDH asserted that NL-TL differences are necessary, but not sufficient, to explain difficulty in acquisition.

One of the most explicit statements of the CAH is the following quotation from Lado (1957, 2):

> (1) "We assume that the student who comes in contact with a foreign language will find some features of it quite easy and others

> extremely difficult. Those elements that are similar to his native language will be simple for him, and those elements that are different will be difficult."

In the decades of research that followed the postulation of the CAH, the results were mixed. Although some studies supported the CAH, many others reported findings that were counter to the hypothesis, leading to the eventual demise of the CAH.

The goal of the MDH, stated in (2), was to remedy some of the empirical counterevidence against the CAH by incorporating the concept of markedness as a measure of degree of difficulty.

(2) The Markedness Differential Hypothesis (Eckman, 1977: 321)
The areas of difficulty that a language learner will have can be predicted such that
(a) Those areas of the TL that differ from the NL and are more marked than the native language will be difficult;
(b) The relative degree of difficulty of the areas of difference of the TL that are more marked than the NL will correspond to the relative degree of markedness;
(c) Those areas of the TL that are different from the NL, but are not more marked than the TL will not be difficult.

The idea behind markedness, which was pioneered by the Prague School of Linguistics (Trubetzkoy, 1939; Jakobson, 1941), is that some, but not all, structural differences or contrasts between linguistic representations (e.g. voiced and voiceless obstruents, definite and indefinite articles, open and closed syllables) are not simply polar opposites. Rather, one member of the opposition or contrast can be shown to be privileged in that it occurs more widely across languages. Imposing a markedness value on this opposition is one way of characterizing this privileged status: the member of the opposition that is more widely distributed than the other is designated as unmarked. This indicates that the structure in question is more basic and more natural than the other member of the opposition, which is defined as the marked member.

The construct of markedness has been developed and employed in descriptions of languages over the ensuing decades by numerous linguistic schools of thought, and has therefore, depending on the school of thought, been characterized in slightly different ways. The concept of markedness that is incorporated into the MDH is defined as in (3).

> (3) A structure X in some language is typologically marked relative to another structure, Y (and Y is typologically unmarked relative to X) if every language that has X also has Y, but every language that has Y does not necessarily have X.
> (Gundel, Houlihan and Sanders, 1986: 108)

As an example of typological markedness, consider the case of voiced and voiceless fricatives in a language (e.g., sounds such as [f], [v], [s], [z], etc.). Voiced and voiceless fricatives are in a markedness relationship, because, across the world's languages, if a language has voiced fricatives in its inventory of sounds, it also has voiceless fricatives, but not vice versa. Therefore, the presence of voiced fricatives in a language implies the presence of voiceless fricatives, but the presence of voiceless fricatives does not necessarily imply the presence of voiced fricatives. Consequently, voiced fricatives are marked relative to voiceless fricatives, and conversely, voiceless fricatives are unmarked relative to voiced fricatives.

The MDH is programmatic with the CAH in that both hypotheses assert differences between the NL and TL are necessary to explain learning difficulty. The MDH is different from the CAH in that the former hypothesis claims that NL-TL differences are not sufficient for an explanation of difficulty; rather, the MDH states that it is necessary also to incorporate typological markedness into the hypothesis as a measure of difficulty. Within the areas of NL-TL differences, marked structures are more difficult than the corresponding unmarked structures.

What follows immediately from the MDH is that not all NL-TL differences will cause equal difficulty. A specific example of this kind of supporting evidence derives from different amounts of difficulty are encountered by learners from diverse NL backgrounds who are all learning the same TL. A study by Anderson (1987) reported that the difficulty in learning onset and coda clusters in English was different for native speakers of Egyptian Arabic, Mandarin Chinese and Amoy Chinese, and that the degree of difficulty associated with this learning corresponded to the relative markedness of the clusters. The markedness principle employed in Anderson's study came from the work of Greenberg (1976) and stated that the existence of an onset cluster of length N in a language implies the occurrence of onset clusters of length N-1 in that language, where N is an integer. For example, a language that allows three consonants in onsets will necessarily allow two-consonant onset clusters, but not vice versa; and a language that allows bi-consonantal onsets will also permit singleton onsets, but not vice versa. The same principle holds also for codas. In short, longer clusters in onsets and codas are more marked relative to, respectively, shorter clusters in onsets and codas. The results of Anderson's study supported the MDH in that the performance of the Chinese-speaking subjects was less target-like than that of the Arabic-speaking subjects on coda clusters, and the difference in performance correlated with degree of markedness associated with the NL-TL difference.

See also: Contrastive Analysis Hypothesis (CAH), cross-linguistic influence, functional-typological linguistics, implicational universals, interlanguage, markedness

References

Anderson, J. (1987). The markedness differential hypothesis and syllable structure difficulty. In G. Ioup and S. Weinberger (eds), *Interlanguage Phonology: The Acquisition of a Second Language Sound System*. New York: Newbury House.

Eckman, F. (1977). Markedness and the contrastive analysis hypothesis. *Language Learning*, *27*, 315–30.

Greenberg, J. (1976). *Language Universals*. The Hague: Mouton.

Gundel, J., K. Houlihan and G. Sanders. (1986). Markedness distribution in phonology and syntax. In F. Eckman, E. Moravcsik and J. Wirth (eds), *Markedness*. New York: Plenum Press.

Jakobson, R. (1941). *Child Language, Aphasia, and Phonological Universals*. The Hague: Mouton.

Lado, R. (1957). *Linguistics Across Cultures: Applied Linguistics for Language Teachers*. Ann Arbor: University of Michigan Press.

Trubetzkoy, N. (1939). *Principles of Phonology*. Paris: Klincksieck.

Wardhaugh, R. (1970). The contrastive analysis hypothesis. *TESOL Quarterly*, *4*, 123 – 130.

Further reading

Battistella, E. (1990). *Markedness: The Evaluative Superstructure of Language*. Albany, NY: The State University of New York Press. (An extended treatment of markedness in numerous linguistic domains.)

Eckman, F. (2004). Universals, innateness and explanation in second language acquisition. *Studies in Language*, *28*, 682–703. (An article on markedness as an explanatory principle.)

Moravcsik, E. and J. Wirth. (1986). Markedness: An overview. In F. Eckman, E. Moravcsik and J. Wirth (eds), *Markedness*. New York: Plenum. (A description of markedness as defined in various ways by linguists.)

Measuring and researching SLA

Andrew Cohen and Ernesto Macaro

University of Minnesota and University of Oxford

What does the measure of SLA encompass at present and how is expertise in its measurement manifested? A useful starting point is to identify the phenomenon in question which is that human beings are capable of learning multiple languages beyond the one they are exposed to at birth (their L1) and that they vary in the way that they learn that L2 in terms of rate of development and final attainment. L2 research, in fact, started as an extension of L1 acquisition research (because the assumption was that the mental processes were similar). By and large this is no longer the case since current L1 acquisition concern is more with specific learning difficulties, especially in the case of literacy. SLA research has therefore concentrated more on the second aspect of phenomenon, rate of learning and final attainment.

This entry explores the following:

- What kinds of research questions have been asked in order to try to explain and predict the phenomenon?
- What populations have been investigated in order to explain the phenomenon?
- What kinds of data have been collected?
- What types of tests have been employed in order to measure SLA?

Explaining and predicting the phenomenon

The variance, in either rate of learning or final attainment levels (or both), has been explored from two main perspectives: the acquisition of linguistic knowledge and the development of linguistic skills. Research into the acquisition of linguistic knowledge can be subdivided into three further categories: the acquisition of the L2 rule system, the acquisition of vocabulary (including larger lexical units), and the acquisition of pragmatic knowledge (both linguistic- and socially related). Until relatively recently it is the first of these sub-categories that has most exercised the minds of researchers. One key concept has been the notion of "constraint" – namely, what stops learners from learning or making progress with the rule system (see the entries for **Morpheme acquisition orders**; **Developmental sequences**; and **Developement in SLA**, this volume). This focus on the rule system sends the message that language acquisition will be best explained once these constraints are understood, rather than focusing, for example, on the relative prowess of memory. This focus suggests that the answer essentially lies in the mechanics of the language, as related to all learners or groups of learners, rather than in the attributes of the individual learner.

Research on the acquisition of words and the development of the mental lexicon has gained pace in recent decades and is no longer a neglected field of study, perhaps because of developments in corpus-based linguistics and a growing interest in lexical approaches to teaching and learning. Here research interest has focused on vocabulary depth and breadth, how words are associated with one another, and the strategies that learners use to acquire vocabulary.

Our review of studies from 2002 to 2007 (see below) suggests that the acquisition of pragmatic knowledge is a field, if not in its infancy, certainly still only in early adolescence. Researchers working in the field of oral interaction (see **Interaction and the Interaction Hypothesis,** this volume) have been more concerned with the acquisition of the mental lexicon and morpho-syntactic development than with the development of the skill of speaking. When it comes to the development of linguistic skills, not surprisingly, there appears to be a division between the receptive skills of listening and reading and the productive skills of speaking and writing. In the former two, there is a close conjoining of research interest in how general knowledge of the world interacts with the text that the learner/participant is listening to or reading. There are differences of emphasis brought on by the two modalities, but in essence the research agenda is similar. In the case of speaking and writing, however, the research agendas have diverged; in oral production the emphasis being on measuring development in fluency, complexity, and accuracy. In the case of writing (whilst these three developmental aspects have certainly not been ignored) there has been a notable interest in the topic of feedback to learners' errors, this being a tool for the exploration of the development of the rule system. Interestingly, the field of speaking research (in the sense of speaking as a skill to be developed) has not concerned itself extensively with what learners do with feedback on their errors (see **Corrective feedback**, this volume), the latter being appropriated by the field of "interaction," a field more concerned with the development of the rule system than skill development.

Exploring the populations of language learners

The macro-population of learners that has been overwhelmingly researched is adults and particularly young adults in their first years of college or university. There are no doubt many practical reasons for this, not least of which: accessibility of participants, sufficient proficiency levels to enable quantities of linguistic data to be collected, ethical and "risk" issues. Even so, some commentators have suggested that the neglect of young and particularly beginner learners is unacceptable and may be ignoring the very investigations which might lead the SLA field to answer its "rate" and "final attainment" research questions (see, for example, Macaro, 2010). Moreover, SLA research has focused on a quite limited number of second languages (English, Spanish, and French) compared to the diversity of languages and L1 learners internationally.

The very nature of SLA as a global phenomenon appears to have led researchers to provide only limited information regarding the context in which the second language acquisition is taking place. Samples of participants are described and, at best, the *procedure* for arriving at those samples is given, but not the *rationale* for arriving at the sample from the population.

Epistemological basis for research

The split in applied linguistic and especially SLA research between more quantitative and qualitative approaches draws from a distinction in educational research between positivist and constructivist approaches. The positivist approach relied on observation and reason as a means of understanding behavior, drawing on the approach to scientific description that called for verification of findings (Shank, 1993). The emphasis was on quantitative research, on empirical science and rational methods, with an emphasis on objectivity.

In contrast, the constructivist view was that the human mind had a role to play in not only understanding but also, crucially, creating behaviour and other phenomena. Constructivists contended that a mechanistic and reductionist view of nature excluded choice, freedom, subjectivity, individuality, and life experiences. Their stance was that reducing researchers to observers, set on discovering general laws governing human behavior, was dehumanizing. Anti-positivist approaches included *phenomenology* – the study of direct experience taken at face value, where behavior is determined by the phenomena of experience rather than by external, objective, and physically described reality. Another anti-positivist approach was that of *ethnomethodology*, dealing with how people make sense of their everyday world: interactions in a social encounter (the assumptions they make, the conventions that they use, and the practices that they adopt) (Cohen and Manion, 1994: 29–32).

These opposing epistemological positions are partly mirrored by the over-arching methodological split between a psycholinguistic approach to understanding SLA (see **Psycholinguistics of SLA**, this volume) and a socio-cultural approach (see **Social and sociocultural approaches to SLA**, this volume). Whether fledgling students or experienced professionals in the field, researchers need to determine for themselves the nature of knowledge before they begin to select research methods for answering their questions of interest.

The traditional way to contrast qualitative and quantitative approaches to research is by providing descriptors for the two (see the entries on **Qualitative research** and **Quantitative research**, this volume), such as the one by Larsen-Freeman and Long (1991: 12), and echoed in Lazaraton (2002):

> **Quantitative Research** – controlled, experimental, objective, inferential, outcome-oriented, reliable, particularistic, hard/replicable data, generalizable, aggregate analysis;
>
> **Qualitative Research** – naturalistic, observational, subjective, descriptive, process-oriented, valid, holistic, real, rich/deep data, ungeneralizable, single-case analysis.

In an effort to clarify this distinction, Johnstone (2000) noted that quantitative studies tend to inquire about how often something happens (e.g., counting instances, computing means, calculating statistics), while qualitative studies focus on *why* and *how* things happen (e.g., by asking about, watching or listening to phenomena of interest).

While Brown (2004) viewed the distinction between quantitative and qualitative research as a matter of degrees on a continuum rather than a clear-cut dichotomy, Dörnyei (2007: 20) argued that although the dichotomous distinction is useful, *mixed-methods research* (namely, hybrid studies that combine qualitative and quantitative methods) helps reduce the inherent weaknesses of individual methods. Dörnyei provided arguments in favor of methodological triangulation through mixed methods – that they can compensate for unrepresentative samples, allow investigations of the problem from different perspectives, and help researchers corroborate findings (pp. 45–46). Dörnyei also provided caveats in that mixed methods can become a substitute for sharp conceptual thinking, and researchers may not have equal methodological skills for doing both kinds of research. Most SLA research theorists would agree that what is to be avoided in mixed methods is a "scattergun approach," where different tools are adopted ad hoc and without being justified by the research questions.

In any effort to determine just how often applied linguists were doing one or another kind of research, Lazaraton (2005) classified all empirical research articles in *Language Learning, Modern Language Journal, Studies in Second Language Acquisition,* and the *TESOL Quarterly* during an 11-year period, 1991–2001. She found 86 per cent of the 524 articles to reflect quantitative research, only 13per cent to be qualitative, and 1per cent to involve mixed approaches. At the time, *TESOL Quarterly* was the most likely of the four journals to publish a qualitative research report.

In order to update this picture, the current authors examined 420 empirical studies in five leading journals from 2002 to 2007 (Cohen and Macaro, 2010). Largely on the basis of the research questions (where available), the overall design, and the instruments, the design types were summarized, along with their frequency and the frequency of the different instruments used. Of the 420 papers, half were either descriptive or experimental studies, and the other half were explorations of relationships. An example of a *descriptive study* is that of Hyland and Tse (2004), who analyzed 240 dissertations by students writing in their L2 in order to understand the range of devices that they deployed in order to organize the texts that they produced and the ways in which they communicated with their readers. Another descriptive study is that of Vickers (2007) who collected naturalistic data from seven team meetings of six university engineering students in order to describe the interactional processes that defined who the expert, socialized participants were, and those interactional processes that worked to socialize novice participants.

Experimental studies, for example, involve exposing learners to a different kind of instruction to what they normally experience and measuring whether this results in better learning, or setting up a situation where one group of learners is exposed to a particular technique and another group to a different technique. The "gold standard" for the experimental study is the randomized control trial where the participants are randomly allocated to the conditions. Experimental study designs in SLA are considered to be the most scientific because they try to emulate the natural sciences' approach to research even though, in SLA, researchers are dealing with processes which ultimately occur in the brain but are predominantly investigated through means other than understanding the functions of the brain. In this type of study, the researcher usually formulates a hypothesis about what the outcomes are likely to be, based on the theory (or past evidence) that underpins the study. The intention is to test the theory, to see if it actually predicts what it claims to predict will happen if the right conditions are established and the situation is manipulated in a particular way.

Explorations of relationships studies look for associations among different variables. These are existing variables, occurring naturally in time and space, and the researcher does not change the nature of these variables nor add to them in any way. In these studies, however, researchers normally have some knowledge of the phenomenon under scrutiny or at least sufficient knowledge for them to ask questions such as:

- What is the impact of phonological awareness on listening ability?
- What is the relationship between teaching styles and learner motivation?
- What most affects success in L2 learning, length of residence in the target country or age of arrival in that country?

In other words, the relationship examined can be between dependent and independent variables or between two or more variables without specifying the direction of impact, or causation.

An example of an exploration-of-relationships study is by Leeser (2004). In this study a number of variables were compared for their potential effect on students' comprehension of L2 texts, as well as their ability to process future tense morphology. So comprehension and ability to process morphology were the dependent variables, the outcome measures that Leeser was trying to investigate. The independent variables were mode (the participants either read or listened to the text), topic familiarity (whether the topic of the text was familiar to the students), and pausing (whether short pauses were inserted in the text or not). Leeser was trying to test the effect of one variable on the other – to show possible causation. In fact, the majority of studies exploring relationships between variables attempt to show a possible causation. A minority of studies take a correlational approach – in other words, investigating whether a higher value for X also means a higher value for Y. Such a study is Griffiths (2003) where strategy use, course level, and age were correlated with one another to see which pair was most strongly linked.

Research instruments in SLA

In the authors' analysis of SLA research articles in leading journals, the finding was that the overwhelming majority of studies (80 per cent) made use of tests or tasks as the primary research instrument (Cohen and Macaro, 2010). This strongly implies that researchers' conceptualization of how to understand the SLA phenomenon is to measure acquisition or learning via actual performance of some kind. Far fewer used questionnaires, still fewer used observation or interviews, and fewer than 5 per cent of the studies had other types of instruments. The scarce use of these instruments would suggest that SLA researchers have been less interested in teaching and learning processes or teacher and learner beliefs, and more interested in isolating or manipulating variables to test outcomes.

Where tests were used, the number of standardized tests adopted was very low and little researcher attention seemed to be devoted to ensuring their validity. Nor was there a stated concern with piloting of these tests and tasks. Bearing in mind that studies sometimes used multiple measures, it was found that well over 50 different types of tests and tasks were used in research studies since 2002. Twenty percent consisted of vocabulary tests, 15per cent were comprehension tests, 9 per cent were oral production tests, 7 per cent were written production tests and grammaticality judgment tests, respectively, 6 per cent were information-gap tests, 5 per cent were tests of oral production, 4 per cent were standardized tests of proficiency, and then there were 28 different types of measures with a more limited frequency in the various studies (appearing in only 2 per cent or fewer of the studies).

In considering these instruments, it is best to refer to them by their generic names, and to focus on their features or attributes, much as co-author Cohen (1994) did some years ago in describing the item-elicitation and item-response formats for language assessment instruments. The advantage of doing this kind of distinctive-feature analysis of research measures is that instruments with dissimilar sounding labels may in fact be relatively similar in nature.

Focus on instrumentation: Tests and tasks

How does one distinguish a *test* from a *task*? In part, the distinction is between measures intended to assess language proficiency as opposed to those intended for the purpose of exploring issues in second language acquisition (see Bachman and Cohen, 1998). If a measure is referred to as a *test*, the implication is that there is a certain level of rigor, presumably established through piloting of the measure and establishing its internal validity. A task, on the other hand, has not necessarily undergone the same rigorous scrutiny in terms of its validity and the results from its use would have a different purpose than for a test.

This brief description of tests and tasks is limited to the discussion of measures of linguistic knowledge and linguistic performance whilst recognizing that linguistic knowledge and performance may overlap. Below a representative sample is provided of recently used measures of competence and performance – involving vocabulary, grammatical control, listening comprehension, oral discourse, reading and writing.

- *Word association as a test of vocabulary knowledge (depth and breadth)*: in a test used by Greidanus, Beks, and Wakely (2005), respondents were given a trigger word in French L2: for example, *jeune*. They then had to tick all the words in a provided list that they thought had a clear connection to the word. For further reading on word association see Meara (2010).
- *A written measure of speech-act production*: this task, used by Cohen and Shively (2007), constituted an indirect means for assessing pragmatic ability in L2 speaking. A multiple-rejoinder discourse completion task (DCT) was designed which included 10 vignettes (five requests and five apologies). Eighty-six college students in a study abroad filled in the blanks of the dialogues that included two to four responses from an interlocutor, in one of three versions: French, Peninsular Spanish, and Latin American Spanish.
- *Inferencing vocabulary from a written context*: this task, used by Paribakht (2005), involved the inferencing of English L2 words from a text that included concepts familiar to educated Farsi speakers but for which no lexical equivalents were found in Farsi L1. The construct being examined here was "knowledge of the world" and its contribution to arriving at the meaning of unfamiliar words.
- *Morphological judgment task*: this task was used to assess morphological awareness in Hebrew L1 and English L2 by Schiff and Calif (2007). Separate task sheets were prepared for each language. All of the morphologically related task word pairs were a base and a linear derivational form. The respondents had to write "yes" where they thought that the meanings of the paired words were related and "no" if they did not.
- *Translation task*: the purpose of this task, used by Bruton (2007), was to investigate the acquisition of new English L2 vocabulary from the act of writing. Using the justification that a translation task reduces the possibility of avoidance in writing, the researcher required participants to translate text from their L1 in order to "push" them to use previously unknown vocabulary, in line with Swain's (1985) Output Hypothesis.
- *Form-recognition task*: this task, used by Leeser (2004), was intended to measure the extent to which learners noticed future tense in Spanish L2, either when they listened to a narrative passage or when they read the same text. The two versions each contained 60 items: 19 future tense forms, five nouns, and 36 distracter items. In the recitation mode, the respondents ticked whether they remembered hearing a given word in the passage. In the reading mode, they ticked words if they remembered seeing them in the passage.
- *Grammaticality judgment tests (GJT)*: a GJT was constructed by Cuervo (2007) to test participants' knowledge of the double-object construction in Spanish L2 and how it differed from its English L1 counterpart in its morphosyntactic properties (case, clitic doubling, word order) and its semantic properties (interpretation of arguments and restrictions on the construction). The respondents were given a list of 38 grammatical sentences and 29 ungrammatical sentences plus 20 distracters, and were asked to judge their acceptability on a Likert scale from –2 for completely unacceptable to +2 for perfectly acceptable, according to first impressions. The subjects took 25–40 minutes to complete the task. For a discussion of how GJTs differentially test implicit or explicit knowledge see Ellis (2004).
- *Input memory task and generalization test*: Williams and Lovatt's (2003) investigation of the noticing of syntactic relationships involved a strict experimental sequence for participants completely new to Italian L2: they were first exposed to determiner-noun relationships in L2 (both oral and written) as a test of phonological working memory. They had to recall the vocabulary presented, recall an L1 noun-phrase following a presented set of Italian phrases, and generate new determiner-noun combinations to demonstrate whether they could generalize the rule to a new lexical item.
- *Sentence conjunction judgment task*: Montrul and Sablakova (2003) used a measure of competence in tense and aspect that specifically tested the semantic implications of the preterite

and imperfect tenses in Spanish L2. The subjects received a list of sentences containing two coordinated clauses conjoined by *y* "and" or *pero* "but." Some of the combinations were contradictory, while others made sense.

- *Phonological awareness*: in order to measure the phonological awareness of young Chinese-L1 children learning English L2, Knell, Qiang, Pei, Chi, Siegel, Zhao, and Zhao (2007) devised two measures, one focusing on awareness of initial sound (onset) and one on rime (the last syllable in the word). To get at awareness of onset each child first heard a stimulus word and afterwards three more words. The children were to indicate which of the three words had the same first sound as the first word.
- *Aural discrimination task*: Arteaga, Herschensohn, and Gess (2003) used an 18-item aural discrimination test with the items pre-recorded by a native French speaker. In the instructions for the test, the English L1 participants were told that French L2 names often sound the same for both males and females, as for example, *Claude*, who may be a man or a woman. All items consisted of a proper name of this type, followed by the copula verb (in positive or negative form), followed by an adjective which in French has to agree.
- *Reading span test of working memory*: in order to determine working memory span in Spanish L2, with a focus on the future tense among beginning learners, Leeser (2007) constructed a computerized reading span test for Spanish L2, based on a reading span test in English. Participants read on a computer screen 80 sentences that varied in length, syntactic complexity, and plausibility, and indicated whether they thought the sentence was plausible or implausible. They were also instructed to remember the last word of each sentence, and after sets ranging between two and six sentences, they had to write down as many of the sentence final words as they remembered.
- *Timed sentence-comprehension test*: this measure was used to study the semantic and syntactic processing of a German L2 text appearing on a computer screen (Jackson, 2007). Twenty-four target sentences were constructed consisting of a main clause, followed by a subordinate clause, with each manipulated to create four different versions in German L2. The key portion of each sentence was in the subordinate clause, which contained a subject, identified by nominative case markings, and a direct object, identified by accusative case markings.
- *Four-stage writing task*: in this English-L2 writing multi-stage task (Hanaoka, 2007), Japanese-L1 students compared their output to native models in two revisions of a story that they wrote, with the focus being on what they noticed about their written production. The question that the researcher asked was whether "noticing" later turned into better performance. The four stages of the task were: writing a story in response to a two-frame picture prompt, writing on a new sheet of paper whatever they noticed as they compared their original text with two native-speaker models, performing an immediate revision of their story on a new sheet based on what they remembered of what they had noticed, and performing another revision two months later.

Mixed-methods studies

Some of the examined studies adopted a mixed-methods approach (see the entry on **Mixed methods research**, this volume), which facilitated the use of alternative instruments. To exemplify, mixed methods were applied in the investigation of all of the following areas:

- *Linguistic knowledge* – including grammatical judgment tests, discourse completion tasks, verbal report data, and reaction time measures.
- *Linguistic performance/skills* – anything from tests of receptive ability using a multiple-choice format to cloze and C-tests, to free-recall protocols or story narration, to role play.
- *Attitudes and perceptions* – including questionnaire/surveys (on- and off-line), interviews (varyingly structured), journals, or use of a "repertory grid" (to get at people's perceptions, assumptions, and concepts).
- *Cognitive processing* – mostly through verbal report measures such as think-alouds, introspective, and retrospective self-observation (also referred to as *stimulated recalls*), and self-report.

While the categories of "linguistic knowledge" and "linguistic performance" would appear to be relatively discrete, a study could be designed that would, say, use a role play to not only measure someone's performance in the L2, but also their knowledge about it. The researcher would use retrospective self-observational data from the learners to find out what they knew about the various forms that they used. By the same token, a grammatical judgment test could be used to determine learners' knowledge of third-person singular *–s* in English, and then to follow it up with elicitation of the form to get at the performance side (Mackey and Gass, 2005: 49–50).

Verbal reports

Two verbal report techniques, in particular, think aloud and stimulated recall (see entries on **Protocol analysis** and **Stimulated recall**, this volume), represent polarities on a continuum because they involve two variables: time and distance from the learning event. In a think-aloud protocol, the participants are given a task to perform and during the performance of that task they are asked to articulate what their thought processes are. The researcher's role is merely to encourage that verbalization through prompting the participants with utterances such as "Please keep telling me what you are thinking" and "please keep thinking aloud if you can." Think-aloud implies no direct inspection of the mental state, but merely reportage.

There is debate as to how feasible it is to reliably capture these inner thought processes and whether the process of thinking aloud might distort the way that the participants would normally go about doing the task (for an update, see Bowles, 2010). For example, trying to think aloud while "concurrently" listening to an audio recording is challenging, and trying to think aloud when carrying out a speaking task is even more so. Consequently, a researcher may choose to stop the recording during, say, a listening task and to ask listeners to verbalize what they were doing in their heads during that segment of the text, or have the respondents select the moment to pause and provide a retrospective verbal report.

There are also situations where it is impossible (or unacceptable) to capture learners' thought processes at the time that the event is taking place. A typical instance would be during a language lesson, where, for example, a researcher may want to know what the learners' reaction was to a specific teacher behavior. Or a researcher interested in investigating the theme of L2 pragmatic ability sets up a role play in a meeting between student and teacher. Here is a situation where employing stimulated recall could be beneficial. For example, the role play can be video-recorded and played back to the participants in order to stimulate what was going through their minds at the time of the event. The more time that has elapsed since the event, the more the learners may have forgotten what they were thinking and/or the more they might be interpreting the event in the light of later events.

In both think-aloud and stimulated-recall situations, there is the methodological issue of whether the researcher pre-selects the episodes to be used as stimuli or has the participants self-selecting them. Further coverage of issues relating to verbal report in L2 research can be found in Green (1998), Brown and Rodgers (2002: 53–78), Mackey and Gass (2005: 75–85), Bowles (2010), and Cohen (2012).

Discussion

SLA research has advanced considerably from use of traditional instruments. Although questionnaires also feature highly on the lists of instruments used, many were adopted for the purposes of providing brief background information about the participants. SLA research has tried to develop a clearly distinctive set of tools, but particularly language tests and tasks. These have been specifically designed to measure the SLA of developing or actual bilinguals. Those bilinguals are often in formal educational contexts. A concern therefore is that the international nature of SLA research (compounded by the global status of English) almost demands that language tests and tasks be lifted and divorced from their original educational context, without taking into account aspects of the learner as an individual, and as a socially situated and creative human being. We would argue for more description of the educational context in which the testing is taking place, and likewise for the researcher to provide adequate information about the tests and tasks so that readers anywhere in the world can understand just what they entailed and their value in the given study. Bachman and Cohen (1998) had raised this issue over a decade ago because it appeared that SLA tasks were (and probably still are) in need of more rigorous evaluation using the tools of language assessment. We speculate that measures currently used in SLA studies may vary in reliability according to the L2 being tested and indeed the first language and culture of the participants. And this fluctuation in reliability would of course have serious implications for the validity of the measures as well.

See also: ethnographic research, meta-analysis, mixed methods research, qualitative research, quantitative research, theoretical constructs in SLA

References

Arteaga, D., Herschensohn, J. and Gess, R. (2003). Focusing on phonology to teach morphological form in French. *Modern Language Journal, 87* (1), 58–70.

Bachman, L.F. and Cohen, A.D. (1998). Language testing – SLA interfaces: An update. In L.F. Bachman and A.D. Cohen (eds), *Interfaces between Second Language Acquisition and Language Testing Research*, pp. 1–31. Cambridge: Cambridge University Press.

Brown, J.D. (2004). Research methods for applied linguistics: Scope, characteristics, and standards (pp. 476–500). In A. Davies and C. Elder (eds), *The Handbook of Applied Linguistics*. Malden, MA: Blackwell.

Bruton, A. (2007). Vocabulary learning from dictionary referencing and language feedback in EFL translational writing. *Language Teaching Research*, *11*(4), 413–31.

Cohen, A.D. (1994). *Assessing Language Ability in the Classroom*, 2nd edn. Boston, MA: Newbury House/Heinle and Heinle.

——(2012). Verbal report. In C.A. Chapelle (ed.), *The Encyclopedia of Applied Linguistics*. Oxford: Wiley-Blackwell.

Cohen, A.D. and Macaro, E. (2010). Research methods in second language acquisition. In E. Macaro (ed.), *Continuum Companion to Second Language Acquisition*, pp. 107–136. London: Continuum.

Cohen, A.D. and Shively, R.L. (2007). Acquisition of requests and apologies in Spanish and French: Impact of study abroad and strategy-building intervention. *Modern Language Journal*, *91*(2), 189–212.

Cohen, L. and Manion, L.(1994). *Research Methods in Education,* 4th edn. London: Routledge.

Cuervo, M.C. (2007). Double objects in Spanish as a second language: acquisition of morphosyntax and semantics. *Studies in Second Language Acquisition*, *29*(4), 583–615.

Dörnyei, Z. (2007). *Research Methods in Applied Linguistics*. Oxford: Oxford University Press.

Greidanus, T., Beks, B. and Wakely, R. (2005). Testing the development of French word knowledge by advanced Dutch- and English-speaking learners and native speakers. *Modern Language Journal*, 89(2), 221–33.

Griffiths, C. (2003). Patterns of language learning strategy use. *System*, *31*(3), 367–83.

Hanaoka, O. (2007). Output, noticing, and learning: An investigation into the role of spontaneous attention to form in a four-stage writing task. *Language Teaching Research*, *11*(4), 459–79.

Hyland, K. and Tse, P. (2004). Metadiscourse in academic writing: A reappraisal. *Applied Linguistics*, *25*(2), 156–77.

Jackson, C. (2007). The use and non-use of semantic information, word order, and case markings during comprehension by L2 learners of German. *Modern Language Journal*, *91*(3), 418–32.

Johnstone, B. (2000). *Qualitative Methods in Sociolinguistics*. New York: Oxford.

Knell, E., Qiang, H., Pei, M., Chi, Y., Siegel, L.S., Zhao, L. and Zhao, W. (2007). Early English immersion and literacy in Xi'an, China. *The Modern Language Journal*, *91*(3), 395–417.

Larsen-Freeman, D. and Long, M.H. (1991). *An Introduction to Second Language Acquisition research*. London: Longman.

Lazaraton, A. (2002). Quantitative and qualitative approaches to discourse analysis. *Annual Review of Applied Linguistics*, *22*, 32–51.

Leeser, M.J. (2004). The effects of topic familiarity, mode, and pausing on second language learners' comprehension and focus on form. *Studies in Second Language Acquisition*, *26*(4), 587–615.

——(2007). Learner-based factors in L2 reading comprehension and processing grammatical form: Topic familiarity and working memory. *Language Learning*, *57*(2), 229–70.

Macaro, E. (ed.) (2010). *Continuum Companion to Second Language Acquisition*. London: Continuum.

Mackey, A. and Gass, S.M. (2005). *Second Language Research: Methodology and Design*. Mahwah, NJ: Lawrence Erlbaum.

Meara, P. (2009). *Connected Words: Word Associations and Second Language Vocabulary Acquisition*. Amsterdam: John Benjamins.

Montrul, S. and Slabakova, R. (2003). Competence similarities between native and near-native speakers: An investigation of the preterite-imperfect contrast in Spanish. *Studies in Second Language Acquisition*, *25*(3), 351–98.

Paribakht, S. (2005). The influence of first language lexicalization on second language lexical inferencing: a Study of Farsi speaking learners of English as a foreign language. *Language Learning*, *55*(4), 701–48.

Porte, G. (2010). *Appraising Research in Second Language Learning: A Practical Approach to Critical Analysis of Quantitative Research*. Amsterdam and Philadelphia, PA: John Benjamins.

Schiff, R. and Calif, R. (2007). Role of phonological and morphological awareness in L2 oral word reading. *Language Learning*, *57*(2), 271–98.

Vickers, C.H. (2007). Second language socialization through team interaction among electrical and computer engineering students. *The Modern Language Journal*, *91*(4), 621–40.

Williams, J.N. and Lovatt, P. (2003). Phonological memory and rule learning. *Language Learning*, *53*(1), 67–121.

Further reading

Dörnyei, Z. (2007). *Research Methods in Applied Linguistics*. Oxford: Oxford University Press. (Dörnyei takes a similar approach to research methods to the one we advocate, though this book is directed at more experienced researchers, looks more broadly at the full range of applied linguistics research and deals with the increasingly common phenomenon of mixed methods research.)

Mackey, A. and Gass, S.M. (2005). *Second Language Research: Methodology and Design*. Mahwah, NJ: Lawrence Erlbaum. (Mackey and Gass innovate in their textbook by dealing early on and robustly with ethical guidelines for research, and by painstakingly describing in detail the kinds of measures that tend to accompany both quantitative and qualitative research studies.)

Seliger, H.W. and Shohamy, E. (1989). *Second Language Research Methods*. Oxford: Oxford University Press. (Seliger and Shohamy take the reader through all the stages of a research project from understanding the epistemological basis for research to reporting and summarizing the results.)

Porte, G. (2010). *Appraising Research in Second Language Learning: A Practical Approach to Critical Analysis of Quantitative Research*. Amsterdam and Philadelphia, PA: John Benjamins. (In his "practical approach to critical analysis of quantitative research" Porte presents a series of questions that the reader of an article should ask themselves when reading it, and presumably, principles and guidelines they should then apply in their own work.)

Meta-analysis

Luke Plonsky and Frederick L. Oswald
Northern Arizona University and Rice University

At its core, meta-analysis is a quantitative procedure for averaging a set of numbers. These numbers are effect sizes extracted from primary studies reflecting a given research domain, and they are usually one of two types: correlation coefficients (*r*) or standardized mean differences between groups or within groups (Cohen's *d*). Meta-analytic averaging enables researchers to estimate the overall relationship between two variables, or the overall effect of a given treatment. Meta-analysis can also be taken a step further to investigate whether a correlation or mean difference is larger or smaller due to subgroup differences (e.g., second vs foreign language) or other study characteristics (e.g., lab vs classroom). This analysis can provide information that no single study can provide by itself. In a thriving culture of research such as SLA, with its immense volume and diversity of designs, measures, and findings accumulating constantly, the set of techniques embodied by meta-analysis has massive potential.

Strengths of meta-analysis

Meta-analysis offers several advantages compared to traditional, qualitative reviews. Since being introduced in the late 1970s (Glass, 1976), these benefits have led fields that share empirical interests and traditions with SLA, such as education and psychology, to adopt meta-analysis as the preferred if not de rigueur approach to synthesizing quantitative research (Dalton and Dalton, 2008).

The first major advantage of meta-analysis is its systematicity. By collecting, refining, and analyzing data in a consistent manner, much of the idiosyncrasy, bias, and human error inherent to traditional narrative reviews is reduced or removed. To be clear, the judgment and expertise of the researcher remain critical; there is no substitute for the expert's understanding of the literature and the nature of the studies being synthesized, as is the case with the narrative review. But unlike narrative reviews, meta-analysis allows for greater transparency and replicability of the review process.

The second major advantage of meta-analysis lies in its use of effect sizes as the primary unit of analysis. Effect sizes estimate the size of the relationship(s) in question, rather than reducing research findings into the yes/no dichotomy of statistical significance or non-significance based on *p* values (see Schmidt, 1996).

Third, meta-analysis enables us to test theories that have not been addressed in the primary literature. For instance, study characteristics were mentioned as important predictors or moderators of study effect sizes. Meta-analysis could also be used to populate a path model of theoretical relationships involving a large set of variables whether or not the model has been tested in any single study (Viswesvaran and Ones, 1995).

The process

It is useful to conceptualize the steps involved in carrying out a meta-analysis as parallel to those of primary research.

(1) *Locating primary studies* (i.e., "the participants"): determine the theoretical and methodological domain from which the study inclusion criteria can then be defined. The meta-analyst then searches for a thoroughly representative if not exhaustive body of studies that meet those criteria.
(2) *Designing and implementing a coding sheet* (i.e., "data collection"): the coding sheet is an instrument to survey each study that meets the inclusion criteria. At least five types of items will be included: study identification (e.g., authors), context (e.g., second/foreign language), design and treatment (e.g., lab vs. classroom, pretesting [Y/N]), measures (e. g., dependent variables, reliability), and outcomes (e.g., effect sizes). Many coded study characteristics are common across SLA meta-analyses, yet each coding sheet also reflects domain-specific variables, measures, and research designs relevant to the domain being investigated. Each study is then processed using the coding sheet. Multiple coders of all studies, or some subset of them, help ensure that coding is performed reliably.
(3) *Meta-analysis phase*: effect sizes from each study are meta-analytically averaged to estimate the overall correlation or standardized mean difference, as appropriate. It is also common practice to adjust or weight study

effects according to sample size, inverse variance, and/or other measures of precision such as instrument reliability, such that effects with larger sample sizes and more reliable measures contribute more to the meta-analytic average. Some of the previous extensions may be incorporated, such as comparing subgroups, examining predictors of study effects, or testing a broad theoretical model.

(4) *Interpretation*: meta-analytic findings must be interpreted with respect to their theoretical and practical importance. These results, also like primary research, are best understood when compared to effects found in similar or related subdomains. In order to encourage field-specific interpretations of effect sizes within SLA, and to provide an alternative to Cohen's (1988) generic benchmarks for d values in the social sciences (d = 0.20 = small, 0.50 = medium, 0.80 = large), Oswald and Plonsky (2010) proposed a tentative set of standards with a d value of 0.40 representing a small effect, 0.70 medium, and 1.00 large. However, these standards provide only a general or initial point of reference; several additional factors to consider when interpreting meta-analytic effects include changes in designs and effects over time, practical significance, and the degree of experimental manipulation involved (Oswald and Plonsky, 2010).

Meta-analysis in SLA

Approximately ten years ago, Norris and Ortega (2000) provided the field with a formal and well-articulated introduction to meta-analysis. Since then, approximately 30 SLA meta-analyses have been carried out on topics such as interaction, strategy instruction, and CALL. Interestingly, this period of growth has covered a surprisingly small number of unique research areas, and approximately two-thirds of SLA meta-analyses to date have been replicated and/or are conceptual replications of previous meta-analyses (Plonsky, forthcoming).

Conclusion

Meta-analysis embodies a set of research synthetic techniques that, when carried out in a manner that is informed by the well-defined principles of meta-analytic methods and the relevant substantive literature, can provide an accurate, reliable, and richly informative summary of previous findings. Beyond summarizing, there is perhaps no better tool than meta-analysis for directing future research, especially in a relatively young field such as SLA. In other words, meta-analysis speaks to and informs on both the past and future of the field. In serving both of these functions, meta-analysis carries immense potential to illuminate both the past and future of SLA.

See also: effect sizes, hypothesis testing, Quantitative research, replication research, significance level, variance

References

Cohen, J. (1988). *Statistical Power Analysis for the Behavioral Sciences*, 2nd edn. Hillsdale, NJ: Erlbaum.

Dalton, D.R. and Dalton, C.M. (2008). Meta-analyses: Some very good steps toward a bit longer journey. *Organizational Research Methods, 11*, 127–47.

Glass, G.V. (1976). Primary, secondary and meta-analysis of research. *Educational Researcher, 5*, 3–8.

Norris, J.M. and Ortega, L. (2000). Effectiveness of L2 instruction: A research synthesis and quantitative meta-analysis. *Language Learning, 50*, 417–528.

Oswald, F.L. and Plonsky, L. (2010). Meta-analysis in second language research: Choices and challenges. *Annual Review of Applied Linguistics, 30*, 85–110.

Plonsky, L. (forthcoming) Replication, meta-analysis, and generalizability. In G. Porte (ed.), *A Guide to Replication in Applied Linguistics*, New York: Cambridge University Press.

Schmidt, F.L. (1996). Statistical significance testing and cumulative knowledge in psychology:

Implications for training of researchers. *Psychological Methods, 1*, 115–29.
Viswesvaran, C. and Ones, D.S. (1995). Theory testing: Combining psychometric meta-analysis and structural equations modeling. *Personnel Psychology, 48*, 865–85.

Further reading

Cooper, H., Hedges, L.V. and Valentine, J.C. (eds), (2009). *The Handbook of Research Synthesis and Meta-analysis*, 2nd edn. New York: Russell Sage Foundation. (Handbook of advanced meta-analytic methods.)
Lipsey, M.W. and Wilson, D.B. (2001). *Practical Meta-analysis*. Thousand Oaks, CA: Sage. (User-friendly introduction to meta-analysis.)
Norris, J.M. and Ortega, L. (2006). *Synthesizing Research on Language Learning and Teaching*. Philadelphia, PA: John Benjamins. (Introduction to meta-analysis and first edited volume of meta-analyses in SLA.)
——(2010). Timeline: Research synthesis. *Language Teaching, 43*, 61–79. (Traces the history of research synthesis and meta-analysis in and outside of SLA.)
Oswald, F.L. and Plonsky, L. (2010). Meta-analysis in second language research: Choices and challenges. *Annual Review of Applied Linguistics, 30*, 85–110. (Survey of L2 meta-analyses.)

Metaphor

Jeannette Littlemore
University of Birmingham

Metaphor is conventionally defined as a figure of speech in which one thing is described in terms of another. For example, in the sentence: *This isn't the end of the road for this team,* which comes from a piece of football reporting, the team's period of success is metaphorically construed as a 'road'. In metaphor terminology, the success rate of the team is the 'topic' and the road is the 'vehicle'. Metaphor performs key functions, such as: the signalling of evaluation; agenda management; mitigation and humour; technical language; reference to shared knowledge; and topic change. Some researchers (e. g. Lakoff, 1993) have argued that metaphor is a cognitive phenomenon as well as a linguistic one and that abstract thought is structured via a series of conceptual metaphors. So the metaphor cited above would be a linguistic manifestation of the conceptual metaphor LIFE IS A JOURNEY. More recently, the rigidity of conceptual metaphors has been challenged and 'metaphoric thinking' has been viewed as a more fluid phenomenon (Gibbs, 1994). The fact that metaphor is a cognitive phenomenon explains why it is ubiquitous in language, extending well beyond expressions that might conventionally be described as 'figures of speech'.

The fact that metaphor is so pervasive in language means that it is likely to be an important component of second language learning. The first person to argue for an inclusion of metaphor awareness in language teaching was Low (1988), who discussed the different levels of metaphor understanding and proposed a number of ways in which metaphor could be introduced into the language classroom. There has since been an explosion of research into the role of metaphor in second language teaching and learning. It has been suggested that ability to use metaphor appropriately can contribute to sociolinguistic, illocutionary, grammatical, textual and strategic competence (Littlemore and Low, 2006) and that the ability to use metaphor well is thus a key component of communicative language ability. Research has been conducted into: the problems that it presents to different types of language learners; the comprehension and production of metaphor by language learners; and the effectiveness of various approaches designed to raise learners' awareness of metaphor.

Metaphor presents both a problem and an opportunity to foreign language learners. It has been found that an inability to understand metaphor in university lectures leads students whose language is not the same as that of the lecturer to misunderstand not only the content of the lecture, but also (perhaps more importantly) what the lecturer actually thinks about the content (Littlemore, 2001). This is because one of the main functions of metaphor is to offer evaluation. On a more positive note, MacArthur and Piquer Píriz (2007) have shown that language learners, including children as young as six are able to reason about the meanings of metaphors in the target language and that this reasoning often leads to successful understanding. They argued that a 'recognition of this ability to reason figuratively about the motivation of polysemous senses of core vocabulary items even in early childhood may suggest ways in which young learners could be helped to expand the semantic possibilities of the words they know' (ibid.: 132). They found however that the willingness to engage in this sort of reasoning decreases with age.

In a similar vein, a series of research studies by Boers and colleagues (e.g. Boers, 2000) showed that where teachers systematically drew the attention of language learners to the vehicles of vocabulary items whose senses had been metaphorically extended, then the students' depth of knowledge of those vocabulary items, and their ability to retain them improved significantly. There is some suggestion from Boers' studies that this explanatory technique also led learners to understand connotations, and to inductively detect what made the words differ from their near-synonyms. The studies all involved university undergraduates with a fairly advanced level of English and focused on immediate learning and short-term retention periods of up to five weeks. Boers (2004) also explored the benefits of what he called 'etymological elaboration' for the teaching and learning of metaphorical idioms in the language classroom. This involves focusing on the more basic sense of the vehicles in the idioms (either via a picture or by simply conjuring up an image in one's own mind) and using this to reach an understanding of the idioms. Like MacArthur and Piriz, Boers found that the strategy was largely beneficial but the success rates varied significantly according to learning style and the imageability of the items. Drawing on this research as well as his own, Holme (2004) proposes a series of interesting, innovative teaching techniques that are designed to help students understand and produce metaphor in the target language.

Research has shown that there are considerable individual differences in terms of language learners' ability to produce and understand metaphor in the target language. These differences have been found to be consistent over time, and to be significantly related to their ability to produce and understand novel metaphor in their native language (Littlemore, 2010) and to variation in terms of cognitive style (Boers *et al.*, 2004; Littlemore, 2001). Learners from different cultures have also been found to experience different problems with metaphor. There is empirical support for a 'continuum of analyzability' which stretches between instances of figurative speech that reflect general universal structures, and instances that reflect specific cultural and historical references. Unsurprisingly, it is the metaphors that fall into this latter category that present the most difficulties to language learners (Bortfeld, 2003). An awareness of these cultural and historical references has been shown to be a key determinant of successful idiom comprehension and retention (Boers *et al.*, 2004). Interestingly, research by Deignan (2003) showed that metaphorical idioms often reflect cultural knowledge from a by-gone era and that there is thus a time-lag between the cultural references involved and their presence in widely used idioms. A further challenge to language learners is the fact that when words are used figuratively, they tend to occur in relatively fixed phraseological patterns, which differ from the phraseological patterns that are used with their more 'literal' senses (Deignan, 2005). Deignan also found that the part of speech often changes when words are used metaphorically. For example, when the word 'squirrel' is used metaphorically, it is nearly always used as a verb, which is never the case when it is used literally. This means that the learning of metaphor involves attending to phraseology as well as meaning and that students need to understand the relationship between them.

The findings from the above studies have shown that both declarative and procedural knowledge are both involved in the development of metaphoric competence in a foreign language, and that it is important to view metaphor as both as a cognitive process and a linguistic product used in real communicative situations. The studies have repeatedly shown that there is a high degree of variation across different learners and different contexts of use. Future research in this area is likely to include: a greater focus on metonymy (a related trope); more consideration of the role of gestural metaphor;

and an increased appreciation of the ways in which patterns of metaphor use vary across different registers and languages.

See also: cognitive linguistics and SLA, communicative competence, formulaic language, idiomaticity, language and the lexicon in SLA, vocabulary learning

References

Boers, F. (2000). Metaphor awareness and vocabulary retention. *Applied Linguistics, 21* (4), 553–71.

——(2004). 'Expanding Learners' vocabulary through metaphor awareness: What expansion, what learners, what vocabulary? In M. Achard and S. Niemeier (eds), *Cognitive Linguistics and Foreign Language Teaching*, pp. 211–32. Berlin and New York: Mouton de Gruyter.

Boers, F., Demecheleer, M. and Eyckmans, J. (2004). Cultural variation as a variable in comprehending and remembering figurative idioms. *European Journal of English Studies, 8* (3), 375–88.

Bortfeld, H. (2003). Comprehending idioms cross-linguistically. *Experimental Psychology, 50* (3), 217–30.

Deignan, A. (2003). Metaphorical expressions and culture: An indirect link. *Metaphor and Symbol, 18* (4), 255–72.

——(2005). *Metaphor and Corpus Linguistics* London: John Benjamins.

Gibbs, R.W. (1994). *The Poetics of Mind* Cambridge: Cambridge University Press.

Holme, R. (2004). *Mind, Metaphor and Language Teaching* Basingstoke: Palgrave MacMillan.

Lakoff, G. (1993). The Contemporary Theory of Metaphor. In A. Ortony (ed.), *Metaphor and Thought*, 2nd edn, pp. 202–51. Cambridge: Cambridge University Press.

Littlemore, J. (2001). The use of metaphor by university lecturers and the problems that it causes for overseas students. *Teaching in Higher Education, 6* (3), 335–51.

——(2001). Metaphoric competence: A possible language learning strength of students with a holistic cognitive style? *TESOL Quarterly, 35* (3), 459–91.

——(2010). Metaphoric competence in the first and second language: Similarities and differences. In M. Putz and L. Sicola (eds), *Cognitive Processing in Second Language Acquisition*, pp. 293–316. Amsterdam: John Benjamins.

Littlemore, J. and Low, G. (2006). *Figurative Thinking and Foreign Language Learning*. Basingstoke and New York: Palgrave Macmillan.

Low, G. D (1988). On teaching metaphor. *Applied Linguistics, 9* (2), 95–115.

MacArthur, F. and Piquer Píriz, A. (2007). Staging the introduction of figurative extensions of familiar vocabulary items in EFL: Some preliminary considerations. *Ilha do Desterro: Metaphor in Language and Thought: Contemporary Perspectives, 53*, 123–34.

Minimalist program

Ianthi Maria Tsimpli
Aristotle University of Thessaloniki

The minimalist program is the most recent approach to the architecture of the human language system within the generative framework, starting with Chomsky (1993, 1995) and subsequently revised with Chomsky (2000 *et seq.*), as put in perspective by Hornstein *et al.* (2005). It is formulated in the spirit of Principles and Parameters in that universal properties together with a set of options along which languages may differ are innate.

Minimalism, similarly with earlier generative approaches, considers Language to be pairings of form and meaning defined by a computational system, the syntactic component. The computation produces hierarchical representations which interface with the 'form' component, that is, the sound interface and the 'meaning' component, that is, the semantic interface. Interfaces are of primary importance in minimalist descriptions: they define language as the main vehicle of thought and communication. Thus, derivations give rise to representations legible by the C-I (conceptual-intentional) interface for higher cognition and the S-M (sensory-motor) interface for production and perception. Convergent representations contain all and only features that are *interpretable* at each interface. Computational operations and constraints on their output representations are universal. Language variation should ideally be restricted to variation in the Lexicon where lexical items and features are contained (cf. Borer, 1984).

Universal properties: the computational system

Derivational processes are dictated but also inherently constrained by the computational system. This component includes operations responsible for structure-building which are, in turn, subject to *economy* and *locality* conditions. Consider displacement, one of the defining characteristics of Language. Displacement allows linguistic elements (words, phrases, clauses) to be interpreted in a position other than the one in which they surface. Displacement is dictated by a simple operation in the derivational component; meanwhile, the distance computed and the choice between alternative derivations depend on *locality* and *economy* considerations (e.g. in terms of *phases*; Chomsky, 2000 *et seq.*).

Minimalism assumes a strongly derivational character of the human computational system in that the generative capacity is dictated by the repeated application of the computational operation *Merge*. Merge combines two elements (lexical items or phrases) as sister nodes; one of these nodes is the head and the resulting structure is the projection of this head. Recursive application of Merge eventually gives rise to sentence formation. Internal merge, or Move, allows an element to be removed from its original position and attach to the top node as a sister, leaving a copy behind. Finally, *Agree* is a process in which abstract morphological features are checked against (Chomsky, 1995), copied (Chomsky, 2000, 2001), or valued (Chomsky, 2004, 2007, 2008) by features borne by another lexical item or category. Agree presupposes *c-command* and *locality,* that is, hierarchical relations between the agreeing elements but not any dedicated AGR(eement) feature or category, as in earlier approaches.

The above sketch helps us look at language acquisition by restricting the domain of inquiry to where language variation is found. Since the computational system and the operations referred to as *Merge* and *Agree* are universal, they are not part of the acquisition task.

Language variation: the Lexicon

Syntactic computations presuppose the selection of a set of features and lexical items (with feature clusters) which enter a *numeration* (Chomsky, 1995) or *lexical array* (Chomsky, 2000 *et seq.*). This selection is drawn from the Lexicon of the language. The computational system recursively applies the operation Merge so that the numeration will eventually be exhausted. Since variation is restricted to the Lexicon, we need to identify the ways in which lexical elements may differ cross-linguistically. In general, variation involves either the set of features a language draws from the universal repertoire or the clustering of these features on lexical items. Consider Gender as a potential source of language variation. Grammatical gender languages include [gender] as a feature in their Lexicon while the others do not. Further variation within the former group distinguishes between the French type, where only nominal elements are specified for an unvalued gender feature, and the Arabic type, where verbs too are specified for the same feature.

Features differ in a number of important ways. Consider agreement relations: the same feature is repeated at least twice in the derivation (e.g. in D-N number agreement), giving rise to the traditional distinction between 'inherent' and 'contextual' features. In minimalism, this redundancy is expressed in two ways, one relevant for the computation and one for interpretation. A feature may enter the derivation as being *valued* (e.g. [number] on N) or *unvalued* (e.g. [number] on D). The computation seeks, via *Agree*, to value the latter feature which then becomes invisible to the resulting representation. In terms of interpretation, a feature may be interpretable or uninterpretable at the semantic or the sound interfaces. In general, features merged in the computation as valued are semantically interpretable. Possible problematic cases could include [gender] which is valued on the noun but lacks interpretability. Which features are interpretable or valued? Usually, features which are inherent on a lexical item such as [number] on the noun are valued and interpretable. Moreover, features which are relevant to interface interpretation are also by definition interpretable.

Parametric variation in minimalism is accordingly perceived as variation in the number and type of features, or feature-clusters, on lexical items, entering the computation and triggering *Agree* or (internal) *Merge* operations. Thus, features are also responsible for word-order variation. An open question in minimalism is the relation between morphological expression and parametric variation: in early minimalism (Chomsky, 1993, 1995), this relation could reflect *feature strength*. Strong features triggered movement, while weak ones had to satisfy computational constraints by Merge (e.g. Inflection in French vs. English). Since morpho(phono)logical expressions are indirect manifestations of syntactic processes and, by extension, provide cues to the language learner, interpretability at the sound interface is of primary importance to language acquisition research. Ultimately, research on cross-linguistic variation should define the repertoire of features available to Language as well as any constraints on their combinations, in order to address questions of learnability.

See also: agreement, functional categories, generative linguistics, inflectional morphemes, theoretical constructs in SLA, Universal Grammar (UG) and SLA

References

Borer, H. (1984). *Parametric Syntax*. Dordrecht: Foris.

Chomsky, N. (1993). A minimalist program for linguistic theory. In K. Hale and S.J. Keyser (eds), *The View from Building 20: Essays in linguistics in honor of Sylvain Bromberger*, pp. 1–52. Cambridge, MA: MIT Press.

——(1995). *The Minimalist Program*. Cambridge, MA: MIT Press.

——(2000). Minimalist inquiries: The framework. In R. Martin, D. Michaels, and J. Uriagereka (eds), *Step by Step: Essays on Minimalist Syntax in Honor of Howard Lasnik*, pp. 89–155. Cambridge, MA: MIT Press.

——(2001). Derivation by phase. In M. Kenstowicz (ed.), *Ken Hale: A Life in Language*, pp. 1–52. Cambridge, MA: MIT Press.

——(2004). Beyond explanatory adequacy. In A. Belletti (ed.), *The Cartography of Syntactic Structures*, vol. 3: *Structures and Beyond*, pp. 104–31. New York: Oxford University Press.

——(2007). Approaching UG from below. In U. Sauerland and H.-M. Gärtner (eds), *Interfaces + Recursion = Language?*, pp. 1–29. Berlin: Mouton de Gruyter.

——(2008). *On Phases*. In R. Freidin, C.P. Otero and M.L. Zubizarreta (eds), *Foundational Issues in Linguistic Theory: Essays in Honor of Jean-Roger Vergnaud*, pp. 134–66. Cambridge, MA: MIT Press.

Hornstein, N., J. Nunes, and K.K. Grohmann (2005). *Understanding Minimalism*. Cambridge: Cambridge University Press.

Mirror neurons

Gregory Hickok
University of California, Irvine

Mirror neurons are cells that respond both during the execution of goal-directed actions and during the observation of similar actions by others (Rizzolatti and Craighero, 2004). They were originally discovered in frontal lobe motor area F5 in the macaque monkey cortex (Gallese, Fadiga, Fogassi, and Rizzolatti, 1996), but have since been reported in the parietal lobe in the same species (Fogassi *et al.*, 2005). The dominant view of the function of these cells is that they support action understanding via a motor simulation mechanism (Rizzolatti and Craighero, 2004), although this view has been challenged (Heyes, 2010; Hickok, 2009; Hickok and Hauser, 2010). Because mirror neurons can only be identified directly by invasive methods, the existence of mirror neurons in humans has been inferred primarily on the basis of functional imaging and transcranial stimulation studies (Rizzolatti and Craighero, 2004), however some direct evidence in humans has been reported (Mukamel, Ekstrom, Kaplan, Iacoboni, and Fried, 2010).

Mirror neurons have been linked theoretically to speech from the earliest publications (Gallese *et al.*, 1996). Specifically, this system has been argued to be the neural basis for a motor theory of speech recognition. According to this motor theory, speech recognition is achieved by mapping the acoustic speech signal onto a neural representation of the motor gestures that produced those sounds (Liberman and Mattingly, 1985). Although it has been found that listening to speech can activate the human motor speech system, and that stimulating the motor system can modulate performance in certain speech tasks (typically syllable discrimination or identification) under certain listening conditions (partially degraded speech) (Pulvermuller and Fadiga, 2010), it has also been shown unequivocally that the motor speech system is not necessary for speech perception (Hickok, 2010). For example, individuals with anarthria (inability to produce articulate speech) due to cerebral palsy, who have never acquired motor speech capacity, are nonetheless able to make fine phonemic discriminations; and complete, acute deactivation of the motor speech system as induced in clinical Wada procedures does not prevent patients from performing well on speech recognition tests (for review see (Hickok, 2010)). Thus, an extreme motor/mirror neuron account of speech perception, in which the motor speech system is necessary for recognition, is empirically untenable.

Most of the debate regarding the possible role of the mirror system has therefore shifted to less extreme views of the function of mirror neurons in speech perception in which the motor system plays a top-down, modulatory role. Some authors argue that the motor system is critical for speech perception under noisy listening conditions where top-down information is particularly helpful (Davis and Johnsrude, 2007; Wilson and Iacoboni, 2006). On this view, motor representations instantiated by mirror neurons would constrain the analysis of incoming auditory information. Evidence for this view comes from studies in which the motor system is stimulated and effects on the speech sound categorization are found (D'Ausilio *et al.*, 2009; Meister, Wilson, Deblieck, Wu, and Iacoboni, 2007).

An alternative view of the role of mirror neurons in speech is that it is part of a feedback control mechanism for speech production (Hickok, Houde, and Rong, 2011). On this view, the goal of the speech production system is to control the vocal tract to reproduce auditory speech targets that have been acquired through exposure to the speech patterns in a linguistic environment. The sensory consequences of motor speech acts are evaluated against the previously learned auditory targets, which acts as an error detection and correction mechanism. In the case of a mismatch between the actual speech pattern produced and the intended target, an error signal is generated which can be used to train the motor speech system. The role of this system in second language acquisition is fairly obvious: the learner must both acquire the acoustic patterns in L2 and learn how to reproduce those patterns with the vocal tract. A feedback control circuit that integrates sensory and motor speech representations is critical for this function.

This feedback control perspective flips the mirror neuron hypothesis on its head. Rather than the motor system being critical for speech perception, the feedback control model holds that the auditory system is critical for speech production in the sense that the targets or goals of speech actions are auditory in nature.

In sum, mirror neurons are likely part of sensorimotor integration circuit for speech that plays a critical role in both L1 and L2 acquisition, as well as online control of motor speech gestures. They may also play a role in some aspects of speech production, although this is still being debated (Gallese, Gernsbacher, Heyes, Hickok, and Iacoboni, 2011).

See also: corrective feedback, Levelt's model of speech production and comprehension, psycholinguistics of SLA, listening, speaking, speech perception

References

D'Ausilio, A., Pulvermuller, F., Salmas, P., Bufalari, I., Begliomini, C. and Fadiga, L. (2009). The motor somatotopy of speech perception. *Curr. Biol., 19*(5), 381–85.

Davis, M.H. and Johnsrude, I.S. (2007). Hearing speech sounds: top-down influences on the interface between audition and speech perception. *Hear Res, 229*(1–2), 132–47.

Fogassi, L., Ferrari, P.F., Gesierich, B., Rozzi, S., Chersi, F. and Rizzolatti, G. (2005). Parietal lobe: from action organization to intention understanding. *Science, 308*(5722), 662–7.

Gallese, V., Fadiga, L., Fogassi, L. and Rizzolatti, G. (1996). Action recognition in the premotor cortex. *Brain*, 119 (Pt 2), 593–609.

Gallese, V., Gernsbacher, M.A., Heyes, C., Hickok, G. and Iacoboni, M. (2011). Mirror neuron forum. *Perspectives on Psychological Science, 6*, 369–407.

Heyes, C. (2010). Where do mirror neurons come from? *Neurosci Biobehav Rev, 34*(4), 575–83.

Hickok, G. (2009). Eight problems for the mirror neuron theory of action understanding in monkeys and humans. *Journal of Cognitive Neuroscience, 21*(7), 1229–43.

——(2010). The role of mirror neurons in speech perception and action word semantics. *Language and Cognitive Processes, 25*, 749–76.

Hickok, G. and Hauser, M. (2010). (Mis)understanding mirror neurons. *Curr. Biol., 20*(14), R593–4.

Hickok, G., Houde, J. and Rong, F. (2011). Sensorimotor integration in speech processing: computational basis and neural organization. *Neuron, 69*(3), 407–22.

Meister, I.G., Wilson, S.M., Deblieck, C., Wu, A. D. and Iacoboni, M. (2007). The essential role of premotor cortex in speech perception. *Curr Biol, 17*(19), 1692–6.

Mukamel, R., Ekstrom, A.D., Kaplan, J., Iacoboni, M. and Fried, I. (2010). Single-neuron responses in humans during execution and observation of actions. *Curr. Biol., 20*(8), 750–6.

Pulvermuller, F. and Fadiga, L. (2010). Active perception: sensorimotor circuits as a cortical basis for language. *Nature Reviews Neuroscience, 11*(5), 351–60.

Rizzolatti, G. and Craighero, L. (2004). The mirror-neuron system. *Annual Review of Neuroscience, 27*, 169–92.

Wilson, S.M. and Iacoboni, M. (2006). Neural responses to non-native phonemes varying in producibility: evidence for the sensorimotor nature of speech perception. *Neuroimage, 33*(1), 316–25.

Mixed methods research

Eunice Eunhee Jang
Ontario Institute for Studies in Education, University of Toronto

At its simplest, mixed methods research (MMR) is an inquiry approach that includes both qualitative and quantitative methods within a single study or program of inquiry. Researchers in second language acquisition (SLA) and social sciences have increasingly adopted mixed methods to better understand the linguistic, psychological and sociocultural characteristics of language process and realities shaped by social, political, cultural and economic values (Abbuhl and Mackey, 2008). Such research combines methods and data analytic strategies to produce findings greater than the sum of their parts. These findings result from: (1) a fluid reasoning (*abductive*) that generates a theory from case-based observations (*inductive*), tests it for generality (*deductive*), and applies it back to the particular, original context; (2) intersubjectivity that uses multiple reference frames and renders the continuity between subjectivity and objectivity; and (3) tacking back and forth dialectically between experience-near (*emic*) and experience-distant (*etic*) knowing to achieve a contextually sensitive yet transferable understanding.

The field is not without debate. As the terms "qualitative," and "quantitative," refer to both technical procedures and epistemological and methodological stances, views on MMR are *mixed.* Methodological purists reject the concept *in toto*, arguing the philosophical differences between qualitative and quantitative inquiry methods are irreconcilable. Alternatively, stances such as pragmatic, dialectic, and transformative MMR endorse methodological pluralism and privilege research problems over philosophical assumptive worlds. These stances suggest that the alleged dichotomy between qualitative and quantitative research grossly oversimplifies both rich research traditions and the nature of human reasoning. For these researchers, research purposes and questions should guide methodological decisions as Greene (2006) states "methodology is ever the servant of purpose, never the master" (p. 97). Ultimately, the goal of MMR is to contribute to broader, deeper, and more inclusive understandings of multi-layered social worlds and human behavior. In doing so, differences are honored and both particularity and generality are dialectically tacked.

In SLA, despite methodological tensions rooted largely in a theoretical divide between cognitive and socio-cultural perspectives (Firth and Wagner, 1997; Lazaraton, 2000), the field has embraced pluralistic perspectives and accordingly adopted complementary and inter-disciplinary inquiry approaches (Swain and Lapkin, 1998). This shift is evident in classroom research (Spada, 2005), research on learner cognition and identity through the juxtaposition of psychological inquiry with socio-cultural approaches (Dewaele, 2005), and transformative inquiry approaches to language problems and the attendant policy decisions that affect the lives of marginalized populations (Valdes, 2005). Such a shift is also supported by reviews of empirical studies published in SLA journals: Lazaraton (2000) found that of all the empirical research articles published in *Language Learning, Modern Language Journal, TESOL Quarterly*, and *Studies in Second Language Acquisition* from 1991 through 1997, 88 percent were quantitative and 10 percent were qualitative. Based on a review of all empirical studies published in *TESOL Quarterly and Modern Language Journal* from 2001 to 2005, Jang and Quinn (2006) reported roughly even numbers of qualitative (42 per cent) and quantitative (45per cent) studies, with mixed methods studies accounting for 13 percent. Clearly the field increasingly employs multiple inquiry methodologies in order to respond to various sociocultural, political, multilingual needs in a global context.

Mixed methods inquiry designs

Mixing occurs at various stages of inquiry, from formulating research questions and collecting and analyzing data, to interpreting and synthesizing findings. As with any other approach, MMR demands a clear rationale for its design, by interconnecting among five components including research purposes, conceptual framework, research questions, methods, and validity considerations for claims made (Maxwell and Loomis, 2003). In practice, MMR is frequently much more complex than any single design typology can adequately capture. Therefore, mixed methods design typologies should not be applied rigidly nor exclusively (Tashakkori and Teddlie, 2010).

One of the most common purposes of MMR is triangulation, in which multiple methods are used to confirm, corroborate, and cross-validate findings, and to further explain contradictory and inconsistent findings. The design of a triangulation study requires consideration of several issues: 1) do different methods elicit the same phenomenon? 2) Does each method recruit an independent sample? 3) Should each method be given equal weight? 4) Is data collection concurrent or sequential? And 5) How can different data sources be prepared for comparative interpretation?

The data collection and analysis in triangulation design is often kept separate for parallel comparison and joint interpretations at a later stage. Parallel comparison may require data transformation or creative displays of results to highlight data comparability: thematic findings from qualitative data can be compared with factor-analyzed survey data, and survey-generated profiles can be placed into a qualitative data pattern matrix. Although convergence is often the goal of triangulation, inconsistent and even contradictory findings can allow for further explorations of the complexity of the phenomenon studied, and construct plausible explanations for contradictory findings (Mathison, 1988).

Another common purpose of MMR is development, with data from one method used to guide subsequent data collection or to substantiate results from preceding data analysis. A developmental MMR design proceeds sequentially in multiple phases. The decision of how to sequence methods may depend on relevant theoretical frameworks. For example, a study of a culturally sensitive construct may prefer an inductive approach that allows researchers to explore participants' emic perspectives, which can be further experimented with a larger sample in the subsequent phase. Alternatively, one can design a confirmatory study in order to deductively test hypothetical theories and find plausible explanations by focusing attention on a small but information-rich sample.

One can also employ mixed methods in nested design, a model that gives priority to one dominant method with a lower priority method placed within. In nested design, one could conduct an experimental study with qualitative methods embedded or nest quantitative methods in a largely ethnographic study. In either case, nested methods can address different aspects of the phenomenon studied, or yield complementary primary data.

One significant challenge researchers face is data integration. Parallel presentations of findings without full integration can limit the ideal yield of mixed methods research – a synergistic and holistic understanding. Puzzling preliminary findings should encourage investigators to integrate multiple sources through various integrative analytic strategies: juxtaposing contrasting evidence; transforming one data set into a form compatible with another; creating blended variables merged from multiple data sets; and by performing in-depth analysis of cases that demonstrate the phenomenon's complexity.

As SLA has widened and deepened its view of language process, it appears MMR best addresses both the elements of language phenomena and the discursive interactions among these elements. Although blending multiple methods does not automatically guarantee stronger claims, fully realized and integrated MMR clearly offers the chance to gain a holistic and contextualized understanding.

See also: factor analysis, measuring and researching SLA, replication research, qualitative research, quantitative research, theoretical constructs in SLA

References

Abbuhl, R. and Mackey, A. (2008). Second language acquisition research methods. In K.A. King and N.H. Hornberger (eds), *Encyclopedia of Language and Education: Vol. 10, Research Methods in Language and Education*, pp. 1–13. Dordrecht: Springer.

Dewaele, J.M. (2005). Investigating the psychological and emotional dimensions in instructed language learning: Obstacles and possibilities. *Modern Language Journal*, *89*, 367–80.

Firth, A. and Wagner, J. (1997). On discourse, communication, and (some) fundamental concepts in SLA research. *Modern Language Journal*, *81*, 285–300.

Greene, J.C. (2007). *Mixed Methods in Social Inquiry*. San Francisco, CA: Jossey-Bass.

Jang, E.E. and Quinn, P. (2006). *Mixed methods research in SLA*, paper presented at 2006 Joint AAAL-ACLA/CAAL 2006 Conference, Montreal, Quebec, June.

Lazaraton, A. (2000). Current trends in research methodology and statistics in applied linguistics, *TESOL Quarterly*, *34*, 175–81.

Mathison, S. (1988). Why triangulate? *Educational Researcher*, *17*, 2, 13–17.

Maxwell, J.A. and Loomis, D.M. (2003). Mixed methods design: An alternative approach. In A. Tashakkori and C. Teddlie (eds), *Sage Handbook of Mixed Methods in Social and Behavioral Research*, pp. 241–71. Thousand Oaks, CA: Sage publications.

Spada, N. (2005). Conditions and challenges in developing school-based SLA research programs. *Modern Language Journal*, *89*, 328–38.

Swain, M. and Lapkin, S. (1998). Interaction and second language learning: two adolescent French immersion students working together. *The Modern Language Journal*, *82*, 3, 320–37.

Tashakkori, A. and Teddlie, C. (2010). *Handbook of Mixed Methods in Social and Behavioral Research*. Thousand Oaks, CA: Sage publications.

Valdes, G. (2005). Bilingualism, heritage language learners, and SLA research: Opportunities lost or seized? *Modern Language Journal*, *89*, 410–26.

Modern Language Aptitude Test (MLAT)

Daniel J. Reed and Charles Stansfield
Michigan State University and Second Language Testing, Inc.

The Modern Language Aptitude Test (MLAT), published by the Second Language Testing Foundation, is a well-known aptitude test that measures how quickly and easily a person would likely be able to learn a foreign language. It is used by churches and missionary organizations, private schools, government agencies, and private corporations for such purposes as deciding who would benefit most from language instruction, how long they would have to study a language to attain an intermediate level of proficiency, and who would be the best candidates for learning difficult languages. It has also been used in the diagnosis of foreign language learning difficulties and in second language acquisition research.

Description of the MLAT

The MLAT is comprised of five parts, the first two of which are controlled by an audio recording. The first part, *Number Learning*, requires examinees to learn a set of numbers and then discriminate different combinations of those numbers. The second part, *Phonetic Script*, asks examinees to learn a set of sound-symbol correspondences. The third part, *Spelling Clues*, asks examinees to quickly read words with alternative spellings and identify from a set of words one whose meaning is closest to the "disguised" word. In the fourth part, *Words in Sentences*, examinees are given a key word in a sentence and asked to select a word in another sentence that functions in the same way. Finally, in the *Paired Associates* part, examinees must quickly learn a set of vocabulary words from another language and memorize their English meanings.

Test development

The MLAT was developed by Harvard psychologist John Carroll and Rochester University linguist Stanley Sapon during a 5-year research project they conducted in the 1950s with support from the Carnegie Corporation of New York. Through these experimental studies, Carroll identified the following four distinct abilities that factored into language aptitude, separate from motivation and verbal intelligence:

> *Phonetic coding ability*—the ability to identify distinct sounds, to form associations between those sounds and symbols representing them, and to retain these associations;
> *Grammatical sensitivity*—the ability to recognize the grammatical functions of words (or other linguistic entities) in sentence structures;
> *Rote learning ability*—the ability to learn associations between sounds and meanings rapidly and efficiently, and to retain these associations; and
> *Inductive learning ability*—the ability to infer or induce the rules governing a set of language materials, given samples of language materials that permit such inferences.

The final version of the MLAT was normed on about 2,900 students in U.S. high school, college, and government language programs. Some of the results of the field test and norming administrations are reported in Carroll (1981) and in the MLAT manual (Carroll, Sapon, Reed and Stansfield, 2010). The general conclusion from the data gathered during the development process was that the MLAT is a very useful instrument for predicting success at FL learning, especially when other relevant considerations, such as motivation, attitude, effort, and quality of instruction, are also taken into account (see also Carroll, 1963, 1973, 1993).

See also: aptitude, cognitive linguistics and SLA, factor analysis, individual differences in SLA, language testing and SLA, measuring and researching SLA

References

Carroll, J.B. (1963). A model of school learning. *Teachers College Record*, *64*(8), 723–33.

——(1973). *The Aptitude-Achievement Distinction: The Case of Foreign Language Aptitude and*

Proficiency. Proceedings of the Second CTB/ McGraw-Hill Conference on Issues in Educational Measurement, pp. 286–311. Monterey, CA: CTB/McGraw-Hill.

——(1981). Twenty-five years of research on foreign language aptitude. In K.C. Diller (ed.), *Individual Differences and Universals in Language Learning Aptitude*, pp. 83–118. Rowley, MA: Newbury House.

——(1993). *Human Cognitive Abilities: A Survey of Factor-analytic Studies*. Cambridge: Cambridge University Press.

Carroll, J.B., Sapon, S.M., Reed, D.J. and Stansfield, C.W. (2010). *Modern Language Aptitude Test Manual*. Rockville, MD: Second Language Testing, Inc.

Modularity

John Truscott

National Tsing Hua University

A recurring idea in discussions of the mind is that it contains or consists of a number of functionally specialized components, or *modules*. Considerable controversy exists on this view, both on its general validity and in regard to specific issues such as the extent to which the mind is modular, the nature of that modularity, and how individual modules are to be identified. The logic of a modular mind is that a system of experts, each specializing in one particular function, can carry out those specialized functions very efficiently and accurately.

In the area of language, modularity is closely associated with the notion of Universal Grammar (UG). From a Chomskian perspective, the human mind includes a "language organ" (module), innately specified by UG. The modularity of language is thus a fundamental background assumption in generative linguistics, the goal of which can be seen as understanding the nature of the language organ, along with its development and use. The term *module* is also commonly used by linguists taking a Principles and Parameters or Minimalist perspective, referring to any of the component systems that are hypothesized to make up the mental grammar.

Modularity is often seen in the context of natural selection, and the concept of a language organ can be readily incorporated in such a view, though fundamental disagreements exist in this area (e.g. Hauser, Chomsky, and Fitch, 2002; Pinker and Jackendoff, 2005). For many, the development of the human mind in general can be explained to a considerable extent in Darwinian terms: certain functions proved to be valuable for survival and reproduction and therefore came to be inherent parts of the mind, that is, modules, through natural selection. This idea has been developed and researched by evolutionary psychologists such as Tooby and Cosmides (1992), who compare the mind to a Swiss army knife with its many functionally specialized parts, such as tool use, face recognition, social reasoning, and grammar acquisition. Perhaps the most accessible presentation of this perspective is Pinker (1997). Gardner's (1983) *multiple intelligences* are also modules of this sort, though Gardner hypothesizes a much smaller number and naturally differs on their identity.

Fodor argues for a more limited notion of the modular mind, rejecting what he calls the "massive modularity" of the evolutionary psychologists in favor of a division between modular *input systems*, including perceptual systems and language, and a non-modular *central* portion of the mind which has the function of fixing beliefs. Fodor's (1983) work also provides the classic treatment of defining features for modules. Notable examples of such features are innate specification, informational encapsulation, and the existence of a unique encoding system. For the case of language, the innate specification is UG. The idea of encapsulation is that a module only deals with specific types of information coming from specific sources and has no access to most of what goes on in the mind. The unique encoding system is often spoken of as a "language" specific to the module and tuned to its specialized function, making it unreadable by other modules. There is, however, no consensus on these points, as can be seen for example in Pinker's skeptical view of informational encapsulation as an essential feature of modularity.

Karmiloff-Smith (1992) argues that modular structure develops through the child's experience, rather than being innately fixed, and also stresses continuing development that results in smooth interaction across domains. Steven Mithen offers a similar view of modularity in the context of human evolution, arguing that natural selection first produced a flexible general-purpose mind, which then became increasingly specialized over a period of a few million years before taking a relatively recent turn to a general, fluid form of intelligence.

Apart from Chomsky's and Fodor's, the most prominent and extensive account of modularity in regard to language is that of Jackendoff (2002), which also falls within the Chomskian tradition. In Jackendoff's *parallel architecture*, syntax and phonology each represent a module, connected to one another and to other modules by *interface processors*. While Fodor speaks of language as an input system, Jackendoff takes a more general processing view, seeing the language module as responsible for production of language as well as comprehension.

In SLA, Fodor's version of modularity has been developed by Schwartz (1986), with the goal of providing a stronger theoretical basis for Krashen's *Monitor Model*. In this reformulation, Krashen's unconscious *acquisition* represents the workings of the module while his conscious *learning* is a product of non-modular central processes. Jackendoff's modularity serves as the foundation for Carroll's *Autonomous Induction Theory* and Truscott and Sharwood Smith's *MOGUL* framework. More generally, most linguistically oriented work in SLA is modular in nature, as it assumes a UG approach, with an inherently modular view of language.

This approach can be contrasted with that derived from cognitive psychology, according to which language in the mind is simply one kind of knowledge or skill, not fundamentally different from others. The implication is that the study of second (and first) language acquisition should be in essence the application of general principles of learning to the area of language. This view can be seen in some prominent approaches to SLA, particularly in traditional skill building and the increasingly influential emergentist approach. Similar implications hold for linguists who accept the notion of UG as an innate module responsible for first language acquisition but hypothesize that the module is not available for the learning of a second language, which therefore relies on more general learning mechanisms (cf. the Fundamental Difference Hypothesis). But while the split between modular approaches and their generalist counterparts is real, the former can and sometimes do seek to incorporate insights of generalist work done within a cognitive psychology approach, as can be seen for example in Towell and Hawkins' (1994) model and in the MOGUL framework.

See also: Autonomous Induction Theory, Fundamental Difference Hypothesis (FDH), MOGUL framework for SLA, monitor model, psycholinguistics of SLA, Universal Grammar (UG) and SLA

References

Fodor, J.A. (1983). *The Modularity of Mind: An Essay on Faculty Psychology*. Cambridge, MA: MIT Press.

Gardner, H. (1983). *Frames of Mind: The Theory of Multiple Intelligences*. New York: Basic Books.

Hauser, M.D., Chomsky, N. and Fitch, W.T. (2002). The faculty of language: What is it, who has it, and how does it evolve? *Science*, *298*, 1569–79.

Jackendoff, R. (2002). *Foundations of Language*. Oxford: Oxford University Press.

Karmiloff-Smith, A. (1992). *Beyond Modularity: A Developmental Perspective on Cognitive Science*. Cambridge, MA: MIT Press.

Pinker, S. (1997). *How the Mind Works*. London: Penguin.

Pinker, S. and Jackendoff, R. (2005). The faculty of language: What's special about it? *Cognition*, *95*, 201–36.

Schwartz, B.D. (1986). The epistemological status of second language acquisition. *Second Language Research*, *2*, 120–59.

Tooby, J. and Cosmides, L. (1992). The psychological foundations of culture. In J.H. Barkow, L. Cosmides, and J. Tooby (eds), *The Adapted Mind: Evolutionary Psychology and the Generation of Culture*, pp. 19–136. New York: Oxford University Press.

Towell, R. and Hawkins, R. (1994). *Approaches to Second Language Acquisition*. Clevedon: Multilingual Matters.

MOGUL framework for SLA

John Truscott
National Tsing Hua University

MOGUL (Modular On-line Growth and Use of Language) is a theoretical framework that aims to provide a means by which research and theory from diverse areas can be productively brought together and more fruitfully developed. The thinking is that SLA is now rich in research and theory but is badly fragmented; if there is to be a good understanding of SLA, the fragments must ultimately be unified. In the shorter term, all areas can be expected to benefit from the cross-fertilization brought about by participation in a common framework. Research in these various areas can also benefit from ideas and findings from outside SLA, and this broader cross-fertilization can be facilitated by a framework designed with such links in mind.

As a framework rather than a theory, MOGUL aims to directly incorporate reasonable (if sometimes controversial) positions on general, fundamental features of SLA and to facilitate the development of theories that can successfully address more specific issues. It does not in itself directly address such issues or make predictions about them. The fundamental features include the gradual, quantitative nature of development and the fact that development does nevertheless have discrete and categorical aspects (Sharwood Smith and Truscott, 2005), the routine appearance in learners' performance of two mutually exclusive grammatical forms (Truscott, 2007), crosslinguistic influence (Sharwood Smith and Truscott, 2006, 2008), access to Universal Grammar (Sharwood Smith and Truscott, 2006), automatization, the role of awareness and the limits of that role (Truscott and Sharwood Smith, 2011), and the nature of metalinguistic knowledge, along with the part that it plays in the use and development of language (Sharwood Smith, 2004).

The orientation of MOGUL is primarily cognitive and linguistic, but it allows for connections to more socially and culturally oriented work as well. Examples involve the social factors in codeswitching and the value of interaction for SLA. More generally, the cognitive representation of social and cultural factors is a natural topic for theoretical development within MOGUL, as are the ways in which such factors influence acquisition and use of language.

MOGUL architecture is loosely based on Jackendoff (2002, for example). The cognitive system consists of processor/information store pairs. An example is syntactic structures (SS), made up of a syntactic processor and a store of syntactic representations. The processor is invariant and consists of all the principles provided by Universal Grammar (UG). The store is made up of the basic structures provided by UG and all the combinations of them that have been constructed through linguistic processing experience. Each such pair can be considered a module, though they vary in the degree to which they have the classic characteristics of modularity. The specifically linguistic component consists of phonological structures (PS), syntactic structures, the interface connecting them, and additional interfaces connecting PS to sensory and motor modules and SS to conceptual structures. Representations in one store are connected to those in others by coindexing, the indexes being assigned by and used by interfaces.

Processing consists of each specialized processor constructing representations on its store, following its own built-in principles. In doing so, it uses those simpler, already-existing representations that are currently active. Initial activation comes from the interfaces, whose function it is to activate representations in one store when coindexed representations in the adjacent store are active. Stimulation from the interface results in a sudden rise in activation level, followed by a gradual decline (during which the representation will exhibit priming effects). Additional representations become available to the processor through spreading activation within the store, based on shared features. Each representation has a current activation level, determining its current availability to a processor. More abstractly, it also has a resting level—how active it is when not subject to external influences.

Sensory processing provides the input for development in the system, including second language acquisition. Each sensory modality is a complex unit consisting of a chain of specialized modules, terminating in a perceptual output module. The information stores of the various output modules—visual structures, auditory structures, tactile structures, etc.—are tightly connected to one another; that is, their representations are richly connected across stores by indexes with high resting activation levels. The result is a strong tendency to synchronization of activity across the perceptual output stores, making it reasonable, and useful, to see the various stores as a single unit—perceptual output structures, or POpS. Active representations on POpS are the input to the linguistic component, and to other portions of the system. POpS is also the de facto seat of consciousness: conscious experience consists primarily of perceptual elements, that is, POpS representations, including those generated internally. MOGUL hypothesizes that the objects of consciousness are representations with sufficiently high activation levels, these levels resulting from the synchronization of activity on the multiple POpS stores (Sharwood Smith and Truscott, 2010, Truscott and Sharwood Smith, 2011). This conceptualization makes possible a theoretically based analysis of the role of awareness in SLA, particularly of noticing, in the context of relatively clear notions of input and intake (Truscott and Sharwood Smith, 2011).

A crucial component of the MOGUL framework is its novel approach to learning: Acquisition by Processing Theory, or APT (Truscott and Sharwood Smith, 2004), which can be summarized as "Acquisition is the lingering effect of processing." MOGUL hypothesizes no mechanisms specifically for learning, seeing it instead as a by-product of processing activity. The function of each processor is to construct a representation consistent with its built-in principles, using active existing representations. Sometimes this necessitates construction of a novel representation, either as the overall representation or as a component. A new representation created in this way lingers in the store, with an initially low resting level which rises with each use in subsequent processing. Extensive use can thus make it a fixture in processing. This is the essence of learning within MOGUL.

See also: awareness, bilingualism and SLA, development in SLA, modularity, theoretical constructs in SLA, Universal Grammar (UG) and SLA

References

Jackendoff, R. (2002). *Foundations of Language*. Oxford: Oxford University Press.

Sharwood Smith, M. (2004). In two minds about grammar: On the interaction of linguistic and metalinguistic knowledge in performance. *Transactions of the Philological Society*, *102*, 255–80.

Sharwood Smith, M., and Truscott, J. (2005). Stages or continua in second language acquisition: A mogul solution. *Applied Linguistics*, *22*, 219–40.

Sharwood Smith, M., and Truscott, J. (2006). Full transfer full sccess: A processing-oriented interpretation. In A. Sorace and S. Unsworth (eds), *Paths of Development*. Amsterdam: John Benjamins.

——(2008). MOGUL and crosslinguistic influence. In D. Gabrys (ed.), *Morphosyntactic Issues in Second Language Acquisition Studies*. Clevedon: Multilingual Matters.

——(2010). Consciousness and language: A processing perspective. In E.K. Perry, D. Collerton, F.E.N. LeBeau, and H. Ashton (eds), *New Horizons in the Neuroscience of Consciousness*. Amsterdam: John Benjamins.

Truscott, J. (2007). Optionality in second language acquisition: A generative processing-oriented account. *International Review of Applied Linguistics*, *44*, 311–30.

Truscott, J. and Sharwood Smith, M. (2004). Acquisition by processing: A modular approach to language development. *Bilingualism: Language and Cognition*, *7, 1–20.*

——(2011). Input, intake, and consciousness: The quest for a theoretical foundation. *Studies in Second Language Acquisition*, *33*, 497–528.

Monitor Model

Ali Shehadeh
United Arab Emirates University

The Monitor Model is one of the most widely discussed and ambitious theories in second language acquisition (SLA). The Model evolved in the late 1970s in a series of articles (e.g., Krashen, 1977), but was developed and modified in subsequent writings by the author himself (e.g., Krashen, 1981, 1982, 1985). The Model consists of the following five hypotheses which together, according to Krashen, constitute a theory that accounts for all phenomena in SLA research and practice.

The acquisition-learning hypothesis

This hypothesis states that adults, unlike children, have two different and independent means for developing ability in L2: the learning ability and the acquisition ability. The former is conscious, the latter is subconscious. Further, what is learned cannot be acquired. It remains separate. Krashen states: "Monitor Theory hypothesizes that adults have two independent systems for developing ability in second languages, subconscious language *acquisition* and conscious language *learning*" (Krashen, 1981: 1). [italics in original]

The natural order hypothesis

This hypothesis states that acquisition in an L2 context (both children and adults) occurs in a predictable order. Krashen and Terrell (1983) cite evidence from morpheme studies (e.g., Dulay and Burt, 1974) that shows that some grammatical forms and structures tend to be acquired early such as (for example)–ing (progressive), plural, and copula (to be), and some tend to be acquired late like third person singular -s and possessive -s. Krashen and Terrell argue that for our instruction in L2 to be effective, we should teach learners along this universal, natural route of acquisition.

The monitor hypothesis

The third hypothesis states that our fluency in L2 performance is due to what we have acquired, not what we have learned. Learning is only available as a Monitor, or editor. Our acquired competence initiates utterances, and later these are referred to the conscious rules in the output system. To use the Monitor, three conditions should be met: (i) time: the learner must have enough time to utilize conscious rules; (ii) focus on form: the learner must be thinking about correctness; and (iii) knowledge of rules.

The input hypothesis

The fourth hypothesis attempts to answer the important question of how we acquire language. It states that a necessary condition for language acquisition to occur is that the acquirer understands input that contains structure "a bit beyond" his or her current level of competence. In other words, if an acquirer is at stage i, the input he or she understands should contain i + 1. Krashen (1985: 2) explains: "humans acquire language only in one way-by understanding messages, or by receiving 'comprehensible input'. ... We move from i, our current level, to i + 1, the next level along the natural order, by understanding input containing i + 1." That is, we acquire only when we understand the language that contains structure a little beyond where we are now.

Krashen (1981: 57) argues that comprehensible input is the only "causative factor" for SLA, claiming that "comprehensible input is responsible for progress in language acquisition" (Krashen, 1982: 61). The role of output is only to provide opportunities for generating more comprehensible input via feedback. Accordingly, speaking itself is not necessary for acquiring an L2. Krashen (1982: 60) states: "It is, in fact, theoretically possible to acquire language without ever talking."

The affective filter hypothesis

The fifth and last hypothesis states that certain personality characteristics predict success, such as self-confidence, motivation, and low anxiety. Conversely, learners with less self-confidence, lack of motivation, and high anxiety are less successful in SLA. The filter, a mental block, with the former group is low, with the latter it is high. Krashen (1985: 3–4) writes: "When the filter is 'up', the acquirer may understand what he hears and reads, but the input will not reach the Language Acquisition Device (LAD). … The filter is 'down' when the acquirer is not concerned with the possibility of failure in language acquisition and when he considers himself to be a potential member of the group speaking the target language."

Krashen (1985: 4) summarizes the Monitor Model in the following way: "We can summarize the five hypotheses with a single claim: 'people acquire second languages only if they obtain comprehensible input and if their affective filters are low enough to allow the input in.' When the filter is 'down' and appropriate comprehensible input is presented (and comprehended), acquisition is inevitable. It is, in fact, unavoidable and cannot be prevented-the language 'mental organ' will function just as automatically as any other organ."

The Monitor Model gained support and raised criticism, at the same time, among language teachers, applied linguists, and researchers. On the one hand, the Model won a lot of support in the 1970s and 80s, in particular from the advocates of an approach to Communicative Language Teaching methodology which postulates that learners need only be provided with comprehensible input whereby they only focus on meaning and communication, receive no or minimal explicit instruction, rules, or error correction. On the other hand, the Model was heavily criticized by other researchers and SLA scholars. In particular, it was argued that the acquisition-learning distinction is artificial rather than real (e.g., Schmidt, 1995), and that the claim that 'learned' knowledge does not convert to 'acquired' is not real either because many people have had their conscious L2 knowledge automatized to become acquired through practice (see, McLaughlin, 1987; Schmidt, 1995).

Similarly, several SLA researchers have also argued the Monitor Model favors the role of comprehension (input) while de-emphasizing at the same time the importance of production, or learner output (e.g., Swain, 1985; Shehadeh, 1999). Swain, in particular, has strongly argued that comprehensible input is not sufficient for successful SLA, but that opportunities for learners to produce comprehensible output are also necessary. Specifically, Swain argued that understanding new forms is not enough and that learners must also be given the opportunity to produce them. Swain therefore doubts that interactions and comprehensible input on their own are sufficient for SLA: "Conversational exchanges … are not themselves the source of acquisition derived from comprehensible input. Rather they are the source of acquisition derived from comprehensible output: output that extends the linguistic repertoire of the learner as he or she attempts to create precisely and appropriately the meaning desired" (Swain, 1985: 252).

See also: input enhancement, morpheme acquisition orders, naturalistic and instructed learning, Output Hypothesis, theoretical constructs in SLA, Universal Grammar (UG) and SLA

References

Dulay, H. and Burt, M. (1974). Natural sequence in child second language acquisition. *Language Learning, 24*/1, 37–53.

Krashen, S. (1977). The monitor model for adult second language performance. In M. Burt, H. Dulay and M. Finocchiaro (eds), *Viewpoints on English as a Second Language*, pp. 152–161. New York: Regents.

——(1981). The 'Fundamental Pedagogical Principle' in second language teaching. *Studia Linguistica, 35*/1, 50–70.

——(1982). *Principles and Practice in Second Language Acquisition*. Oxford: Pergamon.

——(1985). *The Input Hypothesis: Issues and Implications*. London: Longman.

Krashen, S. and Terrell, T. (1983). *The Natural Approach: Language Acquisition in the Classroom*. New York: Prentice-Hall.

McLaughlin, B. (1987). *Theories of Second Language Learning*. London: Edward Arnold.

Schmidt, R. (1995). Consciousness and foreign language learning: A tutorial on the role of attention and awareness in learning. In R. Schmidt (ed.), *Attention and Awareness in Foreign*

Language Learning, pp. 1–63. Honolulu: University of Hawaii Press.

Shehadeh, A. (1999). Non-native speakers' production of modified comprehensible output and second language learning. *Language Learning*, *49*/4, 627–75.

Swain, M. (1985). Communicative competence: Some roles of comprehensible input and comprehensible output in its development. In S. Gass and C. Madden (eds), *Input in Second Language Acquisition*, pp. 235–53. Rowley, MA: Newbury House.

Monitoring

Judit Kormos
Lancaster University

Self-monitoring, which involves checking the correctness and appropriateness of the produced spoken output, is an important component of speech production, which has three additional key components: (1) *conceptualization*, that is, planning what one wants to say, (2) *formulation*, which includes the grammatical, lexical, and phonological encoding of the message, and (3) *articulation*, in other words, the production of speech sounds. One of the basic mechanisms involved in producing and monitoring speech is *activation spreading*. Activation spreading is a metaphor adapted from brain research, which is based on the finding of neurological studies that neural networks consist of interconnected cells (neurons) that exchange simple signals called activations via the connections they have with each other (Hebb, 1949). The speech processing system is assumed to consist of consecutive, hierarchical levels, among which information is transmitted in terms of activation spreading.

The conceptualization of monitoring processes constitutes a major difference between the two major theories of first language (L1) speech production: *spreading activation theory* (the latter name is somewhat misleading because as just mentioned, both models assume that the way information is transmitted in the speech processing system is activation spreading) (e.g., Dell, 1986) and *modular theories* (e.g., Levelt, 1989). Spreading activation theories allow for the backward flow of activation from a lower level of processing to the higher level, whereas in modular theories, activation can only spread forwards. Consequently, in spreading activation theory, if an error occurs in one specific process, a warning signal is immediately issued, and activation flows backwards to the previous level, from which processing will restart. Therefore in this theory, monitoring is assumed to be an inherent feature of the perception and production processes, and no separate monitoring device is postulated (Dell, 1986). The claims of the spreading activation theory concerning monitoring have been subject to serious criticism because if errors were detected automatically, the monitor would perceive all the errors, which, in turn, would all be automatically corrected (Levelt, 1989). Empirical research, however, shows that even L1 speakers do not correct every mistake in their speech (Levelt, 1989).

In modular models of speech production and monitoring such as Levelt's (1989) *Perceptual Loop Theory*, errors are not noticed at the level they are made, but only once the erroneous fragment of speech has been phonologically encoded or later when it is articulated. Hence in this view, bits of message that contain an error need to be encoded again from the level of conceptualization. In this model the same mechanism is applied for checking one's own message as for the perception and checking of other speakers' utterances. In order to avoid the necessity for reduplication of knowledge, in Perceptual Loop Theory the speech comprehension system is used for attending to one's own speech as well as to others. The outcome of the production processes is inspected in three monitoring loops (i.e., direct feedback channels leading back to the monitor). The first loop involves the comparison of the preverbal plan, which contains the conceptual specifications for the message to be conveyed, with the original intentions of the speaker before the plan is linguistically encoded. In this loop the preverbal plan might need modification because the speaker might find that the formulated message is not appropriate in terms of its information content or in the given communicative situation. In the second loop the phonetic plan (i.e., "internal speech") is checked before articulation, which is also called "covert monitoring" (Postma and Kolk, 1993). In this stage the speaker might notice an error such as a wrongly selected word before it is actually uttered. Finally, the generated utterance is also scrutinized after articulation, which constitutes the final, external loop of monitoring. When perceiving an error or inappropriacy in the output in any of these three loops, the monitor issues an alarm signal, which, in turn, triggers the production mechanism for a second time. Studies on the timing of self-repairs have revealed that the sequence of the detection of different types errors and inappropriacies is similar to the order in which the interlocutor's speech is processed, which lends support for the assumption that monitoring involves the same mechanisms as speech comprehension (Levelt *et al.*, 1999; Kormos, 2000b). Additionally, the investigations of the syntactic structure of self-repairs show that speech production does not start from the intermediary level where the error occurred, but from the level of conceptualizing which provides a strong support for modular models of speech production (e.g., Levelt, 1989, Levelt *et al.*, 1999). Thus it can be concluded that both theoretical considerations and the empirical results on monitoring suggest the superiority of Levelt's Perceptual Loop Theory over the spreading activation both in L1 and L2 speech processing.

Mechanisms of L1 and L2 monitoring and self-repair behavior share a number of similarities, in that the distribution and detection of self-repairs display an analogous pattern in the processes of L1 and L2 acquisition and production (Kormos, 2000a; van Hest, 1996). Nevertheless, due to lack of automaticity in L2, monitoring in L1 differs from monitoring in L2 as regards the amount of attention available for error detection. Attentional resources are limited, and because L2 speech processing frequently needs attention at the level of lexical, syntactic and phonological processing (unlike in L1), L2 speakers have little attention available for monitoring. The role of attention in monitoring has been investigated by a number of studies, which suggest that attentional resources for monitoring are constrained by the level of proficiency and the task learners have to perform (for a review see Kormos, 2000a). Furthermore, due to the fact that the L2 speakers' system of knowledge might be incomplete and their production mechanisms are not fully automatic, certain repair mechanisms such as corrections performed in cases when L2 users are uncertain about the correctness of their utterance, occur in L2 speech that are not——or only very rarely—observable in L1 production.

Although attention is limited in capacity, it can be controlled voluntarily. A number of studies suggest that L2 speakers tend to direct their attention to the informational content than to the accuracy of their message. On the other hand, Kormos's (2000a) research revealed that this may not hold for all formally instructed learners. Students in whose instruction grammar teaching plays an important role might devote more attentional resources to accuracy than to lexical appropriacy than learners taught with communicative methods. L2 speakers' attention in monitoring also tends to shift from lower level linguistic errors to problems arising at the discourse level with the development of language proficiency.

Monitoring plays a key role in promoting second language acquisition. As L2 monitoring involves the checking of both internal and external speech against the learner's often unstable existing L2 linguistic system, L2 learners might not always be able to decide with certainty whether the output is error-free. This can contribute to noticing the gap in one's knowledge, and it might trigger further acquisition processes (Schmidt, 1990). Not only perceiving a gap in one's knowledge but also simply noticing an error can promote L2 learning. Robinson (1995) argued that noticing involves "detection plus rehearsal in short-term memory prior to encoding in long-term memory" (p. 296). In the case of monitoring, this means that the erroneous item is detected and the error-free solution is rehearsed before it becomes stored in long term memory, which process can also be conducive to L2 development. Moreover, a self-initiated and self-completed repair in L2 is executed in a similar way as the repairs made in response to the confirmation or clarification requests of interlocutors. The difference between the two processes is only that in the former case, it is the speaker, whereas in the latter case, it is the conversational partner who perceives the error. Instances when corrections or rephrasings of are elicited by the interlocutor have been termed pushed output and might also contribute to the success of L2 acquisition. In sum, just like pushed output, self-initiated self-repairs also serve to test hypotheses about the L2, trigger creative solutions to problems and expand the learners' existing resources (Swain, 1995).

See also: attention, awareness, Levelt's model of speech production and comprehension, speaking, self-repair, Output Hypothesis

References

Dell, G.S. (1986). A spreading activation theory of retrieval in sentence production. *Psychological Review*, *93*, 283–321.

Hebb, D.O. (1949). *The Organization of Behavior*. New York: Wiley.

Kormos, J. (2000a). The role of attention in monitoring second language speech production. *Language Learning*, *50*, 343–84.

——(2000b). The timing of self-repairs in second language speech production. *Studies in Second Language Acquisition*, *22*, 145–69.

Levelt, W.J. M. (1989). *Speaking: From Intention to Articulation*. Cambridge, MA: MIT Press.

Levelt, W.J. M., Roelofs, A. and Meyer, A.S. (1999). A theory of lexical access in speech production. *Behavioural and Brain Science*, *22*, 1–38.

Postma, A. and Kolk, H. (1993). The covert repair hypothesis: Prearticulatory tepair processes in normal and stuttered disfluencies. *Journal of Speech and Hearing Research*, *36*, 472–87.

Robinson, P. (1995). Attention, memory and the 'Noticing' Hypothesis. *Language Learning*, *45*, 283–331.

Schmidt, R. (1990). The role of consciousness in second language learning. *Applied Linguistics*, *11*. 129–58.

Swain, M. (1995). Three functions of output in second language learning. In G. Cook, and B. Seidlhofer (eds), *Principle and Practice in Applied Linguistics: Studies in Honour of H.G. Widdowson*. Oxford: Oxford University Press.

Van Hest, E. (1996). *Self-repair in L1 and L2 Production*. Tilburg: Tilburg University Press.

Further reading

Kormos, J. (2006). *Speech Production and Second Language Acquisition*. Mahwah, NJ: Lawrence Erlbaum. (Provides a detailed and up-to-date overview of second language speech production processes and proposes a new model for encoding speech in second language.)

Postma, A. (2000). Detection of errors during speech production: A review of speech monitoring models. *Cognition*, *77*, 97–131. (An excellent summary of monitoring first language speech.)

Verhoeven, L.T. (1989). Monitoring in children's second language speech. *Second Language Research*, *5*, 141–55. (An exemplary study of how the monitoring behavior of bilingual children changes as a result of linguistic and cognitive development.)

Morpheme acquisition orders

Zoe Luk
University of Pittsburgh

Brown (1973), who conducted a longitudinal study with English-speaking children, was the first to notice that English-speaking children acquire English grammatical morphemes in a relatively fixed order, regardless of their family backgrounds. The acquisition order reported in Brown's study is as follows:

Present progressive *-ing*
Prepositions *in, on*
Plural-*s*
Irregular past
Possessive-*'s*
Uncontractible copular (e.g., *this is a cup*)
Articles
Regular past
3rd person singular regular (e.g., *She smiles*)
3rd person singular irregular (e.g., *She does*)
Uncontractible auxiliary (e.g., *Ross is running*)
Contractible copula (e.g., *He's a student*)

Contractible auxiliary (e.g., *She's smiling*)

Following Brown (1973), Dulay and Burt (1973, 1974) investigated whether a similar fixed order can be found with learners of English as a second language. They found that, despite having different native languages, both Chinese and Spanish learners of English followed a similar order, but the order is different from that of native English-speaking children. They therefore assert that second language learners of English follow a relatively fixed order when acquiring English grammatical morphemes, and the learner's native language has little influence on the order. Numerous subsequent studies have concluded that the order is also followed by native speakers of many other languages, including Japanese, Korean, Greek, Farsi, etc. Although practically speaking the morpheme acquisition order is not unique to English, English as a second language (ESL) is by far the most researched in this area.

Based on the results of Dulay and Burt (1973, 1974) and a number of morphemes studies that followed, Krashen (1977) proposes a universal acquisition order of English grammatical morphemes. The order is as follows:

Group 1: *-ing*, plural-*s*, copula
Group 2: auxiliary, article
Group 3: irregular past
Group 4: regular past, third-person singular-*s*, possessive-*'s*

There are some similarities between the morpheme acquisition order for first language and that for second language. First, the progressive marker and plural-*s* are among the first to be acquired. Second, irregular past markers are learned earlier than regular past markers. Third, third-person singular-*s* is one of the latest acquired.

The universal acquisition order of English grammatical morphemes is important in Generative Linguistics. The idea that the acquisition order is relatively fixed regardless of the learner's first language may suggest that there is an innate language learning mechanism that guides learners through the stages of acquisition, thus lends support to the notion of Universal Grammar. It presents a challenge to Contrastive Analysis Hypothesis, which predicts learners' difficulties in reference to their L1s. The order also has important pedagogical implications in the sense that it should be considered when designing teaching materials.

However, the morpheme acquisition order is not without controversy. Two major issues have been raised. First, it has been argued that the acquisition order is an artifact of the methodology. Several studies (e.g., Bailey, Madden, and Krashen, 1974; Dulay and Burt, 1973, 1974) used Bilingual Syntax Measure as the elicitation method, in which participants view pictures and answer questions asked by the experimenter. Larsen-Freeman (1975) administered a battery of five tasks, including reading, writing, listening, imitating, and speaking to 24 participants with four native language backgrounds. She found that the performance of the participants varied for different tasks. Except for the speaking task, the participants with different native languages did not show a high degree of correlation in other tasks. Rosansky (1976) raised similar concerns. She examined spontaneous speech data from six Spanish learners of English, and found that there was great individual variability that the morpheme acquisition order she obtained correlated with both Dulay and Burt's order, and also de Villiers and de Villiers' (1973) L1 acquisition order. She concluded that such results cannot be "meaningfully interpreted" (p. 423).

Another criticism is that the learner's native language does have an influence on the acquisition order. Luk and Shirai (2009) reviewed 18 morpheme studies that looked at Japanese, Chinese, Korean, and Spanish learners of English. They found that there indeed exists L1 influence, particularly regarding articles, plural-*s*, and possessive-*'s*. Because articles and plural-*s* are absent in Chinese, Korean, and Spanish, learners who speak these language as their first language tend to learn these morphemes later than is predicted by the morpheme acquisition order. On the other hand, the possessive constructions in these languages considerably resemble the NP's NP construction in English. Therefore, learners of these native languages acquire possessive-*'s* earlier than the order predicts. These findings pose challenges to the claim that the morpheme acquisition order is impervious to the learner's native language.

Instead of resorting to an innate mechanism for second language acquisition, an alternative has been proposed by Goldschneider and DeKeyser (2001) to explain the seemingly invariant morpheme acquisition order as a result of properties of the morphemes. They conducted a meta-analysis of 12 ESL studies, and found that percentages of correct grammatical morphemes supplied correlate significantly with properties of the morphemes, including frequency, phonological salience, semantic complexity, morphophonological regularity, and syntactic category, and that these five factors account for a large portion of the total variance in the accuracy score. This implies that it is the external factors (i.e., properties of English grammatical morphemes), instead of internal innate language learning mechanisms, that causes the acquisition order to occur.

See also: inflectional morphemes, development in SLA, developmental sequences, Target-Like-Use (TLU) Analysis, Contrastive Analysis Hypothesis (CAH), Universal Grammar (UG) and SLA

References

Bailey, N., Madden, C. and Krashen, S. (1974). Is there a 'natural sequence in adult second language learning'? *Language Learning*, *24*, 235–43.

Brown, R. (1973). *A First Language: The Early Stages*. Cambridge, MA: Harvard University Press.

de Villiers, J. and de Villiers, P. (1973). A cross-sectional study of the acquisition of grammatical morphemes in child speech. *Journal of Psycholinguistic Research*, *2*, 267–78.

Dulay, H. and Burt, M. (1973). Should we teach children syntax? *Language Learning*, *24*, 245–58.

——(1974). Natural sequence in child second language acquisition. *Language Learning*, *24*, 37–53.

Goldschneider and DeKeyser, R. M. (2001). Explaining the 'natural order of L2 morpheme acquisition' in English: A meta-analysis of multiple determinants. *Language Learning*, *51* (1), 1–50.

Krashen, S.D. (1977). Some Issues Relating to the Monitor Model. In H. Brown, C. Yorio, and R. Crymes (eds), *On TESOL'77*. Washington, DC: TESOL.

Larsen-Freeman, D. (1975). The Acquisition of Grammatical Morphemes by Adult ESL Students. *TESOL Quarterly*. *9*(4), 409–19.

Luk, Z.P. and Shirai, Y. (2009). Is the Acquisition Order of Grammatical Morphemes Impervious to L1 knowledge? Evidence From the Acquisition of Plural-*s*, Articles, and Possessive-*'s*. *Language Learning*, *59*(4), 721–54.

Rosansky, E. (1976). Methods and Morphemes in Second Language Research. *Language Learning*, *26*, 409–25.

Motivation

Robert C. Gardner
University of Western Ontario

The concept of motivation is multifaceted. An individual who is motivated has a goal, expends effort to achieve it, wants to achieve it, has favorable attitudes concerning the activity of doing so, is persistent, is focused and attentive, makes attributions about success and failure, and perhaps has many other characteristics as well. Motivation is a term commonly used to explain many aspects of behavior. A teacher will exclaim that a student isn't doing well in school because of a lack of motivation. A researcher will note that a research animal deprived of food for some period of time runs a maze because it is motivated by hunger, etc … In the history of psychology, motivated behavior has been explained in terms of many concepts such as physiological drives, social motives, needs, presses, etc … In all cases, they are seen to impel an organism to action. Kleinginna and Kleinginna (1981) referenced 102 statements concerning motivation and presented and classified them in terms of nine categories; phenomenological (emphasizing conscious or experiential processes – 7 examples), physiological (internal physical processes – 11), energizing (energy arousal – 9), directional/functional (choice, incentives, goal-directed behavior, or adaptive effects – 15), vector (both energy arousal and direction – 25), temporal-restrictive (immediate or temporary determinants of behavior – 6), process-restrictive (distinguishing motivation from other processes – 11), broad/balanced (emphasizing the complexity of motivation – 8), and all-inclusive (incorporating all determinants of behavior – 10). In addition, they identified four statements that were disparaging (i.e., questioning the term or concept). They note that others may categorize the definitions somewhat differently. It is clear nonetheless that there is interest in the concept of motivation in psychology and related disciplines and that there are different interpretations as to how it should be defined.

A similar observation can be made in the area of second (or foreign) language learning. Most researchers and teachers in this area consider motivation to be an important factor in learning a second language, but often the concepts used and the role played are seen to differ. Motivation has even been postulated to be important in first language learning. Mowrer (1950) proposed that young children come to imitate parents' vocalizations because in the past they were associated with primary drive reduction, and in time took on secondary reinforcing value. That is, as babies they were fed, had diapers changed, etc., by care-givers who vocalized at the same time. The child imitates and ultimately perfects these word-sounds to make them more similar to the care-giver's productions making them more rewarding. Mowrer referred to this tendency to imitate the care-giver as Identification. This concept was adapted by Gardner and Lambert (1972) and extended to the area of second language acquisition who proposed that a similar process could explain instances of superior second language acquisition among students, though it would have a social basis rather than a physical one. They labelled it an "integrative motive" (p. 12). In the original Gardner and Lambert (1959) study, it was referred to simply as motivation "characterized by a willingness to be like valued members of the language community" (p. 271).

Models of motivation in second language acquisition

There are a number of theoretical models of motivation in second language acquisition and many of them include a similar concept. We will focus on eight models that have a series of empirical studies associated with them. One of the earlier models was Lambert's (1974) *social psychological model.* It posits that social attitudes and orientations influence both motivation and proficiency, that motivation and aptitude influence proficiency and that proficiency in the language has an influence on the individual's self-identity. This influence can result in additive or subtractive bilingualism, depending on whether it adds to the individual's growth with respect to both cultures (additive) or loss of one's original cultural identity (negative).

The *socio-educational model of second language acquisition* was initially focused on individuals from a majority cultural background learning a minority language (Gardner, 1985), but has been extended now to consider both second and foreign language learning in any cultural context (Gardner, 2010). The model is concerned with understanding the motivation of a student learning the language primarily in the classroom. It distinguishes between language learning motivation and language classroom motivation directing attention to both the cultural and classroom implications of language learning. It postulates that integrativeness (reflecting the cultural component) and attitudes toward the learning situation (reflecting the classroom context) are two correlated variables that influence the motivation to learn a second language and that motivation and aptitude influence subsequent achievement. In more recent formulations, it is further proposed that other variables such as an instrumental orientation can influence achievement and moreover that achievement (or rather lack of it) can lead to language anxiety which can influence subsequent achievement. Until recently, Gardner has proposed that integrative motivation is characterized by integrativeness, attitudes toward the learning situation and motivation, but now he sees it as also including language anxiety as a negative component. That is, it is proposed that an individual who is integratively motivated to learn a second language will demonstrate high levels of integrativeness, favorable attitudes toward the learning situation, high levels of motivation and low levels of language anxiety (cf., Gardner, 2010).

Clément's (1980) *social context model* proposed a primary motivational process as a contrast of integrativeness and fear of assimilation having both approach and avoidance tendencies depending on the sign of the contrast which could have different implications in unicultural and multicultural contexts. In multicultural contexts the frequency and quality of contact that the student has with the other cultural community would result in differences in self-confidence with the language which would influence the motivation and thus the communicative competence which would eventuate in integration or assimilation depending on the relative status of the first culture. Thus, this model considers motivation to be an important aspect of second language acquisition which differs as a function of the reinforcements engendered by interactions with the other language community provided by the social context and which eventuates in self-confidence with the language. In more recent formulations, there has been an even larger emphasis placed on the role played by language acquisition and self-identity in multicultural contexts (cf., Clément and Noels, 1992) in their studies of situated language identity.

Confidence with the language is also a major feature of the *willingness to communicate model* proposed by MacIntyre (1994). In an initial formulation, he proposed that willingness to communicate in a second language was influenced by communication apprehension and perceived communication competence. In a later development, MacIntyre, Clément, Dörnyei and Noels (1998) presented an heuristic model of variables influencing willingness to communicate, which they propose should be the major goal of language instruction. This model then was one of the first to take the focus off the role of motivation in second language learning and direct it to the use of the language. The model was presented in the form of a pyramid which comprised six layers with variables relating to the social and individual context at the base and use of the second language at the apex. Layers 1 to 3 referred to a number of situation-specific influences on willingness to communicate while layers 4 to 6 were seen to represent more stable influences. Motivation to learn the language was viewed as an aspect of intergroup attitudes at level 5.

Dörnyei's (1994) *framework of L2 motivation* focused on variables similar to those discussed above, characterizing them in three levels. The Language Level comprised both integrative and instrumental motivational subsystems. The Learner Level involved Need achievement and Self-confidence which was comprised of language use anxiety, perceived language competence, causal attributions, and self-efficacy. The Learner Situation Level comprised three classes of variables, course-specific motivational components (e.g., interest in the course, expectancy of success, etc.), teacher specific components (e.g., authority type, task presentation, etc.), and group-specific motivational components (e.g., norm and reward system, group cohesiveness). It is hypothesized that the three motivational levels are independent of each other but in combination are responsible for the individual's overall motivation to learn the language, and that the motivation at any one level can nullify the effects of the other two levels.

Noels (2001) has placed greater focus on orientations and types of motives in a *self-determination model of L2 motivation*. Based on Deci and Ryan's (1985) self-determination theory, this model conceives of motivation as varying along a continuum. At the low end is amotivation while at the upper end is intrinsic orientation; extrinsic motivation is intermediate. At the one end, amotivaion is seen to characterize the approach of the individual who is not at all motivated to learn the language. In the category of extrinsic motivation, there are four subdivisions. In order, these are referred to as external regulation, introjected regulation, identified regulation, and integrated regulation, reflecting respectively higher levels of self-involvement. An intrinsic orientation reflects a higher level of self-determination and is demonstrated in an enthusiastic interest in the knowledge and stimulation associated with learning the language. Research has linked a number of the other variables discussed above to this type of classification of motives (cf., Noels, 2001).

Dörnyei and Ottó (1998) presented another approach to motivation by focusing on factors that influence it over a period of time in their *process model of second language motivation*. In essence, they propose that different motives operate at different stages. In their model, they distinguish between three phases, preactional, actional, and postactional and describe processes operative in each. The preactional phase begins with goal setting followed by the formation of intentions, and terminating with an intention to act, and identifies motivational influences at each stage. This leads to the actional phase which begins with action leading to some specific outcome such as goal achievement or termination of the action. These are governed by executive motivational influences. Lastly, there is the postactional phase which involves evaluation of the experience and inferences about the outcome. A major feature of this approach is that the motives operating at any given phase are relatively independent of those operating at any other one, but that they can influence each other.

Dörnyei (2009) has proposed a motivational model of second language acquisition that focuses on self-perceptions in what is conceived of as a *new L2 motivational self-system*. The model conceptualizes perceptions of the ideal self as a more central feature of what the socio-educational model defines as integrativeness and that links it more closely with current psychological theorizing. There are three dimensions in the model, the ideal L2 self, the ought-to L2 self, and the L2 learning experience. The ideal self refers to one's vision of the self in the future as being facile in the other language (i.e., bilingual or multilingual). The ought-to self is concerned with duties and obligations imposed externally to develop proficiency in the other language. The L2 learning experience relates to one's motivation that is inspired by prior experience interacting with the current language learning environment. This is a cognitive-based model that like many of the others perceives motivation in terms of one's own feelings, pressures from external forces and experiences in the language learning context.

As will be observed in all of these conceptualizations, motivation is a very important attribute of the individual. All of them agree that motivation is positively related to achievement and each would make similar predictions concerning its role in the learning process. With the possible exception of the process model, all of them include a concept that is similar to integrativeness which emphasizes that learning another language is different from most other subjects in that it involves acquiring features of other cultural communities, such as vocabulary, speech-sounds, etc … Some claim to be more education friendly than others in that they use terms that are familiar to teachers, educators, and others concerned with language pedagogy. Some refer to language motivation as a general construct that can vary over time while others focus on situational influences on it. But in the end, their objectives are the same, viz., to explain why some students are more successful than others in learning (and using) a second language.

See also: attitudes to the L2, child second language acquisition, individual differences in SLA, social and sociocultural influences on SLA, theoretical constructs in SLA, Willingness to communicate (WTC)

References

Clément, R. (1980). Ethnicity, contact and communicative competence in a second language. In Giles, H., Robinson, W.P. and Smith, P.M. (eds), *Language: Social Psychological Perspectives*. Oxford: Pergamon Press.

Clément, R. and Noels, K.M. (1992). Towards a situated approach to ethnolinguistic identity: The effects of status on individuals and groups. *Journal of Language and Social Psychology*, *11*, 203–32.

Deci, E.L. and Ryan, R.M. (1985). *Intrinsic Motivation and Self Determination in Human Behavior*. New York: Plenum.

Dörnyei, Z. (1994). Motivation and motivating in the foreign language classroom. *Modern Language Journal*, *78*, 273–84.

——(2009). The L2 motivational self-system. Chapter 3 in Z. Döyei and E. Ushioda (eds),

Motivation, Language Identity and the L2 self. Bristol: Multilingual Matters.

Dörnyei, Z. and Ottó, I. (1998). Motivation in action: A process model of L2 motivation. *Working papers in Applied Linguistics, 4*, 43–69.

Gardner, R.C. and Lambert, W.E. (1959). Motivational variables in second language acquisition. *Canadian Journal of Psychology, 13*, 266–72.

——(1972). *Attitudes and Motivation in Second-language Learning.* Rowley, MA: Newbury House.

Gardner, R.C. (1985). *Social Psychology and Second Language Learning.* London: Edward Arnold Publishers.

——(2010). *Motivation and Second Language Acquisition: The Socio-educational Model.* New York: Peter Lang Publishing.

Kleinginna, P.R. and Kleinginna, A.M. (1981). A categorized list of motivational definitions with a suggestion for a consensual definition. *Motivation and Emotion, 5*, 263–91.

Lambert, W.E. (1974). Culture and language as factors in learning and education. In Aboud, F. E. and Meade, R.D. (eds), *Cultural Factors in Learning and Education.* Bellingham, WA: Fifth Western Washington Symposium on Learning.

MacIntyre, P.D. (1994). Variables underlying willingness to communicate: A causal analysis. *Communication Research Reports, 11*, 135–42.

MacIntyre, P.D., Clément, R., Dörnyei, Z. and Noels, K.A. (1998). Conceptualizing willingness to communicate in a L2: A situational model of L2 confidence and affiliation. *Modern Language Journal, 82*, 545–62

Mowrer, O.H. (1950). *Learning Theory and Personality Dynamics.* New York: Ronald.

Noels, K.M. (2001). New orientations in language learning motivation: Towards a model of intrinsic, extrinsic, and integrative orientations and motivation. In Dörnyei, Z. and Schmidt, R. (eds), *Motivation and Second Language Acquisition.* Honolulu: University of Hawai'i Press.

Multi-competence

Vivian Cook
Newcastle University

"Multi-competence" is the knowledge of more than one language in the same mind or the same community, first proposed in Cook (1991). It treats the first and second languages as parts of a whole: the individual mind of a second language (L2) user has a language system built up out of two or more languages; the multilingual community uses two or more languages alongside each other. The L2 user and the multilingual community are treated as entities in their own right, not as monolingual native speakers or monolingual communities (Brutt-Griffler, 2002). An L2 user is then somebody who is actively using a language other than their first, whatever their level of proficiency, rather than a person learning a second language or a balanced bilingual.

Multi-competence can be regarded in two ways: as a specific testable hypothesis and as a general perspective on second language acquisition.

The multi-competence hypothesis: L2 users are distinct kinds of people from monolingual native speakers.

Research has examined the many ways in which L2 users may differ from native speakers, such as:

- *their knowledge of their first language.* Transfer from the second language to the first is a relatively new area of research (Cook, 2003). Research has revealed that the first language of an L2 user is affected in its phonology, for example Voice Onset Time, in its syntax, for example cues for assigning subjects in the sentence, and in its lexicon, where L2 users seem unable to switch off one language entirely while processing another rather than lowering its level of activation.
- *their uses of language.* L2 users use the second language for functions that differ from monolingual native speakers, such as codeswitching in which speakers effectively use both languages within a sentence or an utterance, and

translation in which they turn one language into another.

- *their awareness of language.* L2 users have a sharpened metalinguistic awareness of language itself, being more aware of its arbitrariness, more readily capable of adapting to less proficient speakers, and more capable of making grammaticality judgments.
- *their ways of thinking.* Compared to their monolingual peers, L2 users think differently (Cook and Bassetti, 2011). They perceive colors slightly differently, categorize objects differently in terms of shape and substance, and convey notions of manner and path differently in the sentence.
- *their greater efficiency in their first language.* Another language helps children to learn to read their first language (Yelland *et al.*, 1993) and to write better essays in it.

The overall conclusion from this first generation of research into the specific nature of L2 users confirms that they are distinct people in their own right (Grosjean, 1989), not pale shadows of monolingual native speakers. Indeed knowing another language delays the onset of Alzheimer's disease (Bialystok *et al.*, 2004) and develops the areas of the brain responsible for control (Green, 2011). The hypothesis of the distinct nature of L2 users has therefore been confirmed by wide-ranging research across several areas.

The multi-competence perspective: L2 users should be seen as people in their own right.

The multi-competence perspective is in part based on the multi-competence hypothesis, in part a free-standing assumption. It claims that any consideration of L2 users should be concerned with them as L2 users, not with their relationship to monolingual native speakers. This goes diametrically against the assumption implicit in most SLA research that L2 users are more or less successful approximations to monolingual native speakers, thus seeing deviation from a native speaker target as constituting failure and the task of SLA research as accounting for this comparative failure vis-à-vis the success of L1 learners. Apart from the specific evidence for the distinctive nature of L2 users presented above there are two broad arguments – the normality of L2 users and the discrimination against particular groups of speakers:

- the L2 user is the rule not the exception
  While it is notoriously difficult to calculate the figures, it is probable that L2 users in the world outnumber monolingual native speakers. This may be seen firstly from the number of countries with multiple official languages such as India, secondly from the number of languages spoken in supposedly monolingual countries, with London for example having 300 languages, thirdly from the vast numbers of students learning English in virtually every country in the globe, a proportion of which become L2 users. A typical human being nowadays uses more than one language in their everyday life. The normal human potential is to acquire more than one language; monolinguals have had a form of language deprivation. The L2 user state is the norm, monolingualism an exception.
- one group should not be measured against the standard for another
  Since the early days of linguistics, there has been a realization that one group of speakers should not be judged against another group to which they cannot belong (Labov, 1969), first speakers of "primitive" languages, then speakers of dialects, Black English, working class English and women's language. The only group whom it is still permissible to measure by standards of another group is L2 users. Yet the argument is the same: L2 users are not native speakers of the target language and should not be measured against them. Any definition of a native speaker necessarily includes a reference to the first language being acquired in early childhood. Under this definition, L2 users cannot become native speakers; their minds have been transformed by the acquisition of the first language and often by the acquisition of literacy. Their language state is necessarily different from an L1 child or adult if only because they already know language itself and one language in particular. Like the other group

comparisons, the alleged deficiency of L2 users is a question of one group asserting power over another group.

Hence the multi-competence perspective suggests that any discussion of L2 users should recognize their independence. They may be good L2 users or bad L2 users but they are not failed native speakers, whatever their proficiency.

Implications of multi-competence

The overall multi-competence idea has profound implications for SLA research and for second language teaching.

- *SLA research*
  Most of the perennial questions of SLA research continue to revolve around whether the L2 user is like a native speaker: "Does age affect L2 acquisition?" comes down to whether older L2 users speak the L2 like native speakers; "Do L2 learners have access to Universal Grammar?" amounts to whether they acquire the same grammars as native speakers. Most current SLA research techniques also depend upon measuring the L2 user against natives whether Error Analysis, reaction times, grammaticality judgments, obligatory occurrences or elicited imitation. At its strongest any SLA research that involves checking the L2 user against the native speaker is wrong – perhaps the majority of extant research. It is of course perfectly possible to use the native speaker as a parallel group and to evaluate the differences and similarities between them and L2 users, so long as L2 users are treated as equals not deficient inferiors.
- *language teaching*
  - *goals of language teaching*
    Several trends across the globe have been moving the goals of language teaching away from a slavish imitation of the native speaker to an elaboration of what an L2 user might need (Cook, 1999), for example the English as Lingua Franca movement. Looked at as external goals, multi-competence suggests that the student needs to learn uses of language appropriate to L2 users, chiefly interacting with fellow L2 users rather than native speakers. Looked at as internal goals, multi-competence reminds teachers that second language learning affects the whole mind of the L2 user and that the students benefit in many ways other than the instrumental use of the second language.
  - *the language teaching classroom*
    Banning the use of the first language in the classroom denies the reality of the classroom as an L2 situation and creates an artificial L1 monolingual situation. It tries to sever the inextricable links between the two languages in the students' minds and deprives them of their single important asset compared to the native child – knowledge of a first language. The multi-competence perspective advocates rational use of the second language in the classroom when it is more efficient to do so (Cook, 2001).
  - *native speaker language teachers*
    Much language teaching around the globe has preferred native speaker teachers over non-native speakers (Llurda, 2005). From the multi-competence perspective, the native speaker is not an appropriate model for the students as they have followed a different route to knowledge of language than the students and they are using the language as monolinguals rather than L2 users. Their asset of fluent native speech is beside the point if native speaker speech is no longer the goal.

Thus multi-competence has raised many issues about second language acquisition that need to be considered. If it were accepted in toto, it would mean ruling out much second language acquisition as irrelevant and much language teaching as inappropriate. The multi-competence perspective is not a model as such but a different angle for looking at second language acquisition, which reveals new research questions and issues and new approaches to language teaching.

See also: bilingualism and SLA, Complex Systems Theory/Dynamic Systems Theory, linguistic relativity, linguistic transfer, native speaker, proficiency

References

Bialystok, E., Craik, F.I., Klein, R. and Viswanathan, M. (2004). Bilingualism, aging, and cognitive control: Evidence from the Simon task. *Psychology and Aging, 19*, 2, 290–303.

Brutt-Griffler, J. (2002). *World English: A Study of its Development*. Clevedon: Multilingual Matters.

Cook, V.J. (1991). The poverty-of-the-stimulus argument and multi-competence. *Second Language Research*, *7*, 2, 103–117.

——(1999). Going beyond the native speaker in language teaching. *TESOL Quarterly*, *33*, 2, 185–209.

——(2001). Using the first language in the classroom. *Canadian Modern Language Review*, *57*, 3, 402–423.

Cook, V.J. (ed.) (2002). *Portraits of the L2 user*. Clevedon: Multilingual Matters.

——(2003). *Effects of the Second Language on the First*. Clevedon: Multilingual Matters.

Cook, V.J. and Bassetti, B. (eds) (2011). *Language and Bilingual Cognition*. New York: Psychology Press.

Green, D. (2011). Bilingual world. In Cook, V.J. and Bassetti, B. (eds), *Language and Bilingual Cognition*. New York: Psychology Press.

Grosjean, F. (1989). Neurolinguists, beware! The bilingual is not two monolinguals in one person. *Brain and Language*, *36,* 3–15.

Labov, W. (1969). The logic of non-standard English. *Georgetown Monographs on Language and Linguistics*, *22,* 1–31.

Llurda, E. (ed.) (2005). *Non-native Teachers*. New York: Springer.

Yelland, G.W., Pollard, J. and Mercuri, A. (1993). The metalinguistic benefits of limited contact with a second language. *Applied Psycholinguistics*, *14,* 423–444.

Further reading

Cook, V.J. (2008). *Second Language Learning and Language Teaching*. Edward Arnold. Fourth edition. (A multi-competence oriented account of second language acquisition and teaching.)

De Bot, K., Lowie, W. and Verspoor, M. (2005). *Second Language Acquisition: An Advanced Resource Book*. Abingdon: Routledge. (An important set of explicated readings.)

Herdina, P. and Jessner, U. (2002). *A Dynamic Model of Multilingualism: Changing the Psycholinguistic Perspective*. Clevedon: Multilingual Matters. (A general model that accommodates multi-competence.)

Ortega, L. (2009). *Understanding Second Language Acquisition*. London: Hodder Education. (A multi-competence view of second language acquisition.)

Scott, V.M. (2009). *Double Talk: Deconstructing Monolingualism in Classroom Second Language Learning*. Upper Saddle River, NJ: Prentice Hall. (A practical book for modern language teachers using multi-competence.)

Multifunctionality

Kathleen Bardovi-Harlig
Indiana University

The principle of multifunctionality allows multiple forms for a single meaning and multiple meanings for a single form. The multifunctionality principle in SLA governs a stage of interlanguage development which follows a period of association of one form to one meaning (see *the one-to-one principle*). Whereas the one-to-one principle guides the development of an interlanguage that is clear and can be easily processed, the multifunctionality principle ushers in a stage which is expressive (Andersen, 1990; Slobin, 1977). The multifunctionality principle is one of seven cognitive operating principles proposed by Andersen (the others are the one-to-one, formal determinism, distributional bias, transfer to somewhere, relevance, and relexification principles) which are based on Slobin's (1973) operating principles for first language acquisition. The principles govern the path a second language learner takes in developing an increasingly target-like and efficient linguistic competence.

The principle of multifunctionality states (Andersen, 1990: 53):

> (a) Where there is clear evidence in the input that more than one form marks the meaning conveyed by only one form in the interlanguage, try to discover the distribution and additional meaning (if any) of the new form.
> (b) Where there is evidence in the input that an interlanguage form conveys only one of the meanings that the same form has in the input, try to discover the additional meanings of the form in the input.

Since mature languages allow many types of multifunctionality, interlanguage stages which admit multifunctionality are less noticeable than stages that are restricted to one form-one meaning.

One of the clearest cases of the development of multifunctionality is found in the acquisition of tense-aspect morphology. Whereas initial stages associate one morpheme to one lexical-aspectual category (the perfective past to achievements and accomplishments, the progressive with activities, and the imperfective with states, following the one-to-one principle), the tense-aspect system expands from the use of past perfective morphology as a marker of completion to a marker of the past, the visible evidence of which is the spread of the perfective past from predicates with inherent endpoints to activities which lack endpoints. Similarly, the imperfect moves from states to activities, to accomplishments, which allows for a range of expression introducing choice and flexibility to the system. Grammatical aspect thus becomes viewpoint aspect (Smith, 1983) which is used by native speakers to encode the same events in different ways depending on their discourse function.

The Japanese durative imperfective aspect marker, *-te i-*, offers an interesting case of multifunctionality. It has an action in progress reading which is acquired first and is used with activities and accomplishments; it also has a resultative state reading when used with achievements, and this is acquired later (Shirai and Kurono, 1998).

Other cases of multifunctionality include multiple means of expressing the same function, such as multiple request forms (an interlanguage stage characterized by monoclausal request forms giving way to a stage that also admits biclausal forms) or multiple thanking expressions (an interlanguage stage characterized by the use of a general conventional expression for thanking giving way to specialized expressions).

See also: acquisition of tense and aspect, development in SLA, form-meaning connections, interlanguage, one-to-one principle, operating principles

References

Andersen, R.W. (1990). Models, processes, principles and strategies: Second language acquisition inside and outside the classroom. In B. VanPatten and J.F. Lee (eds), *Second Language Acquisition-foreign Language Learning*. Clevedon: Multilingual Matters.

Slobin, D.I. (1973). Cognitive prerequisites for the development of grammar. In C.I. Ferguson and D.I. Slobin (eds), *Studies of Child Language Development*. New York: Holt, Rinehart, and Winston.

——(1977). Language change in childhood and history. In J. Macnamara (ed.), *Language Learning and Language Thought*. New York: Academic Press.

Shirai, Y. and Kurono, A. (1998). The acquisition of tense-aspect marking in Japanese as a second language. *Language Learning*, *48*, 245–79.

Smith, C.S. (1983). A theory of aspectual class. *Language*, *59*, 479–501.

Myelination

Helen Carpenter
Upper-Story Educational Services and Consulting

Myelination is the process by which glial cells ensheath the axons of neurons (nerve cells). Myelin is a thin sheet of plasma membrane, composed of lipids and proteins, that is wrapped spirally around one or more axons. Axons are cable-like extensions of neurons that convey electrochemical signals to other cells via synapses. Myelin insulation helps maintain the strength and speed of the signal along the length of axon until it reaches the synapse. At varying intervals, there are gaps in the myelin sheath called nodes of Ranvier. These gaps, which allow contact with external media such as neuromodulators, permit the electrochemical signal to be recharged. The signal "jumps" from node to node through saltatory conduction (from Latin *saltare*). Myelin and the location of nodes of Ranvier contribute to the regulation and timing of the spread of signals across networks of cells, thus promoting or inhibiting the temporal summation of convergent inputs to dendrites (Fields, 2005). Neurons that do not undergo myelination rely on axon diameter (thickness) to regulate signal strength. The signal conduction rate for unmyleIinated axons may be as much as 100 times slower than that of mylenated axons of equal cross-sectional size. Myelination is advantageous because it allows greater neuronal density and cellular connectivity within limited space.

Myelination takes place in the central and peripheral nervous systems. Neurons in the peripheral nervous system are myelinated by Schwann cells, while those in the central nervous system are myelinated by oligodendrocytes. In both cases, cytoplasm is removed between each turn of myelin, leaving only the thin sheathing formed by the plasma membrane.

Neurological disorders occur when there are myelin deficiencies. For example, multiple sclerosis and Guillain-Barre syndrome are characterized by demyelination in the central and peripheral nervous systems, respectively. Symptoms in both disorders arise from impaired intercellular communication caused by degraded signal conduction.

Myelinated axons are sometimes called white matter, while the unmyelinated somas and dendrites of neurons are called gray matter. The developing brain undergoes myelination for several years, becoming complete in the 20s. Myelination initially takes place in the brain stem, then progresses upward and outward into the cerebellum and basal ganglia, and lastly progresses to the cerebrum, with the frontal lobes among the last areas to mature. Myelination can also increase in specific regions in response to activity in children, and possibly in adults, and is thus a source of neural plasticity (Fields, 2005).

Myelination of language-related areas occurs in infancy and then again in adolescence. Around 18 months of age, myelination matures within Wernicke's and Broca's areas, corresponding to an increase in vocabulary development (Pujol *et al.*, 2006). At adolescence, there is a lateralized increase in white matter tracts linking Wernicke's and Broca's areas in the left hemisphere (left arcuate fasciculus; Schmithorst *et al.*, 2002). The maturation of myelin may contribute to adult learners' inability to develop a native-like second language (see Hyltenstam and Abrahamsson, 2003). Nevertheless, no causal link between myelination and language processes has yet been established.

See also: Critical Period Hypothesis (CPH), executive control and frontal cortex, lateralization, mirror neurons, neuroimaging, psycholinguistics of SLA

References

Fields, R.D. (2005). Myelination: An overlooked mechanism of synaptic plasticity? *Neuroscientist*, *11*(6), 528–31.

Hyltanstam, K. and Abrahamson, N. (2003). Maturational constraints on SLA. In C. Doughty and M. Long (eds), *The Handbook of Second Language Acquisition*, pp. 539–88. Oxford: Blackwell.

Pujol, J., Soriano-Mas, C., Ortiz, H., Sebastián-Gallés, N., Losilla, J.M. and Deus, J. (2006). Myelination of language-related areas in the developing brain. *Neurology*, *66*, 339–43.

Schmithorst, V.J., Wilke, M., Dardzinski, B.J. and Holland, S.K. (2002). Correlation of white matter diffusivity and anisotropy with age during childhood and adolescence: A cross-sectional diffusion tensor MR imaging study. *Radiology*, *222*, 212–18.

Squire, L.R., Berg, D., Bloom, F.E., du Lac, S., Ghosh, A., and Spitzer, N.C. (2008). *Fundamental Neuroscience*, third edition. Amsterdam and Boston, MA: Elsevier/Academic Press.

Further reading

Brauer, J., Anwander, A. and Friederici, A.D. (2009). Neuroanatomical prerequisites for language functions in the maturing brain. *Cerebral Cortex*, *21*, 459–66. (Describes differences between adults and children in degree of myelination and its relation to language processing during development.)

Native speaker

Vivian Cook
Newcastle University

A working definition of a native speaker is "a person who has spoken a certain language since early childhood" (McArthur, 1992). Davis (1996) and Cook (1999) deconstructed this into attributes such as: subconscious knowledge of rules, intuitive grasp of meanings, ability to communicate within social settings, range of language skills, creativity of language use, identification with a language community, the ability to produce fluent discourse, and knowing differences between their own speech and that of the standard form of the language. Until the 1990s it was tacitly assumed that the only owners of a language were its native speakers. The objective of L2 learning was therefore to become as like a native speaker as possible; any differences counted as failure. The native speaker construct has however become increasingly problematic in SLA research.

On the one hand it is a highly idealized abstraction. Native speakers of any language vary from each other in many aspects of grammar, pronunciation and vocabulary for dialectal, social and regional reasons. So which native speaker should be used as a model? For French is it an inhabitant of Paris, Marseilles, Geneva, Quebec City, Paramaribo or Ouagadougou? The choice of native speaker is related more to the status of particular varieties than to any properties of language. Additionally any native speaker commands different genres of language rather than possessing a single monolithic form; speech varies from one moment to the next, accommodating to speaker, situation, topic, and other factors. Hence the model of the native speaker in SLA research needs to allow for substantial variation.

On the other hand this has seemed to be one group exercising power over another (Phillipson 1992). Since Boas, linguistics has refrained from value judgments about different groups of speakers. Treating the native speaker as the model for SLA is falling into the same trap of subordinating the group of L2 users to the group of native speakers, to which they could never belong by definition. The alternative is to treat successful L2 users as the model against which L2 users are measured. This led to the description of L2 user speech in its own terms (Jenkins, 2000) and to research on L2 grammar and vocabulary centred around the VOICE project (Vienna Oslo International Corpus of English) into English as Lingua Franca (Seidlhofer, 2004).

SLA research has then been questioning its faith in the native speaker as the only true possessor of language, leading some to reinforce the importance of an idealized speaker of a standard form of a language, others either to a more flexible version of the native speaker or to the establishment of a non-native model. The issue has been closely related to language teaching both in terms of the model that students should be offered in the classroom and of the relative merits of native speaker and non-native speaker teachers.

See also: multi-competence, proficiency, second dialect acquisition, theoretical constructs in SLA, variationist approaches to SLA, World Englishes

References

Davies, A. (1996). Proficiency or the native speaker: what are we trying to achieve in ELT? In G. Cook and B. Seidlhofer (eds), *Principle and Practice in Applied Linguistics*, pp. 145–57. Oxford: Oxford University Press

Cook, V.J. (1999). Going beyond the native speaker in language teaching. *TESOL Quarterly*, *33*, 2, 185–209.

Jenkins, J. (2000). *The Phonology of English as an International Language*. Oxford: Oxford University Press.

McArthur, T. (1992). *Oxford Companion to the English Language*. Oxford: Oxford University Press.

Phillipson, R. (1992). *Linguistic Imperialism*. Oxford: Oxford University Press.

Seidlhofer, B. (2004). Research perspectives on teaching English as a lingua franca. *Annual Review of Applied Linguistics*, *24*, 209–39.

Further reading

Canagarajah, A.S. (ed.) (2005). *Reclaiming the Local in Language Policy and Practice*. Mahwah, NJ: Lawrence Erlbaum Associates.

Phillipson, R. (2010). *Linguistic Imperialism Continued*. London: Routledge.

Naturalistic and instructed language learning

Teresa Pica
University of Pennsylvania

Naturalistic and instructed learning share common features with respect to the cognitive abilities and perceptual processes that underlie them. As such, both naturalistic and instructed learning are grounded in the learner's comprehension of L2 message meaning, and the mapping of L2 form onto that meaning. Both require access to positive evidence of the form, function, and meaning relationships that are possible, acceptable, or appropriate in the L2. Both are believed to require access to negative evidence of the form, function, and meaning relationships that are not possible, acceptable, or appropriate. This is especially so for adult learners.

Naturalistic and instructed learning differ with respect to the labels and terms to which they are referred in the literature, the access to positive and negative evidence on which they depend, the settings in which they occur, the types of intervention they encounter, the interlanguage processes they reveal, and the outcomes to which they might lead. Thus, naturalistic and instructed learning have been distinguished from each other in the following areas:

> Labels and Terms of Reference: Naturalistic and instructed learning processes and contextual features have been described in research studies, review articles, and authored books as "out of the classroom" and "in the classroom" (D'Anglejan, 1970), "implicit" and "explicit" (DeKeyser, 2003), "natural" and "educational" (Ellis, 2009), "spontaneous" and "guided" (Klein, 1986), "untutored" and "tutored" (Klein and Dimroth, 2009), and "informal" and "formal" (Krashen, 1976).

By access to, and mode of delivery for positive and negative evidence

Throughout naturalistic and instructed learning, access to positive evidence is provided through the learner's exposure to, and transaction with L2 input that can be internalized as intake. Access to negative evidence is provided through feedback to learners on the clarity, accuracy, and comprehensibility of their L2 output (e.g., Doughty and Varela, 1998; Long and Robinson, 1998; Schmidt and Frota, 1986).

Positive evidence is abundant in authentic oral and written texts, as well as in texts that are modified through visual and auditory enhancement, repetition, and rephrasing. Instructed learning allows learners to access positive evidence of L2 form, function, and meaning relationships that they might overlook because the forms themselves and/or the meanings and functions they convey are not obvious. Such low salience items are characterized by any or all of the following: They are difficult to notice (e.g., *–s* infections for English 3rd person singular verbs); are found infrequently in everyday social discourse (e.g., English indirect questions); are limited in communicative transparency (articles *the*, *a*, and *zero* that refer to items that vary in specificity and interlocutor familiarity); or are wide ranging in functionality (modal verbs such as *might, can, could, should*, etc. that can be used to advise, argue, and predict).

Negative evidence is abundant in interlocutor signals of feedback on message clarity and comprehensibility during meaningful exchange, and in interlocutor- or learner-initiated attempts to achieve mutual understanding through strategies such as confirmation checks, for example, "Did you say a book?" and clarification requests, for example, "What did you say?" Here, too, instructed learning allows for a broader range of opportunities to access negative evidence in the form of preemptive rules, explicit error correction, and prompts to generate learner output and output modification.

Naturalistic and instructed learning are enhanced by opportunities to participate in communication, interaction, and information exchange, and especially in those transactions that generate the need for mutual understanding, known as the negotiation of meaning. These opportunities are characteristic of naturalistic learning, and can be implemented in instructed learning through teacher intervention, goal-oriented communicative activities, and grammatical form focusing tasks. A further enhancement to both naturalistic and instructed learning is found in the construct of "Learner Involvement" (Hulstijn, 2005) whose constituents include a need to understand meaning, a search for answers, and opportunities to evaluate performance and apply findings to future contexts. The range and breadth of learner involvement can be achieved in naturalistic and instructed learning, particularly during interaction that is oriented toward task completion and goal accomplishment.

Especially important to both naturalistic and instructed learning are learners' abilities to "notice the hole" for L2 form, function, meaning relationships they still need to acquire (Doughty and Williams, 1998), and to "notice the gap" between their interlanguage and the form, function, meaning relationships of their L2 target (Schmidt and Frota, 1986) as they attend to message meaning. These noticing abilities can be activated through different approaches to attention, including those that are incidental, implicit, or explicit to the learning process. Incidental learning processes are typically activated as communication problems arise in the course of conversational exchanges and social interaction (Long and Robinson, 1998). Therefore, they are associated with naturalistic learning more so than with instructed learning. Implicit learning processes are activated in "focused tasks" and activities that require specific linguistic features for their completion (Doughty and Varela, 1998; Doughty and Williams, 1998; Ellis, 2003). Explicit processes are activated through form-focused instruction (described by Spada, 1997), if learners reveal a need for assistance with forms and rules in the context of communication. Because implicit and explicit processes are activated through intervention, they are associated with instructed learning more so than with naturalistic learning.

By setting and type of intervention

Naturalistic learning often takes place in community contexts outside of schools and classrooms. However, many aspects of naturalistic learning can be activated in schools and classrooms that use communicative activities and materials. In naturalistic learning, there is no preset syllabus or pre-planned curriculum. Instead, learners themselves serve as their own instructors, who sample from the vocabulary, structure, and discourse to which they are exposed. They are rarely corrected by their interlocutors for their errors of linguistic structure, grammatical rules, and sentence formation. However, their messages might be questioned by interlocutors who cannot understand them due to clarity of pronunciation and comprehensibility of message meaning. In naturalistic learning, learners can access positive and negative evidence as modified L2 input and feedback in one-to-one conversations and during information exchange. A two-part, learner-interlocutor structure characterizes their discourse.

Instructed learning is associated with classrooms and instructors, trained and/or experienced in input and feedback provision, who often follow a preset syllabus and curriculum. The L2 is presented in a systematic, planned manner by level of difficulty, degree of complexity, and/or communicative importance. Lessons on language form, vocabulary, pronunciation, and discourse features are presented and learners practice their application across different modalities. Assessment occurs through classroom feedback and test instruments such as direct, objective quizzes and exams and holistic essays, interpretive papers, and answers to comprehension questions. A two-part discourse structure can occur during learner and interlocutor exchange, but quite typically, what transpires is a three-part structure in which instructors initiate exchanges with questions and directives, learners respond, and instructors follow up these responses with feedback.

By impact on learning processes and outcomes

Both naturalistic and instructed learning are characterized by the same cognitive processes of attention, awareness, and comprehension and the same developmental sequences and outcomes for sentence and question formation. However, there are several process and outcome distinctions between naturalistic and instructed learning. These are reflected in the rate of learners' progress through the sequences of L2 development, and in the extent of learners' attainment of L2 learning outcomes. This variation in rate and attainment reflects the range and variety of instructional and conversational interventions that are available to the learner.

Instructional interventions have been shown to increase the rate of L2 learning, if their timing is based on learners' readiness to notice relationships of L2 form, meaning, and function they have yet to master. Instructional interventions have also been shown to raise learners' ultimate attainment of complex grammatical constructions, if these interventions are encoded in linguistic input that refers to individuals and items outside the immediate context, poses arguments that integrate multiple claims and assertions, and conveys other, related functions whose communication requires sentence embeddings and dependent clauses.

Naturalistic and instructed learning also exhibit differences in the types of morpheme errors the learner produces. As revealed in Pica (1983), omission is typical of naturalistic learning, in which the learner is likely to say, for example, "one child" and "*two child." This pattern suggests that the naturalistic learner might not have noticed the bound, often phonetically reduced plural *–s* morpheme form in the input and feedback available, nor yet achieved knowledge or control over its application and use. Overgeneralization of grammatical morphemes is typical of instructed learning, as the learner is more likely to say, "one child" and "*two childs." This pattern suggests that the learner has acquired knowledge of the form of the plural *–s* morpheme, but has yet to achieve a firm control over its application and use. It also suggests that the form may have been made available in the classroom, but the learner has not been completely understood in its applications.

Across both naturalistic and instructed learning, conversational and instructional interventions appear to have little impact on the acquisition order of grammatical morphemes or of rules for sentence constituent movement and placement (Ellis, 1984; Pienemann, 1989; and Spada and Lightbown, 1999), but interventions have been shown to accelerate the learner's movement through the stages of these orders. For example, instruction in a rule for sentence formation can be directed at the stage that immediately follows a learner's current stage of development in the acquisition order of these rules. The learner can then apply the rule to the reorganization of the internal grammar, incorporate the rule into the interlanguage system, or use it to reset a specific grammatical parameter.

There is a variable rate of acquisition that can be influenced though natural conditions such as face-to-face and frequent native speaker contact, and responses to learners that repeat, paraphrase, or show relevance to their messages. These conditions are likely to arise during naturalistic learning. Interventions from instructor strategies, pre-planned activities, and materials that provide access to meaningful input and opportunities to produce and modify output can also influence the rate of acquisition, and these are generally characteristic of instructed learning.

Cognitively, naturalistic and instructed learning are highly similar, but with respect to contextual factors and variable features, they differ a great deal. As such, contextual factors have an impact on the learners' L2 acquisition rate and the extent of their learning outcomes, but cognitive processes insure a similar sequence of development.

See also: attention, developmental sequences, explicit learning, input enhancement, implicit learning, positive and negative evidence

References

D'Anglejan, A. (1970). Language learning in and out of the classroom. In J.C. Richards (ed.), *Understanding Second and Foreign Language Learning*. Rowley, MA: Newbury House.

DeKeyser, R. (2003). Implicit and explicit learning. In C. Doughty and M. Long (eds), *The Handbook of Second Language Acquisition*. New York: Blackwell Publishing Ltd.

Doughty, C. and Williams, J. (eds) (1998). *Focus on Form in Classroom Second Language Acquisition*. Cambridge: Cambridge University Press.

Doughty, C. and Varela, E. (1998). Communicative Focus on Form. In C. Doughty and J.Williams (eds), *Focus on Form in Classroom Second Language Acquisition*. Cambridge: Cambridge University Press.

Ellis, R. (1984). Can syntax be taught? A study of the effects of formal instruction on the acquisition of Wh-questions by children. *Applied Linguistics*, *5*, 138–55.

——(2003). *Task Based Language Learning and Teaching*. Oxford: Oxford University Press.

——(2009). *The Study of Second Language Acquisition*. Oxford: Oxford University Press.

Hulstijn, J. (2005). Theoretical and empirical issues in the study of implicit and explicit second-language learning. *Studies in Second Language Acquisition*, *27*, 129–40.

Klein, W. (1986). *Second Language Acquisition*. Cambridge: Cambridge University Press.

Klein, W. and Dimroth, C. (2009). Untutored SLA. In W. Ritchie and T. Bhatia (eds), *The New Handbook of Research on Second Language Acquisition*. London: Emerald Group Publishing Ltd.

Krashen, S. (1976). Formal and informal linguistic Environments in Language Learning and Language Acquisition. *TESOL Quarterly*, *10*, 157–68.

Long, M. and P. Robinson (1998). Focus on Form: Theory, Research, and Practice. In C. Doughty and J. Williams (eds), *Focus on Form in Classroom Second Language Acquisition*. New York: Cambridge University Press.

Pica, T. (1983). Adult acquisition of English as a eecond language under different conditions of exposure. *Language Learning*, *33*, 465–97.

Pica, T., Kang, H. and Sauro, S. (2006). Information gap tasks: Their multiple roles and contributions to interaction research methodology. *Studies in Second Language Acquisition*, *28*, 301–38.

Pienemann, M. (1989). Is language teachable? Psycholinguistic experiments and hypotheses. *Applied Linguistics*, *10*, 52–79.

Schmidt, R. and Frota, S. (1986). Developing basic conversational ability in a second language: A case study of an adult learner of Portuguese. In R. Day (ed.), *Talking to Learn: Conversation in Second Language Acquisition*. Rowley, MA: Newbury House.

Spada, N. (1997). Form-focused instruction and second language acquisition: A review of classroom and laboratory research. *Language Teaching*, *29*, 73–87.

Spada, N. and Lightbown, P. (1999). Instruction, first language influence, and developmental readiness in second language acquisition. *The Modern Language Journal*, *83*, 1–22.

Negotiation of meaning

Jenefer Philp
University of Auckland

Negotiation of meaning (NfM) describes the way in which people adjust how they express meaning in response to communication difficulties. It is during interaction with others that second language (L2) learners build up implicit understandings of how language form conveys particular meanings, and in turn, develop their L2 use (Hatch, 1978). NfM is an important part of this process, and is defined by Pica (1992) as "those interactions in which learners and their interlocutors adjust their speech phonologically, lexically, and morphosyntactically to resolve difficulties in mutual understanding that impede the course of their communication" (p. 200). Research on NfM has its roots in first language (L1) acquisition research. First language acquisition researchers recognized the important role played in acquisition by the speech of caretakers to infants: the language addressed to infants is characterized by features that assist comprehension, and help to make connections between form and meaning more evident. Taking a cue from this research, second language researchers (Hatch, 1983; Long, 1983) found, similarly, that "foreigner talk," the type of language used to address adult non-native speakers, helps to anticipate and repair communication difficulties. Specifically, a native speaker (NS) may modify and simplify language, for example, through stress or pausing before a key word, as in Example 1 (Long, 1983: 135), or through elaboration, substitution of a word, or simplification of a grammatical form.

(1)

NS: Aha What *year* are you? (.) What year in college are you in?

Importantly, it is not only language, but the structure of the conversation itself that changes: negotiation frequently involves clarifying, confirming, and checking what is being communicated (Long, 1983; Pica, 1994), as seen in Example 2 (Mackey, 1999: 558–59). The learner's request for clarification ("A what?", "Glassi?") prompts the speaker (NS) to isolate the problematic word and elaborate upon it. This helps to make the form "reading glasses," and its meaning, more salient to the learner ("ahh glasses to read – you say reading glasses").

(2)

NS: There's there's a a pair of reading glasses above the plant.

LEARNER: A what?

NS: Glasses reading glasses to see the newspaper?

LEARNER: Glassi?

NS: You wear them to see with, if you can't see. Reading glasses.

LEARNER: Ahh ahh glasses glasses to read you say reading glasses.

Research on negotiated interaction has identified four ways in which interaction faciliates acquisition (Pica, 1992; Gass, 1997): by assisting comprehension; supporting learner output; drawing attention to language form and meaning; and providing feedback contiguous with the learner's attention. Firstly, linguistic and interactional modifications that occur in response to communication difficulties assist learners to understand problematic input (Long, 1983). Particular moves characteristic of this process include "comprehension checks," used by the speaker to verify understanding (e.g "do you understand?"); "clarification requests" by the interlocutor to signal a communication problem (e.g. "a what?" "glassi?") and "confirmation checks" – a move in which the interlocutor seeks to confirm a particular interpretation of what was said (e.g "do you mean … ?"). Strategies that anticipate comprehension problems include increased salience of key words through stress, intonation, and the use of left dislocation (putting the topic first in an utterance). Long (1983) hypothesized that, given the necessity of comprehensible input for acquisition (Krashen, 1980), interaction facilitates L2 acquisition through adjustments that make input intelligible (see **Interaction Hypothesis**). The relationship between interactional modifications and comprehension is well supported by early research (see Pica, 1992).

Secondly, negotiation may assist learners to use language that is more coherent, accurate, and/or appropriate (Swain, 1985, **Comprehensible output hypothesis**). Learners may modify their production in response to feedback such as clarification requests, confirmation checks, and "recasts," in which the interlocutor reformulates the learner's utterance in a target-like manner. Thus, in Example 3 (Mackey, 1999: 559), the learner modifies her production ("weep") in response to a clarification request from the interlocutor ("huh?"), and becomes more accurate in L2 use.

(3)

LEARNERS: And one more weep weep this picture.

NS: Huh?

LEARNERS: Another one like gun to shoot them weep weepon.

NS: Oh ok ok yeah I don't have a second weapon though so that's another differ- ence.

In this way, NfM may draw learners' attention to problems in their understanding and use of the L2, a third important benefit of negotiation. Interactional modifications can serve to highlight relationships between form and meaning in ways that are contingent with the learner's own focus (Pica, 1992, 1994). Noticing language form, rather than attending to meaning alone, is critical to interlanguage change. Gass and Varonis (1994: 299) argue that this attention to form in the context of communication is a catalyst for language development:

> [negotiations] crucially focus the learner's attention on the parts of the discourse that are problematic, either from a productive or a receptive point of view. Attention in turn is what allows learners to notice a gap between what they produce/know and what is produced by speakers of the L2. The perception of a gap or mismatch may lead to grammar restructuring.
>
> (Gass and Varonis, 1994: 299)

Finally, an important feature of NfM is the contiguous nature of the interaction: learners receive feedback uniquely attuned to their own production. That is, it is both meaningful and relevant. When a learner receives feedback from an interlocutor, for example a recast of the learner's utterance, or a signal to repeat or rephrase the utterance, this feedback comes just as the learner's attention is focused on what they want to say and how to say it (Long, 1996: 2007).

Research

For these reasons, interaction is a key context for language acquisition. L2 acquisition researchers have sought to describe the nature of such interaction, and outcomes for learning: in terms of comprehended input, modified output, noticing of form, and second language development. Mackey's (1999) empirical study of interaction and acquisition of question forms, for example, demonstrates a relationship between interactional modifications and language development. This finding has since been born out in a wide range of studies, as clear from recent meta-analysis of interaction and L2 development (e.g. Mackey and Goo, 2007). Most recently, researchers have sought to explain how negotiation facilitates learning, and the processes involved, leading to the development of a model of interactionally driven acquisition (Gass, 1997).

Methodology

Typically, research on negotiated interaction tends to analyze interaction through identification of specific sequences of negotiation within a discourse. These are coded as a three-turn unit consisting of a "trigger" utterance, that causes a communication problem; an "indicator" or response turn in which the interlocutor signals the problem; and a "reaction" turn in which the initial trigger may be modified or reformulated to assist comprehension. This final turn may itself become a trigger – thus the sequences can be recursive.

Limitations

While the relationship between interaction and L2 learning is now well established, it should by no means be assumed that NfM offers blanket benefits for language development. Firstly, the learner does not always notice language form or perceive feedback as corrective, in the struggle to understand or be understood. Secondly, not all linguistic features change as a result of conversational modifications for reasons relating to salience, redundancy, and relative difficulty for the learner. Thirdly, NfM is not common to all interaction. Indeed, in many classroom settings, NfM is relatively rare: a shared first language and/or shared context often precludes comprehension problems. Certain task features, and participant-related factors such as gender, relative status, and proficiency level foster greater NfM more than others (Gass, 1997; Pica, 1992, 1994).

More socially oriented researchers have criticized research on negotiation as too narrowly focused, both in theory and methodology. Socio-cultural and socio-cognitive perspectives (e.g. Block, 2003) encourage a view of interaction that is more holistic and considers the relational aspects of interaction in addition to the linguistic. A methodological problem arises where there is an over-reliance on quantitative measures: counting occurrences of negotiation sequences, for example, reduces our ability to see negotiation as part of the whole interaction, or to recognize negotiation of social goals such as solidarity or affiliation as also being at play.

New directions

Research on NfM has moved from description to exploration of how, when, and why negotiation provides learning opportunities. Researchers have identified a variety of learner internal and external factors that appear to mediate the potential of negotiation. These include task-related factors, gender, proficiency pairings, and individual differences in working memory (Gass, 1997; Philp, 2008). The methodology used to explore the benefits and limitations of negotiation has developed and improved, with the use of more fine-grained analysis of discourse and introspective techniques such as stimulated recall to capture learner perceptions and processing of interactional modifications. A deeper understanding of the contribution of interaction to second language learning, includes, but is not limited to the role of NfM. There is now a wealth of research in related areas, including corrective feedback, negotiation of form, and task-based interaction, that reinforces the importance of interaction as a context for acquisition. It is negotiation of meaning research that provided the springboard for these areas, and our current understandings of interaction and L2 development.

See also: Interaction and the Interaction Hypothesis, Focus on Form (FonF), Noticing Hypothesis, Output and the Output Hypothesis, recasts, task-based learning

References

Block, D. (2003). *The Social Turn in Second Language Acquisition*. Washington, DC: Georgetown University Press.

Gass, S. (1997). *Input, Interaction, and the Second Language Learner*. Mahwah, NJ: Lawrence Erlbaum.

Gass, S.M. and Varonis, E. (1994). Input, interaction and second language production. *Studies in Second Language Acquisition*, *16*, 283–302.

Hatch, E. (1978). Discourse analysis and second language acquisition. In E. Hatch (ed.), *Second Language Acquisition: A Book of Readings*, pp. 401–35. Rowley, MA: Newbury House.

——(1983). *Psycholinguistics: A Second Language Perspective*. Rowley, MA: Newbury House.

Krashen, S. (1980). The input hypothesis. In J. Alatis (ed.), *Current Issues in Bilingual Education*, pp. 168–80. Washington, DC: Georgetown University Press.

Long, M.H. (1983). Native speaker/non-native speaker conversation and negotiation of comprehensible input. *Applied Linguistics*, *4*, 2, 126–41.

Long, M. (1996). The role of the linguistic environment in second language acquisition. In W. C. Ritchie and T.K. Bhatia (eds), *Handbook of Second Language Acquisition*, pp. 413–68. San Diego, CA: Academic Press.

——(2007). *Problems in SLA*. Mahwah, NJ: Lawrence Erlbaum.

Mackey, A. (1999). Input, interaction, and second language development: An empirical study of question formation in ESL. *Studies in Second Language Acquisition*, *21*, 557–87.

Mackey, A. and Goo, J. (2007). Interaction research in SLA: A meta-analysis and research synthesis. In A. Mackey (ed.), *Conversational Interaction in Second Language Acquisition: A Collection of Empirical Studies*, pp. 407–52. Oxford: Oxford University Press.

Philp, J. (2008). Epilogue: Exploring the intricacies of interaction and language development. In A. Mackey and C. Polio (eds), *Multiple Perspectives on Interaction. Second Language Research in Honour of Susan M. Gass*, pp. 254–74. New York: Routledge.

Pica, T. (1992). The textual outcomes of native speaker-non-native speaker negotiation: What do they reveal about second language learning? In C. Kramsch and S. McConnell-Ginet (eds), *Text and Context: Cross-Disciplinary Perspectives on Language Study*, pp. 198–237. Lexington, MA: Heath.

——(1994). Research on negotiation: What does it reveal about second language learning conditions processes and outcomes? *Language Learning, 44,* 3, 493–527.

Swain, M. (1985). Communicative competence. Some roles of comprehensible input and comprehensible output in its development. In S. Gass and C. Madden (eds), *Input in Second Language Acquisition*, pp. 235–53. Rowley, MA: Newbury House.

Neuroimaging

Helen Carpenter
Upper-Story Educational Services and Consulting

Neuroimaging broadly refers to the techniques used to observe structural and/or functional properties of the nervous system, particularly the brain, in SLA. Structural components which may be examined include, but are not limited to, the volume and distribution of gray matter, white matter, vasculature, calcification, and bone. Functional aspects which may be examined include, but are not limited to, the timing, location, and scope of blood flow, and metabolic and/or other activities. Researchers may examine intrinsic activity and/or evoked activity that occurs in response to stimuli.

With neuroimaging, researchers examine sensory phenomena, movement, memory, emotions, and the like. Neuroimaging complements cognitive methodologies like behavioral testing, reaction time analyses, and introspective data collection (stimulated recall, think aloud protocols), but specifically allows researchers to link hypotheses to well-established findings on how biophysical processes lead to the acquisition, storage, representation, and retrieval of knowledge. Typically, neuroimaging findings neither fully support, nor fail to support, SLA hypotheses, but instead, offer an additional dimension from which to consider issues.

Initially, much SLA neuroimaging research was insufficiently rigorous. It suffered from, among other issues, inadequate control of confounding variables (*e.g.,* amount- and type-of-exposure) and inadequate assessment of L2 proficiency (de Bot, 2008). Other research reflected inadequate knowledge of cognitive neuroscience and neuroimaging techniques. As SLA researchers have increasingly sought relevant instruction and cross-disciplinary collaboration, the quality of SLA-related neuroimaging has improved.

Neuroimaging techniques

Computed Tomography (CT). CT provides images of the brain's structure using x-rays (ionizing radiation). Images are constructed from multiple locations around the head. CT provides only limited differentiation between gray and white matter. To image vasculature and lesions, researchers use pharmaceutical contrast agents (Park and Gonzalez, 2004).

Electroencephalography (EEG). EEG captures the timing and intensity of neuronal electrical signals. It can be used to examine ongoing, synchronized, and/or dynamic activity (such as that evoked by stimuli). EEG has excellent *temporal resolution*, capturing millisecond-by-millisecond timing information, including automatic linguistic processes, but poor *spatial resolution*, as it does not establish the location of electrical activity (*i.e.*, the *inverse problem*, where one cannot determine the distribution of electric current within the brain from measurements at the skull). EEG does not involve radiation or toxins (Luck, 2005; see EEG Coherence, ERPs).

Magnetic Resonance Imaging (MRI). An array of MRI techniques examine structural, hemodynamic (blood-flow), water diffusion, and metabolic activity within neural tissue and vasculature. MRI images depend on the use of magnets to first manipulate and then detect the activity of protons (see fMRI). MRI produces detailed structural images that look like photographs. Images are presented as "slices" of the brain. MRI can image most, but not all, areas of the brain. MRI does not expose participants to ionizing radiation but there are other safety concerns related to the ferromagnetic properties of foreign bodies within participants. Pharmaceutical agents are typically unnecessary (Buckner and Logan, 2001; Deichmann, 2009).

In MRI, gray matter appears distinct from white matter because of differing water content. Diffusion Tensor Imaging (DTI) examines the direction and rate of water diffusion in these tissues. In gray matter, water diffuses similarly in all directions (*i. e.*, isotropy); in white matter, however, water diffusion is more directional (*i.e.*, anisotropy; Goldstein and Price, 2004). Researchers examine the connectivity of white matter tracts using DTI (see **Myelination**).

MRI may be used to explore blood flow and metabolic processes. Using fMRI, researchers examine blood flow patterns related to cognitive activity (see fMRI; Deichmann, 2009). Using Magnetic Resonance Spectroscopy (MRS), researchers examine metabolic processes to understand processes such as cellular energy consumption (Vink, 1997).

Magnetoencephalography (MEG). MEG is sensitive to magnetic fields generated during brain activity. These are measured by super-conducting quantum interference device (SQUID) detectors (Luck, 2005). MEG, like EEG, provides millisecond-by-millisecond temporal resolution. Moreover, magnetic activity, unlike electrical activity, is not distorted by the skull, so MEG provides better spatial resolution than EEG (nonetheless an "inverse problem" exists; Schmidt and Roberts, 2009). Images are based on Event-Related Magnetic Fields (ERFs), a magnetic correlate to ERPs. MEG does not involve radiation or toxins.

Positron Emission Tomography (PET). PET measures blood flow, glucose metabolism, and neurotransmitter activity. Participants consume or receive injections of radiopharmaceutical agents prior to imaging. These are designed to target specific metabolic processes and tissues. For example, one may target dopamine metabolism in the basal ganglia, while another may target serotonin metabolism in the frontal lobes. Radiopharmaceuticals contain excess protons that contribute to the formation of gamma rays that are detected by a gamma camera or PET scanner. To protect human health and research integrity, radiopharmaceuticals adhere to stringent guidelines; nevertheless, they pose some risks (Daugherty, Rauch, and Fischman, 2004).

Additional Neuroimaging Techniques. Some techniques are used infrequently in SLA research, but are encountered occasionally. (a) Researchers may use *brain stimulation* techniques to activate specific areas of brain tissue during surgery, and then record participant responses. (b) Transcranial Magnetic Stimulation (TMS) allows researchers to temporarily *knock out*, or suspend, activity in proscribed areas via electromagnetic coils. Researchers then observe changes in participant behavior. (c) Optical imaging (and related methodologies, such as Near Infrared Spectroscopy), provides data based on the convergence or dispersion of light that passes through tissue. (d) Single Photon Emission Tomography (SPECT), similar to PET, uses radiopharmaceuticals to examine blood flow and neurotransmitter function.

Data analysis and interpretation

Following data acquisition, researchers convert raw data into "images" via filtering and transformation. These steps improve the *signal-to-noise ratio* by extracting the desired signal from irrelevant signals and artifacts. Final results may rely on a single participant's data or averaging several participants' data.

Interpreting images is based on, but not limited to, the following: intensity of activation, locality, relationship to other data (*e.g.*, combining EEG and fMRI), and relationship to research on human behavior, patient populations, individuals with developmental disorders, pharmaceutical effects, and other phenomena.

Individual brain responses to stimuli vary according to many known factors—and very likely, many unknown factors. To minimize variation due to heterogeneity, participants may be grouped according to medical history, handedness, gender, age, and other criteria. In SLA research, participant groupings account for factors such as age of acquisition, type of exposure, amount of exposure, language transfer, L1, L2, and other relevant criteria.

See also: Declarative Procedural (DP) model, Event Related Potentials (ERP), Functional Magnetic Resonance Imaging (fMRI), measuring and researching SLA, psycholingustics of SLA, theoretical constructs in SLA

References

Daugherty, D.D., Rauch, S.L. and Fischman, A.J. (2004). Positron emission tomography and single photon emission computed tomography. In D.D. Daugherty, S.L. Rauch, and J.F. Rosenbaum (eds), *Essentials of Neuroimaging*, pp. 75–91. Washington, DC: American Psychiatric Publishing.

De Bot, K. (2008). Review article: The imaging of what in the multilingual mind? *Second Language Research*, *24*(1), 111–33.

Deichmann, R. (2009). Chapter 1. Principles of MRI and Functional MRI. In Filippi, M. (ed.), *fMRI Techniques and Protocols*, pp. 3–29. New York: Humana Press.

Goldstein, M.A. and Price, B.H. (2004). Magnetic resonance imaging. In D.D. Daugherty, S.L. Rauch, and J.F. Rosenbaum (eds), *Essentials of Neuroimaging*, pp. 21–73. Washington, DC: American Psychiatric Publishing.

Luck, S.J. (2005). *An Introduction to the Event-related Potential Technique*. Cambridge, MA: The MIT Press.

Park, L.T. and Gonzalez, R.G. (2004). Computed tomography. In D.D. Daugherty, S.L. Rauch, and J.F. Rosenbaum (eds), *Essentials of Neuroimaging*, pp. 1–19. Washington, DC: American Psychiatric Publishing.

Schmidt, G.L. and Roberts, T.P.L. (2009). Second language research using magnetoencephalography: A review. *Second Language Research*, *25*(1), 135–66.

Vink, R. (1997). Magnetic resonance spectroscopy. In P. Riley and R. Bullock, *Head Injury*, pp. 261–68. London: Chapman and Hall.

Further reading

Gullberg, M. and Indefrey, P. (eds) (2006). *The Cognitive Neuroscience of Second Language Acquisition*. Oxford: Blackwell. (An edited collection of papers utilising a variety of neuroimaging techniques—including PET, fMRI and ERP—to examine such issues as second language parsing, and word learning; age effects and Critical Period phenomena; executive control in bilingual processing; the learning of artificial versus natural second languages.)

Sabourin, L. (2009). Neuroimaging research into second language acquisition. *Second Language Research*, *25*, 5–11. (This special issue contains overview papers discussing the latest neuroimaging techniques, and empirical studies illustrating their use during SLA research.)

Noticing Hypothesis

Jenefer Philp
University of Auckland

The Noticing Hypothesis concerns the role of attention in learning, and the observation that, unlike first language acquisition, adult second language acquisition is not predominantly implicit. That is, it requires cognitive effort, focused attention, and the adoption of more explicit modes of learning if high levels of proficiency and grammatical accuracy are the goal. Schmidt's Noticing Hypothesis (1990, 2001, 2010) is fundamental to current understanding of second language learning and is widely used to explain a key step in acquisition processes.

Schmidt noted the failure among adult second language learners to acquire common linguistic forms despite plentiful exposure in the input. He hypothesized that in order for input to become intake for learning, learners needed to "attend to and notice linguistic features of the input" (Schmidt, 2010: 3). That is, in order to process input sufficiently to integrate new linguistic forms with existing knowledge (intake), there must be a degree of conscious registration of that input. Schmidt emphasizes that attention to input is not simply global; learning requires attention to specific properties of language features in the input.

Development of the Noticing Hypothesis

The Noticing Hypothesis is supported by theoretical and empirical work in the cognitive sciences that suggest that learning requires attention, because attention is "the necessary and sufficient condition for long-term storage" (Schmidt, 2001: 16). Further, attentional resources are limited and can be subject to voluntary control. Thus, the learner selectively attends to the elements of the input. Robinson (1995) refined the construct of noticing, with reference to Tomlin and Villa's (1994) description of attention as comprising alertness (readiness to deal with the input); orientation (direction of attentional resources); and detection, the selective "cognitive registration of sensory stimuli" (p. 192). Robinson defines noticing as more than detection: it is detection with awareness, specifically, "detection plus rehearsal in short-term memory" (p. 296). That is, it involves a level of attention sufficient for input to not only be registered, but maintained in memory – it is "rehearsed" in the sense of being persistently activated, and thus made available for further processing.

The level of awareness implicated by the term "noticing" is controversial, and remains unspecified. Awareness cannot always be articulated, and is better described as graded in level, because awareness, or the degree of activation of attentional resources, is unlikely to be equivalent for all linguistic features (Simard and Wong, 2001; Robinson, 1995).

Schmidt's case study research of adult language learners living among target language speakers, very much reflected the argument that learning requires attention. For example, "Wes", an immigrant in the USA, exhibited high pragmatic competence, but lacked use of common grammatical morphemes and syntax, such as articles, possessive pronouns or tense marking; non-salient forms he apparently did not notice. Conversely, Schmidt and Frota's (1986) study of Schmidt's own learning of Portuguese while living in Brazil, demonstrates clear links between what he noticed in the input, as recorded in a learning journal, and forms that subsequently emerged in his interlanguage production. Schmidt's description emphasizes awareness as an essential component of noticing: "I just started hearing[.] reflexives. Maybe I just didn't pay attention to them before, but I never really noticed any. [...] Suddenly I'm hearing those forms" (Schmidt and Frota, 1986: 280–81).

Both Gass (1997) and Schmidt (2001) point out that noticing itself filters the input: we interpret the input through our existing knowledge or schemata. Researchers have posed a range of learner-internal and external factors that influence the availability and allocation of attentional resources. These factors reflect the complex relationship between: past experience and prior knowledge; individual differences; task demands; and the input itself. Noticing linguistic cues can depend greatly on language experience: first language usage, second languages, and proficiency in the target language (Ellis, 2008). Individual differences in working memory and aptitude also impact noticing in terms of orientation and availability of attentional resources. Other factors relate to features in the input: the difficulty level of the feature; the frequency and saliency of the form; familiarity and/or novelty of the input; relevance and contiguity for the learner (Gass, 1997). Finally, the attentional demands of the task itself affects likelihood of noticing language form (Simard and Wong, 2001).

Alternative views

The major area of contention regarding the noticing hypothesis concerns the necessity of awareness for all learning. Along with Tomlin and Villa, some researchers agree that learning requires detection (cognitive registration), but not necessarily conscious awareness (for a review of evidence for implicit (non-attentional) learning, see Simard and Wong, 2001; Leung and Williams, 2011).

A usage-based account of second language acquisition suggests implicit learning of form-meaning relations that reflect probabilities of occurrence is fundamental to linguistic competence. Yet, as Schmidt points out, this competence is often poor. Low salience, redundant forms, bias due to prior knowledge and L1 usage all limit the scope of implicit learning: this is where focused attention is crucial (N. Ellis, 2008). These views acknowledge a central role for noticing, but dispute the stronger claim that all intake is dependant on noticing.

Evidence

The difficulty of testing the Noticing Hypothesis lies in measurement of variables that are internal cognitive constructs. Empirical evidence for the hypothesis varies, and likely reflects inconsistencies in measures of noticing, of intake and/or learning, and diversity of target forms. Noticing and awareness have been variously operationalized through online methods, such as think alouds and eye tracking; and by retrospective report, including diary entries; questionnaires; underlining of written forms; and stimulated recall. A combination of these techniques is likely to provide greater reliability.

The major contribution of Schmidt's Noticing Hypothesis is in specifying noticing as an essential process in language acquisition. In particular, the claim that it is only what the learner consciously *notices* about the input that holds potential for learning (Schmidt, 1990; Gass, 1997) underlies much of the research and theory of form-focused instruction, task-based language learning, and interaction-driven second language acquisition.

See also: attention, awareness, Focus on Form (FonF), Interaction and the Interaction Hypothesis, implicit learning, explicit learning

References

Ellis, N. (2008). The psycholinguistics of the interaction approach. In Mackey, A. and Polio, C. (eds), *Multiple Perspectives on Interaction. Second Language Research in Honour of Susan M. Gass*, pp. 11–40. New York: Routledge.

Gass, S.M. (1997). *Input, Interaction and the Second Language Learner*. Mahwah, NJ: Lawrence Erlbaum Associates.

Leung, J. and Williams, J. (2011). The implicit learning of mappings between forms and contextually derived meanings. *Studies in Second Language Acquisition*, *33*, 33–55.

Robinson, P. (1995). Attention, memory, and the "noticing" hypothesis. *Language Learning, 45*, 283–331.

Schmidt, R. (1990). The role of consciousness in second language learning. *Applied Linguistics*, *11*, 206–26.

——(2001). Attention. In P. Robinson (ed.), *Cognition and Second Language Instruction*, pp. 3–32. New York: Cambridge University Press.

——(2010). Attention, awareness, and individual differences in language learning. In W.M. Chan, S. Chi, K.N. Cin, J. Istanto, M. Nagami, J.W. Sew, T. Suthiwan, and I. Walker (eds), *Proceedings of ClaSIC* 2010, pp. 721–37. Singapore: Singapore. National University of Singapore. Centre for Language Studies.

Schmidt, R. and Frota, S. (1986). Developing basic conversational ability in a second language: A case study of an adult learner of Portuguese. In R. Day (ed.), *Talking to Learn: Conversation in Second Language Acquisition*, pp. 237–326. Rowley, MA: Newbury House.

Simard, D. and Wong, W. (2001). Alertness, orientation, and detection: The conceptualization of attentional functions in SLA. *Studies in Second Language Acquisition*, *23*, 103 24.

Tomlin, R. and Villa, V. (1994). Attention in cognitive science and second language acquisition. *Studies in Second Language Acquisition*, *16*, 183–203.

Further reading

Mackey, A., Philp, J., Egi, T., Fujii, A. and Tatsumi, T. (2002). Individual differences in working memory, noticing of interactional feedback and L2 development. In P. Robinson (ed.), *Individual Differences and Instructed Language Learning*, pp. 181–209. New York: Benjamins. (This study investigates the contribution of individual differences in working memory to noticing of recasts in oral interaction.)

Park, E.S. (2011). Learner-generated noticing of written L2 input: What do learners notice and why? *Language Learning*, *61*, 146–86. (This study investigates the contribution of L1 and current L2 knowledge of beginner learners noticing of forms in written input.)

Philp, J. (2003). Constraints on 'noticing the gap': Non-native speakers' noticing of recasts in NS-NNS interaction. *Studies in Second Language Acquisition*, *25*, 99–126. (This study investigates the contribution of existing knowledge to noticing of recasts in oral interaction.)

Robinson, P. (1996). Learning simple and complex second language rules under implicit, incidental, rule-search, and instructed conditions. *Studies in Second Language Acquisition*, *18*, 27–67. (This study compares conditions of implicit and explicit exposure to simple and complex structures, and the effects of learning under these implicit and explicit conditions.)

Rosa, E. and O'Neil, M.D. (1999). Explicitness, intake, and the issue of awareness. *Studies in Second Language Acquisition*, *21*, 511–56. (This study examines effects of different levels of awareness, and of task conditions on intake.)

One-to-one principle

Kathleen Bardovi-Harlig
Indiana University

The one-to-one principle in SLA states that an interlanguage system "should be constructed in such a way that an intended underlying meaning is expressed with one clear invariant surface form (or construction)" (Andersen, 1984: 79). As Andersen sums up, the one-to-one principle "is a principle of one *form* to one *meaning*" (1984: 79, emphasis original). The one-to-one principle is one of seven cognitive operating principles modeled on Slobin's (1973) operating principles for first language acquisition (the others are multifunctionality, formal determinism, distributional bias, transfer to somewhere, relevance, and relexification; Andersen, 1990). Of the seven principles, the one-to-one and multifunctionality principles are relevant to any analysis that considers form-meaning mappings and their change over time; the principles are an attempt to describe how interlanguage associates a single meaning to a single form (the one-to-one principle) and how the form-meaning associations expand (the multifunctionality principle).

The one-to-one principle applies to a variety of constructs including syntax, morphology, lexis, and pragmatics. For example, in the early expression of futurity by learners of English, learners begin to express the future with *will*, and only later expand their repertoire to include the *going to* future (Bardovi-Harlig, 2004). Although the present progressive may serve as a future (*I'm going to Chicago tomorrow),* longitudinal learner data show that the present progressive is used in less than 2 per cent of future expressions. The present progressive has the primary function of expressing ongoing action, and is thus involved in a one-to-one relationship with another meaning in the interlanguage, and not initially available to express the future.

Additional examples of initial one-to-one associations of form and meaning are found in the development of L2 tense-aspect systems. In initial form-meaning associations, verbal morphology associates with the lexical-aspectual class that most closely shares its meaning. In initial stages of the expression of the past, English simple past, Spanish preterite, or French passé composé appear with verbs that have natural endpoints (achievements and accomplishments); progressive associates initially with activities; and imperfect associates with states (see *acquisition of tense and aspect*).

Andersen (1990) includes examples of syntactic structure, citing the initial invariant use of SVO by L2 learners of German before they admit the structurally conditioned verb-final SOV variant. The interlanguage tendency to admit new forms and functions before variants for the same functions or forms are admitted is an outcome of the one-to-one principle. When learners compared native-speaker and non-native-speaker discourse transcripts, learners who were successful users of monoclausal request forms did not report noticing biclausal request forms in the transcripts (Takahashi, 2005). The instructional activity attempted to lead learners into multifunctionality; however, learners instead reported noticing new forms for which they had no equivalent. Other examples from pragmatics include learners' use of general expressions where specialized expressions are preferred by native speakers.

With time learners expand their systems beyond the initial stage described by the one-to-one principle and move into a stage characterized by multifunctionality, but at the outset they begin with a transparent, invariant, and simple association of form and meaning.

See also: acquisition of tense and aspect, development in SLA, form-meaning connections, interlanguage, multifunctionality, operating principles

References

Andersen, R.W. (1984). The one-to-one principle of interlanguage construction. *Language Learning*, *34*, 77–95.

——(1990). Models, processes, principles and strategies: Second language acquisition inside and outside the classroom. In B. VanPatten and J.F. Lee (eds), *Second Language Acquisition-Foreign Language Learning,* Clevedon: Multilingual Matters.

Bardovi-Harlig, K. (2004). The emergence of grammaticalized future expression in longitudinal production data. In M. Overstreet, S. Rott, B. VanPatten, and J. Williams (eds), *Form and Meaning in Second Language Acquisition,* Mahwah, NJ: Erlbaum.

Slobin, D.I. (1973). Cognitive prerequisites for the development of grammar. In C.I. Ferguson and D.I. Slobin (eds), *Studies of Child Language Development,* New York: Holt, Rinehart, and Winston.

Takahashi, S. (2005). Pragmalinguistic awareness: Is it related to motivation and proficiency? *Applied Linguistics*, *26*, 90–120.

Operating principles

Yasuhiro Shirai
University of Pittsburgh

Operating principles are universal psycholinguistic principles, proposed by Slobin (1973, 1985), that children use in processing linguistic stimuli in L1 acquisition. For example, the principle "Pay attention to the end of words" was proposed because children are sensitive to this information in acquiring grammatical markers across languages.

Extending Slobin's work to SLA, Andersen, in his Cognitive Interactionist Model (1988: 117; see also Ellis, 1994: 378–82) proposed seven cognitive operating principles "that govern the path the learner takes in developing an increasingly more native-like and more efficient and successful linguistic competence in a second language."

(1) The One-to-One Principle: an interlanguage system should be constructed in such a way that an intended underlying meaning is expressed with one clear invariant surface form (or construction).
(2) The Multifunctionality Principle: (a) where there is clear evidence in the input that more than one form marks the meaning conveyed by only one form in the interlanguage, try to discover the distribution and additional meaning (if any) of the new form. (b) Where there is evidence in the input that an interlanguage form conveys only one of the meanings that the same form has in the input, try to discover the additional meanings of the form in the input.
(3) Formal Determinism: when the form:meaning relationship is clearly and universally encoded in the input, the learner will discover it earlier than other form:meaning relationships and will incorporate it more consistently within his interlanguage system.
(4) Distributional Bias: if both X and Y can occur in the same environments A and B, but a bias in the distribution of X and Y makes it appear that X only occurs in the environment A and Y only occurs in environment B,

when you acquire X and Y, restrict X to environment A and Y to environment B.

(5) Relevance: if two or more functors apply to a content word, try to place them so that the more relevant the meaning of a functor is to the meaning of the content word, the closer it is placed to the content word. If you find that a notion is marked in several places, at first mark it only in the position closest to the relevant content words.

(6) Transfer to Somewhere: a grammatical form or structure will occur consistently and to a significant extent in the interlanguage as a result of transfer if and only if (1) natural acquisitional principles are consistent with the L1 structure or (2) there already exists within the L2 input the potential for (mis-) generalization from the input to produce the same form or structure.

(7) Relexification: when you cannot perceive the structural pattern used by the language you are trying to acquire, use your native language structure with lexical items from the second language.

(1), (3) and (2) are the basis for initial simplified form-function mapping and its subsequent complexification. (4) accounts for frequency-based form-function mapping, while (6) concerns the ordering of functors. (6) and (7) predict how the L1 influences L2 development.

See also: Aspect Hypothesis (AH), functional-typological linguistics, linguistic transfer, multifunctionality, one-to-one principle, prototypes

References

Andersen, R.W. (1988). Models, processes, principles and strategies: Second language acquisition inside and outside the classroom. *IDEAL* 3 111–38. (Reprinted in B. VanPatten and J.F. Lee (eds) (1990). *Second Language Acquisition – Foreign Language Learning*. Clevedon: Multilingual Matters.)

Ellis, R. (1994). *The Study of Second Language Acquisition*. Oxford: Oxford University Press.

Slobin, D.I. (1973). Cognitive Prerequisites for the Development of Grammar. In C.A. Ferguson and D.I. Slobin (eds), *Studies of Child Language Development*. New York: Holt, Rinehart and Winston.

——(1985). Crosslinguistic Evidence for the Language-Making Capacity. In D.I. Slobin (ed.) (nd), *The Crosslinguistic Study of Language Acquisition*, Vol. 2: Theoretical Issues. Hillsdale, NJ: Lawrence Erlbaum Associates.

Further reading

Andersen, R.W. (1983). Transfer to Somewhere. In S. Gass and L. Selinker (eds), *Language Transfer in Language Learning*. Rowley, MA: Newbury House. (An extended discussion of TTS (Transfer-To-Somewhere) principles.)

——(1984). The One-to-One Principle of interlanguage construction. *Language Learning, 34*, 77–95. (An extended discussion of the One-to-One Principle.)

Output hypothesis

Shinichi Izumi

Sophia University

The output hypothesis claims that the act of producing language constitutes an important part of the *process* of language learning, not simply the *product* of it. It was originated from Swain's (1985) observation of Canadian French immersion programs, where students, while developing their receptive skills considerably, nevertheless fail to achieve adequate mastery of certain aspects of L2 grammar, despite many years of learning in the program. Swain argued that, in stark contrast to the rich amount of comprehensible input they receive, immersion students lack opportunities for output in two important ways: first, they lack opportunities to produce extended output; and second, they are not pushed to be grammatically more accurate and sociolinguistically more appropriate in their output. Thus, it was argued that L2 learners need more than just comprehensible input, but also "comprehensible output" ("pushed output") to develop their

IL capability fully. Such output is believed to stimulate language development beyond functional levels of L2 proficiency by forcing the learner to move from semantic processing prevalent in input comprehension to syntactic processing that necessitates more focused attention to and more detailed analysis of language features.

In her later publications, Swain (e.g., 1995, 2005) expanded her original hypothesis and advanced three functions of output beyond the obvious function of developing automaticity (i.e., fluency function), which is triggered by repeated accessing of the existing IL knowledge for output production. One proposed function of output is the noticing function. It claims that output prompts learners to notice the gap between what they want to express and what they can express, which results in their greater utilization of their existing knowledge and/or greater noticing of the relevant features in the input. Another function is the hypothesis testing function, which states that output allows the learner to test his/her IL hypotheses. Upon receiving feedback from the interlocutor, learners can judge the comprehensibility and well-formedness of their utterances and modify them accordingly. Output is also claimed to serve a metalinguistic function. As learners use output in dialoging with others, as well as with themselves, they come to reflect on their IL use and knowledge, which may then lead to reshaping and refining of their IL knowledge through output-induced awareness-raising. Output is, thus, believed to play active roles by feeding back to various critical junctures in the dynamic SLA processes, as shown in Figure 9.

While empirical support for the different functions of output has been accumulating (see Muranoi, 2007; Swain, 2005 for summaries of these studies), further issues remain to be investigated. For instance, under what conditions does output promote L2 learning and how? What is the relationship between output and learning of different forms? What differences are there in the way learners with different profiles (e.g., ages, aptitude, proficiency) utilize output in their learning processes? Continued investigation into the roles of output will be fruitful in illuminating the dynamic processes at work in SLA.

See also: grammatical encoding, hypothesis testing, Levelt's model of speech production and comprehension, parsing sentences, semantic processing, task-based learning

References

Izumi, S. (2003). Comprehension and production processes in second language learning: In search of the psycholinguistic rationale of the Output Hypothesis. *Applied Linguistics*, *24*, 168–96.

Muranoi, H. (2007). Output practice in the L2 classroom. In R. DeKeyser (ed.). *Practice in a Second Language: Perspectives from Applied Linguistics and Cognitive Psychology*, pp. 51–84. Cambridge: Cambridge University Press.

Swain, M. (1985). Communicative competence: Some roles of comprehensible input and comprehensible output in its development. In S. Gass and C. Madden (eds). *Input in Second*

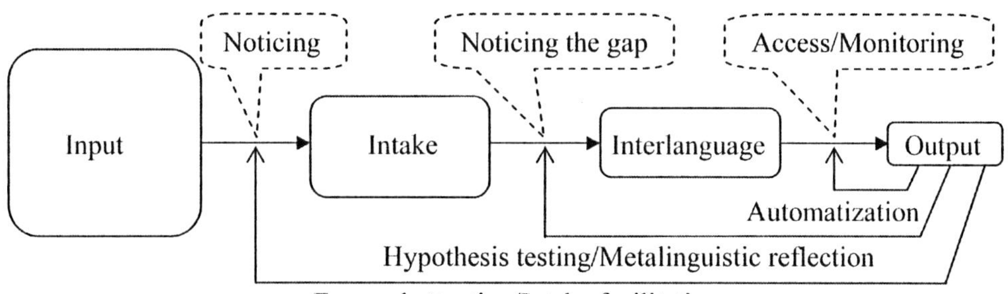

Figure 9 Effects of output on SLA processes (adapted from Izumi, 2003: 188).

Language Acquisition, pp. 235–53. Rowley, MA: Newbury House.

——(1995). Three functions of output in second language learning. In G. Cook and B. Seidlhofer (eds). *Principles and Practice in Applied Linguistics: Studies in Honour of H.G. Widdowson*, pp. 125–44. Oxford: Oxford University Press.

——(2005). The output hypothesis: Theory and research. In E. Hinkel (ed.). *Handbook of Research in Second Language Teaching and Learning*, pp. 471–83. Mahwah, NJ: Laurence Erlbaum.

P

Parallel distributed processing (PDP) models in SLA

Henk Haarmann
University of Maryland

Parallel distributed processing (PDP) or connectionist models are neurally inspired models of human information processing that help theory development in cognitive science. These models have been successfully applied to all major cognitive abilities, including attention, perception, learning, memory, language, reasoning, problem-solving, decision making, and action (Rumelhart and McClelland, 1986).

Structure

In terms of structure, PDP models consist of many simple processors or nodes, which are organized in one or more layers, plus a set of connections or links among nodes, tying them together in a network. A node can represent a specific piece of information (e.g., a particular letter or phoneme), while a layer represents all the information of a particular type (e.g., all letters or all phonemes). Each node has an activation value that reflects its relevance in the current context. Furthermore, each link between a pair of nodes (e.g., a specific letter and a word in which the letter occurs) has a connection strength, reflecting their degree of association. The pattern of connections and their strengths stores the knowledge of the network.

Process

Processing consists of a continuous and parallel determination of the activation values of all nodes and of the connection strengths between nodes according to activation and learning rules. The activation rules determine how activation is propagated between nodes. One frequently employed and biologically plausible learning rule, Hebbian learning, increases the connection strength between pairs of units that are active together. Processing continues until the model has achieved a stable activation pattern and connections or a response deadline, such that an input pattern in the environment (e.g., spoken word) activates an output pattern (e.g., word meaning) and associated internal representations (e.g., word form). The degree of match between the desired and actual output pattern and the time to activate an output pattern can be used to define measures of performance accuracy and response time.

Within this general framework, modelers have considerable freedom in specifying theory-relevant properties. One example involves the nature of the connections between two nodes in different layers. The connections may allow for bi-directional or uni-directional activation propagation, resulting in a mode of processing that is highly interactive and parallel versus more discrete and sequential, respectively. Another example pertains to the mode of representation. A particular piece of information (e.g., word meaning) may be represented by a single node or, alternatively, distributed across several nodes, corresponding to a local versus distributed scheme of representation.

Brain basis

As a result of these properties, both representation and processing are massively parallel and distributed, involving patterns of activations and connections across many nodes and changes in these patterns, akin to the way neurons in the brain process information. Although PDP models are neurally inspired, they reflect brain operation at high levels of abstraction. A single node is typically not thought of as a single neuron (i.e., nerve cell) but instead as reflecting the aggregate firing pattern of many thousands of neurons, such as a cell assembly (e.g., Haarmann and Usher, 2001). PDP models may consist of different interconnected sub-networks of nodes believed to correspond to functions performed by different brain regions (e.g., Van Heuven and Dijkstra, 2010). Increasingly, such models aim to be compatible with data about the location and time course of activation in networks of brain regions.

Desirable features

PDP models have several desirable properties resulting from their neurally inspired approach, particularly, (i) pattern completion (i.e., given only a part of a pattern the model can infer the total pattern), (ii) graceful degradation (i.e., loss of a subset of the nodes and connections results in graded instead of all-or-none decrements in performance), (iii) constraint satisfaction (i.e., processing results from the competitive and facilitatory interactions of many simultaneous constraints across levels of representation, limiting the need for central control mechanisms, e.g., for coordinating syntactic and semantic processing), and (iv) activation-based cognitive control (i.e., cognitive control mechanisms need not incorporate detailed knowledge of the operation of controlled cognitive functions but merely bias the operation of nodes within the networks that implement them through transient increases and decreases in their activation levels, consistent with task goals).

First and second language processing

PDP models of L1 processing have been proposed to explain aspects of language learning (e.g., past tense acquisition), written and spoken word recognition, and sentence processing (for a review see Rohde and Plaut, 2003). PDP models of L2 processing include learning and non-learning models of the bi-lingual mental lexicon and sentence processing (for a review see Li and Farkas, 2002). Prominent PDP models of bi-lingual word recognition that continue to stimulate empirical studies are the Bilingual Interactive Activation model (BIA, Dijkstra and Van Heuven, 1998), its successor BIA+ (Heuven and Dijkstra, 2010), the Bilingual Model of Lexical Access (BIMOLA, Léwy and Grosjean, 2001), and the Self-Organizing Model of Bilingual Processing (SOMBIP, Li and Farkas, 2002). BIA and BIMOLA are non-learning models of visual and spoken word recognition, respectively, while SOMBIP is a model that learns to recognize spoken words in a self-organizing, non-supervised manner. A major goal of these models is to address the issue of how integrated the L1 and L2 mental lexicons are and what neurally inspired mechanisms achieve integration or separation.

The potential of implemented PDP models remains underutilized, which is regrettable. Like other types of cognitive computer models, PDP models enable theory development in domains, such as language processing, in which deriving and understanding predictions without the aid of a computer model is difficult due to the complexity of the activation dynamics and factors involved (e.g., timing, size, and rate of input in L2 learning, proficiency, and working memory capacity) (Li and Farkas, 2002). In addition, PDP modelers are now beginning to understand how to capture computational mechanisms, such as variable binding, which may be crucial for the generative use of language. Finally, PDP models are helpful for understanding how the brain's cognitive abilities, such as working memory, enable aptitude(s) for language learning and for machine learning approaches to mapping patterns of brain activation onto language and thought content.

See also: connectionism and SLA, emergentism, psycholinguistics of SLA, statistical learning, theoretical constructs in SLA, working memory

References

Dijkstra, T. and Van Heuven, W.J. B. (1998). The BIA-model and bilingual word recognition. In J. Grainger and A. Jacobs (eds), *Localist Connectionist Approaches to Human Cognition*, pp. 189–225. Mahwah, NJ: Lawrence Erlbaum Associates Inc.

Haarmann, H.J. and Usher, M. (2001). Maintenance of semantic information in capacity-limited item short-term memory. *Psychonomic Bulletin and Review*, *8*(3), 568–578.

Léwy, N. and Grosjean, F. (2001). *The Computerized Version of BIMOLA: A Bilingual Model of Lexical Access*. Manuscript in preparation, University of Neuchâtel, Switzerland.

Li, P. and Farkas, I. (2002). A self-organizing connectionist model of bilingual processing. In R. Heredia and J. Altarriba (eds), *Bilingual Sentence Processing*. Amsterdam: Elsevier Science Publisher.

Rohde, D.L. T. and Plaut, D.C. (2003). Connectionist models of language processing. *Cognitive Studies*, *10*(1), 10–28.

Rumelhart, D.E., McClelland, J.L. and the PDP Research Group (1986). *Parallel Distributed Processing: Explorations in the Microstructure of Cognition, Vol. 1: Foundations*. Cambridge, MA: MIT Press.

Thomas, M.S. C. and van Heuven, W.J. B. (2005). Computational models of bilingual comprehension. In J.F. Kroll and A.M. B. de Groot (eds), *Handbook of Bilingualism*, pp. 202–225. New York: Oxford.

Van Heuven, W.J. B., and Dijkstra, T. (2010). Language comprehension in the bilingual brain: fMRI and ERP support for psycholinguistic models. *Brain Research Reviews*, *64*(1), 104–22.

Further reading

Dijkstra, T. and Van Heuven, W.J. B. (2002). Modeling bilingual word recognition: Past, present and future. *Bilingualism: Language and Cognition, 5(3)*, 219–24.

Ellis, N.C. (1998). Emergentism, connectionism and language learning. *Language Learning, 48* (4), 631–64.

McClelland, J.L. (2011). *Explorations in Parallel Distributed Processing: A Handbook of Models, Programs, and Exercises*. Second edition, draft. Available from www.stanford.edu/group/pdplab/pdphandbook/

O'Reilly, R.C. and Munakata, Y. (2000). *Computational Explorations in Cognitive Neuroscience: Understanding the Mind by Simulating the Brain*. Cambridge, MA: MIT Press.

Thomas, M. and Van Heuven, W. (2005). Computational models of bilingual comprehension. In J.F. Kroll and A. de Groot (eds), *Handbook of Bilingualism: Psycholinguistic Approaches*. New York: Oxford University Press.

Parsing sentences

Paola E. Dussias and
Rosa E. Guzzardo Tamargo
Pennsylvania State University

Understanding the sentence (1) *The CIA director confirmed the rumor could mean a security leak* involves a set of interconnected processes. Listeners and readers must retrieve the meaning of each word, as well as group words together into syntactic constituents and create dependencies between them to assign the grammatical roles of subject, verb, and complement. In the psycholinguistic literature, the process of classifying word strings in terms of structural categories and of establishing appropriate syntactic relations between them is referred to as "syntactic parsing" (Mitchell, Cuetos, and Zagaand, 1990). Our experience as listeners and readers tells us that the parsing process is very rapid and efficient. The parser computes the syntactic structure of sentences in a remarkably short period of time, allowing us to determine with much success "who did what to whom."

Much of the work toward developing a theory of the architecture of the human sentence parsing mechanism has relied on the operations that the parser follows when it is confronted with temporary structural ambiguity. Why is this so? Because it is assumed that the parser's initial choice when faced with a syntactically ambiguous phrase will provide insight into the processes underlying its architecture. An example is (1) above, taken from Wilson and Garnsey (2009). The ambiguous noun phrase (NP) "the rumor" can initially be interpreted as the direct object (DO) of the verb "confirm" or as the subject of the embedded clause "(that) the rumor could mean a security leak." Past research has shown that English readers incorrectly choose the DO interpretation as the initial analysis and only later, once they encounter the embedded verb phrase "could mean," reanalyze the NP as the subject of the embedded phrase. This example shows that the parser's operations during syntactic analysis are better understood when they are disrupted. In other words, it is because readers erroneously interpret the ambiguous NP as a DO that we infer that the parser has made a decision to attach it to the main verb. Structural ambiguities of this type, then, offer an avenue to study the parsing mechanism.

Several parsing models have been proposed to explain why readers commit to one interpretation of an ambiguous phrase at points in the sentence where two or more alternative interpretations are possible. *Syntax-first* models (e.g., Frazier, 1979) postulate that early parsing decisions are determined by a small set of fixed structure-driven principles, whose function is to increase the speed and efficiency with which the syntactic representation of sentences is built during real-time processing, in order to reduce computational load. One such principle, *minimal attachment*, ensures that the parser constructs the syntactic analysis of a string of words using the fewest number of syntactic nodes. Due to this, in (1) above the prediction is that the parser's initial preference should be to attach the ambiguous NP directly to "confirm." *Constraint-based lexicalist accounts* (e.g., Garnsey, Pearlmutter, Myers, and Lotocky, 1997; MacDonald, Pearlmutter, and Seidenberg, 1994; Trueswell, Tanenhaus, and Kello, 1993) make the same prediction but for a different reason. These theories propose that usage-based and exposure-based factors, such as readers' expectations about the likely complement of a verb (i.e., subcategorization bias), guide the initial interpretation of an ambiguous clause and can ease the difficulty encountered during temporary ambiguity resolution. To illustrate, although *confirm* can be followed by several types of verbal complements, it is most often used with a direct object. Accordingly, processing disruptions arise in structures like (1), where "confirm" is followed instead by an embedded clause.

A critical question in the second language (L2) sentence parsing literature concerns whether the specific sub-processes that learners engage during L2 language comprehension differ from those followed by monolinguals as they process input in their native language. Numerous variables that affect sentence processing among L2 learners have been identified. Some are linguistic in nature in that they are concerned with the specific sources of linguistic information that L2 learners use during L2 sentence comprehension. Others are related to the characteristics of learners and their linguistic experience.

Experimental work in L2 sentence comprehension has investigated similarities and differences between native language (L1) and L2 processing using an array of psycholinguistic methods, ranging from offline tasks and behavioral tasks, which measure reaction times or provide records of eye-movements, to electrophysiological responses recorded through the scalp while participants are exposed to stimuli (e.g., Kroll, Gerfen, and Dussias, 2008 and references therein). This rapidly growing body of work suggests that L2 learners' performance is sometimes strikingly close to that of native speakers, but not always. For example, recent research suggests that the syntactic representations constructed by L2 learners while processing input in their L2 are "shallower" and less detailed than those computed by adult L1 speakers. Whereas monolinguals prioritize on structure-driven strategies and syntactic information, L2 speakers privilege lexico-semantic and pragmatic information (Clahsen and Felser, 2006).

Data in favor of "shallow processing" come from studies that contrast the behavior of L1 and L2 speakers while reading syntactically ambiguous relative clauses, such as (2) *The dean liked the secretary of the professor who was reading a letter.* Attachment preferences concerning these structures have been found to differ cross-linguistically. In languages, such as English, Brazilian Portuguese, and Norwegian, the general preference is to attach the relative clause ("who was reading a letter") to the second noun ("the professor"), resulting in the following interpretation: "the professor was reading the letter." By contrast, in Spanish, German, French, and Greek, readers show a clear preference to attach the relative clause to the first noun ("the secretary"), giving rise to an interpretation where "the secretary was reading the letter." Papadopoulou and Clahsen (2003) asked native speakers of high-attaching languages to read ambiguous constructions in their L2 Greek, a language where high attachment is also the preferred strategy. They found that proficient L2 speakers showed no particular preference for high or low attachment when processing an L2 that, like their L1, favored high attachment. This finding, coupled with results of clear attachment preferences when lexical cues guided attachment decisions, was interpreted as evidence that L2 speakers do not use structure-based information, but rather are guided by lexico-semantic cues (see Felser, Roberts, Gross, and Marinis, 2003 for similar findings, but Frenck-Mestre and Pynte, 1997; Dussias, 2003; Dussias and Sagarra, 2007, for counter-evidence).

There is, however, some indication in the literature that the difficulties L2 speakers experience while parsing some temporarily ambiguous structures could be explained by universal, structure-based principles of parsing. For example, Frenck-Mestre and Pynte (1997) investigated the way in which advanced English-speaking learners of French and native French speakers resolved attachment ambiguities involving prepositional phrases. Records of eye movements revealed that the L2 speakers momentarily experienced greater difficulty than native speakers with verb phrase attachment of the prepositional phrase in sentences, such as (3) *He rejected the manuscript on purpose because he hated its author*. No such difficulty was observed when they read structures in which the correct analysis required attachment of the prepositional phrase to the noun phrase immediately preceding it, as would be the case in (4) *He rejected the manuscript on horses because he hated its author*. In other words, L2 speakers temporarily adopted a strategy of attaching the ambiguous prepositional phrases to the most recently processed constituent. This analysis resulted in an incorrect interpretation in example (3), but not in example (4). To account for this finding, Frenck-Mestre and Pynte proposed that non-native readers may have a general preference for *late closure* (Frazier, 1978), a structure-based locality principle assumed to be operative during monolingual sentence parsing, which effectively reduces the distance between a potential host site and a modifier within the sentence.

A number of other linguistic variables have been shown to affect L2 learners' choices during syntactic ambiguity resolution. Recent studies have produced empirical evidence demonstrating the rapid influence of plausibility information during L2 sentence processing, and have shown that, in this respect, non-natives can behave in a native-like way. For instance, Williams, Möbius, and Kim (2001) explored differences between native and non-native readers of English by asking whether the semantic plausibility of a potential filler modulated the postulation of a gap during parsing. Their study included native English speakers and advanced learners of English whose first languages had overt Wh-movement, such as German, or non-overt Wh-movement, such as Korean and Chinese. They compared the processing of sentences like (5) and (6) using a self-paced, plausibility judgment task:

(5) Which girl did the man push the bike into late last night?
(6) Which river did the man push the bike into late last night?

For the native and non-native English groups alike, when the *wh*-filler was a plausible DO of the verb, as in (5), it was more costly to discard it as the actual gap filler. Conversely, when it was an implausible DO, as in (6), there was less resistance to reanalysis and, therefore, reading times were faster at the position of the actual filler ("the bike"). This indicates that adult learners of English use plausibility information in a manner that is very similar to that of native speakers, even when parallel structures in their native languages look very different (see also Frenck-Mestre, 1997 and Pynte, 1997).

Non-native comprehenders, just like native speakers, have also been shown to use subcategorization information specific to the L2 to resolve syntactic ambiguity during reading. In an early study conducted by Frenck-Mestre and Pynte (1997), French-dominant and English-dominant bilinguals read sentences in both their L1 and their L2 containing temporary subject/object ambiguities, as in (7) *Every time the dog obeyed the pretty girl showed her approval.* In English, *obey* is optionally transitive. Therefore, it is ambiguous whether the NP "the pretty girl" is the object of "obeyed" or the subject of the ensuing clause. In French, however, this syntactic ambiguity does not exist because the French equivalent of *obey* must be interpreted as an intransitive verb. Eye-movement records from both groups failed to show any qualitative differences between the native and L2 speakers at the point of disambiguation, indicating that L2 speakers were able to activate the correct lexical representation of the L2 verbs, even when these lexical representations were different in each language.

Recently, Dussias and Cramer Scaltz (2008) examined the degree to which Spanish-English L2 learners made structural commitments constrained by verb subcategorization bias while reading syntactically ambiguous sentences in their L2. The temporary ambiguity involved the DO/sentential complement ambiguity exemplified in (1). In a monolingual experiment with English participants, the authors replicated the findings reported in other monolingual studies (e.g., Wilson and Garnsey, 2009), demonstrating that native speakers are guided by subcategorization bias. In a bilingual experiment, they then showed that L2 learners also keep track of the relative frequencies of verb-subcategorization alternatives and use this information when building structures in the L2.

Participant variables, such as the availability of processing resources (e.g., Williams, 2006; Dussias and Piñar, 2010; cf. Juffs, 2004) have also been shown to modulate the extent to which L2 learners are able to exploit various sources of information during L2 sentence comprehension. In Williams (2006), participants were required to perform one of two tasks: (a) to press a button as soon as they thought that a sentence displayed on a computer screen stopped making sense or (b) to perform a memory task involving the completion of a sentence with a word that had appeared in a previously displayed sentence. The results showed that L2 speakers processed the input incrementally, just as native speakers did, when the task encouraged such a type of processing (i.e., in the stop-making-sense task). However, when the task imposed memory demands, the non-native readers did not process the input incrementally, most likely because they were not able to allocate sufficient resources to perform such processing. This suggests that availability of processing resources plays a role during L2 sentence comprehension; it also indicates that L2 readers may be able to overcome processing limitations under the appropriate task conditions.

Other findings indicate that proficiency modulates the ability to access syntactic information during L2 sentence comprehension. Hopp (2006), for instance, found that advanced learners of German displayed the same processing preferences as native Germans when reading subject/object ambiguities, but, contrary to native speakers' syntactic reanalysis, they did not show differences in response latencies. The near-native speakers, on the other hand, reliably used syntactic features in phrase-structure reanalysis, and also showed evidence of incremental reanalysis patterns typically found in native speakers.

To conclude, in order to determine the parser's architectural mechanisms during L2 processing, most research has examined how participants resolve syntactic ambiguity. Taken together, proposed parsing models indicate that structural, lexical, semantic, pragmatic, and experience-based factors are accessed during sentence processing. In addition, studies using various methods and tasks have shown that both linguistic and participant variables affect L2 processing. Regarding comparisons between native and learner parsing, research has presented conflicting results: sometimes L2 learner processing is similar to native processing; other times they seem qualitatively and quantitatively different. More research on L2 sentence parsing is needed to further address these diverging findings.

See also: bilingualism and SLA, discourse processing, eye-tracking, psycholinguistics of SLA, reaction time, working memory

References

Clahsen, H. and Felser, C. (2006). Grammatical processing in language learners. *Applied Psycholinguistics*, *27*, 3–42.

Dussias, P.E. (2003). Syntactic ambiguity resolution in L2 learners: Some effects of bilinguality on L1 and L2 processing strategies. *Studies in Second Language Acquisition*, *25*, 529–57.

Dussias, P.E. and Cramer Scaltz, T.R. (2008). Spanish-English L2 speakers' use of subcategorization bias information in the resolution of temporary ambiguity during second language reading. *Acta Psychologica*, *128*, 501–13.

Dussias, P.E. and Piñar, P. (2010). Effects of reading span and plausibility in the reanalysis of wh-gaps by Chinese-English second language speakers. *Second Language Research*, *26*, 443–72.

Dussias, P.E. and Sagarra, N. (2007). The effect of exposure on syntactic parsing in Spanish-English bilinguals. *Bilingualism: Language and Cognition*, *10*, 101–16.

Felser, C., Roberts, L., Gross, R. and Marinis, T. (2003). The processing of ambiguous sentences by first and second language learners of English. *Applied Psycholinguistics*, *24*, 453–89.

Frazier, L. (1979). *On comprehending sentences: Syntactic parsing strategies*. Unpublished doctoral dissertation, University of Connecticut.

Frenck-Mestre, C. and Pynte, J. (1997). Syntactic ambiguity resolution while reading in second and native languages. *Quarterly Journal of Experimental Psychology*, *50*, 119–48.

Garnsey, S.M., Pearlmutter, N.J., Myers, E.M. and Lotocky, M.A. (1997). The contributions of verb bias and plausibility to the comprehension of temporarily ambiguous sentences. *Journal of Memory and Language*, *37*, 58–93.

Hopp, H. (2006). Syntactic features and reanalysis in near-native processing. *Second Language Research*, *22*, 369–97.

Juffs, A. (2004). Representation, processing and working memory in a second language. *Transactions of the Philological Society*, *102*, 199–225.

Kroll, J.F., Gerfen, C. and Dussias, P.E. (2008). Laboratory designs and paradigms in psycholinguistics. In L. Wei and M. Moyer (eds), *The Blackwell guide to research methods in bilingualism*, pp. 108–31. Cambridge, MA: Blackwell Publishers.

MacDonald, M.C., Pearlmutter, N.J. and Seidenberg, M.S. (1994). Syntactic ambiguity resolution as lexical ambiguity resolution. In K. Rayner (ed.), *Perspectives on sentence processing*, pp. 123–153. Hillsdale, NJ: Erlbaum.

Mitchell, D.C., Cuetos, F. and Zagar, D. (1990). Reading in different languages: Is there a universal mechanism for parsing sentences? In D.A. Balota, G.B. Flores d'Arcais, K Rayner (eds), *Comprehension Processes in Reading*, pp. 285–302. Hillsdale, NJ: Lawrence Erlbaum Associates.

Papadopoulou, D. and Clahsen, H. (2003). Parsing strategies in L1 and L2 sentence processing: A study of relative clause attachment in Greek. *Studies in Second Language Acquisition*, *25*, 501–28.

Trueswell, J.C., Tanenhaus, M.K. and Kello, C. (1993). Verb-specific constraints in sentence-processing: Separating effects of lexical preference from garden-paths. *Journal of Experimental Psychology: Learning, Memory, and Cognition*, *19*, 528–53.

Williams, J.N. (2006). Incremental interpretation in second language sentence processing. *Bilingualism: Language and Cognition*, *9*, 71–88.

Williams, J.N., Möbius, P. and Kim, C. (2001). Native and non-native processing of English wh-questions: Parsing strategies and plausibility constraints. *Applied Psycholinguistics*, *22*, 509–40.

Wilson, M.P. and Garnsey, S.M. (2009). Making simple sentences hard: Verb bias effects in simple direct object sentences. *Journal of Memory and Language*, *60*, 368–92.

Pausology and hesitation phenomena in SLA

Michiko Watanabe and Ralph L. Rose
University of Tokyo and Waseda University

Speech by one or more interlocutors may be described as continuous, but a moment's reflection will reveal that it is not really continuous at all. Minimally, speakers must break off their speech to breathe. In extreme cases, their speech may become highly discontinuous, with long breaks, extraneous sounds or words, or reformulations that cause delay in message transfer. These kinds of discontinuities have been studied under the name of pausology and hesitation phenomena (also sometimes called *speech disfluencies*). Studies of pauses and hesitations have focused on several different types of phenomena, though the most common in speech and the most commonly studied are silent and filled pauses. *Silent pauses* (or *unfilled pauses*) are breaks in speech production of any duration. Very short silent pauses below a certain length (e.g., 0.1 seconds, as used in many studies; cf., Griffiths, 1991) are typically regarded as the product of articulatory processes rather than linguistic processes and excluded from pausological studies. Thereafter, silent pauses may be classified into short and long pauses—or more fine-grained analyses may classify short, medium, and long pauses—based on some standards, though these standards have not been consistent across studies. *Filled pauses* (sometimes called *fillers*) involve the articulation of some sound during the delay. The sound may resemble an actual word (e.g., in Spanish, *este* "that" or in Japanese, *ano* "that") or be a non-lexical formation (e.g., in English, *uh* or *um*).

Other hesitation phenomena have been studied somewhat less than pauses, perhaps because they are less frequent. *Lengthenings* (also called *prolongations*) are when the speaker extends the articulation of one or more segments of a word. *Repeats* involve the repetition of one or more words or word segments in an utterance. A repeat which occurs at the beginning of an utterance is called a *restart*. *Self-corrections* involve a sequence of words which are intended to be understood as a repair of a preceding sequence of words. When this occurs at the beginning of an utterance, it is called a *false start*.

Production

Since pausological and hesitation phenomena research began in the mid-twentieth century with work by Howard Maclay, Charles Osgood, and Frieda Goldman-Eisler, many researchers have sought to draw an explicit connection between these phenomena and specific linguistic processes such as lexical access, syntactic processing, or discourse planning. Evidence supporting all of these possibilities has been found in different studies. Hence, the current consensus on pauses and hesitations in first language production is that speakers are making processing decisions (brought upon by high cognitive load or by error, for example) leading to a delay. The complexity hypothesis (Clark and Wasow, 1998), for example, holds that the burden of these processing decisions is related to syntactic complexity: the production of more complex constituents leads to greater processing burden and subsequently the likelihood of greater delay.

Perhaps the most sophisticated model of how second language speakers produce hesitations is based on Levelt's (1983) model of monitoring and error repair. Levelt defined a taxonomy of error types and showed how speakers handle these various errors through the use of editing terms (including silent and filled pauses) and repairs (including restarts and repeats) with respect to rules for well formedness. Research on second-language repairs shows that repairs in second language speech proceed similarly to those in first language speech, though evidence suggests that second language speakers repair error types which are not included in Levelt's original taxonomy (Kormos, 1999) such as message replacement repair—when a speaker completely abandons the original message. For second language learners, processing tasks are much greater and therefore increase the cognitive load, leading to greater chance of error and subsequent repair. Furthermore, limitations in the learners' second language proficiency causes patterns of error and repair which are different from those of native speakers (Temple, 2000).

Studies of pause and hesitation in second language production have also focused on how the speakers' hesitation patterns influence judgments about the speakers' second language proficiency. Many of these studies have used a common experimental design involving organizing a corpus of speech from second language speakers through a controlled elicitation task, and then gathering scaled judgments from listeners (usually native speakers of the target language) on the second language speech. These studies have yielded quite interesting results in such areas as fluency, accentedness, and comprehensibility.

While there are differing views of what constitutes fluency in a second language, one common theme in all of these views is speed: that is, fluent second language speech is rapid, comparable to native speech. Thus, many researchers have investigated the role that pauses and hesitations play in fluency in second language speech production. Results of these studies have not always been consistent but generally show that the length of silent pauses but not filled pauses correlates with perceptions of fluency (Kang, 2010). This result is highly consistent with many previous studies showing that silent pauses and filled pauses, despite their titular similarity, are quite different phenomena.

Along with fluency, many researchers have also focused on accentedness. The question for these researchers has been to what degree pausological and hesitation phenomena influence or determine perceptions of accentedness. Results here show that duration of silent pauses contribute to perceptions of accentedness: the longer the speaker pauses, the more likely their speech will be judged as accented (Trofimovich and Baker, 2006; Kang, 2010). Interestingly, once again, silent pauses and filled pauses show a different behavior. Some research has also focused on how speakers' hesitation patterns influence comprehensibility. Fayer and Krasinski (1987) found that participants in a listening task experiment cited hesitation most frequently as the main barrier to their understanding of second language spoken texts. Kang (2010), however, found that hesitations (specifically, filled pauses) were only marginally correlated with judgments of comprehensibility and were, in fact, less important than other articulation factors (e.g., mean number of words between pauses as well as articulation rate).

One weakness in the studies on perception of fluency, accentedness, and comprehensibility is that the experimental task required native speaker participants to judge the second language speaker's speech directly. This is problematic for two reasons. First, in most of these studies, the judges are not trained judges of these features of speech, and therefore it is not clear what their judgments are based on or even whether their judgments are consistent. The second problem is that the experimental task is not necessarily a task that listeners do in authentic communicative events. For instance, judging the degree to which a speaker is comprehensible is not the same task as actually comprehending the speaker. Work therefore remains to be done to establish the connection between pause and hesitation phenomena and second language speech production.

Perception

First language studies on pause and hesitation show that while listeners are often not aware of the speakers' use of hesitation phenomena, they do make linguistic processing decisions based on them (Reich, 1980; Brennan and Schober, 2001; Arnold, *et al.*, 2004). To date, studies of the perception of pause and hesitation phenomena in second language speech have been somewhat inconsistent. Some studies have shown that pauses and hesitation phenomena provide perceptual barriers for second language listeners, leading to such things as greater transcription errors (Voss, 1979). Other studies have found that pause and hesitation phenomena may actually facilitate comprehension in second language listeners. Blau (1991), for example, observed that listeners comprehended a passage with filled pauses better than if those pauses were converted to silent pauses or deleted entirely. A possible answer to the barrier versus facilitation difference might be found in Watanabe, Hirose, Den, and Minematsu (2008): results showed that listeners with high second language proficiency used filled pauses as cues to the complexity of upcoming phrases, but listeners with low proficiency did not show this result. Future research in the area of second language perception of pause and hesitation may need to carefully control for the proficiency level of second language listeners.

Proficiency development

Based on the many results showing cross-linguistic differences in pausing and hesitation phenomena patterns and possible perceptual difficulties for second language listeners, there have been several calls for greater attention to these phenomena in second language education (Rose, 1998). However, one shortcoming with these proposals is that there has been little discussion, let alone consensus, about the developmental process of second language pausing and hesitation patterns. Under one view, as learners' proficiency in the target language increases, their pausing and hesitation patterns will transfer from their native language and develop naturally in their second language. This view assumes that the cross-linguistic differences that have been observed in these patterns derive from the structure of the language itself. This is certainly possible, but has yet to be shown. An alternate view is that this developmental process can be facilitated by giving learners explicit instruction in target language hesitation patterns. However, at this point, there has been no formal confirmation that such explicit attention is effective.

See also: fluency, Levelt's model of speech production and comprehension, proficiency, self-repair, speech rate, thinking for speaking

References

Arnold, J., Tanenhaus, M., Altmann, R. and Fagnano, M., (2004). The old and thee, uh, new: disfluency and reference resolution. *Psychological Science*, *15*(9), 578–82.

Blau, E., (1991). More on comprehensible input: the effect of pauses and hesitation markers on listening comprehension. Additional information about the document that does not fit in any of the other fields; not used after 2004.*Annual Meeting of the Puerto Rico Teachers of English to Speakers of Other Languages*. San Juan, PR 15 November. (online) Education Resources Information Center (ERIC) database. Available at: www.eric.ed.gov/ERICWebPortal/detail?accno=ED340234 (Accessed 1 October 2010).

Brennan, S. and Schober, M., (2001). How listeners compensate for disfluencies in spontaneous speech. *Journal of Memory and Language*, *44* (2), 274–96.

Clark, H. And Wasow, T., (1998). Repeating words in spontaneous speech. *Cognitive Psychology*, *37*(3), 201–42.

Fayer, J. and Krasinski, E., (1987). Native and nonnative judgments of intelligibility and irritation. *Language Learning*, *37*(3), 313–26.

Griffiths, R., (1991). Pausological research in an L2 context: a rationale, and review of selected studies. *Applied Linguistics*, *12*(4), 345–64.

Kang, O., (2010). Relative salience of suprasegmental features on judgments of L2 comprehensibility and accentedness. *System*, *38*(2), 301–15.

Kormos, J., (1999). Monitoring and self-repair in L2. *Language Learning*, *49*(2), 303–42.

Levelt, W.J.M., (1983). Monitoring and self-repair in speech. *Cognition*, *14*(1), 41–104.

Maclay, H. and Osgood, C.E., (1959). Hesitation phenomena in spontaneous English speech. *Word*, *15*, 19–44.

Reich, S., (1980). Significance of pauses for speech perception. *Journal of Psycholinguistic Research*, *9*(4), 379–89.

Rose, R.L., (1998). *The communicative value of filled pauses in spontaneous speech*. Master's Dissertation, University of Birmingham.

Temple, L., (2000). Second language learner speech production. *Studia Linguistica*, *54*(2), 288–97.

Trofimovich, P. and Baker, W., (2006). Learning second language suprasegmentals: Effect of L2 experience on prosody and fluency characteristics of L2 speech. *Studies in Second Language Acquisition*, *28*(2), 1–30.

Voss, B., (1979). Hesitation phenomena as sources of perceptual errors for non-native speakers. *Language and Speech*, *22*(2), 129–44.

Watanabe, M., Hirose, K., Den, Y. and Minematsu, N., (2008). Filled pauses as cues to the complexity of upcoming phrases for native and non-native listeners. *Speech Communication*, *50*(2), 81–94.

Further reading

Ferreira, F. and Bailey, K.G.D., (2004). Disfluencies and human language comprehension. *Trends in Cognitive Sciences*, *8*(5), 231–37. (Model of disfluency processing in speech perception.)

Kormos, J., (1999). Monitoring and self-repair in L2. *Language Learning*, *49*(2), 303–42. (Review of second language research using Levelt's monitor and self-repair model.)

Lickley, R.J. and Bard, E.G., (1998). When can listeners detect disfluency in spontaneous speech? *Language and Speech*, *41*(2), 203–26. (An experimental study on listeners' ability to detect hesitations in spontaneous speech.)

Shriberg, E.E., (2001). To "errrr" is human: Ecology and acoustics of speech disfluencies. *Journal of the International Phonetic Association*, *31*(1), 153–69. (A compact overview of distributional and acoustic features of hesitation phenomena in American English.)

Person-in-situation approaches to SLA

Ema Ushioda
University of Warwick

Person-in-situation or person-in-context approaches to SLA seek to capture the dynamic interactions between individuals and the evolving social, cultural, and physical environments within which they learn and use an L2, and which both shape and are shaped by their actions and behaviors. A core feature of such approaches is a particular focus on "real persons" with unique histories, identities, goals, motives and personalities, situated in "real contexts," rather than a generic focus on abstract types of L2 learner, individual difference characteristic, or contextual factor. A further key feature of such approaches is the organic and mutually constitutive relationship between person and context, whereby individuals are inherently part of, act upon and contribute to shaping the social, cultural, and physical environments with which they interact. This person-in-situation perspective on the organic nature of the relations between person and context contrasts sharply with more mainstream SLA perspectives which regard contextual factors as external independent variables that may influence L2 learning processes or determine behavior.

Within SLA, person-in-situation approaches represent a fairly recent development, arising out of the growing emphasis on social and sociocultural influences on SLA, and reflecting a stronger concern with issues of context in the SLA field as well as across the social sciences since the turn of the millennium. Outside SLA, person-in-situation (or person-in-environment) concepts are now well established in the field of social work practice (e.g. Cornell, 2006), and learner-in-context perspectives have become increasingly important in the field of motivation theory in educational psychology (e.g. Volet and Järvelä, 2001).

It is probably true to say that, as a relatively new development within SLA, person-in-situation approaches do not constitute or privilege a specific theoretical framework of analysis, but rather define in broad terms what the unit of analysis should be when adopting a holistic and situated perspective on individuals' L2 learning processes and experiences (for further discussion, see Ushioda, 2009). In expanding the unit of analysis beyond the individual to embrace the interaction between the individual and the social context, person-in-situation approaches share much conceptual ground with sociocultural theory (SCT) and sociocognitive approaches to SLA. In particular, they share with these theoretical perspectives a shift from an exclusive focus on learning as an internal cognitive process, towards a view of language and language learning as socially situated and socially constructed processes which, as Atkinson (2002: 525) puts it, take place both "in the head" and "in the world."

In seeking to capture the dynamic and mutually constitutive relationships between individuals and their social and cultural environment, person-in-situation approaches also have close affinities with current ecological perspectives on language learning (e.g. van Lier, 2004), and with theories of second language socialization (e.g. Kramsch, 2002a). Integral to these theoretical perspectives is the adaptive and symbiotic nature of the relations between L2 learner-users and the sociocultural environment, and the difficulty of separating the person from the context, or L2 learning from L2 use, or, as Kramsch (2002b) puts it metaphorically (quoting the poet W.B. Yeats), separating the dancer from the dance.

In taking the person-in-context as an integrated unit of analysis or system, person-in-situation approaches can also potentially be aligned with current perspectives on complexity theory and dynamic systems theory in SLA (e.g. Larsen-Freeman and Cameron, 2008). According to Larsen-Freeman and Cameron (2008: 2) a defining characteristic of a complex system is that its behavior emerges from the interaction of its components, and that this emergent behavior is often non-linear and unpredictable. As Dörnyei (2009: 229) notes, when a dynamic systems perspective is applied to the analysis of learner–environment interactions, the challenge becomes to consider simultaneously the complex multiple influences *between* learner and environmental factors as well as the emerging changes *within* the learner and the environment arising out of these mutual interactions.

In view of the complex, dynamic, mutually constitutive, and non-linear relations between individual and context, person-in-situation approaches to SLA clearly call for alternative strategies of inquiry and research designs than the causal linear models and quantitative methodologies that have traditionally prevailed in the field. In particular, person-in-situation approaches call for richly grounded descriptions of context and detailed analyses of the individual's interactions in this context. However, a key critical issue is how to define and delimit the social, cultural, spatial, historical, and future boundaries of context relevant to the analysis (e.g. a study abroad experience, a single language lesson, a task performance, a brief interactional exchange). Depending on the research focus, one possibility may be to adopt a fairly constrained micro-perspective on those features of context which are explicitly invoked or made relevant during a person's L2 interactions in a specific social situation (e.g. through conversation analysis methods). An alternative strategy may be to focus on those aspects of context which are salient to particular individuals, which they respond to or act upon, or which are experienced as impinging on the situated process of learning and using the L2. Clearly, introspective methods (e.g. stimulated recall) are likely to be instrumental here, perhaps integrating multiple perspectives from the various interacting individuals embedded within the situation under analysis. However, a limitation of introspective methods is that they cannot shed light on situational factors, contextual processes and individual behaviors which are below the level of consciousness. In this regard, it may be that person-in-situation approaches are best suited to exploring the more subjective dimensions of L2 learning and use that have particular salience and perhaps emotional significance for individuals, such as processes of motivation or loss of motivation, situations that arouse anxiety or stress, identity work in L2 interactions, or transitions to new L2 experiences such as migration or study abroad.

See also: Complexity Theory/Dynamic Systems Theory, ecology of learning, identity theory, second language socialization, social and sociocultural influences on SLA, sociocognitive approaches to SLA

References

Atkinson, D. (2002). Towards a sociocognitive approach to second language acquisition. *The Modern Language Journal*, *86*(iv), 525–45.

Cornell, K.L. (2006). Person-in-situation: History, theory, and new directions for social work practice. *Praxis*, *6*, 50–57.

Dörnyei, Z. (2009). *The Psychology of Second Language Acquisition*. Oxford: Oxford University Press.

Kramsch, C. (ed.) (2002a). *Language Acquisition and Language Socialization: Ecological Perspectives*. London: Continuum.

——(2002b). Introduction: How can we tell the dancer from the dance? In C. Kramsch (ed.), *Language Acquisition and Language Socialization: Ecological Perspectives*, pp. 1–30. London: Continuum.

Larsen-Freeman, D. and Cameron, L. (2008). *Complex Systems and Applied Linguistics*. Oxford: Oxford University Press.

Ushioda, E. (2009). A person-in-context relational view of emergent motivation, self and identity. In Z. Dörnyei and E. Ushioda (eds), *Motivation, Language Identity and the L2 Self*, pp. 215–28. Bristol: Multilingual Matters.

van Lier, L. (2004). *The Ecology and Semiotics of Language Learning: A Sociocultural Perspective*. Boston, MA: Kluwer Academic.

Volet, S. and Järvelä, S. (eds) (2001). *Motivation in Learning Contexts: Theoretical Advances and Methodological Implications*. Amsterdam: Pergamon.

Phonological short-term memory (PSTM)

Elena Grigorenko
Yale University

The concept of phonological short-term memory (PSTM) lies at the junction of two wide streams of research in psychology and education—that of phonological sensitivity skills (also referred to as phonological awareness skills) and working memory. The former broadly refers to understanding the system of skills framing the awareness of and ability to manipulate the phonological structures of a language. There is a large and convincing literature suggesting that phonological sensitivity skills are crucial for the acquisition of both spoken and written language, whether native or foreign. Phonological sensitivity skills can be stratified by levels of linguistic complexity—words, syllables, onsets and rimes, and phonemes (Anthony, Lonigan, Driscoll, Phillips, and Burgess, 2003). As language acquisition progresses, the predictive power of different indicators of phonological sensitivity at different levels of linguistic complexity also changes.

The latter theoretical framework, that of working memory (WM), has numerous overlapping representations (i.e., competing, but partially overlapping approaches) in the literature. One such theory (Baddeley, 1986) indicates that WM consists of control processes, the central executive and two lower-level systems, the phonological loop and the visuospatial sketchpad. The phonological loop, also known in the literature as phonological short-term memory (PSTM), is responsible for capturing and maintaining speech-based information in a readily accessible form and supporting long-term phonological learning (Baddeley, Gathercole, and Papagno, 1998), that is, the acquisition of phonological sensitivity skills. This acquisition goes through stages of detection, recognition, and then manipulation of phonological units, with an increased sensitivity to smaller units of phonological data. Along with the skill of differentiating phonemes into smaller units also grows the capacity to increase the amount of consciousness in phonological sensitivity, so that developmental change occurs by transitioning from epilinguistic (i.e., mostly implicit and unconscious) to metalinguistic (i.e., mostly explicit and conscious) types of processing (Gombert, 1992). In other words, in acquiring a language, linguistic units are first thought to be present in implicit format, which subsequently need to be reformatted into explicit format—that is, a representational redescription (Karmiloff-Smith, 1992) or an installation of more fine-grained lexical representations (Metsala and Walley, 1998) should take place. PSTM is crucial in both forming the epilinguistic, then switching to metalinguistic types of processing, which provide both the context and the working tool for phonological maturation within any given language.

PSTM includes a short-term store where the material is held in a phonological code that is subject to rapid decay unless it is refreshed by, for example, a time-based subvocal rehearsal process. The stream of speech that constantly enters PSTM clears up quickly, unless processed immediately. In other words, PSTM can be conceived as an information holder in which sequences of incoming speech are held temporarily so that more demanding tasks (e.g., sentence and paragraph comprehension) can be performed. PSTM has distinct developmental characteristics, being less developed (i.e., smaller) in children, continuing to develop (i.e., enlarging) throughout adolescents, and achieving its maximum in adulthood.

PSTM is also a source of individual differences, especially in early and middle childhood; these differences, in turn, are predictive of children's capacity to acquire new words (Gathercole, 2006), both in their native (e.g., Michas and Henry, 1994) and foreign (Service, 1992) tongues. The specifics of the mechanisms connecting PSTM and word learning are yet not fully understood, and there are numerous theoretical accounts of this connection. In the tradition of Baddeley's work, this connection is linked to the role of the phonological loop in the assembly of robust phonological representations of words in the mental lexicon (Baddeley, *et al.*, 1998). Specifically, it is assumed that across multiple exposures to a novel phonological form, the structure of the form is derived from the temporary phonological representation to serve as the basis for its eventual lexical specification. Correspondingly, the process of acquiring a new word can be compromised in more than one way. First, if its phonological storage is challenged and the derivation of a new phonological form based on repeated exposure is either very slow and/or filled with errors. Second, it can also be compromised if there is not enough exposure to a new word while the word form is being derived. Finally, the word form derivation can be aided by the presence of a strong mental lexicon and, conversely, can be harmed in the absence of such. There are substantive bodies of literature that provide illustrations of the importance, individual and collective, of these three factors for learning new words in native and foreign tongues.

PSTM skills are typically evaluated via the utilization of serial recall tasks such as the alphabet span, digit span, or nonword (pseudoword) repetition. PSTM has been referred to as one of three—along with language analytic capacity and memory ability—main predictors of the acquisition of foreign-language skills such as listening, reading, writing, and speaking (Skehan, 1989). Of interest is that PSTM appears to exert direct (i.e., via the capacity of the store) and indirect (i.e., through long-term phonological knowledge about a foreign language) influences on the acquisition of a foreign language. Also notable is that the level of mastery of a foreign language, in turn, influences the capacity of PSTM. Although most of the research in the field has addressed the connection between PSTM and vocabulary (see above), the literature also contains hypotheses in which PSTM plays a more systematic role in the acquisition of a foreign language. For example, Ellis (1996) hypothesized that, since language learning is mostly sequence learning, and PSTM is chiefly responsible for remembering sequential information, the role of PSTM is much greater than is commonly recognized. Thus, in addition to being an informative predictor of vocabulary acquisition, PSTM has been shown to be a predictor of grammar and syntax acquisition.

In summary, PSTM is an important indicator, predictor, and outcome of the process of language acquisition, whether the language that is being acquired is either native or foreign. PSTM provides a vehicle for the development of phonological sensitivity skills and, reflecting the level of development of these skills, in turn is a predictor of semantic (vocabulary), grammar, and syntactic facets of native- and foreign-language acquisition.

See also: aptitude, executive control and frontal cortex, individual differences in SLA, psycholinguistics of SLA, Linguistic Coding Deficit Hypothesis (LCDH), working memory

References

Anthony, J.L., Lonigan, C.J., Driscoll, K., Phillips, B.M. and Burgess, S.R. (2003). Phonological sensitivity: A quasiparallel progression of word structure units and cognitive operations. *Reading Research Quarterly, 38*, 470–87.

Baddeley, A.D. (1986). *Working memory*. London: Oxford University Press.

Baddeley, A.D., Gathercole, S.E. and Papagno, C. (1998). The phonological loop as a language learning device. *Psychological Review, 105*, 158–73.

Ellis, N.C. (1996). Sequencing in SLA: Phonological memory, chunking, and points of order. *Studies in Second Language Acquisition*, *19*, 91–126.

Gathercole, S.E. (2006). Nonword repetition and word learning: The nature of the relationship. *Applied Psycholinguistics*, *27*, 513–43.

Gombert, J.-E. (1992). *Metalinguistic Development*. London: Harvester Wheatsheaf.

Karmiloff-Smith, A. (1992). *Beyond the Modularity*. Cambridge, MA: MIT Press.

Metsala, J.L. and Walley, A.C. (1998). Spoken vocabulary growth and the segmental restructuring of lexical representations: Precursors to phonemic awareness and early reading ability. In J.L. Metsala and L.C. Ehri (eds), *Word recognition in beginning literacy*, pp. 89–120. London: Erlbaum.

Michas, I.C. and Henry, L.A. (1994). The link between phonological memory and vocabulary acquisition. *British Journal of Developmental Psychology*, *12*, 147–64.

Service, E. (1992). Phonology, working memory, and foreign-language learning. *Quarterly Journal of Experimental Psychology*, *45*A, 21–50.

Skehan, P. (1989). *Individual differences in second language learning*. London: Edward Arnold.

Pidginization and creolization

Silvia Kouwenberg
University of the West Indies

The fields of Creole Linguistics and Second Language Acquisition enjoyed a brief period of mutual interest in the 1980s, and we will begin this overview with it. We then turn to the notion of "transfer" in explanations of creole genesis, followed by a consideration of recent attempts to reengage the fields with each other. First, though, I should note that the distinction between pidgins and creoles is contested, as is the view that creolization is necessarily preceded by pidginization. Nevertheless, I will use the terms here as traditionally understood, whereby pidginization refers to the emergence of a rudimentary contact variety, creolization to the emergence of a full-fledged community language.

Pidginization and early L2 acquisition as simplification

During the 1980s, linguists explored the parallels between processes of pidginization/creolization and second language acquisition (Andersen, 1983). The basis for the comparative discussions were notions of simplification in pidginization and early SLA, and expansion/elaboration in creolization and late SLA. Pidgins and creoles were seen as providing apparent-time models of different interlanguage stages. However, while many discussants seemed to subscribe to the early SLA-as-pidginization view, the relation between creolization and SLA was more contentious. A number of questions were raised even at that stage. Also, the explanatory power of the notion of simplification was questioned (e.g., Meisel, 1983). As research revealed that SLA proceeds through ordered developmental sequences, SLA specialists turned their attention to the internal dynamics of interlanguage development and lost interest in exploring its relation to pidginization and creolization.

At the same time, among creolists, debates focused on creolization rather than pidginization, and centered around the "substrata vs. universals" question: did the characteristics of creole languages derive primarily from the first languages of the substrate populations, or from universals of first language acquisition (Muysken and Smith, 1986)? Moreover, questions were being raised about the assumptions inherent in approaching creole genesis as L2 acquisition. Baker (1990) pointed out that pidgin and creole languages emerged in historical contexts where it is unlikely that the European lexifier constituted a "target language" in the sense in which that term is intended. His argument, that pidgins and creoles should be seen as successful solutions to a problem of communication rather than as failed attempts to learn a European language, was widely accepted.

L1 transfer in creole genesis

Many creolists nevertheless continued to draw on SLA concepts, most notably that of first language transfer. SLA specialists in the 1990s deemphasized transfer, as they found that interlanguage generally fails to replicate properties of the L1 in a transparent manner. Creolists, on the other hand, have continued to use the term, without the benefit of further exchange with SLA specialists, and without making reference to evolving insights in SLA research. As a result, the creolist concept of transfer may strike SLA specialists as decidedly odd.

Creolists apply the notion of transfer to cases where surface characteristics of pidgin or creole grammar resemble those of the relevant substrates, focusing wholly on negative transfer – and ignoring the fact that negative transfer is often considered to be of only minor importance in L2 acquisition. Moreover, what emerges from the SLA literature is that L1 interference is evident in L2 *use* rather than L2 acquisition, as a compensatory strategy in situations of communicative pressure (Siegel, 2008); such transfer is not expected, in L2 acquisition, to become a permanent characteristic of the interlanguage.

Additionally, creolists have considered as transfer cases where superstrate forms have been reinterpreted and given grammatical functions derived from those of a substrate form. Siegel koined the term "functional transfer" for this phenomenon, and makes it clear that it is essentially not found in L2 acquisition – an observation which supports the point made by Kouwenberg (2006) that, paradoxically, the more evidence of substrate patterns is seen, the less it can be assumed that L2 acquisition is involved in creole genesis.

Creole language as early interlanguage

Plag (2008) constitutes an attempt to bring current insights from SLA studies to bear on questions of creole genesis. He adopts Processability Theory (e. g., Pienemann, 2000), which postulates a hierarchy of processing procedures which the L2 learner acquires sequentially, beginning with the lower-order ones: the acquisition of invariant word forms (lemma access, stage 1), and of some syntactic and morphological complexity (category procedures, stage 2). Plag argues that creole languages emerge as fossilized early interlanguages. There are, however, some problems for his claim that creole languages show evidence of acquisition at stages 1 and 2: the morphological complexity acquired at stage 2 includes "inherent" inflections such as number for nouns, comparative degree for adjectives, tense and aspect for verbs. Coming early in the acquisition process, one might expect creoles to contain such inherent inflections from their European "targets." However, this is the case for very, very few creoles. The incorporated plurals which we see in creole forms such as Jamaican *ans* "ant" (English "ants") and Haitian *ze* "eye" (French *les yeux* "the eyes") provide evidence of exposure to plurals in the lexifier during creole genesis; however, they also provide evidence that the relevant inflections were not recognized by the originators of these creoles. Instead, ways of expressing number, etc. were innovated in most creoles (compare Jamaican *di ans dem* [DEF ant PL] "the ants"). This effectively reduces the relevance of L2 acquisition in creole genesis to the acquisition of the surface forms of lexical items (lemma access) – as predicted by Lefebvre's Relexification Model, to which I return below.

On the other hand, there is also evidence that creole development may involve the acquisition of lexifier characteristics at more advanced stages, for instance of productive derivational morphology. That creole genesis takes more from the lexifier than mere lemmas also becomes clear when lexifier-driven differences between creoles are considered. To name but a few things, the postnominal position of the definite determiner in French-lexifier creoles contrasts with its prenominal position in English-lexifier creoles, and whereas attributive APs are strictly prenominal in English-lexifier creoles, French- and Portuguese-lexifier creoles replicate the more variable patterns of their superstrates.

Creolization and L2 acquisition revisited

Simplification, the notion which provided the initial basis for contact between the fields, no longer serves that function: it plays no role in current models of L2 acquisition, and its role in pidgin/creole studies is reduced to a (contentious) descriptive generalization (McWhorter, 2001), not an explanatory principle. Attempts to reengage creolists and SLA specialists in debates about the interface between their fields of study now have to find a different basis for their exchange. We find such attempts in Lefebvre, White and Jourdan (2006) and Kouwenberg and Patrick (2003), while Siegel (2008) assesses the relationship between the fields. Among contributions to Lefebvre *et al.* is Sprouse (2006), who points to convergence between Lefebvre's Relexification model of creole genesis and the Full Transfer/Full Access (FTFA) model of SLA. In relexification, L2 learners replace the phonological shapes of lexical entries by L2 surface forms, while retaining the morphosyntactic and semantic features of the L1 form; applied to creole genesis, the Relexification Hypothesis predicts that creole grammars resemble those of their (dominant) substrates. Like relexification, FTFA predicts that the initial state of the L2 grammar is identical to that of the L1. Sprouse argues that subsequent L2 development allows for resetting of morphosyntactic parameters through target language input, in contrast with creole development, where this input is presumed too limited.

However, the claim that creole languages emerged simply because of lack of access to the lexifier can be challenged. Perhaps Baker's (1990) point, that incipient pidgins and creoles became targets for language learning early in their development, provides a better explanation. This is apparently not so for interlanguages: even where learners have more access to L2 speakers than to native speakers, they appear to be aware of the fact that interlanguage varieties do not constitute a legitimate form of the target. Presuming that the creators of creole languages were similarly aware, it is reasonable to conclude that motivation to acquire the lexifier was lacking. This point is made by Singler (2008), who, speaking of the prototypical context where creole languages emerged, argues that modern sociolinguistic insights point to the unlikelihood that slaves would simply wish to imitate the most powerful in the plantation society.

A very different position is taken by Chaudenson (2001) and Mufwene (2008), who argue that slaves attempted to learn the European lexifier and approximated it as closely as circumstances allowed – presumably motivated precisely by the desire to imitate the most powerful in the plantation society. Since, they argue, each subsequent wave of slave arrivals had access only to the "approximations" of the previous arrivals, the variety spoken by slaves diverged gradually from the European "target," leading to creole genesis. However, since motivation is a powerful force in reaching L2 fluency, one wonders why so few among the enslaved were successful L2 acquirers. The approximations view is compromised further by its reliance on processes of language change in accounting for the oftentimes far-reaching differences between creole and lexifier grammar. Not only is there no clear way in which language change is envisaged in L2 acquisition, there appears to be consensus that where L2 learners do not attain fluency in the target language, their interlanguage version will simply fail to develop any further. Thus, Becker and Veenstra (2003) argue that the Basic Variety, an early interlanguage stage which its users consider to be functionally adequate, fails to use the resources of the target to create independent distinctions. In contrast, creole languages do just that, making innovation rather than approximation characteristic of creole development.

Conclusion

That *some* amount of acquisition of the lexifier takes place in the emergence of creoles is not contested among students of these languages, and this is the basis for the enduring interest among creolists in L2 acquisition. It is fair to say, though, that the reverse is not true. Characterized by innovation, pidgins and creoles are too unlike interlanguage varieties to reignite much interest among SLA specialists in their development.

See also: basic variety, interlanguage, linguistic transfer, pidginization and creolization, simplification, Universal Grammar (UG) and SLA

References

Andersen, R.W. (ed.) (1983). *Pidginization and Creolization as Language Acquisition*. Rowley, MA: Newbury House.

Baker, P. (1990). Off target? [Column] *Journal of Pidgin and Creole Languages*, *5*, 107–19.

Becker, A. and T. Veenstra (2003). The survival of inflectional morphology in French-related creoles: the role of SLA processes. *Studies in Second Language Acquisition*, *25*, 283–306.

Chaudenson, R. (2001). *Creolization of Language and Culture.* London: Routledge.

Klein, W. and C. Perdue (1997). The Basic Variety (or: Couldn't natural languages be much simpler?)" *Second Language Research*, *13*, 301–47.

Kouwenberg, S. (2006). L1 transfer and the cut off point for L2 acquisition processes in creole formation. In C. Lefebvre, L. White and C. Jourdan (eds), *L2 Acquisition and Creole Genesis: Dialogues,* pp. 205–219. Amsterdam and Philadelphia, PA: John Benjamins.

Kouwenberg, S. and P. Patrick (eds) (2003). Special issue on second language acquisition and creolization. *Studies in Second Language Acquisition*, *25* (2).

Lefebvre, C.L. White and C. Jourdan (eds) (2006). *L2 Acquisition and Creole Genesis: Dialogues.* Amsterdam and Philadelphia, PA: John Benjamins.

McWhorter, J. (2001). The world's simplest grammars are creole grammars. *Linguistic Typology*, *5*, 125–66

Meisel, J.M. (1983). Strategies of second language acquisition: more than one kind of simplification. In R.W. Andersen (ed.), *Pidginization and Creolization as Language Acquisition*, pp. 120–157. Rowley, MA: Newbury House.

Mufwene, S. (2008). *Language Evolution. Contact, Competition and Change.* London and New York: Continuum.

Muysken, P. and N. Smith (eds) (1986). *Substrate versus Universals.* Amsterdam and Philadelphia, PA: John Benjamins.

Pienemann, M. (2000). Psycholinguistic mechanisms in the development of English as a second language. In I. Plag and K.P. Schneider (eds), *Language Use, Language Acquisition and Language History: (Mostly) Empirical Studies in Honour of Rüdiger Zimmermann*, pp. 99–118. Trier: Wissenschaftlicher Verlag Trier.

Plag, I. (2008). Creoles as interlanguages. Inflectional morphology. *Journal of Pidgin and Creole Languages*, *23*(1), 114–35.

Siegel, J. (2008). Pidgins/Creoles and Second Language Acquisition. In S. Kouwenberg and J.V. Singler (eds), *Handbook of Pidgin and Creole Studies*, pp. 189–218. Oxford: Wiley-Blackwell.

Singler, J.V. (2008). The sociohistorical context of creole genesis. In S. Kouwenberg and J.V. Singler (eds), *Handbook of Pidgin and Creole Studies*, pp. 332–58. Oxford: Wiley-Blackwell.

Sprouse, R.A. (2006). Full Transfer and Relexification: second language acquisition and creole genesis. In C. Lefebvre, L. White and C. Jourdan (eds), *L2 Acquisition and Creole Genesis: Dialogues*, pp. 169–81.

Planning time

Parvaneh Tavakoli
London Metropolitan University

Investigations of planning time and the impact it has on second language (L2) performance have gained currency in both SLA research and language pedagogy over the past decades. Although this shared interest among SLA researchers and language educators is closely interrelated, there are some differences in why each group invests in examining and researching this topic. From a language pedagogy point of view, planning time is effective in attracting and directing learners' attention to aspects of the L2 form and meaning and in providing them with an opportunity to monitor, plan and/or practice the L2. Planning is also believed to inform the methodology about whether and how L2 learners benefit from the availability of time to plan and the type of planning that is most effective for each pedagogic goal.

From an SLA perspective, planning is of particular significance partly because language production is viewed as a process divided into planning and execution phases, with the planning phase allowing users to scan their linguistic repertoire and select the rules and items needed to reach their communicative goals, and the execution phase entailing production of the language that has been planned (Faerch and Kasper, 1986). It has also been suggested that because planning involves activation and retrieval of knowledge about linguistic forms and their meanings (Hulstijn and

Hulstijn, 1984), it can promote focus on form and encourage learners to notice the gap in their L2 knowledge. The greater significance of planning in SLA studies, however, lies in the contribution it has for information-processing models, already established in cognitive psychology but only recently applied to language learning by Skehan (1998). These models hypothesize that since humans have a limited attentional capacity to process information particularly when engaged in cognitively demanding tasks such as L2 production, planning before an L2 task may release some attentional resources and ease the pressure on the working memory. Skehan (1998) proposes that planning provides learners with an opportunity to access their rule-based system as well as their exemplar-based system and allows them to compensate for inadequacy in one system by drawing on the other. This, Skehan argues, would in turn cause trade-offs since, for example, when a learner takes risks by attempting more complex structures, she/he may not have enough attentional capacity available to attend to L2 accuracy. This claim has been challenged by Robinson's (2003) Cognition Hypothesis that views planning as a resource depleting factor working closely with resource directing factors to determine the complexity of the task and the extent the learners attend to form when they perform the task. Cognition Hypothesis predicts that a no-planning condition will reduce attention and memory resources with negative effects on both complexity and accuracy of performance.

Many of the recent studies on planning time are informed by Levelt's (1989) model of speaking in which the three processing components of Conceptualizer, Formulator, and Articulator depict the process of speech from the moment an intention to speak is formed until when the actual language is produced. While the three processes are assumed to work simultaneously and in parallel in L1 speech, SLA researchers believe that in L2 production they compete for limited attentional resources. A crucial function of planning time in L2 production, therefore, is to increase the attentional resources for the Formulator and Articulator, particularly when the Conceptualizer attracts the primary attention.

Types of planning time

Ellis (2005) distinguishes between pre-task and within-task planning, that is, planning that is conducted prior to task performance and that which takes place during it. With pre-task planning, rehearsal is a type that allows learners to perform the complete task before the main performance, while strategic planning provides learners with an opportunity to plan the content and the language they are going to use. Within-task planning is further divided into pressured and unpressured types, with the former involving learners in rapid planning of what they are going to say and the latter requiring them to engage with careful on-line planning without any time restriction. Ellis (2005) acknowledges that while pre-task and within-task planning constitute distinctive types of planning they should not be seen as mutually exclusive.

Planning can be operationalized as guided or unguided according to whether or not the learners receive instructions about how to plan their performance or what to focus on. Research in this area suggests that the guided planning results in more fluency and complexity of learner performance but the unguided planning leads performance towards more accuracy (Foster and Skehan, 1996). Similarly, Mochizuki and Ortega (2008) investigated whether pre-task planning with embedded grammatical guidance to attend to a specific L2 form had an impact on learner performance, and found that the guided planning time helped learners to produce more accurate target forms.

Depending on its source, planning can also be divided to teacher-led, solitary and group-based. Although planning has traditionally been viewed as a solitary activity, interest in studying planning as a group endeavor has increased on the grounds that group planning is considered as more authentic and pedagogically oriented in language classrooms. Foster and Skehan (1999) reported that while more fluency was associated with solitary planning, more accuracy resulted from teacher-led planning. Troung and Storch (2007) contended that group planning dealt with the content rather than the language of the performance, and it allowed for the largest number of ideas to be generated.

Research on planning time

Unlike many other areas of SLA inquiry, research on planning time has produced relatively consistent results concerning the effects it has on L2 production. Regardless of the differences in interest and focus, there is general consensus among language researchers and educators that presence of planning time helps learners produce language of higher quality, and that planners outperform non-planners with improvement in one or more aspects of their performance.

Research on rehearsal (Bygate, 1996) suggests that rehearsing tasks has a beneficial effect on subsequent performances but this effect cannot be transferred to a different task, even to the same type of task at a different setting. It also implies that although repeated encounters lead learners to optimize their resources and perform at a more sophisticated level, they do not necessarily involve learners in doing the "same" thing. Rather, they work differently on the same thing.

The length of planning time has been a further area of investigation. Mehnert (1998) found that while there were significant differences in fluency of performance between planners and non-planners, the differences caused as a result of 1, 5, and 10 minutes of planning on fluency were largely non-significant. However, with regard to complexity, providing longer planning times, that is, 10 minutes, seemed essential in encouraging learners to increase the complexity of their performance. Interestingly, in Mehnert's study accuracy improved only with 1 minute of planning time but did not increase with the longer planning opportunities.

Measuring performance in planning studies is yet another important area of discussion. Although a number of planning studies have employed more holistic measures of performance including task essentialness and amount and type of interaction to examine the effects of planning on performance, the majority of research in this area has looked into how planning influences L2 performance as measured by analytic measures of complexity, accuracy, and fluency. These three aspects, sometimes known as CAF, are assumed to represent a learner's language proficiency demonstrable through production of language that is accurate, fluent, and syntactically and lexically complex.

Learners and planning time

Wendel (1997) and Ortega (2005) are among the few studies that investigated what learners actually do when they are given time to plan for task performance. The results of Wendel's study suggested that learners varied in what they reported doing during the planning time with many focusing on sequencing the events in the narratives and some attending to content and/or grammar. Reporting on two studies in which the learners were retrospectively interviewed, Ortega (2005) maintains that they used a noticeable and balanced proportion of cognitive and metacognitive strategy types and rarely resorted to the social/affective strategies. In sum, these studies have shown that learners tend to attend to meaning before they think about form.

Learner perceptions of pre-task planning have generally been reported positively with the majority of L2 learners claiming that planning time helped them perform the task better and made them feel less stressed (Ortega, 2005; Tavakoli and Skehan, 2005). Undoubtedly, in order to develop a more in-depth insight into what learners do when they plan, what their feelings and beliefs are and whether their perceptions are contingent on their performance, more research is needed.

The way forward

Despite the fact that research on planning time has been innovative, productive, and fruitful in terms of its impact on L2 production, and has produced consistent and constructive results from which researchers and teachers benefit, it has suffered from some fundamental limitations. First of all, planning research has only been concerned with learner *performance* and has failed to provide sufficient evidence that potentially allows for the development of an L2 *acquisition* model. Without extending its domain to investigations of acquisition and interlanguage development, research into planning time can only present an incomplete and inadequate picture of how second languages are learnt. Another complication that planning research faces is the fallacy of considering "planning" as a unitary construct or as a predetermined process through which different language users proceed similarly. Hence, a major responsibility of planning research is to accommodate an overarching and detailed account of what constitutes planning. Finally, more research is needed to examine planning from different perspectives and in various contexts. At present, there are only few studies, for example, Philp *et al.* (2006) that look into how planning time contributes to learner construction of knowledge and acquisition of language in their social and cultural settings, or how planning impacts on children's interaction and cognitive development in an early language learning settings.

See also: Cognition Hypothesis, fluency, Levelt's model of speech production and comprehension, Limited Capacity Hypothesis, task-based learning, units for analyzing L2 speaking

References

Bygate, M. (1996). Effects of task repetition: Appraising the developing language of learners. In D. Willis and J. Willis (eds), *Challenge and Change in Language Teaching*, pp. 134–46. London: Heineman.

Ellis, R. (2005). *Planning and Task Performance in a Second Language*. Amsterdam: John Benjamines.

Faerch, C. and Kasper, G. (1986). The role of comprehension in second language learning. *Applied Linguistics*, *7*(2): 257–74.

Foster, P. and Skehan, P. (1996). The influence of planning and task type on second language performances. *Studies in Second Language Acquisition*, *18*, 299–323.

——(1999). The influence of source of planning and focus of planning on task-based performance. *Language Teaching Research*, *3*(3), 215–47.

Hulstijn, J. and Hulstijn, W. (1984). Grammatical errors as a function of processing constraints and explicit knowledge. *Language Learning*, *34* (1), 23–43.

Levelt, W. (1989). *Speaking: From Intention to Articulation*. Cambridge, MA: MIT Press.

Mehnert, U. (1998). The effects of different length of time for planning on second language performance. *Studies in Second Language Acquisition*, *20*(1): 83–108.

Ortega, L. (2005). What do learners plan? Learner-driven attention to form during pre-task planning. R. Ellis (ed.), *Planning and Task Performance in a Second Language*, pp. 77–110. Amsterdam: John Benjamins.

Philp, J., Oliver, R. and Mackey, A. (2006). The impact of planning on children's task-based interactions. *System*, *34*(4), 574–65.

Robinson, P. (2003). Task complexity, cognitive resources, and syllabus design: A triadic framework for examining task influences on SLA. In P. Robinson (ed.), *Cognition and Second Language Instruction*, pp. 287–318. Cambridge: Cambridge University Press.

Skehan, P. (1998). *A Cognitive Approach to Language Learning*. Oxford: Oxford University Press.

Tavakoli, P. and Skehan, P. (2005). Strategic planning, task structure and performance testing. In R. Ellis (ed.), *Planning and Task Performance in a Second Language*, pp. 239–77. Amsterdam: John Benjamins.

Troung, A. and Storch, N. (2007). Investigating group planning in preparation for oral presentations in an EFL class in Vietnam. *RELC*, *38*(1): 104–24.

Wendel, J. (1997). *Planning and Second Language Narrative Production*. Unpublished doctoral dissertation, Tokyo: Temple University Japan.

Politeness

J. César Félix-Brasdefer
Indiana University

The concept of politeness, initially conceptualized in the field sociology and later refined in the areas of pragmatics and discourse analysis, refers to the interpersonal or relational function of language where meaning is negotiated between interlocutors that are engaged in social interaction. Politeness is often associated with good manners or rules of etiquette (e.g., say "please" and "thank you"), deference (formality), consideration for others, mitigation or attenuation (e.g., "*could* [vs. can] you *please* call me when you get this message?"), indirectness (e. g., "I was wondering whether you … "), socially appropriate behavior, rapport management, social behavior in excess (e.g., "I'm *really grateful* for your *kind* offer, *thank you so much*"), or behavior that is perceived as polite (or impolite) by others. Polite behavior can be communicated in various ways: it can be conveyed through linguistic expressions (not inherently polite) used in specific situations (e.g., "*thanks* for offering to give me a ride. It's really *kind* of you") or non-verbal signals that may be perceived as polite by the interlocutor (e.g., gaze, body orientation).

This entry is organized as follows. First, I provide an overview of the origins of the notion of politeness. Second, I describe how the concept of politeness has been understood in politeness research, including a description of appropriateness and politeness in interaction. Third, I explain how politeness is realized among second language learners, followed by my conclusion.

The words "polite" and "politeness" can be traced back to concepts related to cleanliness or to smooth, polished, refined, planned, civilized, or courtly activity. In English "polite" is recorded in 1501 with a sense of something elegant or cultured, and in 1762 the word "polite" acquires a sense of "behaving courteously" (Online Etymology Dictionary). The English word "polite" is derived from the Latinate past participle "politus," from the verb "polire," meaning "polished" or "smoothed." The word "courtesy," in German "Höflichkeit," in French "courtoisie," in Portuguese "cortesia," or in Spanish "cortesía," all refer back to this original root, alluding to polite or planned behavior in the court. On the contrary, in Roman society, the notion of politeness does not appear to have a connection to the court, but rather, to the big city ("urbanitas") or the *urb* which stressed the social demands of life and class differences of a civilized but elitist society where hierarchical differences played a role. Overall, the concept of politeness as understood in our modern times still retains remnants of the historical notion of politeness dealing with appropriate social behavior, good manners, etiquette, deference, affect, and consideration for others in social interaction.

Politeness research

The concept of politeness is investigated from two angles, first- and second-order politeness. First-order politeness (or politeness1) as perceived by members of different sociocultural groups (i.e., the folk notion of politeness or politeness-as-practice in everyday interaction), and second-order politeness (or politeness2) as a theoretical construct or the scientific conceptualization of politeness1 (Watts, 2003). The politeness1-politeness2 distinction should be taken with caution and should not be viewed as categorical, as certain models of politeness may comprise features that encompass one or the other dimension.

Politeness as a research object has been examined from different perspectives. The concept of politeness was founded in universal rules of pragmatic competence (e.g., Lakoff's [1973] rule of "be polite"), principles (e.g., Grice's cooperative principle [1975]) or Leech's politeness principle [1983]), maxims in conversation (e.g., Grice's quantity [provide no more no less information than is required] or Leech's maxims of approbation and modesty), as well as in sociological notions of face (our "self") and facework (negotiation of social practices) (Goffman, 1967). Most of these concepts represent the foundation of different frameworks of politeness to date, in particular, Grice's cooperative principle and Goffman's notion of face.

Brown and Levinson's (1987 [1978]) universal model of linguistic politeness has predominated in empirical work on politeness, especially in the field of cross-cultural pragmatics. This model has influenced our understanding of how politeness is strategically used to minimize the degree of imposition in acts that may pose a threat to the interlocutor such as requests or suggestions (Brown and Levinson's notion of Face-Threatening Act). Under this model, Brown and Levinson define face as "the public self-image that every member [of a society] wants to claim for himself" (1987: 61). The foundation of their model is their distinction between positive and negative politeness strategies which they claim to be universal. For example, positive politeness strategies (positive face) refers to the hearer's desire to be appreciated or approved of; this includes seeking agreement, solidarity, reciprocity, or in-group membership markers (e.g., dear, buddy, honey, sweetie, dude). In contrast, negative politeness (negative face) alludes to "the basic claim to territories, personal preserves, and rights to non-distraction, i.e., freedom of action and freedom from imposition" (Brown and Levinson 1987: 61) (e.g., being indirect, giving deference, being apologetic).

Most research on cross-cultural pragmatics utilizes Brown and Levinson's model (or revised versions) and focuses on the inventory of the strategies that are used to convey linguistic politeness. For example, positive and negative politeness strategies are examined through the speech acts of apologies and requests in various languages, such as English (Australian, British, and U.S. English), Argentinean Spanish, and French (Blum-Kulka, House, and Kasper, 1989); England and Spain (Márquez Reiter, 2000), and Russia, Poland, and England (Ogiermann, 2009).

To avoid ambiguity in the terms of positive (for good) and negative politeness (for bad), the concepts of involvement (group orientation: emphasizing common ground and affiliation) and independence (individual orientation: emphasizing the individuality or autonomy of the speaker) are often used instead (Scollon and Scollon, 2001). Further, it is well known that polite behavior is conditioned by at least three factors: social distance (+/-D) (the degree of familiarity/distance with the interlocutor), social power (+/-P) (vertical relationships such as a boss–employee relationship), and the weight of imposition (e.g., can I borrow $10 dollars vs can I borrow $1,000 dollars). In general, while cultures may differ in their positive (Russians, Poles, Spaniards) or negative politeness orientation (U.S. Americans, British), politeness is better understood in terms of a continuum (ranging from more to less polite) within each culture.

It is also important to note that while certain linguistic expressions may express politeness (e.g., "thank you," "please"), it is the situation and the degree of social distance or power that determine whether these expressions are perceived as polite or not by the interlocutor.

Empirical work on linguistic politeness is evident in the production of speech acts such as requests (Márquez Reiter, 2000) and refusals (Félix-Brasdefer, 2008) among native speakers of English (England and U.S.) and Spanish (Uruguay and Mexico), respectively. In these studies politeness is realized through the use of mitigated or indirect requests or refusals with various degrees of tentativity (e.g., "*Could* I borrow ... " / "I'm sorry, but *unfortunately* I will be unable to attend your birthday party").

Appropriateness and politeness in interaction

In politeness research it is common to make the distinction between polite behavior and socially appropriate behavior. For example, politeness is associated with socially appropriate behavior to the extent in which it is understood in terms of a conversational contract (Fraser, 1990); that is, the rights and obligations that participants expect when they participate in social interaction. In this respect, if a person behaves according to the socially expected rules when interacting with a doctor or a stranger, the speaker is said to behave politely. However, Meier (1995) refers to socially appropriate language behavior as behavior that is expected in specific situations. For instance, certain address forms (e.g., "sir," "professor") may not be intrinsically more or less polite than others, but rather, they may express different degrees of deference in particular speech communities and are expected in certain situations. In contrast, overpoliteness alludes to excessive deference in a situation where less deference is expected. In Meier's view, socially appropriate behavior is considered one aspect of the framework of social interaction, where norms of appropriate behavior may vary across cultures.

Other researchers have adopted the post-modern view (the discursive approach) of politeness. Under this view, polite behavior represents one limited component of social interaction which is referred to as relational work that comprises the broader continuum of social interaction, ranging from appropriate (or politic) behavior to inappropriate or impolite behavior (Locher and Watts, 2005). Under the discursive approach, socially appropriate behavior refers to expected behavior that occurs in specific situations, whereas polite behavior refers to social behavior that is excessive (or over politic). For example, routine formulae (e.g., greetings) are considered part of socially appropriate behavior (as in Meier's [1995] view) because the selection of these forms in specific situations (e.g., greeting a friend) represents the expected socially appropriate behavior, and thus, does not represent polite behavior. However, if these forms are over emphasized during the course of an interaction, it is the interlocutor who may infer a polite interpretation. It should be noted that under the post-modern view, it is the hearer who decides whether something was interpreted as polite or not.

On the (revised) post-modern view, politeness represents one aspect of social interaction that emerges in and through interaction (Haugh, 2007). From this perspective, politeness (or impoliteness) is negotiated in social interaction and emerges through the joint participation of the speaker and the interlocutor during co-construction of meaning in social interaction. Politeness is analyzed both within the sequential interaction of talk (sequential context) and outside to include information with respect to the participants' roles and identities and information prior to the contex of the interaction. And, unlike politeness research that is conducted under the Brown and Levinson's universal politeness model, the discursive approach to politeness aims at analyzing natural data with longer stretches of talk, includes both the speaker and the hearer engaged in social interaction, tends to avoid generalizations of universality and normativity, and is mainly restricted to single cases of social interaction.

Politeness in a second language

The ability to behave politely or impolitely in a second language represents one aspect of the learners' communicative competence. The learners' ability to produce or perceive polite (or impolite) behavior is often studied in the field of second language pragmatics or interlanguage pragmatics through the analysis of speech acts such as requests or apologies. The analysis of politeness in a second language has mainly utilized Brown and Levinson's (1987) model of politeness and focuses on the linguistic expressions used to convey positive or negative politeness. For example, one of the earliest cross-sectional studies on the development of L2 requests is Scarcella's (1979) analysis of the emergence of polite features when performing English (role play) requests in two learner groups, one group of beginners and one advanced group. The author found that the learners' use of internal modifiers to express politeness in their requests (e.g., *please, maybe, kind of, I think*) improved with increasing proficiency.

Other studies have examined the learners' ability to produce (polite) refusals across various turns with various degrees of mitigation in interactions with native speakers of the target language (Félix-Brasdefer, 2004; Gass and Houck, 1999). Politeness is also examined in professor–student (non-native) advising sessions (Bardovi-Harlig and Hartford, 1993). In this setting, non-native speakers showed a lack of mitigation devices that soften the negative effects of a direct rejection (e.g., *kind of, probably, maybe)* when refusing a professor's advice, as well as a lack of initiated suggestions that predominated in the non-native speaker data. In this institutional context an unmitigated or direct rejection to advice by non-native speakers may be perceived as rude or impolite by the professor.

In conclusion, polite behavior is a social phenomenon that is realized through communicative and non-communicative actions between at least two interlocutors that engage in social interaction. What counts as polite (or impolite) behavior is the result of the speaker's and the hearer's negotiation of interpersonal meaning that is achieved in social interaction, as well as the hearer's perception of the speaker's utterances. Finally, although politeness research has been the center of attention, impoliteness, its evil twin, represents a central component of social interaction and should be discussed in theoretical and empirical research on politeness.

See also: communicative competence, discourse and pragmatics in SLA, pragmalinguistics, pragmatics, sociopragmatics, speech acts

References

Bardovi-Harlig, K. and B.S. Hartford (1993). Learning the rules of academic talk: A longitudinal study of pragmatic change. *Studies in Second Language Acquisition*, *15*, 279–304.

Blum-Kulka, S., J. House, and G. Kasper (eds) (1989). *Cross-Cultural Pragmatics: Request and Apologies*. Norwood, NJ: Ablex.

Brown, Penelope, and S.C. Levinson (1987). *Politeness: Some Universals in Language Usage*. Cambridge: Cambridge University Press (original publication in 1978).

Félix-Brasdefer, J.C. (2004). Interlanguage refusals: Linguistic politeness and length of residence in the target community. *Language Learning*, *54*(4), 587–653.

Félix-Brasdefer, J. César (2008). *Politeness in Mexico and the United States: A Contrastive Study of the Realization and Perception of Refusals*. Amsterdam: John Benjamins.

Fraser, B. (1990). Perspectives on politeness. *Journal of Pragmatics*, *14*, 219–36.

Gass, S. and N. Houck (1999). *Interlanguage Refusals: A Cross-Cultural Study of Japanese-English*. New York: Mouton de Gruyter.

Goffman, E. (1967). *Interaction Ritual: Essays on Face to Face Behavior*. Chicago, IL: Aldine Publishing Company.

Grice, H.P. (1975). Logic and conversation. In P. Cole and J. Morgan (eds), *Syntax and Semantics 3: Speech Acts*, pp. 41–58. New York: Academic Press.

Haugh, M. (2007). The discursive challenge to politeness research: An interactional alternative. *Journal of Politeness Research*, *3*, 295–317.

Lakoff, R. (1973). The logic of politeness; or, minding your p's and q's. In C. Corum, S. Cedric and A. Weiser (eds), *Papers from the Ninth Regional Meeting, Chicago Linguistic Society*, pp. 292–305. Chicago, IL: Chicago Linguistics Society.

Leech, G. (1983). *Principles of Pragmatics*. New York: Longman.

Locher, M. and R. Watts (2005). Politeness theory and relational work. *Journal of Politeness Research*, *1*, 9–33.

Márquez Reiter, R. (2000). *Linguistic Politeness in Britain and Uruguay: A Contrastive Study of Requests and Apologies* (Pragmatics and Beyond 83). Amsterdam and Philadelphia, PA: John Benjamins.

Meier, A. (1995). Defining politeness: Universality in appropriateness. *Language Sciences*, *17*(4), 345–56.

Ogiermann, E. (2009). *On Apologising in Negative and Positive Politeness Cultures*. Amsterdam and Philadelphia, PA: John Benjamins: Online Etymology Dictionary. Retrieved August 29, 2007, www.etymonline.com/.

Scarcella, R. (1979). On speaking politely in a second language. In C. Yorio, K. Perkins, and J. Schachter (eds), *On TESOL '79: The Learner in Focus* (pp. 275–87). Washington, DC: TESOL.

Scollon, R. and S.W. Scollon (2001). *Intercultural Communication: A Discourse Approach*. (Language in Society 21), 2nd edn. Malden, MA: Blackwell.

Watts, R. (2003). *Politeness*. Cambridge: Cambridge University Press.

Further reading

Bargiela-Chiappini, F. and M. Haugh (eds) (2009). *Face, Communication and Social Interaction*. London: Equinox.

Spencer-Oatey, H. (2000). Rapport management: A framework for analysis. In H. Spencer-Oatey (ed.), *Culturally Speaking: Managing Rapport through Talk across Cultures*, pp. 11–46. London: Continuum.

Positive and negative evidence

Shawn Loewen

Michigan State University

Positive evidence is the language available to learners in the surrounding input. Thus, it provides models and examples to learners of what is linguistically grammatical and acceptable in the target language. In contrast, negative evidence consists of information, either direct or indirect, about what is ungrammatical and unacceptable in the target language. Examples of positive and negative evidence come from White's (1991) study of English adverb placement. Learners of English may receive positive evidence regarding the grammaticality of sentences such as *Mary often watches television* or *John drinks his coffee quickly*. However, positive evidence does not demonstrate the unacceptability of sentences such as **Mary watches often television*. Instead, negative evidence provides information about ungrammaticality through, for example, a recast *Mary often watches television* or overt metalinguistic information *The adverb cannot occur between the verb and direct object*.

The necessity of positive evidence for both L1 and L2 learning is uncontroversial. Learners must receive input for acquisition to occur. However, controversy exists regarding the availability and role of negative evidence. Negative evidence is generally not provided to L1 learners, although some caregivers may reformulate children's erroneous utterances. Nevertheless, negative evidence can occur frequently in L2 learning contexts. As for utility, some theories, such as innatism or Universal Grammar (UG), maintain that positive evidence alone is necessary and sufficient for L2 acquisition; consequently, negative evidence plays no role (Schwartz, 1993). However, within these theories, some positions hold that negative evidence may be useful for learning difficult grammatical structures (White, 1991) or that it may play a role at certain stages of development (e.g., intermediate) but not at others (e.g., beginning or advanced) (Carroll, 2001).

In contrast to the limited role of negative evidence proposed by UG-based theories, other theories, such as the interactionist approach, suggest a more central role for negative evidence, given that positive evidence alone often does not result in target-like L2 proficiency (Long, 1996). Interactionists argue that negative evidence, particularly in the form of corrective feedback, can draw learners' attention to incorrect forms, thereby facilitating L2 acquisition. Research into reactive negative evidence has mushroomed in recent years, with synthetic analyses of existing research demonstrating that corrective feedback can be beneficial for L2 acquisition. However, debate remains regarding the most beneficial types of corrective feedback, with some researchers favoring input-providing feedback such as recasts, and others preferring output-prompting feedback. Furthermore, these various types of feedback differ in the types of evidence they provide learners. Output-prompting feedback offers only negative evidence, while input-providing feedback supplies both positive and negative evidence. At least one study (Leeman, 2003) suggests that the positive evidence provided in feedback may be more beneficial than the negative evidence. Controversy also surrounds the optimal degree of explicitness of negative evidence. Implicit feedback, such as recasts, simply juxtaposes the correct and incorrect forms, assuming that learners will notice the difference between the two forms. On the other hand, explicit feedback involves direct and overt identification of the ungrammatical item. Research into these varying characteristics of negative evidence is ongoing.

See also: corrective feedback, input enhancement, Interaction and the Interaction Hypothesis, Noticing Hypothesis, recasts, Universal Grammar (UG) and SLA

References

Carroll, S. (2001). *Input and Evidence: The Raw Material of Second Language Acquisition*. Amsterdam: John Benjamins.

Leeman, J. (2003). Recasts and second language development: Beyond negative evidence. *Studies in Second Language Acquisition*, *25*, 37–63.

Long, M. (1996). The role of linguistic environment in second language acquisition. In W.C. Ritchie and T.K. Bhatia (eds), *Handbook of Second Language Acquisition*, pp. 413–468. San Diego, CA: Academic Press.

Schwartz, B. (1993). On explicit and negative data effecting and affecting competence and linguistic behaviour. *Studies in Second Language Acquisition*, *15*, 147–63.

White, L. (1991). Adverb placement in second language acquisition: Some effects of positive and negative evidence in the classroom. *Second Language Research*, *7*, 133–61.

Pragmalinguistics

Kenneth R. Rose
City University of Hong Kong

Pragmalinguistics is usually discussed alongside sociopragmatics. As Thomas (1983) notes, this division "parallels Leech's (1983) division of linguistics into 'grammar' (by which he means the decontextualized formal system of language) and 'pragmatics' (the use of language in a goal-oriented speech situation in which S [the speaker] is using language in order to produce a particular effect in the mind of H [the hearer])." Pragmalinguistics, then, is the study of form-function mappings, while sociopragmatics involves the application of social context information to making the most appropriate choice for a specific context/occasion given the options available. For example, linguistic forms in English that comprise the inventory of those items that can be used to perform requests include the modals *can*, *could*, *will*, and *would (you mind)*, among others. Also included are various mitigating devices, such as *please* or supportive moves, which can take an infinite number of linguistic forms. (For a detailed account of the various pragmalinguistic elements of requests and apologies, see the coding manual for these speech acts in Blum-Kulka, House and Kasper, 1989.) So an individual's pragmalinguistic competence is his/her knowledge of these form-function mappings. Sociopragmatic competence, on the other hand, is demonstrated by an individual's deployment of the most appropriate (and thus potentially most effective) linguistic realization of the desired speech act.

Imagine a situation in which you are sitting in class next to a classmate with whom you have a fairly close relationship. Given the context and the relationship, uttering the following request would reflect well on your pragmalinguistic competence, but not so well on your sociopragmatic competence:

> I'm really sorry to bother you, but I had to leave my apartment rather quickly this morning, and I forgot to bring my book bag that has all of my pens and pencils in it, so I don't have anything to write with. Would it be possible to borrow a pen or pencil from you, I mean, if you have an extra one? I'll take good care of it, and give it right back after class, I promise. And I'll remember to bring my book bag next time!

This request is absolutely brimming with evidence of pragmalinguistic competence, while at the same time a signal failure in terms of sociopragmatics—for this context. A simple "Can you lend me a pen?," "Got an extra pen?" or even "Give me a pen" would suffice here. However, if you change the situation to a faculty meeting in which the recently arrived Dean, whom you have never met, takes a seat next to you after introducing a guest speaker, then the request becomes a marvel of sociopragmatic savvy.

While our knowledge of pragmalinguistic and sociopragmatic development in second language acquisition is necessarily limited by the current state of interlanguage pragmatics, which as Bardovi-Harlig (1999) pointed out is "fundamentally not acquisitional" (p. 679), studies to date have yielded one fairly robust finding: pragmalinguistic development appears to precede sociopragmatic development, and often by a large margin. This was established in an early study by Scarcella (1979), who investigated the politeness strategies of beginning and advanced learners of English. She found (among other things) that her participants appeared to acquire politeness forms before acquiring the rules for their appropriate use, thereby putting pragmalinguistics before sociopragmatics. We have also seen little evidence of sociopragmatic development in foreign-language contexts, despite evidence of considerable pragmalinguistic competence. For example, in two cross-sectional studies involving learners of English in Hong Kong at two-year intervals from ages 7 through 17 (six groups altogether), Rose (2000, 2009) found evidence of pragmalinguistic competence in even the youngest learners (e.g., 'Can we McDonalds' as a request to be taken for lunch by their father), as well as evidence of pragmalinguistic development (e.g., movement from reliance on direct requests in the earliest stages to more conventional indirectness later on), but virtually no evidence of sociopragmatic competence or development. There is, however, at least one study in which sociopragmatics appears to have outpaced pragmalinguistics. Bardovi-Harlig and Hartford (1993) conducted a longitudinal study of the development of suggestions and rejections by adult learners of English in academic advising sessions. Over time, their participants more closely approximated native speaker norms for appropriate speech act choice but not for appropriate form, thus favoring sociopragmatics over pragmalinguistics. Tellingly, this study was conducted in an English-speaking environment, where learners have ample opportunity—even the necessity—to communicate in real-world situations with higher stakes than anything found in the classroom, which is something foreign language learners lack.

The lack of sociopragmatic development in foreign language contexts raises the issue of teaching pragmalinguistics and sociopragmatics. To date, such efforts have been hampered by, among other things, our lack of knowledge concerning pragmatics and how learners develop competence in this important aspect of language. Rose (1994, 1997, 1999, 2001) has advocated the use of consciousness-raising/input enhancement approach (Sharwood-Smith, 1981, 1993), assisted by the use of examples from film and television. However, as Thomas (1983) has pointed out, the teaching of sociopragmatics is a far more delicate affair than instruction in pragmalinguistics—where the latter is akin to the learning of grammar rules, the former amounts to teaching people how to behave appropriately, which is something that should be done with delicacy (if at all).

See also: communicative competence, formulaic language, identity theory, linguistic transfer, politeness, second language socialization

References

Bardovi-Harlig, K. (1999). Exploring the interlanguage of interlanguage pragmatics: A research agenda for acquisitional pragmatics. *Language Learning*, *49*, 677–713.

Bardovi-Harlig, K. and Hartford, B. (1993). Learning the rules of academic talk: A longitudinal study of pragmatic change. *Studies in Second Language Acquisition*, *15*, 279–304.

Blum-Kulka, S., House, J. and Kasper, G. (eds) (1989). *Cross-cultural Pragmatics: Requests and Apologies*. Norwood, NJ: Ablex.

Leech, G. (1983). *The Principles of Pragmatics*. London: Longman.

Rose, K. (1994). Pragmatic consciousness-raising in an EFL context. In L. Bouton and Y. Kachru (eds), *Pragmatics and Language Learning*, Monograph Series vol. 5, pp. 52–63. Urbana-Champaign, IL: Division of English as an International Language, University of Illinois, Urbana-Champaign.

——(1997). Pragmatics in foreign-language teacher education: A consciousness-raising approach. *Language, Culture and Curriculum*, *10*, 125–38.

——(1999). Teachers and students learning about requests in Hong Kong. In E. Hinkel (ed.), *Culture in Second Language Teaching and Learning*, pp. 167–80. Cambridge: Cambridge University Press.

——(2000). An exploratory cross-sectional study of interlanguage pragmatic development. *Studies in Second Language Acquisition*, *22*, 27–67.

——(2001). Compliments and compliment responses in film: Implications for pragmatics research and language teaching. *International Review of Applied Linguistics*, *39*, 309–26.

——(2009). A cross-sectional study of pragmatic development in Hong Kong, Phase 2. *Journal of Pragmatics*, *41*, 2345–64.

Scarcella, R. (1979). On speaking politely in a second language. In C. Yorio, K. Perkins and J. Schachter (eds), *On TESOL '79: The Learner in Focus*, pp. 274–87. Washington, DC: TESOL.

Sharwood Smith, M. (1981). Consciousness-raising and the second language learner. *Applied Linguistics*, *7*, 239–56.

——(1993). Input enhancement in instructed SLA: Theoretical bases. *Studies in Second Language Acquisition*, *15*, 165–79.

Thomas, J. (1983). Cross-cultural pragmatic failure. *Applied Linguistics*, *4*, 91–112.

Pragmatics

Kenneth R. Rose
City University of Hong Kong

The first reference to pragmatics is generally attributed to Morris (1938), who in his division of semiotics into syntax, semantics and (of course) pragmatics defined pragmatics as the relation of signs to their users. Mey (1993) defines pragmatics as "the societally necessary and consciously interactive dimension of the study of language" (p. 315), a definition which does not identify any particular objects for study, but rather conceptualizes pragmatics as a perspective on the linguistic enterprise. Crystal (1997) offers a more specific view when he delineates pragmatics as "the study of language from the point of view of users, especially of the choices they make, the constraints they encounter in using language in social interaction and the effects their use of language has on other participants in the act of communication" (p. 301). Pragmatic meanings arise from choices between linguistic forms, such as using one discourse marker or particle over another, or opting for one linguistic form of a communicative act instead of a contextually possible alternative to convey illocutionary force or politeness (e.g., for requests, "Give me a pencil" vs "I don't seem to have anything to write with"). These choices are constrained by social conventions which can be bent to different, contextually varying degrees but ignored only at the risk of loss of face or insider status, or even possible questions about one's sanity. (The next time someone asks "Do you know what time it is?", try answering "Yes" and see what happens.)

In its journey from philosophy (Austin, 1962; Grice, 1975; Searle, 1969), through theoretical linguistics (Bach and Harnish, 1979; Morgan, 1978), and finally on to second language acquisition (Kasper and Rose, 1999, 2002; Rose and Kasper, 2001), pragmatics has been something of a third wheel, never attracting as much attention as areas like phonology or syntax. This is evidenced by the fact that perhaps the most widely used introductory second language acquisition text in the past decade or so—Lightbown and Spada's *How Languages are Learned*—did not include pragmatics as an aspect of learner language development until the third edition was published in 2006. But this is not altogether without reason.

By analogy with interlanguage grammar, interlanguage phonology, and the interlanguage lexicon, pragmatics in second language acquisition is usually referred to as interlanguage pragmatics, which can be roughly divided into two areas. As the study of second language use, interlanguage pragmatics examines how nonnative speakers comprehend and produce action in a target language. As the study of second language learning, interlanguage pragmatics investigates how second language learners develop the ability to understand and perform action in a target language. Second language researchers have been studying nonnative speakers' pragmatic abilities for almost three decades now, but for the most part this has been approached as an issue of second language use, not development. In fact, this state of affairs led Bardovi-Harlig (1999) to observe that "not only [is] interlanguage pragmatics not fundamentally acquisitional, but it [is], in fact, fundamentally not acquisitional" (p. 679). This is undesirable because the importance accorded to pragmatic ability surely must be met with a commensurate curiosity regarding the ways such ability develops, whether to better understand the different uses to which such ability is put, to cultivate second language pragmatic development as a domain within second language acquisition research, or to establish a research basis for instruction in second language pragmatics. Focusing solely on pragmatic production contributes little to any of these goals.

The seminal study largely responsible for putting pragmatics on the radar of second language acquisition researchers was the Cross Cultural Speech Act Realization Project (CCSARP). First reported in Blum-Kulka and Olshtain (1984) and later in Blum-Kulka, House and Kasper (1989), the CCSARP was a large-scale project designed to examine crosscultural and contextual variability in the production of requests and apologies by native and non-native speakers of a wide range of languages, including English (several varieties, native and nonnative), Spanish, French, Danish, German and Hebrew. The breadth of the CCSARP inspired researchers to carry out similar work on languages not covered (e.g., Rose, 1992, 1994), and provided these researchers with a very good "etic" coding manual for requests and apologies. However, one persistent negative impact of the CCSARP is its introduction to a wider audience of the rather unsophisticated use of discourse completion tasks (DCTs) for a single-moment research design (Cook, 1993), an approach that became—and remains to this day—the prevailing model in interlanguage pragmatics research. The resulting glut of single-moment DCT studies cannot provide much useful data in efforts to understand the acquisition of second language pragmatics, and too few interlanguage pragmaticians seem to possess much awareness of this fact. Instead, the debate has often been characterized by clear misunderstandings of research methodology.

As a type of questionnaire, DCTs cannot provide information regarding actual language use. Questionnaires do not directly measure linguistic action, so expecting them to do so, or criticizing them for not doing so, misses the point. Only the observation of action in context can tell us what people actually say and do, whereas DCTs prompt self-reports of (usually hypothetical) action. Of course, this does not mean that they are therefore useless for pragmatics. DCTs are effective in collecting information on language users' pragmalinguistic and sociopragmatic knowledge, which is brought to bear in actual language use. They can provide us with information on the range of conventions of means (semantic formulas) and form by which linguistic acts are carried out in a language and the types and factors of context associated with their use. DCTs could be an effective instrument to investigate, at a more detailed level than has usually been the case thus far, the conventionalized pragmalinguistic functions (both illocutionary and politeness) of morphosyntax and lexis, or pragmatic routines. In languages which rely heavily on routine formulas, such as Arabic or Japanese, DCTs have rich potential for eliciting standard responses to a wide range of situations. Such work would contribute significantly to the pragmalinguistics of individual languages, contrastive pragmatics, and interlanguage pragmatics, both from the perspective of second language use and development. DCTs—preferably in conjunction with other data collection procedures—are useful in examining the relationship between learners' development of L2 grammar and pragmatics, a rather neglected research issue that deserves much more attention, as Bardovi-Harlig (1999) has pointed out. In order to investigate these sorts of issues, then, DCTs are an appropriate and valuable tool. Unfortunately, it seems that most interlanguage pragmaticians employing DCTs as their main (or often only) data collection instrument do not evidence an awareness of these facts. While the literature does offer some signs of progress (e.g., Jucker, 2009; Rose, 2009), these appear to be more concentrated in the assessment of pragmatic competence (e.g., Liu, 2006; Roever, 2008), not the study of its development.

In another early influential paper, Kasper and Schmidt (1996) posited the following key questions about interlanguage pragmatics that would require research for interlanguage pragmatics to warrant inclusion within second language acquisition:

1. Are there universals of language underlying crosslinguistic variation, and if so, do they play a role in interlanguage pragmatics?
2. How can approximation to target language norms be measured?
3. Does the L1 influence the learning of a second language?
4. Is pragmatic development in a second language similar to first language learning?
5. Do children enjoy an advantage over adults in learning a second language?
6. Is there a natural route of development, as evidenced by difficulty, accuracy, acquisition orders, or discrete stages of development?
7. Does type of input make a difference?
8. Does instruction make a difference?
9. Do motivation and attitudes make a difference in level of acquisition?
10. Does personality play a role?
11. Does learners' gender play a role?
12. Does (must) perception or comprehension precede production in acquisition?

Although efforts have been made to answer some of these questions, most of these areas have not provided the object of analysis for many studies in interlanguage pragmatics, and, sadly, when they have the results have often been less than satisfactory. This is despite the fact that more than two decades ago, Schmidt (1983) observed that "what is new, in fact just beginning, is systematic study of the actual acquisition of communicative abilities by nonnative speakers" (p. 138).

There are, however, a few bright spots in the ever-expanding interlanguage pragmatics literature. For example, on the issue of developmental sequences (Kasper and Schmidt's Question #6), Kasper and Rose (2002), based largely on longitudinal work by Schmidt (1983), R. Ellis (1992), and Achiba (2002), identify what appears to be a robust five-stage developmental route for the learning of requests by non-native speakers that be characterized generally as a move from reliance on routine formulas in the earliest stages of development to a gradual introduction of analyzed, productive language use. In the first stage of request development (pre-basic), learners' utterances convey requestive intent through highly context-dependent, minimalist realizations, expressing the intended reference and illocution but no relational or social goals. In the second stage (formulaic), requests are mainly performed by means of unanalyzed routines and imperatives. The third stage (unpacking) brings with it the unpacking of routine formulas that then become increasingly available for productive use, and more frequent use of conventional indirectness, while the fourth stage (pragmatic) brings with it the addition of new forms to learners' pragmalinguistic repertoires, as well as increased use of mitigation, and more complex syntax. The final stage (fine-tuning) is characterized by the fine-tuning of requestive force to participants, goals, and contexts.

However, despite the identification of a possible developmental sequence for requests (and perhaps one or two other pragmatic constructs), it is clear that interlanguage pragmatics has barely come of age as a bona fide subject for second language acquisition researchers. One measure of the coming-of-age of a discipline is when the accumulated research is of a quality and quantity that it allows for productive use of quantitative meta-analysis to establish prevailing trends across studies. Such was the case for the quantitative meta-analysis of studies on the effects of instruction in second language acquisition carried out by Norris and Ortega (2000), who found (among other things) that explicit instruction in second language acquisition yielded durable gains. A similar attempted meta-analysis of research on the effects of instruction in second language pragmatics by Jeon and Tadayoshi (2006) did not yield such promising results. In fact, as they note, "the value of a meta-analysis is dependent on the soundness of the research practices in a given research domain that precede synthesis of that domain. The shortcomings of the present study can be seen as an inevitable result of weaknesses in the practices that predominate in the domain of L2 pragmatic instructional research to date" (p. 202). It is fair to say that these results were—and remain to this day—indicative of the state of the field.

In sum, then, pragmatics as language use in social contexts has attracted some attention in second language acquisition, but nothing yet that is either comparable to other research areas (e.g., phonology, syntax) or commensurate with its importance for communication. And it is also fair to say that the existing literature provides more information concerning the pragmatic production of second language learners, falling far short in the efforts to understand how learners acquire this pragmatic competence they have been observed to deploy. Until researchers in pragmatics shift the focus to pragmatic development and become more savvy regarding research methodology—in particular the (mis)use of DCTs—there is not much indication that the situation will improve.

See also: cross-sectional research, development in SLA, developmental sequences, discourse and pragmatics in SLA, discourse completion tasks, speech acts

References

Achiba, M. (2003). *Learning to Request in a Second Language: A Study of Child Interlanguage Pragmatics*. Clevedon: Multilingual Matters.

Austin, J. (1962). *How to do Things with Words*. Oxford: Oxford University Press.

Bach, K. and Harnish, M. (1979). *Linguistic Communication and Speech Acts*. Cambridge, MA: MIT Press.

Bardovi-Harlig, K. (1999). Exploring the interlanguage of interlanguage pragmatics: A research agenda for acquisitional pragmatics. *Language Learning*, *49*, 677–713.

Blum-Kulka, S., House, J. and Kasper, G. (eds) (1989). *Cross-cultural Pragmatics: Requests and Apologies*. Norwood, NJ: Ablex.

Blum-Kulka, S. and Olshtain, E. (1984). Requests and apologies: A cross-cultural study of speech act realization patterns (CCSARP). *Applied Linguistics*, *5*, 196–213.

Cook, V. (1993). *Linguistics and Second Language Acquisition*. New York: St. Martin's Press.

Crystal, D. (1997). *The Cambridge Encyclopedia of Language*, second edn. New York: Cambridge University Press.

Ellis, R. (1992). Learning to communicate in the classroom: A study of two learners' requests. *Studies in Second Language Acquisition*, *14*, 1–23.

Grice, P. (1975). Logic and conversation. In P. Cole and J. Morgan (eds), *Syntax and semantics, vol. 3: Speech Acts*, pp. 41–58. New York: Academic Press.

Jeon, E. and Tadayoshi, K. (2006). Effects of L2 instruction on interlanguage pragmatic development. In J. Norris and L. Ortega (eds), *Synthesizing Research on Language Learning and Teaching*, pp. 165–211. Amsterdam: John Benjamins.

Jucker, A. (2009). Speech act research between armchair, field and laboratory: The case of compliments. *Journal of Pragmatics*, *41*, 1611–35.

Kasper, G. and Rose, K. (1999). Pragmatics and second language acquisition. *Annual Review of Applied Linguistics*, *19*, 81–104.

——(2002). *Pragmatic Development in a Second Language*. Oxford: Blackwell.

Kasper, G. and Schmidt, R. (1996). Developmental issues in interlanguage pragmatics. *Studies in Second Language Acquisition*, *18*, 149–69.

Lightbown, P. and Spada, N. (2006). *How Languages are Learned*, third edn. Oxford: Oxford University Press.

Liu, J. (2006). *Measuring Interlanguage Pragmatic Knowledge of EFL Learners*. Frankfurt: Peter Lang.

Mey, J. (1993). *Pragmatics: An Introduction*. Oxford: Blackwell.

Morgan, J. (1978). Two types of convention in indirect speech acts. In P. Cole (ed.), *Syntax and Semantics, vol. 9: Pragmatics*, pp. 261–80. New York: Academic Press.

Morris, C. (1938). Foundations of the theory of signs. In O. Neurath, C. Carnap and C. Morris (eds), *International Encyclopedia of Unified Science*, pp. 77–138. Chicago, IL: University of Chicago Press.

Norris, J. and Ortega, L. (2000). Effectiveness of L2 instruction: A research synthesis and quantitative meta-analysis. *Language Learning*, *50*, 417–528.

Roever, C. (2008). Rater, item and candidate effects in discourse completion tests: A FACETS approach. In E. Alcón Soler and A. Martínez-Flor (eds), *Investigating Pragmatics in Foreign Language Learning, Teaching and Testing*, pp. 249–66. Bristol: Multilingual Matters.

Rose, K. (1992). Speech acts and questionnaires: The effect of hearer response. *Journal of Pragmatics*, *17*, 49–62.

——(1994). On the validity of DCTs in non-western contexts. *Applied Linguistics*, *15*, 1–14.

——(2009). A cross-sectional study of pragmatic development in Hong Kong, Phase 2. *Journal of Pragmatics*, *41*, 2345–64.

Rose, K. and Kasper, G. (2001). *Pragmatics in Language Teaching*. New York: Cambridge University Press.

Schmidt, R. (1983). Interaction, acculturation, and the acquisition of communicative competence: A case study of one adult. In N. Wolfson and E. Judd (eds), *Sociolinguistics and Language Acquisition*, pp. 137–74. Rowley, MA: Newbury House.

Searle, J. (1969). *Speech Acts: An Essay in the Philosophy of Language*. Cambridge: Cambridge University Press.

Priming

Pavel Trofimovich and
Kim McDonough
Concordia University

The term "priming" refers to a cognitive repetition phenomenon in which prior exposure to specific language forms or meaning facilitates speakers' subsequent language processing. For example, if a speaker hears a particular word spoken by her interlocutor, she is likely to comprehend and produce this word faster and more accurately when it is used again in the same conversation. Similarly, if a speaker uses a specific grammatical structure, later in the conversation his interlocutor is likely to produce that same structure rather than a different one. In essence, priming shows that prior experience with language shapes a speaker's subsequent language use, which suggests that priming may underlie interactive, communicative uses of language. Because priming usually occurs with little awareness and without much explicit, conscious effort on the part of a language user, researchers often interpret priming as a form of implicit learning.

Priming encompasses a variety of related phenomena, including auditory, phonetic, phonological, morphological, syntactic, semantic, associative, and orthographic priming. Despite differences in the aspect of language that is affected (namely, which meanings or forms), all types of priming explore the influence of prior language use on subsequent performance. Because a comprehensive review of all priming types is beyond the scope of this entry, we briefly outline two types of priming (auditory and syntactic) in more detail and highlight their applications to second language (L2) acquisition and teaching. More detailed information about priming, including additional references to priming research, are available in recent reviews of the priming literature by McNamara (2005), McDonough and Trofimovich (2008), and Pickering and Ferreira (2008).

Auditory and syntactic priming

Auditory priming describes the tendency for people to process a spoken word more quickly and more accurately when they have had previous exposure to that word, compared to a word that was not previously heard. For instance, if speakers hear a word like "hypothesis" in their interlocutor's speech, they will be more likely to understand this word and respond to it more quickly and accurately, compared to a word that their interlocutor did not use. Several studies have shown that L2 learners rely on auditory priming in learning how to pronounce L2 vocabulary (Bird and Williams, 2002; Trofimovich and Gatbonton, 2006). Thus, learners can learn something from their previous experiences with language, and can draw upon this knowledge when they subsequently perceive and produce these words.

Syntactic priming refers to the tendency for speakers to produce a syntactic structure that appeared in the recent discourse, as opposed to an alternative. For instance, if a speaker uses a passive structure (*the votes were tallied*), later in the conversation her interlocutor is likely to produce a new utterance with the passive (*the results were announced*) rather than an alternative structure, such as an active construction (*the officials announced the results*). Several L2 studies have demonstrated that syntactic priming occurs in L2 speech production (Gries, 2005; Schoonbaert, Hartsuiker, and Pickering, 2007) and that it may facilitate the subsequent use of targetlike structures as opposed to simple or erroneous structures (McDonough and Mackey, 2008).

Because both auditory and syntactic priming describe how prior exposure to specific aspects of language influence subsequent language use, they are often described as *repetition* phenomena. In the case of auditory priming, repetition involves the phonological form of words (e.g., the sound sequence and stress pattern of the word "hypothesis"). In syntactic priming, repetition involves the syntactic frame of an utterance (e.g., the word order and verbs in the passive structures). For both types of priming, the benefits of repetition tend to be implicit and represent a form of implicit learning, or learning without much conscious effort and awareness.

Priming and L2 acquisition

As implicit learning phenomena, both auditory and syntactic priming have enormous potential to help researchers understand the processes by which L2 learners acquire vocabulary, pronunciation, and grammar. At the theoretical level, priming can help researchers test claims about the processes involved in L2 learning. For example, one established theoretical view of L2 learning—the Interaction Hypothesis—holds that communication between learners (or between learners and more proficient speakers) facilitates L2 learning in part by engaging cognitive learning mechanisms (Long, 1996). By exploring the relationship between collaborative priming activities and learners' subsequent performance, researchers can test whether priming is one of the cognitive learning mechanisms that may help learners benefit from interaction.

Priming may also be used to test theoretical claims associated with usage-based approaches to acquisition (Bybee, 2008; Goldberg and Casenhiser, 2008), which hold that the learning of language form (sounds, words, and structures) unfolds as learners detect patterns in the input. The complexity of those patterns evolves over time and is influenced in part by the frequency features associated with individual words or structures. With respect to L2 pronunciation, the logic is that certain aspects of speech (e.g., specific sounds, stress patterns) are easier to learn when they occur within and across recurrent familiar words. The more frequently learners experience a given pronunciation pattern in the input, especially across a range of words, the more accurately they will perceive and produce this pattern (Bybee, 2008; Pierrehumbert, 2003). In turn, for L2 grammar, learners initially learn a structure, such as the passive in English, by associating it with a handful of verbs in high-frequency utterances (such as "bear", as in "I was born in … "). Eventually, through exposure to passive sentences with more diverse verbs, learners develop more extensive and abstract knowledge of the passive structure (Goldberg and Casenhiser, 2008). By devising priming activities that manipulate the type and token frequencies of the target structures, researchers can test claims about the acquisition of constructions.

Researchers working within knowledge-based approaches to acquisition can use priming as a tool to explore the acquisition of a complex skill. As summarized by DeKeyser (2007) in his Skill Acquisition Theory, learning of any complex skill proceeds from initial knowledge representation to changes in behavior, and eventually results in fluent, effortless, and highly skilled (proceduralized, automatized) performance. As an implicit phenomenon, priming can contribute to the development of fluent, effortless, and highly skilled L2 comprehension (through repeated exposure to forms and meanings in input) and L2 production (through the elicitation of repeated forms and meanings in output). In sum, researchers who investigate the development of automaticity can use priming as a way to explore the process by which linguistic knowledge becomes proceduralized.

To take another example, priming can be helpful for researchers who investigate the role of attention in L2 acquisition (Robinson, 2003). The idea here is that learners need to attend to certain linguistic forms in the input in order to learn them, and that providing opportunities for learners to attend to formal features of language is beneficial for linguistic development. As a repetition phenomenon, priming may serve as a form-focusing device that underlies learning. In other words, through exposure to repeated forms and meanings in comprehension and production, learners may progressively shift their attention from meaning-related properties of the input (as the meaning of each utterance used becomes progressively more familiar with its every repetition) to its form-related properties. Therefore, priming might help researchers understand how linguistic information is detected and acquired during language comprehension and production.

Priming and L2 teaching

At a more practical level, priming tasks may help L2 teachers create learning opportunities during classroom interaction. For example, teachers could design and use auditory priming tasks to promote the encoding of phonological information in the mental lexicon, or to encourage the acquisition of novel words. And teachers could explore whether the effectiveness of auditory priming activities is influenced by task features, such as the number of times words are spoken or by the use of single or multiple speakers to present novel L2 words. Auditory priming tasks that present forms in larger discourse units (e.g., embedded in phrases or sentences) may be a useful tool for L2 pronunciation training, particularly for forms that are highly variable. Since variation in pitch, accent, and intonation are often context specific, auditory priming tasks that reflect this variation may be an effective way to help learners generalize across multiple, non-identical spoken words.

Similarly, the use of syntactic priming tasks in L2 classrooms has potential to build upon the existing task literature that has compared effectiveness of communicative tasks at eliciting interactional feedback, modified output, and attention to form. Communicative syntactic priming tasks may be useful for L2 learning because they simultaneously model and elicit target structures. By doing so, syntactic priming tasks may help allay concerns that learners will "pick up" interlanguage forms during peer interaction, particularly in large classes where teachers may have more difficulty monitoring and providing feedback. Thus far, few syntactic priming activities have been designed for use in teacher–learner interaction in a whole-class setting or for peer interaction (see McDonough and Chaikitmongkol, 2010, for some examples). These types of tasks might be particularly useful in contexts where peer interaction is difficult to implement, such as in L2 classes with large enrollments.

See also: attention, construction learning, implicit learning, Interaction and the Interaction Hypothesis, L2 phonology, psycholinguistics of SLA

References

Bird, S. and Williams, J. (2002). The effect of Bimodal input on implicit and explicit memory: An investigation into the benefits of within language subtitling. *Applied Psycholinguistics*, *23*, 509–33.

Bybee, J. (2008). Usage-based grammar and second language acquisition. In P. Robinson and N. Ellis (eds), *Handbook of Cognitive Linguistics and Second Language Acquisition*. New York: Routledge.

DeKeyser, R. (2007). Skill acquisition theory. In B. VanPatten and J. Williams (eds), *Theories in Second Language Acquisition*. Mahwah, NJ: Lawrence Erlbaum.

Goldberg, A. and Casenhiser, D. (2008). Construction learning and second language acquisition. In P. Robinson and N. Ellis (eds), *Handbook of Cognitive Linguistics and Second Language Acquisition*. New York: Routledge.

Gries, S. (2005). Syntactic priming: A corpus-based approach. *Journal of Psycholinguistic Research*, *34*, 365–99.

Long, M. (1996). The role of the linguistic environment in second language acquisition. In W. Ritchie and T. Bhatia (eds), *Handbook of Language Acquisition: Vol. 2. Second Language Acquisition*. San Diego, CA: Academic Press.

McDonough, K. and Chaikitmongkol, W. (2010). Collaborative syntactic priming activities and EFL Learners' production of *Wh*-questions. *Canadian Modern Language Review*, *66*, 817–42.

——and Mackey, A. (2008). Syntactic priming and ESL question development. *Studies in Second Language Acquisition*, *30*, 31–47.

——and Trofimovich, P. (2008). *Using Priming Methods in Second Language Research*. New York: Routledge.

McNamara, T.P. (2005). *Semantic Priming: Perspectives from Memory and Word Recognition*. New York: Psychology Press.

Pickering, M. and Ferreira, V. (2008). Structural Priming: A Critical Review. *Psychological Bulletin*, *134*, 427–59.

Pierrehumbert, J.B. (2003). Probabilistic Phonology: Discrimination and Robustness. In R. Bod, J. Hay, and S. Jannedy (eds), *Probabilistic Linguistics*. Cambridge, MA: MIT Press.

Robinson, P. (2003). Attention and memory during SLA. In C.J. Doughty and M.H. Long (eds), *Handbook of Second Language Acquisition*. Malden, MA: Blackwell.

Schoonbaert, S., Hartsuiker, R. and Pickering, M. (2007). The representation of lexical and syntactic Information in Bilinguals: Evidence from Syntactic Priming. *Journal of Memory and Language*, *56*, 153–71.

Trofimovich, P. and Gatbonton, E. (2006). Repetition and Focus on Form in L2 Spanish word processing: Implications for pronunciation instruction. *The Modern Language Journal*, *90*, 519–35.

Further reading

Bowers, J.S. and Marsolek, C.J. (eds) (2003). *Rethinking Implicit Memory*. Oxford: Oxford University Press. (A book which brings together various theoretical views on implicit memory, including priming.)

Kinoshita, S. and Lupker, S.J. (eds) (2003). *Masked Priming: The State of the Art*. New York: Psychology Press. (An edited collection of studies on the use of the masked priming paradigm in language research.)

Trofimovich, P. and McDonough, K. (eds) (in press). *Applying Priming Methods to L2 Learning, Teaching and Research: Insights from Psycholinguistics*. Amsterdam: John Benjamins. (An edited volume featuring a collection of empirical studies employing priming methods to investigate L2 learning and teaching.)

Private speech

María C.M. de Guerrero
Inter American University of Puerto Rico

As distinct from social speech, private speech is speech addressed to oneself, rather to others. It is speech that serves intramental—rather than intermental—cognitive and communicative functions. Usually low in volume (but at times loud enough to be overheard), private speech tends to be elliptical and condensed in form but rich in meaning. Because of its significant role in psycholinguistic activity and development, private speech has become a highly interesting phenomenon in SLA, particularly within the Vygotskyan sociocultural theory approach (Lantolf and Thorne, 2006).

For Vygotsky (1986), private speech—"egocentric speech" in his writings—was a transitional phase between social and inner speech. Characteristic of pre-school children, private speech was for Vygotsky symptomatic of the ongoing process of internalization of external, cultural tools of mediation. In this phase, speech takes on a new, thinking, self-regulatory function, in addition to its former social, communicative one. Eventually, private speech evolves into inner speech as the person is capable of cognitively functioning on the basis of silent verbal thinking. People past the age of childhood, however, continue to resort to overt private speech mediation to regulate themselves, most commonly in situations of cognitive difficulty.

The emergence of private speech has been observed not only among monolingual children but also among bilinguals and learners of additional languages, including children, adolescents, and adults. In other words, there is robust evidence that learners in the process of acquiring an alternate language also self-vocalize in this language. As in monolingual L1 development, it is believed that private speech in the L2 signals the internalization of this language as a tool for individual psychological use.

Researchers (see literature reviews in Guerrero, 2005; Lantolf and Thorne, 2006) have documented several uses of L2 private speech in classroom contexts: responding vicariously to teachers' questions or prompts, close repetition and transformative imitation of others' utterances, manipulation of language forms and meanings, rehearsal before speaking publicly, and display of metalinguistic awareness. These forms of private speech appear to have an internalizing role, providing learners the opportunity to play with and appropriate elements of the L2, reinforce existing knowledge, and creatively extend the L2 to possible or imaginary scenarios. In Ohta (2001), for example, a college student of Japanese selects part of a teacher's utterance to work covertly on verb conjugations:

TEACHER: Ah: ja onaka suite inai n desu ka: Onaka? [*Okay isn't your stomach empty: Stomach?*]

LEARNER: (after a few turns, whispering to himself) Suite inai? (.) Suite imase:n. [*Isn't empty? (uses informal negator 'nai') (.) isn't empty? (uses formal negator 'masen')*] (pp. 61–62, transcription notations slightly adapted from the original)

In addition to the internalizing function, private speech has been found to serve as a self-regulatory mechanism for learners engaged in solving challenging cognitive tasks which require use of the L2 (see, for example, Centeno-Cortés and Jiménez, 2004). This type of private speech provides important insights into the role and nature of the L2 in cognitive activity as well as into the extent to which learners rely on their L1 or L2 to mediate thinking.

See also: awareness, individual differences in SLA, Output hypothesis, social and sociocultural approaches to SLA, sociocognitive approaches to SLA, turn taking

References

Centeno-Cortés, B. and Jiménez, A. (2004). Problem-solving tasks in a foreign language: The importance of the L1 in private verbal thinking. *International Journal of Applied Linguistics, 14(1)*, 7–35.

Guerrero, M.C. M. de. (2005). *Inner Speech – L2. Thinking Words in a Second Language*. New York: Springer.

Lantolf, J.P. and Thorne, S.L. (2006). *Sociocultural Theory and the Genesis of Second Language Development*. New York: Oxford University Press.

Ohta, A.S. (2001). *Second Language Acquisition Processes in the Classroom. Learning Japanese*. Mahwah, NJ: Erlbaum.

Vygotsky, L.S. (1986). *Thought and Language*. Cambridge, MA: MIT Press.

Further reading

Centeno-Cortés, B. (2003). *Private Speech in the Second Language Classroom: Its Role in Internalization and Its link to Social Production*. Unpublished doctoral dissertation, Pennsylvania State University. (In-depth study of the private speech production of three adult learners of Spanish.)

McCafferty, S.G. (1994). Adult second language Learners' use of private speech: A review of studies. *The Modern Language Journal, 78*(4), 421–36. (Reviews research on the functions of adult L2 private speech.)

Saville-Troike, M. (1988). Private speech: Evidence for second language learning strategies during the 'Silent' Period. *Journal of Child Language, 15*(3), 567–90. (A seminal, early study on child L2 private speech.)

Smith, H.J. (2007). The social and private worlds of speech: Speech for inter- and intramental activity. *The Modern Language Journal, 91*(3), 341–56. (Examines the functions of private speech among bilingual school children.)

Yoshida, R. (2008). Functions of repetition in Learners' private speech in Japanese language classrooms. *Language Awareness, 17*(4), 289–306. (Focuses on the role of repetition in the L2 private speech of college learners.)

Procedural memory and knowledge

Kara Morgan-Short
University of Illinois at Chicago

Two types of long-term memory are understood to underlie general human cognition: declarative and nondeclarative memory (Squire and Knowlton, 2000; Eichenbaum and Cohen, 2001). Although the term declarative memory refers to a unitary memory system, nondeclarative memory refers to all other memory systems that are not declarative. These nondeclarative memory systems are dissociable from declarative memory and from each other and include systems that support classical conditioning, priming and perceptual learning, and skill and habit learning. The memory system that underlies skill and habit learning is the procedural memory system (Eichenbaum and Cohen, 2001; Eichenbaum, 2002). Here we define and describe aspects of procedural memory. In addition, a brief overview of the role that procedural memory has been posited to play in second language (L2) acquisition is discussed. (See the **declarative memory and knowledge** entry in the current volume for information on declarative memory.)

Procedural memory underlies human ability to learn and perform skills and habits, such as typing, driving a car, throwing a ball, etc. Often procedural memory is described as "knowledge how" (Ohlsson, 2008). One might consider the execution of these skills to be due to "muscle memory." However, the memory is not stored and accessed in the muscles but rather in the procedural memory system. In addition to motor skills and habits, procedural memory is also known to underlie cognitive skills (Ohlsson, 2008), such as playing chess, computer programming, and managing complex systems such as air traffic control systems. Procedural memory skills are dependent on motor and cognitive programs that are not available to conscious awareness (Eichenbaum and Cohen, 2001). Thus, procedural memory is considered to be one type of implicit memory.

The skills and habits that are supported by procedural memory are learned and improve with practice according to a power law, with larger improvements in performance at early stages of practice and smaller but continuous improvements seen with ongoing practice. Thus, performance is tuned by repeated practice and such tuning continues indefinitely, as long as practice continues. Neither the learning nor the execution of skills and habits is thought to rely on attention. Indeed, procedural memory learning has been shown not to be impaired in dual-task conditions because it is not affected by the diversion of attention to a secondary task (Foerde *et al.*, 2006). Also, when use of procedural memory is triggered, the response is automatic and may be disrupted when attention is paid to the process. This explains why experts sometimes "choke" when trying too hard to perform well: the attentional processes interfere with automatic processes that underlie their skill ability (Beilock and Carr, 2001). Over the lifetime, our ability to learn motor and cognitive skills appears to be fairly stable during childhood and early adulthood but may decline at older ages (Lum *et al.*, 2009, Nilsson, 2003). Importantly, however, older adults have been shown to learn skills as well as younger adults although they require more practice to reach equivalent levels (Hubert *et al.*, 2009).

The development of a skill is believed to occur in three general stages (Ohlsson, 2008), which have been labeled by different researchers as either cognitive, associative, and autonomous (Fitts, 1954) or declarative, procedural, and automatic (Anderson, 1982). The task of the first stage is learning how to get started. Knowledge about how to get started may be acquired through various means, including of observation of others who are performing the skill, inductive or deductive learning, or transfer of prior knowledge. The focus of the second stage is how to improve one's performance so that the skill can reliably be performed correctly. At this stage, both positive and negative feedback play an important role in the process of tuning performance with practice. Once the skill can reliably be performed correctly, the third stage begins. In this stage, performance of the skill gradually improves with continual practice and the ability to perform the skill becomes automatic. The three stages and the learning mechanisms that occur in each of them, should not be thought of as stages that are turned on and off sequentially. Rather, it is likely that all the learning mechanisms are operating continuously and in parallel with the level of input and accessibility of each mechanism varying over time (Ohlsson, 2008).

Once procedural memory has been learned, it is believed to be largely encapsulated, that is, unavailable for use by other memory systems. Moreover, a procedural skill that has been learned in one particular context may not be easily executed when performed in a different context (DeKeyser, 2007). Because procedural memory is unavailable to conscious awareness, it cannot be assessed through measures that depend on explicit recollection. Instead performance measures, such as reaction time, are needed to assess procedural memory.

Procedural memory has been dissociated from other types of memory, and from declarative memory in particular, based on evidence of double dissociations between particular memory systems. Evidence of dissociation among memory systems first came from the patient H.M., who had a large part of his medial temporal lobe removed in a surgery that aimed to remediate his severe epileptic seizures. After the surgery, it was evident that H.M. had lost the ability to form new declarative memories while retaining his ability to perform within normal ranges on experimental tasks associated with procedural memory, such as the mirror drawing task and the Wisconsin card-sorting task. By analyzing the intact and spared domains of H.M.'s memory, researchers were able to identify skills that could be learned without recourse to declarative memory (Eichenbaum and Cohen, 2001). Further research with patients who have suffered some type of trauma- or disease-induced injury to the brain has validated the dissociation between procedural and declarative memory (Poldrack and Foerde, 2008). For example, patients with Parkinson's disease, which is caused by basal ganglia malfunction, have demonstrated that they are impaired on procedural tasks but are able to learn declarative knowledge, whereas amnesic patients with damage to the medial temporal lobe show the opposite pattern.

Procedural memory is supported by a highly complex neural system. Although our understanding of this neural system is far from complete, the primary regions that underlie procedural memory include portions of cortex in the frontal lobe, the striatum, which are part of the basal ganglia, and the thalamus (Eichenbaum, 2002). Information related to procedural memory appears to be processed in the following way: the striatum can receive input from any region of the cerebral cortex. The input that is received is topographically organized and is passed onto the thalamus through both inhibitory and disinhibitory pathways. Finally the thalamus relays the information to appropriate cortical areas of the frontal lobe. The contribution of this neural network to procedural memory is likely to be related to the planning and execution of goal-oriented behavior related to skills and habits (Eichenbaum and Cohen, 2001). This characterization of the neural system that underlies procedural memory is quite simple and does not describe interactions within these brain regions and interactions among other brain regions that are important to the functioning of procedural memory. Nevertheless, even this basic description of the primary neural areas serves to show that this system relies on a different set of neural substrates than other memory systems, such as the declarative memory system, which relies primarily on areas of the medial temporal lobe.

Various perspectives of second language (L2) acquisition have posited that procedural memory and knowledge may play a role in second language acquisition (e.g., Ullman, 2001, 2005; DeKeyser, 2007). An assumption of these perspectives is that L2 acquisition is at least partially a domain-general process, that is, that processes involved in L2 acquisition are the same as cognitive processes involved in the acquisition of other types of skills. The involvement of procedural memory is generally thought to be evident only after initial stages of learning. For example, DeKeyser's skill acquisition theory (2007) maintains that procedural memory is invoked after an initial, declarative stage of learning. Practice is crucial at the procedural stage and serves to transform knowledge about the L2 into "knowledge how," converting it to procedural "programs" that, with a sufficient amount of practice, can be executed automatically. The declarative/procedural model (Ullman, 2001, 2005) also posits a role for procedural memory in L2 acquisition. Under this neurocognitive model, the procedural memory system, which is expected to underlie the mental grammar in L1, may also come to underlie aspects of the mental grammar in L2. Crucially, however, this is expected to happen only at higher levels of L2 proficiency when a learner has had significant amounts or practice and/or exposure to the L2. (See the **Declarative/Procedural Model** entry in the current volume for more information.)

If one assumes that L2 acquisition in adults is a domain-general process, it may be fruitful to explore whether procedural memory can provide an explanatory account for that portion of L2 acquisition that is determined to be implicit. Future research along these lines is likely to prove fruitful to the field of second language acquisition as well as to the field of cognitive science.

See also: automaticity, Declarative/Procedural Model, declarative memory and knowledge, Implicit learning, psycholinguistics of SLA, reaction time

References

Anderson, J.R. (1982) Acquisition of cognitive skill. *Psychological Review*, *89*, 369–406.

Beilock, S.L. and Carr, T. (2001) On the fragility of skilled performance: What governs choking under pressure? *Journal of Experimental Psychology: General*, *130*(4), 701–25.

Dekeyser, R. (2007) Skill acquisition theory. In Vanpatten, B. and Williams, J. (eds), *Theories in Second Language Aquisition: An Introduction*. Mahwah, NJ: Erlbaum.

Eichenbaum, H. (2002) *The Cognitive Neuroscience of Memory: An Introduction*. New York: Oxford University Press, Inc.

Eichenbaum, H. and Cohen, N.J. (2001) *From Conditioning to Conscious Recollection: Memory Systems of the Brain*. New York: Oxford University Press.

Fitts, P.M. (1954). The information capacity of the human motor system in controlling the amplitude of movement. *Journal of Experimental Psychology*, *47*, 381–91.

Foerde, K., Knowlton, B.J. and Poldrack, R.A. (2006) Modulation of competing memory systems by distraction. *Proceedings of the National Academy of Science*, *103*, 11778–83.

Hubert, V. *et al.* (2009) Age-related changes in the cerebral substrates of cognitive procedural learning. *Human Brain Mapping*, *30*(4), 1374–86.

Lum, J., Kidd, E., Davis, S. and Conti-Ramsden, G. (2009) Longitudinal study of declarative and procedural memory in primary school-aged children. *Australian Journal of Psychology*. First published on: 27 August 2009 (iFirst).

Nilsson, L.G. (2003) Memory function in normal aging. *Acta Neurologica Scandinavia Supplementum*, *179*, 7–13.

Ohlsson, S. (2008) Computational models of skill aquisition. In Sun, R. (ed.), *The Cambridge Handbook of Computational Psychology*. Cambridge: Cambridge University Press.

Poldrack, R.A. and Foerde, K. (2008) Category learning and the memory systems debate. *Neuroscience and Biobehavioral Reviews*, *32*, 197–205.

Squire, L.R. and Knowlton, B.J. (2000) The medial temporal lobe, the hippocampus, and the memory systems of the brain. In Gazzaniga, M.S. (ed.), *The New Cognitive Neurosciences*. Cambridge, MA: MIT Press.

Ullman, M.T. (2001) The neural basis of lexicon and grammar in first and second language: The Declarative/Procedural Model. *Bilingualism: Language and Cognition*, *4*, 105–22.

——(2005) A cognitive neuroscience perspective on second language acquisition: The Declarative/Procedural Model. In Sanz, C. (ed.), *Mind and Context in Adult Second Language Acquisition: Methods, Theory and Practice*. Washington, DC: Georgetown University Press.

Processability Theory (PT)

Bruno Di Biase and Satomi Kawaguchi
University of Western Sydney

Processability Theory (PT) is a theory of second language (L2) development which is based on the architecture of the human language processor. On this basis it aims to hypothesize a universal hierarchy of processing resources that can be related to language-specific processing requirements. PT's origins can be traced back to ZISA's work, which found a fixed and cumulative order of acquisition in the development of German L2 (Meisel, Clahsen and Pienemann, 1981), accounted for through "processing strategies" related to saliency and other processing constraints (Clahsen, 1984). Supported by Johnston's Australian migrants' SAMPLE data, this framework was extended to English syntax as well as morphology (Pienemann and Johnston, 1987).

The actual birth of PT occurs in 1998 with the publication of *Language Processing and Second Language Development: Processability Theory*, in which Pienemann abandons Clahsen's (1984) processing strategies in favor of more explicit and broader psycholinguistic foundation by incorporating

Levelt's (1989) speech production model to better characterize the cognitive environment in which language learning takes place. Furthermore, Pienemann adopts Lexical Functional Grammar (LFG, Kaplan and Bresnan, 1982) as a formal, non-derivational representation of linguistic knowledge (e. g., Pickering *et al.*, 2002 would consider a derivational representation incompatible with the formulation of constituent structure). Furthermore, LFG can model the lexical basis of linguistic learning and the principle of information exchange, which is in line with the grammatical encoding requirements of Levelt's Formulator. Being cognitively based and formally explicit, makes PT's application to any language empirically testable and falsifiable. Its "capacity to predict which formal hypotheses are processable at which point in development" (Pienemann, 1998, p. xv) is one of PT's strongest points: its typological plausibility has been successfully tested not only for Germanic languages such as German, English and Scandinavian languages (Glahn *et al.*, 2001), but also "distant languages," such as Arabic (Mansouri, 2005), Chinese (Zhang, 2004), Italian, and Japanese (Di Biase and Kawaguchi 2002). Attesting to theoretical maturity and attracting fresh research, recent work on "Extending Processability Theory" (Pienemann, Di Biase and Kawaguchi 2005) opens up new dimensions for PT beyond obligatory morphological and syntactic defaults towards speakers' linguistic optional constructions at the syntax–pragmatic interface. PT's scope now reaches towards the study of L1-L2 transfer, which is shown to be developmentally moderated (Pienemann, Di Biase, Kawaguchi and Håkansson 2005), the development of pragmatically marked speaker choices, bilingual first language acquisition, automatization, L2 classroom studies, and other areas of SLA and its applications (cf. e.g. Chapters in Kessler, 2008).

Morphological development

PT's essential intuition is that the sequence in which the learner develops the processing routines needed to handle the components of the L2 accords to the time course in which procedures are incrementally activated in speech generation. This occurs in the following sequence (cf. Levelt, 1989: 235–83):

1. lemma,
2. category procedure (lexical category of the lemma),
3. phrasal procedure (instigated by the category of the head),
4. S-procedure and target language word order rules,
5. subordinate clause procedure.

The processing resources to be acquired in the L2 mirror this implicational hierarchy in the grammatical encoding process, whereby the resources at the lower level are prerequisite for the higher level. Yet, whenever the target L2 is not very closely related to the L1 a different Formulator must be built to handle language-specific requirements (cf. Levelt, 1989: 103–4). The L2 learner then will need to construct language-specific processing devices to produce the L2 lexicon and grammar – such as the lexical category of lemmas; diacritic features in the lexicon (e.g. number, case, tense); functorization rules (instigating the activation of free and bound morphemes); syntactic procedures and their specific stores (holding grammatical information over the course of production and making it available when exchange is required); and word order rules (canonical and/or pragmatically optimal) – all of which are overtly expressed variably across languages. Table 11 represents the process of SLA development over time (t1-t5) and progression over stages (bottom-to-top), each characterized by the kind of procedure acquired (leftmost column) and the extent of exchange of information required for the deployment of morphological procedures.

Notice that this progression is hypothesized as universal (not language-specific): each stage represents a hypothesis space for the learner in the target L2. Using an LFG-like representation, Figure 10 illustrates two stages of information exchange which English requires for generating *Peter owns many dogs*. First, the exchange of the value PLURAL over the *many* and *dogs* node instantiates

Table 11 Hypothesized hierarchy of processing procedures (after Pienemann 1998: 79).

STAGE	*t1*	*t2*	*t3*	*t4*	*t5*
S-BAR PROCEDURE	–	–	–	–	interclausal information exchange
SENTENCE PROCEDURE	–	–	–	interphrasal information exchange	+
PHRASAL PROCEDURE	–	–	phrasal information exchange	+	+
CATEGORY PROCEDURE	–	lexical form variation (no information exchange)	+	+	+
LEMMA ACCESS	invariant forms and formulas	+	+	+	+

the exchange of information (unification) and checks compatibility at NP-phrasal level. Second, the interphrasal exchange of information is instantiated in the unification of PERS and NUM feature values between two different phrases, that is, the NP_{SUBJ} (*Peter*) and VP-head (*owns*) at the S node, signalling the assignment of one of the arguments (*Peter*) to sentential subject function. The implicational nature of the hierarchy ensures that this interphrasal stage will be acquired later than the phrasal stage because learners can produce only those L2 forms which the current stage of his/her language processor can handle.

Table 12 summarizes and exemplifies the structural outcomes for English L2 morphology at each stage of development.

Syntactic development

PT now hypothesizes separately developmental sequences in L2 syntax, previously subsumed within the single hierarchy in (2), which could not differentiate active from passive constructions, for instance, or canonical order from pragmatically marked orders. Questions were also problematic as they too require pragmatic-modal information. To account for discourse-pragmatic development connected to speaker choices, PT adopts three hypotheses (Pienemann, Di Biase and Kawaguchi, 2005). First, the Unmarked Alignment Hypothesis accounts for canonical order, the most pervasive order used to organize constituents in c-structure. Canonical order is language-specific, and learners infer it from the input as soon as they start sorting out words into main semantic (e.g., agent, action, patient) and/or grammatical (noun, verb) categories. Second, the Topic Hypothesis accounts for syntactic development from canonical order towards marked alignment, as languages may use word order for topicalizing, highlighting, contrasting or questioning particular c-structure elements. Third, the Lexical Mapping Hypothesis accounts for development towards non-default mapping of semantic roles in argument structure (a-structure) to grammatical functions (f-structure). For instance, in passive constructions patient roles are mapped to subject rather than object in f-structure. Native speakers may choose any of such word order or lexical mapping devices to take perspective and guide the listener's attention, but L2 learners must learn how to deploy these choices in real time. This means that, at least initially, that is, until automatization is achieved, processing such information additional to pure propositional content would require greater processing and memory storage than fixed word order and default mapping

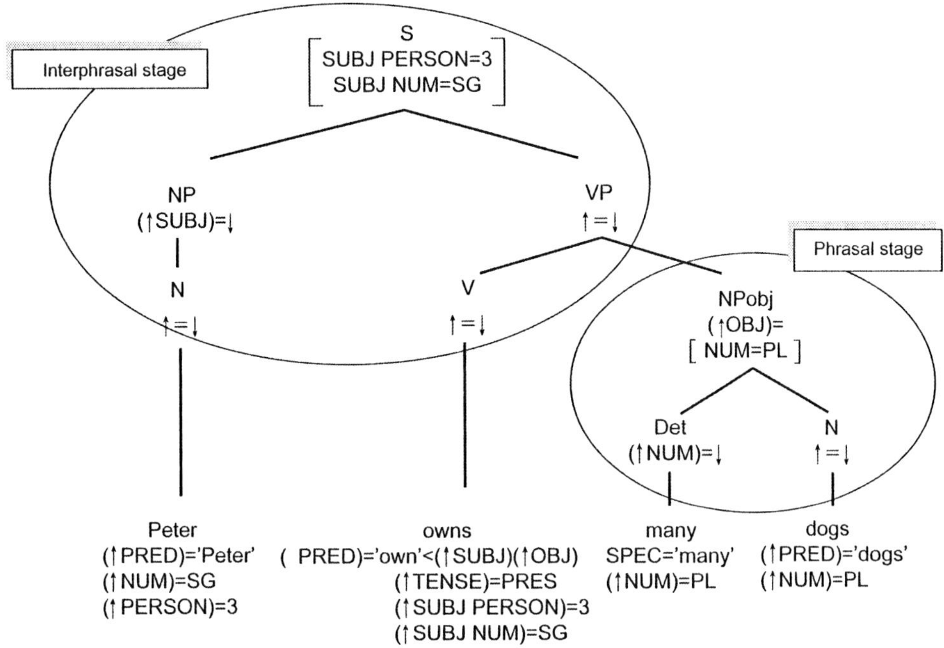

Figure 10 Lexical entries and c-structure for *Peter owns many dogs*

Table 12 Developmental Stages for English Morphology

Procedure	*Morphological outcome/stage*	*English structure*	*Example*
S-BAR PROCEDURE	INTERCLAUSAL MORPHOLOGY	e.g., subjunctive marking in subordination	*I suggest he eat less* *it's time you left*
S- PROCEDURE	INTERPHRASAL MORPHOLOGY	3rd person singular *–s*	*Peter loves rice*
PHRASAL PROCEDURE	VP MORPHOLOGY	AUX V: have V*–ed* MOD V be V*–ing*	*they* ***have studied*** *you* ***can go*** *I* ***am going***
	NP MORPHOLOGY	phrasal plural marking	*these girls* *many dogs* *three black cats*
CATEGORY PROCEDURE	LEXICAL MORPHOLOGY	past *–ed* V *–ing* plural *–s*	*Mary jumped* *he eating* *my brothers working*
LEMMA ACCESS	INVARIANT FORMS	single words; formulas	*station, here* *my name is Pim*

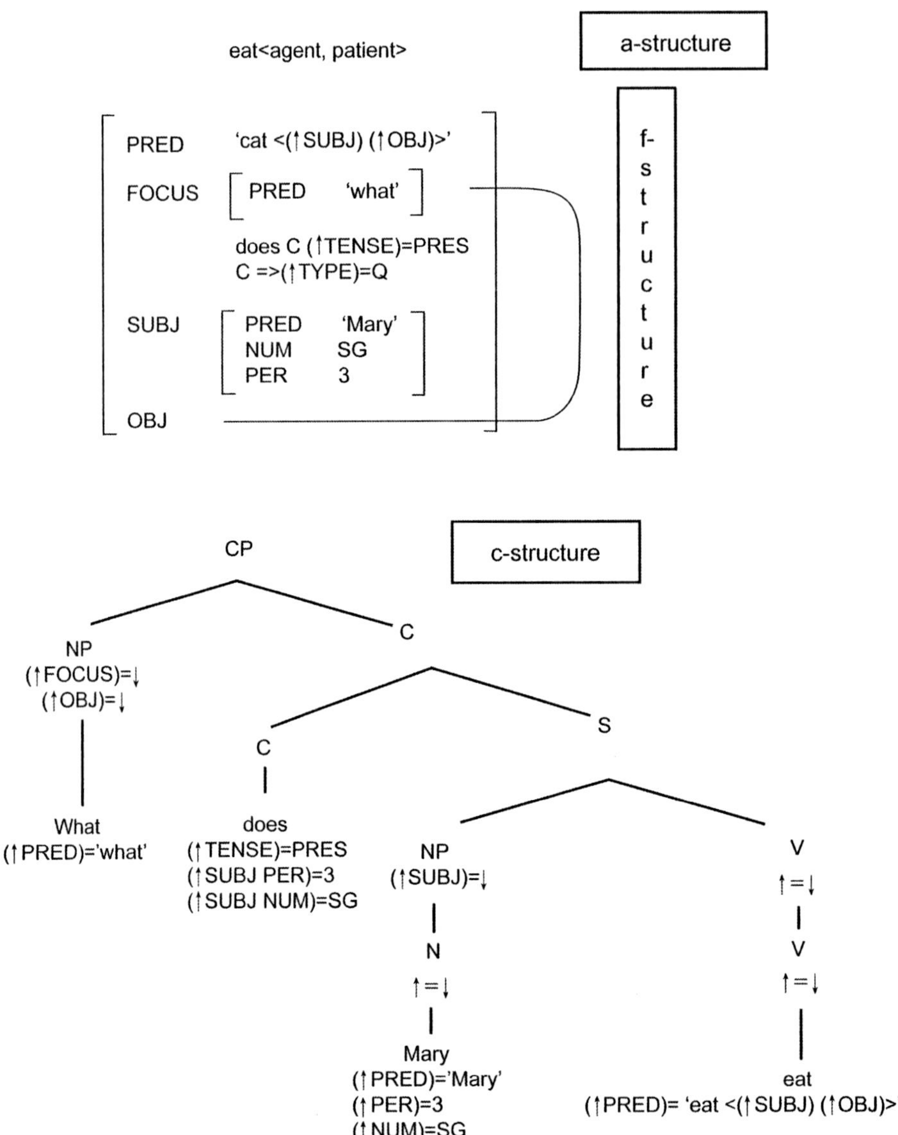

Figure 11 A-structure, f-structure and c-structure for *What does Mary eat?*

frames. The processing resources listed in Table 11 do not guarantee this acquisition but are pre- or co-requisites for syntactic development to occur.

LFG work in grammatical theory – such as on syntacticized discourse functions (Bresnan and Mchombo, 1987), information structure (e.g., on questions, Mycock, 2007), and Lexical Mapping Theory (Bresnan, 2001) – make formal representation of these phenomena possible and typologically plausible. For reasons of space only part of the hypotheses are represented and exemplified for English here. In Figure 11 a content question, representing discourse functions (FOC in this case),

Table 13 Developmental stages for English syntax: constituent questions and Y/N questions

Stage	*Y/N questions*	*Examples*	*Constituent questions*	*Examples*
XP MARKED ALIGNMENT	–	–	wh AUX SUBJ V O ?	*what has he eaten? where did she go? when are they going?*
MARKED ALIGNMENT	AUX SUBJ V O ?	*have you tried pizza? can Mary swim?*	–	–
XP UNMARKED ALIGNMENT	*do* canonical order ?	*do they have cat?*	wh canonical order ?	*what he eat? where you live?*
UNMARKED ALIGNMENT	canonical order?	*Mary jumped? you like pizza?*	–	–
LEMMA ACCESS	single words? formulas ?	*coffee?going?*	single words? formulas ?	*what? what colour? how much is it?*

is shown over the three parallel structures of LFG: a-structure (semantic roles) and c-structure (left-to-right position) mapping both on f-structure (grammatical functions).

Both yes/no and content questions development in English L2 are exemplified in Table 13.

Applications

The popularity of PT is partly due to its universal application to learning any L2, and increasingly also its use in L1-L2 comparison, bilingual L1 acquisition, heritage language maintenance, and L2 in special populations. Once the development of a language is mapped out with PT, this becomes an ideal blueprint for research and applications to learnability, rapid profiling, L2 syllabus construction, assessment and teaching techniques.

See also: development in SLA, developmental sequences, grammatical encoding, Levelt's model of speech production and comprehension, psycholinguistics of SLA, theoretical construicts in SLA

References

Bresnan, J. and Mchombo, S. (1987). Topic, pronoun and agreement in Chichewa. *Language, 63*, 741–82.

Clahsen, H. (1984). The acquisition of German word order: A test case for cognitive approaches to L2 development. In R. Andersen (ed.), *Second Languages: A Cross-linguistic Perspective*, pp. 219–42. Rowley, MA: Newbury House.

Di Biase, B., and Kawaguchi, S. (2002). Exploring the typological plausibility of Processability Theory: language development in Italian L2 and Japanese L2. *Second Language Research*, *18*/3, 274–302.

Glahn, E., Håkansson, G., Hammarberg, B., Holmen, A., Lund, K. and Hvenekilde, A. (2001). Processablity in Scandinavian second language acquisition. *Studies in Second Language Acquisition*, *23*, 389–416.

Kaplan, R.M. and Bresnan, J. (1982). Lexical-Functional grammar: a formal system for grammatical representation. In J. Bresnan (ed.), *The Mental Representation of Grammatical Relations*, pp. 173–281. Cambridge, MA: MIT Press.

Kessler, J.-U. (ed.) (2008). *Processability Approaches to Second Language Development*. Newcastle: Cambridge Scholars Publishing.

Levelt, W.J.M., Roelofs, A. and Meyer, A.S. (1999). A theory of lexical access in speech production. *Behavioral and Brain Sciences*, *22*, pp. 1–75.

Mansouri, F. (2005). Agreement morphology in Arabic as a second language: typological features and their processing implications. In M. Pienemann (ed.), *Cross-linguistic Aspects of Processability Theory*, pp. 117–53. Amsterdam: Benjamins.

Meisel, J.M., Clahsen, H. and Pienemann, M. (1981). On determining developmental stages in natural second language acquisition. *Studies in Second Language Acquisition*, *3*, 109–35.

Mycock, L. (2007).Constituent question formation and focus: a new typological perspective. *Transactions of the Philological Society*, *105*, 192–251.

Pickering, M.J., Branigan, H.P. and McLean, J.F. (2002). Constituent structure is formulated in one stage. *Journal of Memory and Language*, *46*, 586–605.

Pienemann, M. and Johnston, M. (1987). Factors influencing the development of language proficiency. In D. Nunan (ed.), *Applying Second Language Acquisition Research*, pp. 45–141. Adelaide: National Curriculum Research Centre, Adult Migrant Education Program.

Pienemann, M., Di Biase, B., and Kawaguchi, S. (2005). Extending processability theory. In M. Pienemann (ed.), *Cross-linguistic Aspects of Processability Theory*, pp. 199–251. Amsterdam: Benjamins.

Pienemann, M., Di Biase, B., Kawaguchi, S., and Håkansson, G. (2005). Processing constraints on L1 transfer. In J.F. Kroll, and A.M.B. de Groot (eds), *Handbook of Bilingualism: Psycholinguistic Approaches*, pp. 128–53. New York: Oxford University Press.

Zhang, Y. (2004). Categorial analysis, processing demands, and the L2 acquisition of the Chinese adjective suffix-*de* (ADJ). *Language Learning*, *54*/3, 437–68.

Further reading

Bresnan, J. (2001). *Lexical-functional Syntax*. Malden, MA: Blackwell. (An authoritative introduction to the grammar adopted by PT.)

Levelt, W.J.M. (1989). *Speaking. From Intention to Articulation*. Cambridge, MA: MIT Press. (Classic introduction to speech production; the psycholinguistic foundation of PT.)

Pienemann, M. (1998). *Language Processing and Second Language Development: Processability Theory*. Amsterdam: Benjamins. (Comprehensive foundational text of PT.)

Pienemann, M. (ed.) (2005). *Cross-linguistic Aspects of Processability Theory*. Amsterdam: Benjamins. (Chapter 7 is the basis for the current PT extension. Other chapters provide a summary of the original PT as well as a history and bibliography of PT's range of works up to its publication date.)

Processing Instruction (PI)

Bill VanPatten

Michigan State University

Processing Instruction (PI) is a specific type of focus on form or pedagogical intervention for grammatical structures first reported in VanPatten and Cadierno (1993). It has the following characteristics:

* it is predicated on what learners do (and don't do) during input processing (i.e., sentence-level processing strategies);
* it is input oriented (learners don't produce the targeted item during the treatment);
* input is manipulated in particular ways to alter processing strategies and increase better intake for acquisition (structured input);
* it includes explicit information for the learner on both grammatical structure and processing problems;
* it follows certain guidelines for the creation of structured input activities.

We will illustrate with one example. In the model of input processing developed by VanPatten (e.g., VanPatten 2004, 2007, 2009), learners begin processing an L2 using the First-noun Principle: *learners tend to interpret the first (pro)noun they encounter in an utterance as the subject/agent.* This strategy has negative consequences for object-first sentences, English-like passives in which the subject is not the agent, case marking (learners may ignore it), among others. In a typical PI treatment, learners are asked to listen to and read a mixture of sentences with varying word orders and asked to indicate who did what to whom (via picture selection, logical sentence follow-up, translation, and other means). These are called referential activities because they have right and wrong answers. Learners are thus pushed to abandon the First-noun Principle and grapple with other cues that lead to correct interpretation. Following referential activities are affective activities–activities in which learners indicate what is true for them and/or supply information about themselves and the world they live in. These activities reinforce the appropriate processing that has begun with the referential activities.

What processing instruction isn't

Because PI is linked to instructed SLA, a number of misconceptions have occurred over the years. Following is a list of some of the things that PI is not:

* *PI is not a method.* A method implies a more general approach to instruction. PI is better classified as a technique that can be used within a method. It is one type of focus on form or "intervention."
* *PI is not an implicit focus on form.* PI is neutral on the explicit versus implicit debate in language acquisition. Because PI generally involves some kind of explicit information regarding language structures and processing problems, it cannot be regarded as implicit. At the same time, research has shown that this explicit information is not a necessary component of PI (see below) and that structured input activities alone can bring about changes in learner knowledge and performance. However, researchers in the PI framework have never made any claims about explicit or implicit learning within SLA more generally.
* *PI is not simply contextualizing structures in input.* Because PI is informed by a particular model of input processing, the idea behind PI is to manipulate input in specific ways to force processing of a target structure and to alter the actual processing strategies learners take to comprehending input. To this end, it is quite different from such things as text enhancement, input flood, and input-output cycles that merely embed target structures in the input but may not force processing.
* *PI is not predicated on "noticing."* Unlike text enhancement and some other interventions, PI is not based on the noticing hypothesis but instead on a particular model of input processing. PI is neutral on the noticing issue.

What has been researched?

Dozens of studies have been conducted on the effectiveness of PI as well as the factors internal to PI that contribute to that effectiveness. Here are some of the main research findings of PI.

* PI always results in significant gains on a variety of measures, both comprehension and production, sentence-level and discourse-level, and in both oral/aural and writing. Thus, the effects of PI show up on measures that are not part of the treatment itself (e.g., Sanz and Morgan-Short, 2004; Uludag and VanPatten, forthcoming; VanPatten, 2004).
* PI is always as good as if not better than other focus on form techniques (e.g., Uludag and VanPatten, forthcoming; VanPatten, 2004; VanPatten and Cadierno, 1993; VanPatten, Farmer and Clardy, 2009).
* The effectiveness of PI is not dependent on the explicit information given to learners prior to structured input activities; structured input activities seem to be sufficient. However, for some structures in some languages, the effects of PI may be accelerated by explicit information. For example, in OVS structures, processing case marking in German within PI seems to be speeded up by explicit information but not the processing of clitic object pronouns in Spanish. Yet, learners of German do eventually begin to process correctly with PI even without explicit information on case marking (e.g., Henry, Culman, and VanPatten, 2009; Sanz and Morgan-Short, 2004; VanPatten, 2004).

* PI has secondary effects on structures not taught. Learners who have undergone PI have demonstrated the ability to transfer new processing strategies to novel structures not part of the treatment they have received (e.g., Benati and Lee, 2008)

Future directions

The effects of PI are relatively clear, as are its effects compared to a variety of other interventions/ treatments. One area in need of investigation for PI is the role of individual differences, in particular working (phonological) memory and aptitude (grammatical sensitivity). Such variables have been shown to play a role in other treatments but the research agenda in PI has not yet included ids as a variable. It is possible PI may favor particular aptitude profiles or "clusters," but this remains an open question. Given the robustness of findings on PI to date, the role of individual differences within PI seems to be a fruitful avenue to explore.

See also: attention, awareness, Focus on Form (FonF), input enhancement, instructed SLA, theoretical constructs in SLA

References

Benati, A. and Lee, J.F. (2008). *Grammar Acquisition and Processing Instruction: Secondary and Cumulative Effects*. Bristol: Multilingual Matters.

Henry, N., Culman, H. and VanPatten, B. (2009). More on the effects of explicit information in instructed SLA. A partial replication and response to Fernández (2008). *Studies in Second Language Acquisition*, *31*, 559–75.

Sanz, C. and Morgan-Short, K. (2004). Positive evidence vs. explicit rule presentation and explicit negative feedback: A computer assisted study. *Language Learning*, *54*, 35–78.

Uludag, O. and VanPatten, B. (forthcoming). The comparative effects of processing instruction and dictogloss on the acquisition of the English passive by speakers of turkish. *International Review of Applied Linguistics*.

VanPatten, B. (ed.) (2004). *Processing Instruction: Theory, Research, and Commentary*. Mahwah, NJ: Lawrence Erlbaum and Associates.

VanPatten, B. (2007). Input processing in adult second language acquisition. In B. VanPatten and J. Williams (eds), *Theories in Second Language Acquisition*. Mahwah, NJ: Lawrence Erlbaum Associates.

——(2009). Processing matters in input enhancement. In T. Piske and M. Young-Scholten (eds), *Input Matters*. Clevedon: Multilingual Matters.

VanPatten, B. and Cadierno, T. (1993). Explicit instruction and input processing. *Studies in Second Language Acquisition*, *15*, 225–43.

VanPatten, B., Farmer, J.L. and Clardy, C.L. (2009). Processing instruction and meaning-based output instruction: A response to Keating and Farley (2008). *Hispania*, *92*, 124–35.

VanPatten, B., Inclezan, D., Salazar, H. and Farley, A.P. (2009). Processing instruction and dictogloss: A study on object pronouns and word order in Spanish. *Foreign Language Annals*, *42*, 557–75.

Proficiency

Alessandro Benatti

University of Greenwich

The issue of what constitutes proficiency and how it can be measured is still a controversial issue. There is some inconsistency in the way proficiency is defined as the debate on appropriate ways of conceptualising the nature of language has continued for at least half a century. There have been a variety of concepts connected to the term proficiency. Disagreement on the definition of this term is based on different views of language and what it means to know a language. The term proficiency refers overall to the ability for learners to master and use a second language in different contexts. Stern (1992) has argued that the four skills (listening, speaking, reading and writing) remain a useful expression of proficiency in modern language education. Many dictionaries equate proficiency with terms such as 'ability' or 'skill.' Widdowson (1983: 8) associates the term proficiency with the term 'capacity' which he describes as "the ability to produce and understand utterances by using the resources of the grammar in association with features of context to make meaning". Taylor (1988) also describes proficiency as L2 learners' ability to use their language knowledge in specific contexts. Cummins (1980; 2000) has developed two main categories of interpersonal communication skills: Basic Interpersonal Communication Skills, which refers to day-to-day language skills; and Cognitive Academic Language Proficiency (CALP). According to his research, it usually takes language learners three to seven years to develop CALP.

Language proficiency is a term that scholars, theoretical linguists and educators have used for many years and it can often be interchanged with other terms such as competence and performance. Ingram (1985) suggests that proficiency is the ability to apply language knowledge in a specific communication context. Davies (1989) defines 'proficiency' as a part of communicative competence, along with innate ability and performance. Kasper (1997: 345) points out that the best way to express proficiency is to relate this term to the notion of communicative competence.

Is proficiency the same as competence and performance?

Proficiency is very often associated with the term 'language competence'. Proficiency and competence are different terms, yet, they are related terms which merge into one another. Theoretical linguists vary in how they define competence in relation to proficiency. Taylor (1988: 166) views competence as "a static concept having to do with structure, state or form whereas proficiency is essentially a dynamic process, having to do with process and function". Taylor (1988: 166) argues that proficiency is "the ability to make use of competence". Ellis (1994: 697) suggests that the term competence refers to "a language user's underlying knowledge of language, which is drawn on in actual performance". Early models to describe competence included listening, speaking, writing and reading skills. Chomsky's view of competence (1965) is limited to linguistic competence as he believes that the linguistics competence that is innate in children, will lead to internalisation of the rules of the language.

Hymes (1972) reacts to this narrow view on the basis that it concentrates knowledge of the language only, taking no account of the social context in which it takes place. He proposes a broader notion of competence that he called 'communicative competence'. Hymes views language as affected by a variety of social factors in specific contexts. He distinguishes between linguistic (knowledge of grammatical rules) and socio-linguistics competence (knowledge of the rules of language performance).

Canale (1983) has associated proficiency to the concept of communicative competence. This new construct included four aspects of competence: grammatical (knowledge of the linguistic form or structure of a target language); sociolinguistic (knowledge of use of the language in an appropriate way); discourse (knowledge of how sentences connect for discourse, cohesion and coherence); and strategic competence (knowledge of how to cope with the L2 target language when we do not possess a full knowledge of the language). Similarly, Bacham and Palmer (1982) view proficiency as multi-componential in nature. They redefine proficiency in terms of 'communicative proficiency' which includes organizational competence (morphology, syntax, vocabulary, cohesion and organization); pragmatic and sociolinguistic competence.

Stern (1983) argues that proficiency corresponds to the actual learner's performance in second language and it involves the mastery of four aspects: the forms, the various meanings (e.g. linguistics, affective, cognitive and socio-cultural) of those forms, the capacity to use the language for communication purposes and the creativity in language use. Taylor (1988) sees proficiency as the ability to make use of competence and he defines performance as what is done when proficiency is put to use. Ellis (1994) provides a definition of proficiency which entails the ability of L2 learners to use their language knowledge to perform different language tasks.

Can proficiency be measured?

Theorists and practitioners have been struggling in providing a practical framework to assess L2 proficiency. The lack of consensus on what language components should be tested has caused problems in the development of tests that can measure proficiency. Cummins (1984) argued that language proficiency has been understood, by some scholars, of consisting of many language components, and by other scholars as consisting of only few elements. Valdes and Figueroa (1994: 34) viewed knowing a language as something that ". ... goes beyond simplistic view of good pronunciation, 'correct' grammar, and even mastery of rules of politeness. Knowing a language and knowing how to use a language involves a mastery and control of a large number of interdependent components and elements that interact with one another and that are affected by the nature of the situation in which communication takes place."

Language proficiency is a measurement of how well an individual has mastered a language. It is often measured in terms of receptive and expressive language skills, syntax, vocabulary, semantics and other areas that demonstrate language abilities. The ACTFL Proficiency Guidelines represent an attempt from language educators to provide an operational definition of proficiency. The theory of communicative competence is a theory that provides a framework for testing knowledge and ways of using language knowledge. In this sense, a theory of communicative competence is an appropriate tool to measure language proficiency (Spolsky, 1989). However, the challenge has been to develop tests that would constitute a reliable and valid measurement of proficiency. Thomas (1994) has distinguished different ways in assessing language proficiency: impressionistic judgements; institutional status; research design tests; and standardised tests.

One useful description and categorisation of language proficiency testing is the one provided by Oller and Damico (1991) who identified four schools of thought:

- the discrete point approach that it is based on the view that language proficiency is characterised by various components (e.g. phonology, morphology, syntax and so on) and each of these components can be also divided into other elements (e.g. sounds, morphemes, phrase structures). Well-known types of tests of this kind are spelling tests, grammar and vocabulary tests;
- the integrative approach that is based on the assumption that language proficiency should be assessed in a rich context of discourse. Language processing and use entails the simultaneous involvement of more than one language component and skills. Dictation and cloze tests are well-known types of integrative testing;
- the pragmatic approach that is based on the assumption that language proficiency should be assessed in a pragmatic and real life manner;
- the communicative approach that it is based on the assumption that there is a need to formulate a theoretical framework for language proficiency. Various frameworks were proposed (Canale, 1983; Bacham, 1990).

Despite the many attempts to provide a definition of language proficiency and how proficiency is measured, an agreement has not been found yet.

The multidimensional model (Vollmer,1981), both the strong (16 components for the total language proficiency) and the weak version (four language skills), was criticized for the failure to accommodate the relationship among the components and skills and the discourse dimension.

The unidimensional model, the so-called Unitary Competence Hypothesis (Oller, 1978) suggests that one underlying ability (the *g* factor) accounts for language proficiency. This model was criticized for its methodological and theoretical drawbacks. No matter what model is proposed to evaluate and assess proficiency, the main questions which still need to be asked is the one formulated by Briere (1971) over 40 years ago "Are we really measuring language proficiency?"

See also: BICS and CALP, communicative competence, language testing and SLA, measuring and researching SLA, multicompetence, native speaker

References

Bacham, L. and Palmer, A. (1982). The construct validation of some components of communicative proficiency. *TESOL Quarterly*, *16*, 449–65.

Bacham, L. (1990). *Fundamental Considerations in Language Testing*. Oxford: Oxford University Press.

Briere, E. J. (1971). Are we really measuring proficiency with our foreign language tests? *Foreign Language Annals*, *4*, 385–91.

Canale, M. (1983). From communicative competence to communicative language pedagogy. In J. Richards and R.Schmidt (eds), *Language and Communication*, pp. 2–28. London: Logman.

Chomsky, N. (1965). *Aspects of the Theory of Syntax*. Cambridge, MA: MIT Press.

Cummins, J. (1980). The construct of language proficiency in bilingual education. In J. Alatis (ed.), *Current Issues in Bilingual Education*, pp. 81–103. Washington, DC: Georgetown University Press.

——(1984). Wanted. An academic framework for relating language proficiency to academic achievement among bilingual students. In C. Rivera (ed.), *Language Proficiency and Academic Achievement*, pp. 138–61. Avon: Multilingual Matters.

——(2000). Putting language proficiency in its place: responding to critiques of the conversational/academic language distinction. In J. Cenoz, and U. Jessner (eds), *English in Europe: The Acquisition of a Third Language*, pp. 54–83. Clevedon: Multilingual Matters.

Davies, A. (1989). Communicative competence as language use. *Applied Linguistics*, *10*, 157–70.

Ellis, R. (1994). *The Study of Second Language Acquisition*. Oxford: Oxford University Press.

Hymes, D. (1971). Competence and performance in linguistic theory. In R. Huxley and E. Ingram (eds), *Language Acquisition: Models and Methods*, pp. 3–28. London: Academic Press.

Ingram, D. (1985). Assessing proficiency: An overview of some aspects of testing. In K. Hyltenstam and M. Pienemann (eds), *Modelling and Assessing Second Language* Development, pp. 215–76. Clevedon: Multilingual Matters.

Kasper, G. (1997). Beyond reference. In G. Kasper and E. Kellerman (eds), *Communication Strategies*, pp. 345–60. Harlow: Longman.

Oller, J.W. (1978). Pragmatics and language testing. In B. Spolsky (ed.), *Advances in Language Testing, Series*, 2. Arlington: Center for Applied Linguistics.

Oller, J.W. and Damico, J.S. (1991). Theoretical considerations in the assessment of LEP students. In E. Hamayan and J.S. Damico (eds), *Limiting Bias in the Assessment of Bilingual Students*, pp. 77–110. Austin, TX: Pro-ed publications.

Valdes, G. and Figueroa, R. (1994). *Bilingualism and Testing. A Special Case of Bias*. Norwood, NJ: Ablex Publishing Corporation.

Spolsky, B. (1989). *Conditions for Second Language Learning: Introduction to a General Theory*. Oxford: Oxford University Press.

Stern, H.H. (1983). *Fundamental Concepts of Language Teaching*. Oxford: Oxford University Press.

Stern, H.H. (1992). *Issues and Options in Language Teaching*. Oxford: Oxford University Press.

Taylor, D. (1988). The meaning and use of the term 'competence' in linguistics and applied linguistics. *Applied Linguistics*, *9*, 148–68.

Thomas, M. (1994). Assessment of L2 proficiency in second language acquisition research. *Language Learning*, *44*, 307–36.

Vollmer, H. (1981). Why are we interested in 'general language proficiency'? In J. Alderson and A. Hughes (eds), *ELT documents 111 – Issues in Language Testing*, pp. 152–75. London: British Council.

Widdowson, H.G. (1983). *Learning Purpose and Language Use*. Oxford: Oxford University Press.

Protocol analysis

Melissa Bowles

University of Illinois at Urbana-Champaign

Protocol analysis (PA) is a methodology used to gain insight on thought processes. It involves eliciting a research participant's spoken thoughts (verbal reports), which are recorded either during task completion or some time after task completion. Verbal reports elicited during task completion are referred to interchangeably as concurrent verbal reports or think-aloud protocols (TAPs), whereas those elicited after task completion are referred to as retrospective verbal reports. PA originated in cognitive psychology in the 1940s, where verbal reports were first used to investigate problem-solving. Subsequently, PA has emerged as a primary data collection method to investigate strategies, thought processes, and decisions in diverse fields, ranging from health care and behavior analysis, to marketing and software design. In language research, PA has been used since the 1980s to study a range of phenomena, including L1 and L2 reading and writing strategies (Cohen, 1986), interlanguage pragmatics (Kasper and Blum-Kulka, 1993), and language testing (Green, 1998). It has also been used to gauge L2 learners' awareness of features of language input (Leow, 2000), and to provide insight into, among other topics, learners' perceptions of oral corrective feedback (Mackey, Gass, and McDonough, 2000). Prior to the use of PA to elicit such data, researchers and teachers could only speculate about learners' perceptions and beliefs, oftentimes hypothesizing (erroneously) that their perceptions matched those of the learners.

Controversy has always surrounded PA, both in cognitive psychology (Nisbett and Wilson, 1977) and in language research (Jourdenais, 2001). The two main concerns are that verbal reports may 1) provide an inaccurate and/or incomplete account of thought processes (veridicality) and that they may 2) have a (facilitative or detrimental) effect on participants' processing and performance (reactivity) compared to participants who complete the same task silently. In their classic book on PA, Ericsson and Simon (1984; 1993) regard veridicality as an unfortunate but unavoidable feature of verbal reports; verbalization can never capture *all* thoughts, and the authors caution that PA can only reveal thoughts that are verbalizable (i.e., conscious and encoded verbally) and held in working memory. Furthermore, they advise that think-alouds are more accurate and complete than retrospective reports because there is no time delay during which participants can forget. To minimize the veridicality of retrospective reports, they suggest that as short a delay as possible occur between the time the task is completed and the time of reporting. (In addition, when participants in language research are asked to provide retrospective reports, it is generally done by means of a method called stimulated recall, whereby participants watch or listen to a videorecording of themselves performing the task and comment on it.) Reactivity, on the other hand, has been a source of considerable concern and has been the topic of scores of empirical studies in cognitive psychology (Ericsson and Simon, 1984, 1993) and more than a dozen in second language acquisition (Bowles, 2010). Findings have been far from uniform, although the pattern of findings indicates that PA slows task completion but does not tend to affect the outcome of task performance significantly, so long as participants are asked only to think their thoughts aloud and not to provide additional commentary or justify their decisions during the task.

The variables that interact to cause reactivity are, at the present time, not well understood, but are thought to include time of reporting (concurrent vs retrospective), type of report (metacognitive vs non-metacognitive), task type, language of task (L1 vs L2), and language of verbalization (L1 vs L2 vs combination) (Bowles, 2010). In a quantitative meta-analysis of reactivity in studies involving verbal tasks, Bowles (2010) found that think-aloud groups did not consistently perform significantly differently than silent control groups. The results for time on task were more decisive, indicating across the board that thinking aloud increased time on task. She concluded that inferences made on the basis of verbal reports should be taken cautiously and that whenever possible, a small silent (control) group should be included so that, at a minimum, the verbalization group's performance can be compared to that of an otherwise matched group that completes the task silently. Such a procedure serves as a check on reactivity on a study-by-study basis. Bowles advises that if researchers follow guidelines for using PA, it is a valid data collection method that provides insight that could otherwise not be gleaned. See Ericsson and Simon (1984, 1993) and Bowles (2010) for detailed guidelines on using PA.

See also: attention, awareness, measuring and researching SLA, Noticing Hypothesis, psycholinguistics of SLA, stimulated recall

References

Bowles, M. (2010). *The Think-aloud Controversy in Second Language Research*. New York: Routledge.

Cohen, A.D. (1986). Mentalistic measures in reading strategy research: Some recent findings. *English for Specific Purposes*, *5*(2), 131–45.

Ericsson, K.A. and Simon, H.A. (1984). *Protocol Analysis: Verbal Reports as Data*. Cambridge, MA: MIT.

——(1993). *Protocol Analysis: Verbal Reports as Data* (rev. ed.). Cambridge, MA: MIT.

Green, A.J. F. (1998). *Using Verbal Protocols in Language Testing Research: A Handbook*. Cambridge: Cambridge University Press.

Jourdenais, R. (2001). Cognition, instruction, and protocol analysis. In P. Robinson (ed.), *Cognition and Second Language Instruction*. Cambridge: Cambridge University Press.

Kasper, G. and Blum-Kulka, S. (1993). *Interlanguage Pragmatics*. New York: Oxford University Press.

Leow, R.P. (2000). A study of the role of awareness in foreign language behavior: Aware versus unaware learners. *Studies in Second Language Acquisition*, *22*(4), 557–584.

Mackey, A., Gass, S. and McDonough, K. (2000). How do learners perceive interactional feedback? *Studies in Second Language Acquisition*, *22*(4), 471–497.

Nisbett, R.E. and Wilson, T.D. (1977). Telling more than we can know: Verbal reports on mental processes. *Psychological Review*, *84*, 231–259.

Prototypes

Richard Hudson
University College London

In cognitive science a prototype is a concept which is defined in terms of its most typical examples (which may or may not be those which are first in terms of learning or anything else) and the term is associated with a particular view of categories. The alternative 'classical' view is that a category, such as 'dog', is defined by a set of necessary and sufficient conditions; according to this view, something is a dog only if it barks, has four legs and lives indoors or in a kennel. In contrast, the 'prototype' view of categories links each category to a typical case, while allowing the flexibility needed to accommodate less typical, uncertain and exceptional cases such as non-barking, three-legged or outside-living dogs.

Experimental evidence, as well as everyday experience, seems to support the prototype view rather than the classical one, though the latter still has its supporters (see Croft and Cruse 2004: 77–15 for a review of the debate). Since the early experiments of the cognitive psychologist Eleanor Rosch (1978), numerous experiments have shown various 'prototype effects' which support the idea that members of a category may have different degrees of 'goodness' as examples; for instance, a sparrow is better than an ostrich or a penguin as an example of a bird. In short, generalisations allow exceptions, and the logic of generalisation is default inheritance (Hudson 2010: 24–30).

The nature of conceptual categories is important in the study of SLA because almost everything that is learned is a category, in the sense in which this term is used in cognitive science. The categories of language are not only those of word meanings (such as 'dog' or 'bird'), but also those of lexico-grammar, morphology and phonology: words, word-classes, inflections, constructions, morphemes, phonemes. If all these elements of a second language are categories, it matters a great deal whether they are classical concepts or prototypes. If they are classical concepts, then some mechanism has to be found for discovering which features are necessary and which are sufficient, and a theory is needed to explain how learners internalise these features. If, on the other hand, they are prototypes, then what has to be learned is a typical case, with a more or less rich set of features all of which allow exceptions. In the former case, a category can only be learned from multiple examples that reveal which features are always shared; but in the latter case, a single well-chosen example is sufficient to learn the prototype. SLA researchers have drawn on the notion of prototypes to explain various phenomena, such as why prototypical uses of verbs in sentences lead them to be judged more acceptable by L2 learners than sentences containing non-prototypical uses of verbs (Kellerman, 1978), and for why tense is used to mark some aspectual distinctions before others in L2 development (Li and Shirai, 2000).

See also: Aspect Hypothesis (AH), cognitive linguistics and SLA, conceptual transfer, frequency effects, lexical concepts, language and the lexicon in SLA

References

Croft, W. and Cruse, A. (2004). *Cognitive Linguistics*. Cambridge: Cambridge University Press.

Hudson, R. (2010). *An Introduction to Word Grammar*. Cambridge: Cambridge University Press

Kellerman, E. (1978). Giving learners a break: Native language intuitions about transferability. *Working Papers in Bilingualism*, *15*, 59–92.

Li, P. and Shirai, Y. (2000). *The Acquisition of Lexical and Grammatical Aspect*. Berlin: Moutopn de Gruyter.

Rosch, E. (1978). Principles of categorization. In E. Rosch and B. Lloyd (eds), *Cognition and Categorization*, pp. 27–48. Hillsdale, NJ: Lawrence Erlbaum.

Psycholinguistics of Second Language Acquisition

Ping Li and Natasha Tokowicz
Pennsylvania State University and University of Pittsburgh

The study of second language acquisition (SLA) from a psycholinguistic perspective has led to significant discoveries over the last three decades. Psycholinguists are concerned with basic processes and mechanisms underlying the perception, production, and learning of language, whereas second language (L2) learners are faced with the tasks of perceiving and producing utterances and learning to read and write in a new language. Although classical psycholinguistic theories have largely grown out of studies of human linguistic behavior in limited language, recent years have seen several important changes to this tradition. First, psycholinguists have clearly moved away from the study of the "ideal speaker or listener." In Chomsky's (1957) tradition, linguistic competence rather than performance should be the main focus of language science, but today's psycholinguistic models are largely "performance-based." Second, psycholinguists are no longer interested only in language universals based on assumptions and inferences drawn from the study of a single language (often English); instead, they invest in both language universals and language variation to account for psycholinguistic phenomena in diverse languages (see, for example, reviews in Li, Tan, Bates, and Tzeng, 2006). Finally, the field of psycholinguistics has become increasingly intertwined with neurolinguistics and cognitive neuroscience, in that issues of brain mechanisms of language are taking center stage in current psycholinguistic theories (see, for example, Gaskell, 2007). These recent changes have created an exciting environment for studying SLA with new perspectives, new methodologies, and new directions. Below we focus on these new dimensions of psycholinguistics and how they impact our understanding of SLA.

Sensitive periods and beyond

Perhaps no other domain in SLA has generated so much excitement and public attention as well as debate and controversies as the critical period1 hypothesis (CPH) (see **Critical Period Hypothesis (CPH)**, this volume). Understanding of the biological and cognitive bases of child–adult differences in SLA has been listed among the top 125 science questions for the next quarter century in the *Science* magazine (vol. 309, July 2005). According to the original formulation of CPH by Lenneberg (1967), the critical period in language is linked to constraints in brain plasticity, and the endpoint of that period coincides with puberty, at which time a complete acquisition of language as a native speaker will be impossible. This formulation attracted a great deal of interest for its simplicity and conformity to intuition based on folk wisdom.

However, since the 1980s psycholinguistic research has cast doubt on the CPH with respect to learning speed versus outcome for children versus adults, the developmental trajectory in linguistic performance within and beyond the presumed critical period, and the neural and cognitive underpinnings of various sensitive periods for different components of language (see **Age effects in SLA**, this volume). In a series of comprehension and production tasks (e.g., auditory discrimination of sounds, translation), Snow and Hoefnagel-Hohle (1978) showed that a group of older children (12–15 years of age) learned a new language at a faster rate than younger children. In another study, Johnson and Newport (1989) provided evidence that the age of acquisition effects (AoA) are more complex than originally thought: within the early time window of learning (age 2–16), there is a linear decline in performance, but beyond the time window performance is uncorrelated with AoA and is highly variable, with some individuals at or close to native performance at very late AoAs. Liu, Bates, and Li (1992) examined a Chinese–English bilingual group at different AoAs and discovered further nonlinear patterns: in general, late learners showed clear forward transfer, that is, using L1 processing strategies for L2 comprehension, whereas early learners showed either backward transfer (using L2 strategies for L1 comprehension) or distinct patterns for L1 versus L2. Interestingly, in contrast to Johnson and Newport's findings, their data indicated no linear decline even within the so-called critical period, showing that there is no single "critical period" point for language learning and the possibility that a positive outcome can rise and fall at different developmental points. Finally, Weber-Fox and Neville (1996), in an event-related potential (ERP) study of sentence processing by Chinese learners of English, found differences in the timing and distribution of ERP components during the processing of semantic and syntactic violations when learners were compared to native speakers (see **Event-related potential (ERP)**, this volume). Differences between L2 learners and native speakers appeared at different ages depending on whether the violation was syntactic or semantic: for syntactic violations, native-non-native differences appeared as early as 2 years of age for the learners, whereas for semantic violations, differences appeared only after age 11. These data suggest that the age effects may appear at different ages for grammar versus meaning (for further review of this point, see Hernandez and Li, 2007).

Many subsequent studies are consistent with the above-mentioned studies in arguing against the existence of a simple, clearly bounded, and monotonically developing, critical period for SLA. Although both biological and environmental factors must contribute to AoA effects, as in any developmental domains, the causal link between biology and a critical period in human language learning remains contentious (see Bialystok, 2001). One influential theory that does not rely on biology to account for sensitive periods is the "less is more" hypothesis (Johnson and Newport, 1989), according to which the less well-developed cognitive capacity in children actually confers advantage to language learning: young learners tend to be engaged in piecemeal, gradual, and implicit statistical learning whereas adults, because of formal operational abilities, tend to use explicit analytic procedures in dealing with language. When faced with complex linguistic stimuli, children perform only a limited number of componential analyses of the possible form-meaning mappings because they do not have the capacity to compute the complete set of data. Such componential analysis gives children an advantage over adults who use larger cognitive resources (e.g., working memory) in computing complex form-meaning mappings at once. This "less is more" view coincides with patterns from computational modeling (Elman, 1993), according to which connectionist networks are able to learn complex grammar only if the network receives simple sentences first and then gradually move to complex ones, or if the network is provided with limited working-memory windows early on so that initial componential analysis is efficient and successful (see **Connectionism and SLA**, and **Parallel Distributed Processing (PDP) Models**, this volume).

The "less is more" hypothesis remains a hypothesis after 20 years, as no causal links (with negative relationship) have been experimentally established between cognitive resources and the ability to learn new languages. An alternative view is to look at the AoA effects in relation to the competition between the two languages, more specifically to the entrenchment of L2 created by the consolidation of L1 during learning (Hernandez, Li, and MacWhinney, 2005). As knowledge and skill of L1 become more established, the representational structure becomes increasingly resistant to change from new input. Connectionist simulations in which L2 was introduced at different time points relative to L1 have shown that these entrenchment effects are observed in both phonological and lexical representation systems (Zhao and Li, 2010), in that at later stages of AoA, a parasitic L2 representation develops upon the L1 representation (see **Entrenchment**, this volume). This is because when structural consolidation in L1 has reached a point at which further reorganization becomes difficult or impossible, L2 learning will have to tap into existing representational resources as well as its system layout. Furthermore, along with this entrenchment occurs the change in neural plasticity, particularly in sensorimotor integration, which confers an advantage to early exposure because of the highly flexible neural system for the development of motor sequence control and coordination of articulatory actions, skills critical for early phonological processing and grammatical acquisition (Hernandez and Li, 2007). Once the neural system settles into stable patterns for phonology and grammar, additional changes to these patterns become difficult when learning a new language that differs from the established patterns. Connectionist simulations further show that even in lexical learning the overall representation structures of L1 and L2 may differ significantly as a result of AoA (see Figure 12), depending on whether the functional units and connections in the network are fully specified or committed to one versus the other language.

A recent theoretical framework articulated by MacWhinney (2011) as the Unified Competition Model has attempted to account for sensitive periods in L2 by reference to a host of neural, cognitive, and social variables as risk factors of L2 learning (see **Competition Model**, this volume). Consistent with considerations above regarding the dynamic interplay between competing languages, the unified model assumes that the underlying learning mechanisms are not fundamentally different in L1 and L2 acquisition. The differences arise from the risk factors of negative transfer from L1, entrenchment as discussed above, parasitism (dependency of L2 on L1), mismatched connectivity (incorrect connections between processing areas), and social isolation. To achieve successful L2 acquisition, the adult learner must strive to use the same core mechanisms available to

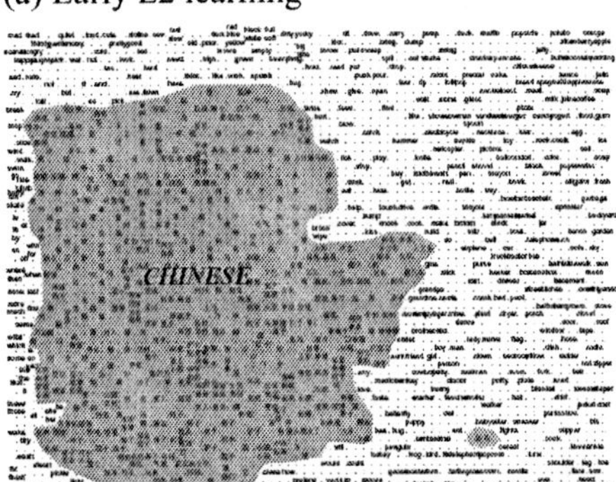

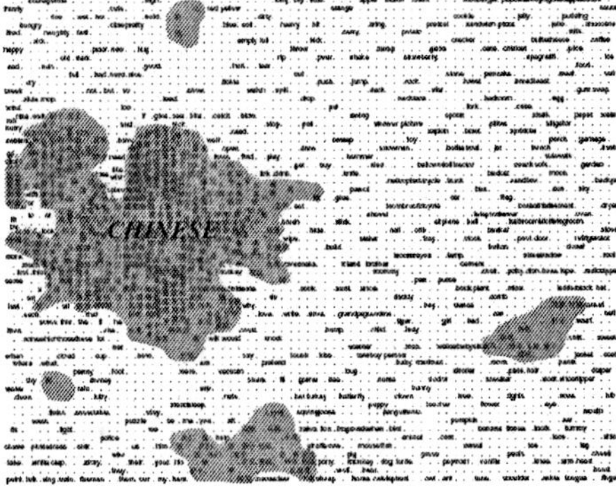

Figure 12 Lexical organization as a function of early vs. late learning of L2. Shaded areas indicate L2 (Chinese) representations

the child, as well as a set of protective factors including positive transfer, social participation or immersion, active thinking in the L2, reorganization through resonance (interactive activation from corresponding sites), and internalization (using L2 for inner speech). Adults who are able to maximize the benefits of these protective factors will show better and faster learning than adults who are disadvantaged on these factors. How the various risk factors unfold in development and how learners can actively use the protective factors will remain to be the major challenges to theories of SLA.

Cognitive executive functions and second language

In contrast to the study of sensitive periods, researchers have only recently become interested in the relationship between the learning of an L2 and cognitive executive functions such as the maintenance and updating of information through working memory and selective attention (see **Attention**, **Executive control and frontal brain**, and **Working memory**, this volume). One integrative discussion of the relationship between multiple languages and executive functions came from Bialystok (2001), where a developmental perspective was taken on the bilingual child, compared with the monolingual child, who learns to juggle between two or more languages, and how this language juggling provides direct benefits in cognitive flexibility. Specifically, children who grow up learning two or more languages are provided with extra opportunities to learn to inhibit irrelevant information or misleading cues when encountering inference, due to the speech task that requires speaking one language while inhibiting the unwanted language(s) (see **Inhibitory control**, and **Language (task) switching**, this volume). Another topic of research with a slightly different focus is learned attention and the accompanying effects of blocking (see **Learned inattention and blocking**, this volume), which could lead to strong positive or negative transfer from L1 to L2. For example, L2 learners whose native language is Chinese tend to explore adverbial cues (e.g., *yesterday*) more than grammatical cues (e.g., tense markers) even when both cues are equally available in the L2, perhaps due to the learned associative attention to adverbial cues as a reliable predictor of temporal reference, hence blocking the learning of tense marking on verbs.

In the past decade the study of bilingual executive functioning has boomed. A general consensus is that bilingualism confers a set of distinct advantages in cognitive abilities, including inhibitory control, selective attention, and working memory, especially in cases in which conflict resolution is required (e.g., making a decision when two relevant cues point in different directions; see a recent review in Bialystok, 2009). To summarize the ever-growing literature, we can make a few quick observations. First, during childhood, bilinguals demonstrate improved executive control. This has been measured using tasks such as the card-sorting task, in which children first sort cards along one dimension and later along another, ignoring the first dimension, and the ambiguous figures task, in which children first see a figure in one way, and then must see the other figure, ignoring the first (see Bialystok, 2009). Second, the cognitive advantages associated with bilingualism can be traced to the need to select one language for production while inhibiting the other because the same advantages are not present for bimodal bilinguals who can speak one language while signing another (Emmorey, Luk, Pyers, and Bialystok, 2008). Finally, the bilingual advantage on tasks that examine inhibitory control such as the Simon task are maintained into adulthood, and in fact are larger for older bilinguals than younger bilinguals. This is likely because an enhanced inhibitory mechanism buffers the effects of aging (see **Cognitive aging**, this volume). Notably, this research also suggests that bilingualism may delay the onset of dementia by approximately four years (Bialystok, Craik, and Freedman, 2007), highlighting the breadth of the cognitive advantages of bilingualism. Such cognitive advantages in older individuals who are bilingual may also confer benefits to later learning of another language.

One issue that is yet to become clear from the SLA perspective is whether and how individual differences in cognitive executive functions impact the learning of an L2: despite the effects of language learning on executive functions, different learners may have different executive functions at the outset. In a number of domains, including reading acquisition and first language acquisition for typically and atypically developing children, there is a tradition to use cognitive variables such as working memory, naming or processing speed, attentional control, and auditory and other perceptual processing abilities to predict children's early and later linguistic skills, to distinguish good readers from poor readers, and to identify children who may be at risk for specific language impairment or other forms of language delay (e.g., Leonard *et al.*, 2007). However, much more work needs to be done in SLA, as in reading acquisition or first language acquisition, to connect the relevant cognitive variables with individual differences in the speed and outcome of L2 learning; an exception in this regard is the promising research on working memory and L2 vocabulary learning (e.g., Service, 1992).

Neurocognitive approaches to SLA

As mentioned at the beginning, in recent years brain mechanisms of language are taking center stage in psycholinguistic theories. The psycholinguistics of SLA has also adopted this trend. An increasing number of SLA studies have employed neuroimaging methods including the Magnetic Resonance Imaging (MRI) and Event-Related Potential (ERP) techniques (see **Neuroimaging**, this volume). Functional MRI (fMRI) involves the use of a very strong magnetic field around the head to measure hemodynamic changes in blood flow, specifically the blood-oxygen-level-dependent (BOLD) signals, in various cortical and subcortical areas of the brain. These hemodynamic changes are taken to reflect neural activity relevant to task performance. The spatial resolution of fMRI is quite good, on the order of several millimeters. Therefore, fMRI has been particularly useful for determining whether similar or distinct neural tissue is used to process L1 and L2, and the factors that affect the extent of such overlap. fMRI can further be used to determine the relative amount of activation of particular areas of the brain during L1 and L2 processing. However, because hemodynamic changes occur relatively slowly, fMRI has relatively poor temporal resolution, only on the order of seconds. ERPs overcome the shortcomings of fMRI in this regard.

ERPs measure the electrical activity of populations of neurons in the brain through electrodes placed at the surface of the scalp. When time-locked to specific events such as the presentation of a stimulus, ERPs fluctuate in voltage, reflecting brain activity that takes place as a result of the event. Evident in the ERP signal are "components" or "brainwaves" that vary in their polarity (positive vs negative), latency (timing), and amplitude (level) of activation, and their distribution of this activity (location) across the surface of the scalp. Several components have been linked to specific cognitive events relevant for language processing (see Kutas *et al.*, 2007, for a review). ERP has excellent temporal resolution (on the order of milliseconds) and is particularly useful in understanding the dynamics of language processing in two languages. However, because of the difficulty in determining the neural source of activity measured at the scalp's surface, the spatial resolution of ERP is not as good as that of fMRI. fMRI and ERP therefore are complementary in their strengths and are used to investigate different questions about SLA, with fMRI focusing on the localization of processing in the brain and ERPs on the timing and extent of the engagement of particular cognitive processes. When combined, these studies can be used to inform theoretical issues regarding how native-like adult L2 processing is and the extent to which age of acquisition influences language learning and processing.

A central question that has attracted the attention of investigators in bilingual neuroimaging is whether the processing of L1 and L2 involves the same (common) or different (distinct) neural systems. Although earlier studies (e.g., Kim *et al.*, 1997) suggested AoA as a determining factor for common versus distinct neural patterns, more recent studies tend to point to largely overlapping systems for L1 and L2 (see Stowe and Sabourin, 2005 for a recent review), mainly in the left frontal and temporal areas. However, a host of variables, such as AoA, L2 proficiency, language-specific characteristics of

L1 and L2 (distinctness of the two languages), task demands (verb generation vs lexical decision vs picture naming), modality (comprehension vs production; spoken vs written language), and the language component being processed (syntax vs semantics), have all been found to modulate neural activities in the bilingual brain, thereby involving either distinct or common systems for the two languages.

One key issue in this debate has been the relative contribution of AoA versus L2 proficiency (see review in Hernandez and Li, 2007). Contrary to the greater emphasis the CPH places on age effects (see earlier discussion), current neuroimaging findings point to a stronger role of L2 proficiency than of L2 AoA. However, many studies, including the Kim *et al.* (1997) study, have confounded effects of AoA with those of proficiency. In a study that de-confounded the two variables, Wartenburger *et al.* (2003) found that neural response patterns in a semantic task differed mainly as a function of L2 proficiency level and not AoA. By contrast, neural response patterns in a grammatical task differed mainly as a function of AoA and not proficiency. Although these results suggest greater influence of AoA in grammatical processing, some findings point to the possibility that explicit judgments of grammaticality lead to greater differences than when such judgments are not explicitly required (e.g., Indefrey, 2006). Indeed, most bilingual imaging studies may be limited by the task demands that are placed on the participants. The most commonly used tasks (e.g., grammatical judgment, semantic categorization, verb generation, and silent sentence generation) may tap into general linguistic skills rather than the linguistic representations in L1 and L2. Moreover, level of analysis is also important because most fMRI data are based on averaged BOLD signals at a group level that neutralizes subject differences. Thus, greater overlap may be found when data are examined at the group level, but not when considered at the individual subject level (Indefrey, 2006). With the latter approach, specific L2 areas may be identified, as observed with electrical stimulation of particular areas during clinical treatment (e.g., Lucas, McKhann, and Ojemann, 2004). Taking these perspectives together, it is clear that there is no simple answer to whether common or distinct neural systems underlie bilingual language processing. It is therefore more meaningful to ask under what conditions, with what variables, and in what fashion the bilingual brain uses shared versud distinct cortical and subcortical structures to support the comprehension and production of the two languages.

The issue of not just *where* in the brain but *how much* neural activity occurs is also important. Various fMRI studies have examined the relative amount of activation of certain brain areas during the processing of L1 versus L2. Interestingly, these studies have found that L2 processing, as compared with L1 processing, is sometimes associated with more blood flow and sometimes with less blood flow to specific brain regions (see review in Abutalebi, Cappa, and Perani, 2005). To account for such seemingly conflicting findings, Abutalebi *et al.* (2005) suggest that in production tasks, higher activation may indicate increased task difficulty and hence more processing effort. By contrast, lower activation in comprehension tasks may indicate better comprehension, which requires less processing effort.

ERP studies of SLA have focused on issues such as the degree to which L2 processing is native-like (see earlier discussion on sensitive period effects). ERPs can be used to examine both quantitative differences (e.g., in terms of timing of events) and qualitative differences (e.g., in terms of types of processing; see van Hell and Tokowicz, 2010, for a review). The research on semantic processing demonstrates that early L2 learners process semantics similarly in L1 and L2, and similarly to native speakers of that language (see **Semantic processing**, this volume). For example, L2 learners demonstrate ERP effects indicative of the detection of semantic anomalies in L2. This detection occurs on a similar timescale as in L1, but only for individuals who were first exposed to L2 before age 11 (Weber Fox and Neville, 1996). However, this latter finding may be due to age of exposure or to lower proficiency because it is often difficult to de-confound these factors.

In relation to morpho-syntactic processing, numerous ERP studies have examined the extent to which processing is similar or different in L1 and L2, not in terms of common versus distinct neural regions as in fMRI studies but in terms of the timing of the ERP components. In some studies, performance is compared in L1 and L2 for a given group of bilinguals. In other studies, the bilingual group is compared to a group of native speakers. Some of these studies use naturalistic language learners (e.g., Chen *et al.*, 2007), whereas others use miniature versions of natural languages or artificial languages (e.g., Friederici, Steinhauer, and Pfeifer, 2002) (see **Artificial language learning**, this volume). Recently, longitudinal studies have also been used to examine learning over time (e.g., McLaughlin *et al.*, 2010). Overall, the results of many studies point to the possibility that adult L2 learners can achieve native-like performance in L2, under certain conditions (see Kotz, 2008; van Hell and Tokowicz, 2010, for reviews): for example, after higher proficiency is obtained, when the stimuli are syntactically simple, or when the types of constructions being tested allow learners to predict more accurately the upcoming information, as in obligatory clauses.

As discussed in the Introduction, cross-linguistic differences are capturing the attention of psycholinguists and cognitive scientists (see **Cross linguistic influence (CLI)**, and **Linguistic transfer**, this volume). ERP studies examining cross-language similarity have shown that cross-linguistically similar features are processed more similarly in the L1 and L2 than cross-linguistically dissimilar features (e.g., Tokowicz and MacWhinney, 2005; see review in Tolentino and Tokowicz, 2011). This line of research focuses on the idea that L1 processing routines may be used for the processing of L2 (e.g., MacWhinney, in press), and that learning features of an L2 that are dissimilar from those of L1 are likely to create competition (Hernandez, Li, and MacWhinney, 2005).

Some fMRI studies of SLA have also focused on the impact of cross-language similarity. Consistent with ERP studies, they demonstrate that features of languages that are cross-linguistically similar are associated with a greater overlap in brain regions during processing, when compared to features that are cross-linguistically dissimilar (see Tolentino and Tokowicz, 2011 for review). Dissimilar features could lead to distinct neural response patterns for the L1 versus the L2, along with the other variables discussed earlier that affect the recruitment of common or distinct neural systems. For example, using lexical decision tasks, researchers have indentified distinct neural patterns in bilinguals' responses to nouns and verbs in English versus Chinese, showing that the differences in how grammatical classes are marked in L1 versus L2 affect areas and degrees of neural activity (e.g., Chan *et al.*, 2008). In neuroimaging studies of English and many Indo-European languages, verbs activate prefrontal regions whereas nouns activate temporal-occipital regions. fMRI evidence from native Chinese speakers, however, showed no such dissociations (Li, Jin, and Tan, 2004). Interestingly, early Chinese–English bilinguals are able to respond to the language-specific properties of both L1 and L2, whereas late bilinguals can only use L1 patterns for L2 processing. In another study of bilingual learners, Perfetti *et al.* (2007) further suggested asymmetric neural patterns in how the learner acquires the reading task in Chinese versus English: English learners of Chinese tend to recruit additional neural structures to handle the high spatial analytic demands of reading Chinese characters, whereas Chinese learners of English can use existing structures for both L1 and L2 reading. Together, these findings suggest that, consistent with the Competition Model, established neural networks of the L1 can significantly shape the neural representation and processing of the L2, depending on the similarity of the two languages under study.

Recently, neuroimaging studies have also attempted to determine whether *structural* changes (e.g., grey-matter density), in addition to *functional* changes (blood flow), occur as a result of learning or using an L2. Structural MRI can be used to examine changes in brain morphology, specifically with a technique called Voxel-Based Morphometry (VBM). This method allows examination of the structural makeup of areas of the brain. Using VBM, Mechelli *et al.* (2004) demonstrated structural plasticity in terms of increased grey-matter density in the left inferior parietal cortex, as a function of both age of acquisition and proficiency (the earlier the L2 is learned, the higher the density; the more proficient the learner, the higher the density). Green *et al.* (2006) further found that simultaneous interpreters had greater grey-matter density in several brain areas as compared to monolinguals or bilinguals who were not simultaneous interpreters. Finally, Stein *et al.* (2012) observed that learning a new language in an immersion context led to increased grey matter density, possibly reflecting an increase in the structural capacity for future learning. Together these data suggest significant neural plasticity as a function of L2 learning, consistent with the overall picture discussed so far that the adult bilingual brain, in both function and structure, is shaped by language-specific experiences and amount of experience with the languages.

In sum, the cognitive neuroscience approach has led to many insights regarding the neurocognitive underpinnings of SLA. Neuroimaging techniques complement behavioral methods in understanding mechanisms and processes of L2 learning, particularly when differences are not evident in behavioral data but are in neuroimaging data (e.g., Chen *et al.*, 2007; McLaughlin *et al.*, 2004; Tokowicz and MacWhinney, 2005). As a final note, although there has been a surge of neuroimaging studies of SLA in recent years, there is a lack of longitudinal research in this domain, which is urgently needed for investigating the adaptive changes triggered during the acquisition of a new language.

See also: cognitive aging, competition model, Critical Period Hypothesis (CPH), Event Related Potentials (ERP), learned inattention and blocking, Functional Magnetic Resonance Imaging (fMRI)

Note

1 In the literature various terms have been used to refer to roughly the same concept though with difference in emphasis, including critical period, sensitive period, age-related differences, age of acquisition (AoA), age of onset (AoO), and age of arrival (AoA).

References

Abutalebi, J., Cappa, S.F. and Perani, D. (2005). What can functional neuroimaging tell us about the bilingual brain? In J.F. Kroll and A.M. B. De Groot (eds), *Handbook of Bilingualism: Psycholinguistic Approaches*, pp. 497–515. New York: Oxford University Press.

Bialystok, E. (2001). *Bilingualism in Development: Language, Literacy, and Cognition.* Cambridge: Cambridge University Press.

Bialystok, E. (2009). Bilingualism: The good, the bad, and the indifferent. *Bilingualism: Language and Cognition, 12*, 3–12.

Bialystok, E., Craik, F.I.M. and Freedman, M. (2007). Bilingualism as a protection against the onset of dementia. *Neuropsychologia, 45*, 459–464.

Chan, A., Luke, K., Li, P., Yip, V., Li, G., Weekes, B. and Tan, L. (2008). Neural correlates of nouns and verbs in early bilinguals. *Annals of the New York Academy of Sciences, 1145*, 30–40.

Chen, L., Shu, H., Liu, Y., Zhao, J. and Li, P. (2007). ERP signatures of subject-verb agreement in L2 learning. *Bilingualism: Language and Cognition, 10*, 161–174.

Chomsky, N. (1957). *Syntactic Structures*. The Hague: Mouton.

Elman, J. (1993). Learning and development in neural networks: The importance of starting small. *Cognition, 48*, 71–99.

Emmorey, K., Luk, G., Pyers, J. and Bialystok, E. (2008). The source of enhanced cognitive control in bilinguals: Evidence from bimodal bilinguals. *Psychological Science, 12*, 1201–1206.

Friederici, A.D., Steinhauer, K. and Pfeifer, E. (2002). Brain signatures of artificial language processing: Evidence challenging the critical period hypothesis. *Proceedings of the National Academy of Sciences of the United States of America, 99*, 529–534.

Gaskell, G. (2007). *Oxford Handbook of Psycholinguistics*. Oxford: Oxford University Press.

Green, D.W., Crinion, J. and Price, C.J. (2006). Convergence, degeneracy, and control. *Language Learning, 56*, 99–125.

Hernandez, A. and Li, P. (2007). Age of acquisition: Its neural and computational mechanisms. *Psychological Bulletin, 133*, 638–650.

Hernandez, A., Li, P. and MacWhinney, B. (2005). The emergence of competing modules in bilingualism. *Trends in Cognitive Sciences, 9*, 220–225.

Indefrey, P. (2006). A meta-analysis of hemodynamic studies on first and second language processing: Which suggested differences can we trust and what do they mean? In M. Gullberg and P. Indefrey (eds), *The Cognitive Neuroscience of Second Language Acquisition*, pp. 279–304. Malden, MA: Blackwell.

Johnson, J. and Newport, E. (1989). Critical period effects in second language learning: The influence of maturational state on the acquisition of English as a second language. *Cognitive Psychology, 21*, 60–99.

Kim, K., Relkin, N., Lee, K.M. and Hirsch, J. (1997). Distinct cortical areas associated with native and second languages. *Nature, 388*, 171–174.

Kotz, S.A. (2008). A critical review of ERP and fMRI evidence on L2 syntactic processing. *Brain and Language, 109*, 68–74.

Kutas, M., Federmeier, K.D., Staab, J. and Kluender, R. (2007). Language. In J.T. Cacioppo, C. G. Tassinary and G.G. Berntson (eds), *Handbook of Psychophysiology*, 3rd edn. New York: Cambridge University Press.

Lenneberg, E. (1967). *Biological Foundations of Language*. New York: John Wiley and Sons, Inc.

Leonard, L., Ellis Weismer, S., Miller, C., Francis, D., Tomblin, J. and Kail, R. (2007). Speed of processing, working memory, and language impairment in children. *Journal of Speech, Language, and Hearing Research, 50*, 408–428.

Li, P., Tan, L.-H., Bates, E. and Tzeng, O. (2006). *The Handbook of East Asian Psycholinguistics* Vol. 1: Chinese. Cambridge: Cambridge University Press.

Li, P., Jin, Z. and Tan, L. (2004). Neural representations of nouns and verbs in Chinese: An fMRI study. *NeuroImage, 21*, 1533–1541.

Liu, H., Bates, E. and Li, P. (1992). Sentence interpretation in bilingual speakers of English and Chinese. *Applied Psycholinguistics, 13*, 451–484.

Lucas, T.H., McKhann, G.M.M. and Ojemann, G. A. (2004). Functional separation of languages in the bilingual brain: A comparison of electrical stimulation language mapping in 25 bilingual patients and 117 monolingual control patients. *Journal of Neurosurgery, 101*, 449–457.

MacWhinney, B. (2011). The logic of the Unified Model. In S. Gass and A. Mackey (eds), *Handbook of Second Language Acquisition*. New York: Routledge.

McLaughlin, J., Osterhout, L. and Kim, A. (2004). Neural correlates of second-language word meaning: Minimal instruction produces rapid change. *Nature Neuroscience, 7*, 703–704.

McLaughlin, J., Tanner, D., Pitkänen, I., Frenck-Mestre, C., Inoue, K., Valentine, G. and Osterhout, L. (2010). Brain potentials reveal discrete stages of L2 grammatical learning. *Language Learning, 60*, 123–150.

Mechelli, A., Crinion, J.T., Noppeney, U., O'Doherty, J., Ashburner, J., Frackowiak, R.S. and Price, C. (2004). Structural plasticity in the bilingual brain. *Nature, 431*, 757.

Perfetti, C.A., Liu, Y., Fiez, J., Nelson, J., Bolger, D. and Tan, L. (2007). Reading in two writing systems: Accommodation and assimilation of the brain's reading network. *Bilingualism: Language and Cognition, 10*, 131–146.

Service, E. (1992). Phonology, working memory, and foreign-language learning. *Quarterly Journal of Experimental Psychology, 45*, 21–50.

Snow, C.E. and Hoefnagel-Hohle, M. (1978). Critical period for language acquisition: Evidence from second language learning. *Child Development, 49*, 1263–1279.

Stein, M., Federspiel, A., Koenig, T., Wirth, M., Strik, W., Wiest, R., *et al.* (2012). Structural plasticity in the language system related to increased second language proficiency. *Cortex, 48*, 458–465.

Stowe, L.A. and Sabourin, L. (2005). Imaging the processing of a second language: Effects of maturation and proficiency on the neural processes involved. *International Review of Applied Linguistics in Language Teaching, 43*, 329–353.

Tokowicz, N. and MacWhinney, B. (2005). Implicit and explicit measures of sensitivity to violations in second language grammar: An event-related potential investigation. *Studies in Second Language Acquisition, 27*, 173–204.

Tolentino, L.C. and Tokowicz, N. (2011). Across languages, space, and time: A review of the role of cross-language similarity in L2 (morpho) syntactic processing as revealed by fMRI and

ERP. *Studies in Second Language Acquisition, 33,* 1–34.

van Hell, J.G. and Tokowicz, N. (2010). Event-related brain potentials and second language learning: Syntactic processing in late L2 learners at different L2 proficiency levels. *Second Language Research, 26,* 43–74.

Wartenburger, I., Heekeren, H., Abutalebi, J., Cappa, S., Villringer, A. and Perani, D. (2003). Early setting of grammatical processing in the bilingual brain. *Neuron, 37,* 159–170.

Weber-Fox, C.M. and Neville, H.J. (1996). Maturational constraints on functional specializations for language processing: ERP and behavioral evidence in bilingual speakers. *Journal of Cognitive Neuroscience, 8,* 231–256.

Zhao, X. and Li, P. (2010). Bilingual lexical interactions in an unsupervised neural network model. *International Journal of Bilingual Education and Bilingualism, 13,* 505–524.

Further reading

Gullberg, M. and Indefrey, P. (eds) (2006). *The Cognitive Neuroscience of Second Language Acquisition*, Malden, MA: Blackwell. (An overview of the use of cognitive neuroscience techniques to the study of second language acquisition.)

Hernandez, A. and Li, P. (2007). Age of acquisition: Its neural and computational mechanisms. *Psychological Bulletin, 133,* 638–650. (Provides an account of age of acquisition versus proficiency effects in first language lexical processing and second language learning centered around general sensorimotor integration.)

Hernandez, A., Li, P. and MacWhinney, B. (2005). The emergence of competing modules in bilingualism. *Trends in Cognitive Sciences, 9,* 220–225. (Describes an emergentist approach to first and second language learning that appeals to the processes of competition, parasitism, resonance, and entrenchment rather than modularity.)

Sabourin, L. and Stowe, L.A. (2008). Second language processing: When are first and second languages processed similarly? *Second Language Research, 24,* 397–430. (An event-related brain potential study that focuses on the similarities and differences between first and second language processing.)

van Hell, J.G. and Tokowicz, N. (2010). Event-related brain potentials and second language learning: Syntactic processing in late L2 learners at different L2 proficiency levels. *Second Language Research, 26,* 43–74. (A review of event-related brain potential studies of adult second language morpho-syntactic and syntactic processing.)

Q

Qualitative research

Richard F. Young
University of Wisconsin-Madison

Qualitative research methods in second language acquisition developed after a change in thinking in the social sciences away from an approach to knowledge, in which researchers took observable behavior and individual mental states as indexes of social and psychological phenomena. In this earlier tradition, if a researcher adopted accepted procedures to generate a hypothesis from a theory of a social psychological phenomenon, and then collected and analyzed data in such a way to ensure the validity and reliability of the process, the results would be replicable by other researchers adopting the same procedures and would be generalizable to similar phenomena. Because much (but not all) of this research involved collecting numerical data and subjecting it to statistical procedures of inference, this approach came to be known as quantitative.

Qualitative research challenges four assumptions of quantitative methods. In qualitative research:

* Participation in L2 learning and use is recognized as subjective and different from one participant to another.
* The relationship between researcher and participant is recognized as collaborative and thus interpretation of data by a researcher is necessarily value-laden.
* Analysis of data involves attention to the particulars and the context of L2 learning and use, a process that often emerges as the study proceeds.
* In presentation of their research to an audience, qualitative researchers aim for an informal style and a personal voice.

Although a large majority of published SLA research continues to be quantitative (Richards, 2009), qualitative approaches have been used in a number of recent studies, exemplifying six distinct ways of researching social context in second language learning: case study, narrative inquiry, grounded theory, ethnography, critically engaged research, and action research.

Case study involves collection and presentation of detailed information about a particular case, which may be a single learner, a small group of learners, a teacher, a classroom, or even a country. Case studies may focus on interlanguage development by learners or on changes in social participation and in the linguistic reflexes of identity. Many case studies in SLA are longitudinal, such as Schmidt's (1983) multi-year study of the acquisition of communicative competence in English by a Japanese artist or Leki's (2007) multi-year study of academic literacy development in English by four international students at a US university. The methodologies of data collection and analysis used in case studies by SLA researchers have been extensively reviewed by Hood (2009).

Narrative inquiry is also a longitudinal methodology but in narrative inquiry the data are a story or set of stories told by learners themselves. Narratives may take different forms including diaries, life histories, learner memoirs, and stories of critical language-learning events, but are first-person accounts. In the anthology of short narratives collected by Nunan and Choi (2010), all contributions were written in this personal voice, as were the book-length learner memoirs and essays reviewed by Pavlenko (2001). In many cases, the narratives themselves and the connections made by their authors among language-learning events, beliefs, and the sense that their authors make of them are the end of analysis, but selections from learner narratives may be used by other researchers to illustrate their own arguments or researchers may provide a full-blown analysis of the narrative. The process of narrative analysis has been described by Murray (2009) as involving six steps: (a) coding the narrative, (b) grouping codes into categories, (c) reconfiguring the narrative according to the emergent categories, (d) sending the reconfigured narrative to the participant for comments, (e) comparing codes of different events in the narrative, and (f) noting the themes that emerge from the narrative.

The process of coding and the emergence of theory from data rather than using pre-existing theories in order to explain language-learning phenomena are well established in qualitative research in the practice of *grounded theory*. Grounded theory emphasizes the meaning of experience for participants while allowing the researcher to generate or discover a theoretical framework within which social processes can be accurately described and fully explained. Thus, theories or ideas about the social and psychological processes of language learning can become "grounded" in data from the field and, more specifically, in the actions, interactions, and social processes of learners. Grounded theory has developed in two different directions depending on the training and epistemology of its practitioners. Objectivist grounded theory falls within a positivist epistemology in which the grounded theorist assumes that data represent facts about a knowable world. The objectivist researcher's task is to "discover" the theory that explains them. An example of objectivist grounded theory is Yan and Horwitz's (2008) study of anxiety in classroom foreign language learning. By contrast, in constructivist grounded theory, data and analysis are considered to arise from experiences shared by the participants, the researcher, and relevant others. Practitioners of constructivist grounded theory inspired by Charmaz (2006) take a reflexive stance toward the research process and consider how their theories evolve. Garrett and Young's (2009) study of one learner's emotional responses to an intensive foreign-language course is one example of this stripe.

Perhaps best known of all qualitative research methods is *ethnography*. Because of its long tradition in anthropology as the study of human cultures and societies, ethnographic researchers in SLA as described by Duff (forthcoming) cast their data net far wider than in other qualitative approaches. Data are often collected over an extended period of participant observation ranging from several months to several years, and the resulting report may be in the form of a monograph. In her two-year ethnographic study of educational reform in the United States as experienced by three second language learners attending a school attempting to transform itself into a high-performance elementary school in California's Silicon Valley, Gebhard (2002/2004) listed three main sources of data: observations of teacher staff meetings, workshops, and open houses; audio and video tapes of classroom interaction, interviews with students, teachers, parents, and administrators; and documents such as student records, reports, correspondence with parents, and textbooks. In the anthropological tradition, the role of the researcher has often been seen as both participant and observer in which the researcher must find a role within the group observed from which to participate in some manner, for instance as a substitute teacher in an ethnography of schooling, as a coordinator in an ethnography of a study-abroad program, or as a bilingual aide in an ethnography of an immersion ESL program. The objective of participant observation is to describe participants' subjectivities from their own perspective and to eschew an outsider's stance.

Some ethnographers choose to study a social group because they perceive social inequity in the materials resources available to the group or in the status of the group in society. In these cases, critical ethnographers do not produce materials for a disinterested audience but write academic policy studies and involve themselves directly in political movements on behalf of the group they are studying. In a stance opposed to the "truth-is-out-there" objectivism of positivist researchers, critical ethnographers work to advance political ends either by writing cultural critiques of American capitalism in schools like Gebhard (2002/2004) or by passionate identification and involvement with the group they are studying like Canagarajah's (1993) critical ethnography of Tamil students' complex and ambiguous responses to learning English in a Sri Lankan classroom.

The desire of researchers to bring about social change harks back to the Marx's affirmation: "Philosophers have only interpreted the world in different ways. What is crucial, however, is to change it." The desire of researchers to bring about change is found in critically engaged research and action research. In neither of these paradigms is there an accepted research method or set of procedures; what distinguishes them from other approaches is the researcher's stance toward its outcome—the use to which research is put.

A *critical approach* to SLA research involves describing and understanding language-learning situations with a view to uncovering the ways in which the context of learning creates, reproduces, and provides opportunities for resistance to dominant power and ideology. In some cases, a researcher's values may be fundamentally pessimistic. For example, some critical researchers may identify the sources of oppression and ground their analyses in the belief that we live in a fundamentally unjust world. For others, critical research may be founded on the view that knowledge of the connections between local educational practices and societal ideologies may further an individual learner's resistance and struggle against the preponderant influence of harmful public policy. Both of these values are exemplified in the essays describing the practice and effects of racism in second language education collected by Kubota and Lin (2009).

The object of criticism in *action research* is a teacher-researcher's own practice and beliefs. As described by Burns (1999), action research is a form of self-reflective inquiry undertaken often by teachers in order to improve the effectiveness of their teaching, their understanding of their teaching practice, and the relation between their own teaching and the institutional context in which they teach. Data for self-reflection may be in the form of journals written by students or the teacher; systematic observations of the teacher-researcher herself, of students and others, and of peers; as well as interviews with the same participants. One example of action research is a project undertaken by five ESL writing instructors to discover how students understand and respond to feedback from their instructors on the students' written work. Data were the students' initial written work, their instructors' feedback, students' revised writing, and interviews with the students aiming to discuss how students understood the instructors' feedback and how (or whether) they acted upon it. Because the researchers were the writing instructors themselves, they aimed to gain greater understanding of students' responses to the feedback that they provide and, perhaps, to modify their feedback on the basis of this new understanding.

"Qualitative research" in SLA is thus an umbrella term used to refer to a complex and evolving research tradition. Despite the apparent contrast with quantitative approaches, what distinguishes qualitative researchers is not a dislike of numbers but a realization that any numerical representation of L2 phenomena limits consideration of the multiple contexts in which languages are learned and limits attention to differences among learners. Because those contexts may have harmful effects on different learners, many qualitative researchers aim to alleviate the harm done by learning and using a new language.

See also: case-studies, context of situation, ethnographic research, longitudinal research, person-in-situation approaches, social and socio-cultural approaches to SLA

References

Burns, A. (1999). *Collaborative Action Research for English Language Teachers*. New York: Cambridge University Press.

Canagarajah, A.S. (1993). Critical ethnography of a Sri Lankan classroom: Ambiguities in student opposition to reproduction through ESOL. *TESOL Quarterly*, *27*(4), 601–26.

Charmaz, K. (2006). *Constructing Grounded Theory: A Practical Guide Through Qualitative Analysis*. Thousand Oaks, CA: Sage.

Duff, P.A. (forthcoming). *Ethnographic Research in Applied Linguistics: Exploring Language Teaching, Learning, and Use in Diverse Communities*. New York: Routledge.

Garrett, P. and Young, R.F. (2009). Theorizing affect in foreign language learning: An analysis of one learner's responses to a communicative-based Portuguese course. *The Modern Language Journal*, *93*(2), 209–26. doi:10.1111/j.1540-4781.2009.00857.x

Gebhard, M. (2002/2004). Fast capitalism, school reform, and second language literacy practices. *The Canadian Modern Language Review/La Revue canadienne des langues vivantes, 59*(1), 15–52. Reprinted in *The Modern Language Journal*, 88(2), 245–64. doi:10.1111/j.0026-7902.2004.00228.x

Hood, M. (2009). Case study. In J. Heigham and R. A. Croker (eds), *Qualitative research in applied linguistics: A practical introduction* (pp. 66–90). Basingstoke: Palgrave Macmillan.

Kubota, R. and Lin, A. (eds) (2009). *Race, culture, and identities in second language education: Exploring critically engaged practice*. New York: Routledge.

Leki, I. (2007). *Undergraduates in a second language: Challenges and complexities of academic literacy development*. New York: Lawrence Erlbaum Associates.

Murray, G. (2009). Narrative inquiry. In J. Heigham and R.A. Croker (eds), *Qualitative Research in Applied Linguistics: A Practical Introduction*, pp. 45–65. Basingstoke: Palgrave Macmillan.

Nunan, D. and Choi, J. (eds) (2010). *Language and Culture: Reflective Narratives and the Emergence of Identity*. New York: Routledge.

Pavlenko, A. (2001). Language learning memoirs as a gendered genre. *Applied Linguistics*, *22*(2), 213–40. doi:10.1093/applin/22.2.213

Richards, K. (2009). Trends in qualitative research in language teaching since 2000. *Language Teaching*, *42*(2), 147–80. doi:10.1017/S0261444808005612

Schmidt, R.W. (1983). Interaction, acculturation, and the acquisition of communicative competence: A case study of an adult. In N. Wolfson and E. Judd (eds), *Sociolinguistics and Language Acquisition*, pp. 137–74. Rowley, MA: Newbury House.

Yan, J.X. and Horwitz, E.K. (2008). Learners' perceptions of how anxiety interacts with personal and instructional factors to influence their achievement in English: A qualitative analysis of EFL learners in China. *Language Learning, 58*(1), 151–83. doi:10.1111/j.1467-9922.2007.00437.x

Quantitative research

Jenifer Larson-Hall

University of North Texas

Quantitative research describes a particular type of scientific investigation that uses numbers to back up its claims. Henning (1986: 702) defines quantitative research as "the kind of research that involves the tallying, manipulation, or systematic aggregation of quantities of data." In the SLA field, such research is typically conducted with human participants from whom some information is obtained. This information is encoded in terms of numbers such as scores on tests, points on attitudinal surveys, reaction times, judgments on performances, and so on. This type of approach is assumed to result in an objective analysis that can be replicated with further groups of participants. It is said to be reliable in this sense.

Quantitative research is often set in opposition to qualitative research. Qualitative research situates an activity or practice by describing it in its naturalistic setting, and thus would not use the laboratory tests and techniques that are often used in quantitative research. Qualitative research is concerned with situating itself in a particular context and developing it from the viewpoint of the participant. Lazaraton (2003) says that the most frequent type of qualitative research conducted in applied linguistics is ethnography and conversation analysis. Although qualitative research has been called subjective as opposed to the supposed objectivity of quantitative research, Lazaraton (2003) notes that conversation analysis is not subjective since it accurately transcribes the actual utterances of persons, but it does not start with research questions (it lets them emerge) and it does not report counts of features or items because it seeks to understand the situation as a whole instead of as a part of a larger unit. Ethnography too is conducted through a rigorous analysis and should be regarded less as subjective than as rooted in one particular situation. Qualitative research is thus said to be valid in that it richly describes a situation.

It would seem that quantitative research is inherently more generalizable than qualitative research. However, the fact that we human beings like to look for patterns and generalize our experiences means that readers will often generalize findings from both quantitative and qualitative research. In fact, we may ask what it might mean to have a quantitative study with reliability but without validity (a qualitative study with validity but without any reliability seems easier to understand—readers should not generalize from it). Authors in the SLA field (Jick, 1984; Lazaraton, 2000; Mackey and Gass, 2005) have called on practitioners to combine both qualitative and quantitative research, or to triangulate by using a number of information-gathering techniques in their reports, and this seems prudent in order to have both reliable and valid research. In addition, Lazaraton (1995) notes that many quantitative studies use questionable statistical practices and small sample sizes so that one should question whether the label of quantitative research automatically implies an imprimatur of 'reliability'.

Notwithstanding this caveat, the field of SLA today is dominated by research articles utilizing quantitative approaches, with Gass (2009) documenting that 61 per cent of empirical research articles from 2001–06 were quantitative (combined qualitative and quantitative made up 7 per cent of the total) and Lazaraton (2005) reporting that 86 per cent of the journal articles she surveyed from 1991–2001 were quantitative.

Since quantitative research reports employ numbers, they almost invariably contain at least descriptive statistics. Descriptive statistics are summary statistics such as counts, mean or median scores and standard deviations or variances. Many quantitative studies also include inferential statistics (also called parametric statistics), which are used to generalize scores from a given sample of participants to a wider population of participants. Usually this wider population is not explicitly named, but perhaps assumed to be all adult (or child) language learners (although this is surely too wide of an implication to be drawn from the average SLA study which may contain 10–30 participants per group). Inferential statistics include statistical tests that look for group differences, such as t-tests or ANOVAs, or tests that examine relationships among variables, such as correlation or multiple regression.

Another potentially problematic issue in quantitative research is how to code data. Whatever is measured in a research study must ultimately be converted into numbers in order to use a quantitative approach. The main topic of interest, such as the accuracy of students' tone on Thai words or their ability to use correct question formation in English, must somehow be measured on a scale with consistent differences between each increase of +1 (a continuous scale). Other factors that affect the main topic, such as language proficiency or teaching method, have no inherent numerical value (they are categorical). For more help with such topics, see Brown (1988) or Larson-Hall (2010).

Many authors in the language acquisition field view quantitative methodology, and the historical expansion of such methodology, as a positive addition to descriptive studies in linguistics. Henning (1986: 702) claims that the advantages to a quantitative approach lie in the ability to generalize beyond specific instances and infer expected frequencies of occurrence, and the application of the scientific method. However, Henning (1986) also notes that without appropriate randomized participant selection procedures, inferential statistics and the ensuing generalizations that result from such statistics are flawed.

Quantitative research reports use a common framework for reporting data. In most cases, the researcher generates a hypothesis based on either previous research or, if there has been no previous research on the topic, on research that touches in some way on the current topic of investigation. The researcher then uses an approach called "null hypothesis significance testing" (NHST) which involves generating a null hypothesis and an alternative hypothesis. The null hypothesis states that there is no difference between groups or relationship between variables. This is a rather confusing way of looking at things, but it fits with the Popperian idea (1959) that empirical claims must be falsifiable. That is, one cannot definitively prove something true, but one way to begin to scientifically examine evidence is by proving that some hypotheses are false. A common example in this area is that one cannot prove that unicorns do not exist, but one could easily disprove the assertion that no horses are brown by bringing forth an actual brown horse.

Using a framework that assumes that the data are distributed according to a normal distribution (a technical term involving the bell-shaped curve) and that the variances of groups are equal, mathematical calculations involving the mean, standard deviation, and sample size are computed, resulting in a statistic. If the probability of obtaining the computed statistic, given that the null hypothesis is true, is small (usually below a p-value of 0.05), one is said to reject the null hypothesis and accept the alternative hypothesis. Otherwise, one in essence keeps the null hypothesis (although it should be noted that this does not prove the null hypothesis; instead, we may say that we have "failed to disprove the null." This is not just semantics—if we fail to find a brown horse in our sample that does not mean that we should once and for all accept the assertion that there are no brown horses).

There are some significant problems with this type of statistical approach (detailed cogently in Kline, 2004), not the least of which is that the results of statistical tests do not tell researchers what they really want to know, which is how likely or how important the results are. Kline (2004) advises researchers to always include effect sizes, which do not depend on sample sizes and do provide information on how important the results are. Researchers would also be well advised to look at and understand effect sizes just as well or better than they understand what p-values mean, since a statistically "non-significant" effect (where the p-value is above a certain threshold, such as 0.05) may still indicate an interesting effect if it has a strong effect size (Kirk, 2001; Kline, 2004). Larson-Hall (2010: 118–19) contains tables which give possible interpretations of various effect size magnitudes.

Lazarton's (2000: 180) essay on current trends in research methods and statistics in applied linguistics ends with a hope that future research will help develop "alternatives to parametric statistics for small-scale research studies that involve limited amounts of dependent data." Although larger sample sizes are still the best remedy for ambiguous statistical results, an alternative to parametric statistics called robust statistics has been developed by the statistical community but is still relatively unknown to those using quantitative methodologies (Wilcox, 1998). Traditionally non-parametric statistics have been viewed as an alternative because they do not require that the data be normally distributed. However, they still require random sampling and equal variances between groups. Robust methods of statistics contain even fewer assumptions about the data; they deal better with outliers, skewed distributions and unequal variances than parametric or non-parametric methods (Larson-Hall and Herrington, 2010; Wilcox, 2001). Larson-Hall (2011) provides information about how to calculate robust alternatives to a variety of statistical tests using the R statistical program. Readers are advised to find out more about such methods as a way of improving their own quantitative research.

See also: Analysis of Variance (ANOVA), correlation, effect size, qualitative research, significance level, T-tests

References

Brown, J.D. (1988). *Understanding Research in Second Language Learning: A Teacher's Guide to Statistics and Research Design*. Cambridge: Cambridge University Press.

Gass, S. (2009) A historical survey of SLA research. In T.K. Bhatia and W.C. Ritchie (eds), *The New Handbook of Second Language Acquisition*. Bingley: Emerald Group Publishing.

Henning, G. (1986) Quantitative methods in language acquisition research. *TESOL Quarterly, 20*(4), 701–8.

Jick, T. (1984) Mixing qualitative and quantitative methods: Triangulation in action. In J. Van Maanen (ed.), *Qualitative Methodology*. Beverly Hills, CA: Sage.

Kirk, R.E. (2001) Promoting good statistical practices: Some suggestions. *Educational and Psychological Measurement, 61*(2), 213–8.

Kline, R. (2004) *Beyond Significance Testing: Reforming Data Analysis Methods in Behavioral Research*. Washington, DC: American Psychological Association.

Larson-Hall, J. (2010) *A Guide to Doing Statistics in Second Language Research using SPSS*. New York: Routledge.

Larson-Hall, J. and Herrington, R. (2010) Examining the difference that robust statistics can make to studies in language acquisition. *Applied Linguistics, 31*(3), 368–90.

Lazaraton, A. (2000) Current trends in research methodology and statistics in applied linguistics. *TESOL Quarterly, 34*(1), 175–81.

——(2003) Evaluative criteria for qualitative research in applied linguistics: Whose criteria and whose research? *The Modern Language Journal, 87*(1), 1–12.

——(2005) Quantitative research methods. In E. Hinkel (ed.), *Handbook of Research in Second Language Teaching and Learning*. Mahwah, NJ: Lawrence Erlbaum Associates.

Lazarton, A. (1995) Qualitative research in applied linguistics: A progress report. *TESOL Quarterly, 29*(3), 455–72.

Mackey, A. and Gass, S. (2005) *Second Language Research: Methodology and Design*. Mahwah, NJ: Erlbaum.

Popper, K. (1959) *The Logic of Scientific Discovery*. New York: Basic Books.

Wilcox, R. (1998) How many discoveries have been lost by ignoring modern statistical methods? *American Psychologist, 53*(3), 300–14.

Wilcox, R. (2001). *Fundamentals of Modern Statistical Methods: Substantially Improving Power and Accuracy*. New York: Springer.

Questionnaire research

Rebekha Abbuhl
California State University at Long Beach

A questionnaire consists of a set of standardized questions in writing designed to gather factual, behavioral, and attitudinal information from respondents. Most questions require respondents to select among a range of presented answers. These "closed-ended" questions include multiple-choice questions, checklists, rank order questions, and likert scales. Questionnaires may also include "open-ended" questions (such as sentence completions, short answers, and clarification questions) that invite respondents to write longer responses. Typically, questionnaires are self-administered, with respondents providing their own answers on paper or online. However, when dealing with less literate respondents, it is also possible for the researcher to ask the questions verbally and record the respondents' answers.

Questionnaires are one of the most commonly employed data collection procedures in second language research and have been used to investigate attitudes to the L2, anxiety, learning styles, learning strategies, motivation and willingness to communicate (WTC). Additional topics include needs analyses, teacher and self-evaluations, learners' beliefs about language learning, and students' preferences concerning feedback and grammar instruction.

In addition to lending themselves to a wide range of topics, questionnaires are valued for their ease of administration and cost-effectiveness. If properly designed and administered, questionnaires can allow researchers to gather detailed information from large samples on phenomena that are not directly observable (such as attitudes, beliefs, and values). Many second language learners may also find it easier to provide answers to questions on written questionnaires rather than in oral interviews, as they are not under the pressure of time constraints or one-on-one discourse processing. In addition, the relative anonymity of the questionnaire may embolden respondents and simultaneously help researchers to avoid interviewer effects (the quality of responses being affected by characteristics of the interviewer).

However, questionnaires are not without their limitations. For example, even native speaker respondents may misinterpret questionnaire items (e.g., Low, 1999) and the problem is compounded when the respondents are not fully literate in the language of the questionnaire (as is often the case with less proficient nonnative speakers). Questionnaires can be translated and validated for another language (see, for example, Brown, Cunha, Frota, and Ferreira, 2001), but it still is common for respondents to (1) answer quickly, superficially engaging with the questionnaire; (2) give socially desirable answers (prestige bias); and/or (3) experience fatigue effects (if the questionnaire is too lengthy). As researchers typically have few opportunities to ask follow-up questions to clarify any vague or conflicting answers, questionnaires are not considered the ideal instrument for probing deeply into an issue (Dörnyei, 2010; Gilham, 2008).

To minimize these problems, second language acquisition researchers in recent years have advised the field to exercise the utmost care when designing, piloting, and administering questionnaires (e.g., Brown, 2001; Dörnyei, 2010; Petrić and Czárl, 2003; Spada, Barkaoui, Peters, So and Valeo, 2009). Areas of concern include the wording of questions, the length and layout of the questionnaire, piloting the questionnaire to identify problematic questions, deciding on sample size and procedures, and employing strategies to maximize the quality and quantity of responses (Dörnyei, 2010; Gilham, 2008). Researchers have also advised the field to present information on the reliability and validity of questionnaire measures (for example, reporting Cronbach alpha coefficients to provide evidence on the internal consistency of the questionnaire and using factor analysis to evaluate construct validity) (e.g., Petrić and Czárl, 2003; Spada *et al.*, 2009). It has also been suggested that questionnaire data be combined with data from other sources (e.g., interviews and observations) to help researchers obtain a deeper understanding of the phenomena under investigation.

With respect to analyzing questionnaire data, a variety of methods can be used. For closed-ended items, researchers can use descriptive statistics such as the mean, median, and standard deviation. Inferential statistics can also be used to compare the responses of different groups (e.g., to see if there is a significant difference in the responses of female and male students) or to examine whether various sets of results are correlated (e.g., to determine whether there is a correlation between various measures of motivation and proficiency in the second language). The results of open-ended questions can be subjected to content analysis, a process that involves transcribing and coding the responses and finding patterns within those responses (Brown, 2001, 2009; see Brown and Bailey, 2008 for an example of a qualitative analysis of open-ended items).

Recent developments

One recent development in second language questionnaire research is the online administration of questionnaires (e.g., the Bilingualism and Emotions Questionnaire employed in Dewaele, Petrides and Furnham, 2008). As noted by Wilson and Dewaele (2010), researchers using web questionnaires, in comparison with those using the traditional pen-and-paper questionnaire, "have the advantage of reaching out to a larger and more diverse pool of potential participants, which may increase the ecological validity of the resulting database" (p. 103). Reviewing recent literature on the topic, Wilson and Dewaele (2010) argue that there is little evidence that the anonymity of the web-based questionnaire leads participants to provide less serious responses than they would on pen-and-paper surveys, and in general, the results of web-based questionnaires are consistent with those from more traditional formats.

At the same time, however, researchers have noted that the sheer diversity of web-based questionnaire participants and the fact they are self-selected may pose problems for the generalizability of the results (e.g., Dörnyei, 2010). To help the field have greater confidence in the findings of web-based questionnaires, Wilson and Dewaele (2010) suggest comparing the results of web-based questionnaires with those from pen-and-paper questionnaires while Dörnyei (2010) raises the possibility of using a "mixed-mode strategy" (using both web- and paper-based questionnaires in a single study to access respondents who lack internet access or computer literacy).

See also: cross-sectional research, measuring and researching SLA, mixed methods research, motivation, quantitative research, qualitative research

References

Brown, J.D. (2001). *Using Surveys in Language Programs*. Cambridge: Cambridge University Press.

——(2009). Open-response items in questionnaires. In J. Heigham, and R. Croker (eds), *Qualitative Research in Applied Linguistics: A Practical Introduction*. New York: Palgrave Macmillan.

Brown, J.D. and Bailey, K. (2008). Language testing courses: What are they in 2007? *Language Testing, 25*, 349–83.

Brown, J.D., Cunha, M., Frota, S. and Ferreira, A. (2001). Development and validation of a Portuguese version of the motivated strategies for learning questionnaire. In Z. Dörnyei, and R. Schmidt (eds), *Motivation and Second Language Acquisition*. Manoa, HI: University of Hawaii at Manoa, Second Language Teaching and Curriculum Center.

Dewaele, J.-M., Petrides, K. and Furnham, A. (2008). Effects of trait emotional intelligence and sociobiographical variables on communicative anxiety and foreign language anxiety among adult multilinguals: A review and empirical investigation. *Language Learning, 58*, 911–60.

Dörnyei, Z. (2010). *Questionnaires in Second Language Research: Construction, Administration, and Processing*. New York: Routledge.

Low, G. (1999). What respondents do with questionnaires: Accounting for incongruity and fluidity. *Applied Linguistics, 20*, 503–33.

Petrić, B. and Czárl, B. (2003). Validating a writing strategy questionnaire. *System, 31*, 187–215.

Spada, N., Barkaoui, K., Peters, C., So, M. and Valeo, A. (2009). Developing a questionnaire to investigate second language learners' preferences for two types of form-focused instruction. *System, 27*, 70–81.

Wilson, R. and Dewaele, J. (2010). The use of web questionnaires in second language acquisition and bilingualism research. *Second Language Research, 26*, 103–23.

Further reading

Brown, J.D. (2001). *Using Surveys in Language Programs*. Cambridge: Cambridge University Press. (Contains an excellent discussion on the quantitative and qualitative analysis of questionnaire data.)

Dörnyei, Z. (2010). *Questionnaires in Second Language Research: Construction, Administration, and Processing*. New York: Routledge. (The most comprehensive overview of questionnaires in second language acquisition research to date.)

Gillham, B. (2008). *Developing a Questionnaire*. London: Continuum. (A slim and accessible volume with practical suggestions on questionnaire development and implementation.)

Oppenheim, A.N. (1992). *Questionnaire Design, Interviewing and Attitude Measurement*. London: Pinter Publishers. (One of the most oft-cited works on questionnaire design, this book provides detailed information on questionnaire design and statistical analysis of results.)

R

Reaction Time (RT)

Theodoros Marinis
University of Reading

Reaction Time (RT) is the time it takes for participants to react/respond to a stimulus. For example, in naming tasks, participants see a picture and have to name it. In naming tasks we can measure two types of information: accuracy and RTs. The accuracy rate shows how accurate participants are in naming the picture; the RTs measure how long it takes for the participants to name the picture. Children typically show longer RTs than adults and several studies have demonstrated that second language (L2) learners show longer RTs than native speakers (Marinis, 2010).

RTs are measured in milliseconds (ms) and can be used in off-line and in on-line tasks. Off-line tasks measure the participants' response after they have encountered a stimulus. Examples of off-line tasks that can have a RT component are picture-pointing and grammaticality judgment tasks. In a picture-pointing task, participants see an array of pictures, listen to a sentence and they have to select which picture corresponds to the sentence they heard. In such a task, we can measure how accurate participants are in pointing to the correct picture, but we can also measure how fast they are in deciding on the picture by using a touch-screen. Grammaticality judgment tasks can also have a RT component, that is, we can measure how fast participants decide about the grammaticality of a sentence by asking participants to press a button on the keyboard or on a button box. The keyboard or the button box records how fast they made their decision. If off-line tasks are not speeded, that is, if participants do not have to respond as fast as possible, then they can make a conscious and controlled decision about the meaning of the sentence by making use of their explicit knowledge and their meta-linguistic abilities.

On-line tasks measure the participants' responses while they listen to or while they read sentences as they unfold. Examples of on-line tasks are self-paced reading (e.g., Marinis *et al.*, 2005) and self-paced listening tasks (e.g., Felser *et al.*, 2003). In a self-paced reading task, participants read a sentence word-by-word or phrase-by-phrase and each time they read a word or a phrase they have to press a button on the keyboard or on a button box to read the next word or phrase. The keyboard or the button box records the RT it takes them to read the word/phrase. In on-line tasks, participants do not have time to think about the words and sentences they encounter. Therefore, they measure the participants' automatic response to language stimuli and they are relatively immune to meta-linguistic abilities. However, if participants are asked to judge the acceptability of sentences, then the task may engage also the participants' meta-linguistic abilities. Based on the RT data in an on-line task we can make inferences about the way participants parse or process words or sentences in real-time. RTs have to be filtered for extreme values and outliers before being analyzed (see Lachaud and Renaud, 2011; Ratcliff, 1993).

See also: automaticity, eye tracking, lexical access and selection in bilingual production, measuring and researching SLA, parsing sentences, psycholinguistics of SLA

References

Felser, C., Roberts, L., Gross, R. and Marinis, T., (2003). The processing of ambiguous sentences by first and second language learners of English. *Applied Psycholinguistics*, *24*, 453–89.

Lachaud, C.M. and Renaud, O., (2011). A tutorial for analysing human reaction times: how to filter data, manage missing values, and choose a statistical model. *Applied Psycholinguistics*, *32*, 389–416.

Marinis, T., (2010). On-line sentence processing methods in typical and atypical populations. In S. Unsworth and E. Blom (eds), *Experimental Methods in Language Acquisition Research*. Amsterdam: John Benjamins.

Marinis, T., Roberts, L., Felser, C. and Clahsen, H., (2005). Gaps in second language sentence processing. *Studies in Second Language Acquisition*, *27*, 53–78.

Ratcliff, R., (1993). Methods for dealing with reaction time outliers. *Psychological Bulletin*, *114*, 510–32.

Further reading

Chondrogianni, V. and Marinis, T., (in press). Production and processing asymmetries in the acquisition of tense morphology by sequential bilingual children. *Bilingualism: Language and Cognition*. (Study comparing production with on-line comprehension in L2 children using a word-monitoring task.)

Dussias, P.E., (2003). Syntactic ambiguity resolution in second language learners: Some effects of bilinguality on L1 and L2 processing strategies. *Studies in Second Language Acquisition*, *25*, 529–57. (Study addressing how the amount and type of exposure may affect on-line RT tasks.)

Felser, C. and L. Roberts, (2007). Processing wh-dependencies in a second language: A cross-modal priming study. *Second Language Research*, *23*, 9–36. (Study using the cross-modal priming technique in SLA research.)

Jackson, C.N., (2008). Proficiency level and the interaction of lexical and morphosyntactic information during L2 sentence processing. *Language Learning*, *58*, 875–909. (Study showing effects of proficiency.)

Marinis, T., 2003. Psycholinguistic techniques in second language acquisition research. *Second Language Research*, *19*, 144–61. (Introduction to using on-line processing tasks in SLA.)

Reading

Keiko Koda
Carnegie Mellon University

The ultimate goal of reading is to construct text meanings based on visually presented information, As such, reading involves three major operations: (a) extracting linguistic information from printed words; (b) integrating the extracted information into text segments; and (c) assembling the integrated segments to uncover the message intended by the author. Reading acquisition, as a dynamic pursuit embedded in a language and its writing system, entails making links between the two systems. Learning to read thus demands a clear grasp of the grapheme-to-language relationships, and in this regard, is heavily constrained by the properties of both language and writing system. Inevitably, the knowledge of those properties is a strong and reliable predictor of reading achievement in monolingual first language (L1) readers.

When learning to read occurs in a second language (L2), the required linkage building becomes exponentially more complex because L2 reading involves two languages. Once developed in one language, reading skills transfer to another, and are assimilated in learning to read in the new language (Koda and Reddy, 2008). Hence, L2 reading skills evolve through cross-linguistic interaction between transferred L1 skills and L2 print input. Evidently, models of monolingual reading development cannot adequately explain how two languages coalesce in shaping, refining and maintaining reading skills within and across linguistically diverse L2 learners.

This entry describes (a) how monolingual reading acquisition is constrained by the grapheme-language relationships; (b) how those constraints engender cross-linguistic variations in learning to read; and (c) how such variations affect L2 reading development.

Linguistic constraints on learning to read: Reading universal and cross-linguistic variations

According to the simple view of reading (e.g., Hoover and Gough, 1990), reading acquisition necessitates the mastery of two abilities: decoding and comprehension. While decoding is unique to reading, comprehension is required for both listening and reading, and much of its ability is acquired through listening in the course of oral language development. Although, in principle, the listening comprehension ability should be fully functional in reading, in actuality, such cross-modal transfer does not transpire automatically until sufficient decoding skills develop. Decoding thus is a vital requisite for learning to read, as it enables children to exploit their listening comprehension ability.

The Universal Grammar of Reading (Perfetti, 2003) also underscores the centrality of decoding in learning to read. The theory posits that writing systems encode spoken language, and therefore, cannot represent meaning directly independent of language. This dependency essentially determines the initial task in learning to read – that is, uncovering how spoken language elements are mapped onto the graphic symbols that encode them. To achieve this, children must recognize *which language element* (e.g., phoneme, syllable, and morpheme) is directly encoded in each graphic symbol (the general mapping principle), and then, learn *how* those symbols encode spoken words (the mapping details).

Although the grapheme-to-language mapping learning is universally demanded, how it is achieved differs from one language to another. To uncover the general mapping principle, for example, children learning to read English need to understand that each letter represents a distinct sound – either a consonant or a vowel. In contrast, children learning to read Chinese must realize that each graphic symbol (character) corresponds to the meaning and sound (single syllable) of one whole morpheme.

In learning *mapping details,* children work out the details of the grapheme-language correspondences in their writing system. For example, Korean and Hebrew writing systems are both alphabetic, but the required mappings vary considerably between the two systems. The Korean Hangul consists of 24 basic symbols, each encoding a single phoneme – either a vowel or a consonant. Unlike English, however, the Korean symbols do not appear individually; instead, they are packaged into square blocks, each corresponding to a distinct syllable. Reflecting the dual-level representation, the ability to manipulate both syllables and phonemes is a strong predictor of early reading development in Korean (Cho and McBride-Chang, 2005). The Hebrew symbols, on the other hand, represent only consonant phonemes. Hebrew vowels are shown in the form of dots and dashes, and placed below, above or to the left of symbols. In the consonantal Hebrew, children are required to develop stronger sensitivity to consonants than vowels and use the sensitivity in learning the mapping details (Geva, 2008).

The Psycholinguistic Grain Size theory (Ziegler and Goswami, 2006) provides a plausible explanation of how variations in decoding development occur in conjunction with the grapheme-phonology relationships in typologically diverse languages. In learning to read, as noted above, children must find out the graphic unit that corresponds most reliably to the salient sound unit in spoken words (e.g., rime, coda, and mora). According to the theory, the optimal size is determined by the amount of orthographic information required for decoding. In phonologically transparent writing systems, such as Spanish and Serbo-Croatian, decoding demands little orthographic information. The grain sizes in these systems are small at the phonemic level. In contrast, in phonologically opaque orthographies, decoding requires far more orthographic information, necessitating larger grain sizes, such as syllables, rimes, and even morphemes.

Over the past three decades, word recognition studies have shown that two forms of linguistic knowledge – orthographic and phonological –

contribute independently to decoding efficiency within each language (e.g., Barker, Torgesen, and Wagner, 1992); and that differences in the grapheme-to-phonology correspondences relate systematically to the procedural variations in decoding across languages (e.g., Katz and Frost, 1992). Such variations have significant implications for L2 reading development.

Learning to read in a second language

It is well documented that reading skills – decoding skills, in particular – transfer across languages (Akamatsu, 1999; Hamada and Koda, 2008). When transferred, those skills are incorporated in learning to read in a later acquired language. Evidently, L2 decoding skills are shaped through continual interaction between transferred skills and L2 print input and their development is jointly, but differently, affected by L1 and L2 orthographic properties (Koda, 2007). While L1 properties, via transferred skills, induce *qualitative* differences in L2 reading behaviors, L2 properties, through L2 print input experience, yield *quantitative* variances in L2 reading efficiency. To capture these and other cross-linguistic phenomena, L2 reading research has explored the subtle ways in which L1 and L2 print processing experiences coalesce in L2 reading development. Three lines of inquiries are particularly germane: (a) cross-linguistic relationships in L1 and L2 reading skills; (b) L1-induced variations in L2 reading behaviors; and (c) L1 and L2 joint impacts on L2 processing performance.

Cross-linguistic relationships

One way of exploring dual-language involvement in L2 reading is to determine how L1 and L2 reading skills are related in school-age children learning to read two languages concurrently. Employing a large battery of tasks in two languages, recent biliteracy studies have examined the functional connections of a wide range of skills between two languages, including phonological awareness (e.g., Wang, Park and Lee, 2006), decoding (e.g., Wade-Woolley and Geva, 2000), syntactic awareness (e.g., Da Fontoura and Siegel, 1995), and working memory (e.g., Abu-Rabia, 1997).

Because the studies listed above focused mainly on biliteracy cases involving two alphabetic languages, it is not clear to what extent the reported cross-linguistic relationships can be generalized to other cases entailing two typologically diverse languages. A small, but growing, body of research suggests that inter-lingual relationships are more complex when two languages are dissimilar (e.g., McBride-Chan, Cheung, Chow and Choi, 2006). Although L1 and L2 phonological awareness (PA) are related in Chinese-English biliteracy learners, PA in one language only minimally contributes to decoding in the other (e.g., Luk and Bialystok, 2008). This sharply contrasts with the strong functional relationship between L1 phonological awareness and L2 decoding skills found among Spanish-English biliteracy learners (e.g., Durgunoglu, Nagy and Hancin, 1993).

Collectively, the cumulative evidence, though still limited in quantity, indicates that L1 and L2 reading skills are variably interconnected between biliteracy learners handling two typologically similar languages and those dealing with two distinct languages; that, as in L1 reading, L2 decoding development depends on phonological awareness within each language; and that such dependency does not always occur across languages particularly when two languages are typologically distant.

L1-induced variations

Because decoding skills are shaped to accommodate the orthographic properties specific to the language in which reading occurs, those skills, when transferred to another language, induce systematic variations in L2 decoding behaviors. A number of L2 reading studies have investigated L1-induced variances in linguistically diverse L2 learners. In those studies, the magnitude of a particular experimental manipulation is compared between two learner groups. For example, L2 learners of English (ESL) with alphabetic and logographic L1 orthographic backgrounds can be contrasted in the degree of their reliance on phonemic analysis during decoding. While alphabetic literacy demands word segmentation and analysis at the phonemic level, the basic unit of logographic mappings is morpheme, and therefore, logographic processing does not require phoneme-level analysis. Because logographic symbols encode phonological information (usually syllable) holistically via morpheme, the ability to distinguish visually complex, and often similar, stroke patterns is vital in logographic literacy.

These comparisons have generated a number of testable hypotheses regarding L1-induced variations in L2 reading behaviors. One such hypothesis is that decoding efficiency among ESL learners with alphabetic and logographic L1 backgrounds is differentially affected when phonological and graphic information is made inaccessible. The hypothesis has been tested using a variety of experimental manipulations, designed to impair phonological decoding. Such manipulations include, for example, heterographic homophones ("eight" and "ate"; Koda, 1988), graphic distortion through case alteration ("ReAd"; Akamatsu, 1999), and pseudowords (pronounceable nonsense letter strings, such as "munt"; Hamada and Koda, 2008). These and other related studies have shown that alphabetic and logographic ESL learners differentially use phonological and graphic information during L2 decoding; and that such disparities are clearly attributable to the qualitatively different demands imposed by the orthographic properties specific to the participants' respective L1s (e.g., Koda, 2000). In sum, L1 orthographic properties have lasting impacts on L2 reading development, and explain significant portions of the variances in L2 decoding performance.

L1 and L2 joint impacts

Of late, interest in the joint impacts of L1 and L2 orthographic properties has arisen sharply. A small, but growing, number of studies have investigated the relative contributions of L1 and L2 factors to L2 reading development, using a variety of experimental tasks, such as semantic category judgment (Wang, Koda, and Perfetti, 2003), associative word learning (Hamada and Koda, 2008), and word identification (Wang and Koda, 2005). To isolate the impact of L1 and L2 orthographic properties, L2 stimulus words were manipulated both graphically and phonologically within each study, and the magnitude of interference stemming from each type of manipulation was compared between two learner groups, each representing a distinct L1 orthographic system. In such a design, the extent that a particular manipulation affects both groups is used as the basis for gauging the L2 impact, and the extent that the effect of the manipulation varies between the learner groups serves as an index of the L1 impact.

The studies have demonstrated that phonological and graphic manipulations both significantly affected L2 decoding efficiency, but the magnitude of the impairment stemming from each type of manipulation varied among learners with alphabetic and logographic backgrounds. These findings clearly indicate that L2 properties have a stronger effect on L2 decoding development, overriding the variance induced by L1 properties. Viewed as a whole, the current database suggests that L2 reading development is guided by insights arising from L1 and L2 print processing experiences, but L2 experience appears to be a dominant force in honing L2 reading skills.

Concluding remarks

In all languages, reading acquisition entails learning to map spoken language elements onto the graphic symbols that encode them. When reading occurs in a second language, the required mappings become exponentially more complex because L2 reading involves two languages and its acquisition is jointly affected by L1 and L2 properties. Such cross-linguistic constraints, inherent in L2 reading development, explain many of the processing behaviors unique to L2 print information processing.

See also: bilingualism and SLA, crosslinguistic influence, instructed SLA, linguistic transfer, Phonological short term memory (PSTM), psycholinguistics of SLA

References

Abu-Rabia, S. (1997). Verbal and working memory skills of bilingual Hebrew-English speaking children. *International Journal of Psycholinguistics*, *13*, 25–40.

Akamatsu, N. (1999). The effects of first language orthographic features on word recognition processing in English as a second language. *Reading and Writing*, *11*(4), 381–403.

Barker, K., Torgesen, J.K. and Wagner, R.K. (1992). The role of orthographic processing skills on five different reading tasks. *Reading Research Quarterly*, *27*, 334–45.

Cho, J.-R. and McBride-Chang, C. (2005). Correlates of Korea Hangul acquisition among kindergarteners and second graders. *Scientific Studies of Reading*, *9, 3–16.*

Da Fontoura, H. A., and Siegel, L.S. (1995). Reading syntactic and memory skills of Portuguese-English Canadian children. *Reading and Writing: An International Journal*, *7*, 139–53.

Durgunoglu, A.Y., Nagy, W.E. and Hancin, B.J. (1993). Cross-language transfer of phonemic awareness. *Journal of Educational Psychology*, *85*, 453–65.

Geva, E. (2008). Facets of metalinguistic awareness related to reading development in Hebrew: Evidence from monolingual and bilingual and bilingual children. In K. Koda and A.M. Zehler (eds), *Learning to Read Across Languages: Cross-linguistic Relationships in First and Second Language Literacy Development*, pp. 154–187. New York: Routledge.

Hamada, M. and Koda, K. (2008). Influence of first language orthographic experience on second language decoding and word learning. *Language Learning*, *58*, 1–31.

Hoover, W.A. and Gough, P.B. (1990). The simple view of reading. *Reading and Writing: An Interdisciplinary Journal*, *2*, 127–60.

Katz, L. and Frost, R. (1992). Reading in different orthographies: The orthographic depth hypothesis. In R. Frost and L. Katz (eds), *Orthography, Phonology, Morphology, and Meaning*, pp. 67–84. Amsterdam: Elsevier.

Koda, K. (1988). Cognitive process in second language reading: Transfer of L1 reading skills and strategies. *Second Language Research*, *4* (2), 133–56.

Koda, K. (2000). Cross-linguistic variations in L2 morphological awareness. *Applied Psycholinguistics*, *21*, 297–320.

Koda, K. (2007). Reading and language learning: Cross-linguistic constraints on second-language reading development. *Language Learning*, *57*, 1–44.

Koda, K. and Reddy, P. (2008). Cross-linguistic transfer of reading skills. *Language Teaching, 41*, 497–508. (invited submission).

Luk, G. and Bialystok, E. (2008). Common and distinct cognitive bases for reading in English–Cantonese bilinguals. *Applied Psycholinguistics*, *29*, 269–89.

McBride-Chan, C., Cheung, B.W. -Y., Chow, C.S.-L., and Choi, L. (2006). Metalinguistic skills and vocabulary knowledge in Chinese (L1) and English (L2). *Reading and Writing*, *19*, 695–716.

Perfetti, C.A. (2003). The universal grammar of reading. *Scientific Studies of Reading*, *7*, 3–24.

Wade-Woolley, L. and Geva, E. (2000). Processing novel phonemic contrasts in the acquisition of L2 word reading. *Scientific Studies of Reading*, *4*, 295–311.

Wang, M. and Koda, K. (2005). Commonalities and differences in word identification skills among learners of English as a second language. *Language Learning*, *55*, 71–98.

Wang, M., Koda, K. and Perfetti, C.A. (2003). Alphabetic and non-alphabetic L1 effects in English semantic processing: A comparison of Korean and Chinese English L2 learners. *Cognition*, *87*, 129–49

Wang, M., Park, Y. and Lee, K.R. (2006). Korean-English biliteracy acquition: Cross language and orthography transfer. *Journal of Educational Psycholgy*, *98*(1), 148–58.

Ziegler, J.C. and Goswami, U. (2006). Becoming literate in different languages: Similar problems, different solutions. *Developmental Sciences*, *9*, 425–36.

Further reading

August, D. and Shanahan, T. (eds) (2008). *Developing Reading and Writing in Second-language Learners: Lessons from the Report of the National Literacy Panel on Language Minority Children and Youth*. New York: Routledge. (This is a comprehensive overview of empirical studies on literacy development of school-age (K-12) second language learners.)

Coulmas, F. (2003). *Writing Systems*. New York: Cambridge University Press. (The book examines the structural makeup of the major writing systems of the world and explains how they work.)

Koda, K. and Zehler, A.M. (eds) (2008). *Learning to Read across Languages: Cross-linguistic Relationships in First- and Second-language Literacy Development*. New York: Routledge. (The volume describes systematic variations in learning to read in typologically diverse languages and explains how those variations affect second-language reading development.)

Li, P. (ed.) (2006). *The Handbook of East Asian psycholinguistics* (Vols I-III). New York: Cambridge University Press. (The three-volume series on East Asian psycholinguistics presents a state-of-the-art discussion of the psycholinguistic study of Chinese (Vol. I), Japanese (Vol. II) and Korean (Vol. III).)

Recasts

Andrea Revesz and Rebecca Sachs
Lancaster University and Georgetown University

Recasts are a form of reactive corrective feedback in which an interlocutor reformulates all or part of a language learner's utterance, modifying its non-target-like aspects while keeping its central meaning intact. This is illustrated in the example below, from Mackey, Gass, and McDonough (2000: 485):

LEARNER: (*utterance*) So one man feed for the birds.
INTERLOCUTOR: (*recast*) So one man's feeding the birds?
LEARNER: (*response*) The birds.

Recasts were first researched extensively in the field of first language acquisition, where findings regarding adults' provision of recasts and children's reactions to them were applied to answering questions about the existence, usability, use, and necessity of negative evidence for language development. In the field of SLA, where the role of negative evidence has also been a matter of longstanding debate, another reason for the interest in recasts from the standpoints of both theory and pedagogy has lain in their potential for promoting Focus-on-Form—drawing learners' attention to form-meaning mappings in natural communicative contexts without interrupting the flow of conversation (Doughty and Williams, 1998). In a variety of classroom settings (e.g., Lyster and Ranta, 1997), recasts have been found to be the most frequently used feedback technique. However, learners have also sometimes been found to mistake them for confirmations of meaning as opposed to corrections (e.g., Mackey *et al.*, 2000). Perhaps to some degree because of these factors, the past decade has witnessed a burgeoning amount of research into their characteristics, functions, and effectiveness for adult L2 learning, with one result being that a facilitative role for recasts in SLA is now well established.

In fact, several meta-analyses have converged on the conclusion that recasts can lead to sustained L2 learning benefits. Mackey and Goo's (2007) meta-analysis of research on negotiated **interaction** in face-to-face and computer-mediated contexts, for example, produced a large positive effect for recasts, not only immediately, but also as measured by delayed post-tests. More recent meta-analyses (e.g., Li (2010) on oral and computer-delivered corrective feedback and Lyster and Saito (2010) on classroom oral feedback) have yielded positive medium-sized effects for recasts, and similar conclusions have been reached in a number of traditional research syntheses (e.g., Ellis and Sheen, 2006; Long, 2007; Nicholas, Lightbown, and Spada, 2000).

In detailing a psycholinguistic rationale for the effectiveness of recasts, Long (2007) has argued that many of their benefits may be attributable to the fact that they juxtapose learners' utterances with more target-like versions of what they have just said, presenting the forms in direct contrast with one another. Learners and their interlocutors are presumed to share a joint attentional focus, and since recasts are contextualized and contingent on the meanings that the learners have just expressed, their content should already be familiar. This may serve to free up attentional resources for learners to notice the gap (Schmidt and Frota, 1986) and conduct cognitive comparisons between their interlanguage and the target language. Moreover, recasts are claimed to be able to promote these processes without diverting attention away from an overarching focus on meaning and, thus, hypothetically, facilitate the recognition of form-meaning connections. As reactions to non-target-like L2 use that simultaneously provide more target-like models, another potential benefit of recasts is that they may serve not only as a source of negative evidence but also (perhaps salient) positive evidence. Finally, depending on the discourse context, recasts may push learners to modify their output (Swain, 1995) and hence may contribute to the automatization and/or extension of their linguistic knowledge.

Although a generally beneficial role for recasts has been established, researchers have also identified a number of factors that may mediate their impact on L2 development, including learners' expectations and orientations to feedback in different classroom contexts (e.g., relatively form-oriented versus meaning-oriented settings); characteristics of the interactional contexts in which recasts occur (e.g., focusing on content, classroom management, communication, or language form); features of the communicative tasks learners are performing (e.g., their cognitive demands and learners' familiarity with their content); the number and types of changes recasts make in relation to learners' original utterances (e.g., substitutions vs. additions); the recasts' linguistic focus (e.g., morphosyntax vs. lexicon vs. phonology); their degree of segmentation or integration into longer stretches of speech (e.g., full vs. partial repetitions, isolated vs. incorporated statements); their prosodic features (e.g., use of interrogative vs. declarative intonation and emphatic stress) and perceived functions (e.g., communicative vs. didactic); their frequency and consistency (e.g., intensive focus on a particular linguistic target vs. extensive provision in response to a variety of errors); learners' immediate **uptake** as well as delayed responses (e.g., simple acknowledgments, exact repetitions, productive reformulations); and a wide variety of individual differences, such as learners' ages, literacy levels, L2 proficiency or developmental readiness for targeted features, affective variables such as anxiety, and cognitive variables such as phonological short-term memory, working memory capacity, grammatical sensitivity, and other aspects of L2 aptitude.

Currently, some especially prolific research agendas (see Ellis and Sheen, 2006; Long, 2007; Mackey, 2007) involve comparing the developmental benefits of recasts against those of other feedback techniques, particularly elicitations (or prompts), which, unlike recasts, require learners to modify their output; exploring whether recasts have differential effects on different types of L2 knowledge (e.g., explicit vs. implicit, declarative vs. procedural) and whether their observed effects are influenced by the type of outcome measure used; and investigating the extent to which the findings obtained for face-to-face recasts in the oral mode may transfer to computer-mediated contexts such as text-based chatting (e.g., Baralt, 2010; Sagarra, 2007). Several authors have called for further examination of how the characteristics of linguistic targets (e.g., salience of form, complexity of meaning, transparency of form-meaning mapping) might influence the usefulness of recasts, how combinations of individual-difference variables might mediate the effects of recasts on SLA processes and outcomes, and, finally, how social factors might shape the incidence and use of recasts by L2 learners. Definitive judgments may not be forthcoming; different kinds of recasts are likely helpful in promoting different kinds of knowledge in learners with different abilities. Nonetheless, this is an increasingly productive area of research which has made and will continue to make important contributions to L2 theory and pedagogy.

See also: corrective feedback, Focus on Form (FonF), Interaction and Interaction hypothesis, negotiation for meaning, positive and negative evidence, uptake

References

Baralt, M. (2010). *Task complexity, the Cognition Hypothesis, and interaction in CMC and FTF envirionments*. Unpublished doctoral dissertation, Georegetown University, Washington, DC.

Doughty, C. and Williams, J. (eds) (1998). *Focus on Form in Classroom Second Language Acquisition*. New York: Cambridge University Press.
Ellis, R. and Sheen, Y. (2006). Reexamining the role of recasts in second language acquisition. *Studies in Second Language Acquisition*, *28*, 575–600.
Li, S. (2010). The effectiveness of corrective feedback in SLA: A meta-analysis. *Language Learning, 60*, 309–365.
Long, M.H. (2007). Recasts in SLA: The story so far. *Problems in SLA*. Mahwah, NJ: Erlbaum.
Lyster, R. and Ranta, L. (1997). Corrective feedback and learner uptake: Negotiation of form in communicative classrooms. *Studies in Second Language Acquisition*, *19*, 37–66.
Lyster, R. and Saito, K. (2010). Oral feedback in classroom SLA: A meta-analysis. *Studies in Second Language Acquisition, 32*, 265–302.
Mackey, A., Gass, S.M. and McDonough, K. (2000). How do learners perceive interactional feedback? *Studies in Second Language Acquisition*, *22*, 471–97.
Mackey, A. and Goo, J. (2007). Interaction research in SLA: A meta-analysis and research synthesis. In A. Mackey (ed.), *Conversational Interaction in Second Language Acquisition: A Collection of Empirical Studies*. Oxford: Oxford University Press.
Nicholas, H., Lightbown, P.M. and Spada, N. (2001). Recasts as feedback to language learners. *Language Learning*, *51*, 719–58.
Sagarra, N. (2007). From CALL to face-to-face interaction: the effect of computer-delivered recasts and working memory o L2 development. In A. Mackey (ed.), *Conversational Interaction in a Second Language*, pp. 229–46. Oxford: Oxford University Press.
Schmidt, R. and Frota, S. (1986). Developing basic conversational ability in a second language. A case study of an adult learner of Portuguese. In R. Day (ed.), *Talking to Learn: Conversation in Second Language Acquisition*. Rowley, MA: Newbury House.
Swain, M. (1995). Three functions of output in second language learning. In G. Cook and B. Seidlhofer (eds), *Principles and Practice in the Study of Language*. Oxford: Oxford University Press.

Further reading

Ellis, R. and Sheen, Y. (2006). Reexamining the role of recasts in second language acquisition. *Studies in Second Language Acquisition*, *28*, 575–600. (A state-of-the-art review, highlighting problems in theoretical and empirical research on recasts.)
Long, M.H. (1996). The role of the linguistic environment in second language acquisition. In W. R. Ritchie and T.K. Bhatia (eds), *Handbook of Second Language Acquisition*. San Diego, CA: Academic Press. (A position paper proposing an updated version of the Interaction Hypothesis, including a discussion of the rationale for using recasts.)
——(2007). Recasts in SLA: The story so far. *Problems in SLA*. Mahwah, NJ: Erlbaum. (A review paper including an in-depth discussion of the psycholinguistic rationale for using recasts.)
Mackey, A. (2007). (ed.), *Conversational Interaction in Second Language Acquisition: A Collection of Empirical Studies*. Oxford: Oxford University Press. (An edited collection including several primary studies of recasts, and a traditional synthesis and meta-analysis of previous research on interactional feedback.)
Nicholas, H., Lightbown, P.M. and Spada, N. (2001). Recasts as feedback to language learners. *Language Learning*, *51*, 719–58. (A review of research on recasts including a discussion of first and second language acquisition findings.)

Rehearsal

Alice F. Healy and James A. Kole
University of Colorado

In learning a foreign language, much memorization is required, especially for acquiring vocabulary. Rehearsal is a strategy typically used for this purpose. The most common rehearsal type is "rote" rehearsal and involves repeating the to-be-remembered material, by saying it or writing it down (e.g., Rundus, 1971). Other types of rehearsal involve more elaboration than simple repetition and involve more attention to either phonology or semantics. The type of rehearsal can vary across many dimensions, with the success on a memory test depending on rehearsal type. Rote rehearsal is often referred to as "maintenance rehearsal" (Craik and Watkins, 1973) because its purpose is primarily to maintain information in working memory (i.e., short-term memory). In contrast, elaborative rehearsal, which usually leads to better retention, can be used to bring information from working memory into a more permanent memory store (i.e., long-term memory).

The type of rehearsal used varies in its effectiveness depending on when and how memory is tested. It is often thought that making learning as easy as possible for students would facilitate acquisition. Indeed assessments of performance during learning itself are consistent with this intuition. However, assessments of performance after a delay or in a new context often yield the opposite conclusion, namely that it is preferable to make learning more difficult to promote greater retention and transfer of the learned material. For example, in a study of English-French vocabulary acquisition by native English speakers (Schneider, Healy, and Bourne, 2002), two different types of rehearsal that varied in translation direction were compared. An easier French-to-English direction was compared to a harder English-to-French direction. Although students responded more accurately in the easy direction while studying, performance on a delayed test was higher when rehearsal involved the harder direction.

One way to lead students to perform more elaboration during vocabulary rehearsal is to force them to generate the vocabulary terms rather than simply read and repeat them. For example, in a foreign vocabulary-learning task, McNamara and Healy (1995) led native English speakers to rehearse the language pairs in one of two ways. In the *read* condition, they saw both the English word and its translation, whereas in the *generate* condition they saw the English word and actively translated it. In both conditions they wrote down both words. Tests followed immediately and after a 1-week delay in which students translated each English word. Performance on the tests was better in the generate than in the read condition, demonstrating that generation helps foreign vocabulary learning.

Another dimension along which rehearsal can vary is the spacing between successive rehearsals either within a single session or across multiple sessions. It has been shown in many studies including some involving foreign vocabulary acquisition (Cepeda, Pashler, Vul, Wixted, and Rohrer, 2006) that a long interval separating successive rehearsals leads to better performance after a delay than does a short interval. The optimal interval between successive rehearsals depends on the retention interval separating the last rehearsal from the test, with longer rehearsal intervals more desirable for longer retention intervals.

See also: attention, declarative memory and knowledge, depth of processing, explicit learning, vocabulary learning and teaching, working memory

References

Cepeda, N.J., Pashler, H., Vul, E., Wixted, J.T. and Rohrer, D. (2006). Distributed practice in verbal recall tasks: A review and quantitative synthesis. *Psychological Bulletin*, *132*, 354–80.

Craik, F.I. and Watkins, M.J. (1973). The role of rehearsal in short-term memory. *Journal of Verbal Learning and Verbal Behavior*, *12*, 599–607.

McNamara, D.S. and Healy, A.F. (1995). A generation advantage for multiplication skill training and nonword vocabulary acquisition. In A. F. Healy and L.E. Bourne Jr. (eds), *Learning and Memory of Knowledge and Skills: Durability and Specificity*, pp. 132–69. Thousand Oaks, CA: Sage.

Rundus, D. (1971). Analysis of rehearsal processes in free recall. *Journal of Experimental Psychology*, *89*, 63–77.

Schneider, V.I., Healy, A.F. and Bourne, L.E. Jr. (2002). What is learned under difficult conditions is hard to forget: Contextual interference effects in foreign vocabulary acquisition, retention, and transfer. *Journal of Memory and Language*, *46*, 419–40.

Further reading

Healy, A.F. and Bourne, L.E. Jr. (eds) (1998). *Foreign Language Learning: Psycholinguistic Studies on Training and Retention*. Mahwah, NJ: Erlbaum. (A summary of specific psychology experiments on foreign language learning.)

Hulstijn, J.H. (2001). Intentional and incidental second language vocabulary learning: A reappraisal of elaboration, rehearsal and automaticity. In P. Robinson (ed.), *Cognition and Second Language Instruction*. pp. 258–86. Cambridge: Cambridge University Press. (A review of incidental and intentional vocabulary learning and the rehearsal regimes and levels of retention they result in).

Kroll, J.F. and de Groot, A.M. B. (eds) (2005). *Handbook of Bilingualism: Psycholinguistic Approaches*. New York: Oxford University Press. (A comprehensive summary of psychology research on bilingualism, including relevant neuroscience.)

Menn, L. (2011). *Psycholinguistics: Introduction and Applications*. San Diego, CA: Plural Publishing. (Introduction to research accomplishments in the psychology of language.)

Roediger, H.L. III (ed.) (2008). *Cognitive Psychology of Memory*. Vol. 2 of *Learning and Memory: A Comprehensive Reference*, 4 vols. (J. Byrne, Editor). Oxford: Elsevier. (A broad summary of cognitive psychology research on memory.)

Relative clauses

Hiromi Ozeki and Yasuhiro Shirai
Reitaku University and University of Pittsburgh

A relative clause (RC) is a clause which modifies a noun or a noun phrase. It can be classified into two broad types – prenominal RCs and postnominal RCs (although there are languages that have head-internal RCs in which the head noun is embedded in the RC).

Although RCs have been studied within a variety of frameworks, including Universal Grammar and emergentism, research on the acquisition of RCs has played an especially important role in identifying the role of typological markedness in SLA. These studies have investigated whether the order of acquisition follows the Noun Phrase Accessibility Hierarchy (NPAH). The NPAH, proposed by Keenan and Comrie (1977) on the basis of their typological work, is a universal hierarchy of relativizability on different NP types determined by the role of the head NP within the RC, often described metaphorically as a "gap." In this hierarchy, subject relatives (SU, e.g. *the man who died*) are the easiest to relativize, then direct object (DO) relatives (e.g. *the book I bought*), indirect object (IO) relatives (e. g. *the man I gave the book*), followed by oblique (OBL) relatives (e.g. *the man I talked with*), genitive (GEN) relatives (e.g. *the man whose father is sick*), and finally object of comparison (OCOMP) relatives (e.g. *the man that I am taller than*). In other words, SU is the most unmarked and OCOMP is the most marked:

SU > DO > IO > OBL > GEN > OCOMP

This is a typological implicational hierarchy; that is, if a language can relativize on a position on the hierarchy, then any other position higher than that position can also be relativized on. Furthermore, Keenan and Comrie proposed that this hierarchy reflects the psychological ease of relativization.

In SLA, many experimental studies of the NPAH have been conducted (e.g. Gass, 1979), most of which employed either sentence combination tasks or grammaticality judgment tasks. A few studies used oral picture-description tasks. In these studies, regardless of elicitation measures or participants' L1, the accuracy order followed the hierarchy of the NPAH, except for genitive (GEN), and therefore the hierarchy was argued to be a universal of SLA. However, most studies have been conducted on postnominal RCs. The results from studies on prenominal RCs in Asian languages such as Japanese, Korean, and Chinese are inconclusive, showing varying orders of accuracy and acquisition (e.g. Tarallo and Myhill, 1983; Ozeki and Shirai, 2007).

Another theoretically important issue concerns the determinants of the difficulty of different types of RCs. One argument is that the difficulty can be predicted by the linear distance between the gap and the head (Tarallo and Myhill, 1983). In postnominal RCs, DO relatives have longer linear distance between the gap and the head NP as shown in (1) and (2).

(1) *The man* who [______ saw me] … (SU)
(2) *The man* whom [I saw ______] … (DO)

Another explanation is that the structural distance between the gap, or the depth of embedding of the gap, is the determinant (e.g. O'Grady, 1999). The claim here is that the RC will be more difficult if the gap is more deeply embedded in the RC. As shown in (1)' and (2)', DO's gap is more deeply embedded than SU's.

(1)' *The man* [who ______ saw me] … (SU)
(2)' *The man* [whom I [saw ______]] … (DO)

Although for postnominal RCs both theories make the same predictions, in prenominal RCs the linear distance hypothesis predicts that DO is easier, while structural distance hypothesis predicts that SU is easier. Here too, conflicting results are observed, Tarallo and Myhill (1983) showing that DO is easier in prenominal languages (Chinese and Japanese) while O'Grady *et al.* (2003) observe that SU is easier in Korean.

Using this implicational hierarchy of RCs, researchers have also investigated the effect of instruction (e.g. Eckman *et al.*, 1988). These studies investigated the effect of instruction on marked items in the hierarchy, and in most studies the results showed that the instruction on a more marked type of RC has a positive effect on the generalization of rules to less marked types. These results support Zobl's (1983) projection hypothesis, which claims that, for certain grammatical features, if L2 learners are provided with instruction on more marked items, the instructional effect will project to the acquisition of less marked items, but not vice versa.

Another syntactic variable which has been proposed as affecting the difficulty of RCs is the position of the head noun in the matrix clause in which the RC is embedded. It is claimed that center-embedding is more difficult than right- or left-embedding (Kuno, 1974). In the case of English, the RC modifying the subject in the matrix clause as in (3) is predicted to be more difficult than the RC modifying the object in the matrix clause as in (4).

(3) The boy [who saw the girl] chased the robber.
(4) The boy saw the girl [who chased the robber].

Although there have not been as many studies focusing on this issue as studies focusing on NPAH, this hypothesis has been supported in several studies. For example, in his longitudinal study, Schumann (1980) found that L2 English learners only very infrequently used center-embedded RCs.

Aside from research focusing on RC acquisition itself, a study that made an important contribution to SLA by investigating RCs is Schachter (1974). Comparing RCs used by L2 learners in their English compositions, Schachter found that native speakers of Chinese and Japanese, whose L1s have prenominal RCs, produced fewer errors than native speakers of Arabic and Persian, whose L1s have postnominal RCs. However, she also found that Chinese and Japanese speakers *used* fewer RCs. Schachter explained that they have difficulty using postnominal RCs in English and that therefore this led to their "avoidance" of RCs. This study is one of the earliest studies to point out that error analysis alone cannot account for the whole picture of the L2 learners' interlanguage.

See also: construction learning, functional typological linguistics, implicational universals, language typology and language distance, markedness, parsing sentences

References

Eckman, F.R., Bell, L. and Nelson, D. (1988). On the generalization of relative clause instruction in the acquisition of English as a second language. *Applied Linguistics*, *9*, 1–20.

Gass, S. (1979). Language transfer and Universal Grammatical relations. *Language Learning*, *29*, 327–44.

Keenan, E.L. and Comrie, B. (1977). Noun phrase accessibility and Universal Grammar. *Linguistic Inquiry*, *8*, 63–99.

Kuno, S. (1974). The position of relative clauses and conjunctions. *Linguistic Inquiry*, *5*, 117–36.
O'Grady, W. (1999). Toward a new nativism. *Studies in Second Language Acquisition*, *21*, 621–33.
O'Grady, W., Lee, M. and Choo, M. (2003). A subject-object asymmetry in the acquisition of relative clauses in Korean as a second language. *Studies in Second Language Acquisition*, *25*, 433–48.
Ozeki, H. and Shirai, Y. (2007). Does the noun phrase accessibility hierarchy predict the difficulty order in the acquisition of Japanese relative clauses? *Studies in Second Language Acquisition*, *29*, 169–96.
Schachter, J. (1974). An error in error analysis. *Language Learning*, *27*, 205–14.
Schumann, J.H. (1980). The acquisition of English relative clauses by second language learners. In R.C. Scarcella and S. Krashen (eds), *Research in Second Language Acquisition: Selected Papers of the Los Angeles Second Language Acquisition Research Forum*. Rowley, MA: Newbury House.
Tarallo, F. and Myhill, J. (1983). Interference and natural language in second language acquisition. *Language Learning*, *33*, 55–76.
Zobl, H. (1983). Markedness and the projection problem. *Language Learning*, *33*, 293–313.

Replication research

Graeme Porte
Universidad de Granada

Replicating a study involves repeating that study in some way. The researcher might apply theory or hypotheses presented in the original study or posterior replications of it to new situations and compare outcomes with the original study and/or other replications of the same. Verifying the results of an experimental study helps us to confirm that what we observe is not an isolated incident or outcome but one which is robust and replicable. As no single study can control for every possible intervening factor in outcomes, repeated replication is one of the few guarantees we have that a "significant" outcome is worth closer attention. Such replications will often aim to verify a finding or determine the generalisability of the observed outcomes in the original study to different subjects, age groups, contexts or similar variables. The comparative scarcity of such work in SLA research has led to the criticism that researchers are being attracted to pursue spurious 'one-off' research enquiry rather than seek more valid, proven lines of investigation (Polio and Gass, 1997).

Types of replication study

'Replication' spans a continuum from doing the same experiment to doing a new experiment, the literature commonly recognising three types of replication study. Repetition of an earlier, methodologically sound study to confirm the original findings is an **exact** (or literal) replication. Many working in the field of SLA use non-experimental research methodology which is difficult or impossible to repeat exactly, particularly since continual shifts in social and historical contexts will inevitably influence outcomes. A more common venture is an **approximate** (or partial) replication, which involves repeating the original study closely in most respects, but changing one or two of the non-major variables (so as to maintain comparability between both studies). This might help us to generalise, for example, from the original study to a new population, setting, or modality. **Conceptual** (also known as constructive) replications test previous hypotheses or results against a different experimental design. Thus, different, but related data collection procedures might be employed, such as observation instead of self-report, or qualitative methods used alongside the original quantitative methods. A successful conceptual replication provides stronger support for the original findings precisely because evidence shows outcomes were not just artefacts of the original methodology.

Interpreting outcomes

Replication studies will always *inform* the field, but results from one study to another can never be *interpreted* without some ambiguity. Exact replications, by their very nature, cannot be exactly the same as the original in all respects. When they obtain equivalent results to an original study, they permit a high degree of confidence in the internal and external validity of the original. It is not a novel outcome, however, and this may have an effect on its perceived value as a potential contribution to the field (see below). Moreover, failure exactly to replicate outcomes might indicate a problem with the original study or errors in the subsequent replication procedure itself. In an approximate replication equivalent results to the original study give us more confidence that the original results can now be generalised to a new population of learners, learning context, or linguistic feature (for example). Failure to replicate outcomes still leaves us with further questions: for example, what aspect of the new study caused this to happen?

Model replication studies in SLA

Despite the increase both in journals and other publications over the last two decades, relatively few replication studies have been published. Among those worthy of mention as models of how to conduct and present such work are Wong's (2001) replication of VanPatten (1990), which lent partial support to the original findings and showed that different outcomes may present with other target languages or modalities. Eckerth (2009) partially confirmed Foster's (1998) results on the negation of meaning. Henry, Culman and VanPatten's (2009) conceptual replication of an original L2 Spanish study (Fernández, 2008) on explicit instruction revealed different results as regards L2 German word order and case markings. There are also replications of researcher's own studies or team work of which they were members. For example, Juff (2008) reinforces his earlier (1998) finding that L2 learners use argument structure in parsing and comprehension. Finally, Crossley and McNamara (2008) help to provide a more thorough understanding of the linguistic features that construct simplified and authentic texts.

Encouraging more replication studies

Whole areas remain, however, where there are doubts about key processes, such as L2 writing, and where replication of key studies is needed. More replication work must be encouraged in a number of ways. Firstly, the data and methodology used in the original study should be made freely available on the web. Secondly, journal contributors or editorial boards might identify key studies in the field and actively encourage their replication and submission. Finally, research tutors at ground roots level need to be seen to value this kind of work. Too many consider this as 'unoriginal' or synonymous with mere repetition of another's work and discourage its production; the discovery of robust empirical consistency, however, is best served by encouraging more replication studies.

See also: effect size, hypothesis testing, measuring and research SLA, meta-analysis, qualitative research, quantitative research

References

Crossley, S.A. and McNamara, D.S. (2008). Assessing second language reading texts at the intermediate level: An approximate replication of Crossley, Louwerse, McCarthy, and McNamara (2007). *Language Teaching*, *41* (3), 409–229.

Eckerth, J. (2009). Negotiated interaction in the L2 classroom. *Language Teaching*, *42* (1), 109–30.

Fernández, C. (2008). Reexamining the role of explicit information in processing instruction. *Studies in Second Language Acquisition*, *30*, 277–305.

Foster, P. (1998). A classroom perspective on the negotiation of meaning. *Applied Linguistics*, *19* (1), 1–23.

Juffs, A. (1998). Main verb vs. reduced relative clause ambiguity resolution in second language sentence processing. *Language Learning*, *48*, 107–47.

——(2006). Processing reduced relative vs. main verb ambiguity in English as a second language: a replication study with working memory. In

R. Slabakova, S. Montrul and P. Prevost (eds), *Inquiries in Linguistic Development in Honor of Lydia White*, pp. 213–32. Amsterdam: John Benjamins.

Henry, N., Culmaan, H. and VanPatten, B. (2009). More on the effects of explicit information in instructed SLA. *Studies in Second Language Acquisition*, *31* (4), 559–75.

Polio, C. and Gass, S. (1997). Replication and reporting: A commentary. *Studies in Second Language Acquisition*, *19*, 499–508.

VanPatten, B. (1990). Attending to form and content in the input. *Studies in Second Language Acquisition*, *12*, 287–301.

Wong, W. (2001). Modality and attention to meaning and form in the input. *Studies in Second Language Acquisition*, *23* (3), 345–68.

Further reading

Hendrik, C. (1991). Replications, strict replications, and conceptual replications: Are they important? In J.W. Neuliep (ed.), *Replication research in the social sciences*, pp. 41–49. Newbury Park, CA: Sage Publications. (Explains the different types of replication approach and the advantages and disadvantages of each.)

Language Teaching Review Panel (1999). Replication studies in language learning and teaching: Questions and answers. *Language Teaching*, *41* (1), January, 1–14. (A set of questions and answers from the review board of this journal covering aspects of replication research method from selecting studies for possible replication to ways of promoting more such research at grass-roots level.)

Mackey, A. and S. Gass (2005). *Second Language Research: Methodology and Design*. Mahwah, NJ: Lawrence Erlbaum. (Chapter 1 provides a useful introduction to different types of research approach and includes a discussion on the importance of replication studies.)

Porte, G.K. (ed.) (2012). *Replication Research in Applied Linguistics*. Cambridge: Cambridge University Press. (An edited collection of papers which illustrate a number of routes into replication research.)

Revised Hierarchical Model (RHM)

Natasha Tokowicz
University of Pittsburgh

The Revised Hierarchical Model is a model of bilingual memory representation proposed by Kroll and Stewart in 1994 (see figure). The model was posited to explain the changes that occur with increased proficiency in an adult-learned second language (L2). The Revised Hierarchical Model incorporates aspects of the Word Association and Concept Mediation Models of Potter, So, von Eckardt, and Feldman (1984). All three of these models are referred to as "hierarchical" because they include separate lexical and conceptual levels of representation that are hierarchically organized. Specifically, these models posit an amodal conceptual store, a first language (L1) lexical store, and an L2 lexical store. The L1 lexical store is larger than the L2 lexical store, because most individuals know more L1 than L2 words. The models vary in terms of the interconnections among these stores, which have consequences for processing. According to the Word Association Model, L2 words gain access to meaning via connections to L1 words, which are directly connected to their concepts. By contrast, the Concept Mediation Model proposes that both L1 and L2 words have direct connections to their concepts and that no lexical associations

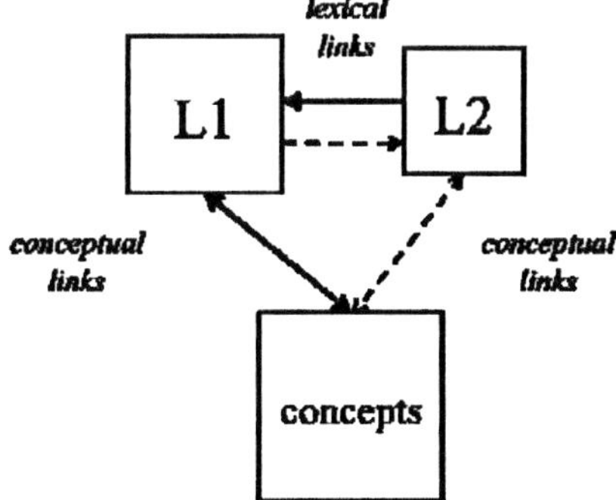

Figure 13 The Revised Hierarchical Model (adapted from Kroll and Stewart, 1994)
L1=first language. L2=second language. Dashed lines indicate weaker connections

exist between words and their translation equivalents. Potter *et al.* reported that it takes a similar amount of time to name pictures in L2 as it does to translate from L1 to L2, both for highly proficient Chinese-English bilinguals and for relatively less-proficient English-French bilinguals, and therefore concluded in favor of the Concept Mediation Model.

The Revised Hierarchical Model incorporates aspects of the Word Association and Concept Mediation Models and makes additional predictions regarding changes in L2 proficiency. In particular, the model posits that L2 words are strongly connected to their L1 translations because L2 initially relies on L1 for access to meaning. However, L1 words are only weakly connected to their L2 translations. Furthermore, both lexicons are connected to concepts, but with links of differing strength: L1 words are strongly connected to concepts (and the reverse), whereas L2 words are only weakly connected to concepts (and the reverse). With increased L2 proficiency, the relatively weak link between L2 words and concepts becomes stronger, leading to more conceptually mediated translation from L2 to L1.

The consequence of these asymmetric connections from L1 and L2 words to concepts is that translation in the two directions (from L1 to L2 and from L2 to L1) will differ in the extent to which they activate concepts. The model posits that initially, translation from L2 to L1 will rely on the lexical connection from L2 words to their L1 translations, and will not involve conceptual mediation. Translation from L1 to L2 will necessarily involve conceptual mediation because of the strong connection between L1 words and concepts and the weak connection between L1 words and their L2 translations. Because this direction of translation would require traversing the weak link between concepts and L2 words, translation in this direction should be slower and more error-prone, in addition to being more sensitive to conceptual factors. Increased L2 proficiency is hypothesized to be accompanied by a shift to more conceptually mediated L2 to L1 translation and by a decrease in the asymmetry in translation time and accuracy between the two directions.

The initial evidence for the Revised Hierarchical Model came from a series of experiments by Kroll and Stewart (1994). They used a categorization manipulation to examine the sensitivity of the two directions of translation to semantic factors. Presenting items in a semantically organized list leads to semantic interference provided that semantics are indeed activated. Therefore, slowed processing in a categorized list as compared to a randomly organized list can be taken as evidence that processing occurred at a conceptual level. Although L1 to L2 translation was susceptible to category interference, L2 to L1 translation was unaffected by the organization of the list. These findings were taken as evidence that only L1 to L2 translation necessarily involves conceptual activation (see also Sholl, Sankaranarayanan, and Kroll, 1995).

The link between L2 words and concepts is thought to be the connection that changes most with increased proficiency, such that it is initially weak but later becomes stronger. In particular, beginning L2 learners have difficulty retrieving L2 words from their concepts, although they seem to have less difficulty in retrieving meaning from L2 words. Thus, although not a part of the original model, this weak link may be stronger in one direction than the other such that it is more difficult to lexicalize concepts into L2 words than it is to activate meanings from L2 words (see Kroll, van Hell, Tokowicz, and Green, 2010).

A study by Talamas, Kroll, and Dufour (1999) used a translation recognition task to explore the extent to which less and more proficient bilinguals relied on form and meaning in processing L2 words. In particular, they manipulated the "no" trials to include words that were related to the correct translation in either form or meaning. Talamas *et al.* found that less-proficient bilinguals were more susceptible to form distractors and more-proficient bilinguals were more susceptible to meaning distractors. Subsequent research by Sunderman and Kroll (2006) showed that only less-proficient bilinguals activate the translation equivalent, similar to the findings of Talamas *et al.* However, even the less-proficient bilinguals were affected by the meaning distractor, demonstrating an early ability to process L2 words meaningfully. Thus, there may be access to meaning even for less-proficient bilinguals (see also Dufour and Kroll, 1995), but only less-proficient speakers rely on the translation equivalent, as proposed by the Revised Hierarchical Model.

The Revised Hierarchical Model has been extremely influential in the field of bilingualism and second language acquisition, leading to numerous citations. Notably, Kroll and DeGroot (1997) posited a distributed lexical/conceptual feature model that incorporates aspects of the Distributed Feature Model (De Groot, 1992) and the Distributed Representation Model (Van Hell and De Groot, 1998) into the Revised Hierarchical Model to consider lexical and conceptual overlap.

See also: bilingualism and SLA, conceptual transfer, language and the lexicon in SLA, linguistic transfer, semantic processing, vocabulary learning and teaching

References

De Groot, A.M. B. (1992). Determinants of word translation. *Journal of Experimental Psychology: Learning, Memory, and Cognition*, *18*, 1001–18.

Dufour, R. and Kroll, J.F. (1995). Matching words to concepts in two languages: A test of the concept mediation model of bilingual representation. *Memory and Cognition*, *23*, 166–80.

Kroll, J.F. and De Groot, A.M. B. (1997). Lexical and conceptual memory in the bilingual: Mapping form to meaning in two languages. In De Groot, A.M. B. and Kroll, J.F. (eds), *Tutorials in Bilingualism: Psycholinguistic Perspectives*. Mahwah, NJ: Lawrence Erlbaum Publishers.

Kroll, J.F. and Stewart, E. (1994). Category interference in translation and picture naming: Evidence for asymmetric connections between bilingual memory representations. *Journal of Memory and Language*, *33*, 149–74.

Kroll, J.F., Van Hell, J. G., Tokowicz, N. and Green, D.W. (2010). The revised hierarchical model: A critical review and assessment. *Bilingualism: Language and Cognition*, *13*, 373–81.

Potter, M.C., So, K.-F., Von Eckardt, B. and Feldman, L.B. (1984). Lexical and conceptual representation in beginning and proficient bilinguals. *Journal of Verbal Learning and Verbal Behavior*, *23*, 23–38.

Sholl, A., Sankaranarayanan, A. and Kroll, J.F. (1995). Transfer between picture naming and translation: A test of asymmetries in bilingual memory. *Psychological Science*, *6*, 45–49.

Sunderman, G. and Kroll, J.F. (2006). First Language activation during second language lexical processing: An investigation of lexical form, meaning, and grammatical class. *Studies in Second Language Acquisition*, 28, 387–422.

Talamas, A., Kroll, J.F. and Dufour, R. (1999). From form to meaning: Stages in the acquisition of second language vocabulary. *Bilingualism: Language and Cognition*, *2*, 45–58.

Van Hell, J. G. and De Groot, A.M. B. (1998). Conceptual representation in bilingual memory: Effects of concreteness and cognate status in word association. *Bilingualism: Language and Cognition*, *1*, 193–211.

Further reading

Kroll, J.F. and Sholl, A. (1992). Lexical and conceptual memory in fluent and nonfluent bilinguals. In Harris, R.J. (ed.), *Cognitive Processing in Bilinguals*. Amsterdam: Elsevier Science Publishing. (Compares performance on several tasks as a function of second language proficiency.)

Kroll, J.F. and Tokowicz, N. (2001). The development of conceptual representation for words in a second language. In Nicol, J.L. (ed.), *One Mind, Two Languages: Bilingual Language Processing*. Malden, MA: Blackwell Publishers. (Describes the developmental trajectory for adult L2 learners.)

——(2005). Models of bilingual representation and processing: Looking back and to the future. In Kroll, J.F. and De Groot, A.M. B. (eds), *Handbook of Bilingualism: Psycholinguistic Approaches*, New York: Oxford University Press. (Provides an overview of models of bilingual memory representation and processing.)

Kroll, J.F., Michael, E. and Sankaranarayanan, A. (1998). A model of bilingual representation and its implications for second language acquisition.

In Healy, A.F. and Bourne Jr., L.E. (eds), *Foreign Language Learning: Psycholinguistic Studies on Training and Retention*. Mahwah, NJ: Lawrence Erlbaum Associates, Inc. (Describes several adult second language vocabulary training studies.)

Kroll, J.F., Michael, E., Tokowicz, N. and Dufour, R. (2002). The development of lexical fluency in a second language. *Second Language Research*, *18*, 137–71. (Compares performance on several tasks as a function of second language proficiency and working memory.)

S

Scaffolding

Pauline Gibbons
University of Technology Sydney

Originally coined by Wood, Bruner and Ross (1976) in their examination of one-to-one adult–child talk, the metaphor of scaffolding is now used more broadly to describe the nature of assisted performance in first and second language pedagogical contexts. However, the term is now so variously used that it risks becoming indistinguishable from generalized notions of supportive teaching (Michell and Sharpe, 2005). To take account of these broader contexts, this paper redefines the metaphor through an account of its theoretical bases and educational significance.

Within Vygotskian perspectives human development is viewed as a social and collaborative endeavor where both "expert" and "apprentice" are engaged in shared, goal-oriented activity. Central to this view of learning is Vygotsky's notion of the zone of proximal development (Vygotsky, 1978), broadly defined as the distance between the actual developmental level of a learner (determined by what a learner can achieve alone) and their level of potential developmental (determined by what a learner can achieve collaboratively with someone more skilled). Within this collaborative learning context, scaffolding is the task-enabling support that is required if a learner is to participate in learning in their ZPD. Thus scaffolding and a learner's ZPD are two sides of the same coin, since it can be argued that it is only *when* scaffolding is needed that learning will take place.

In formal pedagogical contexts two levels of scaffolding can be identified: *designed* scaffolding, and *interactional* scaffolding (Gibbons, 2006, 2009). Designed scaffolding is planned; for example, a teacher may choose to deconstruct a model text in order to provide a basis for students to later write a text in the same genre themselves. But designed activities are usually enacted through a teacher's interactional scaffolding in the talk between teacher and learner, which is always contingent on what a learner has just said. For example, a teacher may recast what a learner says, so as to provide a more technical and registrally appropriate term, or prompt the student to do this. In such negotiated meaning-making contexts the student is afforded opportunities for self-repair and more appropriate and comprehensible output (Gibbons, 2006).

Whether designed or contingent, scaffolding leads to learners moving to new levels of knowledge, concepts and skills, and a greater level of independent learning. It is increased or withdrawn according to the developing competence of a learner, varies between learners and is tied to the specific task being attempted. It also represents, in microcosm, an instance of Vygotky's notion of "cultural apprenticeship," through which novices become members of the specific community into which they are being apprenticed (Michell and Sharpe, 2005).

This perspective on scaffolding has implications for all pedagogical contexts. It challenges teachers to hold high expectations of learners while providing high levels of scaffolding, so that students engage in worthwhile learning. Students are thus set up for success. And it challenges notions of individual "readiness" and "educational failure," focusing instead on the strengths, appropriateness, and success of the scaffolding frameworks within which a student is learning.

See also: affordance, Interaction and the Interaction Hypothesis, negotiation of meaning, output hypothesis, recasts, social and sociocultural approaches to SLA

References

Wood, D., Bruner, J. and Ross, G. (1976). The Role of Tutoring in Problem Solving. *Journal of Child Psychology and Psychiatry*, *17*(2), 89–100.

Gibbons, P. (2009). *English Learners, Academic Literacy and Thinking: Learning in the Challenge Zone*. Portsmouth, NH: Heinemann.

——(2006). *Bridging Discourses in the ESL Classroom: Teachers, Students and Researchers*. London: Continuum.

Michell, M. and Sharpe, T. (2005). Collective Instructional Scaffolding in English as a Second Language Classrooms. *Prospect, An Australian Journal of TESOL* 20 (1) *Re-thinking ESL pedagogy: Socio-cultural Approaches to Teaching and Learning*, 31–58.

Vygotsky, L. (1978). *Mind in Society: The Development of Higher Psychological Processes*. Cambridge, MA: Harvard University Press.

Further reading

Donato, R. (2000). Sociocultural contributions to understanding the foreign and second language classroom. In J. Lantolf (ed.), *Sociocultural Theory and Second Language Learning*, pp. 27–50. Oxford: Oxford University Press. (A description of how the interpretive tools of sociocultural theory can be used to examine the classroom, including an examination of peer scaffolding.)

Hammond, J. and Gibbons, P. (2005). Putting scaffolding to work: The contribution of scaffolding in articulating ESL education. *Prospect, An Australian Journal of TESOL* 20 (1) *Rethinking ESL pedagogy: Socio-cultural approaches to teaching and learning*, 6–30. (Describes a detailed model of scaffolding as a way of informing educational practice.)

Mercer, N. (1994). Neo-Vygotskian theory and classroom education. In B. Stierer and J. Maybin (eds), *Language, Literacy and Learning in Educational Practice*. Clevedon: Multilingual Matters. (Describes the central features and concepts of a Vygotskian approach to talk and learning in the classroom.)

van Lier, L. (2004). *The Ecology and Semiotics of Language Learning: A Sociocultural Perspective*. New York: Springer. (An overview of an ecological approach to language learning, including a discussion of three-level model of scaffolding.)

Schemata

Hossein Nassaji
University of Victoria

Schema (or its plural *schemata*) is a notion that has been used in cognitive psychology to describe the organization of knowledge in the human mind. There are different perspectives on schema and different researchers have used different terminologies to describe its nature. In general, however, *schema* can be defined as the generic knowledge structure people store in their mind of what they know and experience. Such knowledge structures of previously stored information are used in acquiring and interpreting new information.

The concept of schema was originally proposed by Bartlett (1932) to account for how information in stories and events is represented in memory. Bartlett's thinking was somewhat influenced by Gestalt theory that emphasized holistic perception and the idea that people make sense of materials by making a coherent pattern of what they perceive.

According to Bartlett, understanding and recall take place mainly in the context of past experience and with reference to the relevant information in memory. He then used the term *schema* to refer to the organization of such past experiences.

Bartlett conducted a number of experiments to demonstrate how people's knowledge of past events influenced their subsequent recall. However, he did not elucidate the nature of such knowledge. It was later on, and as a consequence of advances in computer science and interests in modeling human cognition in the field of artificial intelligence, that schema theory was emerged as a theoretical framework to explain the mental representation of knowledge. Influential works in this area were those of Minsky (1975) and Schank (e.g., Schank and Abelson, 1977) in computer science and then Rumelhart (e.g., Rumelhart, 1980; Rumelhart and Ortony, 1977) in cognitive psychology. Minsky (1975) used the notion of *frame* to explain how knowledge is organized and stored in memory and then used in machines to simulate human-like behavior. He defined *frame* as "a data-structure for representing a stereotyped situation, like being in a certain kind of living room, or going to a child's birthday party" (p. 212). Schank and Abelson (1977) used the notion of *script* to describe such generic knowledge structures. According to these authors, a script consists of slots and information about how to fill those slots. Rumelhart (e.g., Rumelhart, 1980; Rumelhart and Ortony, 1977) elaborated on these notions by further refining and also extending their application to other areas of cognitive science, including discourse comprehension and interpretation.

Rumelhart's work contributed considerably to the development of schema theory in its contemporary understanding. He defined schemata as "the building blocks of cognition" (1980: 33), and then described the theory of schema as a theory about "how knowledge is presented and about how that representation facilitates the use of the knowledge in particular ways" (p. 34). In his speciation of schemata, Rumelhart (1980) listed six major features for schemata: (1) schemata have variables; 2) schemata can be embedded, one within another; 3) schemata represent knowledge at all levels of abstraction; 4) schemata represent knowledge rather than definition; 5) schemata are active processes; and 6) schemata are recognition devices whose processing is aimed at the evaluation of their goodness of fit to the data being processed (pp. 40–41).

The schema view of knowledge as described above provided new and exciting developments in the field of cognitive psychology, leading to a theoretical framework that was used to explain and interpret a host of cognitive processes, such as inferencing, remembering, reasoning, problem-solving, and text comprehension and recall. These developments also greatly influenced the field of second language (L2) reading comprehension and instruction. An important contribution of the schema theory to reading was its drawing attention to the constructive nature of the reading process and the idea that readers interpret and understand the meaning of texts according to the knowledge (or schema) they bring to text. In this respect, researchers who applied schema theory to reading have distinguished between different kinds of such schemata such as *formal schemata*, *content schemata*, and *cultural schemata*. Formal schemata refer to the prior knowledge that people have about the formal and rhetorical structure of a text whereas content schemata is people's prior knowledge of the content and subject-specific domain of a text. Cultural schemata embraces the shared knowledge people have of a particular culture. It is this kind of schema that is used in understanding and interpreting particular social and cultural events. A number of studies have investigated the role of different schemata in reading and have found that readers' recall and understanding of texts are greatly influenced by such preexisting knowledge structures (see Carrell, 1987).

However, despite the important contributions of schema theory to our understanding of how knowledge is represented in the mind, the theory has been criticized as having significant limitations. One major problem has been taken to relate to the oversimplified view that it represents of the mental knowledge structure. For example, the idea that schemata exist in preexisting formats in the mind has been criticized as providing a static and inflexible view of the role of knowledge, "which is at variance with the dynamic nature of knowledge in human cognition" (Nassaji, 2002: 444). Other problems concern the lack of specificity of the theory and also attempts to attribute existence to conceptual notions (Sadoski, Paivio, and Goetz, 1991). Sadoski *et al.* argued that "schemata are, by most accounts, abstractions derived from experience that exist in a potential, nonspecific state, awaiting input (p. 467)." Such notions, they argued, are problematic because they do not allow operationalization of variable and formulations of alternatives that could be adequately investigated in empirical research. Such problems of schema theory have led researchers to explore alternative theoretical frameworks to explain the role of knowledge in comprehension and human cognition. This, for example, includes theories within a connectionist perspective such as Kintch's construction-integration model (e.g., Kintsch, 1988) and Sedoaki *et al.*'s (1991) dual coding theory or theories that present a social conception of human mind such as the Vygotskian sociocultural theory (see Nassaji, 2002, for a more detailed discussion of schema theory, its contributions, and limitations).

See also: connectionism and SLA, declarative memory and knowledge, depth of processing, listening, reading, semantic processing

References

Anderson, R.C. and Pearson, P.D. (1984). A schema-theoretic view of basic processes in reading comprehension. In P.D. Pearson (ed.), *Handbook of Reading Research*, pp. 255–92. New York: Longman.

Bartlett, F.C. (1932). *Remembering: An Experimental and Social Study*. Cambridge: Cambridge University Press.

Carrell, P.L. (1987). Content and formal schemata in ESL reading. *TESOL Quarterly*, *21*, 461–81.

Kintsch, W. (1988). The role of knowledge in discourse comprehension: A construction-integration model. *Psychological Review*, *92*, 163–82.

Minsky, M. (1975). A framework for representing knowledge. In P.H. Winston (ed.), *The Psychology of Computer Vision*, pp. 211–77. New York: McGraw-Hill.

Nassaji, H. (2002). Schema theory and knowledge-based processes in second language reading comprehension: A need for alternative perspectives. *Language Learning*, *52*, 439–81.

Rumelhart, D.E. (1980). Schemata: The building blocks of cognition. In R.J. Spiro, B.C. Bruce and W.F. Brewer (eds), *Theoretical Issues in Reading Comprehension*, pp. 33–58. Hillsdale, NJ: Erlbaum

Rumelhart, D.E. and Ortony, A. (1977). The representation of knowledge in memory. In R.C. Anderson, R.J. Spiro and W.E. Montague (eds), *Schooling and the Acquisition of Knowledge*, pp. 99–135. Hillsdale, NJ: Erlbaum.

Sadoski, M., Paivio, A. and Goetz, E.T. (1991). Commentary: A critique of schema theory in reading and a dual coding alternative. *Reading Research Quarterly*, *26*, 463–84.

Schank, R.C. and Abelson, R.P. (1977). *Scripts, Plans, Goals and Understanding: An Inquiry into Human Knowledge Structures* (Vol. 2). Hillsdale, NJ: Lawrence Erlbaum Associates.

Further reading

Adams, M.J. and Collins, A. (1979). A schema-theoretic view of reading. In R.O. Freedle (ed.), *New Directions in Discourse Processing*, Vol. 2, pp. 1–22. Norwood, NJ: Ablex. (This paper discusses schema theoretic models of language comprehension and their application to the study of reading comprehension.)

Anderson, R.C. (1984). Role of the reader's schema in comprehension, learning, and memory. In R. C. Anderson, J. Osborn and R.J. Tierney (eds), *Learning to Read in American schools: Basal Readers and Content Texts*, pp. 243–58. Hillsdale, NJ: Erlbaum. (This paper defines schema theory, examines the supporting research evidence, and explains the application of the theory for classroom teaching.)

Carrell, P.L. (1984). The effects of rhetorical organization on ESL readers. *TESOL Quarterly*, *18*, 441–69. (This article reports the results of an empirical study of the effects of rhetorical organizations (formal schemata) of different expository texts read by different ESL learners, with the results showing effects for the overall rehtorical patterns and learners' L1 backgrounds.)

Carrell, P.L. and Eisterhold, J.C. (1983). Schema theory and ESL reading pedagogy. *TESOL Quarterly*, *17*, 553–73. (This article discusses the role of prior knowledge in models of L2 reading and the implications of schema theory for the ESL/EFL reading pedagogy.)

Rumelhart, D.E. (1984). Schemata and the cognitive system. In R.S. Wyer and T.K. Srull (eds), *Handbook of Social Cognition*, Vol. 1, pp. 161–88. Hillsdale, NJ: Lawrence Erlbaum Associates. (In this paper, Rumelhart discusses in some detail the notion of schemata and its characterists as well as the various psychological domains in which a schema theoretic view can be applied.)

Scope

Hye-Young Kwak and William O'Grady
University of Hawai'i

Scope is the term used for the relationship between operators (quantifiers, *wh* expressions, negation) and other parts of a sentence, including other operators. A simple example of the interpretive consequences of a scope relation comes from the sentence in (1), which is ambiguous.

(1) All the students didn't pass the exam.

This sentence can mean either that all the students failed the exam (the *all* > *not* reading), or that just some of the students fell short (the *not* > *all* reading, in which the negative affects the interpretation of the quantifier).

The relevance of scopal phenomena to the study of language acquisition stems largely from the fact that the governing principles are thought to be highly abstract, whereas the relevant input (i.e., sentences containing two or more operators) appears to be relatively sparse (e.g., O'Grady, 2008). Scope has been used to support at least three separate ideas in the literature on second language acquisition.

First, it has been argued that second language learners have access to subtle scopal contrasts in a second language that have no counterpart in their first language. For example, Dekydtspotter, Sprouse and Swanson (2001) have shown that advanced English-speaking adult learners of French (but not their intermediate-level counterparts) recognize the subtle difference exemplified in (2). One can respond to a question such as (2a) either by counting the number of books that each student is buying, or by counting only the books that all the students buy (that is, just the purchases they have in common). In contrast, (2b) permits only the first response.

(2) a. [Combien de livres] est-ce que les étudiants achètent tous?
How.many of books is it that the students buy all
'How many books are the students all buying?'

b. [Combien _i] est-ce que les étudiants achètent tous [de livres]i?

Dekydtspotter *et al.* interpret their finding as evidence for the view that SLA is constrained by the same domain-specific and informationally encapsulated mental architecture relevant to L1 acquisition. Dekydtspotter and Outcalt (2005) carried out a detailed investigation of on-line processing that supports the same conclusion for a slightly different scopal ambiguity.

Second, Marsden (2009) makes use a cross-linguistic difference in scope to argue that L2 learners are able to reset the parametric values of their native language. A representative contrast in this regard involves the fact that whereas an English sentence such as *Someone stroked every cat* is ambiguous (a single person stroked all the cats, or different people stroked each cat), the equivalent Japanese sentence permits just the first interpretation.

(3) Dareka-ga dono neko-mo nadeta.
someone-Nom which cat-Focus stroked
'Someone stroked every cat.'

Marsden reports that advanced English-speaking learners of Japanese restrict the interpretation of (3) in the appropriate way, but that less proficient learners incorrectly permit the interpretation in which different people stroke each cat (as happens in English). Marsden takes this result to indicate that second language learners initially transfer the (lexically based) parameter settings of their L1 to the L2, but are eventually able to make the appropriate adjustment thanks to ongoing access to Universal Grammar, consistent with the Full Transfer/Full Access theory of SLA.

Third, O'Grady, Lee and Kwak (2009) make use of scopal data to argue for a processing-based theory of transfer built around the hypothesis in (4).

(4) L2 learners will transfer the dominant scopal interpretation of their first language, unless there is a less costly interpretation in the second language.

The contrast on which they focus involves the difference between English and Korean with respect to sentences containing a negated verb and a universally quantified direct object, as illustrated in (5). Whereas the preferred interpretation of the English sentence is 'Mary read fewer than all the books' (*not* > *all*), the Korean sentence is usually taken to mean 'All of the books were unread by Mary' (*all* > *not*).

(5) a. Mary didn't read all the books. (*not* > *all* strongly preferred)

b. Mary-ka **motun** chayk-ul **an** ilkessta. (*all* > *not* strongly preferred)
Mary-Nom all book-Acc not read
'Mary didn't read all the books.' (in the sense of 'All of the books were unread by Mary.')

Drawing on psycholinguistic and developmental data, O'Grady *et al.* argue that processing considerations strongly favor the *all* > *not* interpretation in Korean, but impose no preference at all in English. (Pragmatic factors and input are responsible for the *not* > *all* preference in that language.) Thus Korean speakers should transfer the preferred *all* > *not* interpretation of their native language, since the alternative is no less costly in English. On the other hand, English speakers should FAIL to transfer the English-favored *not* > *all* interpretation to Korean, as the alternative reading (*all* > *not*) IS less costly in that language. Experimental work with adult English-speaking learners of Korean and adult Korean-speaking learners of English bear out these predictions.

See also: cross-linguistic influence, modularity, parsing sentences, semantic processing, Universal Grammar (UG) and SLA, Wh-questions

References

Dekydtspotter, L., Sprouse, R. and Swanson, K. (2001). Reflexes of mental architecture in second-language acquisition: The interpretation of *Combien* extractions in English-French interlanguage. *Language Acquisition*, *9*, 175–227.

Dekydtspotter, L. and Outcalt, S. (2005). A syntactic bias in scope ambiguity resolution in the processing of English-French cardinality interrogatives: Evidence for informational encapsulation. *Language Learning*, *55*, 1–36.

Marsden, H. (2009). Distributive quantifier scope in English-Japanese and Korean-Japanese interlanguage. *Language Acquisition*, *16*, 135–77.

O'Grady, W. (2008). Does emergentism have a chance? In H. Chan, H. Jacob and E. Kapia (eds), *The Proceedings of the 32nd Annual Boston University Conference on Language Development*. Somerville, MA: Cascadilla Press.

O'Grady, W., Lee, M. and Kwak, H.-Y. (2009). Emergentism and second language acquisition. In W. Ritchie and T. Bhatia (eds), *The New Handbook of Second Language Acquisition*. Bingley: Emerald Publishing Group.

Second dialect acquisition

Jeff Siegel
University of New England

Second dialect acquisition (SDA) refers to the learning of another dialect of a language as opposed to learning a separate language. Dialects are defined here as varieties that speakers perceive as belonging to the same language. One dialect differs from another in vocabulary, pronunciation and/or morphosyntax, and in its association with a particular geographic region or social group. SDA is concerned mainly with three broad types of dialects: (1) national dialects such as Canadian and Australian English and Mexican and European Spanish; (2) regional dialects such as Yorkshire and Liverpool English in England, and Swabian and Bavarian in Germany; and (3) ethnic dialects such as Aboriginal English in Australia and African American English and Chicano Spanish in the USA.

As in second language acquisition (SLA), the study of SDA can be divided into two broad contexts: naturalistic and educational. Naturalistic SDA refers to learning a new dialect without any instruction. This most often occurs when people who speak a particular regional dialect as their first dialect (D1) migrate to another part of the same country where a different regional dialect (D2) is spoken – for example, Norway (Kerswill, 1994) and China (Stanford, 2007). Naturalistic SDA also occurs when people migrate to another country where a different national dialect is spoken – for example, Canadians and Americans to Australia (Foreman, 2003). Studies of SDA in this context have been conducted by dialectologists or variationist sociolinguists looking mainly at phonological variables, but they vary widely in their methodology and analysis – for example, in their criteria for measuring attainment in the D2. Nevertheless, some overall explanations of differential attainment emerge which are similar to those of SLA. Age is the most important factor, with sensitive periods for acquisition identified as 7 years or younger for complex phonological features, and the mid-teens or younger for lexical and morphological features (see Chambers, 1992). Other significant sociolinguistic factors concern degree or social interaction and identification with the D2 speakers.

These studies also reveal many differences between SDA and SLA. First, SDA is generally replacive rather than additive, and therefore true bidialectalism is rare. Learners often end up with mixed or "hybrized" dialects, containing many intermediate forms (Trudgill, 1986). The close linguistic similarity between the D1 and D2 compared to an L1 and L2 is also significant. There is generally no communicative reason to use D2, and learners are often unaware of subtle differences between the dialects. Furthermore, the small linguistic distance results in greater negative transfer. Various sociolinguistic factors are also more important for SDA. According to folk views about identity, a person's dialect is part of their "true self," and speaking another dialect is often seen as being fake or pretentious. In addition, there is the matter of ownership: when a dialect is a crucial marker of group identity, outsiders trying to speak it may provoke strong negative reactions.

Educational SDA involves formal training in one of three different educational contexts. Dialect coaching involves teaching actors to speak in various national, regional, or ethnic dialects for the purpose of dramatic performance. Accent modification (or accent reduction) training is aimed at speakers of regional or ethnic dialects who want to acquire a particular national "standard" variety in order to improve their prospects in education or employment. This standard is the abstracted and idealized version of a particular dialect originally spoken by the upper middle classes of one dominant region of the country, and later "standardized" in written form – for example, standard British English and High German. This is often considered to be the only correct or legitimate form of the language. Both of these contexts normally involve adults with instruction one-to-one or in small groups and an emphasis on pronunciation.

The third and most common educational context for SDA is the classroom in the formal education system. The D2 is the standard variety, and the emphasis is on grammar and vocabulary, rather than pronunciation. The learners are initially children who come to school speaking unstandardized dialects markedly different from this standard. These include regional dialects – for example, Swabian D1 and High German D2 (Ammon, 1989) – and ethnic dialects – for example, African American English D1 and standard American English D2 (Isaacs, 1996). Classroom SDA is also prevalent in countries with diglossic situations, where the standard is very different to the variety spoken colloquially by most of the population – for example, in Cyprus with the Greek Cypriot dialect D1 and standard Modern Greek D2 (Yiakoumetti, 2006). SDA in "heritage language learning" settings in the USA involves older students – for example, Chicano Spanish D1 and standard Spanish D2 (Fairclough, 2005).

The term SDA is also applied to classroom settings involving a creole language and the standard form of the language which provided most of its vocabulary – for example, Hawai'i Creole D1 and standard American English D2. While most linguists would say these are separate languages, a large proportion of their speakers view them as varieties of the same language. Classroom SDA is thus relevant to most students in creole-speaking countries such as Jamaica and Guyana (Lacoste, 2009), and to creole-speaking immigrants in countries such as Canada and the USA (Calchar, 2005).

Teaching programs specifically for classroom SDA have existed in the past (see Siegel, 2003), but D1 speakers today are rarely given any special instruction to help them acquire the D2. The reasons for this include the greater similarity between the D1 and D2 compared to that between an L1 and L2. Also, the view persists that dialects are simply careless speech or incorrect forms of the standard variety. In addition, there is the belief that using the students' D1 in the classroom as a bridge to learning the D2 would disadvantage students by exacerbating interference and by wasting time that could be devoted to the standard. (See Siegel, 2006 for a rebuttal of these and other arguments.) However, students who speak unstandardized dialects or creoles are truly disadvantaged in other ways. First, they have to learn how to read and write in a variety of languages that they do not already know (the D2). Second, since their D1 is often denigrated and considered inappropriate for the classroom, they face the frustration of constant correction and not being allowed to express themselves in their own way of speaking. Unstandardized dialect and creole speakers in mainstream programs are faced with the additional disadvantage of having to compete with classmates who already speak the D2. Other obstacles include uninformed teachers, who often cannot distinguish errors caused by systematic differences between the D1 and the D2 from those caused by carelessness. There are also issues of social identity, as students may be averse to learning and using the D2 because it is seen as closely associated with a different social group. With regard to linguistic factors, students may not notice some of the subtle linguistic differences between the D1 and the D2.

Three approaches exist which attempt to deal with these disadvantages and utilize the students' D1 to help them acquire the D2. The instrumental approach uses the students' D1 as a medium of instruction to teach initial literacy and sometimes content subjects such as mathematics. This approach has been implemented in situations where the D1 is clearly distinguished from the D2 and where all students in the classroom are speakers of the D1 – for example, in creole-speaking countries such as Haiti and the Seychelles, and in some communities in Australia and Papua New Guinea. The accommodation approach does not adopt the D1 for instruction but allows students to speak or write in it, or makes use of students' own interactional patterns, stories and/or music. This approach can be used in a mainstream classroom with other students who speak varieties closer to the standard. This approach has had successful results with speakers of African American English and Hawai'i Creole. The awareness approach involves at least two of the following three components. The accommodation component accepts aspects of the students' D1 in the classroom in various ways, as just described. The sociolinguistic component teaches students about variation in language and different varieties, such as types of dialects and creoles. Students also find out about the socio-historical processes that lead to a particular variety becoming accepted as the standard. The contrastive component helps students to discover the rule-governed nature and linguistic characteristics of their own varieties and the differences from the varieties of other students and from the standard. This approach can also be used in classrooms where students have a variety of linguistic backgrounds.

Evaluations of these approaches (e.g. Murtagh, 1982 in Australia; Boggs, 1985 in Hawai'i; Yiakoumetti, 2006 in Cyprus) demonstrate that they lead to greater interest and motivation and better rates of participation. In addition, they result in higher scores in tests measuring reading, writing or oral skills in the standard D2 and in some cases to increases in overall academic achievement.

See also: age effects in SLA, attitudes to the L2, heritage language acquisition, identity theory, pidginization and creolization, variationist approaches

References

Ammon, U. (1989). Aspects of dialect and school in the Federal Republic of Germany. In J. Cheshire, V. Edwards, H. Münstermann and B. Weltens (eds), *Dialect and Education: Some European Perspectives*, pp. 113–38. Clevedon: Multilingual Matters.

Boggs, S.T. (1985). *Speaking, Relating, and Learning: A Study of Hawaiian Children at Home and at School.* Norwood, NJ: Ablex Publishing

Calchar, A. (2005). Creole-English speakers' treatment of tense-aspect morphology in interlanguage written discourse. *Language Learning*, *55*, 275–334.

Chambers, J.K. (1992). Dialect acquisition. *Language*, *68*, 673–705.

Fairclough, M. (2005). *Spanish and Heritage Language Education in the United States: Struggling with Hypotheticals*. Madrid and Frankfurt am Main: Iberoamericana and Vervuert.

Foreman, A. (2003). *Pretending to Be Someone You're Not. A Study of Second Dialect Acquisition in Australia*. PhD thesis. Monash University. Melbourne.

Isaacs, G.J. (1996). Persistence of non-standard dialect in school-age children. *Journal of Speech and Hearing Research*, *39*, 434–41.

Kerswill, P. (1994). *Dialects Converging: Rural Speech in Urban Norway*. Oxford: Clarendon.

Lacoste, V. (2009). *Learning the Sounds of Standard Jamaican English: Variationist, Phonological and Pedagogical Perspectives on 7-Year-Old Children's Classroom Speech*. PhD dissertation. University of Essex and Université Paul Valery, France. UMI/ProQuest Dissertations Database.

Murtagh, E.J. (1982). Creole and English as languages of instruction in bilingual education with Aboriginal Australians: Some research findings. *International Journal of the Sociology of Language*, *36*, 15–33.

Siegel, J. (2003). Social context. In C.J. Doughty and M.H. Long (eds), *Handbook of Second Language Acquisition*, pp. 178–223. Oxford: Blackwell.

——(2006). Keeping creoles and dialects out of the classroom: Is it justified? In S.J. Nero (ed.), *Dialects, Englishes, Creoles, and Education*, pp. 39–67. Mahwah, NJ: Erlbaum.

Stanford, J.N. (2007) *Dialect contact and identity: A case study of exogamous Sui Clans*. PhD dissertation. Michigan State University.

Trudgill, P. (1986). *Dialects in Contact*. Oxford: Blackwell.

Yiakoumetti, A. (2006). A bidialectal program for the learning of standard modern Greek in Cyprus. *Applied Linguistics*, *27*(2), 295–317.

Further reading

Nero, S.J. (ed.). (2006). *Dialects, Englishes, Creoles, and education*. Mahwah, NJ: Erlbaum. (A collection of studies on dialects of English and creoles in classroom contexts in the USA.)

Siegel, J. (2010). *Second Dialect Acquisition*. Cambridge: Cambridge University Press. (A comprehensive survey of field of SDA, including studies in both naturalistic and classroom contexts.)

Second language socialization

Steven Talmy

University of British Columbia

Language socialization is the process through which children or novices, in interaction with more proficient caregivers or experts, develop the social, cultural, and communicative competencies needed to participate in the everyday life of particular (sub) cultural groups and communities of practice, including those in which languages other than a learner's first language (L1) are used. Second language (L2) socialization is thus an "alternative" (Atkinson, 2011) "paradigm" (Watson-Gegeo, 2004) for the study of second/additional language and culture learning. It is typically longitudinal, ethnographic in design, and favors analytic frameworks that allow for the examination of microgenesis and ontogenesis in (L1 and L2) linguistic and other social practices, as well as how such practices relate to matters of extra-situational, or macro, cultural and sociological significance. This allows language socialization researchers to examine the contingent, multidirectional processes of socialization *in situ*, while simultaneously remaining attentive to social and cultural continuity, change, and disjuncture across time scales.

From the "first generation" to the "second wave"

Language socialization in North America originated in the late 1970s and 1980s in the work of Elinor Ochs, Bambi Schieffelin, Shirley Brice Heath, Karen Watson-Gegeo, and colleagues. It developed as a response both to previous anthropological studies of child socialization, which "proceeded as if language was irrelevant," and to the "invisibility," in psycholinguistic studies of L1 acquisition, of culture "as a principle that organized speech practices and their acquisition" (Kulick and Schieffelin, 2004: 349; also see Schieffelin and Ochs, 2008). Research in the "first generation" (Garrett and Baquedano-López, 2002) of language socialization studies examined how children in comparatively monolingual communities in Samoa, Papua New Guinea, the Solomon Islands, and in the U.S., learned the first language and other social practices of everyday life through interaction with parents, caregivers, and older siblings (see, e.g., Ochs, 1988; Schieffelin, 1990; Schieffelin and Ochs, 1986a, 1986b, 2008). "Second wave" (Bronson and Watson-Gegeo, 2008) L1 socialization researchers have continued to build upon the insights of earlier work by bringing an expanding range of disciplinary interests, theoretical lenses, and empirical foci to complement those of prior studies (see Duff and Hornberger, 2008; Garrett and Baquedano-López, 2002). Thus, studies increasingly concern the socialization not just of children, but of youth and adults in multilingual, transnational learning contexts in addition to those that are, at least seemingly, more homogeneous. Conceptions of *Culture* have shifted, as well, from those that appear to be relatively static, monolithic, or essentialistic (cf. Ochs, 1999), defined along lines of nation-state or "speech community," to more local, variable, dynamic conceptions of (small "c" and plural) *cultures* (e.g., of particular classrooms or communities of practice). School and workplace contexts of socialization are also more frequently featured, as is socialization through multiple modalities rather than primarily face-to-face interaction. The inherent multidirectionality of language socialization is also more often included in analysis, that is, the consequences of socializing processes not only for novices and newcomers, but for experts or oldtimers as well. Finally, studies are increasingly highlighting the contingent, contested character of socialization, by examining not only "successful" cases of socialization, when social and cultural reproduction occur, but when it is unsuccessful, or results in outcomes that are unanticipated, out of the ordinary, and/or unwelcome.

Studies of L2 socialization have played a formative (though by no means exclusive) role in this latter stream (i.e., second wave) of language socialization inquiry, no doubt because L2 socialization by definition concerns bi- and multilingual learners, who are often older, are perhaps learning the L2 in a school or other formal setting, and have often unique configurations of (first and additional) language and literacy abilities, backgrounds, life experiences, investments, desires, and identities that can come into play as they attempt to gain access to and participate in the language and other social practices of communities that are in some way new or unfamiliar to them (see, e.g., Duff, 2010; Duff and Kobayashi, 2010).

What is learned

Language socialization can be distinguished from other theories of (language) learning by its theorization of the learning object, or language. Variously reflecting influences from phenomenology, symbolic interactionism, cultural historical psychology, pragmatics, ethnography of communication, and functional linguistics, language is conceptualized as one of an array of dynamic, contested, and changeable social practices that constitute and are constituted by particular sociohistorically-, socioculturally-, and sociopolitically situated communities. This is in contrast to a decontextualized view of language as a neutral, referential medium composed of morphemes, phonemes, syntax, and lexis, as is common in many other (e.g., cognitivist) theories, including those that have predominated in SLA (see Duff and Talmy, 2011; Watson-Gegeo and Nielsen, 2003; Watson-Gegeo, 2004). Thus, L2 socialization research involves far more than investigating whether and what kinds of word endings, or grammatical structures, or vocabulary, or speech acts are (or are not) acquired – although this will likely be *part* of an L2 socialization study. For language socialization researchers, the crucial analytic move involves: accounting for the *social and cultural meanings* that are indexed by or associated with particular morphemes, syntactic constructions, lexical items, ways of apologizing or requesting or displaying respect, and so forth; how those meanings simultaneously produce, reproduce, and/or transform the orientations, values, mores, traditions, and ways of being-in-the-world of the community they both constitute and are constituted by; as well as the language-user's identity as a (particular kind of) member of that community. That is, (L2) learning in language socialization is viewed not simply as the acquisition of a *code*, but of becoming a particular kind of person in society, of accommodating (or resisting) certain ways of being, of transforming identities, of learning new or additional ways of knowing, sense-making, and self-presentation; in short, of the many kinds of cultural knowledge and social relations that are learned both in and through language.

Methods

Language socialization research is typically longitudinal, and, true to its ethnographic principles, aims for persistent, prolonged on-site researcher engagement, drawing on methods such as participant observation, field notes, interviews, audio/video recordings of socializing interactions, and analysis of site artifacts. Data generated from such sources are used to produce in-depth, thick descriptions both of a given culture or community of practice, as well as apprentices' development in one or more focal social practices, speech events, or other (language-mediated) activities. Data analysis is intensive, iterative, and begins at the commencement of data generation, continuing through to the final write-up of the study. Analytic methods are diverse, ranging from thematic coding or even content analysis, to, more commonly, some form of discourse analysis. The aim, whatever analytic framework is adopted, is to examine processes of language socialization (see, e.g., Watson-Gegeo and Nielsen, 2003).

Paradigmatic debates

Although the methods described above are commonly acknowledged as hallmarks of language socialization, some studies may not utilize them all, or may utilize them differently, even if there remain substantive questions concerning the extent to which such studies qualify as language socialization research. This issue recalls a series of debates that have arisen recently concerning the scope, orientation, and foci of research conducted under the mantle of language socialization (see Duff and Talmy, 2011: 95–116 for an overview). One outcome of these debates has been the formulation of taxonomies to describe the extent to which research conforms to the theoretical and methodological principles articulated by the originators of the language socialization paradigm. In one such taxonomy, developed by Bronson and Watson-Gegeo (2008), "language socialization as topic" is not longitudinal, ethnographic, nor does it utilize methods such as those described in the previous section. Rather it draws on "thin data sets," such as retrospective accounts of participants' socialization experiences (e.g., generated in interviews) while providing little "intensive analysis of primary discourse data" (p. 48). "Language socialization as approach" adopts the theoretical, philosophical, and methodological commitments of the paradigm, but "does not necessarily follow a longitudinal design" (p. 49). In contrast, the "gold standard" is "language socialization as method," which "adhere[s] to the highest standards, including full-blown longitudinal ethnographic research and discourse analyses of relevant data" (p. 48).

Duff and Talmy (2011) have maintained that such debates as this are testament to the strength and vitality of language socialization as a paradigm. At the same time, they caution that the "unequivocal demarcation of paradigmatic boundaries" in the current moment of language socialization's historical development may be premature, noting that it could "foreclose ... [and] delimit investigation into the diverse, variable, and ever-changing means and social practices that novices/newcomers and experts/old-timers may be socialized through and into" (p. 102–103).

Conclusions

Language socialization has proven over the years to be among the most enduring and productive of the so-called "alternative approaches to SLA" (Atkinson, 2011). As the contemporary "second wave" generates a third, there is little doubt that the paradigm's rich empirical tradition will continue to expand, promising more and greater insights into the complex phenomenon commonly known as "L2 learning."

See also: discourse and pragmatics in SLA, ecology of learning, ethnographic research, longitudinal research, qualitative research, social and sociocultural influences on SLA

References

Atkinson, D. ed., (2011). *Alternative Approaches to Second Language Acquisition*. New York: Routledge.

Bronson, M.C. and Watson-Gegeo, K.A., (2008). The critical moment: Language socialization and the (re)visioning of first and second language learning. In P.A. Duff and N.H. Hornberger, eds *Encyclopedia of Language and Education*, Volume 8: Language Socialization, pp. 43–55. Boston, MA: Springer.

Duff, P.A., (2010). Language socialization. In N.H. Hornberger and S.L. McKay (eds), *Sociolinguistics and Language Education*, pp. 427–52. Bristol: Multilingual Matters.

Duff, P.A. and Hornberger, N.H. (eds) (2008). *Encyclopedia of Language and Education*, Volume 8: Language Socialization. Boston, MA: Springer.

Duff, P.A. and Kobayashi, M., (2010). The intersection of social, cognitive, and cultural processes in language learning: A second language socialization approach. In R. Batstone (ed.), *Sociocognitive Perspectives on Language Use and Language Learning*. Oxford: Oxford University Press, pp. 75–93.

Duff, P.A. and Talmy, S., (2011). Language socialization approaches to second language acquisition: Social, cultural, and linguistic development in additional languages. In D. Atkinson (ed.), *Alternative Approaches to Second Language Acquisition*, pp. 95–116. New York: Routledge.

Garrett, P. and Baquedano-López, P., (2002). Language socialization: Reproduction and continuity, transformation and change. *Annual Review of Anthropology*, *31*, 339–61.

Kulick, D. and Schieffelin, B.B., (2004). Language socialization. In A. Duranti (ed.), *A Companion to Linguistic Anthropology*, pp. 349–68. Malden, MA: Blackwell.

Ochs, E., (1988). *Culture and Language Development: Language Acquisition and Language Socialization in a Samoan Village*. Cambridge: Cambridge University Press.

Schieffelin, B.B., (1990). *The Give and Take of Everyday Life: Language Socialization of Kaluli Children*. Cambridge: Cambridge University Press.

Schieffelin, B.B. and Ochs, E., (1986a). Language socialization. *Annual Review of Anthropology*, *15*, 163–91.

——(1986b). *Language Socialization across Cultures*. Cambridge: Cambridge University Press.

——(2008). Language socialization: An historical overview. In P.A. Duff and N.H. Hornberger (eds), *Encyclopedia of Language and Educa-*

tion, Volume 8: Language Socialization, pp. 3–15. Boston, MA: Springer.

Watson-Gegeo, K.A., (2004). Mind, language, and epistemology: Toward a language socialization paradigm for SLA. *Modern Language Journal*, *88*, 331–50.

Watson-Gegeo, K.A. and Nielsen, S., 2003. Language socialization in SLA. In C. Doughty and M.H. Long (eds), *Handbook of Second Language Acquisition*, pp. 155–77. Oxford: Blackwell.

Self-repair

Roger Gilabert

University of Barcelona

As part of our language production system, self-repair is a widespread phenomenon both in first and second language production and it involves noticing trouble in either our speech plan or our overt speech, interrupting the flow of speech, and providing the needed repair. When communicating, speakers find problems in their processing of messages to which they typically apply a series of problem-solving mechanisms, and they do so a lot less in the L1 than in the L2. As Levelt (1983) pointed out, as humans we are capable of monitoring both the speech of others as well as our own inner and overt speech. In Levelt's (1989, 1993) model of speech production, which is the most widely accepted one in the applied linguistics literature, the conceptualizer is responsible for monitoring the whole speech production system. Monitoring plays both a matching function and one which creates instructions for adjustment. Regarding the former function, parsed aspects of either inner or overt speech are revised by means of three monitor loops: one that checks the message against the speaker's intentions; one that checks the articulatory plan against the overall plan; and one that monitors overt speech by means of the acoustic-phonetic processor. These problems may involve both the content and the form of the message. The second function of the monitor is to generate instructions for adjustment which typically cause speakers to apply a series of problem-solving mechanisms.

Taxonomy of self-repairs

The most exhaustive taxonomy of problem-solving mechanisms related to perceived deficiencies in one's own production is the one proposed by Kormos (1999). Kormos adopts Levelt's perceptual loop theory and her framework brings together theories about psycholinguistic processes of production, L2 research findings regarding the development of automaticity, as well as theories of consciousness, awareness, and noticing. In agreement with Van Hest (1996), Kormos suggests that perceptual loop theory can be used to explain monitoring in the L2 with no major qualitative changes. Following previous classifications of repairs (Kormos, 1998; Levelt, 1983; Van Hest, 1986) Kormos distinguishes between different repairs (D-repairs), appropriateness repairs (A-repairs), and error repairs. A D-repair is the consequence of error with the conceptualization of the message, either because the information has not been organized properly or because there has been inadequate encoding in the preverbal plan. This type of error therefore requires a reconceptualization of the speech plan. This basic classification which was originally proposed by Levelt (1983) was extended by Kormos (1998) to include inappropriate information repairs, different order repairs, and message abandonment repairs. In inappropriate-information A-repairs the speaker detects a problem with the information content and repairs it. In the case of different-order repairs, the speaker changes the order of the different parts of the message. In message abandonment repairs, the speaker replaces the originally intended message by a new one. Appropriateness repairs are meant to resolve ambiguity, achieve precision, and maintain coherence with previously used words. Kormos distinguishes among five different types of A-repairs: appropriate-level-of-information repairs, with which the speaker decides to be more precise or specific; ambiguous-reference repairs, in which the speaker repairs the referring expression to avoid ambiguity; coherent-terminology repairs, which are employed to be more coherent with the terms used in previous discourse; pragmatic appropriacy repairs, in which the speaker repairs part of the message to make it more pragmatically appropriate in a specific situation; and repairs for "good language," in which the speaker modifies his or her message in order to use more sophisticated language. Finally, error repairs are the result of wrong formulation, and may be used to correct an inappropriate syntactic structure, a lexical problem, faulty morphology, or a phonetic error. Typically the identification of the reasons behind different and appropriate repairs (i.e. the type of error they are correcting) requires the use of retrospective protocol analysis for their identification. Conversely, overt error repairs are more easily identified and do not require introspection for their identification and classification.

Findings in the self-repair literature

Findings in the L2 self-repair literature (Kormos, 2006: 131) have identified a number of facts that are now widely accepted. Firstly, there are a number of factors which may affect the speaker's decision to self-repair, such as the accuracy demands of a specific communicative situation (i.e. an oral exam), the assessment of the speaker regarding how seriously a specific error may prevent communication, and whether repairing an error may slow down the production of the utterance. Secondly, while in the L2 it is often the case that speakers prioritize the correction of content (i.e. lexical repairs) rather than form (i.e. morphosyntactic repairs), certain types of L2 learners may devote a similar amount of attention to both content and form because their formal and grammar-oriented training in such L2. Thirdly, as learners become more proficient in the L2, rather than increasing or reducing the global frequency of self-repairs they shift from simple error-repairs to more complex ones at the level of discourse (Kormos, 2006: 133). In the fourth place, studies on self- repairs in the L2 have demonstrated that the "well-formedness" rule applies when errors are repaired, with studies reporting that over 80% of repairs are being well formed. There are at least two phenomena that are still unexplained by the perceptual loop theory. Firstly, despite having sufficient underlying L2 knowledge, L2 speakers do not notice a lot of the errors in their speech. Secondly, certain types of errors go undetected. In Kormos' view, differences in monitoring are explained by the fact that monitoring needs attentional control. Because attentional capacity is limited, attention used to compensate for the non-automatic processes in the L2 (e.g. grammatical and phonological encoding) limits the amount of monitoring that takes place. The assumption here is that because a lot of attentional resources are being employed to encode messages both grammatically and phonologically in the L2, fewer resources are available for self-monitoring which, as a consequence, is reduced. An additional explanation by Kormos is that attention to monitoring depends on individual differences, which display different working memory capacities among speakers (Harrington and Sawyer, 1992). The verbal component of working memory combines attention control with phonological loop storage capacity (Baddeley, 1986). Differences in both attention control and storage can be expected to affect the amount of self-repairs. However, studies in the area are urgently needed. Thirdly, in Kormos' view, increasing task demands deviates attention from monitoring. There are, however, opposing views about how task demands affect second language production in general, and monitoring in particular. Skehan (1998, 2009), for example, suggests that as language tasks are made more demanding by, for example, giving learners less time to plan them, they consume capacity which deviates attention from monitoring form, with negative consequences for accuracy. Robinson (1995b; 2001a; 2001; 2003; 2005) agrees with Skehan that increasing task demands along planning time, as well as other "resource-dispersing" dimensions of tasks, deviates attention from monitoring. He argues, however, that increasing task demands along other dimensions, such as the number of elements in a task or the reasoning demands they impose on speakers, actually draws learners' attention to the way they encode messages with positive consequences for accuracy.

Self-repairs and SLA

Self-repairs, whether other-initiated or self-initiated (Schegloff *et al.*, 1977), have attracted the interest of SLA researchers because they denote students' awareness of form and can be interpreted as learners' attempts at being accurate (Kormos, 1999). Lyter and Ranta (1997: 57), for example, suggest repairs generated by learners as a result of corrective feedback lead them both to automatize the retrieval of target language knowledge they already have and to revise their hypotheses about the target language. Swain (1998: 66) has also hypothesized that noticing a hole in their own interlanguage may lead learners to notice the gap by directing their attention to relevant input. All these functions of self-repairs have been said to potentially lead to acquisition, and they have been pointed out in order to defend the benefits of certain types of corrective feedback. Self-initiated repairs, on the other hand, serve the same purposes as other-initiated repairs only that they are not the result of corrective feedback but rather are spontaneously generated by learners themselves. Thirdly, the amount of self-repair may be sensitive to task conditions. Language performance studies, such as the one by Yuan and Ellis's (2003: 17), have reported a higher frequency of reformulations and self-corrections when they are given sufficient time 'during' (as opposed to 'before') performance. Gilabert (2007), has also shown that increased task demands in a narrative task and in a map task led learners to self-repair more often when task demands were high than when they were low.

Finally, while our understanding of the phenomenon of second language self-repair has increased in the last two decades, further longitudinal studies and studies into individual differences (e.g. working memory capacity, attention control) will help us understand the phenomenon more accurately in relation to second language acquisition.

See also: attention, Levelt's model of speech production and comprehension, monitoring, Limited Capacity Hypothesis, speaking, Monitor Model

References

Baddeley, A.D. (1986). *Working Memory*. Oxford: Oxford University Press.

Gilabert, R. (2007). Effects of manipulating task complexity on self-repairs during L2 oral production. *International Review of Applied Linguistics in Language Teaching (IRAL)*, *45*(3), 215–40.

Harrington, M. and Sawyer, M. (1992). L2 working memory capacity and L2 reading skills. *Studies in Second Language Acquisition*, *14*, 25–38.

Kormos, J. (1998). A new psycholinguistic taxonomy of self-repairs in L2: a qualitative analysis with retrospection. *Even Yearbook, ELITE SEAS Working Papers in Linguistics*, *3*, 43–68.

——(1999). Monitoring and self-repair in L2. *Language Learning*, *49*(2), 303–42.

——(2006). *Speech Production and Second Language Acquisition*. Mahwah, NJ: Lawrence Erlbaum.

Levelt, W.J. M. (1983). Monitoring and self-repair in speech. *Cognition*, *14*, 41–104.

——(1989). *Speaking: From Intention to Articulation*. Cambridge, MA: Massachusetts Institute of Technology Press.

——(1993). Language use in normal speakers and its disorders. In G. Blanken, J. Dittmann, H. Grimm, J.C. Marshall and C.W. Wallesch (eds), *Linguistic Disorders and Pathologies*, pp. 1–15. Berlin: de Gruyter.

Lyter, R. and Ranta, L. (1997). Corrective feedback and learner uptake. *Studies in Second Language Acquisition*, *19*, 37–66.

Robinson, P. (2001). Task complexity, cognitive resources, and syllabus design: A triadic framework for examining task influences on SLA. In P. Robinson (ed.), *Cognition and second Language Instruction*, pp. 287–318. Cambridge: Cambridge University Press.

——(2003). The cognition hypothesis, task design, and adult task-design language learning. *Second Language Studies*, *21*, 45–105.

——(2005). Cognitive complexity and task sequencing: Studies in a Componential Framework for second language task design. *International Review of Applied Linguistics in Language Teaching*, *43*(1), 1–32.

Schegloff, E., Jefferson, G. and Sacks, H. (1977). The preference of self-correction in the organization of repair in conversation. *Language, 53*, 361–82.

Skehan, P. (2009). Modelling second language performance: Integrating complexity, accuracy, fluency, and lexis. *Applied Linguistics, 30*(4), 510–32.

——(1998). *A Cognitive Approach to Language Learning.* Oxford: Oxford University Press.

Swain, M. (1998). Focus on form through conscious reflection. In C. Daughty and J. Williams (eds), *Focus on form in classroom SLA*, pp. 64–81. New York: Cambridge University Press.

Van Hest, E. (1996). *Self-repair in L1 and L2 Production.* Tilburg, The Netherlands: Tilburg University Press.

Yuan F. and Ellis, R. (2003). The effects of pre-task planning and on-line planning on fluency, complexity, and accuracy in L2 monologic oral production. *Applied Linguistics, 24*(1), 1–27.

Semantic processing

Jeanette Altarriba and
Donald F. Graves
University at Albany, State University of New York

Semantic memory refers to memory for generalized knowledge about the meaning and understanding of concepts that are unrelated to specific events in a person's life. Semantic memory can therefore be thought of as knowledge of factual information, as might be learned in school. Recalling semantic information gives a person a feeling of "knowing," unlike recalling episodic information (information about *specific* events and episodes in a person's life) which gives a person a feeling of "remembering." Semantic memory is linked to *semantic processing*, which describes the process of determining relationships between concepts in order to ascertain meaning from phrases or narratives (Rindflesch and Aronson, 1993). Thus, understanding semantic processing requires some understanding of how semantic memory is represented in the mind.

In the field of psychology, several models of semantic memory have been proposed over the years. Some of the most influential are the network models (see e.g., Collins and Loftus, 1975), the feature models (see e.g., Smith, Shoben, and Rips, 1974), and the associative models of semantic memory and processing (see e.g., SAM; Raaijmakers and Shiffrin, 1981). The technical aspects of each model make them distinctive, but herein, each class of model will be applied to semantic processing, in general.

The network models have some common design features, for example, concepts are represented by nodes that are connected to other concept nodes by links. These links represent a semantic connection between the concepts. Items that are highly related are viewed as having shorter links between concept nodes and sharing many common connections. Thus, the more closely related the concepts are, the easier it is for one concept to "activate" the other concept. For example, accessing the word "cat" from memory may lead easily to the activation of the related word "dog." This activation process is referred to as spreading activation. Thus, when processing semantic information, different nodes will be activated during the process of inputting information, which results in the spread of activation to related nodes. The interaction created by having activation spread across nodes results in overall access of meaning for the concepts involved. More will be said below as to how semantic processing in this vein can describe cross-language processing.

Associative models of semantic memory assume that semantic concepts are stored in memory with associative connections that are based on shared context of use, co-occurrence, or defined relationships between concepts. For example, in the Search of Associative Memory (SAM; Raaijmakers and Shiffrin, 1981) model of memory items that co-occur or that share similar processing contexts are given higher association strengths than items that do not share those features, thus semantic relationships are captured as a result of frequent co-uses of semantically related materials (e.g., the words "bird" and "feathers"). The Adaptive Control of Thought (ACT; Anderson, 1983) model captures semantic relationships by connecting concepts with propositional statements. Thus, when a concept is activated during an attempt to process semantic material it activates concepts that are linked with it, and as semantic processing continues, more and more concepts are activated within the propositional network eventually leading to a group of related concepts that have enough activation to cross into conscious awareness. When concepts attain enough activation to become conscious, it is said that semantic processing is complete and meaning is attained.

Feature models of semantic memory are based on the assumption that semantic categories (e.g., furniture) are stored as lists of features that explain a concept (e.g., used for sitting, reclining, sleeping, or resting materials upon, etc.). These feature lists become active when the individual begins processing a concept, feature by feature, and the feature lists grow in recognition. Once one or more feature lists are activated, they are compared for similarity and when some is found, the overlap is used as evidence for the appropriate meaning of the material that is being processed. Thus, semantic processing is the result of feature overlap between active feature lists.

The organization of words and concepts in monolingual as well as bilingual semantic memory has been previously explored mainly by examining priming effects in lexical decisions (Meyer and Schvaneveldt, 1971; Meyer, Schvaneveldt, and Ruddy, 1975; Neely, 1977). This type of experimental paradigm often used in cognitive psychology research involves presenting a participant with one or two letter strings on a computer screen. Participants are then instructed to decide as quickly and as accurately as possible whether or not the letter string composes a real word. This is often done by pressing one key if the letter string is a real word and a second key if a nonword (e.g., *blit*) is presented. The response times to each target item are then recorded for each participant. A priming paradigm involving a naming task would require participants to pronounce the target word aloud so that reaction time could also be recorded and examined. The concept behind semantic priming is that as a word is presented (e.g., light), automatic access to its meaning results in activation of both that concept, as well as other concepts that are related to it (e.g., dark; lamp; light, etc.). One of the most common effects that have been found to occur in lexical decision tasks is the semantic priming effect. This effect occurs when prime and target words are semantically related, thereby producing faster reaction times than if they were unrelated. For example, the word *dog* semantically primes the word *cat* better than the word *box, per se.* This result is predicted by semantic network theories (as described above) suggesting that the activation of a prime word such as *dog* results in the spread of activation to related nodes and concepts (i.e., *cat*), making cat more available for processing. Indeed, when cat appears as following the word dog, responses are speeded up or facilitated, given the semantic connection between these words, in memory. In monolingual studies, semantic priming has proven to be a robust effect, found under several different experimental manipulations (see McNamara and Holbrook, 2003; Neely, 1991, for reviews).

Since the semantic priming paradigm has proven to be an extremely informative experimental technique, it is not surprising that it has been expanded to examine bilingual memory representation by using between-language stimuli. For example, participants in a cross-language priming experiment can be presented with the prime word *cat* followed by the target word *perro*, the Spanish translation of *dog*. Word stimuli can also be created such that the prime and target words appear in the opposite language direction, like *gato-dog,* for example (*gato* is the Spanish word for cat). This allows one to measure priming effects in the L1-L2 (i.e., dominant language-nondominant language) or L2-L1 direction. Translation (or repetition) priming can also be examined by presenting a prime word followed by its translation in the opposing language. Therefore, word pairs can be presented as either *gato-cat* or *cat-gato* (the Spanish translation of *cat*). During the past three decades, there has been a plethora of studies conducted on bilingual memory representation and the way in which two or more languages are stored in memory. A review of this literature reveals that nearly one dozen of these studies have used the semantic priming paradigm with between-language stimuli (Altarriba and Basnight-Brown, 2007; Basnight-Brown and Altarriba,

2007). In general, these studies have revealed that semantic processing proceeds more quickly and easily from the more dominant language (L1) to the nondominant or subordinate language (L2), rather than the other way around. That is, when presented with a word in one's stronger language, semantic activation tends to spread more quickly to related words in the same and the *other* language, as opposed to when a word is presented in one's weaker language. This asymmetry in semantic representation and processing has been documented in bilinguals who are not quite balanced in their fluency and proficiency in their two languages. Additionally, the more polysemous a word is (i.e., the more meanings it has, for example, the word head can refer to a body part, the "head of the class," or the eraser part of a pencil), the more likely it is to prime a word with fewer meanings (Finkbeiner, Forster, Nicol, and Nakamura, 2004).

In a recent demonstration of second language learning and the acquisition of semantic concepts, Altarriba and Knickerbocker (2011) presented English-speaking monolinguals with Spanish words in one of three formats—paired with either their English word translation; a black-and-white picture; or a color picture. Participants were given a series of quizzes and tests that required writing down the newly acquired Spanish word to its English translation or using the word to complete a phrase or sentence emphasizing semantic, orthographic, and phonological features. A priming task was then administered to participants with English-Spanish word pairs they had learned as a related condition (e.g., *clock-reloj*) and repairings of those words in a control or unrelated condition (e.g., *building-reloj*). Results indicated that the semantic information or association that had been learned for these new words produced significant priming across experiments for the word-word conditions and the black-and-white picture-word conditions. The effect was strongest for the word-word learning condition. The color picture-word conditions did not seem to facilitate semantic processing, as the other two did. Thus, in terms of second language acquisition of semantic concepts, as tested via a priming paradigm, it appears as though the best situation is to have individuals learn new words as paired with the words they already know, rather than pairing those new words with color pictures or images. The matching of the format of learning to the testing format appears to facilitate semantic processing of newly acquired words (i.e., transfer appropriate processing; Morris, Bransford, and Franks, 1977).

See also: bilingualism and SLA, lexical access and selection in bilingual production, lexical concepts, priming, psycholinguistics of SLA, transfer appropriate processing

References

Altarriba, J. and Basnight-Brown, D.M. (2007). Methodological considerations in performing semantic and translation priming experiments across languages. *Behavior Research Methods*, *39*, 1–18.

Altarriba, J. and Knickerbocker, H. (2011). Acquiring second language vocabulary through the use of images and words. In P. Trofimovich, and K. McDonough (eds), *Applying Priming Methods to L2 Learning, Teaching and Research: Insights from Psycholinguistics*, pp. 21–48. Amsterdam: John Benjamins Publishing Company.

Anderson, J.R. (1983). A spreading activation theory of memory. *Journal of Verbal Learning and Verbal Behavior*, *22*, 261–95.

Basnight-Brown, D.M. and Altarriba, J. (2007). Differences in semantic and translation priming across languages: The role of language direction and language dominance. *Memory and Cognition*, *35*, 953–65.

Collins, A.M. and Loftus, E.F. (1975). A spreading activation theory of semantic processing. *Psychological Review*, *82*, 407–28.

Finkbeiner, M., Forster, K., Nicol, J. and Nakamura, K. (2004). The role of polysemy in masked semantic and translation priming. *Journal of Memory and Language*, *51*, 1–22.

McNamara, T.P. and Holbrook, J.B. (2003). Semantic memory and priming. In A.F. Healy, and R.W. Proctor (eds), *Handbook of Psychology: Experimental Psychology*, Vol. 4, pp. 447–74. New York: John Wiley and Sons, Inc.

Meyer, D.E. and Schvaneveldt, R.W. (1971). Facilitation in recognizing pairs of words: Evidence of a dependence between retrieval operations. *Journal of Experimental Psychology*, *90*, 227–34.

Meyer, D.E., Schvaneveldt, R.W. and Ruddy, M.G. (1975). Loci of contextual effects on visual word recognition. In P.M. A. Rabbitt, and S. Dornic (eds), *Attention and performance V*, pp. 98–118. New York: Academic Press.

Morris, C.D., Bransford, J.D. and Franks, J.J. (1977). Levels of processing versus transfer appropriate processing. *Journal of Verbal Learning and Verbal Behavior*, *16*, 519–33.

Neely, J.H. (1977). Semantic priming and retrieval from lexical memory: Roles of inhibitionless spreading activation and limited-capacity attention. *Journal of Experimental Psychology: General*, *106*, 226–54.

——(1991). Semantic priming effects in visual word recognition: A selective review of current findings and theories. In D. Besner, and G. Humphreys (eds), *Basic Processes in Reading: Visual Word Recognition*, pp. 264–336. Hillsdale, NJ: Erlbaum.

Raaijmakers, J.G. W. and Shiffrin, R.M. (1981). Search of associative memory. *Psychological Review*, *8*, 98–134.

Rindflesch, T.C. and Aronson, A.R., (1993). *Semantic processing in information retrieval*. In the Proceeding of the 17th Annual Symposium on Computer Applications in Medical Care (SCAMC'93), Washington, DC, pp. 611–15.

Smith, E.E., Shoben, E.J. and Rips, L.J. (1974). Structure and process in semantic memory: A featural model for semantic decisions. *Psychological Review*, *1*, 214–41.

Further reading

Altarriba, J. (2003). Does *cariño* equal "liking"? A theoretical approach to conceptual nonequivalence between languages. *International Journal of Bilingualism*, *7*, 305–22.

Altarriba, J. and Heredia, R.R. (eds) (2008). *An Introduction to Bilingualism: Principles and Processes*. New York: Lawrence Erlbaum Associates.

Altarriba, J. and Mathis, K.M. (1997). Conceptual and lexical development in second language acquisition. *Journal of Memory and Language*, *36*, 550–68.

Illes, J., Francis, W.S., Desmond, J.E., Gabrieli, J.D. E., Glover, G.H., Poldrack, R., Kee, C.J. and Wagner, A.D. (1999). Convergent cortical representation of semantic processing in bilinguals. *Brain and Language*, *70*, 347–63.

Pillai, J.J., Araque, J.M., Allison, J.D., Sethuraman, S., Loring, D.W., Thiruvaiyaru, D., Ison, C.B., Balan, A. and Lavin, T. (2003). Functional MRI study of semantic and phonological language processing in bilingual subjects: Preliminary findings. *NeuroImage*, *19*, 565–76.

Significance level

Hossein Nassaji
University of Victoria

Significance level or what is also called alpha (α) *level* is a concept used in statistical studies to determine whether or not certain results are statistically significant in a given study. The concept is used in the context of *significance tests*, which are statistical methods used to test what is called the *null hypothesis* (the assumption that there is no significant relationship or difference between or among variables in the study). There are different kinds of significance tests. Some of the most commonly used ones are t-tests, f-tests, and chi-square tests. Significance tests assess the likelihood of the data, assuming that the null hypothesis is true for the population based on a given sample size.

In null hypothesis testing, there is no way to know for certain whether the null hypothesis is true. Therefore, one major issue that the researcher is confronted with is to decide at what level the null hypothesis should be rejected. To this end, the researcher uses a criterion level called significance level. This is a cut-off point to decide whether or not to reject the null hypothesis. In other words, it is the probability level at which a decision is made about accepting or rejecting the null hypothesis. This level is arbitrary and decided on based on the agreement of researchers and statisticians in a given discipline. In social sciences, the significance level is conventionally pre-set at 0.05. This set level shows that the maximum acceptable risk that the null hypothesis is wrongly rejected is 5 per cent.

The procedure for rejecting or accepting the null hypothesis is as follows. In statistical analyses, based on the distributional characteristics of the sample data, the significance test used computes a value called *test statistic*. The test also calculates another value called the *probability value* (*p-value*), which indicates how likely it is that the test statistic obtained is due to chance (note the difference between the *significance level,* which refers to a preset probability and the *p-value*, which indicates the probability calculated by the statistical test of getting the results under the assumption of a true null hypothesis). To reject or accept the null hypothesis, the researcher compares the p-value with the significance level. If the observed p-value is equal to or lower than the set significance level, the researcher rejects the assumption that the null hypothesis is true. If the null hypothesis is rejected, the results are considered to be statistically significant; otherwise, they are not statistically significant. For example, if the calculated p-value is 0.04 and the set significance level is 0.05, the researcher rejects the null hypothesis because the observed p-value is lower than 0.05.

In statistics, the error in rejecting a null hypothesis is called *type I error*. Thus, the significance level is the probability of making type I error, that is, the probability of making an error in rejecting the null hypothesis when it is assumed to be actually true. Thus, the lower the significance level, the lower the chance of making that error. To minimize this error, the researcher may use a more conservative significance level, such as 0.01 instead of 0.05, in which case the null hypothesis is rejected if the observed p-value is less than or equal to 0.01.

See also: effect size, hypothesis testing, measuring and research SLA, meta-analysis, quantitative research, T-tests

Further reading

Ary, D., Jacobs, L.C., Razavieh, A. and Sorensen, C. (2010). *Introduction to Research in Education*, 8th edn. Belmont, CA: Wadsworth. (This book offers an excellent introduction to various research methods in education along with numerous exercises illustrating fundamental research elements and concepts.)

Brown, J.D. (1988). *Understanding Research in Second Language Learning: A Reacher's Guide to Statistics and Research Design.* New York: Cambridge University Press. (This book, addressed to teachers, provides a very readable introduction to basic statistical analyses and key concepts in research on second language teaching and learning.)

Hatch, E. and Lazaraton, A. (1991). *The Research Manual: Design and Statistics for Applied Linguistics.* New York: Newbury House. (This book offers a detailed guide to the various research designs and statistical analyses in applied linguistics along with numerous activities to enhance deeper understanding of fundamental research ideas and skills.)

Larson-Hall, J. (2010). *A Guide to Doing Statistics in Second Language Research Using SPSS.* New York: Routledge. (This book provides a clear description of statistical concepts and how to conduct a variety of most commonly used statistical tests in second language research using the SPSS (Statistical Package for the Social Sciences) program.)

Seliger, H. and Shohamy, E. (1989). *Second Language Research Methods.* Oxford: Oxford University Press. (This book provides an excellent overview of the major research components and steps involved in conducting second language research.)

Simplification

Ronald P. Leow
Georgetown University

Simplification in second language acquisition (SLA) may be viewed from two perspectives: as an internal learner process and as external manipulated

L2 input. As an internal learner process, simplification forms part of several processes that L2 learners employ as they develop their interlanguage. Found among early stage language learners, this process is exemplified by the use of minimal language to convey meaning. Given that not much research has been conducted on this internal L2 learner process, the rest of this chapter focuses on simplification as external manipulated L2 input, a strand of research that has been well investigated.

External simplification has its origins in the concepts of motherese and caretaker's speech that are purposely employed with babies and young children during the early years of language development. Motherese and caretaker's speech are characterized by its simpler syntax, morphology, phonology, and lexicon when compared to the standard language and used exclusively in a here and now context. The underlying premise for such a simplified language is the belief that the young child is incapable of processing more complex structures etc. due to his/her developing and immature language system and simplified language will facilitate better comprehension of the messages being conveyed.

Research interest in the role of simplified language or input in second or foreign language (L2) comprehension arguably began in the 70s with the effort to understand the relationship between more qualitative features of the input to which L2 learners were exposed and their output. To this end, several studies examined communicative interactions between native speakers and L2 learners, both in the natural (foreigner talk) and classroom (teacher talk) settings. Foreigner talk generally refers to the register used by native speakers when addressing L2 learners while teacher talk refers to a similar register used by teachers when addressing different levels of classroom L2 learners. In most cases, studies reported that native speakers usually made some kind of simplification or modification when addressing L2 learners in an effort to facilitate comprehension, be it in the natural setting (e.g., Ferguson, 1975) or in the classroom setting (e.g., Henzl, 1973). Once the characteristics of simplified input were established, mainly in the areas of phonology, lexis, syntax, and discourse, empirical investigation into the potential effects of such simplified input began in earnest in the early 80s.

One early theoretical postulation for the importance of simplified input was the view that simplified input makes the input more comprehensible to L2 learners (e.g., Hatch, 1983). By making the input more comprehensible, it was further postulated that this increased comprehensibility would affect language acquisition by providing more linguistic information to the L2 learner's developing linguistic system (e.g., Krashen, 1985). In the written mode, it is also assumed that exposure to simplified texts provides some preparation for interacting with more advanced and authentic texts in upper classes.

A more recent premise fits neatly within cognitive theory in terms of the postulated limited cognitive capacity of L2 learners (McLaughlin, 1987) and the role of attention in L2 learning (e.g., Schmidt, 2001). An L2 listener or reader, viewed from this limited capacity processing perspective, may be cognitively overloaded when attempting to process authentic input (with their inherent lexical and syntactic complexities) geared for native speakers of that language. Reduced cognitive effort allows the L2 learner to reallocate some of his/her attention to linguistic information in the input, which is argued to be crucial for such information to be taken in by the learner and subsequently processed further. Simplifying the L2 input, then, is one technique postulated to overcome some of L2 learners' cognitive limitations while processing L2 input with the aim of primarily facilitating comprehension followed by the potential of affecting learning.

A concise review of studies that have empirically investigated the effects of aural and written simplification in SLA reveals that the baseline input selected for simplification in the experimental designs were mainly both original and authentic. Typical features of aural simplification included slower rate, redundancy, decreased sentential complexity, paraphrases, repetition of subject nouns, etc. The simplification of written texts typically included modifications for vocabulary (e.g., high frequency vocabulary, fewer idioms, fewer pronoun forms of all kinds, high use of names for *one*, *they*, *we*, marked definitions, lexical information in definitions), syntax (e.g., short, propositional syntax, repetition, restatement), and length of input. The lengths of simplified input when compared to the original, authentic input, topics and genres (for written texts), and amount of exposure time were varied.

The research design employed to measure the effects of simplified input on L2 comprehension was the following: exposure to either a simplified, elaborative, or unsimplified input followed usually by a comprehension test after exposure. Post-tests employed to measure comprehension included written recalls, cloze tests, written composition, multiple-choice questions, and comprehension questions.

Studies have found empirical support for aural simplification (e.g., Long, 1985) while others have reported either a mixture of results (e.g., Ellis, Tanaka, and Yamazaki, 1994) or no difference between aural simplified and unsimplified input (Loschky, 1994). For written simplification, the research reveals that there appears to be evidence for the effects of simplified input on L2 comprehension (e.g., Leow, 1993), although this benefit was not reported in other studies (e.g., Young, 1999). However, in spite of the empirical support found for the simplification of L2 input on L2 comprehension in several published studies, it is not surprising that there remains doubt raised years ago (e.g., Honeyfield, 1977) as to the efficacy of such simplification on comprehension and, more specifically, on learning. Concerns about the efficacy of simplifying the L2 include the unnaturalness of the discourse, its effect on the its cohesion and coherence, the potential for actually making the input more difficult to process, the removal of important features in the input that are deemed necessary for learning and so forth. There are several plausible explanations to account for these misgivings, which include what constitutes simplification in the research field, the inability to control methodologically text type, level of language experience, length of input, amount of time of exposure, type of post-reading comprehension test, learner approach, prior knowledge, to name a few variables that could have played a role in the findings. The multitude of variables that need to be considered when addressing the issue of simplified input clearly warrants further empirical investigation into their effects on comprehension in the SLA field.

On the issue of learning from exposure to simplified input, a few studies have investigated the input to intake phenomenon in order to arrive at a clearer understanding of the relationship between the nature of the input L2 readers are exposed to and how such input is processed (e.g., Leow, 1993). These studies addressed specific linguistic items in the L2 input and reported no benefits for simplification of both aural (Leow, 1995) and written input (Leow, 1993) on learners' subsequent intake of new grammatical information in the input. In other words, they reported finding no evidence to support the premise that, by reducing the cognitive load of processing the L2 via making the input more comprehensible, learners would reallocate their attention to targeted grammatical forms in the input. One plausible explanation for the absence of an impact on L2 readers' intake may be that L2 adult readers approach the L2 text with the purpose of extracting meaning and not form (grammar) from the input.

Interestingly, there has been a resurgence of studies that have begun to address once again the qualitative and descriptive aspects of simplification to include, for example, the linguistic features of both simplified and authentic texts (Crossley, Louwerse, McCarthy, and McNamara, 2007) and discourse analysis of the linguistic and sociolinguistic authenticity of simplified (scripted dialogs) and unsimplified conversations (Granena, 2008).

Conclusion

The simplification of L2 input remains arguably one of the more popular pedagogical practices that still persists in many classroom settings. During the early stages of any language program, many foreign language teachers purposely use teacher talk (characterized, for example, by slower rate of speech, pauses, sentential length, and so on), and both listening and written texts are carefully selected based on, for example, difficulty level, syntactic structures, and vocabulary ostensibly to promote listening and reading comprehension. Whether the use of simplified input to promote increased comprehension of the L2 in the classroom setting appears to be beneficial, future studies addressing this issue are certainly warranted. At the same time, research findings revealing that such simplifications appeared not to have any impact on the intake of new grammatical data suggests that care should be taken not to extrapolate these findings to the area of learning of grammatical information. The literature also appears to support the use of authentic and original materials in the L2 to be used as the baseline before simplification is performed in an effort, minimally, to preserve some of the inherent features of authentic input written for native speakers.

See also: attention, development in SLA, intake, interlanguage, pidginization and creolization, teacher talk

References

Crossley, S.A., Louwerse, M., McCarthy, P.M. and McNamara, D.S. (2007). A Linguistic Analysis of Simplified and Authentic Texts. *The Modern Language Journal*, *91*, 15–30.

Ellis, R., Tanaka, Y. and Yamazaki, A. (1994). Classroom Interaction, Comprehension and the Acquisition of L2 Word Meanings. *Language Learning*, *44*, 449–91.

Ferguson, C. (1975). Toward a Characterization of English Foreigner Talk. *Anthropological Linguistics*, *17*, 1–14.

Granena, G. (2008). Elaboration and Simplification in Spanish Discourse. *IRAL*, *46*, 137–66.

Hatch, E. (1983). Simplified Input and Second Language Acquisition. In R.W. Anderson (ed.), *Pidginization and Creolization as Language Acquisition*, pp. 64–86. Rowley, MA: Newbury House.

Henzl, V. (1973). Linguistic Register of Foreign Language Instruction. *Language Learning*, *23*, 207–22.

Honeyfield, J. (1977). Simplification. *TESOL Quarterly*, *11*, 431–40.

Krashen, S. (1985). *The Input Hypothesis*. Oxford: Pergamon Press.

Leow, R.P. (1993). To simplify or not to simplify: A look at intake. *Studies in Second Language Acquisition*, *15*, 333–55.

——(1995). Modality and intake in SLA. *Studies in Second Language Acquisition*, *17*, 79–89.

Long, M. (1985). Input and second language acquisition theory. In S.M. Gass and C.G. Madden (eds), *Input in Second Language Acquisition*, pp. 377–93. Rowley, MA: Newbury House.

Loschky, L. (1994). Comprehensible input and second language acquisition: What is the relationship? *Studies in Second Language Acquisition*, *16*, 303–23.

McLaughlin, B. (1987). *Theories of Second Language Learning*. London: Edward Arnold.

Schmidt, R.W. (2001). Attention. In P. Robinson (ed.), *Cognition and Second Language Instruction*, pp. 3–32. Cambridge: Cambridge University Press.

Young, D. (1999). Linguistic simplification of SL reading materials: Effective instructional practice? *Modern Language Journal*, *83*, 350–66.

Further reading

Leow, R.P. (2009). Simplified Written Input and its Effects on L2 Comprehension: What the Research Reveals. In A. Cirocki (ed.), *Extensive Reading in English Language Teaching*, pp. 129–41. Munich: LINCOM EUROPA. (A more in-depth report of empirical studies addressing the effects of written simplification on comprehension and learning.)

Social and socio-cultural approaches to SLA

Dwight Atkinson
Perdue University

Second language acquisition (SLA) researchers have historically conceptualized social phenomena, if at all, as *influencing* the cognitive processes considered by many to be at the heart of SLA. This "social influence" approach is described by Ellis (1994):

> Social factors have a major influence on L2 proficiency but probably do not influence it directly. Rather, their effect is mediated by a number of variables. One … is learner attitude. Social factors help to shape learners' attitudes, which, in turn, influence learning outcomes. Social factors also influence L2 learning indirectly in another way. They determine the learning opportunities which individual learners experience. For example, the learner's socio-economic … and ethnic background may affect the nature and extent of the input to which they are exposed.
>
> (Ellis, 1994: 197)

While opinion has differed as to how strong or direct the influences may be, the social influence approach dominated socially oriented SLA studies for many years, while the main interest in the field overall continued to be the mental system, deemed responsible for taking in, storing, and producing linguistic forms and representations. Over the past two decades, however, social concerns have moved closer to the heart of SLA studies, and the cognitive-social divide has been questioned. After briefly describing the cognitivism underlying mainstream SLA studies, this entry first reviews social influence and other longer-lived approaches to SLA, and then moves to more recently innovated SLA theories, some of which give a more integrative place to the social.

Cognitivism at the heart of SLA studies

Understanding the place of the social in SLA studies requires first understanding the place of the cognitive. The field emerged in the 1960s and 1970s under the influence of the "cognitive revolution"—actually a rebirth of ideas dating back to Plato. In stating, "I think therefore I am, or exist," Descartes gave these ideas their modern formulation, arguing that the human essence was purely cognitive. The cognitive revolutionaries of the mid-twentieth century likewise sought to demonstrate the priority and autonomy of cognitive processes in human nature and development, but they did so in response to the then-dominant school of psychology: behaviorism. Behaviorists had denied the possibility of studying the "intervening [i.e. cognitive] variables" between the input/stimulus and output/response because these variables were hidden and therefore inaccessible to empirical analysis, leading them to construct an "anti-mentalistic" psychology.

The cognitive revolution opposed behaviorism with its own radical philosophy—*cognitivism.* The mirror-image of behaviorism in some ways, cognitivism regards mind as a thing-in-itself, largely cut off from the surrounding environment except through the reception of narrow-gauge input, which contributes to but by no means fully explains the mental system's products—an active, constructive mental apparatus is invoked. Such "lonely cognition" is well represented in Chomsky's competence-performance distinction, wherein humans have (in a sense) perfect tacit knowledge of their L1s, or *competence,* which is, however, only weakly reflected in their linguistic *performance.* Chomsky (1965) described the assumptions underlying this distinction:

> Linguistic theory is concerned primarily with an ideal speaker-listener, in a completely homogeneous speech community, who knows its language perfectly and is unaffected by such grammatically irrelevant conditions as memory limitations, distractions, shifts in attention and interest, and errors (random or characteristic) in applying his knowledge of the language in actual performance.
>
> (Chomsky, 1965: 3)

This statement's exclusivity is breathtaking: real people, real social groups, real linguistic knowledge, and real conditions of language production are eliminated, leaving a highly idealized and abstract cognitive system. The extraction of language from social life is likewise reflected in Chomsky's views on language use:

> The general fact about language, which is not really in doubt, is that primarily we use it for thought. Secondarily, we use it for interactions with others. And a pretty small part of that interaction … is communication in any independent sense of the term. … If by

> communication you really mean something fairly definite, and try to specify it—like, say, transfer of information or something like that—a very small amount of even the external use of language is communication. And of course, the overwhelming mass ... is internal.
>
> (Chomsky, cited in Andor, 2004:109)

Such views powerfully impacted the genesis of SLA studies. Thus, in what is widely considered the field's founding manifesto, Corder (1967/1981) hypothesized that systematic L2 errors, as distinguished from mere "errors of performance," would reveal the nature of learners' developing interlanguage, or "transitional competence" (1967: 168). Also reflected in Corder's manifesto was a second cognitivist principle—learners are disembodied information processors: "The internal structure of the (language acquisition) device, i.e., the learner, has gone relatively unexplored" (1967: 12, quoting Saporta). Other SLA pioneers, including Dulay and Burt, Selinker, and Krashen, were equally influenced by cognitivist thinking, and cognitivism continues to dominate SLA studies today:

> Much current SLA research and theorizing shares a strongly cognitive orientation. The focus is firmly on identifying the nature and sources of the underlying L2 knowledge system, and on explaining developmental success and failure. Performance data are inevitably the researchers' mainstay, but understanding underlying competence, not the external verbal behavior that depends on that competence, is the ultimate goal. Researchers recognize that SLA takes place in a social context., and accept that it can be influenced by that context. However, they also recognize that language learning.is ultimately a matter of change in an individual's internal mental state.
>
> (Doughty and Long, 2003: 4)

Social influence approaches to SLA

Three socially oriented approaches appeared early in the history of SLA studies: 1) sociolinguistic variationism; 2) social psychology-inspired models; and 3) Schumann's acculturation hypothesis. All three continue to exist in updated versions, as described in the entries devoted to them in this encyclopedia (see below). They are social influence approaches to the degree that they distinguish the social from the cognitive, and see the former as exerting contextual influence on the latter, still regarded by many as the core of SLA.

SLA variationism was inspired by the pioneer sociolinguist Labov, who, against Chomsky's homogeneous linguistic competence, sought to demonstrate the rule-governedness of linguistic variation. Noting that variability is endemic to interlanguage, SLA scholars began to apply variationist methods and insights (see the entry on **Variationist approaches to SLA**, this volume). Tarone (1983) posited that interlanguage could be represented as a "capability continuum"—a continuous scale of variable competences for speech styles, organized according to how much learners monitored their output for form, or paid "attention to speech." She hypothesized that new forms enter interlanguage either through "careful (speech) style" and then spread toward less attentive "vernacular style," or develop spontaneously via universal principles in the latter and spread to the former. Ellis (1985) proposed that interlanguage variants occur first in free (i.e., non-systematic) variation, and then become systematized. Preston (1989) offered a complex model in which three interacting dimensions—planning, depth, and stability—accounted for the character of individuals' interlanguage, with social and linguistic factors influencing the acquisition of new forms. Additional variationist research using Variable Rule (VARBRUL) analysis showed how multiple social and linguistic factors combined to shape learner language. Variationism continues to make an active and significant contribution to SLA studies in the present day.

Social psychology-inspired approaches to SLA include Gardner's "socio-educational model" and work based on Giles' speech/communication accommodation theory (see entries on **Attitudes and Motivation Test Battery (AMTB)**, and **Accommodation**, this volume). The former seeks to determine underlying attitudes motivating learners to acquire an L2. Historically, these attitudes were studied via questionnaires, with Anglophone Canadian French learners as the target population. For Gardner (1985), "motivation involves four aspects, a goal, effortful behaviour, a desire to attain the goal, and favourable attitudes toward the activity in question" (50). The theory's main claim to being social is that certain kinds of attitudes—for example, Anglophone Canadians' attitude of social superiority vis-à-vis Francophones—are socially shared, and negatively or positively influence SLA.

Speech/communication accommodation theory highlights the variable adjustment of speech styles to those of interlocutors. Characteristics of the learner's cultural-linguistic group, including its ethnolinguistic vitality, relative status, and boundedness, predict learners' convergent or divergent linguistic behavior. In SLA, learners' linguistic convergence with native speaker (NS) norms has been argued to promote acquisition (Beebe and Giles, 1984), while Zuengler (1991) used accommodation to explain the presence or absence of Foreigner Talk—why NS speakers do or don't adjust their language to match the (assumed) proficiency level of non-native speaker (NNS) interlocutors.

The acculturation model (see **Acculturation Model**, this volume) was developed by Schumann (1978) to explain the lack of grammatical morpheme acquisition by "Alberto," a Costa Rican immigrant to the US, over a 10-month period. Schumann attributed Alberto's feeble progress to two variables—social and psychological distance—which together comprised degree of acculturation to the NS community. Social distance signifies the NNS community's degree of separation/difference from that of the NS, and consists of sub-variables like relative community size and status, leading to lack of exposure to the target language. Psychological distance signifies individual factors such as negative L2-using experiences or discomfort with the dominant culture, explaining non-acquisition when social distance is low and therefore insignificant.

Other early social approaches to SLA

In the 1960s, linguistic anthropologist Dell Hymes developed the concept of communicative competence (see **Communicative competence**, this volume). Although it has had a greater impact on L2 teaching than SLA studies proper, the concept deserves mention here. Communicative competence was an attempt to broaden the competence notion beyond Chomsky's narrow vision. Its most influential applied linguistics version has four components: grammatical competence, roughly equivalent to Chomsky's notion; sociolinguistic competence, or knowledge of communicative appropriateness in social context; strategic competence, or ability to compensate for gaps in knowledge; and discourse competence, or principles of extended discourse. Hyme's concept has undergirded SLA research in several areas, although grammatical competence is still widely regarded as SLA's core domain.

Hymes also inspired the SLA approach known as second language socialization, which examines how novices are socialized both to use language itself and to the sociocultural values inculcated through language (see **Second language socialization**, this volume). Early L2 socialization research examined L2 socialization in both informal settings and classrooms; more recently, it has focused on mutual socialization of novice and expert, and issues of power and inequality across educational settings. While not exactly a social influence approach, language socialization research often draws a line between the social and the cognitive, Watson-Gegeo (2004) being an important exception.

SLA theory wars

The 1990s saw a battle for "the heart and soul of SLA" (Block, 1996), at least at the meta-theoretical level. It began with calls for rational criteria whereby SLA theories could be evaluated and their number thereby reduced (see **theoretical constructs in SLA**, this volume). SLA studies, it was argued, needed to become a "normal science" in which cumulative progress could be made.

Block (1996) and others rejected this proposal, advocating continued theoretical pluralism and faulting the proposers for trying to model SLA studies on the hard sciences while fearing relativism. But the debate's watershed event from a social perspective was the appearance of Firth and Wagner (1997). These authors criticized mainstream SLA studies for: 1) highlighting individual grammatical competence while "at best marginaliz[ing], and at worst ignor[ing], the social and … contextual dimensions of language" (288); 2) privileging language learner over language user identities while viewing learners as "defective communicator[s]" vis-à-vis an NS ideal; 3) neglecting "emic" (i.e. participant) understandings of interactions; and 4) lacking awareness that discourse is negotiated. They concluded by calling for SLA studies to embrace the use-based, non-deficit, outward-looking "bio-social" nature of learning.

While Firth and Wagner's influence on SLA studies generally is debatable, it unquestionably served to galvanize dissatisfaction with its mainstream version at the end of the twentieth century, thus contributing to a "social turn" (Block, 2003) in at least part of the field. This turn is described in the following section.

Newer social and sociocultural approaches to SLA

Starting in the 1980s, socially oriented approaches to SLA appeared which departed from the social influence tradition. From around 2000, and synergistically with Firth and Wagner's critique, they helped to alter the landscape of SLA studies, although cognitivism still dominates the field (Atkinson, 2011). Six such approaches are described below.

Neo-Vygotskyan sociocultural theory

As its name denotes, neo-Vygotskyan sociocultural theory (SCT) was inspired by Lev Vygotsky, the Soviet psychologist who died at age 37 in 1934. Vygotsky's views have strongly influenced Western educators and educational researchers over the past three decades, especially in the U.S. Their application to SLA studies has been championed by James Lantolf and his colleagues and students.

Vygotsky investigated how human beings develop consciousness, our most consequential trait in his view because it enables voluntary self-control over our activities. He posited that *mediation*—the use of culturally constructed *psychological tools*, and particularly language, to constitute and regulate our cognition—was how consciousness develops. For Vygotsky, language and other semiotic media start wholly external to children, but through intrinsically meaningful co-participation with more experienced social others they are gradually internalized. SCT is therefore best described as a "sociogenetic cognitive theory" (Kinginger, 2002: 240) rather than a more straightforwardly social or sociocognitive one.

Early SCT-L2 research focused on how learners use their L2s to *self-regulate*, that is, mediate their language learning, and how they perform in the *zone of proximal development* (ZPD), the metaphorical space between what a learner can achieve independently and with the aid of an expert. Thus, Saville-Troike (1988) found that L2-learning children use *private speech* to mediate their learning although appearing to be in the "silent period," while Aljaafreh and Lantolf (1994) identified 12 points on an implicit-to-explicit continuum of feedback types which teachers provide students when working within the ZPD, adjusting their level as students move forward (see **Private speech**, this volume). More recently, SCT-L2 research has taken a pedagogical turn, focusing especially on dynamic assessment and concept-based instruction. Dynamic assessment integrates assessment with instruction based on the ZPD concept, while concept-based instruction adapts scientific explanations of language for pedagogical purposes (see **Dynamic assessment**, this volume). Substantial attention is also being paid to conceptual metaphors and gestures as semiotic mediators (see **Gestures in SLA** and **Metaphor**, this volume).

Complexity theory/dynamic systems theory

Complexity theory (CT) and its close sibling dynamic systems theory (DST) represent a second recent socially oriented SLA approach (see **Complexity Theory/Dynamic Systems Theory**, this volume). CT/DST originated in mathematical and biological descriptions of complex systems—systems in which components interact non-linearly, causing a variety of distinctive phenomena including self-organization, emergent behavior, holism (i.e. the non-decomposability of systems into parts), and non-predictability. The pioneer SLA researcher Diane Larsen-Freeman and a group of researchers based at the University of Groningen, Netherlands have been the chief proponents of CT/DST in SLA studies.

Dynamics systems are by definition in flux—variability is therefore the central concept in CT/DST. CT/DST seeks to explain the trajectories of dynamic systems, operating according to no predetermined overall design. Thus, in SLA "there is no end and there is no state" (Larsen-Freeman, 2005: 189)—a dynamic system in which equilibrium prevails is no longer dynamic. Dynamic systems are social in that, depending on the level of analysis, they incorporate progressively larger chunks of the ecosocial environment. The mental and the social can therefore be seen as dynamically integrated—there is *co-adaptation* between learner and ecosocial environment.

Evidence of SLA as a dynamic system is currently being developed. Larsen-Freeman (2006) described the written language production of five Chinese learners of English over a six-month period, finding that while they showed modest linear progress *as a group* on fluency, accuracy, and complexity measures, their individual development was anything but linear, and in fact quite idiosyncratic. These differences were attributed to the different "initial conditions" underlying each participant's language learning experience, as well as to unique interactions among the interlanguage system's components. Other CT/DST studies of SLA have used computer modeling to simulate L2 learning profiles.

Conversation analysis

A third recent socially oriented approach to SLA is conversation analysis (CA) (see **Conversation Analysis (CA)**, this volume). CA is a theory/method complex based on ethnomethodology, a non-mainstream sociological tradition. It seeks to describe the micro-structures and strategies which organize conversation and other forms of interaction. Sequential micro-analysis is the primary CA method, yielding rich transcripts of talk-in-interaction.

CA's application to SLA has been spearheaded by, among others, Kasper, Markee, Mori, and Wagner. Social interaction is treated as the crucible of SLA—interaction is both the basis and product of learning. Cognition is seen as public and shared, because interactors work to achieve intersubjectivity by displaying their orientation to what is expressed through talk and other modalities. The public nature of cognition supports learning, as with the sociocognitive approach (see below).

CA-SLA studies have focused mainly on the moment-by-moment unfolding of interaction rather than longer-term learning profiles. Mori and Hayashi (2006) investigated the use of *embodied completions*—gestures used to complete utterances (e.g. "Let's go … " followed by a locative pointing gesture)—in "conversation table"-type interactions among Japanese NSs and NNSs. The NSs were found to monitor NNSs' moment-to-moment comprehension levels, adjusting their language in highly sensitive ways. In doing so, they incidently produced opportunities for learning—for example by providing embodied completions which the NNSs then sought to verbalize and elaborate on.

Ecology

A fourth recent socially oriented approach to SLA is the ecological approach, as developed especially by van Lier (see **Ecology of language learning**, this volume). More loosely organized and metatheoretical, perhaps, than other approaches reviewed here, the ecological approach emphasizes the relationality of learners to their ecosocial environments, and how this affects acquisition. It holds that SLA is anything but a dry computational process—rather, learner engagement based on values, experience, personal relationships, identity construction, and individual aims and intentions underlie language development: "Acquisition is bound up with the totality of our social, cultural, and personal experience" (Leather and van Dam 2003: 24). Emphasis is also placed on learners' phenomenological experience—how they personally construe their language learning.

The ecological approach to SLA has affinities with language socialization—it studies learning situations and learners from an up-close, often ethnographic perspective, wherein the interpretative lens is designed to at least partly reflect that of the learners themselves. Ecological validity—the correspondence of research methods and procedures to the phenomenological experience of those being studied and their ecosocial situations—takes center stage in this approach.

Empirical studies taking an ecological approach have often focused on classrooms—van Lier in particular has been a vocal proponent of the need to look at classrooms as ecological systems. van Dam (2002) provides a rich account of teacher-student discourse on the first day of a Dutch secondary EFL class, showing how the teacher highlighted certain socioeducational practices as she "bootstrap [ped] a classroom culture" (p. 239).

Poststructuralist identity approach

A fifth recent approach, known simply as "the identity approach" by socially oriented SLA researchers, will here be called "the poststructuralist identity approach" to distinguish it from other SLA identity research (see **Identity Theory**, this volume). Innovated by Bonny Norton, this approach highlights: 1) the dynamic, unstable, and multiple nature of language learner identities; 2) the role of power and inequality in the formation and social valuing of such identities; and 3) the social structuring of language learning opportunities. The result is a perspective in which "every time learners speak, they are negotiating and renegotiating a sense of self in relation to the larger social world, and reorganizing that relationship in multiple dimensions of their lives" (Norton and McKinney, 2011: 73).

Two crucial concepts in the poststructuralist identity approach are *investment* and *imagined communities*. Investment was developed as a more social alternative to the motivation construct (see above)—it treats learner engagement in particular language learning/using situations as the complex result of learner-community member relations, typically having a power dimension (see **Community of practice** and **Investment**, this volume). The Canadian immigrants in Norton (2000), for instance, were highly motivated to learn English, but generally found learning difficult because they were treated as socially marginal or undesirable. In response, they negotiated identities which gave them value or at least legitimate senses of self in their local contexts.

Borrowed from the field of international studies, imagined communities foregrounds the fact that the immediate situational context of SLA is not the only context relevant to how and what a learner learns: Understanding of self and one's future life can also profoundly affect SLA. Middle class young people throughout the world, for instance, may have at least an intuitive understanding of the likely future importance of English in their lives, causing them to orient to it quite differently than others, no matter how it is locally taught or used.

A substantial amount of SLA research adopting a poststructuralist identity perspective has been undertaken in recent years (see Norton and McKinney, 2011 for review). In an exemplary study, Kinginger (2004) described the language learning experience of a desperately poor American woman trying to escape her menial existence by becoming an educated and urbane speaker of French.

Sociocognitive approach

The final socially oriented SLA approach to be described here—the sociocognitive approach—was developed by Atkinson and colleagues (see **Sociocognitive approaches to SLA**, this volume). The term "sociocognitive" itself conveys the approach's distinctive claim—that the social and the cognitive are functionally integrated. This claim is based on the notion of adaptive intelligence—that human cognition has developed evolutionarily to help us adapt to our varied and ever-changing environments, and continues to retain this characteristic in the present day. This is a fundamentally different understanding of cognition than that adopted by cognitivism, wherein the mind is a disembodied, disembedded information processor.

The guiding concept in the sociocognitive approach is *alignment* (Atkinson *et al.* 2007), the complex means by which living beings dynamically adapt to the environments they depend on for their survival. From this perspective, we learn L2s to operate adaptively in L2 worlds, and we do so substantially *by* doing so—that is, L2s are learned in moment-by-moment attempts to perform social action. Against deficit-oriented cognitivist approaches, learners bring an array of largely innate interactional skills to the learning task, from intention-reading abilities to cooperative skills to turn-taking to eye-gaze to repair to "natural pedagogical" abilities like Foreigner Talk. Cognition thus becomes (in part) publicly "visible"—others instruct us in meaning-making through their semiotic actions and intentions, that is, by how they act in/in relation to the world. Eye-gaze, for example, is a primary indicator of cognitive focus, and powerfully aids SLA as a result (Yu *et al.*, 2005). In this sense, language learning takes place not in the head, but in the integrated mind-body-world.

Evidence supporting a sociocognitive approach is modest. To date, studies reveal the intense, multi-layered sensitivity and alignment of moment-to-moment interaction, both learning-focused and otherwise, with a few studies (e.g. Atkinson *et al.* 2007; Yu *et al.*, 2005) showing actual development. There is extensive work in anthropology and cognitive science, however, which supports the general approach.

Conclusion

This overview has described some—but certainly not all—socially oriented perspectives on SLA. It has taken a quasi-historical approach, beginning with "social influence" viewpoints and then moving to more recently innovated frameworks. A distinctive feature of several of the latter is that they attempt to bring the social and the cognitive closer together, in some cases even treating them as an integrative whole. This trend is likely to continue, potentially leading to SLA studies in which the social and cognitive are no longer separated by a "great divide." At the same time, basically *all* the socially oriented approaches described here continue to contribute substantially to our understanding of the extremely complex and multi-faceted phenomenon known as SLA.

See also: activity theory and SLA, alignment, Conversation Analysis (CA), Complexity Theory/ Dynamic Systems Theory, ecology of language learning, identity theory

References

Andor, J. (2004). The master and his performance: An interview with Noam Chomsky. *Intercultural Pragmatics*, *1*, 93–111.

Aljaafreh, A. and Lantolf, J. (1994). Negative feedback as regulation and learning in the zone of proximal development. *Modern Language Journal*, *78*. 465–83.

Atkinson, D. (ed.) (2011). *Alternative Approaches to Second Language Acquisition*. Oxford: Routledge.

——, Churchill, E., Nishino, T. and Okada, H. (2007). Alignment and interaction in a sociocognitive approach to second language acquisition. *Modern Language Journal*, *91*, 169–88.

Beebe, L. and Giles, H. (1984). Speech accommodation theories: A discussion in terms of second language acquisition. *International Journal for the Sociology of Language*, *46*, 5–32.

Block, D. (1996). Not so fast! Some thoughts on theory culling, relativism, accepted findings, and the heart and soul of SLA. *Applied Linguistics*, *17*, 65–83.

——(2003). *The Social Turn in Second Language Acquisition*. Edinburgh: Edinburgh University Press.

Chomsky, N. (1965). *Aspects of a Theory of Syntax*. Cambridge, MA: MIT Press.

Corder, S.P. (1967/1981). The significance of learners' errors. Reprinted in S.P. Corder, *Error Analysis and Interlanguage*. Oxford: Oxford University Press.

Doughty, C. and Long, M. (2003). The scope of inquiry and goals of SLA. In C. Doughty and M. Long (eds), *Handbook of Second Language Acquisition*. Malden, MA: Blackwell.

Ellis, R. (1985). Sources of variability in interlanguage. *Applied Linguistics*, *6*, 118–31.

——(1994). *The Study of Second Language Acquisition*. Oxford: Oxford University Press.

Firth, A. and Wagner, J. (1997). On discourse, communication, and (some) fundamental concepts in SLA research. *Modern Langage Journal, 81*, 285–300.

Gardner, R. (1985). *Social Psychology and Second Language Learning: The Role of Attitude and Motivation*. London: Arnold.

Kinginger, C. (2002). Defining the zone of proximal development in US foreign language education. *Applied Linguistics, 23*, 240–61.

——(2004). Alice doesn't live here anymore: Foreign language learning and identity reconstruction. In A. Pavlenko and A. Blackledge (eds), *Negotiation of Identities in Multilingual Contexts*. Clevedon: Multilingual Matters.

Larsen-Freeman, D. (2005). Second language acquisition and fossilization: There is no end and there is no state. In Z.-H. Han and T. Olden (eds), *Studies of Fossilization in Second Language Acquisition*. Clevedon: Multilingual Matters.

——(2006). The emergence of complexity, fluency and accuracy in the oral and written production of five Chinese learners of English. *Applied Linguistics, 27*, 590–619.

Leather, J. and van Dam, J. (2003). Towards an ecology of language acquisition. In J. Leather and J. van Dam (eds), *Ecology of Language Acquisition*. Dordrecht: Kluwer.

Mori, J. and Hayashi, M. (2006). The achievement of interculturality through embodied completion: A study of interactions between first and second language speakers. *Applied Linguistics, 27*, 195–219.

Norton, B. and McKinney, C. (2011). An identity approach to second language acquisition. In D. Atkinson (ed), *Alternative Approaches to Second Language Acquisition*. Oxford: Routledge.

——(2000). *Identity and Language Learning: Gender, Ethnicity, and Educational Change*. Harlow: Pearson Education.

Preston, D. (1989). *Sociolinguistics and Second Language Acquisition*. Oxford: Blackwell.

Saville-Troike, M. (1988). Private speech: Evidence for second language learning strategies during the "silent" period. *Journal of Child Language, 15*, 567–90.

Schumann, J. (1978). Social and psychological factors in second language acquisition In J. Richards (ed.), *Understanding Second and Foreign Language Learning: Issues and Approaches*. Rowley, MA: Newbury House.

Tarone, E. (1983). On the variability of interlanguage systems. *Applied Linguistics, 4*, 143–63.

van Dam, J. (2002). Ritual, face, and play in a first English lesson: Bootstrapping a classroom culture. In C. Kramsch (ed.), *Language Acquisition and Language Socialization*. London: Continuum.

Watson-Gegeo, D. (2004). Mind, language, and epistemology: Toward a language socialization paradigm for SLA. *Modern Language Journal, 88*, 331–50.

Yu, C., Ballard, D. and Aslin, R. (2005). The role of embodied intention in early lexical acquisition. *Cognitive Science, 29*, 961–1005.

Zuengler, J. (1991). Accommodation in native-nonnative interactions: Going beyond the 'what' to the 'why' in second-language research. In H. Giles, N. Coupland, and J. Coupland (eds), *Contexts of Accommodation: Developments in Applied Sociolinguistics*. Cambridge: Cambridge University Press.

Further reading

Atkinson, D. (ed.) (2011). *Alternative Approaches to Second Language Acquisition*. Oxford: Routledge.

Batstone, R. (ed.) (2010). *Sociocognitive Perspectives on Language Use and Language Learning*. Oxford: Oxford University Press.

Bayley, R. and Preston, D. (eds) (1996). *Second Language Acquisition and Linguistic Variation*. Amsterdam: Benjamins.

Lantolf, J. and Thorne, S. (2006). *Sociocultural Theory and the Genesis of Second Language Development*. Oxford: Oxford University Press.

Larsen-Freeman, D. and Cameron, L. (2008). *Complex Systems and Applied Linguistics*. Oxford: Oxford University Press.

Sociocognitive approaches to second language acquisition

Dwight Atkinson
Purdue University

Mainstream approaches to second language acquisition (SLA) view it as:

> in large part an internal, mental process: *the acquisition of new (linguistic) knowledge.* ... SLA is a process that (often) takes place in a social setting, ... but ... that neither obviates the need for theories of those processes, nor shifts the goal of inquiry to a theory of the settings.
>
> (Long, 1997: 319)

Mainstream SLA approaches thus assume a "great divide" between the cognitive and (eco)social while privileging the cognitive. In Sharwood Smith's (1991) terms, cognition is the cake in L2 learning while social context is the icing. Due to such assumptions, mainstream SLA approaches have sometimes been called *cognitivist. Sociocognitive* approaches to SLA reject the mentalist assumptions of cognitivism. Instead, they regard the cognitive and ecosocial as functionally integrated. Below, I describe the theoretical basis for this viewpoint.

Cognition as adaptive intelligence

Cognitivism views the mind as a computer, which, based on narrow sensory input, constructs context-independent inner representations of the external environment. Cognition thus becomes the mechanical, largely uniform process whereby the mind forms and uses knowledge-containing representations (Boden, 2006).

Sociocognitive approaches, in contrast, view cognition as *adaptive ecological intelligence.* Ambient organisms need to successfully navigate their complex environments to survive—for example, to avoid predators and other dangers, or to locate (including via communication) food, shelter, or mates. For some animals, an important evolutionary outcome of such adaptive pressures is cognition. Yet while many animals are pre-adapted (cognitively and otherwise) to specific ecological niches, humans are cognitively *pre-adapted to adapt* (Shore, 1996)—we find, create, and master our *own* niches. This adaptive intelligence perspective opposes cognitivism in that: 1) adaptive action rather than knowledge creation/storage becomes cognition's primary evolved function; 2) organism and environment become functionally integrated instead of separate; and 3) learning, rather than being competence-oriented, ecologically insensitive, and exceptional, becomes performance-oriented, adaptive, and continuous.

From adaptive intelligence to SLA

From a sociocognitive perspective, learning is therefore an ongoing existential condition: we learn in order to survive, and to survive we must continuously and dynamically adapt to our environment. Cognition and learning are thus tightly linked, with learning being any (non-genetic) result of adaptive action that enables different/better adaptation in the future.

SLA in this view is an adaptive response to contingencies in the ecosocial environment – the need to execute joint action via communication with those one shares no common language with. Finding and maintaining safe and efficient living conditions, buying, selling, and developing goods and services, establishing social networks, and locating potential partners are examples of adaptive action facilitated by SLA. An important sociocognitive claim is that individuals with stronger adaptive needs will generally learn L2s better (where "better" is defined in terms of real-world performance, not tests of abstract knowledge).

Conceptual principles

Atkinson (2010) proposed three principles of sociocognitive SLA. The first or *inseparability principle* claims that cognition and learning are ecological—that they occur, functionally speaking, only as part of an ecological circuit comprised of mind, body, and world. This is a necessary consequence of viewing cognition as adaptive intelligence: studying SLA as the product of disembodied, environmentally disembedded computational minds violates the inseparability principle.

Although little research has explored SLA as the outcome of mind-body-world (inter)action, consider the place of gaze and gesture in SLA. Yu *et al.* (2005) found that novice L2 Mandarin learners acquired more vocabulary and segmented words better when tracking the gaze of a Mandarin speaker orally composing a story based on a picture book. Similarly, Churchill *et al.* (2010) examined how a single recurring "symbiotic gesture" prompted and organized cognition/learning in an L2 teaching/learning interaction, leading the learner to "outperform her competence."

The second, or *learning-is-adaptive principle* of sociocognitive SLA recapitulates the assumption that learning is environmentally adaptive. Including such a truism here might seem unnecessary, but by radically severing learning from its real-world functions cognitivist views demand it. Thus, Chomsky, the innnovator of cognitivism's all-important competence-performance distinction, believes that "the overwhelming mass of [language] is internal"—"primarily we use it for thought. Secondarily, we use it for interactions with others" (in Andor, 2004: 109). For Chomsky, then, language is fundamentally cognitive and incidentally social.

If the primary purpose of language, however, is to get along in the ecosocial world, then its learning is by definition adaptive. This certainly seems true for children vis-à-vis their first language—non-speaking children are seriously disadvantaged in almost every ecosocial sense. Learning L2s can be viewed somewhat similarly: no matter how facilitative their L1-speaking communities, immigrant non-speakers of their adopted home's dominant language are commonly regarded as ecosocially limited.

The third, or *alignment principle* of sociocognitive SLA holds that an essential requirement for all communication and learning is person-to-person or person-to-environment alignment. For instance, loss of interlocutor eye contact commonly causes speakers to restart and repair their utterances in face-to-face interaction (Goodwin, 2006), and a major sign that learning is not occurring is lack of physical orientation to the learning activity.

Alignment undergirds learning in at least four ways: 1) efforts to teach and learn centrally involve alignment—teachers seek to share with learners their understanding of selected aspects of the world, just as learners seek to join that world; 2) more specifically, teaching activities structure and simplify the world so that learners can participate/align in ways they otherwise couldn't; 3) learners therefore learn by attempting to align, relying on humans' profound and largely innate interactive abilities (Levinson, 2006). This is crucial in SLA, where, without a common language, some pre-existing means of understanding on which to build one is necessary; and 4) alignment takes place in sociocognitive space, which is semi-public by its very nature. In Goodwin's (2003) terms, "the positioning, actions, and orientation of the body in the environment are crucial to how participants understand what is happening and build action together" (20)—a view which can be broadened to incorporate elements of the inanimate environment.

Example

The following example (from Atkinson *et al.* 2007) suggests how alignment may work in SLA. "A" is a Japanese junior high school student completing an English grammar-translation homework exercise, while "T" is her aunt and tutor, an experienced English teacher. The interaction is transcribed using conversation-analytic conventions (Ochs *et al.*, 1996: 461–5):

01 A: ((Quietly reads first part of exercise item to be translated)) > °Anata wa ima made ni eigo de tegami° < (2.0) Ima made ni =
[Lit: You (Top) until now in English letter] *Until now*

02 T: ((Mirroring A's volume, intonation, and body orientation)) = °Un ima made°
Right, until now

03 A: [Ne:ba:
Never

04 T: [>Sakki no tsukaeba iin janai?
Why not use the one you used before?

05 A: Ima made (.8) n- e:va ka
Until now ne- ever?

06 T: Have you ever toka nantoka =
Have you ever blank
07 A: Have you eva writu, written =
Have you ever write, written

In line 1, A reads aloud from the item to be translated, then repeats the adverbial *ima made ni*—literally *until now*, or *ever*—a crucial element because it cues the correct verb form, the main pedagogical focus of the exercise. By reading the item and repeating the adverbial, A publically focuses/aligns the participants' shared attention on the part of the exercise immediately to be addressed, thus initiating and organizing shared cognition.

In line 2, T responds in multiple ways——each viewable from a sociocognitive/ alignment perspective—by: 1) "latching" (i.e. following with no perceptible gap) A's utterance; 2) providing an agreement marker (*un*); 3) repeating the adverbial; 4) speaking in the same quiet tones as A; 5) closely mirroring A's intonation; and 6) adopting a near-identical physical orientation (see Atkinson *et al.* 2007, Picture 1.1). T thus encourages and enhances mutual alignment, sociocognitively co-constructing the beginnings of an answer to the problem, in effect saying, "You're on the right track."

In line 3, A makes an initial attempt to translate the adverbial, exactly as T (line 4) suggests that, rather than trying to construct the answer "in her head," A rely on an already-completed exercise item, thus sharing the cognitive problem-solving load with the environment. Although T's subsequent search for the item is unsuccessful, this is a classic example of (potential) distributed cognition, where the functional cognitive unit includes T, A, and the inanimate environment.

In line 5, A provides the correct translation of the adverbial—*ever*. T then restructures the task by building A's answer into a fill-in-the-blank frame: *Have you ever blank*, with the blank to be filled by the correct principal part of the verb, the main focus of the exercise. By so doing, T reduces the sociocognitive "problem space" of the activity dramatically, refocusing their shared cognition on determining the correct verb form.

In line 7, A immediately supplies a targetlike answer—*write*—which, while not correct, seems to provide an in-the-world platform for the correct answer to be developed on. She then produces the correct answer—*written*.

Conclusion

From a sociocognitive viewpoint, SLA is an ecological process involving mind, body, and world. Learning is seen as *relational*—as connecting the learner more fully and adaptively to the ecosocial environment. Such a view, while by no means renouncing cognition, does renounce *cognitivism,* assuming instead that language, learning, and cognition function primarily to help us align with the world, and thereby survive and prosper.

See also: affordance, alignment, communities of practice, ecology of learning, person-in-situation approaches to SLA, social and sociocultural approaches to SLA

References

Andor, J. (2004). The master and his performance: An interview with Noam Chomsky. *Intercultural Pragmatics*, *1*, 93–111.

Atkinson, D. (2010). Extended, embodied cognition and second language acquisition. *Applied Linguistics*, doi:10.1093/applin/amq009.

——Churchill, E., Nishino, T. and Okada, H. (2007). Alignment and interaction in a sociocognitive approach to second language acquisition. *Modern Language Journal*, *91*, 169–88.

Boden, M. (2006). *Mind as Machine: A History of Cognitive Science*. Oxford: Clarendon.

Churchill, E., Nishino, T., Okada, H. and Atkinson, D. (2010). Symbiotic gesture and the sociocognitive visibility of grammar. *Modern Language Journal*, *94*, 234–53.

Goodwin, C. (2003). The body in action. In J. Coupland and R. Gwin (eds), *Discourse, the Body, and Identity*. New York: Palgrave-MacMillan.

——(2006). Human sociality as mutual orientation in a rich interactive environment: Multimodal utterances and pointing in aphasia. In N.J. Enfield and S. Levinson (eds), *Roots of Human Sociality*. Oxford: Berg.

Levinson, S. (2006). On the human 'interaction engine'. In N.J. Enfield and S. Levinson (eds), *Roots of Human Sociality*. Oxford: Berg.

Long, M.H. (1997). Construct validity in SLA research: A response to Firth and Wagner. *Modern Language Journal, 81*, 318–23.

Ochs, E., Schegloff, E. and Thompson, S. (eds) (1996). *Interaction and Grammar*. Cambridge: Cambridge University Press.

Sharwood Smith, M. (1991). *Second language acquisition and the cognitive enterprise*. Plenary presentation, Second Language Research Forum. Los Angeles, CA, March 2.

Shore, B. (1996). *Culture in Mind: Cognition, Culture, and the Problem of Meaning*. New York: Oxford University Press.

Yu, C. Ballard, D., and Aslin, R. (2005). The role of embodied intention in early lexical acquisition. *Cognitive Science, 29*, 961–1005.

Further reading

Atkinson, D. (In press). A sociocognitive approach to second language acquisition: How mind, body, and world work together in learning additional languages. In D. Atkinson (ed.), *Alternative Approaches to Second Language Acquisition*. London: Routledge.

——(2010). Sociocognition: What It can mean for second language acquisition. In R. Batstone (ed.), *Sociocognitive Perspectives on Language Use and Language Learning*. Oxford: Oxford University Press.

Batstone, R. (2010). Issues and options in sociocognition. In R. Batstone (ed.), *Sociocognitive Perspectives on Language Use and Language Learning*. Oxford: Oxford University Press.

Clark, A. (1997). *Being There: Putting Mind, Body, and World Together Again*. Cambridge, MA: MIT Press.

Sociopragmatics

Satomi Takahashi
Rikkyo University

Sociopragmatics is one of the several research areas in pragmatics. It is described as "the sociological interface of pragmatics" (Leech, 1983: 10) or as dealing with "the social conditions placed on language in use" (Thomas, 1983: 99). Specifically, in sociopragmatics, we investigate relationships between communicative action and contextual factors such as social status/power, social distance, rights and obligations, and the degree of imposition arising from communicative action; thus, it essentially involves *social* issues in pragmatics without analyzing actual wordings used in verbal behaviors. Sociopragmatics has traditionally been paired with pragmalinguistics, which refers to "the particular resources which a given language provides for conveying particular illocutions" (Leech, 1983: 11). In other words, the form-function relationships relevant for particular sociocultural contexts are explored in pragmalinguistics; thus, it fundamentally concerns *linguistic* issues in pragmatics.

In interlanguage pragmatics (ILP), the sociopragmatics/pragmalinguistics distinction has been treated in the framework of *sociopragmatic failure* (communication breakdown due to the application of different contextual assessment from native speakers (NSs) by learners) versus *pragmalinguistic failure* (communication breakdown due to the application of different form-function mappings from NSs by learners) (Thomas, 1983). These two types of failures have been investigated intensively in speech act realization and pragmatic transfer research. By concentrating on the outcomes related to L2 sociopragmatics, an attempt will be made to provide more specific empirical findings of past ILP research with respect to speech act realization, pragmatic transfer, pragmatic development, and pragmatic intervention (instruction).

Past L2 speech act realization research comprehensively documented the cases in which learners' realization patterns differed from those of NSs for the target language. One interpretation of these findings could be that learners may rely on sociopragmatic knowledge, distinctive from NSs, in formulating L2 speech acts, thereby possibly leading to sociopragmatic failure. Bergman and Kasper (1993) empirically verified this interpretation. They focused on an English apology attempted by Thai learners of English, who were asked to rate apology situations on a five-point rating scale for six contextual factors. Their contextual assessment was analyzed in correlation with the number of apology strategies. A notable finding was that learners used IFID (illocutionary force indicating device; e.g., "I'm sorry") contingent on perceived "obligation to apologize," and this tendency was not observed in the performance of English NSs or Thai NSs. This clearly demonstrates that learners' realization of apology was influenced by their L2-distinctive assessment of contextual factors.

In pragmatic transfer research, instances of possible sociopragmatic failures have been reported in different configurations. Sociopragmatic transfer may occur as a result of learners implementing an inappropriate linguistic action in an L2 sociocultural context. Robinson (1992) collected the verbal protocol data from Japanese ESL learners and realized their confusion about the applicability of Japanese sociopragmatic knowledge of refusing to L2 contexts. The learners stated that they felt reluctant to refuse in English, because refusing is not considered polite in the Japanese society. Sociopragmatic transfer is also triggered by learners' inaccurate assessment of contextual factors. Takahashi and Beebe (1993) demonstrated that Japanese ESL learners employed different correction strategies according to the interlocutors' status, which deviates from English norms. They argued that these different speech act realization patterns were induced by transfer of Japanese style-shifting; that is, "they style-shift in English according to the status of the interlocutor in a manner similar to the style-shifting typical of native Japanese" (p. 152). In the same situation, English NSs are more likely to think that politeness can be conveyed by denying that status differences exist. Preferences in communication styles in L1 could also be the sources of sociopragmatic transfer. For instance, Al-Issa (2003) investigated refusal realization patterns by Jordanian EFL learners and found that lengthier refusal responses in L2 were a result of transfer of Arabic speakers' communication style—expressive and exaggerated language use in everyday conversations—to L2 contexts.

Parallel to the mainstream SLA research, efforts have also been made to explore the developmental and interventional aspects of L2 pragmatics. With respect to sociopragmatic aspects of pragmatic development, Rose (2000) provides us with insightful findings. In the framework of cross-sectional research, he explored pragmatic development among three groups of primary school students in Hong Kong by focusing on speech acts of request, apology, and compliment response. He identified a number of developmental patterns in the choices of pragmatic strategies; however, little evidence was obtained regarding the learners' sensitivity to situational variation. According to Rose, this indicates a precedence of pragmalinguistics over sociopragmatics. This further demonstrates that sociopragmatic competence is more difficult to acquire than pragmalinguistic competence. However, pragmatic intervention research substantiated that sociopragmatic knowledge could be acquired through "explicit" interventions featured with the provision of metapragmatic information. Rose and Ng Kwai-fun (2001), for example, reported that sociopragmatic knowledge governing decisions on whether to accept, deflect, or reject the responses to compliments in L2 English was more successfully acquired through the deductive (explicit) method than the inductive one. Furthermore, Liddicoat and Crozet (2001) illustrated the case where sociopragmatic knowledge was more sustainable than pragmalinguistic knowledge as a result of explicit intervention. Specifically, they investigated the effect of explicit intervention on Australian learners' learning of the French interactional norm that an elaborated response should be provided to the greeting question "Did you have a good weekend?" The delayed posttest administered one year after the treatment revealed that only the content was retained, whereas the forms for responses were not.

Thus, the previous ILP studies reviewed above clearly demonstrate that the acquisition of L2 sociopragmatic competence is crucial for realizing the appropriate speech acts and conversational styles in L2. Explicit teaching of L2 sociopragmatic features may contribute to this goal. However, there should be caution against this approach. While pragmalinguistic failure is basically a linguistic problem, sociopragmatic failure is a sociocultural problem; developing L2 socio-pragmatic competence may trigger sensitive issues as the learners' L1 identities, values, and beliefs may be negatively affected in the process of learning (Kasper, 2001; Thomas, 1983). Therefore, it would be best to leave it to the learners to decide what aspects of L2 sociopragmatics they should acquire.

See also: crosslinguistic influence, instructed SLA, politeness, pragmalinguistics, pragmatics, speech acts

References

Al-Issa, A. (2003). Sociocultural transfer in L2 speech behaviors: Evidence and motivating factors. *International Journal of Intercultural Relations*, *27*, 581–601.

Bergman, M.L. and Kasper, G. (1993). Perception and performance in native and nonnative apology. In G. Kasper and S. Blum-Kulka (eds), *Interlanguage Pragmatics*, pp. 82–107. Oxford: Oxford University Press.

Kasper, G. (2001). Classroom research on interlanguage pragmatics. In K.R. Rose and G. Kasper (eds), *Pragmatics in Language Teaching*, pp. 33–60. Cambridge: Cambridge University Press.

Leech, G. (1983). *Principles of Pragmatics*. London and New York: Longman.

Liddicoat, A.J. and Crozet, C. (2001). Acquiring French international norms through instruction. In K.R. Rose and G. Kasper (eds), *Pragmatics in Language Teaching*, pp. 125–44. Cambridge: Cambridge University Press.

Robinson, M.A. (1992). Introspective methodology in interlanguage pragmatics research. In G. Kasper (ed.), *Pragmatics of Japanese as Native and Target Language*, pp. 27–82. Honolulu: University of Hawaii, Second Language Teaching and Curriculum Center.

Rose, K.R. (2000). An exploratory cross-sectional study of interlanguage pragmatic development. *Studies in Second Language Acquisition*, *22*(1), 27–67.

Rose, K.R. and Ng Kwai-fun, C. (2001). Inductive and deductive teaching of compliments and compliment responses. In K.R. Rose and G. Kasper (eds), *Pragmatics in Language Teaching*, pp. 145–70. Cambridge: Cambridge University Press.

Takahashi, T. and Beebe, L.M. (1993). Cross-linguistic influence in the speech act of correction. In G. Kasper and S. Blum-Kulka (eds), *Interlanguage Pragmatics*, pp. 138–57. Oxford: Oxford University Press.

Thomas, J. (1983). Cross-cultural pragmatic failure. *Applied Linguistics*, *4*(2), 91–112.

Further reading

Kasper, G. (1992). Pragmatic transfer. *Second Language Research*, *8*(3), 203–31. (An extensive review of pragmatic transfer research.)

LoCastro, V. (2001). Individual differences in second language acquisition: Attitudes, learner subjectivity, and L2 pragmatic norms. *System*, *29*, 69–89. (Exploration of the norms issues in interlanguage pragmatics.)

Takahashi, S. (2010). Assessing learnability in second lLanguage pragmatics. In A. Trosborg (ed.), *Pragmatics Across Languages and Cultures (Handbooks of Pragmatics)*, Volume 7, pp. 391–421. Berlin and New York: De Gruyter Mouton. (An extensive review of pragmatic intervention research.)

Speaking

Diana Boxer
University of Florida

A focus on the acquisition of spoken competence in L2 has gradually increased in importance over the past 50 years. The current state of affairs is that we have a highly developed field of Discourse Analysis and a highly developed body of research in SLA that have begun to inform each other. Early SLA of the mid twentieth century emphasized the ability to *read* foreign language texts, speaking competence was widely held to have secondary importance. We could, at best, hope to develop an ability to decipher reading material.

However, the world as we knew it then began to rapidly change during the second half of the twentieth century. Globalization and transnationalism urged a rethinking of the need for spoken competence in the world's lingua franca, English. Thus, since the 1980s we have seen a uniting of research on SLA with studies in the area of spoken discourse analysis. Scholars at this intersection now study language users' speaking competence in a variety of contexts and from a variety of theoretical, epistemological, and methodological perspectives. This focus on spoken discourse enables teachers and other experts to create curriculum, materials, and assessment instruments based on mother tongue users, bilinguals, and language learners.

SLA and early focus on speaking

Dating back to the late 1970s and for a decade beyond, early SLA research studied spoken discourse to ascertain the *interactional* features important to language learning (e.g. Hatch, 1978; Long, 1983; Pica, 1988). This research showed that negotiated interaction encourages language learners to stretch their linguistic abilities in L2 by means of checking their understanding of the discourse until mutual comprehension is achieved.

This thrust was later viewed by some as an overly psycholinguistic approach. Firth and Wagner (1997) opened up a controversial debate on this issue, in which they called for a reconceptualization of SLA in order to address what they saw as an imbalance biased toward a *cognitive* perspective on SLA that neglected *social interactional* perspectives. They asserted that ultimately, it is the social interactional that affords speaking ability in L2. Their major claim was that SLA research has viewed L2 development as one of learners traversing an "interlanguage" continuum that has, at its hypothetical end point, the abstract notion of the idealized "native speaker." Movement toward the "target" proceeds along the linguistic dimensions of phonological, morphological, syntactic, lexical, and semantic growth. Even pragmatic considerations have been studied in terms of "interlanguage pragmatics," a concept viewing the acquisition of norms of appropriate speech behavior largely through a lens of movement from L1 norms to L2 norms, with particular attention to pragmatic transfer (e.g. Blum-Kulka, House-Edmondson, and Kasper 1989).

Nonetheless, regarding spoken acquisition at least, some early work in SLA did indeed take into account more sociolinguistically relevant points of view: Labovian sociolinguistic perspectives on SLA (see, for example, the early work on variation and SLA of Tarone, 1985), accommodation theory perspectives on SLA (e.g. Beebe and Giles, 1984), acculturation theory perspectives (e.g. Schumann, 1978), and classroom discourse and interaction perspectives (e.g. Stubbs, 1983). Notwithstanding these early efforts, the tension between psycholinguistic and sociolinguistic perspectives in the intersection of discourse and SLA persists.

Most SLA researchers now would agree that with the state of English as a Lingua Franca (ELF) in today's world, spoken English is of primary importance for international commerce, trade, and diplomacy. Communication in the English language occurs, more often than not, among speakers none of whose first language (L1) is English. The constructs of "native speaker," "learner," and "interlanguage" have consequently changed from how they were seen in early SLA research, at least for English. Spoken language competence for lingua franca users is now the main focus for an SLA perspective on successful communication. Thus, discourse studies in recent years have enabled applied linguists to view language learning, especially speaking competence, as more than a purely cognitive phenomenon, as the issue of the native speaker is obfuscated in a shrinking planet (cf. Boxer, 2002).

Theoretical frameworks

Innovative perspectives within which to investigate the acquisition of L2 speaking competence are congruent with a postmodernist view of the world as it presently exists. Three theoretical frameworks now lend new insights into this issue: 1) language identity, 2) language socialization, and 3) sociocultural theory.

Language identity

The notion of discourse communities as "communities of practice" (Le Page and Tabouret-Keller, 1985) has engendered among SLA researchers an interest in the relationship between identity and second language development (e.g. Norton-Pierce, 1995; Pavlenko and Lantolf, 2000). These researchers have been interested in studying how incorporating an additional language and culture impacts on one's sense of who one is in the world. Adding a spoken language to one's verbal repertoire necessarily entails modifying one's self perception in relationship to others in the world.

It seems likely that the first and foremost resource of those involved in additional language learning is social and interactional, involving face-to-face spoken discourse. Individuals involved in acquiring additional languages must grapple with fluid and shifting identities—individual, social, and relational—and come to terms with the power relations inherent in them. Whether or not those in the position of taking on new linguistic and cultural identities choose to appropriate or reject the "affordances" of the new language/culture may depend largely on the lived histories of the individuals, the contexts of their interactions, and the power relationships inherent in these contexts.

Language socialization

The language socialization framework of studying linguistic and cultural development emanates from the early work of Schieffelin and Ochs (e.g. 1986), who focused on L1 socialization (e.g. Samoa). Socialization practices of L2 learning communities, however, are by and large reflected in the classroom discourse and interaction of second language classes in which talented teachers take on the role of socializing agent, much in the fashion of adults vis a vis children for L1 acquisition (cf. Ohta, 2001). The applications of socialization theory to SLA are principally in the realm of discourse and pragmatic development (see Kasper, 2001 for an overview of this research).

These two frameworks, language identity and language socialization, are clearly overlapping and compatible with each other.

Sociocultural theory

A contingent of SLA researchers has been actively engaged in adopting the theoretical perspectives of Vygotsky (e.g. 1986) to the acquisition of language (first and subsequent) as a sociocultural phenomenon linking the social/interactional with the cognitive. Sociocultural theory, in contradistinction to the language identity and language socialization models just described, specifically connects the role of discourse as a mediating tool between social interaction and the development of higher order mental processes. This theoretical perspective calls for elucidating the connection between internal, mental representations of learning and language development stemming from interactions between and among interlocutors of differing levels of expertise. Vygotsky's notion of "Zone of Proximal Development" (ZPD) is useful in envisioning how the expert/novice paradigm of sociocultural interaction leads to new mental representations in learners.

Sociocultural theory is a lens through which we can view more clearly both tutored and untutored second language development. Scaffolding occurs through the various configurations of social interaction between the expert and novice. In contrast to a more traditional SLA view of the learner as a "deficient version of an idealized monolingual expert in linguistics" (Hall, 1997: 303), a sociocultural theoretical view of SLA treats the learner as "an active and creative participant in what is considered a sociocognitively complex task" (ibid.).

Epistemological and methodological issues

Since 2004, research employing qualitative methodologies for SLA speaking studies has been at the cutting edge of providing crucial information on how speaking is best developed in L2. Notwithstanding, major difficulties persist in applying discourse analysis to SLA. The principal epistemological problem is what counts as evidence of spoken language *acquisition*. An outgrowth of this problem is that of ascertaining how best to track language development as it takes place. A major issue is the distinction between L2 *use* and actual *learning*.

A close look at recent developments in the SLA/discourse intersection reveals new methodologies taking *emic* perspectives (e.g. ethnographic, interactional sociolinguistic, and conversational analytic methods). This latter approach, widely known as CA, is evident in a strand of research claiming it to be a very effective means for studying moment-by-moment second language speaking development. Indeed, a 2004 special issue of the *Modern Language Journal* (Volume 88, number 4) edited by Numa Markee and Gabriele Kasper, was devoted to a series of articles using CA for L2 research. These scholars overviewed how far the field has come since the 1997 debate begun by Firth and Wagner. These essays deal with the very real problem that research showing evidence of spoken *participation* in L2 conversational exchanges does not necessarily give evidence of *acquisition*. Indeed, the growing body of research deriving from contextually rich approaches lends insights into language *use*. Claiming that language *learning* has taken place is much more problematic.

Of critical importance among the essays in the special edition are the four commentaries by applied linguists Susan Gass, Diane Larsen-Freeman, Joan Kelly Hall, and Johannes Wagner. Each assesses the role played by CA while taking to task some specific claims made by the individual papers in the collection. Gass comes from a psycholinguistic tradition in SLA research, that of negotiated interaction. Thus, as in the 1997 MLJ debate, she continues to question how CA can demonstrate acquisition. Larsen-Freeman, who espouses a chaos/complexity perspective on SLA, questions the CA conception of *emic* in these studies. Hall's work is firmly rooted in a Vygotskyan sociocultural (SCT) perspective, and thus while noting the pros of CA, also outlines what SCT can offer to L2 language development; Wagner, the sole CA representative of the group, reasserts his stance that classroom discourse may not be the best site for studying language learning.

Spontaneous spoken discourse data for SLA

As we have seen, the language *use vs. learning* dichotomy is something that Applied Linguists have grappled with over the past 15 years. While some of these methods of data collection and analysis have lent important insights into language *use* for decades, their applications to language *learning* contexts, however, are more recent. A collection of studies by Boxer and Cohen (2004) provides examples of recent in-depth studies on second language speaking development. The volume offers a dozen contextually rich analyses of talk-in-interaction that reveal important information about spoken language development. The studies employ methods ranging from the ethnography of speaking, conversation analysis, and interactional sociolinguistics, offering cutting-edge examples of social/interactional approaches to analyzing second language speaking (e.g. see chapters by Lazaraton and Brown for CA approaches; chapters by Hamilton, Hall, Taylor-Hamilton, and Halmari for ES and IS approaches).

Conclusion

The theoretical, epistemological, and methodological frameworks described herein have been instrumental over the past 20 years for studying spoken second language development. Given a world of more fluid boundaries owing to globalization and transnationalism, the notion of language use in communities of practice has become the relevant focus for weaving together a picture of speaking in SLA.

Research at the intersection of discourse and SLA can help us develop the best practices for fostering L2 speaking competence. These findings are crucial for situations in which novice language users are acquiring and employing an L2 in any domain and in variously configured communities and interactions. Such varied contexts include: bilingual language practices such as code alternation and switching; sensitivity to the constraints of the sociolinguistic variables (e.g., gender, social distance, and social status) in the L2; sensitivity to domains of usage (e.g., workplace, education, and social interaction); and understanding how to carry out transactional and interactional discourse (Brown and Yule, 1983).

Highly contextualized, *emic* approaches to applied linguistics research are increasingly important in current analyses of spoken SLA, not only within native speech communities, but in multilingual contexts of interaction as well. Critical discourse analysis will continue to be an important thrust in such analyses, since issues of power and dominance necessarily come into play. Yet we are still left with nagging questions of how best to view language acquisition as well as use. The perspectives outlined here have only recently begun to lend insights into these questions.

See also: communities of practice, Conversation Analysis (CA), discourse and pragmatics in SLA, ethnographic research, pragmatics, qualitative research

References

Beebe, L. and Giles, H. (1984). Speech accommodation theories: A discussion in terms of second language acquisition. *International Journal of the Sociology of Language*, *46*, 5–32.

Blum-Kulka, S., House-Edmonson, J. and Kasper, G. (eds) (1989). *Cross-cultural Pragmatics: Requests and Apologies*. Norwood, NJ: Ablex.

Boxer, D. (2002). Discourse issues in cross-cultural pragmatics. *Annual Review of Applied Linguistics*, *22*, 150–67.

Brown, G. and Yule, G. (1983). *Discourse Analysis*. Cambridge: Cambridge University Press.

Firth, A. and Wagner, J. (1997). On discourse, communication, and (some) fundamental concepts in SLA research. *Modern Language Journal*, *81*(3), 285–300.

Hall, J.K. (1997). In response to Firth and Wagner: A consideration of SLA as a theory of practice. *Modern Language Journal*, *81*(3), 301–6.

Hatch, E. (ed.) (1978). *Second Language Acquisition*. Rowley, MA: Newbury House.

Kasper, G. (2001). Four perspectives on L2 pragmatic development. *Applied Linguistics*, *22*(4), 502–30.

Lantolf, J. (2002). *Sociocultural and Second Language Learning Research: An Exegesis*, Paper presented at the 9th annual Sociocultural Theory Workshop, November 1, 2002, Tallahassee, Florida.

Le Page, R.B. and Tabouret-Keller, A. (1985). *Acts of Identity*. Cambridge: Cambridge University Press.

Long, M. (1983). Native speaker/non-native speaker conversation and the negotiation of comprehensible input. *Applied Linguistics*, *4*(2), 126–41.

Norton Peirce, B. (1995). Social identity, investment, and language learning. *TESOL Quarterly*, *29*(1), 9–31.

Ohta, A. (2001). *Second Language Processes in the Classroom: Learning Japanese*. Mahwah, NJ: Lawrence Erlbaum.

Pavlenko, A. and Lantolf, J. (2000). Second language learning as participation and the (re) construction of selves. In J. Lantolf (ed.), *Sociocultural Theory and Second Language*, pp. 155–77. New York: Oxford University Press.

Pica, T. (1988). Interlanguage adjustments as an outcome of NS-NNS negotiated interaction. *Language Learning*, *38*(1), 45–73.

Schieffelin, B. and Ochs, E. (1986). Language socialization. *Annual Review of Anthropology*, 15, 163–91.

Schumann, J. (1978). The acculturation model for second language acquisition. In. R. Gingras (ed.), *Second Language Acquisition and Foreign Language Teaching*. Arlington, VA: Center for Applied Linguistics.

Stubbs, M. (1983). *Discourse Analysis: The Sociolinguistic Analysis of Natural Language*. Chicago, IL: University of Chicago Press.

Tarone, E. (1985). Variability in interlanguage use: A study of style-shifting in morphology and syntax. *Language Learning*, *35*(3), 373–403.

Vygotsky, L.S. (1986). *Thought and Language*. Cambridge, MA: MIT Press.

Further reading

Boxer, D. and A.D. Cohen (eds) (2004). *Studying Speaking to Inform Second Language Learning*. Clevedon: Multilingual Matters. (Ethnographic, interactional sociolinguistic, and conversational analytic studies on speaking in SLA).

Modern Language Journal (1997). (Volume 81, number 3) A. Firth and J. Wagner (eds). (The entire debate on psycholinguistic vs. social/ interactional research in SLA.)

Modern Language Journal (2004). (Volume 88, number 4) N. Markee and G. Kasper (eds). (Studies on Conversation Analysis for SLA.)

Speech acts

J. César Félix-Brasdefer
Indiana University

Although the idea that language is used to express social action was initially conceptualized in Plato's *Cratylus* (1875), our current understanding of language, speech act theory, and communicative action, dates back to modern philosophical thinking (Austin, 1962; Searle, 1969; Wittgenstein, 1953/ 1957). These philosophers stated that the function of language is to perform speech acts or actions (or Wittgenstein's concept of "language-games"), such as describing or reporting the weather, requesting a letter of recommendation from a professor, apologizing for arriving late, or complaining to our boss about an unfair work load. This view of language rejected the ideas of logical positivism of the 1930s that believed that the main function of language was to describe true or false statements. However, it was in the mid-1950s that philosophical thinking brought speech act theory to life with the seminal work on speech acts by J.L. Austin and John Searle, two language philosophers who were concerned with meaning, use, and action. Speech acts represent a key concept in the field of pragmatics which can be broadly defined as language use in context taking into account the speaker's and the addressee's verbal and non-verbal contributions to the negotiation of meaning in interaction.

This entry is organized as follows. First, I present an overview of the main concepts of speech-act theory and Searle's influential classification of speech acts. Then, I review the central contributions of speech-act research to pragmatics in first and second language contexts, followed by the conclusion.

Speech act theory: An overview

Austin's first attempts to formalize a theory of communicative action began during the William James lectures that he presented at Harvard University (1956) and that were later published posthumously in his seminal work *How to do Things with Words* (1962). The British philosopher initially observed that language serves to accomplish two things: on the one hand, it is used to describe or report things in the world by means of true or false statements (constatives); on the other, speakers can use utterances to accomplish communicative actions simultaneously (performatives). However, toward the end of these lectures, the constative-performative distinction no longer held; instead, Austin realized that all utterances have qualities that are characteristic of both constatives and performatives. To avoid confusion, the term "performative" was adopted by Austin to suggest that in saying something we perform an action, and these actions can be realized with (e.g., *I promise* I'll come to your party) or without a speech act verb (e.g., I'll come to your party). Further, Austin proposed a three-way taxonomy of speech acts: 1) a locutionary act refers to the act of saying something meaningful, that is, the act of uttering a fragment or a sentence in the literal sense (referring and predicating); 2) an illocutionary act is an act performed by saying something that has a conventional force such as informing, ordering, complaining, or refusing; and, 3) a perlocutionary act refers to what we achieve "by saying something such as convincing, persuading, deterring, and even, say, surprising or misleading" (1962: 109). Austin noted that for an illocutionary act to be successfully performed, it needs to secure an uptake (i.e., an effect must be achieved on the audience), it must take effect (e.g., I pronounce you husband and wife), and it invites a response or a sequel (1962: 116–17). As a result, in the pragmatics literature the term speech act is often associated with illocutionary force.

Austin's speech act theory was solidified and further developed by the American philosopher John Searle. Inspired by Austin's original classification of illocutionary forces, Searle (1969, 1977, 2010) proposed a five-way taxonomy of speech acts (representatives, directives, commissives, expressives, and declarations) along four dimensions: 1) illocutionary point or speech act type; 2) direction of fit; 3) expressed psychological state; and 4) propositional content. Representatives express the speaker's belief and the speaker commits himself to the truth expressed in the content of the proposition (e.g., describing, reporting, concluding). Here, words are used to describe the world. Directives express the speaker's desire/wish to get hearer to perform an action (e.g., requests, advice, questions); in this case, the world matches the words through the hearer. Commissive acts commit the speaker to a future action and create an obligation on the part of the speaker to do something. In this case, the world matches the words through the speaker (e.g., promising or refusing). Expressive speech acts express a psychological attitude or an inner state of the speaker which says nothing about the world (e.g., apologies, congratulations, compliments). Thus, there is no direction of fit for this speech act type. Finally, declarations include speech acts in which declarative statements are successfully performed and no psychological state is expressed (e.g., declaring war, excommunication, or baptism). Since these actions are institutionalized, the actions performed by the speaker produce a change in the current state of affairs. In this case, the direction of fit can be bidirectional, that is, the words are used to match the word, or the world can be used to describe the words.

Searle proposed a set of felicity conditions that must be met before a speech act can be said to have a particular illocutionary force. First, the propositional content concerns the reference and predication of an act of a certain type. Second, preparatory conditions must be fulfilled prior to the performance of the act. Third, the sincerity condition refers to the speaker's true intention or belief in performing an illocutionary act. And fourth, the essential condition indicates how an utterance is considered; for example, a request is classified as an attempt to get the hearer to perform an action. Each of these conditions highlights a different aspect of an utterance: the propositional content focuses on the textual or referential content; the preparatory conditions refer to the background circumstances; the sincerity condition reflects the speaker's psychological state; and, the essential condition centers on the illocutionary point of what is said.

Speech-act research

The aforementioned theoretical contributions by Austin and Searle represent the foundation for current speech-act research in first and second language contexts. The primary objective of speech-act research lies in the pragmalinguistic-sociopragmatic distinction (Leech, 1983; Thomas, 1983). Pragmalinguistics refers to the linguistic resources (or strategies) necessary to express speech acts (e.g., *I apologize* for my behavior; I *love* your house; I'm sorry, *I can't come* to your party), while sociopragmatics refers to the appropriateness of those expressions or knowledge of social conventions at the perception level, such as an awareness of the differences in social distance (+/-D) or social power (+/-P) among interlocutors. It includes the knowledge of what expressions are appropriate (or are not appropriate): 1) when insulting a coworker (-P,-D), 2) when refusing a professor's advice to take a class (+P, +D), or 3) when asking a stranger for directions (-P, +D). Overall, most empirical speech-act research is based on the foundation of speech act theory (Austin, 1962; Searle, 1969), Brown and Levinson's (1987) dichotomy of positive (e.g., approach-based, solidarity) and negative politeness (e.g., distance-based, deference), and Grice's (1975) inferential concept of conversational implicature that attempts to explain indirectness in communication.

Emerging with cross-cultural pragmatics research conducted by Wierzbicka (1985), speech-act research developed with the Cross-Cultural Speech Act Realization Project (CCSARP) initiated by Blum-Kulka, House, and Kasper (1989). These authors contrasted the realization patterns of requests and apologies from university-level students in seven countries (Australia, Britain, Canada, Denmark, Germany, Israel, and the United States) and five different language varieties (Australian English, American English, British English, Canadian French, Danish, German, and Hebrew). The editors proposed a classification of the pragmalinguistic strategies to describe the speech-act set of requests and apologies and used a written questionnaire (Discourse Completion Task) to elicit samples of speech acts. In addition to requests and apologies, the realization patterns of refusals were investigated in first (Félix-Brasdefer, 2008) and second language contexts (Beebe, Takahashi, and Uliss-Weltz, 1990; Gass and Houch, 1999).

Speech act sequences can also be examined in natural settings such as retail service encounters. In the following example taken from a transaction that took place in a delicatessen in a supermarket in the United States, the customer and the clerk negotiate a request for service that is realized by means of sequences of speech acts:

(1) Delicatessen in US supermarket
(Male clerk / Female Customer)
((Clerk turns to customer who is waiting on the other side of the counter))
01 Clerk: alright, can I help whoever's next? (Starts at 71:09 [minutes; seconds])
02 Customer: uh, I guess that's me.
03 Um, can I have a half a pound of the honey-smoked turkey?↑
04 Clerk: OK. Do you want the uh: maple or the plain?
05 Customer: the – the honey smoked
06 Clerk: how much would you like and how would you like it cut?
07 Customer: half a pound, please, and thin, – pretty thin
08 Clerk: thin↑
09 Customer: yeah
10 How about this? ((clerk shows thickness of product))
11 Customer: that's fine ((referring to the thickness)) (72:15)
12 Clerk: would you like a piece while you wait?
13 Customer: no, that's OK
14 Clerk: and that was a half a pound?↑ (72:23)
15 Customer: yeah
16 Clerk: OK. It's a shade under.
17 I can add another piece or leave it as is. (72:39)
18 Customer: oh, that's fine
19 ((clerk seals bag and affixes price sticker))
20 Clerk: there you go (73:12)
21 Customer: thanks
22 Clerk: is there anything else?
23 Customer: no, that's it↓
24 Clerk: thank you. Have a good day.
25 Customer: you too.

This transaction is realized by means of a series of sequences of speech acts. The transaction begins with the clerk's offer for service that aims at getting the customer's attention (line 01), followed by the customer's acknowledgment (line 02). The request–response sequence is negotiated across multiple turns and sequences of speech acts. The customer's request is realized through a conventional indirect request (e.g., can I have …) (line 03), followed by the clerk's acceptance ("Okay"), the clerk's request for further information (line 04), and the customer's response (line 05). The next four-turn sequence includes the clerk's request for additional information (line 06) and the customer's specific response (line 07), followed by the clerk's clarification signal with a rising intonation ("thin↑", line 08) and the customer's acknowledgment (line 09). This sequence is completed with the clerk's clarification request (line 10) and the customer's acknowledgment (line 11). Then, the clerk initiates three sequences to complete the negotiation of the transaction: an offer–response sequence (lines 12–13), a clarification request–response sequence (lines 14–15), and a request for further information followed by the clerk's response (lines 16–18). This transaction concludes with the clerk sealing the bag and affixing a price sticker to the product, which is followed by the customer's acceptance of the item with an expression of gratitude (lines 19–21). A pre-closing sequence signals the completion of the transaction by the clerk and the customer, an offer of additional service and a negative response (lines 22–23). The terminal exchange consists of the clerk's "thank-you" and good wishes, followed by the customer's reciprocity which signals the completion of the transaction (lines 24–25).

Recent speech-act research has proliferated with fine descriptions of speech acts in cross-cultural and interlanguage pragmatics (e.g., Usó-Juan and Martínez-Flor, 2010; Trosborg, 2010) and research-based pedagogical proposals for the learning and teaching of speech acts in second and foreign language contexts (e.g., Tatsuki and Houck, 2010; Ishihara and Cohen, 2010). There are also web-based pedagogical proposals for the teaching of speech acts through web-delivery tools accessed directly in the classroom (e.g., Cohen, 2011; Félix-Brasdefer, 2011). These websites contain detailed descriptions of speech acts with regard to their pragmalinguistic structure, namely, advice, apologies, complaints, compliments and compliment responses, thanking expressions, invitations, refusals, and suggestions.

In conclusion, speech-act research has advanced our understanding of how action is negotiated and accomplished in social interaction. It has set the foundation to study communicative action in cross-cultural and inter-cultural settings and in interlanguage pragmatics among second language learners. And because speech acts are ubiquitous in everyday conversation as well as in formal (e.g., professor-student advising sessions) and non-formal institutional settings (e.g., travel agencies, service encounters), it is essential that they be represented in the language curriculum and in second/foreign language teaching. Future work in speech-act research awaits more refined methods of data collection and analysis in both experimental and ethnographic studies, and descriptions of speech acts at the discourse level.

See also: discourse completion tasks, interlanguage, politeness, pragmalinguistics, pragmatics, turn taking

References

Austin, J.L. (1962). *How to Do Things with Words*. Cambridge, MA: Harvard University Press.

Beebe, L.M., T. Takahashi, and R. Uliss-Weltz (1990). Pragmatic transfer in ESL refusals. In R. C. Scarcella, E.S. Andersen, and S.D. Krashen (eds), *Developing Communicative Competence in Second Language*, pp. 55–73. New York: Newbury House.

Blum-Kulka, S., J. House, and G. Kasper (eds) (1989). *Cross-Cultural Pragmatics: Requests and Apologies*. Norwood, NJ: Ablex.

Brown, P. and S.C. Levinson (1987). *Politeness: Some Universals in Language Usage*. Cambridge: Cambridge University Press (original publication in 1978).

Cohen, A. (2011). Dancing with words. *Center for Advanced Research on Language Acquisition* (CARLA). http://www.carla.umn.edu/speechacts/sp_pragmatics/home.html. Retrieved on February 21, 2011.

Félix-Brasdefer, J.C. (2008). *Politeness in Mexico and the United States: A Contrastive Study of the Realization and Perception of Refusals*. Amsterdam: John Benjamins.

——(2011). *Speech Acts* http://www.indiana.edu/~discprag/spch_acts.html. Retrieved on February 21, 2011.

Gass, S.M. and N. Houck. (1999). *Interlanguage Refusals: A Cross-Cultural Study of Japanese-English*. New York: Mouton de Gruyter.

Grice, H.P. (1975). Logic and conversation. In P. Cole and J. Morgan (eds), *Syntax and Semantics 3: Speech Acts*, pp. 41–58. New York: Academic Press.

Ishihara, N. and Cohen A. D. (2010). *Teaching and Learning Pragmatics: Where Language and Culture meet*. London: Pearson.

Leech, G.N. (1983). *Principles of Pragmatics*. New York: Longman.

Plato (1975). Cratylus. In *The Dialogues of Plato*, Volume II. Translated by Benjamin Jowett. Oxford: Oxford Clarendon Press.

Searle, J.R. (1969). *Speech Acts*. London: Cambridge University Press.

——(1977). A classification of illocutionary acts. In A. Rogers, B. Wall, and J. Murphy (eds), *Proceedings of the Texas Conference on Performatives, Presupposition, and Implicatures*, pp. 27–45. Washington, DC: Center for Applied Linguistics.

Searle, J. (2010). *Making the Social World: The Structure of Human Civilization*. Oxford: Oxford University Press.

Tatsuki, D.H. and N.R. Houck (eds) (2010). *Pragmatics: Teaching Speech Acts*. Alexandria, VA: TESOL.

Thomas, J. (1983). Cross-cultural pragmatic failure. *Applied Linguistics*, *4*(2), 91–112.

Trosborg, A. (ed.) (2010). *Pragmatics across Languages and Cultures*. Berlin: Walter De Gruyter

Usó-Juán, E. and A. Martínez-Flor (eds) (2010). *Speech Act Performance: Theoretical, Empirical, and Methodological Issues*. Amsterdam: John Benjamins.

Wierzbicka, A. (1985). Different cultures, different languages, different speech acts. *Journal of Pragmatics*, *9*, 145–78.

Wittgenstein, L. (1957). *Philosophical Investigations*. (G.E.M. Anscombe, Trans.). London: The Macmillan Co. (Original Work published 1953).

Speech perception and SLA

Wander Lowie
University of Groningen

Speech perception is the process during which listeners meaningfully interpret a complex acoustic signal. The process of speech perception involves several sub-processes, namely hearing the acoustic signal (audition), extracting the phonological information (phonological decoding), and matching the phonological information with semantic information in the lexicon (word recognition). Research into speech perception in second language (L2) learning has mainly concentrated on phonological decoding, and especially on the way in which the learner's mother tongue (L1) affects the perception of the L2. When L2 learners perceive the L2 speech stream using L1 phonetic cues, this may lead to unsuccessful or ambiguous phonological decoding. Unnoticed or misinterpreted L2 phonological contrasts may subsequently affect the production of L2 sounds.

Categorical perception

One of the most crucial steps in the development of human cognition is categorization. While stimuli may be located along a physical continuum, like a color on the color spectrum from blue to green, people tend to make categorical distinctions. The same applies to the categorization of sounds; although there may be an acoustic continuum for the front vowels [i] to [a], we perceive a limited number of different vowels, which is language-specific.

Applied to the acquisition of phonology, babies are still able to perceive speech sounds in continuous mode. However, perception research shows that from around 10 to 12 months, babies' perception of speech sounds starts to concentrate almost exclusively on phonetic cues that occur in the L1 (Ohala, 2008), which is often referred to as evidence for the emergence of L1 phonology. By the end of the first year, children start to show language-specific patterns of phonetic perception, and after three to four years, the perceptual phonetic cues will have developed into patterns that resemble adult native speakers (Nittrouer and Miller, 1997). These patterns of multiple acoustic cues enable the recognition of language-specific phonological categories, which create minimal meaning differences within a language. Once the language-specific categories have been established for the language humans have been exposed to, it becomes increasingly difficult to disregard these categories when perceiving linguistic information (Werker and Tees, 1999). This finding has important consequences for the perception of languages other than the mother tongue.

A commonly used test for categorical perception serves to illustrate how language-specific categorical perception works. In an identification task, listeners are presented with stimuli that represent several steps in a sound contrast continuum. For instance, to test the categorical perception of the /p/-/b/ voicing contrast, Abrahamson and Lisker (1970) used a continuum in which the Voice Onset Time (VOT) increased in steps of 10 ms ranging from −150ms to +150ms. Typically in these tasks, learners do not consciously perceive steps, but just hear either /p/ or /b/. Depending on the L1 of the listener, the cut-off point between /p/ and /b/ can be expected to occur at different points on the VOT continuum. In prevoicing languages, 0–30ms VOT is perceived as /p/, while in aspirating languages a stop within the same VOT range is perceived as /b/.

Categorical perception and second language development

Categorical perception forms the basis of the three major models of the acquisition of second language sound systems, Best's Perceptual Assimilation Model (PAM) (Best, 1994), Flege's Speech Learning Model (SLM) (Flege, 1995), and Kuhl's Native Language Magnet Model (Kuhl, 1992). All of these models point to the difficulty of creating new phonetic categories. One of their main premises that follow logically from the crosslinguistic influence of phonetic categories is that phonetic characteristics that are similar in L1 and L2, but not identical can be expected to cause more problems for L2 learners than phonetic properties that are obviously different between languages. The reason is that the similar sounds may be perceptively assimilated to an existing native category. This explains why Japanese learners of English have problems perceiving the difference between the acoustically similar sounds /ɹ/ and /l/ and why Dutch and German learners of English have problems perceiving the difference between /ɛ/ and /æ/. In both cases there is an L2 phonological contrast for phonetically similar sounds, which cannot be distinguished using L1 phonetic cues.

The emergence of categorical perception is often referred to in accounting for age-related issues in second language phonology (see the Encyclopaedia entry on **Second Language Phonology**). Most researchers agree about the general influence of existing language-specific phonetic cues and language-specific phonological categories on the perception of L2 sound contrasts, and about the fact that this contributes to our understanding of age-related differences in L2 phonological development. The longer people have been exposed to the categories of one language, the more difficult it becomes to perceive certain non-native contrasts. However, there is less consensus about the degree to which adult listeners are still able to perceive non-native sound contrasts. If after the categorization of speech sounds it were no longer possible to perceive (and produce) L2 sounds accurately, authentic, native-like sound perception would simply be impossible after age four. This is indeed what is claimed by advocates of a strong critical period hypothesis (Scovel, 1988). However, based on a range of empirical studies, Flege's SLM claims that the mechanisms necessary to perceive new phonetic categories remain intact across the lifespan. Whether or not a learner is able to create new L2 categories depends, according to Flege, on the combination of a number of factors, like the age of onset of acquisition, the length of residence in an L2 context, the amount of daily L2 use, the typological distance between L1 and L2, and the nature of the sound difference; for similar sounds assimilation to existing L1 categories is more likely (Piske, Mackay, and Flege, 2001). In addition to this, factors like a high degree of motivation and explicit training are likely to affect this process positively.

New developments in second language speech perception research

Research into categorical perception in L1 and L2 research has used a variety of methods and techniques, which have sometimes caused contradictory results. Choices in the use of stimulus materials as well as the phonetic and phonotactic context in which speech sounds are presented can yield different results. The same is true for the task condition, depending on the memory load and cognitive demands involved in the task (for an overview of perception techniques, see Strange and Shafer, 2008). Recently, the focus of attention has shifted from strongly idealized and reduced speaking situations to perception research that takes real, casual speech into account. For instance, Tuinman (2011) argues that the perception of casual L2 speech remains one of the biggest challenges for L2 learners. After the introduction of the major models of L2 phonology in the 1990s, this again emphasizes the relevance of L2 perception research.

See also: age effects in SLA, Critical Period Hypothesis (CPH), intelligibility in SLA, L2 phonology, listening, speech rate

References

Abrahamson, A. and Lisker, L. (1970). Discriminability along the voicing continuum: Cross-language tests. In B. Hála, M. Romportl, and P. Janota (eds), *Proceedings of the 6th International Congress of Phonetic Sciences*, pp. 569–73. Prague: Academia.

Best, C.T. (1994). The emergence of native-language phonological influences in infants: A perceptual assimilation model. In C. Goodman, and H.C. Nusbaum (eds), *The Development of Speech Perception: The Transition from Speech Sounds to Spoken Words*, pp. 171–204. Cambridge, MA: MIT Press.

Bohn, O., Munro, M.J. and Flege, J.E. (2007). *Language Experience in Second Language Speech Learning: In Honor of James Emil Flege*. Amsterdam: Benjamins.

Flege, J.E. (1995). Second language speech learning. theory, findings and problems. In W. Strange (ed.), *Speech Perception and Linguistic Experience*, pp. 233–77. Timonium, MD: York Press.

Kuhl, P.K. (1992). Psychoacoustics and speech perception: Internal standards, perceptual anchors, and prototypes. In L. Werner, and E. Rubel (eds), *Developmental Psychoacoustics*, pp. 293–332. Washington, DC: American Psychological Association.

Nittrouer, S. and Miller, M.E. (1997). Predicting developmental shifts in perceptual weighting schemes. *The Journal of the Acoustical Society of America*, *101*(4), 2253–66.

Ohala, D.K. (2008). Phonological acquisition in a first language. In J.G. Hansen Edwards, and M. L. Zampini (eds), *Phonology and Second Language Acquisition*, pp. 19–39. Amsterdam and Philadelphia, PA: Benjamins.

Piske, T., Mackay, I.R. A. and Flege, J.E. (2001). Factors affecting degree of foreign accent in an L2: A review. *Journal of Phonetics*, *29*(2), 191–215.

Scovel, T. (1988). *A Time to Speak: A Psycholinguistic Inquiry into the Critical Period for Human Speech*. Rowley, MA: Newbury House.

Strange, W. and Shafer, V.L. (2008). Speech perception in second language learners. In J.G. Hansen Edwards, and M.L. Zampini (eds), *Phonology and Second Language Acquisition*, pp. 153–91. Amsterdam and Philadelphia, PA: Benjamins.

Tuinman, A.E. (2011). *Processing Casual Speech in Native and Non-Native Language*. PhD, Radboud Universiteit Nijmegen.

Werker, J.F. and Tees, R.C. (1999). Influences on infant speech processing: Toward a new synthesis. *Annual Review of Psychology*, *50*, 509–35.

Speech rate

Minna Toivola and Mietta Lennes
University of Helsinki

The speech rate (also referred to as *tempo*) is one of the most frequently studied temporal properties of speech. The speech rate is measured as the average number of words per minute, syllables per second, syllables per minute or sounds per second within a particular speech sample, including pauses. The *articulation rate* is a similar measure, but it is calculated by excluding the pauses within the sample. The most important factors affecting the speech rate are the number and duration of pauses (Goldman-Eisler, 1968), whereas the articulation rate reflects the time spent in producing speech.

In spontaneous speech, pauses occur more often and they are longer than in read-aloud speech. Moreover, spontaneous speech contains more filled pauses (e.g., *um, er*) and feedback utterances (e.g., *mm*), which are not always counted as syllables. Consequently, the measured speech rate is usually lower in spontaneous than in read-aloud speech, whereas the articulation rate may not vary as much. For conversational speech, the speech rate is difficult to interpret, since the pauses arise from the interaction between all the participants.

When comparing the speech rates for two different languages, it is usually necessary to count units that are smaller than a word, since languages may differ in their average word length. A similar problem appears in syllable-based speech rate comparisons, since the average complexity of syllables may differ between languages. For instance, some languages may only allow for short CV syllables, whereas other languages may exhibit different consonant clusters or vowel length contrasts.

The speed of speech production varies for individual speakers and languages. Moreover, people vary their speech rate in different situations either consciously or unconsciously. Changes in the emotional state or the arousal of the speaker affect the speech rate. Excitement may increase the speech rate, whereas sadness tends to decrease it. People may also speak more slowly to a child or to a language learner. Poetry tends to be read aloud at a lower pace than news. Changes in speech rate may also be used for highlighting specific portions in speech. During conversation, words and syllables may be lengthened in order to hold turn or to gain time to think.

Depending on the language and the analysis procedure, the speech rates in newsreading typically range between 4 and 6 syllables per second, the articulation rates being slightly higher. In other speaking styles, rates of over 7 syll/s have been reported. For native English, the normal speech rate corresponds to two–three words per second. The extreme limits of speech rate are determined by the properties of the speech production system, which may vary slightly between individuals. At a maximum, it is possible to articulate at least 15 phonemes per second (Levelt, 1989).

In fast speech, the amount of articulatory reduction tends to increase. The reduction processes often change the qualities of individual sounds. It is relatively common for sounds, syllables, and even whole words to "merge" or to be dropped completely in casual speech. These issues should be considered when measuring speech rate.

Research on L2 speech rate

The speech rate is generally considered as one of the most important temporal features that can be used to measure fluency in the second and foreign language (see, e.g., Towell, Hawkins and Bazergui,1996; Kormos and Dénes, 2004). A deviant speech rate has often been considered as an indication of non-native speech (Anderson-Hsieh and Koehler, 1988). The speech rates for second or foreign language learners and native speakers have been compared in both read-aloud and spontaneous speech. Most of the L1-L2 research has been performed on the different varieties of English. Consequently, some results cannot be generalized to other languages. However, L2 learners have generally been found to exhibit smaller speech rates than the native speakers, especially at the initial stages of learning. The lower speech rates of language learners may be due to articulatory difficulties as well as the higher cognitive demands associated with, for example, phonological processing.

A large proportion of the available research on L2 fluency and foreign accent is based on listening experiments. One important object of study has been the effect of speech rate on intelligibility. In such experiments, speech stimuli have been created by instructing either native or non-native speakers to speak faster or slower than their normal rate, or by manipulating the speech samples. Either native or non-native listeners have then been asked to judge the stimuli. It appears that in order to be maximally intelligible, the speech rate of the L2 learner should fall within an ideal range. Speaking too fast may increase the number of pronunciation errors, and fast speech tends to impede comprehension especially when the speaker has a strong foreign accent. (See, e.g., Anderson-Hsieh and Koehler, 1988.) On the other hand, very slow speech may sound tedious for the native listener.

The speech rate tends to increase during language learning, and the learning context appears to play a role in this process. L2 learners tend to increase their speech rates when studying abroad (Lennon, 1990; Towell *et al.*, 1996; Segalowitz and Freed, 2004), although they do not reach native-like speech rates. Advanced learners tend to clearly exceed the rates of low-intermediate learners (Riggenbach, 1991; Kormos and Dénes, 2004).

The age of acquisition is one of the most important factors affecting L2 pronunciation, including the speech rate (Guion, Flege, Liu, and Yeni-Komshian, 2000; Trofimovich and Baker, 2006). Early learners tend to have higher speech rates than late learners. In addition, the length of residence in the target country appears to have a lesser effect on L2 speech rate. Significant improvements in the L2 speech rate have been observed after a stay of at least six months in the target country. However, even several decades of residence cannot guarantee a native-like pronunciation. The time period during which the L2 speech rate may develop is not yet known.

See also: age effects in SLA, development in SLA, fluency, longitudinal research, pausology and hesitation phenomena, speaking

References

Anderson-Hsieh, J. and Koehler, K. (1988). The effect of foreign accent and speaking rate on native speaker comprehension. *Language Learning*, *38*, 561–613.

Goldman-Eisler, F. (1968). *Psycholinguistics: Experiments in Spontaneous Speech*. London: Academic Press.

Guion, S.G., Flege, J.E., Liu, S.H. and Yeni-Komshian, G.H. (2000). Age of learning effects on the duration of sentences produced in a second language. *Applied Psycholinguistics*, *21*, 205–228.

Kormos, J. and Dénes, M. (2004). Exploring measures and perceptions of fluency in the speech of second language learners. *System*, *32*, 145–164.

Lennon, P. (1990). Investigating fluency in EFL: A quantitative approach. *Language Learning*, *40*, 387–417.

Levelt, W.J.M. (1989). *Speaking: From Intention to Articulation*. Cambridge, MA: MIT Press.

Munro, M.J. and Derwing, T.M. (1995). Processing time, accent, and comprehensibility in the perception of native and foreign-accented speech. *Language and Speech*, *38*, 289–306.

Riggenbach, H. (1991). Toward an understanding of fluency: A microanalysis of nonnative speaker conversations. *Discourse Processes*, *14*, 423–441.

Segalowitz, N. and Freed, B.F. (2004). Context, contact, and cognition in oral fluency acquisition: Learning Spanish in at home and study abroad contexts. *Studies in Second Language Acquisition*, *26*, 173–199.

Towell, R., Hawkins, R. and Bazergui, N. (1996). The development of fluency in advanced learners of French. *Applied Linguistics*, *17*, 84–119.

Trofimovich, P. and Baker, W. (2006). Learning second language suprasegmentals: Effect of L2 experience on prosody and fluency characteristics of L2 speech. *Studies in Second Language Acquisition*, *28*, 1–30.

Further reading

Trouvain, J. (2004). *Tempo Variation in Speech Production: Implications for Speech Synthesis*, Doctoral Dissertation, Saarland University. (An extensive overview of the sources of variation and the measurement methods for speech rate.)

Statistical learning

Patrick Rebuschat
University of Wales, Bangor

Recent years have witnessed a strong interest in empiricist approaches to language acquisition (Ellis, 2006). This development was driven, in part, by two observations, namely that (i) infants' environment is considerably richer in linguistic and nonlinguistic cues than previously anticipated and that (ii) infants are able to make extensive use of these cues when acquiring language. Both findings suggest a greater role for learning than traditionally assumed by nativist approaches to language development. Among empiricist approaches, research conducted on *statistical learning*, that is, our ability to make use of statistical information in the environment to bootstrap language acquisition, has been particularly fruitful. This entry briefly describes key characteristics and major findings in statistical learning research. It concludes with suggestions for future research.

Statistical learning: Methodology and results

Statistical learning research was sparked by the work of Jennifer Saffran and colleagues (Saffran,

Aslin and Newport, 1996; Saffran, Newport and Aslin, 1996) and developed into a major topic in developmental psychology (see Gómez, 2007; Saffran, 2003, for reviews). Statistical learning involves computations based on units or patterns, which can include linguistic elements such as speech sounds, syllables, syntactic categories and form-meaning mappings. The types of statistical computation range from simple frequency counts to the tracking of co-occurrence information and conditional probability. Research in statistical learning generally focuses on infant or child language acquisition, though studies with adult subjects are also common. In terms of methodology, the most distinctive features of statistical learning research are the careful manipulation of statistical information in the input and the use of artificial languages (see Gómez and Gerken, 2000, for a review).

In their seminal study, Saffran, Aslin, and Newport (1996) investigated whether 8-month-old infants could use statistical information to solve the problem of word segmentation, that is, to discover word boundaries in running speech. Infants were exposed to two minutes of a continuous speech stream that contained four three-syllable nonsense words (e.g., *tupiro*, *padoti*). The "words" were repeated in random order, and a speech synthesizer was used to generate a continuous auditory sequence (e.g., *bidakupadotigolabubidakupadotigolabubidakutupiro* ...). The sequence contained no pauses, stress differences or any other acoustic cues between words, so that the only cues to word boundaries were the transitional probabilities between syllables. The transitional probability *within* words was 1.0, given that the first syllable of a word was always followed by the second, and the second syllable by the third (e.g., *tu*–was always followed by *–pi–*, and *–pi–* followed by *–ro*). The transitional probability *between* words was 0.33 because the final syllable of a given word could be followed by the initial syllable of three different words (e. g., *–ro* could be followed by *go–*, *bi–*, or *pa–*). Infants were then tested by means of the head-turn preference procedure to determine whether they could recognize the difference between trained items (*tupiro*, *golabu*) and novel items (*dapiku*, *tilado*). Saffran, Aslin and Newport (1996) found that the 8-month-olds successfully discriminated between familiar and unfamiliar stimuli, which suggests that infants are highly sensitive to statistical information (here, transitional probabilities) and that they can use this information to succeed in a complex learning task (word segmentation).

This early research on statistical learning was important for demonstrating that infants are "intuitive statisticians" (Ellis, 2006), who are able make extensive use of environmental cues when acquiring language. Importantly, subsequent research has shown that the capacity for statistical learning is maintained throughout adulthood (e.g., Saffran, Newport, and Aslin, 1996) and that statistical learning is not restricted to the task of word segmentation. After more than a decade of experimental research, there is ample evidence that both infants and adults can exploit the statistical structure of their environment in order to succeed in a wide variety of linguistic tasks, including phonological learning (e.g., Maye, Weiss, and Aslin, 2008), word learning (e.g., Hamrick and Rebuschat, submitted) and syntactic development (e.g., Thompson and Newport, 2007). Gómez (2007) provides an extensive review of what can and cannot be acquired by means of statistical learning.

There is also evidence that the cognitive mechanism involved in statistical learning is not specific to language acquisition but rather domain-general in nature, that is, the learning mechanism applies to statistical information in the environment, irrespective of the nature of the stimulus (auditory, visual, tactile, etc.; see Saffran and Thiessen, 2007, for discussion). For example, several experiments have demonstrated that infants and adults can track sequential statistics in non-linguistic auditory stimuli (e.g., Saffran, Johnson, Aslin, and Newport, 1999) and visual stimuli (e.g., Fiser and Aslin, 2002). Studies on nonhuman primates, including cotton-top tamarin monkeys and rodents (e.g., Toro and Trobalón, 2004), further suggest that basic aspects of statistical learning are not unique to human learners. Finally, it is widely accepted that the process of statistical learning can occur incidentally, that is, subjects can acquire the statistical structure of language without the conscious intention to learn, making the process of statistical learning analogous to that of implicit learning.

Future directions

While there is a general consensus that human learners can make use of statistical cues in the input, research on statistical learning has raised a number of intriguing questions that remain to be answered (Gómez, 2007). It is clear, for example, that language learners make use of multiple cues in the process of natural language acquisition, and it remains to be fully determined how statistical information interacts with other types of cues (e.g. prosodic, semantic, etc.). Another challenge is to determine what cognitive processes are involved in statistical learning. For example, what is the role of attention and working memory? Yet another open question refers to the primitives of learning (Yang, 2004). In order to perform statistical computations learners must first know what kind of units are relevant (phonemes, syllables, etc.). How learners come to possess these primitives is a key question that needs to be addressed. Finally, with respect to second language learning, the question arises of how previous knowledge affects statistical learning of a novel language. More empirical research is required before the precise role of statistical learning in language acquisition can be fully specified.

See also: artificial language learning, competition model, connectionism, frequency effects, implicit learning, psycholinguistics of SLA

References

Ellis, N.C. (2006). Language acquisition as rational contingency learning. *Applied Linguistics*, *27*, 1–24.

Fiser, J. and Aslin, R.N. (2002). Statistical learning of new visual feature combinations by infants, *Proceedings of the National Academy of Sciences*, *99*, 15822–26.

Gómez, R. (2007). Statistical learning in infant language development, In M. Gaskell (ed.), *The Oxford Handbook of Psycholinguistics*, pp. 601–16. Oxford: Oxford University Press.

Gómez, R.L. and Gerken, L. (2000). Infant artificial language learning and language acquisition. *Trends in Cognitive Sciences*, *4*(5), 178–86.

Hamrick, P. and Rebuschat, P. (submitted). Statistical learning of second language vocabulary.

Maye, J., Weiss, D.J. and Aslin, R.N. (2008). Statistical phonetic learning in infants: Facilitation and feature generalization. *Developmental Science*, *11*, 122–34.

Saffran, J.R. (2003). Statistical language learning: Mechanisms and constraints. *Current Directions in Psychological Science*, *12*, 110–4.

Saffran, J.R. and Thiessen, E.D. (2007). Domain-general learning capacities. In E. Hoff and M. Schatz (eds), *Blackwell Handbook of Language Development*, pp. 68–86. Oxford: Blackwell Publishing.

Saffran, J.R., Aslin, R.N. and Newport, E.L. (1996). Statistical learning by 8-month-old infants. *Science*, *274*, 1926–28.

Saffran, J.R., Newport, E.L. and Aslin, R.N. (1996). Word segmentation: The role of distributional cues. *Journal of Memory and Language, 35, 606–21.*

Thompson, S.P. and Newport, E.L. (2007). Statistical learning of syntax: The role of transitional probability. *Language Learning and Development*, *3*, 1–42.

Toro, J.M. and Trobalón, J.B. (2005) Statistical computations over a speech stream in a rodent. *Perception and Psychophysics*, *67*, 867–75.

Yang, C. (2004). Universal Grammar, statistics, or both. *Trends in Cognitive Sciences*, *8*, 451–56.

Further reading

Perruchet, P. and Pacton, S. (2006). Implicit learning and statistical learning: One phenomenon, two approaches. *Trends in Cognitive Sciences*, *10*, 233–38. (An interesting comparison of implicit and statistical learning research.)

Rebuschat, P. and Williams, J.N. (2011). *Statistical Learning and Language Acquisition*. Berlin: Mouton de Gruyter. (A collection of articles that focuses on the role of statistical learning in first and second language acquisition.)

Stimulated recall

Susan Gass
Michigan State University

Stimulated recall is a methodology used to discover cognitive processes while performing a proscribed task. In essence, a stimulus from a task is used as the basis for asking participants about their thoughts during that task. As such, it is a complement to production data which are limited in that they do not reveal the thought processes underlying those data.

Stimulated recall is a subset of a wider set of methodologies referred to as verbal reports (see Bowles, 2010) which include concurrent reports (e.g., think-alouds) and retrospective reports, of which stimulated recall is a frequent type in second language research particularly in oral interaction.

Verbal reports, in general, have been discussed by Ericsson and Simon (1984, 1993), all of which are designed to provide information about cognitive processes. They divide reports according to 1) temporal characteristics (concurrent or retrospective) and 2) whether they require participants' actual thoughts or whether they ask participants to provide additional information. In this scheme, stimulated recall is retrospective and requires thoughts about a prior task.

Stimulated recalls are often part of research on oral interaction given the virtual impossibility of gathering concurrent reports. In second language research, learners (see Gass and Mackey, 2000 for a fuller description) complete some sort of oral communication task, with a researcher or with another learner or learners. The task itself is recorded (audio or video) and the audio/video serves as the subsequent stimulus. The learner, generally together with a researcher, watches the video or listens to the audio and is asked to comment on what they were thinking about at the time of the task.

There are two important characteristics to a stimulated recall: 1) there is a stimulus and 2) the learner is asked to verbalize what she or he was thinking about at the time of the original task. The stimulus serves as a reminder of the event—a video/audio in the case of oral research or a piece of writing in the case of writing research.

It is important in stimulated recall research to ensure to the extent possibility that learners are truly verbalizing their thought processes which occurred at the time of the original event. Having a stimulus as a reminder is one way to maximize this as it helps triggers actual memories of the event thereby minimizing the problem of veridicality. A second way of increasing validity is through the immediacy of the recall. Stimulated recalls that are conducted immediately following the original production of data (either oral or written) are less likely to suffer from memory decay. Yet another way to lessen the problem of inaccurate thought processes is through the actual questioning. Thus, a question such as "What were you thinking about when you said/wrote x?" is appropriate because it asks about thoughts at the time of doing. A question such as "What are you thinking?" is not appropriate because it is not clear if the time frame being asked about is the actual time of data production or the time of the recall.

See also: attention, awareness, declarative memory and knowledge, instructed SLA, measuring and researching SLA, protocol analysis

References

Bowles, M. (2010). *The Think-aloud Controversy in Second Language Research*. New York: Routledge.

Ericsson, K.A. and Simon, H.A. (1984). *Protocol Analysis: Verbal Reports as Data*. Cambridge, MA: MIT Press.

——(1993). *Protocol Analysis: Verbal Reports as Data*, revised edition. Cambridge, MA: MIT Press.

Gass, S. and Mackey, A. (2000). *Stimulated Recall Methodology in Second Language Research*. Mahwah, NJ: Lawrence Erlbaum Associates.

Structural equation modeling (SEM)

Yasuyo Sawaki
Waseda University

Structural equation modeling (SEM) is a multivariate statistical technique that is used to test hypotheses about interrelationships among a set of observed and latent (unobservable) variables. SEM is confirmatory in nature. In an SEM application, the investigator defines one or more models reflecting a hypothesis (or hypotheses) about underlying relationships among variables of interest based on substantive theory and previous empirical research results. Then, statistical analyses are conducted to examine how well the proposed model(s) fits the data. A main goal of an SEM analysis is to identify a well-fitting model that offers a theoretically meaningful explanation to the relationships among a set of variables. An early application of SEM in SLA research is Gardner, Tremblay, and Masgoret's (1997) study on the relationships among SLA, L2 learning motivation, and other learner variables. Recent SEM applications include Schoonen, van Gelderen, de Glopper, Hulstijn, Simis, and Snelling's (2003) investigation into the relationships among linguistic knowledge, metacognitive knowledge, and fluency in L1- and L2-writing abilities and Phakiti's (2008) research on how L2 reading comprehension test performance relates to relevant strategy knowledge and use.

In a typical SEM analysis, a covariance matrix is analyzed to simultaneously test a series of regression equations that define direct and indirect relationships among variables of interest. A major strength of SEM over other familiar statistical techniques, such as multiple regression analysis and path analysis, is that it allows examination of underlying relationships among latent variables, which are unaffected by measurement error. While SEM is often used to analyze a covariance structure on a single dataset in cross-sectional research, it can also be used to compare both covariance and mean structures across groups. Change of performance over time can be investigated in longitudinal studies as well.

A full SEM model contains two types of models. Figure 14 shows a graphical representation of a sample SEM model. One is a measurement model, which defines predictive relationships between latent variables (ovals in Figure 14) and their indicators (observed variables; rectangles in Figure 14). The other is a structural model, which depicts predictive relationships among latent variables. The single-headed arrows connecting the variables denote regression paths, while the arrows labeled E1 through E5 and D1 show residuals. Once an SEM model is developed, a mathematical function is fit to data to estimate model parameters. Then, model fit is examined based on multiple criteria, including (1) substantive interpretability of model parameters, (2) values of various model fit indices, and (3) the extent to which a model is mathematically simple, involving

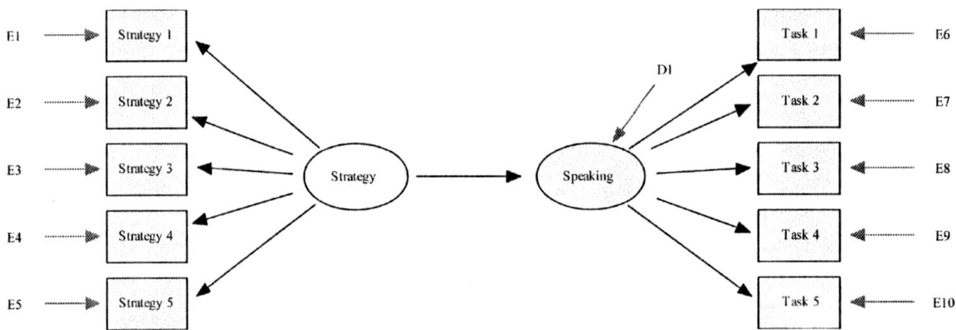

Figure 14 A sample SEM model showing a predictive relationship between strategy use (based on responses to a 5-section strategy survey) and performance on a speaking test comprising five tasks.

a relatively small number of freely estimated parameters, and yet explains the underlying relationships among a set of variables sufficiently well (model parsimony).

The investigator needs to carefully examine a variety of substantive and measurement issues when determining whether applying SEM to his/her own investigation is appropriate. Interested readers should refer to introductory texts on SEM, such as Raykov and Marcoulides (2006) and Ullman (2007), on various issues of consideration, including data requirements, steps for developing and testing SEM models, and reporting analysis results.

See also: correlation, cross-sectional research, factor analysis, hypothesis testing, longitudinal research, quantitative research

References

Gardner, R.C., Tremblay, P.F. and Msgoret, A.-M. (1997). Towards a full model of second language learning: An empirical investigation. *The Modern Language Journal*, *81*, 344–62.

Phakiti, A. (2008). Construct validation of Bachman and Palmer's (1996) strategic competence model over time in EFL reading tests. *Language Testing*, *25*, 237–72.

Raykov, T. and Marcoulides, G.A. (2006). *A First Course in Structural Equation Modeling*, 2nd edn. Mahwah, NJ: Erlbaum.

Schoonen, R., van Gelderen, A., de Glopper, K., Hulstijn, J., Simis, A., Snellings, P. and Stevenson, M. (2003). First language and second language writing: The role of linguistic knowledge, speed of processing, and metcognitive knowledge. *Language Learning*, *53*, 165–202.

Ullman, J.B. (2007). Structural equation modeling. In B.G. Tabachnick and L.S. Fidell (eds), *Using Multivariate Statistics*, 5th edn. Boston, MA: Pear.

Study abroad and SLA

Margaret A. DuFon
California State University, Chico

Study abroad (SA) continues to be popular with nations around the globe sending high numbers of students abroad for education. One reason students go abroad is to learn a foreign language because it is generally assumed that living in an environment where the language is spoken is the best way to learn it.

Indeed research has repeatedly demonstrated that learners who SA can make gains in all skill areas – listening, speaking, reading and writing – during their term abroad. Their best performance, however, is in speaking skills including oral fluency, oral proficiency, vocabulary, pragmatics, discourse, and narrative abilities, where they not only make gains over the course of a term abroad but also typically outpace learners who remain at home in foreign language classes. Yet a closer look reveals a more complex picture. SA learners sometimes compare unfavorably, particularly when compared with learners in intensive immersion programs particularly on measures of linguistic accuracy. (See Churchill and DuFon, 2006 and Collentine, 2009 for reviews.) This is not surprising given that classroom instruction puts more attention on linguistic accuracy than is typically found in naturalistic interactions (e.g. McMeekin, 2006). Yet differences in gains cannot be attributed to program qualities alone since even within the same program there is a high degree of variation among learners. In fact, some learners even regress in some skills during the course of their stay (Kinginger, 2008). Therefore a careful look at both program variables and individual characteristics is needed to see how they affect the language acquisition process.

Program variables

One program variable that affects SLA abroad is length of stay. While even short stays abroad can result in language acquisition, longer stays typically yield better results (e.g., Llanes and Munoz, 2009). Yet even longer stays do not guarantee language gains or a reduction in ethnocentrism and improved attitudes toward the host culture. Just spending more time is not the answer; rather learners need training to raise awareness of language use and cultural differences and then given strategies for dealing with these differences (Paige, Cohen and Shively, 2004) as well as tools for developing self-understanding and *identity competence* (Aveni, 2005) so that they remain open to the host culture, less likely to negatively evaluate and disengage from their hosts, and thus increase their potential for language gains.

How learners spend their time and who they spend it with while abroad also affects acquisition. Programs that are scheduled so that learners spend more time in activities with each other or living together limit access to hosts and thus to language practice with native speakers. In contrast, programs that integrate students with their hosts in classes, internships or living arrangements build in opportunities to access and interact with hosts, thus facilitating acquisition. Yet even programs designed to place students in close proximity to native speakers on a daily basis can fail to provide opportunities for interaction if not carefully planned and implemented so as to provide true social integration into the existing community (see Churchill and DuFon for review, 2006).

Learner characteristics

Even among students in the same program, there is differential success in language acquisition, which can be traced to learner differences. One difference is learner goals. Language learning, while desirable, is not every learner's top priority and realizing other goals may steal time and attention away from language learning (Hassall, 2006). Yet even students for whom language learning is a top priority can encounter roadblocks that interfere with acquisition. For example, when a learner is studying an ingroup code, practice can be difficult since hosts may insist on using the language of interethnic communication with the learner (Trosset, 1986). In such situations only the most tenacious learners continue to use the target language with their hosts. Another roadblock occurs when language learners experience negative interactions with their hosts. In such cases, even initially "highly motivated" learners often disengage from the host culture (e.g. Wilkinson, 1998). This has been particularly true for females, who often do not receive the same "respect" they are used to in their home culture (e.g. Dierdre in Kinginger, 2008).

This leads us to ask: which learners are more likely to make gains while abroad? Which are more likely to have positive experiences with their hosts even under unfavorable conditions? One factor that might create more positive interactions is that of proficiency. A higher initial level of proficiency has been found to positively influence the nature and intensity of out of class contact with hosts, linguistic improvement, and motivation. This makes sense in that higher proficiency learners have more processing space available to focus their attention on linguistic form and employ metalinguistic strategies such as self-monitoring and thus increase their linguistic accuracy (cf. Collentine, 2009). Along with linguistic competence, greater cultural knowledge and intercultural competence (Aveni, 2005) facilitates their adjustment to the foreign environment. That said, other learner factors such as self-perception (e.g. self-perception of communicative competence) (Yashima, Zenuk-Nishide, and Shimizu, 2004), and self-understanding (e.g. a stable self-identity) (Aveni, 2005) affect their willingness to communicate and to remain open to their hosts, which is a necessary pre-requisite for building social networks and expanding the types of discourse one engages in, and thus affects SLA (Isabelli-Garcia, 2006). Thus while higher proficiency learners may be the best candidates for SA, even lower proficiency learners who remain open to their hosts can make good gains while abroad and in areas like pragmatics can even outpace some of the more proficient learners (e.g., DuFon, 2000).

Summary

The research so far indicates that SA is a conducive environment for SLA for high school and college students and that they can improve both accuracy and fluency while abroad depending on their own learning goals and whether they are equipped with the personal and linguistic skills and the motivation to invest their time and attention on achieving those goals, to engage in quality interactions with their hosts, and to self-monitor.

Directions for future research

Further research is needed to determine how to identify those learners who are most likely to succeed. This entails taking into account learners' goals for SA. Where language acquisition is a primary goal, research is needed to determine how to adequately measure personal traits necessary for success including: 1) their level of investment in language acquisition such that those selected remain committed even when they encounter negative experiences; 2) their level of cultural and pragmatic knowledge such that they more easily adjust to and recognize the value of the target culture; 3) their knowledge of strategies for language learning and cultural adjustment; and 4) their level of self-understanding and identity competence in the L2 (Aveni, 2005).

Self-understanding and identity competence have received little attention in the field of SLA. Additional research is needed into methods for assessing and fostering the development of self-understanding and identity competence prior to and during SA. The effect of contemplative practices, such as meditation, which have helped students come to know themselves better by strengthening their capacities for self-observation as well as producing other benefits such as reduced stress and increased empathy (Shapiro, Brown, Astin and Duerr, 2008), all of which would have potential benefit for learners abroad, is another promising area of research.

Further research is also needed to refine our knowledge about how programs can be structured to: 1) focus learner's attention on particular aspects of language while abroad; 2) provide more quality interactions between learners and hosts; and 3) support learners' linguistic and cultural development prior to and during SA. One area that holds promise both for focusing attention and cultural adjustment is that of strategy training. Qualitative research has demonstrated potential benefits of strategy training to help learners cope with adjustment to the culture and its ways of speaking, but research focused both on strategy training and on measuring its effects is needed (Paige, Cohen and Shively, 2004). Such training could facilitate improved interactions with hosts.

Further research is needed not only on learner characteristics such as proficiency (and the thresholds of particular cognitive or linguistic abilities that must be crossed to fully participate in and benefit from the SA experience with respect to SLA (Collentine, 2009)), but also on how these characteristics interact. For example, what is the intercultural competence threshold needed to fully benefit from SA and how does intercultural competence interact with proficiency in determining readiness for SA?

While we have obtained a clearer picture of how SA benefits language acquisition during the sojourn, only a few studies have delved into its after effects, and even at multiple points in time fewer (e.g. Matsumura, 2007) following the sojourn.

Finally, SA research to date has focused mainly on high school and college students. Little is known about the language acquisition of children of international students and ex-patriots with respect to their rate or patterns of acquisition or the variables that facilitate their language learning abroad. Research into these areas would provide greater depth and breadth to our understanding of SLA during SA.

See also: identity theory, individual differences and SLA, learning strategies, proficiency, social and sociocultural influences on SLA, Willingness to communicate (WTC)

References

Aveni, V.P. (2005). *Study Abroad and Second Language Use: Constructing the Self.* New York: Cambridge University Press.

Churchill, E. and DuFon, M.A. (2006). Evolving threads in study abroad research. In M.A. DuFon and E. Churchill (eds), *Language Learners in Study Abroad Contexts*. Clevedon: Multilingual Matters.

Collentine, J. (2009). Study abroad research: Findings, implications and future directions. In C. Doughty and M. Long (eds), *Handbook of Language Teaching*. Malden, MA: Blackwell Publishing, Ltd.

DuFon, M.A. (2000). The acquisition of linguistic politeness in Indonesian by sojourners in naturalistic interactions. PhD thesis, University of Hawai'i, 1999, *Dissertation Abstracts International*-A, 60:11, 3985.

Hassall, T. (2006). Learning to take leave in social conversations: A diary study. In M.A. DuFon and E. Churchill (eds), *Language Learners in Study Abroad Contexts*. Clevedon: Multilingual Matters.

Isabelli-García, C. (2006). Study abroad social networks, motivation, and attitudes: Implications for second language scquisition. In M.A. DuFon and E. Churchill (eds), *Language Learners in Study Abroad Contexts*. Clevedon: Multilingual Matters.

Kinginger, C. (2008). Language learning in study abroad: Case studies of Americans in France. *Modern Language Journal Winter2008 Supplement*, *92*, 1–124.

Llanes, A. and Munoz, C. (2009). A short stay abroad: Does it make a difference? *System*, *37*, 353–65.

Matsumura, S. (2007). Exploring the aftereffects of study abroad on interlanguage pragmatic development. *Intercultural Pragmatics*, *4*, 167–92.

McMeekin, A. (2006). Negotiation in a Japanese Study abroad setting. In M.A. DuFon and E. Churchill (eds), *Language Learners in Study Abroad Contexts*. Clevedon: Multilingual Matters.

Paige, M. Cohen, A.D. and Shively, R.L. (2004). Assessing the impact of a strategies-based curriculum on language and culture learning sbroad. *Frontiers* (X), pp. 253–76. [Online], Available: http://www.frontiersjournal.com/issues/vol10/vol10–15_PaigeCohenShively.pdf [20 January 2005].

Shapiro, S.L., Brown, K.W. Astin, J.A. and Duerr, M. (2008). *Toward the Integration of Meditation into Higher Education: A Review of Research*, [Online] Available: http://www.contemplativemind.org/programs/academic/MedandHighered.pdf [11 March 2009].

Trosset, C. (1986). The social identity of Welsh learners. *Language in Society*, *15*, 165–92.

Wilkinson, S. (1998). On the nature of immersion during study abroad: Some participants' perspectives. *Frontiers: The Interdisciplinary Journal of Study Abroad*, IV, 21–138 [Online] Available: http://www.frontiersjournal.com/issues/vol4/vol4–05_Wilkinson.pdf [17 July 2004].

Yashima, T., Zenuk-Nishide, L. and Shimizu, K. (2004). The influence of attitudes and affect on willingness to communicate and second language communication. *Language Learning*, 54, 119–52.

Symbolic mediation

Claire Kramsch
University of California, Berkeley

SLA researchers agree that language acquisition is about the acquisition of symbols that mediate our thoughts and actions in an L2 context. This mediation enables us to order the unshaped mass of our thoughts and those of others, and to act upon the world through the symbolic system of an L2. But there are two ways of conceiving of mediation depending on how symbolic systems like language are conceptualized.

A structuralist view sees language as a closed linguistic system and as a mode of action that leads to linguistic and cognitive development. Inherited from Saussure, this view continues to be prevalent in post-Vygotskian sociocultural and activity theory. Signifiers supplement objects in the world and make them into signifieds. We impose our grammars and vocabularies on phenomena that exist out there, independent of our symbolic forms. Our symbols make these phenomena as well as our knowledge of them and the emotions we associate with them communicable, shareable, because the symbolic forms through which culture gives voice to nature are arbitrary. For example, the fact that there existed out there a t-r-e-e before we even named it so reinforces the irreducible identity and truth of that tree, irrespective of whether we call it a tree, *ein Baum* or *un arbre*. As Jim Lantolf describes it: "Just as humans do not act directly on the physical world but rely, instead, on tools and labor activity, which allows us to change the world … we also use symbolic tools, or signs, to mediate and regulate our relationships with others and with ourselves and thus change the nature of these relationships … Humans use symbolic artifacts to establish an indirect, or mediated, relationship between ourselves and the world" (Lantolf, 2000: 1).

This way of describing symbolic mediation – *tools, labor activity, regulation, change, relationships between ourselves and the world* – presupposes a stable reality to which human activity is applied by means of symbols that represent that reality and are more easily manipulated than reality itself. This view finds its ultimate expression in computer-mediated communication. While Saussure saw knowledge as declarative and language as referring to how the world is, computer scientists like Abelson and Sussman (1985) view computer knowledge as procedural, that is, it acts upon the world, models it, manipulates it, in an attempt to solve its problems. In structuralist accounts of SLA, mediation is seen as a semiotic process that supplements and gives meaning to stable structures in a given world, either in a descriptive or in a constructive way, through arbitrary symbolic forms that ultimately aim to change the world.

More recently, under the influence of post-structuralism, applied linguists are interested in the way symbols not only represent or even construct existing reality, but how they constitute meanings, perceptions, memories, real or imagined identities, and ideologies. They draw on the work of anthropologists and psychologists who have adopted a more constitutive view of symbolic mediation. In the anthropologist Ernst Cassirer's account, (Cassirer, 1953) symbols do not supplement anything. "[They] partake in the very constitution of the object as an object … They are spliced onto the phenomenon to form a graft; they are implanted into the 'ground' of sensibility and make the phenomena grow beyond themselves; they are rooted but always transcend their point of departure" (Hoel, 2009: 5,16). For example a tree does not mean anything to us, it has no signification without the mediation of symbols (visual, verbal, semiotic) that make it differently meaningful to us than the sky or the earth. Stories, pictures, paintings, films, utterances about trees have constructed the natural object called *tree*, an object that is thus for a human being neither purely nature nor purely culture, but a condensation of meaning through "intellectual articulation" (Cassirer, 1953: 87). The way this condensation takes place is through human play with the signifiers we have created. According to psychologists like Vygotsky, children who realize that not all desires are immediately realizable find in play "the imaginary … realization of unrealizable desires" (Vygotsky, 1966: 4). For instance, by calling a stick "a horse" the child emancipates the word *horse* from its object and gains control over his desire to ride a horse – "a novel form of behavior in which the child is liberated from situational constraints through his activity in an imaginary situation" (ibidem: 13). Cassirer and Vygotsky were precursors of a new way of viewing symbolic mediation, namely as the imaginary relations constructed through symbolic forms and their subjective resonances in the sensibilities of the users.

The renewed interest in the Sapir-Whorf hypothesis (Lucy, 1992; Gumperz and Levinson, 1996) is evidence of a concern for the way the words we use mediate, that is, construct and channel the way we think. Advances in cognitive linguistics (e.g., Lakoff, 1987) and cognitive psychology (e.g., Boroditsky, 2003) make us aware that learning German, for example, might mean that we learn to attribute feminine qualities to a bridge (*die Brücke*), masculine qualities to death (*der Tod*), whereas for learners of French it is the other way around. The world mediated through German would, then, be different from the world mediated through French, and so would our perceptions and memories of bridges and death.

In post-structuralist accounts of SLA, the advent of computer-mediated communication is complexifying our view of symbolic mediation in language learning. The computer's subversion of time, space, and reality makes it into a structuralist tool with post-structuralist effects (Kramsch, 2009). Networked computers and their digital interfaces are effectively transforming the way we think, speak, and act. It is blurring the lines between the foreign and the familiar, the local and the global, the quantitative and the qualitative. We can no longer think of SLA as an input-output affair, or even as a communicative challenge; nor can we conflate language acquisition and language socialization. In the ecological world of symbolic mediation, symbols evoke other symbols; memories, emotions, identities emerge; symbolic systems leak into one another – English meanings in French, Chinese meanings in English, creating new meanings with different forms of symbolic power.

See also: cognitive linguistics and SLA, computer-assisted language learning (CALL), ecology of language learning, linguistic relativity, social and socio-cultural approcahes to SLA, thinking for speaking

References

Abelson H. and G.J. Sussman with J. Sussman. (1985). *Structure and Interpretation of Computer Programs*. Cambridge, MA: MIT Press.

Boroditsky, L. (2003). Linguistic relativity. In Nadel, L. (ed.), *Encyclopedia of Cognitive Science*, pp. 917–21. London: McMillan Press.

Cassirer, E. (1953). *The Philosophy of Symbolic Forms. Vol.1 Language*. Trsl. R. Manheim. New Haven, CT: Yale University Press.

Gumperz, J.J. and S.C. Levinson (eds) (1996). *Rethinking Linguistic Relativity*. Cambridge: Cambridge University Press.

Hoel, A.S. (2009). Thinking 'difference' differently: Cassirer versus Derrida on symbolic mediation. *Synthese*. Published online 31 July, 1–17 Springer.

Kramsch, C. (2009). *The Multilingual Subject*. London: Oxford University Press.

Lakoff, G. (1987). *Women, Fire and Dangerous Things. What Categories Reveal about the Mind*. Chicago, IL: University of Chicago Press.

Lantolf, J. (2000). *Sociocultural Theory and Language Learning*. Oxford: OUP.

Lucy, J. (1992). *Language Diversity and Thought: A Reformulation of the Linguistic Relativity Hypothesis*. Cambridge: Cambridge University Press.

Vygotsky, L. (1966). Play and its role in the mental development of the child. Trsl. C. Mulholland. *Voprosy psikhologii*, No.6. Retrieved December 22, 2010 at www.all-about-psychology.com

Systemic Functional Linguistics

Heidi Byrnes
Georgetown University

Systemic Functional Linguistics (SFL) belongs to the family of functionally oriented theories of language. Its assumptions about the nature of language and the goals of theorizing about it as well as its own contributions focus on the use and meaning of oral and written texts as these occur in specified sociocultural contexts.

SFL is closely associated with the work of the British-Australian linguist M.A. K. Halliday, who laid out its global parameters in the late 1950s and has since then formalized and expanded them with a focus on their 'appliability' in wide-ranging domains of language-in-culture (Halliday and Matthiessen, 2004; Webster 2002–7). Researchers working within an SFL framework have filled in its architecture through studies in: child language acquisition, particularly the link between linguistic and socio-cognitive development and literacy; translation studies, including machine translation; multisemiotic studies that explore the relation between language and other semiotic systems; meaning-oriented typological studies that yield topographies of language families; corpus-linguistic inquiry in the continuum between more lexically and more syntactically oriented phenomena; critical discourse analysis; institutional linguistics (e.g., health care); and educational linguistics through the construct of genre, primarily addressing L1 literacy development (Christie and Martin, 1997; Martin and Rose, 2003, 2008) but increasingly also L2 learning and teaching in ESL and FL environments (Byrnes, 2009, 2011; Byrnes, Maxim, and Norris, 2010).

The intellectual origins of SFL lie in mid-twentieth century British linguistic empiricism as espoused by J.R. Firth, which rejected a duality of mind and body, idea and word, and placed language in the matrix of experience for its users. These include insights by the Danish linguist Hjelmslev who proposed overcoming the Saussurean split between *langue* and *parole* through the notion of *realization* or manifestation; by the anthropologist Malinowski, who suggested the concepts of *context of situation* and *context of culture* in order to link the particularities of language form and use with their occurrence in cultural and historical contexts; and from Prague School Linguistics with its strong textual and meaning orientation.

To better theorize a use-orientation Halliday privileged the system-related, meaning-oriented paradigmatic "choice" axis over the structure-related and rule-oriented syntagmatic "chain" axis: the syntagmatic organization of language is but the realization of the paradigmatic, unordered system networks that characterize a particular language. In freeing linguistic analysis from the "constraints" orientation characteristic of formal theorizing that approach also facilitated the incorporation of dimensions of time and depth, evolution and dynamic change, development and learning, inasmuch as the system networks can be understood as ordered in terms of scales of delicacy or granularity, moving from left to right from the most fundamental resources within the overall meaning-potential of a particular language system (e.g., polarity; tense/aspect; mood; transitivity) to ever more nuanced ways of meaning-making that are deployed by particularly competent users of a language who have honed their performance abilities over a life-time.

For historical, ideological, and intellectual reasons, the considerable contributions of SFL to an understanding of semogenesis (in a particular instance of language use), ontogenesis (a particular user's evolving abilities over a life-time), and phylogenesis (the gradual change of a language system over time) have been differentially recognized in theoretical and applied linguistics. However, most recently, its close affinity to innovative proposals within dynamic and adaptive systems thinking, emergentism, cognitive semantics, usage-based approaches, language ecology, literacy development, sociocultural theory, and language use in professional and institutional settings heralds the possibility of a substantive contribution by SFL to the much-needed specification, operationalization, and detailed investigation of language use and development under particular conditions (Matthiessen, 2007, 2009).

Taking language to arise from social acts of meaning-making, SFL asserts that the organization of the grammar of a language, not just its lexicon or language use, is fundamentally functional: particular "wordings" bear a "natural" orientation to sociocultural contexts rather than a logical, much less an arbitrary one. That solidary relationship is investigated through three metafunctions, the ideational, the interpersonal, and the textual metafunctions, where FIELD construes our experience in the world, TENOR enacts various social roles and relationships and their valuation, and MODE refers to the textual features that present the construed and enacted meanings as a flow of discourse in oral and written texts. As a meaning-making resource, grammar becomes the engine of a language. By exploring the link between context of situation and highly probable bundles of lexicogrammatical features, one can specify the construct of "register" as an in-between region between social context and language use. When such functional varieties of language occur in particular situation contexts, we refer to them as textual genres, understood as staged, goal-oriented social processes.

Language is a probabilistic system with *inherent and necessary* indeterminacies that respond to sociocultural givens *and* their gradual change: variation is built into the system. Because every text is multifunctional, there is no need for (indeed, a theoretical prohibition against) a separate pragmatics, literal versus derived/metaphorical meanings, discourse meanings versus sentence-level meanings.

Language is a hierarchical, non-arbitrary stratified system where its semantics is realized in a single stratum of lexicogrammar that, in turn, is realized in phonology/graphology. The core relationship is one of construal: users transform experience in their social and physical world into meaning through the available lexicogrammatical resources. Construal takes place in two strongly developmental ways. Congruent construal follows the previously mentioned "natural" relationships; non-congruent or metaphorical construal skews the alignment of lexicogrammatical resources and semantics in a process aptly called grammatical metaphor. Language learning to advanced ability levels amounts to continued expansion of registerial and generic capacities.

Language is not a "thing" but a meaning-making potential. Learners work only with instances of texts, themselves part of subsets of possible texts and their meaning potential. By positing a cline of instantiation between instance and language system and specifying it for its registerial, generic, and lexicogrammatical features, SFL contributes to a much-needed principled understanding of the long-term development of naturalistic and instructed L2 learners as they infer the capacities of the system from individual texts and, in turn, generate texts on the basis of their access to the system's semogenic resources.

See also: development in SLA, discourse and pragmatics in SLA, emergentism, functional linguistics, multifunctionality, sociocognitive approaches to SLA

References

Byrnes, H. (2011). Conceptualizing FL Writing Development in Collegiate Settings: A Systemic Functional Linguistic Approach. In R.M. Manchón (ed.), *L2 Writing Development: Multiple Perspectives*. Berlin: de Gruyter Mouton.

——(ed.) (2009). Instructed Foreign Language Acquisition as Meaning-making: A Systemic-functional Approach. *Linguistics and Education*, *20* (1), 1–79.

——Maxim, H.H. and Norris, J.M. (2010). Realizing Advanced FL Writing Development in Collegiate Education: Curricular Design, Pedagogy, Assessment. *Modern Language Journal*, *94* (Monograph Issue).

Halliday, M.A.K. and Matthiessen, C.M.I.M. (2004) *An Introduction to Functional Grammar*, 3rd edn. London: Edward Arnold.

Hasan, R., Matthiessen, C.M.I.M. and Webster, J.J. (eds) (2005, 2007) *Continuing Discourse on Language: A Functional Perspective*, 2 volumes. London: Equinox.

Martin, J.R. and Rose, D. (2003). *Working with Discourse: Meaning beyond the Clause*. London: Continuum.

——(2008). *Genre Relations: Mapping Culture*. London: Equinox.

Matthiessen, C.M.I.M. (2007). The 'Architecture' of Language According to Systemic Functional Theory: Developments since the 1970s. In R. Hasan, C.M.I.M. Matthiessen, and J.J.Webster (eds), *Continuing Discourse on Language: A Functional Perspective*, pp. 505–61. London: Equinox.

——(2009). Meaning in the Making: Meaning Potential Emerging from Acts of Meaning. *Language Learning*, *59* (Suppl.1), 206–29.

Webster, J.J. (ed.) (2002–2007) *The Collected Works of M.A. K. Halliday*, 10 volumes. London: Continuum.

Further reading

Christie, F. and Derewianka, B. (2008). *School Discourse: Learning to Write across the Years of Schooling*. London: Continuum. (Application of SFL constructs to understanding writing development in terms of genre, from the primary grades to the end of secondary education.)

Christie, F. and Martin, J.R. (1997). *Genre and Institutions: Social Processes in the Workplace and School*. London: Continuum. (Examines genres as instances of social processes, enacting diverse institutional practices.)

Eggins, S. (2004). *An Introduction to Systemic Functional Linguistics*. London: Continuum. (Good introductory textbook, with exercises.)

Halliday, M.A.K. and Martin, J.R. (1993). *Writing Science: Literacy and Discursive Power*. London and Washington, DC: The Falmer Press. (Use of SFL constructs, particularly the notion of grammatical metaphor, to understanding the nature of scientific discourse.)

——and Matthiessen, C.M.I.M. (1999). *Construing Experience through Meaning: A Language-based Approach to Cognition*. London and New York: Continuum. (Comprehensive discussion of the link between language and consciousness through meaning-making.)

T

T-tests

Jenifer Larson-Hall
University of North Texas

The t-test is a statistical test which compares the mean scores and variances of two groups and tests the hypothesis that there is no difference between the groups. The t-test is the simplest statistical test of group differences; it can also be used when more than two groups exist just by comparing only two groups at a time. However, one must take care when using a t-test to note whether the scores come from entirely separate groups of people or whether the scores measure the same people. If the participants in the groups do not overlap, an independent-samples t-test should be used; if the same participants have contributed information for both scores, a paired-samples t-test should be used.

In the field of second language acquisition, t-tests are most often conducted on data collected from human beings, although this does not have to be the case (the test data could come from widgets or animal reactions, for example, in other fields). The data collected should consist of interval-level data, meaning that a difference in one point in one part of the scale is equal to a difference of one point in another part of the scale. The groups will be split by a categorical (nominal) variable, which might include group membership, time of test (pretest/posttest), type of item (phonology vs syntax, or two different phonemic contrasts), experimental condition, proficiency level, or type of condition that a language was learned in.

The mathematical formula for calculating a t-test is not difficult and involves calculations with the mean, standard deviation, and number of participants in each group. However, t-test calculators are readily available online or in standard statistical packages like SPSS or R. Here are two online sites where t-tests can be reliably calculated:

www.graphpad.com/quickcalcs/ttest1.cfm
http://studentsttest.com

One important assumption for the independent-samples t-test is that the variances of the groups are equal. The standard deviations for the two groups should be roughly equal, given the total number of points available. If they are not, the Welch correction can be used to correct for unequal variances (some authors, like Dalgaard, 2002 recommend always using this correction). If variances are highly unequal or data are highly skewed, differences which actually exist may be obscured (Larson-Hall and Herrington, 2010; Wilcox, 1998). In these cases, robust t-tests may more accurately reflect the true situation (see online R companion files to Larson-Hall, 2010 for more information on how to conduct robust t-tests).

Report the results of a t-test by giving the t-value, degrees of freedom (df), p-value, and confidence interval (if possible). Additionally, the effect size of the difference between means should be calculated and can be reported as Cohen's d (on online calculator to use if variances are equal is www.uccs.edu/~faculty/lbecker/). Here is an example:

A t-test between participants on the pre-test and post-test found a statistically significant difference, $t(21) = 3.78$, $p = 0.028$, 95% CI [–15.3, –3.7], $d = 1.4$. This is a large effect size and indicates considerable difference between testing times.

See also: correlation, effect size, Factor Analysis (FA), quantitative research, significance level, variance

References

Dalgaard, P. (2002). *Introductory Statistics with R.* New York: Springer-Verlag.

Larson-Hall, J. (2010). *A Guide to Doing Statistics in Second Language Research using SPSS.* New York: Routledge.

Larson-Hall, J. and Herrington, R. (2010). Examining the difference that robust statistics can make to studies in language acquisition. *Applied Linguistics, 31*(3), 368–90.

Wilcox, R. (1998). How many discoveries have been lost by ignoring modern statistical methods? *American Psychologist, 53*(3), 300–14.

Further reading

Hatch, E.M. and Lazaraton, A. (1991). *The Research Manual: Design and Statistics for Applied Linguistics.* New York: Newbury House. (Uses examples from SLA; Chapters 9 and 10 cover t-tests.)

Howell, D.C. (2009). *Statistical Methods for Psychology*, 7th edn. Pacific Grove, CA: Duxbury/Thomson Learning. (Thorough statistical coverage; Chapter 7 covers t-test design.)

Larson-Hall, J. (2010). *A Guide to Doing Statistics in Second Language Research using SPSS.* New York: Routledge. (Uses examples from SLA and shows how to use SPSS and R statistical software; Chapter 9 covers t-test design.)

Wilcox, R. (2001). *Fundamentals of Modern Statistical Methods: Substantially Improving Power and Accuracy.* New York: Springer. (Chapter 5 covers t-tests; the entire book explains why robust methods are useful.)

TalkBank

Brian MacWhinney
Carnegie Mellon University

The TalkBank system is an international resource for the study of written and oral productions in second language learning and bilinguals. The system can be accessed over the Internet at http://talkbank.org. The goal of TalkBank is to make available materials that can further the empirical study of language. The three core principles upon which the system is based are data sharing, open access, and interoperability. The principle of data sharing holds that researchers have the responsibility to make the results of their research available to the full scientific community. The principle of open access holds that both transcripts and recordings should be available to researchers without restrictions or licenses. Passwords are only required in cases where participants have requested limited access. The principle of interoperability holds that data should be in a uniform format that can be transformed for analysis using a wide variety of analysis tools and methods.

Use of TalkBank materials is open to all researchers who agree to follows basic guidelines for respecting the participants and data contributors. TalkBank includes a wide range of subcomponents, ranging from child phonology (PhonBank) to aphasia (AphasiaBank). Of these various components, two are particularly relevant to the study of second language acquisition. The first component, called BilingBank, includes over a dozen major corpora from adult bilinguals and language learners. This component is located at http://talkbank.org/BilingBank. The second component is the collection of data from childhood bilinguals which is located within the Biling folder of the CHILDES database at http://childes.psy.cmu.edu.

All TalkBank corpora are transcribed using the CHAT transcription format that is designed for analysis using the CLAN programs. The CLAN program and the manuals for CHAT and CLAN can be freely downloaded from http://childes.psy.cmu.edu. Many of the corpora in both components have transcripts that are directly linked to audio or video which can be played back directly over the web.

Currently, there are 21 corpora in the Biling component of the CHILDES database. These corpora include childhood bilinguals and their caregivers with these configurations: Arabic-Dutch, Turkish-Dutch, Mandarin-English, Cantonese-English, Dutch-English, Spanish-English, French-English, Danish-Japanese, Russian-English, Italian-German, English-Polish, Swedish-Portuguese, Hungarian-English, Spanish-Catalan, and Dutch-Italian.

Within the BilingBank database, there are currently these 17 corpora:

1. Bangor: Welsh-English bilinguals speaking primarily Welsh.
2. BELC: Studies of Catalan speakers learning English at ages 8, 11, 14, and 18+.
3. BlumSnow: Hebrew-English bilingual families in Israel and the United States.
4. Connolly: Japanese teenages learning English through peer-to-peer dialogs.
5. Diaz: Adult learners of Spanish in Barcelona.
6. Dresden: German 9-year-olds learning English, French, and Czech.
7. Eppler: Austrian Jews who had emigrated to London before World War II, speaking German and English in informal conversations.
8. ESF: The large European Science Foundation study of guest workers in 10 bilingual configurations.
9. FLLOC: Classroom learners of French in England.
10. Hatzidaki: Greek-French bilinguals in Paris.
11. Køge: Danish-Turkish adolescent bilinguals.
12. Langman: Chinese-Hungarian bilinguals.
13. PAROLE: Young adult learners of English, French, and Italian.
14. Qatar: Spoken interviews with Qatari learners of English.
15. Reading: Oral interviews of English school children learning French.
16. SPLLOC: Classroom learners of Spanish in England.
17. TCD: Adolescent learners of French in Paris.

Several new corpora are being added each year to the databases on both childhood and adult bilingualism.

See also: code-switching, corpus analysis, error analysis, European Science Foundation (ESF) project, measuring and researching SLA, qualitative research

References

http://talkbank.org
http://childes.psy.cmu.edu

Target-Like-Use (TLU) Analysis

Teresa Pica
University of Pennsylvania

Target-Like-Use (TLU) Analysis is an approach to examining interlanguage data that includes (1) coding and quantifying the data with respect to correspondence between inflectional morphemes and functors in the data and their standard L2 counterparts, and (2) calculating a percentage score that takes into account linguistic contexts in the data where their suppliance is required (aka obligatory) and linguistic contexts in the data where suppliance occurs, but is not required.

TLU Analysis was introduced by Pica (1983), as an extension of Suppliance in Obligatory Context (SOC) Analysis. Whereas SOC Analysis determines the percentage score of particular morphemes and functors solely on the basis of their accurate suppliance in required contexts, TLU Analysis further reduces the percentage score each time these morphemes and functors are supplied in non-required contexts.

TLU (and SOC) Analyses are typically applied to inflectional morphemes and functors that characterize the "Natural Order" of second language acquisition (Krashen, 1976), and first language acquisition (Brown, Cazden, and Bellugi, 1973). These include: English progressive *–ing*, plural *–s*, copula, articles, personal pronouns, prepositions, progressive *aux*, regular and irregular past, possessive *–s*, and third person singular *–s*.

To compute TLU, researchers take the following steps:

1 Identify linguistic contexts that require suppliance of a specific inflectional morpheme or functor, for example, noun plural *–s*. Use structural, semantic, and discourse clues, for example, speakers' use of numerals or pre-modifiers such as "a few," or "many," in referring to several items, or interlocutors' questions that refer to these items. Disregard contexts where suppliance is ambiguous, for example, "the book."
2 Calculate the total number of required contexts identified in Step 1. Make that number the first of a two-part denominator that will be used to obtain the TLU percentage score. Do not count ambiguous contexts, for example, those lacking contextual clues.
3 Determine if the morpheme or functor was supplied in these required contexts.
4 Calculate the total number of correctly supplied morphemes and functcrs. Make that number the numerator of the TLU percentage score.
5 Identify linguistic contexts in which the morpheme or functor was supplied, but was not required, for example, "*the childrens," "*one books."
6 Calculate the total number of non-required contexts identified in Step 5. Make that number second part of the denominator of the TLU percentage score.
7 Calculate the sum of the two parts of the denominator.
8 Divide the denominator into the numerator. The quotient is the TLU percentage score.

Example: TLU Analysis/English noun plural *–s*:

"I have three sons. Two are doctor. One is a teachers. We live in different city but not far. They visit my home two days a week and stay for few hour." (See Table)

Table 14 A TLU Analysis of English noun plural *-s*

Context	*N*	*Items*
Required contexts for noun plural *–s* suppliance:	4	three sons two are doctor two days *few *hour
Required contexts with suppliance	2	three sons *two days
Non- required contexts with suppliance:	1	*one is a teachers
Ambiguous contexts for suppliance:	1	different city

TLU Computation:
2 suppliance/4 required contexts +1 non-required context = 2/5 = 40% TLU

See also: error analysis, inflectional morphemes, grammatical encoding, morpheme acquisition orders, units for analyzing L2 speaking, units for analyzing L2 writing

References

Brown, R., Cazden, C. and Bellugi, U. (1973). The Child's Grammar from I to III. In C. Ferguson and D. Slobin (eds), *Studies of Child Language Development*. New York: Holt Rinehart and Winston.

Krashen, S. (1976). Formal and Informal Linguistic Environments in Language Learning and Language Acquisition. *TESOL Quarterly*, 157–68.

Pica, T. (1983). Methods of Morpheme Quantification and their Effect on the Interpretation of Second Language Data. *Studies in Second Language Acquisition*, *6*, 69–78.

Task-based language teaching and learning

Kris Van den Branden
Katholieke Universiteit Leuven

Task-based language teaching (TBLT) starts from the basic premise that most second and foreign language learners aim to acquire a new language to use it for functional purposes. In TBLT, the term "task" first of all refers to the numerous things that people aim to do to reach goals that are relevant to their personal lives, and which involve (or even necessitate) the use of language (Van den Branden, Bygate and Norris, 2009). To develop functional language proficiency, learners will need to be given ample opportunity to try and perform the tasks that are relevant to their learning needs. So, rather than first having to learn a language explicitly in order to use it later, language learners learn language while using it.

Task-based language teaching, then, aims to engage students in authentic (or semi-authentic) acts of communication in the classroom. Being holistic and functional in nature, tasks are constructed in such a way as to create wide potential for learners to be presented with authentic stretches of natural discourse, relevant chunks and formulas, and thus to cater for exemplar-based learning that underlies spontaneous language use. Rather than focusing on the explicit, discrete knowledge of specific aspects of language in isolation, and building up proficiency in an incremental, step-by-step fashion, task-based work aims to feed the learner's internal syllabus while engaging the learner in holistic communicative use of language.

To launch the learner into action, tasks will preferably be interesting and motivating for their own sake, and include strong stimuli for learners to engage in genuine social interaction. Such stimuli may be provided by reasoning or information gaps that students can close by communicating, the challenge of working towards a well-defined outcome, the selection of highly interesting topics and methodological formats stimulating joint problem-solving, negotiating and lively discussion (Bygate, Skehan, and Swain, 2001; Ellis, 2003; Norris, 2009; Samuda and Bygate, 2008). The extent to which the learner is interactionally supported while trying to comprehend task-related input and producing output, is of paramount importance. In this respect, task-based classroom work has been claimed to result in rich learning opportunities if students are provided with rich positive evidence of language in use, and with opportunities to negotiate about the meaning of the input. Such task-based interaction pushes learners to produce more adequate output and offers them chances to incorporate implicit negative feedback, for example, in the form of recasts, into their interlanguage system (Swain, 1995; Mackey, 2007). In the end, not the task in itself, but the richness of the interaction to which it gives rise, and the extent to which interactional support can dynamically enrich the learner's interlanguage development, will determine the impact of task-based classroom work on language learning.

As mentioned above, TBLT syllabuses will often be targeted towards the needs of specific groups of language learners. Through needs analyses, syllabus designers aim to identify the tasks specific groups of language learners need or want to be able to perform in their personal, professional or societal lives, and fine-tune the development of classroom tasks to the results of those analyses (Long, 2005). TBLT syllabuses, then, basically consist of a collection of tasks that are increasingly complex approximations of the target tasks that are relevant to the students' needs.

There are quite a number of challenges that a task-based approach will need to deal with, some of which have been formulated as criticisms. First, there have been claims that TBLT is not appropriate as the foundation for classrooms of beginners, because the latter allegedly need to acquire basic vocabulary and grammar rules first before they can start using the kind of language task performance requires. Second, if the predetermined order of grammar-based syllabuses is given up, TBLT syllabus designers will need to devise an alternative framework for sequencing tasks and gradually raise the complexity of tasks in a balanced and structured way that does not violate students' inner syllabuses. Third, there have been criticisms, mainly based on the results of studies into immersion education, that students may develop high levels of receptive skills and become highly proficient in conveying their meaning intentions, yet fail to acquire sophisticated levels of accuracy. Finally, a task-based syllabus will need to include a suitable approach to testing and assessment. We will deal with these challenges in the sections below.

Tasks for beginners ... and beyond

Most of the examples that are provided in research articles and pedagogical literature to illustrate the concept of "task" in a task-based syllabus are of the jigsaw, information gap or opinion exchange kind: students are required to exchange information (e.g. route instructions, descriptions of cartoons or pictures) or discuss various alternatives to solve a challenging problem. As illustrative of the basic principles of TBLT as these prototypical examples may be, they do raise the impression that TBLT is typically geared at students who have already reached advanced stages of language development, and the performance of tasks systematically requires the production of relatively complex output. Tasks, however, can equally address the language learning needs of beginners. On the one hand, in the beginning stages, listening and reading tasks, in which the input is made comprehensible by use of visualization, accompanying actions or high levels of contextualization will be predominant. In task-based second language classrooms, for instance, beginners may quickly pick up chunks, basic expressions and structures while trying to understand instructions for (and the language use accompanying) play, chores, handiwork, and the performance of tricks and scientific experiments. On the other hand, output demands will be relatively low in beginner tasks, and interactional support accompanying student speech relatively high.

In the above, the main parameters for describing tasks at the beginner end of the learning continuum refer to (a) the context-embeddedness of task performance (tasks typically being situated in the here-and-now and in a physical context that provides many clues for the comprehension of input); (b) the learner's familiarity with the topic that is being discussed; (c) the linguistic complexity of vocabulary and syntax (highly frequent vocabulary and simple syntactic constructions predominating); (d) the level of interactional support that is being offered. Congruent with the fact that task performance requires the establishment of form-function relationships in view of reaching real-life goals in a particular social setting, lists of parameters aiming to determine task complexity should not be restricted to linguistic aspects of the language involved, but also relate to contextual and social features of the communication situation, the reasoning demands task performance requires, the multi-dimensionality of the goals that need to be reached, and the kind and range of topics that need to be covered (for examples of such frameworks, see Duran and Ramaut, 2006; Robinson's Cognition Hypothesis, 2011).

Through the separate or combined manipulation of these parameters, tasks in a syllabus should be sequenced in a way to increasingly approximate the performance of real-world tasks, while also gradually extending the range of tasks that the learner will be able to perform, and stepping up the levels of accuracy, adequacy, fluency, and complexity of the language that these tasks involve. Evidently, the above-mentioned parameters can also be manipulated by teachers while engaging with tasks in the classroom. In fact, the teachers' dynamic manipulation of these parameters in response to the students' successes and failures to cope with the demands of challenging tasks will strongly determine the degree to which the syllabus developer's preparatory work can maximally pay off in terms of creating optimal learning opportunities for individual learners, or groups of learners (Van den Branden, 2006, 2009).

Focus on form

Task-based classroom activity starts from, and builds upon, students' attempt to develop communicative behavior. This, however, does not mean that TBLT should be equated with a "meaning-only" approach. As a matter of fact, during task-based work students will often run into comprehension problems and find themselves unable to express their meaning intention in adequate or accurate terms. Equally, while performing tasks, students may notice a gap in their current interlanguage knowledge, or notice a difference between their written output and the written input, or between their verbalization of a certain meaning intention and their interlocutor's. These are moments that have been singled out in the TBL-related literature as being particularly fit for paying attention to form (Long and Robinson, 1998; Norris and Ortega, 2000). Focus on form in TBLT, then, is typically reactive (responding to learners' requests, signals, and problems), and functional (meaning that the focus on form should not entirely destroy the natural flow of communication and that forms which are particularly relevant for the performance of the task have stronger appeal to be explicitly discussed than forms that are of marginal importance for task performance). Furthermore, focus on form in TBLT is not associated with immediate mastery and perfect reproduction; as with other aspects of language development, the acquisition of formal aspects of the target language system will need repeated exposure and practice, and sufficient amounts of recycling for true incorporation of new forms in the interlanguage system to take shape.

Paying attention to formal linguistic features in a task-embedded way may increase the chance that students will find the explicit form-focus relevant to their personal needs, and will also be able to link explicit knowledge to actual exemplars of language use (and thus associate form with meaning and function). In this way, the effectiveness and efficiency of language teaching may be strongly enhanced. As such, task-based language teaching has been claimed to harness the benefits of a focus on meaning while simultaneously, through use of focus on form (not forms), to deal with its known shortcomings, particularly rate of development and incompleteness where grammatical accuracy is concerned (Long and Norris, 2000).

Task-based assessment

In TBLT, tasks are used not only as a basic unit for the description of goals and for the organization of educational activity in the classroom, but also for the assessment of students' language skills and the progress they are making. For assessment purposes as much as for teaching purposes, a task-based approach focuses on what learners are able to do with the language (Norris, 2009). Using a wide variety of instruments and procedures (that range far beyond the mere use of tests, and also include observations of tasks-in-action, portfolios, peer and self-assessment procedures), learners will be invited to perform tasks that generate authentic language use and strongly resemble the kinds of tasks that students are expected to perform outside the classroom. As such, task-based syllabi are characterized by a strong coherence with regard to the selection of target tasks (goals), classroom tasks (education), and assessment tasks (evaluation).

The students' performances of these tasks will preferably be rated according to the criteria that reflect the norms of task accomplishment in the target discourse communities (Norris, Brown, Hudson and Bonk, 2002). The rating thus primarily focuses on the extent to which the student can perform tasks to criterion as established by insiders or experts in the field, rather than on the students' ability to complete discrete-point grammar items. For productive tests, assessment grids accompany the assessment tasks, carefully describing what items are required to meet the preset quality standards, and what formal demands need to be met.

Assessment directly feeds back into educational activity. Assessment not only informs the students about the progress they have made or the current interlanguage level they have acquired, but also provides teachers and school administrators with rich information about the effectiveness of the educational support they have offered to individual learners, and the gaps in the students' current interlanguage system that require more intensive treatment. As such, in task-based language teaching, evaluation and interactional support are inextricably entwined: observing learners while they are performing tasks, exploring the problems they encounter when trying to meet task demands, and dynamically supporting them in ways that do not deprive the student of the chance to take an active role in coping with the challenge raised by the task, will richly inform the teacher about the current state of learners' target language development, and guide the teacher into fine-tuning interactional support to the learners' needs and internal syllabus.

Conclusions

In task-based language education, "task" is the basic unit of analysis at the levels of the goals and objectives of a syllabus, the classroom activities that are organized to enhance language development, and the assessment practices aimed to gather information (and take decisions) about the learner's progress and the most optimal ways of further promoting it. Over the past 15 years, empirical research underpinning the basic tenets of TBLT has been accumulating. Yet one of the major challenges TBLT faces today has to do with implementing this promising approach in mainstream classrooms. In addition to the development of task-based curricula and coursebooks, and the development of task-based assessment instruments, what seems to be needed to stimulate the implementation of TBLT are coherent and intensive training and coaching programmes that will allow teachers (and teacher trainers) to build up the confidence, beliefs, and skills to stimulate the experiential, learning-by-doing, and learning-by-interacting approach to classroom learning that TBLT seeks to enhance, and to interactionally support learners in a way that is consistent with their learning needs.

See also: classroom interaction research, Focus on Form (FonF), form-meaning relations, instructed SLA, Interaction and the Interaction Hypothesis, language testing and SLA

References

Bygate, M., Skehan, P. and Swain, M. (eds) (nd). *Researching Pedagogic Tasks: Second Language Learning and Testing*, pp. 23–48. Harlow: Longman.

Ellis, R. (2003). *Task-Based Language Learning and Teaching*. Oxford: Oxford University Press.

Long, M. (2005). *Second Language Needs Analysis*. Cambridge: Cambridge University Press.

Long, M. and Robinson, P. (1998). Focus on Form: Theory, research and practice. In C. Doughty and J. Williams, (eds), *Focus on Form in Classroom Second Language Acquisition*, pp. 15–41. New York: Cambridge University Press.

Mackey, A. (ed.) (2007). *Conversational interaction in SLA*. Oxford: Oxford Unversity Press.

Norris, J. (2009). Task-based teaching and testing. In M. Long and C. Doughty (eds), *The Handbook of Language Teaching*. Cambridge: Blackwell.

Norris, J. and Ortega, L. (2000). Effectiveness of L2 instruction: a research synthesis and quantitative meta-analysis. *Language Learning, 50*, 417–528.

Norris, J., Brown, J., Hudson, T. and Bonk,W. (2002). Examinee abilities and task difficulty in a task-based second language performance assessment. *Language Testing, 19*, 395–418.

Robinson, P. (ed.) (2011). *Second Language Task complexity. Researching the Cognition Hypothesis of Language Learning and Performance*. Amsterdam: John Benjamins.

Samuda, V. and Bygate, M. (2008). *Tasks in Second Language Learning*. Basingstoke: Palgrave MacMillan.

Swain, M., (1995). Three functions of output in second language learning. In G. Cook and B. Seidlhofer (eds), *Principle and Practice in Applied Linguistics: Studies in Honour of H.G. Widdowson*, pp. 125–44. Oxford: Oxford University Press.

Van den Branden, K. (ed.) (2006). *Task-Based Language Teaching: From Theory to Practice*. Cambridge: Cambridge University Press.

Van den Branden, K. (2009). Mediating between predetermined order and chaos: The role of the teacher in task-based language education. *International Journal of Applied Linguistics, 19*/3, 264–85.

Van den Branden, K, Bygate, M. and Norris, J. (2009). Task-based language teaching: introducing the reader. In K. Van den Branden, M. Bygate, and J. Norris (eds), *Task-Based Language Teaching: A Reader*, pp. 1–13. Amsterdam: John Benjamins Publishing.

Teacher talk

Roy Lyster
McGill University

Teacher talk is the speech used by teachers to enhance and structure classroom discourse in ways that facilitate language learning. Although considerable variability in teacher talk can be found across instructional settings in accordance with program type and objectives as well as cultural norms, common across most contexts is that teacher talk usually exceeds student talk in terms of quantity and yet still plays a pivotal role in determining the overall quality of classroom discourse. Of concern here are two variable aspects of teacher talk with potential to contribute to second and foreign language development across a range of instructional settings: teacher input and teacher scaffolding.

Teacher input

For learners to notice target features in the input in order to process them as intake (a crucial first step in second language learning; see Schmidt, 1990), instructional input can be enhanced through teacher talk. For example, teachers are known to modify their speech by emphasizing key words or phrases and by using cognates, restricted vocabulary, and shorter phrases, and also by speaking more slowly, at least with beginners. Redundancy permeates teacher talk in the form of discourse modifications such as self-repetition, modeling, and paraphrase, as well as multiple examples, definitions, and synonyms. Teachers also rely extensively on body language, including gestures and facial expressions.

Emphasizing comprehension in this way enables learners to benefit from comprehensible input, which contains structures that are a bit beyond their current abilities yet made accessible through pragmatic and situational cues. Krashen (1985) claimed that, when input is understood in this way, information about second language syntax is automatically available to the learner and acquisition occurs. Teacher talk consisting of language just ahead of learners' current level of ability, rather than only language they already know, is still considered essential to effective language instruction. There is now a consensus, however, that comprehensible input engages comprehension strategies that enable students to process language semantically but not necessarily syntactically, allowing them to bypass structural information otherwise essential for continued second language development. In addition, even in content-based classrooms presumed to be input-rich because of their focus on subject-matter content, teacher talk has proven restricted in the range of language forms and functions it contains (Swain, 1988). On its own, therefore, teacher talk does not provide sufficiently varied input to ensure continued language development and is most effectively delivered in contexts of interaction and in ways that complement the current focus of instruction.

Teacher scaffolding

Scaffolding is what "enables a child or novice to solve a problem, carry out a task or achieve a goal which would be beyond his unassisted efforts" (Wood, Bruner, and Ross, 1976, p. 90). The scaffolding of verbal exchanges is a helpful metaphor for understanding the central role played by teacher talk replete with questions and feedback designed to support language learning while fostering students' engagement in a language they know only partially.

In their seminal study of classroom discourse, Sinclair and Coulthard (1975) found that the most typical teaching exchange consists of an initiating (I) move by the teacher, a responding (R) move by the student, and a follow-up (F) move by the teacher. The IRF sequence has been criticized for engaging students only minimally and for maintaining unequal power relationships between teachers and students, yet continues to permeate classroom discourse. Mercer (1999) suggested that teachers' reliance on IRF sequences and frequent questions serves to monitor students' knowledge and understanding. By assessing their students in an ongoing manner in the course of interaction, teachers are better equipped to plan and evaluate their teaching.

Teachers' initiating moves in the IRF exchange are usually epistemic questions considered to be either display questions (to which the teacher knows the answer) or referential questions (to which the teacher does not know the answer). Referential questions can be either open (with many possible answers) or closed (with only one possible answer). Display questions are generally thought to limit the students' possibilities to try out their own ideas, but teachers have been observed using both display and referential questions with equal effectiveness (Haneda, 2005). This is partly because, as the focus of instruction moves toward substantive content other than language itself and away from language rehearsal, it becomes less feasible for teachers to ask only questions to which they do not know the answers.

Arguably more important than the teacher's initial question in the IRF exchange is the teacher's choice of follow-up move and the extent to which it allows the teacher to work with the student's response in a variety of ways. Nassaji and Wells (2000) found that IRF exchanges beginning with a display question "can develop into more equal dialogue if, in the follow-up move, the teacher avoids evaluation and instead requests justifications, connections or counter-arguments and allows students to self-select in making their contributions" (pp. 400–401; see also Haneda, 2005). As they work dialogically with students in this way, teachers need also to give students appropriate "wait time" to interpret questions and formulate responses.

In addition to various questioning techniques, teacher follow-up moves include a range of corrective feedback types involving negotiation of both meaning and form. Negotiation for meaning includes semantically contingent responses such as recasts, repetition, and expansions, as well as conversational modifications such as confirmation checks, comprehension checks, and clarification requests (Long, 1996). Negotiation for meaning aims primarily to achieve comprehensibility of message meaning and is especially useful in teacher-student interaction if used mutually by teacher and students alike to request clarification and confirmation. Because experienced teachers are often able to understand their students in spite of non-target forms, however, they need to promote more than just mutual comprehension and also to negotiate form with students by using various elicitation moves and metalinguistic clues to prompt them to self-repair as a means to develop more accurate representations of the target language. Research is increasingly suggesting that teacher talk that incorporates a range of corrective feedback types in contexts of communicative interaction contributes significantly to second language development (Lyster and Saito, 2010).

See also: classroom interaction research, corrective feedback, input enhancement, negotiation of meaning, noticing hypothesis, scaffolding

References

Haneda, M. (2005). Functions of triadic dialogue in the classroom: Examples for L2 research. *The Canadian Modern Language Review*, *62*, 313–33.

Krashen, S. (1985). *The Input Hypothesis: Issues and Implications*. London: Longman.

Long, M. (1996). The role of the linguistic environment in second language acquisition. In W. C. Ritchie and T.K. Bhatia (eds), *Handbook of Second Language Acquisition*, pp. 413–68. San Diego, CA: Academic Press.

Lyster, R. and Saito, K. (2010). Oral feedback in classroom SLA: A meta-analysis. *Studies in Second Language Acquisition*, *32*, 265–302.

Mercer, N. (1999). Classroom language. In B. Spolsky (ed.), *Concise Encyclopedia of Educational Linguistics*, pp. 315–19. Oxford: Pergamon.

Nassaji, H. and Wells, G. (2000). What's the use of 'triadic dialogue'?: An investigation of teacher-student interaction. *Applied Linguistics, 21*, 376–406.

Schmidt, R. (1990). The role of consciousness in second language learning. *Applied Linguistics*, *11*, 129–158.

Sinclair, J. and Coulthard, R.M. (1975). *Towards an analysis of discourse: The English used by teachers and pupils*. Oxford: Oxford University Press.

Swain, M. (1988). Manipulating and complementing content teaching to maximize second language learning. *TESL Canada Journal*, *6*, 68–83.

Wood, D., Bruner, J. and Ross, G. (1976). The role of tutoring in problem solving. *Journal of Child Psychology and Psychiatry*, *17*, 89–100.

Theoretical constructs in SLA

Geoff Jordan
Leicester University

Theoretical constructs in SLA include such terms as interlanguage, variable competence, motivation, and noticing. These constructs are used in the service of theories which attempt to explain phenomena, and thus, in order to understand how the term "theoretical construct" is used in SLA, we must first understand the terms "theory" and "phenomena."

A theory is an attempt to provide an explanation to a question, usually a "Why" or "How" question. The Critical Period hypothesis (Lenneberg,1967; see Birdsong, 1999, for an appraisal) attempts to answer the question "Why do most L2 learners not achieve native-like competence?" Processability Theory (Pienemann, 1998) attempts to answer the question "How do L2 learners go through stages of development?" In posing the question that a theory seeks to answer, we refer to phenomena: the things that we isolate, define, and then attempt to explain in our theory. In the case of theories of SLA, key phenomena include transfer, staged development, systemacity, variability and incompleteness (see Towell and Hawkins, 1994: 15).

A clear distinction must be made between phenomena and observational data. Theories attempt to explain phenomena, and observational data are used to support and test those theories. The important difference between data and phenomena is that the phenomena are what we want to explain, and thus, they are seen as the result of the interaction between some manageably small number of causal factors, instances of which can be found in different situations. By contrast, any type of causal factor can play a part in the production of data, and the characteristics of these data depend on the peculiarities of the experimental design, or data-gathering procedures, employed. As Bogen and Woodward put it:

> Data are idiosyncratic to particular experimental contexts, and typically cannot occur outside those contexts, whereas phenomena have stable, repeatable characteristics which will be detectable by means of different procedures, which may yield quite different kinds of data.
>
> (Bogen and Woodward, 1988: 317)

A failure to appreciate this distinction often leads to poorly defined theoretical constructs, as we shall see below.

While researchers in some fields deal with such observable phenomena as bones, tides, and sun spots, others deal with non-observable phenomena such as love, genes, hallucinations, gravity, and language competence. Non-observable phenomena have to be studied indirectly, which is where theoretical constructs come in. First we name the non-observable phenomena, we give them labels and then we make constructs. With regard to the non-observable phenomena listed above (love, genes, hallucinations, gravity, and language competence), examples of constructs are romantic love, hereditary genes, schizophrenia, the bends, and the Language Acquisition Device. Thus, theoretical constructs are one remove from the original labeling, and they are, as their name implies, packed full of theory; they are, that is, proto-typical theories in themselves, a further invention of ours, an invention made in our attempt to pin down the non-observable phenomena that we want to examine so that the theories which they embody can be scrutinized. It should also be noted that there is a certain ambiguity in the terms "theoretical construct" and "phenomenon." The "two-step" process of naming a phenomenon and then a construct outlined above is not always so clear: for Chomsky (1986), "linguistic competence" is the phenomenon he wants to explain; to many it has all the hallmarks of a theoretical construct.

Constructs are not the same as definitions. While a definition attempts to clearly distinguish the thing defined from everything else, a construct attempts to lay the ground for an explanation. Thus, for example, while a dictionary defines motivation in such a way that motivation is distinguishable from desire or compulsion, Gardener (1985) attempts to explain why some learners do better than others, and he uses the construct of motivation to do so, in such a way that his construct takes on its own meaning, and allows others in the field to test the claims he makes (see **Motivation**, this volume). A construct defines something in a special way: it is a term used in an attempt to solve a problem, indeed, it is often a term that in itself suggests the answer to the problem. Constructs can be everyday parlance (like "noticing" and "competence") and they can also be new words (like "interlanguage"), but, in all cases, constructs are "theory-laden" to the maximum: their job is to support a hypothesis, or, better still, a full-blown theory. In short, then, the job of a construct is to help define and then solve a problem.

Criteria for assessing constructs used in theories of SLA

There is a lively debate among scholars about the best way to study and understand the various phenomena associated with SLA. Those in the rationalist camp insist that an external world exists independently of our perceptions of it, and that it is possible to study different phenomena in this world, to make meaningful statements about them, and to improve our knowledge of them by appeal to logic and empirical observation. Those in the relativist camp claim that there are a multiplicity of realities, all of which are social constructs. Science, for the relativists, is just one type of social construction, a particular kind of language game which has no more claim to objective truth than any other. This article rejects the relativist view and, based largely on Popper's "Critical Rationalist" approach (Popper, 1972), takes the view that the various current theories of SLA, and the theoretical constructs embedded in them, are not all equally valid, but rather, that they can be critically assessed by using the following criteria (adapted from Jordan, 2004):

1. **Theories should be coherent, cohesive, expressed in the clearest possible terms, and consistent.** There should be no internal contradictions in theories, and no circularity due to badly defined terms.
2. **Theories should have empirical content.** Having empirical content means that the propositions and hypotheses proposed in a theory should be expressed in such a way that they are capable of being subjected to tests, based on evidence observable by the senses, which support or refute them. These tests should be capable of replication, as a way of ensuring the empirical nature of the evidence and the validity of the research methods employed. For example, the claim "Students hate maths because maths is difficult" has empirical content only when the terms "students." "maths," "hate," and "difficult" are defined in such a way that the claim can be tested by appeal to observable facts. The operational definition of terms, and crucially, of theoretical constructs, is the best way of ensuring that hypotheses and theories have empirical content.
3. **Theories should be fruitful.** "Fruitful" in Kuhn's sense (see Kuhn, 1962: 148): they should make daring and surprising predictions, and solve persistent problems in their domain.

Note that the theory-laden nature of constructs is no argument for a relativist approach: we invent constructs, as we invent theories, but we invent them, precisely, in a way that allows them to be subjected to empirical tests. The constructs can be anything we like: in order to explain a given problem, we are free to make any claim we like, in any terms we choose, but the litmus test is the clarity and testability of these claims and the terms we use to make them. Given its pivotal status, a theoretical construct should be stated in such a way that we all know unequivocally what is being talked about, and it should be defined in such a way that it lays itself open to principled investigation, empirical and otherwise. In the rest of this article, a number of theoretical constructs will be examined and evaluated in terms of the criteria outlined above.

Krashen's Monitor Model

The Monitor Model (see Krashen, 1985) is described elsewhere (see **Monitor Model**, this volume), so let us here concentrate on the deficiencies of the theoretical constructs employed. In brief, Krashen's constructs fail to meet the requirements of the first two criteria listed above: Krashen's use of key theoretical constructs such as "acquisition and learning," and "subconscious and conscious" is vague, confusing, and, not always consistent. Furthermore, in conflict with the second criterion listed above, there is no way of subjecting the set of hypotheses that Krashen proposes to empirical tests. The Acquisition-Learning hypothesis simply asserts that two distinct systems exist, but gives no means of determining whether they are, or are not, separate. Similarly, there is no way of testing the Monitor hypothesis: since the Monitor is nowhere properly defined as an operational construct, there is no way to determine whether the Monitor is in operation or not, and it is thus impossible to determine the validity of the extremely strong claims made for it. The Input Hypothesis is equally mysterious and incapable of being tested: the levels of knowledge are nowhere defined and so it is impossible to know whether $i + 1$ is present in input, and, if it is, whether or not the learner moves on to the next level as a result. Thus, the first three hypotheses (Acquisition-Learning, the Monitor, and Natural Order) make up a circular and vacuous argument: the Monitor accounts for discrepancies in the natural order, the learning-acquisition distinction justifies the use of the Monitor, and so on.

In summary, Krashen's key theoretical constructs are ill-defined, and circular, so that the set is incoherent. This incoherence means that Krashen's theory has such serious faults that it is not really a theory at all. While Krashen's work may be seen as satisfying the third criterion on our list, and while it is extremely popular among EFL/ESL teachers (even among those who, in their daily practice, ignore Krashen's clear implication that grammar teaching is largely a waste of time), the fact remains that his series of hypotheses are built on sand.

Schmidt's Noticing Hypothesis

Schmidt's Noticing Hypothesis (see Schmidt, 1990) is described elsewhere (see **Noticing Hypothesis**, this volume). Essentially, Schmidt attempts to do away with the "terminological vagueness" of the term "consciousness" by examining three senses of the term: consciousness as awareness, consciousness as intention, and consciousness as knowledge. Consciousness and awareness are often equated, but Schmidt distinguishes between three levels: Perception, Noticing, and Understanding. The second level, Noticing, is the key to Schmidt's eventual hypothesis. The importance of Schmidt's work is that it clarifies the confusion surrounding the use of many terms used in psycholinguistics (not least Krashen's "acquisition/learning" dichotomy) and, furthermore, it develops one crucial part of a general processing theory of the development of interlanguage grammar.

Our second evaluation criterion requires that theoretical constructs are defined in such a way as to ensure that hypotheses have empirical content, and thus we must ask: what does Schmidt's concept of noticing refer to exactly, and how can we be sure when it is, and is not, being used by L2 learners? In his 1990 paper, Schmidt claims that noticing can be operationally defined as "the availability for verbal report," "subject to various conditions," He adds that these conditions are discussed at length in the verbal report literature, but he does not discuss the issue of operationalization any further. Schmidt's 2001 paper gives various sources of evidence of noticing, and points out their limitations. These sources include learner production (but how do we identify what has been noticed?), learner reports in diaries (but diaries span months, while cognitive processing of L2 input takes place in seconds and making diaries requires not just noticing but also reflexive self-awareness), and think-aloud protocols (but we cannot assume that the protocols identify *all* the examples of target features that were noticed) (see **Protocol analysis**, this volume).

Schmidt argues that the best test of noticing is that proposed by Cheesman and Merikle (1986), who distinguish between the objective and subjective thresholds of perception. The clearest evidence that something has exceeded the subjective threshold and been noticed is a concurrent verbal report, since nothing can be verbally reported other than the current contents of awareness. Schmidt adds that "after the fact recall" is also good evidence that something was noticed, providing that prior knowledge and guessing can be controlled.

For example, if beginner level students of Spanish are presented with a series of Spanish utterances containing unfamiliar verb forms, and are then asked to recall immediately afterwards the forms that occurred in each utterance, and can do so, that is good evidence that they noticed them. On the other hand, it is not safe to assume that failure to do so means that they did not notice. It seems that it is easier to confirm that a particular form has *not* been noticed than that it has: failure to achieve above-chance performance in a forced-choice recognition test is a much better indication that the subjective threshold has not been exceeded and that noticing did not take place.

Schmidt goes on to claim that the noticing hypothesis could be falsified by demonstrating the existence of subliminal learning, either by showing positive priming of unattended and unnoticed novel stimuli, or by showing learning in dual task studies in which central processing capacity is exhausted by the primary task. The problem in this case is that, in positive priming studies, one can never really be sure that subjects did not allocate any attention to what they could not later report, and similarly, in dual task experiments, one cannot be sure that *no* attention is devoted to the secondary task (see **Attention**, and **Awareness**, this volume).

In conclusion, it seems that Schmidt's noticing hypothesis rests on a construct that still has difficulty measuring up to the second criteria of our list; it is by no means easy to properly identify when noticing has and has not occurred. Despite this limitation, however, Schmidt's hypothesis is still a good example of the type of approach recommended by the list. Its strongest virtues are its rigour and its fruitfulness; Schmidt argues that attention as a psychological construct refers to a variety of mechanisms or subsystems (including alertness, orientation, detection within selective attention, facilitation, and inhibition) which control information processing and behaviour when existing skills and routines are inadequate. Hence, learning in the sense of establishing new or modified knowledge, memory, skills and routines is "largely, perhaps exclusively a side effect of attended processing" (Schmidt, 2001: 25). This is a daring and surprising claim, with similar predictive ability, and it contradicts Krashen's claim that conscious learning is of extremely limited use.

Variationist approaches

An account of these approaches is given elsewhere (see **Variationist approaches to SLA**, this volume). In brief, variable competence, or variationist, approaches, use the key theoretical construct of "variable competence," or, as Tarone calls it, "capability." Tarone (1988) argues that "capability" underlies performance, and that this capability consists of heterogeneous "knowledge" which varies according to different factors. Thus, there is no homogenous competence underlying performance but a variable "capacity" that underlies specific instances of language performance. Ellis (1987) uses the construct of "variable rules" to explain the observed variability of L2 learners' performance: by successively noticing forms in the input which are in conflict with the original representation of a grammatical rule learners acquire more and more versions of the original rule. This leads to either "free variation" where forms alternate in all environments at random, or "systematic variation," where one variant appears predictably in one linguistic context, and another variant in another context.

The root of the problem with the variable competence model is the weakness of its theoretical constructs. The underlying "variable competence" construct used by Tarone and Ellis is nowhere clearly defined, and is, in fact, simply asserted to "explain" a certain amount of learner behavior. As Gregg (1992: 368) argues, Tarone and Ellis offer a *description* of language use and behavior, which they confuse with an *explanation* of the acquisition of grammatical knowledge. By abandoning the idea of a homogenous underlying competence, Gregg says, we are stuck at the surface level of the performance data, and, consequently, any research project can only deal with the data in terms of the particular situation it encounters, describing the conditions under which the experiment took place. The positing of any variable rule at work would need to be followed up by an endless number of further research projects looking at different situations in which the rule is said to operate, each of which is condemned to uniqueness, no generalization about some underlying cause being possible.

At the center of the variable competence model are variable rules. Gregg argues cogently that such variability cannot become a theoretical construct used in attempts to explain how people acquire linguistic knowledge. In order to turn the idea of variable rules from an analytical tool into a theoretical construct, Tarone and Ellis would have to grant psychological reality to the variable rules (which in principle they seem to do, although no example of a variable rule is given) and then explain how these rules are internalized, so as to become part of the L2 learner's grammatical knowledge of the target language (which they fail to do). The variable competence model, according to Gregg, confuses descriptions of the varying use of forms with an explanation of the acquisition of linguistic knowledge. The forms (and their variations) which L2 learners produce are not, indeed cannot be, direct evidence of any underlying competence – or capacity. By erasing the distinction between competence and performance "the variabilist is committed to the unprincipled collection of an uncontrolled mass of data" (Gregg, 1990: 378).

As we have seen, a theory must explain phenomena, not describe data. In contradiction to this, and to criteria 1and 2 in our list, the arguments of Ellis and Tarone are confused and circular; in the end, what Ellis and Tarone are actually doing is gathering data without having properly formulated the problem they are trying to solve, that is, without having defined the phenomenon they wish to explain. Ellis claims that his theory constitutes an "ethnographic, descriptive" approach to SLA theory construction, but he does not answer the question: how does one go from studying the everyday rituals and practices of a particular group of second language learners through descriptions of their behavior to a theory that offers a general explanation for some identified phenomenon concerning the behavior of L2 learners?

Variable Competence theories exemplify what happens when the distinctions between phenomena, data, and theoretical constructs are confused. In contrast, Chomsky's UG theory, despite its shifting ground and its contentious connection to SLA, is probably the best example of a theory where these distinctions are crystal clear. For Chomsky, "competence" refers to underlying linguistic (grammatical) knowledge, and "performance" refers to the actual day to day use of language, which is influenced by an enormous variety of factors, including limitations of memory, stress, and tiredness. Chomsky argues that while performance data are important, they are not the object of study (they are, precisely, the data): linguistic competence is the phenomenon that he wants to examine (see **Generative linguistics**, and **Universal Grammar (UG) and SLA**, this volume). Chomsky's distinction between performance and competence exactly fits his theory of language and first language acquisition: competence is a well-defined phenomenon which is explained by appeal to the theoretical construct of the Language Acquisition Device. Chomsky describes the rules that make up linguistic competence and then invites other researchers to subject the theory that all languages obey these rules to further empirical tests.

Aptitude

Why is anybody good at anything? Well, they have an aptitude for it: they're "natural" piano players, or carpenters, or whatever. This is obviously no explanation at all, although, of course, it contains a beguiling element of truth. To say that SLA is (partly) explained by an aptitude for learning a second language is to beg the question: what is aptitude for SLA? Attempts to explain the role of aptitude in SLA illustrate the difficulty of "pinning down" the phenomenon that we seek to explain. If aptitude is to be claimed as a causal factor that helps to explain SLA, then aptitude must be defined in such a way that it can be identified in L2 learners and then related to their performance (see **Aptitude**, this volume).

The CANAL-F theory of foreign language aptitude, which grounds aptitude in "the triarchic theory of human intelligence," argues that "one of the central abilities required in FL acquisition is the ability to cope with novelty and ambiguity" (Grigorenko, Sternberg and Ehrman, 2000: 392).

But, however successfully the test might predict learner's ability, the theory fails to explain aptitude in any causal way. The theory of human intelligence that the CANAL-F theory is grounded in fails to illuminate the description given of FL ability; we do not get beyond a limiting of the domain in which the general ability to cope with novelty and ambiguity operates. The individual differences between foreign language learners' ability is explained by suggesting that some are better at coping with novelty and ambiguity than others. Thus, whatever construct validity might be claimed for CANAL-F, and however well the test might predict ability, it leaves the question of what precisely aptitude at foreign language learning is, and how it contributes to SLA, unanswered. There is an obvious circularity to the claim that those who score well on any test for aptitude for second language learning do better at second language learning than those who score badly. The question is: how can we step outside the reference of aptitude and establish more than a simple correlation between the construct and the phenomenon we are trying to explain?

Robinson (2007) comes to the rescue. Robinson uses aptitude as a construct that is composed of different cognitive abilities. His "Aptitude Complex Hypothesis" claims that different classroom settings draw on certain combinations of cognitive abilities, and that, depending on the classroom activities, students with certain cognitive abilities will do better than others. Robinson adds the "Ability Differentiation Hypothesis" which claims that some L2 learners have different abilities than others, and that it is important to match these learners to instructional conditions which favor their strengths in aptitude complexes. This is an admirable attempt to pin down aptitude, and the hypotheses are clear and testable. If we refine Robinson's construct (too much description destroys a construct) and take it further than the classroom context, then his hypotheses have the makings of a daring and fruitful theory of differential success in SLA, where "aptitude" is the key.

Conclusion

The history of science offers many examples of theories that began without any adequate description of what was being explained. Darwin's theory of evolution by natural selection (the young born to any species compete for survival, and those young that survive to reproduce tend to embody favorable natural variations which are passed on by heredity) lacked any formal description of the theoretical construct "variation," or any explanation of the origin of variations, or how they passed between generations. It was not until Mendel's theories and the birth of modern genetics in the early twentieth century that this deficiency was dealt with. But, and here is the point, dealt with it was: we now have constructs that pin down what "variation" refers to in the Darwinian theory, and the theory is stronger for them (i.e. more testable). Theories progress by defining their terms more clearly and by making their predictions more open to empirical testing.

Theoretical constructs lie at the heart of attempts to explain the phenomena of SLA. Observation must be in the service of theory: we do not start with data, we start with clearly defined phenomena and theoretical constructs that help us articulate the solution to a problem, and we then use empirical data to test that tentative solution. A rationalist methodology, which gives priority to the need for clarity, logic, and empirical content, offers the best possibility for making progress. Popper (1972) argues that progress is made in science by subjecting the logic and the evidence of theories to strict and empirical tests. In SLA, theories must use terms that are defined in such a way that it is possible to challenge their internal consistency, and the theories themselves must be stated in such a way that they are open to empirical tests. All those who attempt to explain SLA must pin down the slippery concepts they work with, convert these concepts into well-defined terms and theoretical constructs, and then offer us a testable theory.

See also: development in SLA, individual differences and SLA, instructed SLA, measuring and researching SLA, psycholinguistics of SLA, social and sociocultural approaches to SLA

References

Birdsong, D. (ed.) (1999). *Second Language Acquisition and the Critical Period Hypothesis*. Mahwah, NJ: Lawrence Erlbaum Associates.

Bogen, J. and Woodward, J. (1988). Saving the phenomena. *Philosophical Review*, *97*, 303–52.

Cheesman, J. and Merikle. P. M. (1986). Distinguishing conscious from unconscious perceptual processes. *Canadian Journal of Psychology*, *40*, 343–67.

Chomsky, N. (1986). *Knowledge of Language: Its Nature, Origin and Use*. New York: Prager.

Ellis, R. (1987). Interlanguage variability in narrative discourse: style-shifting in the use of the past tense. *Studies in Second Language Acquisition*, *9*, 1–20.

Gardner, R.C. (1985). *Social Psychology and Second Language Learning: The Role of Attitudes and Motivation*. London: Edward Arnold.

Gregg, K.R. (1990). The Variable Competence Model of second language acquisition and why it isn't. *Applied Linguistics*, *11*, 1, 364–83.

Grigorenko, E., Sternberg, R. and Ehrman, M. (2000). A theory-based approach to the measurement of foreign language learning ablity: The Canal-F theory and test. *The Modern Language Journal*, *84*, iii, 390–405.

Jordan, G. (2004). *Theory Construction in SLA*. Benjamins: Amsterdam.

Kuhn, T. (1962). *The Structure of Scientific Revolutions*. Chicago, IL: University of Chicago Press.

Krashen, S. (1985). *The Input Hypothesis: Issues and Implications*. New York: Longman.

Lenneberg, E.H. (1967). *Biological Foundations of Language*. New York: Wiley.

Pienemann, M. (1998). *Language Processing and Second Language Development: Processability Theory*. Amsterdam: John Benjamins.

Popper, K.R. (1972). *Objective Knowledge*. Oxford: Oxford University Press.

Robinson, P. (2007). Aptitudes, abilities, contexts and practice. In DeKeyser, R. (ed.), *Practice in Second Language Learning: Perspectives from Applied Linguistics and Cognitive Psychology*, pp. 256–87. Cambridge: Cambridge University Press.

Schmidt, R. (1990). The role of consciousness in second language learning. *Applied Linguistics*, *11*, 129–58.

——(2001). Attention. In Robinson, P. (ed.), *Cognition and Second Language Instruction*, pp. 3–32. Cambridge: Cambridge University Press.

Tarone, E. (1988). *Variation in Interlanguage*. London: Edward Arnold.

Towell, R. and Hawkins, R. (1994). *Approaches to Second Language Acquisition*. Clevedon: Multilingual Matters.

Further reading

Gregg, K. (2003). SLA theory: Construction and assessment. In Doughty, C. and Long, M. (eds), *The Handbook of Second Language Acquistion*, pp. 831–65. Malden, MA: Blackwell. (The foremost scholar in this area offers a lucid and eloquent discussion of the main issues.)

Gregg, K.R., Long, M.H., Jordan, G. and Beretta, A. (1997). Rationality and its discontents in SLA. *Applied Linguistics*, *18*, 4, 539–59. (The authors defend a rational approach to SLA research against the relativists.)

McLaughlin, B. (1987). *Theories of Second Language Learning*. London: Edward Arnold. (A good overview for beginners with an excellent introductory chapter.)

Mitchell, R. and Myles, F. (2004). *Second Language Learning Theories*. London: Arnold. (A more up-to-date introduction to the main theories of SLA.)

Thinking for speaking

Henriëtte Hendriks
University of Cambridge, RCEAL

Thinking for speaking is a term first used by the psycholinguist Dan Slobin to describe "The expression of experience in linguistic terms" (Slobin, 1991). According to Slobin (1991) thinking for speaking is a special form of thought that is mobilized for communication. It involves picking the characteristics of objects and events that 1) fit some conceptualization of the object or event and that 2) are readily encodable in the language one is speaking. Many a word has been written about the relation between language and thought. Can we think without language? Are our thoughts controlled by the language we speak? Questions of this type arise in areas in which it is evident that, although the issues one tries to communicate are similar across languages and cultures, the language-specific means available to talk about the issues can be very different.

Earlier linguistic studies, from the mid-nineteenth and early twentieth century, showed that, when taking a given event in the world outside us, the information regarding this event can be expressed by a myriad of different ways across different languages. They also showed that not all information is systematically expressed in every single language. Otherwise said, some languages tend to express one part of the semantic information, whereas other languages tend to express another part of it. Studying these phenomena in the very early days were von Humboldt (1836/1988) and Boas (1911), the latter studying diversity in American-Indian languages at the start of the twentieth century. He found that there is an important level of variation across languages in terms of what is obligatorily expressed (grammaticized information) versus what can be left out from a certain account of an event across languages. Lexicalization patterns across languages were also found to be very different.

> The diversity tells us that languages are not neutral coding systems of an objective reality. Rather, they are "a subjective orientation to the world of human experience, and this orientation affects the ways in which we think while we are speaking."
>
> (Slobin, 1991)

Given the linguistic diversity with respect to the expression of similar information, researchers tried to understand the influence such diversity might have on the world view of speakers of different languages. Von Humboldt, Sapir and Whorf all proposed different levels of influence of language on thought. In its strongest version, speakers are proposed to be "trapped" by their language, and confined to a particular world view that they cannot change as it is determined by the language they speak. In a less strong version, speakers are thought to merely be guided by their language to observe the world in different ways. Slobin's thinking for speaking is overall seen as a more moderate version of the Sapir-Whorf hypothesis.

Relevance for first language acquisition

If languages show a high level of diversity, and frequently express only part of the features of a full event or object, how do children learn what is expressed in their language and what is not expressed? The first language acquisition context is the one in which Dan Slobin first coined the expression "thinking for speaking." In the context of high linguistic relativity, he proposes that it is language itself that trains children to pay attention to certain aspects of an object or event only. Slobin is not claiming (as Sapir or Whorf might) that speakers have an essentially different experience of the world, but rather that they pay attention to different elements of an event as picked out by their language to be expressed. For example, when English and French native speakers observe a motion scene in which a girl cycles across the railroad tracks, both groups are likely to notice the fact that the girl is at one side of the tracks at time A, and at the other side of the tracks at time B (the path of motion). Moreover, they are likely to both notice that the girl is not walking but using a bike (manner of motion). However, when the English speaker organizes his thinking for speaking, he will have to focus on the manner of motion (cycling) as this information is systematically expressed in the verb in his language. Hence, it is awkward to talk about the event without mentioning the cycling. In contrast, when the French speaker organizes his thoughts for speaking, he needs to only focus on the path of motion, as in French speakers express the crossing event in the verb: "traverser" (to cross). Thus, whereas both speakers observe the same event, and can probably remember most facets of the event they observed, when talking about it, the English person is very likely to state that "the girl *cycled* [manner] *across* [path] the railroad tracks" whereas the French speaker is much more likely to say that the "girl crossed [path] the tracks." A mention of the manner of motion, in French, is optional and even more "complex" to achieve as the verb is already taken up by the path of motion. At the same time, however, Slobin very clearly states, as do all linguists, that although not all is said, all can be said in any given language.

The mystery to be solved in terms of acquisition is then: how do children know what aspects to focus on and express in their native language? The mystery is particularly intriguing given the fact that children have been shown to recognize situations in a target-like manner from a very young age onward (Bowerman and Choi, 2001; Choi and Bowerman 1991). Does this mean that children initially focus on all facets of events, and eliminate some aspects when learning their mother tongue? Slobin argues that this is not very likely, as children would have to pay attention to a multitude of facets, many of which are not systematically expressed across languages but only occasionally by a sub-group of languages. The only other explanation is that children learn the language simultaneously with the facets on which to focus.

Relevance for second language acquisition

Slobin's proposal that the training is carried out in childhood implies that it will, over time, become exceptionally resistant to restructuring. If this is indeed the case, then adult second language learners of an entirely differently structured L2 should have difficulty shaking off the thinking for speaking of their first language when acquiring a second one. As Slobin mentions in his 1991 article, "much of value could therefore be learned from a systematic study of those systems in particular second languages that speakers of particular first languages find especially difficult to master." Slobin feels that these systems have something important in common: they cannot be experienced directly in our perceptual, sensori-motor and practical dealings with the world, but rather can only be discovered through acquiring the language in which the information is expressed.

Studies taking this direction have recently started in second language acquisition (von Stutterheim, 2003; Cadierno, 2004; Cadierno and Lund, 2004; Hendriks *et al.*, 2008; Hendriks and Hickmann, 2010). They look at second language acquisition from a cognitive linguistics point of view. They analyze the linguistic means acquired, but also the meaning learners associate with these linguistic expressions, and ask if these meanings correspond to the meanings associated with the expression in the target language.

One could propose that an (often adult) second language learner should have a solid understanding of the world. When observing an event (such as a girl cycling across the tracks) he should understand that such an event involves a manner of motion (cycling), and a path of motion (crossing). The second language learning task should therefore be completely straightforward for such a learner: he only needs to find the words in the L2 that correspond to cycling and crossing, in whatever grammatical form such words may come about in the second language. But what if that adult learner follows the focus that corresponds to his native language? Taking the example of the French native speakers, given that they are used to focusing mainly on the path of motion in their thinking for speaking process, they may not even look to express the cycling (manner) part of the event in their second language, or if they do, it will not be in an automatized way. If Slobin is right that the way of focusing becomes exceptionally resistant to restructuring, the adult L2 learner suddenly has more problems than the child L1 learner, in that he does not only need to find new linguistic means for already known concepts, but he also has to adapt a completely new way of focusing on the information available in a given event. Results of studies researching this particular hypothesis will therefore enlighten the question: how do speakers learn what information to talk about amongst the multitude of possible information given one particular event? Slobin's hypothesis has thus importantly contributed to the field of second language acquisition, in terms of questions he asked and in terms of other research resulting from his work.

See also: acquisition of motion expressions, cognitive linguistics and SLA, conceptual transfer, cross-linguistic influence, interlanguage, language typology and language distance

References

Bowerman, M. and Choi, S. (2001). Shaping meanings for language: Universal and language-specific in the acquisition of spatial semantic categories. In M. Bowerman, and S. Levinson (eds), *Language Acquisition and Conceptual Development*, pp. 475–511. Cambridge: Cambridge University Press.

Cadierno, T. (2004). Expressing motion events in a second language: A cognitive typological perspective. In M. Achard, and S. Niemeyer (eds), *Cognitive Linguistics, Second Language Acquisition, and Foreign Language Teaching*, pp. 13–49. Berlin and New York: Mouton de Gruyter.

Cadierno, T. and Lund, K. (2004). Cognitive linguistics and second language acquisition: motion events in a typological framework. In B. van Patten, J. Williams, S. Rott, and M. Overstreet (eds), *Form-Meaning Connections in Second Language Acquisition*, pp. 139–54. Mahwah, NJ: Lawrence Erlbaum.

Choi, S. and Bowerman, M. (1991). Learning to express motion events in English and Korean: The influence of language-specific lexicalization patterns. *Cognition*, *41*(1–3), 83–121.

Hendriks, H., Hickmann, M. and Demagny, A.C. (2008). How English native speakers learn to express caused motion in English and French. *Acquisition et Interaction en Langue Étrangère*, *27*, 15–41.

Hendriks, H. and Hickmann, M. (2010). Space in second language acquisition. In V. Cook and B. Bassetti (eds), *Language and Bilingual Cognition*, pp. 315–39. Hove: Psychology Press.

Hickmann, M., Taranne, P. and Bonnet, P. (2009). Motion in first language acquisition: Manner and path in French and English child language. *Journal of Child Language*, *36*, 4, 705–42.

Von Stutterheim, C. (2003). Linguistic structure and information organization: The case of very advanced learners. In S. Foster-Cohen, and S. Pekarek-Doehler (eds), *EUROSLA Yearbook*, pp. 183–206. Amsterdam: John Benjamins.

Slobin, D.I. (1991). Learning to think for speaking: Native language, cognition, and rhetorical style. *Pragmatics*, *1*, 7–26.

Further Readings

Cook, V. and Bassetti, B. (2011). *Language and Bilingual Cognition*. Hove: Psychology Press. (A collection of papers on the relationship between language and cognition, or, thinking and speaking.)

Gumperz, J.J. and Levinson, S.C. (1996). *Rethinking Linguistic Relativity*. Cambridge: Cambridge University Press. (A collection of papers illustrating earlier and current ideas on linguistic relativity and phenomena of linguistic relativity).

Han, Z. and Cadierno, T. (eds) (2010). *Linguistic Relativity in SLA: Evidence of Thinking for Speaking*. Bristol: Multilingual Matters. (A collection of papers examining whether and to what extent first languages constrain thinking for speaking in a second language.)

Slobin, D.I. (1997). Mind, code, and text. In J. Bybee, J. Haiman, and S. Thompson (eds), *Essays on Language Function and Language Type: Dedicated to T. Givón*, pp. 437–67. Amsterdam and Philadelphia, PA: Benjamins. (Evidence from translation that speakers describe motion in typologically distinct ways, and may think differently for speaking.)

Third language acquisition

Björn Hammarberg
Stockholm University

Third language acquisition (L3 acquisition, TLA) takes place in a situation in which a language learner has prior knowledge of two or more languages, usually including at least one other non-native language. In trilingual settings, the term third language (L3) usually refers to the speaker's chronologically third language, but in a more general sense where the number of languages involved may vary, it has been used for the language currently being acquired by a multilingual learner, not necessarily number three in acquisition order. L3 learners are distinguished from those who acquire a non-native language (L2) for the first time both by their previous experience of L2 acquisition and their more varied and complex knowledge of languages. TLA research investigates the nature and effects of such complex language backgrounds.

Third language acquisition as a discipline in the making

Research on TLA is closely associated with two wider areas of study. On the one hand, TLA is the acquisitional aspect of *multilingualism*, which is then understood in the sense that three or more languages are involved. The study of TLA is usually conducted in the context of individual or societal multilingualism. On the other hand, TLA research has branched off from the mainstream of studies within the wider discipline of *second language acquisition* (*SLA*), where all learners are viewed, in a broader sense, as second language learners. Research on third language acquisition as a phenomenon in itself has developed from the late twentieth century on and gained momentum in the years around 2000 along with a growing interest in multilingualism and multilingual speakers. This has given rise to a rapidly expanding literature on multilingualism and TLA as well as efforts to organize regular scientific exchange in this area. Thus, a series of biannual *International Conferences on Third Language Acquisition and Multilingualism* has been arranged since 1999, leading to the formation of the *International Association of Multilingualism* in 2003 (http://www.iamultilingualism.org) and the establishment of the *International Journal of Multilingualism* in 2004. For an extensive account of resources for research on multilingualism and TLA, see Ecke (2009).

Multilingualism and third language acquisition

Multilingualism, and hence third language acquisition, is extremely frequent across the world. Many linguists believe that individual bi- or multilingualism is more frequent in the world than monolingualism. All humans have the potential of acquiring several languages; a precise upper limit cannot be fixed. In this sense, multilingualism is natural to human speakers and an integral part of the human language faculty, and it is rather (adult) monolingualism that has to be explained. There are certain situations which contribute to keeping people monolingual, as for example:

- if you are a native speaker of an international *lingua franca*;
- if you are a speaker of your country's majority language;
- if your language is spoken by a large population;
- if your everyday contacts do not cross language borders;
- if you stay in the language area where you have acquired your first language.

By contrast, in a variety of cases where conditions such as these do not apply or apply only in part, the acquisition of two or more languages is commonplace. Third language acquisition becomes a need in many types of sociolinguistic settings and occurs both as naturalistic acquisition and through foreign language study. There are areas in the world (for example, Papua New Guinea or many parts of Africa) where local linguistic populations live in close contact and the alternate use of several languages is a regular part of daily life. In the modern society, the growing importance of national or majority languages in multilingual countries and of languages of wider currency such as English in international communication furthers the learning of languages, as does the increased mobility between countries. For example, in continental Europe, the increased role of English as the dominant *lingua franca* has had a dual effect: on the one hand, other languages of international significance, such as German, French and Spanish, tend to be studied in schools as third languages after English, although the dominance of English also counteracts the study of additional foreign languages. On the other hand, for speakers of regional minority or immigrant languages who already have to deal with a national majority language as L2, English as a foreign language takes on the role as L3 (Cenoz and Jessner, 2000; Extra and Gorter, 2008).

Issues in third language acquisition

The study of TLA is basically an extension of research on SLA, making use of the same research methods and theoretical frameworks and applying insights about language acquisition gained in the field of SLA. However, with the multilingual perspective on language acquisition and use, certain key issues have come in focus.

Cross-linguistic influence. Studies of TLA have shown that L3 learners are often influenced not only by their L1, but also by prior L2s, contrary to a common assumption in earlier SLA research. This has motivated research on cross-linguistic influence in multilinguals with various combinations of languages. Typical forms of reliance on background languages in speech are switching, that is, temporary insertions of words or short sequences from a background language, and cross-linguistic influence on the lexicon, grammar or pronunciation of the learner's L3 (transfer). The question arises: what causes transfer from a particular background language (L1 or L2) rather than from another? Various factors that favor such influence have been suggested, such as *proficiency*, *recency of use*, *typological similarity to the L3*, and *L2 status* (Williams and Hammarberg, 2009). Of these, cross-linguistic typological similarity is the factor most often considered in the literature; see the extensive treatment in Ringbom (2007). Although it has been emphasized that the relevant criterion here is similarity as perceived or assumed by the learner, the "*psychotypology*" (Kellerman, 1983), rather than factual typological similarity, most studies have in practice relied on the latter or simply on degree of genetic relatedness. The factor L2 status, that is, the notion that a non-native language has a favored role as a source language for transfer into L3, has also attracted considerable attention and debate. Suggested reasons for this factor are (i) a different acquisition mechanism for L2s as opposed to L1s, and hence a reactivation of the L2 type mechanism in L3 acquisition, (ii) greater ease to suppress L1 as it forms a stronger network than the more loosely organized L2s, and (iii) a desire to suppress L1 so as not to sound like a speaker of that language.

Language production in multilinguals. A central concern is to investigate and model L3 speech in order to increase our understanding of the speaking process, especially with respect to how the multilingual speaker controls the choice of language and how L1 and L2 knowledge becomes activated in the process. Levelt's (1989) modular, lexically driven model of the mature monolingual speaker has been particularly influential as a point of departure. Adaptations of this model have been proposed for the bilingual speaker (see full discussion in Kormos, 2006) and for the multilingual speaker (de Bot 2004, with particular reference to the lexicon and the control of language choice). An approach also taken into account is Green's (1986) *inhibitory control model*, which posits three states of activation for a language: *selected* (chosen for speaking), *active* (non-selected, but potentially influencing ongoing processing), and *dormant* (known but exerting no effects), and the possibility to control and inhibit activation. A dimension connected with the character of the speech situation is Grosjean's (2001) differention of language modes which a speaker may adopt: *monolingual* (striving to adhere to the selected language), or *bi/tri/multilingual mode* (allowing activation of other languages more freely in the form of switching or cross-linguistic influence on the target language).

The beneficial effect on TLA of prior language knowledge. It is generally recognized today that prior linguistic experience is an asset in language acquisition. Bi- or multilingualism does not stand in the way, but tends to support the acquisition of further languages. Studies comparing bilinguals with monolinguals and L3 learners with first-L2 learners predominantly confirm this (for a review of studies see Cenoz, 2003). Positive effects have been found on the *language proficiency* attained, on *linguistic awareness* (Jessner, 2006) and on the use of *learning strategies*. For a study of the positive influence of various types of prior L2 experience (including the number of and proficiency in prior L2s) on various kinds of strategic learning behavior, see Missler (2000).

Third language in education. The various aspects mentioned above all have implications for the organized study and teaching of third languages. Although TLA is nothing new in practice, the possibilities of exploiting insights about multilingualism and TLA in study, teaching and teacher training is a recent concern. This includes taking advantage of the degree of bilingualism already attained by the students in training their observance of language similarities and differences and enhancing their metalinguistic awareness and strategic learning techniques. Jessner (2008) gives an overview of issues in multilingual education, also including several educational projects in this area.

See also: awareness, bilingualism and SLA, cross-linguistic influence, learning strategies, linguistic transfer, speaking

References

Cenoz, J. (2003). The additive effect of bilingualism on third language acquisition. *International Journal of Bilingualism*, *7*, 71–87.

Cenoz, J. and U. Jessner (2000). *English in Europe: The Acquisition of a Third Language*. Clevedon: Multilingual Matters.

de Bot, K. (2004). The multilingual lexicon: Modelling selection and control. *International Journal of Multilingualism*, *1*, 17–32.

Ecke, P. (2009). Multilingualism resources: Associations, journals, book series, bibliographies and conference lists. In L. Aronin and B. Hufeisen (eds), *The Exploration of Multilingualism: Development of Research on L3, Multilingualism and Multiple Language Acquisition*. Amsterdam: John Benjamins.

Extra, G. and D. Gorter (eds) (2008). *Multilingual Europe: Facts and Policies*. Berlin: Mouton de Gruyter.

Green, D.W. (1986). Control, activation and resource: A framework and a model for the control of speech in bilinguals. *Brain and Language*, *27*, 210–23.

Grosjean, F. (2001). The bilingual's language modes. In J.L. Nicol (ed.), *One Speaker, Two Languages: Bilingual Language Processing*. Oxford: Blackwell.

Jessner, U. (2006). *Linguistic Awareness in Multilinguals: English as a Third Language*. Edinburgh: Edinburgh University Press.

——(2008). Teaching third languages: Findings, trends and challenges. *Language Teaching*, *41*, 15–46.

Kellerman, E. (1983). Now you see it, now you don't. In S. Gass and L. Selinker (eds), *Language Transfer in Language Learning*. Rowley, MA: Newbury House.

Kormos, J. (2006). *Speech Production and Second Language Acquisition*. New York: Lawrence Erlbaum.

Levelt, W.J. M. (1989). *Speaking: from Intention to Articulation*. Cambridge, MA: The MIT Press.

Missler, B. (2000). Previous experience of foreign language learning and its contribution to the development of learning strategies. In S. Dentler, B. Hufeisen, and B. Lindemann (eds), *Tertiär-und Drittsprachen: Projekte und empirische Untersuchungen*. Tübingen: Stauffenburg.

Ringbom, H. (2007). *Cross-linguistic Similarity in Foreign Language Learning*. Clevedon: Multilingual Matters.

Williams, S. and B. Hammarberg (2009). Language switches in L3 production: Implications for a polyglot speaking model. In B. Hammarberg (ed.), *Processes in Third Language Acquisition*, Edinburgh: Edinburgh University Press. (Originally in *Applied Linguistics*, *19*, 295–333 (1998).)

Further reading

Cenoz, J. and F. Genesee (eds) (1998). *Beyond Bilingualism: Multilingualism and Multilingual Education*. Clevedon: Multilingual Matters. (Perspectives on multilingualism as a world phenomenon, aspects of education towards multilingualism and examples of educational programs in different parts of the world.)

Cenoz, J., B. Hufeisen and U. Jessner (eds) (2001). *Cross-linguistic Influence in Third Language*

Acquisition: Psycholinguistic Perspectives. Clevedon: Multilingual Matters. (An influential collection of papers on a number of key issues in third language acquisition.)

De Angelis, G. (2007). *Third or Additional Language Acquisition.* Clevedon: Multilingual Matters. (An excellent introduction to major issues in third language acquisition.)

Hammarberg, B. (ed.) (2009). *Processes in Third Language Acquisition.* Edinburgh: Edinburgh University Press. (A set of case studies of an adult multilingual learner in action, exploring her acquisitional activity and the influence of her background languages in relation to current models of the speaking process.)

Todeva, E. and J. Cenoz (eds) (2009) *The Multiple Realities of Multilingualism: Personal Narratives and Researchers' Perspectives*, Berlin: Mouton de Gruyter. (Here a variety of often highly multilingual speakers report and comment on their personal histories of acquiring languages.)

Threshold hypothesis

Jim Cummins
Ontario Institute for Studies in Educatiuon, University of Toronto

The threshold hypothesis was originally proposed by Cummins (1976) to account for apparently contradictory findings relating to the cognitive and academic consequences of bilingualism. The hypothesis proposed that the level of bilingual proficiency that students attained mediated the effects of bilingualism on their cognitive and academic development. Thus, the apparent contradiction between early studies (1920s to 1950s) reporting negative cognitive and academic consequences associated with bilingualism and more recent studies (1960s and 1970s) highlighting the potential cognitive benefits of bilingualism could be resolved by positing two thresholds of proficiency that students needed to attain (a) to avoid the negative effects associated with instruction through a weaker language, and (b) to experience the enhancement of cognitive and linguistic functioning that knowledge of two or more languages confers on the developing child. In other words, the threshold hypothesis argued that language proficiency acts as an intervening variable in explaining the different educational and cognitive outcomes associated with bilingualism. In contexts where students are enabled (either through sociolinguistic circumstances or educational provision) to develop functional proficiency and literacy in two languages, bilingualism confers cognitive and academic advantages; however, when students are required to learn through a second/weaker language without being given the support to develop strong academic skills in that language (or in their home language), then bilingualism (or lack thereof) is likely to be associated with negative cognitive and academic consequences.

The hypothesis that language proficiency acts as an intervening variable in explaining the different educational and cognitive outcomes associated with bilingualism should be distinguished from a related but different use of the term "threshold" in the context of second language reading research (e.g., Bernhardt and Kamil, 1995). This "threshold hypothesis" has also been labeled the "short-circuit" hypothesis (Clarke, 1980) and it proposes that first language (L1) reading proficiency can begin to positively influence the acquisition of second language (L2) reading proficiency only after a certain threshold of L2 proficiency has been attained. Lack of L2 knowledge "short-circuits" positive transfer from L1 reading to L2 reading. Hulstijn (1991) points out that "these two distinct threshold notions do not rule out each other; they are evidently compatible with each other" (p. 10).

Since the original formulation of the threshold hypothesis in 1976, the research evidence relating to the impact of bilingualism on children's cognitive, linguistic, and academic development has expanded significantly (see Bialystok, 2001 for a review). Specifically, research has reported that high levels of proficiency in both L1 and L2 are associated with higher levels of metalinguistic awareness, greater executive control of cognitive functions, enhancement of additional language learning, and stronger mathematical reasoning skills. Numerous researchers have interpreted their findings as consistent with the threshold hypothesis (see Cummins, 2000 for a review).

One difficulty in empirically testing the threshold hypothesis lies in our limited ability to specify and operationalize the linguistic thresholds that the hypothesis proposes. This reflects a more general issue regarding the nature of the construct "language proficiency" and how it should be measured. When we talk about linguistic thresholds, what aspects of the language actually constitute those thresholds?

In light of the vagueness association with the notion of threshold, Cummins (2000) suggested that the major contribution of the threshold hypothesis might be heuristic. It stimulated research into the broader consequences of bilingualism and drew attention to the problematic situation of students learning through a weaker language who are insufficiently supported in gaining access to comprehensible input in that language and acquiring the academic language proficiency necessary to succeed academically. While many minority language students do catch up academically when the instructional conditions are favourable, the gap between learners and native speakers may widen in classroom contexts where students' language proficiency is not sufficient to comprehend poorly delivered (non-scaffolded) instruction in that language.

The threshold hypothesis has engendered controversy on the grounds that specifying "language proficiency" as an intervening variable in determining academic success or failure effectively attributes minority group students' underachievement to linguistic deficits (MacSwan, 2000). In response to this critique, Cummins (2000) pointed to the broader framework within which the threshold hypothesis was embedded that assigned a causal role to the coercive relations of power that minority groups experienced in educational contexts (Cummins, 1986). These societal power relations express themselves both in the structures of schooling (curriculum, assessment, language of instruction, etc.) and in the patterns of identity negotiation that educators orchestrate with students from subordinated minority groups. The interactions that students experience in school exert a major influence on the extent to which they will expand their academic language and literacy skills in L2 (and L1), which, in turn, will affect their ability to profit from instruction.

In summary, there is extensive evidence that developing proficiency in two or more languages exerts a positive (albeit subtle) influence on children's linguistic, cognitive, and academic growth. There is also extensive evidence that many immigrant and minority group students experience significant levels of underachievement academically in some social contexts (e.g., Stanat and Christensen, 2006). The threshold hypothesis proposes that students' academic language development (in L1 and L2) is relevant to understanding these patterns of academic outcomes. It is not clear whether there are specific "thresholds" associated with students' metalinguistic, academic, and cognitive outcomes. However, the issue may be of only academic interest since the practical implication of the research data is the same: schools should attempt to encourage minority students to develop their L1 abilities to as great an extent as possible both to develop bilingualism and to stimulate transfer of concepts and skills to L2.

See also: analysis-control model, BICS and CALP, bilingualism and SLA, proficiency, reading, scaffolding

References

Bernhardt, E.B. and Kamil, M.L. (1995). Interpreting relationships between L1 and L2 reading: Consolidating the linguistic threshold and linguistic interdependence hypotheses. *Applied Linguistics*, *16*, 15–34.

Bialystok, E. (2001). *Bilingualism in Development: Language, Literacy, and Cognition*. Cambridge: Cambridge University Press.

Clarke, M.A. (1980). The short-circuit hypothesis of ESL reading – or when language competence interferes with reading performance. *The Modern Language Journal*, *64*, 203–9.

Cummins, J. (1976). The influence of bilingualism on cognitive growth: A synthesis of research findings and explanatory hypotheses. *Working Papers on Bilingualism*, *9*, 1–43.

——(1986). Empowering minority students: A framework for intervention. *Harvard Education Review*, 15, 18–36.

——(2000). *Language, Power and Pedagogy: Bilingual Children in the Crossfire.* Clevedon, England: Multilingual Matters.

Hulstijn, J.H. (1991). How is reading in a second language related to reading in a first language? In J.H. Hulstijn and J.F. Matter (eds), *Reading in Two Languages*, pp. 5–14. Amsterdam: AILA.

MacSwan, J. (2000). The threshold hypothesis, semilingualism, and other contributions to a deficit view of linguistic minorities. *Hispanic Journal of Behavioral Sciences, 22*, 3–45.

Stanat, P. and Christensen, G. (2006). *Where Immigrant Students Succeed: A Comparative Review of Performance and Engagement in PISA 2003.* Paris: Organisation for Economic Cooperation and Development.

Time-series design

J. Dean Mellow
Simon Fraser University

Time-series designs (TSDs) utilize the repeated, quantitative measurement of an individual's language abilities over time to investigate language use and/or development. To investigate language comprehension or production, the time period of investigation can be seconds and milliseconds, as in spoken discourse research that measures stages in speech planning and production (e.g., Roberts and Kirsner, 2000). To investigate second language acquisition, the time period of investigation can be days, weeks, and months (e.g., Mellow, Reeder and Foster, 1996). TSDs can be (i) descriptive, precisely specifying temporal trends; or (ii) quasi-experimental, assessing the effect of a specific variable or session of learning on use or acquisition.

TSDs require careful methodological choices to validly address the intended research questions (e.g., Glass, Willson, and Gottman, 2008; Kratochwill and Levin, 1992; Mackey and Gass, 2005). First, TSDs require a relatively large number of data points to adequately reveal temporal patterns (e.g., gradual or sudden changes in accuracy or range of use). The number of data points that are practical varies according to the research issues. In Roberts and Kirsner's (2000) study of speech production, 30-second monologues were divided into 200-millisecond segments, yielding 150 data points. Mellow *et al.* (1996) reported an acquisition study that had 10 observation sessions, once per week, resulting in 10 data points. Second, TSDs require that these multiple measurement instances or instruments are sufficiently similar to each other so that any variation exhibited by learners is not likely due to differences in measurement procedures. Because variability is a common characteristic of second language use, the properties of the measurement procedures must be carefully planned and the order of instruments should be randomized.

Third, to assess the effect of a specific variable or session of learning on use or acquisition, the design must attempt to eliminate other variables as possible causes of changes in scores. For a longitudinal case study of one learner, a number of baseline or pretest data samples before the change in variable (or learning event) can indicate whether the expected patterns were affected by the change in variable. The systematic inclusion of multiple learners can increase the internal validity of a design. If several learners randomly receive an experimental treatment session at different points in time, then these replications of the single-case design are called a multiple-baseline design. Fourth, when a TSD has a small number of data points, a visual examination of a scatterplot is often the best approach for interpreting the results. If a large number of data points per learner is obtained, a variety of statistical models can be used to interpret the data.

In contrast to a TSD, a cross-sectional design investigates acquisition by including learners at different proficiency levels and inferring that these different learners validly represent sequential stages in the acquisition process. A TSD provides a direct assessment of temporal patterns. However, the results from TSDs that have small numbers of research participants cannot be generalized. Thus, TSDs can complement other types of research designs for investigating second language acquisition.

See also: case-studies, cross-sectional research, longitudinal research, measuring and researching SLA, quantitative research, variationist approaches to SLA

References

Mackey, A. and Gass, S. (2005). *Second Language Research: Methodology and Design*. Mahwah, NJ: Lawrence Erlbaum Associates.

Mellow, J.D., Reeder, K. and Forster, E. (1996). Using the time-series design to investigate the effects of pedagogic intervention on SLA. *Studies in Second Language Acquisition, 18*, 325–50.

Roberts, B. and Kirsner, K. (2000). Temporal cycles in speech production. *Language and Cognitive Processes, 15*, 2, 129–57.

Glass, G., Willson, V. and Gottman, J. (2008). *Design and Analysis of Time-Series Experiments*. Charlotte, NC: Information Age Publishing.

Kratochwill, T. and Levin, J. (eds) (1992). *Single-case Research Design and Analysis: New Directions for Psychology and Education*. Hillsdale, NJ: Lawrence Erlbaum.

Topicalization

Bryan Donaldson
University of Texas at Austin

Topicalization is treated here as a synonym of topic-marking, making reference to the notions *topic* (what an utterance is about) and *focus* (new information about the topic). Topicalization is the process by which a speaker signals that a constituent or segment of an utterance constitutes its topic. Crosslinguistically, topicalization operates via syntactic, lexical, morphological, or phonetic means. In (1), *John* constitutes the topic, about which new information (focus) is provided. *John* is topicalized lexically by the expression *as for*. Syntactically, *John* represents the grammatical subject, frequently associated with topic.

(1) As for John, he loves Mary.

In (adult) SLA, learners possess knowledge of discourse organization (acquired in L1)—including the notion of topic—but must acquire the specific mechanisms by which the L2 signals these relations.

The topicalization strategies available in the L2 may differ from those of the L1, and L1 preferences for discourse organization—including topicalization strategies—may influence L2 production. Schachter and Rutherford's seminal (1979) study of Japanese and Chinese learners of English revealed mismappings between discourse function (topicalization) and L2 form (extrapositions, existentials). In both Japanese and Chinese, utterances typically exhibit topic-focus order, and this L1 principle underlay certain L2 pragmatic infelicities. The Japanese learners (over)produced extraposition structures like (2) as a means of topicalizing (in this example, *sweet flag leaves*).

(2) It is believed that sweet flag leaves contain the power to expel sickness and evil.

Likewise, the Chinese learners infelicitously used English existential constructions (e.g., *there is* ...) as topicalizations. In both cases, the learners appropriated an available utterance-initial syntactic construction in English as a topicalization strategy. Neither construction possessed a direct counterpart in the L1. Rather, the interlanguage form-function mapping represented an attempt to preserve L1 discourse principles with available L2 syntactic forms.

Trévise (1986) reported a similar effect of L1 topicalization strategies on L2 production. In her data, however, the L2 word order directly reflected that of the L1. Trévise's French learners of English produced utterances like (3):

(3) I think it's very good the analysis.

The word order calques a French right-dislocation, in which a topic (*the analysis*) appears to the right of the main clause, which contains a resumptive pronoun (*it*). Hendricks (2000) examined Chinese learners of French. As in Schachter and Rutherford (1979), L1 topicalization strategies did not transfer directly. The learners acquired French topicalization strategies, but incompletely, as evidenced by both formal and functional errors.

A topic of current interest concerns the ability of L2ers, even at advanced proficiency levels, to coordinate discourse-pragmatic knowledge with other types of linguistic knowledge (syntax, morphology, phonology, etc.). Valenzuela's (2006) findings support the claim that, although core syntax may be fully acquired, related interpretive properties remain problematic, even at endstate. Valenzuela's near-native speakers of Spanish mastered the syntax of clitic left-dislocation but not a more subtle constraint on how left-dislocations topicalize specific versus non-specific referents. On the other hand, Donaldson (2011) provided evidence of nativelike acquisition of a range of properties related to topicalization by clitic left-dislocation by near-native speakers of French.

See also: discourse and pragmatics in SLA, pragmatics, form-meaning relations, cross-linguistic influence, communicative competence, speaking

References

Donaldson, B. (2011). Left-Dislocation in near-native French. *Studies in Second Language Acquisition*, *33*, 399–432.

Hendricks, H. (2000). The acquisition of topic marking in L1 Chinese and L1 and L2 French. *Studies in Second Language Acquisition*, *22*, 369–97.

Schachter, J. and Rutherford, W. (1979). Discourse function and language transfer. *Working Papers on Bilingualism*, *19*, 1–12.

Trévise, A. (1986). Is it transferable, topicalization? In E. Kellerman, and M. Sharwood Smith (eds), *Crosslinguistic Influence in Second Language Acquisition*. New York: Pergamon.

Valenzuela, E. (2006). L2 end state grammars and incomplete acquisition of Spanish CLLD constructions. In R. Slabakova, S.A. Montrul, and P. Prévost (eds), *Inquiries in Linguistic Development: In Honor of Lydia White*. Amsterdam: John Benjamins.

Further reading

Bohnacker, U. and Rosén, C. (2008). The clause-initial position in L2 German declaratives. *Studies in Second Language Acquisition*, *30*, 511–38. (Acquisition of preferences for topic versus focus information in the German clausal first position.)

Callies, M. (2009). *Information Highlighting in Advanced Learner English: The Syntax-Pragmatics Interface in Second Language Acquisition*. Amsterdam: John Benjamins. (A corpus-based and experimental study of information structure marking, including topic-marking, by German learners of English.)

Lambrecht, K. (1994). *Information Structure and Sentence Form: Topic, Focus and the Mental Representations of Discourse Referents*. Cambridge: Cambridge University Press. (A detailed treatment of topic- and focus-marking and discourse organization.)

Gregory, M.L. and Michaelis, L.A. (2001). Topicalization and left-dislocation: A functional opposition revisited. *Journal of Pragmatics*, *33*, 1665–1706. (A corpus-based investigation of topic- and focus-marking in English.)

Reinhart, T. (1981). Pragmatics and linguistics: An analysis of sentence topics. *Philosophica*, *27*, 53–94. (A seminal discussion and definition of the notion of topic.)

Transfer appropriate processing

Patsy M. Lightbown

Concordia University

Transfer appropriate processing (TAP) refers to the relationship between the kinds of cognitive processing that are used during learning and those that are needed during retrieval. TAP is consistent with the principle of "encoding specificity" which suggests that "encoding will be specific to the set of conditions prevailing at the time of intake" (Segalowitz, 2010: 62). Thus, encoding (learning) of skills and information takes place within a particular context, using particular cognitive processes. In a number of experiments, researchers have found that retrieval is more successful if the cognitive processes and even some of the environmental conditions present at the time of learning are also present during retrieval. Recently, neuroimaging research has provided evidence that the same neural areas that are active during learning are also active during retrieval of information. Such findings provide some explanation for the behavioral findings of TAP experiments (see Segalowitz, 2010).

Research on TAP developed partly in response to earlier research on *levels of processing* (LOP). A number of LOP studies had shown that learning a word while focusing on its meaning was associated with more success in remembering the word than learning while focusing on its form. For example, Craik and Tulving (1975) had participants read a series of words in a list. During learning, the participants were asked "orienting" questions such as "Is the word a type of flower?" or "Does the word rhyme with train?" before seeing each word. The participants were then asked – unexpectedly – to look at words on a new list and to indicate which of the words they had seen in the original list. Words that had been learned when the orienting question drew attention to semantic properties (e.g., whether it was a type of flower) were more successfully identified than those that were learned when the orienting question drew attention to form (e.g., whether the word rhymed with train). This was interpreted as showing the superiority of "semantic" encoding. TAP studies suggested that the effect might be due to the nature of the retrieval task rather than to the inherent superiority of semantic encoding. In one of the first TAP studies, Morris, Bransford, and Franks (1977) used learning conditions that were similar to those in the Craik and Tulving study described above. However, they used additional retrieval tasks. They found that when the retrieval task required participants to identify words that rhymed with those from the original lists, words that had been learned in the rhyming condition were retrieved more successfully than those that had been learned in the semantic condition.

Most of the research on TAP has been done in cognitive psychology laboratories where the material to be learned consists primarily of word lists in the participants' native language. While this research has implications for second language acquisition (SLA), there is also research that relates more directly to SLA. Barcroft has proposed a model of second language processing that is consistent with the principles of TAP. He calls his model Type of Processing-Resource Allocation (TOPRA) and emphasizes the competition for cognitive resources that occurs when learners try to learn different things at the same time (see VanPatten, 1990). In one study, Barcroft (2006) told English L1 learners of Spanish L2 to "try to learn" new words. Participants looked at a sequence of computer screens, each one showing a simple line drawing accompanied by the Spanish word that labeled it. One group were told simply to study the picture/word pairs; the other group were instructed to write each word as they saw it. The retrieval task was to write each word when the associated picture appeared on the screen. Participants who had written the words during the learning phase were *less* successful at the retrieval task than those who had merely "studied" the words and pictures. This led Barcroft to propose that, in addition to semantic processing and form processing, "form-meaning mapping" requires a specific kind of processing. Barcroft's TOPRA model suggests that when the learning condition led participants to focus their attention on the strictly formal aspects of each word (how it was written), they had been less able to (also) focus on the form-meaning connection that linked the words and pictures. When the learning condition encouraged a focus on the form-meaning connection alone, learners were better able to remember the words associated with the pictures.

In another study related to SLA, Trofimovich (2005) investigated how the effects of lexical priming varied according to what participants were told to pay attention to when listening to spoken words. English L1 learners of Spanish L2 listened to recorded lists of English words and lists of Spanish words whose meaning they already knew. The participants heard the words in one of three conditions: (1) Just Listen, (2) Semantic (assign each word a rating according to its "pleasantness"), and (3) Auditory (rate each word according to the clarity of the recording). When the words were played again, the participants were asked to repeat each word as quickly and accurately as possible. They heard both words that were on the original lists (primed) and others that were not on the original lists (new). The effects of priming were assessed in terms of the difference in the speed (measured in milliseconds) with which participants began their repetition of primed versus new words. For English (L1), primed words were repeated faster than the new words, regardless of the experimental condition. In Spanish (L2), priming also resulted in faster repetition for the Just Listen and Auditory groups but not for the Semantic group. Emphasis on listening to what the words sounded like was associated with more rapid retrieval of their acoustic properties but emphasis on the words' meaning did not facilitate that retrieval.

L2 learners need to retrieve what they have learned in a variety of conditions, from multiple choice tests to rapid fire conversations. These different retrieval conditions will require many different cognitive processes. For this reason, Lightbown (2008) suggests that successful L2 learning can be enhanced by increasing "the number of settings and processing types in which learners encounter the material they need to learn" (p. 43).

See also: attention, depth of processing, priming, psycholinguistics of SLA, reaction time, rehearsal

References

Barcroft, J. (2006). Can writing a new word detract from learning it? More negative effects of forced output during vocabulary learning. *Second Language Research*, *24*, 487–97.

Craik, F.I. M. and Lockhart, R.S. (1972). Levels of processing: A framework for memory research. *Journal of Verbal Learning and Verbal Behavior, 11*, 671–84.

Lightbown, P.M. (2008). Transfer appropriate processing as a model for classroom second language acquisition. In Z. Han (ed.), *Understanding Second Language Process*, pp. 27–44. Clevedon: Multilingual Matters.

Morris, D.D., Bransford, J.D. and Franks, J.J. (1977). Levels of processing versus transfer appropriate processing. *Journal of Verbal Learning and Verbal Behavior, 16*, 519–33.

Segalowitz, N. (2010). *Cognitive Bases of Second Language Fluency*. New York: Routledge.

VanPatten, B. (1990). Attending to form and content in the input: An experiment in consciousness. *Studies in Second Language Acquisition, 12*, 287–301.

Further reading

DeKeyser, R.M. (2007). Introduction: Situating the concept of practice. In R.M. DeKeyser (ed.), *Practice in a Second Language: Perspectives from Applied Linguistics and Cognitive Psychology*. Cambridge: Cambridge University Press. (This chapter discusses the role of practice in SLA, recognizing that the "specificity of practice" can limit the transfer of knowledge from one context to another and suggesting that declarative knowledge can improve transferability.)

Lockhart, R.S. (2002). Levels of processing, transfer-appropriate processing, and the concept of robust encoding. *Memory, 10*, 397–403. (A look back at 30 years of research on LOP and a discussion of how both LOP and TAP interpretations can be further understood in terms of "robust encoding," that is, encoding that maximizes the number of cues for retrieval.)

Nairne, J.S. (2002). The myth of the encoding-retrieval match. *Memory, 10*, 389–95. (A review of TAP and LOP approaches, concluding that the most important factor in facilitating retrieval is in ensuring that learning opportunities provide multiple associations with the learning target.)

Roediger, H.L., Gallo, D.A. and Geraci, L. (2002). Processing approaches to cognition: The impetus from the levels-of-processing framework. *Memory, 10*, 319–32. (This article is a widely cited and thorough review of research based on cognitive processing approaches to learning and memory.)

Schmidt, R.A. and Bjork, R.A. (1992). New conceptualizations of practice: Common principles in three paradigms suggest new concepts for training. *Psychological Science*, *3*, 207–17. (A discussion of training protocols that may have implications for classroom learning. The writers argue that learning conditions that make performance easy may be less effective for long-term retention and retrieval than those conditions that make the "acquisition phase" more difficult.)

Triarchic Theory of intelligence

Robert Sternberg
University of Oklahoma

The Triarchic Theory of intelligence (Sternberg, 1985, 1997, 2003) views intelligence in a somewhat broader way than do conventional theories (e.g., Carroll, 1993). As in the case of Gardner's (2006) theory of multiple intelligences, the Triarchic Theory suggests that general ability (*g*) and abilities nested hierarchically under it do not fully capture the range of skills that should be viewed as intelligence. Both of these theories suggest that conventional tests of intelligence do not adequately capture the full range of abilities that constitute human intelligence.

The structure of the Triarchic Theory

According to the Triarchic Theory in its original form (Sternberg, 1985), intelligence comprises three sets of abilities: *creative abilities*, which are used to generate new ideas and to adapt to novel tasks and situations; *analytical abilities*, which are used to evaluate ideas and to reason with relatively abstract problems; and *practical abilities*, which are used to apply one's own and others' ideas and also to persuade others of the value of ideas. In its more recent forms (Sternberg, 2003), the theory also posits *wisdom-based abilities,* which are used to ensure that ideas help to serve a common good.

To be more specific, creative abilities are important to create, invent, discover, suppose, and imagine. Analytical abilities are essential to analyze, evaluate, critique, assess, and compare and contrast. Practical abilities are needed to use, utilize, implement, put into practice, execute, and persuade. Wisdom-based abilities are indispensable to balance interests, apply to the common good, take into account multiple points of view, realize that what is true sometimes can change over time, and think ethically.

The mental processes underlying the different kinds of abilities are highly overlapping. For example, seven executive processes are common to all the abilities: recognizing the existence of a problem, defining the problem, mentally representing the problem, allocating resources to the solution of the problem, setting up a strategy to solve the problem, monitoring solution of the problem, and evaluating the solution after it is done. What differs is how the processes are applied. Creative abilities are needed to formulate or solve problems that are relatively novel or familiar problems presented in relatively novel contexts. Analytical abilities are needed when problems are relatively abstract and unfamiliar. Practical abilities are involved when problems are relatively concrete and familiar. Wisdom-based abilities are involved in matters of human relations and long-term planning.

Evidence favoring the Triarchic Theory

Sternberg and his colleagues have collected evidence over the years supporting the Triarchic Theory, as reviewed in Sternberg (1985, 1997, 2003, 2010; Sternberg, Jarvin, and Grigorenko, 2011). The evidence has been of different kinds. Factor-analytic studies have shown that creative and practical abilities can be measured relatively independently of analytical abilities. Developmental studies have shown that development of component processes can be traced over time. Validity studies have shown that triarchically based tests can reliably and validly measure the abilities posited by the theory. Cultural studies have shown the relevance of the theory across various cultures. And instructional studies have shown that teaching based on the Triarchic Theory is superior to various alternative forms of teaching (see Sternberg, Grigorenko, and Zhang, 2008). Most importantly, these studies have shown that students have different learning and thinking styles and hence must be taught through a variety of modalities for them to learn in the most effective way possible.

Relevance to second language acquisition

The theory was applied to second-language learning in the construction of an assessment to measure second-language learning ability (Grigorenko, Sternberg, and Ehrman, 2000). A test was constructed that involved dynamic assessment (Sternberg and Grigorenko, 2002): students learned an artificial language at the time of the test and were assessed throughout the test on various aspects of their learning abilities. The test proved to be an effective predictor of second-language learning abilities. Moreover, it showed satisfactory reliability and other psychometric properties required for successful utilization of a test. A limitation of the test, as constructed, is that it assumed English as a first language. Other versions could be constructed that are based upon other native languages.

The theory has relevance not only for assessment of second-language learning abilities, but also for instruction and assessment of learning. Because students learn in different ways, they profit most if foreign languages are taught in variegated ways. For example, a learner who is memory-oriented might profit from typical mimic-and-memorize instruction. An analytical learner might profit more from instruction that involves analysis of the grammatical and syntactical structure of the language. A creative learner might profit especially from instruction that involves inventing novel scenarios that one might encounter in a new environment in a country speaking the foreign language. A practical learner might profit most from learning that occurs in the everyday contexts of the cultures in which the foreign language is embedded. Wrong conclusions might be drawn if teaching does not correspond to the ability pattern of the learner, as, according to the Triarchic Theory, students learn best when they capitalize on strengths and compensate for or correct weaknesses.

Conclusion

The Triarchic Theory of intelligence provides a differentiated way of viewing human intelligence. Applied to second-language learning, it suggests that it is important to teach and assess learning in variegated ways that take into account students' patterns of analytical, creative, and practical abilities. Such teaching is directed not only to students' strengths. Rather, it helps students to capitalize on these strengths while at the same time compensating for or correcting weaknesses. Incorrect conclusions may be drawn about students' second-language learning abilities if it is assumed that intelligence is basically one-dimensional, and if students are not taught in ways that enable them best to utilize their strengths.

See also: aptitude, aptitude-trait complexes, Aptitude-treatment Interaction (ATI) research, dynamic assessment, individual differences and SLA, vocabulary learning and teaching

References

Carroll, J.B. (1993). *Human Cognitive Abilities: A Survey of Factor-Analytic Studies*. New York: Cambridge University Press.

Gardner, H. (2006). *Multiple Intelligences: New Horizons in Theory and Practice*. New York: Basic.

Grigorenko, E.L., Sternberg, R.J. and Ehrman, M. E. (2000). A theory-based approach to the measurement of foreign language learning ability: The CANAL-F theory and test. *The Modern Language Journal*, *84*(3), 390–405.

Sternberg, R.J. (1985). *Beyond IQ: A Triarchic Theory of Human Intelligence*. New York: Cambridge University Press.

——(1997). *Successful Intelligence*. New York: Plume.

——(2003). *Wisdom, Intelligence, and Creativity Synthesized*. New York: Cambridge University Press.

——(2010). *College Admissions for the 21st Century*. Cambridge, MA: Harvard University Press.

Sternberg, R.J. and Grigorenko, E.L. (2002). *Dynamic Testing*. New York: Cambridge University Press.

Sternberg, R.J., Grigorenko, E.L. and Zhang, L.-F. (2008). Styles of learning and thinking matter in instruction and assessment. *Perspectives on Psychological Science*, *3* (6), 486–506.

Sternberg, R.J., Jarvin, L. and Grigorenko, E.L. (2011). *Explorations in Giftedness*, New York: Cambridge University Press.

Triggering

María del Pilar García-Mayo
Universidad del País Vasco

Triggering is a term referring to the different cues a learner receives when learning a language. Like a child learning his/her first language (L1), the second language (L2) learner has to establish form-meaning mappings on the basis of the input. All second language acquisition (SLA) theories acknowledge the need for input but they differ in the importance attached to it and, therefore, in what they consider triggering evidence (Ortega, 2007 for a review).

From the perspective of a formal theory like generative theory input is important but only to the extent that it works as triggering evidence that sets off language processing. The initial state of children acquiring their L1 is hypothesized to be Universal Grammar (UG), an innate mechanism consisting of invariant principles and some options referred to as parameters. Positive input guides the child in the fixing of parameters, that is, positive input triggers properties of UG (Lightfoot, 1989) and negative input (i.e. information about ungrammatical utterances) is not supposed to play a role. In L2 acquisition, input is also essential but the situation is a bit different: the L2 learner already has an L1 in place which, together with the L2 input, plays a role in the development of the L2 interlanguage. Interlanguage is by definition a dynamic system changing over time and the key question is what motivates that change from one stage to the other. White (2003: 157ff) places triggering as the crucial concept here because positive evidence will determine the choice of the various parameters As White points out not any utterance serves as a trigger but, rather, a structured and predetermined stream of speech. The findings regarding the role of negative evidence in triggering SLA are mixed, although some researchers argue that it does not play any role (Schwartz, 1993).

From a functional perspective, like the one adopted by cognitive interactionist approaches (Long, 1996), different conversational adjustments (confirmation checks, comprehension checks, clarification requests, negotiation of meaning) serve as triggers that facilitate the L2 acquisition process. Input from this perspective plays a much more crucial role than in UG-based theories but together with the learner's internal mechanisms. Within the interactionist approach, learners' production, referred to as output, has been claimed to raise the language learners' awareness of form-meaning connections in the target language and to trigger cognitive processes that have been claimed to be involved in L2 learning. Current approaches within the interactionist approach consider not only cognitively oriented research but also socially oriented work: in both cases, verbal interaction is the trigger for L2 learning.

See also: interaction and the Interaction Hypothesis, form-meaning connection, positive and negative evidence, theoretical constructs in SLA, Universal Grammar (UG) and SLA

References

Lightfoot, D. (1989). The child's trigger experience: Degree-0 learnability. *Brain and Behavioral Sciences*, *12*, 321–75.

Long, M.H. (1996). The role of the linguistic environment in second language acquisition. In W. Ritchie and T. Bhatia (eds), *Handbook of Research on Second Language Acquisition*, pp. 413–68. New York: Academic Press.

Ortega, L. (2007). Second language learning explained? SLA across nine contemporary theories. In B. VanPatten and J. Williams (eds), *Theories in Second Language Acquisition. An Introduction*, pp. 225–50. Mahwah, NJ: Lawrence Erlbaum.

Schwartz, B.D. (1993). On explicit and negative date effecting and affecting competence and 'Linguistic Behavior'. *Studies in Second Language Acquisition*, *15*, 147–63.

White, L. (2003). *Second Language Acquisition and Universal Grammar*. Cambridge: Cambridge University Press.

Turn taking

Numa Markee
University of Illinois at Urbana-Champaign

Turn taking is one of the three major foci of the method-theory complex known as conversation analysis (CA) – the other two are repair and sequence organization – which analyzes how participants "do" ordinary conversation and institutional varieties of talk in real time. Collectively, these varieties of talk are known as talk-in-interaction (Schegloff, 1987). Ordinary conversation is the kind of naturally occurring, everyday chitchat that habitually occurs among friends and acquaintances, and is the default speech exchange system against which all institutional forms of talk (such as debates or classroom talk) must be compared. The foundational publication on turn taking is Sacks, Schegloff and Jefferson (1974). I henceforward refer to this article as SSJ. In what follows, I summarize how turn-taking works in L1 talk-in-interaction. I then talk about how CA has been applied to L2 talk. Finally, I close by considering why turn taking in L2 talk might be an interesting topic for second language acquisition (SLA) researchers to pursue in more detail.

Turn taking organization in L1 talk

SSJ propose that turn-taking involves participants orienting to separate "turn-constructional" and "turn-allocation" components, from which a powerful set of more or less abstract rules of turn-taking behavior may be deduced. Turn-constructional units (TCUs) include sentential, clausal, phrasal, and lexical constructions that speakers use as building blocks to construct turns (see Fragment 1 for empirical examples of lexical and sentential TCUs). In terms of turn allocation, transfer of speakership occurs when a so-called transition-relevance place (TRP) is reached, based on speakers' grammatically and/or phonologically based projections of when a turn-as-a-course-of-action becomes complete. Thus, in contrast with turn-constructional component, turn allocation techniques enable: 1) a current speaker to allocate next turn to another speaker; or 2) a currently silent participant to select him or herself as next speaker. Alternatively, current speaker may self-select and produce another turn. Fragment 1 below illustrates how these various components simultaneously come into play:

Fragment 1

```
1 DESK:   What is your last name [Loraine.
2 CALLER:                        [Dinnis.
3 DESK:   What?
4 CALLER: Dinnis
```

(SSJ, p. 702)
[= overlap
period = low fall intonation
Question mark = high rising intonation

More specifically, we can see that in lines 2, 3, and 4, each turn is composed of single lexical TCUs, while the utterance "What is your last name" in line 1 is a sentential TCU. Note that, in line 2, Caller projects that Desk has reached a grammatical TRP in line 1 after this initial sentential TCU is complete. This real time analysis by Caller turns out to be wrong, as Desk observably continues his/her turn in line 1 with the lexical TCU "Loraine." Thus, Caller's lexical TCU in line 2 ("Dinnis.") is in unintentional overlap with the final lexical increment of Desk's turn ("Loraine.") in line 1. Finally, in line 2, Caller mistakenly self-selects as next speaker. This action leads Desk to initiate a repair sequence in line 3, which Caller self-completes in line 4 by repeating her surname "Dinnis." (Note that although this is an unspecified service call, the way in which the turn-taking machinery exemplified in Fragment 1 works is typical of ordinary conversation.)

Based on this and many other empirical examples, SSJ propose a set of participant relevant, recursive rules that specify a "simplest systematics" of turn-taking behavior (see SSJ, p. 704 for details). Briefly, if a "current speaker selects next" technique is used, the person so selected by current speaker has the right and obligation to speak next. If current speaker does not designate next speaker, any first starter acquires the right to speak next. Alternatively, current speaker may continue to produce another turn. Finally, if neither of the first two rules has operated and current speaker continues speaking, the three rules above are recycled in the same order until a change in speakership is achieved.

In contrast with this rule set that describes turn taking in ordinary conversation, Mehan (1979) has proposed that teacher fronted classroom talk is organized in terms of Question-Answer-Comment (also known as Initiation-Response-Feedback) sequences in which teachers have the right and obligation to ask students questions, students to answer these questions, and teachers to comment on the quality of students' responses. Similarly, McHoul (1978: 188) has proposed a modified set of rules for teacher-fronted classroom interaction that is closely modeled on SSJ's work. These institutionally relevant rules differ from those that obtain in ordinary conversation in that ordinary conversation is a locally managed speech exchange system (i.e., it is a system of peers), while institutional talk is asymmetrical (i.e., teachers and students do not have equal rights and obligations to talk).

Turn taking in L2 talk

Turn taking in L2 talk-interaction works in similar ways. However, at least two important differences between the L1 and L2 literatures exist: 1) L2 researchers have to work harder than L1 researchers to make their arguments stick because L2 speakers are often not fully competent in the L2 (Wong and Olsher, 2000); and 2) the majority of the CA literature on L2 talk focuses on classroom talk (see Markee, 2000, but see also Kurhila, 2006). In addition, it is important to note that the application of CA techniques to issues in SLA has always been, and will doubtless continue to be, highly controversial for the foreseeable future (see Firth and Wagner, 1997; Lafford, 2007). In particular, there is considerable disagreement about what specific role(s), if any, turn taking and other interactional practices play in the traditionally psycholinguistic domain of (second) language learning (see Ortega, 2009 for a balanced treatment of this issue).

I do not have the space to address these issues here. Instead, let me sketch out how TCUs may function as participant-relevant building blocks for SLA. In Markee (2000), I analyze some ESL classroom data to show how a learner first understands and then learns the word "coral," at least in the short term. The crucial finding here is that the learner in question cannibalizes TCUs that occur in seven preliminary fragments of small group work-based interaction, and then recycles these TCUs in a novel, complex definition of the word "coral" that she presents to the rest of the class in the final eighth fragment.

Similarly, Markee and Kunitz (2011) show how, during the course of some out-of-class planning talk that is spread out over several days, three learners in an Italian as a second language class formulate and develop the opening line of a restaurant skit that they present in class at a later date. The final version of this opening line in the in-class presentation is "bienvenuti al nostro ristorante Pasta Hut" (= welcome to our restaurant Pasta Hut). The focus of this presentation is on how, over time, the participants fix the grammatical gender of the word "ristorante" (a masculine noun in Italian), but which the students at first incorrectly mark as a feminine noun via article and adjective agreement. As shown below, these participants also cannibalize and recycle several closely related TCUs from four fragments in two speech events (SE1 and SE2):

Fragment 1 (SE1):
bienvenuti-welcome to our restaurant
Fragment 2 (SE2):
*bienvenuti *alla ristorante*
welcome to-**the(F)** restaurant**(M)**
Fragment 3 (SE2):
*bienvenuti to **our** restaurant*
Fragment 4 (SE2):
*bienvenuti ****alla*** *****nostra*** *ristorante*
welcome to-**the(F) our(F)** restaurant**(M)**
↓
repair sequence (first on *nostra*, then on *la*)
↓
In-class presentation:
*bienvenuti **al** nostro ristorante*

welcome to-**the(M) our(M)** restaurant**(M)**
Prepositions with article:
a + la (F) = alla
vs a + il (M) = al

These findings suggest that cannibalization/recycling practices are one of several empirically observable resources that participants use not just in the context of vocabulary-related "language learning behavior" (Markee, 2008). They are also relevant to learners as they grapple with incorporating gender-related morphology into their talk. If further research confirms the robustness of such practices, we may eventually be able to address much "bigger" theoretical issues concerning what an interface between behavior and cognition actually looks and sounds like.

See also: alignment, context of situation, Conversation Analysis (CA), institutional talk, pragmatics, social and socio cultural approaches to SLA

References

Firth, A. and Wagner, J. (1997). On discourse, communication, and (some) fundamental concepts in SLA research. *The Modern Language Journal*, *81*, 285–300.

Kurhila, S. (2006). *Second Language Interaction*. Amsterdam and Philadelphia, PA: John Benjamins.

Lafford, B. (ed.) (2007). *The Modern Language Journal*, Focus Issue, *91*.

Markee, N. (2000). *Conversation Analysis*. Mahwah, NJ: Lawrence Erlbaum Associates.

——(2008). Toward a learning behavior tracking methodology for CA-for-SLA. *Applied Linguistics*, *29*, 404–427.

Markee, N. and S. Kunitz (2011). *Doing planning: A non-cognitive perspective*. Paper presented at the American Association of Applied Linguistics Conference, March 26, 2011, Chicago, IL.

McHoul, A. (1978). The organization of turns at formal talk in the classroom. *Language in Society*, *7*, 183–213.

Mehan, H. (1979). *Learning Lessons: Social Organization in the Classroom*. Cambridge, MA: Harvard University Press.

Ortega, L. (2009). *Understanding Second Language Acquisition*. London: Hodder Education.

Sacks, H., E.A. Schegloff, and G. Jefferson (1974). A simplest systematics for the organization of turn-taking for conversation. *Language*, *50*, 696–735.

Schegloff, E.A. (1987). Between macro and micro: Contexts and other connections. In J. Alexander, B. Giesen, R. Munch, and N. Smelser (eds), *The Micro-macro Link*, pp. 207–34. Berkeley: University of California Press.

Wong, J. and D. Olsher (2000). Reflections on conversation analysis and nonnative speaker talk: An interview with Emanuel A. Schegloff. *Issues in Applied Linguistics*, *11*, 111–28.

Type and token frequency in SLA

Soren Eskildsen
University of Southern Denmark

In modern linguistics, especially due to the dominating status of generative grammar, notions of frequency have been largely ignored. However, the functionalist assumption that grammar emerges from language use, and the advent of usage- and exemplar-based models of language (e.g., Barlow and Kemmer, 2000) have given rise to an interest in how specific expressions and structures are used and learned, by children as well as adults. Here, notions of frequency, especially type and token frequency, have become an essential point of interest.

Primarily associated with Bybee's (e.g., 2007) work on how frequency of use influences diachronic language change, the notions of type and token frequency refer to two different ways of counting linguistic occurrences in a body of text. Token frequency refers to the occurrence of a specific item, be it a morpheme, a phoneme, a syllable, or a specific word or phrase. Type frequency, on the other hand, refers to the number of different instantiations representing a given morphological, phonological, or syntactic pattern or construction.

The two kinds of frequency have different effects. Token frequency is key in processes of entrenchment of specific items, whereas type frequency determines the degree of productivity of a construction. In studies on language change, high-frequency irregular tokens have been found to have a tendency to remain unchanged over time, whereas less frequent irregular tokens are more susceptible to paradigmatic change. This has been especially evident in studies on inflectional morphology which have revealed that, for example, irregular past tense forms with a high frequency retain their status as irregular, whereas less frequent irregular tokens tend to evolve regular forms over time, sometimes used by speakers alongside the irregular forms. Examples include *keep* – *kept*; *sleep* – *slept* versus *creep* – *creeped/crept*; *leap* – *leaped/leapt* (Bybee, 2007).

Leaped and *creeped* can be said to be two new additions to the *-ed* past tense construction. Such additions are possible because of the high degree of productivity of the construction, and this high degree of productivity is in turn brought about by a high type frequency, that is, the existence of a large number of different instantiations of the construction. Type frequency, then, determines productivity because to be productive (i.e., sanction the use of a high number of lexical items in a given slot) a construction is dependent on recurrence which helps entrench its representational schema. The construction, however, is also dependent on token frequency as recurrent exemplars of high frequency help establish the categorical boundaries of the construction (Bybee, 2007). For example, the double object construction (*he gave her flowers*) is semantically dependent on high-frequency exemplars containing the verb *give* which prototypically associates with the general meaning of the construction.

Implications for language acquisition

In recent usage- and exemplar-based language learning research, L1 and L2, type and token frequency have been found to play an important role. This research proposes a developmental learning trajectory from exemplars towards an increasingly varied and schematized linguistic inventory that is crucially dependent upon type and token frequency (e.g., Ellis, 2002, Tomasello, 2003). Token frequency is the frequency of a concrete, specific linguistic element, for example, a specific expression. The higher the token frequency of this expression in the language learner's experience, the more likely it is to become entrenched in his/her mind. The expression may then subsequently form the experiential basis from which the emergence of the more productive construction is made possible. However, token frequency is only half the story; in order for the construction to emerge in learning, the learner, child or adult, needs access to a variety of types, that is, different instantiations of the same pattern. In experimental studies, it has been shown that children and adults learn a construction faster if they are exposed to one high frequency token as well as several types exemplifying the construction (Goldberg and Casenhiser, 2008). Type frequency, then, here refers to the number of different instantiations of the same construction, and it is key in determining the schematicity of that construction.

In second language acquisition, the role of frequency has been a matter of controversy. Introductory textbooks to the field have usually put forward cautious statements that neither promoted nor dismissed the importance of frequency (e.g., Larsen-Freeman and Long, 1991). In the influential input-interaction model, frequency has been considered a factor among many in the ways in which interaction is a source of L2 learning (Gass, 1997). It is in connection with usage- and exemplar-based models of language and language learning that frequency is given a more prominent role. Here, the role of type and token frequency has been investigated in terms of Zipfian distribution in input and learner production, in terms of the evolution from exemplar to construction in individual learners, and in terms of the interplay of vocabulary productivity and other linguistic subsystems in a Dynamic Systems approach to SLA. For example, Ellis and Ferreira-Jr. (2009) showed that learners first learned high frequency prototypical exemplars of the constructions under investigation – exemplars based on the the verb *put* in the Verb Object Locative-construction and exemplars based on the verb *give* in the double-object construction. Eskildsen (e.g., 2011) has used type and token frequency counts in learner production. This research has confirmed the initial use of high-frequency exemplars, but it has also shown in two longitudinal case studies how learners, in development, tend to display an increase in type frequency of the constructions under investigation, and that productivity within the construction gradually expands, albeit in a nonlinear fashion, as displayed through an increase in type-token ratios. Finally, SLA research from a Dynamic Systems Theory perspective (Verspoor, Lowie and Van Dijk, 2008) has applied type-token ratios to investigate variation in learner text production over time in order to investigate how vocabulary productivity interplays with other subsystems in L2 learning.

See also: collostruction, construction learning, Complex Systems Theory/Dynamic Systems Theory, development in SLA, entrenchment, frequency effects

References

Barlow, M. and Kemmer, S. (2000). *Usage-Based Models of Language*. Stanford, CA: CSLI Publications.

Bybee, J. (2007). *Frequency of Use and the Organization of Language*. Oxford: Oxford University Press.

Ellis, N.C. (2002). Frequency effects in language processing: A review with implications for theories of implicit and explicit language acquisition. *Studies in Second Language Acquisition*, *24*, 143–188.

——and Ferreira-Junior, F. (2009). Construction learning as a function of frequency, frequency distribution, and function. *The Modern Language Journal*, *93* (3) 373–85.

Eskildsen, S.W. (2011). The linguistic inventory in action: Conversation analysis and usage-based linguistics in second language acquisition. In G. Pallotti and J. Wagner (eds), *L2 Learning as Social Practice: Conversation-analytic Perspectives*. Honolulu, HI: National Foreign Language Resource Center.

Gass, S. (1997). *Input, Interaction, and the Second Language Learner*. Mahwah, NJ: Erlbaum.

Goldberg, A. and Casenhiser, D. (2008). Construction learning and second language acquisition. In P. Robinson and N.C. Ellis (eds), *Handbook of Cognitive Linguistics and Second Language Acquisition*. New York: Routledge.

Larsen-Freeman, D. and Long, M.H. (1991). *An Introduction to Second Language Research*. London: Longman.

Tomasello, M. (2003). *Constructing a Language*. Cambridge, MA: Harvard University Press.

Verspoor, M., Lowie, W. and Van Dijk, M. (2008). Variability and second language development from a dynamic systems perspective. *The Modern Language Journal*, *92* (2) 214–31.

Further reading

Bybee, J. and Hopper, P. (eds) (2001). *Frequency and the Emergence of Linguistic Structure*. Amsterdam: John Benjamins.

Ellis, N.C. (2003). Constructions, chunking, and connectionism: The emergence of second language structure. In C.J. Doughty and M.H. Long (eds), *The Handbook of Second Language Acquisition*. Malden, MA: Blackwell.

——and Ferreira-Junior, F. (2009). Constructions and their acquisition: Islands and the distinctiveness of their occupancy. *Annual Review of Cognitive Linguistics*, *7*, 187–220.

Gries, S. Th. And Wulff, S. (2009). Psycholinguistic and corpus-linguistic evidence for L2 constructions. *Annual Review of Cognitive Linguistics*, *7*, 163–86.

U

U-shaped learning and overgeneralization

Niclas Abrahamsson
Stockholm University

A common phenomenon in both first language (L1) and second language (L2) acquisition is that the child or adult learner who earlier has produced a newly acquired linguistic form in a targetlike manner then begins systematically using a non-targetlike form instead, only to return to the target form at a later stage. This phenomenon is frequently called *U-shaped learning* (see Figure 15) or *restructuring* of the interlanguage system (cf. Lightbown, 1985: 177; Sharwood Smith, 1994: 209). A typical example is the development of irregular preterits by English L1 children as well as by L2 learners of English. Initially, learners pick up words like *ate* and *went* from input as unanalyzed items and use them accordingly. Later, when the learner discovers the linguistic rule for regular preterits, this rule is automatically used for all verbs, including irregular ones, and forms like **eated* and **goed* are systematically produced. Finally, when the learner discovers that there are irregular verbs that do not undergo the acquired rule, the irregular preterit forms – that is, *ate* and *went* – re-enter the system, this time as analyzed forms.

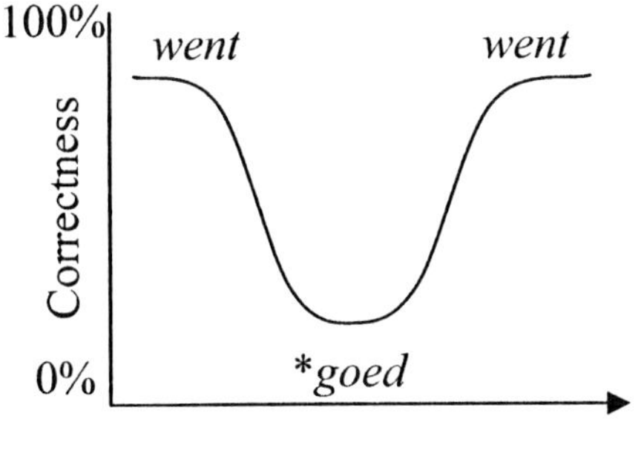

Figure 15 U-shaped learning curve

The primary reason for the U-shaped learning curve – thus called because initially there are high rates of correctness, followed by low rates of correct forms, and then high correctness rates again – is generally the phenomenon of linguistic *overgeneralization* (although other sources for U-shaped language behavior can be identified, as will be exemplified below). *Overgeneralization* was listed by Selinker (1972) in his *Interlanguage Theory* as one of the five central processes responsible for adult L2 learners' development and potential fossilization of interlanguage forms. Overgeneralization occurs when language learners systematically extend the use of some acquired linguistic element to contexts where it, according to the target-language norm, does not apply. The object of overgeneralization may be:

- morphological rules, for example, Eng. regular preterit: *go* → **goed*; Eng. regular plural: *fish* → **fishes*; Eng. regular comparative: *good* → **gooder*;

- syntactic rules, for example, post-verbal NEG placement to subordinate clauses in Swedish, **Jag vet att hon spelar inte / I know that she playes not*, 'I know that she doesn't play'; SUBJ/V (over-)inversion in Eng. subordinate clauses, **I know where is she*;
- phonological rules/patterns, for example, word intonation in Swedish, accent 1 → accent 2, *'havet* (with one F0 peak) 'the sea' → **æha-vet* (with two F0 peaks);
- lexicon/semantics, for example, when children use the word *dog* for cats and other four-legged animals as well, or when Swe. learners of L2 Eng. incorrectly use *house* when referring to a tall multi-store building; or
- pragmatics, for example, L2 learners of Eng. using *Miss* or *Mrs.* to all women, regardless of their age and marital status.

Some overgeneralizations lead to errors, while others, such as overgeneralization of idiomatic expressions to situational contexts where they do not apply, do not always result in overt errors, but rather in a certain degree of awkwardness or deviance from the target-language norm in terms of native/adult-speaker usage.

U-shaped patterns of development are not always the result of overgeneralization but may surface for a variety of reasons. One example is the number of phonological errors made over time in second language acquisition. Our intuition might tell us that beginner learners would in all likelihood begin with a very high number of pronunciation errors and that the number of errors would decrease in a linear fashion with increased learning/time. However, in reality this is not typically the case. Instead, both L1 and L2 development is characterized by relatively little pronunciation deviance in early phases – phases during which the child or adult learner carefully tries out new lexical items by repetition and imitation, and by speaking at a slow rate of speed. Later on, when the learner has gained a large enough vocabulary, the focus of attention shifts from the pronunciation of isolated words to the conveyance of messages with meaning, and with increased communicative fluency, the ratio of correct to incorrect pronunciations tends to shift, too, from low to high. Only when actual mastery of the phonological system takes place, allowing for correct pronunciation even at high speaking rates and even when focusing on communication and meaning, does the error rate return to lower frequencies. In other words, an overall pattern of high-low-high frequencies of correct pronunciation is usually found without overgeneralization being the principal process causing the U-shaped development (see, e.g., Abrahamsson, 1999, 2003; Sato, 1987).

In cases of U-shaped learning, whether caused by overgeneralization or by some other linguistic aspect (such as fluency, efficiency, etc.), the decrease in nativelikeness/targetlikeness/correctness must not be interpreted as a sign of back-sliding or developmental regression – on the contrary, the temporary dip in correct utterances is some of the clearest evidence of learner creativity and of the systematicity and advancement of interlanguage systems. As for the example with **eated* and **goed*, the error comes about because the learner has *discovered* and actually *acquired a rule* that was not part of the interlanguage system before. Armed with this new rule, inferred from the input perceived so far, the learner will systematically and automatically try to apply it wherever possible. It is only later, when the learner discovers that the regular preterit rule does not apply to all verbs (just the regular ones), that the initially correct, irregular form re-appears in the system. At the same time, the U-shaped learning curve and overgeneralizations of forms or rules (such as **eated* and **goed*) are strong evidence against the behaviorist view that language acquisition results from imitation of adult/native-speaker utterances.

See also: acquisition of tense and aspect, development in SLA, error analysis, form-meaning relations, fossilization, interlanguage, morpheme acquisition orders

References

Abrahamsson, N. (1999). Vowel epenthesis of /sC (C)/ onsets in Spanish/Swedish interphonology: A longitudinal case study. *Language Learning, 49*, 473–508.

——(2003). Development and recoverability of L2 codas: A longitudinal study of Chinese/Swedish interphonology. *Studies in Second Language Acquisition*, *25*, 313–49.

Lightbown, P. (1985). Input and acquisition for second language learners in and out of classrooms. *Applied Linguistics*, *6*, 263–73.

Sato, C. (1987). Phonological processes in second language acquisition: Another look at interlanguage syllable structure. In G. Ioup and S.H. Weinberger (eds), *Interlanguage Phonology. The Acquisition of a Second Language Sound System*. Cambridge: Newbury House.

Selinker, L. (1972). Interlanguage. *International Review of Applied Linguistics*, *10*, 209–31.

Sharwood Smith, M. (1994). *Second Language Learning: Theoretical Foundations*. London and New York: Longman.

Units for analysing L2 speaking

Pauline Foster

St. Mary's University College

In contrast to writing, which tends to be edited, monologic and made up of complete units (i.e. sentences), speech tends to be unedited, to involve more than one person and to have a high proportion of false starts, repetitions and elliptical fragments. These characteristics make the task of dividing it reliably into units for analysis rather difficult. To illustrate, here is an example of second language (L2) speech, taken from a conversation between two adult learners of English discussing suitable prison terms for a list of offenders:

1A: which which what is your opinion?
2B: . ... maybe er. he.
3A: long time? or it's for for you it's a major mistake or a small mistake?
4B: maybe three months
5A: three months for this one okay for me it's ten
6B: ten?
7A: ten years
8B: yeah ten years oh very long

(data from Foster and Skehan, 1996)

The simplest way to analyse this is to divide it into units called *turns,* of which there are clearly eight. A speaker's contribution to any interaction under analysis can be measured by the number of turns he or she makes in, say, a minute. However, as shown in our example, a turn can be as short as a single word, so a speaker whose contribution was characterised by many short turns would not be distinguishable from a speaker who made many long ones. The way round this is to calculate the *mean length of turn* for each speaker by dividing the total number of words by the total number of turns. This usually involves *pruning* the speech of extraneous repetitions and false starts, so that the hesitant first line in the example above would be pruned of its first two words. Nevertheless, an analysis of turns is limited. It can tell us only about relative complexity of performance, and it can only be used with interactional speech.

Other units of analysis can be applied equally well to non-interactional speech. These can be categorised broadly as semantic, intonational or syntactic. Segmenting speech into semantic units operates by dividing it into parcels of information, called either ideas or propositions. A *proposition* is defined as a 'semantic unit consisting of at least one major argument and one or more predications about this argument' (Sato, 1988: 375). An *idea* is 'a chunk of information ... viewed by the speaker/ writer cohesively as it is given a surface form. ... related ... to psychological reality for the encoder' (Kroll, 1977: 85). In practice, the identification of units based on parcels of information or meaning is not always easy and can be impossible to establish with certainty. In the example above, 1A seems unproblematically one unit of meaning, while 8B could be one or two, depending on whether the speaker meant 'ten years is a very long time', or 'I understand that you want ten years. For me that is too long.' Ellis and Barkhuisen (2005: 154) argue that a segmentation into semantic units like these works best if the L2 performance is pre-specified (as would be the case in a picture description), and which can be matched to a native-like performance. Because it is so hard for the analyst to work reliably with semantic measures, in the research literature they are often supplemented by syntactic and intonational ones.

Intonational units include the *tone unit* and the *utterance.* Crystal and Davy (1975: 16) define the tone unit as 'a distinctive configuration of pitches, with a clear center, or nucleus … which carries the greatest prominence'. The tone unit boundary is signalled by a rise or fall in intonation, often followed by a pause. The utterance is defined similarly as a single semantic unit under one intonational contour with pauses at the boundaries (Crookes, 1990). While the focus of both these definitions is intonational, we can see that semantic features play their part, as do pausing patterns. The line 8B above, which a semantic analysis might determine as either one or two units, could more confidently be coded once its intonational contour is taken into account. For example, it would be two units if there were two nuclei, and/or the speaker's intonation fell at the word 'years', and/or there was a pause here before the next word. However, the intonation of L2 speakers can be unpredictable and hard to account for. Their pauses are not necessarily at unit boundaries, and it can be difficult to distinguish between a pause that occurs at the end of a unit and one that occurs in the middle due to a lexical search.

Syntactic units of speech are based on the grammatical plan that underpins the speaker's formulation of thought. The *T-unit,* which was conceived by Hunt (1966) for the analysis of writing, is defined essentially as a main clause plus any other clauses which are dependent upon it. It has been used extensively in the analysis of spoken data, though researchers have often reported difficulties. Tarone (1985) for example remarks that she was unable to divide some of her recorded speech data in T-units because it was so dysfluent and full of fragments. The example given above would also be hard to analyse as T-units; lines 3A, 4B, 5A, 6B, 7A, and 8B all contain or comprise elliptical elements which do not fit Hunt's definition. If this is followed closely, only lines 1A, and parts of 3A and 5A can be described confidently as T-units; the rest must be regarded as fragments. To avoid discarding so much potentially valuable data, researchers choosing to use the T-unit for oral data have needed to adapt it. Young (1995) for example reported the ad hoc modifications he made to the definition of the T-unit that allowed him to include elliptical elements, exclude discourse markers such as 'OK' and 'good', and to incorporate false starts into the following unit.

Related to the T-unit and designed specifically for dealing with oral data, is the communication unit or *c-unit* (Loban, 1966: 5–6). This starts with definition of the T-unit and builds upon it by including "answers to questions which lack only the repetition of the question elements to satisfy the criterion of independent predication", and also single word answers to questions such as "have you ever been sick?" This goes some way to solving the problem of what to do with the widespread and entirely natural choice of answering questions elliptically or with one word. It means that line 4B above is a c-unit because it is an elliptical answer to the question in line 1A. But the definition does not specifically address elliptical constructions that do not link with an interlocutor's question, such as line 6B and the first two words of line 3A.

The Analysis of Speech unit or *AS-unit* (Foster *et al.*, 2000) is a syntactically based unit that is similar to the c-unit, but which has a fuller definition. It includes sub-clausal elements such as the first two words of 3A where the full clause can be recovered from the context of the discourse. It also includes units that cross turn boundaries where the interlocutor interupts or else supplies part of the speaker's utterance. Topicalised noun phrases, which abound in speech, are regarded as belonging to the AS-unit of which they are the topic, rather than as fragments. The AS-unit makes use of intonational and pausing phenomena where segmentation problems arise. For example, in line 8B, because the speaker's intonation falls after the word 'years' and rises afterwards with the word 'oh' a unit boundary is drawn between them. Another feature of the AS-unit is that it can be applied on three levels, depending on the researcher's needs. A level one analysis works on all the data, such that even minimal discourse markers such as 'OK' (line 5A) and 'yeah' (line 8B) count as units. A level two analysis excludes these and verbatim echoic responses such as 'ten?' in line 6B. A level three analysis further excludes anything involving ellipsis of elements of the interlocutor's speech, such as when a speaker replies, 'I think so' to a question beginning 'Do you think … ?'

Once segmentation of speech data is completed, using whatever unit the analyst regards as the most valid and reliable, it is possible to determine the frequency of discourse features such as self-corrections and clarification requests, or grammatical features such as tense and gender markers. The relative syntactic complexity and fluency of individual speakers can also be calculated and expressed quantitatively as, for example, mean number of clauses per unit, or mean number of false starts per unit. Grammatical accuracy can be expressed as mean number of errors per unit, or proportion of units that are error-free. A unit for the segmentation of oral data is thus an essential tool in second language acquisition research.

See also: classroom interaction research, quantitative research, scaffolding, speaking, speech rate, turn taking

References

Crookes, G. (1990). The utterance, and other basic units for second language discourse analysis. *Applied Linguistics*, *11*, 183–99.

Crystal, D.C. and Davy, D. (1975). *Advanced Conversational English*. London: Longman.

Ellis, R. and Barkhuizen, G. (2005). *Analysing Learner Language*. Oxford: Oxford University Press.

Foster, P. and Skehan, P. (1996). The influence of planning on performance in task based learning. *Studies in Second Language Acquisition*, *18*, 299–324.

Foster, P., Tonkyn, A. and Wigglesworth, G. (2000). A unit for all reasons: the analysis of spoken interaction. *Applied Linguistics*, *21*, 354–74.

Hunt, K. (1966). Recent measures in syntactic development. *Elementary English*, *43*, 732–39.

Kroll, B. (1977). Combining ideas in written and spoken English: a look at subordination and coordination. In E. Ochs and T. Bennett (eds), *Discourse across Time and Space*. SCOPIL (Southern California Occasional Papers in Linguistics) no. 5.

Loban,W. (1966). *The Language of Elementary School Children*. (Research Report no. 1). Champaign, IL: National Council of Teachers of English.

Sato, C. (1988). Origins of complex syntax. *Studies in Second Language Acquisition*, *10*, 371–95.

Tarone, E. (1985). Variability in interlanguage use: a study of style-shifting in morphology and syntax. *Language Learning*, *35*, 373–405.

Young, R. (1995). Conversation style in language proficiency interviews. *Language Learning*, *45*/1: 3–45.

Further reading

Bygate, M. (1988). Units of oral expression and language learning in small group interaction. *Applied Linguistics*, *9*, 59–82. (An extended treatment of the topic.)

Units for analyzing L2 writing

Charlene Polio
Michigan State University

Research on second language (L2) writing that takes a quantitative approach to analyzing writers' texts must determine the most appropriate units and measures to use. Such measures are used in experimental studies, which may ask questions about the effects of a given treatment on L2 writers' texts, or in causal-comparative research, which examines how different groups of writers' texts differ from one another or from native speakers' texts. The way that writers' texts are analyzed varies greatly from study to study depending on the research question.

The units used in L2 writing fall roughly into five categories: word or phrases; errors; clauses and T-units; entire texts; and changes across texts. Each of these units may be used in measures for a variety of constructs. For example, T-units maybe used in measuring both accuracy and complexity. Furthermore, the same constructs may be measured using different units. For example, accuracy may be assessed by counting the number of errors or by counting error-free T-units. Other studies have examined less quantifiable features such as functions, rhetorical moves, and intertextuality (in the form of citations). These are discussed below as well, but studies using these units tend to be more qualitative because the units are more difficult to isolate.

Words can be used as units to measure a variety of constructs. The number of words written in a certain amount of time, for example, can measure fluency. Words can also be used to measure a variety of vocabulary-related constructs (Wolfe-Quintero, Inagaki, and Kim, 1998). Lexical complexity, for example, can be measured using a type/token ratio. Using this measure, the number of different words is divided by the total number of words. Thus, a writer whose vocabulary is not diverse would receive a lower lexical complexity score. The frequency of a lexical item may also be considered in determining lexical complexity so that writers using less common words will receive higher lexical complexity scores (e.g., Laufer and Nation, 1995).

Words can also be used as a unit in measuring discourse features of texts. For example, lexical cohesion, developed in work by text linguists such as Hasan (1984) and Hoey (1991), is a construct describing relationships between sections of a text and can be measured using the repetition of words or synonym use. Automated measurement of this construct has been attempted through latent semantic analysis (Landauer, Foltz, and Laham, 1998). Crossley and MacNamara (2009) used Coh-Matrix software to describe several dimensions of writers' texts based on the word as a unit.

Recently, learner language has been analyzed in terms of formulaic sequences or chunks. A sequence can be a unit of two or more words and can be identified and classified in a variety of ways. For example, an idiom can be considered a sequence, or words that naturally co-occur (i.e., lexical bundles) found through analyses of learner corpora can be used. These sequences are of particular interest in academic writing and can illuminate differences in the writing of novices and second language learners from the writing of experts or published research. Hyland (2008), for example, conducted a corpus analysis of students' theses and dissertations to determine the occurrence of formulaic sequences.

Some studies that measure accuracy use the error as the unit of analysis and often report the number of errors per words and some of these studies classify each error, which can be morphological, syntactic, or lexical. Counting and classifying errors can lead to inevitable coder disagreements. For example, what appears to be a subject-verb agreement error can sometimes be classified as a singular/plural error. If detailed guidelines are written, however, intercoder reliability can be achieved, and using errors as the unit provides a more fine-grained measure of accuracy than measures based on the T-unit.

Clauses and T-units are commonly used units in second language writing research. A T-unit is an independent clause and all its associated dependent clauses. This unit is based on earlier research on children writing in their first language, who often string together sentences using coordinating conjunctions (Hunt, 1965). Although there has been some discussion about the appropriateness of T-units (Bardovi-Harlig, 1992), they remain more commonly used than sentences. A T-unit can be used in a number of measures. The most common are: error-free T-units/total T-units, to measure accuracy; clauses/T-units, to measure complexity; and words/T-units, which has been used to measure fluency (Wolfe-Quintero *et al.*, 1998) or complexity (Norris and Ortega, 2009). Defining a T-unit is quite straightforward and very high intercoder reliability can be easily achieved. Clauses within a T-units are defined differently among studies, so researchers need to carefully identify how they count clauses. As for using T-units to measure accuracy, the identification of an error-free T-unit can be problematic as coders will often not agree on whether or not a T-unit includes an error.

The entire text of a piece of writing may be examined to evaluate the overall quality of the text or components of the text. In this case, the entire piece of writing is the unit in that the text is not broken down for analysis. The text can be evaluated by assigning a holistic score to the entire essay for overall quality or an analytic scale can be used to assess individual characteristics such as organization, language use, content, and so on.

While rating, a rater may indeed be focused on smaller units such as errors or vocabulary use but these units are not analyzed beyond how the rater views them in the text as a whole.

Sometimes writers' texts are analyzed for change from a prior draft. This may be done in studies that investigate, for example, the effect of peer review on revision. Such studies are particularly difficult because a unit of analysis that indicates type of change is not immediately obvious. Because a variety of units can be changed (e.g., word, sentence, paragraph) operationalizing change is problematic. Several systems of coding changes have been devised. One commonly used one was developed by Faigley and Witte (1981). It codes what they call meaning-preserving changes (such as changes in grammar or spelling) as well as larger-scale changes (such as the deletion or addition of sentence). Such an analysis is problematic in that the units vary with different types of changes making the coding difficult to quantify. Other studies have coded changes relevant to their research questions. For example, Ferris (1997) coded changes or lack thereof in response to a teacher's comment. Again, the exact unit of what a change is is still a bit unclear, but the focus, in this case, is narrower.

Finally, many studies analyze texts according to units that are more difficult to quantify. Hinkel (2002) describes features of learners' texts according to the function that certain words, phrases, or sentences fulfill. For example, exemplification can be manifested in a variety of words or phrases. Hedging, too, has also been described in L2 writers' texts (Hyland and Milton, 1997; Hinkel, 2002).

Another possible unit of analysis is based on the genre analysis work of Swales (1990) who analyzes texts with regard to rhetorical moves. Rhetorical moves are units that refer to various functions of a segment of text. For example, in a research article, a move can be to state the limitations of a study. Research on rhetorical moves is more commonly applied to published texts but can also be applied to L2 writing to better understand how second language writers' texts differ from those of native speakers or those written by experts and published writers.

Intertexuality, the relationship between the writers' text and other texts, has been described using a variety of units. Inappropriate textual borrowing, or plagiarism, is, of course, hard to quantify, but some researchers have used the paraphrase as a unit (e.g., Keck, 2006) to identify types of paraphrases in writers' texts. Others have examined the forms that citations take in writers' texts (Thompson and Tribble, 2001).

Because research on L2 writing is so diverse and takes into account linguistic features such as word choice and grammar as well as more global issues such as text organization, a large variety of ways to analyze texts exists. Researchers have a wide array of units to choose from and while there is no right or wrong way to analyze a text, clarity in the choices made during the analysis is essential for evaluating and interpreting the research.

See also: cohesion and coherence, formulaic language, interrater reliability, type and token frequency in SLA, units for analyzing L2 speaking, writing

References

Bardovi-Harlig, K. (1992). A second look at T-unit analysis: Reconsidering the sentence. *TESOL Quarterly*, *26*, 390–95.

Crossley, S.A. and McNamara, D.M. (2009). Computational assessment of lexical differences in L1 and L2 writing. *Journal of Second Language Writing*, *18*, 119–35.

Faigley, L. and Witte, S. (1981). Analyzing revision. *College Composition and Communication*, *32*, 400–414.

Ferris, D. (1997). The influence of teacher commentary on student revision. *TESOL Quarterly*, *31*, 315–52.

Hasan, R. (1984). Coherence and cohesive harmony. In J. Flood (ed.), *Understanding Reading Comprehension*, pp. 181–219. Newark, NJ: International Reading Association.

Hinkel, E. (2002). *Second Language Writers' Text.* Mahwah, NJ: Erlbaum.

Hoey, M. (1991). *Patterns of Lexis in Text.* New York: Oxford University Press.

Hunt, K. (1965). *Grammatical Structures Written at Three Grade Levels*. Champaign, IL: National Council of Teachers of English.

Hyland, K. (2008). Academic clusters: text patterning in published and postgraduate writing. *International Journal of Applied Linguistics, 18* (1), 41–62.

Hyland, K. and Milton, J. (1997). Hedging in L1 and L2 student writing. *Journal of Second Language Writing, 6*, 183–206.

Keck, C. (2006). The use of paraphrase in summary writing: A comparison of L1 and L2 writers. *Journal of Second Language Writing, 15*, 261–78.

Landauer, T.K., Foltz, P.W. and Laham, D. (1998). Introduction to latent semantic analysis. *Discourse Processes, 25*, 259–284.

Laufer, B. and Nation, P. (1995). Vocabulary size and use: Lexical richness in L2 written production. *Applied Linguistics, 16*, 307–22.

Norris, J. and Ortega, L. (2009). Towards an organic approach to investigating CAF in instructed SLA: The case of complexity. *Applied Linguistics, 30*, 555–578.

Swales, J. (1990). *Genre Analysis: English in Academic and Research Settings*. Cambridge: Cambridge University Press.

Thompson, P. and Tribble, C. (2001). Looking at citations: Using corpora in academic English. *Language Learning and Technology, 5* (3), 91–105

Wolfe-Quintero, K. Inagaki, S., and Kim, H.Y. (1998). *Second Language Development in Writing: Measures of Fluency, Accuracy, and Complexity. (Technical Report #17)*. Honolulu, HI: National Foreign Language Resource Center.

Further reading

Housen, A. and Folkert, K. (eds) (2009). Special issue: Complexity, accuracy, and fluency (CAF) in second language acquisition research. *Applied Linguistics, 30*. [Entire issue] (This special issue includes six articles on defining and measuring complexity, accuracy, and fluency in spoken and written language.)

Leki, I., Cumming, A. and Silva, A. (2008). *A synthesis of research on second language writing*. New York: Routledge/Taylor & Francis. (This book is a comprehensive review of second language writing research and includes a section on analyzing writers' texts.)

Norris, J. and Ortega, L. (2009). Towards an organic approach to investigating CAF in instructed SLA: The case of complexity. *Applied Linguistics, 30*, 555–578. (This discussion of the challenges of measuring complexity, accuracy, and fluency in spoken and written language focuses on measures of complexity.)

Polio, C. (2001). Research methodology in second language writing research: The case of text-based studies. In T. Silva and P. Matsuda (eds), *On second language writing*, pp. 91–116. Mahwah, NJ: Erlbaum. (This chapter classifies studies that analyze writers' texts in a variety of ways.)

Wolfe-Quintero, K. Inagaki, S. and Kim, H.Y. (1998). *Second Language Development in Writing: Measures of Fluency, Accuracy, and Complexity. (Technical Report #17)*. Honolulu, HI: National Foreign Language Resource Center. (This book reviews 39 studies that examine measures of writing development.)

Universal Grammar (UG) and SLA

Lydia White
McGill University

A tenet of generative linguistic theory is that certain principles of language structure are innately present in first language (L1) acquirers, taking the form of Universal Grammar (UG), which constrains the linguistic competence of native speakers during the course of acquisition and thereafter. Arguments for UG stem from a consideration of the *logical problem of language acquisition*, the issue being that young children come to know highly complex and subtle linguistic phenomena which are not transparent in the input (e.g. Chomsky, 1981). UG includes universal principles, which predetermine the form and functioning of natural language grammars, as well as parameters, which allow for circumscribed variation across languages.

Determining the precise nature and content of UG is the domain of linguistic theory; proposals have been changed and refined over the years. Along with such changes, there have been shifts in perspective on the role of UG in second language (L2) acquisition. The earliest UG-oriented research (starting in the 1980s) pursued two major themes: (i) access (or lack of access) to principles of UG; and (ii) possibility (or impossibility) of resetting UG parameters. In the 1990s, there was a change in emphasis. Parameters were now largely conceived of as being associated with grammatical features and L2 research focused on the extent to which adult learners are able to access features not instantiated in the L1. More recently, there has been yet another shift in focus, involving a consideration of linguistic interfaces, the idea being that L2 learners/speakers (henceforth L2ers) might have particular difficulties in the integration of certain kinds of grammatical phenomena.

Principles and parameters

The debate on L2 access to UG principles was couched in the following terms: if L2ers demonstrate unconscious knowledge of constraints operating on the L2 grammar, especially if these could not be derived from the L1, this provides evidence for the continuing functioning of UG (White, 1989). In contrast, if L2ers fail to observe such constraints, this suggests that UG is no longer accessible (e.g. Bley-Vroman, 1989). Accordingly, much early research focused on L2 constraints which happen, for independent reasons, to be inactive in the L1. A much studied example involves restrictions on wh-movement in languages like English. *Subjacency* is a constraint which predetermines what kind of wh-movement is and is not possible; this constraint is vacuous in languages without wh-movement, such as Japanese, Chinese, or Korean. The test case, then, is whether native speakers of such languages observe restrictions on *wh*-movement when acquiring L2 English.

One of the original studies investigating this issue was by Schachter (1990), who showed that adult L2ers of English with Korean or Chinese L1s were significantly less accurate than native speakers in rejecting ungrammatical sentences that are ruled out by this UG principle. Furthermore, L2ers whose L1 (Dutch) was a wh-movement language had no such difficulty, suggesting access to UG principles only via the L1. In contrast, other researchers have found no evidence of failure of Subjacency in L2. For example, White and Juffs (1998) report that Chinese speakers who learned the L2 as adults were not significantly different from English native speakers in their ability to reject Subjacency violations.

While investigation of UG principles tried to control for potential L1 effects in order to determine the operation of principles in isolation, investigation of UG parameters was explicitly focused on the question of how language transfer might interact with UG. The hypothesis was that learners might, at least initially, transfer parameter settings from L1 to L2, followed by subsequent resetting to the appropriate L2 value, a position subsequently formulated as the Full Transfer Full Access Hypothesis (Schwartz and Sprouse, 1996). In this context, a number of UG parameters were investigated, starting with the pro-drop or null subject parameter (White, 1985). White compared learners of English whose L1s either were or were not pro-drop languages. She found (i) significant differences between groups, with Spanish speakers (pro-drop L1) much more likely than French speakers (non pro-drop) to accept null subjects in the L2; (ii) a decline in acceptance of null subjects with increasing proficiency level; and (iii) a failure of linguistic properties associated with each parameter value to cluster together in learner grammars.

Another influential paper on parameter resetting was a small study by Finer and Broselow (1986), looking at parameters related to the Binding Theory (Chomsky, 1981). This paper reported that Korean-speaking learners of English adopt a parameter setting for choice of possible antecedents of reflexive pronouns which is that neither of the L1 (which allows long distance antecedents) nor L2 (which requires local antecedents) but which is possible in other natural languages, such as Russian (where tense is crucial in determining antecedent choice).

In summary, it is now fairly generally accepted that L2ers demonstrate unconscious knowledge of abstract and subtle syntactic properties of the L2, implicating the involvement of UG principles, either directly or indirectly (via the L1). As for parameters, while there is evidence for L1 transfer followed by resetting, this resetting is not necessarily appropriate for the L2 and does not necessarily involve all linguistic properties associated with the parameter.

Categories and features

In the 1990s, the relationship between UG and the L1 remained a major consideration. However, the focus changed, with attention now devoted to a consideration of the nature of the initial state in L2 acquisition, as well as subsequent development and ultimate attainment (Schwartz and Sprouse, 1996). Theories were couched in terms of functional categories and their projections (such as IP, CP, and DP), as well as grammatical features (such as tense and agreement). UG is assumed to contain an inventory of grammatical features, with different languages selecting different features from the full set. In other words, the L1 and the L2 might differ as to which features are represented, raising the question of whether L2ers start off restricted to the set exemplified in the L1 and whether they are able to acquire other features required to appropriately represent the L2.

A related consideration involved recognition of the fact that, in contrast to performance implicating abstract syntactic properties, L2ers are often remarkably unsuccessful when it comes to L2 inflectional morphology implicating functional categories and features (e.g. Lardiere, 2000; White, 2003). Inflections marking tense, agreement, number, case, gender, etc., as well as function words like determiners, auxiliaries and complementizers, are used variably in L2 spontaneous production, in circumstances where they would be obligatory for native speakers. Furthermore, when morphology is present, it is not necessarily appropriate; certain forms can be over-used, occurring in contexts where they would not be used by native speakers.

Hawkins and colleagues claim that the full UG feature inventory is no longer accessible. Instead, the grammars of adult L2 speakers are restricted to certain formal features found in the L1. In the case of tense, for example, Hawkins and Liszka (2003) argue for the absence of a tense feature in L1 Chinese, resulting in a corresponding lack of tense in the interlanguage grammar of Chinese-speaking learners of English, thus accounting for variable production of past tense morphology. Originally termed the Failed Functional Features Hypothesis (FFFH), this position has come to be known as the Representational Deficit Hypothesis (RDH).

The claim that problems with past tense and other types of inflection are attributable to lack of the relevant feature in the interlanguage grammar has been challenged. Instead, the Missing Surface Inflection Hypothesis proposes that morphosyntactic features can be represented in a grammar despite lack of corresponding overt morphology (Haznedar and Schwartz, 1997; Prévost and White, 2000). Along these lines, in a detailed case-study, Lardiere (1998) demonstrated that, even in the absence of appropriate morphology, her Chinese-speaking subject had command of many syntactic properties associated with tense. Lardiere suggests that, when inflection is missing in L2 production, there is a problem mapping between the underlying morphosyntactic structure and the associated overt morphological forms.

Semantic factors have also been under investigation in the context of features. For example, in the case of article acquisition, Ionin, Ko and Wexler (2004) have shown that L2ers whose L1s lack articles (Korean and Russian) fluctuate between two settings of an Article Choice Parameter, being uncertain of whether [±definite] or [±specific] is the relevant feature that determines English article choice. In contrast, learners whose L1s have articles with [±definite] features, such as Spanish, show no such fluctuation.

Yet another approach is advanced by Goad and White (2004) who propose a prosodic account of L2ers' omission or mispronunciation of inflection, couched within the Prosodic Transfer Hypothesis (PTH). According to the PTH, the problems that L2ers have with production of inflection result from difficulties associated with constructing prosodic representations required for the L2 but disallowed in the L1. As a result, L2 functional material may be omitted, variably produced or subject to certain substitutions, all dependent on phonological considerations. Difficulties that are apparently due to morphology turn out to be attributable to prosodic representations.

To summarize, the investigation of UG in terms of availability of grammatical features has resulted in a somewhat different perspective on transfer (L1 features rather than L1 parameter settings), on parameter resetting (new features are/are not acquirable), and on deficits (features are/are not represented in the interlanguage grammar). This line of research also emphasizes the need to distinguish between underlying forms and their surface manifestations.

Interfaces

The most recent shift in focus involves consideration of how different aspects of the grammar relate to each other. The linguistic system mediates between sounds and meanings, hence the grammar must interface with external domains, such as discourse. Furthermore, the grammar includes several different components which must interface with each other (lexicon, morphology, phonology, semantics, syntax). Recent L2 research has centered on such interfaces. There is active consideration of whether: (i) the failure of adults to acquire a fully native-like L2 grammar can be attributed to problems integrating material at various interfaces; (ii) such problems arise even when L2ers can otherwise be shown to be observing UG constraints and resetting parameters; and (iii) all interfaces are equally problematic.

For purposes of illustration, we will consider one grammar-internal interface, namely the syntax/semantics interface, and one external interface, namely the syntax/discourse interface, although these are by no means the only interfaces currently being investigated (see White, 2009). Tsimpli and Sorace (2006) propose the Interface Hypothesis, whereby the syntax/discourse interface is hypothesized to be the more problematic, leading to persistent problems (such as L1 transfer and residual optionality), even for near native L2ers.

Achievement of native-like competence relating to the syntax/semantics interface appears to be relatively unproblematic. L2ers prove to be highly sensitive to subtle semantic distinctions which arise as a result of word order differences between the L1 and the L2. Dekydtspotter and colleagues have shown, for the acquisition of French by English speakers, that once L2ers acquire L2 word order alternations which are not found in the L1, they also acquire the associated subtle interpretive distinctions that hold only for the L2 and that are derived from properties of UG (e.g. Dekydtspotter, Sprouse and Swanson 2001).

The syntax/discourse interface appears to be more problematic. A much-studied case involves crosslinguistic differences in how the topic of discourse is realized. In null subject languages like Italian, discourse plays a role in pronoun choice, such that null subjects are strongly preferred when there is no change in topic, while overt subjects imply a change of topic. While L2 Italian speakers acquire syntactic properties of null subjects, successfully resetting the null subject parameter, at the same time they fail to fully appreciate the effects of discourse in determining appropriate pronoun choice (e.g. Belletti, Bennati and Sorace 2007).

Conclusion

In conclusion, there have been a number of recurring themes in research that has investigated the role of UG in L2 acquisition over the past 25 years. These include: (i) the extent to which the L1 grammar has effects and the extent to which transfer can be overcome; and (ii) how similar or different the L2ers' unconscious representation of grammar is from native speaker knowledge of language. As research has become more nuanced and sophisticated, the preoccupation with UG access as such has lessened. Instead, the focus has turned to the nature of linguistic representations in L2 acquisition (both child and adult), including the role of grammatical features and the influence of interfaces in determining not only what is acquired but also how it is used.

See also: age effects in SLA, crosslinguistic influence, fossilization, generative linguistics, initial state, minimalist program

References

Belletti, A., E. Bennati and A. Sorace. (2007). Theoretical and developmental issues in the syntax of subjects: evidence from near-native Italian. *Natural Language and Linguistic Theory*, *25*, 657–89.

Bley-Vroman, R. (1989). What is the logical problem of foreign language learning? In S. Gass and J. Schachter (eds), *Linguistic Perspectives on Second Language Acquisition*. Cambridge: Cambridge University Press.

Chomsky, N. (1981). *Lectures on Government and Binding*. Dordrecht: Foris.

Dekydtspotter, L., R. Sprouse and K. Swanson. (2001). Reflexes of mental architecture in second-language acquisition: the interpretation of *combien* extractions in English-French interlanguage. *Language Acquisition*, *9*, 175–227.

Finer, D. and E. Broselow. (1986). Second language acquisition of reflexive-binding. In S. Berman, J.-W. Choe and J. McDonough (eds), *Proceedings of NELS* 16. University of Massachusetts at Amherst: Graduate Linguistics Students Association.

Goad, H. and L. White. (2004). Ultimate attainment of L2 inflection: effects of L1 prosodic structure. In S. Foster-Cohen, M. Sharwood Smith, A. Sorace and M. Ota (eds), *Eurosla Yearbook Vol*, 4. Amsterdam: John Benjamins.

Hawkins, R. and S. Liszka. (2003). Locating the source of defective past tense marking in advanced L2 English speakers. In R. van Hoet, A. Hulk, F. Kuiken and R. Towell (eds), *The Lexicon-Syntax Interface in Second Language Acquisition*. Amsterdam: John Benjamins.

Haznedar, B. and B.D. Schwartz. (1997). Are there optional infinitives in child L2 acquisition? In E. Hughes, M. Hughes and A. Greenhill (eds), *Proceedings of the 21st Annual Boston University Conference on Language Development*. Somerville, MA: Cascadilla Press.

Ionin, T., Ko, H. and Wexler, K. (2004). Article semantics in L2 acquisition: The role of specificity. *Language Acquisition*, *12*, 3–69.

Lardiere, D. (1998). Case and tense in the 'fossilized' steady state. *Second Language Research*, *14*, 1–26.

——(2000). Mapping features to forms in second language acquisition. In J. Archibald (ed.), *Second Language Acquisition and Linguistic Theory*. Oxford: Blackwell.

Prévost, P. and L. White. (2000). Missing surface inflection or impairment in second language acquisition? Evidence from tense and agreement. *Second Language Research*, *16*, 103–33.

Schachter, J. (1990). On the issue of completeness in second language acquisition. *Second Language Research*, *6*, 93–124.

Schwartz, B.D. and R. Sprouse. (1996). L2 cognitive states and the full transfer/full access model. *Second Language Research*, *12*, 40–72.

Tsimpli, I.-M. and A. Sorace. (2006). Differentiating interfaces: L2 performance in syntax-semantics and syntax-discourse phenomena. In D. Bamman *et al.* (eds), *Proceedings of the 30th Annual Boston University Conference on Language Development*. Somerville, MA: Cascadilla Press.

White, L. (1985). The pro-drop parameter in adult second language acquisition. *Language Learning*, *35*, 47–62.

——(1989). *Universal Grammar and Second Language Acquisition*. Amsterdam: John Benjamins.

——(2003). *Second Language Acquisition and Universal Grammar*. Cambridge: Cambridge University Press.

——(2009). Grammatical theory: Interfaces and L2 knowledge. In W. Ritchie and T. Bhatia (eds), *The New Handbook of Second Language Acquisition*. Leeds: Emerald Group Publishing Limited.

White, L. and A. Juffs. (1998) Constraints on wh-movement in two different contexts of non-native language acquisition: competence and processing. In S. Flynn, G. Martohardjono and W. O'Neil (eds), *The Generative Study of Second Language Acquisition*. Mahweh, NJ: Lawrence Erlbaum.

Uptake

Shawn Loewen
Michigan State University

Upake refers to several different constructs in SLA research. The most common usage comes from interactionist research and refers to learners' optional, immediate responses to the provision of linguistic feedback, as shown in example 1 in which the student repeats the correct form provided in the teacher's recast.

Example 1 (Lyster and Ranta, 1997: 50)
S: *Là, je veux, là je vas le faire à pied.*
T: *...avec mon pied.* [Recast]
S: *...avec mon pied.* [Uptake]

From this definition of uptake, there are several important issues to consider. First, regarding the immediacy of uptake following feedback, the majority of studies have operationalized uptake as occurring in the turn adjacent to the feedback. In this way, uptake serves as a response to the feedback. Production of the corrected form more than one or two turns after the feedback has not generally been viewed as uptake, however, Smith (2005) has suggested that in synchronous, written computer-mediated communication contexts, uptake may occur multiple turns after the provision of feedback.

Another important issue pertaining to the definition of uptake is its optionality. Learners are not obligated to respond to feedback. Instead, they may simply continue to discuss the topic at hand, as illustrated in example 2.

Example 2
S: to her is good thing
T: yeah, for her it's a good thing [Recast]
S: because she got a lot of money there [Topic continuation]

Additionally, learners may not have the opportunity to respond to the feedback if the interlocutor who provided the feedback continues his or her turn or advances the discourse (Oliver, 2000), as seen in example 3. In this instance, the teacher asks a follow-up question after the recast; consequently, the student responds to the question rather than to the feedback itself.

Example 3 (Loewen, 2004, 168)
S: otherwise only one part go bust
T: goes bust, okay, so you're thinking about some financial protection [Recast plus Topic Advancement]
S: yes

If learners do respond to feedback, the resulting uptake may be characterized in several ways. Lyster and Ranta (1997), in their study of French immersion classes in Canada, categorized uptake as repair or needs-repair, depending on whether or not the learners produced the correct linguistic form in their uptake. Similarly, Ellis, Basturkmen and Loewen (2001), investigating private language school classes in New Zealand, distinguished between successful and unsuccessful uptake, also based on learner production of the correct form. An example of repair/successful uptake occurs above in example 1. Example 4 illustrates needs-repair/unsuccessful uptake as the learner acknowledges the teachers' feedback but does not reformulate his initially ungrammatical utterance.

Example 4 (Ellis *et al.*, 2001: 299)
S: I was in pub
T: in the pub?
S: yeah and I was drinking beer with my friend

One final term, modified output, overlaps with uptake. Similar to uptake, modified output includes learner production that reformulates an ill-formed utterance following feedback. However, in contrast to uptake, modified output may include learner self-corrections, and it may occur multiple turns after the provision of feedback.

In addition to identifying different types of uptake, interactionist research has investigated which types of feedback result in both more uptake and more successful uptake. There is general consensus that output-prompting feedback, such as elicitations or prompts, (e.g., Example 5) is more likely to result in uptake than is input-provided feedback, such as recasts (e.g. Examples 1, 2, 3, and 4). However, studies investigating differential levels of successful uptake following input-providing and output-prompting feedback have found conflicting results.

Example 5 (Lyster and Ranta, 1997, 50)
S: *La marmotte c'est pas celui en haut?*
T: *Pardon?* [Elicitation]
S: *La marmotte c'est pas celle en haut?* [Repair/ Successful Uptake]

The importance of uptake in SLA has been promoted based on several theoretical claims. Although successful uptake cannot be viewed as proof of successful L2 learning, it has been argued to be a possible indication of noticing and a potential facilitator of acquisition. Successful uptake arguably provides some evidence that learners have noticed the gap between their initial erroneous utterance and the target-like form. For example, Egi (2010) found a positive relationship between learners' perception of feedback and production of successful uptake. Given that noticing is essential for L2 acquisition, the relationship between noticing and uptake can provide insights into the acquisition process.

As well as being a potential indication of noticing, successful uptake is considered by many to be facilitative of learning as learners are pushed to produce syntactically more accurate language. Such a position is supported by Swain's (1995) output hypothesis. Several studies (Loewen, 2005; McDonough, 2005) concluded that the production of successful uptake does contribute to L2 learning; however, at least one study (Mackey and Philp, 1998) found that learners were able to benefit from corrective feedback even if they did not produce uptake. Another aspect of the debate surrounding the efficacy of uptake involves the cognitive processes that are involved depending upon the type of feedback that uptake follows. Uptake following input-providing feedback such as recasts may involve simple mimicking of the correct form. In contrast, uptake following output-prompting feedback may require deeper cognitive processing by learners since they must produce the correct form on their own. Of course, output-prompting feedback assumes learners possess some knowledge of the linguistic form and are thus able to produce the correct form. Given the conflicting nature of these issues, further investigation into the relationship between uptake and L2 learning is necessary.

The second use of uptake in SLA research is to refer to what learners are able to report noticing from a lesson (Allwright, 1984). Studies investigating this type of uptake have provided learners with uptake charts in which they are asked to write down what they remember learning from a given lesson. This alternative definition of uptake is less commonly used in SLA research.

See also: corrective feedback, input enhancement, interaction and the interaction hypothesis, noticing hypothesis, output hypothesis, recasts

References

Allwright, B. (1984). Why don't learners lean what teachers teach? The interaction hypothesis. In D. Singleton and D. Little (eds), *Language Learning in Formal and Informal Contexts*, pp. 3–18. Dublin: IRAAL.

Egi, T. (2010). Uptake, modified output, and learner perceptions of recasts: Learner responses as language awareness. *The Modern Language Journal*, *94*, 1–21.

Ellis, R., Basturkmen, H. and Loewen, S. (2001). Learner uptake in communicative ESL lessons. *Language Learning*, *51*, 281–318.

Loewen, S. (2004). Uptake in incidental focus on form in meaning-focused ESL lessons. *Language Learning*, *54*, 153–88.

——(2005). Incidental focus on form and second language learning. *Studies in Second Language Acquisition*, *27*, 361–86.

Lyster, R. and Ranta, L. (1997). Corrective feedback and learner uptake: Negotiation of form in communicative classrooms. *Studies in Second Language Acquisition*, *19*, 37–66.

McDonough, K. (2005). Identifying the impact of negative feedback and learners' responses on

ESL question development. *Studies in Second Language Acquisition*, *27*, 79–103.
Oliver, R. (2000). Age differences in negotiation and feedback in classroom and pairwork. *Language Learning*, *50*, 119–51.
Smith, B. (2005). The relationship between negotiated interaction, learner uptake, and lexical acquisition in task-based computer-mediated communication. *TESOL Quarterly*, *39*, 33–58.
Swain, M. (1995). Three functions of output in second language learning. In G. Cook and B. Seidlhofer (eds), *Principles and Practice in the Study of Language*, pp. 125–44. Oxford: Oxford University Press.

V

Variance

Jenifer Larson-Hall
University of North Texas

The statistical number of variance, which is the square of the standard deviation, gives a measure of the shape of a distribution. The mean, or average score, gives a measure of location of the typical score. The variance indicates how wide the spread of scores around this mean score is. The larger the variance, the less confidence there is that the mean score is an accurate representation of what is typical of the group of scores.

Variance and standard deviation are unbiased estimators of population variance. An unbiased estimator is one whose "average sampling error is zero" (Bachman, 2004, p. 71), meaning that it may overinflate or underinflate the variance in specific instances but over time these differences will average out to zero. They are thus excellent choices to use in calculating inferential statistics.

To understand how the standard deviation (the square root of the variance) is calculated, think first about how the average is calculated. One calculates an average by adding up all of the scores in a group, then dividing by the number of scores in the group:

Group A = {5, 7, 13, 12, 6, 9, 9, 10, 14, 9}
Average of Group A = (5 + 7 + 13 + 12 + 6 + 9 + 9 + 10 + 14 + 9)/10 = 94/10 = 9.4

To calculate the standard deviation, the difference between each point and the average is added together. In other words, the distance that the actual data point varies from the average is examined. Then this number is divided by the number of scores in the group, minus one (this is a better estimate of the sample than just the number of scores). Thus, you can see how the standard deviation is something like the average of the deviation of each point away from the mean. However, because the data points may be greater than or less than the average, and thus both positive and negative numbers are added up, this distance is squared to avoid coming out to zero.

Here is how the variance for the scores in Group A is calculated:

Variance of Group A = $((5–9.4)^2 + (7–9.4)^2 + (13–19.4)^2 + (12–19.4)^2 + (6–9.4)^2 + (9–9.4)^2 + (9–9.4)^2 + (10–19.4)^2 + (14–19.4)^2 + (9–9.4)^2) / (10–11) = 8.7$

The standard deviation (sd) of this group is the square root of the variance, so $\sqrt{8.7} = 2.95$.

There is a rule of thumb relating the sd to the population distribution: approximately 68 per cent of the population falls within one sd of the mean, 95 per cent falls within two sds, and 99.7 per cent falls within three sds. In the example, this means that 68% of the participants received a score between 6.45–12.35 (6.45 = 9.4–2.95 and 12.35 = 9.4+2.95). Following the rule, six of the 10 scores fell in this range. This fact has been used by some authors to set limits for performance; for example, Flege, Yeni-Komshian and Liu (1999) proposed that non-native speakers had nativelike performance if their scores fell within two sds of the native speaker average.

See also: correlation, effect size, factor analysis (FA), quantitative research, significance level, T-tests

References

Bachman, L. (2004). *Statistical Analyses for Language Assessment*. Cambridge: Cambridge University Press.

Flege, J.E., Yeni-Komshian, G. and Liu, S. (1999). Age constraints on second-language acquisition. *Journal of Memory and Language, 41*, 78–104.

Variationist approaches to SLA

Robert Bayley and Elaine Tarone

University of California, Davis and University of Minnesota

Variationist approaches to second language acquisition can be traced to the beginnings of the field. Studies in this tradition build upon model of variation in native languages developed by William Labov (1966, 1972) in research in the lower East Side and Harlem in New York City. Labov showed that rather than being random, much of the variation observed in language is highly systematic. That is, language is characterized by orderly or "structured" heterogeneity (Weinreich, Labov, and Herzog, 1968). For example, coronal stop deletion such that *mist* or *missed* becomes *mis/Ø/*, a feature observed in all English dialects studied to date, is not random. Rather, it is constrained both by linguistic factors such as the features of the following segment or grammatical category, and by non-linguistic factors such as the amount of attention paid to speech. Thus final /t/ or /d/ is more likely to be deleted from a monomorpheme followed by another consonant than from a past tense verb followed by a vowel. It is also more likely to be deleted in informal than in formal speech.

At about the same time that Labov's work on variation was becoming widely known, scholars in second language acquisition began to focus on the variability evident in learner speech. Selinker (1972), for example, posited that a learner's linguistic system, or "interlanguage," was variable, in that learner utterances could be expected to vary dramatically depending on whether the learner was trying to communicate meaning, or was focused on form, as when responding to classroom drills and exercises or providing grammaticality judgments. Three years later, Dickerson (1975) published the first variationist study of interlanguage, showing systematic shifts in the accuracy of Japanese learners' production of English *l* and *r* depending on task (e.g., reading a passage vs reading a word list). The following decade saw the publication of a number of studies of variation in SLA including Huebner's (1983) study of a Hmong speaker acquiring English, Wolfram's (1985) study of tense marking by Vietnamese learners of English, and Tarone and Parrish's (1988) study of Japanese and Arabic speakers enrolled in a U.S. university.

Despite a promising beginning, for a number of years variationist studies of second language acquisition enjoyed relatively little influence. Formal models, with their focus on competence rather than performance, tended to dominate SLA research (Preston and Bayley, 2009). Studies were conducted with university students for whom the standard variety of the target language was, perhaps, the only relevant variety. However, beginning in the 1990s and continuing in the twenty-first century, an increasing number of studies focused on L2 variation. Many of these studies focused on Type I variation, or variation in forms that are considered obligatory in the target language. Young (1991) is among the best known examples. Young used VARBRUL, a specialized application of logistic regression developed to model variation in L1 speech communities (see Bayley, 2002 for details), to examine the acquisition of /s/-plural marking by Chinese learners of English. The results showed a rich patterning of constraints, with animacy, features of the phonological environment, and proficiency all achieving statistical significance. Of particular interest was the finding that redundancy favored plural marking, so that a phrase like "two apples" was more likely to be marked for plurality than "I ate apple/Ø/" (Young, 1991).

Beginning with work by Adamson and Regan (1991) and Bayley (1996), who examined the acquisition by learners of English of alverolarization of /ŋ/ and-t,d deletion, respectively, scholars began to focus on the acquisition of Type II variation, or the acquisition of native-like patterns of variation. This research was motivated by the concern that in order to function effectively in the target language society, learners need to acquire not only grammatical competence, but sociolinguistic competence as well. That is, like native speakers, L2 speakers need to be able to shift from the relatively formal style characteristic of classroom discourse to the more informal styles characteristic of everyday life.

To date, much of the work on Type II variation has focused on French. Regan, Howard, and Lemeé (2009), for example, report on the acquisition of sociolinguistic competence in L2 French. Regan *et al.* studied the acquisition of target-like patterns of deletion of *ne* (the first particle of negation), /l/ deletion, and other variables by Irish university students before and after study in France. As expected, students were considerably more likely to use vernacular forms after residence abroad. In Ontario, Mougeon and his associates have carried out a series of studies with French immersion students on a range of variables including *ne* deletion, schwa deletion, and *nous/on* alternation (see Mougeon, Rehner, and Nadasdi 2010 for a full discussion). Overall their results show that students tend to underuse mildly marked variants and to avoid marked variants. An analysis of textbooks used in the immersion program as well as teachers' speech also shows a general avoidance of vernacular forms. Students who had spent some time in a Francophone environment, however, were more likely to use informal forms than their counterparts who had not spent time in a French-speaking area. Studies such as those by Mougeon *et al.* (2010) are valuable because they provide an indication of why, despite years of study in French immersion programs, students often fail to achieve native-like abilities in French and frequently speak English in all environments except the classroom. As Bayley and Tarone (in press) observe, the classroom does not provide the opportunity for students to acquire the informal register needed for communication with adolescent peers. For immersion students, French remains a language for formal environments, while English is the vernacular to be used with fellow students.

Type II variation has also been investigated in recent studies of languages other than French including English and Mandarin. Wolfram, Carter, and Moriello (2004), for example, examined monopthonization of /ai/, a feature of U.S. southern English, by Spanish-speaking immigrants in North Carolina. Through a detailed phonetic analysis, Wolfram *et al.* show that the majority of Latino participants were reluctant to accommodate to the general southern vowel system. Possible reasons for this lack of accommodation included the insularity of newly formed ethnic communities, whose members have very limited interactions with the long-time residents of the area, as well as the constant influx of Spanish-speaking newcomers, whose presence contributes to maintaining Spanish as the main means of communication within the Latino community. The authors also note that most of the ESL teachers who serve as models for Latino immigrants are from outside of the region and do not follow the local southern norm.

Li (2010) studied the acquisition, by speakers of English, Japanese, Korean, and Russian residing in China, of variable patterns of the multi-functional Mandarin morphosyntactic particle *de* (?), which is variable in some environments and required in others. *De* serves a variety of grammatical functions. It can function as a genitive marker (e.g. *tā de lí* "his pear"), an attributive marker (e.g. *xīnqín de lǎonóng* "hardworking farmer") and a nominalization marker (e.g. *wǒ bǐjiào xǐhuān de shì yóuyǒng* "What I like very much is swimming"). Used in combination with *huà* (?), *de* can also indicate a conditional clause. Li (2010) showed that in native speech *de* is always used in conditional clauses and never in lexicalized terms. For other functions, however, native speakers sometimes omit *de*, including from relative clauses. And, as is the case with other instances of morphosyntactic variation, presence or absence of *de* is systematically conditioned by linguistic factors, including grammatical function, and by social factors, with men more likely than women to omit *de*. In addition, as we might expect from the fact that omission of *de* is characteristic of informal speech, *de* is more likely to be present in teachers' classroom discourse and in language teaching materials than in casual conversation.

Variationist SLA studies have shown, convincingly in our view, that much of the variation that we see in L2 is systematic. However, as Bayley and Tarone (in press) note, a number of questions remain to be resolved. First, relatively few longitudinal studies have been undertaken. Rather, researchers have used cross-sectional designs, with the assumption that learners of different proficiency levels follow the same path. Although we have abundant empirical evidence that members of the same L1 speech community are subject to the same constraints on variable processes, the evidence for speakers of an L2 is not yet sufficiently robust. Thus, we need more longitudinal studies to establish the extent to which individual learner patterns do indeed match group patterns (such as Tarone and Liu, 1995). Finally, as is the case generally with SLA research, too few variationist studies have focused on immigrant communities (but see, e.g., Tarone, Bigelow and Hansen, 2009). Rather, research has focused on university students. To fully understand SLA, including acquisition by learners with low literacy levels, we need to shift our attention from the university and, like our colleagues in variationist sociolinguistics, enter minority communities where a majority of language learners reside.

See also: cross-sectional research, longtitudinal research, quantitative research, social and sociocultural approaches to SLA, sociocognitive approaches to SLA, theoretical constructs in SLA

References

Adamson, H.D. and Regan, V. (1991). The Acquisition of Community Speech Norms by Asian Immigrants Learning English as a Second Language: A Preliminary Study. *Studies in Second Language Acquisition*, *1*, 1–22.

Bayley, R. (1996). Competing constraints on variation in the speech of adult Chinese learners of English. In R. Bayley and D.R. Preston (eds), *Second Language Acquisition and Linguistic Variation*, pp. 97–120. Amsterdam: John Benjamins.

——(2002). The quantitative paradigm. In J.K. Chambers, P. Trudgill, and N. Schilling-Estes (eds), *The Handbook of Language Variation and Change*, pp. 117–41. Oxford: Blackwell.

——and Tarone, E. (2012). Variationist perspectives. In S.M. Gass and A. Mackey (eds), *Handbook of Second Language Acquisition*, pp. 41–56. New York: Routledge.

Dickerson, L. (1975). The learner's interlanguage as a system of variable rules. *TESOL Quarterly*, *9*, 401–7.

Huebner, T. (1983). *A Longitudinal Analysis of the Acquisition of English*. Ann Arbor, MI: Karoma.

Labov, W. (1966). *The Social Stratification of English in New York City*. Arlington, VA: Center for Applied Linguistics.

——(1972). *Language in the Inner City: Studies in the Black English Vernacular*. Philadelphia, PA: University of Pennsylvania Press.

Li, X. (2010). Sociolinguistic variation in the speech of learners of Chinese as a second language. *Language Learning*, *60*, 366–408.

Mougeon, R., Rehner, K. and Nadasdi, T. (2010). *The Sociolinguistic Competence of Immersion Students*. Clevedon: Multilingual Matters.

Preston, D.R. and Bayley, R. (2009). Variationist linguistics and second language acquisition. In W.C. Ritchie and T.K. Bhatia (eds), *The New Handbook of Second Language Acquisition*, pp. 89–113. Bingley: Emerald.

Regan, V., Howard, M. and Lemée, I. (2009). *The Acquisition of Sociolinguistic Competence in a Study Abroad Context*. Clevedon: Multilingual Matters.

Selinker, L. (1972). Interlanguage. *IRAL*, *10*, 209–41.

Tarone, E., Bigelow, M. and Hansen, K. (2009). *Literacy and Second Language Oracy*. Oxford: Oxford University Press.

——, and Liu, G.-Q. (1995). Situational context, variation and SLA theory. In G. Cook and B. Seidlhofer (eds), *Principle and Practice in Applied Linguistics: Studies in Honour of H.G.*

Widdowson, pp. 107–24. Oxford: Oxford University Press.

——, and Parrish, B. (1988). Article usage in interlanguage: A study in task-related variability. *Language Learning*, *38*, 21–44.

Weinreich, U., Labov, W. and Herzog, M. (1968). Empirical foundations for a theory of language change. In W.P. Lehmann and Y. Malkiel (eds), *Directions for Historical Linguistics: A Symposium*, pp. 95–188. Austin, TX: University of Texas Press.

Wolfram, W. (1985). Variability in tense marking: A case for the obvious. *Language Learning*, *35*, 229–53.

——, Carter, P. and Moriello, B. (2004). Emerging Hispanic English: New dialect formation in the American South. *Journal of Sociolinguistics*, *8*, 339–58.

Young, R. (1991). *Variation in Interlanguage Morphology*. New York: Peter Lang.

Further reading

Adamson, H.D. (2009). *Interlanguage Variation in Theoretical and Pedagogical Perspective*. New York: Routledge. (A clear account of variation theory as applied to first and second languages, with consideration of pedagogical implications.)

Geeslin, K. and Gudmested, A. (2010). An exploration of the range and frequency of occurrence of forms in potentially variable structures in second language Spanish. *Studies in Second Language Acquisition*, *32*, 433–64. (A study of the use of a number of sociolinguistic variables by English L1 learners of Spanish and native-Spanish speakers.)

Hansen, J.G. (2006). *Acquiring a Non-Native Phonology: Linguistic Constraints and Social Barriers*. London: Continuum. (A longitudinal study of the acquisition of several phonological variables by Vietnamese immigrants to the United States.)

Walker, J.A. (2010). *Variation in Linguistic Systems*. New York: Routledge. (An up-to-date and accessible account of principles of variation theory and analysis.)

Vocabulary learning and teaching

Paul Nation
Victoria University of Wellington

A vocabulary teacher has four main jobs. The first job is to plan. That is, to ensure that the right vocabulary is focused on and that opportunities for vocabulary learning occur in all of the four equally balanced strands of meaning-focused input, meaning-focused output, language-focused learning, and fluency development (Nation, 2007). The second most important job is to help learners develop skill in the four strategies of guessing from context, learning using word cards, learning using word parts, and learning from dictionary use. These strategies help learners deal with the many unknown words that they will meet in their use of the language. The third most important job is to test in order to use the results to see where learners are in their vocabulary development, to plan future learning, and to motivate learning. The teacher's fourth most important job vocabulary is to teach, giving attention to high-frequency words and academic words where appropriate, and to multiword units.

Teaching is rated fourth in the list of jobs because the deliberate teaching of vocabulary is relatively inefficient compared to other ways of learning, and a word is not fully learned through one meeting with it, even if this meeting involves substantial deliberate teaching. This is because:

1 there are numerous things to know about a word, namely its form (spoken, written, and its component affixes and stem), its meaning (underlying concept, particular instantiations, and associations), and its use (collocations, grammatical patterns, and constraints on its use).
2 there are several strands through which knowledge of a word needs to develop.
3 teaching can usefully deal with only a limited amount of information at a time – too much confuses.

Because of this, we should expect only limited learning from single meetings with a word and should bear this in mind when we plan or carry out those meetings and not spend too much time on vocabulary teaching.

Teaching words

Research has established several useful guidelines for the teaching of vocabulary.

1 Only high-frequency vocabulary (the first 2000 words and the AWL) and vocabulary learning strategies should be systematically taught, and teachers should know where the learners are in their knowledge of these words (Nation, 2001: Chapter 1). The justification for this guideline is that only the high-frequency words of the language occur often enough to deserve valuable classroom time. Low-frequency words need to be dealt with in the classroom through training in vocabulary strategies. Similarly, high-frequency multiword units also deserve deliberate attention, but the learning of the lower-frequency collocations can be left to learning through input and fluency development activities.
2 The amount and strength of learning depends on the quality of mental processing. The quality of mental processing can be increased by giving attention to a range of aspects involved in knowing a word, by spaced retrieval, generative use and instantiation, and by giving attention to word parts and helpful etymology. Knowing a word involves knowing aspects of its form, meaning, and use. This involves both receptive and productive knowledge (Nation, 2001: 27). There is an enormous amount of research which shows that repetition is very important to learning and that the most effective repetition involves spaced recall (retrieval) of the item to be learnt (see for example, Pyc and Rawson, 2007). There is also considerable research showing that the more deeply and thoughtfully a word is processed the better its retention is likely to be (Pyc and Rawson, 2009). Doing spaced retrieval is one way of getting more thoughtful processing. Meeting or using a word in contexts which are not exactly the same as those in which it has been met or used before is also another important way of deepening the processing (Joe, 1998). This means that teachers should come back to a previously met word in a different collocation from which it has been met before. There is also good value in drawing attention to the morphological structure of words. There are around 15 very useful high-frequency prefixes, such as *pre-*, *un-*, *mis-*, *com-*, *ad-*, *dis-*, *in-*, *non-*, *pro-*, that learners should be able to recognize and provide a meaning for. In addition, it is useful if a teacher can show learners that an unknown word shares a stem with an already known word, for example that *rank* is related to *arrange*, and that *neglect* and *negate* are related to *negative*. Connecting new learning to old knowledge is a useful mnemonic device.
3 There are many ways of communicating word meanings. The best are clear, simple, and brief. Where possible, the first language translation should be given. Several studies have shown that when different methods of communicating meaning are compared first language translation typically comes out as the most effective (Laufer and Shmueli, 1997). There is also evidence that in the early and intermediate stages of learning a language, the first language and the second language share the same lexicon (De Groot, 1993). Thus, even if words are not directly translated by the teacher, they will be stored with their L1 translation in the brain of the learner. Pictures have also been shown to be effective, partly because they provide what is called dual encoding of the meaning (D'Agostino, O'Neill, and Paivio, 1977). That is, it is stored both linguistically and visually.
4 The meaning given should describe the underlying meaning that includes most of the word's uses and senses.
5 Words should not be taught with others that belong to the same lexical set, are near synonyms, or are opposites (Nation, 2000; Erten and Tekin, 2008). Words which are closely related in meaning make learning around 50 to 100 per cent more difficult if they are learnt together. That is, grouping by lexical sets has negative effects on learning. Grouping items

thematically (Tinkham, 1997) where the words are related as if they were part of the story helps vocabulary learning.

6 There should be repeated opportunities for spaced retrieval of each word. Later meetings with a word are more important than the initial presentation and teaching may be more useful then.
7 Direct teaching is only part of one of the four strands that a word should be met in, and is only one way of giving deliberate attention. The language-focused learning strand of a course should make up only one-quarter of learning time. The deliberate teaching of vocabulary has to share this time with the development of vocabulary strategies, intensive reading, vocabulary learning activities and exercises, and learners' use of the word card strategy for deliberate learning. This means that vocabulary teaching should only make up a small proportion of a well-planned vocabulary course.
8 Learners should take control of their own vocabulary learning. Learners should be taught how to learn vocabulary and how to choose vocabulary to learn. In order to cope with unsimplified texts, learners need a vocabulary size of around 8000 words (Nation, 2006). Vocabulary teaching of individual words can only deal with a very small proportion of this substantial figure. This is why the second most important job of the vocabulary teacher is to train learners in the use of vocabulary learning strategies. An important part of this training is encouraging learners to take responsibility for their own vocabulary learning and to become autonomous vocabulary learners. Learners are typically reluctant to take on this role (Moir and Nation, 2002).

Evaluating vocabulary learning activities

Laufer and Hulstijn (2001) devised a checklist for measuring what they called "the involvement load" of vocabulary learning activities. Involvement load depends on three criteria – the learners' *need* to learn a particular word, whether they have to *search* for the formal meaning of that word in some way, and whether they had to make an *evaluation* of the context or use of that word. The higher the involvement load score for an activity, the more likely the activity will result in useful learning. There have now been several pieces of research on the involvement load hypothesis (Folse, 2006; Keating, 2008) with mixed results, but the strength of Laufer and Hulstijn's hypothesis is that it not only encourages the experimental investigation of vocabulary learning activities, but provides a guide to designing such activities. Nation and Webb (2010) have designed a more complicated scheme which largely gives different results than involvement load analysis. This may provide a useful focus for future research on vocabulary learning activities. Barcroft (2006) has looked closely at the effect of the focus of learning on the actual learning that occurs, largely finding that we learn what we focus on and that multiple or unwanted focuses may detract from learning. This simple but very useful finding is a very helpful guide to the teaching of vocabulary and to the design of vocabulary learning activities. There are many commonly used vocabulary learning activities, such as form and meaning matching activities, writing a sentence using a given word, filling in a word part table, analyzing semantic features of words, and looking up words from a text in a glossary, that have started to become the focus of analysis and experimental research. Such research will undoubtedly improve the teaching of vocabulary.

What vocabulary should teachers focus on?

All vocabulary is not created equal and roughly in agreement with Zipf's law in any text or collection of texts there is a relatively small number of high-frequency words (traditionally around 2000) and a very large number of low-frequency words. The 2000 highest frequency word families cover from 80 per cent to 90 per cent of the running words in a text, depending on the nature of the text. It takes around a total of 6000 to 9000 word families plus proper nouns to reach 98 per cent coverage of a text.

The high-frequency/low-frequency distinction is made largely for teaching and curriculum design purposes. The high-frequency words need to be learned first and they deserve classroom time. The vocabulary teacher can feasibly and usefully give attention to individual high-frequency words. The low-frequency words, however, are so numerous, and have such a low frequency that individual words do not deserve attention. Instead, the vocabulary teacher should focus on strategy training for dealing with those words. Thus, when a learner asks the teacher for the meaning of a low-frequency word, this can be dealt with by using the opportunity to guess it from context clues and thus practise the guessing strategy, or to look it up in the dictionary and thus practise the dictionary use strategy. An alternative is to quickly give the meaning of the word using the L1 or some other means and to move on with the lesson.

For learners with special purposes there are specialised word lists. The words on these lists can be dealt with in much the same way as high-frequency words because these words are like high-frequency words for such users. The 570 word family Academic Word List (Coxhead, 2000) is the best known of these and is designed for students studying in high school or university. It assumes knowledge of the first 2000 words. It provides around 10% coverage of academic text. Technical vocabulary also deserves attention but this is best done during the study of the specialized area. Technical vocabulary can make up from 20% to 30% of the running words in a specialized text, such as an economics text. The Vocabulary Levels Test (Schmitt, Schmitt and Clapham, 2001) is designed to find out what vocabulary individual learners need to focus on. Vocabulary teaching is the least important of the vocabulary teacher's jobs, but it needs to be done in a principled way both when selecting what vocabulary to focus on and when deciding how to focus on it.

See also: depth of processing, frequency effects, instructed SLA, involvement load hypothesis, rehearsal, word knowledge

References

Barcroft, J. (2006). Can writing a word detract from learning it? More negative effects of forced output during vocabulary learning. *Second Language Research, 22*(4), 487–97.

Coxhead, A. (2000). A new academic word list. *TESOL Quarterly, 34*(2), 213–38.

D'Agostino, P.R., O'Neill, B.J. and Paivio, A. (1977). Memory for pictures and words as a function of level of processing: depth or dual coding? *Memory and Cognition, 5*, 252–56.

de Groot, A.M. B. (1993). Word-type effects in bilingual processing tasks: support for a mixed-representational system. In R. Schreuder and B. Weltens (eds), *The Bilingual Lexicon*, pp. 27–51. Amsterdam and Philadelphia, PA: John Benjamins.

Erten, I.H. and Tekin, M. (2008). Effects on vocabulary acquisition of presenting new words in semantic sets versus semantically unrelated sets. *System, 36*, 407–22.

Folse, K. (2006). The effect of type of written exercise on L2 vocabulary retention. *TESOL Quarterly, 40*(2), 273–93.

Joe, A. (1998). What effects do text-based tasks promoting generation have on incidental vocabulary acquisition? *Applied Linguistics, 19*(3), 357–77.

Keating, G. (2008). Task effectiveness and word learning in a second language: The involvement load hypothesis on trial. *Language Teaching Research, 12*(3), 365–86.

Laufer, B. and Hulstijn, J. (2001). Incidental vocabulary acquisition in a second language: the construct of task-induced involvement. *Applied Linguistics, 22*(1), 1–26.

Laufer, B. and Shmueli, K. (1997). Memorizing new words: Does teaching have anything to do with it? *RELC Journal, 28*(1), 89–108.

Moir, J. and Nation, I.S. P. (2002). Learners' use of strategies for effective vocabulary learning. *Prospect, 17*(1), 15–35.

Nation, I.S. P. (2007). The four strands. *Innovation in Language Learning and Teaching, 1*(1), 1–12.

——(2006). How large a vocabulary is needed for reading and listening? *Canadian Modern Language Review, 63*(1), 59–82.

——(2001). *Learning Vocabulary in Another Language*. Cambridge: Cambridge University Press. http://uk.cambridge.org/elt/nation/

——(2000). Learning vocabulary in lexical sets: dangers and guidelines. *TESOL Journal*, 9, 2: 6–10.

Nation, I.S. P. and Webb, S. (2010). *Researching and Analysing Vocabulary*. Boston, MA: Heinle Cengage Learning.

Pyc, M.A. and Rawson, K.A. (2009). Testing the retrieval hypothesis: Does greater difficulty correctly recalling information lead to higher levels of memory? *Journal of Memory and Language, 60*, 437–47.

——(2007). Examining the efficiency of schedules of distributed retrieval practice. *Memory and Cognition, 35*(8), 1917–27.

Schmitt, N., Schmitt, D. and Clapham, C. (2001). Developing and exploring the behaviour of two new versions of the Vocabulary Levels Test. *Language Testing, 18*(1), 55–88.

Tinkham, T. (1997). The effects of semantic and thematic clustering on the learning of second language vocabulary. *Second Language Research, 13*(2), 138–63.

Further reading

Boers, F. and Lindstromberg, S. (2009). *Optimizing a Lexical Approach to Instructed Second Language Acquisition*. Basingstoke: Palgrave Macmillan. (A detailed and well-researched analysis of the teaching and learning of multiword figuratives.)

Nation, I.S.P. (2008). *Teaching Vocabulary: Strategies and Techniques*. Boston, MA: Heinle Cengage Learning. (A practical coverage of teaching and learning techniques and activities.)

Schmitt, N. (2008). Review article: Instructed second language vocabulary learning. *Language Teaching Research, 12*(3), 325–63. (A clearly presented, up-to-date review of recent research.)

Wh-questions

Barbara Schulz
Goethe-Universität Frankfurt am Main

Due to their cross-linguistic properties, wh-questions have received a substantial amount of attention in second language acquisition research. While their cross-linguistic variation enables investigations of native-language transfer, their universal constraints can be used to investigate linguistic universals in interlanguages, and the wh-dependency has been of use to look at second language processing.

Along with yes/no-questions (see [1]) and echo-questions (see [2]), wh-questions (see [3]) are one form of cross-linguistically attested questions.

(1)	Will Martha play poker tonight?	Yes/no-question
(2)	Martha will play **which game/what** tonight?	Echo-question
(3)	**Which game/what** will Martha play __ tonight?	Wh-question

While yes/no questions elicit (dis-)agreement ("yes"/"no"), and while echo-questions function as clarification requests, wh-questions are asking for some informative content. They derive their name from the fact that, in English, the word that introduces them (mostly) starts with a *wh-*.

Wh-phrases can either consist of only a wh-word ("what" in [3]) or be more complex (like "which game"). Syntactically, the wh-phrase is replacing the constituent that the question is about (which is the direct object in [2]/[3]). For forming a regular wh-question, English requires the wh-phrase to be placed in clause-initial position, leaving a "gap" in the original position of the constituent. Thus, the wh-phrase forms a dependency that can either be conceptualized as a lexical dependency between the wh-phrase and the verb, or as a syntactic dependency between the wh-phrase and its gap. This dependency has been referred to as a filler-gap dependency, a wh-dependency, or as wh-movement dependency. Depending on the syntactic framework, the gap position is either truly empty, or it may contain a silent "trace" or an unpronounced copy of the wh-phrase.

Cross-linguistically, not all languages require clause-initial placement of wh-phrases; wh-in-situ languages like Japanese allow wh-phrases to remain in their base position making them structurally similar to English echo questions.

In addition to the above mono-clausal questions, wh-questions can also occur in complex sentences. Here, we can distinguish between embedded questions in which the question constitutes an embedded clause (see [4]), and long-distance/complex wh-questions in which the wh-dependency holds across two (or more) clauses (see [5]).

(4) Jason wondered [**which game** Martha will play __].

(5) **Which game** did Jason say [that Martha will play __]?

While English mono-clausal questions require subject-auxiliary inversion, embedded questions prohibit it. Many languages, however, do not show such an asymmetry between mono-clausal and embedded wh-questions.

Long-distance questions have received a lot of attention since wh-movement out of complex clauses (also called "extraction") is subject to universal restrictions (usually called "island constraints" [Ross, 1967] or "Subjacency" [Chomsky, 1977]) which seem to be instantiated in all languages. Thus, some syntactic contexts (such as embedded questions) do not allow wh-extraction. While we can see in (5) that wh-movement from an embedded *that*-clause to clause-initial position is possible, such extraction is impossible, if the clause is an embedded question. This is illustrated in (6b) (the asterisk indicating ungrammaticality).

(6) a. Jason wondered [when Martha will play **poker**.]

b. *__What__ did Jason wonder [when Martha will play __]?

See also: construction learning, development in SLA, developmental sequences, implicational universals, linguistic transfer, Universal Grammar (UG) and SLA

References

Chomsky, N. (1977). On Wh–movement. In P. Culicover, T. Wasow, and A. Akmajian (eds), *Formal syntax*, pp. 71–132. New York: Academic Press

Ross, J.R. (1967). *Constraints on Variables in Syntax*. Unpublished PhD dissertation, Cambridge: MIT.

Further reading

Belikova, A. and White, L. (2009). Evidence for the fundamental difference hypothesis or not? Island constraints revisited. *Studies in Second Language Acquisition, 31*, 199–223. (An investigation of island constraints in interlanguage development.)

Eckman, F.R., Moravcsik, E.A. and Wirth, J.R. (1989). Implicational universals and interrogative structures in the interlanguage of ESL learners. *Language Learning, 39*, 173–205. (An investigation of the instantiation of implicational universals in interlanguage development.)

Hawkins, R. (2001). *Second Language Syntax*. Malden, MA: Blackwell. (Chapter 7 provides a nice summary about the acquisition of complex wh-questions by second language learners.)

Omaki, A. and Schulz, B. (in press) Filler-gap dependencies and island constraints in second language sentence processing. *Studies in Second Language Acquisition*. (An investigation of the processing of long-distance wh-questions by second language learners.)

Williams, J.N., Möbius, P. and Kim, C. (2001). Native and non-native processing of English wh-questions: Parsing strategies and plausibility constraints. *Applied Psycholinguistics, 22*, 509–40. (An investigation of processing of wh-dependencies by second language learners.)

Willingness to communicate (WTC)

Peter D. MacIntyre
Cape Breton University

The concept of willingness to communicate (WTC) represents the probability of initiating communication when free to do so. Studies of WTC began in the first language (L1) communication literature in the United States (McCroskey and Richmond, 1991) where WTC was originally described as a cognitively based personality trait that reflects differences among persons in their predisposition toward oral communication. The concept is based on the observation that some people are willing to initiate conversation and others tend to avoid it, or at least wait for others to initiate communication. McCroskey and Richmond (1991) originally proposed five factors contributing to WTC: introversion, self-esteem, communication competence, communication apprehension, and cultural diversity. Each of these five factors has been found to be related to WTC. McCroskey and Richmond (1991) also suggest that an individual's perception of his or her own competence might influence WTC more than that person's actual level of competence, because the perception guides a person's choices in communicative situations. Further, the authors argue that communication apprehension is likely the factor most strongly associated with WTC in native language.

The notion of cultural diversity in WTC raises the question of communicating in languages other than a person's native language (L1). MacIntyre, Clément, Dörnyei and Noels (1998) adapted the WTC concept to refer to second-language communication (target language or the L2). They proposed a heuristic model (see Figure 16) that captures a number of relevant individual difference factors that can influence WTC, integrating and expanding on the factors identified by McCroskey and Richmond (1991). MacIntyre *et al.* (1998) made another key modification in conceptualizing WTC. They proposed a situated model, one that is based on a feeling of being willing to communicate on a specific occasion with a specific person. The distinction between trait-WTC and situated or state-WTC mirrors the long-standing distinction made with respect to trait and state anxiety. State-WTC can be viewed as the final psychological step in being prepared to (or intending to) communicate in the L2.

WTC has been the subject of a number of studies involving a wide variety of language learners, different learning environments, quantitative and qualitative methods, inside and outside the language

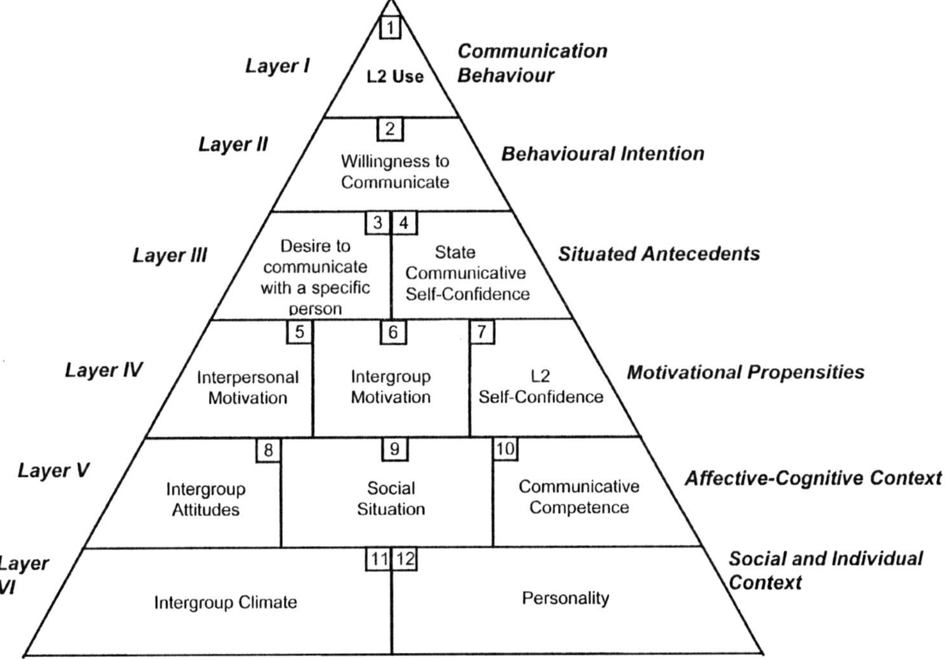

Figure 16 The Pyramid Model of willingness to communicate
Note: P. D. MacIntyre, R. Clément, Z. Dörnyei, and K. Noels (1998). Conceptualizing Willingness to Communicate in a L2: A Situational Model of L2 Confidence and Affiliation. *Modern Language Journal*, *82*, 547. Reprinted with permission.

classroom. In general, research has shown that WTC tends to be higher when learners have greater opportunities for contact with speakers of the L2, such as in an immersion classroom (MacIntyre, Baker, Clément, and Donovan, 2003) or in a travel abroad program (Yashima, 2002). Research also shows that self-confidence, or the combination of low levels of anxiety and high levels of perceived communication competence, is the most reliable predictor of L2 trait-WTC. When a more microscopic approach is taken, splitting self-confidence into its constituent concepts, perceived competence tends to better predict trait-WTC among novice learners but anxiety seems to be a better predictor among advanced learners. When a more macroscopic approach is taken, examining the wider communication context, there appears to be considerable diversity in the factors identified as increasing or decreasing WTC. Studies have shown that cultural background, for example the Confucian philosophy of many Chinese learners, is relevant to the ways in which WTC is enacted (Wen and Clément, 2003). In addition, being in a majority or minority group position, or in a second-language versus foreign-language context, has been shown to affect WTC. Clément, Baker and MacIntyre (2003) argue that WTC is most relevant when there is free choice to use the target language or avoid it, implicating the individual's sense of volition over L2 communication.

Language learners who are willing to communicate in the L2 choose to place themselves in an awkward communicative situation. Among adults learning another language, speaking the L2 often requires setting aside another language (e.g., L1) that is very well known. Learners have described a willingness to talk in order to learn (MacIntyre *et al.*, 2003). Compared to L1 proficiency, L2 skill shows a far greater range, with some people at the very earliest stages of the learning process and others being fluent bilinguals. The willingness to engage in communication under various conditions requires a supportive attitudinal and motivational subsystem.

Motivation for language learning has been associated with both instrumental/pragmatic goals as well as a genuine interest in other peoples and cultures (Yashima, 2002). Yet learners often find themselves in an ambivalent state, both wanting to speak in the L2 and wanting to avoid it. Perhaps, then, it is not surprising that subtle features of the situation have a dramatic effect on WTC (MacIntyre, Burns and Jessome, in press). For example, error correction might be welcome from some peers but not from others, or welcome from a teacher in one context but not another.

Dynamic fluctuations in WTC present an interesting avenue for investigation. Kang (2005) argued that L2 WTC results from a combination of individual psychological conditions and situational variables. Studies of classroom processes indicate that WTC can be affected by various types of activities and supportive teachers (Cao and Philp, 2006; Peng and Woodrow, 2010). Moreover, as L2 communication unfolds, WTC can show remarkable fluctuation over a very short period of time. MacIntyre and Legatto (in press) propose a dynamic systems perspective to explain increases and decreases in WTC as a communication event takes its twists and turns. From this perspective, WTC is evaluated and re-evaluated on the fly and may be affected by factors such as memory for vocabulary and grammar, interpersonal reactions from interlocutors, and meta-linguistic knowledge.

Communication is a broad topic encompassing much more than spoken dialog. WTC has not been widely explored in areas other than speech, but certainly can be conceptualized with respect to writing, reading, and comprehension skills. Future research is required in each of these areas. Given that WTC may be seen as both (1) an individual difference factor facilitating L2 acquisition, especially in a pedagogical system that emphasizes communication, and (2) as an outcome of the language learning process, the concept has wide applicability in second language acquisition.

See also: anxiety, aptitude-trait complexes, emotion, individual differences in SLA, instructed SLA, motivation

References

Cao, Y. and Philp, J. (2006). Interactional context and willingness to communicate: A comparison of behavior in whole class, group and dyadic interaction. *System*, *34*(4), 480–93.

Clément, R., Baker, S.C. and MacIntyre, P.D. (2003). Willingness to communicate in a second language: The effects of context, norms and vitality. *Journal of Language and Social Psychology*, *22*, 190–209.

Kang, S.-J. (2005). Dynamic emergence of situational willingness to communicate in a second language. *System*, *33*, 277–92.

MacIntyre, P.D. and Legatto, J.J. (in press). A dynamic system approach to willingness to communicate: Developing an idiodynamic method to capture rapidly changing affect. *Applied Linguistics*.

MacIntyre, P.D., Burns, C., Jessome, A. (in press). Ambivalence about communicating in a second language: A qualitative study of French immersion students' willingness to communicate. *Modern Language Journal*.

MacIntyre, P.D., Baker, S.C., Clément, R. and Donovan, L.A. (2003). Talking in order to learn: Willingness to communicate and intensive language programs. *The Canadian Modern Language Review*, *59*, 587–605.

MacIntyre, P.D., Clément, R., Dörnyei, Z. and Noels, K.A. (1998). Conceptualising willingness to communicate in a L2: A situational model of L2 confidence and affiliation. *Modern Language Journal*, *82*, 545–62.

McCroskey, J.C. and Richmond, V.P. (1991). Willingness to communicate: A cognitive view. In M. Booth-Butterfield (ed.), *Communication, Cognition, and Anxiety*, pp. 19–37. Newbury Park, CA: Sage.

Peng, J.-E. and Woodrow, L. (2010). Willingness to communicate in English: A model in the Chinese EFL classroom context. *Language Learning*, *60*, 834–76.

Wen, W.P. and Clément, R. (2003). A Chinese conceptualization of willingness to communicate in ESL. *Language, Culture and Curriculum*, *16*, 18–38.

Yashima, T. (2002). Willingness to communicate in a second language: The Japanese EFL context. *Modern Language Journal*, *86*, 54–66.

Word knowledge

Charles Browne

Meiji Gakuin University

The concept of word knowledge is one that has been much discussed by second language acquisition researchers and practitioners. Thornbury (2002) asks the question "What does it mean to 'know a word?'", before going on to explain that beyond the most basic level of knowing (1) its form and (2) its meaning, it also involves a wide variety of knowledge types ranging from receptive to productive knowledge, with these knowledge links being stored in the mind in a way that less resembles a dictionary than it does a highly organized interconnected network or web, referred to as the *mental lexicon*.

Paul Nation (2001) describes the receptive/productive distinction in much more detail, identifying close to 20 different aspects of word knowledge with the basic assumption that receptive knowledge of a word such as recognizing it as a word or recognizing its meaning, is easier, and thus precedes productive knowledge of a word such as being able to pronounce, spell or use it in a sentence. This range of knowledge from receptive to productive is often described as occurring along a kind of continuum (Palmberg, 1987; Melka, 1997). Nation identifies three key aspects that need to be considered (1) word form, and (2) the meaning of the word, which are similar to Thornbury's categories, with the addition of a third, (3) the use of the word.

With regard to the aspect of word form, Nation distinguishes between:

1) the spoken form
2) the written form, and
3) word parts

For the *spoken form*, Nation considers receptive ability to be the ability to recognize what a word sounds like, whereas productive ability is being able to pronounce a word correctly. For the *written form*, receptive ability is being able to recognize what a word looks like, while productive ability is being able to write and spell the word. For *word parts*, receptive ability is being able to recognize various parts of the word such as word roots, prefixes and suffixes, while productive ability is being able to use the parts of the word that are needed to express its meaning.

With regard to the aspect of word meaning, Nation distinguishes between:

1) form and meaning
2) concepts and referents, and
3) associations

For *form and meaning*, receptive ability is being able to understand what the word form signals, while productive ability is being able to express meaning using the word form. For *concepts and referents*, receptive ability is being able to understand what is included in the concept of this word, while productive ability is knowing which concepts this word can refer to. For *associations*, receptive ability is the other words this word makes us think of, while productive ability is the ability to use other, similar words in its place.

With regard to the aspect of word use, Nation distinguishes between:

1) grammatical functions
2) collocations, and
3) constraints on use (such as register or frequency)

For *grammatical functions*, receptive ability is being able to understand the grammatical patterns within which this word occurs, while productive ability is the ability to use those patterns correctly. For *collocations*, receptive ability is knowing what words or types of words occur together with the key word, while productive ability is the ability to correctly produce them in speech or writing. For *constraints on use*, receptive ability is being able to understand where, when, and how often the word could be expected to be seen, while productive ability is being able to correctly use the word where, when, and how it is expected to be used.

Schmitt (2000) also reviews the receptive/productive distinction, rightly pointing out that although most researchers assume that receptive knowledge precedes productive knowledge, there are actually many exceptions to this rule such as when learners are able to use a word's spoken form (productive knowledge) before being able to write it (receptive knowledge).

Another concept often discussed with regard to word knowledge is that of learning burden, which, simply put, is how easy or difficult it is to learn a word. Nation (1990) argues that different words have different learning burdens depending on a variety of factors not only including the different aspects of word knowledge discussed above, but also the learner's own language background, the way a word is learned or taught, and the intrinsic difficulty of a word. With regard to the learner's previous language background, the general principle is that the more a vocabulary word represents patterns and knowledge that the learner is already familiar with (such as knowledge of their L1 or other L2's), the easier the learning burden will be. Meara (1980) reviewed several studies of bilingual learners and found evidence that beyond recall of the phonetic form of the word, first and second language knowledge seem to be interrelated and potentially stored in the same part of the brain. Yoshida (1978) in a study of a Japanese child learning English in the United States as a second language, found evidence that knowledge of English loanwords in Japanese seemed to help the child to learn and remember these words in English more quickly.

There is evidence that learners of different levels learn and store the meanings of words differently. Henning (1973) found that while low-level learners tended to store the meaning of words by their sound, higher-level learners tend to do so by their meaning. The implication for classroom practice is that words that are similar in sound or spelling should not be introduced together as they will tend to interfere with each other. This supports earlier findings by Higa (1963) on word associates, which showed that word sets which were strongly related to each other such as opposites, free associates, or synonyms were much harder to learn than word sets containing unrelated or loosely related words.

Repetition is another factor that is often discussed when considering word difficulty. Both findings in mainstream memory research (Baddeley, 1966) as well as second language vocabulary research (Leitner, 1972; Mondria, 1994) have found that spaced repetition of vocabulary learning over increasing periods of time is far more effective than massed repetition over short periods of time, helping word knowledge to move from short-term to long-term memory. They describe elaborate systems of physical boxes and flashcards to help learners with this kind of spaced repetition, but in recent years, researchers have used computer adaptive technology to smart phones and computers to help automate and make the process more efficient (Browne and Culligan, 2008).

Other researchers believe that a factor even more important than repetition is attention (Schmidt, 2001). In their seminal criticism of "multistore" approaches to explaining human memory, Craik and Lockhart (1972), proposed the Depth of Processing Theory. Until that time, most research had been concerned with the distinction between short-term and long-term memory, with the assumption that the longer a new piece of information was held in short-term memory, the better chance there was of it becoming part of long-term memory (Baddeley, 1966). Craik and Lockhart argued that the most important factor is actually the shallowness or depth by which a new piece of information is initially processed, a process related to attention. The authors point out that shallow, sensory levels of depth might be characterized by processing the stimuli simply in terms of its visual or acoustic properties, whereas deeper, more semantic levels of processing might involve analysis of meaning, compatibility with the analyzing structures, and processing time.

Browne (2003) compared three kinds of vocabulary learning tasks with differing depths of processing in an attempt to establish baseline quantitative date on the effectiveness of pushed output (Swain, 1985) for vocabulary learning. With time on task controlled for all these conditions, participants in the study attempted to learn 10 previously unknown words by either extensive reading containing multiple occurrences of each target word (condition 1), typical vocabulary learning games and tasks such as crossword puzzles (condition 2), or a pushed output task that required learners to write the new words in original sentences (condition 3). Results indicated that regardless of the language level of the learner, significantly more words were learned by the pushed-output condition, followed by condition 2, vocabulary learning games. In other words, the more deeply the learners were required to process information about the new vocabulary words, the longer they were able to remember them.

In an experiment that looked at short- and long-term retention of new vocabulary words for three types of classroom learning tasks, Hustijn and Laufer (2001) propose the Involvement Load Hypothesis in an attempt to explain the higher retention rate for vocabulary learning tasks which required deeper levels of mental processing. Their model consists of three motivational-cognitive constructs: need, search, and evaluation. Need refers to whether the motivation to complete a task is extrinsic or intrinsic, search to the attempt by the learner to find the meaning of a new word through dictionaries or other means, and evaluation to the learner's attempt to compare how the new word will fit together with the other word. Although time on task was vastly different for the three conditions in their experiment, Hulstijn and Laufer found that tasks with greater involvement loads (that is, deeper levels of processing) resulted in greater learning.

Automaticity of word knowledge is another area that has been much discussed in the literature. Eskey (1988) points out that the rapid and accurate decoding of language is an extremely important basis for any kind of reading and especially important for second-language readers. Earlier work by LaBerge and Samuels (1974) argues that fluent readers tend to be able to automatically recognize most of the words they read. In a discussion of the various processes involved in reading comprehension, Abdullah (1993) argues that it appears that humans have a finite amount of processing ability and that the automaticity of lexical access can free up cognitive processing capacity which can be devoted to the comprehension of text. In other words, fast decoders of a language will have a better chance to be a good reader.

See also: depth of processing, instructed SLA, Involvement Load Hypothesis (ILH), language and the lexicon in SLA, lexical concepts, vocabulary learning and teaching

References

Abdullah, K.I. (1993). Teaching reading vocabulary: From theory to practice. *TESOL Forum, 31*,10.

Baddeley, A.D. (1966). Short term memory for word sequences as a function of acoustic, semantic and formal similarity. *Quarterly Journal of Experimental Psychology, 18*, 362–65.

Browne, C. (2003). *Vocabulary aquisition through reading, writing and tasks: A comparison.* Doctoral dissertation, Temple University Japan.

Browne, C. and Culligan, B. (2008). *The JALT CALL Journal, 4*(2), 3–16.

Craik, F.I.M. and Lockhart, R.S. (1972). Levels of processing: A framework for memory research. *Journal of Verbal Learning and Learning Behavior, 11*, 671–84.

Eskey, D. (1988). Holding in the bottom: An interactive approach to the language problems of second language readers. In P. Carrell, J. Devine, and D. Eskey (eds), *Interactive Approaches to Second Language Reading*, pp. 93–100. Cambridge: Cambridge University Press.

Higa, M. (1963). Interference effects of intralist word relationships in verbal learning. *Journal of Verbal Learning and Verbal Behavior, 2*, 170–75.

Hulstijn, J. and Laufer, B. (2001). Some empirical evidence for the Involvement Load Hypothesis in vocabulary acquisition. *Language Learning, 51*, 539–58.

LaBerge, D. and Samuels, J. (1974). Towards a theory of automatic information processing in reading. *Cognitive Psychology, 6*, 293–323.

Meara, P. (1980). Vocabulary acquisition: A neglected part of language learning. In V. Vinsella (ed.), *Surveys I*, pp. 100–126. New York: Cambridge University Press.

Melka, F. (1997). Receptive vs. productive aspects of vocabulary. In Schmitt, N. and M. McCarthy (eds), *Vocabulary: Description, Acquisition and Pedagogy*, pp. 84–102. Cambridge: Cambridge University Press.

Mondria, J. (1994). Efficiently memorizing words with the help of word cards and "hand computer": Theory and applications. *System, 22*, 47–57.

Nation, P. (2001). *Learning Vocabulary in Another Language.* Cambridge: Cambridge University Press.

——(1990). *Teaching and Learning Vocabulary.* New York: Heinle and Heinle.

Palmberg, R. (1987). Patterns of vocabulary development in foreign language learners. *Studies in Second Language Acquisition, 9*, 201–20.

Pimsleur, P.A. (1967). Memory schedules. *Modern Language Journal, 51*, 73–75.

Schmidt, R. (2001). Attention. In P. Robinson (ed.), *Cognition and Second Language Instruction*, pp. 3–32. Cambridge: Cambridge University Press.

Schmitt, N. (2000). *Vocabulary in Language Teaching.* Cambridge: Cambridge University Press.

Swain, M. (1985). Communicative competence: Some roles for comprehensible input and comprehensible output in its development. In S. Gass and C. Madden (eds), *Input and Second Language Acquisition* (pp. 235–57). Rowley, MA: Newbury House.

Yoshida, M. (1978). The acquisition of English vocabulary by a Japanese speaking child. In E. M. Hatch (ed.), *Second Language Acquisition*, pp. 91–100. Rowley, MA: Newbury House.

Working memory

Henk Haarmann,
University of Maryland

Working memory is an effortfully controlled, capacity-limited system for the transient storage and processing of information (Engle, Kane, and Tuholski, 1999). The storage component of working memory may be viewed as a short-term memory (STM), which maintains codes in long-term memory (LTM) in a highly activated state in or near the focus of conscious awareness (Cowan, 2001). The storage is transient and lasts only on the order of a few seconds unless the information is actively updated by focusing attention on it again or by rehearsing it with code-specific mechanisms, such as sub-vocal rehearsal and visual-spatial imagery in the case of phonological and non-verbal spatial codes, respectively (Baddeley, 2007). The information loss over time results from storage capacity limitations due to a passive process of time-based decay and/or displacement of weakly activated information by more strongly activated information. The displacement process is sometimes described with the technical term interference, but this is a misnomer since in the memory literature the term interference refers to similarity-based retrieval errors during recall from a relatively inactive LTM state (Haarmann and Usher, 2001). In fact, there is evidence that the highly activated part of the storage component of WM or STM protects against such interference and that semantic similarity promotes storage in STM instead of hindering it (Davelaar, Goshen-Gottstein, Ashkenazi, Haarmann, and Usher, 2005). In addition to storage, WM also has a processing function. WM is a mental workspace, which allows for the integration and/or manipulation of information that is stored in it and for its encoding in LTM. Examples of processing in WM in the verbal domain include associating a word in the second language (L2) with its translation equivalent and meaning in the first language (L1) and figuring out who did what to whom from the presentation of the words in a sentence. A non-verbal, visual-spatial example of processing in WM involves determining whether and when to switch lanes while driving a car based on stored knowledge of the position of one's own car and other surrounding cars stored in STM. The storage and processing in working memory involve the deployment of effortful attention to select task relevant content and suppress task irrelevant and potentially distracting information. These are core functions of the central executive system of which WM is a major part (Baddeley, 2007).

Historical perspective

The history of the construct of working memory in academic psychology (for reviews see Baddeley, 2007; Davelaar *et al.*, 2005) goes at least back to the distinction that William James (1890) made between primary memory (i.e., working memory) and secondary memory (i.e., long-term memory). William James equated the contents of primary memory with consciousness (cf. Baddeley, 2007). This is conceptually related to the proposal by Donald Hebb of a dual-store memory with an activation-based (STM or storage component of WM) and weight-based component (LTM), which are two functionally interacting but distinct memory properties operating over the same neurophysiological substrate. The identification of the contents of STM with consciousness was revived more recently in Nelson Cowan's proposal according to which STM is the highly active part of WM in or near the focus of conscious awareness, which in turn is a subset of the contents of a much larger LTM in which most memory traces are not activated above threshold (see Robinson, 2003, for an application of this proposal to issues in second language acquisition). The ramifications of associating consciousness with STM remained to be explored. Such an exploration could prove to be critical for understanding and fostering second language learning, because conscious awareness of deviations from automatically activated, previously established, habitual patterns is crucial for novel learning (i.e., for the ability to overcome and change habits). Working memory storage was also a major feature of the modal model of memory in contemporary cognitive psychology, in the form of an STM system whose major function it was to transfer information to LTM. However, for a number of reasons, including the discovery of recency effects (i.e., better recall of list final than list initial items) under both short- and long-term retrieval conditions, the concept of a unique STM separate from LTM was abandoned and considered somewhat taboo for a while in cognitive psychology (for a revival see Davelaar *et al.*, 2005). Meanwhile, the concept of STM was incorporated into the larger construct of working memory with its combined storage and processing function. Many studies in the last few decades have explored the nature and role of individual differences in working memory (e.g., Engle, Kane, and Tuholski, 2099; Haarmann, Davelaar, and Usher, 2003) and the de-composition of WM into component operations and sub-systems, using well-established task paradigms to assess this cognitive function.

Task paradigms

Working memory is typically assessed with tasks that require immediate recall of a list of items, either in the form of a simple span or complex span task (for a review see Haarmann, Davelaar, and Usher, 2003). In a simple span or storage-only tasks, the testee is instructed to perform only one task and that is to retain each item for immediate recall. In a complex span or storage-plus-processing task, the testee is instructed to retain each item for immediate recall and to perform an information manipulation task in between each consecutive two items, involving those items themselves and/or additional materials. Recall is typically serial recall, requiring recall of items in the order presented, or free recall, involving recall of items in any order regardless of the order of presentation. Sometimes the recall procedure involves cued recall, such that on each test trial the testee has to recall only a single item that corresponds to or is related to some cue presented after the list. Cued recall has the advantage of minimizing response interference at recall.

Frequently used simple span tasks in the verbal domain include word span, digit span, and non-word span, involving the presentation of a list of words, digits, and non-words (e.g., pseudo-words which are pronounceable but have no meaning), respectively. Sometimes non-word repetition is used as a substitute for non-word span. Simple span tasks can also involve non-verbal materials, as is the case for example in tests using visual-spatial materials, such as dots or faces occurring successively in different locations of a grid.

Frequently used complex span tasks include reading span and variations of it, especially listening span and operation span. In reading span, the testee is presented with a set of sentences and has to read aloud each sentence as it is presented (processing), while also trying to recall the final word of each sentence or a separate word presented in between every two sentences (storage). In listening span, verbal materials are presented in spoken form and the processing task involves judging a property of the sentence (e.g., whether it contains a semantic anomaly or not), while the storage portion of the task is the same as in reading span. In operation span, the subject is presented with a series of words or other items for immediate recall (i.e., storage) and with problems that have to be solved in between every two consecutive items (e.g., an arithmetic problem). In addition to a storage measure (e.g., longest size of set of sentences for which the sentence-final words are recalled correctly), complex span measures may also yield a measure of the processing portion of the task (e.g., speed and/or accuracy of anomaly judgment). Another frequently used WM task is the n-back task. In this task, the subject is presented with an ongoing series of items (e.g., letters) and has to detect a repetition of an item that occurred n positions previously (e.g., two positions previously in the two-back version of the n-back task). In order to perform this task, the testee has to engage not only in storage but also in processing, since the subject must continuously update his or her record of which letters are in the last n+1 positions. Yet another WM task is the running span task. In this task, the subject is presented with a list of items that stops unpredictably and has to recall the last few items, for which individuals either use a storage-only strategy or a storage-plus-processing strategy that involves continuous updating using rehearsal (Bunting, Cowan, and Saults, 2006).

Many of these WM tasks have been used in SLA research into such issues as the relationship between L1 and L2 WM capacity and attained levels of second language reading skill (Harrington and Sawyer, 1992); the relationship of WM capacity to successful uptake of orally delivered corrective recasts (Mackey *et al.*, 2002); the contribution of cognitive abilities to succesful implicit Artificial Grammar versus incidental natural second language learning (Robinson, 2010); and the sensitivity of measures of protocol analysis to SLA processes (Goo, 2010).

One of the most well-known properties assessed with these tasks is designated as a person's span, which is an index of the number of independent chunks of information they can hold in working memory, also known as the storage capacity. A chunk is a memory representation whose internal complexity does not contribute to the memory load (e.g., the frequently practised month-day-year sequence representing one's birthday). The storage capacity of working memory has been estimated at four items plus or minus one item, when contributions from rehearsal and LTM encoding are minimized or absent (Cowan, 2001). The neural basis of this capacity limitation is not yet understood. An alternate viewpoint is that there is no such thing as a maximum storage capacity of working memory. Accordingly, the attention control system can distribute activation in different ways over varying number of items and their associated detail, rather than activating only items within a fixed limit.

Working memory components

Many researchers agree that working memory consists of a domain-independent or central attention control system that interacts with separate domain-specific storage and processing systems in the verbal and non-verbal domain (Engle *et al.*, 1999). Within the verbal domain a distinction can be made between phonological (Baddeley, 2007) and semantic working memory (Haarmann and Usher, 2001; Martin, Shelton, and Yaffee, 1994), which store and process the speech sounds and meanings of words, respectively. A separate orthographic buffer for maintaining written codes has been proposed as well. It is not yet clear whether there is also a domain-specific working memory for syntactic information. Within the non-verbal domain, there are separate but interacting WM components for identity (what) and location (where) information. The executive control system needs to be able to store and process goals and information about task context and might recruit semantic WM to achieve these functions. Episodic LTM, while not a part of working memory proper, may contribute to various degrees to task performance on WM tasks, since episodic or time- and context-specific information associated with presented items may be encoded in and retrieved from LTM to aid WM recall (Haarmann and Usher, 2001; Davelaar *et al.*, 2005).

Variability in working memory capacity

Individuals show systematic differences in their WM capacity. Numerous studies have assessed and demonstrated correlations between WM capacity and performance on more complex cognitive and language tasks in order to determine the role of WM for performance on these tasks. A general finding that has emerged from this type of research is that WM plays a role whenever a person's available WM capacity is surpassed by the WM demands, for example when sentences are syntactically complex or syntactically or semantically ambiguous. Individual differences in WM with first language (L1) materials have been found to correlate positively with individual differences in WM second language materials, (L1) suggesting that different languages rely on a general WM (Osaka, Osaka, and Groner, 1993). A majority of studies on WM in simultaneous interpreters, have revealed a WM advantage for these foreign language professionals compared to individuals who do not have professional interpreting experience but are matched in terms of their L2 proficiency (Signorelli, Haarmann, and Obler, in press). This finding could indicate that individuals with good WM self-select into a profession that places high demands on WM or that experience with such a profession improves WM. Several (but not all) studies have shown that individuals can increase their WM capacity through intense behavioral practice involving performance of WM tasks. This finding opens up exciting vistas. For example, fluid intelligence, which refers to a person's ability to reason about abstract patterns and which is known to rely on WM (Engle, Kane, and Tuholski, 1999), may improve after WM training. It is an open question whether second language learning benefits from WM training. Such an outcome is to be expected because WM helps a person cope with difficulty not only in L1 but also in their L2, especially since L2 tends to be less automated than L1. Nevertheless, it is not clear that WM is important and beneficial for all types of language learning. Somewhat puzzling in this regard is the well-known observation that children acquire foreign languages much better than adults, even though their WM is still developing and functionally impaired compared to adults. A related and still open question is whether a person's WM is functionally impaired when testing is done with L2 compared to L1 materials. In healthy aging, there is well-known cognitive decrement including reduced working memory functioning. This finding may have implications for older language learners who may want to consider cognitive training to improve their WM or engage in a version of task-based learning that does not overtax their more limited WM abilities (e.g., first learning new L2 vocabulary or L2 constructions before applying them in communicative tasks, such as a phone conversation).

See also: aptitude, attention, conceptual span, individual differences in SLA, psycholinguistics of SLA, rehearsal

References

Baddeley, A.D. (2007). *Working Memory, Thought and Action*. Oxford: Oxford University Press.

Bunting, M., Cowan, N. and Saults, J.S. (2006). How does running memory span work? *Quarterly Journal of Experimental Psychology, 59* (10), 1691–1700.

Cowan, N. (2001). The magical number 4 in short-term memory: A reconsideration of mental storage capacity. *Behavioral and Brain Sciences, 24*, 87–185.

Davelaar, E.J., Goshen-Gottstein, Y., Ashkenazi, A., Haarmann, H.J. and Usher, M. (2005). The demise of short-term memory revisited: empirical and computational investigations on recency effects. *Psychological Review, 112* (1), 3–42.

Engle, R.W., Kane, M.J. and Tuholski, S.W. (1999). Individual differences in working memory capacity and what they tell us about controlled attention, general fluid intelligence and functions of the prefrontal cortex. In Miyake, A. and Shah, P. (eds), *Models of Working Memory: Mechanisms of Active Maintenance and Executive Control*. London: Cambridge Press.

Goo, J. (2010). Working memory and reactivity. *Language Learning, 60*, 712–52.

Haarmann, H.J. and Usher, M. (2001). Maintenance of semantic information in capacity-limited item short-term memory. *Psychonomic Bulletin and Review, 8*(3), 568–78.

Haarmann, H.J., Davelaar, E.J. and Usher, M. (2003). Individual differences in semantic short-term memory capacity and reading comprehension. *Journal of Memory and Language, 48*, 320–45.

Harrington, M. and Sawyer, M. (1992). L2 working memory capacity and L2 reading skill. *Studies in Second Language Acquisition, 14*, 25–38.

Mackey, A., Philp, J., Egi, T., Fujii, A. and Tatsumi, T. (2002). Individual differences in working memory, noticing of interactional feedback and L2 development. In P. Robinson (ed.), *Individual Differences and Instructed Language Learning*, pp. 181–209. Amsterdam: Benjamins.

Martin, R.C., Shelton, J.R. and Yaffee, L.S. (1994). Language processing and working memory: Evidence for separate phonological and semantic capacities. *Journal of Memory and Language, 33*, 83–111.

Osaka, M., Osaka, N. and Groner, R. (1993). Language-independent working memory: evidence from German and French reading span tests. *Bulletin of the Psychonomic Society, 31* (2), 117–18.

Robinson, P. (2003). Attention and memory during SLA. In C. Doughty and M.H. Long (eds), *Handbook of Second Language Acquisition*, pp. 631–78. Oxford: Blackwell.

——(2010). Implicit Artificial Grammar and incidental natural L2 learning: How comparable are they? *Language Learning, 60* (Supplement 2), 245–63.

Signorelli, T., Haarmann, H.J. and Obler, L.K. (2010, in press). Working memory in professional interpreters. *International Journal of Bilingualism*.

Suggested reading

Baddeley, A.D., Gathercole, S. and Papagno, C. (1998). The phonological loop as a language learning device. *Psychological Review, 105*, 158–73. (Discusses the role of phonological working memory in language learning.)

Fukuda, K., Vogel, E., Mayr, U. and Awh, E. (2010). *Quantity, not Quality: The Relationship between Fluid Intelligence and Working*

Memory Capacity, *17*(5), 673–79. (Presents evidence that the storage-capacity of working memory is an important contributor to fluid intelligence.)

Jaeggi, S.M., Buschkuehl, Jonides, J., and Perrig, W.J. (2008). Improving fluid intelligence with training on working memory. *Proceedings of the National Academy of Sciences*, *105*(19), 6829–33.

Osaka, N., Logie, R.H. and D'Esposito, M. (eds) (2007). *The Cognitive Neuroscience of Working Memory*. Oxford: Oxford University Press. (Discusses the state-of-science on the neurobiological basis of working memory.)

Williams, J. (2011). Working memory. In S. Gass and A. Mackey (eds), *Routledge Handbook of Second Language Acquisition*. New York: Routledge. (An extended review of the role of working memory in experimental and classroom-based studies of second language acquisition.)

World Englishes

David Stringer
Indiana University

The study of World Englishes is largely concerned with the linguistic nature and sociopolitical contexts of second language varieties of English that have emerged in postcolonial societies, although it also encompasses research on the spread of English as a global lingua franca, and general relationships between standard and nonstandard varieties. The plural form *Englishes* is now conventional for many researchers in this thriving and expanding field of inquiry, as it emphasizes increasing diversity and suggests a pluricentric view of language norms. Speakers of the so-called "New Englishes" collectively constitute the largest population of users of English as a second language in the world. Many attain extremely high levels of proficiency and can provide insight into the nature of ultimate attainment in second language acquisition. Most use English together with other languages as they communicate in multilingual societies, and thus may shed light on psycholinguistic and sociolinguistic questions of bilingualism. Yet studies of such populations are notable primarily by their absence in mainstream second language research, and second language theory has only intermittently been drawn upon in the research tradition of World Englishes. Nevertheless, the possibilities for cross-pollination are manifold, and contemporary developments in both fields favor the germination of new interdisciplinary research.

In the following overview, a summary of several influential models of World Englishes is followed by observations on both the diversity and common features of the most investigated varieties. Sociopolitical issues are then examined, with reference to language planning in South Asia and Africa amid ongoing debates over how to move beyond the colonial legacy. Finally, discussion turns to the ways in which the distinct research traditions of World Englishes and SLA can each contribute to a more profound understanding of the other.

Perhaps the most influential categorization of World Englishes is Kachru's (1985a, 1988) Three Circles model. On this account, the Inner Circle comprises the countries where English is the primary language, and is acquired mostly as a first language: it includes the UK, Ireland, the USA, Canada, Australia, and New Zealand, and contains about 400 million people. The Outer Circle consists of countries which, having emerged from British (and later, American) colonialism, continue to give special status to English as an institutionalized variety, in education, law or politics: it includes India, Pakistan, Sri Lanka, Nigeria, Ghana, Kenya, Tanzania, Malaysia, Singapore, and the Philippines, among many other countries and territories, in which there are also about 400 million speakers of English. Perhaps the most crucial observation is that in the Outer Circle, English as a second language is used primarily for communication within the country, with other second language users, most people never having significant contact with native speakers. The Expanding Circle involves those countries that recognize the importance of English as an international language and teach it in their public school systems, while not according it any official status or using it to any degree for internal purposes: it includes China, Japan, Korea, Russia, Israel, Egypt, Indonesia, and the non-English-speaking countries of the European

Union, among many others. Estimates for number of speakers vary widely, but are usually around 6–700 million (all population figures from Crystal, 2006). The Three Circles model intuitively captures the distinction between English as a Native Language (ENL), English as a Second Language (ESL), and English as a Foreign Language (EFL). (Note that in the UK and in the World Englishes literature, ESL usually refers to the acquisition and use of English in countries where the second language variety has official status for purposes of intranational communication; in the USA, it refers to the acquisition of English in the target-language environment in contrast to classroom learning in learners' home countries). The model can also be used to capture attitudes toward standards: the Inner Circle is "norm-providing," the Outer Circle is "norm-developing," and the Expanding Circle is "norm-dependent" (Kachru, 1985a). This general categorization has proven very useful and influential, but is not without its problems. The analysis is at the level of nation states, none of which are homogenous in terms of a variety of English: the cline of English in India is dramatic, including people who speak only a few words, those who can converse in limited fashion, those who can communicate fluently according to developing national norms, and those whose English is almost indistinguishable from British English (phonological differences aside). As such, Inner, Outer, and Expanding Circle characteristics may be present in a single country. Characterizing Inner Circle varieties can prove equally problematic; many places such as Northern Ireland subscribe to local as well as international norms (Henry, 1995); it is not clear how varieties such as African-American English or Chicano English fit into the model; and certain postcolonial Inner Circle countries such as Canada or Australia may also be described as norm-developing, looking to American or British English while developing and codifying their own standards. In one of a growing number of attempts to move beyond this model, Bruthiaux (2003) argues for a less historical approach, characterizing World Englishes in terms of synchronic factors such as geopolitical power, size of population, multicultural versus monocultural ethos, and the status of the language in political administration.

Another influential characterization is McArthur's (1987) "wheel model." In the center of the wheel is a circle denoting World Standard English. Around the hub is another circle representing both established and emerging standards, such as British/Irish and South Asian. The rim of the wheel comprises localized varieties, such as Welsh English and Ulster Scots grouped outside Britsh/Irish, and Pakistani and Bangladeshi English grouped outside South Asian. This model is useful in that it helps to visualize the centripetal force of the desire for intelligibility at national and international levels, and the centrifugal force of the desire for identity at the level of the community (Crystal, 2003: 113). However, the center is in reality a void: World Standard English cannot be characterized in terms of lexicon, syntax or morphology; it is spoken by nobody, and arguably never will be. In the outside wheel, ENL, ESL, and EFL varieties are conflated: differences between Pakistan (where English exists as an indigenized variety) and Bangladesh (where English is a foreign language) slip through the spokes of the wheel. More recent models of the development of World Englishes include Schneider's (2007) Dynamic Model, which proposes that uniform sociolinguistic processes at work in language contact situations may be used to explain common patterns of patterns of development in countries that differ in their particular histories and geographies. Another perspective is offered by Chew (2009), who maintains that World Englishes are best analyzed in terms of the evolution of lingua francas more generally. While the general narrative in the World Englishes literature is one of English tied to an unprecedented, Western-inspired form of globalization, Chew considers that the same forces are at work in other languages, and have been present throughout human history, as evidenced in the spread of Ancient Greek, Arabic, Russian, and Mandarin, and in her own case study of the history of lingua francas in Fujian province, China. Indeed, while some researchers anticipate or even embrace the idea that English will one day be a global lingua franca, it seems highly unlikely that it will replace the existing national languages in multilingual countries such as China or Russia anytime soon. Some researchers, notably Jenkins (2006, 2009) reserve the term World Englishes for

Outer Circle varieties, and develop the notion of English as a Lingua Franca (ELF) in the context of the Expanding Circle.

In terms of comparative linguistics, it is possible to focus on the diversity of distinct varieties of English, and emphasize the particularity and independence of regional or social dialectal forms; but it is equally possible to highlight the commonalities, and examine different varieties with a view to furthering our understanding of language universals. Platt, Weber and Ho (1984), Schneider (2007), and Mesthrie and Bhatt (2008) provide intriguing summaries of common features and similarities in ostensibly very different varieties of English, including, in phonology: shortening of long vowels, weakening or loss of diphthongs, consonant cluster reduction, and syllable-timed speech; and in syntax: marking of specificity rather than definiteness in noun phrases; pluralization of mass nouns; use of progressive aspect with stative verbs; and use of perfective morphemes instead of *have* + past participle. The consensus is that both first language transfer and universal processes appear to be in play, much as in second language varieties more generally.

Sociolinguistic issues are at the heart of much research on World Englishes, and many in the field feel that investigation of language in postcolonial societies is unavoidably political in nature (e.g. Phillipson, 1993). For example, the choice of a foreign language as the medium of education carries implications for the whole of society, with direct effects on literacy rates, political (dis) enfranchisement, and the locus of socioeconomic power in the population. However, researchers with similar hopes for the promotion of equality and opportunity in postcolonial societies may come to opposite conclusions concerning the effects of English as an official language. Mahboob (2002) argues that the only way to challenge the status of English in Pakistan as the preserve of the political and economic elite is to make it obligatory as a national lingua franca and the compulsory basis of the school curriculum. Yet Obeng (2002), in his survey of education policies in seven Sub-Saharan countries, comes to the opposite conclusion, arguing that the choice of one indigenous language (linguistically related to others spoken in the country) is necessary to promote literacy, political engagement, and socioeconomic progress.

The question remains as to how to bridge the "paradigm gap" (Sridar and Sridar, 1986) between the distinct research traditions of World Englishes and SLA. The study of World Englishes calls into question several concepts that usually go unchallenged in the SLA literature. One such concept is that of the "target language": the target is not the Western monolingual ideal of a single language used for all social functions, but more often knowledge of multiple languages with distinct social functions. Another concept is that of "success" as an approximation of native speaker competence: if English is used intranationally, and most speakers never interact with native speakers of English, then native speaker norms are in some sense irrelevant for these populations. Another vexing issue is the elusive definition of a "native speaker": language knowledge in bilinguals is never identical to that in monolinguals, yet if this term is synonymous with "monolingual," then we reach the absurd conclusion that there may be no native speakers of any human languages in cities such as Capetown, Delhi, Kuala Lumpur, Lagos, Lahore, Manila, or Singapore. While SLA research may certainly glean insights from the World Englishes perspective, the reverse is certainly also true: for many years, World Englishes research proceeded largely uninformed by SLA theory, resulting in lists of typological observations, often anectodotal, with little theoretical underpinning. For example, many researchers are aware of the role of specificity in article use in World Englishes, following observations by Platt, Weber, and Ho (1984), and this phenomenon is regularly cited in textbooks. Yet no recent studies appear to recognize that this might be a phenomenon found in second language acquisition more generally, and none make significant reference to the influential work on this topic in SLA (e.g. Ionin *et al.*, 2004), despite the exciting implications of this research for our understanding of second language knowledge. Similarly, while challenges to the notion of the native speaker are nothing new in World Englishes (Kachru, 1985b), future research might benefit from insights gleaned from SLA investigations of multi-competence (Cook, 2002, 2003). Given the shared interests of researchers in both disciplines, it is to be hoped that future work will take inspiration from our collective knowledge of second language environments involving a broader range of population types than those that have dominated previous SLA research. The foundations are already in place for the two separate traditions of World Englishes and SLA to serve as a common platform for research, leading to enriched understanding in both fields.

See also: bilingualism, multi-competence, multilingualism, native speaker, social and sociocultural influences on SLA, Universal Grammar (UG) and SLA

References

Bruthiaux, P. (2003). Squaring the circles: Issues in modelling English worldwide. *International Journal of Applied Linguistics*, *13*(2), 159–78.

Chew, P.G.L. (2009). *Emergent Lingua Francas and World Orders: The Politics and Place of English as a World Language*. New York: Routledge.

Cook, V.J. (ed.) (2002). *Portraits of the L2 User*. Clevedon: Multilingual Matters.

——(2003). *Effects of the Second Language on the First*. Clevedon: Multilingual Matters.

Crystal, D. (2003) *The Cambridge Encyclopedia of the English Language*, 2nd edn. Cambridge: Cambridge University Press.

——(2006). English worldwide. In R. Hogg and D. Denison (eds), *A History of the English Language*. Cambridge: Cambridge University Press.

Henry, A. (1995). *Belfast English and Standard English: Dialect Variation and Parameter Setting*. Oxford: Oxford University Press.

Ionin, T., Ko, H. and Wexler, K. (2004). Article semantics in L2-acquisition: The role of specificity. *Language Acquisition*, *12*(1), 3–69.

Jenkins, J. (2006). Current perspectives on teaching World Englishes and English as a Lingua Franca. *TESOL Quarterly*, *40*(1), 157–81.

——(2009). *World Englishes*, 2nd edn. London: Routledge.

Kachru, B.B. (1985a). Standards, codification and sociolinguistic realism: The English language in the outer circle. In R. Quirk and H. Widdowson (eds), *English in the World: Teaching and Learning the Languages and Literatures*. Cambridge: Cambridge University Press and the British Council.

——(1985b). The sacred cows of English. *English Today*, *16*, 3–8.

——(1986). *The Alchemy of English: The Spread, Functions and Models of Non-native English*. Oxford: Pergammon Press. (Reprinted 1990, University of Illinois Press.)

Mahboob, A. (2002). No English, nọ future: Language policy in Pakistan. In S.G. Obeng and B. S. Hartford (eds), *Political Independence with Linguistic Servitude: The Politics about Languages in the Developing World*. New York: NOVA Science.

McArthur, T. (1987). The English languages? *English Today*, *11*, 9–11.

Phillipson, R. (1992). *Linguistic Imperialism*. Oxford: Oxford University Press.

Platt, J.T., Weber, H. and Ho, M.L. (1984). *The New Englishes*. London: Routledge and Kegan Paul.

Obeng, S.G. (2002). 'For the most part they paid no attention to our native tongues': The politics about languages in Sub-Saharan Africa. In S.G. Obeng and B.S. Hartford (eds), *Political Independence with Linguistic Servitude: The Politics about Languages in the Developing World*. New York: Nova Science Publishers Inc.

Schneider, E.W. (2007). *Postcolonial English: Varieties Around the World*. Cambridge: Cambridge University Press.

Sridar, K.K. and Sridar, S.N. (1986). Bridging the paradigm gap: Second language acquisition theory and indigenized varieties of English. *World Englishes*, *5*(1), 3–14. (Reprinted in B.B. Kachru, 1996, 2nd edn, *The Other Tongue: Englishes Across Cultures*, Urbana: University of Illinois Press.)

Further reading

Kachru, B.B. (1986). *The Alchemy of English: The Spread, Functions and Models of Non-native English*. Oxford: Pergammon Press. (Reprinted

1990, University of Illinois Press.) (A classic work that ignited modern research in the field.)

Kachru, B.B., Kachru, Y. and Nelson, C.L. (eds) (2006). *The Handbook of World Englishes*. Oxford: Blackwell. (Edited volume providing excellent coverage of various theoretical approaches.)

Kortmann, B., Schneider, E.W., Burridge, K., Mesthrie, R. and Upton, C. (2008). *Varieties of English, Vol. 1: The British Isles*; *Vol. 2: The Americas and the Carribean*; *Vol. 3: The Pacific and Australasia*; *Vol. 4: Africa, South and Southeast Asia*. New York: Mouton de Gruyter. (The paperback version of the most comprehensive linguistic survey of World Englishes to date, with 132 articles on almost 70 varieties, and an accompanying CD-ROM.)

Mesthrie, R. and Bhatt, R.M. (2008). *World Englishes: The Study of New Linguistic Varieties*. Cambridge: Cambridge University Press. (A lucid overview of World Englishes as a field of research, with comparative linguistic analysis and a focus on Outer Circle varieties.)

Schneider, E.W. (2007). *Postcolonial English: Varieties Around the World*. Cambridge: Cambridge University Press. (A socio-historical account of the emergence of World Englishes.)

Writing

Alister Cumming
Ontario Institute for Studies in Education, University of Toronto

Three fundamental purposes have dominated inquiry into writing in second languages: (a) describing learners' development of writing abilities in second languages; (b) identifying the variables and contexts that influence that development; and (c) promoting effective educational policies and practices for teaching, curricula, and assessment. These purposes are complementary in serving to inform each other, to illuminate the multifaceted complexity of writing, and to offer pedagogical guidance for the increasing numbers of educational programs around the world that involve learners of all ages acquiring literacy in international languages such as English, Arabic, Chinese, French, Japanese, or Spanish as well as in diverse heritage, ancestral, or regional languages.

Writing abilities stand out in second language acquisition because they symbolize individual and group identity, are a primary means to express knowledge in education or work, and produce fixed texts that can be readily analyzed and assessed (in contrast to the fleeting, interactively embedded discourse of spoken conversation). Writing abilities in second languages are also highly variable, multifaceted, and challenging to master. The latter qualities—variability, complexity, and difficulty—may help to explain why most research on second language acquisition has focused on oral discourse in conversation or classrooms, neglecting writing as a medium or source of language learning, as Harklau (2002) has neatly demonstrated. Conversely, the symbolic, knowledge-oriented, and text-based characteristics of writing may help to explain why educational programs, language tests and other formal assessments, as well as new multi-media communications have continued to emphasize, and even renewed interests in, writing and related literate abilities in second languages. For these reasons, and in response to increasing demands by educators to cope with the global spread of international languages and mobility, research on writing in second languages has burgeoned over the past few decades, as documented in recent book-length syntheses by Leki, Cumming and Silva (2008) and Manchon (2009) as well as earlier volumes by Kroll (2003) among others.

Second-language writing development

Writing development occurs in three interrelated dimensions, each of which has multiple aspects. Writing involves (a) processes of composing to (b) produce texts that are (c) socially situated activities. Each of these three dimensions of writing development have been researched extensively in recent decades from a range of theoretical orientations and with diverse research methods. For detailed documentation on this research, see Leki, Cumming and Silva (2008).

The textual aspects of writing range from micro-levels of vocabulary, spelling, punctuation, and grammatical morphology to more macro-levels of syntactic complexity, discourse structure, and genre or text types. Research on the development of second-language written texts has drawn on various linguistic, rhetorical, or learning theories, utilizing both cross-sectional and longitudinal designs. One research option has been to address a single language sub-system from a theoretically informed perspective, such as the acquisition of tense-aspect in written English analyzed in Bardovi-Harlig (2000). A second research option has been to investigate language learners' acquisition of a particular genre in academic or workplace contexts, conceptualized through theories of systemic-functional linguistics (e.g., Hyland, 2004; Schleppegrel and Colombi, 2002) or rhetorical analyses of apprenticeship into specific communities of practice (e.g., Parks and Maguire, 1999; Tardy, 2009). A third research option has been to evaluate corpora of written texts for indicators of text development—such as fluency (e.g., represented by lexical variety), accuracy (e.g., represented by grammatical errors), and complexity (e.g., represented by syntactic and discourse complexity)—to analyze skill-learning theories or task conditions, as in Wolfe-Quintero, Inagaki and Kim (1998).

Early research on composing processes drew on theories of cognitive problem-solving and think-aloud protocols to describe language learners' planning, text production, revising, and uses of information sources while writing (e.g., Cumming, 1989). Such research identified differences between novice and skilled writers in respect to the sophistication, complexity, and effectiveness of their composing strategies or evaluated the impact of focused instruction on these behaviors. More recently, inquiry has adopted socio-cultural theories to analyze the mental and peer-collaborative aspects of writing as sources for learning a language (e.g., Swain *et al.*, 2009), goal-oriented processes of self-regulated learning (e.g., Cumming, 2006), or the development of literate abilities spanning first and second languages (e.g., Albrechtsen, Haastrup, and Henriksen, 2008).

Extending this sociocultural orientation, the most illuminating of recent inquiry has involved long-term, ethnographic case studies of individuals' socialization into specific academic or workplace settings, demonstrating how individuals develop writing abilities to adapt to prevailing norms and practices in these contexts, to accommodate or resist group membership, to extend multilingual repertoires, and to mark and express personal identities (Duff, 2010; Gentil, 2005; Leki, 2007). Along with theories of language socialization, much inquiry has also taken up critical, political stances, and Freierian theories to view writing development in second languages as a means to challenge prevailing norms and empower socially disadvantaged groups (e.g., Auerbach, 1992; Benesch, 2001; Bigelow, 2010). As the publications cited above indicate, the theories informing research on second-language writing and the issues addressed in this research represent a broader range of perspectives than have conventionally appeared in research on the oral or psycholinguistic processing aspects of second language acquisition. Writing in second languages has been studied as much as a process of literacy, sociocultural, or academic or professional skills development as it has been considered an aspect or medium of language learning.

Variable contexts of second-language writing

Rather than positing uniform developmental sequences, the conclusions from research on second-language writing are that it is highly variable and dependent on the contexts in which learners write, live, and learn. Even the text characteristics of effective writing in a single writing test prove to vary on many dimensions (Jarvis, Grant, Bikowski, and Ferris, 2003). Even the learning trajectories of students from the same cultural background are better explained by complexity rather than by predictability (Larsen-Freeman, 2006). In addition to the multifaceted dimensions of second-language writing (described above), two explanations appear for this prevailing variability and complexity.

The first explanation concerns the institutional contexts in which different populations of learners acquire writing abilities in second languages. Research on second-language writing has emerged as relatively distinct sets of inquiries and issues related to certain learner populations: either young children in primary or pre-schools, adolescents with minority or migrant backgrounds in secondary schools, young adults in university or colleges, or mature adults in graduate education, workplace or professional situations, or immigrant settlement programs (Leki, Cumming, and Silva, 2008). Findings about second-language writing development for each of these populations tend to differ. Children seem to acquire literacy in multiple languages readily if provided appropriate opportunities and significance for doing so. Adolescents tend to struggle with issues of identity, marginalization, and relocation. Adults gradually adopt, resist, or express ambivalent motivations for acquiring new forms of and approaches to writing as they cope with changing contexts for studies, work, or settlement.

The second source of variability and complexity concerns the diverse status of languages and purposes of writing in societies, the many point(s) in learners' lives when second-language writing may be acquired in relation to individual literacy development or maturation, and the relative proximity and potential for transfer between literacy practices and language structures in first, second, or additional languages. All of these factors vary extensively for societies, subcultures, individuals, and combinations of languages. Most discussions of second-language writing distinguish between the acquisition of writing in settings where the second language is dominant (e.g., for recent immigrants or students studying abroad, e.g., studies reviewed in Leki, Cumming and Silva, 2008) or is "foreign" in the sense of primarily being an object of study in language classrooms or used only in certain workplace or institutional contexts rather than for routine communications in society or in homes (e.g., studies reviewed in Manchon, 2009). But numerous other contexts for language teaching and learning commonly exist and also promote variable conditions for writing development, such as immersion or bilingual education (e.g., Perez, 2004), maintenance of heritage or ancestral languages, societal situations of diglossia, or communications for work. Synthesizing these matters, Hornberger (2003) developed an elegant conceptual framework to account for the main sources of variation in the development of what she called biliteracy (i.e., writing and reading abilities in two or more languages), demonstrating how many different factors interact in the development of second-language writing across different populations, points in the lifespan, combinations of languages or literate forms, or societal contexts. At the same time, these variables need to be understood and addressed for policies and practices to be effective in particular educational circumstances.

Educational policies and practices

The impetus for most research and theories about second-language writing has been pragmatic: to better understand and improve educational policies and practices. Curricula, instruction, and assessment for writing in second languages have numerous variable options for their organization and foci, arising from the complexity and multi-faceted nature and purposes for writing development as well as the institutional formats of educational programs (Leki, Cumming and Silva, 2008).

Curricula for second-language writing can be organized as courses focused primarily on writing, as in many university or college courses, writing centers, or online tutorials or resources. Or writing can be taught in conjunction with other language abilities, with varying degrees of emphasis, as in most comprehensive or intensive language programs, many immersion or bilingual programs, or conventional courses for foreign language studies in schools or higher education. Curricula and teaching may emphasize any or all of the multiple aspects of writing development described above: macro-characteristics or written genres, micro-systems of grammar and vocabulary, integral stages and strategies for composing, knowledge construction, acculturation into scholarly or work roles, community development or empowerment, or individual expression, identity, or voice.

Instructional practices fundamentally involve modeling, scaffolding, practicing, and then assessing any or all of these aspects of second-language writing. The modes of doing so may include—or involve combinations of—lectures delivered to large classes, workshop types of interaction, or individual, small-group or computer-mediated tutorials. Tasks for second-language writing instruction similarly vary in their complexity, sequencing, utilization of information sources (including expression of personal opinions, responses to readings or other stimuli, or diverse types of research in libraries or local communities), and modes of interaction (i.e., personal compositions, group reports, or ongoing communications such as dialogue journals, diaries, or computer-mediated exchanges).

Formative assessments of students' writing are a conventional expectation for teaching and learning second languages, though controversies still abound about appropriate methods for responding to second-language writing and their impact on writing or language development (as reviewed comprehensively in Hyland and Hyland, 2006). The sheer variety of possible ways for teachers or others (such as peers or friends) to respond to students' written texts—which aspects of their writing or language to address? Which stages in their composing processes? Defy generalizations because curricula, teaching approaches, and learning opportunities vary so much but are also crucial to learners' being able to make use of such responses for their writing or language development. The widespread perception that teachers' responses to second-language writing are integral for learning has prompted innovative methods for organizing such responses, for example, through portfolios of students' drafts or collected compositions, computer-based feedback systems, or one-on-one oral conferences. Little research or development, however, has been conducted on other educational purposes for writing assessments, such as diagnostic or achievement purposes, although the bases to develop these arise through the increasing adoption in curricula of benchmark or competency standards, such as the Common European Framework of Reference for Languages, which describe expected writing competencies with a certain degree of precision (though limited empirical validation or generalizability across populations and contexts).

Formal, standardized tests of second-language writing have assumed an increasingly important role for two purposes related to institutional policies and increased global mobility and communications: decisions regarding admission into programs at universities or colleges or certification of language abilities for occupational credentials, employment, or immigration. In response, a small number of internationally administered tests of English and French have come to serve as gatekeepers for these decisions which have high-stakes consequences for individual life circumstances. This situation has prompted increased technical sophistication and research into the design, validation, and administration of these tests, particularly their writing components. Such inquiry has involved needs assessments to identify the types of writing tasks most important for academic or occupational success, key indicators of proficient written texts, and the crucial role of raters and rating scales in interpreting and scoring written compositions.

See also: communities of practice, developmental sequences, Instructed SLA, output hypothesis, social and socio-cultural approaches to SLA, task-based learning

References

Albrechtsen, D., Haastrup, K. and Henriksen, B. (2008). *Vocabulary and Writing in First and Second Languages: Processes and Development*. Houndmills: Palgrave Macmillan.

Auerbach, E. (1992). *Making Meaning, Making Change: Participatory Curriculum Development for Adult ESL Literacy*. Washington, DC: Center for Applied Linguistics and Delta Systems.

Bardovi-Harlig, K. (2000). *Tense and Aspect in Second Language Acquisition: Form, Meaning, and Use*. Malden, MA: Blackwell.

Bigelow, M. (2010). Mogadishu on the Mississippi: Language, racialized identity, and education in a new land. Supplement 1 to *Language Learning, 60*.

Benesch, S. (2001). *Critical English for Academic Purposes: Theory, Politics, and Practice*. Mahwah, NJ: Lawrence Erlbaum.

Cumming, A. (1989). Writing expertise and second language proficiency. *Language Learning, 39*, 81–141.

Cumming, A. (ed.). (2006). *Goals for Academic Writing: ESL Students and Their Instructors*. Amsterdam: John Benjamins.

Duff, P. (2010). Language socialization into academic discourse communities. *Annual Review of Applied Linguistcs, 30*, 169–92.

Gentil, G. (2005). Commitments to academic biliteracy: Case studies of francophone university writers. *Written Communication, 22*, 421–71.

Harklau, L. (2002). The role of writing in classroom second language acquisition. *Journal of Second Language Writing, 11*, 329–50.

Hornberger, N. (ed.) (2003). *Continua of Biliteracy: An Ecological Framework for Educational Policy, Research, and Practice in Multilingual Settings*. Clevedon: Multilingual Matters.

Hyland, K. (2004). *Genre and Second Language Writing*. Ann Arbor: University of Michigan Press.

Hyland, F. and Hyland, K. (2006). Feedback on second language students' writing. *Language Teaching, 39*, 83–101.

Jarvis, S., Grant, L., Bikowski, D. and Ferris, D. (2003). Exploring multiple profiles of highly rated learner compositions. *Journal of Second Language Writing, 12*, 377–403.

Kroll, B. (ed.) (2003). *Exploring the Dynamics of Second Language Writing*. New York: Cambridge University Press.

Larsen-Freeman, D. (2006). The emergence of complexity, fluency, and accuracy in the oral and written production of five Chinese learners of English. *Applied Linguistics, 27,* 590–619.

Leki, I. (2007). *Undergraduates in a Second Language: Challenges and Complexities of Academic Literacy Development*. Mahwah, NJ: Lawrence Erlbaum.

Leki, I., Cumming, A. and Silva, T. (2008). *A Synthesis of Research on Second Language Writing in English*. New York: Routledge.

Manchon, R. (ed.) (2009). *Writing in Foreign Language Contexts: Learning, Teaching, and Research*. Bristol: Multilingual Matters.

Parks, S. and Maguire, M. (1999). Coping with on-the-job writing in ESL: A constructivist-semiotic Perspective. *Language Learning, 49*, 143–75.

Perez, B. (2004). *Becoming Biliterate: A Study of Two-way Bilingual Immersion Education*. Mahwah, NJ: Lawrence Erlbaum.

Schleppegrell, M. and Colombi, M. (eds) (2002). *Developing Advanced Literacy in First and Second Languages*. Mahwah, NJ: Lawrence Erlbaum.

Swain, M., Lapkin, S., Knouzi, I., Suzuki, W. and Brooks, L. (2009). Languaging: University students learn the grammatical concept of voice in French. *Modern Language Journal, 93*, 6–30.

Tardy, C. (2009). *Building Genre Knowledge*. West Lafayette, IN: Parlor Press.

Wolfe-Quintero, K., Inagaki, S. and Kim, H.-Y. (1998). *Second Language Development in Writing: Measures of Fluency, Accuracy and Complexity*. Honolulu: University of Hawai'i at Manoa.

Z

ZISA project

Jürgen M. Meisel
University of Hamburg and University of Calgary

The ZISA project was initiated in 1974 at the University of Wuppertal (Germany) by a group of students (including Harald Clahsen and Manfred Pienemann) directed by Jürgen M. Meisel, professor of Romance linguistics. The acronym stands for *Zweitspracherwerb italienischer (portugiesischer) und spanischer Arbeiter* (Second Language Acquisition by Italian (Portuguese) and Spanish Workers), referring to a project investigating naturalistic acquisition of German by migrant workers from Italy, Portugal, and Spain. P(ortuguese) is missing because recruiting informants from the small local Portuguese community initially seemed impossible.

Originally conceived as a sociolinguistic investigation of the predicted emergence of a German pidgin, the project was redesigned as a study of non-tutored SLA, for it became soon apparent that this prediction failed (Meisel, 1977). Its new goal was the search for principles and mechanisms determining development and use of natural SLA. A grant proposal for a *longitudinal* study submitted to the Ministry of Science and Research of the State of North Rhine-Westphalia was partially successful, obtaining funds (1977–1978) for a *cross-sectional* study to be done first. The longitudinal study was carried out subsequently, funded 1978–1982 by the Volkswagen Foundation. The data for both studies were collected from 1977 through 1980 in Wuppertal and neighboring cities. The two corpora consist of audio-recorded interviews with Italian, Portuguese, and Spanish immigrant workers, 45 (age range 15–65) in the cross-sectional, 12 (age range 14–37) in the longitudinal study. The latter were recorded for a minimum of 57 weeks up to over 80 weeks, starting shortly after the subjects' arrival in Germany. In 1980, the project was relocated to the University of Hamburg when the principal investigator (Meisel) took up the chair of Romance linguistics. The other members of the Hamburg ZISA project were Harald Clahsen, Klaus-Michael Köpcke, Howard Nicholas, and Maryse Vincent.

The ZISA team developed the multidimensional model of SLA, first presented at the *German-Scandinavian Symposium on Migrant Workers* (1978) and published in Meisel, Clahsen and Pienemann (1981). It is based on the observation that differences in learners' speech need not reflect different acquisition stages, contrary to what was frequently assumed. Rather, they may indicate varying approaches to SLA, characterizing different learner types. The model therefore distinguishes between a *developmental* and a *learner-specific* dimension. For example, the omission of obligatory elements of the target system, for example, articles, is more likely to reflect learner-specific variation than phases of acquisition. The model's third dimension refers to *causal* factors. The invariant order of acquisition stages at the developmental dimension is explained in terms of increasing processing complexity of the constructions to be acquired, cf. Pienemann (1998) for a more elaborated treatment of this problem. The learner-specific variation is argued to be caused by social-psychological factors. An in-depth investigation of the latter, including a multivariate factor analysis of attitudes and motivations of the L2 learners', can be found in Clahsen, Meisel and Pienemann (1983). This model and the corpora were the foundation for subsequent research, including comparisons of first and second language acquisition, e.g. Meisel (2011).

See also: attitudes to L2, cross-sectional research, development in SLA, longitudinal research, pidginization and creolization, simplification

References

Clahsen, H., Meisel, J.M. and Pienemann, M. (1983). *Deutsch als Zweitsprache: Der Spracherwerb ausländischer Arbeiter*. Tübingen: Narr.

Meisel, J.M. (1977). Linguistic simplification: A study of immigrant workers' speech and foreigner talk. In S.P. Corder and E. Roulet (eds), *The Notions of Simplification, Interlanguages and Pidgins and their Relation to Second Language Pedagogy*, pp. 88–113. Geneva: Droz.

——(2011). *First and Second Language Acquisition: Parallels and Differences*. Cambridge: Cambridge University Press.

Meisel, J.M., Clahsen, H. and Pienemann, M. (1981). On determining developmental stages in natural second language acquisition. *Studies in Second Language Acquisition*, *3*, 109–35.

Pienemann, M. (1998). *Language Processing and Second Language Development: Processability Theory*. Amsterdam: John Benjamins.

Index